TEXAS BUSINESS LAW

Texas Business Law

Don Alan Evans, J.D., B.F.T.
*Professor of Administrative Services
Stephen F. Austin State University*

Pelican Publishing Company
Gretna 1980

DETROIT COLLEGE
OF LAW

Copyright © 1980
By Don Alan Evans
All rights reserved

Library of Congress Cataloging in Publication Data

Evans, Don Alan.
    Texas business law.

    Includes index.
    1. Commercial Law—Texas.   2. Law—Texas.
I. Title.
KFT1352.E8   346.764'07   80-17836
ISBN 0-88289-251-7

Manufactured in the United States of America

Published by Pelican Publishing Company, Inc.
1101 Monroe Street, Gretna, Louisiana 70053

TO MY STUDENTS,
Who have taught me so much.

Table of Contents

Preface   ix

Part I Introduction to Law   1

1. Nature of the Legal System; The Legal Profession   3
2. Texas Family Law   22
3. Texas Criminal Law   36
4. Federal Criminal Law   61
5. Torts   73

Part II Courts and Court Procedures   89

6. Texas and Federal Court Systems   91
7. Texas Criminal Procedure   99
8. Texas Civil Procedure   127
9. Special Court Procedures   153
10. Administrative Law and Procedure   177

Part III Contracts   189

11. Introduction to Contracts; Offer and Acceptance   191
12. Mutual Assent; Consideration   202
13. Contractual Capacity; Illegal Contracts   213
14. Statute of Frauds; Parol Evidence Rule   228
15. Joint Obligations; Third-Party Beneficiary Contracts; Assignment of Contract Rights   238
16. Performance and Discharge of Contracts   253
17. Remedies for Breach of Contract   270

Part IV Personal and Property Relationships   279

18. Agency   281
19. Employment   292
20. Union-Employer Relations   311
21. Bailments   322
22. Personal Property   331
23. Co-Ownership of Property   340
24. Suretyship and Guaranty   350

Part V Commercial Paper   361

25. Money and the Law; Types, Negotiability, Interpretation, and Transfer of Commercial Paper   363
26. Holder in Due Course; Defenses to Payment   380
27. Liability of Parties; Discharge of Commercial Paper   396
28. Checks and Bank Deposits   410

viii   Table of Contents

Part VI Sale and Transportation of Goods   427

29. Formation of Contracts for Sale of Goods; Title, Risk of Loss, and Insurable Interest   429
30. Documents of Title   444
31. Transportation of Goods   457
32. Bulk Sales; Sale of Goods by Nonowners; Performance of Contracts for Sale of Goods; Letters of Credit and Credit Cards   479
33. Warranties; Product Liability   503
34. Remedies for Breach of Contract for Sale of Goods   518

Part VII Secured Transactions; Motor Vehicles; Business Regulation   525

35. Secured Transactions   527
36. Consumer Protection   546
37. Motor Vehicle Law   566
38. Intellectual Property   588
39. Regulation of Business Practices   608

Part VIII Business Organizations   627

40. Partnerships   629
41. Formation and Powers of Corporations   645
42. Corporation Finance; Investment Securities   653
43. Rights and Duties of Shareholders, Directors, and Officers   671
44. Texas and Federal Securities Regulation   684
45. Close Corporations; Creditors' Rights; Corporate Combinations and Divisions   704
46. Dissolution and Liquidation of Corporations; Foreign Corporations; Texas Corporate Franchise Tax   721

Part IX Real Property   733

47. Estates in Land   735
48. Transfer of Ownership of Real Property   751
49. Landlord and Tenant   764
50. Liens on Real Property   775
51. Public Rights in Private Property   786

Part X Trusts; Wills; Estates; Bankruptcy   799

52. Trusts   801
53. Wills and Decedent Estates   812
54. Estate Planning   831
55. Bankruptcy   845

Index   859

Preface

Since I began teaching business law in 1967, I have wished for a textbook which included rules of Texas law. Since it is difficult to teach the specifics of many areas of business law without going into the rules of state law, and since the majority of Texas students who study business law will spend most of their lives in Texas, I have felt that the content of business law courses taught in Texas could be made much more meaningful to the student if taught from the Texas perspective.

The realities of textbook publishing being what they are, I finally realized that, if a business law textbook from the Texas perspective were ever to be written, I would probably have to do the job myself. I deeply appreciate the confidence of Dr. Milburn Calhoun and of Pelican Publishing Company in my ability to create such a work.

The business law textwriter of today finds himself caught up in the great debate over the proper content of the undergraduate business law course from the time he begins to contemplate his task.

Should he concentrate upon producing a volume fit for use as a CPA law review text, in order to satisfy the needs of accounting majors and accounting departments? Or should he concentrate upon the "law and society" approach, so heartily recommended by the American Assembly of Collegiate Schools of Business?

There is much to be said for both approaches. Ideally, schools of business should offer courses taught from both perspectives. It has always seemed to me that the student better understands the nature of the law of contracts and the law of the Uniform Commercial Code if he understands the nature of the legal system which applies this law. We should commence by examining the environment of the legal system, and then proceed to a study of the substantive law.

However, the reality of curriculum construction works against this. The business major must learn so much—and so little may be squeezed into 130 semester hours. The hours available for law courses may be few indeed. Smaller schools of business, particularly, may have to choose between the traditional approach to business law and the environmental approach. Some have apparently chosen tradition, others environment. Since this is the case, a text devoted to the business law of one state must include elements of both approaches, as this one does.

For the traditionalists, there is coverage of contracts, the Uniform Commercial Code, and the other subjects covered on the business law portion of the CPA examination. For the environmentalists, there is material on court organization and procedure, including administrative law and that hazy area lying between the criminal and the civil—guardianship, civil commitment of the mentally ill, and so on. There are also materials on the relationship between government and business.

This work also touches upon other areas of the law not often included in business law texts. I have included a chapter on family law for two reasons. First, no one can have a true understanding of the law of community property, or of wills and estates, without some understanding in this area. Secondly, no informed, educated citizen should be lacking in knowledge of this area.

I have also included in many areas of the text materials on international trade and foreign legal systems. Most business law texts lack materials in this area. I find this to be unfortunate. The Houston area is an area of very active international trade; thus many Texas business school graduates may well find work in the international department of a firm engaged in foreign commerce. In addition, many Texans engage in international travel, if only to cross the Rio Grande from El Paso to Juarez, from Laredo to Nuevo Laredo, or from Brownsville to Matamoros.

I have discovered no business law text which prefaces its discussion of the law of commercial paper with a discussion of the law of money. Yet I have found that my students find the concept of negotiability of commercial paper much more comprehensible once they understand the negotiability of money. I hope that the discussion in this area will prove as helpful to other students as it has to mine.

This work contains a chapter on the law of motor vehicles. This is an area of law which is important to all would-be businesspersons, and indeed to all citizens. It is also an area of great interest to most students.

It is rather difficult to assemble up-to-date materials on the law of consumer protection; every regular session of the Texas legislature is likely to bring new changes. Nevertheless, the necessity for knowledge in this area justifies the effort to paint a picture of the state of consumer protection law as of a particular point in time.

The materials in this work should be useful in either an environmentalist or a traditionalist business law course. They would also be useful in a course designed to give non-business majors some fundamental knowledge of the law. Lastly, there is sufficient material here for an elementary course in government and business.

PART I

Introduction to Law

1

Nature of the Legal System
The Legal Profession

Nature of the Legal System

In the beginning, perhaps, was the family. Later families combined into clans. Still later clans combined into tribes. Civilization arose and tribes combined into states. Finally, states became nations.

Man is a social animal; being a social animal, he must live in groups. Man is also an individualistic creature. He possesses intelligence. He also possesses will power—the desire to do what he wants to do when he wants to do it. Since possession of strong will is a necessity for survival in an insecure world, and since a strong desire for self-preservation is also a necessity for survival in such a world, man must of necessity have a powerful element of selfishness in his make-up.

For a social group to survive as a group, the selfishness of individual human beings must be subordinated to some degree. Here arises one of the basic paradoxes of the human condition: the individual cannot prosper if his group does not prosper, while the group will not prosper unless the individuals who comprise the group also prosper. The well-being of the group demands the suppression of the ego of individuals to a degree; but the individual, being an individual, cannot completely suppress his ego. Rules must therefore be made by the group for the government of individuals. In nations and states, we call these rules law.

Law, however, is a companion of civilization. It is also a companion of formal government. Organized society can exist without civilization, without formal government, and without formal law. Human societies have existed in this primitive state throughout most of human history. There are societies in out-of-the-way corners of this planet today which still exist in this state.

In the clan or tribe the unit of society is small enough to enable all members to be personally acquainted with all other members. As they mature, all members are indoctrinated in the social rules governing the society. Though there is no formal law, there are customs aplenty. In all human societies there must be rules governing marriage and the family. The human child is helpless for a long period; therefore society must provide for the care of the young. Since human beings require food and shelter (and clothing too, in most societies), property exists in all societies, and rules are necessary for determining ownership of it. (Artifacts must belong to someone. If the group does not believe in private ownership of property, then all existing property must belong to the group.)

Since human beings are passionate creatures, they will quarrel. Since human beings are violent, they will commit acts of physical violence against each other. They will kill if passions escape too far beyond control. Rules are therefore necessary in order to control these passions, and to provide punishment for transgressors and remedy for the wronged.

In the tribal society there is usually no writing; therefore the customs are passed down from generation to generation as a part of the group's oral traditions. The customs change little because the condition of society remains static for generation after generation and no necessity for change exists.

Since the young are so well indoctrinated in the rules of the group, and since the social stigma attached to those who do not conform is generally so unpleasant, most members of such societies behave as they are expected to do. Loss of status is a dreaded punishment in any society, and in a society where everyone personally knows everyone else status once lost is very difficult to regain.

With the advent of civilization, social groups became so large that all members of the group did not know all other members. Custom became an unsatisfactory cement for holding such societies together, because the individual members of society now had only an impersonal attachment to the social group. The old personalized sanctions for ignorance of the customs no longer were effective; more impersonal and powerful methods of insuring order became needed.

Impersonal government therefore came into being. Since writing was invented at about the same time as government, the customs were reduced to writing. And since civilization brings with it changes in the conditions of human existence and a more complex way of life—commerce, formal religion, and the like—governments find it necessary to exercise the power to make law, the power to legislate. Governments also find it necessary to train specialists in knowledge of the law, and to train other specialists in its enforcement.

In order to insure that the law of a state could be known to all who could read, rulers acquired the idea of promulgating a written code of law, containing the entire law of the realm. The first monarch to do this was King Hammurabi of Babylon, in about 2,000 B.C. His code governed the city of Babylon and those parts of Mesopotamia (modern Iraq) which were subject to Babylonian rule. As the size of the empires of ancient times grew, the complexities of the legal systems of these empires grew also. And as the level of material prosperity grew and the varieties of commerce expanded, the subject matter of law also expanded.

In due course the Babylon of Hammurabi became a part of the greater empire of Assyria. The empire of Assyria gave way to the new Babylon of Nebuchadnezzar, who ruled from Jerusalem to the borders of Persia. Babylonia yielded to Persia, which ruled from India to the borders to Greece. Persia yielded to an even larger Macedonia, which yielded to imperial Rome.

Under Rome the entire Mediterranean world was subjected to one government and became one vast trading area. A huge mass of written statutes of the Roman republican government and written decrees of the later emperors served as the law of this vast area, and a court system of unparalleled sophistication grew up to interpret and enforce this law. Some of this ancient Roman law seems cruel and barbaric to us today. Since so much of the labor of the Roman world was done by slaves, much of the Roman law dealt with the institution of slavery, the right of some persons to own other persons.

The law of the family began in a stern manner, the head of a family exercising almost absolute power over other family members, and the father having, among other rights, the right to kill his children for their misdeeds. As time passed, the law mellowed in this area, wives acquiring the right to own property and, later, the right to divorce their husbands and to live their own lives to a degree.

The law of commerce was to a great extent based upon the law of contract, and the complexity of the Roman law of contract and of property was not exceeded until modern times.

As the military power of Rome began to wane her law continued to grow in complexity, and famous legal scholars such as Ulpian and Papinian wrote voluminous treatises that sought to bring order to the complexities. Ultimately, however, the Germanic conquest of Italy in the fifth century A.D. put an end of this development in western Europe. As commerce contracted and the Dark Ages began, Roman law faded from the memory of most West Europeans, to be replaced by the more primitive law of the barbarian conquerors.

The magnificent Roman law did not utterly perish, however. The Emperor Justinian of the eastern half of the Roman Empire (which survived for another thousand years) ordered his legal scholars to reduce the huge body of the Roman law to writing. These men, working with the writings of the Roman scholars of earlier times and the huge mass of statutes and decrees, brought order out of confusion and produced the most systematic scheme of written law yet seen in the world. In a few areas this law still lives today. Provisions of the Code of Justinian may still influence the outcome of lawsuits in Scotland and the Republic of South Africa.

Justinian's massive work became and remained the basis of the law of the Byzantine Empire until that relic of ancient times was destroyed by the Turks in 1453. Copies of it found their way into western Europe, but were ignored in the chaos of the Dark Ages. In only a few areas, such as Provence in the south of France, did the ancient, written Roman law continue to be honored.

With the revival of commerce and intellectual life of the eleventh and twelfth centuries, the shortcomings of Germanic tribal law became apparent, and scholars rediscovered the work of Justinian. Some of the principles of Roman law again found their way into the living legal systems of western Europe, and this fusion of Roman and Germanic law started western European law upon the road to its present state of development.

At this point in history, the legal development of England began to diverge from that of the European continent. The destruction of the centralizing influence of the Roman Empire and the rise of feudalism so fragmented political power that, for most of the Dark Ages, the only effective government was the local government of the feudal lord. The only effective law was local law, which could vary considerably within the space of a few hours of travel. On the Continent, this did not begin to change until the fifteenth and sixteenth centuries in France and Spain, and until even later in other parts of Europe.

The same situation prevailed in England before the Norman Conquest. However, William the Conqueror and his successors created in England a centralized monarchy of a power unknown on the Continent. They gave to royal judges the power to enforce and interpret law throughout the realm, and these judges created through their decisions a unified national system of law—the English Common Law. From the beginning this system was based upon judicial decisions and the doctrine of "stare decisis"—that is, that courts must follow the precedents set by other courts in deciding cases. Royal and later parliamentary legislation became incorporated into the system, and by the fourteenth century the use of the jury as a decision-maker had become common. So unique were these English developments that the English judges had little interest in the rediscovery of Roman law; very little of it has found its way into the common law. The Roman influence is limited to the law of the nations of continental Europe and those nations elsewhere whose law has been influenced by continental Europe.

The legal unification of the nations of continental Europe did not come until the late eighteenth and nineteenth centuries—and when it came, it came through legislation. One of the first of these great legislators was King Frederick the Great of Prussia, who ordered the legal scholars of his realm to draft a code of law for the entire kingdom of Prussia. Their creation, the Allgemeine Landrecht, became effective in 1792.

The legislation of this nature which has had, and still has, the greatest influence in the world is that codification of French law which was done by command of Napoleon Bonaparte. The "Code Napoleon" became the law of France in 1804, and was carried into other European lands upon the bayonets of Napoleon's armies. It is still the basic civil law of France. In amended form it governs Belgium and the Netherlands, and is the basis of civil law in the French-speaking nations of Africa.

The law of Germany was not unified until 1900, when the "Buergerliches Gesetzbuch" became law. Swiss law was unified in 1912 by the "Zivilgesetzbuch." Other non-English-speaking nations unified their law through similar legislation. Most of the non-English-speaking nations of the world, however, base their legal systems upon the French, German, or Swiss codes, or upon a combination of ideas derived from them.

The common law brought unification to England without the necessity for comprehensive legislation. Wherever English-speaking settlers went during the age of colonization, they took the common law—and most of the ex-colonies of England have legal unity under the common law. This includes, of course, our own United States of America.

Fundamental characteristics of the common law. The common-law system has several characteristics which separate it from other world legal systems.

First, judicial decisions—decisions by courts deciding cases—are probably the most important part of the system. Many areas of law contain little or no legislation in common-law countries—contracts, agency, and torts, for example. Other areas have been codified through legislation, criminal law being the major example. However, even in those areas governed by legislation, the judges have the power to interpret the legislation in the course of deciding cases. The common-law lawyer cannot be certain as to the meaning of a legislative enactment until he does some research upon the question of how the courts have interpreted it.

Secondly, the judges, in the course of deciding cases and interpreting statutes and constitutions, have the power to make law themselves. The rule of "stare decisis" is not inflexible. It requires lower courts in a judicial hierarchy to follow decisions handed down by higher courts, but it does not require higher courts to follow their own decisions. Most of the time, of course, higher courts do follow their own decisions, in order to keep the law stable and predictable. But if the judges believe that an old decision is outmoded and obsolete they will overrule it, thus changing the law.

Thirdly, common-law judges are not very numerous, and they generally enjoy a high status. In the United States, state court judges are generally elected (as they are in Texas); thus they are a part of the political system and they are chosen through a very conspicuous part of that system. Federal judges are appointed for life by the president upon the advice and consent of the Senate. The selection of federal judges is also a part of the political system, but the selection process is not very conspicuous. However, once the judge is appointed and confirmed, his life tenure insulates him from further concern with politics. In most other common-law nations, judges are appointed for life under ground rules which tend to greatly reduce political influence over their appointment and tenure. American judges are thus the most political of common-law judges.

Fourthly, common-law judges rise to their positions from the ranks of the legal profession, except for those of lowest rank. They are generally educated as lawyers and have practiced as lawyers before being called to the bench.

In the fifth place, the jury is the decision-maker in many common-law courtrooms. In the United States, juries are almost universally used in criminal cases, and are very commonly used in civil cases, though the use of the jury in civil matters is declining somewhat. The use of the jury in criminal matters is very common throughout the common-law world, but its use in civil matters is far less common outside the United States.

Finally, and perhaps most important, common-law courts operate on the adversary system. The principle of this system is that if you have the parties to a controversy represented by zealous, competent lawyers who will do everything legally possible to bring before the court all the facts which will help their cause, all important evidence will be dug up and produced. If the decision-maker—judge or jury—has all of the facts at hand, it will know the truth in the controversy and be able to make a proper decision.

Since it is the responsibility of the lawyers to dig up and introduce this evidence, it follows that the lawyers must be left in control of the conduct of the trial. They decide which witnesses are to be called and what evidence is to be presented. They question the witnesses. The proceeding is, as has been suggested, a judicial duel between the lawyers. The judge serves as umpire or referee, making certain that the combat is conducted according to the rules.

Fundamental characteristics of the civil-law system. The civil law system is that system based upon the fusion of Germanic and Roman law which developed upon the European continent.

First, legislation is the most important part of that system. The comprehensive codes enacted by legislatures cover all areas of law. The judges have little or no power to make binding interpretations of the written law. The major interpretations are done by legal scholars in learned treatises.

Secondly, judges have much less power to make law in civil-law nations. The rule of "stare decisis" either does not apply at all under this system, or it applies only in limited areas. So judges deciding a case may be influenced by the decisions of other judges in similar cases, but they need not follow the other decisions if they do not want to.

Thirdly, judges are more numerous in civil-law nations—and they generally enjoy lower status than do common-law judges. A civil-law judge is generally a member of the national civil service, so he is a sort of government employee. If the procedure for making civil service appointments in a civil-law country is nonpolitical, the making of judicial appointments will also be nonpolitical. Matters of pay, promotion to higher courts, and the like are also matters of civil service regulation. Thus, a judge in any of these countries is in essence a nonpolitical bureaucrat.

Fourthly, civil-law judges in most countries choose the judiciary as a profession before or during their study of law. Very rarely does a practicing lawyer become a judge in a civil-law country. A candidate for the judiciary in these countries enters a rigorous training program after receiving his degree in law. If he performs well and passes his final exam, he will then be appointed to a minor judicial post and his judicial career begins. Thus, the profession of lawyer and the profession of judge are two separate entities.

In the fifth place, juries are not commonly used in civil-law nations, and when they are used they function differently from those in nations governed by common law. In most civil-law lands, juries are not used at all in civil matters: one judge or a panel of judges hears the evidence and decides the case. When juries are used in criminal matters, the jurors do not decide the case alone. The judges deliberate on the outcome of the case with the jurors, and the vote of judges and jurors combined determines the result.

Finally, civil-law courts operate upon the inquisitorial system. The principle of this system is that it is the duty of the court to discover the truth in the controversy before it. Since the judges are the only impartial persons in the courtroom, it is their duty to guide the proceedings in directions necessary for discovery of the truth. Thus, the judges decide the course of the trial. They call the witnesses, they determine which evidence shall be presented, and they question the witnesses. The lawyers may make suggestions, and they may question witnesses after the judges finish, but the function of the lawyer in the courtroom is very limited.

Respect for individual rights under the civil-law system. In common-law systems, the criminal justice system operates upon the theory that it is better if some guilty criminals escape punishment if punishment of one innocent person for a crime he did not commit is avoided. Thus common-law criminal justice systems are filled with procedural rights for persons accused of crime, such as the right to a speedy trial, the right to be released on reasonable bail (unless accused of a very serious crime), the privilege against self-incrimination, and the right to be informed of the charges when arrested.

The civil-law system seems to operate upon the principle that it is better for a few innocents to suffer for crimes they did not commit so that no guilty person may escape just punishment. Thus, the civil law permits the practice of investigative detention. When the authorities believe that a person may have committed a serious crime, they may take him into custody and question him, meanwhile conducting a police investigation of the matter. They are under no obligation to inform him exactly why he is being detained, although the person can guess from the nature of the questioning. Generally, the investigative detainee is not entitled to legal representation unless he is detained for an unreasonable time, or until charges are finally brought against him. There is also no right to bail in such a situation. The investigative detainee may remain in jail for several months while the investigation proceeds.

The detainee is under no obligation to answer questions during his detention, though he is very well aware that lack of cooperation on his part could prolong his detention. Anything he says during this questioning may later be used against him.

The defendant in a criminal case in a civil-law court may not refuse to testify. However, he normally is not put under oath upon the witness stand, as are other witnesses. (The idea is that if he is really guilty, an oath to tell the truth probably would not mean anything to him anyway.) His testimony is thus unsworn, and the court may evaluate it for whatever it is worth. If the defendant lies, well, that is what criminals normally do; the lies will not subject him to charges of perjury.

In common-law nations an acquittal of the defendant results in dismissal of the charges against him. The prosecution may not appeal an acquittal. In civil-law nations acquittal does not necessarily mean dismissal of charges, since the prosecution may appeal an acquittal.

In the United States a criminal defendant is entitled to a free appeal after conviction, and, even if his conviction is affirmed, he may forever challenge the lawfulness of his conviction through habeas corpus petitions and other means. Other common-law nations allow the defendant his appeal, but if the conviction is affirmed, that ends the argument. Civil-law nations also allow the free appeal, but a civil-law appellate court may increase the defendant's sentence—something the common-law system does not permit.

The severity of the criminal law and the harshness of the prison system will vary from country to country. The laws of the nations of Latin America are generally harsher than ours, and prison conditions seem barbaric to us. In connection with this, it must be remembered that Mexico is a civil-law land. Her criminal law is in many respects harsher than ours—particularly with respect to drug violations. Her prisons do not pretend to be institutions of rehabilitation; they exist for purposes of punishment, and that is all.

On the other hand, many nations of northern Europe have more lenient criminal codes. In some of these, there is no death sentence and no life imprisonment; also, serious efforts are made to rehabilitate the offender.

Common and civil law compared. Both of the world's major legal systems seek to do justice. Within the limitations imposed upon all systems of justice by the frailties of human nature, both succeed reasonably well. Both have their advantages and their drawbacks.

It has happened in the United States that a confessed murderer is released from custody because he had not been informed of his privilege against self-incrimination at the time he made his confession, and no other evidence of his guilt was available. This could not happen in, let us say, Switzerland. On the other hand, it has happened in Switzerland that a person suspected of a crime has been taken into investigative detention and retained in prison for a year while the charges against him were investigated, and that he has then been released because the authorities decided not to bring charges. This could not happen in the United States.

Under our adversary system, good legal representation is essential to a litigant's success in court. If your lawyer is incompetent or corrupt, no one else will help you. Under the inquisitorial system, on the other hand, an incompetent lawyer cannot do so much harm, because the judge, in his effort to find the truth, remedies the deficiency. Under our system, money, or the ability to buy the best legal talent available, can create inequality in the courtroom. Under the civil law, the power of the judge may be the equalizer.

A corrupt or dishonest judge in the U.S. has the potential to severely disrupt the administration of true justice. His potential for mischief is limited, however, by the power of the dedicated lawyer and the power of the jury—particularly in criminal matters. On the other hand, under the inquisitorial system, there is little protection against the corrupt or dishonest judge; he may so dominate the courtroom that no one may obstruct his will.

Since human nature is weak, no human judiciary is insulated from corruption and political influence. Money and political "pull" have been used to assure injustice in the past, and they will continue to be so used in the future. Persons have been convicted and punished for crimes more because of political belief than for the severity of the crimes allegedly committed. This too will continue in the future. However, the American jury is notoriously wary of convicting persons of crimes upon the basis of political belief or prejudice—the acquittal of Angela Davis was a good example.

Since the civil-law judiciary is a part of the national civil service, on the other hand, any political movement with the power to control the civil service may also control the judiciary. Maintenance of judicial independence is impossible under such conditions. For that reason Benito Mussolini had little difficulty in subjecting the Italian judiciary to the political demands of Fascism, or Adolf Hitler in subjecting the German judiciary to the demands of Nazism. Once a civil-law judiciary is subjected to the commands of a totalitarian ideology, it can be used as one of the arms of the ideology, and woe be unto the political dissenter who falls into its clutches.

There is no doubt that the power of the civil-law judge exceeds that of his common-law colleague in many respects. But the civil-law system can hardly be said to be inferior for that reason. The power of the civil-law judge, as is true with all power, can be used either for good or for evil; everything depends upon the political system of the nation which he serves.

Other legal systems. In the Soviet Union a third legal system has been created since the Bolshevik Revolution of 1917. Prerevolutionary Russia had a civil-law system, but the Communist rulers of the USSR have adapted the civil law to the needs of the Soviet society which they have created. Since no private ownership of large-scale economic enterprise exists in the USSR, and since no private ownership of land is permitted, wide areas of law so important to the operation of capitalist economies no longer exist in the Soviet Union.

The concept of equal justice under law is not a part of the Soviet system, since one of the purposes of Soviet law is the molding of the character of Russian man into "Soviet Man," the ideal citizen of the coming Soviet new world. Thus, in the administering of Soviet justice, the court must take into account the individuality of the persons before the court—specifically, how close these persons are to being ideal Soviet citizens. Attitude, in this sense, is all-important.

We tend to think of Soviet society as being a lawless society. This is of course not true. Much of the day-to-day activity of human beings in a totalitarian country has nothing to do with politics. Soviet citizens marry and divorce, they make contracts with each other and they breach them, they commit torts and crimes against each other, and they die and leave personal property behind for heirs to squabble over. Law must exist in the Soviet Union to govern these universal human affairs—and that law is not very different from law on those subjects in other countries.

There are crimes in the USSR which do not exist in many other lands. Not to have gainful employment is to be a "parasite," which can earn one a prison term. To buy goods with intent to resell them at a profit is to be a "speculator," which is a more serious offense. (To wish to do this shows that you have an element of capitalist ideology in your make-up; Soviet citizens must have no such motivations.) To criticize the government is to "slander the Soviet state," which is a very serious offense indeed.

Some elements of Soviet law have been transplanted into the legal systems of the Soviet's East European satellites—many elements in Bulgaria, Czechoslovakia, and East Germany; fewer in Poland, Hungary, and Rumania; and still fewer in Yugoslavia.

In most nations where Islam is the national religion, much of the national legal system is based upon the Shari'a, the Islamic religious law. In Western legal systems, both common and civil law, a divorce took place long ago between the sacred law of the church and the profane law of the state. For a long period Western church courts applied sacred law in matters of family relations and inheritance; these matters were considered not to be the business of the state. But these separate church courts were abolished long ago and these areas of sacred law passed under the control of the state. Christianity in the West is a source of moral commandments, but nothing in the Bible is a legal commandment enforceable by the state.

In Islamic nations, however, traditionalists believe that the only true lawgiver is God, and the only true source of law is the Koran, the holy scripture of Islam. Thus, there can be

1/ Nature of the Legal System

no distinction between religious law and secular law, and no distinction between religion and the state.

Since the Koran is as old as Islam itself—over 1,300 years old—the Shari'a provisions cannot deal with legal problems caused by modern technological and economic development. Islamic lands have reacted to this in several ways. Some, like Turkey, have completely westernized their legal systems and eliminated the religious influence. Most of the law of Turkey is based upon the Swiss codes; Turkey is now a full-fledged civil-law nation. Other countries, like Saudi Arabia, try to keep the old Shari'a law strictly in force, modifying it only where absolutely necessary. Most Islamic countries, like Tunisia, Egypt, and Iraq, try to steer a middle ground, creating a "Western" law for business and economic relationships, but retaining traditional Islamic law in matters of family property, inheritance, and the like.

In India the Hindu religion has from time immemorial provided rules for the conduct of life. Much traditional Hindu law has been changed by legislation enacted by the parliament of India and adapted to modern conditions, but for believers in Hinduism religious precept is still the basis of much of the law under which they live.

In China, Japan, and other parts of the Far East, a Western type of law prevails—civil law in non-communist areas, Soviet-style law in communist areas. However, the application of the law is colored by the unique attitude toward law possessed by peoples influenced by Chinese culture.

The Chinese have not been adherents of formal religion in the Western sense. The philosophy of Confucianism—the strongest moral element of Chinese culture—is in essence a moral philosophy. It sets forth rules of right conduct which the superior person should obey. Unless people adhere to these rules of conduct, a virtuous society cannot exist and the purposes of life cannot be fulfilled. Thus, man has an inescapable moral obligation to behave properly. Human beings must be taught these moral imperatives, and taught that the soul of virtue is obedience to them. If this job of education is properly performed, law is not necessary, because people will do right out of moral obligation, not out of fear of the law. Thus, law is to be used only where the better sanction—that is, morality—breaks down.

The exceedingly strong sense of obligation which Far Eastern cultures impose upon their members make this way of doing things effective. Because of it, China under the Communists has not found it necessary to erect the formal edifice of law which is found in the USSR; the strong discipline of the people of China is maintained without it. Also because of it, the elaborate law of Japan has not caused the courts of that country to be swamped with business. To the Japanese it is still somehow disgraceful to become involved with law and courts; to become so involved is to confess that the web of moral obligation has somehow been torn asunder.

In black Africa the governments of many newly independent nations seek to adapt Western systems of law inherited from European colonial administrations to the realities of non-Western, non-industrialized societies. The Western law is necessary for governing the newborn industries of these nations, and their urbanized populations, but has little relevance for the farmers of the hinterlands. The task facing these new governments is to combine modern law with the best of the ancient tribal customs into legal systems which advance into the twentieth century.

Our study of law will naturally be limited to that version of the common law which applies in the state of Texas. But an educated person must know that law is an element of culture, and that the nature of law varies from nation to nation and from people to people.

Texans especially should realize that a very different legal system prevails on the other side of the narrow Rio Grande, and that the visitor to Mexico who does not respect the laws of our southern neighbor may learn about the differences between their system and ours the hard way. Many of the American inhabitants of Mexican prisons can testify to the rigors of that educational experience.

The nature of the Texas legal system. Texas lived under the Romanized law of Spain during the period of Spanish sovereignty here. The same law, modified by the government of Mexico, essentially prevailed during the period of Mexican sovereignty. The American settlers in Texas brought with them their attachment to the common-law system of England and the United States, but the common law had no legal force.

After the attainment of Texan independence from Mexico, there was no necessity for the retention of Mexican law, although its retention was a possibility—it must be remembered that the inhabitants of Louisiana decided to continue to live under the French law of the Louisiana colony after they became a part of the United States as a result of the Louisiana Purchase. A code of civil law based upon the Code Napoleon was enacted by an early Louisiana legislature, and to this day many elements of French civil law are found in the state law of our eastern neighbor.

The Congress of the Republic of Texas chose not to follow this Louisiana precedent, however. An act of this congress in 1840 declared that the common law of England was to be the basis of the legal system of Texas, and it has remained so ever since.

A little of our Spanish and Mexican heritage can still be found in Texas law, most notably in our community property system. In Texas, most property acquired by a married person after marriage is co-owned by both partners. This is also true in seven other American states; but in the other forty-two states the common-law rule prevails that the property of a married person is strictly his or hers.

Since Texas became a state of the United States, the fundamental law here has of course been the Constitution of the United States and the statutes and administrative regulations enacted thereunder. The fundamental law of the state of Texas is the Texas Constitution of 1876 and the statutes and administrative regulations enacted thereunder. The fundamental law of an incorporated home rule city is its home rule charter, and the city ordinances and administrative regulations enacted thereunder. In case of conflict, of course, federal law takes precedence over state law and state law takes precedence over municipal law. A constitutional provision takes precedence over a conflicting statute, and a statute takes precedence over a conflicting administrative regulation.

Constitutions, statutes, and administrative regulations. A constitution is the fundamental law of a political organism. It is enacted by a special procedure, and it must be amended by special, extraordinary procedure. The charter of an incorporated city is essentially that city's constitution.

A statute is a legislative enactment by a duly constituted legislative body, enacted in accordance with the procedure set forth in the constitution which created the legislative body.

An administrative regulation is a piece of written law enacted by an administrative body or agency. Administrative regulations are not enacted by elected lawmakers. In fact, most administrative agency members are not elected to anything by anybody. They are appointed to their positions by the president of the United States or the governor of Texas for the purpose of administering the area of the economy, the profession, or whatever is entrusted to their jurisdiction by the constitutional provision or statute creating the agency. Though these regulations are not enacted by elected lawmakers, they have the force of law.

Statutory law vs. judge-made law. In many areas in which the legislature has chosen not to enact statutes, the only existing law is the case law made by judges. The law maintains its force because of the power of the doctrine of "stare decisis," as described earlier. It may be changed by the judges when they decide to overrule formerly decided cases.

A legislative body may change case law by enacting a statute. However, the interpretation of a statute is in the hands of the judges. Written law means essentially what the judges say it means. Thus, the judges in a sense possess the last word when it comes to a determination of what the law means.

Criminal law vs. civil law. When a person violates the criminal law, he is charged with a criminal offense by the government which enacted the law which was violated. He is brought to trial with the object of subjecting him to punishment if he is found guilty. If he is found guilty, he may be deprived of his life (capital punishment), of his liberty (imprisonment), or of some of his property (fines), in accordance with the punishments set by law for those committing a particular offense.

Only those officials authorized by law to prosecute may commence criminal prosecutions. If the victim of a crime desires to see the criminal punished, he may do no more than report the offense to the proper authorities. Only the authorized prosecuting authority may actually bring formal charges. Fines levied as a result of conviction are not paid to the victim of the offender's criminal conduct; they are paid to the prosecuting government. Normally the criminal process does not require the offender to make any sort of restitution to his victim, though under modern criminal procedure an offender may be found guilty and sentenced to probation on condition that he make appropriate restitution to his victim.

If the criminal act of an individual causes damage to another individual, the crime is also a tort. The perpetrator may be criminally prosecuted for the crime and punished, and he may also be sued for damages by his victim because of the tort. The objective of the ordinary civil suit is normally recovery of money from the person being sued. The plaintiff—the person bringing the suit—wants compensation for the wrong that was done him. If a person desires to file an action for civil damages against someone, he may do so. However, he is then strictly on his own. Government prosecutors are not in the business of helping citizens with civil lawsuits.

Thus, one wrongful act by an individual, such as running a stop sign and causing an accident, may subject him to two legal proceedings—a criminal prosecution for running the stop sign, and a civil lawsuit for causing the accident.

Law vs. equity. In medieval England, the royal judges had the power to command that a defendant pay damages to a plaintiff. They also had the power to determine the ownership of property, both real and personal. However, they had no authority to command a person to do something (other than to pay money or the like) or to decide cases involving family relations. Matters of family relations were under the jurisdiction of the ecclesiastical (church) courts, and for much of this period there was no acceptable way to get a judicial body to order someone to do something (or not to do something).

Those who had problems that the law courts would not handle began to appeal to the royal chancellor for justice, and the chancellor began to hear such petitions and to award remedies. The chancellor's court became known as the Court of Chancery, and the body of law that developed there became known as equity. When the ecclesiastical courts passed from the scene later, their power over family relations became vested in the court of chancery, to a degree.

Thus, two co-existing civil court systems grew up in England: the law courts which handled damages and property cases, and the chancery or equity courts, which had the power to decree that a defendant do something or not do something.

These two coexisting courts were brought to America by the English settlers, and for a while most states had separate courts of law and equity. Eventually the separate equity courts were abolished, but differences still existed between law procedure and equity procedure. The biggest difference was that, since no juries were ever used in the Court of the Royal Chancellor in England, no juries were used at all in equity cases.

The difference between law procedure and equity procedure is still meaningful in the federal court system, and in most state systems. However, the Congress of the Texas Republic which adopted the English common law as the basis of Texas law also provided that Texas courts should recognize no distinction between law and equity. Texas courts may thus award damages, as the old law courts could, or hand down injunctions, as the old equity courts could. Juries are available in Texas in both types of cases.

Administrative adjudication and administrative law. Much of the law contained in administrative regulations is not enforced in the regular law courts. The statutes which create administrative agencies and give them the power to enact legislation in the form of regulations usually also give the agencies the power to enforce the regulations which they have made and to try violations of the regulations in their own administrative tribunals.

Most administrative regulations deal with regulation of business conduct, licensing of trades or professions, and the like. The average citizen is not very likely to get involved in an administrative judicial proceeding. However, as society becomes more complex, and legal and administrative regulation invades more areas of our lives, the likelihood of the citizen having dealings with administrative agencies increases. Since the typical agency exercises all three governmental powers—legislative, executive, and judicial—outside the classic political framework, it has the potential for exercise of enormous power.

Finding the law. The mass of statutes, court decisions, and administrative regulations which comprise the law of the United States and of the state of Texas must of course be published and organized in comprehensible form in order for citizens to be able to know what the law is.

Acts of the Congress of the United States are published in the order in which they are enacted, and they are numbered in that order. For instance, the Federal Real Estate Settlement Procedures Act of 1974 was Public Law 93-533—that is, the 533rd piece of legislation enacted by the Ninety-third Congress. It was amended in 1976 by Public Law 94-205.

Since the public laws are published in order of enactment, and are not classified by subject matter, a more efficient system of organization of federal statutes is necessary. The classification is provided by the United States Code. Federal statutes are codified into fifty titles; each title deals with a particular subject matter. The Real Estate Settlement Procedures Act is codified as part of the twelfth title of the United States Code, the title dealing with banks and banking. It is found beginning at Section 2601 of Volume 12 of the Code. Lawyers would say that this act is found at 12 USC 2601 et seq.

Texas state statutes are published in the order in which they are enacted. These publications are called session laws, and each individual statute comprises a chapter of the session laws. For instance, the Alcoholic Beverages Code, enacted by the Texas legislature in 1977, was Chapter 194 of the Acts of 1977, or the Session Laws of 1977.

Some Texas state statutes are classified as separate codes dealing with broad subject-matter areas, such as the Alcoholic Beverages Code mentioned above. There also exist, for example, the Taxation Code, the Insurance Code, the Education Code, the Election Code, the Business and Commerce Code, and others.

1/ Nature of the Legal System 15

Other session laws deal with subject matter which does not lend itself to organization into codes. For instance, Chapter 700 of the Session Laws of 1969 provides that when unsolicited goods are delivered to a recipient, he may either refuse to accept delivery of them, or he may treat them as a gift and use and dispose of them as he pleases. This sort of legislation is codified as a part of the Texas Revised Civil Statutes. This particular piece of legislation was codified as Article 29c-1 of these statutes. The legislation is cited by layers as RCS 29c-1.

Federal administrative regulations are published for the first time in the *Federal Register*. Here there is no classification by subject matter. The regulations are then codified in the Code of Federal Regulations (CFR), which is organized in the same manner as is the U.S. Code. Since the total number of federal administrative regulations far exceeds the number of federal statutes, the CFR is a huge set of volumes. Though many businesses, libraries, and law offices possess complete sets of the U.S. Code, far fewer possess complete sets of the Code of Federal Regulations.

Texas administrative regulations are published in the *Texas Register*, the Texas equivalent of the *Federal Register*. There exists, however, no Texas publication similar to the CFR. If one wishes to obtain a complete set of regulations issued by a particular Texas agency, one's best bet is to contact the agency itself.

Decisions of the Supreme Court of the United States are published in the *United States Reports*. These are referred to by the volume of the *Reports* in which a particular decision is published, and the page number upon which the report of the case begins. The title of the case is also a part of a proper citation, the first party named being the party who appealed the case to the Supreme Court, the second party named being the other party to the case. The appealing party, called the appellant, is not necessarily the plaintiff in the case. If the plaintiff won in the trial court and the court of appeals, the defendant is the appellant; thus his name appears first in the title of the case.

A Supreme Court case may then be cited as, for instance, *Brown vs. White*, 496 US 742.

Decisions of the federal courts of appeal are collected in the *Federal Reporter*, published by West Publishing Company of St. Paul, Minnesota. These cases are cited in this manner: *Green vs. Blue*, 202 F. 2d 404. The case may be found on page 404 of the 202nd volume of the second series of the *Federal Reporter*.

Some federal district court decisions are published, others not. Those which are published appear in the *Federal Supplement*, another publication of West Publishing Company. These are cited as, for instance, *Gray vs. Pink*, 226 F. Supp. 902.

Decisions of the Supreme Court of Texas were formerly published in the *Texas Reports* and cited 109 Tex. 933, for instance. However, *Texas Reports* is no longer published. All published decisions of all Texas courts appear in the *Southwestern Reporter*, another West publication, along with all published court decisions from the state courts of Arkansas, Missouri, Kentucky, and Tennessee. These are cited as, for instance, *Able vs. Baker*, 409 SW 2d 784.

Some states still publish an official series of court decision reports. Others do not. All published state court decisions are published in West Publishing Company publications, however. There is a *Pacific Reporter* containing decisions from California and the other Far Western states, a *Southern Reporter* containing decisions from Louisiana and other states of the Deep South, and so forth.

Court decisions are reported only in the order of publication; they are not classified in these reports according to subject matter of cases decided. Therefore, various legal publishing companies market a wide variety of digests, law reports, etc., which classify information from court decisions by subject matter.

Ability to use these publications is essential for the lawyer. It is small wonder that the most important of law courses is the course in legal research.

Uniform laws. Much of the statutory business law of the United States is state law. However, since the growth of interstate business makes it advantageous to have uniform law throughout the nation, efforts have been made to induce the states to enact uniform legislation on many subjects, so that the law may be harmonized throughout the nation.

The most successful and far-reaching of these uniform laws has been the Uniform Commercial Code. It was drafted by a panel of experts in business law during the late 1940s and early 1950s, and was submitted to the states for consideration by the Commissioners on Uniform State Laws in 1952. It was adopted in Pennsylvania in 1954. Since then it has been adopted by the legislature of every state except Louisiana.

The almost universal adoption of this code has made the law on contracts for the sale of goods, commercial paper, checks and bank deposits, letters of credit, documents of title, investment securities, and secured transactions in personal property virtually uniform throughout the nation.

Several chapters of this work will deal with the law of the Uniform Commercial Code. It will be referred to for the most part as the UCC, though the Texas legislature has added the UCC to a longer code of business regulation—the Texas Business and Commerce Code. The non-UCC portions of the Business and Commerce Code will generally be referred to as the TB&CC.

The Legal Profession

The practice of law is limited to those who have a license. The licensing of practitioners of the law is done at the state level. At the moment no federal regulation of the legal profession exists.

In Texas the profession is regulated by the State Bar of Texas, an organization sanctioned by act of the Texas legislature. In order to practice law in this state, one must have a license issued by the Supreme Court of Texas, upon the recommendation of the Board of Bar Examiners.

In this state an integrated bar exists—that is, in order to practice law in this state one must be a member of the State Bar of Texas. In those states which do not have integrated bars, membership in the state bar organization is not required. The Texas bar has been integrated since 1939. More and more state legislatures are adopting legislation requiring members of the profession to belong to state bar associations.

Qualifications for admission to the Texas bar. An aspiring member of the Texas bar must meet three qualifications in order to be admitted to the practice of the profession in this state. These are:

1. Possession of a J.D. degree or the equivalent from a university accredited by the American Bar Association.
2. Good moral character.
3. A passing grade on the Texas Bar Examination, or seven years of practice in a state other than Texas or in a nation the basis of whose legal system is the English common law.

In the state of Texas there are seven universities which offer programs leading to the J.D. degree. These are the University of Texas at Austin, Texas Tech University, the University of Houston, Southern Methodist University, Baylor University, St. Mary's University, and South Texas University.

One must, of course, qualify for admission to an accredited university in order to obtain the J.D. degree. All seven Texas universities offering this degree are accredited by the American Bar Association, as are most such universities in the nation. However, a minority of the nation's law schools are not so accredited. A Texan desiring to earn the J.D. degree in a university or other law school outside this state should be certain that the school is properly accredited. If it is not, the state of Texas will not recognize the degree.

In order to obtain admission to most law schools, one must hold a bachelor's degree or the equivalent. Six of the seven Texas law schools require this. The one exception is Baylor University, which will admit a person to the study of law who has completed three years of undergraduate education.

Because the number of applicants for admission to the study of law far exceeds the number of available places in freshman law school classes, possession of an undergraduate degree does not guarantee admission. Schools of law generally consider two criteria for admission: the undergraduate grade-point average and the student's performance on the Law School Admission Test (LSAT). The LSAT was devised by the Educational Testing Service of Princeton, New Jersey, and is administered in many locations throughout the country. It is a test that measures the student's general knowledge and also his aptitude for legal reasoning. The aspiring law student should take this test before applying for admission to law school. A good score on this will to an extent offset a GPA which does not sparkle. In these days of affirmative action programs, female applicants for admission to law school will have some advantage over male applicants, and minority applicants will likewise have an advantage over caucasian applicants.

After obtaining the J.D. degree, one must apply for permission to take the state bar exam. At this time one must file a completed, detailed questionnaire on one's life history, designed to determine whether or not the applicant is a person of good moral character. Of supreme importance here is the record one has compiled (if any) of brushes with the law, particularly felony convictions. It is of the utmost importance that the applicant state the truth, the whole truth, and nothing but the truth in answer to the questions propounded in this questionnaire. Most matters having an important bearing upon the question of whether or not one is a person of good moral character are matters of public record, particuarly brushes with the criminal law. Such matters cannot very well be hidden.

The bar exam is given three times a year in Texas. Over 80 percent of all examinees pass each time that it is given. If one fails on the first try, one may try again the next time; if one fails the second time, a third attempt is allowed. If one fails three times in a row, one must wait a year before making the fourth attempt.

A person who has practiced law for seven years or more in another state may be admitted to practice in this state without taking the bar exam.

LEGAL ETHICS

Texas lawyers are governed by a Code of Professional Responsibility, the violation of which may subject members to disciplinary action. A brief discussion of the canons of the code follows.

Maintaining the integrity and competence of the profession. An applicant for admission to the bar must not make false statements upon his application for membership. Nor shall such an applicant deliberately fail to disclose a material fact in his application.

A bar member must not further in any way the application for admission to the bar of a person he knows is not qualified for admission.

A bar member must not engage in illegal conduct involving moral turpitude; engage in conduct involving fraud, deceit, misrepresentation, or dishonesty; obstruct the administration of justice; or violate the disciplinary rules of the profession.

A lawyer who knows of misconduct by another lawyer must report his knowledge to the proper authority, unless he is bound by the rules of privilege not to disclose it (if, for example, the information was disclosed by a client in confidence).

Making legal counsel available. A lawyer must not recommend the employment of himself or his associates through any means other than those types of advertising authorized by the State Bar of Texas. The client must seek out the lawyer; the lawyer must not seek out the client. The lawyer may speak upon legal topics or write books or articles about them, so long as he does not use the occasion to emphasize his expertise and availability for employment.

A lawyer must not charge excessive fees. Whether or not a fee is excessive is to be determined by the opinion of a lawyer of ordinary prudence, taking into account the nature of the case. Members of the profession should keep in mind that there are those who are unable to pay a reasonable fee for needed legal representation; lawyers should be willing on occasion to represent such persons, despite their inability to pay.

Acceptance of employment by a lawyer on a contingent fee basis is acceptable in most civil matters, except that one may not accept a divorce case on a contingent fee basis if the basis for the fee is the property settlement obtained. One may also not accept a criminal case upon a contingent fee basis. Contingent fees in civil litigation are acceptable because they provide access to the legal process for persons otherwise unable to pay; if the lawyer's efforts on behalf of the client are unsuccessful, he does not get paid.

A lawyer must not accept employment if he knows that his client is attempting to harass or maliciously injure a person. He also must not present a claim in litigation, or a defense in litigation, unless it is warranted in existing law or it can be justified by a good-faith argument for changing existing law. In short, a lawyer must not advance arguments in favor of his client which are bound to fail.

Once a lawyer has accepted employment, he must not withdraw from it without refunding unearned portions of his fee, returning all papers and other property of his client, and giving the client time to find another attorney.

The lawyer must withdraw from a matter if he learns that the client is merely seeking to harass or injure another party, if the lawyer is physically or mentally unable to do his best for the client, if the client discharges him, or if the lawyer's continued employment will require him to perform unethical acts. A lawyer may withdraw from a matter if his client insists upon performing illegal acts himself or insists that his lawyer perform unethical acts, if his client refuses to follow his lawyer's advice, if the client breaches an agreement with the lawyer relative to expenses or fees, or if the client otherwise makes it unreasonably difficult for the lawyer to represent him. Thus, the lawyer must give great thought to the matter before giving up an employment, but his duty to the law and to his profession comes before his duty to his client.

Until very recently all that the lawyer could do by way of advertising was to have himself listed as an attorney in the yellow pages of the telephone directory, to announce the opening or relocation of his office in the newspaper, and to have business cards giving his professional address and telephone number. Other sorts of advertising are now permissible, but the boundaries of permissible advertising have not yet been definitely determined.

Preventing unauthorized practice of law. A lawyer must not aid a non-lawyer to practice law. A lawyer may not form a partnership with a non-lawyer if part of the work of the partnership is to consist of the practice of law, nor may a lawyer share legal fees with a non-lawyer.

The borderline of the practice of law is sometimes difficult to determine. Accountants may advise their clients upon problems of taxation. Abstractors search public records in order to determine the status of real estate titles. Both do something which lawyers also do, but neither engages in the unauthorized practice of law. It is sufficient for our purposes to say that the lawyer must not share fees or offices or membership in a partnership with a non-lawyer.

Preservation of the client's confidence. Generally, a lawyer must not disclose anything that his client tells him in confidence unless the client consents to the disclosure. He also must not use such confidences for his own benefit or for the benefit of a third party. He may find it necessary to disclose such information to his law partners, or to employees of his office. He must exercise strict control over these employees to be certain that they do not make unauthorized disclosures.

This obligation does not end when the attorney-client relationship ends. In essence, the obligation of nondisclosure is a permanent one.

The obligation to honor such confidences does not apply when the client tells his lawyer of his intent to commit a crime. The lawyer then owes a duty to his profession to disclose the client's intent and to divulge such information as may prevent the crime. Confidences also may be divulged in order to establish the lawyer's right to a fee, or to collect said fee. They may also be divulged in order to protect the lawyer or his associates from charges of misconduct.

Avoiding conflict of interest. A lawyer must not accept employment in a matter in which his personal interest may affect his relationship with his client, unless he makes full disclosure of the possible conflict to his client and the client still insists upon his employment. Thus, if the lawyer is a shareholder of a corporation with which the client has a dispute, if the lawyer is a relative or friend of the party with whom the client has a dispute, or if the lawyer owns an interest in property which is the subject matter of his client's dispute with another, the lawyer should make full disclosure.

A lawyer should not agree to represent a client when his testimony, or the testimony of a member of his firm, will be essential evidence in the case. If the evidence to be given by the lawyer or member of his firm relates only to such matters as legal services provided, no conflict of interest is present. However, if the evidence is important to the outcome of the case, the lawyer must choose between the roles of advocate and witness.

A lawyer must not acquire an interest in the outcome of litigation, other than by contracting for payment of a contingent fee in a civil case or by asserting a lien upon judgment proceeds.

An attorney must not enter into a business relationship with his client unless the interests of attorney and client are identical. If the interests of attorney and client diverge, the divergence may interfere with the lawyer's representation of his client.

A lawyer should not agree to represent a client in a matter in which another client is adversely involved. So long as the interests of multiple clients are substantially the same, no problem arises. When the interests of the multiple clients diverge, the lawyer cannot represent all of them effectively due to their conflicting interests. In order to avoid this problem, the lawyer must choose which client to represent in the matter or refuse to represent any of them.

The lawyer must not allow his judgment in a case to be influenced by a person other than his client. Thus, he must not accept compensation from a non-client without the consent of his client. He must not accept gifts from non-clients under any circumstances.

Representing the client competently. An attorney must continuously study new developments in the law, so that he keeps his legal knowledge up to date. He is not under any obligation to accept any employment offered him; in fact, he must refuse to handle a matter which he knows he is not competent to handle.

Once the lawyer accepts employment, he must use his best efforts to bring the matter to a successful conclusion. He must not neglect any matter he has agreed to handle.

Under no circumstances may an attorney attempt to limit his liability to his client for malpractice. He may not escape the obligation to do the best job of which he is capable.

Limitations upon representing the client. The lawyer must do everything that he can, within the bounds of law and ethics, to help his client secure his rights. There are limitations upon what the attorney may do in representing the client, however.

The lawyer must not do anything that serves no purpose except harassing or maliciously injuring another. He must not make false statements of law or fact. He must not use false evidence, or false testimony of witnesses. He must not assist his client in the commission of fraud, or in the commission of illegal acts. If his client perpetrates a fraud upon a person or tribunal, he must try to get the client to make amends. If the client refuses to do so, the lawyer must reveal the fraud to the person or tribunal affected. Thus, the attorney-client privilege does not obligate the lawyer to conceal the illegal act or fraud of his client.

On the other hand, the attorney defending his client in a criminal prosecution is not obligated to reveal statements of his clients, even if the client has admitted guilt.

If the lawyer knows that a person with interests adverse to those of his client is represented by counsel, he must communicate with that person only through his counsel; he must not make personal contact with the other counsel's client without the counsel's knowledge and consent.

In trial work, the lawyer must abide by all rules of procedure and evidence, and he must behave in a gentlemanly manner. He must be discreet in making comments to the press or other communications media about cases in which he is involved; such comments should generally be limited to matters of public record.

The lawyer may not contact potential jurors before a trial, nor may he communicate with any member of the jury during the trial. After the trial he may contact jurors, but he must not harass or embarrass them in any way.

An attorney may not suppress evidence. He must not conceal witnesses, or offer to pay compensation to a witness if a case turns out in a specified manner. The only legitimate compensation payable to a witness is:

1. Payment of expenses incurred by testifying.
2. Compensation for time lost in testifying, lost salary, etc.
3. A reasonable professional fee for an expert witness.

Generally, the lawyer may not contact a judge outside the courtroom about a case over which the judge is presiding and in which the attorney is participating.

The lawyer may not threaten anyone with criminal prosecution merely in order to obtain an advantage in a civil matter.

A prosecuting attorney is not to act merely as an advocate for the state and to seek as many convictions as possible. He must not bring charges against someone unless he believes in the guilt of the accused. Should he discover evidence that tends to prove the innocence of the accused, or which tends to mitigate his guilt, this evidence must be revealed to the defense.

Improving the legal system. Since members of the bar administer the legal system, they should serve as models of good citizenship. As citizens they should seek to improve the operation of the legal system. When called upon to act as lobbyists, they must keep in mind the public welfare as well as the wishes of the lobbying organization. When serving as a public official, a lawyer must always place the public good above the good of himself, his family, and his former clients.

Avoidance of appearance of impropriety. The ex-judge or ex-public official who resumes the private practice of law must not accept employment in a matter upon which he has acted judicially or in his capacity as a public officer.

With respect to the handling of the money or property of his client, the lawyer must not mix funds belonging to himself or his firm with funds belonging to his clients. He must maintain a separate trust account in a bank for deposit of client funds.

He must maintain a safe deposit box or other safe depository for securities and valuables belonging to clients. He must notify clients immediately upon receipt of property belonging to them. He must keep accurate records of all client property in his possession, and he must return such property to the client upon request. It goes without saying that he must not use his client's funds or other property for personal use.

Penalties for violation of ethical rules. A violation of these rules subjects the lawyer to disciplinary action, and may cause his disbarment—the loss of his right to practice law. If the violation is also a criminal offense, he is of course also subject to criminal prosecution.

2

Texas Family Law

Some understanding of the law of the family is essential to the understanding of several aspects of business law, including the law of property, of wills and estates, and, to a degree, of contracts and agency.

In the United States, family law is almost exclusively a matter of state law. In broad outline, American family law is substantially the same in all fifty states, but in detail state laws in this area differ.

The Texas law of the family is found in the Texas Family Code and in the court decisions interpreting that legislative enactment. In this section we shall consider the law relative to the marriage relationship and to the parent-child relationship.

Texas recognizes two forms of marriage: the ceremonial marriage and the common-law marriage. We shall first consider the requisites of a valid ceremonial marriage.

Ceremonial marriage age requirements. Texas Family Code (TFC) Section 1.51 provides that a person eighteen years of age or older may marry without parental consent. Such a person must be issued a marriage license if he or she meets the other requirements.

TFC 1.52 provides that a marriage license may not be issued to a person between the ages of fourteen and eighteen unless permission to marry is given by a parent or guardian. Only one parent's consent is required, but the parent must appear in person before the county clerk and acknowledge that he or she is a parent of the applicant and that he or she is giving permission for the applicant to marry.

Sex requirements. TFC 1.01 provides that a man and a woman shall apply for a marriage license. It further states that a marriage license shall not be issued to two persons of the same sex. Thus, Texas does not recognize homosexual marriage.

The marriage license. A ceremonial marriage may not be validly performed in Texas unless the applicants possess a valid marriage license. Texas Family Code Section 1.01 (TFC 1.01) provides that such a license may be obtained from the county clerk of any county in the state.

Persons applying for a license should appear in person before the county clerk and submit the following (as per TFC 1.02):
1. Proof of identity and age, and
2. The medical examination certificate required by law, and
3. The required parental or judicial permission to marry (if the applicant is under the age of eighteen).

The applicants must complete an application for a license. The application must be in the form provided by TFC 1.03. It inquires, among other things, whether the applicant is presently married, or whether he or she has obtained a divorce within thirty days of the application; and whether or not the applicants are such close blood relatives that their marriage would be void. The applicants must swear to the truth of all information disclosed in the application.

If one of the applicants is unable to appear in person before the county clerk, he or she must submit a written affidavit answering the required questions and disclosing the required information (TFC 1.05).

The county clerk shall not issue a marriage license to the couple if:
1. Required proof of age or identity has not been submitted by one of the applicants, or
2. One or both applicants did not meet the medical examination requirements, or
3. One of the applicants is under fourteen and has not submitted a court order authorizing the marriage, or
4. One of the applicants is between the ages of fourteen and eighteen and has submitted neither parental consent to the marriage nor a court order authorizing it, or
5. One of the applicants discloses in his application that he or she is already married to someone other than the other applicant, or
6. One of the applicants discloses that he or she has been divorced within thirty days of the making of the application.

TFC 1.07 provides that the license shall be issued unless one of the above-named reasons exists for not issuing it. If one of the applicants will be unable to attend the ceremony, that person may appoint a proxy to represent him in the ceremony. If this is to be done, the name of the proxy must be noted upon the license.

The medical examination. The required medical examination consists of two parts: a physical examination by a physician licensed to practice medicine in this state, and a serological exam (blood test) done by an approved laboratory in this state. TFC 1.31 provides that the examining physician must not issue a medical certificate to an applicant if he finds that the applicant suffers from syphilis or other venereal disease. TFC 1.32 provides that the physician must state in his certificate that the applicant does not suffer from any of these diseases.

TFC 1.35 provides that the Texas Department of Public Health may require testing of female applicants to determine their immunity or lack thereof to rubella (German measles). Such testing need not be required of an applicant over fifty, or one who has undergone surgical sterilization.

The public policy justification for these requirements requires little comment. The dangers of permitting a person with active VD to marry are obvious. The danger to an unborn child when the mother contracts German measles certainly justifies the test for immunity to that disease.

TFC 1.37 provides that it is a misdemeanor to give false information in any medical exam or lab report done under the Family Code. A violator may be fined no more than $500 and no less than $200.

It is also a misdemeanor for a county clerk to issue a marriage license to persons not complying with the medical exam requirements of the Family Code. The penalties provided by TFC 1.38 are the same as above—a fine of no less than $200 nor more than $500.

Underage applicants. An applicant between the ages of fourteen and eighteen must present to the county clerk either the consent of a parent to his or her marriage, or a court

24 Introduction to Law/ I

order issued by the judge of a court of competent jurisdiction giving consent to the marriage.

TFC 1.52 provides that one parent may give the required consent; but the consent must be in writing and sworn to in person by the parent before the county clerk. An acknowledgment of the consent before an officer other than the county clerk is permissible only when the parent cannot appear before the county clerk to do it because of illness, physical incapacity, or the like.

If the parent giving consent lives out of state, the consent must be in writing and sworn to before an official of the state of residence who is authorized to administer oaths. If the parents of the applicant are deceased, or their whereabouts are unknown, a court-appointed guardian may give the required permission.

TFC 1.53 provides that the underage applicant for a marriage license may obtain such a license if he has permission to marry from a judge of a Texas district court. Such permission cannot be obtained without going through a rather lengthy process.

A petition must be filed in the county of residence of one of the petitioner's parents (or in the county of the petitioner's residence if he or she has no parent or guardian), asking for permission to marry and stating the reasons why the petitioner wants to marry. A copy of the petition must be served upon the parents or guardian. A hearing then must be held before the judge, in which the petitioner can argue why he or she should be given permission to marry and the parents or guardian may argue why such permission should not be granted. The court must appoint a guardian "ad litem" to speak for the petitioner during the hearing. No jury is used in these hearings; the hearing itself is held behind closed doors and the record of it is confidential.

The judge alone, then, decides whether or not to grant the petition for permission to marry.

An applicant for a marriage license who is under fourteen may not be granted such a license unless he or she has the permission of a Texas district judge. Parental consent is not enough to permit issuance of a marriage license to a person under fourteen years of age.

The marriage ceremony. TFC 1.83 provides that the following persons may conduct marriage ceremonies in Texas:

1. Licensed or ordained Christian ministers or priests.
2. Jewish rabbis.
3. Officers of religious organizations who are authorized by the organization to conduct marriage ceremonies.
4. Any judge of any Texas state court, excluding municipal judges but including justices of the peace, and any federal judge sitting in the state.

The marriage must be conducted within twenty-one days of the earliest medical examination of one of the applicants, according to TFC 1.81. A proxy may stand in for one of the parties, according to TFC 1.82. After the ceremony, the person conducting it should take the marriage license from the couple, note upon it the time and place of the marriage, sign it, and return it to the county clerk who issued it for recording.

It is a misdemeanor to marry persons who have no marriage license, or persons who have an expired marriage license. It is also a misdemeanor not to return the license to the county clerk who issued it for recording. The penalties for noncompliance are a fine of not less than $200 nor more than $500.

The common-law marriage. TFC 1.91 provides that a couple may prove that they are married by proving that they agreed to marry, and, after so agreeing, lived together as husband and wife and represented to the world that they were married. Thus, essentially, persons may enter into a common-law marriage by agreeing to marry and then acting as if they have married.

Because of the difficulty of proving a common-law marriage after the death of one of the spouses, TFC 1.92 provides a procedure for registering the existence of a common-law marriage with the county clerk of the county where the spouses reside. In order to accomplish the registration, the couple must fill out applications in the office of the county clerk, who asks for essentially the same information that is requested on an application for a marriage license, except that no parental or judicial permission is required for underage persons (this would serve no useful purpose since the parties are already married in common law) and no medical examination is required.

If the county clerk finds from the applications that the applicants are validly married, he will record the certificate. If he finds that they are not (because, perhaps, one "spouse" admits that he is married to someone else), there is no legal marriage and thus nothing to record.

Void, voidable, and valid marriages. Persons who marry enter into a valid marriage if no legal impediment exists to the marriage. Such a marriage is valid until terminated by the death of one of the spouses, or by divorce.

The TFC provides that a marriage is voidable if entered into under one of six circumstances, which will be discussed later. A voidable marriage is a marriage until terminated by the death of one of the spouses, by divorce, or by annulment.

When a voidable marriage is terminated by annulment, it is in a sense expunged from the record, so that legally neither party to it was ever married. A voidable marriage may not be declared invalid by a court except in a suit for divorce or annulment brought by a proper party.

The TFC provides two grounds for declaring a marriage void. A void marriage is in many respects no marriage at all; it will terminate by the death of a spouse, or by divorce, or by annulment. It may also be declared void by a court in proceedings other than divorce or annulment proceedings. Thus, in probate proceedings, a court may deny the supposed widow of the deceased the right to inherit from her supposed husband because her marriage to him was void.

Void marriage—one spouse already married to someone else. Human beings have devised several forms of marriage during their habitation upon this earth. Monogamy, the marriage of one man to one woman, is the only form which has received legal sanction in Western society, including Texas. A person may be married to only one spouse at a time.

Once contracted, a marriage continues to exist until it is dissolved. The only permissible means of dissolution are the death of a spouse and termination by court action—divorce or annulment. This rule is true even of common-law marriages. For that reason it is much easier to contract a common-law marriage than it is to dissolve one. Thus, TFC 2.22 provides that a marriage entered into during the existence of a prior marriage is void.

Two rules mitigate the severity of this, however. If Betty marries Bill before her former marriage to Paul is terminated, her marriage to Bill is void. However, if Paul dies, and Bill and Betty have been living together as husband and wife up to that time, they now enter into a common-law marriage; their marriage is now valid.

The second mitigating rule may be illustrated by an example. Pete and Polly married in 1935. They broke up housekeeping and separated in 1946. Pete thought Polly was going to divorce him. Polly thought Pete was going to divorce her. Neither actually divorced the other. In 1951 Pete married Sandra, thinking he was free to do so because, surely, Polly had divorced him by now. In 1976 Pete died, by will leaving all his property to Sandra. Polly, still alive, still undivorced, and still not associating with another man, reads of Pete's death in the newspapers, and finds out that Pete had become well-to-do. So, Polly now shows up and declares that she is Pete's true widow, and that she is entitled to a large slice of his estate. If it is true that Pete and Polly were never divorced, Polly is absolutely correct.

However, TFC 2.01 provides that in a case like this, where two persons claim to be married to the same spouse, the later marriage is presumed to be valid. The burden of proof lies upon the party claiming the later marriage is void. Thus, in our example Polly must prove that Pete's marriage to Sandra is void. If she cannot do this, Sandra is Pete's lawful widow, not Polly.

Polly may have some problems. She could prove that she did not divorce Pete, but to prove that Pete never divorced her would be much harder. If she could provide a complete history of Pete's life since he left her, including all his addresses, and could prove that Pete never filed for divorce against her in any of his localities of residence, she could win. If she could not fill in all the gaps in Pete's history, she could not win. Sandra will get the benefit of any doubts.

Putative marriages and meretricious relationships. The doctrine of putative marriage to a degree lessens the harshness of the general rule that a second marriage is void if entered into before the death of a first spouse or the dissolution of a first marriage. If, in the above example, Polly can prove beyond a doubt that Sandra's marriage to Paul was void, but Sandra can prove that she married Paul in the true belief that she contracted a valid marriage, the court will treat the marriage between Sandra and Paul as a putative marriage. Sandra will to a degree be treated as Paul's widow.

Parties to a putative marriage are not legally married. However, the courts consider that the parties do accumulate community property. Thus, in the above example, Sandra would have an interest in Paul's earnings after the commencement of their putative marriage; she would be entitled to half of any bank accounts containing such earnings, and to at least half of the value of any assets purchased with such earnings. A putative widow thus will not be denied the right to inherit from her putative husband's estate if he died intestate.

On the other hand, had Sandra known that her "marriage" to Paul was void, the courts would consider the "marriage" to be a meretricious relationship. In such a case, Sandra and Paul would not be said to have accumulated community property, and Sandra would normally be entitled to inherit nothing from Paul if he died intestate. However, if the rigor of this rule would work hardship on Sandra, the courts might, through use of mental gymnastics, consider the Paul-Sandra relationship to be a form of partnership, thus granting Sandra an interest in assets which would be considered community assets of a married couple.

Thus, a partner to a void marriage may under some circumstances have property rights in the estate of a deceased partner.

Presumption of death. RCS 5541 states that a person absenting himself for seven years consecutively shall be presumed to be dead, unless proof is made that he was alive within that time. This article also states that when a certificate is issued by any branch of the armed forces declaring a person to be dead, the person in question is presumed to have died on the date stated in the certificate.

A spouse may take advantage of the provisions of this statute to have the estate of the presumed decedent probated. In the course of this process, of course, the probate court will declare the absent spouse to be dead. This declaration will have the effect of removing legal impediments to the remarriage of the petitioning spouse. Thus, if the spouse has religious scruples against divorce, the marriage may in a sense be terminated without the necessity of divorce proceedings, and remarriage could take place with an almost clear conscience.

Though the remarried spouse could not be guilty of bigamy even if the person who was declared dead returned, some very sticky personal and legal problems could arise in such a case. The second marriage would in all probability be void because the original spouse was still alive—and the original spouse would have the right to reclaim at least some of his or her property.

Fortunately, such "Enoch Arden" situations are rare.

Void marriage: consanguinity. TFC 2.21 provides that marriages between persons who are very close blood relatives are void. The marriages forbidden under this section include marriages between:

1. Ancestors and descendants, by blood or adoption. This includes marriages between mother-son, father-daughter, grandmother-grandson, grandfather-granddaughter. An adoptive father may also not marry an adoptive daughter. The reason here is that the Family Code treats adoptive children as natural children.
2. Brothers and sisters, by whole blood, half blood, or adoption.
3. A parent's brother or sister, of the whole or half blood. Thus, an uncle may not marry his niece, nor may an aunt marry her nephew.
4. A son or daughter of a brother or sister, by whole or half blood or by adoption.

The Texas rules on consanguinity are less restrictive than the rules existing in some other states. Marriages between first cousins are forbidden in some states, but not in Texas. Thus Bob may marry Jean, the daughter of his uncle Tom. Marriages between in-laws are forbidden in some states, but not in Texas. Thus, if Tom's wife Sylvia dies and Tom would like to marry Sylvia's sister Bonita, he may do so.

Voidable marriage: underage. The marriage of a person who is under the age of fourteen is voidable unless the person had obtained a court order permitting the marriage. The marriage of a person between the ages of fourteen and eighteen is voidable if that person did not obtain parental permission for the marriage or a court order permitting it. Such marriages may be annulled under the provisions of TFC 2.41.

The following persons may bring suit to annul a marriage of a person fourteen years of age or younger:

1. The underage person himself (or herself), acting through an adult next friend, if the suit is brought within ninety days after the fourteenth birthday of the underage party.
2. A parent, guardian, or managing conservator of the underage party; such suit must be brought any time before the fourteenth birthday of the underage person, or, if brought after said person's fourteenth birthday, must be brought within ninety days after the petitioner knew or should have known of the marriage.

The following persons may bring suit to annul a marriage of a person between the ages of fourteen and eighteen contracted without proper consent:

1. The underage party himself (or herself), acting through an adult next friend, if the suit is brought within ninety days after the date of the marriage.
2. The parent, guardian, or managing conservator of the underage party, if the suit is brought within ninety days after the petitioner knew or should have known of the marriage.

The adult spouse in a marriage involving an underage person has no right to annul.

The judge hearing a suit to annul a marriage due to the underage of one of the spouses need not decree an annulment, if in his discretion he feels that annulment is not in the best interest of all parties. Among the factors he may take into account in exercising his discretion is the matter of whether or not the wife is pregnant.

Voidable marriage contracted under influence of alcohol or narcotics. TFC 2.42 provides that a party may sue to annul a marriage if, at the time of the marriage, he was so under the influence of drugs or alcohol that he (or she) had no capacity to consent to the marriage; and if, after the effects of the alcohol or narcotics ended, he or she did not voluntarily cohabit with the other party.

Only the spouse who was under the influence at the time of the marriage may sue to annul, and then only if the alcohol or drug had so deprived him of his senses that he did not know what he was doing at the time of the ceremony.

Such a marriage is ratified if the party under the influence at the time of the marriage acts like a spouse after his senses return.

Voidable marriage: impotency. Under TFC 2.43, a marriage may be annulled if:
1. Either spouse is permanently impotent at the time of the marriage, and
2. Petitioner did not know this at the time of the marriage, and
3. Petitioner has not voluntarily cohabited with the other spouse since learning of the impotency.

Voidable marriage: fraud, duress, or force. TFC 2.44 provides that a person who is tricked into marriage through fraud, or who is forced into it, may sue for annulment if he or she has not voluntarily cohabited with the other party since learning of the fraud, or has not voluntarily cohabited after the duress or force has been relieved.

The type of fraud that will justify annulment of a marriage must relate to the essentials of the marriage relationship. If the fraud involves pregnancy, ability to procreate, concealment of venereal disease, concealment of homosexuality, or concealment of an intent to marry for a limited purpose (such as ease of immigration into the U.S. or ease of access to the money of the other spouse), the fraud may well justify annulment. If the fraud is a matter of lesser import—lies about age, concealment of the fact that one wears dentures, lies about one's financial status, etc.—annulment will be much more difficult.

When duress or force is claimed as grounds for annulment, the duress or force must consist of something more than a threat to do what one has a right to do. Thus, if John marries Mary because Mary told John, "If you don't marry me I'm going to file a paternity suit against you and have you declared to be the father of the child I'm carrying," John is not a victim of duress. He could be a victim of fraud, though, if he is not the father of the child and Mary knows it.

On the other hand, if John marries Mary because Mary's father pointed a .45 automatic at him and said, "You agree to marry my daughter or else I pull the trigger," this of course is duress.

Voidable marriage: mental incompetency. TFC 2.45 provides that either party to a marriage may seek an annulment when one of the parties suffers from a mental disease or defect.

The incompetent party may sue when:
1. He or she did not have the mental capacity to consent to marriage or to understand the nature of the marriage relationship, and
2. He or she has not cohabited with the other spouse during periods of lucidity when he or she understands the nature of marriage.

Normally the incompetent party will sue through a next friend. He or she would not have the capacity to conduct a lawsuit on his or her own.

The competent party may sue when:

1. At the time of the marriage the incompetent party did not have the mental capacity to consent to marriage or to understand the nature of the marriage relationship, and
2. At the time of the marriage the petitioner neither knew nor reasonably should have known of the other's incompetence, and
3. Petitioner has not voluntarily cohabited with the other party since he or she knew or should have known of the other's mental disease or defect.

Obviously, it is difficult for the competent spouse to meet this burden of proof.

Voidable marriage: concealed divorce. TFC 2.46 provides that a marriage is voidable if one of the parties to it was divorced from a third party within the thirty-day period preceding the day of the marriage ceremony, if at the time of the ceremony the other party did not know, and a reasonably prudent person would not have known, of the divorce; and if, after discovery of the concealed divorce, the innocent party did not voluntarily cohabit with the other party.

A suit for annulment on this ground must be brought by the innocent party within one year of the date of the marriage.

Irregularities not rendering a marriage void or voidable. TFC 2.01 declares it to be state policy to presume the validity of existing marriages. Thus, irregularities in the obtaining of a marriage license or in the conduct of a marriage ceremony will not affect the validity of a marriage.

Any fraud, mistake, or illegality involved in the obtaining of a marriage license will not render the marriage itself invalid, unless the fraud, mistake, or illegality was of a nature which concealed a void or voidable marriage (TFC 2.02).

A ceremonial marriage conducted by a person with no authority to conduct it is valid if the person reasonably appeared to have the required authority, and if at least one party to the marriage ceremony went through it in good faith and treated the marriage as valid.

In any event, if the parties live together as husband and wife, and if the marriage is not void because of a prior marriage or consanguinity, a valid common-law marriage will exist.

Effect of the death of a spouse upon a voidable marriage. TFC 2.47 provides that the death of a party to a voidable marriage will in essence validate the marriage. As a result, the following may occur: Bonnie, age sixteen, marries Jack, age twenty-one, without the consent of her parents. The day after the wedding, Jack is killed in an auto accident. Bonnie's parents claim that Bonnie is not Jack's widow because the marriage was voidable. They are wrong. Though they could have sued to annul the marriage while Jack lived, they cannot dispute the validity of the marriage after he is dead.

If, on the other hand, Jack had been validly married to Mary at the time he married Bonnie, Bonnie's parents could still claim that Bonnie was not Jack's widow. Since the marriage in this situation is void, not voidable, its validity may be questioned even after Jack's death.

Divorce, in general. The only way to terminate a valid marriage while both spouses are alive is through divorce. The only way a party to a voidable marriage who cannot sue for annulment may terminate his marriage is through divorce. The Texas Family Code enumerates seven grounds for divorce, the meaning of which will now be discussed.

Divorce: insupportability. This is by far the most commonly used ground for divorce. TFC 3.01 provides that either party to a marriage, without regard to fault, may petition for divorce if the marriage has become insupportable because of discord or conflict of personalities that destroys the legitimate ends of the marriage relationship and prevents any reasonable expectation of a reconciliation.

This is the Texas version of no-fault divorce. It amounts to legitimizing divorce on demand; if a married person is unhappy with his or her marriage he or she can well argue that there is such discord or personality conflict within the marriage relationship that the relationship no longer serves its legitimate purpose.

It may well be that this ground is more attuned to human nature than are the more traditional grounds based upon supposed wrongdoing by one of the spouses. Discord and personality conflict need not arise from the wrongdoing of one spouse: they may arise from wrongs committed by neither or both.

Divorce: cruelty. This was probably the most common ground for divorce in the days before no-fault divorce. TFC 3.02 provides that cruel treatment by a spouse is grounds for divorce if it is of such a nature as to render further living together insupportable.

Traditionally, cruelty consisted of acts of physical violence or abuse. The meaning of the concept has progressively broadened, however, until deliberate inconsiderate behavior by one spouse toward the other could be defined as cruelty. Of course, only the victim of the alleged cruelty could sue for divorce upon that ground. It would be a defense of the charge if the defendant could prove lack of cruel treatment of the plaintiff.

Divorce: adultery. Traditionally this has been a permissible ground for divorce in even the most conservative of jurisdictions. TFC 3.03 provides that this is a ground for divorce without going into any detail. Plaintiff must prove an act of adultery by defendant. It is a defense if defendant can prove the alleged adultery never occurred.

Divorce: conviction of felony. TFC 3.04 provides that a spouse may obtain a divorce upon this ground when:

1. The defendant has been convicted of a felony, and
2. He or she has been imprisoned in a state or federal penitentiary for at least one year, and
3. He or she has not been pardoned.

However, the defendant in such a case must not have been convicted of the felony on the testimony of the plaintiff. Thus, Jane cannot get rid of Jim as a husband by making certain that he gets convicted of a felony and sent to Huntsville, and then divorcing him after he has been there for a year. (If Jane can get him sent to Huntsville without the necessity of her testimony aiding in the conviction, though, this can be done.)

Divorce: abandonment. TFC 3.05 provides that a spouse has grounds for divorce if the other spouse moves out with the intent to abandon the relationship and remains away for at least one year. Thus, if John takes off in July 1977 and tells Mary, "Goodbye forever—you'll never see me again!" and he has not shown up again by July 1978, Mary has grounds for divorce.

Divorce: living apart. TFC 3.06 says that when spouses have lived apart for three years without cohabitation, either spouse may obtain a divorce. In a sense this is a no-fault ground, because it does not matter why the parties have lived apart for three years.

Divorce: confinement in a mental hospital. According to TFC 3.07, a person may obtain a divorce when his or her spouse has been confined in a public or private mental hospital for at least three years, if it appears that the nature of the mental disorder is such that the spouse will not adjust, or, if he does adjust, that he will suffer a relapse. In short, the mental disorder which has caused the confinement must be virtually incurable.

Some aspects of divorce and annulment litigation. Matters regarding jurisdiction and venue in divorce and annulment litigation will be discussed in the materials on civil procedure. Matters regarding marital property will be discussed in the materials on co-ownership of property. Other aspects of the litigation will be discussed here.

A petition for divorce must state whether or not there are children under the age of eighteen born or adopted of the marriage. If there are, the fate of the children is to be considered during the litigation, as per TFC 3.55.

The court may require, in its discretion, that the spouses consult a marriage counselor during the pendency of the proceedings. The judge may also grant a continuance of the court proceedings if he feels that there is a possibility of reconciliation. These powers are granted by TFC 3.54.

During a divorce or annulment case, either spouse may request an inventory and appraisement of property in the hands of another party—usually property in the possession of the other spouse, though the possessor need not necessarily be the other spouse if the property in question is the marital property of the spouses. A party may also request and obtain an injunction forbidding the other spouse or another named party from disposing of alleged marital property. These matters are enumerated in TFC 3.56.

According to TFC 3.57, while divorce or annulment litigation is pending a spouse may not transfer community property nor create a debt encumbering community property if the purpose would be to injure the rights of the other spouse.

While divorce or annulment litigation is pending the court may order the husband to make temporary payments for support of the wife. The wife may also be ordered to make temporary payments for the support of the husband, if the husband cannot support himself. TFC 3.59 covers these matters. TFC 11.05 authorizes temporary child support orders at this time also.

According to TFC 3.60, a decree of divorce shall not be granted until at least sixty days after the filing of the divorce petition.

When the divorce decree is granted, the court may divide the marital property of the spouses as it deems proper, considering the ability of the parties to support themselves and the custody of the children of the marriage, as per TFC 3.63. TFC 3.64 also authorizes the court to restore to the wife the use of her maiden name, if she so wishes.

Nature of the husband-wife relationship. Every married person in the state of Texas is an adult, at least for the purpose of making contracts (TFC 4.03).

Each spouse has the duty to support his or her minor children. The husband has the duty to support the wife, and the wife has the reciprocal duty to support her husband when he cannot support himself. A spouse who does not abide by his duty to support is liable to any third person who furnishes necessities to those he is obligated to support.

Nature of the parent-child relationship. TFC 12.04 provides that the parent of a child has the following rights, privileges, duties, and powers:

1. The right to physical possession of the child, and the right to establish its domicile (legal residence).
2. The duty of care, control, protection, moral and religious training, and reasonable discipline.
3. The duty to support, including the provision of clothing, food, shelter, medical care, and education.
4. The duty to manage the child's property, except when a guardian of the child's estate has been appointed.

5. The right to the services and earnings of the child.
6. The power to consent to marriage, enlistment in the U.S. armed forces, and to medical, psychiatric, and surgical treatment.
7. The power to represent the child in legal actions, and the power to make other legal decisions of significance to the child.
8. The power to receive and give receipt for payments for the support of the child and to hold or disburse funds for the benefit of the child.
9. The right to inherit from and through the child.

Thus, parents are given control over most aspects of the lives of their children, and also have many duties with respect to the present and future well-being of their children.

Legitimacy. The concept of legitimacy is important in two respects. An individual has no duty to support an illegitimate child, and an individual may not inherit from or through an illegitimate child. Neither may the illegitimate child inherit from or through its father.

A mother, strictly speaking, may not bear an illegitimate child. TFC 12.01 flatly provides that any child is the legitimate child of its mother. A male may well father an illegitimate child, however. A child is the legitimate child of the father if:

1. The child is born or conceived during or before the marriage of its father and mother, or
2. The child's father and mother have attempted to marry, though the marriage is or might be declared to be void, and the child is born or conceived during or before the attempted marriage, or
3. Court action has determined that the father is indeed the father of the child, or the father has filed a statement of paternity.

Of course, if the child is not legitimate by the above definition (TFC 12.02), it is illegitimate.

A somewhat common plot complication in soap operas—and, perhaps, an occasional happening in the real world—is the case of the married woman who has a child fathered by a man other than her husband while she is married. Is such a child illegitimate?

The answer is that the child of a married woman is presumed to be the child of her husband. If the husband could prove that the child is not his, then, perhaps, it would be branded illegitimate with respect to him. The difficulty of doing this would be so great, however, that it would almost certainly not be worth the effort. The law will bend far, far backward in order to avoid branding the child of a married woman as illegitimate.

Conservatorship, possession, and support of children. Chapter 14 of the TFC contains the law here. It is too complex to cover in detail, but a summary is necessary. When the parents of a child commence litigation to dissolve their marriage, the court must appoint a managing conservator for this child, the conservator being in essence the person or agency having custody of the child. TFC 14.01 mandates the appointment of the conservator, and further provides that the conservator shall be a parent unless the court finds that appointment of a parent would not be in the child's best interests. The sex of the parent shall have no weight in the decision as to which to appoint as conservator. If the parents have voluntarily agreed who should be conservator, the court will go along, if the agreement is in the child's best interests. A non-parent or an agency may be appointed conservator when the court feels that neither parent is qualified.

TFC 14.05 provides that either or both parents may be ordered to support the child. The duty to support will terminate upon court order, or when the child reaches the age of eighteen or marries. It will also terminate upon the death of the parent ordered to furnish the support. If the child is possessed of such disabilities that it cannot support itself after it reaches adulthood, continued support may be ordered, even though the child is now an adult.

A child fourteen years of age or older may choose his or her own managing conservator, according to TFC 14.07, subject to the approval of the court. Refusal to pay child support as per a court order is punishable as contempt of court. A claim for unpaid child support may also be reduced to a judgment and collected as other judgments are, as per TFC 14.09.

Termination of the parent-child relationship. A parent may, by following proper procedure, terminate his relationship to a child, if a court feels this to be in the child's best interest. The parent-child relationship may also be involuntarily terminated if the court feels that involuntary termination is in the child's best interest.

Involuntary termination. A petition for involuntary termination of a parent-child relationship may be granted if:

1. The parent has left the child alone or in the possession of another person not the parent and has expressed an intention not to return.
2. The parent has voluntarily left the child alone or with another person not the parent without expressing intent to return and without providing adequate support for the child, and has remained away for at least three months.
3. The parent has voluntarily left the child alone or with another not the parent, and has expressed an intent to return, but has not provided adequate support and has remained away for at least six months.
4. The parent has knowingly placed or knowingly allowed the child to remain in conditions or surroundings which endanger the physical or emotional well-being of the child.
5. The parent has engaged in conduct or knowingly placed the child with persons who engaged in conduct endangering the physical or emotional well-being of the child.
6. The parent has failed to support the child in accordance with his ability for a period of one year ending within six months of the filing of the petition.
7. The parent has abandoned the child without identifying the child or furnishing it with a means of identification, and the child's identity cannot be ascertained by exercise of reasonable diligence. (Here, of course, the defaulting parent will be unknown and unidentifiable.)
8. The father voluntarily and with knowledge of her pregnancy abandoned the mother of the child before birth and has remained apart from mother and child since, not supporting the mother before birth and not supporting mother and child after birth.
9. The parent has been the major cause of the child not being enrolled in school.
10. The parent has been the major cause of the child running away from home without the consent of its parents or guardian for a substantial length of time, or without intent to return.
11. The parent has executed an affidavit of relinquishment of parental rights.
12. A report of abuse of the child has been received, and the parent refuses to obey a court order relevant to an investigation of the alleged abuse.

The above is provided for by TFC 15.01.

A petition for involuntary termination of parental rights may be filed before the birth of a child after the first trimester of the mother's pregnancy. No hearing may be held on the petition until the child is at least five days old, however (TFC 15.021).

Voluntary termination. A parent desiring to relinquish parental rights in a child must file an affidavit after the birth of the child, witnessed by two credible persons, and verified before an officer authorized to take oaths, containing the information required by TFC 15.03. No parent who is under a court order to support the child may normally file such an affidavit. The affidavit may name a person or state agency as managing conservator of the child. It may also contain a consent for the child to be placed for adoption by a proper state agency.

If the child is illegitimate with respect to the father, the mother shall execute an affidavit of status of the child, providing the information required by TFC 15.04, including information as to the name and whereabouts of the father, if known. This affidavit may be executed any time after the first trimester of pregnancy.

A father may execute an affidavit of waiver of interest in a child. He may as a part of the affidavit deny paternity and/or sexual relationship with the mother. This affidavit cannot be used, however, as evidence of non-paternity in a suit filed for the purpose of establishing that the affiant is the father of the child. The above provisions are found in TFC 15.041.

TFC 15.05 declares that the parent-child relationship may be terminated only by court decree. If the relationship is terminated with respect to both parents, or with respect to the only living parent, the court must appoint a managing conservator for the child. The parent whose rights are being terminated must be mentioned by name, except in the case of the child of an unknown father. The rights of such a father in the child may in effect be terminated in absentia.

The handing down of a decree severing a parent-child relationship severs all legal relations between parent and child except the right of the child to inherit from and through the parent, unless the decree severs this relationship also, as provided by TFC 15.07.

Involuntary termination of a parent-child relationship may come about because of the unwillingness or inability of the parent to care for the child, or it may happen because of the desire of outside parties to adopt the child. If the termination is sought by the state, the child will most likely become a ward of the state for a period. If it is sought by an individual, it will probably result in adoption. The rights of the father of an illegitimate child may be terminated upon the initiative of the mother incidental to giving up the child for adoption.

Voluntary termination is, more often than not, a result of the effort of a mother to give the child up for adoption. It often occurs also when the child's father and mother are divorced, if the mother obtains custody, later remarries, and her new husband desires to adopt.

Adoption. Any child residing in Texas may be adopted, and any adult residing in Texas may adopt, as per TFC 16.01 and 16.02.

A person desiring to adopt need not be married. However, if a married person desires to adopt, his or her spouse must join in the petition to adopt. Adoption may take place only through court action.

A petition for adoption of a child will not be granted unless the rights of the parents in the child to be adopted have been terminated. If these rights were terminated before the filing of the adoption petition, this must be alleged and proven in court. If the rights of the parents have not been terminated at the time of the filing of the petition, said petition must ask for the termination of these rights. In case one of the parents is married to the petitioner for adoption (which is the case when, for instance, a stepfather seeks to adopt the child of his wife and her husband by a prior marriage), that parent's rights will of course not be terminated. The above provisions are found in TFC 16.03.

Normally a petition for adoption will not be granted until the child has lived with the petitioner for at least six months, as per TFC 16.04. However, the residence requirement can be waived if the court feels the waiver to be in the child's best interest.

If the child has a managing conservator, that person's consent to an adoption is required, unless it is withheld or revoked for no good cause. If the child is twelve years of age or older, his consent to the adoption is also necessary, unless the court feels that the adoption is in his best interest even if he does not consent (TFC 16.05).

According to TFC 16.09, the effect of an adoption decree is to establish the same parent-child relationship between the child and the adoptive parents that would have existed had the child been born to the adoptive parents during marriage.

It must be emphasized that the only way to adopt a child is through court proceedings. The fact that a child has grown up in the home of adults and the adults have treated the child as their own does not mean that the child has been adopted. Legally, such a child is still the child of his biological parents. He may inherit from and through his biological parents, but he may not inherit by and through his foster parents.

It must also be emphasized that a child may not legally have two sets of parents. This means that the adopted child has had all relations severed with his biological parents; a decree of adoption will at the same time sever the right of the adoptive child to inherit from and through his biological parents.

Adoption of adults. Any Texas adult may adopt any other Texas adult. The consent of the person being adopted is essential to the process. No termination of the relationship of the adoptee to his biological parents is required. The adoptee may inherit from both his adoptive parents and his biological parents, but his biological parents may not inherit from or through him. TFC sections 16.51 through 16.55 govern adoption of adults.

Children conceived through artificial insemination. TFC 12.03 provides that a child conceived through artificial insemination is the legitimate child of the mother's spouse, no matter who the donor of the semen was. The donor has no parental rights in the child. This has been a sore spot in litigation in some other states, but the Texas legislature has provided a clear solution to any problems.

3

Texas Criminal Law

Criminal law affecting business has been enacted at both the federal and state levels. Most of the criminal law of Texas is found in the Texas Penal Code (PC). The federal law is scattered through the many Congressional enactments on various subjects. In this chapter basic provisions of Texas criminal law will be presented.

Classification of offenses. The Penal Code divides crimes into two major categories: misdemeanors and felonies. It further divides misdemeanors into three subcategories: Class A, Class B, and Class C. It divides felonies into four subcategories: capital, first degree, second degree, and third degree.

The range of punishments authorized by the PC for the various classifications of offenses is as follows:

Capital felony: life imprisonment or death. (PC 12.31).

First-degree felony: imprisonment for no more than ninety-nine years and no less than five years and/or a fine not to exceed $10,000 (PC 12.32).

Second-degree felony: no more than twenty years and no less than two years imprisonment, and/or a fine not to exceed $10,000 (PC 12.33).

Third-degree felony: imprisonment of no more than ten years and no less than two years, and/or a fine not to exceed $5,000 (PC 12.34).

Class A misdemeanor: jail for term not to exceed one year and/or a fine not to exceed $2,000 (PC 12.21).

Class B misdemeanor: jail for term not to exceed 180 days, and/or fine not to exceed $1,000 (PC 12.22).

Class C misdemeanor: fine not to exceed $200 (PC 12.23).

Imprisonment for felonies must be in an institution of the Texas Department of Corrections. Imprisonment for misdemeanors must be in a county jail or similar institution. Notice that the PC provides a mandatory minimum felony sentence, but provides no such mandatory minimum for misdemeanors.

PC 12.42 provides for heavier sentences for repeat and habitual felony offenders. If a person already convicted of one felony is convicted of another, the following rules apply:

1. If the second offense is a third-degree felony, punishment shall be for a second-degree felony.

2. If the second offense is a second-degree felony, punishment shall be for a first-degree felony.
3. If the second offense is a first-degree felony, punishment shall be imprisonment for no more than ninety-nine years and no less than fifteen years.

If a person already convicted of two felonies is convicted of another, and he was convicted of the second after his conviction for the first became final (that is, after all appeals had been considered), punishment shall be life imprisonment.

PC 12.43 provides for heavier penalties for repeat misdemeanor offenses. If a person convicted of a Class A misdemeanor has already been convicted of another Class A misdemeanor or of a felony, his punishment shall be jail for no more than one year and no less than 90 days. If a person convicted of a Class B misdemeanor has already been convicted of another Class B misdemeanor, Class A misdemeanor, or felony, his punishment shall be jail for no more than 180 days and no less than 30 days.

PC 12.44 provides that a court may set aside a verdict of guilt of a third-degree felony and substitute for it a judgment of guilt of a Class A misdemeanor if the court feels that this would best serve the ends of justice, considering the background and rehabilitation potential of the defendant.

Murder. PC 19.02 provides that a person commits murder if:
1. He intentionally or knowingly causes the death of a person, or
2. He intends to cause someone serious bodily injury and commits an act dangerous to human life which results in the death of someone, or
3. He kills someone by committing an act dangerous to human life in the course of committing or attempting to commit a felony other than manslaughter, or in the course of flight from the commission of a felony or attempt to commit one.

Murder is a first-degree felony.

Capital murder. Murder is capital murder when:
1. The victim is a peace officer or fireman doing his duty, and the murderer knows that, or
2. The murder is intentionally committed in the course of committing or attempting to commit kidnapping, burglary, robbery, aggravated rape, or arson, or
3. The murderer killed for remuneration or promise of remuneration; or the accused paid or promised to pay the murderer to kill, or
4. The murderer was escaping or attempting to escape from a penal institution, or
5. The murderer was a prisoner and killed an employee of the prison.

Capital murder is a capital felony (PC 19.03).

Voluntary manslaughter. A person commits voluntary manslaughter if he kills under the influence of sudden passion for adequate cause. In short, the killer loses his head because he was angered or enraged by some cause that would anger or enrage a normal person. The killing is thus not premeditated.

PC 19.04 declares this to be a second-degree felony.

Involuntary manslaughter. A person is guilty of involuntary manslaughter when he:
1. Recklessly causes the death of another, or
2. Kills another by accident or mistake while guilty of driving while intoxicated.

PC 19.05 declares this to be a third-degree felony.

Criminally negligent homicide. He who kills another through negligence is guilty of criminally negligent homicide. PC 19.07 declares this to be a Class A misdemeanor.

Kidnapping. A person is guilty of kidnapping if he intentionally or knowingly abducts another, unless:
1. There was no intent or threat to use deadly force, or

2. The person abducted was a relative, and
3. The abductor's sole purpose was to assure lawful conduct by the victim.

PC 20.03 declares this to be a third-degree felony.

Aggravated kidnapping: Intentional and knowing abduction of a person is aggravated kidnapping if done with intent to:
1. Hold victim for ransom or reward, or
2. Use victim as a shield or hostage, or
3. Facilitate commission of a felony or flight from commission of a felony, or
4. Inflict bodily injury or sexual abuse upon victim, or
5. Terrorize victim or a third person, or
6. Interfere with performance of a governmental or political function.

This is a first-degree felony unless the actor voluntarily releases the victim alive and in a safe place, in which case it is a second-degree felony (PC 20.04).

False imprisonment. Anyone who intentionally or knowingly restrains another without abducting him commits this offense. Such restraint is lawful when:
1. The person restrained is under fourteen years of age, and
2. The actor is a relative of the child, and
3. The restraint is solely to permit the actor to assume lawful control over the victim.

Detention in the course of effecting a lawful arrest or in the course of detaining a lawfully arrested person is lawful.

The offense is a Class B misdemeanor, unless the actor recklessly exposed the victim to substantial risk of severe bodily injury, in which case it is a third-degree felony (PC 20.02).

Sexual offenses. Chapter 21 of the Penal Code defines numerous sexual offenses. Without exploring this in detail, the following may be said:

Sexual intercourse with an adult woman not one's wife without her consent is rape, a second-degree felony.

Rape accompanied by severe bodily injury to the victim, or by attempt to cause such injury, or by threat to cause such injury, or by threat of kidnapping, is aggravated rape, a first-degree felony.

Homosexual conduct is a Class C misdemeanor.

This chapter of the Penal Code describes numerous other sexual offenses, the details of which we shall not pursue.

Arson. PC 28.02, which contains the law on this offense, was completely rewritten by the 1979 session of the legislature. The revision considerably broadened the definition of the offense.

A person commits arson when he starts a fire or causes an explosion with intent to destroy any building, habitation, or vehicle when he knows that:
1. It is within the limits of an incorporated city or town, or
2. It is insured against damage or destruction, or
3. It is subject to a mortgage or other security interest, or
4. It is located on property belonging to another, or
5. It has within it property belonging to another.

If the person causing the fire or explosion is careless about whether the burning or explosion endangers the person or property of another, he is also guilty of this offense.

The burning or demolition of a building located within the limits of an incorporated city or town is not arson just because of the building's location if the actor has a proper city permit for destruction of the building.

In the past, only the burning of buildings could be arson. Under the revised Texas statute, one can also commit arson by burning a motor vehicle.

Traditionally, one could not commit arson by burning down one's own building. Now, burning one's own building is arson if the building is insured or mortgaged, or if it contains the property of others, or if it is located in an incorporated city or town and is burned without possession of a proper permit.

The offense is a second-degree felony unless someone is injured by the fire or explosion, in which case it is a first-degree felony.

Criminal mischief. PC 28.03 defines criminal mischief as the intentional or knowing damaging or destruction of the tangible property of another, or the intentional or knowing tampering with the tangible property of another which causes substantial pecuniary loss or substantial inconvenience to the owner of the property or to a third person.

The degree of the offense depends upon the type and value of property involved. The offense is:

A Class C misdemeanor if pecuniary loss is less than $5.
A Class B misdemeanor if pecuniary loss is less than $20 but more than $5.
A Class C misdemeanor if pecuniary loss is less than $200 but more than $20.
A third-degree felony if:
  Pecuniary loss is less than $10,000 but more than $200, or
  Impairment of public service was caused, or
  Injury to one or more head of cattle, sheep, swine, or goats was caused, or
  A fence used for production of above animals was involved, or
  One or more head of the above animals was branded.
A second-degree felony if amount of pecuniary loss was more than $10,000.

Intentional horseplay resulting in property damage is hereby made a criminal offense. Such "fun and games" as tampering with another person's automobile so that it won't start is a commission of this offense, if the owner suffers pecuniary loss or inconvenience because of it.

Reckless damage or destruction. PC 28.04 provides that a person guilty of reckless damage to or destruction of property of another commits a Class C misdemeanor.

It is of course no criminal offense to destroy one's own property. But if the property is co-owned by the actor and another person an offense is committed, unless all co-owners participate in or consent to the destruction (PC 28.05).

Theft. PC 31.03 provides that a person commits theft if he unlawfully appropriates property with the intent to deprive the owner of it. The appropriation is unlawful if it is done without the owner's consent, or if the property is stolen and the actor appropriates it knowing that it was stolen by another.

The classification of the offense depends upon the value and nature of the stolen property. The offense is:

A Class C misdemeanor if value is under $5.
A Class B misdemeanor if value is less than $20 but $5 or more.
A Class A misdemeanor if value is less than $200 but $20 or more.
A third degree felony if:
  Value is less than $10,000, but $200 or more, or
  Property includes cattle, horses, sheep, swine or goats of value under $10,000, or
  Property is stolen from the person of another, or from a corpse, or from a grave, or

Value of property is under $200, but defendant has already been convicted of theft two or more times (regardless of degree).

A second-degree felony if value is $10,000 or over.

The Penal Code definition of theft is now very broad. It encompasses several formerly separate offenses, such as theft by false pretext, conversion by bailee, theft from the person, shoplifting, acquisition of property by threat, swindling, swindling by worthless check, embezzlement, extortion, receiving or concealing embezzled property, and receiving or concealing stolen property.

Anyone who sneakily takes another's property from his yard is of course a thief. So are pickpockets and shoplifters, confidence men, and persons who borrow items and never return them (after the owner has demanded their return).

The thief may be guilty of a felony or he may not, depending on the value of the stolen property. Notice, however, that the pickpocket, the grave robber, the livestock thief, and the habitual thief are felons no matter what the value of the property stolen.

Notice also that the "fence"—the knowing buyer of stolen property—is a thief, even though he personally steals nothing from anyone. He may not even hire anyone to steal anything. In short, anyone who knowingly acquires stolen property is a thief.

Theft of service. PC 31.04 provides that he who secures performance of services normally provided for compensation without intent to pay is guilty of theft of service if he obtains performance by deception, threat, or false token, or if he diverts services intended for someone else to his own benefit.

The classification of the offense depends upon the value of the services stolen, the scale being the same as that set forth with respect to theft.

Anyone who eats a meal in a restaurant and walks out without paying for it, who sleeps in a motel and sneaks away without paying the bill, or who cons a dentist into filling an aching tooth without intending to pay the bill is guilty of this offense.

Theft of trade secret. PC 31.05 provides that a person who steals a trade secret, or makes a copy of an article representing a trade secret, or communicates a trade secret knowingly, is guilty of theft of trade secrets. A trade secret for this purpose is defined as the whole or any part of any scientific or technical information, design, process, procedure, formula, or improvement that has value and that the owner has taken measures to prevent from becoming available to persons other than those selected by the owner to have access for limited purposes.

The offense is a third-degree felony.

Industrial spies may well be guilty of commission of this offense.

Theft by check. Anyone who buys goods and pays for them with a bad check may be guilty of theft. A person who obtains services and pays for them with a bad check may be guilty of theft of services. When a person pays for goods or services with a bad check and does not make the check good, he is presumed to have written the check with the intent not to make it good if:

1. He had no checking account in the bank the check was written upon at the time he wrote it, or
2. The check was presented for payment within thirty days of issue, the drawee bank dishonored it, the holder gave notice to the writer that the check had been dishonored, and the writer has not made the check good within ten days of receipt of notice of dishonor.

The writer could still escape conviction of the crime of theft of goods or services if he could prove that his act of writing the bad check and his actions in not making the bad check good were not intentional, but proving that could be difficult.

The severity of the offense here will again depend upon the amount of the check (PC 31.06).

Unauthorized use of vehicle. Anyone who intentionally and knowingly operates the motor vehicle, boat, or airplane of another without the effective consent of the owner commits this offense, as per PC 31.07. This is a third-degree felony.

If the unauthorized use is a misappropriation with intent to deprive the owner of the vehicle, and the value of the vehicle is $10,000 or more, the charge could be theft, a second-degree felony.

However, a person may be guilty of unauthorized use of a vehicle without the intent to permanently deprive the owner of it. In this case all that is necessary is the intent to take a joyride and bring the vehicle back.

Robbery. Under PC 29.01, a person commits robbery if, in the course of committing theft, he intentionally, knowingly, or recklessly causes bodily injury to another, or intentionally and knowingly threatens another or places another in fear of bodily injury or death. This is a second-degree felony.

Aggravated robbery is committed, according to PC 29.03, when a person committing robbery uses or exhibits a deadly weapon, or causes serious bodily injury to another. This is a first-degree felony.

Of course, if the robber uses a deadly weapon to kill someone in the course of the robbery, he commits both aggravated robbery and capital murder.

Burglary. According to PC 30.01, burglary is committed if a person:
1. Enters a building or habitation not then open to the public, without the consent of the owner, with intent to commit a felony or theft, or
2. Remains concealed without the consent of the owner in a building or habitation with intent to commit a felony or theft, or
3. Enters a building or habitation without the consent of the owner and commits or attempts to commit a felony or theft.

The offense is a second-degree felony, unless:
1. The premises are a habitation, or
2. Any party to the offense is armed with explosives or a deadly weapon, or
3. Any party to the offense injures someone or attempts to injure someone in effecting entry to the building or while in the building or in immediate flight from the building.

If any of these three circumstances prevails, the offense is a first-degree felony.

It is not necessary to steal anything in order to be guilty of burglary. If the burglars are successful in stealing something, they are not only guilty of burglary but also of theft. The burglar of a house commits a more serious offense than does the burglar of an office building. The safecracker who takes explosives into the target building to blow the target safe commits a first-degree felony.

Burglary of coin-operated machines. A person breaking into or entering a coin-operated machine, contrivance, or apparatus, or any coin-operated equipment, without the consent of the owner and for the purpose of obtaining property or services, commits a Class A misdemeanor (PC 30.03).

Included in this offense would be the theft of money from vending machines, washing machines in laundromats, pinball machines, public telephones, etc. It would also include theft of goods from vending machines and manipulation of the mechanism of a public telephone so that one may make free phone calls. Imagination will provide other examples.

Burglary of vehicles. A person commits this offense if, without the consent of the owner, he breaks into or enters a vehicle or any part of a vehicle with intent to commit theft or felony. "Entry" here means intrusion with any part of the body, or intrusion with any object connected to the body.

This means that an unauthorized person who uses a coat hanger to unlock a locked vehicle with the intent of stealing the contents thereof commits this offense, even if he is caught before he puts a finger into the vehicle. PC 30.04 declares this to be a third-degree felony.

Criminal trespass. A person commits this offense if he enters or remains on property or in a building belonging to someone else without effective consent, and if he either had notice that the entry was forbidden or had been given notice to depart and had not done so. PC 30.05 declares this to be a Class C misdemeanor unless committed in a habitation, in which case it is a Class A misdemeanor.

Forgery. A large number of possible actions may constitute forgery according to PC 32.21. In general, a person commits the crime of forgery when he forges a writing with the intent to defraud or harm another. A forged writing is one that has been altered, made, completed, executed, or authenticated so that it purports:
1. To be the act of another who did not authorize the act, or
2. To have been executed at a time or place or in a numbered sequence other than was in fact the case, or
3. To be a copy of an original when no such original exists.

The forger himself commits this offense. So does the person who issues, transfers, registers the transfer of, publishes, or otherwise utters a forged writing, and the person who possesses a forged writing with the intent to utter it.

Forgery is a second-degree felony if the writing is or purports to be part of an issue of money, securities, postage or revenue stamps, or other instruments issued by a government, or part of an issue of stocks, bonds, or other instruments representing interests in or claims against another person.

Forgery is a third-degree felony if the writing is or purports to be a will, codicil, deed, trust deed, mortgage, security instrument, security agreement, credit card, check, contract, release, draft payable on sight, or other commercial instrument.

Any other forgery is a Class A misdemeanor.

We normally think of forgery as being the unauthorized writing of the name of another person with intent to defraud that person. The offense encompasses much more than that. Material alteration of a writing with evil intent is forgery, as are unauthorized completion (the filling in of blanks in the original writing) and counterfeiting.

The counterfeiting of money, postage stamps, government bonds, and the like is of course also a federal criminal offense.

Criminal simulation. Anyone who commits one of four prohibited acts with intent to defraud or harm another commits the crime of criminal simulation (PC 32.22). The forbidden acts are:
1. Making or altering an object, in whole or part, so that it appears to have value because of age, antiquity, rarity, source, or authorship that it does not have, or
2. Selling, passing, or otherwise uttering such an item, or
3. Possessing such an item with intent to sell, pass, or otherwise utter it, or
4. Authenticating or certifying that such an item is genuine with the knowledge that it is not.

This offense is a Class A misdemeanor.

Persons who commit this offense are primarily those who make furniture and other artifacts in the style of a century or two ago and artificially age their creations so that they appear to be valuable antiques. Also guilty of the offense are those who knowingly sell such creations as antiques, and the so-called "experts" who certify these to be genuine antiques.

Credit card abuse. PC 32.31 declares eleven types of conduct to be a commission of this offense. These are:

1. Presenting a credit card not issued to the user, or a revoked, expired, or cancelled credit card, with intent to fraudulently obtain property or services.
2. Using a fictitious credit card, or the pretended number or description of a fictitious credit card, with intent to obtain property or services.
3. Receiving property or services one knows have been obtained by use of fictitious, revoked, cancelled, or expired credit cards.
4. Stealing a credit card, or knowingly receiving a stolen credit card with intent to use it, sell it, or transfer it to someone other than the true owner.
5. Buying a credit card from someone known not to be the issuer.
6. Selling a credit card when one is not the issuer.
7. Inducing a cardholder to obtain goods or services for the actor's benefit for which the cardholder is unable to pay.
8. Signing one's name or someone else's name on a credit card without being the cardholder, and without the permission of the cardholder.
9. Possessing two or more incomplete credit cards with the intent to complete and use them, though they have not been issued to the possessor by the issuer.
10. Being authorized by an issuer to furnish goods or services to cardholders, with intent to defraud the issuer or the cardholder furnishing goods and services upon presentation of a credit card obtained or retained in violation of this section, or upon a credit card which is forged, expired, or revoked.
11. Being authorized by an issuer to furnish goods or services to cardholders, and representing to the issuer that one has furnished goods or services which he has truly not furnished.

This offense is a third-degree felony. The provisions of this section are broad enough to cover almost every conceivable fraudulent misuse or abuse of credit cards.

False statement to obtain property or credit. Anyone who knowingly or intentionally makes a materially false or misleading statement in writing in order to obtain property or credit for himself or for another commits this offense (PC 32.32). The credit sought may include a loan of money; a purchase of goods or services on credit; extension of the due date of an obligation; or cosigning or otherwise endorsing or guaranteeing commercial paper, a line or letter of credit, or a credit card.

The offense, a Class A misdemeanor, essentially encompasses lying to a creditor in a written credit application in order to defraud. To avoid committing this offense, the applicant must tell the truth, the whole truth, and nothing but the truth when answering questions on a credit application.

Hindering secured creditors. This offense may be committed by a person who has given a creditor a mortgage upon real estate, or by a person who has given a creditor the right to repossess his personal property if an obligation is not paid as agreed.

According to PC 32.33, such a person commits this offense if, with intent to hinder enforcement of the mortgage lien or repossession, he destroys, removes, conceals, encumbers, transfers, or otherwise harms or reduces the value of the collateral real estate or personal property. One is presumed to have intended to hinder the creditor when one has not paid the part of the debt which is due and has not delivered possession of the secured property to the creditor.

If the debtor removes the property which is the collateral, by taking it away from the place where it is normally found, selling it, giving it away, lending it, hiding it, or any similar action, the offense is a third-degree felony. If the property has not been removed, the offense is a Class A misdemeanor.

It is not an offense, however, to resist an unlawful repossession. Suppose, for example, that Squoze Finance Company has a lien upon your car, and you are behind a couple of payments. You keep the car locked up in a garage which is attached to your home. Agents of the finance company try to pick the lock on your garage and to break in at midnight in order to repossess, but you stop them and refuse to let them take the car. You have committed no criminal offense—not if you have not used excessive force to stop the repossessors. On the other hand, if you park the car on the street in front of your house and you catch the company agents preparing to tow your car away some evening, you may not interfere—this is a lawful repossession.

If the finance company people are after a color TV set on which you have missed payments and they want to walk into your house and repossess, you have the right to refuse them admittance—until they go to court and obtain a Writ of Sequestration. If you are behind on your payments and you have no legally sufficient reason for being behind, though, you might as well let them repossess. If you make them go to court and obtain the Writ of Sequestration, you will have to pay the court costs of that proceeding.

Fraud in insolvency. A debtor may commit this offense when he is involved or about to become involved in a receivership, assignment for benefit of creditors, or liquidation for benefit of creditors. If such a debtor hides his assets to keep them away from creditors, or if he destroys or removes them, he has committed the offense. If he deliberately falsifies his records, or if he deliberately misrepresents or refuses to disclose to his receiver or assignee the existence, amount, or location of some or all of his assets, he has also committed this offense. PC 32.34 declares this to be a Class A misdemeanor.

When a person who is involved in a federal bankruptcy proceeding does this sort of thing he commits the federal crime of bankruptcy fraud, a more serious offense.

Issuance of a bad check. A person commits this offense if he issues or passes a check knowing that the check will be dishonored. The offense as described in PC 32.41 is a Class C misdemeanor. The writer is presumed to have known that the check would be dishonored if he had no account in the bank upon which the check was written when he wrote it, or if the check was presented for payment within thirty days of issue, it was dishonored, the holder gave the writer notice of dishonor, and the writer did not make the check good within ten days.

Remember that if the bad check is given in payment for goods or services, the writer may be charged with theft. If the check is given in payment of a debt, however, the writer may only be charged with passing a bad check.

If the writer makes the check good when charged with this offense, the charges will normally be dropped. However, the law does not require that the charge be dropped. That matter lies within the discretion of the holder of the check and of the county attorney, who prosecutes misdemeanor cases.

Deceptive business practice. PC 32.42 declares twelve types of conduct by a businessman to be deceptive trade practices. A person commits a Class A misdemeanor if he

knowingly, intentionally, or recklessly:
1. Uses, sells, or possesses for use or sale a false weight or measure, or a device for falsely determining or recording any quality or quantity.
2. Sells less than the represented quantity of a good or service.
3. Takes more than the represented quantity when he is a buyer and furnishes the weight or measure.
4. Sells an adulterated or mislabeled commodity. A commodity is adulterated if its composition varies from the standard of composition or quality set by law or business custom. It is mislabeled when the label is not in accordance with the standard of disclosure set by law or by business custom.
5. Passes off property or service as that of another.
6. Represents that a product is new if it is really deteriorated, altered, rebuilt, reconditioned, reclaimed, used, or secondhand.
7. Represents that a commodity or service is of a particular style, grade, or model if it is of another style, grade, or model.
8. Advertises property or services with the intent not to sell as advertised, or not to supply a reasonably expectable public demand, unless the advertising discloses a time or quantity limit.
9. Represents the price of property or service falsely or in a way tending to mislead.
10. Makes a materially false statement or materially misleading statement of fact concerning the reason for, existence of, or amount of a price or price reduction.
11. Conducts a deceptive sales contest. A deceptive sales contest is one in which the nature and number of prizes are not disclosed, or in which the odds on winning a certain prize are misstated, or in which the outcome is rigged.
12. Makes a materially false or misleading statement in an advertisement for the purchase or sale of goods or services, or otherwise in connection with purchase or sale of goods or services.

This section of the Penal Code makes criminal a wide spectrum of deceptive practices. Anyone who uses such practices—not only businessmen—may violate this Penal Code section, but most of the offenses described here are unlikely to be committed outside the business context.

Commercial bribery. A person who is a fiduciary—that is, an agent, employee, trustee, guardian, custodian, administrator, executor, conservator, receiver, assignee for benefit of creditors, lawyer, physician, accountant, appraiser, or other professional adviser—or an officer, director, partner, manager, or other participant in the affairs of a corporation, partnership, or association, who intentionally or knowingly solicits, accepts, or agrees to accept a benefit as consideration for violating his fiduciary duty to a beneficiary or otherwise harming a beneficiary by act or omission, commits a third-degree felony. The person offering the bribe is also guilty of a third-degree felony. Essentially, anyone who occupies a fiduciary capacity commits this offense if he accepts a bribe to violate his fiduciary duties, and anyone who offers to bribe or does bribe a fiduciary also commits the offense (PC 32.43).

Rigging a publicly exhibited contest. A person commits this offense if, with intent to influence the score or outcome of a publicly exhibited contest, he:
1. Offers to confer a benefit upon, or threatens harm to, a participant in the contest in order to induce him not to use his best efforts, or does the same to an official or other person associated with the contest to influence his actions, or

2. Tampers with a person, animal, or object in a manner contrary to the rules of the contest.

Anyone soliciting a benefit for taking any action which is an offense also commits this crime, which is a Class A misdemeanor unless it is committed in connection with betting or wagering on the contest. If betting or wagering is involved, it is a third-degree felony.

A person who pays off an athlete not to do his best in a contest violates this section (PC 32.44), as does the athlete who solicits a payoff for not doing his best. Anyone who pays an official to call things against a certain team commits the offense, as does the official who solicits such a payoff. It does not matter whether the purpose of the rigging is to influence the margin by which the winner wins, or whether it is to influence the identity of the winner.

Misapplication of fiduciary property or property of financial institution. According to PC 32.45, this offense is committed by any fiduciary who intentionally, knowingly, or recklessly misapplies property he holds as a fiduciary or property of a financial institution in a manner that involves substantial risk of loss to the owner of the property or to the person for whose benefit the property is held.

This section is most commonly violated by a fiduciary using the property in question for his own benefit. A trustee or any guardian of funds could also commit the offense by lending out trust assets to a bad credit risk.

The offense is classified as:

1. A Class A misdemeanor if the property involved is worth less than $200.
2. A third-degree felony if the property involved is worth $200 or more but less than $10,000.
3. A second-degree felony if the property involved is worth more than $10,000.

Securing execution of a document by deception. A person commits this offense if, with intent to defraud or harm another, he uses deception to cause someone to sign or execute a document affecting property, service, or the pecuniary interest of any person. PC 32.46 declares this to be a third-degree felony.

The offense is committed by any person who fraudulently induces another to sign a contract or other document. It apparently does not matter whether the deception consists of a misrepresentation of the nature of the document being signed, or whether it is a misrepresentation of the reasons for signing.

Fraudulent destruction, removal, or concealment of writing. PC 32.47 declares that a person who, with intent to defraud or harm another, destroys, removes, conceals, alters, or otherwise impairs the verity, legibility, or availability of a writing, other than a government record, commits this offense.

For purposes of this section of the Penal Code, "writing" is defined as anything we normally consider to be writing, as well as symbols of value, right, privilege, or identification, and labels, price tags, or markings on goods.

If the offense is committed with respect to a deed, mortgage, or other document for which the law provides public recording, it is a second-degree felony. If it is committed with respect to a will or codicil, it is a third-degree felony. Otherwise, it is a Class A misdemeanor.

Notice that anyone who alters a trademark, price tag, or label is guilty of this offense.

Endless chain scheme. Anyone who contrives, prepares, sets up, proposes, operates, promotes, or participates in an endless chain is guilty of a Class B misdemeanor.

The definition of an endless chain scheme in PC 32.48 essentially coincides with the familiar chain letter scheme, in which one person receives a letter asking him to send money to one other person and to make two copies of the letter to send on to still other persons, the idea being that if the chain extends far enough, the sender will recover his expenditure many times over. Anyone taking any part in such a scheme commits the offense.

Bribery. Anyone who offers, confers, or agrees to confer any benefit upon a public servant or party official, with intent to influence him in a specific exercise of his official powers or a specific performance of his official duties; or upon a voter with intent to influence him to vote or not to vote in a particular manner, commits this offense. The party official, public servant, or voter who solicits, accepts, or agrees to accept the benefit also commits the offense.

PC 36.02 declares this to be a third-degree felony, except in the case of the public servant or party official who solicits or accepts or agrees to accept the bribe; such persons are guilty of a second-degree felony.

Anyone who offers to pay a policeman for tearing up a traffic citation, or who pays a voter one dollar to vote for Joe Doakes for sheriff, commits the offense. The building inspector who demands that he be paid off not to report an alleged infraction of the city building code also commits the offense. In all cases where a bribe is offered and accepted, at least two persons are guilty of the offense—the giver and the taker.

Coercion of public servant or voter. A person violates PC 36.03 if by coercion he influences or attempts to influence a public servant in a specific exercise of his public duties or in a specific performance of his official duty, or if he influences or attempts to influence a voter to vote or not to vote in a particular manner. The offense is a Class A misdemeanor, unless the coercion is a threat to commit a felony. In the latter case, it is a third-degree felony.

The landowner who tells his farmhand employee, "You vote for Zilch for sheriff, otherwise you're fired," commits this offense. So does the motorist who tells the policeman who is about to write him a traffic citation, "The chief of police is my cousin, and he doesn't take kindly to his relatives getting traffic tickets. If you write that ticket I'll tell him, and he'll remember."

Improper influence. Anyone who privately addresses a representation, entreaty, argument, or other communication to a public servant who exercises or will exercise discretion in any adjudicatory proceeding with intent to influence the outcome of the proceeding on a basis of considerations other than those authorized by law commits a Class A misdemeanor (PC 36.04). An adjudicatory proceeding is a court proceeding or a judicial-type administrative proceeding.

The person who writes to a judge presiding over a criminal prosecution, "If the jury convicts Slunk, go easy in sentencing him; you know you wouldn't be sitting on the bench now if it hadn't been for his financial support of you in the last election campaign," would commit this offense.

Tampering with a witness. A person commits a third-degree felony if he offers, confers, or agrees to confer a benefit upon a witness or prospective witness in an official proceeding, or if he coerces such a witness or prospective witness, to:
1. Testify falsely, or
2. Withhold testimony, information, or any document or thing, or
3. Elude legal process summoning him to testify or supply evidence, or
4. Absent himself from an official proceeding to which he has been summoned.

The witness also commits the offense if he knowingly solicits, accepts, or agrees to accept such a benefit (PC 36.05).

Retaliation. PC 36.06 provides that any person who knowingly or intentionally harms or threatens to harm another by an unlawful act in retaliation for or on account of the service of the other as public servant, witness, or informant commits a third-degree felony.

Compensation for past official behavior. Any person who intentionally or knowingly offers, confers, or agrees to confer a benefit upon a public servant for having officially acted favorably toward the actor or another commits this offense. The public servant who intentionally or knowingly solicits, accepts, or agrees to accept the benefit also commits the offense, a Class A misdemeanor (PC 36.07).

The person who presents the municipal judge with a case of scotch for acquitting him of a speeding charge has committed this offense, as has the judge himself if he accepts the gift.

Gift to public servant by person subject to his jurisdiction. PC 36.08 is a very lengthy section of the Penal Code which essentially makes it unlawful for a public servant to solicit, accept, or agree to accept a benefit from a person with whom he may have official dealings in the course of the performance of his official duties. PC 36.09 makes the offering of such a gift a Class A misdemeanor.

Perjury and aggravated perjury. A person commits perjury if, with intent to deceive and with knowledge of the statement's meaning, he makes a false statement under oath or swears to the truth of a false statement previously made, and the statement is required or authorized by law to be made under oath.

If the statement is made during an official proceeding or in connection with an official proceeding and is material, the offense is aggravated perjury. PC 37.02 declares ordinary perjury to be a Class A misdemeanor; PC 37.03 declares aggravated perjury to be a third-degree felony.

A person who makes a false statement under oath believing that he is telling the truth is not guilty of perjury.

A person who deliberately lies on the witness stand, whether in court, before a grand jury, before an administrative tribunal, or before a committee of the state legislature or similar body commits aggravated perjury if his lie could influence the outcome of the proceeding. A person who deliberately lies while giving a deposition would also commit aggravated perjury if the lie could influence the outcome of the proceeding in which the deposition is to be used.

False report to peace officer. Anyone who reports an offense or incident to a peace officer within that officer's concern who knows that this offense or incident did not occur commits a Class B misdemeanor (PC 37.08).

Tampering with or fabricating physical evidence. A person who knows that an investigation or official proceeding is in progress and:
1. Alters, destroys, or conceals any record, document, or thing with intent to impair its verity, legibility, or availability as evidence in the investigation or official proceeding, or
2. Makes, presents, or uses any record, document, or thing with knowledge of its falsity and with intent to influence the course or outcome of the investigation or official proceeding commits a Class A misdemeanor (PC 37.09).

Anyone concealing, destroying, or fabricating evidence is guilty of this offense.

Tampering with governmental record. PC 37.10 makes it an offense to:
1. Knowingly make a false entry in, or false alteration of, a government record, or

2. Make, present, or use any record, document, or thing with knowledge of its falsity and with intent that it be taken as an official government record, or
3. Intentionally destroy, conceal, remove, or otherwise impair the verity, legibility, or availability of a government record.

If this is done with intent to defraud or harm another, it is a third-degree felony. Otherwise, it is a Class A misdemeanor.

Impersonating a public servant. Anyone who impersonates a public servant with intent to induce another to submit to his pretended authority or to rely upon his supposedly official acts commits a Class A misdemeanor, unless the impersonation is of a peace officer, in which case a third-degree felony is committed (PC 37.11).

Failure to identify as a witness. A person who, when lawfully stopped by a police officer and asked for information, refuses to supply information or gives the officer a false name and address, commits a Class C misdemeanor (PC 38.02).

Resisting arrest or search. A person commits this offense if he intentionally prevents a person he knows is a peace officer (or a person he knows is acting in a peace officer's presence and at his direction) from effecting an arrest or search of the actor or of another person, or if he obstructs such an arrest. It does not matter whether or not the search or arrest was lawful. If a deadly weapon is used to resist the arrest or search the offense is a third-degree felony; otherwise it is a Class A misdemeanor, as per PC 38.03.

Evading arrest. A person evades arrest if he flees from a peace officer who is attempting to arrest him. If the attempted arrest is unlawful, the flight is justified. If the actor does not know that the person pursuing him is a peace officer, no offense is committed. PC 38.04 declares this to be a Class B misdemeanor.

Hindering apprehension or prosecution. A person commits a Class A misdemeanor if, with intent to hinder the arrest, prosecution, conviction, or punishment of another, he:
1. Harbors or conceals the other, or
2. Provides or aids in providing the other with means of avoiding arrest or effecting escape, or
3. Warns the other of impending discovery or apprehension.

If the warning is given in an effort to bring the other into compliance with the law— "The police are coming, you'd better give up because you'll never get away"—no offense is committed. PC 38.05 describes this offense.

Compounding. A witness who has filed a complaint is guilty of compounding if, after criminal proceedings have been initiated, he solicits, accepts, or agrees to accept any benefit in consideration for abstaining from, discontinuing, or delaying the prosecution of another for the offense. PC 38.06 declares this to be a Class A misdemeanor.

If Mama pays Victim $1,000 not to cooperate with prosecuting authorities who have brought charges of assault against Son for having beaten up Victim, and Victim now refuses to cooperate with the authorities, he has committed this offense.

Escape. A person who has been arrested for, charged with, or convicted of an offense commits this additional offense if he escapes from custody. According to PC 38.07, the severity of the additional offense depends upon the circumstances under which it is committed.

If a deadly weapon is used in the escape, or if the escapee threatens to use such a weapon, it is a second-degree felony. If the escapee uses no deadly weapon, but he escapes from a penal institution or he is under arrest for, charged with, or convicted of, a felony, it is a third-degree felony; otherwise it is a Class A misdemeanor. PC 38.09 provides that it does not matter if the custody from which he escapes is unlawful.

Bail jumping and failure to appear. A person lawfully released from custody with or without bail on condition that he subsequently appear commits this offense if he knowingly or intentionally fails to appear as required. This does not apply to appearances incident to probation or parole.

If the offense for which the appearance was required is a felony, the failure to appear is a third-degree felony. If the offense for which the appearance was required is one punishable by fine only, the offense is a Class C misdemeanor. Otherwise it is a Class A misdemeanor (PC 38.11).

Barratry. PC 38.12 declares that a person commits this offense if, with intent to obtain benefit for himself or to harm another, he:

1. Institutes any suit or claim in which he knows he has no interest, or
2. Institutes any suit or claim he knows is false, or
3. Solicits employment for himself or another to prosecute or defend a suit or to collect a claim, or
4. Procures another to solicit employment for him to prosecute or defend a suit or collect a claim.

Persons who can be guilty of barratry, then, are persons who begin groundless lawsuits against others in order to harass them or in order to get out-of-court settlements or courtroom judgments to which they are not entitled; attorneys who solicit employment for themselves; or attorneys who hire agents to solicit employment for themselves. The offense is a Class A misdemeanor.

Official misconduct. A public official commits a Class A misdemeanor if, with intent to obtain a benefit for himself or to harm another, he knowingly or intentionally:

1. Exercises his official power in an unauthorized manner, or
2. Exceeds his power by committing an act under color of his office, or
3. Does not perform a duty imposed upon him by law or one that is clearly a part of his job, or
4. Violates a law with respect to his office or employment.

An official of this sort commits a third-degree felony if he takes or misapplies any government property of which he has custody by virtue of his job, if he secretes it with intent to take it or misapply it, or if he pays or delivers it to a person he knows is not entitled to receive it. PC 39.01 describes this offense.

Official oppression. A public official commits a Class A misdemeanor if he intentionally subjects another to mistreatment or arrest, detention, search, seizure, dispossession, assessment, or lien that he knows is unlawful, or intentionally impedes another in the exercise or enjoyment of any right, privilege, power, or immunity, knowing that his conduct is unlawful.

Peace officers may commit this offense by conducting unreasonable searches and seizures, by making unlawful arrests, or by committing similar acts. Tax collectors may commit the offense by exceeding their authority on the job, and tax assessors may do so by making unlawfully high property assessments (PC 39.02).

Misuse of official information. PC 39.03 declares that a public servant commits a Class A misdemeanor if he uses information available to himself in his official capacity, but not made public, to:

1. Acquire, or to aid another in acquiring, a pecuniary interest in any property, transaction, or enterprise that may be affected by the information, or
2. Speculate or aid another to speculate on the basis of the information.

Obstructing a highway or other passageway. PC 42.03 makes it a Class B misdemeanor to:

1. Obstruct a highway, street, sidewalk, railway, waterway, aisle, elevator, hallway, entrance, or exit to which the public or a substantial group of the public has access, or any other place used for the passage of persons, vehicles, or conveyances, regardless of the means of creating the obstruction and of whether the obstruction arises from his acts alone or from his acts and the acts of others, or
2. Disobeys a request or order to move issued by someone the actor knows to be a peace officer, fireman, or other person with authority to control the use of the premises to prevent obstruction of a public way or to maintain public safety by dispersing those gathered in dangerous proximity to a fire, riot, or similar occurrence.

In order to constitute an offense, the obstruction must be created intentionally, knowingly, or recklessly, and without legal privilege or authority. Property owners, delivery men, spectators, and many others may commit the offense. So long as a person accused is guilty of causing any part of the obstruction, he may be prosecuted.

False alarm or report. PC 42.06 makes it a Class A misdemeanor to knowingly initiate, communicate, circulate or broadcast a report of a present, past, or future bombing, fire, or other emergency which he knows is false and baseless and which he knows would ordinarily:

1. Cause action by an official or volunteer agency organized to deal with emergencies, or
2. Place a person in fear of serious bodily injury, or
3. Prevent or interrupt the occupation of a building, room, assembly place, place to which the public has access, or of an aircraft, automobile, or other mode of conveyance.

Harassment. PC 42.07 declares that a person commits a Class B misdemeanor if he intentionally:

1. Communicates by telephone or in writing in vulgar, profane, obscene, or indecent language or in a coarse or offensive manner intended to annoy or alarm the recipient, or
2. Threatens by telephone or in writing to take unlawful action against a person (not necessarily the recipient), thereby annoying or alarming the recipient, or
3. Places one or more anonymous telephone calls at unreasonable hours, in an offensive and repetitious manner, or without a legitimate purpose of communication, thereby annoying or alarming the recipient.

Debt collectors may commit this offense if they become overzealous.

Under this section a phone call is placed by completing the dialing of a number, whether any conversation ensues or not. The ringing of a telephone, particularly at 3 A.M., is just as annoying as is any conversation—hence the provision that completion of dialing constitutes completion of the call.

Commercial obscenity. It is an offense under PC 43.23 to:

1. Sell, commercially distribute, commercially exhibit, or possess for sale, commercial distribution, or commercial exhibition any obscene material, or
2. Present or direct an obscene play, dance, or performance, or participate in that portion of the play, dance, or performance which makes it obscene, or
3. Hire, employ, or otherwise use a person seventeen years of age or younger to accomplish any of the above.

The offense is a Class B misdemeanor, unless minors are made participants. In such a case, it is a Class A misdemeanor.

When obscene material is sold, distributed, or displayed to minors, the offense escalates a degree under PC 43.24, and becomes that of sale, display, or distribution of harmful material to minors. It is then a Class A misdemeanor unless minors are used in the project, in which case it becomes a third-degree felony.

It is lawful to sell, distribute, or exhibit obscene material for scientific, educational, or governmental purposes. It is also lawful to sell, distribute, or exhibit obscene material to a minor accompanied by a consenting parent, guardian, or spouse to the extent that the grade of offense may be reduced to commercial obscenity rather than sale, distribution, or display of harmful material to minors.

It should be remembered that community notions of what is and is not obscene will vary from locality to locality. What is totally unacceptable in Funk's Thickett, population 1,000, might be quite unobjectionable in Podunk, population 500,000.

Unlawful transfer of firearms. PC 46.07 declares it to be a Class A misdemeanor to:
1. Sell, rent, lease, loan, or give a handgun to a person knowing that the person intends to use the weapon unlawfully or to perform an unlawful act, or
2. Intentionally sell, rent, lease, or give, or offer to sell, rent, lease, or give any firearm to a child under the age of eighteen, or
3. Intentionally, knowingly, or recklessly sell any firearm or ammunition for a firearm to an intoxicated person.

It is no offense to transfer a firearm to a minor if the parent or guardian of the minor has given written permission for a purchase, or effective consent to any other type of transfer.

Gambling. PC 47.02 declares that a person commits a Class C misdemeanor if he:
1. Makes a bet on the partial or final result of a game or contest, or on the performance of a participant in a game or contest, or
2. Makes a bet on the result of any political nomination, appointment, or election, or on the degree of success of any nominee, appointee, or candidate, or
3. Plays and bets for money or other things of value at any game played with cards, dice, or balls.

No offense is committed if a person engages in gambling in a private place where no person receives any economic benefit other than personal winnings, when, except for the luck factor, all participants have an equal chance to win. Thus, a poker game in a private residence is not unlawful gambling, so long as the game is honest, the homeowner does not take a cut from each pot to compensate himself for being host, and no admission fee is charged.

Gambling promotion. According to PC 47.03, a person commits a third-degree felony if he intentionally or knowingly does any of the following:
1. Operates or participates in the earnings of a gambling place, or
2. Receives, records, or forwards bets or offers to bet, or
3. For gain, becomes a custodian of anything of value bet or offered to be bet, or
4. Sells chances on the partial or final result of or on the margin of victory in any game or contest; on the performance of any participant in a game or contest; on the result of any political nomination, appointment, or election; or on the degree of success of any candidate for nomination, appointment, or election, or
5. For gain, sets up or promotes any lottery, sells or knowingly offers to sell or

knowingly possesses any card, stub, ticket, check, or other device designed to serve as evidence of participation in any lottery.

The casino operator, the bookie, the seller of chances on the outcome of all sorts of contests, and the lottery operator may be guilty of this offense. The businessman who operates a giveaway contest as a promotion device for his business, and requires all participants to pay consideration for a chance or insists that they buy merchandise from him in order to get a "free chance" is an operator of a lottery, and is thus guilty of this offense.

Keeping a gambling place. Under PC 47.04 it is a third-degree felony to use, permit another to use, or to rent out for use as a gambling place any real estate, building, room, tent, vehicle, boat, or other property. However, if no one is guilty of gambling under PC 47.02 because the place is a private place, the game is honest, and the house takes no cut, there is no offense committed.

Communicating gambling information. PC 47.05 makes it a third-degree felony to communicate information with respect to bets, betting odds, or changes in betting odds, or to knowingly provide equipment for transmission or reception of such information, if this is done to further gambling.

Possession of gambling device, equipment, or paraphernalia. It is a third-degree felony to possess, own, manufacture, or transfer gambling devices, equipment, or paraphernalia in order to further gambling. This would include slot machines, pinball machines that pay off in cash, crap tables, blackjack tables, wheels of fortune, lottery tickets, books for recording bets, blackboards for recording betting odds, etc.

Technically, possession of playing cards or dice with the intent to further gambling would also be a violation, but proving the required intent with respect to these would be difficult, to say the least.

PC 47.06 and 47.07 describe these offenses.

Unlawful carrying and possession of weapons. PC 46.06 makes it unlawful to possess, manufacture without proper permit, transport, repair, or sell the following weapons:

1. Explosive weapons, such as bombs, grenades, rockets, or mines.
2. Machine guns.
3. Short-barreled firearms, such as sawed-off shotguns.
4. Firearm silencers.
5. Switchable knives.
6. Knuckles.

Violation with respect to switchblade knives and knuckles are third-degree felonies. Violations with respect to the others are second-degree felonies. Law enforcers and military personnel of course may possess and use weapons in the line of duty. Registered dealers may buy and sell some of these weapons in accordance with the terms of their permits. Antique collectors and dealers may deal in short-barreled firearms and switchblade knives.

It is unlawful to intentionally, knowingly, or recklessly carry a handgun, illegal knife (knife with blade over 5½ inches long, throw knife, bowie knife, dagger, sword, or spear), or club (blackjack, mace, nightstick, tomahawk, or the like) unless one is traveling; engaging in lawful hunting, fishing, or sporting activity; on one's own premises; or discharging one's official duty as a peace officer or member of the armed forces. Violation is a Class A misdemeanor unless committed on premises licensed for sale or service of alcoholic beverages, in which case it is a third-degree felony.

It is unlawful for a person other than a peace officer, on-duty national guard member, or on-duty member of the armed forces to carry a firearm onto the premises of an educational institution, or onto the premises of a polling place on election day. Violation is a Class A misdemeanor (PC 46.04).

A person convicted of a felony involving violence or threatened violence commits a third-degree felony when he possesses a firearm away from the premises where he lives (PC 46.05).

Assault and aggravated assault. A person commits an assault if he:

1. Intentionally, knowingly, or recklessly causes bodily injury to another, including his spouse; or
2. Intentionally or knowingly threatens another, including his spouse, with imminent bodily injury, or
3. Intentionally causes physical contact with another when he knows or should reasonably know that the other person will regard the contact as offensive or provocative.

An assault is aggravated if:

1. It causes serious bodily injury to another, including the actor's spouse, or
2. It causes bodily injury to a peace officer in lawful discharge of his official duties when the actor knows or has been informed that the person assaulted is a peace officer, or
3. It causes bodily injury to a participant in a court proceeding (judge, attorney, grand juror, trial juror, or witness) when the perpetrator knows or has been informed that the person he is assaulting is a participant in a court proceeding, or
4. A deadly weapon is used in its commission.

An assault is a deadly assault upon a peace officer or participant in a court proceeding if the actor uses a firearm or prohibited weapon to inflict serious bodily injury upon a peace officer or participant in a court proceeding while the victim is performing his official duty or in retaliation for acts performed by the victim in performance of his official duty.

Deadly assault upon a peace officer or participant in a court proceeding is a first-degree felony.

Aggravated assault is a third-degree felony.

Assault causing bodily injury is a Class A misdemeanor.

Assault not causing bodily injury committed against a classroom teacher, counselor, principal, or instructional or administrative employee of an accredited educational institution or committed by an employee of a state hospital against an inmate or patient of said hospital is a Class B misdemeanor.

Assault not causing bodily injury committed against persons other than the above is a Class C misdemeanor. PC sections 22.01, 22.02, and 22.03 detail these offenses.

PC 22.06 provides that an accused has a defense to a charge of assault of any degree when:

1. The conduct did not threaten or inflict serious bodily injury, or
2. The victim knew that the conduct complained of was a risk of his occupation, or of recognized medical treatment, or a scientific experiment conducted by recognized methods.

We generally think of assault inaccurately, as a deliberate physical attack by one person upon another, with malice aforethought. Intent is an element of the offense, but malice is not. Thus, the physician who performs surgery upon a patient without the patient's consent, the dentist who pulls a patient's tooth without his full consent, or the boy who kisses a girl he knows does want to be kissed commits the offense. The boy who kisses the girl could not be found guilty, however, because the kiss does not threaten or inflict bodily injury. The physician or dentist must obtain permission from the patient before performing the surgery or pulling the tooth if the patient is in good enough condition to give it, or from a spouse, parent, or guardian if he is not.

The boxing referee who is KO'd by the heavyweight champ cannot complain of assault; it is a risk of his occupation. The same is true of the pro football quarterback who has bones broken in a pile-up on the field, and of the subject who gets hurt in the course of a scientific experiment, if he was warned of the danger in advance.

Bigamy. A person commits this offense under PC 25.01 if:
1. He is legally married to one person and marries another, or
2. He is legally married and he lives with another person not his spouse and presents himself as being married to that person he lives with, or
3. He knows that a person is already married and goes through a valid marriage ceremony with that person or lives with that person as a spouse, the couple presenting themselves as married.

A person is not guilty of bigamy if, when he marries for the second time, he reasonably believes that his first marriage has been dissolved or was void. But there is no defense for a single person who marries someone he knows is already married.

Bigamy is a third-degree felony.

Interference with child custody; enticing a child. An offense is committed by a person who, with intent to interfere with the lawful custody of a child, entices, persuades, or takes the child from the parent or guardian or the person standing in the stead of the parent or guardian. This is the offense of enticing a child.

Interference with child custody takes place when the actor takes the enticed child out of Texas and does not bring it back into Texas within seven days, knowing that the taking is a violation of a court order disposing of the child's custody, or when the actor has not been awarded custody by a court of competent jurisdiction and knows that a divorce suit or similar litigation to dispose of the child's custody has been filed.

PC 25.03 declares interference with custody to be a third-degree felony. PC 25.04 declares enticement of a child to be a Class B misdemeanor.

The parent who is angry because his ex-spouse got custody of a child in divorce proceedings is usually the person who commits these offenses. Once the marriage has split up, it is wisest not to interfere with custody of a child until a court changes the custody award.

Criminal nonsupport. A person commits this offense if he intentionally or knowingly fails to provide support he can provide and he is legally obligated to provide for his minor children, or for his spouse who is in need. Inability to pay is a good defense to such a charge.

PC 25.05 provides that this is normally a Class A misdemeanor; it becomes a third-degree felony, however, if it is a second or subsequent offense under this section of the Penal Code, or if the offense is committed while residing in another state.

Criminal attempt. A person who, with intent to commit an offense, perpetrates an act amounting to more than mere preparation for it but fails to effect the commission of the offense is guilty of criminal attempt. The punishment upon conviction is the punishment for an offense one category lower than that of the offense attempted (PC 15.01).

Criminal conspiracy. PC 15.02 declares that if, when there is intent to commit a felony, one or more persons agree that some, one, or all of them shall commit the offense, and one or more of the group perform an overt act in performance of the agreement, a criminal conspiracy exists.

It is no defense that one or more of the conspirators has been acquitted if two or more have not been acquitted.

Conspiracy may be—and often must be—proven by circumstantial evidence, which makes it a very difficult crime to prove.

Conspiracy is one category of offense lower than the felony which was the object of the conspiracy. Conspiracy to commit a third-degree felony is a Class A misdemeanor.

Punishments for corporations and associations. A corporation convicted of an offense for which the punishment is a fine may be fined as an individual. A corporation convicted of a crime for which the punishment is imprisonment may be sentenced to a fine not to exceed $10,000 for a felony or $2,000 for a Class A or Class B misdemeanor. If the corporation gained money or property through the commission of the offense, the fine may be as much as double the illicit gain, without regard for the above limitations (PC 12.51).

Effect of age upon criminal liability. PC 8.07 provides that adults (those seventeen years and older) shall be punished as directed in the sections of the Penal Code so far covered. Fifteen- and sixteen-year-olds may be tried and punished for their crimes either by the juvenile court or as adults. The juvenile court has jurisdiction over such minors unless it waives said jurisdiction.

Fourteen-year-olds and younger children cannot be tried as adults, except for perjury or aggravated perjury, driving while intoxicated, or violations of local traffic ordinances.

General defenses to criminal charges. PC 8.01 provides that insanity is a defense to prosecution if the accused, due to mental disease or defect, either did not know that his conduct was wrong, or was incapable of conforming his conduct to the requirements of the law he allegedly violated. The term "mental disease or defect" does not include an abnormality manifested only by repeated criminal or antisocial conduct.

Texas has thus abolished the McNaghten rule for determining insanity, under which a person was insane if he did not know right from wrong when he committed the criminal act. In Texas, there must be some good medical or psychiatric reason why the defendant did not know right from wrong in order for him to be able to claim that he was insane.

Under PC 8.01, the kleptomaniac cannot escape punishment for his thefts by claiming that he has an irresistible impulse to steal. The pyromaniac cannot escape punishment for his arson by claiming that he has an irresistible impulse to set fires. And the hothead cannot escape punishment for his assaults by claiming that he cannot stand frustration or insult, that he has an irresistible impulse to use violence upon those who frustrate him.

PC 8.04 provides that voluntary intoxication is no defense to a criminal charge, unless it caused temporary insanity. Involuntary intoxication might be a defense, but it would be hard to convince a jury that intoxication was involuntary.

PC 8.05 provides that duress is a defense under limited circumstances. When the charge is a misdemeanor, it is a defense that the defendant did what he did because threatened with force or because force was used upon him. If the charge is a felony, the alleged duress must be a threat of death or imminent bodily injury to the actor or to another.

Justifiable use of force as defense. PC sections 9.31 through 9.44 spell out the circumstances under which use of force is justifiable in defense of person or property. The provisions are too elaborate to go into in detail; in general, however, use of force against another is not justified in response to verbal provocation, when the actor provoked his antagonist to use force, or when the actor is being searched or arrested by a peace officer or by a person acting under the direction of a peace officer.

One may, however, use force in resisting an arrest or search when the person doing the arresting or searching uses greater force than necessary. It is dangerous to use force even here, however, because it might be the actor's word against the officer's as to just how much force the officer used.

One may use deadly force in self-defense when faced with an antagonist using deadly force, or to protect oneself against murder, rape, robbery, or some other aggravated offense. Force may be used to protect a third person when the actor feels that his intervention is necessary. Deadly force may be used to protect the third person, then, if it could be used by the actor to protect himself.

One may use force in defense of property to the extent necessary to terminate an unlawful trespass on land or unlawful interference with personal property. Deadly force may be used to protect property when it can be used to protect the person, as well as to protect against arson, burglary, robbery, nighttime theft, or nighttime criminal mischief; it may also be used to stop a person from fleeing who has committed the above offenses, when the actor reasonably believes that the use of deadly force is necessary to protect his property, or that the use of less than deadly force would subject him to the risk of death of serious bodily injury.

The Texas Controlled Substances Act. The Texas Controlled Substances Act makes criminal the unlawful manufacture, delivery, and possession of very dangerous drugs. The act, RCS 4476-15, divides these drugs into four penalty groups and provides penalties for unlawful manufacture, delivery, and possession of each. It also contains special provisions for marijuana.

Controlled substances may not be manufactured without a proper permit issued by the U.S. Food and Drug Administration or a similar agency. They may not be delivered except to medical practitioners, pharmacists, or laboratory facilities authorized to dispense or use such drugs; and medical practitioners may not deliver them to members of the general public for other than medical purposes. Pharmacists may not deliver them to the general public without a prescription. Persons other than medical practitioners, pharmacists, or lab personnel may not possess these drugs unless they possess a legitimate prescription for them.

Penalty Group 1 consists of a very lengthy list of opiate-type drugs, including raw opium, codeine, heroin, morphine, cocaine, and LSD. Unlawful manufacture and delivery of these is a first-degree felony. Unlawful possession is a second-degree felony.

Penalty Group 2 is a small group of hallucinogenic drugs with very long chemical names, including mescaline and psilocybin. Unlawful manufacture or delivery of these is a second-degree felony; unlawful possession is a third-degree felony.

Penalty Group 3 is a group of drugs used as stimulants or depressants of the central nervous system. Amphetamines are examples of the former, barbiturates of the latter. Peyote is also included here. Unlawful manufacture or delivery of these is a third-degree felony. Unlawful possession is a Class A misdemeanor.

Penalty Group 4 consists of combinations of codeine or the like with non-narcotic drugs of medicinal value. Unlawful manufacture or delivery of these is a Class A misdemeanor. Unlawful possession is a Class B misdemeanor.

With respect to marijuana, delivery of any quantity amounting to more than a quarter of an ounce is a third-degree felony. Delivery of a quarter-ounce or less for remuneration is also a third-degree felony. Delivery of less than a quarter-ounce for no remuneration, is a

Class B misdemeanor (for example, giving a marijuana cigarette to a friend). Possession of four or more ounces of marijuana is a third-degree felony. Possession of between two and four ounces is a Class A misdemeanor, and possession of less than two ounces is a Class B misdemeanor.

A first offender under this act may be placed upon probation for a period of up to two years after a plea of guilty or of nolo contendere, or upon a jury finding of guilt, within the court's discretion. The court may decide not to enter a conviction upon the defendant's record if he completes his probation successfully.

The possession of a hypodermic syringe with traces of a drug of Penalty Group 1 or 2 on it is a Class A misdemeanor.

The Texas Dangerous Drug Act. The Dangerous Drug Act, RCS 4476-14, makes unlawful the delivery or possession of drugs defined in the act as dangerous. Included in this category are tranquilizers, drugs of which federal law prohibits dispensing without a prescription, and a few other drugs. Drugs regulated under the Controlled Substances Act are not subject to this act.

These drugs may be delivered only to practitioners of medicine, pharmacists, authorized laboratories, hospitals, or similar institutions. They may be possessed lawfully only by dealers, dispensers, practitioners, pharmacists and the like, or by persons in possession of lawful prescriptions for them.

For unlawful sale or delivery, or for offers to make unlawful sale or delivery, the penalty is two to ten years imprisonment, and in addition a possible fine of up to $5,000. For first offense possession the maximum penalty is six months in jail and/or a fine of $1,000. For second and subsequent offenses the maximum is one year in jail and/or a $2,000 fine.

ALCOHOLIC BEVERAGE REGULATIONS

The Texas statute on regulation of alcoholic beverages is the Alcoholic Beverage Code, enacted by the Sixty-fifth Legislature in 1977. The law is so voluminous that a detailed description of it would be inappropriate here; however, there are some aspects of it that are worthy of brief mention.

Dry areas. Section 101.32 of the Alcoholic Beverages Code provides that no person in a dry area may, among other things, transport, distribute, solicit or take orders for, or possess with intent to sell an alcoholic beverage.

ABC 101.32 says that possession of more than one quart of hard liquor in a dry area is prima facie evidence of possession with intent to sell. Possession of more than twenty-four twelve-ounce bottles of beer (one case) is likewise prima facie evidence of possession with intent to sell.

Thus a person stopped by police in a dry area who has more than a quart of liquor or case of beer in his possession may be charged with intent to sell alcoholic beverages in a dry area. The accused may escape conviction by proving that he had the liquor or beer in his possession for his own consumption, but the burden of proof rests upon him.

Sale of alcoholic beverages to habitual drunkards, intoxicated persons, or insane persons. ABC 101.63 provides that a person (including a bartender or waiter) who sells an alcoholic beverage to a habitual drunkard, an intoxicated person, or an insane person may, for a first offense, be imprisoned for up to a year and/or be fined between $100 and $500.

For a second or subsequent offense the punishment is up to one year and/or a fine of $500 to $1,000.

Hours of sale of alcoholic beverages. ABC 105.01 forbids the sale of packaged liquor on Christmas Day, on Sunday, and between 9 P.M. and 10 A.M. on other days.

On weekdays mixed drinks may be sold between 7 A.M. and midnight. On Sundays such drinks may be sold between midnight and 1 A.M., and between noon and midnight, as per ABC 105.03.

In counties with over 300,000 population, and in other areas that adopt extended hours by ordinance, mixed drinks may be sold between midnight and 2 A.M. any day.

ABC 105.05 applies the same rules to the sale of beer.

ABC 105.06 provides that it is an offense to possess alcoholic beverages with intent to consume them in a public place between fifteen minutes after the close of the legal sale of alcoholic beverages in the area in question and the hour of resumption of sale. Consumption of the beverage during the forbidden hours must be proven before a person may be convicted of this offense. The punishment is a fine of up to $50. Thus, anyone who stands on a street corner drinking beer at, say, 12:30 A.M. in a small town, or at 2:30 A.M. in a large city, could be charged with this offense.

Alcoholic beverages and minors. ABC 106.02 declares that a minor commits an offense if he purchases an alcoholic beverage. For a first offense, the penalty is a fine of between $25 and $200. For a second or subsequent offense, the penalty is a fine of no less than $100 or more than $500.

It is also an offense to knowingly sell alcoholic beverages to a minor. If the minor falsely represents himself to be eighteen or older and displays an apparently valid Texas driver's license with an accurate physical description, and the seller knows nothing about the falsity of the license, no offense is committed by the seller. ABC 106.03 declares the penalty for a first offense to be imprisonment of up to one year, and/or a fine of no less than $100 or more than $500. For a second or subsequent offense, the penalty is imprisonment of up to one year, and/or a fine of no less than $500 nor more than $1,000.

ABC 106.04 declares consumption of alcoholic beverages by a minor to be unlawful, unless he is in the visible presence of an adult parent, guardian, or spouse. The penalties are the same as those for purchase of alcoholic beverages by a minor.

Possession of alcoholic beverages by a minor is declared to be an offense (ABC 106.05), unless the minor is employed on the premises of a licensed seller of such beverages and his employment is lawful; or unless he is in the presence of an adult parent, guardian, spouse, or other person to whom he has been committed by a court. The penalties are the same as those for purchase of alcohol by a minor. Under ABC 106.09, sellers of alcoholic beverages may lawfully employ minors to work in any capacity other than the selling of any alcoholic beverage or the preparation or serving of mixed drinks.

Any adult, other than an adult parent, guardian, spouse, or person to whom a minor's custody has been committed by a court, commits a violation of ABC 106.06 if he purchases an alcoholic beverage for a minor or he gives or knowingly makes available such a beverage to a minor. The penalty is a fine of no less than $100 nor more than $500.

The minor who falsely misrepresents his age to a seller of alcoholic beverages violates ABC 106.07. For a first offense he may be fined no less than $25 and no more than $200. For a second or subsequent offense he may be fined no less than $100 nor more than $500.

Other alcoholic beverage offenses. The Alcoholic Beverage Code subjects all phases of the business of the manufacture, distribution, and retailing of alcoholic beverages to comprehensive regulation. Persons or firms engaged in all phases of the business are required to possess proper permits, licenses, or other authorizations. Engaging in some aspect of the business without the required permit or license is of course an offense.

In addition, licenses or permits may be administratively suspended or revoked due to violations; illegally manufactured or possessed beverages may be seized, along with the vehicles transporting them; and injunctions may be obtained and enforced against violators.

Traffic offenses. Though the contact of most persons with the criminal law comes about because of traffic law violations, the subject is too broad for detailed consideration in this work. Some discussion of this area is found in the chapter on motor vehicle law.

Most of the traffic law of Texas is found in the Texas Uniform Traffic Act, RCS 6701d. Most violations of traffic law, such as speeding, running a stop sign, failing to yield the right-of-way, and the like are Class C misdemeanors. Fines are the only punishment for these violations.

However, there are some traffic violations which are more serious than Class C misdemeanors. Among the most serious are:
1. Driving while under the influence of intoxicating liquor (DWI).
2. Driving while under the influence of drugs (DWD).
3. Failure to stop at the scene of an accident, if you were involved in it.
4. Negligently killing someone while driving a motor vehicle.

4

Federal Criminal Law

The subject of federal criminal law is so broad that it cannot be adequately covered in these materials. The general federal criminal law is contained in Title 18 of the United States Code. It is this area which will be discussed briefly in this chapter. In addition, many other federal criminal statutes are distributed throughout the other titles of the U.S. Code; it is these specialized statutes which deal with various aspects of business regulation. A few of them will be mentioned in passing.

General federal criminal jurisdiction. In general, the federal government has jurisdiction over interstate commerce. Thus, federal criminal law is applicable to interstate criminal transactions. In addition, the United States possesses special maritime and territorial jurisdiction as defined by 18 USC 7. This jurisdiction extends to:

1. The high seas, any waters within the admiralty and maritime jurisdiction of the United States and not within the jurisdiction of any state, and any vessel belonging to an American citizen, an American corporation, or to the government of the United States while that vessel is within the admiralty and maritime jurisdiction of the United States and outside the jurisdiction of a particular state. (In general, the jurisdiction of the state extends to 3 miles off the coast. The jurisdiction of the United States extends to 200 miles off the coast.)
2. Any American flag vessel operating on the Great Lakes or waters connecting them, or on the St. Lawrence River where it constitutes the international boundary line.
3. Any lands reserved or acquired for the use of the United States and under her exclusive or concurrent jurisdiction, or lands acquired or purchased by the United States with the consent of the state legislature where the lands are located for use as a fort, dockyard, etc. (Included here are military installations, national parks, national forests, federal buildings, and related facilities.)
4. Any aircraft belonging in whole or in part to an American citizen, an American corporation, or to the United States government, while it is in flight over the high seas, or over any waters within the admiralty or territorial jurisdiction of the United States and outside the jurisdiction of a state.

Misprision of a felony. Anyone who, knowing of the commission of a federal felony, conceals this knowledge and does not make same known to a judge or other person in authority, violates 18 USC 4 and is subject to imprisonment for up to three years and/or a fine of up to $500.

Bankruptcy fraud. Anyone who conceals property of a bankrupt which is subject to the jurisdiction of the bankruptcy court, makes false oaths or claims in a bankruptcy proceeding, or offers or accept a bribe with respect to any portion of a bankruptcy proceeding, violates 18 USC 152 and is subject to imprisonment for up to five years and/or a fine of up to $5,000.

Bribery of public officials and witnesses. Anyone who promises or pays anything to a federal public official to influence an official act of the official, to induce the official to commit or aid in committing fraud upon the United States, or to induce the official to violate his lawful duty; any federal official who demands payment to do any of the above; anyone paying or offering to pay a witness to testify falsely in an official federal proceeding; or any witness demanding payment to so testify, shall be imprisoned for no more than fifteen years, and/or fined no more than $20,000 or three times the bribe or payoff, whichever is greater.

Anyone who promises or pays anything to a federal official to do his duty, any federal official who demands a payoff to do his duty, anyone who offers to pay or does pay a witness for testifying in an official proceeding (other than a legitimate fee for so testifying), or any witness demanding to be paid more than a legitimate fee for so testifying, shall be imprisoned for no more than two years, or fined no more than $10,000, or both.

These provisions are found in 18 USC 201.

Bribery in sporting contests. Any person or persons carrying into effect, attempting to carry into effect, or conspiring to carry into effect a scheme in interstate commerce to influence the outcome of a sporting event or to influence the event in general violates 18 USC 224 and is subject to imprisonment for no more than five years, or a fine of no more than $10,000, or both.

A person who commits this offense in Texas could violate Texas as well as federal law. The bribery need not be to influence the victory in the event: it is sufficient to be a violation if the bribery is merely intended to influence the margin of victory—the point spread.

Conspiracy against civil rights of citizens. If two or more persons conspire to injure, oppress, threaten, or intimidate any citizen in the free exercise of his constitutional rights, they violate 18 USC 241 and may be imprisoned for no more than ten years or fined no more than $10,000, or both. If death results from the conspiracy, the penalty may be life imprisonment or any shorter period of imprisonment.

Interference with federally protected activity. 18 USC 245 makes it a crime, by force or threat of force, to willfully injure, intimidate, or interfere with a person because:

1. He is trying to vote, run for public office, or otherwise engage in lawful political activity, or
2. He is participating in or enjoying a benefit, facility, service, privilege, program, or activity provided or administered by the United States, or
3. He is applying for, or enjoying, federal employment, or
4. He is attending court as a juror or possible juror, or
5. He is receiving federal financial assistance, or
6. He is trying to do business lawfully in the midst of a riot or civil disorder, or
7. Because of his race, color, national origin, or religion, an effort is made to harass him or stop him from attending a public school or college; applying for or enjoying private employment or membership in a labor union, or public employment; traveling by any common carrier; or obtaining food or lodging in any hotel, motel, restaurant, or public facility.

If no bodily injury is caused by this the penalty is imprisonment for up to one year or a fine of up to $1,000, or both. If bodily injury is caused, the penalty is imprisonment for up to ten years or a fine of up to $10,000, or both. If death is caused, the penalty is life imprisonment or any lesser term of imprisonment.

The two statutes described above cover a multitude of offenses. They are powerful additions to the arsenal of legal weapons devised for the protection of civil rights.

Dealing in explosives. 18 USC 841–848 is a complex group of provisions regulating the importation, manufacture, transportation, and use of explosives in interstate commerce. Importers, manufacturers, and dealers in explosives must obtain licenses from the Treasury Department. It is unlawful to use explosives unless one has a user's permit issued by the Treasury Department, or unless one's use is permitted under state law.

It is unlawful to deal in, manufacture, or transport explosives without a license. It is also unlawful to distribute them to persons other than holders of federal licenses or permits, especially to:

1. Persons under twenty-one years of age.
2. Convicted felons.
3. Persons under indictment for felony.
4. Fugitives from justice.
5. Drug addicts.
6. Mental defectives.

These sections of 18 USC describe many other offenses with respect to explosives. For violation, the penalty is a fine of no more than $10,000, or imprisonment of no more than ten years, or both.

Firearms. 18 USC 921–924 contains provisions relative to transportation, sale, manufacture, and importation of firearms. Importers, manufacturers, and dealers of and in interstate commerce of firearms and ammunition must have appropriate licenses issued by the secretary of the Treasury. A collector of firearms must also have a federal license if he wishes to ship and receive weapons in interstate commerce. The business of manufacture, transportation, and importation of ammunition is subject to the same statutory provisions.

18 USC 922 makes unlawful a lengthy list of activities, including (but not limited to):

1. Transportation of firearms and ammunition by an unlicensed person across a state line except for purposes of hunting, engaging in marksmanship contests, or similar events.
2. Transportation by unlicensed persons of machine guns and other specified weapons across a state line without a special permit issued by the Treasury Department.
3. Sale or delivery of firearms by a licensed person when:
    a. The sale or delivery is to a person under twenty-one years of age.
    b. The sale or delivery is in violation of state law.
    c. The sale is of a machine gun or short-barreled shotgun or short-barreled rifle, unless the sale is authorized by the Treasury Department.
    d. The buyer or transferee does not furnish to the licensed person his name, address, and age, and, if buyer or transferee is an agent, the same information with respect to his principal.
    e. The buyer or transferee is a convicted felon, or is under indictment for felony.
    f. The buyer or transferee is a fugitive from justice.
    g. The buyer or transferee is a drug addict or unlawful user of drugs.
    h. The buyer or transferee is mentally defective.

Of course, a sale or delivery is not a violation here unless the licensed person knows or should know that the buyer or transferee is a minor, fugitive, convicted felon, etc. On the other hand, the licensed person is expected to know the state law governing the sale of firearms. Persons under indictment for felony, convicted felons, fugitives from justice, drug addicts, and mental defectives may neither ship nor transport firearms in interstate commerce nor receive firearms shipped in interstate commerce.

Remember that the above prohibitions apply as much to ammunition as they do to firearms.

In addition, any person who uses a firearm to commit a felony for which he may be prosecuted under federal law, or carries a firearm unlawfully during the commission of such a felony, may be sentenced to no less than one year nor more than ten years imprisonment in addition to the penalty for the felony. For a second or subsequent offense the imprisonment shall be no less than two nor more than twenty-five years in addition to the penalty for the felony.

Blackmail. If Smith believes that Jones has violated federal law in some way, and demands that Jones pay him money or some other thing of value so that he will not report the violation to the authorities, Smith is guilty of blackmail. If Jones pays up in response to the threat, Smith is still guilty of blackmail. 18 USC 873 defines this crime, and provides a penalty of imprisonment for no more than one year, or a fine of no more than $2,000, or both.

Mailing threatening communications. Whoever deposits in the mail a communication threatening the physical well-being, economic well-being, or reputation of the recipient or his loved ones or of a deceased person unless the addressee pays consideration in the form of money or some other thing of value, violates 18 USC 876. The penalty is imprisonment for no more than two years or a fine of no more than $500, or both. If the communication contains a threat to kidnap, or is a demand for payment of ransom for release of a kidnap victim, the penalties are much higher.

Making extortionate extensions of credit. 18 USC 891 et seq. contain criminal provisions relative to the practice commonly known as "loan-sharking." An extension of credit is presumed to be extortionate if the amount lent is over $100 and:

1. The annual interest rate is in excess of 45 percent, and
2. The debtor's promise to repay is unenforceable, and
3. The debtor reasonably believed when he borrowed the money that the creditor had collected from others of his debtors through violence, threats of violence, or other criminal means; or the creditor had a reputation of collecting loans through violence, threats of violence, or other criminal means.

The lender in such a transaction is subject to a fine of no more than $10,000, imprisonment of no more than twenty years, or both. The collectors of such loans, and the financers of such loans, are subject to the same penalty. Despite the existence of this statute, it can be expensive—not to mention dangerous—to do business with loan sharks.

Enlistment in foreign service. 18 USC 959 makes it a criminal offense for an American citizen to enlist in the armed forces of a foreign nation, unless that nation is at war with a nation with which the United States is at war. The penalty is a fine of no more than $1,000, imprisonment for no more than three years, or both. At one time such an action would also be grounds for forfeiture of the enlistee's American citizenship, but this is no longer the case.

Transmission of wagering information. When a person who is in the business of illegally betting or wagering uses a wire communication facility (telephone or telegraph) for interstate or foreign transmission of bets or wagers—or for transmission of information regarding bets or wagers—involving sporting contests, a violation of 18 USC 1084 takes place. This is true unless the betting and wagering business is legal under the law of the locality where it takes place. The penalty for violation of this section is a fine of no more than $10,000, or imprisonment for no more than two years, or both. Since all businesses of this nature are illegal in Texas, any such activity in this state violates 18 USC 1084.

Riots. 18 USC 2101 provides that anyone traveling in interstate commerce or using any facility of interstate commerce for any of the following purposes shall be fined no more than $10,000 or imprisoned for no more than five years, or both:

1. Inciting a riot.
2. Organizing, promoting, encouraging, participating in, or carrying on a riot.
3. Committing any act of violence in furtherance of a riot.
4. Aiding or abetting any person in doing any of the above.

Damage to or destruction of aircraft or motor vehicles. Whoever willfully sets fire to, damages, destroys, disables, tampers with, or wrecks any aircraft or motor vehicle in interstate commerce; whoever willfully places any explosive or destructive substance on board or near to such an aircraft or motor vehicle; whoever willfully incapacitates an aircraft crew member or a motor vehicle driver; or whoever tampers with, damages, or defaces any terminal facility or housing for motor vehicles or aircraft, shall be fined no more than $10,000, or imprisoned no more than twenty years, or both. If the death of any person is caused by the above activity, the penalty shall be death or whatever lesser penalty of imprisonment the court may prescribe.

Civil disorders. Whoever teaches or demonstrates to another the use, application, or making of any firearm, explosive, or incendiary device, or any other technique for causing injury or death to persons, knowing or having reason to know or intending that the same will be used in, or in furtherance of, a civil disorder; or whoever obstructs the activity of firemen or law enforcement officers during a civil disorder; or whoever transports or manufactures for transport in interstate commerce firearms, explosives or incendiary devices for use in civil disorders violates 18 USC 231. The penalty for such violation is imprisonment of no more than five years, or a fine of no more than $10,000, or both. The transport of firearms for such purposes would of course also violate 18 USC 924, unless the violator had a license to transport firearms.

False claim for postal losses. Whoever makes a false claim with the U.S. Post Office for loss of a registered letter or insured parcel violates 18 USC 288. If the false claim is for more than $100, the penalty is imprisonment for no more than one year, a fine of no more than $500, or both. If the false claim is for less than $100, the penalty is a fine of no more than $500.

Counterfeiting. Anyone who, with intent to defraud, falsely makes, forges, counterfeits, alters, or similarly passes the obligations or other securities of the United States (including currency, government bonds, and Treasury bills) violates 18 USC 471.

Anyone counterfeiting such government paper probably does so with intent to defraud. Why else would one do such a thing? It should be noted, on the other hand, that the person who unknowingly passes counterfeit currency does not do so with intent to defraud. However, anyone passing counterfeit currency who knows that it is counterfeit could be said to do so with intent to defraud. Since we are all presumed to know the law, we should know that counterfeit money is not true money.

The penalty for counterfeiting is a fine of no more than $5,000, imprisonment for not more than fifteen years, or both.

Anyone who, with intent to defraud, passes, utters, publishes, or sells, or attempts to pass, utter, publish, or sell such forged, falsely made, or counterfeited obligations or securities, violates 18 USC 472 and is subject to the same penalties as provided in 18 USC 471.

Anyone who buys, sells, exchanges, receives, or delivers any such false security or obligation with the intent that the same be passed, published, or used as true and genuine (but does not pass these on to an innocent party) may be imprisoned for up to ten years, or fined up to $5,000, or both, as per 18 USC 473.

Anyone who, with intent to defraud, counterfeits or forges foreign money may be fined up to $2,000 or imprisoned up to two years, or both, under 18 USC 482. For knowingly passing such forged or counterfeited foreign money one may be fined up to $1,000 or imprisoned up to one year, or both (18 USC 483).

This portion of the U.S. Code also contains provisions punishing the counterfeiting and forging of foreign securities and the knowing passing of the same. It also contains provisions forbidding possessing, making, selling and using plates and stones used for counterfeiting, or tools used in making plates and stones for counterfeiting.

18 USC 500 forbids the counterfeiting of U.S. postal money orders, the forgery of official signatures to such orders, the material alteration of genuine orders, the issuing of genuine orders without having received proper payment for them, and the knowing cashing of such orders as described above, if done with intent to defraud. The penalty is a fine of no more than $5,000, imprisonment of no more than five years, or both.

Customs violations. Anyone who makes false statements to U.S. Customs officers in the process of bringing imported goods into the United States with intent not to pay the full customs duty due on the goods—whether the statements deal with the quantity or the nature of the goods—violates 18 USC 541 and/or 542. The penalty is a fine of no more than $5,000 or imprisonment for no more than two years or both.

A customs officer who knowingly admits goods into the U.S. without charging proper customs duty violates 18 USC 543 and is subject to the above penalties and removal from office.

Anyone who brings goods into the United States the importation of which is forbidden by law, who smuggles or clandestinely introduces into the United States goods which are subject to customs duty, or who knowingly receives, conceals, buys, sells, or facilitates the transportation, concealment, and sale of such goods violates 18 USC 545. The penalty is a fine of no more than $10,000 or imprisonment for no more than five years or both.

Possession of such smuggled goods is sufficient evidence for conviction of this offense, unless the defendant can show that his possession was unknowing and innocent.

18 USC 546 makes it unlawful to smuggle goods into a foreign country if by the law of that country the smuggling of goods into the United States would be unlawful. Only the owners of vessels under the U.S. flag may be convicted for this. The penalty is a fine of no more than $5,000 or imprisonment of no more than two years, or both.

A person who carries merchandise through any building on the boundary line between the United States and another country contrary to law violates 18 USC 548 and may be fined no more than $5,000 or imprisoned not more than two years, or both. Anyone who buys dutiable goods in Mexico and brings them into the United States without making them known to Customs could violate this statute.

Fugitives from justice. A person who harbors or shelters someone for whom a federal arrest warrant is outstanding violates 18 USC 1071 if he knows of the warrant. If the charge involved is a felony, the penalty is a fine of no more than $5,000 or imprisonment of no more than five years, or both. If the charge involved is a misdemeanor, the penalty is a fine of no more than $1,000 or imprisonment for no more than one year, or both. Anyone who harbors or conceals an escaped federal prisoner violates 18 USC 1072 and may be imprisoned for no more than three years.

Anyone who moves or travels in interstate commerce to avoid prosecution or imprisonment for a felony under the law of the place where the crime was committed, or to avoid giving testimony in a prosecution for such a felony, violates 18 USC 1073. The penalty is a fine of no more than $5,000 or imprisonment for no more than five years, or both. Note that the felony involved may be a state crime.

Mail fraud. Anyone depositing anything in the U.S. Mail as part of a scheme or artifice to defraud, as part of a scheme to obtain money or property through false pretenses, or as part of a scheme to distribute false or counterfeit money or obligations, violates 18 USC 1341. Any person receiving any matter in the U.S Mail as a participant in such a scheme also violates this statute.

Any person giving the Post Office a false name or address as part of a scheme declared to be unlawful under 18 USC 1341, or as part of any other unlawful business, violates 18 USC 1342. The penalty for violation of either statute is a fine of no more than $1,000 or imprisonment for not more than five years, or both.

Bank robbery. Anyone entering or attempting to enter a bank, savings and loan association, credit union, or any building used in whole or in part as a bank, savings and loan association, or credit union with intent to commit a felony against the institution or with intent to commit any larceny, violates 18 USC 2113a. Also, any person taking from another by force, violence, or intimidation property belonging to or in the care, custody, control, possession, or management of a bank, savings and loan association, or credit union, violates this statute. The penalty is a fine of no more than $5,000 or imprisonment for no more than twenty years, or both.

Anyone taking or carrying away, with intent to steal or purloin, property or money or any other thing belonging to, or in the care, custody, control, management, or possession of a bank, savings and loan association, or credit union, violates 18 USC 2113(b). If the value of the property involved is more than $100, the penalty is a fine of no more than $5,000 or imprisonment for no more than ten years, or both. If the value of the property involved is less than $100, the penalty is a fine of no more than $1,000 or imprisonment for no more than one year, or both.

A person who knowingly receives, possesses, conceals, sells, or disposes of property taken in violation of 18 USC 2113(b) is subject to the same penalties as the taker thereof. If a person violating this statute assaults any person or puts in jeopardy the life of any person by use of a dangerous weapon or device, the violator may be fined up to $10,000 or imprisoned for up to twenty-five years, or both.

Transporting and receiving stolen goods. Anyone transporting in interstate or foreign commerce goods, wares, merchandise, or money of the value of $5,000 or more, knowing the same to be stolen, converted, or taken by fraud; anyone causing a person to travel in interstate commerce for the purpose of defrauding that person of $5,000 or more in money or property; anyone knowingly transporting counterfeit or forged securities; anyone transporting in interstate commerce travelers checks, or a traveler's check bearing a forged countersignature; or anyone who knowingly transports tools and implements for counterfeiting in interstate commerce, violates 18 USC 2314. Such persons may be fined no more than $10,000, imprisoned no more than ten years, or both.

Anyone who knowingly transports a stolen motor vehicle or aircraft in interstate or foreign commerce may be fined no more than $5,000, imprisoned no more than five years, or both (18 USC 2312).

A person who knowingly receives, conceals, sells, or disposes of a stolen motor vehicle or aircraft in interstate commerce violates 18 USC 2313 and is subject to the same penalty as provided in 18 USC 2312.

Perjury. Anyone who lies under oath in a proceeding before a United States court or a United States grand jury may be fined no more than $10,000 and imprisoned for no more than five years, or both, as per 18 USC 1623. Anyone who lies under oath as part of a proceeding before other federal tribunals—administrative agencies and legislative committees, for example—may be fined no more than $2,000 or imprisoned for no more than five years, or both (18 USC 1621).

Business crimes. In the other volumes of the United States Code are found many statutes which regulate all sorts of business practices. Many of these statutes contain criminal provisions. A short list of some of the business practices which are rendered criminal by federal law includes:

1. Price-fixing by mutual agreement of competitors.
2. Price discrimination—selling goods to two different customers for two different prices for no justifiable reason.
3. Selling adulterated or misbranded foods, drugs, and cosmetics in interstate commerce.
4. Selling unregistered securities in interstate commerce.
5. Selling consumer products that do not comply with safety standards set by the Consumer Product Safety Commission.
6. Selling drugs or pesticides in interstate commerce which have not been approved for marketing by the proper federal authority.
7. Not paying the federally mandated minimum wage to employees when required by law.
8. Not withholding federal income tax and social security payments from wages of employees when required by law, and not paying over these withholdings to the IRS at the proper time.
9. Dumping pollutants into waterways and emitting pollutants into the air in contravention of regulations of the Environmental Protection Agency.

This list is in no way exhaustive; it merely suggests the vast scope of federal criminal regulation of business activity.

Federal drug abuse legislation. The federal drug abuse legislation is in some ways similar to the Texas state legislation; in fact, the Texas law is to some extent based upon the federal law. 21 USC 812 establishes five federal categories or schedules of controlled substances.

The attorney general is given authority to move a drug from one schedule to another, to remove a drug from the schedules altogether, or to add new drugs to the schedule through administrative action. The particular drugs named below under the various schedules are those listed there by Congress when this statute was enacted in 1970. To obtain the current content of the schedules, consult 21 CFR 308, Chapter II.

The criteria for inclusion of a drug in the five categories are as follows:
1. Schedule I. The drug has a high potential for abuse; it has no currently accepted medical use in the U.S.; and it is not safe to use even under medical supervision.

Included in this schedule, among other substances, are:
   a. Heroin
   b. Codeine
   c. Morphine
   d. LSD
   e. Marijuana
   f. Mescaline
   g. Peyote
2. Schedule II. The drug has high potential for abuse; it has current medical use in the U.S., but with severe restrictions; use of the drug may lead to severe psychological or physical dependence. Included here, among other substances, are:
   a. Opium and opiates, except derivatives in Schedule I.
   b. Opium poppy and poppy straw.
   c. Coca leaves and cocaine.
   d. Methadone.
3. Schedule III. The drug has less potential for abuse than those in Schedules I and II; it has current medical use in the U.S.; use of the drug may lead to moderate or low physical dependence or high psychological dependence. Included here, among other substances, are:
   a. Amphetamine and its derivatives.
   b. Barbituric acid and its derivatives (barbiturates).
   c. Other stimulants (uppers) and depressants (downers).
   d. Fairly weak compounds of narcotic drugs.
4. Schedule IV. The drug has less potential for abuse than those in Schedule III; it has accepted medical use in the U.S.; and abuse may lead to limited physical or psychological dependence. The schedule contained only eleven drugs when enacted, the most common of which are:
   a. Chloral hydrate.
   b. Meprobamate.
   c. Phenobarbital.
5. Schedule V. Compounds, mixtures, and preparations containing limited quantities of narcotic drugs plus non-narcotic active ingredients conferring upon them valuable medicinal qualities other than those possessed by the narcotic alone. The maximum permissible quantity of each narcotic is specified in the schedule.

21 USC 822 requires that every person who manufactures, distributes, or dispenses controlled substances must register each year with the attorney general. Since the controlled substances in Schedule I by definition have no medical value, it is unlawful to dispense these.

The registration requirements for drugs are set forth in 21 USC 823. They are too complex to go into in detail; essentially, manufacturing firms, drug wholesalers, physicians, pharmacists, researchers, and all other involved persons must register. (The researcher need not do so if he keeps the controlled substances within his laboratory.) Any sort of medical practitioner who is not permitted to dispense drugs according to state law may not register as a dispenser under federal law.

The penalties for unlawfully manufacturing, distributing, or dispensing a controlled substance, or for possessing with intent to unlawfully distribute or dispense, are:

For narcotic drugs in Schedules I or II: for the first offense, imprisonment of no more than fifteen years or fine of no more than $25,000, or both. For a second or subsequent offense, imprisonment of no more than thirty years or a fine of no more than $50,000, or both.

For a non-narcotic drug in Schedule I or II (such as peyote or marijuana), or any controlled substance in Schedule III: for the first offense, imprisonment of no more than five years or a fine of no more than $15,000, or both. For a second or subsequent offense, imprisonment for no more than ten years, a fine of no more than $30,000, or both.

For a controlled substance in Schedule IV: for the first offense, imprisonment for no more than three years, a fine of no more than $10,000, or both. For a second or subsequent offense, imprisonment for no more than six years, a fine of no more than $20,000, or both.

For a controlled substance in Schedule V: for a first offense, imprisonment for no more than one year or a fine of no more than $5,000, or both. For a second or subsequent offense, imprisonment for no more than two years or a fine of no more than $10,000, or both.

For dispensing a small amount of marijuana for no compensation, the penalty is the same as for possession, which will be discussed later.

The above penalties are set forth in 21 USC 841. Under 21 USC 842, certain unlawful acts by distributors and manufacturers are described and penalties for commission are set forth, which need not concern us here. 21 USC 843 forbids, among other things, acquisition of controlled substances through the use of fraud, forgery, misrepresentation, deception, or subterfuge, and forbids the use of a registered number which is fictitious, issued to another person, revoked, or suspended, in order to obtain controlled substances. The use of the mail, telephone, wire, or radio to commit a felony under this act is also forbidden by this section, each such use being a separate offense. For the first offense the penalty is imprisonment of no more than four years and a fine of no more than $30,000, or both. For a second or subsequent offense the penalty is imprisonment for no more than eight years or a fine of no more than $60,000, or both.

21 USC 844 provides that the knowing or intentional possession of a controlled substance is unlawful unless it was obtained from a practitioner in the course of his practice (dispensed by a physician, for instance) or pursuant to a valid prescription, or unless the possessor is a licensed distributor or dispenser. For first offense of unlawful possession, the penalty is imprisonment for no more than one year, fine of no more than $5,000, or both. For a second or subsequent offense, the penalty is imprisonment for no more than two years, fine of no more than $10,000, or both. For a first offender who has no other federal drug convictions under this or other sections of the drug-control law, the court may place the defendant on probation for a year; if he does not violate the probation, the charges will be dismissed and no conviction will appear on the defendant's record. If the defendant so placed on probation is under twenty-one years of age and does not violate his probation, all records of his arrest and subsequent proceedings against him will be expunged from the record.

Any person engaged in a continuing criminal enterprise in violation of federal drug-control legislation violates 21 USC 848. A person violates this section if he violates other provisions of the drug-control laws of the United States and if this violation is part of a continuing series of violations undertaken by him in concert with five or more other persons with respect to whom he occupies a position as organizer, supervisor, or other position of management, and from whom he obtains substantial income or resources.

For a first violation of this section the penalty is imprisonment of no less than ten years and no more than life, a fine of no more than $100,000, and forfeiture of all profits realized in the enterprise and all interest in the assets, contractual rights, or other property of the enterprise. For a second or subsequent offense the penalty is imprisonment for no less than twenty years nor more than life, and a fine of no less than $200,000, as well as the forfeitures mentioned above.

Thus, federal drug-control legislation in many ways is more stringent than the Texas state legislation. A drug violation may well be both a federal and a state offense.

Federal tax offenses. Section 7201 of the Internal Revenue Code declares that a willful attempt to evade or defeat any tax imposed by the Internal Revenue Code is a felony, for which the punishment is a maximum of five years in prison and a fine of $10,000.

IRC 7202 declares that a willful failure to collect or to account for and pay over a tax imposed by the Internal Revenue Code is a felony, for which the maxiumum sentence again is imprisonment for five years and a fine of $10,000.

Under IRC 7203 it is a misdemeanor for a person who is required to file a tax return, keep records, or supply information by provisions of the IRC or by Treasury regulations to willfully fail to file the return, keep the records, or supply the information. It is also a misdemeanor under this statute for a person (such as someone self-employed) who is required to pay an estimated tax to willfully fail to pay the tax. The maximum sentence for a violation of this statute is one year imprisonment and a fine of $10,000.

IRC 7201 is the most important of these statutes. Generally, a person willfully attempts to evade or defeat a tax either by failing to file required tax returns or by filing false and fraudulent returns.

The violator of IRC 7202 is most likely to be an employer who withholds income tax and the like from the wages of his employees and then willfully fails to pay over the withholdings to the IRS. The violator of IRC 7203 is apt to be a small taxpayer who does not bother to file returns or keep records.

The Internal Revenue Code contains some other criminal provisions, but they will not be explored here.

The citizen should realize that most efforts by the Internal Revenue Service to enforce the Internal Revenue Code are civil in nature, not criminal. The major interest of the IRS is to compel taxpayers to pay their tax liabilities, not to punish them for not paying.

The most commonly used IRS enforcement device is the tax return audit. This is performed by office auditors, or by Internal Revenue agents. The auditor compels the taxpayer to produce documentation to verify the information disclosed on his tax return, in order to substantiate claimed income, deductions, and the like. If the information produced causes the auditor to believe that the taxpayer understated his tax liability, he may assess a tax deficiency. The taxpayer may then either pay the deficiency or appeal the determination of the auditor to higher levels within the IRS and, if he wishes, to the Tax Court of the United States. The proceeding is at all levels a civil proceeding, the subject matter of the argument being money.

Should an IRS auditor, in the course of a routine audit, discover information which leads him to believe that the taxpayer is making a willful effort to defraud the government, he may alert the special agents of the Intelligence Division of the IRS, the division of the IRS charged with criminal enforcement of the Internal Revenue Code. Whenever a taxpayer learns that the Intelligence Division is investigating him, he should realize that criminal charges against him are being contemplated. The Intelligence Division may also begin a special investigation of the taxpayer unaccompanied by any civil audit.

Since the routine tax return audit is a civil matter, the taxpayer may not refuse to provide records and information requested by the auditor. The Intelligence Division investigation being a criminal matter, however, the taxpayer may invoke his right against self-incrimination to avoid furnishing information to the special agent.

Criminal prosecutions for IRC violations are conducted by Justice Department prosecutors, not by attorneys of the IRS. Such prosecutions therefore require close collaboration between the Treasury Department and the Justice Department. The Treasury Department investigators must assemble a strong case against a taxpayer before the Justice Department will undertake criminal prosecution.

Willful attempt to evade a tax is a crime which is very difficult to prove by direct evidence. This is particularly true when the taxpayer is suspected of having understated taxable income on his tax return. The government must be able to convince a jury in a tax evasion case of this nature that the taxpayer had taxable income which he did not report on his returns. How can this be proven?

F. Lee Bailey and Henry B. Rothblatt point out in *Defending Business and White Collar Crimes* (pp. 315-21) that prosecutors may, and do, use three methods to prove receipt of unreported taxable income by the taxpayer.

The simplest of these is the bank-deposit method. The government discovers bank accounts owned or controlled by the taxpayer. It then examines the records of activity in the accounts for the tax period in question (which it may do through subpoena of bank records). If more money is run through these accounts during the taxable period than the taxpayer reported as taxable income, and if these funds are not nontaxable gifts, inheritances, or the like, good evidence of evasion exists.

The net-worth method involves computation of the taxpayer's net worth at the beginning of the taxable period in question and at the end of that period. If the taxpayer's net worth increased during the period by an amount exceeded by his reported income less expenditures, and the increased net worth cannot be accounted for by gifts, inheritances, etc., good evidence of evasion exists.

The cash-expenditure method involves determination of how much money the taxpayer spent during the taxable period in question. If it can be proven that the taxpayer spent more money than his reported taxable income and that the excess expenditure was not of funds acquired through gifts, inheritances, savings, etc., evidence of evasion exists.

Determined investigators may assemble a comprehensive picture of a person's financial status without much assistance from the person himself. We conduct our financial transactions in a goldfish bowl these days—evidence of the sources and application of our personal funds lies about everywhere. The Internal Revenue Code makes all of this the business of the IRS. It is not wise to lie to the IRS about such things; the truth is available for discovery when the government chooses to seek it.

5

Torts

A tort is a wrong committed against someone which interferes with or causes harm to his person, his property, or his business or personal relationships. It could be committed deliberately, or it could be done inadvertently. It could be wrongful because the common law declares it to be so, or because a statute declares it to be so. Most of the torts to be discussed in this chapter are common-law torts. Statutory torts in the area of consumer protection will be discussed in the section on consumer law.

The law makes an important distinction between wrongs caused by torts and wrongs caused by breach of contract. In essence, a tort is a wrong committed in violation of a duty which society or the state has imposed upon the wrongdoer. The wrong which caused the tort may also be a crime, although it need not be. The wrong caused by a breach of contract is caused by one party's violation of his solemn bargain with another party. It could be said that a violation of a private duty has occurred, not a violation of a public duty. With respect to damages recoverable, time available after the wrong within which suit can be commenced, and so forth, the distinction between tort and breach of contract is very important.

Effect of age upon tort responsibility. In general, a person fifteen years of age or older is fully responsible for his torts. A child ten years of age or older is generally considered to be responsible for his torts, though an immature child between the ages of ten and fourteen might be excused from responsibility, depending upon the individual case. A child between the ages of five and nine is too young to be negligent, but might possibly be held responsible for his deliberate torts. A child four years of age or younger cannot be held responsible for torts.

Battery. The tort of battery is committed when a person is the victim of unwanted, unpermitted, and unprivileged bodily contact with another. The contact need not cause injury or be hostile; but the more unwanted, hostile, avoidable, and injurious it is, the more likely it is to be considered battery. Of course, undesired bodily contact is privileged under certain conditions—disciplining of a child by its parents, effecting a lawful arrest, responding to a physical threat by another person, or similar actions.

Assault. The tort of assault is committed when the crime of assault is committed. Remember that no bodily contact is required for assault to occur; threatened bodily contact under circumstances in which such contact is feared or very unwelcome is enough to constitute assault. On the other hand, the uttering of offensive words is not in and of itself assault: the tort must have a physical element. An assault which results in bodily contact is also a battery: the result is commission of assault and battery.

False imprisonment. Whenever the crime of false imprisonment is committed, the tort of false imprisonment is also committed. The same defenses apply in the tort situation as apply in criminal prosecutions.

Negligent confinement. The tort of negligent confinement is a close relative of false imprisonment. It has no criminal counterpart.

If, when a shopkeeper locks up his business for the night, he negligently confines a customer inside his shop, he has committed this tort. The person closing up owes a duty to customers to warn them that it is closing time. Of course, if the customer is in a part of the store in which the clerk or shopkeeper does not expect him to be, the customer is partly to blame for his confinement and may be unable to recover anything.

The major difference between false imprisonment and negligent confinement is, then, that false imprisonment is deliberate, while negligent confinement is unintentional.

Infliction of mental distress. A person who commits the crime of harassment is probably committing the tort of infliction of mental distress, if his harassment causes mental suffering to his victim. For damages to be recoverable, though, the mental distress should cause medically identifiable damage—either physical damage (such as a miscarriage), or psychological damage identifiable by a psychologist or psychiatrist.

Usually the commission of this tort is deliberate. However, it is also possible to commit it through negligence. This may be done by unthinkingly committing an act in the presence of another that greatly disturbs the other person, or by unthinkingly allowing a situation to arise which greatly disturbs another person. For instance, in *Western Union Telegraph Co. vs. Hinson*, 222 S.W. 2d 636, Hinson's son had been killed in action during World War II. The War Department sent Hinson a telegram notifying him that his son's body would be sent home, and would arrive at a named time. Western Union negligently did not deliver the telegram. The body of the son arrived totally unannounced and unexpected, greatly upsetting Hinson. Hinson was allowed to recover damages from Western Union.

Debt collectors have often committed this tort in the past. Now, however, federal and Texas statutes regulate their conduct; their torts are now statutory. These statutes will be covered in the portion of this book on consumer protection.

Malicious prosecution. The tort of malicious prosecution is committed when a person maliciously and without legal grounds causes criminal charges to be brought against another, or begins civil proceedings against another. Before the victim can complain of malicious prosecution, the criminal charges must be dropped or defeated, or the civil suit must be dropped or defeated. In addition, if the court procedure complained of was civil, the victim must have suffered interference with his person or property.

If the victim was convicted of the criminal charge or found liable in the civil suit, there was no malicious prosecution. If the victim was acquitted or found not liable, this is not in itself proof of malicious prosecution. If the defendant in a malicious prosecution case can prove that he acted in good faith when he began court proceedings against the plaintiff, he escapes liability.

Abuse of process. When a person uses the courts and court procedures for an ulterior purpose, he may commit the tort of abuse of process. The misused process may either be criminal or civil. It does not matter whether the defendant in the process was found guilty or liable; the determining factor here is the motive of the plaintiff or complaining witness in beginning the court procedure in the first place. If the purpose was something other than recovery of the relief asked for in a civil case or punishment of the defendant for crime in a criminal case, the court process has been abused.

Conversion. Whenever a person commits the crime of theft, he also commits the tort of conversion. This tort essentially consists of depriving a person of his property without his consent. One may commit conversion in the following ways:

1. By stealing another's property.
2. By borrowing another's property and not returning it when asked.
3. By deliberately destroying or damaging another's property.
4. By attempting to sell, mortgage, or give away property which belongs to another, without permission of the owner.
5. By misdelivering another's property to a third party.
6. By receiving someone else's property from a person unauthorized to transfer it.

Usually the person who commits conversion does it deliberately. However, it can be done negligently, as when Ace Delivery Service delivers to Trey a package addressed to Deuce. Ace is guilty of conversion here by delivering to the wrong party. If Trey accepts delivery he is also guilty of conversion; he should know that the package is not his.

Conversion may also be innocent. Thus, if Clubb steals goods from Spade and sells them to Hart, Clubb commits conversion because he is a thief. Hart also commits conversion because he has bought stolen property—even though he may honestly have believed that Clubb was the true owner of the stolen property.

Damages recoverable for conversion are generally limited to the value of the converted property, plus interest.

Trespass. Generally, anyone who comes upon another's land without the consent of the owner is guilty of trespass. The trespasser incurs no liability to the landowner, however, unless he causes damage to the owner's property during the course of the trespass.

The trespass is usually direct—the trespasser physically invades the owner's property. It may, however, also be indirect, as when Jones engages in blasting upon his property and the blasting causes rock fragments and other materials to fall upon Smith's property.

Pilots of low-flying aircraft are guilty of trespass if they violate Federal Aviation Administration regulations. If they cause mental harm to the landowner or members of his family—or if they interfere with the egg production of the landowner's chickens, for example—they will be liable to him for damages.

Trespass is justified under some conditions. Thus, peace officers may come onto a person's property in performance of their duties. Also, a person may come onto another's land in order to recover personal property of his which has been taken there, so long as the entry is peaceable and causes no damage.

Injury by animals. The owner of animals may be held liable for injury caused by them. The owner of wild animals is absolutely liable for any injury they may cause, while the owner of domestic animals is liable for any injury they may cause if they are known to be vicious.

A domestic animal is known to be vicious if it has injured someone in the past. Hence, it is said that "every dog is entitled to one free bite." The dog is assumed not to be vicious so long as it is not known to have bitten anyone. The first bite victim of the animal has no cause to sue, because he has been bitten by a nonvicious domestic animal. However, after the first bite the dog is now known to be vicious, and his second and subsequent victims may sue his owner for damages.

In those localities which have leash laws—where it is unlawful for a pet owner to permit his animals to run at large—the dog owner who allows his animal to run loose commits a misdemeanor. He assumes liability for any harm his animal does while running loose in violation of the law.

Nuisance. Any occupier of land who uses the land in such a way as to damage his neighbor's enjoyment of *his* land commits a nuisance. There are two categories of nuisances—public and private. The only recourse against a public nuisance is a suit for an injunction. If a private nuisance causes damage to a neighbor, the injured neighbor may sue to recover his losses. Even if the nuisance causes no damage, the neighbor may sue for an injunction to abate it.

RCS 4667 declares that the actual, threatened, or contemplated use of any premises, place, building, or part thereof for any of the following purposes is a public nuisance:
1. Gambling, gambling promotion, or communicating gambling information prohibited by law.
2. Promotion of prostitution, or compelling prostitution.
3. Commercial manufacturing, commercial distribution, or commercial exhibition of obscene material.
4. Commercial exhibitions depicting any type of sexual intercourse.
5. Staging fights between a man and a bull.

The citizen suing for an injunction against a public nuisance need not prove that he has been damaged by it in any way.

The following sorts of activity may constitute a private nuisance:
1. Burning items which continuously causes noxious smoke to drift onto the victim's property.
2. Raising animals which continuously cause noxious odors to invade the victim's property.
3. Doing work on one's property which often causes loud noises to be made.
4. Keeping on one's property wild animals which make loud noises and cause neighbors to live in fear of what might happen if the animals escape.
5. Allowing a pond to exist upon one's property where mosquitoes breed.
6. Allowing an overflowing cesspool to exist upon one's property.
7. Storing explosives in an unprotected area of one's property.

In essence, anyone who suffers damage from a private nuisance which is a menace to health, such as a cesspool or mosquito pond, may complain about it. With respect to those nuisances created by business activity, zoning legislation may play a role in determination of legality. One of course may not conduct commercial or industrial activity upon property which is zoned residential, and one may not conduct industrial activity upon property which is zoned commercial. But if the property is zoned for industry it will be difficult to have industrial activity declared to be a nuisance.

No two private nuisance cases are alike. In deciding a case a court must take into account the social value of the nuisance as well as the disturbance caused to the plaintiff. Mosquito ponds have no social value, of course, but a business does: the business provides jobs and tax revenue. The court will also consider whether or not other individuals or firms in the area engage in the same activity as the defendant. If they do, why should the plaintiff choose to complain about the defendant and not about the others? The court will also consider how long the alleged nuisance has been present. The longer it has been around, the more likely the court is to find for the defendant. Lastly, it will consider whether the plaintiff moved into the neighborhood after the nuisance came into existence. If he did, this factor may also weigh in favor of the defendant.

If the plaintiff can prove that the nuisance has caused him to suffer damage, he may recover damages. Or the plaintiff may sue for an injunction forbidding the defendant to continue the activity complained of or making the defendant "abate" the nuisance—that is, remove it.

Fraud (or deceit). The tort of fraud is a common-law tort in most areas. However, Texas Business & Commerce Code 27.01 makes it a statutory tort when committed in real estate and stock transactions. In these transactions, fraud may take two forms.

The first form consists of a false representation of a past or existing material fact, when the representation is made for the purpose of inducing another to enter into a contract, and its truth is relied upon by the other person in entering into the contract.

The second form consists of a promise to perform an act which is a false promise. For this to be fraud, the false promise must be material, it must be made with the intention of not fulfilling it, it must be made for the purpose of inducing another to enter into a contract, and it must be relied upon by that person in entering into the contract.

In real estate and stock transactions, the plaintiff's measure of damages is the difference between the promised value of the land or stock and its actual value at the time it was delivered to the plaintiff. The person who makes the false representation is liable for the damages; if any other person benefitted from the fraud even if he did not participate in it, he is jointly and severally liable to the victim along with the maker of the false representation. Persons willfully making a false representation in a land or stock sale, and persons knowingly benefitting from the false representation, are jointly and severally liable to the victim for exemplary (punitive) damages of double the actual damages caused by the fraud.

The requirements for fraud in transactions other than stock and real estate are essentially the same as under the statute. A false statement of material fact must be made with the intent to induce the victim to enter into a contract, and the victim must enter into the bargain in justifiable reliance upon the truth of the statement. Reliance is not justifiable when the victim's own eyes, his own common sense, or his own professional knowledge tell him that he is being deceived.

The measure of damages is different in the common-law fraud situations. The plaintiff recovers compensatory damages only—the difference between the promised value of what he got and its actual value at the time the jury decides his case. The plaintiff can recover punitive damages only when the defendant's conduct was willful and malicious. Fraud also provides the victim with the opportunity to rescind the contract he was tricked into making. This aspect of fraud will be covered in the materials on contracts.

Libel. Libel, as defined by RCS 5430, is a defamation expressed in printing or writing, in signs and pictures, or in drawings, tending to smear the reputation of someone dead, or tending to injure the reputation of someone who is alive and thereby expose him to public hatred, contempt, ridicule, or financial injury. It is also libelous to impeach the honesty, integrity, or virtue of anyone, or to publish the natural defects of anyone, and thereby expose him to public hatred, ridicule, or financial injury.

Libel is thus a defamation transmitted in writing (or on radio or television) as opposed to slander, which is a defamation transmitted by word of mouth. In common law, libel and slander were governed by the same principles, but since the Texas statutes (RCS 5430 et seq.) govern libel and not slander, the law governing the two forms of defamation is no longer quite the same.

If a person can prove that he is a victim of libel as defined above, he is entitled to recover "general damages" for his loss of reputation, injury to feelings, or mental suffering, without any necessity to prove that he has actually suffered damages. However, if the victim desires to recover "special damages" for loss of employment, loss of health, or other sorts of damage that may be caused by matters other than libel, he must prove the actual amount of such damages.

A publication by a newspaper or other periodical is privileged (RCS 5432) and may not be made the basis of any action for libel if:
1. It is a fair, true, and impartial account of court proceedings or any other official proceedings, unless the publication has been forbidden by a court.
2. It is a fair, true, and impartial account of legislative or executive proceedings of the federal, state, and local governments or of state-supported institutions.
3. It is a fair, true, and impartial account of the proceedings of a public meeting.
4. It is a reasonable and fair comment or criticism of official acts of public officials and of other matters of public concern published for general information.
5. It is a republication of matter which was originally privileged, unless the republication occurs after the matter has ceased to be one of public interest, and is done out of malice.

Thus, the law of libel is limited by the right of the news-gathering media to report what is newsworthy. A person who does something newsworthy is likely to find himself in the news; the more of a public figure he is, the more likely he is to be in the news.

There are two defenses to liability for libel other than that of privilege, discussed above. These are truth and lack of publication.

An unpublished defamatory statement is not libelous. The plaintiff in a libel action must prove that some third party has actually read or seen the defamatory material.

If the allegedly defamatory statement is true, there is no defamation. Legally and logically, one should not be penalized for printing or speaking the truth, even though compassion sometimes dictates that the truth should be forgotten. Thus, many a libel action resolves itself into a question of fact as to whether or not the allegedly libelous statement is true. It becomes the duty of the jury to decide this question.

Under RCS 5433a, radio and TV broadcasting station owners are not liable for libelous statements broadcast by persons who are not employees of the station in question, unless the station's employees were negligent in allowing the broadcast. Thus, the station would not be liable for a libelous statement uttered by a political candidate in the course of a live TV debate. It might be liable, however, for broadcasting a videotaped libelous statement, since the station could have edited the tape and deleted the libelous material.

Slander. Slander is oral defamation of character, which is not governed by any statutes. In order for an oral statement to be slanderous, it must be:
1. Untrue.
2. Published—that is, third parties must have heard it.
3. The cause of provable damage, unless it is slanderous "per se."

Two types of slanderous statements are now generally regarded as being slanderous "per se." These are:
1. Statements that the victim has committed a crime involving moral turpitude—including any crimes involving abuse of person or property.
2. Statements injurious to the victim's reputation in his trade, office, profession, or business.

The victim of slander "per se" may recover damages without the necessity of proving that he suffered any special damage. The mere fact that he has been slandered entitles him to recovery. If the defamatory statement is not slanderous "per se," however, the victim must prove that he suffered special damages before he may recover anything.

As with libel, the defendant in a slander case may escape liability by proving that the allegedly slanderous statement was true.

The common law has developed several sorts of privilege which insulate the maker of a defamatory statement from liability. These common-law rules of privilege apply in cases of libel as well as in cases of slander.

Statements made by judges, jurors, and witnesses in the course of judicial proceedings are absolutely privileged. You cannot defame anyone in the courtroom.

Statements made by legislators on the floor of the legislature or in committee are absolutely privileged. However, statements by legislators in press conferences, campaign speeches, and the like are not so privileged.

Statements made by executive members of governments in the line of duty are absolutely privileged—but, again, not statements made in press conferences, campaign speeches, and so on.

If the victim gave his consent to the making of the statement before it was made, it is absolutely privileged.

A statement made by a married person about his or her spouse is absolutely privileged, no matter how defamatory. (But a statement made by a formerly married person about his or her ex-spouse is not privileged at all.)

Any statement contained in professional communications, reports of corporate officers to shareholders, or the like is qualifiedly privileged; the statement is not defamatory unless maliciously uttered.

Statements made in the course of the management of the internal affairs of a church, club, or similar private organization are qualifiedly privileged.

Statements exchanged between parties with a mutual interest—employees, lending institutions, employers, and so on—are qualifiedly privileged if they promote the mutual interest in question.

Communications to persons acting in the public interest on matters of public interest, such as the reporting of suspected crimes to the police, are qualifiedly privileged.

Finally, statements made in defense of one's own reputation, or in defense of the reputation of a third party who cannot defend himself, are qualifiedly privileged.

Thus, the notion of privilege covers many sorts of statements which would otherwise be considered defamatory. Essentially, privilege applies in those areas of life and business where it is to society's advantage to encourage people to speak their minds freely, without fear of consequences.

Disparagement. This particular sort of defamation involves the making of false statements by one businessman intended to damage the reputation of his competitor or his competitor's product in the eyes of the public. It is a deceptive business practice under the Texas Deceptive Trade Practices Act: the victim may recover triple damages from the utterer of the disparaging statement. This has also been branded an unfair trade practice under the Federal Trade Commission Act. The FTC may take administrative action against the disparager.

Invasion of privacy. The tort of invasion of privacy is one of recent invention, a product of the technological progress of the twentieth century. It was not recognized by Texas courts until the early 1970s, and its boundaries within this state are still imperfectly defined.

In general, those states which have a well-developed law of invasion of privacy consider the following sorts of conduct to be such an invasion:

1. The appropriation of the victim's name or likeness without his consent.

2. Intrusion upon the victim's private life or property without justification.
3. Disclosure of private facts about the victim for no good reason.
4. Giving the victim publicity which makes him appear in a false light.

So long as a person is not a public, newsworthy individual, his private affairs should remain private. Thus, for example, his photograph should not be used in advertising campaigns without his consent. The fact that he owes a debt which he has not paid should not be made public knowledge, nor should the fact that he has been married six times.

However, a person's right to privacy diminishes as the public becomes aware of and interested in him. The fact that a person was involved in an auto accident will cause his name to be in the newspaper. The person who becomes first-string quarterback for the local high school football team will often find his name in the newspaper. The local football coach will be even more newsworthy. Of course, nationally known entertainers, sports figures, politicians, and such figures will be almost constantly in the news.

The communications media have the right to report the news. Thus, when a person does something newsworthy, his privacy will be diminished. When the person himself is deemed newsworthy, he has very little privacy. One of the penalties one pays for being a public person is that one lives one's life in a goldfish bowl. As time goes on the bowl becomes more and transparent, since the personal and private lives of public persons attract more of the attention of the communications media.

Interference with contractual relations. An individual has the right to conduct his business affairs without outside interference, so long as he does not violate the law. He has the right to make whatever legal contracts he sees fit to make, and his contractual relationships should not be interfered with by outsiders.

Of course, a person who breaches a contract is liable to the other parties to the bargain for damages. A person who induces another to breach a contract is also liable to the other party to the contract for damages. The extent of the damage depends, of course, upon the nature of the breached contract, and upon the nature of the damage suffered.

If Brown Company has a contract with Green Company to buy all of its requirements of an essential raw material from Green, and Blue Company induces Green to breach the contract, Brown may suffer considerable damages, especially if the raw material is in short supply.

On the other hand, if Black has rented an apartment from White under a one-year lease, and Gray induces Black to breach the lease, and White at once rents the apartment to Redd for the same rental he would have collected from Black, White has suffered no great damage.

If a person induces another not to make a contract with a third party, the third party may be a victim of this tort. However, the seriousness of this conduct depends upon who is perpetrating it. If the victim is a businessman and the perpetrator is one of his competitors, there may be nothing wrong, since competition does involve taking customers away from competitors. After all, if Black induces Brown to contract with him rather than with White by offering Brown a better price, better credit terms, a better guarantee, or quicker delivery, that is the way the game of business competition is played. If, however, Black snatches the Brown contract from White through commercial bribery, disparagement of White's product or service, or similar trickery, White does have a legitimate complaint.

If Black is not a competitor of White, but he induces Brown not to deal with White because he dislikes White and wants to harm his business, White also has a legitimate complaint; Black is acting maliciously in this situation.

Defenses in intentional tort cases. There are certain defenses which will relieve a defendant of liability in many sorts of situations. Since these may be applicable to a wide variety of torts, it is best to consider them all at once.

The first of these is self-defense. A person is not guilty of assault or battery if he uses force to defend himself against an actual or threatened attack.

The second is defense of real property. A person may use deadly force to protect his home against burglary, robbery, or similar intrusion. He may use deadly force to protect any other real property he owns against such felonies. He may also arm himself to evict trespassers, but he may use no more force than is necessary to evict them.

The third is defense of personal property. In order to retain possession of one's personal property one may use any force necessary against someone who would unlawfully take it. One may also use force to retake possession of such property while in hot pursuit of a thief or similar unlawful taker. Use of excessive force is of course not justified.

The fourth is consent. If the plaintiff agreed to the defendant's actions but later claims that the actions were wrongful, he has no case. (Of course, if the plaintiff can prove that the defendant exceeded the bounds of his consent, he may prevail.) Thus, a boxer cannot charge assault and battery when his opponent knocks him out, and a patient cannot charge his surgeon with assault and battery if the patient consented to the surgeon's performing an appendectomy upon him.

The fifth is privilege. This has already been discussed in the matter of defamation and invasion of privacy, but it applies elsewhere also. The policeman who searches a house under a valid search warrant cannot be sued for trespass. The parent who spanks his young child in the interest of discipline is not guilty of assault and battery. The parent who denies his teenaged daughter the privilege of socializing after dark is not guilty of false imprisonment.

The sixth and last is necessity. A person may commit a tort if the commission is necessary in order to save himself from suffering damage. He may be liable for the actual damage his tort causes, though, if he is acting to protect only himself or a few others; this is merely a private emergency. Thus, if water coming from Gray's land flows onto White's land, and White diverts the water onto Black's land to save his own from damage, Black could recover damages from White. (Of course, he may recover damages from Gray if he wishes, too, because Gray is the cause of the problem.) Or, if Blue's hog escapes and begins destroying Redd's garden, and Redd injures the hog in his efforts to drive it out of his garden, Blue would have a claim against Redd for the injury. (Redd will of course also have a claim against Blue for the injury to his garden.)

However, if the emergency is a public emergency—that is, if action is needed to protect the general public from a hazard—a person who commits a tort in the process of ending the emergency is not liable for damages he causes. Thus, if a cobra escapes from Spade's carnival and Clubb kills it, Spade has no claim against Clubb, since society cannot afford to have cobras crawling loose. If a fire is advancing toward a populated area, buildings may be destroyed in order to create a firebreak. The owner of these buildings will have no claim against those who carried out the destruction.

Liability of owners and occupiers of land. Owners and occupiers of land owe certain duties to persons outside the premises. They owe other duties to those who come onto the premises.

The duties owed to persons outside the premises can be summarized briefly. Nuisances must not be permitted to exist upon the premises. If negligent acts committed upon the premises cause damage to persons outside, the owner or occupier of the premises will be liable. Thus, if a person negligently permits dynamite to explode upon his property and the concussion breaks his neighbors' windows, he will be liable for the damage. If a person uses his land in a way that trespasses upon his neighbor's land, such as permitting the eaves of his roof to overhang his neighbor's land, he will be liable for the trespass. If the landowner makes an excavation so close to the border of his neighbor's land that the neighbor's land caves into the excavation, the landowner is liable for removing the lateral support. If the owner uses his land in such a way as to make streets and sidewalks nearby unsafe, he will be liable for any damage caused. Thus, if Jones allows water to flow onto the land of his neighbor Smith and onto the sidewalk adjoining Smith's land, and this water freezes in winter, anyone injured by slipping on the ice will be able to sue Jones.

The nature of the duty owed to persons coming onto premises depends upon the status of the injured person. There are three categories of persons who come onto another's property:

1. Trespassers—persons who have no right to come upon the property.
2. Licensees—persons who have a right to come onto the property to benefit themselves, such as door-to-door salesmen, neighbors dropping in uninvited, and the like. Texas courts also consider policemen and firemen performing their duties to be licensees.
3. Invitees—persons invited to come onto the premises, or those who come for the benefit of the owner or occupier. Included here are customers of businesses, guests invited into a home, repairpersons invited into a home, postmen, meter readers, milkmen, etc.

The duty owed a trespasser depends in part on whether the trespasser is an adult or a child. The only duty owed to the adult trespasser is a duty not to set traps or similar obstructions which will cause injury. Since the trespasser has no legal right to trespass, the landowner has no duty to keep the premises safe to protect him. He merely must not deliberately create a condition which might injure the trespasser. With respect to the child trespasser, the law recognizes that young children may not understand the obligation not to go onto other people's land without their consent. The landowner must therefore not have anything on his land which would be dangerous to children and which they would find attractive: in short, there must be no "attractive nuisances" about. Attractive nuisances can take many forms—they include swimming pools, abandoned wells, gravel pits, dangerous animals, old rotten trees, old refrigerators, abandoned, decrepit houses, or other such things. Children could find all of these very interesting, and they all can also be very dangerous. The only way to avoid injury to curious children caused by attractive nuisances is to have no such nuisances on the premises. Children will ignore signs, and they have ways of getting by the strongest and highest fences.

When a licensee is injured by a dangerous condition on the premises which is not obvious to any observer, but of which the landowner or occupier is aware, the owner or occupier is liable for the injury. Such known hazards should be removed or repaired as soon as they are discovered. If this cannot be done, warning signs should be posted, or known licensees should be given oral warnings of the danger. Of course, the owner or occupier is also liable for injury caused a child licensee by an attractive nuisance.

The owner or occupier will be liable to an invitee if he is injured on the premises by a dangerous condition, whether the condition was known or not. The only exception to this is if the invitee, as a reasonable person, should have known of the danger, but took no steps to avoid it, in which case he has no claim. Thus, the landowner or occupier owes the invitee not only the duty to warn him against all known dangers, but also to keep the property under close enough observation to spot unknown dangers before they cause injury and to remedy them.

The tenant is usually responsible for dangerous conditions on rented property. The landlord could be held liable if a dangerous condition existed upon the property when he rented it to the tenant, and the tenant did not know of it and therefore could not correct it. If the landlord did know of it and neither corrected it nor informed the tenant of it, he will be responsible for any injury. If the landlord rents out the premises to a tenant knowing the tenant will maintain a nuisance there, the landlord may be held liable for any damage done by the nuisance.

The seller of property will be liable to third parties for any nuisances which exist upon the property until the buyer has a reasonable time to abate them. If the seller knows of a dangerous condition upon the property when he sells it, but he does not inform the buyer of its existence and the buyer cannot discover it at once, the seller will be liable for any harm done to outsiders. Otherwise the seller gives up responsibility to outsiders for the condition of the property.

NEGLIGENCE

Negligence in general consists of carelessness, behavior which does not show proper regard for the safety of others. It is probably the most commonly committed of torts, and, far more often than not, it is committed in connection with the operation of a motor vehicle.

Standard of care required to be free of negligence. In general, a person should behave toward others as a "reasonable man" would. However, the "reasonable man" standard is not applied uniformly. More is expected of some persons under certain circumstances than is expected of others. Thus, children are held to a lesser standard of care than are adults: children under ten years of age are generally regarded as being too immature to be negligent. On the other hand, children fourteen years of age and older are held to the same standards as adults.

Skilled craftsmen or professionals are held to a high degree of care when performing within their skill or profession; they are expected to perform as a reasonably skilled member of the trade or profession would perform. Professional malpractice essentially consists of the negligent failure to perform according to this high standard.

Sometimes one standard of care is owned to one class of persons and another to another. Thus, as we have seen, in the case of owners and occupiers of land, one duty is owed to the trespasser, another to the licensee, and another to the invitee. The aged and the infirm are of course held to a lower standard of care than the young and the vigorous.

RCS 1a provides that a person who administers emergency care at the scene of an emergency without expectation of compensation shall not be liable for his negligence in administering such emergency care unless his negligence is willful and wanton. The purpose of the statute is, of course, to encourage persons to act as good Samaritans at the scene of an accident without fear of incurring legal liability for any errors in treatment they commit. Of course, anyone performing such emergency aid with the expectation of compensation would not be given the advantage of this reduction of potential liability.

The person who is unexpectedly thrust into an emergency situation in which a quick reaction is necessary is also held to a lower standard of care, on the theory that human beings do not act as rationally under sudden stress as they do when time exists for calm, rational thought.

Proof of negligence. When a person violates a statute enacted to protect the public, and this violation causes injury to a member of the public, violation of the statute is said to be "negligence per se." Proof of the violation of the statute is proof of negligence in and of itself. Generally, if the person accused of negligence has pleaded guilty to the criminal charge of violating the statute, or if he was tried and convicted for the violation, proof of the guilty plea or of the conviction is proof of negligence. On the other hand, if the person pleads nolo contendere to the criminal charge, that plea is not proof of negligence.

If the statutory violation is the traffic offense of speeding, however, proof of a guilty plea or of conviction does not constitute proof of negligence. Thus, exceeding the speed limit while driving a motor vehicle is not negligence per se.

An acquittal upon a charge of violating a statute is of course proof that no violation took place. However, it must be remembered that one may be guilty of negligence without violating any statutes. If a civil defendant has not violated a statute, the plaintiff must prove his negligence the hard way—by essentially proving that the defendant did not behave toward the plaintiff with the degree of care he owed the plaintiff as a reasonable man.

Sometimes the plaintiff in a negligence case must prove that he held a status under which the defendant owed him a certain duty of care. In auto accident cases this might not be necessary, because drivers of motor vehicles owe a duty to members of the public not to be negligent. But when the suit is against an owner or occupier of land and the plaintiff is claiming to have been injured by an unknown hazard upon the property, he will generally have to prove that he was an invitee before he can recover.

Proximate cause. Before the defendant may be held liable for injuries to the plaintiff due to his negligence, the plaintiff must prove that the negligence in question was the proximate cause of the injuries. Thus, the defendant may escape liability if the plaintiff cannot prove that the defendant's negligence caused the injury, or if the defendant can prove that there was another cause of the plaintiff's injury.

If the cause of the injury is not obvious, or if there are two or more possible causes, the jury may well be called upon to decide the cause of the injury. Failure by the plaintiff to convince the jury that the defendant's negligence was the proximate cause of the accident will cost the plaintiff his recovery of damages.

Res ipsa loquitur. Sometimes an injury occurs under circumstances in which there are no witnesses and no one can prove for certain what caused the injury. If under such circumstances there is only one logical explanation for the injury—negligence by the defendant—the rule of *res ipsa loquitur*, ("the matter speaks for itself") will be applied. The defendant will be held to be negligent unless he can prove that something other than his negligence caused the injury.

Assume, for example, that Owner moved into a new house Builder had just erected for him. A week after he moved in, he was injured when the roof collapsed. There had been no rain, snow, earthquake, nearby explosion, or landslide between the time Owner moved in and the time of the collapse, and Owner had engaged in no activity which could have damaged the house. The only logical explanation for such a catastrophe is negligence by the contractor in erection of the building. The matter speaks for itself: the law will presume that Builder's negligence caused the catastrophe unless Builder can prove otherwise.

Unavoidable accident. If a defendant accused of negligence can prove that there was no way he could avoid causing the plaintiff's injury, the defendant escapes liability. Thus, Green has just put four new tires on his automobile. They have been properly mounted and inflated. He is driving on a freeway at 55 MPH when a front tire blows out. Green loses control of the vehicle and it collides with a vehicle driven by Brown. Brown's vehicle is badly damaged, and he demands damages from Green. Green may escape liability, since there is no way he could have foreseen the accident, and no way he could have avoided it.

The probable cause of this incident is a defect in the tire; Brown may be able to recover damages in a suit against the manufacturer of the defective tire.

Sometimes the victim of such an accident will have no one to blame for his injury. Thus Ace drives his auto along a residential street. Ace has never missed a day of work during his forty years of working life. He is sixty-four and appears to be in perfect health. However, he suffers a serious heart attack while driving. He naturally loses control of the car; it runs up onto the sidewalk and strikes Deuce, a pedestrian, injuring him badly. Ace was driving within the speed limit, and his car was in good operating order. Ace can hardly be accused of negligence here—and no one else is guilty of any wrongdoing. Deuce has had the misfortune of being at the wrong place at the wrong time—he has no recourse against anyone.

Assumption of risk and incurred risk. When a person makes a contract to perform services for another as an independent contractor—and he knows that there are certain risks of injury involved in the performance of the contract—he assumes the risk of such injury. If he is injured by one of these known perils, he has no claim against his employer unless his employer was more negligent than he. (If he is an employee rather than an independent contractor, though, he will be able to file a Workers' Compensation claim for his injury.)

When there is no employer-employee or employer-independent contractor relationship, Texas courts do not talk about assumption of risk. When a person goes into an area where there is danger and he knows of the danger, he incurs the risk of being injured. Thus, a person who walks across a railroad bridge over a stream incurs the risk that a train might arrive before he reaches the other side. Anyone who sits in the bleachers to watch a baseball game incurs the risk of being hit by a foul ball. A person who borrows his friend's automobile knowing that it has a defective steering mechanism incurs the risk that the steering gear will fail while he is driving and cause him injury. Someone who goes onto premises ignoring a conspicuous sign warning him of danger there and is injured by the described danger incurred the risk of his injury. Anyone who is injured by an incurred risk has no recourse unless the other party was more negligent than he.

Contributory and comparative negligence. In Texas before 1973, and in many other states now, if an accident occurs and both parties involved are negligent, neither may recover from the other. Contributory negligence was thus an absolute defense to liability. It still is in those states recognizing it. The Texas legislature, however, abolished the absolute defense of contributory negligence in 1973. By its enactment of RCS 2122, it established in this state the rule of comparative negligence. Under that rule, when an accident or other mishap involving two or more persons occurs, and both or all are possibly guilty of negligence, the jury is asked to determine how negligent all of the parties were and how much damage each complaining party suffered. The least negligent may then recover a portion of their damages from the more negligent. The arithmetic involved will be discussed later.

Last clear chance. When both parties to an accident were negligent, but one of them had the last chance to avoid the mishap and did not make use of it, the party with the last clear chance was held to be totally liable under the rules of contributory negligence. Assume that Clubb, driving along a country highway in a rainstorm, has a flat tire. He stops on the road and seeks to change the tire. He does not pull off onto the unpaved shoulder because he does not want to wallow in the mud there. He leaves his lights on, but he has no fusees to make enough light to warn other vehicles of his presence in a more effective manner. He is right in the middle of a two-mile straightaway. Spade comes along later, driving 80 MPH in the rain. When he becomes aware of Clubb's presence ahead, it is too late for him to stop, and a bad collision occurs. Of course Clubb was negligent to obstruct the highway, but Spade obviously had the last clear chance to avoid the wreck. In those states following the rule of contributory negligence, Spade would be totally responsible for this accident. Whether the adoption of comparative negligence in Texas has changed that rule here has not yet been decided.

The rescue doctrine. Viejo, age eighty, starts walking across a street at a traffic light while the light favors him. He gets three-fourths of the way across when the light changes. But Viejo is not aware of this change; he keeps walking slowly on his way. Rash approaches the intersection where the light is now green for him, driving 45 MPH, although the speed limit is 35 MPH. Young, a bystander, observes Viejo's slow progress and the approach of Rash, and knows that Rash will run Viejo down unless something is done. Young rushes into the street and pushes Viejo out of the path of Rash's oncoming car—but Young doesn't get out of Rash's path in time and is injured. Young in due course sues Rash for damages. Rash's defense is that Young was negligent to rush into the street to try to save Viejo. This defense will almost certainly fail: a rescuer such as Young will not be held responsible for his negligence in such a situation, unless he acted wantonly and recklessly. If Young's action saved Viejo from death or serious injury, his actions could hardly be said to have been wanton or reckless.

Damages in negligence cases. A plaintiff in a negligence action is entitled to seek three types of compensation, perhaps, depending upon the circumstances. He is certainly entitled to seek compensatory damages, including compensation for damage to his property and, if he suffered personal injury also, his medical and hospital bills, plus the wages or salary he lost due to his injury. If personal injury was caused, the plaintiff may seek damages for his pain and suffering. There is no objective measure for this: the plaintiff may recover what the jury is willing to award.

In addition, if the plaintiff was injured due to the willful and wanton misconduct of the defendant (such as his driving while under the influence of alcohol), the plaintiff may seek punitive or exemplary damages. The object here is to punish the defendant for his wrongdoing.

Apportionment of damages under comparative negligence. The rules for apportionment of damages when two parties are involved in the case are simple. When three or more are involved, they get more complex.

The complexity of the situation will also be influenced by the matter of whether or not the defendant or defendants have filed counterclaims against the plaintiff. In essence, if an accident results in damage to both parties, each party must make his claim against the other in the same lawsuit. Thus, if the plaintiff has filed suit against the defendant, but the defendant thinks he should be the one doing the suing, he must file a counterclaim against the plaintiff for his injuries. If he does not do this, he forfeits all claim against the plaintiff for damages arising from the incident.

If the defendant claims that the plaintiff was negligent in the incident in which the plaintiff was injured, the jury must apportion the negligence between the parties on a percentage basis. It must also determine how much damage the plaintiff suffered. If the defendant has made a counterclaim, the jury must also decide how much damage the defendant suffered. The judge will determine the recovery on the basis of the jury's answers to these questions.

Take first a two-way accident in which there is no counterclaim: if the jury decides that the plaintiff's damages are $100,000, the plaintiff's negligence is zero percent, and the defendant's is 100 percent, it is all the defendant's fault and the plaintiff recovers $100,000. If damages are $100,000, and the apportionment of negligence is plaintiff 40 percent, defendant 60 percent, the plaintiff recovers $60,000. The logic is that since the defendant is 60 percent responsible, he should pay 60 percent of the damages.

If damages are assessed at $100,000 and the negligence is apportioned plaintiff 51 percent, defendant 49 percent, the plaintiff recovers nothing; the defendant is liable only if he was more negligent than the plaintiff. Thus, under the Texas comparative negligence system, if the plaintiff recovers anything, he will recover 50 percent of his damages at least. There is no way he can recover less than 50 percent.

Compare this to the former Wisconsin system of comparative negligence. Under that system, if the jury found both parties negligent the two assessments of negligence were subtracted from each other and the difference was the basis of recovery. Thus, in Wisconsin, if damages were $100,000, and negligence was apportioned 40 percent to plaintiff and 60 percent to defendant, the plaintiff recovered $20,000 only (60-40=20; therefore plaintiff recovered 20 percent of his damage). This Wisconsin plan has more internal consistency than the Texas plan, which was recently adopted in Wisconsin.

If the defendant has filed a counterclaim, the jury must determine the damages of both parties as well as apportion the negligence. If the jury determines that the plaintiff's damages are $100,000 and the defendant's are $10,000, and that the plaintiff's negligence is 55 percent and defendant's 45 percent, the results are as follows: Plaintiff recovers nothing, because he was more negligent than defendant; defendant recovers 55 percent of his damages, or $5,500.

If the jury assesses the damages as $100,000 to the plaintiff and $100,000 to the defendant, and the negligence 50 percent to plaintiff and 50 percent to defendant, no one recovers anything. The parties are equally to blame, so each is responsible for his own loss.

If the plaintiff sues two or more defendants, the possible negligence may be divided three ways. Assume that White sues Black and Gray for damages, and the defendants claim that White was also negligent. There are no counterclaims. Suppose the jury says White suffered $100,000 in damages, and assesses the negligence as White zero percent, Black 30 percent, and Gray 70 percent. The result is that White gets a judgment against Black and Gray for $100,000. White may collect all of it from either one, or in any proportion from either, since Black and Gray are jointly and severally liable for the $100,000. If Black pays the entire judgment, he will have a claim for $70,000 against Gray, since between themselves the defendants are liable in proportion to their negligence.

If the damages are $100,000 and the negligence is assessed White 55 percent, Gray 30 percent, and Black 15 percent, White recovers nothing. He was more to blame than the other two combined.

If the damages are $100,000, and the negligence is assessed White 30 percent, Gray 10 percent, and Black 60 percent, White recovers $70,000. Though Gray was less negligent than White, he is still liable to White because the two defendants combined were more negligent than the plaintiff. White has a judgement against Gray for $10,000, and against Black, essentially, for $60,000 to $70,000. The most he may collect from Gray is $10,000, but he could collect the entire amount from Black. If he does, Black may recover only $10,000 from Gray.

If the damages are $100,000, and the negligence is assessed White 45 percent, Gray 35 percent, and Black 20 percent, White recovers $55,000. This is true even though he is the most negligent, because Gray and Black together are more negligent than he. In this case the judgment is a several judgment—White may recover $35,000 from Gray, and $20,000 from Black.

If in the three-way case each party files counterclaims against the others, a very complex situation may arise. Consider one example:

White, Gray, and Black are involved in litigation which began with White suing Gray and Black, and progressed to all parties filing counterclaims against each other. The jury asseses the damages as White $1,000,000; Gray $100,000; and Black $10,000. It assesses the negligence as White 48 percent, Gray 32 percent, and Black 20 percent. Since no party was more than 50 percent responsible, each has some sort of claim against the other.

White's recovery is 52 percent of $1,000,000, or $520,000. Of this, Gray is liable for $320,000, and Black for $200,000. Gray's recovery is 68 percent of $100,000, or $68,000. Of this, the most he may collect from Black is $20,000, since Black was less negligent than he. He may collect between $48,000 and $68,000 from White. Black's recovery is 80 percent of $10,000. For this White and Gray are jointly and severally liable, since both were more negligent than Black. Black's claim against White and Gray is for $8,000.

Gray therefore owes White $320,000, and White owes Gray between $48,000 and $68,000. On balance, Gray owes White between $252,000 and $272,000.

Black owes White $200,000. White owes Black a maximum of $8,000. On balance, Black owes White between $192,000 and $200,000.

Black owes Gray $20,000, and Gray owes Black a maximum of $8,000. On balance, Black owes Gray between $12,000 and $20,000.

The "big winner" is of course White, because he suffered the most damage. The final settlement will depend upon who is willing to pay what, and (if it comes to that) upon who can be forced to pay what.

Survival of right to sue for tort damages. If a person who has a personal injury claim against another dies, whether the claim be for injury to health or to reputation, the claim does not die. The estate of the deceased may sue upon the claim or, if the estate is settled before suit is filed, the heirs of the deceased may sue.

If the person who has caused the injury to the health or reputation of another dies, his estate will be liable for the claim. The injured party may therefore file suit upon the claim against the estate of the guilty party.

All of the above is provided for by RCS 5525.

Actions for wrongfully causing death. The Texas Wrongful Death Act comprises RCS 4671–4678. When a person dies of injuries wrongfully inflicted upon him by another whom he could have sued for damages had he lived, his spouse, children, or parents may sue for damages caused them by the death of the deceased. The damages recoverable are essentially for those things lost due to the death of the deceased. Thus, minor children may recover for loss of support, possibility of education, and so forth. A spouse may recover for loss of services and companionship.

The possibility of recovery is limited to actual damages suffered, unless the defendant was guilty of willfulness in causing death, or of gross negligence—that is, carelessness of a degree above and beyond ordinary carelessness. The two-year statute of limitation upon this action starts to run as of the time of death of the deceased, not as of the date of the injury which caused his death. The right to sue for wrongful death does not survive the death of the parties entitled to sue. If there are no surviving children, parents, or spouse of the deceased, there can be no action for wrongfully causing death.

PART II

Courts and Court Procedures

6

Texas and Federal Court Systems

Since the United States has a federal system of government, law is made and enforced at two levels. Most of the nations of the world possessing a federal form of government have their courts organized so that the lower courts of the nation exist under the law of the states or provinces, while only the highest courts of the nation exist under federal law. It is done this way in Canada, Australia, Switzerland, and West Germany.

The United States has chosen not to organize its court system in this manner, however. In this nation, two hierarchies of courts coexist—federal courts and state courts. In order to understand the organization of the system, then, an understanding of two court systems is necessary.

The Texas Court System

The organization of the Texas court system is provided for in the constitution and statutes of the state of Texas. The Texas system is one of the more complex systems of the United States, but for all that it is not too difficult to understand. We shall begin our consideration of it at the bottom of the hierarchial pyramid, and work from there toward the top.

Small claims court. The small claims court is not a constitutional court. It was created by statute, the governing statute being RCS 2460a. There are as many small claims courts as there are justice of the peace (JP) courts. The JP in essence wears two hats: he serves as judge of the small claims court for his precinct and also as judge of the JP court.

The small claims court is strictly a civil court; it may hear only contract cases. The upper monetary limit for its jurisdiction is $150, unless the case involves wages or compensation for services rendered, in which case the upper limit is $200. Commercial lenders and assignees of rights to collect money may not sue in small claims court.

The advantage of using this court is that the procedure is very simple, and no lawyer is necessary. The court costs are thus very low. All pleadings and arguments are oral.

This court has final jurisdiction over cases involving less than $20. Cases involving $20 or more may be appealed from here to the county court.

Justice of the peace court. Each Texas county is divided into no less than four and no more than eight justice precincts, each of which elects one or two justices of the peace, as per Article 5, Sec. 18 of the Texas Constitution.

Art. 5 Sec. 19 provides that the JP court shall have both criminal and civil jurisdiction. The civil jurisdiction extends to Class C misdemeanors and other offenses for which the punishment is a fine of $200 or less. The JP may also conduct examining trials in criminal matters, and may exercise other criminal and quasi-criminal jurisdiction. Persons convicted of misdemeanors in JP court may appeal to the county court.

JP courts have civil jurisdiction over cases where the amount in controversy is $500 or less. The limit used to be $200, until the adoption of an amendment to Art. 5 Sec. 19 during the November 1978 general election. The amendment also gives the legislature authority to increase the limit to $1,000.

These courts also have jurisdiction to hear forcible entry and detainer cases, and suits to remove persons (such as holdover tenants) who are in unlawful possession of real estate. They further have authority to issue writs of attachment, garnishment, and sequestration in proper cases.

They do not have authority to decide cases involving title to land. They may not issue injunctions or exercise other equity powers. They may not hear libel or slander cases.

The statutory jurisdiction of the JP court in civil matters is contained in RCS 2385. The court has final jurisdiction over civil cases involving less than $20. Cases involving $20 or more are appealable from this court to the county court.

Justices of the peace also have the power to punish for contempt of court. The power is limited to the levying of a fine of $100 and commitment to jail for three days.

Municipal courts. Municipal courts are statutory courts, created by RCS 1194 et seq. Every incorporated city, town, or village has such a court, which is strictly a criminal court; it exercises jurisdiction over all cases involving violation of local ordinances. It also has concurrent jurisdiction with the JP courts to try Class C misdemeanor cases arising within the city limits, or other misdemeanor cases involving maximum fines of $200 or less.

Municipal court decisions are appealable to the county court, and municipal court judges have the same contempt powers as do JPs.

County courts. Each county in Texas has a county court; larger counties have more than one. This court may be the constitutional county court created by Art. 5 Sec. 16 of the constitution, or it may be a county court at law created by the legislature under authority granted in Art. 5 Sec. 22 of the constitution. RCS 1949 et seq. detail the jurisdiction of these courts.

Both types of county courts have the same criminal jurisdiction. These courts have authority to try all misdemeanor cases except those under the jurisdiction of the JP and municipal courts. In larger counties this criminal jurisdiction may be exercised by specially created county criminal courts.

Both types of county courts exercise probate jurisdiction, and jurisdiction to appoint guardians and the like. Again, however, in larger counties the legislature may create special probate courts to exercise this jurisdiction—and in a few counties the legislature has granted this jurisdiction to the local Texas District Court.

The upper limit upon the monetary jurisdiction of the constitutional county court is $1,000. The upper limit for the county court at law is $5,000. These courts may hear civil actions involving from $200.01 up to the upper limit. Jurisdiction over cases involving more than $200 but less than $500 is now concurrent with the JP court, while jurisdiction over cases involving $500 or more is now concurrent with the district court.

County courts may issue writs of attachment, garnishment, and sequestration only in cases involving less than $500. These courts may not hear cases involving title to real estate, but they may hear equity cases within their monetary jurisdiction. They may not hear cases of libel or slander.

Both types of county courts have appellate jurisdiction over cases from the three lower courts, as described earlier. Under RCS 1911a, county court judges may punish contempt by a fine of up to $500, or by imprisonment for up to six months, or both.

District courts. Each Texas county is part of a Texas judicial district. Some of these districts comprise more than one county. Larger counties comprise more than one district, though no district comprises a smaller area than one county. In large counties, several district courts share concurrent jurisdiction over the entire county.

Art. 5 Sec. 8 of the constitution outlines in general the jurisdiction of the district court, while the provisions of RCS 1906 et seq. add to the outline. In criminal matters, the district court tries all felonies and all misdemeanor cases involving official misconduct. In civil matters, the district court has concurrent jurisdiction with the county courts over cases involving between $500 and $1,000, or $5,000, as the case may be. It has exclusive jurisdiction over all cases involving sums of money over and above the upper jurisdictional limit of the county court.

The district court also has exclusive jurisdiction over the following civil matters:
1. Issuance of writs of attachment, garnishment, and sequestration when more than $500 is involved.
2. Appointment and supervision of receivers.
3. Injunctions and other equity cases beyond the monetary jurisdiction of the county court.
4. Divorce and other domestic relations cases (child custody, etc.).
5. Libel and slander.
6. Title to real estate, and foreclosure of liens upon real estate.
7. Eminent domain cases—government condemnation of land for public use.
8. Election contest cases.
9. Suits on behalf of the state to recover penalties, forfeits, and escheats.

The district court has a small amount of probate appellate jurisdiction; anyone unhappy with a county court decision in a probate matter may appeal it to the district court. The district court also exercises the same contempt power as does the county court.

Court of civil appeals. The state of Texas is divided into fourteen districts for purposes of appeal of civil cases. Each of these districts has a court of civil appeals. Each of these courts has three judges, but a constitutional amendment adopted at the November 1978 general election permits the expansion of some of these to six judges. Civil cases involving $100 or more are appealable from the county courts or district courts to these courts. Note that appeals of most civil cases from the county courts lie to the court of civil appeals.

These courts exercise a small amount of original jurisdiction, which does not concern us here.

Court of criminal appeals. The state of Texas has one court of criminal appeals. Texas is one of a very few states which has seen fit to establish a special court to hear criminal appeals. This court, which consists of nine judges, sits in Austin. All criminal convictions in county court or district court are appealable here. It is the court of last resort for criminal matters in this state.

Supreme Court of Texas. The Supreme Court of Texas is the highest civil court in the state. It hears appeals of civil matters from the court of civil appeals. It also may hear appeals directly from a district court when the constitutionality of a statute or the validity of an order of an administrative agency is involved. It will not hear divorce, election contest, or defamation cases unless statutory interpretation is involved.

If a civil case involves a federal question, it is possible to appeal from the Supreme Court of Texas to the Supreme Court of the United States. It is rare that a civil case heard in state court contains such a federal question, however, and it is even more rare for the United States Supreme Court to agree to hear such a case.

The Supreme Court of Texas also possesses a small amount of original jurisdiction, which is not of concern in this course.

Jurisdiction of Federal Courts

The federal court system contains a hierarchy of regular trial and appellate courts, as well as several special courts of limited jurisdiction. We shall first consider the regular courts.

United States Magistrate's Court. The federal district courts may appoint a number of U.S. magistrates to serve within a judicial district. They have authority to hear certain preliminary matters in civil litigation, and to try "minor offenses" committed under federal criminal law. 18 USC 3401(f) defines such an offense as one for which the maximum allowable punishment does not exceed a $1,000 fine or a year in prison, or both, except for certain specified offenses.

A person accused of commission of such a minor federal offense has the right to be tried by jury in federal district court. He need not submit to trial by a U.S. magistrate. The accused may be tried by the magistrate if he agrees in writing to be so tried, after the magistrate has carefully informed him of his right to trial by a district judge. There is no trial by jury in the magistrate's court: the accused who agrees to be tried there thus waives his right to trial by jury.

The magistrate may also accept pleas of "not guilty" and "nolo contendere," and may impose appropriate sentences. These magistrates have no trial jurisdiction in civil matters.

Federal district courts. Each state contains within its borders at least one federal judicial district, and at least one federal district court. Larger states are divided into multiple districts; in many cases, these districts are subdivided into smaller divisions.

The district courts are the trial courts of the federal court system. They have original jurisdiction over all criminal offenses committed under federal law. As noted above, they also have concurrent jurisdiction with the U.S. magistrate's courts to try minor criminal offenses.

The district courts may try two sorts of civil cases:
1. "Federal question" cases, where the subject matter involves federal law.
2. "Diversity of citizenship" cases, where plaintiff and defendant reside in different states.

Federal question jurisdiction. Generally, the district courts may not hear a case involving a federal question unless the amount in controversy exceeds $10,000 (28 USC 1331). However, some types of cases may be brought in federal district court if they involve federal law even if the amount in controversy is less than $10,000. These include:
1. Admiralty cases—cases involving the law of the sea or the law of navigable waterways.
2. Patent and copyright cases.
3. Taxation cases arising under federal law, except for matters under the jurisdiction of the customs court.
4. Cases in which the United States is a plaintiff or defendant.
5. Antitrust cases.
6. Civil rights cases.
7. Election contests involving a federal office.
8. Certain other cases not of concern to us here.

It should be noted, then, that some cases involving federal law may be heard in state courts. In fact, some such cases *must* be heard in state court, including all cases under federal law which cannot be heard in federal court because they do not involve $10,000 or more and do not fall into any category in which the $10,000 jurisdictional limit does not apply.

Diversity of citizenship jurisdiction. 28 USC 1332 provides that the federal district courts shall have original jurisdiction over cases in which the sum in controversy exceeds $10,000, if the parties are citizens of different states, or of foreign states. For purposes of this jurisdiction, an individual is generally a citizen of the state in which he maintains his permanent residence. A corporation is considered to be a citizen of the state where it is incorporated, or of the state where it has its principal place of business.

If there are multiple parties on one or both sides of litigation, the case is a diversity case if even one of the parties involved is a citizen of another state. Thus, if a Texan sues six other Texans and one Oklahoman for $50,000 in damages, the case is a diversity case because of the Oklahoma defendant.

If a Texan wants to sue an Oklahoman for $5,000 in damages, then, he must sue in state court, unless the matter is an antitrust case or some other sort of federal case where the $10,000 limitation does not apply. If the Texan sues the Oklahoman for $20,000 damages in federal court, the case is a good diversity case and it stays in federal court.

If the Texan sues the Oklahoman for $20,000 in an Oklahoma state court, the case stays there. The plantiff in a diversity case is not obligated to sue in federal court; he may sue in state court if he wishes. Since the Oklahoman is being sued in his home state, he has no complaint. If the Texan sues the Oklahoman for $20,000 in a Texas state court, however, the Oklahoman has the right to remove the case to federal court. Thus, the defendant in a diversity case need not submit to suit in a state court if he is being sued outside his state.

Equity in federal courts. The vast majority of cases tried in federal district courts are heard by one judge and, perhaps, a jury. However, the federal court system follows the tradition of the English common law, under which there is no trial by jury in equity cases. When the plaintiff seeks an injunction or some other equitable remedy, the case will be heard by a judge alone. When the plaintiff seeks certain kinds of injunctions, the case may be heard by a panel of three district court judges sitting without a jury. The majority of these judges may render a decision.

The federal courts of appeal. The normal route of appeal from the federal district court is to one of the federal courts of appeal. Appeals from Texas federal district courts are made to the Fifth Circuit Court of Appeals in New Orleans; this level of federal court exercises jurisdiction similar to that of the courts of civil appeal and the court of criminal appeals in the Texas court system.

The Supreme Court of the United States. The nine judges of the Supreme Court of the United States comprise the highest court of the nation. The vast bulk of the business of this court consists of cases appealed from lower courts, both federal and state.

Cases may reach the Supreme Court through appeal or through writ of certiorari. The high court must hear cases reaching it by appeal; it has a choice as to whether or not to hear a case arriving via the writ of certiorari. In general, if at least four of the judges of the court are not in favor of hearing a case appealed via writ of certiorari, the case will not be heard. In that case, the decision of the court from which the case is appealed will stand.

In general, the Supreme Court may hear an appeal directly from a federal district court when:

1. The district court has held an act of Congress unconstitutional in an action in

which the United States government, an agent of the same, or an officer or employee of the same is a party (28 USC 1252).

2. The case was heard by a panel of three district judges (28 USC 1253).

The Supreme Court may hear a case on appeal from the federal courts of appeal when the court of appeal has held a state statute to be unconstitutional with respect to the Constitution of the United States. Other cases from the courts of appeal are sent to the Supreme Court on writs of certiorari (28 USC 1254).

The Supreme Court may hear a case on appeal from the highest court of a state when:

1. The state court has held an act of Congress or a treaty of the United States to be unconstitutional, or

2. The state court has held an act of a state legislature not to be in conflict with the Constitution of the United States, when a party to the case has challenged the consitutionality of that statute.

Since far more cases are sent to the Supreme Court on writs of certiorari than are sent there on appeal, the court may exercise its discretion to deny a hearing with respect to most cases sent up for consideration. The court is asked to hear many more cases than it has the time or manpower to consider; thus, most cases sent there on certiorari are returned to the courts from which they came with no action. A litigant may count himself fortunate when the Supreme Court agrees to hear his case.

The Court of Claims. The Court of Claims is a special court established for the purpose of hearing claims other than tort claims brought by persons against the government of the United States. The court ordinarily sits in the District of Columbia, but it may sit elsewhere.

If the case involves the right to a federal pension, the Court of Claims has no jurisdiction. If the case involves a contract claim or the like for less than $10,000, the federal district courts have concurrent jurisdiction over it. In essence, the plaintiff in such a case may sue either in the Court of Claims or in a federal district court.

No juries are used in cases heard by this court; a plaintiff using this court thus waives all rights to trial by jury.

The Customs Court. The Customs Court hears arguments between importers of goods and the U.S. Customs Service over appraisal of goods imported into the United States, and over the amount of customs duty due upon such imported goods.

If the Customs Service renders an administrative decision in these matters which the importer feels is erroneous, and if the importer has exhausted all administrative remedies within the Customs Service, he may appeal the matter to this special federal court. No right to trial by jury exists in this court.

The Court of Customs and Patent Appeals. The Court of Customs and Patent Appeals has authority to hear appeals on the following matters:

1. Decisions of the Customs Court upon matters under the jurisdiction of that court.

2. Decisions of the U.S. Patent Office denying patents to patent applicants, or decisions of Patent Office boards of interference, so long as the petitioner has exhausted administrative remedies within the Patent Office.

3. Decisions of the U.S. Patent Office in matters involving registration of trademarks, so long as the applicant has exhausted all Patent Office administrative remedies.

4. Decisions of the United States Tariff Commission (now the International Trade Commission) involving unfair practices in import trade.

Military court-martials. The person who dons the uniform of one of the armed services of the United States (army, navy, air force, marine corps, or coast guard) subjects himself to the military law of the United States. This law is contained in the Uniform Code of Military Justice (UCMJ).

The UCMJ is essentially a code of criminal law. Many of its provisions are similar to the provisions of civilian law; many ordinary criminal offenses (such as murder, rape, robbery, burglary, assault, and so forth) are also violations of military law. However, many sorts of conduct which are quite acceptable in civilian society (at least in the eyes of the criminal law) are offenses in military law.

For instance, a civilian has the right to quit his employment at any time. If the civilian does not want to work for his boss any longer, he does not have to do so. If he was working under a valid employment contract, he might have to pay damages for breach of contract if he quits, but that is the worst penalty he may suffer. The military person who is tired of being a soldier or sailor may not quit, however. He must serve until the end of his enlistment. If he quits and disappears, he is guilty of desertion, a serious military offense.

If a civilian does not feel like going to work in the morning, he need not go. His pay might be docked because of this—and, in an extreme situation, he might be fired—but no worse can befall him. The military person who does not arrive for work and has no good excuse is guilty of absence without official leave (AWOL), an offense equivalent to a civilian misdemeanor.

If the orders given a civilian employee by his boss "bug" him, the employee can refuse to obey; the worst that can happen to him is that he will be fired. The military person who refuses to obey the orders of his boss (or anyone else of higher rank) commits the offense of refusal to obey a direct order of a superior, a quite serious violation of the UCMJ. The civilian "bugged" by the manner of his boss may tell the boss off, at the risk of being fired. The military man who tells off his boss shows disrespect to a superior, another serious offense under the UCMJ.

The military justice system may administer six sorts of punishment, three of which are unknown to civilian law. These six are:

1. Death.
2. Imprisonment.
3. Fine.
4. Forfeiture of pay. (This amounts to a reduction in pay, or a confiscation of pay by the government. A fine takes away money the convicted person possesses; a forfeiture takes away pay before the military person receives it.)
5. Punitive discharge. (This amounts to firing of the military person, but the consequences of punitive discharge are far more serious than the consequences of being fired from a civilian job. The dishonorable or bad conduct discharge may well brand the dischargee for life as an undesirable and a misfit.)
6. Reduction in pay grade. (This amounts of a reduction in pay, but it is more serious than that. Being "busted" in pay grade by a court-martial may ruin a military career.)

The military person may be imprisoned by order of his commanding officer and without any form of trial for a period of up to thirty days for violation of certain UCMJ provisions.

Before the military man may be imprisoned for more than thirty days, he must be tried by court-martial for his offense. He need not submit to imprisonment at the order of his commander: he has the right to demand trial by court-martial. There are three types of court-martial provided for by the UCMJ:

1. The summary court, consisting of one officer. It may imprison for up to thirty days.

2. The special court, consisting of up to five officers. It may imprison for up to six months.

3. The general court, consisting of a military law judge and a military jury. It may sentence to death in a proper case, or assess any lesser punishment.

The appeal of a court-martial conviction runs as follows:

1. Automatic review of conviction and sentence by the commanding officer who ordered the convening of the court.

2. Appeal to a court of military review, an appellate court composed of military law officers.

3. Appeal to the Court of Military Appeals, the civilian court which is the Supreme Court of the military law system. Very seldom may a Court of Military Appeals decision be appealed to a civilian court. Ordinarily the military court system is a closed system, insulated from civilian influence.

Decisions of civilian courts have tended to narrow the jurisdiction of court-martials, however. Thirty years ago civilian dependents of military personnel living on military bases outside the continental United States were subject to court-martial jurisdiction; this is no longer true. Formerly, civilian employees of the Department of Defense working outside the continental United States were also subject to court-martial jurisdiction, but because of civilian court decisions they are no longer so subject.

Formerly, military personnel were subject to court-martial for civilian-type violations of the criminal law committed off-base. Now, such personnel are not subject to court-martial for offenses committed off-base which are unrelated to their military duties. So, the military man who assaults a civilian in an off-base bar will be tried by the local civilian court for his wrongdoing.

The Tax Court. The Tax Court is the special court with which ordinary Americans are most likely to become acquainted. When the IRS audits an income tax return, the auditor may well decide that the taxpayer owes additional tax. The taxpayer has the right to appeal the auditor's decision to higher levels within the IRS, but he may well appeal as far as he can within the IRS without getting the decision of the auditor changed to any degree. The taxpayer must then decide whether to throw in the towel and pay up, or whether to fight on.

If the taxpayer wants to continue fighting without paying up, his recourse is to appeal to the Tax Court. If the government seeks to recover $1,500 or less in additional tax from the taxpayer, the case will be heard by one of the sixteen judges of the Tax Court in a large city near the taxpayer's residence. If the argument involves more than $1,500, the case will be heard by the entire court in Washington, D.C.

There is no trial by jury before the Tax Court; the judge or judges decide the matter. Since these judges are trained in accounting as well as law, the decision will in all probability turn upon fine points of law and accounting.

The taxpayer who wants a trial by jury in a civil tax dispute may obtain one, but he may find the required method rather objectionable. He must first pay the tax the IRS claims is owed, then sue the government to recover his money in federal district court. There is no way to get a jury trial on the issue before paying.

The Bankruptcy Court. Formerly bankruptcy cases were filed in the federal district courts. However, the Bankruptcy Reform Act enacted by Congress at the close of the 1978 session provided, among other things, for the creation of a new, special federal court to handle bankruptcy matters. Since October 1, 1979, bankruptcy matters have been heard by special bankruptcy courts in each federal judicial district. The ordinary federal district courts no longer exercise jurisdiction over such cases.

7

Texas Criminal Procedure

The law of criminal procedure applied in the state courts of Texas is found in the Code of Criminal Procedure (CCP), enacted by the legislature in 1965. It governs virtually all aspects of the Texas criminal process, from arrest to execution of a person sentenced to death and release of a person after serving his term of punishment.

Arrest. In many cases the criminal process begins with the arrest of a person suspected of having committed a criminal offense. An arrest is usually made by a peace officer pursuant to a warrant of arrest, but peace officers may arrest without a warrant, as may private citizens under certain circumstances.

A peace officer may arrest without a warrant when:

1. An offense is committed in his presence or within his view (CCP 14.01), or
2. A felony or breach of the peace has been committed in the presence or within the view of a magistrate, and the magistrate orders the officer to make the arrest (CCP 14.02), or
3. A person is found in a suspicious place and under circumstances which show reasonably that he has been guilty of some felony or breach of the peace, or that he threatens or is about to commit some offense against the law (CCP 14.03), or
4. The officer knows that a felony has been committed, and that the offender is about to escape, and that there is no time to procure an arrest warrant (CCP 14.04).

The arresting officer must inform the accused why he is being arrested. He may use all reasonable force to carry out the arrest, but may not use excessive force. He may, in case of felony, break down the door of a house if he is refused admittance after stating his business (CCP 15.24-15.26).

Although peace officers are paid by the state to enforce the law, a large element of discretion enters into their decisions in matters of making arrests. If Officer Smith observes two citizens engaged in a loud argument on a street corner, he could conclude that they are guilty of disorderly conduct and charge them with that offense. He could on the other hand decide that this is merely a harmless argument and ignore the whole incident.

If Officer Blatz's trusty radar set shows Zilch driving 37 MPH in a 35 MPH speed zone, Blatz could stop Zilch and cite him for speeding. In most localities he is not likely to do this, since Zilch is barely exceeding the speed limit. But 37 MPH is definitely speeding in a 25 MPH speed zone.

If, while Blatz is writing up a citation for Quatz for driving 47 MPH in a 35 MPH speed zone, Schnell zips past at 55 MPH, Blatz might decide he is too busy finishing up with Quatz to go chase Schnell. In such a case, Schnell in a sense has been lucky.

Officer Ruhig might observe Sotz happily consuming a bottle of sherry on a street corner at 3 A.M. Sotz is breaking the law for consuming alcohol in public at that hour. But Ruhig might decide that Sotz is really a harmless wino and that running him in for this offense would not benefit anyone; he might then choose to ignore the situation.

All of these situations involve peace officers exercising discretion in performing their jobs. If an officer chooses not to act against a law violator, no one may do his job for him (unless a citizen's arrest may be made). If the officer ignores violators, he is in a sense not doing what he was paid for, and a concerned citizen may complain to the chief of police, the city council, or other authority. But such complaints are political matters.

Exercise of discretion may also be a factor in law enforcement because police departments do not have the manpower to be everywhere at once: police manpower is deployed where it will do the most good. Thus, law enforcement is to a degree selective. If the Podunk City Police have only six traffic enforcement units, they may deploy these in only six places. So, they may almost always have a unit stationed somewhere along Main Street, where there is always heavy traffic, but never along Shady Street, a quiet residential street. Thus, someone who speeds along Main Street runs an appreciable risk of being cited for speeding, but someone who speeds along Shady Street has an excellent chance of getting away with it. This is a form of selective enforcement which is quite legitimate.

Private individuals normally do not get involved in law enforcement. However, a private person may make a citizen's arrest when a felony or an offense against the public peace is committed within his presence or within his view (CCP 14.01). In all other cases, arrests may be made only by peace officers pursuant to arrest warrants. An arrest warrant is issued by a magistrate and is directed to a peace officer, ordering the taking of a named person into custody.

The procedure for obtaining an arrest warrant begins with the filing of a complaint before a magistrate or before a district or county attorney. The complainant may be a policeman or other peace officer or a private citizen. The procedure may also commence when a citizen complains to the police.

The complaint must contain the following, as per CCP 15.05:

1. The name of the accused, or a reasonably definite description of him if his name is not known, and
2. An allegation that the accused has committed a described offense, and
3. The time and place of the commission of the offense, and
4. The signature of the complainant.

If the complaint is made to the county or district attorney, he must ask a magistrate to issue a warrant. If the complaint is made directly to the magistrate, he decides himself upon the issuance of a warrant or citation. There exists an element of discretion in this procedure, also. The police, the prosecuting attorney, or the magistrate, as the case may be, must evaluate the complainant's story to determine if he has a valid complaint.

If there are weaknesses in the complainant's story, the authorities may seek to discourage him from proceeding with his complaint. They may even refuse to take his complaint, if they feel that it is unfounded. If they do refuse, the complainant has no legal recourse unless he can make a citizen's arrest; his only recourse would be political.

If the authorities do listen to the complaint and set the machinery of the criminal process in motion, the complainant may well find that control over the proceeding is out of his hands. After filing his complaint, he may regret having done so and ask the authorities to "drop the charges." The authorities may do as the complainant asks, but they are under no obligation to do so. If the complainant's testimony is essential to the prosecution of the accused, demonstration by the complainant of unwillingness to cooperate may cause the authorities to drop the matter. However, if they believe that the administration of justice requires them to proceed against the accused even if the complainant is unwilling to cooperate, they will not drop the charges. Control of these matters rests in the hands of the authorities, not in the hands of the complainant.

The magistrate before whom a complaint is made has the option of issuing a warrant in response to it, or of issuing a summons. Under a warrant the accused must be taken into custody; therefore a peace officer must seek him out. Under a summons the accused is merely required to appear before the issuing magistrate at a named time and place. A summons may be served by an officer upon the accused in person, it may be left at the accused's residence with a person of suitable age, or it may be served by mail.

The magistrate uses his discretion with respect to deciding whether to issue a summons or a warrant. The more serious the offense is, the more likely it is that the warrant will be issued.

If the accused responds to the summons as directed, the process continues from there. If he does not respond, an arrest warrant will be issued (CCP 15.03).

The peace officer who cites a person for a misdemeanor instead of arresting him is also issuing a form of summons. The most common form of such summons is, of course, the traffic ticket. The peace officer has the same powers and duties in arresting under a warrant as he does when he arrests without a warrant.

After the arrest has been made, the accused must be brought before the magistrate who issued the warrant, or another magistrate, without unnecessary delay. The magistrate must inform the accused of the following (CCP 15.17):

1. Of the accusation against him.
2. That he has the right to retain counsel.
3. That he has the right to remain silent.
4. That he has the right to have an attorney at his side during interviews with peace officers or attorneys representing the state.
5. That he has the right to terminate such interviews at any time.
6. That he has the right to have counsel appointed for him at state expense if he cannot afford to hire his own counsel.
7. That he has the right to an examining trial.
8. That any statement he makes may be used against him.

Peace officers should of course not question the accused until his appearance before the magistrate. Should they desire to do so they must first inform the accused of his right to counsel, his right to remain silent, and his other rights.

Bail. The magistrate must at this point in the procedure consider the question of whether or not the accused is entitled to bail. If the accused is charged with murder, the magistrate has the option of not granting bail. If he is charged with capital murder, there can be no bail. If the accused is charged with a noncapital felony and has also been accused of or convicted of other felonies, he may be denied bail under three distinct sets of circumstances, but a bail hearing must be held before a Texas district judge before bail may be denied.

Article III, Section 11a of the Constitution of the State of Texas, approved by the voters of the state on November 8, 1977, provides that a district judge may deny bail to a person accused of a noncapital felony if:

1. The accused has already been convicted of two felonies in this state, the second

being subsequent to the first both with respect to time of commission and time of conviction, or

2. At the time of the alleged felony for which arrested, the accused has been indicted for commission of another felony for which he is out on bail, or

3. The felony of which the person is accused involves the use of a deadly weapon, and he has already been convicted of a felony.

The order denying bail must be issued within seven days of the incarceration of the accused, and is immediately appealable to the Texas Court of Criminal Appeals. If the accused is not brought to trial within sixty days of his incarceration, the order denying bail will automatically be set aside unless the delay is due to the granting of a continuance sought by the accused.

When bail is granted it must be set high enough to assure that the accused will not jump bail, but the ability of the accused to make bail and the nature of the accusation must be taken into account. The magistrate may also release the accused upon personal bond, which is the accused's promise to be available when required (CCP 17.15, 03).

Examining trial. Unless the accused waives his right to it, he is entitled to an examining trial as soon as possible after his arrest and to representation by counsel at the trial. He must therefore be given time to procure counsel (or counsel must be procured for him) and counsel must have time to prepare for the hearing. The hearing is conducted before a magistrate to determine whether or not the state has sufficient evidence against the accused to warrant further legal action against him.

Witnesses testify and are cross-examined under the same rules of evidence that apply in trials to determine guilt or innocence. The accused need not testify, but he does have the right to make an informal statement to the magistrate before any witnesses are examined. Generally only prosecution witnesses are heard.

When the witnesses have testified, the magistrate does one of three things:

1. Discharges the accused.
2. Commits him to jail without bail.
3. Releases him on bail.

The bail question, even if gone into before the examining trial, may be reopened at the examining trial.

CCP Chapter 16 contains the provisions of law applicable to examining trials.

Indictment. A person accused of a felony must be indicted for it by a grand jury before being tried, unless the accused waives such indictment. Texas grand juries are selected under the provisions of Chapter 19 of the CCP. They conduct proceedings under the provisions of Chapter 20, and the indictments which they hand down must be handed down under the provisions of Chapter 21.

Potential grand jurors are chosen from the list of registered voters of a county; fifteen to twenty persons are summoned to appear before the local district judge. A person so summoned may be excused from the duty to obey if:

1. He is over sixty-five years of age, or
2. He has children ten years of age or younger at home who must be cared for, or
3. He is a high-school student, or
4. He is a college or university student.

The judge questions those summoned to determine whether or not they are qualified to be grand jurors. They must meet five qualifications:

1. The grand juror must be a qualified voter in the county where he serves.

2. He must be of sound mind and good moral character.
3. He must be able to read and write.
4. He must not have been convicted of any felony.
5. He must not be under indictment or any other legal accusation for theft or felony (CCP 19.08).

During the questioning any person, including persons confined in the county jail, may challenge any potential grand juror. CCP 19.31 provides that there are only two legal grounds for challenging a potential grand juror:

1. That he is not a qualified grand juror under CCP 19.08.
2. That he is the prosecutor upon an accusation against the person making the challenge.

CCP 19.30 also permits a person to challenge the entire grand jury panel. This is called making a challenge to the "array." There are two legal grounds for this:

1. The persons summoned as grand jurors are not in fact those selected.
2. Corruption was present in the summoning of one or more of the grand jurors.

Challenges to the array must be in writing, while challenges to individual grand jurors may be oral. The judge decides all challenges on the spot. The first twelve persons found to be qualified and not challenged are the grand jury. The body is then sworn in, and is ready to do its work.

Most of the grand jury's work consists of hearing matters brought before it by the district attorney regarding accusations against persons thought to have committed felonies within the county. The attorney general of Texas and the county attorney may also appear before the grand jury.

Both the prosecuting attorneys and the grand jury itself may subpoena and interrogate witnesses. The proceedings of the body are held in secret. Any witness testifying before a grand jury who divulges any matter about which he has been questioned other than when required to give evidence in due course is guilty of contempt of court and may be fined $500 and imprisoned for up to six months (CCP 20.16).

A witness who refuses to obey a subpoena to testify before the grand jury, or a witness who refuses to answer questions legitimately asked before the grand jury, is also guilty of contempt. For evading service of a subpoena, the witness may be fined $500. For refusing to testify, a witness may be fined $500 and imprisoned until he decides to testify (CCP 20.14, 20.15).

A person accused of commission of an offense has no right to appear before the grand jury or to testify before it. Such a person also has no right to have an attorney represent him before the grand jury.

The grand jury is not limited to consideration of matters brought before it by attorneys representing the state. It may investigate other suspected wrongs on its own motion, subpoena its own witnesses, etc. When all of the available evidence on any criminal accusation has been heard, the grand jury votes whether or not to indict the accused. The affirmative votes of nine grand jurors are necessary to indict (CCP 20.19).

The indictment itself is a formal document drawn up by the district or other state attorney after the grand jury has voted to indict. It must state, among other things (CCP 21.02):

1. The name of the accused, or that his name is unknown and give a reasonably accurate description of him.
2. The time and place of the commission of the offense.

3. A description of the offense in plain and intelligible words.

The indictment must also be signed by the foreman of the grand jury, but it need not be signed by other grand jurors.

Information. Misdemeanor proceedings are often begun by the filing of an information in the proper court—usually the county court or the JP court—by the county attorney charging the accused with commission of an offense. Informations are based upon filed complaints, the same type of complaint which leads to the issuance of an arrest warrant or summons. The information must contain the same items as the indictment, except of course that it is signed by the county attorney rather than by the foreman of a grand jury.

Post-indictment or information proceedings. If the accused is already in custody, CCP 25.02 requires that a copy of the indictment be given him. If the accused is out on bail, a copy of the indictment must be furnished to him or to his counsel at the earliest possible time. In misdemeanor cases, no copy of the information need be furnished to the accused unless he or his counsel demands a copy.

It may well be that, when the indictment or information is handed down, the accused has not yet been taken into custody. This is often the case in white-collar offenses. In such a case, the district or county attorney will request that a capias or summons be issued against each accused; the capias is in effect the equivalent of an arrest warrant. The accused is taken into custody and brought before a magistrate primarily for the purpose of fixing bail. A person arrested under a capias is not entitled to an examining trial, since he is already formally charged with commission of an offense.

When a summons is used at this stage of the proceedings, accused is ordered to appear before a magistrate at a named time and place. If the accused does not appear, a capias will then be issued for him.

Discovery. Once an indictment or information is handed down against an accused, he will be required to defend himself in open court if he is to escape punishment for his offense. The preparation of an intelligent defense requires the assembly of evidence and discovery of at least a portion of the state's case. The rules of discovery are to aid the accused in this process.

The defense may well desire that depositions be taken from certain witnesses. The usual procedure is to have the witness appear before an officer authorized to preside over the taking of depositions and to have him subject himself to questioning by the attorneys in the case, just as if he were testifying on the witness stand in court. A court reporter records or takes down in shorthand what is said. The reporter's notes are later transcribed, the resulting document being the deposition. This gives a good idea of what the witness will testify to if summoned to give testimony at the trial.

The accused must ask for and get the permission of a court to take a deposition. If the permission is granted, CCP 39.03 authorizes the appointment of one of the following five persons to preside over its being taken:

1. A district judge.
2. A county judge.
3. A notary public.
4. A district clerk.
5. A county clerk.

The order authorizing the taking of the deposition must name the presiding officer and specify the time and place of the taking. Refusal by a witness to obey a summons to give a deposition, or refusal by the witness to answer a legitimate question at the taking of the deposition is punishable as contempt.

CCP 39.06 authorizes the taking of a deposition by written interrogatories. In such a case, a list of written questions is given to the witness by both the accused and the state (should the state wish to participate), and the witness must answer these questions in writing.

A deposition may not be read to the jury at a trial as a substitute for the in-person testimony of a witness, unless the witness cannot testify in person. The main use of the deposition is to find out what the witness would say if he were called upon to testify. A secondary use is for impeachment, which will be discussed later.

CCP 39.14 permits the defense to inspect and copy certain evidence in the hands of the prosecution. The defense may ask the court for permission to inspect and copy the following materials which are in the hands of the state:

1. Documents and papers.
2. Written statements by the defendant.
3. Books, accounts, letters, and photographs.
4. Objects and other tangible things.

If the items desired for inspection and copying are in the hands of the state, and if they are material to the defendant's case, the court will set a time and place for the inspection and copying. The inspected materials may not be removed from state custody, and a representative of the state may be present throughout the inspection and copying.

The defense may not inspect and copy the following:

1. Written statements of witnesses.
2. Work that is a product of the counsel for the prosecution.
3. Reports of state investigators.
4. Raw work that is a product of state investigators.
5. Written communication between the state and its agents or employees.

Arraignment. After indictment or information is handed down, the defendant must appear in court and plead to the indictment or information, except in misdemeanor cases, when the defendant may make certain pleas by mail. At the arraignment, the defendant must make one of three direct pleas to the indictment or information, and he may also make certain other pleas. The three direct pleas to the indictment or information, as described in CCP 27.02 (3), (4), and (5), are:

1. Guilty—"I did it."
2. Not guilty—"I'm innocent."
3. Nolo contendere—"I won't say whether or not I did it, but I won't defend myself and I throw myself upon the mercy of the court."

If the defendant refuses to make a plea, the court must enter a plea of "not guilty" for him. Since the "not guilty" plea is a denial of guilt, a trial must be held if the defendant is to be found guilty of the charged offense and punished. The "guilty" plea, being an admission of guilt, essentially results in the waiver of a right to trial by the defendant. However, a defendant may not waive his right to trial by jury for a capital offense, so, in effect, there cannot be a plea of guilty to a capital felony. The "nolo contendere" plea is, as some characterize it, "the gentleman's plea of guilty." It is a waiver of trial, but it is not an admission of guilt which can be used against the defendant in a civil lawsuit arising out of the same transaction as the criminal charge.

When defendant pleads "guilty" or "nolo contendere," he has the right to ask that a jury determine his sentence. When such a request is made, a "mini-trial" will be necessary, for sentencing purposes only. If no request is made for the jury to assess punishment, the judge may do so himself.

The majority of criminal complaints are disposed of after "guilty" and "nolo contendere" pleas. In some cases one of these pleas is entered because the prosecution's evidence of guilt is so strong that the defense has no chance of victory at a trial. In other cases the plea is entered as a result of plea bargaining.

It may be that the prosecution has a fairly strong case against the defendant but not strong enough to ensure conviction. The defense knows that if it pleads "not guilty" and goes to trial there is a chance for acquittal and victory. However, the case is closely enough balanced between prosecution and defense that the outcome of a trial is not predictable.

Since prosecution staffs often have more work than they can efficiently handle, and since criminal trials may be very time-consuming, the prosecution may be reluctant to take a questionable case to court and run the risk of a lot of effort going down the drain due to an acquittal. The defense, on the other hand, must balance the chances for acquittal against the chances of conviction and the handing down of a very heavy sentence. The door is therefore open to the prosecution to offer the defendant the chance of a light sentence if he will plead "guilty" and save the state the time and expense of trying him; or the defense may offer the prosecution a plea of "guilty" to a lesser offense and thus save the prosecution from the risk of taking a questionable case to trial. Plea bargaining thus exchanges a sure thing for potentially unpleasant possibilities, and is the equivalent of settlement out of court in a civil case.

The other pleadings and motions which the defendant may make at the arraignment include:

1. Motion to set aside the indictment.
2. Exceptions to the substance or form of the indictment.
3. A plea of double jeopardy.
4. A motion to disqualify the judge.
5. A motion for change of venue.
6. A motion for discharge because of delay in commencing trial.
7. A motion for suppression of evidence.
8. An application for probation.
9. An election to have the jury determine punishment if found guilty.
10. A motion for continuance.

Motion to set aside indictment. CCP 27.03 provides that an indictment is defective if:
1. It was not agreed to by at least nine grand jurors, or
2. An unauthorized person was present in the jury room when the indictment was handed down, or
3. The grand jury was improperly impaneled, and the defendant had no chance to challenge the array when it was impaneled.

Exception to substance of indictment. CCP 27.08 provides that an indictment is defective as to substance if:
1. It does not show upon its face that a criminal offense was committed, or
2. It shows that the statute of limitation has run out upon the prosecution of the offense, or
3. It shows that the offense was committed after the date of indictment, or
4. It shows that a good defense to the charge exists, or
5. It shows that the court trying the case has no jurisdiction to try it.

Exception to form of indictment. CCP 27.09 provides that an indictment is defective in form when:
1. It has not been presented in a proper court, or
2. It is improperly drawn.

Plea of double jeopardy. A defendant has been subjected to double jeopardy when he has already been tried for the offense for which indicted and his trial resulted in acquittal, conviction, or improper termination; or when his trial was terminated by final order or judgment that has not been reversed, set aside, or vacated, showing a determination inconsistent with a fact that must be established to secure conviction.

A defendant has not been subjected to double jeopardy when:
1. His first trial for an offense results in a hung jury.
2. His first trial results in a mistrial due to misconduct.
3. He has not yet been tried for the offense, but a prior indictment for it was set aside.
4. He was discharged by a magistrate at an examining trial due to lack of evidence against him.
5. He was tried for the offense and convicted, he then appealed, and the appellate court reversed and remanded the case for a new trial.
6. The offense for which he stands indicted is both a federal and a state offense and he has already been convicted and punished for the offense by a federal court.

A person is subjected to double jeopardy when:
1. His first trial resulted in acquittal.
2. His first trial resulted in conviction, and all appeals have been exhausted.
3. His first trial was declared a mistrial when it should have been permitted to continue. Perhaps, for example, the judge unreasonably cut short the jury's deliberations.

Another double jeopardy problem is the situation in which the defendant has committed two or more offenses and is tried for them one at a time. If the offenses were committed at different times or in different places, different evidence is required in order to prove guilt. Therefore, separate trials are no violation of the prohibition against double jeopardy.

If the offenses were committed at the same time and place, problems may arise. If the offenses were all committed as part of the same criminal episode, they should be prosecuted together. If this is not done, the defendant may not be tried in a second proceeding for offenses he was not tried for in the first.

Motion to disqualify the judge. CCP 30.01 provides that a justice of the peace or judge shall be disqualified to preside over a criminal trial when:
1. He is the party injured, or
2. He has been involved in the case as legal counsel, either for the prosecution or for the defense, or
3. He is a bood relative or in-law of the injured party within the third degree of relationship (great grandparent, great uncle, second cousin, or any closer relationship).

Disqualification of the judge does not mean that the trial must be moved to another county. CCP 30.02 provides that a judge shall be brought in from another judicial district to preside over the trial.

Motion for change of venue. Defendant may move for change of venue for two reasons:
1. The proceeding has been commenced in an improper county, or
2. The defendant cannot be assured a fair trial in the county.

Chapter 13 of the CCP sets forth the venue rules for criminal prosecutions. These rules are too complex to go into in detail here; generally, however, the proper county for trial of an offense is the county where the offense was committed (CCP 13.18). Forgery may be prosecuted in the county where the writing was forged, or in the county where it was used or passed. Theft may be prosecuted in any county through which the stolen property was transported. Hindering a secured creditor may be prosecuted in the county from which the collateral was taken, in the county to which it was taken, or in the county where the financing statement (if any) was filed. Conspiracy may be prosecuted in the county where the conspiracy agreement was made, in the county where the objective of the conspiracy was to be carried out, or in any county where any act which was a part of the conspiracy was committed.

In order to obtain a change of venue when the proceeding is brought in the proper county, the defendant must be able to produce affidavits by two credible residents of the county that:

1. So much prejudice exists against the defendant in the county that he cannot obtain a fair trial there, or
2. Such a dangerous combination exists against the defendant, actuated by influential persons within the county, that he cannot get a fair trial there (CCP 31.03).

The state may also ask for a change of venue when the state cannot get a fair trial in the county, or when the life of the defendant is in danger in the county. The presiding judge may also order a change of venue upon his own motion if he believes that fair trial cannot be had in the county.

Motion for discharge due to delay. CCP 32A.01, added to the CCP by the 1977 session of the Texas legislature, provides that the state must be ready for trial of a defendant within:

1. One hundred twenty days of commencement of criminal action if defendant is accused of a felony, or
2. Ninety days of commencement of criminal action if defendant is accused of a misdemeanor for which he can be imprisoned for more than one hundred eighty days, or
3. Sixty days of commencement of criminal action if defendant is accused of a misdemeanor punishable by imprisonment for one hundred eighty days or fewer, or
4. Thirty days of commencement of criminal action if defendant is accused of a misdemeanor punishable by fine only.

Criminal action commences with the indictment, information, or complaint unless the defendant was detained in custody or released on bail before the indictment, in which case criminal action begins with arrest or response to a summons. A motion for delay may be made after arraignment and prior to trial. The ramifications of this will be discussed later.

Motions for suppression of evidence. If the defendant believes that some of the evidence to be used against him at the trial was acquired by the state as a result of an unlawful search and seizure, he may move to have that evidence suppressed. Evidence may be seized as a result of a lawful search of a person, or pursuant to a lawful search warrant. A peace officer may lawfully search the person and immediate vicinity of an individual being arrested. Anything which is evidence of the commission of an offense found on the person of the individual or within his immediate vicinity may be seized. When a person in frisked by a peace officer exercising his power to search suspicious persons, any evidence of commission of a crime may be seized.

Search warrants are issued in Texas only by magistrates, in response to applications for their issuance. The magistrate must not issue the warrant unless probable cause for the search is shown to exist—that is, that an offense has probably been committed and that evidence of its commission of a specified nature can probably be found in the place to be searched.

A search warrant is valid for only three days, and the issuing magistrate may shorten that period if he so desires. The warrant must describe with particularity the premises to be searched and the things to be seized. The warrant may also authorize the arrest of a named individual or individuals.

The officer executing the warrant must give notice of his possession of a warrant to the person having charge of the premises. The officer may then search the named premises and seize the property called for in the warrant if he finds it. He may also seize any other evidence of commission of a crime which he finds there.

If the defendant believes that any evidence that the prosecution proposes to use against him was seized in contravention of these rules, he may move for its suppression.

Court action upon motions and pleadings. If the defendant pleads "guilty" or "nolo contendere," the next step in the procedure is sentencing. If he pleads "not guilty," trial is necessary. These pleas may be oral.

An oral motion may also be introduced, but the defendant must reduce it to writing within ten days after making it. Should the state wish to contest a motion, it is entitled to a hearing upon the question of whether or not the indictment or the charge should be dismissed upon such grounds as double jeopardy. The judge will hear evidence upon the matter and make his decision without a jury.

Statutes of limitation in criminal prosecutions. CCP 12.01 provides the following periods of limitation for prosecution of felonies:

1. For murder and manslaughter—none.
2. For theft by a fiduciary of property entrusted to his control, theft by a public servant of government property over which he has control, or for forgery—ten years.
3. For other theft, burglary, robbery, and arson—five years.
4. For other felonies—three years.

Indictments and informations must be presented during the limitation period. The clock starts to run when the offense is committed; it stops when the defendant leaves the state, and starts again when he returns (CCP 12.05).

CCP 12.02 provides that misdemeanor prosecutions must be begun within two years of the commission of the offense.

Effect of speedy trial statute upon trial. When the criminal process begins with indictment or information, the time periods provided in the speedy trial act start to run with the indictment or information. If the defendant is going to avail himself of his rights under this act he must complain about a delay before he comes to trial. Undue delay is cause for the making of a motion to dismiss an indictment: dismissal will normally be granted in case of trial delay beyond the prescribed time limits.

Delays caused by continuance requested by the defense are not considered part of the prescribed period. Continuances requested by the state also stop the clock if they are obtained because of the unusual nature of the case or because of efforts to locate evidence the state is diligently attempting to find. Delays caused by the state's inability to locate the defendant also stop the clock, if the search for him has been diligent.

If an indictment is dismissed and a new indictment is handed down, a new period for entitlement to speedy trial begins as of the handing down of the new indictment. In the scheduling of trials, CCP 32A.01 requires that criminal matters be given precedence over civil matters, and that criminal actions against defendants who are in jail be given precedence over other criminal trials.

Jury selection. The defendant will be tried by a jury unless he specifically chooses to be tried by a judge only. In felony cases the state and the judge must agree to this waiver of jury trial. In a capital felony case the defendant may not waive trial by jury: he will have it whether he wants it or not.

In district court the jury will consist of twelve persons. In county court, JP court, or municipal court it will consist of six persons (CCP 33.01).

In district court cases a panel of fifty or so potential jurors is summoned. A potential trial juror may claim the same exemptions available to the potential grand juror; the basic qualifications of the trial juror are also the same as those for grand jurors.

The judge and the attorneys will question the potential jurors to determine if any are disqualified from sitting upon the jury. If either the state or the defense feels that a juror is not qualified, it may challenge the juror for cause; CCP 35.16 deals with the permissible grounds for such a challenge. The prosecution or the state may challenge a juror for the following reasons:

1. He is not a qualified voter.
2. He has been convicted of theft or of a felony.
3. He is under indictment or legal accusation of theft or felony.
4. He is physically or mentally incapable of being a juror.
5. He is a witness in the case.
6. He served on the grand jury which found the indictment.
7. He served on the trial jury in a previous trial of this case.
8. He has bias or prejudice in favor of or against the defendant.
9. He has already made up his mind as to the defendant's guilt or innocence.
10. He cannot read or write.

In addition, the state may challenge for cause if:

1. The juror is related to the defendant by blood or is an in-law within the third degree of relationship (great grandparent, great uncle, second cousin, or closer).
2. In capital cases, the juror is opposed to infliction of the death penalty.
3. The juror is opposed to the existence of the law the defendant is accused of violating.

In addition, the defense may challenge for cause if:

1. The juror is a blood relative or in-law within the third degree of relationship to the person injured in the commission of the offense or to any of the prosecutors, or
2. The juror has bias or prejudice against the law providing for the defense upon which the defendant hopes to avoid conviction.

When challenge for cause is made, the judge decides whether or not to sustain it. If he does sustain it, the juror is dismissed. If he does not, the juror is not dismissed.

The parties have an unlimited number of challenges for cause. In addition, each side is given a number of peremptory challenges, under which jurors may be dismissed without any necessity for justification or explanation. In a capital case each side has fifteen peremptory challenges. In other felony cases each side has ten such challenges. In misdemeanor cases tried in district court each side has five. In county court and JP or municipal court each side has three.

These challenges are exercised in the following manner: The clerk hands to each attorney the list of jurors who have not been challenged for cause, in the order in which they were questioned. Each attorney then crosses off the list those jurors he wishes to challenge. The lists are then handed back to the clerk. The first twelve names which have not been crossed off by either side are the jury in district court. The first six names not crossed off are the jury in county, municipal, and JP courts.

Order of procedure. CCP 36.01 specifies the order of procedure in a Texas criminal trial as follows:

1. Indictment or information is read to the jury.
2. Defendant's plea is disclosed.

3. Prosecutor makes his opening statement, telling the jury what he expects to prove.
4. Prosecution calls its witnesses.
5. Defense makes its opening statement, telling the jury what it expects to prove.
6. Defense calls its witnesses.
7. Prosecution may present rebuttal evidence.
8. Defense may present rebuttal evidence.
9. Attorneys make closing arguments.
10. Judge charges jury as to the law governing the case.
11. The jury begins its deliberations.

Burden of proof. The prosecution must prove the guilt of the defendant beyond a reasonable doubt. Thus, if the defense can create such a reasonable doubt in the minds of the jurors, the result of the trial should be an acquittal.

In jury criminal trials, only the jury may convict, but the judge acting alone may acquit. If after the prosecution presents its case, the defense feels that the state's evidence standing alone does not prove guilt beyond a reasonable doubt, the defense may move for a directed verdict of acquittal. Should the judge agree that guilt has not been proven, he may grant the motion, thus ending the trial.

If, at the end of the presentation of evidence, the defense feels that it has created such doubt of guilt that no reasonable juror could vote to convict, a motion for directed verdict of acquittal may be made. If the judge agrees that no reasonable juror could convict, he will grant the motion. On the other hand, if the defense is so weak that the prosecutor feels that no reasonable juror could vote to acquit, he may not ask for a directed verdict of conviction. The jury must do the convicting if there is to be a conviction.

Summoning of witnesses. The clerk of the court where a criminal trial takes place has the duty of issuing subpoenas for witnesses upon the request of the attorney desiring to call the particular witness. When it is desired that the witness bring with him items of physical evidence, a subpoena duces tecum is obtained for that witness, describing with certainty the items he is to bring with him.

An officer of the court then serves the subpoena upon the witness by reading it to him. At that point the witness knows the time and place at which he is to testify and what physical evidence, if any, he is to bring with him.

A subpoena may be served upon a witness anywhere in the state of Texas (CCP 24.16). It is also possible to subpoena a witness from out of state, if that state has adopted the Uniform Act to Secure the Attendance of Witnesses from Without the State in Criminal Proceedings, which Texas has incorporated into the CCP as Section 24.28.

A subpoenaed witness may be required to post bail to insure his obedience to the subpoena. Should the party calling him fear that he may take steps to avoid obedience to the subpoena, the party may require that the witness be attached—that is, taken into custody and forced to attend the trial.

An initial attachment is possible only for a witness who is a convict, or for a witness residing in the county of trial. However, should a witness refuse to obey a subpoena, an order for his attachment may be issued even if he is residing outside the county of trial. A witness in a felony case who refuses without cause to obey a subpoena may be fined up to $500. A witness disobeying a subpoena in a misdemeanor case may be fined up to $100. The witness is entitled to a hearing before the judge imposing the fine, however. If he has a good excuse for his disobedience, he may get out of paying the fine.

Questioning of witnesses. The party calling a witness gets the first opportunity to question him. This questioning is called direct examination. During direct examination, the examining attorney must not ask leading questions—that is, he must not ask questions

which suggest their own answers. Questions asked on direct examination must be of this nature:
1. Where were you at 6:10 P.M. on January 23, 1980?
2. What did you see there?
3. Are you acquainted with the defendant, Red Ruffneck?

Normally, the following sorts of questions may *not* be asked on direct examination:
1. You saw Red Ruffneck run the red light at the corner of First and Washington, didn't you?
2. Isn't it true that you consumed three martinis before you left Beeno Boozer's house on the night of July 26?

The asking of leading questions on direct examination is permitted only when the witness is hostile to the party calling him. If the witness is obviously hostile, leading questions will be allowed from the beginning of direct examination. If the witness is supposedly friendly, but shows by his answers to questions that he is in fact hostile, the attorney conducting the direct examination must obtain court permission to ask leading questions.

The scope of direct examination is limited only by the knowledge of the witness and the requirement of relevancy—that is, witnesses may be questioned only about matters directly relevant to the case in question.

When the direct examination is completed, the attorney for the opposing party may cross-examine. The asking of leading questions is quite proper during cross-examination. The asking of questions to which the required answer is merely "yes" or "no" is also proper.

A witness may be cross-examined about any material relevant to the case. Thus, if on direct examination a witness is questioned about where he was and what he did on the evening of July 20, 1979, a cross-examiner may inquire where he was or what he did on the morning of July 20, 1979.

The cross-examiner may also inquire into matters outside the scope of the direct examination for purposes of impeaching a witness. The objective of impeachment may be to show bias on the part of the witness, to show that his reputation for truth and veracity is not good, or to show that his direct testimony was misleading or included lies. The cross-examiner may therefore inquire about the relationship between the witness and the defendant or between the witness and the injured party. He may inquire into matters which call the powers of observation of the witness into question. He may also compare the testimony the witness gave during direct examination with his testimony in a prior deposition; if inconsistencies are found, he may question the witness about them. This is one of the most devastating forms of impeachment.

The attorneys are mainly responsible for keeping the examination of witnesses within the legal bounds. When an attorney hears what he believes to be an improper question, he objects to it and states the reason for his objection. The judge will either sustain the objection, in which case the witness is excused from answering the question, or he will overrule it. in which case the witness must answer.

The privilege against self-incrimination. Both the defendant in a criminal prosecution and the witnesses testifying in the case may make use of this privilege. The defendant may use it as a reason for not testifying at his trial. If he chooses not to testify, the prosecution may not call him as a witness, nor may the prosecution make any comment on his failure to testify to the jury. If the defendant waives the privilege and chooses to testify, however, he thereby subjects himself to cross-examination at the hands of the prosecution. He may then be questioned on cross-examination in the same way as any other witness.

It must be noted here, however, that corporations, partnerships, associations, and the like are not permitted to claim a privilege against self-incrimination. The officers, members, and associates of defendant organizations called upon to testify in criminal prosecutions of their organizations may not claim the privilege against self-incrimination on behalf of the organization. As witnesses they have the same right to claim the privilege as do other witnesses.

A witness may not use the privilege against self-incrimination as an excuse not to testify. He may use it as an excuse for not answering certain questions, however, or as an excuse for not obeying a subpoena duces tecum calling for production of physical evidence.

Essentially, a witness cannot be compelled to answer a question if the answer could be used against him in a criminal prosecution. When a witness is asked such a question, he may refuse to answer on the grounds that the answer may tend to incriminate him. The judge usually calls the witness and the attorneys to the bench and asks the witness why he claims self-incrimination. After the witness has explained and the attorneys make their comments on the situation, the judge will either excuse the witness from answering or order the witness to answer. If the court denies the privilege, the witness is in the uncomfortable position of either answering a question he feels is incriminating or undergoing punishment for contempt for refusing to answer.

The reluctant witness may be stripped of his privilege against self-incrimination by the grant of immunity from prosecution for named offenses. In prosecutions of coconspirators, for example, the prosecution may induce or force one coconspirator to testify against his cohorts by granting him immunity from prosecution for the conspiracy. The grant may be made only by a judge, and it must spell out clearly the area of immunity. Since the person so given immunity cannot be prosecuted for any crimes encompassed by the grant, his answering of questions in the area of the grant cannot incriminate him and the privilege is not available to him.

The use of the privilege as an excuse for nonobedience to a subpoena duces tecum is limited. The production of incriminating evidence may be compelled by subpoena duces tecum, despite the existence of the privilege against self-incrimination, in five situations:

1. When the defendant is a corporation, partnership, or other organization, since the privilege is not available to organizations.
2. When the evidence called for in the subpoena consists of records required by law to be kept. The accounting records of a business, the prescription files of a drug store, the payroll records of an employer, the on-the-job injury records of an employer—all these records and many more are required to be kept by law and are subject to subpoena.
3. When the record of a person's banking transactions is subpoenaed from his bank. Banks are required by law to keep microfilm records of a person's cancelled checks. When these are the object of a subpoena duces tecum served upon the bank, no self-incrimination objection to their production may be raised. The bank, being a corporation, may raise no objection, and the bank's customer may also raise no objection, because these records are not his property: they are the property of the bank, as per the decision of the U.S. Supreme Court in the case of *California Bankers' Assn. vs. Schultz,* 416 US 21.
4. When the items subpoenaed are working papers for preparation of financial statements in the possession of an accountant. These working papers of course contain information from the customer's accounting records, but they are not themselves a part of the records. Therefore, the accountant's customer cannot object to

their production in court, because they are not his property, and the accountant cannot object to their production upon the grounds that they might incriminate his customer. The only objection the accountant can have is if they might incriminate him (Fissher vs. U.S. 425 US 391).

5. When the items subpoenaed are personal records of the defendant in the possession of someone else, the privilege does not apply. The U.S. Supreme Court stated in the case of *Couch vs. United States*, 409 US 322, that the privilege against self-incrimination is essentially personal: it adheres more to the person of the defendant than to information which may tend to incriminate. If such information is outside the control of the defendant, it is fair game for a subpoena.

It is clear from all of this that the scope of the privilege against self-incrimination is narrower than one might have believed. It extends primarily to protecting a person from testifying verbally against himself, and not so much to protection against self-incrimination through documentary evidence.

The husband-wife privilege. What spouses say to each other while they are married is privileged. The parties must have been married to each other when the allegedly privileged words were spoken. If they were, the privilege survives the dissolution of the marriage.

There are two sets of circumstances under which privileged husband-wife conversations may be revealed. A wife, for example, may testify about conversations with her husband if her husband consents, or if he is the defendant in a criminal action which she has brought against him. An eavesdropper may also testify to a husband-wife conversation if it can be categorized as an admissible form of hearsay.

The attorney-client privilege. As discussed in the materials dealing with the legal profession, communications between an attorney and his client are privileged. The privilege actually belongs to the client, not to the attorney; the attorney may not invoke it to keep the client from testifying about a communication.

For the privilege to exist, there must actually have been a professional relationship between attorney and client at the time the communication was made. The privilege is not terminated by the termination of the relationship; what was communicated during the relationship remains privileged. Such communications which are overheard by an eavesdropper may be revealed by the eavesdropper.

The clergyman-penitent privilege. This privilege is governed by statute in Texas. RCS 3715a provides that no ordained minister, priest, rabbi, or accredited practitioner of any established church or religious organization may be required to disclose information confidentially communicated to him in his professional capacity if disclosure is objected to by the communicant and disclosure would violate a sacred moral trust. However, the statute also provides that the presiding judge of a court may compel such disclosure when he feels that disclosure is necessary to the proper administration of justice.

Other privileges. Texas law permits no other privileges similar to those discussed above. Many states recognize a physician-patient privilege, and some states also recognize an accountant-client privilege, but Texas recognizes neither.

The opinion evidence rule. Generally, witnesses are permitted to testify only about what they know. They are not permitted to testify as to what they believe. However, experts may express opinions on the meaning of evidence which is within the scope of their expertise. Thus:

1. A medical doctor may express an opinion as to the state of a person's physical health or well-being.
2. An auto mechanic may express an opinion as to the mechanical condition of an automobile.

3. A psychiatrist or psychologist may express an opinion as to the state of a person's mental health.
4. A real estate appraiser may express an opinion as to the value of a tract of land.
5. A handwriting expert may express an opinion as to the genuineness of a signature.

Lay witnesses are permitted to express opinions only with respect to matters that are within the competence of ordinary human beings. Thus:

1. A person may testify as to another person's mental state—calm, disturbed, angry, depressed, etc.
2. A person may testify as to his own physical injuries, so long as he sticks to observable facts. (A person could not, for instance, try to interpret x-ray pictures taken of himself.)
3. A person may testify as to the speed a motor vehicle was traveling, in terms such as "fast" or "very fast."
4. A person may testify as to the nature of a relationship between two other persons in such terms as "loving," "full of enmity," etc.

Thus, when technical interpretation of evidence is needed, an expert must be called upon to do the interpreting.

Hearsay evidence. It is not permissible for Brown to testify that Green told him that Black said such-and-such, if the object of the testimony is proof of the truth of what Black allegedly said. Black's statements are being offered third-hand, and could obviously have been distorted in the transmission; they are therefore inadmissible hearsay.

Under most circumstances it would not be permissible for Green to testify as to what Black said since even second-hand hearsay is normally inadmissible. However, there may exist circumstances under which hearsay testimony is admissible. One of the most important types of admissible hearsay is the admission of a party which is contrary to his interest. Such an admission in a criminal matter would not be admissible unless it can be shown that the accused was aware of his constitutional right to remain silent at the time he made the admission. A declaration which is contrary to the personal or financial interest of the person making it is also admissible.

Since both admissions and declarations against interest are of more importance in civil matters than they are in criminal, they will be discussed more fully in the section on civil procedures.

Statements uttered by the accused or by other persons at the scene of a crime just after or soon enough after commission of the crime so that they are clearly spontaneous utterances not made as a result of forethought or planning are admissible as part of the res gestae (the matter in question). The statement need not be that of the accused; it could be made by a victim of the crime, or by a witness. Thus, Brown could testify that just after a bank robbery Green said to him, "That was Bill Black who robbed that place!"

Statements made by a third party in the presence of the accused are admissible, even if the person making the statement did not participate in the alleged criminal activity. Dying declarations are a form of admissible hearsay, if the person who made the declaration knew that he was dying and believed that there was no hope of recovery. Thus, if Black is on trial for the murder of Green, Blue could testify that Green told him "Black shot me" just before he died. Statements of age and pedigree are another form of admissible hearsay which will be discussed in the chapter on civil procedure. There are also several other forms of admissible hearsay, but those discussed here are the most important.

Demonstrative evidence. Demonstrative evidence consists of tangible items usable for proving part of the case of the plaintiff, prosecution, or defense. All sorts of articles or objects are admissible as demonstrative evidence, including weapons used for commission of the crime, weapons taken from the defendant as a result of a legal search, articles or objects which tend to prove the defendant's guilt (such as marijuana cigarettes taken from him as a result of a lawful search), items found at the scene of the crime, clothing allegedly worn by accused at the scene of the crime, clothing allegedly worn by the victim of the crime, and so forth. Of course, all of this must be authenticated before it becomes admissible: someone must testify as to what it is, to whom it belongs, its connection with the case, etc.

Photographs, x-rays, and motion pictures are admissible if they can be authenticated. Again, the taker of these items must be identified, and the time and place of the taking must be proven. Tape recordings may also be admitted, but since their reliability is more open to question than is that of other sorts of demonstrative evidence, more authentication is necessary. Generally, it must be shown that the recorder operator knew how to operate the device, that no tampering with the recording has occurred since it was made, and that the person or persons whose voice or voices were recorded consented to the making of the recording. The results of lie detector tests are inadmissible in Texas criminal prosecutions and in civil cases. Evidence that a person refused to take a lie detector test is also inadmissible.

Documentary evidence. Documents are generally admissible forms of evidence. They must normally be authenticated—that is, someone must testify as to when, where, by whom, and under what circumstances the document was written. If the document is signed, proof of the genuineness of the signature is needed; at least, someone must testify that the signer signed it. If the document is witnessed, one of the witnesses must testify to corroborate the making of the document. This requirement is waived if no witness can be produced.

Certain types of documents are admissible without authentication. These include:
1. Documents admitted to be genuine by the other party to the case.
2. Recorded documents which have, generally, been on record for at least ten years, the genuineness of which have not been disputed, as per RCS 3726, 3726a, and 3726b.
3. "Ancient documents," documents which are thirty years old or older, and which have been in proper custody for that period of time.

Business records are admissible under RCS 3737e. Such a record is admissible as proof of the happening of the transaction recorded if it is proven that:
1. The record was made in the normal course of business.
2. It was the regular course of that business for a record to be made of this sort of transaction.
3. The record was made at or near the time of the transaction.

The testimony of the custodian of the records in question on these matters is enough to secure admissibility. The custodian need not be the person who made the entry in question. He may not even be able to identify the person who did make the entry in question; this does not affect the admissibility of the records, but it may affect their credibility.

Photocopies of records are admissible if filed with the clerk of court at least fourteen days before trial, if notice is given to the other parties to the case that these will be used, and if the photocopies are authenticated properly.

Hospital x-ray pictures are also admissible under the provisions of RCS 3737e, so long as they are authenticated by the head of the radiology department of the hospital where they were taken, or by his partner or partners.

Depositions, affidavits, and testimony at other hearings. In general, a witness whose evidence is desired by a party to a case must testify in person if his testimony is to get before the court. Written testimony is not admissible in lieu of personal testimony unless it is impossible to have the witness testify in person.

So, if the witness in question is dead; has become insane, incompetent, or physically disabled; has disappeared and his whereabouts are unknown; or has fled beyond the jurisdiction of the court, his written testimony may be read to the jury in lieu of oral testimony in person. In such a case, the deposition of the witness may be read to the jury, or the testimony of the witness at a previous hearing may be read to the jury. However, testimony at a previous hearing is not admissible unless the issues of the former hearing are substantially the same as those in the present trial, and unless the opposite party at this trial had the opportunity to cross-examine the witness.

Remember that the deposition of a witness may be used for impeachment purposes when the statement of the same witness in court contradicts a statement in his deposition. The contradiction may be brought to the attention of the court and the witness may be asked to explain it, if he can.

An affidavit, which is the sworn statement of a witness, is inadmissible as proof of the truth of its contents, except in certain sorts of preliminary proceedings. It is not a substitute for the personal testimony of the witness or for a deposition, because there has been no opportunity for cross-examination.

Prejudicial evidence. In criminal cases, the prosecution cannot get evidence before the jury soley for the purpose of inflaming the jury against the defendant. Thus, no demonstrative evidence (such as photographs of the victim) is admissible unless it helps to prove that the defendant is guilty of the offense of which he stands accused.

Also, the prosecution may not offer evidence of a defendant's prior criminal convictions. Obviously, the fact that he committed other crimes does not prove that he committed the offense of which he stands accused. Furthermore, the prosecution may not seek to prove that the defendant has a bad character, although the defense may seek to prove that he has a good character.

The presumption of innocence. The criminal defendant is presumed to be innocent. Before he can be convicted, the state must prove his guilt beyond a reasonable doubt.

Charge to the jury and final arguments. After all the evidence has been presented and the attorneys for the two sides have rested their cases, they deliver their closing arguments. The prosecution always has the last word in these, the purpose of which is essentially to sum up the evidence in the case and interpret it from the point of view of the party involved.

The prosecutor must be careful in his summation. He must limit his commentary to the evidence introduced during the trial. He must not refer to evidence not admitted, and he must not make remarks prejudicial to the defendant, such as referrals to previous convictions. If the prosecutor makes improper or prejudicial remarks during his closing argument, the defense may move for a mistrial. If the judge agrees that the remarks may have unduly prejudiced the jury, he may declare a mistrial, which would end the trial and make necessary either a new trial or dismissal of the charges.

The defense counsel is under no such limitations. Courts will not declare a mistrial because of prejudicial remarks by the defense counsel. The only limitation upon the defense in its closing argument is that too prejudicial an argument may call down upon the attorney the displeasure of the presiding judge, who might order some restraint. Further disobedience would be cause for punishment for contempt of court.

When final arguments are completed, the judge instructs the jury on the law applicable to the case. In Texas state courts, the judge must confine his remarks to the law; he may not comment upon the evidence in any way. This principle does not hold true in federal criminal prosecutions: in federal court the judge is permitted to comment upon the evidence while charging the jury. Of course, improper comment by the judge during his charge will be a ground for appeal by the defense if the jury convicts. If the improper comment damages the prosecution, and the jury acquits, there is no legal recourse.

Jury deliberation and verdict. At this stage in a criminal trial, the jury retires to determine the guilt or innocence of the defendant. The sentence is not considered at this point. The jurors must also not consider the question of the defendant's sanity unless he has pleaded "not guilty by reason of insanity." In the absence of an insanity plea, the possible verdicts are "guilty," "not guilty," or "guilty of a lesser included offense." If there are multiple charges against the defendant, the jury must render a verdict upon each charge.

The jurors deliberate alone; no other person may be present with them. The bailiff may contact them to see to the satisfaction of their wants—the jurors communicate with the outside world only through him while deliberating.

All of the jurors must agree upon a verdict. They must be allowed ample time within which to come to an agreement. They may freely discuss all of the evidence in the case, the credibility of the witnesses, and so forth. They may also use their knowledge of the ways of the world, and their common sense. However, they should not use as evidence the personal knowledge of one or more jurors as to aspects of the case not covered by the evidence introduced in court. The jurors must of course not use coercion upon any of their number. There must be no alcoholic beverages brought into the jury room; a verdict influenced in any way by alcoholic consumption must be overthrown. No element of chance may enter into the deliberation, and no bribery or similar conduct is tolerated.

If the jury cannot agree upon a verdict within a reasonable time, the judge may declare a hung jury and a mistrial. The length of time to be given the jury will depend upon the length and complexity of the trial. If the trial lasted for three hours, three hours is probably ample time for jury deliberation. If the trial lasted three days, however, the jury should be given one day or perhaps more. Once a reasonable time has passed, the judge may declare a mistrial, or he may require the jury to keep deliberating. He may keep them deliberating until all hope of agreement is gone.

Far more often than not, however, the jury will agree upon a verdict. If the verdict is "not guilty," the defendant is discharged, since there is no state appeal from an acquittal. If the verdict is "not guilty by reason of insanity," the charges against the defendant are dropped, but the defendant is not necessarily discharged. What will happen to him next depends upon his present mental condition as evaluated by the judge. If he is without a doubt sane and competent, he will be set free. If there is any doubt about his present sanity or competence, he will be held for possible civil commitment to a state mental institution, or at least for observation.

If the verdict is "guilty," the next step is sentencing.

Sentencing. In misdemeanor cases in JP court and municipal court, the jury may assess a sentence at the same time as it finds the defendant guilty. Otherwise, CCP 37.07 requires a separate hearing upon the question of sentencing. If the defendant is found guilty of a capital felony, CCP 37.071 provides for a special sentencing procedure.

In noncapital cases, evidence may be introduced at the sentencing hearing on the previous criminal record of the defendant, and on his character. Here, evidence of the bad character of the defendant is admissible, as well as evidence of his good character.

The sentence is assessed by the judge, unless the defendant has asked that the jury assess it. When sentencing is to be by the jury, the same jury that assessed guilt assesses the sentence. The judge must instruct the jury as to the maximum and minimum sentence permissible. If the defendant filed a proper motion for probation at the beginning of the proceeding the jury must be instructed as to its option to grant probation.

The decision of the jury with respect to the sentence must be unanimous. If there is a hung jury with respect to the sentence, the entire proceeding ends in a mistrial, and a complete new trial becomes necessary.

CCP 42.12 Sec. 3 provides that the jury may grant probation to the defendant for any term authorized by law for the crime for which he has been convicted, but in no case can the probation period exceed ten years. The jury, however, may grant probation only when:
1. The defendant has moved for probation at his arraignment or at other permitted times, and
2. The defendant has never been convicted of a felony in this or any other state, and
3. The jury did not assess punishment of more than ten years.

In all cases in which the jury does not assess a sentence of more than ten years for an offense, the judge may suspend the sentence imposed by the jury and grant probation for a specified period. However, the judge may not grant probation if the defendant is convicted of any of the following:
1. Capital murder.
2. Aggravated kidnapping.
3. Aggravated rape.
4. Aggravated sexual abuse.
5. Aggravated robbery.

The judge may also not grant probation if the defendant used or exhibited a deadly weapon in the course of commission of the crime, or in flight from the scene thereof. The judge may, however, grant probation to a person who has been convicted of another felony.

CCP 42.12 Sec. 3f(b) provides that, if the jury grants probation to a person convicted of a second-degree or higher felony who used or exhibited a deadly weapon during the commission of the crime or during his flight from the scene thereof, the judge may order the defendant confined in the Texas Department of Corrections for no less than 60 days and no more than 120 days.

In those cases in which the defendant elects to have the judge impose sentence, the judge decides whether or not to grant probation, but he cannot grant probation in case of the defendant's use or exhibit of a deadly weapon or if the defendant is convicted of one of the five offenses mentioned above.

Sentencing procedure in a capital case. When a defendant is convicted of a capital offense, the two possible sentences are death and life imprisonment; the jury must decide between the two. CCP 37.071 provides that the jury shall be required to answer "yes" or "no" to two—or possibly three—questions.
1. Did the defendant deliberately commit the acts which caused the death of the deceased with the reasonable expectation that these acts would cause the death of either the deceased or another person?
2. Is it probable that the defendant would commit criminal acts of violence which would constitute a continuing threat to society?
3. If raised by the evidence in the case, was the act of the defendant in killing the deceased unreasonable in response to the provocation, if any, by the deceased?

The third question would only be asked when the question of self-defense or some similar issue was raised during the trial.

In order to answer "yes" to these questions, all jurors must agree. In order to answer "no," ten of the twelve must agree. Failure to agree means a hung jury and a mistrial. All submitted questions must be answered in the affirmative to justify a death sentence. If even one is answered in the negative, the sentence is life imprisonment.

New trial. The only way the defendant may avoid having sentence pronounced after conviction is to move for a new trial under CCP 40.03 or to move for arrest of judgment under CCP 41.01. The defendant may also appeal the conviction to the court of criminal appeals, but making this appeal would not stop the pronouncing of sentence.

CCP 40.03 provides the following grounds for a new trial:

1. Defendant was tried in absentia, or had no legal counsel.
2. The court's charge to the jury misstated the law.
3. The jury reached a verdict by lot, or by other nondeliberative means.
4. A juror was bribed to convict, or was guilty of other corruption.
5. A material witness was by force, threats, or fraud prevented from testifying, or evidence was destroyed or removed.
6. New evidence has been discovered.
7. The jury considered evidence not introduced in court, or a juror had an unauthorized conversation with an outsider about the case during deliberation, or a juror became intoxicated during deliberation.
8. The jury was guilty of other misconduct.
9. The verdict is contrary to law and evidence.

The judge may hold a hearing upon the motion for a new trial, and must use his discretion in deciding whether or not to grant the motion. Normally, such motions are denied. A motion in arrest of judgment is a contention that the proceedings against the defendant have been unlawful in some way.

Granting of a motion for a new trial throws out the result of the old trial. Granting of a motion in arrest of judgment throws out both the results of the trial and the indictment under which the defendant was tried. Both motions must be filed within ten days of conviction.

Pronouncing of sentence. In case the defendant is sentenced to death by the trial court, sentence is not to be pronounced until the court of criminal appeals has considered the case. This review is mandatory, under the provisions of CCP 37.071(f).

In other cases, sentence is pronounced even though an appeal to the court of criminal appeals has been filed by defendant.

If the defendant is to be imprisoned in a Department of Corrections institution, and his sentence is more than the minimum provided by law for the offense, the sentence shall be an indeterminate one (CCP 42.09). It shall be at least the minimum provided by law for the offense, and at most the punishment assessed by judge or jury. If the defendant has been in jail pending the trial of his case, he gets credit against his sentence for his jail time (CCP 42.03). If the defendant is convicted of two or more offenses, he must be sentenced separately for each. The sentences for the offenses may then be served concurrently (all together) or consecutively (one at a time) at the discretion of the trial judge. A defendant sentenced to jail may be permitted to serve his time during off-duty hours or on weekends. Bail may be required of such a defendant, and his travel may be restricted, as per CCP 42.03 sec. 5.

If the defendant is fined, CCP 42.15 permits the court to require payment of the fine:
1. Immediately upon sentence, or

2. At some specified later date, or
3. In designated installments.

If the defendant does not pay the fine as directed, he may be imprisoned in lieu of payment (CCP 43.03). CCP 43.07 authorizes issuance of writs of execution against the defendant's property for collection of fines, as is done to collect civil judgments.

If a fine is levied against a defendant in JP or municipal court, and the defendant does not pay, he may be imprisoned in the county jail and work off the fine at the rate of five dollars per day of imprisonment. Such a defendant may be discharged under the provisions of CCP 45.53 by writ of habeas corpus, showing that he is too poor to pay the fine and he has served enough time to pay it at the rate of five dollars per day.

When a defendant is granted probation for a felony, he may be required to spend up to thirty days or one-third of his sentence in prison, whichever is less. A probationer is placed under the supervision of a probation officer, and is required to report to that officer at stated times. He is also required to abide by certain conditions of probation as imposed by the court. These may include (CCP 42.12 Sec. 6):

1. Not violating the law in any way.
2. Working faithfully in suitable employment as far as possible.
3. Remaining within a specified area.
4. Allowing the probation officer to visit him at home and elsewhere.
5. Paying his fine and court costs, and making such restitution as the court may direct to the victim of his offense.
6. Supporting his dependents.

Other conditions of probation may also be imposed by the court. Violation of the terms of probation may, after a proper hearing, cause revocation of the probation and commission of the defendant to prison. There is no right to a jury in such a hearing. Revocation of probation is not mandatory in such a case; it is a matter of the judge's discretion. If a probationer leaves the state of Texas, he is to be considered a fugitive from justice.

A revocation of probation is appealable to the court of criminal appeals, but the defendant may be imprisoned pending resolution of the appeal.

A person convicted of a misdemeanor other than a Class C misdemeanor may be granted probation under the terms of CCP 42.13. The terms and conditions of misdemeanor probation are very similar to those of felony probation. One difference is that CCP 42.13 Sec. 3A permits the judge of the court which sentences a defendant to jail for a misdemeanor to suspend sentence and put the defendant on probation, if he does so not less than ten days nor more than ninety days after the defendant begins serving his sentence.

The 1979 session of the Texas legislature amended the adult misdemeanor probation statute (CCP 42.13) to permit the granting of community-service probation to persons pleading guilty or nolo contendere to Class B or Class A misdemeanor charges, if the offense is a first offense and if the misdemeanor did not involve bodily injury or a threat of bodily injury to any person. The court may place such persons on community-service probation without entering adjudication of guilt on the court records.

If the court grants an application for community-service probation, it shall require that the probationer work a specified number of hours without compensation on a community-service project for an organization named in the court order.

If the probationer committed a Class B misdemeanor, his hours of work shall be no less than twenty-four and no more than one hundred. If he committed a Class A misdemeanor his hours of work shall be no less than eighty and no more than two hundred.

The work imposed must be within the capabilities of the probationer. His work schedule may be arranged so that the required community service work does not interfere with paid employment or school hours.

The terms of the probation are otherwise similar to the terms imposed upon all probationers. Successful completion of the probation will result in the dismissal of the charges against the probationer, with no record of conviction for the offense existing. Violation of the terms of the probation may well result in revocation of the probation and commitment to jail.

Appeals. Appeal from municipal court and JP court is to the county court. To make an appeal, notice of appeal should be given; the most important item required for perfection of the appeal is the filing of the appeal bond required by CCP 44.13. This bond shall be double the fine and court costs levied in the case, but no less than $50. It must be filed within ten days of sentencing; if this is not done, no appeal is possible.

CCP 44.17 provides that, in the case of such an appeal, an entire new trial is to be held in the county court. The witnesses who testified in municipal court or JP court may be required to testify again in county court. No new service of subpoena upon these witnesses is necessary.

The appeal from the county court and district court is to the court of criminal appeals. Notice of such appeal must normally be filed within ten days after pronouncement of sentence or ten days of the overruling of a motion for a new trial (CCP 44.08).

If the defendant has been sentenced to less than fifteen years imprisonment, he is entitled to bail pending his appeal, but proper bail must of course be posted if this has not already been done. CCP 44.04 permits adjustment of the bail at this point in the proceedings.

There is no new trial in the court of criminal appeals. The bases for appeal are similar to the bases for requesting a new trial. The court examines the record of the trial and briefs filed by the attorneys to determine whether such prejudicial error occurred during the trial that the defendant was not accorded a fair trial. The attorneys also may appear before the judges of the court to make oral arguments.

There are nine judges sitting upon the court of criminal appeals bench. All nine must hear the appeal in a capital case. In noncapital cases appeals are heard by panels of three court of criminal appeals judges. Two of these three may decide the appeal. CCP 44.24(b) provides that the judges may dispose of the case in one of four ways:

1. Affirm the conviction—let the trial decision and sentence stand.
2. Reverse and remand—send the case back to the trial court for a new trial.
3. Reverse and dismiss—throw out the conviction and discharge the defendant.
4. Reform and correct the sentence (only if the sentence is unlawful).

The court of criminal appeals, then, has no power to review the sentence imposed upon the accused. It may only review the conviction itself, and the lawfulness of the sentence.

If the three-judge panel affirms the defendant's conviction, his only remaining recourse is to seek review of the decision by all nine judges of the court of criminal appeals sitting "en banc." The judges are under no obligation to grant this sort of rehearing, but the rules of the court do permit it under certain conditions. Normally, however, there will be no rehearing, and the affirmation by the three-judge panel is final. Of course, the affirmation of the decision results in the withdrawal of bail and the commitment of the defendant to prison, if he was sentenced to prison.

In rare cases, the defendant may wish to make one final appeal, to the Supreme Court of the United States. If that court agrees to hear the appeal—which it ordinarily will not do—the defendant might again be able to obtain bail.

Parole. All prisoners confined to Department of Corrections institutions are eligible for parole after serving a portion of their sentences, except those prisoners sentenced to death. According to CCP 42.12 Sec. 15(b), prisoners serving terms for capital murder, aggravated rape, aggravated sexual abuse, aggravated kidnapping, or aggravated robbery, or those prisoners who used or exhibited a deadly weapon during commission of the crime or flight from the scene thereof, are eligible for parole after serving one-third of their maximum sentence, or twenty years, whichever is less.

Other prisoners become eligible for parole when the time served plus good conduct time equals one-third of the maximum sentence or twenty years, whichever is less. Good conduct time is awarded by the Department of Corrections in accordance with the directive of RCS 6181-1. Under that section trusties are awarded one day of good conduct time for each day served. Other prisoners are divided into three classifications: those in the first category obtain twenty days of good conduct time for each thirty days served; those in the second obtain ten days of good conduct time for each thirty days served; and those in the third class receive no good conduct time. The assignment of prisoners to the various classes may be changed by Department of Corrections administrators. Good conduct time credits may also be revoked if a prisoner is guilty of misconduct.

A person who is eligible for parole may apply for it to the Board of Pardons and Paroles. The board is under no obligation to grant a parole to anyone; the decision to grant or not to grant is entirely at its discretion.

If a prisoner is granted parole, he is released from custody and placed under the supervision of a parole officer, subject to the same sorts of conditions applicable to persons on probation. The parole will endure until the end of a prisoner's sentence, unless he is pardoned earlier.

A prisoner who has not been granted parole is eligible for release on mandatory supervision when his time served plus good conduct time add up to the term of imprisonment. He will then be treated, essentially, as a parolee until the actual term of his sentence expires.

A prisoner who has 180 days or less remaining on his sentence, not counting good conduct time, may also be released under mandatory supervision.

Thus, good conduct time will not serve to shorten a prisoner's sentence. It will, however, help to qualify him for early parole or release under mandatory supervision.

Defendant's sanity. Whenever questions arise about the sanity of the defendant, it must be remembered that such questions can take more than one form. The contention might be raised that the defendant was insane at the time the alleged crime was committed. In that case, he may plead "not guilty by reason of insanity." Proof of his insanity as of that time will result in his acquittal.

The contention might also be raised that the defendant is incompetent to stand trial. In such a case, he cannot participate in his own defense or understand what is happening to him, so the proceedings against him might be postponed until he recovers his sanity. The question of his competency to stand trial has nothing to do with that of his guilt or innocence. It has everything to do with the right of the state to try and punish him.

Incompetency to stand trial. CCP 46.02 contains the law relative to the question of the defendant's competency to stand trial. It also contains the rules of procedure for determining his competency.

The question of competence to stand trial may be raised before the date of trial by the defendant, his counsel, or by the court itself. A person is incompetent to stand trial if:
1. He does not have sufficient present ability to consult with his lawyer with a reasonable degree of rational understanding, or
2. He does not have a rational as well as factual understanding of the proceedings against him (CCP 46.02 Sec. 1).

When the question of competency to stand trial is raised, the court may have the defendant examined by disinterested experts in the mental health field. For this purpose the defendant may be sent to a facility of the Texas Department of Mental Health and Mental Retardation for a period of up to twenty-one days. The experts must submit reports of their findings to the court, including findings as to whether the defendant is mentally ill or mentally retarded, and whether or not he is competent to stand trial.

If the reports of the experts convince the court that there is evidence of the defendant's incompetence to stand trial, a special hearing must be held to resolve the question. The hearing must be held before a jury specially impaneled for this purpose; it must not be the jury which would determine the defendant's guilt or innocence.

The jury is asked to answer two questions:
1. Is the defendant competent to stand trial?
2. If the defendant is incompetent to stand trial, is there a substantial probability that he will regain competence to stand trial in the foreseeable future?

In this hearing, the jury must unanimously answer these questions. If the jury cannot agree unanimously, it is a hung jury and a new jury must be impaneled to decide the question. The witnesses must then testify again.

If the jury's answer to the first question is "yes," the trial of the defendant will be scheduled, and normal procedure will be followed. If the answer to the first question is "No," and the answer to the second "Yes," the defendant will be confined to the maximum security unit of a state mental hospital for observation and treatment for an observation period of up to eighteen months. If the defendant recovers his competence, he will be sent back to stand trial. If he does not recover his competence, steps will be taken toward his permanent commitment to a mental institution.

If the answer to both questions is "No," steps will be taken to commit the defendant civilly to an appropriate institution. The procedures to be followed are set forth in Sections 4(h), 4(i), 6, and 7 of CCP 46.02.

The insanity defense. The defendant may plead "not guilty by reason of insanity" at his arraignment. He may also give notice of his intent to offer evidence of insanity any time up to ten days prior to the trial date. If the defendant claims that he is incompetent to stand trial earlier than ten days prior to trial, he shall also file notice of his intent to use the insanity defense (RCS 46.03 Sec. 2).

The defendant must be examined by experts in the area of mental health, and may be committed to a state mental hospital for a period of up to twenty-one days for observation. The examining experts shall file reports with the court, and may of course testify as expert witnesses when the defendant is brought to trial. No special hearing is necessary on the insanity defense as such: evidence upon it will be heard during the trial of the case.

The defendant who seeks to escape punishment through use of the insanity defense must remember that, although a jury verdict of "not guilty by reason of insanity" is an acquittal and will spare him from confinement in a Texas Department of Corrections institution, it will not guarantee that he will be able to walk the streets as a free man. If the evidence on the insanity question shows that the defendant is presently mentally ill or mentally retarded, his acquittal of the charges against him due to insanity may be the preliminary to commencement of civil proceedings to have him confined to an institution of the Texas Department of Mental Health and Mental Retardation. Thus, though he may escape confinement in prison, he may simultaneously assure his confinement in a mental hospital.

Conflict of laws in criminal matters. It is a general principle in common-law jurisdictions that the criminal jurisdiction of a state or nation extends only as far as its political jurisdiction and no farther. Therefore, Americans are subject to federal criminal law only so long as they are within the jurisdiction of the United States. Uniformed military personnel are subject to the Uniform Code of Military Justice anywhere in the world. Civilians of American citizenship are subject to federal laws if they are on any land reserved or acquired for the use of the United States and under the exclusive or concurrent jurisdiction thereof, including military bases, consulates, and embassies located abroad.

The criminal jurisdiction of the state of Texas applies only within the borders of Texas. An offense committed outside the borders of Texas cannot be a criminal offense under Texas law.

The courts of a state or nation will not undertake to enforce the criminal law of another state or nation. Thus, Texas courts would not try a person for a murder committed in Ohio. Courts of one state or nation will, however, assist other states or nations in the enforcement of their criminal law. Thus, if Hass is wanted in Ohio for the murder of Buckeye, and the police of Podunk, Texas, know that Hass is in Podunk, they may arrest him by following proper procedure.

The procedure for getting Hass back to Ohio is contained in the Texas Uniform Criminal Extradition Act, PC 51.13. In essence, Hass has the right to a hearing after his arrest to inform him of what he is being arrested for. At that point, he is entitled to demand a more formal hearing on the legality of his extradition to Ohio. If he makes this demand, he stays in custody in Texas until the hearing, when it must be shown that there is good cause for sending him back to Ohio. Of course, if the Texas court decides that there is no good cause, he will be released.

More often than not, though, a person in Hass's position knows that there is good cause for sending him back to the state where he is wanted. The defendant normally waives extradition and is sent back quickly.

The courts of the United States and of Texas also do not enforce foreign criminal legislation. American police do collaborate with the police of other nations in enforcing each other's criminal laws.

If, for example, the French police desire the cooperation of American police in arresting of a fugitive from French justice believed to be in America, the American police will probably lend assistance. If the fugitive is apprehended, he will be extradited to France under procedures provided for in federal law. There are some limitations upon international criminal extraditions, however. The duty of the United States to extradite a fugitive wanted by the police of another nation will depend, first of all, upon whether or not a treaty of extradition exists between this nation and the requesting nation, and, secondly, upon whether or not the offense for which the fugitive is wanted is an extraditable offense under the treaty.

The United States has entered into extradition treaties with most of the nations of the world. However, the nature of extraditable offenses varies widely from treaty to treaty. In general, civilized mankind agrees as to the seriousness of the most heinous offenses against persons and property. Murder, armed robbery, and such offenses are almost universally extraditable. However, economic and political offenses are almost universally not extraditable. A foreign government would have no obligation to return to the United States a person wanted for criminal violations of the federal antitrust laws, for instance. No nation is interested in helping another catch its tax evaders. Nor is any nation interested in helping another catch, for example, draft evaders or traitors.

Thus, though international cooperation in the enforcement of criminal law does exist, there are limitations upon this cooperation. It is therefore possible to escape some sorts of criminal liability by crossing an international frontier.

8

Texas Civil Procedure

The procedure by which civil cases are processed through the Texas courts is mandated partly by statutes enacted by the legislature and partly by the Texas Rules of Civil Procedure (TRCP), procedural rules enacted by the judges of the Supreme Court of Texas. The general rules of civil procedure are the same throughout the United States, in federal courts as well as in state courts. But the details differ from state to state, and the details of the federal rules differ from those of state rules; this discussion will therefore be limited primarily to Texas state rules.

When Texas courts may decline jurisdiction over civil cases. A Texas court may not decline to hear a criminal prosecution. If a valid information or indictment is returned against an accused person, the courts must process the case, if only to hear a plea of guilty and impose sentence, or to dismiss a defective indictment.

A Texas court has much more leeway in the matter of deciding whether or not to hear a civil matter; it may decline to hear a civil matter, or dismiss a pending civil matter, when it becomes apparent that:

1. The case involves no real controversy, or
2. The case is moot, or
3. The dispute is not ripe for judgment, or
4. The plaintiff has no standing to sue, or
5. The law offers no remedy for the wrong the plaintiff complains of, or
6. An administrative agency has primary jurisdiction over the subject matter of the dispute, or
7. The plaintiff has not exhausted his administrative remedies in the dispute, or
8. The plaintiff and the defendant have made a binding contract to submit their differences in the disputed matter to arbitration, but they have not done so, or
9. The plaintiff seeks an advisory opinion.

Case or controversy. Courts generally will not hear a civil suit unless there is a genuine dispute between plaintiff and defendant.

For instance: The City Commission of Podunk, Texas, amends its zoning ordinance to change the zoning of several city lots from residential to commercial. This was done to please Moneybags, owner of several of the lots in question. It displeases Patt, another owner of a rezoned lot. It also displeases Ruhig, owner of a lot—adjoining Patt's lot—which remains zoned residential. Neither wants Moneybags erecting commercial buildings in the area, so they decide to try an indirect method of frustrating him.

Patt applies for a building permit to erect a commercial building. Ruhig files suit against him for an injunction against the building, alleging that the zoning law amendment is unlawful because it is contrary to the city's master zoning plan. Patt has agreed in advance to put up a very weak defense to this charge, in the hope that a court will declare the amendment void.

If the court discovers what Patt and Ruhig have in mind, it will dismiss the case, since the plaintiff and defendant have identical interests.

The uncontested divorce is a similar sort of case, but it will of course not be dismissed by the court, which will ignore the absence of a case or controversy in the knowledge that most divorces these days are obtained by mutual consent of the spouses.

Moot cases. A legal dispute is moot if circumstances have changed so that there is no point to resolution of the dispute. For instance: Jager keeps a lion in his back yard. Angst, his next-door neighbor, files suit against Jager for an injunction to compel him to get rid of the lion, his argument being that the lion is a nuisance. Before the case comes to trial Jager's lion dies, so his attorney asks the judge to dismiss the case. The judge will probably do just that. The death of the lion has given Angst what he was suing for—the court could do no more for him.

If Angst and the judge were very anxious to set a legal precedent that it is a nuisance for a person to keep a lion in his back yard, the court might not dismiss the case, but that would be a most unusual situation. Courts usually do not waste time setting precedents in moot cases.

Case not ripe for decision. A court will not entertain a complaint until the plaintiff can demonstrate that he is presently being damaged by the defendant's actions. For instance, Nachbar hears that his neighbor Hambre is thinking of selling his property to Bau Corporation, which owns apartment buildings all over town. Though Nachbar's and Hambre's lots are presently zoned single-family residential, Bau Corporation seems to have no trouble getting the zoning changed on property it buys. Nachbar does not want an apartment complex for a neighbor, so he files suit for an injunction forbidding Hambre to sell his property to Bau Corporation. Hambre responds by asking for summary judgment in his favor, a dismissal of the complaint.

He will succeed. Nachbar here is "hollering before he's hurt." It is doubtful that he could stop Hambre from selling to Bau. He might be able to get a hearing when Bau reveals its plans for an apartment—that is, after Hambre has sold to Bau if Bau does plan to erect an apartment building.

Plaintiff has no standing to sue. A plaintiff cannot complain about a defendant's actions unless those actions damage him in some way. If the defendant's actions do not damage the plaintiff but do damage someone else, that is not the plaintiff's concern.

Assume Kismet is badly injured by Boozer in an auto accident. Kismet does not sue for damages because he feels that the wreck was God's will, and who is to question the will of the Almighty? Spitz feels that it is a shame that Boozer is allowed to escape paying for his negligence, so he files suit against Boozer asking the court to award Kismet damages for his injuries. Boozer's attorney asks for summary judgment for his client, and gets it. If Kismet wants to collect damages from Boozer because of his injuries, he will have to sue for them himself. The matter is none of Spitz's business.

The law offers no remedy for plaintiff's wrong. Ernest frequently asks Bonita for a date. Bonita always refuses him. Ernest cannot understand why this should be—he is sure Bonita will like him if she will just let herself get to know him. Therefore, Ernest files a petition in court for an injunction ordering Bonita to go out with him on a named evening. Bonita's attorney asks for summary judgment and dismissal. She will obviously get it—she has the right to choose her own dates. The law does not care whether or not Bonita wants to date Ernest.

Primary jurisdiction of an administrative agency. Workman is injured on the job. He reports his injury to Boss, his employer, and files a Worker's Compensation claim. Boss, who is self-insured under the Worker's Compensation law, refuses to pay. Workman files suit against Boss to force him to pay. Boss's attorney asks for dismissal of the complaint.

The complaint will be dismissed. Workman's remedy here is to file a complaint against Boss with the Industrial Accident Board (IAB), the administrative agency which initially adjudicates Texas Worker's Compensation claims. The law gives the IAB, not the courts, primary jurisdiction over such matters.

In short, whenever the law requires one to file a complaint with an administrative agency rather than with the courts, the courts have no original jurisdiction over the matter.

Exhaustion of administrative remedies. Zink asks the proper authority of the City of Podunk for a building permit to alter his residence. The authority refuses the permit, saying the alteration Zink has in mind is contrary to the municipal zoning ordinance. Zink thinks this decision is wrong, and wants to appeal it in court.

In most Texas cities, he cannot do this yet. Most zoning ordinances provide that such appeals must be filed with the Board of Adjustment, an administrative tribunal established in part to hear such appeals. Since the law provides an administrative remedy for the wrong Zink thinks he has suffered, he must make use of this administrative remedy before he goes to court.

Prior agreement to arbitrate. Seller and Buyer make an elaborate contract for the sale of some very expensive goods. The contract provides that, if Seller and Buyer have any disagreement about the terms or performance of their bargain, they will submit their differences to binding arbitration. Thus, the dispute would be submitted to an impartial arbitrator, who would render a decision binding upon both parties.

Buyer accuses Seller of delivering defective goods. Seller believes the goods were not defective. Seller files suit against Buyer to force him to pay contract price for the goods. Buyer asks for dismissal of the suit.

This suit would be dismissed, since Seller has violated the terms of the contract by filing suit rather than submitting his gripe to arbitration. Under most circumstances, an agreement to arbitrate is binding—one may not take a dispute covered by such an agreement to court before attempting arbitration.

Advisory opinions. Belinda would like to divorce her husband Burt, but one small matter holds her back. She wants to live as well after she leaves Burt as she is living now as his wife. She does not want to divorce him unless she can get all, or nearly all, of the marital property owned by them as a couple.

So, she files a petition with the local district court which says, in essence, "My husband and I own the following property as community property: (A list follows.) Our marriage is insupportable. I want a divorce. If I file for divorce and you grant me a divorce, how much of the above-listed property would be granted to me in the property settlement?"

The court would of course refuse to answer this question. The position of a court when faced with such a question is, "File your complaint, commence your suit, and we shall see."

In some areas, however, including interpretation of contracts and evaluation of land titles, courts will hand down what are essentially advisory opinions; the technical name for them is declaratory judgments.

Declaratory judgments. The Texas Legislature has enacted the Uniform Declaratory Judgments Act, RCS 2524-1. Section 2 of the act permits a person to have determined questions of the validity of a deed, will, written contract, statute, ordinance, or franchise; or to have his rights, status, or other legal relations under them clarified.

Section 3 authorizes a court to construe a contract either before or after a breach has occurred.

Section 4 permits an interested person to obtain from a court a declaration of rights or legal relations with respect to:
1. Ascertainment of classes of creditors, heirs, next of kin, and the like.
2. Administration of property and the like by fiduciaries.

The great limitation upon the power of a court to grant a declaratory judgment is that if the judgment would not end the controversy or uncertainty which caused it to be requested, the court would not hand down any such judgment. In case of any uncertainty about this, the court would refuse to hear the matter.

Of course, no declaratory judgment will be rendered before all parties involved in the matter are brought before the court to make their arguments. Jury trials are permitted in declaratory judgment cases.

PROCEDURE IN ORDINARY CIVIL SUITS

The complaint. The civil action begins when the plaintiff files his complaint with the clerk of the court which is to hear the matter. The complaint is generally oral when filed in small claims or justice of the peace court. It must be a formal written document if filed in county court or district court.

The complaint must contain the names and addresses of the plaintiff(s) and defendant(s). It must also contain, as per Rule 47 of the Texas Rules of Civil Procedure (TRCP):
1. A short statement of the cause of action sufficient to give fair notice of the claim involved (in other words, an explanation of why plaintiff is suing defendant, a description of what defendant has done to cause plaintiff to sue).
2. If the claim of plaintiff is liquidated (a promissory note, check, promise to pay a fixed sum of money, or written contract), the amount being sued for.
3. If the claim is unliquidated (a tort claim, for example), a statement that the damages sought exceed the minimum jurisdiction of the court. Thus, if suing on a tort claim in district court, one must merely state that one seeks damages of more than $500. Liquidated claims are closed-ended, unliquidated claims are open-ended. One may seek as much as one can get in a tort case.
4. A demand for judgment for relief—damages, an injunction, divorce, title to disputed property, etc.

Service of citation. The defendant must be given notice that he is being sued. If he knows that he is being sued and he wants to keep court costs down, he may notify the court that he waives service of citation. If he does not do this, service of citation will be necessary.

It is the responsibility of deputy sheriffs and constables to serve civil citations. The officer given the task of serving a citation might first see if the defendant is listed in the local telephone directory. If he is, the officer may telephone him and ask him to come to the courthouse and pick up the citation. If the defendant agrees, this will save the officer time and trouble, and keep costs down.

If the defendant cannot be located in this manner, or if he refuses to come to pick up the papers, personal service of citation becomes necessary. TRCP 106 provides that personal service may be accomplished in one of two ways:

1. The officer may deliver to each defendant in person a copy of the citation with the complaint attached. The service here must be upon the defendant personally. Service upon a member of his family or an employee, or service by shoving the papers under his front door or into his mailbox is improper.

2. The officer may mail the papers to the defendant by registered or certified mail, with delivery restricted to the addressee only. It is not required that a return receipt be requested of the post office, but such a receipt would provide proof of time of service.

If it is impracticable to obtain service by the above-mentioned methods, or if these have been tried unsuccessfully, the plaintiff may ask the court to authorize service in other ways. With court permission the papers may be served by:

1. Leaving a copy at the defendant's place of business, or
2. Leaving a copy with some person over sixteen years of age at the defendant's residence, or
3. In any other reasonable manner the court may authorize.

The serving officer must inform the court of his success in serving the citation or lack thereof. His return becomes part of the record in the case. TRCP 107 provides that the plaintiff cannot get a default judgment against a defendant unless proof of service of citation is on file in the case, and has been on file for at least ten days.

If the whereabouts of the defendant remain unknown despite diligent efforts by the plaintiff and his attorney to locate him, the defendant may be "served" by publication. In such a case, notice of the suit, containing the information contained in the citation and complaint, is published in a local newspaper which carries legal advertising. If the action is a divorce action, TFC 3.521 authorizes service by one printing. If the action is of another sort, the ad must run for four consecutive weeks on the same day of the week. Of course, if the ad was published in the Nacogdoches *Sentinel* and the defendant is working on an oil rig in Moose Pass, Alaska, the defendant would not see the ad and would not know that he was being sued. This causes no legal problem: so long as the mechanics of publication have been carried out properly, the plaintiff and his attorney have diligently tried to locate the defendant, and the court has properly authorized service by publication, all is in order.

Service upon defendants outside the state of Texas. American state courts may exercise only limited authority over defendants resident in other states. Normally, out-of-state defendants are not subject to the jurisdiction of a state court. However, since persons are so much more mobile now than in the past, and since so much interstate business is transacted these days, the jurisdiction of state courts over out-of-state persons has been broadened considerably.

For example, a Texas plaintiff may obtain a divorce or annulment from an out-of-state defendant; the Texas probate court may adjudicate the rights of out-of-state heirs to estates of deceased Texans, except for real property located outside the state of Texas; and the Texas district court may adjudicate the rights of nonresidents with respect to ownership of Texas real estate.

Under the Texas "Long Arm" statute, RCS 2031b, a nonresident association or individual who makes a contract with a Texan in Texas, or who commits a tort against a Texan in Texas, is deemed to be doing business in this state. He (or it) may be served by a citation served upon the resident agent of the corporation or organization in Texas, by a citation mailed registered mail to the out-of-state office or residence of the defendant, or by service upon the secretary of state of Texas. Thus, the nonresident doing business in Texas may be sued in Texas state courts by any Texan having a claim.

Under the Texas nonresident motorist statute (RCS 2039a), any non-Texan who operates a motor vehicle on the highways of Texas appoints the chairman of the Texas Highway Commission as his agent for service of citation in case he becomes involved in Texas litigation by causing an accident on a Texas state highway or by other means. Thus, the out-of-stater may be sued in a Texas state court for damages for his negligence even if he resides in Hawaii. All fifty states have similar statutes. Thus the Texan who causes an accident on an Alaska state highway may find himself being validly sued in an Alaska state court.

Service of citation upon out-of-state defendants may thus be accomplished by service upon an agent within Texas, by registered mail, or by dispatch of an agent (other than a Texas sheriff or the like) to the defendant's locality to make personal service.

Limitations upon right to sue nonresidents in Texas courts. Because of the Long Arm statute and the Non-Resident Motorist Statute, it is generally now possible to sue a non-Texan in a Texas state court for wrongs he has committed in Texas. However, if a Texan is wronged by a non-Texan outside Texas, he will probably not be able to sue in Texas unless the non-Texan does business or has assets here. He would be required to go to the defendant's state to sue, unless the case can be gotten into federal court as a diversity case.

"In rem" jurisdiction over assets. Texas courts have jurisdiction over all property, real and personal, located within the borders of Texas. Thus, if a Texan has cause to sue a non-Texan, but has no grounds for suit in a Texas court although he knows that the non-Texan owns assets within Texas, he may file his suit in the Texas county where the assets are located. He may then obtain an attachment upon these assets, serve the defendant with citation, and obtain a judgment which will be good against the attached assets. It will not be good otherwise, unless the defendant came to Texas to defend himself and thus submitted himself to the jurisdiction of the Texas courts. If the attached assets are sufficient to satisfy the plaintiff's judgment if he wins the case, the matter is ended. If the attached assets are insufficient, the plaintiff must sue the defendant somewhere else for the balance.

Prejudgment remedies of the plaintiff. Once the plaintiff has filed his complaint and citation has been properly served upon the defendant, the plaintiff may be able to obtain certain prejudgment remedies before the defendant has a chance to defend himself. The possible prejudgment remedies are attachment, sequestration, receivership, and preliminary injunction.

Attachment. The plaintiff may seek an attachment either when he is suing upon a liquidated claim or when the defendant is a nonresident of Texas and is not subject to the jurisdiction of the Texas court in the plaintiff's case but does own assets in Texas.

A plaintiff is suing upon a liquidated claim when it is obvious that, if he has a claim, he has one for a specific sum of money. Thus, suits to collect checks, drafts, and promissory notes are suits on liquidated claims, as are suits for breach of written contracts. Not all contract claims are liquidated claims, however. In the situation where Doctor performs services for Patient, and the parties did not agree upon Doctor's fee in advance, an unliquidated claim might arise. If Doctor sends Patient a bill and Patient claims the bill is excessive, there exists a legitimate dispute about the amount of the debt. If Doctor really performed the agreed services, he has a claim, but it is an unliquidated claim.

All tort claims are of course unliquidated. There is no way to evaluate a personal injury claim, for example, in advance.

The plaintiff must apply to the court hearing his case for a writ of attachment.

RCS 275 states that the plaintiff must allege in his application one or more of eleven grounds for issuance of the writ. Among the grounds for issuance are:
1. Defendant is about to move out of state, or
2. Defendant is about to take his property out of state, or
3. Defendant has secreted his property for purposes of defrauding creditors, or
4. Defendant is about to dispose of his property with intent to defraud his creditors.

All of the grounds essentially involve the fear that, if the plaintiff does not now get control over some of the defendant's assets, the defendant will not have any assets within reach once the plaintiff gets his judgment.

The court cannot issue the writ before holding a hearing, at which the plaintiff must prove his entitlement to the writ (TRCP 592). The plaintiff must post bond with the court of an amount to be set by the judge. The judge may, in issuing the writ, limit the amount and value of the property to be attached. No property may be attached which is exempt by law from claims of creditors.

When the writ is issued, it is addressed to a sheriff or constable. This official then serves the writ upon the defendant in the same manner in which citations are served. At the same time, the property attached (if it is personal property) is taken into custody. If real property is attached, notice of the attachment is filed in the public records of the county where the land is located.

The writ must inform the defendant that he can regain the attached property by posting a replevy bond with the issuing court in an amount to be set by the court. The writ must also state that the defendant may challenge the validity of the writ by filing a motion to dissolve it. When such a motion is filed, a hearing upon it must be held. The writ will be dissolved if the defendant convinces the court that the plaintiff had no grounds for obtaining the writ in the first place. A motion to dissolve the writ may also be filed by a third party who claims an interest in the attached property. Naturally, if the third party can show that the defendant owns no interest in the property and that he (the third party) does, the attachment is wrongful and the writ will be dissolved.

If the plaintiff ultimately wins his case, the attached property will be sold under writ of execution. If the defendant has posted a replevy bond to get the property back, the plaintiff may apply the bond to his judgment.

If the writ is dissolved, or if the defendant ultimately wins the case, he has of course been damaged by the wrongful attachment and may therefore sue the plaintiff for these damages. He may collect his claim from the attachment bond originally posted by the plaintiff.

Sequestration. RCS 6840 permits a plaintiff to seek a prejudgment writ of sequestration when:
1. Plaintiff is suing to obtain title to personal property in the defendant's possession, and there is danger that the defendant will damage, destroy, or dispose of the property.
2. Plaintiff is suing to repossess personal property upon which he has a security interest or similar lien, and the property is not amenable to self-help repossession, and

there is a danger that the defendant might damage, destroy, or dispose of the property.

3. Plaintiff is suing for title or possession of real property, or to foreclose a lien thereon, and there is danger that defendant will destroy, damage, or dispose of the property.

The procedure in sequestration cases is essentially the same as that in cases of attachment. The writ is not issued without a hearing; the plaintiff must post the same sort of bond as with the attachment. The writ is served upon the defendant by a sheriff or constable, and the property is taken into custody. The defendant may get it back by posting a replevy bond, and may also move to dissolve the writ, as may an interested third party.

RCS 6840(d) provides that when consumer goods are wrongfully sequestered, the defendant may recover from the plaintiff a reasonable attorney's fee, plus his actual damage or $100, whichever figure is greater.

Receivership. RCS 2293 provides that a plaintiff may have a receiver appointed for property in the possession of the defendant before judgment is rendered when:

1. Plaintiff is a seller seeking to set aside a fraudulent purchase of property from him, or
2. A creditor is seeking to subject property or a fund to his claim, or
3. Plaintiff is seeking to foreclose a mortgage upon named property, and
4. There is danger that the property in question may be removed, lost, or materially injured.

This statute also provides that a receiver may be appointed for a corporation which is insolvent or in danger of insolvency. It also provides that receivers may be appointed under other circumstances.

Generally, there is no reason to appoint a receiver when taking the property into official custody would serve to preserve it. A receivership serves a useful purpose when the property is not movable and requires some management, such as would an apartment or office building. The litigation must of course involve a great deal of money or valuable property for this rather extraordinary remedy to be justified.

A receiver of course must post a bond, as must the party asking for his appointment as a prejudgment remedy. The receiver will be given specific management power by the appointing court; he must confine his activities within the bounds of this authority. The receivership will continue until termination by the appointing court.

Preliminary injunction. When a plaintiff sues for an injunction, his objective is to force the defendant to do something he is not now doing, or to force him to stop doing something he is now doing. In the former case, the plaintiff may be seeking to enforce a contract; in the latter, the defendant may be operating a nuisance, with the plaintiff wanting him to stop.

A plaintiff may also seek injunctive relief in connection with some other remedy that he is seeking in court. The plaintiff might be suing the defendant to have himself declared to be the owner of a racehorse which is in the defendant's possession, and he may not want the defendant to run the horse in any races pending the resolution of the litigation. The plaintiff therefore might seek an injunction to prevent the defendant from using the horse in a race.

The ultimate result of a suit for injunction is a permanent injunction, which in theory permanently forbids the defendant to do something or orders him to do something in accordance with the terms of the injunction. No permanent injunction will be issued until a complete trial has been held on the merits of the case. Preliminary injunctions are issued before there is a trial. Since they are issued before the trial, good reason must exist before they can be issued—generally an imminent threat to life or property, or to the status quo.

There are two sorts of preliminary injunction: the temporary restraining order and the temporary injunction. A temporary restraining order is issued by the court without hearing. A temporary injunction may be issued only after a hearing.

Anyone who desires a temporary restraining order must allege in his application that grave risk of harm to life or property exists unless the order is issued. If the court agrees, the order will be issued at once. The seeker of the temporary restraining order will also seek a temporary injunction. At the time the restraining order is issued, a date will be set for a hearing on the request for temporary injunction. The restraining order is effective only until the date of the hearing on the motion for temporary injunction, or for ten days (TRCP 680).

The applicant must also post an injunction bond with the court, in an amount to be set by the court. The amount of the bond must of course be sufficient to compensate the defendant for any damage he suffers if it turns out that applicant had no right to the injunction.

TRCP 681 provides that a plaintiff may not receive a temporary injunction unless he can prove his right to it at a hearing, where the defendant has the right to be present. The plaintiff at this hearing must convince a judge that he will suffer great and irreparable injury if he does not get his temporary injunction. He does not have to prove that he will be the ultimate winner at the trial to decide the issue. If the court decides to grant a temporary injunction, it may change the terms of the bond (if the plaintiff has already posted one because of a temporary restraining order). The temporary injunction remains in effect until the court proceeding which gave rise to it ends.

Time limits upon response to complaint by defendant. The defendant who is served a civil citation must know that he must take action within a relatively short time. Otherwise default judgment will be taken against him.

If the plaintiff's complaint is filed in small claims or justice of the peace courts, the defendant must respond by 10 A.M. on the first Monday ten days after service of citation. Thus, if the citation is served on Monday, June 1, the deadline for response is 10 A.M. Monday, June 15. If the citation were served as late as Thursday, June 4, the deadline would be the same, but if the citation were served on Saturday, June 6, the deadline would be at 10 A.M. Monday, June 22. If the complaint is filed in county or district court, the deadline is 10 A.M. on the first Monday twenty days after service of citation. Thus, if citation is served on Monday, June 1, the deadline is 10 A.M. Monday, June 22. If citation is served on Thursday, June 4, the deadline is 10 A.M. Monday, June 29.

The moral of all this is, if you are served with a civil citation, consult an attorney quickly. If the citation concerns an auto accident and you are covered by liability insurance, get the papers to your insurance company immediately; delay may be fatal to your defense.

Responses to citation. The ultimate response to a citation, when the defendant means to defend himself, is the filing of an answer. However, other matters may be raised in response to the complaint. The defendant may move for dismissal of the complaint because the court has no jurisdiction to hear it. Thus, it is useless to file a divorce complaint in county court since a county court cannot hand down a divorce decree.

The defendant may move to quash service of citation because it was not properly performed. Thus, if he found the citation stuffed in his mailbox one day, and he then discovers that the court did not authorize service in that particular manner, he may have the service quashed as improper. This maneuver serves only to stall, though; if the court quashes service of citation, it deems that the defendant was properly served as of the date of the quashing, so the plaintiff need not have a new citation served.

The defendant may complain that essential plaintiffs or defendants have not been joined as parties to the case. Assume Black signed a promissory note promising to pay $3,000 to Blue and Green on demand. Black did not pay at maturity, and Blue is suing him to collect. Black may object because Green is not a party plaintiff. Since Black owes both Blue and Green, if he owes anyone, then both parties should be before the court here.

Defendant may also complain that he is being sued in an improper county. Questions of the proper county in which to commence a lawsuit are questions of venue. RCS 1995 provides most of the rules in such a case. In general, venue rules are:

1. If title to real estate is involved in the case, the case must be filed in the county where the land is.
2. Divorce cases may be filed in the county of plaintiff's residence, or in the county of defendant's residence.
3. Breach of contract cases may be filed in the county of defendant's residence, or in the county where the contract was made.
4. Tort cases may be filed in the county of defendant's residence, or in the county where the tort was committed.

There are other rules for other sorts of cases. In general, if anything other than land is involved, the plaintiff cannot go wrong by suing in the county of the defendant's residence.

A defendant objects to the venue by filing a plea of privilege to get the case moved to another county. If the plaintiff wants to argue about this, he files a controverting plea and a hearing is held on the matter. If the judge finds that venue is improper, he may move the case to the county the defendant suggested in his plea. If he finds that the venue is proper, the case stays in his court, and the defendant must file an answer. In cases where two or more counties constitute proper venue, it is the plaintiff's choice as to county of suit.

The parties may agree to have the suit heard in a county which would ordinarily be improper venue. If so, the courts will respect the agreement. If the defendant files an answer without complaining about venue, he has waived his right to complain and the case stays in the county where it was filed.

If either party feels that he cannot get a fair trial in the county where the case was filed, he may move for change of venue to another county. This could occur, for example, because of great publicity given the case in the county where filed. If the judge feels that good grounds exist for the change, he may grant the motion.

If the defendant feels that the statute of limitations has run out upon the plaintiff's claim or that he did not sign the contract the plaintiff says he signed, he may file a plea in abatement to the complaint. Ultimately, though, the defendant will probably have to file an answer in order to defend himself. The answer is his statement as to why he is not liable to the plaintiff. It may consist of a general denial, in which the defendant says, essentially, "I didn't do what the plaintiff says I did, and I deny the truth of everything he says in his complaint." This requires the plaintiff to prove in court the truth of what he alleges in his complaint.

The answer may also consist of an affirmative defense. The pure affirmative defense answer says, in essence, "I admit that what the plaintiff says in his complaint is true. However, even so, I'm not liable to the plaintiff because...." In such a case, the plaintiff need not prove what he alleged, because the defendant has admitted its truth, but the defendant must prove the truth of what he has alleged in his answer.

The usual answer is a combination of denial and affirmative defense.

Counterclaims. It may well be that, in an auto accident, both autos were damaged and both drivers were injured. Each thinks the wreck was the other's fault. Finally, Jones sues Smith for damages, Jones and Smith being the two drivers involved. Smith thinks he should be the one suing Jones. Smith may make his claim by filing, as part of his answer, a counterclaim against Jones. If Smith files such a counterclaim as part of his answer, Jones must then file an answer to the counterclaim.

Smith's counterclaim here is a mandatory counterclaim. That is, if he wants to make a legal claim against Jones for his injuries he must make it by way of counterclaim, since Jones has filed suit against him. If Smith does not raise his counterclaim in the case of *Jones vs. Smith*, he has thrown it away and he cannot raise it later.

If Jones owes Smith an overdue debt based upon a contract, Smith may want to make this claim as a counterclaim in the case of *Jones vs. Smith*. Smith may do this if he wishes, but he is not required to do it. This sort of counterclaim, a claim arising out of a different transaction than that giving rise to the plaintiff's claim, is a permissive counterclaim. The defendant may raise it if he wishes, but he will not lose his claim if he does not raise it here.

A tort claim arising out of a transaction other than that giving rise to the plaintiff's claim may not be raised as a counterclaim; it must be settled in a separate suit. Thus, if Jones sues Smith for personal injury damages, and Smith has a slander claim against Jones, Smith cannot file a counterclaim for the slander. He will have to save that for a separate suit.

Default judgment. If the defendant does not file a timely answer to the plaintiff's complaint, he subjects himself to a default judgment. The plaintiff may apply for default judgment if the deadline for the defendant's response has expired, defendant has made no response to the complaint, and the return of service by the sheriff or constable has been on record with the court for at least ten days.

The plaintiff is not entitled to default judgment for the asking. He must first prove three things to the court:

1. That proper service of citation was made upon defendant, and
2. Defendant did not make proper response to the citation within the time limit, and
3. Plaintiff has a valid claim against defendant.

Proving a valid claim is sometimes very easy, and sometimes more difficult. If plaintiff is suing upon an item of commercial paper, or upon a written contract, he proves his right to collect by showing the document to the court. Signatures on written documents are presumed valid until proven otherwise, so the document itself proves the defendant's liability.

If the plaintiff's suit is upon an unwritten contract, he will have no document at hand to ease his burden of proof. He will need evidence that a contract containing specific terms was made, that the defendant breached it, and that because of the breach he, the plaintiff, suffered a specified amount of damage. If the plaintiff's suit is a tort claim, he will have to prove that the defendant committed the tort, that he was damaged by it, and that the damage amounted to a specific sum. Since the defendant is not present to contradict the plaintiff's evidence, fulfillment of that burden of proof is not very difficult.

Vacation of default judgment. Once a default judgment has been entered against a defendant, it is a good, valid judgment. The defendant may challenge the validity of it for only two reasons:

1. The court which handed down the judgment had no jurisdiction over the subject matter of the case, or
2. The court had no jurisdiction over the person of the defendant because citation was not properly served upon him.

If White obtains default judgment for $6,000 against Black in the County Court-at-Law of Podunk County, then Black may have this vacated because the county court-at-law has no jurisdiction over cases involving more than $5,000.

If White obtains default judgment against Black for $6,000 in the Texas District Court of Podunk County, and Black was not served with citation in the suit, Black may have this vacated by proving that he was not properly served. Proving this will be more difficult, because the return of service filed by the sheriff or constable responsible for service of citation will no doubt show that service was properly made. Black must, then, show that the return of service was incorrect. He will need some powerful evidence to accomplish this. If he can convince the court of the truth of what he alleges, the judgment will be vacated.

Dismissal for want of prosecution. If the plaintiff and his attorney take no steps to further their case after the defendant files an answer, the court will mail a notice to them that the case will be dismissed unless action is taken within fifteen days. If nothing is heard during the fifteen-day period, dismissal follows.

The plaintiff's attorney may get the case reinstated within thirty days after dismissal by convincing the court that the inaction was not due to negligence, but to unavoidable circumstances, or mistake. If the plaintiff or his attorney does not show up for a scheduled hearing or trial, this too can trigger the sending of notice to dismiss. The attorney who misses a hearing or trial must have a very good explanation for his default.

Statutes of limitation in civil matters. Complaints in civil actions must be filed before the appropriate statute of limitations runs out upon the plaintiff's claim. The clock starts to run when the plaintiff acquires the right to sue upon his claim. Under RCS 5524, actions of the following sorts must be commenced within one year of the accrual of the right to sue:

1. Malicious prosecution.
2. Libel.
3. Slander.
4. Breach of promise to marry.

RCS 5526 provides that the following sorts of actions must be commenced within two years of accrual of the right to sue:

1. Trespass.
2. Conversion.
3. Breach of unwritten contract (except an unwritten contract for sale of goods).
4. Personal injury.
5. Wrongfully causing death (the two years beginning upon the death of the deceased).
6. Forcible entry and forcible detainer.

RCS 5526b provides that a suit for overcharges against a carrier of property must be commenced within three years of the carrier's delivery or tender of delivery of the article for which the overcharge was levied.

RCS 5527 et seq. list several actions upon which suit must be brought within four years of the accrual of the cause of action. Included here are:

1. Suits upon written contracts.
2. Suits upon any contract for the sale of goods (UCC 2-275).
3. Actions for settlement of accounts between partners or merchants.
4. Actions on the bond of an executor, administrator, or guardian.
5. Actions for specific performance of a contract to sell real estate.
6. Actions to contest a will (period starts when the contested will is admitted to probate).
7. Action to cancel a will for forgery or fraud (period starts when the forgery or fraud is discovered).
8. Any other action for which the law specifies no definite statute of limitations.

RCS 5536a provides that any action against an architect, engineer, contractor, or other person playing a part in designing or building a structure or improving a structure must be brought within ten years of the completion of the structure or improvement thereto. If a claim for damages is made in writing during the ninth or tenth year of this limitation period, the period is extended until the expiration of two years after the making of the claim.

RCS 5535 provides that if, when a right to sue accrues, the would-be plaintiff is a minor, a prisoner, or a person of unsound mind, the clock will not start upon the limitation period until the minor reaches his twenty-first birthday, the prisoner is released from prison, or the person of unsound mind becomes competent again. Once the clock has started to run, however, imprisonment of the person with the claim, or his loss of competence, will not stop it again.

According to RCS 5537, when the person against whom a claim could be asserted is outside the state of Texas when the claim accrues, the clock will not start upon the limitation period until he returns to Texas. If the person against whom a claim may be asserted leaves the state, the clock stops; when he returns, the clock starts again.

RCS 5538 provides that when a claimant dies, or when the person against whom a claim may be made dies, the clock stops on the limitation period until an executor or administrator is appointed for the estate of the deceased, or until twelve months after the death, whichever occurs first.

If a complaint is filed at the last minute, just before expiration of the limitation period, and the defendant has a mandatory counterclaim subject to the same statute of limitations, he may file his counterclaim despite the expiration of the statutory period. If the last-minute complaint is dismissed because of lack of jurisdiction of the trial court, the plaintiff may file again in a proper court, unless he deliberately filed his original complaint in an improper court.

Conflict of laws. Whenever an action is filed in one state involving an occurrence in another state or another nation, a conflict of laws problem may arise. Which law does the court apply to the case—the law of the location of the court (the law of the forum) or the law of the place of the wrong (the law of the locus)?

This situation may arise more often than one might think. For instance, if Straw of Houston and Berry of Baytown are involved in an auto accident near Lake Charles, Louisiana, a conflict of laws arises. If litigation arises over this incident, the parties would naturally want to litigate in Texas. Since the accident happened in Louisiana, would liability be determined by Texas law? The answer is no. In tort matters, liability will be determined by the law of the place of commission of the tort; the Texas court would apply Louisiana law in order to determine liability. If Rojo of Harlingen and Verde of McAllen have a collision on a street in Matamoros, Mexico, the parties would want to litigate matters in Texas, since both live in Texas. But since the accident happened in Mexico, the Texas court would apply Mexican law to determine liability.

In contract cases the matter gets more complex. If Hack Company of Houston contracts with Zilch Company of New York, and the contract is breached by Hack, Zilch may file suit against Hack in a Texas court. As to the law which would be applied, the Texas court would apply, generally, the law of "the center of gravity of the contract" in order to determine liability. In other words, if most of the contract was to be performed in New York, New York law will govern. If most is to be performed in Texas, Texas law will govern. In contract situations, the parties may specify in their contract which law will apply in case of breach. If the choice of law is reasonable, the courts will go along with it.

Normally, courts do not hesitate to apply foreign law in conflict cases. However, if the law the plaintiff is asking the court to enforce is so alien to the forum's legal system that its enforcement is repugnant to the court, the court may refuse to enforce it. Thus, if Able of Dallas sues Baker of Houston to collect a gambling debt incurred in the Republic of Ruritania, under whose law gambling debts are enforceable, Able still would in all probability not collect in Texas. The Texas court might well say that enforcement of gambling debts is contrary to Texas public policy and choose not to enforce the Ruritanian law.

In procedural matters, the law of the forum applies. What may puzzle the student here is the notion that statutes of limitations are matters of procedure. Thus, any case heard in a Texas court is governed by the Texas statute of limitations, even though liability in the case may be determined according to the law of another state or of another nation. Two Texas statutes modify this statement, however. RCS 5542 provides that when a person moves into Texas from another state or nation, no one may make a claim against him here which is barred by the statute of limitations of his former state or nation. Also, if he was discharged from payment of a debt by the law of his former state or nation, he may not be sued upon that debt here.

On the other hand, if a person moves to this state just before the statute of limitations runs out upon a claim against him in his old state or nation, the claim against him will not be barred here until he has been here for twelve months (RCS 5543). For instance, in Louisiana the statute of limitations for suit upon a written contract is six years. If a Louisiana debtor moves here four and a half years after he incurred his debt, he could still be sued upon the debt in Louisiana. He could not be sued upon it if he were a Texan, because it has been more than four years since the debt was incurred, but as a Louisianan he will nevertheless be liable upon this debt for a year after he moves to Texas.

Forum non conveniens. A Texas court may refuse to hear a case when, because of difficulty in bringing witnesses to Texas to testify, it would be inconvenient to have the case tried here. An example of such a situation would be this: A Texan vacations in Europe and buys an automobile to drive there. While driving in Austria, he negligently collides with an auto belonging to a New Yorker. The parties are unable to settle this matter amicably in Europe and it is still hanging fire when they return to the United States, so the New Yorker comes to Texas to sue the Texan for damages here.

The Texas court would have jurisdiction of the subject matter and over the person of the defendant. If there were no witnesses to the accident other than the parties involved, the court could well enough decide the case. Its only difficulty might be the application of Austrian law to determine the liability of the parties. However, if there were Austrian witnesses to the accident, and Austrian documents which would be vital evidence in the case, problems might arise as to how the testimony of the witnesses and documents could be obtained. If the Texas court decided that the difficulties of obtaining the evidence are so great that it is inadequately equipped to make a fair decision in the controversy, it could dismiss the case on the ground that Texas is an inconvenient place to decide the matter.

Discovery in civil cases. The rules of civil procedure give parties in civil litigation every opportunity to discover the evidence of the other party. It is most important, of course, that one's attorney be familiar with the rules of discovery. If he asks the right questions, he can learn very interesting information in response. If he does not think to ask, however, he will get no answers.

Each party has the right to copy relevant documents and data in the possession of the other. The defendant in a physical injury case may require the plaintiff to submit to a physical examination at the hands of an impartial doctor. Each party may propound interrogatories to the other—that is, each may give to the other a list of written questions and demand that the other answer these in writing. Each party may take the other's deposition in essentially the same way that depositions are taken in criminal matters.

Depositions may also be taken from witnesses. However no witness may be compelled to give a civil deposition who lives more than 100 miles from the courthouse where the case is to be tried, or who lives outside the state of Texas. A reluctant witness who lives within 100 miles of the courthouse where the case is to be tried may be compelled by subpoena to give a deposition if he lives in Texas. The reluctant out-of-state witness, or the reluctant Texan who lives more than 100 miles from the courthouse, must be induced to voluntarily give a deposition if his deposition is to be taken. For instance, an El Paso witness in a Houston litigation might be willing to give a deposition if the deposition could be taken in El Paso. If so, the attorneys could travel to El Paso to take the deposition.

Pretrial conference. The judge who is to hear the case may want to hold a pretrial conference with the parties, their attorneys, or both. The purpose of such a conference is to attempt to get the parties to agree to settle out of court. If this cannot be done, then the judge tries to get the parties and the attorneys to agree to as many facts in the case as possible. The more facts the parties agree to, the fewer witnesses must testify at the trial, and the less they must testify about. The facts the attorneys can agree to are stipulated by them, and the stipulation can then be read to the jury at the trial. For instance, the parties to an auto accident case may be able to agree on the time and place of the accident, the persons involved, the prevailing weather conditions, and, perhaps, the damages to the vehicles. Of course they probably will not agree on the exact cause of the accident or the extent of the injuries to the parties.

Trial: the jury. In civil litigation there will be a trial by jury if either party wants it. There will be none only if both parties agree to dispense with a jury.

The qualifications for trial jurors are the same in civil matters as they are in criminal matters: The district court jury consists of twelve members, while the county, small claims or JP court juries consist of six members.

Potential jurors are summoned and questioned as in criminal matters. They may be challenged for cause if they show by their answers to questions that they are not qualified jurors because of conviction of a felony, because of blood or affinity relationship to one of the parties to the case, because of an employer-employee relationship to a party to the case, or because of bias in favor of or against a party to the case.

When twenty-four jurors have passed muster in district court, or twelve in the other courts, the questioning of jurors stops. The clerk of the court gives each attorney a list of jurors who have not been challenged for cause, arranged in the order of questioning, and the attorneys make their peremptory challenges. In district court each attorney has six such challenges: he may cross six names off the list. In the other courts each attorney has three such challenges: he may cross three names off the list. In district court the first twelve names not crossed off are the jury; in the other courts, the first six names not crossed off are the jury.

Trial procedure. The trial procedure in a civil case is similar to that in a criminal matter. Both sides may make opening statements to the jury, the plaintiff then presents his evidence; the defendant presents his evidence; the plaintiff may present rebuttal evidence; the defendant may present rebuttal evidence; and so forth. Presentation of evidence ends when both sides have presented everything they wish.

The plaintiff must present evidence sufficient to convince the jury that everything in the complaint is true. The plaintiff, we therefore say, has the burden of proof with respect to everything in his complaint. After he has presented all of his evidence, the defendant may ask the judge for a directed verdict in favor of the defense. If the plaintiff has not presented sufficient evidence to convince a reasonable juror of the truth of his claim, the defendant is entitled to such a directed verdict. A directed verdict for the defense at this point of course ends the trial.

Most trials do not end at this point in directed verdicts for the defense; if the plaintiff had a strong enough case to warrant going to trial, the evidence should be strong enough to convince a reasonable juror of the truth of what is stated in the complaint, especially when one considers that the defense has not yet had a chance to contradict this evidence. After all evidence is in, both sides have the opportunity to ask for a directed verdict. If the evidence is so one-sided that no two reasonable jurors could differ in their interpretation of it, a directed verdict may be granted. Normally, however, there is enough evidence on both sides to give the jurors something to think about, and the decision will be left to the jury.

Evidence in civil cases. For the most part, the same rules of evidence apply in civil cases as in criminal trials. There are differences which are worthy of mention, however.

Subpoenaing of witnesses. In a civil case, a party may not invoke the Fifth Amendment to the U.S. Constitution and refuse to testify. A party can refuse to testify for himself; but he cannot refuse to testify if he is called to the stand by the attorney for the opposing party. No witness may be compelled to testify if he lives more than 100 miles from the courthouse where the trial is taking place, or if he lives out of state. If a witness cannot be forced to give a deposition, he cannot be forced to testify in person either.

No witness in civil matters may be forced to post bail to insure his attendance. Also, no civil witness may be attached to compel his testimony. Of course, refusal to obey a civil subpoena is punishable as contempt, but there is no way to really insure that a civil witness will show up to testify.

The privilege against self-incrimination. The civil witness must testify if called to the stand. He may claim the privilege against self-incrimination as a reason for not answering a question only if the answer to the question could be used against him as evidence in a criminal prosecution. The defendant in civil litigation cannot refuse to answer a question on the stand because the answer might compel him to admit liability in the case at hand. In short, one may not claim civil incrimination as grounds for not answering a question in a civil proceeding.

Hearsay in civil litigation. Hearsay is just as inadmissible in civil litigation as it is in criminal matters, but further discussion of some admissible forms of hearsay is required.

The statement of a party to the case is admissible in civil litigation, whether it tends to incriminate him in the litigation in question or not. No harm is done by this. The party can tell his side of the conversation himself, if he desires. Also, any statement made by another in the presence of a party to the case is generally admissible hearsay. If the party overheard the remark, he may relate his understanding of the incident.

Statements contrary to the personal or pecuniary interest of the speaker are admissible, as are spontaneous exclamations under the influence of great excitement.

The Dead Man Statute. RCS 3716 provides, in essence, that in actions by or against executors, administrators, and guardians, and in actions by or against the estate of a deceased or incompetent person, no one may testify as to what the deceased or incompetent person said unless called by the opposing party to the case. Thus, if Vorn Vogel sues the estate of Malachi Mort for breach of an oral contract, Vogel cannot testify to the conversation between himself and Mort which led to the making of the contract unless he is called as a witness by the defense, which of course would not happen.

If the estate of Malachi Mort is suing Don Dumbo for damages for breach of an oral contract, Melinda Mort, widow of the deceased, cannot testify for the estate about the conversation between Malachi and Don which led to the making of the contract. If Melinda is called by the defense as a witness, she could answer questions about this, but the defense would never call her as a witness.

Depositions and affidavits as civil evidence. A deposition may be read to the jury as proof of the truth of its contents only if the witness who gave the deposition is not available to testify in person. This is more likely to happen in civil matters than in criminal cases, because the range of the civil subpoena is so limited. The deposition may be read to the jury as a substitute for the in-person testimony of the witness when:

1. The witness is beyond the range of a subpoena, or
2. The witness is disabled, or
3. The witness is dead, or
4. The witness has disappeared, and no one knows his whereabouts, or
5. The witness is otherwise unavailable to testify in person.

An affidavit—a sworn statement of a witness—is normally inadmissible as evidence of the truth of its contents. No one has the opportunity to cross-examine the maker of an affidavit, so the truth of its subject matter is open to question.

Prejudicial information. Certain items of information must not reach the ears of the jury in a civil case. If they do, due to the indiscretion of the opposing party in the case or his attorney, these are immediate grounds for mistrial. These forbidden matters in civil cases are:

1. The fact that the defendant has liability insurance.
2. The fact that one of the parties has offered to settle the case out of court, but the offer was refused.
3. The litigation record of one of the parties to the case.

It is felt by Texas courts that juries might be more likely to find against insured defendants than against uninsured defendants, because they feel that insurance companies are wallowing in cash while individuals are usually lacking in that commodity. Whether this feeling is logical is open to question. In Louisiana, Wisconsin, and some other states the plaintiff who sues an insured defendant may name the insurer as a defendant. These states do not find it objectionable that everyone knows of the insured status of the defendant, and insurance companies still manage to exist there. Nevertheless, in Texas the mention of insurance is forbidden. The rationale for discouragement of mention of offers to compromise is easier to understand. The jury may well interpret a willingness to settle out of court as a confession of weakness by the party involved.

The previous litigation record of a party can be just as prejudicial to that party in civil litigation as prior conviction of crime could be to the criminal defendant. The fact that Pobre has filed ten suits for personal injury damage prior to his suit against Rich, and has lost eight of them, has nothing to do with the validity of this eleventh claim.

The judge's charge to the jury and the closing arguments. The Texas civil jury is not asked to decide in so many words who wins the case. Instead, it is given a list of questions about the facts of the case, and asked to answer these questions. The judge's charge to the jury involves his explanation of these questions and the jury's obligations to answer them. The closing arguments of the attorneys are essentially discussions of the evidence, but the attorneys must not disclose prejudicial information, refer to facts not introduced into evidence, or hint to the jury that certain questions must be answered in certain ways for the attorney's client to win the case. A misstep by an attorney in his closing argument may cause a mistrial.

The verdict. The jury's deliberation in the civil matter is subject to the same limitations as in criminal matters, though the civil jury debates factual matters rather than the broad issue of guilt or innocence of the defendant as such.

Most of the questions to be considered by the civil jury may be answered "yes" or "no." Some of them may not be so answered—particularly those dealing with the amount of damages suffered by the parties and those dealing with the percentages of negligence chargeable to the parties. Ten out of twelve, or five out of six, of the jurors must agree to answer any question. When all have been answered, ten of twelve or five of six must sign the verdict. Thus, the required majority must agree to the answers to all of the questions. If the required majority will not sign a verdict, the result is a mistrial.

The judgment. If the jury can agree upon a verdict, the document is handed to the judge, who reads it to the courtroom. If either side is opposed to the verdict, its attorney may at this point make one, or both, of the following motions:

1. Motion to set aside the verdict of the jury, or
2. Motion for judgment notwithstanding the verdict.

A motion to set aside the verdict of the jury is essentially a request to the judge to throw out not only the verdict of the jury but the entire trial. The reason might well be misconduct on the part of the jury in arriving at a decision (e.g., unauthorized contact with outsiders); a "quotient verdict" with respect to damages (where each juror writes down his figure for damages, the figures are added together, and divided by the number of jurors, all jurors agreeing to be bound by the result); or something similar. If the motion is granted, the result is a mistrial.

A motion for judgment notwithstanding the verdict is a request to the judge to ignore the answers of the jurors to some or all of the questions, and to enter a judgment which is not consistent with these answers. The ground for such a motion is that, considering the evidence, no reasonable juror could have answered the question or questions as these jurors have done. If the motion is granted, the trial concludes, but with a judgment inconsistent with the decision of the jury.

If neither of these motions is made and granted, the judge hands down judgment in accordance with the jury's answer to the special verdict questions. At this point the trial ends. Those who are unhappy with the judgment may now do one of two things: ask the judge of the court hearing the case for a new trial, or appeal the case to a higher court.

Motion for a new trial. Formerly it was necessary to make a motion for a new trial in order to lay the groundwork for an appeal. That is no longer necessary: one may now appeal without first making such a motion.

The motion for a new trial requests the judge of the court deciding the case to void the judgment handed down and to call for a new trial. The ground for a new trial must be a matter of law, not a matter of fact. Generally, the decision of the jury on questions of fact, if not overthrown by the granting of a judgment notwithstanding the verdict, is final. One may not obtain a new trial by arguing that the jury decided questions of fact erroneously, that it was wrong, for example, to believe witness Jones rather than witness Smith. One may not obtain a new trial by arguing that the jury decided questions of fact contrary to the weight of the evidence, if there is some evidence on both sides of the issue. Thus, if six witnesses testify that Jones ran a stop sign at the scene of the accident and two witnesses testify that he did not, the jury could choose to believe the two. If they do, and if the two are credible witnesses, no one may complain about the decision. If ten witnesses testify that Jones ran the stop sign, but only Jones himself testifies that he did not—and

Jones is a convicted perjurer—one might perhaps argue that the jury was in error. In such a case, though, the opponent of Jones should have moved for judgment notwithstanding the verdict when the jury handed in its verdict. His failure to raise the matter at that point in the proceedings could stop him from raising it now.

The motion must be based upon questions of law—perhaps allegations that the judge erred by admitting evidence that was objected to or excluding evidence that was objected to; or that the judge should have granted the motion of plaintiff's attorney for a mistrial because of prejudicial remarks by the defense attorney; or something similar.

A judge almost always makes errors in the conduct of a trial, since human nature is fallible. But the fact that the judge made an error of law does not in and of itself justify the granting of a motion for a new trial. The errors complained of must have been prejudicial—that is, they must have deprived the complaining party of justice.

Since judges do not often admit to committing prejudicial error in the conduct of a trial, motions for new trial are almost always denied. Since these are no longer necessary to lay the groundwork for appeal, they are not as common as they used to be.

Appeal. The loser of a trial, be he plaintiff or defendant, may wish to appeal the result. The ostensible winner may also choose to appeal. For instance, when plaintiff sues defendant for personal injury damages, hoping to recover a judgment for $100,000, but the jury awards him $1,000, the plaintiff may consider himself the loser of the litigation. It is even possible for both parties to appeal. When plaintiff expected a judgment for $100,000 and gets one for $25,000 instead, he might feel that the judgment was too small while the defendant feels that it was too large. If both sides feel that errors were made in the conduct of the trial, both may appeal.

No party may appeal before filing one bond with the trial court, or perhaps two bonds. All appealing parties must file a cost bond with the trial court, to cover the court costs of the trial plus the estimated costs of the appeal. The only way the appealing party may escape that obligation is by filing a pauper's affidavit with the court, alleging in essence that he is too poor to post such a bond. The mere filing of the affidavit is not enough to permit the appealing party to escape posting the bond. If the other party to the case or the court doubts the veracity of the affidavit, a hearing in the trial court will be necessary to establish the truth of the appealing party's claim of poverty. If the claim is upheld, he need not post the bond. If it is not upheld, he must post it.

If the appealing party had a judgment for money awarded against him, he must also post with the court a supersedeas bond of the amount of the judgment. One may not escape the obligation to post this with a pauper's affidavit; the rules of civil procedure and the Texas statutes do not authorize one to do so. The situation here is: no bond, no appeal. A judgment cannot be collected if the defendant perfects a proper appeal. This fact provides the main justification for the requirement of the posting of the supersedeas bond before appeal will be permitted.

If the appeal is from small claims court or JP court to the county court, a new trial takes place in the county court. The witnesses must all testify again, with no necessity for serving new subpoenas. If the appeal is to the court of civil appeals, the review of the case is similar to that which the court of criminal appeals accords a criminal conviction. It is essentially a review of the record of the trial.

The court of civil appeals may do one of four things to the lower court decision:
1. Affirm—let the decision stand.
2. Modify—change the decision in some respects. This is most likely to be done in injunction cases; money judgments are not often modified.
3. Reverse and remand—send the case back to the trial court for a new trial.

4. Reverse and render—declare the loser below the winner.

Any party unhappy with the court of civil appeals decision may of course appeal to the Supreme Court of Texas, which may do one of the above four things with the court of civil appeals decision.

Finality of judgment. When a decision has been appealed to the highest possible court and that court has rendered a decision, that decision is final. If a lower court renders a decision and the parties let the deadlines for filing appeal expire, the decision also becomes final. Once a judgment for money becomes final, the defendant must either pay or become subject to forcible collection methods.

Sometimes the collectability of the judgment is guaranteed in advance. If the claim was a liquidated claim and the plaintiff levied attachment upon sufficient goods of the defendant, the plaintiff merely has the sheriff sell the goods. If the defendant has recovered the goods by posting a replevy bond, the plaintiff may collect the judgment out of this bond. If the plaintiff has obtained a judgment in the trial court and the defendant posted a supersedeas bond and appealed, but lost this appeal, the plaintiff collects out of the supersedeas bond.

If the defendant has liability insurance, the insurance company will probably pay off the judgment. If it does not, either the plaintiff or the defendant may sue to force the company to perform its duty. If the defendant is affluent, he may well pay in order to avoid further controversy. Affluent defendants have great difficulty in escaping the payment of judgments.

If the defendant posted no bonds, has no insurance, and is not affluent, however, the plaintiff may have trouble in collecting. The fact that the plaintiff has obtained a judgment is no guarantee that he will be able to collect that judgment.

What must defendant pay, and what does plaintiff collect? The defendant must of course pay off the judgment rendered against him. That is not his only obligation, however. Since the loser of litigation usually pays the court costs, the defendant must pay these also. If he has appealed and posted a cost bond, these costs will be collected out of the bond. But if there was no appeal, the defendant must pay when the judgment becomes final.

If the plaintiff collected so little on his claim that he is the real loser of the litigation, the court might assess part or all of the costs to him, but this is a rare happening. If the defendant was represented by an attorney, he must of course pay his attorney's fee.

If the suit was a suit on a "sworn account"—that is, a suit on a contractual liquidated debt—the defendant may be forced to pay the plaintiff's attorney. He will also be obligated to do this if the plaintiff was suing under consumer protection legislation which obligates a losing defendant to pay the plaintiff's attorney. TRCP 185 authorizes collection of the plaintiff's attorney fee in sworn account cases. In personal injury litigation, however, the plaintiff must pay his own attorney.

The plaintiff has the right to collect his judgment. Out of this, in most cases, he must pay his attorney. In personal injury cases the attorney may well have agreed to represent the plaintiff on a contingent fee basis. If so, the plaintiff must pay the attorney an agreed percentage of the judgment—if litigation was necessary, normally 25 percent or more. (Legal ethics frown upon the attorney taking more than 30 percent of the recovery.) In such a case the attorney will not be paid if the judgment is not collected, so the attorney has an incentive to help his client collect.

If the attorney has agreed to handle the case on a flat-fee basis, or on an hourly charge basis, the fee will not be based upon the amount of the judgment. In such a case the attorney might have collected his fee, or a part of it, in advance. Also, the attorney might not be willing to wait until the judgment is paid to collect his fee.

Forcible collection of judgments—exemptions. If the defendant will not pay the judgment, the plaintiff and his attorney must force him to pay, essentially by seizing and selling some of his property. However, Texas law provides that certain property of a debtor may not be taken by his creditors. We shall now consider the nature of these exemptions, the most valuable of which is the homestead exemption. The provisions of law governing these exemptions are found in Article 16, Sections 50 and 51, of the Texas Constitution, and in RCS 3833. Personal property exemptions are provided for in RCS 3836.

Homesteads. A homestead is the property where a person resides, or the property where a person conducts his business activity. Before 1974 only a married person could claim a homestead exempt from claims of creditors. Since 1974 a single adult has been entitled to the same privilege.

The extent of the homestead depends upon whether the debtor resides in the country or in the city. A rural homestead must be located outside the city limits of a city, town, or village according to RCS 3833(a)(1) and (2). A rural homestead for the married debtor may consist of up to 200 acres, in one or more parcels, with all improvements thereon (mainly buildings). A single debtor may claim a rural homestead of up to 100 acres, in one or more parcels, with all improvements thereon.

Property inside the city limits of a city, town, or village cannot be a rural homestead. The city or town dweller must be content with an urban homestead, which consists of a lot or lots not to exceed $10,000 in value, not counting the value of improvements. The extent of the urban homestead exemption is the same whether the debtor is married or single. The debtor must of course own the homestead for the exemption to be of value to him. He also must either reside there or conduct his business there.

The extent of the rural homestead exemption is easy enough to define, since it is a matter of counting acres of land. The extent of the urban homestead is more difficult to define, since it depends upon the value of a lot, not counting the value of improvements. When a debtor buys a lot and erects a house upon it, if he paid $10,000 or less for the lot the house he builds upon it will be totally exempt, no matter what its value. If the debtor acquires the lot with the house already erected, the value of the exemption depends upon the value of the lot as appraised without the value of the house.

If the lot is worth more than $10,000 when acquired, the whole property is not exempt as a homestead. This raises the problem of how one determines that portion of the value which is not exempt. The arithmetic used is the rule of *Hoffman vs. Love*, 494 SW 2d 591. The value of the lot at the time of acquisition is compared to $10,000. The excess is nonexempt. If the lot has appreciated in value since the acquisition, the appreciation is not totally nonexempt; it is apportioned between exempt and nonexempt according to the original ratio. The value of the improvements is totally exempt.

Suppose that Huchler bought a city lot in Podunk, Texas, for $12,500 in 1974. He built a house on the lot, which cost him $25,000. In 1980 Grinch obtains a judgment against him and seeks to get to the excess value of the property, upon which Huchler still resides. The property now has an appraised value of $65,000, of which $25,000 is attributable to the house and $40,000 to the lot. The house, being improvement, is totally exempt. The lot was exempt to the tune of $10,000 in 1974 and nonexempt to the tune of $2,500. It was thus 20 percent nonexempt. So, by the rule of *Hoffman vs. Love*, 20 percent of its present value is nonexempt. Since 20 percent of $40,000 is $8,000, the nonexempt portion of the property is $8,000. Huchler must either obtain $8,000 for Grinch, or the creditor could have the homestead sold and take his $8,000 from the proceeds.

If Huchler had paid $10,000 for the lot in 1974, and had it now been worth $40,000, the entire property would be exempt. Appreciation in property value since acquisition of the homestead does not destroy any part of the exemption if the property was totally exempt when acquired.

Four types of creditors may reach an otherwise exempt homestead:

1. The IRS for delinquent federal taxes, since the federal government does not recognize the Texas homestead exemption for this purpose.
2. Governments levying real property tax upon the homestead, to the extent of the tax due upon the homestead.
3. Lenders holding purchase-money liens upon the homestead—essentially lenders from whom the debtor borrowed the money to buy the homestead.
4. Contractors and others who hold mechanic's liens upon the property due to construction or repair work performed upon it.

The extent of these liens will be discussed in the materials on real property later in this work.

If the debtor sells his homestead, the proceeds are exempt from his creditors for six months in order to give him the chance to invest in a new homestead. If the homestead is destroyed by fire and the debtor collects fire insurance proceeds, or if the homestead is condemned in eminent domain proceedings, the proceeds are likewise exempt for six months. However, if the debtor moves into another homestead before disposing of his current homestead, the proceeds would not be exempt because a person cannot have two homesteads at one time.

Personal property exemptions. RCS 3836 provides that a married person may keep $30,000 worth of exempt personal property out of the hands of his creditors. A single person may keep $15,000 worth of such property. The sorts of property which may be exempt are the following:

1. Home furnishings, including heirlooms.
2. Implements, tools, equipment, apparatus, and books used in a trade or profession, if reasonably necessary to its practice.
3. Wearing apparel if reasonably necessary.
4. Two firearms and athletic and sporting equipment.
5. Any two means of travel from the following categories (one from each):
   a. Horses, colts, mules, or donkeys.
   b. A bicycle or motorcycle.
   c. A wagon, cart, or dray.
   d. An automobile or station wagon.
   e. A truck cab.
   f. A truck trailer.
   g. A camper truck.
   h. A truck.
   i. A pickup truck.
6. Livestock and fowl as follows:
   a. Five cows and their calves.
   b. One bull of breeding age.
   c. Twenty hogs.
   d. Twenty sheep.
   e. Twenty goats.
   f. Fifty chickens.
   g. Thirty turkeys.

h. Thirty ducks.
i. Thirty geese.
j. Thirty guineas.
7. A dog, cat, and other household pets.
8. The cash surrender value of a life insurance policy in force for more than two years if the beneficiary is a dependent of the debtor or a member of his family.
9. Current wages for personal service.

The debtor may claim only $30,000 worth of all such property as exempt if he is married or $15,000 worth if he is single. All home furniture appears to be exempt if within the dollar limits. "Reasonably necessary" wearing apparel may not include jewelry, fur coats, and the like, depending upon the social status of the debtor. The transportation exemption extends to one mode of each class and two modes altogether; thus, a car and a pickup truck would be exempt, but two cars would not be. All of the categories of livestock are exempt. The wage exemption is defined narrowly; only employees earn wages. The income (accounts receivable) of the self-employed businessman is not exempt.

The following sorts of creditors may take exempt personal property:
1. The IRS, for delinquent federal taxes.
2. Creditors holding security interests in such property.
3. Creditors holding mechanic's liens, artisan's liens, landlord's liens, etc. upon such property.

Only the IRS may levy upon wages for personal services. Even the IRS may not take an entire paycheck—$50 of the net weekly pay of the debtor is exempt, plus $15 of the net weekly pay for each of his dependents.

Forcible collection of judgments. Plaintiff may have the court which gave him his judgment issue a writ of execution under it thirty days after the judgment becomes final. Under the writ the sheriff may seize any nonexempt property in the hands of the debtor. The property must be sold by the sheriff under the procedure provided by the rules of civil procedure.

The sheriff may sell only the debtor's equity in seized property. The buyer at the sale generally gets the debtor's interest and no more. Thus, if security interests exist in the seized property, the buyer at the sale will buy subject to them.

In order to establish a judgment lien upon a debtor's real property, the plaintiff should record an abstract of his judgment in the public records of each county in which the debtor owns real estate. If the property is later seized under a writ of execution, the judgment lien will be superior to liens recorded after it. The execution sale will wipe out such junior liens and the buyer at the sale will not buy subject to them.

If the plaintiff wants to reach assets of the debtor held by third parties, such as bank accounts and accounts receivable, he may have a writ of garnishment served upon the third party. When such a writ is so served, the third party (garnishee) must file an answer in the court issuing the writ disclosing how much (if any) property belonging to the debtor the garnishee has in his possession. Thus, the garnishee must disclose how much money is in the debtor's bank account, how much garnishee owes the debtor, or the like. Once the amount of the debtor's property held by the garnishee is determined, the court will order the garnishee to deliver the property into its custody.

Discovery in aid of judgment. If the plaintiff has difficulty in locating assets of the debtor, he may use all the weapons of discovery against the debtor (TRCP 621a). Thus, the debtor may be forced to answer interrogatories about his assets or to give depositions with respect to them.

Benefit of the abstract of judgment. The filing of an abstract of judgment in the public records of the county of the debtor's residence serves several useful purposes, even if the debtor owns no nonhomestead real estate in the county.

First, if the debtor's homestead ceases to be a homestead, the judgment lien will meaningfully attach to the property. It would no longer be exempt property. Secondly, if the debtor later acquires more real estate in the county through purchase, inheritance, etc., the judgment lien will attach it when it is acquired. Thirdly, if the debtor wants to sell nonhomestead property to which the lien attaches, he cannot give his buyer clear title until the lien is discharged, i.e. paid.

Fraudulent conveyances. It may be that the debtor has tried to dispose of valuable property in order to keep it out of the hands of the plaintiff. The plaintiff may be able to recover such property from the transferees.

If the debtor has sold an asset for a fair price to a buyer who has no knowledge of the debtor's problems, the sale is not fraudulent, and the third party has good title to the asset. If the debtor sells the asset for a fair price, but the buyer knew why he was selling, the conveyance is fraudulent and the plaintiff may reach the asset. If the debtor sold the asset for less than a fair price, the sale is fraudulent and the debtor clearly intended to put the asset out of reach. In this case it does not matter whether or not the buyer knew of the debtor's intentions.

If the debtor gives the property away with intent to keep it away from creditors, the transfer may of course be avoided. In addition, a creditor may avoid any purported gift of property by his debtor unless the subject matter of the gift is actually given into the possession of the donee, or a deed showing the making of the gift has been recorded, or a will showing the gift has been probated.

If the debtor seeks to prevent a creditor from seizing property in his possession by claiming that he has merely borrowed the property from someone else, the law will deem the possessor to be the owner (so far as the creditor in the matter is concerned) if he has had possession of the property in question for two years, the so-called owner has made no demand for its return, and no writing exists to authenticate the so-called loan.

If the person to whom a fraudulent conveyance of property is made sells the property in question to a bona fide purchaser (a person who pays fair value and knows nothing of previous conveyances), the purchaser gets good title and the creditor has no claim.

The law described here is found in Sections 24.01 through 24.05 of the Texas Business & Commerce Code.

Duration of a judgment. The Texas judgment is valid for ten years, subject to renewal. Affirmative action must be taken during the last year of the life of a judgment to renew it. If no action is taken before the tenth anniversary, it will expire. When the judgment is renewed, new abstracts of it must be filed in the public records in order to keep the judgment lien in force against the debtor's real estate.

Federal court judgments handed down in Texas are also good for ten years, subject to renewal.

Out-of-state judgments. The Constitution of the United States requires each state to give full faith and credit to the judicial acts of all other states. Thus, each American state must recognize the validity of judgments issued by the courts of sister states.

However, this does not mean that the Texan who has a Texas judgment against an Ohioan may have an Ohio sheriff levy execution upon the debtor's Ohio property. The Ohioan who has an Ohio judgment against a Texan likewise cannot ask a Texas sheriff to levy execution upon the Texan's property under the Ohio judgment. The Ohioan may gain

access to the Texan's Texas assets, but first he must obtain a Texas judgment. He should have no difficulty in doing this. He must file a complaint against the Texan in a proper court upon his judgment; but if citation is properly served upon the Texan, he may use only two defenses to escape liability:
1. The Ohio court had no jurisdiction under Ohio law to hand down the judgment (the case was heard by an improper court).
2. The Ohio court had no jurisdiction over the person of the debtor, perhaps because he was not properly served with citation under Ohio law.

Thus, the Texan cannot relitigate the case. That matter is settled. If he cannot dispute the validity of the judgment, he has no defense.

If the original judgment was in rem—that is, obtained against the debtor's assets without any sort of valid service of citation on the debtor himself—the judgment is unenforceable in another state. In such a case, the debtor has not yet had a chance to defend himself, so he may raise any defense he has to liability on the plaintiff's claim.

If the judgment the plaintiff seeks to enforce was handed down by the courts of another nation, a Texas court is under no obligation to accord the judgment full faith and credit. Texas courts generally do recognize judgments of the courts of other nations, though, so long as the other nation has a civilized legal system, and so long as the Texas court is convinced that the debtor got a fair trial in the other nation.

With respect to statutes of limitation on out-of-state judgments, the Texas approach is as follows: Space obtains a judgment against Clubb in California in 1970. Clubb moves to Texas in 1976 without paying. Spade follows him here and sues to obtain a Texas judgment against him in 1978. Clubb claims Spade cannot do this because a judgment is only good for five years in California and the five years have expired. Clubb's statement about the California statute of limitation on a judgment is correct, and his conclusion is also correct. If the judgment is no longer valid in the state where it was handed down, Texas will not recognize it.

Suppose Ace obtains a judgment against Deuce in Ohio in 1960. Deuce moves to Texas in 1967 without paying. Ace follows him here in 1978 and sues for a Texas judgment. Deuce says he is not liable because he has been in Texas more than ten years. Ace says that this does not matter because an Ohio judgment is good for twenty-one years. Ace is right about the Ohio statute of limitation, but Deuce is right about the Texas law. Since he has been in Texas more than ten years, Texas will not enforce the Ohio judgment, though it is still good in Ohio. If Ace had sued on the Ohio judgment in 1976, though, he would have succeeded, since Deuce had not yet been in Texas for ten years.

Escape from judgment liability. If a judgment is validly obtained, the debtor may escape paying only through expiration of the statute of limitations or by filing bankruptcy. Bankruptcy law will be discussed in some detail in the last chapter of this book, but it should be mentioned here that not all judgments may be avoided in bankruptcy.

Ordinary judgments obtained because of breach of contract or commission of negligent torts are dischargeable. However, judgments obtained because of fraud, violation of fiduciary duties, deliberate torts, and the like are not dischargeable. Judgments for taxes, alimony, and child support are also not dischargeable.

Res judicata. Once a civil matter goes to a final decision, it is settled for all time. The loser may not reopen the matter, not even if he discovers new evidence, finds out that his perception of the facts was all wrong, or the like. Each party to the case must present all available evidence, and be sure that he understands the facts completely.

Thus: Pauvre sues Reich for personal injury damages. The medical evidence shows

Pauvre's injuries to be moderately severe, with long-term temporary disability. Pauvre wins a judgment for a moderate sum on this evidence, and Reich pays it. It later turns out that Pauvre is permanently disabled; he therefore wants to sue for more damages. He cannot. He has already had his day in court.

The notion is in a sense the civil equivalent of the criminal prohibition against double jeopardy: the defendant may be subjected to only one suit by a plaintiff upon the plaintiff's claim. If there are multiple parties involved, each is usually entitled to his day in court, but this will depend to a degree upon the nature of the case.

9

Special Court Procedures

In the chapter on criminal procedure we considered the rules of court procedure which must be followed when the state seeks to punish someone for having violated criminal law. In the chapter on civil procedure we considered the rules which must be followed when a citizen seeks the aid of a court in obtaining private redress from another who has wronged him in some way.

This chapter will deal with the rules governing court procedures in proceedings which are neither typically civil nor criminal. We shall consider the following:

1. Guardianship proceedings, intended to restrict the power of a person to make contracts and to manage his property.
2. Civil commitment proceedings, intended to remove a person from society for his own good although he has not violated the criminal law.
3. Habeas corpus proceedings, in which a person who feels that he or another has been wrongfully deprived of his liberty may invoke the aid of the courts to test the legality of the deprivation.
4. Contempt proceedings.
5. Arbitration, in which parties to a dispute may seek to settle their differences through nonjudicial proceedings.
6. Paternity and juvenile proceedings.

Permanent guardianship proceedings. Permanent guardians may be appointed for minors and for incompetent persons. A minor must of course have a guardian because of his youth. Probate Code Section 109 (PrC 109) provides that the parents of a minor are his natural guardians. The courts need not become involved in appointing guardians for minors unless they are orphans.

Permanent guardians may be appointed for the following nonminors:
1. Incompetents.
2. Habitual drunkards.
3. Persons for whom a guardian is necessary in order for them to receive funds from a governmental source.

Any person desiring to have a guardian appointed for an individual may file a petition for appointment of a guardian in the county court of the county of residence of the proposed ward. The petition must state, according to PrC 111:

1. The name, sex, residence, and date of birth (if a minor) of the person for whom the guardian is to be appointed.
2. If a minor, the names of the parents or next of kin, and whether either or both parents are deceased.
3. A general description of the property belonging to the person, if appointment of a guardian for the estate is sought.
4. The reasons for requesting appointment of a guardian.
5. The name, relationship, and address of the person applicant seeks to have appointed guardian.
6. Whether guardianship of person, guardianship of estate, or both, is sought.

PrC 112 permits the county judge to file an application for appointment of a guardian for a minor, person of unsound mind, or habitual drunkard who resides in his county.

The guardian of the person of a ward has responsibility for providing housing and the necessities of life for his ward. The guardian of the estate of a ward is responsible for managing the ward's property. The same person may serve as both guardian of the person and guardian of the estate, or two persons may serve as guardian—one of the person, and the other of the estate (PrC 116). PrC 130 provides that a copy of the application must be served upon the ward-to-be, unless he has been declared by a court to be of unsound mind or an habitual drunkard within six months of the application.

The ward-to-be may contest the application, or any other interested person may contest. The contest may be over the necessity for appointment of a guardian, over the identity of the person to be appointed guardian, or both. PrC 115 provides that the ward-to-be need not be present at the hearing upon the application. It also provides that there is no right to trial by jury in the matter; the county judge decides the matter alone.

The person appointed as guardian must be qualified under PrC 110 to so serve. The following sorts of persons may not serve as guardians:

1. Minors.
2. Persons whose conduct is notoriously bad.
3. Incompetents.
4. Persons indebted to the ward.
5. Persons unable to read or write in English.
6. Persons without the education or experience to be guardians.
7. Persons who are parties to a lawsuit involving the welfare of the ward or his estate.

The capacity of a minor with a guardian to make contracts is governed by the general law of contracts. If a guardian of his estate has been appointed, only the guardian may make contracts regarding the estate. The contractual capacity of an adult with a permanent guardian is nil; he cannot make any contract. Any contract he makes may be voided by his guardian or by the other party to the bargain.

The guardian of the estate stands in a fiduciary relationship with his ward; the nature of this relationship will be discussed in the materials on contracts and trusts. In general, the guardian must manage the ward's assets for the benefit of the ward, must not use such assets for his own purposes, and must not profit at his ward's expense.

The guardianship of a minor terminates when the minor becomes an adult. The guardianship of an adult can be terminated only by the death of the ward or by court decree. PrC 426 provides that a court proceeding to terminate the guardianship of an adult of unsound mind or of an adult habitual drunkard must begin when any person alleges in writing and under oath before the county probate court that the ward is no longer of unsound mind, or is no longer an habitual drunkard. The court must then set a date for a hearing on the matter, and must cite the guardian to appear before it on that date to show cause why the guardianship should not be terminated. If there is no doubt that the ward is now of sound mind and/or sober habits, the judge himself may terminate the guardianship. If there is some doubt about the ward's condition, a jury trial is held upon the question of whether or not the guardianship should be terminated, and the jury decision settles the issue.

Limited guardianship. The Texas legislature added Sections 130a through 130o to the Probate Code in 1977, authorizing the appointment of limited guardians for mentally retarded persons. The ward of a limited guardian retains limited contractual capacity. The limited guardian does not obtain total control over the ward's person and property. Anyone may file a petition for appointment of a limited guardian for a mentally retarded person. However, no such guardian may be appointed for a ward of a permanent guardian.

The application must be filed with the probate court of the ward's county of residence. It must contain the information required in an application for permanent guardian, and, in addition, the nature of the authority the applicant desires for the limited guardian and the limitations to be placed upon the capacity of the ward to manage his life. The application must be served upon the ward-to-be. Within thirty days of the filing of the application the ward-to-be must be examined by experts at a facility of the Texas Department of Mental Health and Mental Retardation. The result of this examination must be reported to the court, as per PrC 130F. A hearing must then be held on the application. The ward-to-be is entitled to attend, unless the court decides attendance is not in his best interest. In any event, he is entitled to representation by counsel and to trial by jury if he wishes.

No limited guardian shall be appointed if it is decided at the hearing that the ward-to-be is capable of caring for himself and managing his property as a prudent person does. Nor shall a limited guardian be appointed if it is decided that the ward-to-be is totally incapable of caring for himself or managing his property. Thus, a limited guardian will be appointed only if the retarded person is lacking in capacity to do some, but not all, the things necessary for caring for himself and his property. PrC 130H provides that the guardian's authority shall be strictly limited to doing for the ward what the ward cannot do for himself. The order appointing the guardian must spell out in detail exactly what the guardian shall have power to do and exactly which property of the ward the guardian shall have authority to manage.

PrC 130M provides that a limited guardianship shall terminate when:
1. The ward dies, or
2. The ward acquires full capacity to manage himself and his property, or
3. A permanent guardian is appointed for the ward, or
4. The ward applies for removal of the guardian, and the court decides that this removal is in the ward's best interest.

A ward of a limited guardian is not necessarily legally incapable of making a contract, nor is he necessarily a person of full contractual capacity. His capacity in this area depends upon the authority of his limited guardian. In those areas where the guardian has authority, the capacity of the ward is limited; in those areas where the guardian has no authority, the capacity of the ward is not limited. The contracts of a person with a limited guardian may well be voidable, though, even if the ward has capacity to make them. This issue will be discussed at more length in the material on contracts.

Commitment of mentally ill persons. The law relative to the commitment of mentally ill persons to mental hospitals is contained in the Texas Mental Health Code (MHC), RCS 5547.

A mentally ill person's first admission to a state mental hospital is likely to come about pursuant to an order of temporary hospitalization issued by the county judge of the patient's county of residence, or the county in which he is found.

Any adult may file an application for temporary hospitalization of a patient with the county court. The application must state the name and address of the patient, and further must state that (MHC 31):

1. The person is mentally ill, and
2. The person is not charged with a criminal offense, and
3. The person requires observation and treatment in a mental hospital for his own welfare and protection and/or for the protection of others.

MHC 33 requires that the county judge schedule a hearing upon the application within fourteen days of the filing of the application. Notice of the filing of the application and of the time and place of hearing must be served upon the patient.

The hearing upon the application may not be held before the patient is examined by two physicians, one of whom must be a psychiatrist if one is available within the county. These examining physicians must file certificates of mental examination for mental illness with the court before the hearing. If the examination has taken place before the filing of the application for hospitalization, the certificates must be filed with the application. If no examination has taken place before the application is filed, the court will order the patient to submit himself to the required examination before his hearing (MHC 32). The patient is entitled to be represented by counsel in these proceedings. As in criminal proceedings, he is entitled to counsel at state expense if he cannot afford to hire his own (MHC 33).

The application for hospitalization must be dismissed by the court unless the examining physicians both certify that the patient is mentally ill and that he requires observation and treatment; the required certificates are part of the case file of the court. The patient is normally at liberty pending his hearing, unless he has already been admitted to a mental hospital, or unless he is placed under protective custody, which will be discussed later.

MHC 36 provides that the hearing need not take place in a courtroom. The patient need not be present, though he has the right to be present if he desires; his attorney must of course be present. The hearing is to be as informal as is consistent with orderly procedure. No jury trial is required, although the applicant for hospitalization, the patient, or the judge may require a jury.

Since there can be no hearing unless the examining physicians have certified the patient to be mentally ill, the patient will be committed unless he or someone else can produce evidence to contradict the contents of the certificates. If the court finds that commitment is necessary, it shall order commitment for a period not to exceed ninety days. If it finds commitment to be unnecessary, it will dismiss the application (MHC 38).

A decision of denial of the application is final, but an order of commitment is appealable to the district court. Notice of appeal must be filed by the patient within five days of the entry of the order for temporary hospitalization. Upon appeal, there must be a new trial (trial de novo) in the district court, where the patient may request a trial by jury. The county judge may release the patient from custody pending the appeal (if he was in custody before), provided that he files a proper appeal bond.

MHC 27 provides a procedure for the emergency involuntary commitment of a mentally ill person. If a health or peace officer believes that a person is mentally ill and may injure himself or others if not immediately restrained, he may apply to a magistrate for a warrant of commitment. Once the warrant is issued, the officer may take the patient into custody and transport him to the nearest hospital. MHC 28 requires that the medical officer on duty at the hospital immediately examine the patient for symptoms of mental illness and likelihood that he could cause injury to himself or others if not restrained. If the examining medical officer finds no such symptoms, the patient must be released. If he does find such symptoms, the warrant of commitment is in order, and the committing officer truly believes that the patient is a menace to himself or to others—or if an order for protective custody of the patient has been duly issued—the patient must be admitted.

The patient may not be detained under this authority for more than twenty-four hours. During that time he must be thoroughly examined by a physician who must issue a certificate of medical examination for mental illness. The authorities may detain the patient for a longer period if a court order permitting this is obtained from the county judge during the twenty-four-hour custody period. If the patient is taken into custody on a Saturday or Sunday or a holiday, however, the authorities have until 9 A.M. on the first business day thereafter to obtain the court order.

Should the examining physician certify the patient to be mentally ill and in need of hospitalization, an application for temporary hospitalization will of course be filed. Under the authority of MHC 66, the county court may issue an order of protective custody authorizing the detention of a patient in a mental hospital pending a hearing upon an application for temporary hospitalization. This may be issued if a certifying physician states that the patient may injure himself or others if not restrained. Such an order may be used to keep the patient originally involuntarily committed under the emergency procedure in custody until an order of temporary commitment is obtained.

After the patient has been under temporary observation in a mental hospital for sixty days or more, application may be filed for his indefinite commitment (MHC 40). The applicant may be any person interested in the welfare of the patient. The application must be accompanied by a certificate of a physician who has examined the patient within fifteen days of the filing, certifying that the patient is mentally ill and requires hospitalization in a mental hospital. A hearing on the application must be held within thirty days of its filing. The patient is entitled to representation by counsel at the hearing, at state expense if necessary. The patient is entitled to trial by jury at his hearing if he wants it, as per MHC 48. If the patient does not want a jury trial, he must sign a written form waiving this right.

The hearing is to be conducted in essentially the same manner as the hearing on application for temporary hospitalization. At least two physicians who have examined the patient within fifteen days of hearing must testify. The patient may not be indefinitely committed unless there is some medical or psychiatric evidence that he should be committed (MHC 50). The court or jury must answer three questions (MHC 51):

1. Is the patient mentally ill?
2. If so, does he require hospitalization in a mental hospital for his own protection and welfare, or for the protection of others?
3. If so, is he mentally incompetent?

If the answers to the first two questions are affirmative, indefinite commitment is mandatory. The affirmative answer to the third question would justify proceedings to appoint a permanent guardian for the patient, but would have no bearing upon his commitment.

MHC 54 provides that the patient may appeal an order of indefinite commitment to the district court within thirty days after it is handed down. The appeal will result in an entire new trial in the district court. MHC 80 provides that the head of a mental hospital may at any time discharge a patient if he determines that the patient no longer requires hospitalization. He may also furlough a patient without discharge—that is, let him live at home or under some other arrangement. When a patient has been on continuous furlough for eighteen months, he is discharged.

MCH 82 provides that a patient or his next friend (legal representative) may petition the county judge of the county where the patient is hospitalized for reconsideration of the question of whether he should be confined. The hospital must be notified of the petition. It must examine the patient to determine the current state of his mental health. If the result of the examination is a determination that the patient no longer requires hospitalization, the patient is discharged. If the result is a determination that hospitalization is still required, the court must be notified of this fact.

A hearing will the be scheduled, and the court will set up an examination of the patient by a physician not on the staff of the confining hospital, a physician of the patient's choice if he has one. The court holds the hearing without a jury. The judge will, at the end of the hearing, either order the patient to be discharged, or dismiss the petition.

Such a petition may be filed at any time. However, petitions of this nature filed before one year of indefinite commitment, or within two years of the rejection of a similar petition, do not require the county judge to order reexamination and hearing. Thus, indefinite commitment may result in the patient spending the remainder of his life in a mental hospital. Release from the hospital comes only when the head of the hospital so determines or the patient assembles enough evidence of his restoration to mental health to convince a judge that he should be released.

Commitment of alcoholics. RCS 5561c provides the Texas statutory law governing commitment of alcoholics to institutions. RCS 5561c Section 9 provides that the county judge may remand an alcoholic to the custody of the Texas Commission on Alcoholism by following specified procedure. A county health officer, spouse, or close relative of the patient may file a petition with the county judge for remand of the alcoholic. The petition, or a copy of it, must be served upon the patient. A hearing must be held no less than five days after filing of the petition, nor more than fourteen days afterward. The hearing may be held without the patient's presence, so long as it is held at least three days after the service of the petition upon him.

The court may (but need not) order the examination of the patient by a physician prior to the hearing. After examination by a physician, but before the hearing, the judge may order the patient taken into protective custody if the patient's alcoholism causes him to be a danger to himself or to others.

If the patient admits that he is an alcoholic and that he requires treatment, no hearing is necessary. Otherwise, a hearing is necessary, and evidence must be heard. The statute does not require a jury at this hearing, but the patient is entitled to representation by an attorney. If the court decides that the patient is an alcoholic in need of treatment, it must remand him to a proper institution for no less than fifteen days and no more than ninety days.

RCS 5561c Sec. 10 provides that a decision of commitment may be appealed by the patient to the district court within five days of the handing down of the decision. As usual, there is a new trial in the district court, where the patient has the right to trial by jury.

RCS 5561c Sec. 12 authorizes the judge of a criminal court who convicts a defendant of a misdemeanor resulting from his habitual or chronic use of alcohol to sentence the defendant to an institution of the commission on alcoholism for a period not to exceed ninety days in lieu of sentence to jail. This should not be done with feebleminded or psychotic defendants, or defendants exhibiting criminal tendencies. If the offense was committed with criminal intent, not because of the influence of the alcohol, the defendant should of course go to jail. If personnel at alcoholic treatment facilities determine a patient to be mentally ill, the commission on alcoholism may start the appropriate commitment proceedings.

A person committed to an alcoholic treatment facility may be discharged before the expiration of the period of commitment. Such a person may also be released on probation before expiration of the period of commitment. These matters are discretionary with the commission on alcoholism and its authorized representatives.

Commitment of drug addicts. RCS 5561c-1 contains the statutory law on commitment and treatment of drug addicts in Texas.

RCS 5561c-1 Sec. 1 provides that any person found to be addicted to narcotics shall be committed to a mental hospital for such period of time as may be necessary to arrest that person's drug addiction.

Section 2 of the statute provides that any adult person may file a petition with the county court having jurisdiction over commitments, asking for commitment of the addict. The county attorney of the county in question may also file such a petition. The petition must be accompanied by the sworn statements of two physicians who have examined the patient within five days of the filing of the petition, stating that in their professional opinions the patient is addicted to narcotic drugs. The statements should include the medical opinions of the physicians as to whether or not hospitalization of the patient is necessary and whether or not immediate restraint of the patient is necessary to prevent injury to himself or to others. A hearing must be held upon the petition within fourteen days of its filing. Notice must be served on the patient, who is entitled to representation by counsel in the proceeding, at state expense if necessary.

Section 3 of the statute grants the patient the right to trial by jury, unless he waives his right by signing a proper written document. Section 4 provides that the patient may remain at liberty pending the hearing unless he is taken into protective custody on the recommendation of the examining physician to protect himself and others.

The patient may not be committed unless medical or psychiatric evidence that commitment was necessary was admitted at the hearing. Commitment, if decided upon, is for an indefinite time, or until the patient is discharged from the hospital.

The procedure for appeal of an order of commitment to the district court is essentially the same as the procedure for appeal of an order of indefinite commitment to a mental hospital, as per Section 9 of the statute.

Commitment of the mentally retarded. In 1977 the Texas legislature enacted the Mentally Retarded Persons Act (MRPA), codified as RCS 5547-300, which became effective January 1, 1978. This statute now contains the statutory law relative to treatment of mentally retarded persons in this state.

The rationale of the new statute on care of the mentally retarded is that these unfortunates should be allowed to participate in society to the extent of their abilities. They should not be removed from society unless they are unable to function within it; therefore, most of the treatment provided for under the statute is voluntary and noncoercive. Since the mandated treatment is generally noncoercive, the authorities should become aware of the identity of most mentally retarded persons in the state.

A discussion of the voluntary benefits available under the statute is beyond the scope of this chapter, which will be limited to the removal of the retarded from society through involuntary commitment. Most of the law here is found in MRPA 37.

Any interested person may file a petition with the county court of the county of residence of the retarded person, asking for his commitment to a residential care facility. The petition must of course state reasons for the retarded person's removal from society. The judge must order an immediate diagnosis and evaluation of the patient's condition by a diagnosis and evaluation team of experts from the Texas Department of Mental Health and Mental Retardation, unless such a procedure has been conducted within the past six months. A hearing must also be scheduled on the petition. Notice must be served upon the patient not less than ten days before the hearing. The notice, besides informing the patient of the filing of the petition and of the date of hearing, must inform him that:

1. He has the right to learn the recommendations of the diagnosis and evaluation team in his case.
2. He has the right to independent diagnosis and evaluation (if he can afford to obtain it).
3. He has the right to be represented by counsel, at state expense if necessary.
4. He has the right to a trial by jury at the hearing.

If the person may cause injury to himself or to others if not restrained, he may be taken into protective custody pending the hearing.

At the hearing, the patient has the right to be present unless the court decides that his presence would be detrimental to his well-being. The proponents of commitment must prove beyond a reasonable doubt that commitment is in the best interest of the patient. If the court or jury finds the patient to be mentally retarded, and if it finds commitment to be in his best interest, it may order commitment for an indefinite period. If the court or jury finds the patient to be mentally retarded, but decides that outpatient services would enable him to function in society to a degree, it may decide not to commit but to recommend that the patient make use of some of the voluntary outpatient services provided by the state.

Any party may appeal the decision of the court in this hearing. The appeal here lies to the court of civil appeals (not, notice, to the district court) and is governed in all respects by the Texas Rules of Civil Procedure. Thus, an appeal may not result in a new trial; it may however result in a review of the record of the hearing.

The superintendent or director of a facility for the care of the mentally retarded may discharge a patient on the ground that he is not truly mentally retarded. This of course is not likely to happen with respect to a patient who was involuntarily committed. If the facility providing service to the patient decides that the patient could be better treated at another facility, or if it decides that discharge from the facility is in the patient's best interest, it may suggest transfer or discharge under MRPA 39.

MRPA 40 provides that the patient himself, or his parent or guardian, may apply for transfer or discharge. The treating facility may grant or decline the application. If the patient or his parent or guardian disapproves of a proposed transfer or discharge under MRPA 39, or if these parties feel aggrieved by a decision not to grant transfer or discharge under MRPA 40, any one of them may request an administrative hearing on the matter. All must be informed that they have the right to request an administrative hearing.

Such a hearing is conducted according to the provisions of MRPA 43. It must be held within thirty days of the making of the decision which caused the hearing to be requested. It is presided over by a hearing officer of the Department of Mental Health and Mental Retardation. All persons interested in the matter have the right to attend and the right to representation by counsel. They also have the right to inspect any departmental records on the patient containing material relevant to the subject matter of the hearing.

There is no right to trial by jury in administrative hearings. The hearing officer decides the matter himself and prepares a written decision describing his action and explaining his reasons for so deciding. Any party unhappy with the decision may appeal it within thirty days to either the county court of the county where the patient resides, or to the county court of Travis County. A new trial is then held in that county.

Committed patients may be given leaves of absences or furloughs by the superintendent or director of their residential care facilities. Should a committed patient develop symptoms of mental illness, the director or superintendent of his facility may transfer him to a mental hospital for a period not to exceed thirty days for observation and evaluation. If, in the belief of the experts commitment to a mental hospital is necessary, MRPA 46 requires that court proceedings be initiated to approve the transfer.

If the patient was originally committed as mentally retarded, the petition for transfer must be filed with the court which originally committed him. If he was not committed by court order, the petition may be filed in the county court of the county in which the patient is committed. The procedure in the hearing is very similar to those procedures which have already been discussed. Two physicians must certify that the patient is mentally ill and requires treatment. The patient is entitled to representation by counsel and to trial by jury (unless he waives jury trial in writing). If the court or jury decides that the patient is mentally ill, he will be transferred from the institution for the mentally retarded to the institution for the mentally ill. If the court or jury decides that he is not mentally ill, he will remain where he is —in the institution for the mentally retarded.

A patient committed to a mental institution under these provisions is in essence committed permanently, or until discharged. When such a patient no longer requires care in an institution for the mentally ill, he may be discharged back into society, or he may be sent back to an institution for the mentally retarded. A transfer from the institution for the mentally ill to the institution for the mentally retarded may only be accomplished by the obtaining of a court order approving the transfer from the court that originally committed the patient to the institution for the mentally ill.

General comments upon civil commitment. The statutes creating all these civil commitment procedures emphasize that a patient caught in the toils of these procedures is not a criminal and is not to be treated as a criminal. Any patient taken into protective custody under any of the procedures described above should therefore not be confined in jail if another place of confinement is available. Generally, though, confinement in jail is authorized for a period of up to seven days when no other suitable place exists. Persons accused of criminal offenses who are under observation in mental facilities should generally be confined separately from other patients, since these persons will be treated as criminals to a degree.

There is of course a difference between the removal of a person from society because he has violated the criminal law and the removal of a person from society because he is mentally ill. In the former instance, the person is removed because of his grievous fault. He has broken the law; therefore he must be punished. In the latter instance, the person is not removed because of his conscious wrongdoing, or indeed because of any wrongdoing at all (except for alcoholics and drug addicts). Rather, he is removed because his removal is in his, and society's, best interests.

The difference in emphasis is subtle but important. The complex mechanisms built into the criminal process to protect the innocent have not been built into the civil commitment process. To be sure, the civil commitment statutes provide for a right to counsel and generally for a right to trial by jury. They also provide that proof beyond a reasonable doubt of a patient's disability is required for commitment. Otherwise, the rules of the civil courts prevail.

The lawyer is at home in the realm of criminal law. He has studied it at some length in law school. The average juror does not find the law involved in the ordinary criminal law case too complex. His task is often enough the very human task of deciding which persons to believe. But frequently in civil commitment cases neither the lawyers nor the jurors feel at home. The commitment statutes emphasize that no person may be committed except upon competent medical or psychiatric testimony; this is necessary, of course, because the question of whether or not a person is mentally ill or mentally retarded is a question of medicine, not a question of law. Lawyers have little, if any, professional training in the disciplines of medicine and psychiatry; most of them therefore have little understanding of the issues involved in such matters. If the lawyer feels himself ignorant when confronted by such a case, the average juror will feel even more ignorant. The civil commitment case may simply boil down to this in the minds of the laymen involved: Is the patient so abnormal that he should be deprived of his liberty for the good of himself and of society? What is the meaning of "normality" in this context? The medical and psychiatric experts of course strive to define it within the boundaries of their professional knowledge. But, in the civil commitment case, these experts must strive to give lawyers, judges, and jurors the benefit of their many years of specialized study within the span of a short court hearing. Can it be done?

Another side of the matter is this: There is probably no such creature as the perfectly normal man or woman. We all carry around, as a part of the baggage of our psyches, behavior traits that the experts might label "neurotic." Perhaps these weaknesses do not crop up in our normal daily routine since we try to arrange our affairs to minimize stress. When we are not living under stress most of us behave normally and rationally. Sometimes, though, we become subject to great stress, through our own fault or due to circumstances over which we have no control. When this occurs, we may "go to pieces" and begin behaving irrationally. When we behave so, have we become mentally ill?

These questions are perhaps more philosophical than medical or legal. They are nevertheless most worthy of consideration. In one sense it does not matter whether a person is confined at Huntsville because he is a criminal or at Rusk because he is mentally ill; either way, he has lost his liberty. We often show more concern for the Huntsville inmate because he is being punished while he is there and is worthy of release when he has "paid his debt to society." We may not concern ourselves with the Rusk inmate so much; we put him there to treat him, not to punish him, and treatment is considered good by definition. The patient should therefore have no objection to being in the hospital, we think; it is best for him, and it is best for us. He is in the hands of the experts who understand his condition best. But does the patient see it that way? We too often choose not to concern ourselves with that question.

Habeas corpus proceedings. The law governing the writ of habeas corpus at the state level is found in Chapter 11 of the Code of Criminal Procedure (CCP). The law here is a part of the law of criminal procedure because the majority of habeas corpus cases involves persons accused or convicted of violations of the criminal law. However, habeas corpus is not exclusively a criminal matter.

CCP 11.01 provides, simply, that the writ of habeas corpus is the remedy available to a person who has been deprived of his liberty. The writ itself is a court order directed to the person depriving another of his liberty, directing him to produce his prisoner in court at a named time and to show cause for the justifiability of this deprivation of liberty.

CCP 11.05 provides that the writ may be granted in Texas by the court of criminal appeals, the district courts, the county courts, or any individual judge of any of these courts. Note, then, that justices of the peace and judges of the courts of civil appeals and the Supreme Court of Texas have no authority in this area.

A petition for a writ may be filed with any judge having power to issue the writ. The person deprived of liberty may file the application for the writ on behalf of himself, or it may be filed by an interested person on behalf of the one so deprived. CCP 11.14 provides that the petition must contain the name of the person being unlawfully confined, and the names of the person or persons unlawfully confining him. If the detainee is confined under a writ, order, process, or the like, a copy of the same must be attached to the petition, or an explanation must be given as to why this cannot be done. If the confinement is not as a result of a writ, order, or process, the petition may state merely that the detainee is being unlawfully deprived of his liberty by the persons named in paragraph 1 above. The petition must ask for a writ of habeas corpus, and the petitioner must swear that the contents of the petition are true.

CCP 11.5 provides that the judge may issue the writ immediately upon receipt of the application, without hearing, unless it is evident from the petition that the confinement of the detainee is lawful. If there is any question as to the lawfulness of the detention complained of, the writ should be issued. The issued writ may be given to any person competent to testify in court as a witness, and that person should immediately serve the writ upon the person or persons unlawfully detaining the detainee. The service should be done in person if possible, but CCP 11.27 provides that if the writ cannot be served personally upon the detaining party because he will not accept it, or because he hides himself, or for similar reasons, the writ may be posted upon a conspicuous part of the building where he resides or conceals himself. CCP 11.28 provides that the party who served the writ must file a return stating exactly how he served it, including time, place, and manner of service.

CCP 11.29 provides that the person upon whom the writ is served must immediately respond to it. CCP 11.30 says that the response must contain the following in writing (on the served copy of the writ, or on some paper attached to it):
1. Whether or not it is true that he has the detainee in custody.
2. For what reason he detains the detainee.
3. If he has transferred the detainee to someone else's custody since issuance of the writ, to whom detainee has been transferred, and why.
4. The writ or warrant authorizing him to have detainee in his custody (if any).

The detainee must be brought before the court issuing the writ within three days of service unless the writ itself allowed more time (CCP 11.36). Failure to make immediate response to the writ, or failure to produce the detainee within three days, is cause for the issuing judge to order the arrest of the person to whom the writ was directed. That person may then be committed to jail until he decides to obey the writ (CCP 11.34).

The court which issued the writ will hear evidence upon the lawfulness of the detention of the detainee; the detainee opens the case. There is no right to a jury in such a case. The judge hears the evidence alone and makes his decision. If he decides that the detention was unlawful, he will order the detainee released immediately. If he decides that the detention was lawful, he will not order release.

If the proper criminal procedure has been followed with respect to the detainee in a criminal matter, the detention is lawful. If proper commitment procedure has been followed with respect to a detainee in a commitment case, the detention is also lawful.

If the detaining party has some lawful reason for depriving the detainee of his liberty (because he is a guardian protecting his ward, for example), the detention is proper. A decision that detention is lawful is appealable to the court of criminal appeals, under CCP 44.34. The procedure is normal appellate procedure, except that it is accelerated. The decision of the court of criminal appeals is final in the matter.

Generally, a detainee is permitted to use habeas corpus as a test of the lawfulness of his detention only once. Once the detention is held to be lawful in such a proceeding, it cannot be contested in this manner again. The only exception to this general rule is in the situation where the detainee finds new evidence on the unlawfulness of his detention and wants to bring it before a court.

CCP 11.63 provides that a Texas habeas corpus petition may not be used to question the lawfulness of the detention of a person by federal authority, either by civilian courts or by the military. The only review possible here is through federal habeas corpus proceedings. It is possible to obtain habeas corpus review of state actions in federal court under limited circumstances. The law on this is contained in 28 USC 2254. The only possible reason for federal habeas corpus review of state action is that the petitioner is in custody in violation of the constitution, treaties, or laws of the United States.

A petition for federal writ of habeas corpus may be made to any Supreme Court judge, circuit court judge, or district judge, or to the Supreme Court itself. The writ will not be granted unless the petitioner has exhausted all remedies available to him under state law, unless he can show the court that no remedies are available to him under state law (which could not be shown with respect to Texas state law), or that circumstances render the state process ineffective to protect his rights. The determinations of the state court in the petitioner's case are presumed to be accurate, unless the petitioner can prove one or more of the following:

1. That he did not get a fair and full hearing in state court, or
2. That the state court had no jurisdiction over his person or over the subject matter of his case, or
3. That he was indigent and the state did not furnish him counsel at the state court proceeding, or
4. That he was otherwise denied due process of law, or
5. That the merits of the case were not developed in state court, or
6. That the factfinding procedures used by the state court were inadequate, or
7. That the facts were not fully developed during the state proceeding, or
8. That the decision in the state proceeding was contrary to the evidence.

Proof of these matters is quite difficult. Of course, if the state court acted properly, proof is impossible. Very seldom will a state prisoner gain anything through this federal habeas corpus proceeding. In situations involving serious miscarriages of justice, however, the procedure may be the petitioner's last chance to obtain justice.

Contempt of court. It is necessary for court judges to have at their disposal a simple mechanism for enforcement of their orders. This mechanism is the contempt process. Judges have the power to punish those who disobey their orders. For purposes of administering punishment, the law recognizes two types of procedure. Which is to be used depends upon where the contempt was committed.

When the contempt is committed in the courtroom, in the presence of the judge, summary procedure is used. The judge warns the party that his conduct is contemptuous and will be punished if he does not mend his ways. If the warning is not heeded, the judge may punish on the spot. In-court contempt may involve the refusal of a witness to answer a question when ordered to do so by the judge, the creation of disorder within the courtroom, improper conduct by an attorney, refusal of a witness to produce physical evidence called for in a subpoena duces tecum without good cause, or the like. The only appeal from such summary punishment is an application for a writ of habeas corpus.

When the contempt is committed outside the judge's courtroom, punishment cannot be imposed without a hearing. Since the judge did not see the commission of the contempt, he is not bound to take the word of the party asking him to impose punishment. The defendant is allowed his chance to present evidence that he is not guilty. There is no right to trial by jury in such a case; and there is no right to an appeal. The court must, however, give the contemnor notice that he is being charged with contempt, and of the nature of the contempt, so that he may prepare a defense.

The most common sort of contempt committed outside the courtroom is probably the violation of the terms of an injunction. Another common sort is refusal by the contemnor to obey a court order performable outside the courtroom.

Arbitration. The parties to a contract may agree in writing to submit any differences which arise between themselves under the contract to arbitration. Parties to a noncontractual dispute may also agree in writing to submit their differences to arbitration. Submission of disputes to arbitration may be advantageous because:

1. Arbitration is less costly than litigation.
2. Arbitration is generally less formal than litigation.
3. The arbitrators may be specialists in the subject matter of the dispute and thus able to render a more intelligent decision than lay judges or jurors. Jurors are usually knowledgeable neither in the law nor in the subject matter of the dispute. Judges are trained in the law, but usually have little specialized knowledge of commercial practices.

Courts were formerly very hostile to agreements to arbitrate, feeling that court is the only proper place for resolution of legal disputes. Today, however, in this era of crowded court dockets, judges are quite willing to permit some types of disputes to be resolved by arbitrators.

In the past, Texas was more hostile to arbitration agreements than the majority of other states. A 1979 amendment to RCS 224 and 224-1, the Texas general arbitration statute, eliminated some of this hostility. Texas courts now enforce any written agreement to submit an existing controvery to arbitration. They also enforce agreements in written contracts to submit controversies arising under said contracts to arbitration, unless:

1. The agreement to arbitrate is unconscionable, or
2. The contract is for the acquisition by an individual person or persons (as opposed to a corporation, trust, partnership, estate, or other such legal entity) of real or personal property, services, money, or credit for $50,000 or less, and the parties have no written agreement to arbitrate signed by themselves and by their attorneys, or
3. The dispute involves a claim for personal injury and no written agreement to arbitrate signed by the parties and their attorneys exists.

No agreement to arbitrate differences arising out of performance of a contract is enforceable unless it is clearly noted on the first page of said contract that such differences are subject to arbitration. Arbitration in intrastate labor disputes is governed by a special statute, RCS 239-249.

Before 1979, agreements to arbitrate in insurance and construction contracts were not enforceable unless they were in writing and signed by the parties and their attorneys. Under the new law, the requirement would still seem to hold for agreements to arbitrate insurance controversies involving personal injury. However most construction contracts (except small contracts for individual property owners) would now seem to be covered by the general law.

When an enforceable agreement to submit a dispute to arbitration exists, the courts will not accept jurisdiction over the resolution of the dispute until the arbitration proceeding has run its course. When an effort is made to sue rather than to arbitrate, the complaint will be dismissed. When a party refuses to submit a dispute to arbitration in breach of an enforceable contract to arbitrate, courts will compel the reluctant party to arbitrate.

There may be one arbitrator, or there may be more than one. The arbitration agreement should spell out the procedure for arbitration, including the number of arbitrators to be chosen, and the method of their choice. If the contractual method of appointment breaks down, or if no appointment method is provided for, the parties may apply to a court for appointment of an arbitrator.

The arbitrators must give adequate advance notice of the time and place of hearings, where all parties are entitled to be represented by counsel. The parties are entitled to be present at all hearings and to cross-examine witnesses. The arbitrators may administer oaths to witnesses, authorize the taking of depositions, issue subpoenas, and so forth. Arbitrators have no power to punish for contempt.

The decision of the arbitrators is called an award. The award may be made by the majority of the arbitrators. It must be in writing and must state the grounds for its making. The fees of the arbitrators and the costs of the arbitration shall be paid as the award directs. Generally each party pays his own attorney, unless the agreement to arbitrate authorizes the arbitrators to include this in the award.

A party unhappy with an award may ask a court to vacate it. The only grounds for vacation of an award of Texas arbitrators are:

1. The award was obtained through fraud or corruption.
2. A supposedly neutral arbitrator was biased. (Often, it is provided in the contract that each party shall choose one arbitrator, and that these two shall choose the third. In such a case, only the third arbitrator is neutral—bias by the first two appointed is to be expected.)
3. The arbitrators exceeded their powers. (These are stated in the agreement to arbitrate.)
4. The rights of a party were prejudiced by the way the arbitrators conducted the proceeding (as by refusal to hear relevant evidence, or the like).
5. There was no arbitration agreement to begin with.

The application to vacate must be filed within ninety days of the handing down of the award. If the award is vacated because there was no agreement to arbitrate, the proceeding is ended. If it is vacated for other reasons, the court will order a rehearing—either before the same arbitrators, or before new ones, within the court's discretion.

If no objection is made to the award, a party may ask a court to confirm it as a matter of routine. The confirmation of an arbitration award converts it into a court judgment, enforceable as such. An unconfirmed arbitration award is not enforceable through the courts.

Arbitration under federal law. Any agreement to arbitrate which is a part of a maritime transaction or which involves interstate commerce is governed by the Federal Arbitration Act, 9 USC 1-13. 9 USC 2 provides that an agreement to arbitrate is valid, irrevocable, and enforceable if in interstate commerce or part of a maritime transaction, unless the agreement is void or voidable under the general law of contracts. Thus, interstate insurance or construction contracts containing agreements to arbitrate differences would be enforceable under federal law.

Under 9 USC 3, whenever a party sues in court upon an issue referable to arbitration under federal law, the defendant may seek to have the court proceeding stayed pending arbitration as per the agreement to arbitrate. If the court is convinced that the dispute should be arbitrated, it will stay the proceeding. 9 USC 4 provides that a party may sue in federal court to compel arbitration when a party to a maritime or interstate contract who has agreed to arbitrate differences refuses to arbitrate as agreed.

The procedure for enforcing an arbitration award under federal law is essentially the same as that provided under state law, except of course that application must be made to a federal district court to have the arbitration award reduced to judgment.

Paternity suits. The law governing paternity suits is contained in Chapter 13 of the Texas Family Code. The purpose of a paternity suit is to obtain a declaration by a court that a named person is the father of a child, and that the named father is responsible for supporting said child.

The petitioner in the paternity suit is generally the mother of the child in question. Under TFC 13.01, a paternity suit must be filed before the child is one year old. Should the respondent in the suit file an answer, the court must order the alleged father, the mother, and the child to submit to blood tests. Should the petitioner refuse to submit to the test, the petition will be dismissed. Should the respondent refuse to submit, he is subject to punishment for contempt of court, as per TFC 13.02.

Under TFC 13.03, the court may appoint two experts to take the blood tests and study the samples so taken. These experts may then present their findings to the presiding judge in the case. After the taking of the blood tests, all parties appear in person or by counsel at a pretrial hearing to be called by the judge (TFC 13.04). The examiners then present the results of the blood tests.

The blood tests cannot conclusively prove that the respondent is the father of the child. They can, however, conclusively prove that the respondent is not the father. If the blood tests show that he is not the father, the petition must be dismissed (TFC 13.05). If they show that the respondent could be the father, however, a trial must be scheduled.

If a trial is necessary, it will be trial by jury if either party wants it. If all parties submitted to blood tests, the results of the tests are admissible as evidence. They will show, of course, that it is possible that the respondent is the father of the child. If the respondent refused to take the test, evidence to this effect is also admissible. Refusal to take a blood test is naturally not proof of paternity.

Since a trial would not be held in a paternity case unless the respondent refuses to take a blood test or the blood test results show that he could be the father, the respondent has not much chance of showing that he is not the father unless he can prove that someone else might be the father. Therefore, a contested paternity case may well involve an exposure of the personal life of the mother of the child, a matter which could become very unpleasant for her.

If the jury or court finds that the respondent is not the father of the child, the matter ends, unless the petitioner has grounds for appeal. If the court or jury decides that the petitioner is the father, a parent-child relationship comes into existence and the respondent will be required to support the child unless he can get the decision reversed upon appeal.

Delinquent children. A child between the ages of ten and seventeen is considered to be delinquent if he violates a criminal law of the state for which the penalty is imprisonment or confinement in the county jail, or if he violates certain orders of the juvenile court.

A child is in need of supervision if he is between the ages of ten and seventeen and:
1. He commits three Class C misdemeanors or violations of municipal ordinances, or
2. He is unexcusedly absent from school for ten days or parts of days within six months, or for three days or parts of days within four weeks, without such justification as bad weather or quarantine, or
3. He is absent from his home without consent of his parent or guardian for a substantial length of time without intent to return, or
4. He is guilty of driving while intoxicated or driving while under the influence of drugs (TFC 51.03).

Delinquent children and children in need of supervision come under the jurisdiction of the juvenile court of the county. If a county has a juvenile board (as large counties do), this board may designate a district or county judge as the local juvenile judge. If a county has no juvenile board, the state court judges other than justices of the peace within the county designate one of their number to be the county juvenile judge (TFC 51.04).

A child apparently guilty of delinquent conduct or conduct causing him to be in need of supervision may be taken into custody by (TFC 52.01):
1. A peace officer acting under the law of arrest, or under an order of a juvenile judge, or who observes the child committing delinquent conduct or conduct showing the child to be in need of supervision, or
2. A probation officer, when the child has violated conditions of probation imposed by a juvenile judge.

When a child is taken into custody, he is not being arrested. The child may be warned and released without further action, he may be released to his parent or guardian with notice to bring the child before the juvenile court at a named time and place, he may be brought before an administrative official designated by the juvenile judge to handle such matters, or he may be placed in detention pending action by proper authority (TFC 52.02). If the child is placed in detention, he must not be detained in jail or in a similar law-enforcement institution (TFC 52.03).

When action is begun against a child, a preliminary investigation is to be conducted by the intake officer or other administrative officer charged by the juvenile court with this responsibility. If the officer finds that the person taken into custody is not a child, that there is no probable cause to believe that he is delinquent or in need of supervision, or that further action is not in the public interest, the matter is to be dismissed and the child released from custody (TFC 53.01). Even if there is cause to take further action, the child must not be detained unless:
1. He is likely to abscond or be removed from the jurisdiction of the court, or
2. Suitable care or supervision is not being provided for him by anyone, or
3. He has no parent, guardian, or relative to care for him.

If one of these three grounds for detention does not exist, the child must be released into the custody of his parent, guardian, or custodian pending further proceedings.

If the decision is made to take the child into detention, or to keep him in detention, a detention hearing must be held before the juvenile judge or before a referee appointed by the juvenile judge or the juvenile board of the county no later than the second working day after the child is taken into custody. The child is entitled to representation by an attorney at this hearing. There is no right to a jury trial at this hearing, but the child does have the right not to testify. The judge or referee must order the child released into the custody of his parent or guardian unless he is convinced that one of the three grounds for detention exists.

If the child is not taken into detention, but he has apparently committed violations of the law or engaged in conduct causing him to be in need of supervision, the administrative officer may propose to the child's parents that he be subjected to informal rehabilitation proceedings under the supervision of a probation officer without any court action. This is in a sense the equivalent of a guilty plea in an adult criminal action. The parent or guardian need not agree to this—a court hearing may be requested. Of course, if the child appears to be guilty of serious delinquency, the administrative officer may turn the matter over to the local prosecuting attorney for commencement of appropriate action. The prosecuting attorney then files with the juvenile court a petition requesting either adjudication by the court that the child is a delinquent or requires supervision, or requesting that jurisdiction over his case be transferred to adult criminal court. Once the petition is filed the court may order the child to be taken into custody if one of the three grounds for detention appears to exist. If this is done, a detention hearing will be necessary, as described above. Normally, however, the child is not taken into custody. The court sets a date for a hearing on the petition, and a summons is then served upon the child and his parent or guardian, informing them of the time and place of the hearing and commanding that they be present. If there has been no detention before now, the child's right to an attorney begins at this point.

The prosecutor may request that the juvenile court transfer its jurisdiction over the child to the adult criminal court when (TFC 54.02):

1. The child is accused of commission of a felony, and
2. He was fifteen years of age or older when he committed the offense, and no juvenile adjudication hearing has been held on it.

The transfer hearing is held before the juvenile judge without a jury. The judge is required to order a complete investigation of the child and the circumstances surrounding the commission of the offense before the hearing. The attorney for the child is entitled to examine this before the hearing, after which the judge must decide whether to transfer the case to the adult criminal court. He must base his decision upon the following matters, among others, as per TFC 54.02(f):

1. Whether the offense was committed against property or against a person, offenses against a person being more serious.
2. Whether the offense was allegedly committed in a premeditated and aggressive manner.
3. Whether the evidence of the child's guilt is or is not probably sufficient for a grand jury indictment.
4. The sophistication and maturity of the child.
5. The record and previous history of the child.
6. Prospects of rehabilitation of the child and protection of the public through the procedures, services, and facilities available to the juvenile court.

If the juvenile court decides to transfer the case to the adult courts, the judge must hand down a written decision explaining why this is being done. The transfer is considered to be an arrest and the normal adult criminal procedure begins, the child being entitled to an examining trial before a magistrate as soon as possible after the transfer. At the examining trial, the magistrate may refuse to accept jurisdiction over the child and may return jurisdiction to the juvenile court.

If the grand jury refuses to indict the child, this fact must be made known to the juvenile authorities. The juvenile court may then take appropriate action on the case. The refusal of the grand jury to indict does not necessarily result in the discharge of the child from court jurisdiction.

If the juvenile judge refuses to transfer jurisdiction of the case to the adult courts, the child may not later be criminally prosecuted for his offense. When the juvenile court retains jurisdiction in a felony case, and in cases where transfer of jurisdiction over the child to the adult courts is not authorized or informal rehabilitation procedures are not used, an adjudication hearing must be held in juvenile court under the provisions of TFC 52.03.

The procedure in the hearing is similar to that in a criminal trial. The child must be represented by an attorney, who has the normal right to cross-examine witnesses and to present testimony. There will be a trial by jury if the child wants it. The child may refuse to testify in his own defense. No out-of-court statement made by the child is admissible as evidence against him. He cannot be found guilty of delinquency, for example, upon the basis of the content of such a confession unless the prosecuting attorney can present corroborating evidence. The confession standing alone cannot constitute proof of guilt.

The guilt of the child must be proven beyond reasonable doubt. The decision of the jury in the case must be unanimous, one way or the other. The jury has no say in the disposal of the case; it must merely decide whether or not the child is guilty of any or all of the offenses with which he is charged. If the child is found not guilty, the case against him ends. If he is found guilty, a disposition hearing must be held in his case.

The statute governing disposition hearings is TFC 54.04. This hearing is before the juvenile judge alone: there is no right to a jury here. The court hears evidence relative to the character and background of the child, and also hears reports of the investigation of the case by probation officers and the like. If the court decides that the child does not require any sort of rehabilitation, it may release him, even if he was found guilty at the adjudication hearing.

If the child is found guilty of delinquent conduct at the adjudication hearing, the court may commit him to the Texas Youth Council for confinement in a juvenile institution. If the child is found guilty of conduct requiring supervision only, or if the court feels that the child's delinquent conduct does not warrant commitment to the Texas Youth Council, the court may place the child on probation for a period of up to one year. During that year the child may be placed in the custody of:

1. His parent(s) or guardian, or
2. Foster parents in a foster home, or
3. A public or private institution or agency, other than the Texas Youth Council.

This probation may be extended from year to year for successive one-year periods if it is felt that the child is not sufficiently rehabilitated. In any event, juvenile jurisdiction over the child ends upon the child's eighteenth birthday.

TFC 54.04 provides that any disposition of a child's case may later be modified by the juvenile court, except a commitment to the Texas Youth Council. The child himself; his parent, guardian, attorney, or probation officer; an appropriate state officer; or the court itself may suggest modification. The modification may be accomplished without a hearing if the child and his parent, guardian, or attorney agree. If the proposed modification is a revocation of probation and commitment of the child to the Texas Youth Council, a hearing is mandatory. In no such hearing to modify the disposition of a juvenile's case is there a right to trial by jury.

If the question of the child's mental capacity arises in a juvenile case, Chapter 55 of the TFC applies. The question of mental capacity may be raised by the court itself, or by any interested party. As soon as the question is raised, the court may have the child examined by a physician, psychiatrist, or psychologist, and may be guided by the result of this examination.

If the child's mental incapacity seems to be so great that he does not understand what is happening to him or is incapable of assisting in his own defense, a hearing similar to the hearing to determine capacity to stand trial in adult criminal procedure must be held (TFC 55.04). The sole issue at this hearing is the capacity of the child to understand what is going on and to assist in his own defense. There is a right to a jury at this hearing. If court or jury decides that the child is incapable of understanding the proceedings or of assisting in his own defense, the juvenile proceeding stops and steps are taken to assure that the child receives treatment. The procedure is similar to that used in adult criminal proceedings when the defendant is found to have no capacity to stand trial. If court or jury decides that the child is capable of understanding the proceedings and of assisting in his own defense, the proceeding continues under normal procedure.

If the child appears to have such mental disease or defect that he is not responsible for what he does, this matter must be raised at the adjudication hearing. The effect of raising this issue is the same as the adult criminal plea of not guilty by reason of insanity. The court or jury at the adjudication hearing must decide, among other things, whether or not the child has such mental disease or mental incapacity that he is not responsible for what he does. If this issue is raised at the adjudication hearing, then, the court or jury must decide whether or not the child did what he was accused of doing, and whether or not he is mentally responsible for what he does. If he is found not to have done what he was accused of doing, he goes free. If he is found to have done that which he was accused of, and to have been mentally responsible for it, the procedure runs its usual course: the disposition hearing will be held to determine the disposal of the case. If he is found to have done what he was accused of doing, but also to be so mentally diseased or deficient that he is not responsible for what he did, there will be no disposition hearing. Rather, the matter will be handled in roughly the same way as the case of the adult criminal defendant who is found not guilty by reason of insanity. The court must consider whether the child is so mentally ill or mentally retarded that steps should be taken to commit him.

The procedure for commitment of the mentally ill or mentally retarded child is essentially the same as the adult procedure, except that all court hearings are held in juvenile court.

All detention hearings, adjudication hearings, and disposition hearings may be held before referees appointed by the juvenile judge rather than before the juvenile judge himself if the parties agree. However, the child and the child's attorney have the right to insist upon a hearing before the juvenile judge himself. When the hearing is held before a referee, the referee transmits his findings and recommendations to the juvenile judge, who may modify the decision within twenty-four hours of its handing down. If a jury is to be used in these hearings, the juvenile judge himself or a designated substitute must preside.

Under TFC 56.01, all juvenile court decisions in transfer hearings, adjudication hearings, disposition hearings, and modification orders or hearings are appealable to the court of civil appeals, and ultimately to the Supreme Court of Texas. These appeals are processed as are civil appeals in general.

Powers of the Texas Youth Council. The authority of the Texas Youth Council (TYC) is set forth in RCS 5143d. It is the Texas agency charged with caring for delinquent children committed to its jurisdiction by the juvenile courts of the state. When a court commits a child to the custody of the TYC, it may order him conveyed forthwith to a youth institution, or it may notify TYC of the commitment but leave the child at liberty until TYC takes custody.

When TYC takes custody, its experts examine and study the child in order to determine what sort of treatment to administer. It may, after this examination and study, confine the child to an institution, it may release the child under supervision, or it may discharge him (RCS 5143d-17).

TYC has wide authority over the lives of its charges. It may place physically fit boys in park maintenance camps, forestry camps, or boys' ranches within the state, and require them to perform conservation and maintenance work. It may require its charges to participate in moral, academic, vocational, physical, and correctional training and activities (RCS 5143d-18). RCS 5143d-24 permits TYC to require all of its physically fit charges to attend a religious service (denomination of the child's choice) on Sunday.

The child committed to TYC is, then, totally under the jurisdiction of that organization until he becomes an adult or until TYC discharges him. TYC has almost complete discretion as to whether to keep a charge confined in an institution, to release him on probation, or to revoke the probation and reconfine.

Protective order against family violence proceedings. Of increasing concern to persons interested in the well-being of the family is the problem of violence committed by one member of a family against another. Existing legal procedures have been somewhat inadequate to deal with the problem. The 1979 session of the Texas legislature therefore added Chapter 71 to TFC, establishing a special procedure under which it is hoped that protective orders may be obtained to protect weak family members against violence committed by stronger family members.

This procedure may not be used when a suit for dissolution of marriage is pending and one of the spouses commits family violence against the other. The victim of the violence may then seek protection as a part of the divorce or annulment proceeding.

Any member of a household may file a petition for a protective order for the protection of himself or of another family member. Any adult may file an application for an order for the protection of a child member of a family or household (TFC 71.04). A former member of a household may also file for protection under this chapter; thus, the ex-wife who is subjected to violence by her ex-husband may make use of this procedure.

The procedure is begun by the filing of an application for protective order with the clerk of the county court, or the clerk of the court having jurisdiction over proceedings involving the parent-child relationship. The application may be filed in the county of the applicant's residence, or in the county where the respondent (the party alleged to have committed family violence) resides (TFC 71.03).

The application must contain, among other things:
1. The names and addresses of all applicants.
2. The names and addresses of all individuals alleged to have committed family violence.
3. The facts and circumstances of each alleged commission of family violence.
4. The relationship between the applicant(s) and the respondent(s).

The application may also contain an application for a temporary ex parte protective order. This may be requested if the applicant believes that there exists a clear and present danger of family violence. If a temporary ex parte order is requested, the judge of the court will examine the application immediately after filing. If he is convinced that a clear and present danger of violence exists, he will immediately issue the temporary ex parte order and direct the respondent(s) to do or restrain from doing specified acts. The order must of course be served upon the respondents. It is valid for the time specified, but the period of validity may not exceed twenty days (TFC 71.15). If no temporary ex parte order is issued, a citation will be served upon the respondents, as per TFC 71.07.

Upon the filing of the application, a hearing must be scheduled at a date and time no more than twenty days after the date of filing. The citation must be served upon the respondents at least forty-eight hours before the date of the hearing, and must notify the respondents of the time and place of the hearing. If respondents are not served at least forty-eight hours before the hearing, it must be rescheduled unless the respondents waive rescheduling (TFC 71.09).

The hearing is apparently before the judge alone—the statute makes no mention of the use of a jury. The judge will issue a permanent protective order if he finds that the respondents have committed family violence in the past, and that such violence is likely to recur in the future. An order may only be issued against a respondent who has been found to have committed family violence in the past or who consents to the entry of an order against him (TFC 71.10).

TFC 71.11 provides that the court handing down a protective order may:
1. Prohibit a respondent from:
   a. Committing family violence;
   b. Directly or indirectly communicating with a member of the family or household;
   c. Going to or near the residence, place of employment, or place of business of a member of the family or household, or any other place a member of the family or household may be;
   d. Removing a child member of the family or household from the possession of a person named in the court order or from the jurisdiction of the court;
   e. Transferring, encumbering, or otherwise disposing of property mutually owned or leased by the parties, except in the ordinary course of business.
2. Grant exclusive possession of a residence to a party and, if appropriate, direct one or more parties to vacate the residence if:
   a. The residence is jointly owned or leased by the party receiving exclusive possession and by some other party denied possession;
   b. The residence is owned or leased by the party retaining possession; or
   c. The residence is owned or leased by the party denied possession and that party has an obligation to support the party granted possession or the child of the party granted possession.
3. Provide for possession of and access to a child of a party.
4. Require payment of support for a party or for the child of a party if the respondent has a duty to support such party or child.
5. Require one or more parties to obtain specified counseling.
6. Award a party use and possession of specified community or jointly-owned property.
7. Prohibit a party from doing specified acts or require a party to do specified acts necessary or appropriate to prevent or reduce the likelihood of family violence.

TFC 71.12 permits parties to agree to mutually satisfactory protective orders out of court. If the court approves such orders, they become orders of the court. The maximum duration of such a family protective order is one year (TFC 71.13).

A copy of a duly issued protective order must be served upon the respondent(s). The order must contain in bold type a warning of the punishments which may be levied for its violation (TFC 71.16). Violation of either a permanent or ex parte order is punishable as contempt of court. After a hearing the contemnor may be punished by up to six months in jail and/or a fine of up to $500. In addition, violation of a permanent order is a Class A misdemeanor, carrying a maximum punishment of a year in jail and a $2,000 fine.

The power granted to courts under this chapter goes far beyond a simple power to order a person not to commit violence. A court may in essence separate the violent person from the remainder of his family, to the extent of expelling him from his residence, depriving him of custody of his victimized children, and forbidding him personal contact with his potential victims. At the same time the violent person may be compelled to continue to support his victims, though he may not live with them or otherwise contact them.

One must of course also remember that the perpetrator of family violence may well commit the crime of assault (or sometimes a more serious offense) against his victims. The remedy against family violence provided by this chapter is a civil remedy. It supplements but does not replace the sanctions against violent conduct contained in the criminal law.

As burdensome as the sanctions which a court may impose under this chapter are, they are not as burdensome to the violator as a sojourn in jail might be.

Compensation for victims of crime. The criminal law defines in detail the types of conduct rendering citizens liable for criminal punishment. It also defines in the greatest detail the punishment which will be levied against the criminal wrongdoer. Under the criminal law the offense for which punishment is levied is an offense against society, and society levies the punishment.

We sometimes forget that most crimes are not only committed against society itself, but also against individual members of society. The criminal law makes little provision for compensation of the individual victim for the wrong he has suffered. To be sure, the person who commits a crime against society also commits a tort against his victim. The law permits the victim to seek compensation through the mechanism of a civil lawsuit against the criminal. All too often, however, the right to sue the criminal for damages is an empty one, because the criminal possesses no assets from which a civil judgment may be collected. Until very recently the citizen damaged by commission of a crime could receive no compensation for his loss if the criminal was not amenable to civil suit.

In order to provide a remedy for this situation, the 1979 session of the Texas legislature enacted the Crime Victim's Compensation Act, CCP 1084. The act went into effect on January 1, 1980. Under it, the state of Texas will pay compensation to those damaged by the commission of crime if the crime causes financial loss to the victim which cannot be made up for in any manner. The program is to be administered by the Texas Industrial Accident Board.

In order for the victim to be eligible for state assistance, he must report the crime which damaged him to the appropriate law enforcement agency within 72 hours of the commission of the offense. The victim must then file an application for benefits with the Industrial Accident Board (IAB) within 180 days after the commission of the crime. The application must contain, among other things:

1. A description of the crime.
2. A complete financial statement, including:
   a. Applicant's assets and liabilities.
   b. Cost of medical care and burial expenses incurred as a result of the crime.
   c. Loss of wages or support incurred, or to be incurred.

9/ Special Court Procedures

    d. The extent to which applicant has been or will be indemnified for these losses from collateral sources (such as insurance).
3. A statement of disabilities incurred from the crime, if any.
4. Authorization to the attorney general of Texas to verify any information contained in the application (CCP 1084-4).

The IAB must review filed applications at once to make certain that they are complete. Incomplete applications will be returned to the applicant with a request for the missing information. A copy of the application is sent to the attorney general's office. The attorney general may, if he desires, investigate the truth of the application and participate in the ensuing administrative proceedings before the IAB. His participation is not mandatory, however. One member of the IAB is assigned to examine and evaluate the application for assistance. This member may grant the application without hearing, or he may decide that a hearing is necessary to determine the merit of the claim. Before the hearing, the board may order that an autopsy be performed upon the body of a deceased crime victim. It may also order that living victims submit to medical and, if necessary, psychiatric examination.

CCP 1084-6(b) provides that compensation shall be awarded if, as a direct result of criminally injurious conduct, the victim suffered physical injury (or death) resulting in a pecuniary loss which the victim (or his dependents) can not recoup from any collateral source or without suffering financial stress.

CCP 1084-6(c) provides that an application shall be denied if:
1. The crime causing the injury was not reported to proper authority within 72 hours, or the application for assistance was not filed within 180 days of the commission of the crime, or
2. The victim or the applicant for assistance participated in the commission of the criminally injurious conduct, or
3. The claimant will not suffer financial stress because of the incident, or
4. The victim resided in the same household as the offender or his or her accomplice.

An award may be reduced or denied if:
1. The victim has not cooperated with law-enforcement agencies, or
2. The victim bears some responsibility for the criminally injurious conduct, even if he did not participate in it, or
3. The pecuniary loss is recouped in part or in full from a collateral source.

The pecuniary losses for which compensation may be payable include:
1. For personal injury:
    a. Medical, hospital, nursing, or psychiatric care and counseling expenses, physical therapy expenses, and
    b. Actual loss of past earnings and anticipated loss of future earnings up to a maximum of $150 per week, and
    c. Funds for care of minor children in order that the victim or his spouse may continue gainful employment, at a rate not to exceed $30 per child per week, or $75 for all minor children per week.
2. As a consequence of death:
    a. Funeral and burial expenses, and
    b. Support of a dependent or dependents for as long as the dependency would have existed had the victim lived, at a rate of no more than $150 per week for all dependents, and
    c. Funds for care of minor children so that surviving spouse may accept gainful

employment, up to $30 per minor child per week or $75 for all minor children per week.

3. No compensation for pain and suffering is payable.

The sources of recoupment of pecuniary loss for which an award may be reduced or denied include:

1. Restitution payable from the offender himself under a court order imposed by a court as a condition of probation, and
2. Social Security, Medicare, and Medicaid, and
3. Worker's Compensation, and
4. Employer wage continuation programs (e.g. sick leave), and
5. Insurance proceeds, and
6. Benefits payable under health insurance policies, etc.

A victim is under financial stress only if he cannot maintain his customary level of health, safety, and education and that of his dependents without undue financial hardship.

No award is payable under this act to victims of criminal conduct by ownership or operation of a motor vehicle, aircraft, or water vehicle, unless the vehicle or aircraft was operated in a manner intended to cause personal injury or death.

In short, auto accident victims normally are not entitled to benefits under this act. Those victims of criminal conduct who are so affluent that the criminal conduct causes them no financial stress are not entitled to compensation, and those victims whose financial stress can be reduced or eliminated by insurance, government aid programs, etc., are also not entitled to compensation. The maximum award may not exceed $50,000 in the aggregate, including payments to the victim and all of his dependents.

A final IAB decision is appealable to the courts, either by the applicant or by the attorney-general on behalf of the state. An appealing party must file notice of his or its dissatisfaction with the IAB within twenty days of the rendition of the decision. Suit must then be filed in the proper Texas district court within twenty days of the filing of the notice of dissatisfaction. A complete new trial of the matter is then held in the district court.

Awards under this act are exempt from claims of creditors of the recipients, except for creditors furnishing products or services the cost of which are included in the award (such as doctors, hospitals, and morticians). When an award is paid, the state of Texas acquires rights by subrogation in all claims the victim might have against collateral sources of compensation for his injury. If the claimant then files suit to collect benefits from such a source, the state must be informed. The state may then join the action. If the action succeeds, the state may recover its award from the proceeds of the payment by the collateral source.

It is far too early to evaluate the operation of this compensation scheme. It appears to be an effort to do for Texans what the legislatures of other states have done for their citizens, to provide assistance for the forgotten man in the criminal process—the victim.

10

Administrative Law and Procedure

In the early days of our nation, all governmental functions were conducted by the three constitutional branches of government at both the federal and state levels. The legislative branch enacted the laws, the executive enforced them, and the judiciary interpreted them and decided the litigation involving them. This changed when Congress enacted the Interstate Commerce Act in 1887, creating the first of the federal independent administrative agencies, the Interstate Commerce Commission (ICC). Shortly thereafter, in 1891, Texas created her first independent administrative agency, the Texas Railroad Commission.

Both of these agencies were created to regulate the railroads. The rationale for creating them was the notion that railroads should be subject to government regulation, but that the regulation should be as nonpolitical as possible. The regulatory bodies were therefore constituted in such a way as to insulate them from the constitutional branches of government.

Texas accomplished this by making the railroad commission an elected body. Thus, it is in a sense a political creature, but it exists outside the framework of the three constitutional branches of government. The members of the Interstate Commerce Commission are appointed by the president for a fixed term, subject to confirmation by the Senate. Once a commissioner assumes office, he cannot be removed except for misconduct.

Administrative agencies have proliferated at both the federal and the Texas levels of government since the turn of the century. At the federal level, there exist many independent agencies which are not a part of the three constitutional branches. There also exist many other agencies which are a part of one of the constitutional branches.

The independent agencies are all organized in a manner similar to the ICC. The members are appointed for fixed terms subject to the advice and consent of the Senate, and are not subject to removal after confirmation except for cause. They generally serve longer terms than does the president, and their terms are staggered so that the president may only appoint one member in a year. Usually the statute creating the agency also requires that the members of the agency be balanced as equally as possible between the political parties.

The agencies are not required to take orders from the president; the only influence he exercises over them (unless one takes into account his moral influence, which is sometimes great) is the power to appoint their members.

The Congress is of course the arm of government which exercises the most control over these agencies. Congress originally created them; it may also abolish them (which it hardly ever does). Congress also appropriates the operating funds of the agencies: it may starve for funds those agencies which have incurred its disapproval, and reward those agencies which meet with its approval.

Some of the important independent federal agencies are the Interstate Commerce Commission, the Federal Trade Commission, the board of governors of the Federal Reserve System, the Securities and Exchange Commission, the National Labor Relations Board, the Federal Communications Commission, the Civil Aeronautics Board, the Federal Maritime Commission, the Environmental Protection Agency, the Nuclear Regulatory Commission, the Consumer Product Safety Commission, and the Equal Employment Opportunity Commission.

Other federal administrative agencies are a part of one of the constitutional branches of government. Most of these are a part of the executive branch, and are under the supervision of a member of the president's cabinet. Among these agencies are the Internal Revenue Service (Treasury), the Customs Service (Treasury), the Secret Service (Treasury), the Federal Bureau of Investigation (Justice), the Immigration and Naturalization Service (Justice), the Social Security Administration (Health, Education, and Welfare), and the Food and Drug Administration (HEW). These agencies are in part under the control of the president, and are obligated to accept direct orders from him. However, the heads of some of them are appointed to a fixed term by law. Some of these have more independence than others.

One rather important agency exists which is a part of the legislative branch: the General Accounting Office (GAO). The GAO supervises the operation of other agencies of the government for the benefit of the Congress. It has the power to investigate the operation of other agencies and to report upon its findings to the Congress and to the public.

At the state level, virtually all administrative agencies are independent. Some are created to be independent by the legislature, others are independent by constitutional provision. Since the major state officials are elected by the voters in this state (rather than appointed by the governor), most of the executive branch of the state government operates independently of gubernatorial influence.

Among the independent agencies of importance in Texas are the Texas Industrial Accident Board, the Texas Employment Commission, the Texas Insurance Board, the Texas Securities Board, the Texas Alcoholic Beverage Commission, the Texas Banking Board, the Texas Department of Corrections, the Texas Consumer Credit Commissioner, the State Department of Highways and Public Transportation, the Texas Department of Mental Health and Mental Retardation, the Texas Department of Public Safety, the Public Utility Commission of Texas, the Railroad Commission of Texas, the Texas Water Quality Board, the Texas Youth Council, and the Texas Air Control Board. There also exist many licensing boards created to supervise the many trades and professions for which licensing of practitioners is required. Examples of these are the State Board of Pharmacy, the Texas State Board of Plumbing Examiners, the Texas Cosmetology Commission, and a host of others.

There are also seventeen separate boards of regents to operate the Texas university system, and the Texas College and University System Coordinating Board to supervise the entire system. Space considerations prevent the listing of many other agencies which are part of the Texas state government.

Powers of administrative agencies. The specific authority of an administrative agency is set forth in the statutory or constitutional provision creating it. The agency may do no more than it has statutory or constitutional authority to do.

The general operation of administrative agencies is also limited by general administrative procedure acts. The federal Administrative Procedure Act, 5 USC 551-559, 701-706, and scattered other sections of 5 USC, was first enacted in 1946. The Texas Administrative Procedure and Texas Register Act (APTRA, RCS 6252-13a) was enacted in 1975, taking effect on January 1, 1976. There are minor differences between the two acts, but their general provisions are very similar. Statutory or constitutional provisions often exempt certain functions of certain agencies from general Administrative Procedure Act requirements. Such exemptions are legitimate, particularly if the statute granting the exemption specifically provides that Administrative Procedure Act provisions are superseded by the exemption in question.

Administrative agencies, though they may be a part of the legislative or executive branch of government, may exercise all three governmental functions: legislative, executive, and judicial. They may legislate by enacting administrative regulations. They may enforce the regulations which they enact. They may bring charges against violators of their regulations, and may adjudicate the resulting cases in their own tribunals. The legitimacy of this power was settled long ago as a matter of expediency: if agencies are to be given the power to regulate areas of human conduct in a way that is to relieve the consitutional branches of government from that particular regulatory burden, the agency must have the authority to do its job. So long as the final results of agency action are subject to judicial review, no harm should be done.

Agency legislation. It may seem peculiar that members of administrative agencies, who for the most part are not elected to anything by anyone, should have the power to enact regulations having the force of law. However, they do have such power.

Of course, this power is circumscribed by constitutional and statutory provisions. Administrative regulations, to be valid, must be within the scope of the rule-making authority granted to the agency by the legislation which created it. They must also be consistent with the regulatory policy of the legislature as set forth in the authorizing statute.

The scope of the power to legislate will vary from agency to agency. For instance, the power of the Internal Revenue Service to legislate is rather limited; its regulations provide for interpretation of complex sections of the Internal Revenue Code. In this area, Congress provides the policy down to minute details, and the agency may by regulation only refine the policy. On the other hand, the Occupational Safety and Health Act simply provides that the Occupational Safety and Health Administration of the Department of Labor shall provide for the safety of all of the nation's workplaces through a system of regulations. The broad matter of how the workplaces are to be made safe is left for the agency to decide.

The federal taxpayer may get some idea of the nature of the tax law he is expected to obey from the Internal Revenue Code. The employer will get no idea at all of the safety standards he is expected to obey by reading the Occupational Safety and Health Act. He must have access to the relevant regulations.

Most administrative agencies at both the federal and Texas levels legislate through the "notice and comment" procedure. The Texas procedure is outlined in APTRA 5, the federal procedure in 5 USC 553. The agency publishes notice of its intention to legislate in the *Federal Register* at the federal level and in the *Texas Register* at the state level. The notice normally contains the text of the proposed rule. Interested parties then have the right to submit comments on the proposed rule to the agency. Usually, the comments are in writing, and no hearing is held on the matter. However, the agency may hold hearings if it desires, and, under the Texas act, interested parties may force a hearing if specified procedures are followed.

The agency is under no obligation to pay any attention to the comments, but normally the comments are of value. They may well point up difficulties in the interpretation or enforcement of the proposed rule. The agency may, after comment, hearing, or both, withdraw the proposed regulation and enact nothing; it may amend the proposed regulation; or it may adopt the proposed regulation without change.

The new regulation, when finally adopted, must be published in the *Federal Register* if it is a federal regulation, or in the *Texas Register* if it is a Texas state regulation. Federal regulations normally become effective thirty days after publication, while Texas regulations become effective twenty days after publication. However, both administrative procedure acts provide that emergency regulations and the like may be made effective immediately upon publication.

Some agencies are required by law to hold formal hearings as a part of their rule-marking. For instance, the federal Food and Drug Administration (FDA) must do this when considering certain types of regulations; its rule-making process may therefore be long, involved, and expensive.

Executive powers of agencies. Administrative procedure acts do not contain provisions relative to agency exercise of executive power. Much agency power here is exercised on a discretionary basis.

The typical agency is given much more authority and responsibility than it can effectively exercise. The ability of the agency to carry out its mission depends upon the amount of manpower it has at its disposal and upon the size of the agency budget. Usually, both funds and manpower are limited. Therefore, the agency must decide how and where it can use its resources to best advantage. Such decisions are of course political rather than legal; courts will not second-guess agency decisions in this area.

Agencies generally possess a different sort of law enforcement authority from that of the police. The police may not take action against a suspected law violator unless proximate cause to suspect him of a violation exists. They may not search the suspect's person or property without cause to arrest, or possession of a proper search warrant. Those agencies which have license-granting authority, and those which have authority to regulate business conduct, generally have the power to require the regulated businesses to maintain certain records, so that they can demonstrate compliance with agency commands. Often the agency requires that the regulated business file periodic reports which show compliance. Often, too, the agency has the authority to inspect these records, which are required to be kept, if it has reason to believe that violation of the law or of applicable regulations is being committed or has been committed.

Some agencies, such as the IRS, have authority to conduct "canvassing" operations, in which enforcement personnel visit businesses which may be subject to tax collection chores (because they have employees, or because they sell goods subject to federal excise taxes) or to tax payments (because, for example, they possess pinball machines or jukeboxes which are subject to federal taxation) just to see if the businesses are in compliance with the Internal Revenue Code. No advance notice of such a visit is necessary, no search warrant is necessary, and no proximate cause for belief that the business is violating the law is necessary. The operation is essentially a "fishing expedition." Generally, such fishing expeditions by other than tax-collection agencies are frowned upon, however.

When an agency discovers a violation of law or regulation by the regulated person or business, it must take the proper steps to bring formal charges against the violator—in the courts, in its own administrative tribunals, or in other ways provided by law. How the agency will proceed is in part a matter of law, but sometimes it is also a matter of discretion. In any event, the operating principle is usually "argue first and act later." The violator cannot be deprived of property without due process of law. Some tribunal must find that he is guilty of violation and impose a sanction upon him.

When the Equal Employment Opportunity Commission charges an employer with unlawful discrimination with respect to employees, it must take court action against the violator. The EEOC has no administrative tribunals to handle such charges. When the National Labor Relations Board decides to charge an employer or a union with an unfair labor practice, on the other hand, the charge is heard by an administrative tribunal of the NLRB.

When the Federal Trade Commission decides to charge a businessman with commission of an unfair trade practice, it may have a choice as to how to handle the matter. It may file an administrative complaint against the accused in its own administrative tribunals, or it may sometimes go to court to seek an injunction against the violator.

Under rare circumstances, agencies are permitted to "act first and argue later." This may be done when the public welfare demands instant action by the agency. Thus, public health officials could shoot a suspected rabid dog without going to court first. The FDA may seize misbranded or adulterated foods, drugs, and cosmetics, wherever and whenever discovered. The Texas Alcoholic Beverages Commission may seize quantities of illegal alcoholic beverages wherever and whenever found.

It should be remembered, also, that agencies conduct a lot of business through simple informal action. The pensioner who applies to the Social Security Administration for social security benefits is usually granted them with no difficulty if he can prove entitlement. The same thing is true of the laid-off employee who applies to the Texas Employment Commission for unemployment compensation. Many sorts of professional licenses are also granted through informal procedures. The would-be life insurance salesman must merely file application forms in good order and pass the examination given by the insurance board, and the license is issued as a matter of course.

Agency adjudication. 5 USC 554–558 contains the provisions of the federal Administrative Procedure Act relative to adjudications. APTRA 13–19 contain the Texas statutory provisions on this matter. We will consider here the matter of adjudication of disputes in administrative tribunals—that is, by tribunals conducted by the agency itself.

Far more often than not, agency adjudication involves a dispute between the agency and an outside party. It may be that the agency accuses the respondent (the "defendant" in such a case) of violating its regulations, and seeks to impose sanctions upon him. Thus, the Federal Trade Commission may seek a cease-and-desist order against a businessman committing an unfair trade practice, or the Texas Board of Medical Examiners may seek to revoke the license to practice medicine of a medical doctor because of unethical conduct.

It may also be that an applicant has applied to the agency for a license or privilege, and the agency has denied the application. The applicant may feel the denial was wrongful and seek adjudication of his claim. Thus, a person applies to the Social Security Administration for benefits, and his application is denied; he applies for a hearing on his claim. Or, a person applies to the Texas Employment Commission for unemployment compensation, and his application is denied; he applies for a hearing upon his claim.

Very rarely, an administrative adjudicatory proceeding may involve two parties, neither of which is the adjudicating agency. The most applicable example of this is the

Worker's Compensation claim filed with the Industrial Accident Board. The dispute being adjudicated is a dispute between an employer or his insurance company and an employee who was injured on the job. The IAB has nothing to do with the dispute until the employee files his claim.

Some dispute adjustment procedures are so informal that it is questionable whether or not they should be called adjudication. For instance, when the IRS audits the income tax return of a taxpayer, the matter involves dealings between the IRS auditor and the taxpayer, without the intervention of any third-party decisionmaker. There does exist an adversary relationship between auditor and taxpayer. If the auditor disallows claimed deductions, he will claim that the taxpayer owes more tax, which makes the relationship more adversary. But if the auditor and the taxpayer agree that a tax deficiency of a certain amount exists, no true adjudication is necessary; the taxpayer must pay. Adjudication of a sort enters the picture only if the taxpayer and auditor agree to disagree and the matter is carried to a higher level within the IRS.

Procedure under the Occupational Safety and Health Act (OSHA) also begins informally. The OSHA inspector inspects the employer's workplace to see if violations of OSHA safety standards exist. If he finds such violations, he will issue a citation to the employer for each one. He may do this on the spot, or at a later time (up to six months after the violation was discovered). The citation may contain a recommended civil penalty against the employer. If the inspector feels that the violation is serious, he must propose a penalty.

The employer who receives such a citation may not argue about it with the inspector. He might have been able to talk the inspector out of issuing the citation before it was issued, but once it is issued, the issuance is final. The employer now has two choices: he may pay the penalty suggested in the citation (and correct the violation), or he may appeal the citation to the Occupational Safety and Health Review Commission. In most cases, the employer pays, so no adjudication occurs. (The Occupational Safety and Health Act establishes a rare system for adjudication of matters arising under it: the OSHRC is a special administrative tribunal set up to hear OSHA adjudications. In these disputes, there is no doubt that an independent tribunal is deciding the case.)

Most administrative judicial-type proceedings are resolved by use of the examiner system. The workings of the system will vary from agency to agency, but it will more often that not operate this way: The initiating party files a complaint with the agency (unless the initiating party is the agency itself) which is similar to a complaint in a civil suit. It explains what the respondent is charged with and states what the initiating party wants by way of remedy. The complaint is served upon the respondent, who must then file an answer within a specified time. There may then be negotiations between initiating party and respondent, seeking to settle the matter without a hearing. Some of the discovery methods used in civil litigation may be available to the parties. Which methods and how they must be used depend upon the agency involved.

If the matter cannot be resolved through negotiation, a hearing is necessary. If a hearing is needed, it will be held before one person; this person is called an administrative law judge in federal procedure, and a hearing examiner in Texas procedure. He will normally be an employee of the agency involved. No jury will be used in the hearing: the examiner is the presiding officer and initial decisionmaker. Since one of the parties to the dispute being adjudicated is normally the agency, and since the examiner is an employee of the agency, the outside party may wonder whether or not his case is being heard by an impartial tribunal.

10/ Administrative Law and Procedure

The administrative tribunal is less obviously impartial than is the judge and jury in a court of law. In court, every effort is made to insure that judge and jury have no institutional relationship with either party to the case (though, of course, if a suit involving the state of Texas is tried in a Texas district court, the presiding judge has an institutional relationship to one of the parties because the state of Texas pays his salary). The normal situation in the administrative hearing is essentially the above situation: the decisionmaker is on the payroll of one of the parties.

In courts as well as in administrative proceedings, the law distinguishes between personal bias and institutional bias. If the decisionmaker has a personal relationship with one of the parties—love, hatred, blood relationship, etc.—personal bias can exist. A decisionmaker may be disqualified for personal bias. If the decisionmaker may be hostile to one of the parties because of a bias that pervades the agency, because of the policy which caused the creation of the agency, or the like, institutional bias exists. Against this the law provides no remedy.

In the law court context, complaints about institutional bias are most often heard from criminal defendants on trial for commission of subversive activities, or from radical defendants on trial for unlawful civil disobedience. The radical engaging in unlawful civil disobedience does this in protest against the wrongdoings of "the establishment." When charges are brought against him, they are brought by an establishment prosecutor, and he is then tried by an establishment judge and jury. Says the radical, "I haven't got a chance in this court; they're all against me. There's no way to get a fair trial in this country." It is in a sense true: no one can truly understand and sympathize with a radical nonconformist except a radical nonconformist. But, on the other hand, the only sorts of persons the radical would accept as unbiased are radicals like himself—and, before such a tribunal as that, society would not get a fair trial. In law courts, the reality is that the more unpopular are the views and conduct of a person, the more likely it is that society will be biased against those views and conduct, and the more difficult it will be to keep that bias out of the courtroom. Ultimately, it comes to this: All courts have an institutional bias in favor of enforcing the law (after all, that is what courts are for). If an individual believes that the law (or a major portion of the law) is evil, he really cannot expect understanding from the courts.

If one can comprehend this concept, one may also understand why courts have not been too disturbed by institutional bias within administrative agencies. With respect to so many administrative agencies, an adversary relationship between regulator and regulated is almost inevitable. One hears charges that the Industrial Accident Board is pro-employee and anti-employer. One hears that the National Labor Relations Board is pro-union and anti-employer. One hears that OSHA is anti-employer. One hears this also about the EEOC. On the other hand, one hears that the Civil Aeronautics Board is pro-airline and anti-passenger, and that the FDA is pro-food processor and drug company and anti-consumer. Some of these charges may be true, and some may not be. Because of the adversary relationship between regulator and regulated, how can such institutional bias be totally avoided? Human beings being imperfect, we have no way of doing so.

The administrative hearing is conducted as a court trial in most respects. All parties are entitled to be present at all sessions of the hearing. They are entitled to be represented by counsel also, but, as in civil litigation, each must hire his own counsel. The agency will not furnish counsel at agency or taxpayer expense. All parties are entitled to cross-examine witnesses. The rules of evidence applicable in the courts generally apply, though court standards on admissibility of hearsay are relaxed to a degree. Since the examiner is thought to be more competent to evaluate evidence than the typical juror, courts are not much disturbed by this.

Whether or not the parties to an administrative proceeding have the power to subpoena witnesses depends upon the agency and the governing law. Most agencies have this power. Problems may exist, however, in the enforcement of these subpoenas. Almost no agencies have power to punish for contempt—and without such power the agency cannot directly enforce its subpoena. It must apply to a court for enforcement, which is cumbersome and time-consuming. This lack of contempt power also reduces to an extent the power of the examiner to control what goes on in his hearing room. However, since most parties to administrative adjudications behave in a civilized manner, there is usually no big problem here.

The examiner hands down an initial decision sometime after the conclusion of the hearing. The decision should be in writing, it should contain findings of facts and law, and it should explain why the examiner decided as he did. The decision must of course be based upon evidence introduced at the hearing.

The remedies which the examiner may award will depend upon the nature of the agency and of the case. No agency may administer criminal punishment. Thus, no agency may imprison or levy fines. Some agencies, though, do have the power to order a respondent to pay money to the agency. Though this power sounds like a power to levy a fine, the payment is generally labeled a civil penalty, so that it can be argued that the agency is really not levying a criminal punishment.

Most agencies have no power to order a respondent to pay money to a third party. The IAB can do this in adjudicating Worker's Compensation claims, however. The National Labor Relations Board (NLRB) can order an employer to rehire persons unlawfully fired for union activity, and to pay these persons back pay, but agencies possessing such powers are few.

The examiner may or course order an agency to pay money to a claimant. Whenever the agency has power to adjudicate claims for benefits filed against itself, the examiner can do this.

Many agencies have the power to hand down cease-and-desist orders against respondents (orders to the respondent to stop doing something that he has been doing). The cease-and-desist order is the administrative equivalent of the court injunction. It is not a very effective weapon, however, because of the agency's lack of contempt power.

The most powerful agency weapon is the power to grant or revoke licenses. Some agencies, in fact most license-granting agencies, may grant licenses without holding hearings. However, no agency may revoke a license without a hearing. The license-granting agency has great control over the economic life of those it regulates. The owner of an FCC broadcasting license, or of an Alcoholic Beverage Commission liquor distribution license, for example, owns a very valuable piece of property. Loss of the license means a considerable financial loss and can mean the death of a profitable business. The holder of a license to practice a profession has in a sense an even more vital piece of property. The holder of an M.D. degree has the ability to earn a substantial sum of money in medical research, for instance; but he may earn much more if he has a license to practice medicine. He needs that license to be able to deal with patients, and it is in dealing with patients that the big money is found in medicine. Loss of his license to practice medicine may severely damage the M.D.'s standard of living.

Administrative appeals. The examiner's initial decision is not likely to be a final one. If either party to it is unhappy with it, that party may appeal to the agency itself. Also, the decision is sent to the agency for cursory review in any case. If the members of the agency themselves wish to subject the case to full review, they may do so on their own motion. It is as if the court of criminal appeals received a copy of all cases involving criminal convictions in Texas, and could call up any case for appellate review, even if the defendant himself did not care to appeal; or as if the Texas Supreme Court reviewed all civil cases decided by the courts of civil appeals, and could call up any case it chose for appellate review even if the parties did not desire it.

If the agency calls up the case, or if the decision is appealed, there may be a new hearing before the agency, or the agency may exercise an appellate-type review of the hearing record. If the agency itself hears more evidence, its eventual decision must be based upon the evidence at the hearing and the evidence before the agency. If the agency hears no more evidence it may change the examiner's decision, but the change must be based upon the evidence in the hearing record. The agency members are forbidden by statute to consult any of the parties to the case, or their attorneys, outside the hearing room. They are, however, permitted to consult their staff members about the case. Because this is permitted, the "institutional decision" exists in administrative proceedings. If the members of the agency are political appointees (as they often are), and if they do not have much technical knowledge of the agency's business, they may not feel competent to decide cases on the basis of their own reactions to the evidence. They may well seek advice from high-ranking civil servants in the agency who are more knowledgeable than they. The decision may well be made, ultimately, by these senior civil servants, persons unknown to the outside party or parties to the case. The agency members sign the decision, of course, and legally they are responsible for it. But no answer may ever be found to the question of who actually decided the case.

Some agencies use other mechanisms for appeal. Some do not provide for automatic review of the examiner's decision by the agency; rather, the agency gets the case only if someone appeals.

With respect to other agencies, the examiner's decision is only a proposed decision. All cases are reviewed by the agency and the agency itself makes the original decision, with no administrative appeal allowed.

Small local agencies may not use the examiner system at all. The initial hearing is before the agency itself, and the agency decision is final.

Judicial review of administrative decisions. Judicial review of agency decisions is normally similar to appellate court review of trial court decisions. There is normally a right to review, but the review is a review on questions of law based upon the record of the proceeding. The court hears no witnesses and does not concern itself with questions of fact.

In one connection, there is review of questions of fact. The factual determinations in the agency decision must be based upon substantial evidence in the record—that is, there must be some persuasive evidence in the record to justify the agency's findings of fact.

How strict the reviewing courts are with respect to questions of law depends upon the nature of these questions. In matters of due process and interpretation of nontechnical statutes and regulations, courts do not hesitate to second-guess the agencies. But with respect to interpretation of technical regulations, the courts defer to the expertise of the agency.

Occasionally a statute is enacted which provides that decisions of a certain agency are final and not subject to judicial review. The courts reserve the right to ignore such statutes, particularly where questions of due process arise with respect to an agency decision. The statutes creating a few Texas agencies provide for trial de novo in court of appealed agency decisions. That is, the court throws out the decision of the agency and hears the evidence all over again, making its own decision.

Primary jurisdiction. When a party makes application to an agency for a benefit and the agency denies it, there is a temptation to take the agency to court in order to force it to do its duty, as the party sees it. This cannot be done if the agency possesses its own machinery for adjudication, or if an administrative tribunal exists in another agency for the consideration of such cases. Thus, the injured worker whose Worker's Compensation claim is denied by his employer's insurer may not sue the employer or the insurer to collect; he must file a claim with the Industrial Accident Board. The applicant for Social Security disability benefits whose claim is denied by office personnel of the Social Security Administration must file for a hearing before the administrative tribunals of the Social Security Administration.

Some kinds of dispute adjudication not involving claims are subject to similar exclusion from the courts. The employer who receives what he thinks is an unjustified OSHA citation must appeal it to the OSHRC, not to the courts. The union which accuses its employer of unfair labor practices must complain to the NLRB, not to the courts. In short, if an agency has primary jurisdiction over a matter, disputes involving that matter must first be heard by the agency, not by the courts.

Exhaustion of administrative remedies. Only final administrative decisions are subject to judicial review. Thus, if a party does not like the decision of a hearing examiner, but the agency permits him to appeal the examiner's decision to the agency itself, the party must take advantage of that right of appeal. He cannot appeal the examiner's decision directly to court.

If there exists a method of obtaining administrative review of an administrative decision, that method must be used. It is only when no further administrative recourse exists that the courts will consent to review the agency decision.

Stare decisis in administrative law. The principle that examiners must follow precedents set in adjudications of cases by their agency is generally followed in administrative law. Since the decisions of examiners are generally reviewed by the agency, this only makes sense. The examiner whose decisions are often reversed by his superiors would not be likely to get favorable consideration at promotion time.

Just as the highest court of a nation or state is not bound to follow its own precedents, the agency is also not bound to follow its precedents. The following of precedent is advisable in order to keep agency policy predictable, but this is a matter of pragmatism, not law.

Res judicata in administrative law. Whether the same matter may be adjudicated twice or more is a question which has arisen on numerous occasions in administrative law. Though courts follow a rigid policy of not litigating a matter twice, even if someone is severely damaged thereby, agencies do not follow this principle quite so strictly.

Generally, relitigation of an administrative matter will be allowed if new evidence is discovered, or if the basic circumstances of the matter in question have changed (if an applicant whose request for disability benefits was denied becomes more disabled, or the like). Relitigation of a matter will not be allowed just because the loser in the proceeding did not like the outcome of it, however.

Administrative rate-making. One of the responsibilities of certain administrative agencies is the determination of the price that the industry regulated by the agency may charge for its service. The Public Utility Commission of Texas is one of the most important of these.

The public utilities subject to Public Utility Commission jurisdiction (which include most of the gas, electric, and telephone companies in the state) may not change the price they charge consumers for their services without approval from the commission. The procedure involved in changing public utility rates is contained in the Texas Public Utility Regulatory Act, RCS 1446c. Rate-making is a legislative matter, but contested rate-making procedures must be handled as adversary procedures, with open hearings, cross-examination of witnesses, and so forth.

Flexibility of administrative procedures. Since administrative agencies exercise all three functions of government, they have great flexibility in accomplishment of their mission. Since law may be made under our governmental system both by legislatures enacting statutes and by judges deciding cases, administrative agencies may make use of both of these methods of lawmaking. They may legislate by enacting regulations, or they may make law by setting precedents in adjudication and then following the precedents in subsequent adjudications.

It is generally simpler for the agency to make law by enacting regulations, since, in most cases, the regulation may be enacted without holding a public hearing. However, it can be argued that lawmaking by adjudication is a more sensitive process, since the law so made develops through responses to concrete problems faced by the parties regulated.

Most agencies do most of their lawmaking by regulation. One agency which chooses to use adjudication instead is the National Labor Relations Board (NLRB). Perhaps the eternal adversary relationship between the clients of the NLRB—labor unions and employers—has caused this. NLRB adjudication involves disputes between two independent parties; most agency adjudication involves disputes between the agency itself and an outside party.

There exists, of course, a fine line between legislation and adjudication. The line does not disturb legislatures and judges, since judges cannot enact statutes and legislatures cannot adjudicate. Since agencies can both legislate and adjudicate, they sometimes try to legislate an answer to an essentially judicial problem.

If a county assessor-collector decides to evaluate taxable real estate within his county at 70 percent of fair market value for taxation purposes rather than at 60 percent, this is a legislative decision; it affects all taxable property in the county in the same way. If, on the other hand, the assessor decides that the fair market value of John Jones's property is $100,000 rather than $80,000, this could become a judicial problem. The public is not entitled to a public hearing on legislative matters, but an individual whose property rights will be affected by a decision involving himself and himself only is entitled to a hearing in order to protect his rights.

PART III

Contracts

11

Introduction to Contracts
Offer and Acceptance

Contracts

Contractual obligations arise when two or more parties make a legal agreement binding themselves to do something or not to do something. By making such an agreement, the parties have in a way enacted a statute containing private law applicable to themselves. If one or more of the parties does not abide by his agreement, the other(s) may seek the aid of the courts in its enforcement.

When the parties enter into a contract in the full knowledge and understanding that they are doing so, it is said that they are entering into an express contract. The vast majority of all contractual obligations are created by express contracts.

It happens on occasion that two parties enter into a contract and one of them is so immature, senile, mentally deficient, or ignorant that he does not know the law surrounding the making of express contracts. The other, knowing of the weakness of his opposite number, gets him to agree to a bargain which is not an enforceable express contract. The strong party then breaches the agreement, because he finds it to his advantage to breach. The weak party threatens suit for damages, only to be told that he has no case because the bargain he made was not legally enforceable.

It may be that a sympathetic court would permit the weak party to recover damages here by implying that a valid contract existed, even though in fact it did not. The existence of a valid contract would not be implied, however, when both parties to the bargain involved are reasonably competent, well-educated adults. Thus, if Uncle orally tells Niece, age sixteen, that if she will care for him until she becomes twenty-one he will give her $5,000, an unenforceable contract is created. Since this contract requires more than a year to perform, it must be in writing. Niece does not know this, so she cares for Uncle until she turns twenty-one. Uncle then refuses to pay off because the bargain was not put into writing. A sympathetic court may well imply the existence of a written contract and order the uncle to pay here, in order to stop him from taking advantage of the niece's immaturity.

It also happens sometimes that one person performs some personal services for another under circumstances in which the recipient is in no position to request the services, although the services performed confer great benefit upon him. The provider bills the recipient, but the recipient refuses to pay because he had no contract with the provider. If the provider provided the service with the expectation of being paid, and if the recipient will be unjustly enriched if he is not made to pay, a court will order him to pay as if there had been a contract. This is quasi-contractual liability.

The classic example is this: Skinch is involved in an auto accident at a street intersection. He is knocked unconscious, and his car is totally disabled. Dr. Goodman sees the accident, renders first aid to Skinch, calls an ambulance, rides with Skinch in the ambulance to the hospital, and in general sees Skinch through this bad period. Meanwhile the police summon a tow truck, which hauls Skinch's disabled auto away to Fixit Garage. In due course Skinch is on his feet again. He finds awaiting him in his mail two bills, one from Dr. Goodman, and one from Fixit Garage. Goodman has billed for the services he provided while Skinch was unconscious—the garage bill is a towing bill. Skinch claims he does not have to pay either one, since he has made no enforceable contract with either party.

In a way he is right. Nevertheless, he must pay the bills unless he can convince a court that they are unreasonably high. Goodman may well have saved Skinch's life, and Fixit has preserved the existence of his car. Both have good quasi-contractual claims here.

If Goodman had made a medical error in his first-aid treatment of Skinch, so that Skinch's condition was made worse by the aid, Skinch might have a claim against Goodman for medical malpractice. Whether he would have such a claim depends upon other factors, but there would possibly be enough of a doctor-patient relationship here to justify such a claim if Goodman's mistake was serious enough.

If, on the other hand, first aid had been rendered to Skinch at the accident site by Jager—a boy scout with a first-aid merit badge—and Jager had billed Skinch for his services, Skinch would not have to pay. One could assume that Jager was merely acting as a boy scout should in such a situation, with no expectation of pay. If Jager's first aid harmed rather than helped Skinch, Skinch would have no claim against Jager. The Texas "Good Samaritan Statute," RCS 1a, immunizes him from liability. Under that statute, anyone rendering first aid at the scene of an accident (other than a medical professional) cannot be held liable for any harm done the victim by his ministrations, so long as he acted in good faith.

Quasi-contractual liability may arise in two other ways. One is illustrated by this example: Habitant comes home from work to observe Sauber mowing his lawn. Habitant asks his next-door neighbor Hilf what Sauber is doing. He, Habitant, had never asked Sauber to mow the lawn. Hilf says that Sauber told him that Habitant's lawn looked awful, so he was going to mow it and he wanted to be paid $5 for his work. Habitant had paid other people $5 to mow his lawn in the past. Habitant tells Hilf that Sauber can mow the lawn if he wants, but he, Habitant, will not pay a dime for it. Habitant then enters his house, totally ignoring Sauber. When Sauber finishes, he demands $5 of Habitant. Habitant refuses to pay. Sauber threatens to sue; he has a good claim.

Habitant knew he was doing the work here and expecting to be paid for it. Habitant let him continue. Thus Habitant unjustly enriched himself at Sauber's expense. Had Habitant told Sauber he would not pay right after his conversation with Hilf, of course, he would have escaped liability. Also, had Habitant not returned until Sauber had finished the work, Sauber would have had no claim. Had Sauber asked Habitant if he wanted the lawn mowed for $5 before Sauber started work; had Habitant told him not to start, but had Sauber done the job anyway, Sauber would have no claim.

The other quasi-contract situation is illustrated by this example: Bonhomme owes Grinch $1,000, and cannot afford to pay it now, though the debt is overdue. Freund tells Bonhomme he will pay the debt, and Bonhomme can pay him when he gets the money later. Bonhomme does not tell Freund to do this—but he does not tell him *not* to do it either. He simply says, "If you want to do that, that's really nice of you." Freund pays. A year later Bonhomme is prosperous, but he refuses to repay Freund. Freund threatens to sue. He may well win, since Bonhomme knew Freund meant to be repaid when he paid Grinch—and Bonhomme really did not try to stop Freund's good deed.

Of course, had Bonhomme told Freund, "I appreciate your help, but it's my debt and I'll take care of it when I can. You stay out of it!" Freund would have no claim. And, had Freund paid Grinch without saying anything to Bonhomme about it in advance, Freund would have no claim against Bonhomme. (However, had Freund bought Grinch's claim against Bonhomme for $1,000, that would be another situation entirely. If Freund pays off simply to discharge Bonhomme's debt, he is making a gift to Bonhomme. If he buys Grinch's claim, he is buying an account receivable with the intent to collect it himself.)

In all quasi-contract situations, the provider of the service or the like is entitled to be paid fair value for what he did. He is not automatically entitled to collect the amount of his bill: if the bill is unreasonable, he must be satisfied with less.

Offer and Acceptance

There can be no binding contract unless the parties involved have agreed to enter into a contract. The contract comes into being when a valid offer is made by the offeror and is accepted by the offeree.

Nature of an offer. An offer may take the form of either an act or a promise. The offer in the form of an act is rare. An example: Able Grocery orders a dozen cases of Spade Canned Peas from Baker Grocery Wholesalers. Baker has no Spade peas in stock, so it ships a dozen cases of Clubb Canned Peas to Able and writes him, "We regret that we have no Spade Canned Peas in stock. We are therefore shipping you a dozen cases of Clubb Canned Peas as an accommodation. The price is $11.11 per case. Please remit at once if you wish to accept. Otherwise, please return the Clubb peas to us at our expense." The offer here is Baker's act of shipping the Clubb peas. Able may accept them and pay for them, or he may reject them and send them back.

The offer in the form of a promise is far more common. A statement is not an offer, though, unless it is clearly a promise to buy or sell. The following conversation is an example:

Ace: Do you want to sell your bloodhound?
Deuce: Maybe. How much is he worth to you?
Ace: Trey sold one like him for $75. Your mutt's worth that.
Deuce: I guess so. If Trey's mutt's worth $75, mine's worth $100.
Ace: You're awfully sure of that.
Deuce: Well, I don't have to sell him if I don't want to.
Ace: What would you think of taking $90 for him?
Deuce: That's not enough.
Ace: Well, your dog's a good dog. If I have to pay $100 to get him, I'll have to pay it.
Deuce: You don't have to pay anything. He's not for sale.

Result: No contract, because Deuce never said, "I'll sell."

The sorts of statements that leave no doubt in the mind of the hearer as to their nature as offers are statements such as the following:
1. "I'll sell you my dog for $50."
2. "I'll mow your lawn tomorrow morning for $10."
3. "I'll buy your record player for $50."
4. "I'll pay $50 to whoever returns my lost ring to me."

The following sorts of published statements are not considered by the law to be offers:
1. Price tags upon merchandise.
2. Advertisements quoting prices for goods.
3. Goods advertised for sale in catalogs.
4. Goods put up for sale at auctions.
5. Invitations for bids published by government agencies.

Responders to the above essentially make offers to the merchant, advertiser, or government agency. The offeree then decides which offers, if any, to accept.

The following sorts of responses to the above are considered to be offers:
1. The store customer pointing to an item on the shelf and saying, "I'll take that, please."
2. The customer ordering goods out of the catalog.
3. The bidder at the auction.
4. The person submitting a written bid to a government agency in response to an invitation to bid.

Although advertisements are generally not offers, there is one exception to this rule: the ad offering a reward for performance of an act. Reward ads are considered to be offers of unilateral contracts. The offer is accepted when a person who knows of the offer performs the desired act.

A statement definite enough to be an offer will not be construed as one if it is obvious that the offeror does not mean what he is saying. For instance:
1. An intoxicated person offers to give his twenty-one-jewel watch to whoever will buy him another fifth of bourbon.
2. Able laughingly offers to buy Baker's twenty-one-jewel watch for $20. It is obvious from his manner that he is joking.
3. Charles, watching his house burn down, shouts that he will pay $5,000 to the person who rescues his cat from the flames, Charles being a factory worker.

When offer becomes effective. An offer becomes effective when it is communicated to the offeree. When the parties are talking face-to-face or over the telephone, there is no communication problem—the offer is communicated as soon as it is uttered. Under other circumstances the offer would not be effective until communicated to the offeree at the direction of the offeror. Thus, the offer may be validly transmitted by:
1. Offeror mails a letter to Offeree containing the offer, which Offeree receives.
2. Offeror tells Agent to tell Offeree of the offer, which Agent does.
3. Offeree reads the ad in the newspaper by which Offeror offers to pay $50 to the person returning his lost dog.

If offeree learns of the offer in an unauthorized manner, the offer is not effective. Thus, the offer would not be effective if:
1. Friend knows Offeror is going to make an offer to Offeree, and tells Offeree about it, Offeror not having told him to do this.
2. Offeror has written a letter to Offeree containing the offer, but has not mailed it.

Offeree sees the letter lying on Offeror's desk and reads it. Offeror changes his mind about making the offer and tears up the letter.

3. Offeree overhears a conversation between Offeror and Buddy in which Offeror describes the offer he is going to make Offeree—but Offeror decides not to make the offer after all.

TERMINATION OF OFFERS

When a valid offer has been validly communicated to the offeree, the offeree may accept it at any time before it is terminated. Once an offer has been terminated, it may no longer be accepted. An offer may be terminated in one of four ways:
1. Revocation by offeror.
2. Rejection by offeree.
3. Expiration of time.
4. Termination by operation of law.

A discussion of these follows.

Revocation. Most offers may be revoked by the offeror any time before acceptance. There are, however, two types of offers which are at least somewhat irrevocable.

An option is an offer which the offeror has agreed not to revoke for a specified time. The offeree has given consideration for the promise of the offeror not to revoke. In essence, an option is a contract in and of itself. The offeror may not revoke his offer, then, without breaching his contract.

A firm offer is a type of irrevocable offer created by Section 2-205 of the UCC. When a merchant of goods makes a written offer to an offeree and promises to keep the offer open for a specified time, the offer is irrevocable for the duration of that time, unless the offer is for a period of more than three months, the maximum duration of a UCC firm offer. The offer becomes revocable after that time. Remember, however, that only a merchant may make a UCC firm offer, and that the offer must be in writing. An oral firm offer may be revoked any time before acceptance, as may any sort of firm offer made by a nonmerchant.

Other offers may be revoked by the offeror at any time before acceptance. The revocation must be communicated to the offeree to be effective. If the revocation is made in a face-to-face conversation or in a telephone conversation, it is effective when uttered. If it is communicated by mail, telegraph, or messenger, it is effective only when received by the offeree. If offeror asks a third party to tell offeree of the revocation, it is effective when the third party delivers the message.

A revocation also becomes effective when offeree learns something which would indicate to a reasonable person that the offer has been revoked. For example: Offeror has offered to sell his one-and-only record player to Offeree. Before Offeree has accepted the offer, he visits Friend—and Friend shows him the record player he has just bought from Offeror. Offeree recognizes it as the one Offeror has offered to sell him. Offeree now knows that Offeror's offer is revoked. Offeror obviously does not have the record player to sell any more.

An offer of a reward must be revoked in the same way in which it was made. Thus, if the offer took the form of a quarter-page newspaper ad, the revocation must also take that form. When a reward offer is validly revoked, it is revoked as to the whole world—even as to those who know of the offer but do not know of the revocation.

Rejection. An offer is rejected when offeree makes a statement that he will not accept, or when offeree makes a counteroffer. The statement of rejection must be so definite that it leaves no doubt as to his intention. "I don't think I want it" would be too indefinite to be a rejection; "I don't want it" leaves no room for doubt. A statement is not a counteroffer unless it would be definite enough to be an offer standing alone. It is quite possible for an offeree to try to get an offeror to modify his offer without rejecting it, as in the following example:

Able: I'll sell you my watch for $100.
Baker: That's a lot of money for that watch. Wouldn't you take $85?
Able: No way would I sell for $85.
Baker: Would you take $90?
Able: No, my price is $100.
Baker: OK, I'll take it.
Able: I don't think you really want it. Forget it.

This conversation results in the making of a contract. Baker's dickering never took the form of making a definite counteroffer. And Able never revoked his offer. On the other hand, consider the following conversation:

Able: I'll sell you my watch for $100.
Baker: That's too much for that watch. I'll buy it for $90, though.
Able: It's worth more than $90. I won't sell for that price.
Baker: I'll buy it for $95.
Able: No way.
Baker: OK, I'll give you $100 for it.
Able: No thanks. I don't want to sell after all.

Here there is no contract. Baker's series of counteroffers rejected Able's original offer. By the time Baker decided that he would take the watch for $100, Able's offer was no longer open. Baker thus offered to buy for $100, and Able rejected the offer.

Lapse of time. If the offer contains a time limit upon acceptance, it means what it says; it automatically terminates when the time limit expires. It is wise to include a time limit for acceptance in an offer. That way everyone knows for certain the duration of the lifetime of the offer.

If the offer contains no such time limit, it is open for a reasonable time. The duration of a reasonable time is often open to question. In case of a difference of opinion between offeror and offeree about this, litigation might result. The length of a reasonable time will depend upon the nature of the subject matter of the offer. The most long-lived of offers are offers of rewards. A reasonable time to accept these might be measured in years. The most short-lived of offers are those involving securities traded on stock exchanges, or commodities traded on commodity exchanges. The prices of these things may change so rapidly that a reasonable time to accept an offer may be measured in hours. With respect to offers involving other types of subject matter, definition of a reasonable time depends upon the demand for the subject matter, and upon the volatility of its price.

The sooner the offeree seeks to accept one of these offers without time limits, the more likely it is that he is accepting within a reasonable time. The longer he waits, the more likely it is that the offeror will claim that the acceptance is too late. If the offeror thinks the acceptance is too late, he must notify the offeree at once that he will not perform. It is then up to the offeree to sue for breach if he wants to argue. The offeror's defense will be that a reasonable time had passed before acceptance. Probably, a jury would then have to decide the matter.

Termination of offers by operation of law. Several sorts of occurrences may cause the automatic termination of an offer. The death of either the offeror or the offeree will cause such termination: the right to accept an ordinary offer is not transferable. The unaccepted offer of a deceased person cannot be converted into a contract binding upon his estate. Loss of contractual capacity by either offeror or offeree will terminate an offer. Such loss of capacity is usually evidenced by the appointment by a court of a guardian for the afflicted person. Since a person with an appointed guardian may not make contracts, he may do nothing which could create a contractual obligation.

An option will not be terminated by the above circumstances, however.

A change in the law which makes a potential contract illegal will terminate an offer, since courts will not enforce an illegal contract. The same principle applies to an option. A change in circumstances which renders performance of a potential contract impossible will also terminate an offer or option. Thus, when offeror offers to sell his car to offeree, and, before offeree accepts the offer offeror wrecks the car, the offer is terminated. It is now impossible for offeror to sell the car in good running order.

THE ACCEPTANCE

An acceptance may take the form of either an act or a promise. More often than not, acceptance in the form of a promise is required. However, there are circumstances under which a valid acceptance must take the form of an act.

The most common sort of offer which must be accepted by act is the offer of a reward. The offeror is not bound to a contract with any offeree until the offeree performs the act for which the reward is offered. A promise to perform that act is not of course an adequate acceptance.

Another sort of offer which must be accepted by performance of an act is the offer of this type: "I'll pay you $5 at 4 P.M. Saturday if you mow my lawn before that time." Here, the offeror does not seek the promise of the offeree to mow the lawn on Saturday; he seeks instead the actual mowing of the lawn. The acceptance must be the actual act of mowing the lawn before 4 P.M. Saturday.

Some sorts of offers may be accepted either by the performance of an act or by the making of a promise. A very common offer of this sort is the letter reading, "Please ship me 100 #6 widgets as soon as possible." The literal interpretation of such an offer of course is that acceptance of it must take the form of the shipment of 100 #6 widgets as soon as possible. However, if a promise by the offeree to ship the widgets as soon as possible is a commercially reasonable response to such an offer, the promise to ship would also be a valid acceptance. UCC 2-206 codifies this notion with respect to contracts for sale of goods.

For performance of an act to constitute a valid acceptance of an offer, the act must be the exact act called for in the offer. If Able offers a $50 reward for return of his lost dog, Baker's act of delivering to Able a stray dog other than Able's lost dog will not be a valid acceptance.

However, when an offeree responds to an order for immediate shipment of goods by shipping nonconforming goods (goods differing from those specified in the offer), UCC 2-206(1)(b) provides that the shipment is an acceptance of the offer and at the same time a breach of the resulting contract. The only way the offeree may avoid this result is to inform the offeror that the shipment is not an acceptance of an offer but merely an accommodation. In such a case the shipment constitutes a counteroffer only.

Content of the acceptance by promise. When the subject matter of the offer to be accepted is services, real estate, securities, intangible property, or anything else other than goods, the effectiveness of the acceptance is judged by the "mirror image" rule. The terms of the acceptance must be identical with the terms of the offer. If the acceptance is not an acceptance of all of the terms of the offer, it is not an acceptance at all and will be treated as a counteroffer. As a result, when offer and acceptance are not in total agreement as to terms, there is no contract, even if the parties truly believe that they do have a contract.

When the subject matter of the deal is goods, Article 2 of the UCC is applicable; and UCC 2-207 has abrogated the mirror-image rule in contracts for the sale of goods. Here, if the parties show by their behavior that they believe they have a contract, they do have a contract. Of course, if offer and acceptance are not identical with respect to the terms of the contract, there is a question as to what these terms are. The UCC provides rules for resolution of this problem, which will be considered in detail in the chapters on contracts for the sale of goods.

Communication of the acceptance. An acceptance must be validly communicated to the offeror before a contract is formed. If the offer specifies the manner in which acceptance is to be made, the offer means what it says. Thus, if the offer says, "If you wish to accept, your written acceptance must be received by me on or before 12 noon on Friday, May 18," an acceptance must be in writing and it must be received by the offeror on or before noon on Friday, May 18.

If the offer specifies a medium of communication for submitting an acceptance, that medium must be used. An acceptance transmitted by any other medium will not be valid. If the offer is the offer of a unilateral contract, such as a reward offer, it may be accepted only by performance of the required act. A promise to perform the required act will not be acceptance. If the offer does not specify that the acceptance must be received to be valid, acceptance may be valid when sent. If the offer does not specify that a certain medium be used for communication of the acceptance, any reasonable medium may be used.

If the offer does not state otherwise, then, an acceptance is good when sent if a reasonable medium of communication is used. Generally, the use of the same medium for communication of an acceptance as was used for communication of the offer is reasonable. If the offer was sent by mail, the acceptance may be sent by mail. The use of a faster medium for communication of acceptance than was used for communicating the offer is also reasonable. If the offer was sent by mail, acceptance by telegraph would be acceptable. On the other hand, the use of a slower medium for communication of the acceptance would not be acceptable. If the offer is sent by wire and an acceptance is sent by mail, this would not be valid until received. If the medium used to communicate is absurdly slow, the acceptance will not be valid even if received.

If the acceptance is improperly dispatched so that it is slowed down in transit, for example, it would not be good until received. Thus, when the acceptance is sent by mail with insufficient postage or no postage at all, it would not be delivered by the post office. This acceptance will never be valid. When a mailed acceptance is sent to the wrong address, it would not be valid if not received. The same is true when a wired acceptance is sent collect, or sent to a wrong address—unless a collect reply is authorized in the offer.

Notice of exercise of an option—the acceptance of the offer contained in the option—must be received before the option expires.

Crossing of acceptance and revocation. Since a revocation is not valid until received, while a reasonable acceptance is good when sent, when a good revocation and a good acceptance cross in the mail a good contract results.

When, however, the acceptance must be received to be valid, the existence of the contract will depend upon which is received first.

Revocability of rejections and acceptances. Sometimes offeree rejects the offer, then changes his mind and seeks to accept. Or he accepts, then changes his mind and seeks to reject. Essentially, a rejection can be countermanded, if done in time. An acceptance cannot be countermanded very easily. When offeree dispatches an acceptance which is valid when sent, he is committed to a contract; he cannot countermand such an acceptance.

When offeree dispatches a rejection, this will not terminate the offer until it is received by the offeror. Thus, the rejection can be countermanded *if* the offeree can get an acceptance to the offeror before the rejection arrives. *Note* that the acceptance sent after dispatch of a revocation must be *received* before the rejection is received to be valid. The same rule applies when an acceptance is dispatched that is not valid until received. This can be countermanded if the offeree gets a rejection to the offeror before the acceptance arrives.

Silence as acceptance. Normally, silence by the offeree will not be construed as acceptance of an offer. For example: Able writes Baker, "I offer to sell you my watch for $100. If I don't hear from you within ten days I'll assume you've accepted." Baker receives the letter but does not reply to it. There is no contract.

Silence will be construed as acceptance when certain unusual circumstances prevail. Most common is when a buyer and seller agree to do business on a "silence is acceptance" basis, as in book and record club memberships. Standard procedure here is that the club mails an offer to its members to sell the book or record of the month. If the member does not want the book he must send notice to the club that he does not want it. His silence is acceptance of the club offer.

Silence will also be construed as acceptance when parties have dealt with each other for a long period on a "silence is acceptance" basis. This usually occurs when a farmer, trapper, fisherman, or the like sends his product to a buyer and the buyer pays for it over a period of years. Then, one year, the seller sends the product and the buyer sends it back, refusing to pay for it because he does not want it. This may well be a breach of contract on the buyer's part. He should have told the seller in advance that he was not going to buy this year.

Auctions. At an auction the auctioneer invites offers when he puts an item up for bids. The bids are offers. The auctioneer accepts the high bid by letting the hammer fall and stating, "Sold!" Since bids are offers, it follows that a bid may be withdrawn anytime before the hammer falls. Since no offeree is normally required to accept an offer, it follows that the auctioneer normally does not have to accept the high bid. The normal auction, then, is "with reserve," and the goods need not be sold to the high bidder. If the auction is advertised as being "without reserve," the auctioneer *must* accept the high bid; the goods must be sold. But auctions are not without reserve unless advertised to be so.

UCC 2-328 also provides some rules for auctions involving sales of goods. At such an auction, normally, the seller may not bid, either by himself or through an agent, unless he announces in advance his intent to bid. Should the seller bid in violation of this understanding, the high bidder has two options. He may either refuse to buy the goods, or he may buy for the last good-faith bid, the last bid made before the seller or his agent intervened in the bidding.

Should the auction be a forced sale—a sale by a foreclosing lienholder, sheriff, or tax-collecting agency—the above rule does not apply. Anyone is permitted to bid at such a sale.

Occasionally, auctions are held by sealed bid rather than by open bid. In such auctions, the announcement of the auction specifies the goods to be sold and the deadline for submitting bids. The bids are of course submitted in writing; any bid received after the deadline for submission will not be opened. The sealed bids are offers. The party conducting the sale opens the bids at a specified time and announces which bid he chooses to accept. Acceptance takes place when the announcement of acceptance is made. Sealed-bid auctions may be with reserve or without reserve. If the announcement of the auction specifies that the goods will be sold to the high bidder, the acceptance, if any, must be of the high bid. If the announcement does not specify that the goods will be sold to the high bidder, the offeree—the party conducting the auction—may accept any bid he chooses.

Construction contract bids. When a property owner invites general contractors to submit bids on a construction contract, the resulting process is in a sense a sealed-bid auction. The bids submitted by the contractors are offers. The bids must be submitted before the deadline for bid submission. The owner then opens the bids and chooses which, if any, to accept.

If the owner is a private individual or corporation, he is under no obligation to accept the low bid. He will take into account in evaluating a bid not only the amount of the bid but also the reputation and financial standing of the contractor submitting the bid. The offeree may accept any submitted bid, or he may accept none.

If the owner is a government or government agency, it may be required by law to accept the low bid. Bids submitted to a government may be irrevocable for a period of time after submission, if this is required by statute or administrative regulation. Bids submitted to a private owner are generally revocable any time prior to acceptance.

When a general contractor receives an invitation to make a bid on a large construction contract, he often will not submit a bid before he invites subcontractors to make bids to him on specialized portions of the work which must be farmed out to specialists. The general contractor is of course not obligated to accept any subcontractor bid unless he is awarded the construction contract.

The general contractor will use the prices bid by subcontractors for their specialized work in computation of his bid. Since this is so, the general contractor may well specify in his invitations to bids sent to subcontractors that subcontractor bids will be irrevocable after a specified date, perhaps the date the general contractor submits his bid.

The general contractor may use his discretion in deciding which subcontractor bids to accept. He is not bound to accept the low bid.

Contracts of adhesion. When parties of disproportionate bargaining power enter into a contract, the strong party far more often than not gives the weak party a prepared contract form and asks him to sign. An offer and acceptance are exchanged, but the weak party may well not know all of the terms of the bargain that he has made. However, the law normally presumes that the weak party has read and understood his contract before he signs. He is thus expected to know the nature of the bargain that he has made.

Once a party has signed such a contract, he will be normally stuck with his bargain even if it contains some harsh terms.

If the contract is one between a merchant and a consumer for sale of goods or services, and the merchant uses his superior bargaining power to force an unconsionable contract upon the consumer, the consumer may well be able to escape. This matter of unconscionability will be discussed in the next chapter.

If the contract is one of bailment, where the consumer has no time to read the small print on the back of his claim check, he may well be able to escape from provisions buried in the small print on the back of the claim check by which the bailee seeks to escape liability for his own negligence in the care of his customer's goods. However, the general rule is that when one signs a contract of adhesion, he is bound to the whole package of provisions it contains. Ignorance of the contents of such contracts is no excuse for not living up to these provisions.

Unsolicited merchandise. RCS 29c-1 provides that, when a person receives unsolicited merchandise by mail or otherwise, he may treat it as a gift. Thus, the recipient has no obligation to pay for such merchandise, nor does he have any obligation to return it. On the other hand, if the merchandise is received in response to an order but is nonconforming, it is not really unsolicited, so the recipient may not treat it as a gift.

Thus, if Gluck receives in the mail a box of Shino cigars, along with a letter reading, "We want to introduce you to the pleasure of smoking Shino cigars. You may keep this introductory package by remitting to us the sum of three dollars," Gluck is under no obligation to send the three dollars. He is also under no obligation to return the cigars. He may acquaint himself with the pleasures of smoking Shino cigars, with no necessity for a cash outlay on his part.

On the other hand, suppose Scharf orders a pair of size 36 green wash slacks by mail from Gritz Company. Gritz sends him a pair of size 44 green wash slacks. Scharf has the slacks altered so that they fit him. When Gritz sends the bill, though, Scharf refuses to pay because he never ordered size 44 slacks. He says that they were unsolicited, and so were a gift. Scharf is wrong: he could have rejected the size 44 slacks and returned them for an adjustment, but he cannot just keep them and not pay for them. After all, they were sent, even if by mistake, in response to his order.

12

Mutual Assent

Consideration

Mutual Assent

A contract does not become binding upon a person unless he entered into it of his own free will, without excessive pressure or deception being applied to him, and without undue advantage being taken of his lack of bargaining power. A party who has been taken advantage of in these ways may rescind his contract and escape being bound by it.

A party may rescind, then, if he can show that he is a victim of one or more of the following: fraud, misrepresentation, violation of fiduciary relationship, undue influence, duress, mutual mistake, or unconscionability.

Fraud. Generally speaking, a person may rescind a contract on grounds of fraud if he has been a victim of the tort of fraud or deceit. Before one may rescind due to fraud, one must be able to prove the following:
1. A deliberate misstatement of a material fact by the other party.
2. Justifiable reliance upon the truth of the statement by the victim, and
3. Damage caused to the victim by this reliance.

There can be no fraud without deliberate intent to deceive by the perpetrator. The deception may consist of the telling of a deliberate lie, or it may consist of a deliberate decision by the perpetrator not to tell the whole truth. If, in order to induce Baker to buy 100 shares of Zilch Corporation common stock, Able does any of the following things, he commits fraud:
1. Able tells Baker that Zilch had earnings of $7 per share last year. The earnings were actually $2 per share, and Able knows this.
2. Able knows that Quatch Company is suing Zilch for hefty damages for patent infringement. He also knows that if Quatch wins, the prospects of Zilch will be considerably dimmed. Able believes that Baker knows nothing about this, so he does not mention it in his sales pitch.
3. Able says that Zilch will get a $7 million government contract next year. Actually, Zilch has merely made a bid to get this contract, but at this point no one knows to whom the government will award it. Able knows this well, but feels that Baker does not know it.

4. Able gets Baker to agree to deliver his payment on Wednesday. Able agrees to deliver the stock certificate on Friday. But Able intends to collect Baker's money on Wednesday, skip town on Thursday, and deliver no stock on Friday.

Baker will not be able to rescind his stock purchase contract with Able unless he can show that he justifiably relied upon the truth of Able's fraudulent statements. If Zilch Corporation is a public corporation, Baker will have trouble proving reliance in some of the above situations.

1. The earnings of Zilch will be a matter of public record. Baker could check out the true earnings for himself and discover Able's lie.
2. The patent infringement suit of *Quatch vs. Zilch* would certainly be a newsworthy item. Information about it could be found in financial publications and perhaps in the financial statements of the corporations involved. Baker could learn about this if he keeps up with Wall Street news.
3. Baker could probably verify the making of the bid by Zilch; he should also know that no one knows who will get the contract.
4. Baker can show reliance here quite easily. Why should he disbelieve Able's promise to deliver the stock on Friday?

But if Zilch is not a publicly held company, its financial affairs will be confidential. Baker would have trouble verifying all of these statements by Able about Zilch's affairs. He could quite likely justifiably rely upon the truth of all of these in that case.

Baker's last hurdle in his fraud case is the necessity to prove that his justifiable reliance upon the truth of Able's false statements caused him to suffer damage. In the first three situations his damage claim will depend upon whether the market price of Zilch is lower now than it was when he bought it (if Zilch is publicly traded) or if the intrinsic value of the Zilch stock has declined since he bought it. In the fourth situation, of course, his damage is obvious: he did not get the stock which he paid for.

Remember that fraud is a tort as well as a ground for rescission of a contract. One must make a tort claim in order to collect damages for fraud; the making of a tort claim alone will not justify rescission of the contract.

Misrepresentation. A person who is induced to make a contract due to a false material statement made unknowingly by the other party may rescind, if he justifiably relied upon the truth of the statement to his detriment. To prove misrepresentation does not require proof of intent to deceive. Misrepresentation may well be totally innocent. The misrepresenter may be guilty of no more than negligence, or overenthusiasm.

In contracts for the sale of goods, any verifiable statement of material fact made with respect to the goods is an express warranty. If the statement is false, there exists a breach of express warranty, which provides grounds for rescission. This concept of express warranty is not found in the law of land sales, for example. But in all types of contract negotiations it should be remembered that negotiators are responsible for the accuracy of their statements of verifiable fact with respect to the contract subject matter.

The only exception to this general rule is the notion that a few exaggerated, glittering generalities by way of sales talk—a little "puffing"—are permissible. The used car salesman's boast, "This is the best deal in town," is almost certainly not literally true; but the customer knows that in his heart and should not be so gullible as to take it at face value.

Violation of a fiduciary relationship. Most of the rules of legal ethics exist to define the nature of the fiduciary relationship between an attorney and his client. They are intended to discourage the attorney from using his superior knowledge to take undue advantage of his client.

The attorney-client relationship is not the only fiduciary relationship recognized by law. Among other such relationships are the following:
1. Principal—agent.
2. Trustee—beneficiary.
3. Guardian—ward.
4. Broker—client.
5. Partner—partner.
6. Corporate director or officer—corporation.
7. Corporate promoter—corporation.
8. Corporate director—corporate shareholder.

Most of these relationships are in a sense unequal relationships, because one of the parties has specialized skill or knowledge which the other does not have. A trustee is appointed to manage investments for the beneficiary because of his expertise in management of investments; a judge appoints a guardian for a ward because he has confidence in the ability of the guardian to care for a person who cannot care for himself; and a principal appoints an agent because he trusts the agent to do whatever it is that he, the principal, wants done. Other types of fiduciary relationships are relationships between equals—persons who voluntarily decide to establish a very intimate business relationship among themselves. Most typical here is the relationship between partners in a partnership.

Because of the intimate nature of the fiduciary relationship, persons having such a relationship to each other do not deal with each other at arm's length. In their contractual relationships, all cards must be laid upon the table. All material facts must be disclosed. Neither party may do anything which would even suggest an intent to profit at the expense of the other party. Conflicts of interest must be strictly avoided. Nondisclosure of a material fact is grounds for avoidance of a contract between parties in a fiduciary relationship, as is any unfairness in the contract. The injured party need not concern himself with justifiable reliance on the truth of an untrue statement, or with detriment. The mere fact of the violation of the relationship is enough to justify termination of the contract.

Undue influence. Whenever a contract is made between persons who have an intimate personal relationship which does not qualify as a fiduciary relationship, the possibility of the use of undue influence is present. In many of these relationships, one of the parties is a very dependent person who needs the relationship for some compelling reason, while the other is independent and can survive very well without the relationship.

Many family relationships are like this—particularly relationships between old, feeble, lonely persons and younger, more vigorous persons. Such a relationship may also exist between a very ill person and his health-care providers—doctors, nurses, etc. It could also exist between a dependent employer and his more independent domestic servants. Whenever the independent party to such a relationship takes advantage of the infirmity or dependence of the other party to make an unfair bargain with him, there exists undue influence. The weak party may use this as a reason for rescinding the contract.

Another situation in which undue influence may arise occurs when a person is under great stress because of some personal problem or family or business problem. He is so preoccupied with this problem that his business sense is impaired. If another person takes advantage of this opportunity to make an unfair contract with him, undue influence exists. When the victim recovers his common sense, he may rescind the contract.

Duress. A person is a victim of duress when he enters into a contract through compulsion. The thought of duress calls to mind the person who signs a contract because the other party is pointing a revolver at his head and telling him, "You sign on the dotted line or else!"

This is only one example of duress. Among other threats which will constitute duress are some of the following:
1. "Sign, or I'll shoot your wife (brother, son, fiancee, etc.)."
2. "Sign, or I'll have you prosecuted for theft!"
3. "Sign, or I'll have your husband (son, brother, etc.) prosecuted for theft!"
4. "Sign, or I'm striking this match and setting your house on fire!"
5. "Sign, or I'll tell the world how you cheated your Aunt Margie out of her life savings!"
6. "Sign, or I'll tell the world about your son being married to two women at the same time!"
7. "Sign, or I'll tell my brother (victim's employer) to fire you!"
8. "Sign, or I'll fire your wife!"

Thus, all sorts of threats may constitute duress. If the threat is credible in the mind of the victim, it is duress. Note that where the duress consists of a threat of criminal prosecution, it does not matter whether or not the threatening party has a legitimate criminal complaint. Even when he does, he must not use this as a lever to force the victim to make a contract.

Not all threats are duress. The following are not:
1. "Sign, or I'm going to sue!"
2. "Sign, or I'm going to foreclose my trust deed on your house!"
3. "Sign this property settlement agreement, or I'll give you trouble when you file for divorce from me!"

Essentially, then, a threat to sue or a threat to do what one has a legal right to do—other than to have someone criminally prosecuted, firing an employee, or the like—does not constitute duress.

Some types of threats are duress when made to some persons but not to others. For example: Blanco and White are involved in an auto accident. Both know it is Blanco's fault. White says, "It's a crime to cause an auto accident here. If the police come, you'll go to jail for sure. Pay me $500 now and I won't tell a soul." Blanco pays. Was he under duress?

If Blanco was born and raised in the U.S., the answer is no. He should know he committed no serious crime here (unless he was guilty of DWI or something similar). If he is a recent immigrant from Mexico, he was perhaps under duress; in Mexico one can be imprisoned for causing an auto accident. He might find White's threat all too credible.

Mutual mistake. Upon occasion a fundamental mistake by the parties as to the nature of the subject matter of the contract will be grounds for rescission. For such a mistake to be grounds for rescission, there must have been no meeting of the minds between the parties as to the true subject matter. An example of such a situation might be:

Able bought a 1977 Ford when the 1977 models first appeared on the market. He drove this car hard during the first part of 1977, putting 15,000 miles on it. Then, just before the 1978 models came out, Able won another 1977 Ford in a raffle, a new one. Able then let it be known that he would sell his old car. Baker heard that Able had a 1977 Ford for sale. He knew Able had won the new Ford at the raffle, but he did not know that Able already had a 1977 Ford. So, Baker made a written offer to Able to buy his 1977 Ford for a price which was somewhat lower than the dealer's price on a new car. He figured that Able might be willing to sell the new car for less than dealer's price. Able at once accepted the offer, because it was for a slightly higher price than he had hoped to get for his used car. Baker first learned of the used car when Able delivered it. He refused to take the used car because he thought he was buying a new car. Able refused to sell the new car because he had never offered it for sale. The probable result is no contract, because Able and Baker did not have the same car in mind when this bargain was made.

Rescission for mutual mistake will not be possible, however, when one of the parties is aware of the other's misconception of the true nature of the subject matter, and tries to take advantage of it. This, of course, would be a form of fraud. Where a true mutual mistake exists, either party may avoid the contract. Where fraud is involved, only the victim may rescind.

If the mistake involves the value of the subject matter, not the essential identity of it, the contract is binding unless fraud is involved. For example: Able sells a tract of land to Baker, both parties assuming that no valuable minerals lie under the land. Six weeks after Baker takes possession, a large uranium deposit is found under the land. Able wants to rescind his sale and get the land back. He cannot—unless Baker had reason to know that the uranium was there and he did not mention this to Able.

A unilateral mistake, a mistake by only one party to the contract, is not a ground for rescission if the other party could not be expected to know of the mistake. For example: Able intends to offer to sell 1,000 bushels of wheat to Baker for $2.80 per bushel. Able's secretary erroneously types the offering price as $2.70 per bushel. The offer is transmitted to Baker, who accepts it, not knowing of the error. Able must in all probability sell the wheat for $2.70 since the erroneous price is so near the intended price. However, if the secretary typed the offering price as $1.80 per bushel and Baker accepted the offer as written, Able could escape from the contract. Assuming $2.80 to be a reasonable price for a bushel of wheat, $1.80 would be unreasonably low. When an offer is "too good to be true," the offeree should be on notice that there might have been a mistake made in the preparation or transmission of the offer.

Unconscionability. Unconscionability is essentially a statutory concept. UCC 2-302 provides that a court may refuse to enforce an unconscionable contract; it may also refuse to enforce unconscionable portions of otherwise enforceable contracts. This section of the UCC does not define unconscionability, however. This task was left to the courts by the draftsmen of the UCC.

The Texas legislature, however, has significantly broadened the concept. Section 17.50 of the Texas Business & Commerce Code declares that a consumer may maintain an action for violation of the Texas Deceptive Trade Practices Act if he has been "adversely affected by...any unconscionable action or course of action by any person." In TB&CC 17.45(4), "consumer" is defined as "an individual, partnership, corporation, or association or governmental entity who seeks or acquires by purchase or lease, any goods or services." Under this broad definition, any buyer or lessor of goods or services, whether for personal, commercial, or governmental use, may complain of an unconscionable practice.

In 1977 the legislature added a definition of "unconscionable action or course of action" to the Deceptive Trade Practices Act. This definition, in TB&CC 17.45(5), is as follows:

"Unconscionable action or course of action means an act or practice which, to a person's detriment:

(A) takes advantage of the lack of knowledge, ability, experience, or capacity of a person to an unfair degree; or

(B) results in a gross disparity between the value received and consideration paid, in a transaction involving transfer of consideration."

This definition is consistent with the definition of unconscionability developed by the courts of the nation in their interpretation of UCC 2-302. The imposition of an extremely

one-sided bargain by a party with very strong bargaining power upon a weak party is the essence of unconscionability, whether the one-sidedness is with respect to the price of the subject matter of the contract or with respect to other contract provisions of it. Unconscionable actions as defined have included the following:
1. Inducing a buyer to purchase an item on credit that he probably cannot afford to pay for.
2. Inducing a buyer to buy goods or services that he will get little or no benefit from.
3. Representing to the buyer that he is getting something for virtually nothing.
4. Denying the buyer basic consumer rights, like the right to redeem repossessed goods by paying off the balance due plus repossession costs.
5. In consumer purchases where creditor retains a security interest in the goods purchased, requiring a security interest in goods already paid for along with the security interest in the purchased goods.

The victim of an unconscionable contract provision may seek rescission of the offending contract or provision. He also has available other remedies under TB&CC 17.50, including the right to sue for triple damages and the right to seek restitution of all consideration paid under the objectionable contract.

It must be remembered, though, that the law of unconscionability does not protect against all bad bargains. The more equal the bargaining power of the parties, the more each party is on his own. Also, the more education a person has, the more he is expected to be able to take care of his own interests.

Consideration

Normally, a party is not bound to a contract unless he receives something in exchange for obligating himself, or unless the other party gives up something. Thus, there must be consideration on both sides before a contract becomes binding.

Consideration may take one of four forms:
1. An act.
2. A promise to perform an act.
3. A forbearance—that is, a promise not to do something.
4. A promise to a third party.

Examples of forms of consideration follow:
1. Able sells Baker his watch for $100 cash. Able's consideration to Baker is the act of giving Baker the watch. Baker's consideration to Able is the payment to him of $100 cash.
2. On Monday Able agrees to sell Baker his watch for $100. Able gives Baker possession of the watch at the time the bargain is made. Baker promises to pay $100 cash for it on Friday. Able's consideration to Baker is the delivery of the watch; Baker's consideration to Able is the promise to pay $100 cash on Friday.
3. On Monday Able agrees to sell Baker his watch for $100, Able to give Baker the watch on Friday, and Baker to pay $100 cash for it on Friday. Able's consideration to Baker is the promise to deliver the watch on Friday; Baker's consideration to Able is the promise to pay $100 cash for it on Friday.
4. On Nephew's eighteenth birthday Uncle promises to pay him $10,000 on his twenty-first birthday if Nephew will not smoke during those three years. Nephew

agrees. Uncle's consideration to Nephew is the promise to pay him $10,000 on his twenty-first birthday. Nephew's consideration to Uncle is the promise not to smoke between his eighteenth and twenty-first birthdays.

5. On Monday Able agrees to give Charles his watch on Friday, if Charles will pay Davis, a third party, $100 on Friday. Able's consideration to Charles is his promise to deliver the watch on Friday; Charles' consideration to Able is his promise to pay Davis $100 on Friday.

Adequacy of consideration. The value of consideration is immaterial. So long as some consideration exists on both sides of the bargain, courts will not void the bargain because of lack of consideration. Thus, a contract under which Able agrees to sell his watch to Baker for $1 will not be void for lack of consideration. However, inadequacy of consideration may well be evidence of fraud, duress, undue influence, unconscionability, or some similar condition.

There is also no requirement that the number of considerations on each side of a contract be equal. Thus, Able may promise Baker that he will be paid $100 on Friday, if, between Monday and Friday, he will mow Able's lawn, trim Able's hedge; clean Able's garage; paint Able's doghouse; and, wash, wax, and polish Able's limousine. Baker agrees. Able's single promise to do one thing is good consideration for Baker's promise to do five things.

Promises which are not good consideration. Some types of promises are not good consideration for contracts. A promise to perform an illegal act is not good consideration.

An example: Meanfellow promises to pay $100 to Bully on Friday, if Bully will beat up Puffer on Thursday. Bully agrees. Since Bully has promised to commit the tort and crime of assault, his promise is illegal, and no consideration for Meanfellow's promise to pay $100.

An illusory promise, a promise which does not really bind the promisor to do anything, is no consideration. Examples follow:

1. On Monday Able offers to pay Baker $100 for his watch, payment due Friday, delivery of the watch also due Friday. Baker agrees to sell Able the watch for $100 on Friday if he feels like it on Friday. Obviously, there is no contract. Baker is not bound to sell the watch if he does not want to, so Able is not bound to buy it.

2. Supplier offers to sell Professor all of the fertilizer he needs during 1978 at a very reasonable price. Professor accepts the offer. Professor is not a farmer or gardener—he does own his own house, but he does not fertilize his lawn every year, as Supplier knows. Supplier is not bound to a contract here, because Professor may choose not to fertilize his lawn this year; thus, Professor's promise is illusory. Of course, if Professor is a professor of horticulture and runs a nursery on the side, he will have need of fertilizer. His promise would not be illusory in that case.

3. Dairyman offers to sell Grocer all of the milk he needs for his grocery for the year 1980 at an agreed price. Grocer accepts the offer, on condition that he may cancel the contract at any time, without notice. Dairyman is bound to no contract here. If Grocer can cancel at any time without prior notice he is not bound to buy any milk. But, if Dairyman is to start delivering milk the day after the contract is made, and Grocer retains a right to cancel upon the giving of ten days notice, there is a good contract. Grocer has in effect obligated himself to buy milk for at least ten days.

A promise to do that which one is already legally obligated to do, or to perform an act which one is already legally obligated to perform, is not good consideration. Examples follow:

1. Able advertises a $50 reward for the return of his lost dog. Baker, the city dogcatcher, picks up the dog in the course of making his rounds. He identifies the dog as Able's from its license and returns it, claiming the reward. He cannot force Able to pay since he was in essence just doing his job when he found and returned the dog.
2. Plaintiff wants Witness to testify for him in his suit against Defendant. He could subpoena Witness and make him testify, but instead, he promises to pay Witness $100 if he will come to court and tell the truth on the witness stand. Plaintiff has gotten no consideration for his promise to pay the $100 since Witness is already legally obligated to tell the truth on the witness stand. (The legality of this is also quite questionable.)
3. Owner hires Driver to drive his racing car in a big race. Bettor promises to pay Driver $10,000 if he wins the race. If Driver wins, Bettor need not pay. Driver already owes the duty to Owner to do his best to win the race.

A promise to pay for a service which has already been performed is not binding. Past consideration is no consideration. For example: Girlfriend tutors Boyfriend for his business law final exam, Girlfriend asking no pay for this and Boyfriend not offering to pay. Boyfriend gets an A on the exam. He is so happy at this that he tells Girlfriend he will pay her $20 for her help next payday. He does not pay. She cannot collect, because he promised to pay after the tutoring job was finished.

Voidable and conditional promises as consideration. A voidable promise is good consideration. Anyone who makes a contract with a minor should know that the minor may disaffirm his contract if he wishes, under normal circumstances. But the minor may hold the adult to the contract if he chooses to do so.

A conditional promise is also good consideration. For example: Owner agrees to sell his racehorse Whirlwind to Buyer if Whirlwind finishes in the money at the Podunk Derby. Buyer is obligated to buy if the horse finishes third or better in the race. If it finishes fourth or worse he is not obligated to buy. This is a good contract.

The promise not to sue as consideration. A promise not to sue is good consideration for payment of money to compromise a claim, so long as the person giving up the right to sue thought in good faith that he had a good claim. It does not matter whether the party giving up the right to sue truly had a good claim, so long as he truly believed that he did. If the party giving up the right had no claim, and knew for a certainty that he did not, the other party may recover his payment due to lack of consideration.

This being the case, it pays not to be too hasty in settling claims which others may assert against you. One should obtain competent legal advice as to the merits of the other person's claim before settling. On the other hand, it may pay to settle a claim out of court when the chances of victory for the defense in court are doubtful. The settlement will at least spare one the expense and nervous tension which accompany litigation.

Compromise of debts—the partial payment as consideration for release of the balance. Whether the partial payment in return for release of the balance is a true release depends primarily upon whether the debt in question is liquidated or unliquidated (the difference between these was discussed in the materials on civil procedure). Remember that the main types of liquidated debts are judgments, matured commercial paper, promissory notes, and the like. Unliquidated debts are debts the amount of which is in dispute.

Payment of part of an unliquidated debt in exchange for a release of the balance is a valid consideration. The debtor is doing something he may not be obligated to do, paying part of a debt he may not owe. Thus the creditor gets consideration for his release. Payment of a portion of a liquidated debt in exchange for the creditor's release of the balance will normally not constitute a valid consideration. When the debtor pays a portion of the liquidated debt he is merely doing that which he was already obligated to do, so creditor gets no consideration for the release. Thus, the release is in essence meaningless and the creditor may proceed to collect the balance of the debt later.

There are ways in which liquidated debts may be compromised, however. Some examples follow.

1. Debtor owes Creditor $1,000 as a result of the maturing of a promissory note by which Debtor promised to pay $1,000 to Creditor's order on May 1. It is now May 15, and Debtor has paid none of the obligation. Debtor offers Creditor $500 and a fifth of scotch in exchange for Creditor calling the debt even. Creditor accepts the offer. The debt is cleared. Since Debtor owed Creditor money, he was not obligated to pay in scotch. By paying a portion in scotch, he did that which he was not obligated to do. So Creditor got consideration for the release.

2. Same situation. On May 15, Buddy offers to pay Creditor $500 in exchange for Creditor's release of his $1,000 claim against Debtor. Creditor agrees, and Buddy pays. The debt is cleared. Assuming that Buddy was not already indebted to Creditor, Buddy did something he was not obligated to do, i.e. paid part of Debtor's debt. So Creditor got consideration for release of the balance.

3. Same situation, except that Debtor's promissory note does not mature until June 1. On May 15, Debtor offers to pay Creditor $500 in exchange for Creditor releasing the balance. Creditor agrees, and Debtor pays. The debt is cleared. Here again Debtor did a thing which he was not obligated to do—he paid off part of the debt early.

4. Debtor owes four overdue liquidated debts—$10,000 to Lender, $10,000 to Pal, $20,000 to Contractor, and $40,000 to Ex-Wife. He does not know where he can get $80,000 in the near future, but he has $40,000 now. He proposes to his creditors that he give them 50 cents per dollar of their debts in exchange for their calling all even. His sob story is so convincing that the creditors agree to his proposition. He pays; the creditors sign releases. The debts are all cleared. Each creditor is said to have gotten consideration for his release here because the other creditors also signed releases. This type of bargain is called a *composition of creditors*.

5. Debtor owes Creditor $5,000 on a promissory note which matured back in June of 1975. Creditor has not pressed because Debtor has had very few assets. Debtor comes to Creditor in June of 1978 and says that his finances are so bad that he will soon be forced to file bankruptcy and if he does, Creditor will not get much on his note. Debtor says he will give Creditor $1,000 and a promise not to file bankruptcy, plus a promissory note for $1,000 due January 1, 1980, if Creditor will release the rest of the debt. Creditor agrees. This is binding; by promising not to file bankruptcy, Debtor has promised to give up a legal right. So long as debtor does not file bankruptcy the release remains in force.

When the debtor owes the creditor more than one debt, and some of the debts are liquidated and some are not, other problems arise with respect to a compromise. Suppose that Debtor owes Creditor an overdue liquidated debt of $1,000. He also owes Creditor an unliquidated debt, which Creditor claims is $1,000 and Debtor claims is only $500. Examples of the problems follow.

1. Debtor sends Creditor a check for $1,000, not specifying to which account it applies, but intending it to pay off the liquidated debt. Creditor cashes the check and says he has applied it to the unliquidated debt, which is now paid in full. Debtor says that is wrongful. It is not. In such a situation, Creditor may apply the payment in any way he sees fit.

2. Debtor sends Creditor a check for $500, writing upon it, "Payment in full of

_____ (the unliquidated debt)." Creditor cashes it, and claims Debtor still owes him $1,500—$1,000 on the liquidated debt and $500 on the unliquidated debt. Creditor is right. Since Debtor beyond a doubt owes $1,000 on the liquidated debt, Debtor was only doing a part of what he had to do by sending $500. Creditor got no consideration for the purported release.

3. Debtor sends Creditor a check for $1,500, writing upon it, "Payment in full of all accounts between us." Creditor cashes the check. The accounts are settled. Debtor here did more than he had to do.

4. Creditor cashes the $1,500 check in #3 above, then writes Debtor, "I've applied your check $1,000 to our unliquidated account and $500 to our liquidated account. Please remit the $500 balance as soon as possible." Creditor cannot collect the other $500. If he cashes this check, he cashes it upon Debtor's terms. Thus, if Creditor wants to try to force Debtor to pay $1,000 on the unliquidated debt, he cannot cash this check.

Substitutes for consideration. Occasionally courts will enforce promises given to discharge a moral obligation, even though no consideration is present. This is done so seldom, however, that no one should count upon a court making moral obligation the equivalent of consideration.

Courts will also sometimes equate extreme hardship with consideration, allowing the enforcement of a promise for which no consideration was given in order to preserve the promisee from suffering great hardship. Here again, this is done so seldom that no one should count upon the court equating hardship with consideration. It will all depend upon who the promisee is and upon the nature of the hardship he may suffer if the promise is not enforced.

Promissory estoppel is the most commonly used substitute for consideration. A typical promissory estoppel situation is something like the following: Secretary worked for Broker for thirty years. She has reached age sixty-five and decides to retire. Broker has no retirement plan for his employees. Nevertheless, upon the day of her retirement, he promises to pay her $300 per month for the rest of her life. He keeps his promise for six years, Secretary adjusting her life style to her Social Security income plus this $300 per month. Broker's business then falls upon hard times, so he decides to cut off Secretary's pension in order to reduce costs. He claims he can do it because he got no consideration for his promise to pay. Secretary says he cannot do it. She is probably right. It is true that he got no consideration for his promise to pay; her consideration to him was past consideration. However, since she has adjusted her life-style to the expectation of this income, the court probably would not allow Broker to deny that he got consideration for the promise to pay.

Promises to make gifts. In general, a promise to make a gift is totally unenforceable, since the person making the promise got no consideration for making it. If the donee did give the donor consideration for his promise, the promise is no longer a promise to make a gift; it is a simple contractual obligation.

However, in the situation where Boyfriend mows Buddy's lawn in exchange for Buddy's promise to give Girlfriend $10, an enforceable promise to make a gift does exist. Buddy did get consideration, Boyfriend's act of mowing the lawn. Girlfriend is a donee beneficiary of the Boyfriend-Buddy contract and has enforceable rights. This will be discussed further in the chapter on third-party beneficiaries.

Once a gift is completed, which occurs when donor delivers the gift to donee, the transaction is normally irrevocable even though donor got no consideration for making the gift. This concept will be discussed at greater length in the chapter on personal property.

Contracts enforceable without consideration. Several types of promises are enforceable without consideration. The most common of these is the promise to make a charitable contribution. Promises to make gifts to organizations such as the Red Cross or the United Fund are enforceable. Among other sorts of organizations defined as charitable are churches, private educational institutions, nonprofit research foundations, etc.

A promise to pay a debt which has been discharged in bankruptcy is enforceable without consideration. For such a promise to be enforceable, though, it must be made after the debtor has received his discharge from the debt. If the promise is made before the debtor gets his discharge, it is not enforceable without consideration.

A promise to pay a debt upon which the statute of limitations has run out is enforceable without consideration. However, such promises must be in writing and signed by the debtor. It must be remembered that this applies only to contractual obligations: a tort claim upon which the statute of limitations has run out cannot be revived by a promise to settle without consideration.

A promise to perform a voidable duty is enforceable without consideration. For example: Able's innocent misrepresentation induces Baker to make a contract with him. Baker learns of the misrepresentation, but tells Able that he will perform anyhow.

A promise to pay a usurious debt is enforceable when the interest rate is reduced to a legal level. For example: Lender lends Borrower $1,000 for a year at 20 percent interest, Lender being a private lender. Borrower finds out the maximum interest rate a Texas private lender can charge is 10 percent. So he tells Borrower he will not repay the loan unless the interest is reduced to 10 percent. It is so agreed. Borrower can no longer complain about usury.

An agreement to modify a contract for the sale of goods is enforceable without consideration, as per the provisions of UCC 2-209. Generally, in order to modify a contract involving something other than goods, the obligations of both parties must be changed; otherwise the modification would not be valid. Examples follow.

1. Workman contracts to mow the lawn of Owner's mansion for $20. This turns out to be more work than he thought, so he tells Owner he will not finish the job unless Owner pays him $30. Owner agrees. Workman finishes. Owner pays him $20 and says that is all he will pay. That is all he has to pay. He got no consideration for his promise to pay $30. Workman just promised to finish the job, which he was already obligated to do.
2. Same situation—but Workman agreed to water the lawn after mowing it in exchange for Owner's promise to pay him $30. This is enforceable, since Workman's obligation was increased.
3. Seller contracts to sell his 1947 Cadillac to Buyer for $300. Buyer later asks Seller to reduce the price to $280. Seller agrees. The price is now $280, even though Seller got no consideration for his promise to reduce the price. Since the car is goods, the modification is binding if agreed to, consideration or no.

13

Contractual Capacity

Illegal Contracts

Contractual Capacity

Most persons have unlimited capacity to make binding contracts. Other persons have limited capacity to do so, and still others have no capacity to do so. Some types of organizations have unlimited contractual capacity, but the capacity of most organizations is limited. This chapter deals with the limitations that exist on contractual capacity.

Governments and government organizations. Governments and government organizations are created by constitutions or acts of legislative bodies. Their powers are limited by these same constitutions or legislative acts. A governmental body can make no contracts other than those authorized. Any unauthorized governmental contract is said to be ultra vires and void.

Private corporations. Private corporations are also creatures of statutory law. They must be created in accordance with the procedures contained in state business corporation acts. Their powers are limited by these acts, and also by their articles of incorporation. The contractual limitations imposed by Texas state law upon corporations will be considered at length in the materials on corporation. For now, it is sufficient to state that any corporate contract which is not authorized by state law or by the articles of incorporation or bylaws of the corporation is ultra vires.

A corporation may nevertheless not escape the consequences of an ultra vires contract. It may not rescind the bargain, nor may the other party rescind. However, a shareholder of the corporation may file suit against the corporation to force rescission. If the contract is truly ultra vires, the shareholder will succeed—unless performance of the contract has already begun. If performance has already begun, the contract is perfectly enforceable.

If the ultra vires contract causes a loss to the corporation, the directors who approved it may be held liable to the corporation for damages. Also, the state of Texas may seek to revoke the charter of a corporation that makes such contracts.

Aliens. Aliens are persons who are not citizens of the United States. Texas state law does not limit the contractual capacity of aliens, but federal law does limit their contractual capacity to an extent.

Under federal law, two classes of aliens exist: those who are legally present in the United States and those who are illegally present in this country. Generally, an alien must have some kind of federal permit to be here legally—a visa, a border-crossing card, or similar documentation.

The alien who is illegally here is subject to immediate deportation upon detection. Though in theory he may make any contract which other aliens may make, he may well get himself into difficulty when he tries to enforce his rights. If, in his effort to enforce these rights, he comes to the attention of the U.S. Immigration and Naturalization Service, he will be deported. He is therefore in the sad situation of being obligated to perform his contractual obligations toward others, while they may take advantage of his status and not perform their legal obligations toward him.

The alien who is legally here has most of the contractual rights of American citizens. His visa may impose certain limitations upon him; for instance, aliens holding some types of student visas are forbidden to work in this country. Violation of such a visa restriction is grounds for deportation.

Also, federal law forbids aliens to own certain types of businesses and to accept certain types of employment. Aliens may not own businesses engaged in:

1. Exploitation of mineral deposits upon U.S. Government land.
2. Use of nuclear energy.
3. Coastal or fresh-water shipping.
4. Radio and television broadcasting.
5. Domestic air transport.

Aliens are barred from some types of government employment, and may also be barred from sensitive jobs in defense industries for which security clearances are required.

Convicts. Convicts are persons confined in state penal institutions. Some states limit the contractual power of convicts, while others declare them to be "civilly dead," with no capacity to make contracts. Texas does neither of these things: in this state, a convict has the same contractual capacity as any other competent adult.

Married women. In the early days of American independence, contractual capacity in the family could be characterised by the saying, "Husband and wife are one, and the husband is the one." The rights of married women to make contracts and to own property were severely restricted.

As time passed, the legal disabilities of married women were whittled away until they have all disappeared. A married woman now has the same contractual capacity as does any other competent adult.

Intoxicated persons. An intoxicated person obviously does not have the mental capacity of a sober person. An intoxicated person is in his condition of limited mental capacity because he wants to be; nearly all intoxication is voluntary.

The law takes account of these realities by holding that contracts made by intoxicated persons are perfectly valid if they are reasonable. If a contract made by an intoxicated person is so unreasonable and unfavorable to him that he was obviously not in full possession of his reason when he made it, the intoxicated person is permitted to rescind when he recovers his reason. If he does not rescind as soon as he discovers what he did, he ratifies the bargain and loses his rescission right. The sober party to such a contract is bound to it, so long as the intoxicated party sees fit to enforce it.

Incompetent or insane persons. The capacity of these persons to make a contract depends upon two factors. First, does the incompetent or insane person have a guardian? If he does, he has absolutely no contractual capacity; any contract he makes is void. Thus, his guardian may disaffirm such a bargain, or the other party may disaffirm.

Guardians are appointed pursuant to an order of a court, at the request of a close relative or at the request of the state. The reason for appointment may be insanity, senility, mental retardation, or something similar. The contractual capacity of the ward will not be terminated until a court officially appoints the guardian. The person who is mentally abnormal may have limited contractual capacity, even though no guardian has been appointed. The extent of his capacity depends upon the second important factor: How obvious is his abnormality?

When such an abnormal person makes a contract with another who knows or should know of his abnormality, the contract is voidable by the person suffering from mental problems. He may rescind, but the normal party is bound. If the unfortunate is obviously abnormal, all of his contracts will be voidable. If he appears to be normal, however, all of his contracts will be valid, except those he makes with persons who know of his abnormality.

When a person with these problems contracts for a necessity (food, clothing, shelter, medical care, or other necessities), the contract is totally unenforceable against the person with a guardian, though the guardian may be made to pay on a quasi-contract theory of liability. If the person has no guardian, he may disaffirm his contract, perhaps, but he will be required to pay fair market value for the necessity.

Minors. Minors are persons who have not become adults. An adult is a person who has:

1. Reached his eighteenth birthday, or
2. Married, or
3. At one time been married, or
4. Enlisted in the armed forces of the United States, or
5. Had his disability of minority removed by court decree.

The contracts of a minor are voidable, except to an extent those for necessities. The minor may escape his contracts by giving notice to the other party that he is disaffirming. If the minor has received consideration for the contract he made, he must return it when he disaffirms—if he still has it. He may return it in its present condition, without the necessity of paying for depreciation, damages, or the like. He is entitled to recover his total consideration from the other party. Examples:

Minor, age sixteen, buys a car from Adult for $1,000 cash. A week later he wrecks the car and disaffirms his purchase. He must return the wreckage to Adult, and in return he recovers his $1,000.

Minor, age sixteen, borrows $1,000 from Adult for a year. He loses the money in a poker game, so he informs Adult that he is disaffirming his obligation to repay the loan. Adult must return to him the promissory note he signed, if one exists. Minor need return no money, because he does not have it any more.

A minor who desires to rescind a contract must do so on, before, or shortly after his eighteenth birthday, or before or shortly after becoming an adult. The longer he waits to disaffirm after becoming an adult, the more likely it is that a court would say that his delay in disaffirmance was ratification, agreement to be bound.

Generally, the minor who has contracted to buy something on credit, and who is making monthly payments, will be said to ratify his purchase contract if he makes a payment after he becomes an adult. The minor who sells land is subject to a slightly different rule. He may not disaffirm his sale while he is a minor, but when he becomes an adult he may disaffirm, if he acts quickly.

Remember, however, that a minor may not disaffirm tort liability. Whenever a minor unjustly enriches himself at the expense of the other party to a contract by disaffirming the contract, the other party may be able to recover the unjust enrichment by suing upon a quasi-contract. In essence, quasi-contract liability is said to be a tort liability rather than a contractual liability.

It also follows from this that the minor who induces an adult to make a contract with him by lying about his age commits the tort of deceit. He also leaves the doorway open for the adult to rescind the contract because of the fraud involved.

The contracts of a minor for necessities are to an extent enforceable. The minor may rescind his obligation to pay contract price for the necessity, but he can be required to pay fair value for it. If fair value equals contract price, the contract is in essence wholly enforceable. Necessities are generally considered to be food, clothing, and shelter. But what is a necessity for one person may not be a necessity for another. A $1,000 per month apartment is certainly not a necessity for a mechanic's daughter, but it might be for the daughter of a millionaire. A $10,000 mink coat is no necessity for a professor's daughter, but it may be for the daughter of the president of a large corporation. Social status is a large determining factor as to what is and is not a necessity. Education, medical care, dental care, and legal services are generally considered to be necessities, though we have not yet arrived at the point where automobiles are so recognized.

A contract to borrow money for purposes of buying necessities is enforceable, though the courts do not consider money itself to be a necessity. The Texas Insurance Code provides that a contract of a minor fourteen years of age or older to purchase life insurance is enforceable, if the minor's parents give their consent to the purchase. Appearance bonds in criminal cases are enforceable, even though given by minors. Since a minor may not disaffirm responsibility for a crime, this is a logical ruling.

Marriages and contracts of enlistment in the armed forces may not be rescinded. The logic of this is obvious when one keeps in mind that the act of marriage or enlistment in the armed forces makes a minor an adult, in and of itself. It should be remembered, however, that a promise to marry will not make a minor an adult. Therefore a minor may disaffirm that promise without liability.

Illegal Contracts

Numerous types of contracts are illegal. As a general rule, courts will not touch cases seeking to enforce illegal contracts. The defendant sued for breach of an illegal contract may respond to the complaint with a motion for summary judgment for the defense, on the ground of illegality. If the judge agrees that the bargain is illegal, he will grant the motion, thus ending the suit. Such suits arising out of illegal contracts almost inevitably end in a summary judgment for the defendant.

The major difficulty in these cases is determining which contracts are legal and which are not. Common sense is very often a good guide, but not always.

Contracts to commit crimes. These are illegal for obvious reasons. It would be illogical to enforce Able's promise to pay Baker $10,000 for murdering Charles, or to enforce Dudley's promise to pay Edwards $5,000 to burn down a building owned by Franks. To enforce such contracts would be to encourage the commission of the crimes contracted for.

Contracts to commit torts. These are unenforceable for the same reasons as are contracts to commit crimes. It would be ridiculous to enforce Green's contract to pay Hawes $5,000 to defame the character of Ingalls.

Contracts in violation of licensing laws. Practitioners of certain trades and professions are required by state law to have licenses before they may practice. It is a criminal offense to practice these trades or professions without the required license, and unlicensed practitioners may not use the courts in order to collect fees from clients. Among those trades and professions for which Texas state law requires a license are:
1. Public accountants.
2. Architects, both general and landscape.
3. Attorneys.
4. Barbers.
6. Chiropractors.
6. Cosmetologists.
7. Dentists.
8. Employment agencies.
9. Hearing aid fitters and dispensers.
10. Insurance agents.
11. Medical doctors.
12. Morticians.
13. Nurses, both registered and vocational.
14. Optometrists.
15. Osteopaths.
16. Exterminators (operators of pest control businesses).
17. Real estate brokers and sales representatives.
18. Securities account executives.
19. Surveyors.
20. Veterinarians.
21. Beer retailers.
22. Liquor retailers.

In general, a license is required by all of the above in order to protect the public from unqualified practitioners. Licenses for these trades and professions issued by the state of Texas only authorize practice of the trade or profession within the borders of this state. An insurance agent licensed in Texas to sell life insurance could not sell insurance in Louisiana. By the same token, a medical doctor licensed to practice medicine in Louisiana could not set up an office in Texas.

Usually, there is no problem when a licensed professional gets involved in an interstate transaction. A Texas real estate broker could lawfully contract to sell Texas land to an Ohioan. Should a Texas real estate broker contract to sell Oklahoma land to an Arkansan on behalf of an Oklahoman, however, that would be a most questionable transaction.

When a license is required of a businessman solely for revenue-raising purposes, contracts made by nonlicenseholders are not illegal. Thus, some retailers who sell merchandise subject to the Texas state sales tax go into business without first obtaining a permit from the Texas state comptroller. To do this is a misdemeanor, but the sales of goods by such retailers are valid.

Wagering contracts. Most contracts which involve gambling are unenforceable. Such unenforceable contracts would include the following:
1. Alfred and Bill play gin rummy for 10¢ per point. Alfred wins by 206 points, so he claims Bill owes him $20.60. He cannot collect.
2. Charlie and Dave play a chess game, the winner to pay the loser $20. Dave wins. He cannot make Charlie pay.
3. Ed and Frank make a bet on the outcome of the Cleveland Browns-Pittsburgh

Steelers football game. Ed bets on the Steelers and Frank bets on the Browns. The stake is $20. The Browns win. Frank cannot make Ed pay.

It is irrelevant whether or not the gambling involved is criminal. Even if the gambling is not criminal, the wager agreement is unenforceable.

A lottery is a special form of illegal wager. Here, the promoter sells chances on a raffle and the winner is determined by luck (by a pretty young lady picking a number out of a hat, or whatever). If participants must buy their chances, or if they must purchase goods or services in order to get a chance—with luck determining the winner—an unlawful lottery exists. If on the other hand the promoter gives his chances away, the game is quite legal. This is why promoters of such giveaways advertise that no purchase is necessary to obtain a chance. If no consideration is required, no lottery exists.

Another type of illegal wager is made when someone takes out insurance on a person or piece of property in which he has no interest. When this is done, the insurer is betting that something unfortunate will happen to the insured person or property. If misfortune occurs, the person who took out the insurance will profit by it because, if he has no interest in it, he will suffer no loss from the misfortune.

Thus, no one may insure a person or property in which he has no insurable interest. With respect to life insurance:

1. I may insure my own life. In a real sense my life is my most valuable possession.
2. I may insure the life of my spouse. If her life ends I obviously stand to suffer loss.
3. I may not insure the life of my next-door neighbor. If his life ends, what do I lose?
4. I may or may not be able to insure the life of my brother. If we live together, I may stand to suffer an economic loss if he dies. If we live apart, we have no economic relationship, so I could not insure his life.

With respect to property insurance:

1. I may take out collision insurance on my automobile, because I will suffer loss if it is damaged.
2. I may take out collision insurance on my brother's automobile if I lent him the money with which to buy it, and I have obtained a lien upon it, until my brother repays me. If the car is damaged, my collateral is damaged.
3. I may not take out collision insurance on my neighbor's automobile if I have no lien upon it. I do not stand to suffer a loss if it is damaged.

An insurer will not pay off a claim if the insured person had no insurable interest in the insured life or property. The insurer's only obligation is to refund the paid-in premiums.

Some types of contracts which amount to wagers are perfectly legal. Some buyers of futures contracts on commodities are engaging in gambling. Anyone who "goes long" on a commodity is betting that its price will rise in the near future, while anyone who "goes short" is betting that the price will fall. Such speculation serves an economically useful purpose, because it permits dealers in the commodities in question to hedge against future price changes. They may shift the risk of loss on these changes from themselves to speculators who are willing to gamble.

The short seller of a security is making another legal wager. He sells a security he has borrowed from someone else, hoping the price will go down in the near future. If the price falls, he can buy back the borrowed security for less than he sold it, thus making a profit.

Some states have legalized other types of wagers which most would regard as pure gambling. Legal gambling casinos exist in Nevada, and in Atlantic City, New Jersey. California permits draw poker palaces to exist because the state does not regard draw poker as a gamble; California courts have held that this game is one of skill rather than luck. Several states operate lotteries under special statutes or constitutional provisions. Most states permit pari-mutuel betting on horse and dog racing—that is, betting at the track—and a few states have also allowed off-track betting on horses. However, none of these types of legal gambling exists in Texas.

Contracts in restraint of trade. Any sort of contract which damages or suppresses business competition is unlawful, with a few minor exceptions. Many such contracts constitute violations of the federal and Texas antitrust laws. Some examples of such contracts follow:

1. Green, Redd, and Brown supermarkets agree to sell Grade A milk for $1.61 per gallon to consumers. This is horizontal price-fixing.
2. Black Motor Company tells all of its dealers to sell Model Q-75 pickup trucks to buyers for $7,999.99—no more, no less. This is vertical price-fixing.
3. Gray Company and Blue Company compete against each other in both Texas and Louisiana. Gray and Blue contract that Gray will acquire all Blue outlets in Louisiana and Blue will acquire all Gray outlets in Texas. In effect the companies are agreeing not to compete any more in the two states. This is horizontal market division.
4. Ball Company gives Batt Company a franchise to market Ball products in Podunk County, Texas, telling Batt that it must sell only to residents of Podunk County. This is vertical market division.
5. Pink Company and Gray Company, wholesalers, agree not to do business with Orange Company, a retailer, because Orange also does business with their competitors. This is a horizontal group boycott.
6. Black Company, a manufacturer, forbids all of its wholesalers to deal with Redd Company, a retailer, if they want to continue to wholesale Black products. This is a vertical group boycott.
7. Silver Distillery manufactures Silver Fox Vodka, a very popular beverage. It also manufactures Silver Dollar Gin, which is not selling too well. So Silver refuses to sell the vodka to wholesalers unless they order an equal quantity of the gin. This is a tying arrangement.

All of the above contracts are violations of the antitrust laws. Other types of illegal contracts to suppress competition are agreements to submit identical bids on government contracts, agreements between bidders on government contracts as to who will submit the low bid, agreements between potential competing bidders at an auction as to who will bid what, and the like.

Lawful types of contracts to suppress competition include:

1. The contract obligating the seller of a business not to compete against the buyer within a named territory for a named length of time. So long as the area restrictions do not exceed the trading area of the sold business, and the time restrictions do not unduly restrict the seller's right to make a living while giving the buyer time to get established, these are lawful.
2. The contract obligating a retiring partner not to compete against his partnership, if time and area restrictions are reasonable.
3. A contract obligating an active partner not to compete against his firm. Since this in essence restates the fiduciary duty of one partner to his partners and to his firm, this is perfectly lawful.
4. The contract by the buyer of property not to use said property to compete against a business owned by the seller.

5. The contract obligating an agent or employee not to work for a competitor of his employer after leaving his job with the employer. This is lawful if the employee is some sort of "key man" with the employer, but it is not lawful with respect to employees who do not possess trade secrets of the employer.

Contracts injurious to governmental processes. This category includes a multitude of sins. Among them are the following:

1. Influence-peddling—contracts to procure government contracts for consideration. Ex-general Black promises Green Company that he will get Green a contract with the Defense Department, in return for Green Company's paying Black consideration.
2. Contracts regarding election or appointment of public officials. Redd donates $1,000 to the "Brown for Mayor" campaign, in return for Brown's promise to appoint Redd director of public works if he is elected.
3. Contracts obstructing the administration of justice. Junior Blue has been arrested for DWI. Papa Blue pays the district attorney $100 to drop the charges. The DA does so. Also included here are such matters as bribery of jurors and payment of witnesses to commit perjury. Also included here are contracts not to prosecute: e.g., Junior Brown burglarizes Pink's house and Pink catches him. Papa Brown pays Pink $500 not to call the police or otherwise report the burglary.
4. Contracts of champerty, maintenance, and barratry. Champerty is a bargain to split the proceeds of a lawsuit. When such a bargain is made between attorney and client, it is lawful—otherwise, it is at least questionable. Maintenance is a bargain to finance another person's lawsuit. If the transaction is a loan which is to be repaid, win or lose, it is lawful. If it is a gift, it is lawful. But if the consideration for the financing is a share in the proceeds of the suit, it is unlawful. Barratry occurs when an attorney seeks out a client and induces the client to sue someone, or in general when the crime of barratry is committed.

Contracts which are contrary to public policy. This category of illegal contracts also covers a multitude of sins. Included are the following:

1. Contracts by which fiduciaries are induced to breach their trust. Included are all sorts of commercial bribery and the like.
2. Contracts promoting immorality. The determining factor here is the court's definition of morality, which changes with the times. Certainly, a contract by which Shade leases a building to Crooks for use as a gambling casino, opium den, or bookie joint would be illegal.
3. Contracts exonerating from liability for torts—usually negligence. Such contracts are illegal when the parties have very unequal bargaining power, such as when an auto rental agency puts a clause in its rental contract stating that it is not responsible for injuries to its customers caused by its negligence in maintaining its cars. If the parties have equal bargaining power and they agree to a provision like this, the courts will go along with it and interpret it as meaning what it says.
4. Contracts injurious to the marriage relationship. A contract to break up a marriage would not be enforced; a bargain by which Father-in-law promises to pay Husband to divorce Wife is illegal. A contract to prevent a marriage may be illegal and it may not, depending upon the reason for the marital restraint. If the main purpose of the contract is to prevent a marriage, the contract is illegal. If the main purpose is not prevention of marriage, and the prevention of marriage is incidental to this main purpose, the legality of the contract depends upon the reasonableness of the main purpose. Thus, if Dad promises to pay Margie, age eighteen, $5,000 on her twenty-

fifth birthday if she does not marry Joe, this would be illegal because the main purpose is to keep Margie from marrying Joe. If he promises to pay Margie's way through medical school on condition that Margie not marry until she completes her medical education, that might well be lawful; the main purpose here is to help Margie complete her education, which is a reasonable and praiseworthy purpose. If Uncle promises Margie that he will pay her $10,000 on Grandma's death if she cares for Grandma and does not marry before her death, and if at the time the contract is made Margie is twenty and Grandma is seventy-five, this would probably hold up. Grandma should not live long enough to prevent Margie from marrying. But if Margie is to live with Auntie and to care for Auntie until she dies, not marrying in the meantime, and if at the time of contracting Auntie is forty-two and Margie is twenty, this might well not hold up, since Margie might well be too old to marry when Auntie dies. In short, a contract which will have the effect of stopping a person from marrying altogether will probably be declared unreasonable and illegal. Most contracts which encourage marriage, on the other hand, are valid.

5. Marriage brokerage contracts. The marriage broker is a valuable institution in some of the world's cultures, particularly those where marriage is for purposes of procreation and cementing family alliances rather than for love. Marriage brokerage is quite incompatible with marriage for love. Therefore, in the U.S., a contract by which Bill promises to pay Agatha $1,000 if Agatha introduces him to the girl he marries would be totally unenforceable.

6. Contracts for the sale of children, or of an interest in children. In some cultures, child purchase is a means of adoption and is looked upon as praiseworthy; our culture detests the practice. Such contracts are totally unenforceable here.

7. Contracts to perform marital duties. Our culture holds that the state of being married obligates partners to perform duties for their mates and offspring without the expectation of payment. Thus, if Wife threatens to leave Husband, Son, and Daughter to care for themselves; Husband promises to pay Wife $50,000 on Daughter's eighteenth birthday if Wife does not leave and continues to perform her wifely and motherly duties; Daughter is the younger child; Wife sticks around and performs to collect the reward; and Husband refuses to pay off on Daughter's eighteenth birthday, Wife cannot collect.

8. Contracts to buy votes in private elections. Vote-buying in public elections is a criminal offense, of course. Buying votes for fraternity president, or for corporate director, will not earn one a trip to Huntsville, but contracts to purchase votes for such offices are unenforceable.

9. Contracts corrupting the objectivity of communications media. Since the communications media have great power to influence public opinion, he who has the power to sway the media may acquire great power over the public. Therefore, members of the media should be free to call the shots as they see them in reporting public affairs. Any contract to influence the media in reporting the news, or to induce the media to endorse a political candidate for consideration, is unenforceable.

Usury. Usury is the charging by a lender of excessive interest upon a loan. Originally, prohibitions of usury applied only to loans of money, not to purchases of goods on credit. In modern times, the growth of consumer credit has rendered this distinction somewhat illogical, because the buyer of goods on credit is most certainly borrowing money with which to make purchases, directly or indirectly.

Article 16 Section 11 of the Texas Constitution grants to the legislature the authority to define interest and fix maximum rates of interest. The legislature has, under the power granted by this provision, enacted the Texas Consumer Credit Code, RCS 5069. This statute imposes maximum interest rates for many sorts of transactions, including the purchase of various sorts of goods on credit. It also provides uniform penalties for the charging of excessive interest.

Article 16 Section 11 of the constitution provides that the maximum rate of interest in Texas shall be 10 percent per annum, unless the legislature authorizes a higher rate. RCS 5069-1.02 restates this constitutional provision.

RCS 5069-1.03 provides that when parties make a contract calling for the payment of interest, but no interest rate is specified, the rate shall be 6 percent per annum. RCS 5069-1.05 provides that judgments shall bear interest at the rate of 9 percent per annum, unless the contract upon which the judgment was handed down calls for a higher interest rate; but under no circumstances shall the interest rate upon a judgment be more than 10 percent per annum.

The Consumer Credit Code generally permits only lenders licensed by the Consumer Credit Commissioner to charge interest in excess of 10 percent per annum on loans to individual borrowers. Such interest may be charged only on the types of loans for which the legislature has authorized higher rates of interest. On the other hand, the legislature has decreed that the 10 percent per annum interest maximum does not apply to profit-making corporate borrowers. RCS 1302-2.09 (the Miscellaneous Business Corporation Act) provides that a corporate borrower may be charged interest of up to 1.5 percent per month. It is settled law in Texas that, if an individual cosigns a loan to a corporation as surety or guarantor, and is forced to pay off the loan, he is not a usury victim if he is charged the maximum corporate interest rate.

Thus, on loans by one private lender to another individual, the maximum interest rate shall be 10 percent. On loans by any lender to any private profit-making corporation borrower, the maximum interest rate shall be 1.5 percent per month. On loans by commercial lenders to individual borrowers for purposes for which higher interest rates are not authorized by law (such as loans for business purposes), the maximum interest rate shall be 10 percent per year.

Until recently the maximum interest rate on real estate loans secured by a first mortgage lien or the equivalent on a family dwelling was 10 percent per year. The rapidly increasing interest rates of mid-1979 rendered this maximum obsolete. The 1979 legislature therefore amended RCS 5069-1.07 to create the following maximum rate upon such loans:

1. 12 percent per annum, or
2. The per annum market yield rate on ten-year United States Treasury notes and bonds for the second preceding calendar month, adjusted for constant maturities, plus 2 percent per annum, rounded off to the nearest one-quarter of one per cent, whichever is less.

The new statute thus creates a floating maximum rate on these loans. Under present law the rate cannot go higher than 12 percent. This floating maximum was to remain in effect until September 1, 1981. However, at a time when the prime interest rate for large corporations (the "going" annual rate for large loans to large corporate borrowers) is 15¾ percent, it makes no economic sense for savings and loan associations or banks to borrow at 15 percent and lend at 12 percent. It also makes no economic sense for small savers to deposit their savings with savings and loan associations when their spare funds earn a greater return invested in money-market funds and the like. Thus, under present law, the supply of lendable funds available to real estate financers could dwindle to almost nothing, as it did before the enactment of the present statute; the maximum might then be revised upward again.

In another 1979 amendment to RCS 5069-1.07, the legislature permitted lenders of $250,000 or more to charge individual borrowers interest of up to 18 percent per annum, unless the loan is to be secured by a lien on land to be used primarily for ranching or agricultural purposes, or as a site for a one-to-four-family residence.

Upon loans of $25,000 or more, a bank may charge an interest rate of the maximum permitted by state law, or a rate 1 percent per year higher than the Federal Reserve rediscount rate in effect on the date of the making of the loan, whichever is higher. The Federal Reserve rediscount rate has normally hovered around 6 percent per annum and has thus had no effect on bank maximum interest rates. However, since the rediscount rate now exceeds 10 percent, banks may justifiably charge interest rates of more than 10 percent on loans exceeding $25,000. When, for instance, the rediscount rate is 11.5 percent, a bank may charge 12.5 percent annual interest on a loan of over $25,000.

Credit unions may charge their borrowers no more than 1 percent per month. The interest payable on brokerage firm margin loans is subject to regulations of the Securities and Exchange Commission. Under present law, brokers may not charge their margin account borrowers more than 1.5 percent per month interest.

On loans from $100 to $2,500 granted by commercial lenders licensed by the Texas Consumer Credit Commissioner, the following maximum interest rates apply:

On the first $300 of principal—$18 per $100 per year.

On all principal over $300—$8 per $100 per year.

Note that this maximum is expressed in terms of dollars per hundred per year rather than in terms of an annual percentage rate. This is an "add-on" rate: the lender adds the interest to the principal in the computation of the amount the borrower is to repay. Anyone who borrows $300 from a finance company for a year will thus be required to repay $354 if the finance company charges the maximum permissible interest. The annual percentage rate of interest upon such a loan will be nearly double the dollars per hundred; in essense the borrower will have the use of approximately $150 of the finance company's money for the one-year life of the loan since the borrower must begin to repay only one month after borrowing.

RCS 5069-3.21 provides that the maximum duration of a loan of $1,500 or less shall be thirty-six months. The maximum duration of a loan of more than $1,500 shall be forty-two months.

Upon loans of $100 or less, RCS 5069-3.16 establishes the following maximum interest rates:

Up to $29.99—$1 per $5 lent.

$30.00-$35.00—10 percent of the principal, plus $3 per month.

$35.00-$70.00—10 percent of the principal, plus $3.50 per month.

$70.00-$99.99—10 percent of principal, plus $4 per month.

The maximum life of such a small loan is one month per $10 lent, with a maximum of six months. If a borrower borrows $80 for six months from a finance company, he could be charged interest of $32. Ten percent of the principal is $8; $4 for six months equals $24; $32 is 40 percent of $80. Since the duration of the loan is six months, the borrower would be paying interest on this loan at an annual percentage rate of 80 percent. Obviously, it does not pay to borrow such small amounts from a finance company.

On installment loans, RCS 5069 Chapter 4 permits a maximum interest charge of $8 per $100 per year, when the principal exceeds $2,500. Chapter 5 of RCS 5069 provides the same maximum for second mortgage loans on real estate.

RCS 5069-6.02 provides the maximum interest rates to be charged on purchases of goods on credit, if no revolving charge account or credit card is involved, and if the goods are not motor vehicles or manufactured housing. The maximums are:

On the first $500 of the price financed—$12 per $100 per year.

On the second $500 of the price financed—$10 per $100 per year.

On all of the price financed which exceeds $1,000—$8 per $100 per year.

This schedule is applied to purchases of furniture, TV sets, power tools, and other consumer goods when a separate purchase contract is negotiated for the purchase in question.

The legislature added Chapter 15 to RCS 5069 in 1979 to govern credit card and revolving charge account interest charges. RCS 5069-15.02 provides that a creditor may use one of two maximum interest rates on such accounts. One option is to levy an annual rate of 14.4 percent on the average daily debit balance of the account. The other option is to use the following sliding scale of maximum rates:

On that portion of the average daily balance not exceeding $1,500—18 percent per year.

On that portion of the average daily balance above $1,500 and not above $2,500—12 percent per year.

On that portion of the average daily balance exceeding $2,500—10 percent per year.

The 1979 amendment substantially raised the maximum interest rate on these accounts; the old maximum was 1.5 percent per month on the first $500 and 1 percent per month on all in excess of that. The amendment also did a favor to consumers. The old law did not specify the method the creditor was to use in computing the balance in the account upon which interest was to be charged. The new law mandates the use of the average daily balance method for computation of the maximum.

Creditors use a monthly billing cycle for revolving charge accounts and for credit card accounts—that is, consumers are expected to make monthly payments upon these accounts. Interest is assessed every month and added to the account balance. The problem is this: since consumers may charge purchases to such an account during the month, and since the consumer should make at least one payment upon the account per month, how does one choose the debit balance upon which to charge interest? Before the 1979 amendments to RCS 5069, creditors could make use of many methods, among them the beginning balance method, the ending balance method, and the average daily balance method.

The beginning balance method uses the debit balance in the account on the first day of the billing cycle. Under this method, a payment made during the month would not reduce the interest charge for that month. Also, of course, a purchase made during the month would not increase the interest payable for the month. The ending balance method uses the debit balance in the account on the last day of the billing cycle. Under this method, a payment made during the month will decrease the interest payable for the month. A purchase charged during the month will increase the interest payable for the month; a large charge on the next-to-last day of the month will accrue interest for the entire month.

Under the average daily balance method, the debit balances at the close of each day of the month are added together and the total is divided by the number of days in the month. The result is influenced by all charges to the account during the month and all payments made during that period. This method is the most equitable, but the method of computation is so complex that access to a computer is necessary in order to use it.

Under the new law, it is still possible for a creditor to use one of the methods other than average daily balance to determine interest payable for the month. However, the interest charged under the method used must not exceed the maximum chargeable under the average daily balance method.

The 1979 legislature also added Chapter 6A to RCS 5069, establishing maximum interest rates for contracts for the sale of manufactured housing (mobile homes and other housing assembled at a factory and transported to the lot upon which it is to be set up). The maximum add-on rate for new manufactured housing is $7.50 per $100 per year. For used housing of this sort—that is, housing being sold at retail for a second or subsequent time—the maximum rate is $10 per $100 per year.

If the buyer is to be given more than sixty months to pay for manufactured housing, interest may be charged on an annual percentage rate basis, but the interest may not exceed the maximum add-on interest as described above (RCS 5069-6A Sec. 3).

For credit sales of motor vehicles, Chapter 7 of RCS 5069 establishes the following maximum interest rates:

For Class 1 vehicles—new vehicles designated by the manufacturer by a model year not earlier than the year of sale, not including heavy commercial vehicles—$7.50 per $100 per year. (This includes, for example, 1980 and 1981 vehicles sold in 1980.)

For Class 2 vehicles—including new vehicles not in Class 1, new heavy commercial vehicles, and any used vehicle designated by the manufacturer with a model year not more than two years prior to the year of sale—$10 per $100 per year. This class would include used 1980 vehicles and 1978 and 1979 vehicles sold in 1980, and all heavy commercial vehicles, new or used.)

For Class 3 vehicles—used vehicles not in Class 2 and any vehicle designated by the manufacturer with a model year not more than four years prior to the year of sale—$12.50 per $100 per year. (Included would be 1976 and 1977 vehicles sold in 1980.)

For Class 4 vehicles—used vehicles not in Class 2 or Class 3—$15 per $100 per year if the amount financed is over $300. If the amount financed is $300 or less, the maximum is $18 per $100 per year.

Whatever the amount financed, the lender or seller may charge interest of at least $25.

With respect to foreign vehicles not designated by a manufacturer's year model, a new vehicle is Class 1. A used vehicle less than two years old is Class 2. A used vehicle more than two years old but less than four years old is Class 3. A vehicle four years old or older is Class 4.

Whenever an installment payment upon a contract governed by RCS 5069 becomes delinquent, a penalty of five cents per dollar of the delinquent payment may be charged. The penalty becomes collectable only if the payment in question is ten or more days overdue. Only one such penalty per installment may be collected.

RCS 5069-51.12 imposes special maximum interest rates upon pawnbrokers. These are:

For loans of $30 or less—20 percent of principal.
For loans of $30.01 up to $100—15 percent of principal.
For loans of $100.01 up to $300—2.5 percent of principal.
For loans of $300.01 or more—1 percent of principal.

A pawnbroker may not lend more than $2,500 to a customer, and maximum duration of a pawnbroker loan is one month. However, the pawnbroker and his customer may by mutual agreement extend the maturity date of a loan for additional periods of one month, provided that the extension is evidenced by a written memorandum, one copy of which is in the hands of the customer.

Any borrower has the right to pay off all or a portion of his loan early. Should he do so, he is entitled to a proportional reduction in the amount of interest payable. The reduction is generally figured by the "rule of 78." Should the loan be paid off one month early, the interest reduction is 1/78 of the annual interest payable. Should it be paid off two months early, the reduction will be 3/78. Should it be paid three months early, the reduction will be 6/78. Should it be paid four months early, the reduction is 10/78. In short, the reduction fraction is one of which the denominator is 78 (the sum of all numbers from 1 through 12) and the numerator is the sum of the digits of the number of months by which the loan is paid early.

A failure by the creditor to permit this reduction in the amount of interest payable may render the lender guilty of usury, if he was charging maximum or near maximum interest.

RCS 5069-1.06 and 8.01 provide the penalties for usury. The penalties in RCS 5069-1.06 apply to usurious loans by private lenders, usurious real property first mortgage loans, and loans of over $250,000 to private borrowers. This penalty is the amount of interest charged in excess of the legal maximum, but no less than $2,000 or 20 percent of the principal, whichever is smaller. Should the interest charged be double or more than double the maximum, the lender forfeits both principal and interest. In addition, a prevailing claimant of usury in litigation may recover a reasonable attorney fee.

RCS 5069-8.01 provides the penalties for usury with respect to regulated loans by commercial lenders to consumers, revolving charge accounts, credit cards, motor vehicle purchases, and the like. The penalty here is double the total interest charged. In addition, if double or more than double the maximum interest is charged, the lender forfeits all principal and interest. If less than double the maximum interest is charged, the penalty may not exceed $2,000 in a transaction involving $5,000 or less, or $4,000 if the transaction involves more than $5,000. Attorney fees are also recoverable under this section. RCS 5069-1.06 also provides that no usury penalty may be collected when usurious interest is charged due to accidental and bona fide (good-faith) error.

RCS 5069-8.01 provides that no usury penalty is collectable if:
1. The charge was unintentional and resulted from a good-faith error, despite maintenance of procedures designed to keep such errors from occurring, or
2. The charge was made in good-faith compliance with an administrative regulation, or
3. The violation is discovered and corrected within sixty days of said discovery, so long as the borrower has not called the attention of the lender to the violation in writing.

Enforceability of illegal contracts. As mentioned above, the ordinary lawsuit involving an illegal contract results in a victory for the defendant upon a motion for summary judgment. However, on occasion the plaintiff may prevail in such a suit.

If the illegality complained of is a violation of a statute enacted to protect consumers or members of the general public, members of the protected class may enforce the contract. Thus, a seller of goods on credit who commits usury could not use his wrongdoing as an excuse to avoid his contract.

When the parties to the illegal contract are not equally responsible for the illegality, the less responsible party might be able to prevail against the more responsible. Thus, if Venge pays Tuff $100 to beat up Dupe, and Venge then changes his mind and tells Tuff not to do this foul deed, and Tuff does not beat up Dupe but does keep Venge's money, Venge could quite possibly sue to get his money back and prevail. His timely repentence would count in his favor.

13/ Illegal Contracts

When a contract is partially legal and partially illegal, the legal part is enforceable if it can be separated from the illegal. If, however, the legal cannot be separated from the illegal, the entire contract is unenforceable. So, if Student mows Mann's yard and also draws up a will for Mann, and Mann agrees to pay $100 for these two services, the resulting contract is partly legal (the lawn-mowing) and partly illegal (the will-drawing), since the only way Student could collect for the will-drawing would be if he were a licensed attorney). If Student can prove how much of the $100 contracted for is compensation for the lawn-mowing, he may collect that amount. If he cannot prove this he collects nothing.

14

Statute of Frauds

Parol Evidence Rule

Statute of Frauds

In order to prevent fraud, the law requires that certain types of contracts must be put in writing before they become enforceable. Four major provisions of the Texas Business and Commerce Code are relevant here. Of these, TB&CC 26.01 will be considered first, since it applies to the generality of contracts, not only to specifically commercial contracts. This section states that seven types of contracts shall not be enforceable unless the promise or agreement, or a memorandum of it, is in writing, and signed by the person to be charged with the promise or agreement, or by his authorized agent.

Promises by executors or administrators. A promise by the executor or administrator of an estate to pay a debt owed by the deceased—or to pay a claim asserted against the estate of the deceased—out of his own funds must be in writing.

Upon the death of a person, an individual must be appointed by a court to settle the deceased's estate. Since a person's obligations do not die with him, these must be satisfied after his death. The personal representative of the deceased is called an executor if the deceased left a will appointing him as such. If the deceased left no will, or if the executor appointed by a will refuses to serve or is disqualified from serving, the personal representative is called an administrator.

The personal representative collects the assets of the deceased. He then is responsible for paying off the deceased's obligations out of these assets. After these obligations are satisfied, the personal representative then distributes the remainder of the estate to the deceased's heirs. The procedure for accomplishment of this will be discussed in the materials on wills and estates.

At this point it must be noted that the personal representative is not personally liable for the obligations of the deceased. However, if the estate of the deceased has more liabilities than assets, and if the executor or administrator is a close relative of the deceased, he may feel that it is an important matter of family honor that all of the deceased's obligations be paid. He may therefore promise to pay some of these obligations out of his own funds. This sort of promise must be in writing.

Contracts in consideration of marriage. Any agreement involving a promise to marry on one side and some other sort of consideration on the other side must be in writing to be enforceable. Such contracts usually take one of two forms:

1. Ron Rich, age sixty-five and not very handsome, promises to pay Pat Prettygirl, age twenty-two and beautiful, $100,000 as her separate property upon the day she marries him.
2. Tina Upright and Cass Creeper have been going together for six years, but Cass has never "popped the question." In order to induce Cass to do right by his daughter, Bolt Upright promises to pay Cass and Tina $100,000 upon their wedding day.

Remember, though, that a contract to pay consideration to a marriage broker for finding a spouse is illegal and unenforceable, even if put in writing.

A simple agreement to marry is not a contract in consideration of marriage, however, and need not be put in writing. Breach of an agreement to marry may subject the breaching party to liability for breach of promise to marry; though most state legislatures have enacted legislation outlawing this type of lawsuit, Texas has not seen fit to do so. If the bridge-to-be is guilty of breach, the groom-to-be may sue to recover the engagement ring. If the groom-to-be does the breaching, the bride-to-be may sue to recover her expenses in arranging the wedding (if any) and also to recover balm for her broken heart and damaged reputation.

A promise to answer for the debt, default, or miscarriage of another. An agreement involving a promise to be responsible for an obligation incurred by another is sometimes required to be in writing to be enforceable. However, oral promises of this nature are more often than not enforceable.

Such promises must be in writing if:
1. The promisor is promising to pay if the debtor does not, and
2. Promisor is promising to pay for the debtor's benefit, not for his own, and
3. Promisor makes the promise to the creditor, not to the debtor.

Such promises which do not meet the above three requirements need not be in writing. Examples illustrating these rules follow.

1. Able tells Baker, "You sell Charles $1,000 worth of goods, and I'll pay for them." No writing is needed. Able is creating his own debt here.
2. Charles owes Baker $100. For consideration, Able promises Charles that he will pay this. No writing is needed—Able made the promise to the debtor, Charles.
3. Charles owes Baker $100. For consideration, Able promises Baker that he will pay this, because he wants to keep his friend Charles from legal difficulty. This must be in writing, because Able's promise is to the creditor Baker, and the promise was made to help the debtor Charles.
4. Charles owes Baker $1,000. Charles also owes Able $1,000. Charles has few assets, and Baker is talking about inducing other creditors of Charles to file involuntary bankruptcy against him. Able fears that if Charles is forced into bankruptcy he will not collect his $1,000. For this reason Able promises Baker that he will pay this $1,000, if Baker will give up his plan to file bankruptcy against Charles. No writing is necessary; Able made this bargain to benefit himself.
5. Charles owes Baker $1,000. Able, Baker, and Charles make a three-way agreement that Able will pay Baker this $1,000, and that Charles no longer owes the debt. This is a novation, which need not be put into writing.
6. Charles owes Baker $1,000. Able promises to pay Baker $900 in exchange for Baker's assigning to Able the right to collect the $1,000 from Charles. Baker is making

this deal because he is not sure he can collect this $1,000 from Charles. This is essentially an assignment of an account receivable, not a payment of a debt, and it need not be in writing.

Contracts which cannot be performed within a year. A contract which cannot be performed within a year must be in writing; a contract which can be performed within a year need not be in writing. If it is possible to perform within a year, no writing is necessary, even if the contract allows more than a year for performance. The year begins as of the date the contract is made, not as of the date performance begins. Examples illustrating these points include:

1. On April 1, 1977, Boss hires Workman to manage his drugstore for a year, beginning at once. This need not be in writing: the year will end on March 31, 1978.
2. On April 1, 1980, Boss hires Workman to manage his drugstore for a year, Workman to commence the job on April 10, 1980. This must be in writing: the contract will not terminate until April 9, 1981.
3. For consideration, Rich promises to pay Earnest $300 per month for the rest of Earnest's life. This need not be in writing: Earnest might die within a year and terminate the contract. Thus, it is possible for this to be performed within a year.
4. On March 31, 1979, Rich hires Workman to clear timber off forty acres of land he owns, Workman agreeing to finish the job by November 30, 1980. This probably does not have to be in writing. If Workman could finish this job in less than a year by hiring a work crew, it would be possible to perform this contract in less than a year.

Contracts for the sale of land or of an interest therein. Any contract for the sale of real estate, or of an interest in a piece of real estate, must be in writing. Anything which is attached to the realty is considered to be a part of the realty. Thus, the following must be in writing:

1. Seller agrees to sell to Buyer Lot 2 of Zilch Addition, Podunk.
2. Seller agrees to sell to Buyer a 50 percent interest in Lot 2 of Zilch Addition.
3. Seller agrees to sell to Buyer the right to live on Lot 2, Zilch Addition, for the rest of his (Buyer's) life.
4. Seller agrees to sell to Buyer all of the coal underlying Lot 2 of Zilch Addition.
5. Seller agrees to grant to Buyer an oil and gas lease for the oil and gas underlying Lot 2 of Zilch Addition.
6. Seller grants to Buyer the right to build a road across Lot 2 of Zilch Addition.
7. Seller grants to Buyer the right to cut the timber off Lot 2 of Zilch Addition.
8. Seller grants Buyer the right to dig gravel out of Lot 2 of Zilch Addition.

The following need not be in writing:

1. Seller sells Buyer the tomato crop he is growing on Lot 2 of Zilch Addition. (Crops are not considered to be attached to the land.)
2. Seller sells to Buyer the haystack located upon Lot 2 of Zilch Addition.
3. Seller sells to Buyer the portable building located upon Lot 2 of Zilch Addition.
4. Seller grants to Buyer the right to hunt upon Lot 2 of Zilch Addition.

Leases of real estate for more than one year. Oral leases of real estate for one year or less are enforceable. A lease with a duration of more than one year must be in writing.

Promises to pay commissions for the sale or purchase of mineral interests. Any promise or agreement to pay a commission for the sale or purchase of the following must be in writing:

1. An oil or gas lease.

2. An oil or gas royalty.
3. Minerals.
4. A mineral interest.

Contracts for the sale of goods. The statutory provisions with respect to contracts for the sale of goods are found in TB&CC (UCC) 2-201. This section provides that contracts for the sale of goods for more than $500 must ordinarily be in writing. Thus, oral contracts for the sale of goods for less than $500 are enforceable. In addition, oral contracts for the sale of goods for more than $500 are enforceable, when:

1. The contract is for the sale of nonresellable or custom-made goods and the seller has commenced performance of the contract to the extent that he will suffer grave loss if buyer rescinds the bargain.
2. Seller has delivered the goods to Buyer.
3. Buyer has paid for the goods in full.
4. The party accused of breach admits in court that an oral contract existed.

In addition, partial payment by buyer will make an oral contract involving more than $500 at least partially enforceable. If the contract is for the sale of nonfungible goods (such as one automobile) the making of a down payment by buyer makes the entire contract enforceable. If the contract is for the sale of fungible goods (like bushels of corn or gallons of gasoline) a down payment by buyer makes the contract enforceable to the extent of the down payment.

A partial delivery of goods by the seller under an oral contract involving more than $500 will also make the contract partially enforceable. A good contract will exist for the sale of the goods delivered. Thus, a delivery or payment under an oral contract involving more than $500 will make the contract at least partially enforceable. In the case of the oral contract for sale of custom-made goods for more than $500, the contract will become enforceable before completion of the making of the goods by the seller. The mere ordering and receipt of raw materials for the making of the goods would not render the contract enforceable unless the seller has no other possible use for the raw materials. However, once the seller begins the process of transforming the raw materials into the finished goods, the contract will normally become enforceable.

In case there is no partial performance, and the contract does not involve custom-made goods, the victim of breach of an oral contract for sale of goods for more than $500 may be able to recover. He may always file suit against the breaching party and try to force him to admit the making of the oral contract. If he can accomplish this, and he can prove the existence of a breach, he may then recover his damages.

Contracts for the sale of securities. The statutory provisions with respect to contracts for sale of securities are found in TB&CC 8-319. This section provides that all contracts for the sale of securities, regardless of price, must be in writing unless:

1. The security has been delivered to the buyer, or
2. The buyer has paid the agreed price, or
3. The party accused of breach admits in court that there was a contract.

A partial delivery of the securities in question, or a partial payment of the agreed price, renders the contract enforceable only to the extent of the delivery or payment.

Contracts for the sale of intangibles. A statutory provision governing contracts for the sale of intangibles—such as commercial paper, contract rights, documents of title, and so on—is found in TB&CC 1-206. This provides that all contracts for the sale or purchase of intangibles for more than $5,000 must be in writing.

Other contracts which must be in writing. Many other types of contracts must be in writing in order to be enforceable. To begin with, several sorts of formal contracts must be written, including the following:
1. Deeds to real estate.
2. Mortgages upon real estate.
3. Commercial paper (checks, drafts, promissory notes).
4. Documents of title (bills of lading, warehouse receipts, delivery orders).
5. Investment securities (stocks, bonds, debentures).
6. Corporate articles of incorporation.

Several sorts of assignments of contract rights must be in writing to be enforceable. These include:
1. Assignments of real estate mortgages.
2. Assignment of all or a major part of the accounts receivable of a business.
3. Assignment of rights under a judgment.
4. Assignment of the right to all or part of the proceeds of a lawsuit (when legal).
5. Assignment of patents, copyrights, or trademarks.

Lastly, several sorts of informal contracts not yet discussed must be in writing to be enforceable. These include:
1. Contracts to pay a commission to a real estate broker.
2. Contracts to pay obligations upon which the statute of limitations has run out.
3. Contracts creating security interests in personal property (unless the creditor takes physical possession of the collateral).

Adequacy of the required writing. With respect to formal contracts which are required to be in writing, the entire contract must be reduced to writing and put into proper form. With respect to informal contracts, the writing in question need not consist of an entire contract. What is required is the existence of a document containing enough of the details of the bargain so that a court may determine the subject matter of the contract.

It is not necessary that the writing exist at the time of litigation over the contract. It is sufficient if the required contract or writing had at one time existed, but of course the party who claims that the required writing had at one time existed must prove both that the writing did exist and that it cannot now be produced in court. It also is not necessary that the writing in question have been delivered to the other party to the contract. What counts is the existence of the writing.

With respect to signatures, normally the writing must be signed by the party to be charged with the breach of contract—that is, the defendant in the case. If the contract is required by law to be in writing, and the defendant has not signed anything, the defendant ordinarily cannot be charged with a breach.

However, in contracts for the sale of goods for more than $500 a defendant who has signed nothing, admitted nothing, and made no partial or full payment or delivery may be charged with a breach if he is a merchant who made an oral contract with another merchant, he received a letter of confirmation of the oral bargain signed by the other merchant, and he did not object to the existence of the bargain described in the confirmation within ten days of his receipt of it. For this rule to apply, then, both parties to the bargain must be merchants, the letter of confirmation must have been received by the defendant, and the defendant must not have objected to its contents within ten days of receipt.

A similar rule applies with respect to contracts for the sale of securities, but in this case it does not matter whether the parties involved are merchants. The defendant charged with breach of an oral contract for the purchase or sale of securities who has signed nothing, admitted nothing, paid nothing, and delivered nothing can be held liable for breach if he received a letter of confirmation of the oral bargain from the other party, and made no objection to the existence of the contract within ten days of receipt of the confirmation.

The required writing need not necessarily consist of just one document. A combination of two or more documents may prove the existence of the contract. The best example of such a situation is the contract entered into by the exchange of a written offer and a written acceptance. The offer standing alone would not prove the existence of the contract; neither would the acceptance standing alone, but the two documents together would be excellent proof of the contract.

Equitable estoppel as a substitute for a writing. Generally, oral contracts for the sale of real estate are not enforceable, even though partial performance has been given by one of the parties. However, when a buyer of real estate under such an oral contract takes possession of the property and makes valuable improvements upon it in reliance upon the validity of his oral contract of purchase, a court may well order the seller to deliver a deed to the property to the buyer. To deny enforcement of the contract under such circumstances would be to allow the unjust enrichment of the seller at the expense of the buyer.

Parol Evidence Rule

If parties are not careful about choosing the words they incorporate into their written contracts, problems of interpretation may arise; these are as numerous as the differences between human minds. Since so many possible problems of interpretation exist, it is very difficult to set forth general rules for resolving difficulties of this nature. However, judicial experience has devised several general rules which may be of help when problems of interpretation arise.

Courts will interpret contracts in accordance with the purpose the parties had in mind when the contract was made. Contracts are made in order to carry out the common objective of the parties, and they will be interpreted in a manner which will expedite the accomplishment of this common objective.

A written contract is generally meant to be internally consistent—that is, persons who draft contracts do not deliberately insert contradictory provisions. In case of doubt as to the meaning of a provision, courts will assume that the meaning of an ambiguous provision is consistent with the meaning of unambiguous portions of the document.

In case of doubt as to the meaning of a word used in the contract, it makes a difference whether the word is a technical word with an accepted technical meaning, or whether it is an ordinary word often used in day-to-day life. If the word has an accepted technical meaning which should be known to all parties, it will be given this technical meaning. If it has no such technical meaning, or if the technical meaning is obviously unknown to the parties, it will be given its everyday meaning.

If there are obvious errors of grammar or spelling, these will be corrected in the course of interpretation. The context of the whole document will prevail over an error which contradicts the context. In case provisions of the contract are mutually contradictory, a typed provision will prevail over a printed provision. A handwritten provision will prevail over either a typed or printed provision.

If none of these rules of interpretation will resolve a conflict, the contract will be interpreted against the party who drafted it and in favor of the other party. If the parties to the contract had unequal bargaining power, the strong party probably insisted upon the weak party's acceptance of his terms. The strong party should therefore have employed precise enough language in drafting the contract so that there is no doubt of its meaning. If the strong party did not do this, he should suffer the consequences.

Problems of interpretation may only be avoided by precise use of language in the drafting of contracts. The parties should be in absolute agreement as to the terms of their bargain. No one should sign a written contract until he is absolutely certain what he has agreed to and also absolutely certain that the written contract expresses completely and accurately the bargain between the parties.

Additional problems of interpretation will arise with respect to contracts for international sales of goods if the parties involved speak different languages. Such problems may even arise when the parties speak the same language. For instance, when an American makes a contract for the sale of goods to an Australian, the contract will doubtless be written in English, since English is the language of both parties. But the parties should be aware that there are differences between Australian English and American English. Extra care must be taken to insure that both parties are in agreement as to the meaning of the words used in the agreement.

When, for example, an American makes a contract for the sale of goods to a Mexican, additional problems will arise. Should the contract be written in Spanish, or in English, or in both languages? The Mexican party may be reluctant to have the contract in English, because if litigation arises over it he will either become involved in what to him is a strange common-law legal procedure in a language somewhat foreign to him; otherwise, translation of the contract into Spanish will be necessary in cases of litigation in a Mexican court. The American party will have similar objections to a contract written in Spanish.

A possible solution is to have the contract drafted in both English and Spanish. However, the solution is also not completely satisfactory, because it is very difficult to draft two documents in two languages which have exactly the same meaning. No matter how careful the drafting and translation, it may well be that the English and Spanish versions of the contract will be slightly different in meaning. In such a case, which contract contains the true agreement of the parties? The law provides no pat answer. If the contract is drafted in both languages, the parties should agree that one of the two versions is the official one. If they do not, the court hearing litigation on the contract is likely to go by the version in the language used in that court.

The American engaged in international trade must also be aware of the fact that most of the world uses the metric system of weights and measures, not the English system. Thus, our neighbors to the south measure liquids in liters rather than in gallons; they measure solids by the gram and the kilogram rather than by the ounce and the pound; they measure length by the meter rather than by the foot and the yard. If weights and measures under contracts with nationals of other countries are expressed in metric terms, the American must know the English system equivalents. If the weights and measures are expressed in English terms, the American should make certain that the non-American party knows the metric equivalents.

In negotiation of international contracts the currency of payment is also a matter to be negotiated. The American buying goods from a Mexican could pay in U.S. dollars, but he could also pay in Mexican pesos. If the transaction is to be a cash transaction, it may not make a great deal of difference which currency is chosen as the medium of payment, so long as both parties know the current exchange rate between U.S. dollars and Mexican pesos. It must be remembered, though, that banks and other financial institutions charge a small commission to convert one currency into another. It should also be remembered that this charge is smaller for commercial paper than it is for currency.

If the seller is granting credit to the buyer, another factor of uncertainty enters in. In this era of floating currency exchange rates, the value of one currency in terms of another does not remain stable. The American buying goods on credit from a Mexican must not only know the current value of the U.S. dollar in terms of Mexican pesos; he must also speculate to a degree upon the future value of the dollar in terms of pesos, particularly the value of the dollar at the time payment becomes due. If the buyer feels that the value of the dollar in terms of the peso is likely to rise before payment becomes due, he may want the contract to specify payment in pesos, while if the seller sees the future in the same way he may want to specify payment in dollars.

In summation, the sources of ambiguity in written contracts for the sale of goods are legion. The more of these sources of ambiguity that are identified and dealt with in the process of drafting a contract, the fewer are the chances of differences of opinion arising later over the interpretation of the agreement.

The parol evidence rule. The principle of the parol evidence rule may be stated very simply. When parties have reduced their bargain to written form, normally they may not use oral evidence in court in an effort to prove that the contract does not mean what it says. If the parties went to the trouble to put their bargain in writing, the writing is the bargain.

However, the writing does not always constitute the only evidence of the bargain between the parties. In the first place, it makes a difference whether or not the written contract is integrated. A contract is integrated if it contains the entire bargain. If the written contract contains all of the provisions that one would normally expect to find in such a contract, a court would consider it to be integrated. Also, if the contract itself provides that it is integrated—if it contains a provision such as, "This written document contains the entire bargain between the parties"—a court will treat it as integrated.

Among the provisions that one would expect to be present in, say, a contract for the sale of real estate, would be the following:

1. The name and address of the seller.
2. The name and address of the buyer.
3. The legal description of the realty being conveyed.
4. The price.
5. The date upon which seller must deliver a deed.
6. The method by which buyer must pay the price, including number and amount of payments, and the due date of each payment.
7. A description of the type of deed seller must deliver to buyer—quitclaim, warranty, etc.

The typical contract for the sale of realty will contain many other provisions in addition to those mentioned above. However, a contract that does not contain at least those provisions listed above would not be considered to be integrated, because, essential elements are obviously missing. Since this is so, oral evidence is always admissible to "fill in blanks" in an obviously unintegrated contract.

A contract which appears to be integrated may not contain the entire agreement between the parties. It may, in fact, actually contradict the oral agreement made between the parties. When an agreed-upon term is left out of the written contract, or if an agreed-upon term is changed in the written contract, the party who claims that the written contract does not contain the true bargain between the parties will have great difficulty proving his assertion.

Courts presume that a party to a written contract has read it before he signed it, and that a reasonable person will not sign a contract that does not contain the actual bargain between the parties. It is therefore of the utmost importance that one never sign a contract before one is absolutely certain of its contents. Otherwise one may not be absolutely certain, for example, that a written contract contains all of the fine-sounding promises contained in the oral sales pitch of the persuasive salesman.

All too often the salesman makes wonderful-sounding promises with respect to the item he is seeking with might and main to sell; then, when his fish has swallowed the bait, he asks the "fish" to sign a prepared-in-advance contract of sale containing a provision such as: "This contract contains the entire bargain between the parties. No warranties, express or implied, are made with respect to the within-described merchandise, and THE IMPLIED WARRANTY OF MERCHANTABILITY AND ALL OTHER IMPLIED WARRANTIES ARE HEREBY EXPRESSLY DISCLAIMED." This sort of contract provision in essence says that the merchandise is in no way guaranteed, despite what the salesman might have said to the contrary.

Oral evidence may be admitted in court which seeks to vary the meaning of an integrated written contract when:

1. The parties have made two contracts, one written and one oral. The fact that the written contract is integrated would not prevent an effort to prove the existence of the separate oral contract.

2. The contract says certain consideration has been paid, but one of the parties claims said consideration has not been paid. Some contracts begin, "In consideration of two thousand dollars in hand paid by buyer to seller, seller hereby sells to buyer _____."
If this means what it says, buyer has already paid the $2,000. However, seller may use oral evidence to try to show that the buyer has not actually paid.

3. One of the parties claims the contract contains a clerical error. The contract might state that buyer agrees to pay seller $3,300 for the 1972 Cadillac which is the subject matter of the bargain, but seller claims the true agreed price is $3,500 and that the person who typed up the contract made an error when she typed in the price. Seller may use oral evidence in an effort to make this point.

4. One of the parties claims that the written contract was later amended orally. This can be done if the contract could be validly amended orally, but if the contract is one of those required by law to be written, an oral amendment would not be valid. Thus, an oral amendment to a contract for the sale of real estate would not be valid. Neither would an oral amendment changing the price of an automobile from $1,000 to $950 because, since the contract involves a sale of goods for more than $500, it must be in writing. On the other hand, an oral amendment changing the price of a car from $525 to $475 would be valid because the price is being reduced below $500. An oral amendment changing the price of a car from $400 to $425 would also be valid because a contract for the sale of a car for such a price need not be oral. In short, oral evidence of an oral amendment to a written contract is admissible if the contract as amended would be valid if oral.

5. One of the parties claims that the contract has been rescinded. Any written contract may be orally rescinded. Therefore any party who claims that rescission has taken place is entitled to try to prove it.

6. One of the parties claims that the enforceability of the contract was made to depend upon the occurrence of a condition precedent, which never occurred. For instance, seller and buyer make a written contract for the sale of seller's racing car to buyer for $25,000. After the written contract was signed, seller and buyer agreed that buyer would not be obligated to buy if the car did not finish fifth or better in the Podunk 500-mile race. The car finished seventh, so buyer does not want to buy.

He can seek to prove by oral evidence the agreement about the condition precedent, and the fact that the car did not finish better than fifth in the Podunk 500.

7. One of the parties claims that he was a victim of fraud, duress, undue influence, mutual mistake, or violation of a fiduciary relationship. Oral evidence of this is always admissible.

In addition, oral evidence is always admissible for the purpose of defining ambiguous terms contained in the contract, so long as the difference of opinion over the meaning of the term in question is reasonable.

The Uniform Commercial Code statement of the parol evidence rule is essentially the same as the rule applicable to ordinary contracts. However, in the process of interpreting the UCC, courts may be a bit more liberal about permitting the use of oral evidence to contradict the meaning of a written contract. Generally speaking, when a written contract does not contain a term the buyer felt to be important when he negotiated the contract with his seller, a court will be likely to let the buyer prove the existence of the oral term when:

1. He and seller had grossly unequal bargaining power (which is the situation in the context of most consumer transactions—buyer must sign seller's contract on a "take it or leave it" basis if he wants seller's goods), and
2. Buyer was not well enough educated to understand that the written contract he signed did not contain all of the terms of the bargain which he thought he had made, and
3. Buyer would never have signed the contract if he had understood that the term which was very important to him was not included. In other words, buyer must show that the omitted term was a part of the basis of the bargain he thought he had made.

15

Joint Obligations

Third-Party Beneficiary Contracts

Assignment of Contract Rights

Joint Obligations

There may be more than two parties to a contract. There may be one party on one side and two on the other, one party on one side and ten on the other, six on one side and nine on the other, or any other mathematically possible combination.

When there are multiple parties on one side of a contract, problems may arise with respect to enforcement of the rights involved. There is one set of problems when multiple parties seek to enforce a right against one party, and another when one party seeks to enforce his rights against multiple parties.

Duties owed to multiple parties. When a duty is owed to multiple parties, all of these must join in enforcing it if possible. If all obligees do not join in the suit to enforce the duty, the defendant may demand that those who have not joined as plaintiffs be added as parties to the case. This will be done, unless one or more of the obligees is outside the state of Texas or is otherwise beyond the jurisdiction of the court. Generally, all persons to whom a duty is owed must join in enforcing it, if at all possible.

Duties owed by multiple parties. The required procedure in enforcing duties owed by multiple parties depends upon the type of obligation owed. The multiple parties may owe the obligation only as a group; if so, it is a joint obligation. They may owe the obligation only as individuals, and not as a group; in this case, it is a series of several obligations. Or, they may owe the obligation both as a group and as individuals, in which case it is a joint and several obligation.

Joint obligations. Generally, any contractual obligation of multiple parties is a joint obligation where the contract of the parties says "We promise" with respect to the obligations of the multiple parties, unless the obligation is evidenced by commercial paper. Commercial paper obligations are always joint and several, unless the parties agree otherwise.

In suits to enforce joint obligations, all of the obligors are essential defendants. The defense may ask that those obligors that have not been joined as defendants be joined. The only excuse for nonjoinder of joint obligors is the impossibility of obtaining court jurisdiction over them. Thus, if one or more obligors is outside the state of Texas, for example, or is dead, there will be excuse for nonjoinder.

If the defense does not demand the joinder of all joint obligors in the suit, the suit may go to a conclusion without them. However, the obtaining of a judgment against the obligors joined as defendants will discharge those joint obligors not joined as defendants. Thus, in suits to enforce joint obligations, the plaintiff must name all obligors as defendants who are within the jurisdiction of the court. Failure to do this may result in the discharge of those not joined.

The person or persons to whom a joint obligation is owed must also be careful about compromising the obligation with some of the joint debtors. In general, a release given to one joint obligor will discharge all of the other obligors. However, a contract or covenant not to sue one joint obligor will not discharge the other obligors.

The creditor to whom a joint obligation is owed may collect the entire obligation from only one of the joint obligors; any one of the obligors may therefore be forced to pay the entire obligation. If this occurs, the paying obligor has a right of reimbursement against the other joint obligors. He may force each of the obligors to pay their share of the obligation in question. The following examples illustrate the application of these rules:

1. Able and Baker owe Charles $1,000 on an overdue loan. Charles files suit against Baker for the $1,000. Baker demands that Able be joined as a party. Able is living in the same county as Baker and Charles. Baker's demand will be granted.
2. Franks sold goods to Drake and Eaves for $1,000. Drake and Eaves claim that the goods were defective. Franks denies this. Drake and Eaves refuse to pay the $1,000. Drake offers $350 to Franks in exchange for Franks's releasing him from liability upon this obligation. Franks accepts the offer and gives Drake his release. Franks then demands $650 from Eaves. He would not collect. Eaves now owes Franks nothing. The release given to Drake released Eaves also.
3. In the above case, suppose Drake was given a promise by Franks not to sue him upon the joint obligation, not a release. Franks could now seek to collect $650 from Eaves. The promise not to sue one joint debtor does not discharge the other joint debtors.
4. Goff and Hanks owed Ilich $1,000 on an overdue loan. Goff paid Ilich the entire $1,000. Goff then demanded $500 from Hanks. Goff could collect. Hanks is responsible for half of the obligation, even though Goff paid it all. Goff is exercising his right of reimbursement.

There are ways in which individual joint debtors may escape liability to the creditor without discharging the balance of the debt. If one of the joint debtors is a minor, he may exercise his right as a minor to disaffirm liability upon the debt. This discharges him as an individual, but it will not discharge the debt. (Of course, if the debt is for necessities, the minor cannot disclaim.)

A joint debtor may file bankruptcy and obtain a discharge from his portion of the debt if the debt is dischargeable in bankruptcy. Again, the other joint debtors remain liable.

If all of the joint debtors did not become liable upon the obligation at the same time, it is possible for one debtor's statute of limitations to expire before another's. In such a case, each debtor will be discharged as his personal statute of limitations runs out.

Remember, any individual discharge of this nature discharges only the individual. It discharges no part of the debt. Thus: Monk, Nunn, and Ott owe Patz $900. Before any part of this is paid Ott files bankruptcy and is discharged from his part of the obligation. Patz can still collect the $900 from Monk and Nunn since they are still jointly liable upon the entire debt. If they are compelled to pay it, they will have no recourse against Ott.

Joint and several obligations. Joint and several obligations are created in two ways:
1. By commercial paper. Co-obligors on checks, drafts, and promissory notes have joint and several liability, unless otherwise agreed.
2. By contracts which state, "We and each of us promise——" wherever obligations of the co-obligors are mentioned.

In order to enforce a joint and several obligation, the creditor need not sue all obligors at once. He may sue only some of them, or just one of them. Those obligors named as defendants may not object to the omission of other obligors. If the creditor obtains a judgment against one or some of the obligors, the others are not discharged. Should the creditor be unable to collect his judgment, he may sue others of the obligors later. Thus, the creditor may "pick his victim" (or victims) among the obligors.

The creditor may compromise the obligation with some of the obligors without discharging the rest of them. He may therefore deal with each as an individual, without fear as to the result of any compromise upon his rights against the other obligors. Of course, any joint and several obligor who pays more than his share of the obligation has his right of reimbursement against the other obligors. As is the case with joint obligors, an obligor may obtain an individual discharge from liability upon the debt through a claim of minority (if justified) or a discharge in bankruptcy. As is the case with joint obligors, this will not only discharge the obligor from liability to the creditor; it will also discharge him from liability to his fellow debtors.

It must be remembered, however, that a discharge or release given to a joint and several obligor by the creditor does not release the obligor from liablilty to his co-obligors. Since the co-obligors are still liable to the creditor, the creditor may force one or more of them to pay the entire obligation. Those who pay still have their right of reimbursement against those discharged by the creditor.

Several obligations. Several obligations are owed by co-obligors as individuals, not as a group. They are evidenced by contracts which state that "Each of us promises——" wherever duties of the co-obligors are concerned. Each several obligor is liable only for his share of the obligation; no obligor can be forced to pay more than his share. Each must be dealt with by the creditor as an individual.

Third-Party Beneficiary Contracts

A problem may arise when Jones and Smith make a contract from which Brown will benefit, Brown learns of the existence of the contract, and the contract is then not performed, causing Brown not to obtain his benefit. Could Brown sue either Jones or Smith because he lost his benefit, even though he had nothing to do with the negotiation of the Jones-Smith contract? This is the problem of the third-party beneficiary. The answer to the question is that sometimes Brown may sue, sometimes he may not. It all depends upon why the Jones-Smith contract was made, and upon Brown's relationship to Jones and Smith.

In general, Brown may recover if he is an intended beneficiary of the Jones-Smith contract, but he may not recover if he is only an incidental beneficiary of that contract. A third party is an intended beneficiary if the contract in question was made at least partially for his benefit. If the contract was made only for the benefit of the two parties directly involved, and the third party's benefit is only incidental to the making of the bargain, then the third party is only an incidental beneficiary.

There are two types of intended beneficiary, and their rights will vary. There are creditor beneficiaries and donee beneficiaries. The creditor beneficiary was a creditor of one of the parties to the contract in question before it was made, and the purpose of the contract is at least in part the payment of his claim against his debtor. The donee beneficiary was not a creditor of either party of the contract before it was made; the main purpose of the contract is the making of a gift to the donee beneficiary.

Creditor beneficiaries. The typical situation creating a creditor beneficiary is the following: Jones owes Smith $1,000. Jones sells Brown a car for $2,000, agreeing to pay $1,000 of the purchase price to Jones and the other $1,000 to Smith. Since Jones made this bargain at least in part to get Smith paid, Smith is an intended beneficiary. And since Smith was a creditor of Jones at the time of the making of the contract, he is a creditor beneficiary.

If Brown does not pay Smith the $1,000 as he agreed to do, Smith may sue to collect it, even though he is not a party to the Jones-Smith bargain. Also, if Brown does not pay Smith as agreed, Smith may sue Jones for his $1,000. After all, Smith still has his claim against Jones no matter what Brown does. If Smith does not get paid by Brown, Jones may sue Brown to force him to do as he had promised to do—pay Smith. And, if Brown does not pay Smith, so that Smith has to collect from Jones, Jones may then recoup his $1,000 from Brown. After all, Brown was guilty of a breach of contract.

Then, this problem may arise. Jones owes Smith $1,000. On Monday Jones agrees to sell a car to Brown, Brown to pay $2,000 for the car, $1,000 to Jones and $1,000 to Smith. Jones is to deliver the car on Friday, and Brown is to pay then. On Tuesday Jones tells Smith about this bargain. On Thursday Jones regrets making this deal and asks Brown to pay him the entire $2,000 on Friday; Brown agrees. Jones then tells Smith on Thursday that he will not be getting $1,000 from Brown after all. Smith claims Jones and Brown cannot cut him out of their bargain in that way. Is he right? In all probability, he is not. The rights of a creditor beneficiary are not normally vested when a contract is made for his benefit. The creditor beneficiary may vest his rights only by suing to enforce them before they're changed, or by changing his position in reliance upon their existence. Since Smith did neither of these things here, his rights could be taken away, and he could do nothing about it. Of course, had Jones and Brown provided in their contract that Smith was to have vested rights to the $1,000, then Smith's rights would have been irrevocable. They could not have been taken away without his consent.

Had Smith made a contract with Gray on Wednesday for the purchase of a city lot, Smith intending to use the $1,000 from Brown as a down payment upon the purchase, Smith would have vested his rights. He would have changed his position by incurring a legal obligation in reliance on his expectation of receipt of Brown's $1,000.

Donee beneficiaries. A common situation creating a donee beneficiary is the following: Gray wants to make a gift of $1,000 to Pink, but he does not have $1,000 cash with which to do it. Gray owes Pink absolutely nothing. One Monday, Gray contracts to sell 100 shares of Blue Company stock to Green for $1,000, Green to pay the $1,000 to Pink. Delivery of the stock and payment of the $1,000 are to occur on Friday. On Tuesday Gray gives Pink the good news. On Friday Gray gives Green the stock, but Green does not pay Pink. If Pink sues Green for the $1,000, he may collect. The donee beneficiary may enforce the promise made for his benefit against the promisor.

Suppose that Pink sued Gray for the $1,000. He could not collect. Gray owes Pink nothing. All Gray gave Pink was a promise to have a gift of $1,000 made to him. Since Gray has not himself promised to pay Pink anything, Pink has no rights against Gray.

If Gray sues Green for the $1,000, Gray cannot win. The reason for this is that Green owes Gray nothing, and Green has promised to pay Gray nothing. However, Gray may sue Green and ask the court to direct Green to pay $1,000 to Pink. The basis of this action is to make Green do the thing which he has promised to do—pay $1,000 to Pink. Thus, Gray may get nothing for himself out of this bargain, but he may enforce the bargain as it was made.

Now, suppose that, after the making of the same Gray-Green contract on Monday and Gray's giving Pink the good news on Tuesday, Gray decides on Wednesday that he would like to keep the $1,000 consideration for the stock himself. So he tells Green to pay him rather than Pink, and Gray agrees. Pink learns on Friday that he will get no $1,000; Pink therefore sues Green for $1,000 on the basis that Green had no right to take away his right to receive $1,000. Pink will win. The rights of a donee beneficiary become vested at the moment the contract creating his rights is made, whether he knows about it or not. Thus, the donee beneficiary's rights, once given, cannot be changed or revoked without his consent.

The only way in which this can be avoided is to provide in the agreement creating the donee beneficiary's rights that these are not vested. If the contract creating the rights provides that they are not vested, there is no way the donee may vest them.

Probably the most common type of contract creating rights for a donee beneficiary is the ordinary life insurance policy. The ordinary life policy is a contract between the insured and the insurer providing that, in the event of the death of the insured, the insurer will pay the face value of the policy to the beneficiary named in the policy. (The contract can involve other parties, but that will be considered later in this book.) The rights of the beneficiary of a life insurance policy are vested, unless the policy provides otherwise. The vast majority of such policies do provide otherwise, so the rights of the beneficiary are not vested. The insured normally has the right to change his beneficiary as he wishes.

In order to validly change the beneficiary of a life policy, the insurer must be informed, so that the name of the beneficiary on his records may be changed. A change of beneficiary which is not communicated properly to the insurer is ineffective. On the other hand, a change of beneficiary may be effected without notice to either the old beneficiary or to the new. It is quite possible to deprive the beneficiary of such a policy of his rights without his knowledge. In short, the rights of beneficiaries of life policies are not vested. The legitimate beneficiary is that person carried upon the insurer's records as such.

Incidental beneficiaries. Incidental beneficiaries are not intended beneficiaries; they therefore have no enforceable rights under contracts from which they may indirectly benefit.

For instance: Charles owns real estate adjoining a vacant lot owned by Baker. Baker contracts to sell his lot to Able, who intends to erect an office building there. Charles is happy to learn of this, since the erection of the building will increase the value of his lot. However, later Able and Baker agree to rescind their contract, so that the office building will not get built and Charles will not realize his anticipated appreciation after all. Charles wants to claim damages from Able and Baker. Of course, he cannot. Able and Baker did not have the welfare of Charles in mind when they made their bargain. It was strictly for the benefit of themselves.

Another example: Eaves owes Franks $1,000, Gross $1,000, and Hamm $2,000. Eaves contracts to borrow $5,000 from Dobbs, intending to use $4,000 of the proceeds of this loan to pay off his three creditors and the other $1,000 as a down payment on a new automobile. Dobbs breaches his contract with Eaves and does not make the loan as agreed. Franks, Gross, and Hamm want to sue him for damages for the breach. They cannot. Dobbs did not promise to pay them anything. He promised to pay money to Eaves, which

Eaves intended to pay them. Therefore they are only incidental beneficiaries of this bargain. Of course, had Dobbs contracted to pay money directly to the three creditors, they would have been creditor beneficiaries of the bargain, and would have acquired enforceable rights.

A final example: Mars owes Neep $5,000. Mars promises to give Neep a new Ford Pinto in full payment of this debt, and Neep promises to take it as full payment. Neep is to have the right to choose any Ford Pinto on the Ott Ford lot as his consideration, and Ott is informed of this. Before this bargain is ever performed, Neep decides he would rather have the cash than the car, so he and Mars agree to rescind their deal. Ott claims this is a breach of contract. Of course, if Mars had made a contract to buy the Pinto from Ott there would be a breach. But if the only existing contract here is the Mars-Neep contract, Ott is out of luck. This bargain was clearly made to adjust the debt Mars owed Neep, not to confer any benefit upon Ott. Ott is rather obviously merely an incidental beneficiary.

In summation, the test for determination of whether a contract is made for an intended beneficiary is: Whose benefit did the parties have in mind when they made their bargain?

Assignment of Contract Rights

Contract rights are quite freely assignable. One must remember, however, that the average contract is a two-way bargain. What one party has the right to receive, the other has the duty to deliver. Thus, when seller contracts to sell his car to buyer for $1,000, seller has the right to collect $1,000 from buyer on the agreed payment date. However, seller has the corresponding duty to deliver his car upon the agreed delivery date, and buyer has the right to receive seller's car on the agreed delivery date and the duty to pay seller $1,000 on the agreed payment date. Thus, for each right there exists a corresponding duty, and for each duty there exists a corresponding right.

When a contract has not yet been performed in any way, we say that it is an executory contract. Whenever assignment of any rights under such a contract is contemplated, the parties must not forget the existence of the corresponding duty. When, however, the contract has been partially performed, rights may exist for which the corresponding duties have already been performed. Such rights are far easier to assign.

When rights are assigned under an executory contract, the assignment should make some provision with respect to the corresponding duty. If no such provision is made, an assignment of a right under such a contract is presumed to include a delegation of the corresponding duty. If the parties do not wish to have the duty delegated, the contract of assignment must say so.

Thus: Able and Baker have a contract under which Able is to sell Baker 1,000 bushels of hard red winter wheat for $3 per bushel, delivery due July 5, payment due July 31, the contract having been made on June 3. On June 15, Able wants to assign the right to receive the $3,000 from Baker to Charles. Able of course has every right to do this. But what effect will Able's assignment of the right to collect the $3,000 to Charles have upon Able's duty to deliver 1,000 bushels of wheat to Baker? If the assignment says nothing about this, Able will also delegate to Charles the duty to deliver 1,000 bushels of wheat to Baker upon delivery day. The UCC provision upon assignment of rights and delegation of duties—TB&CC (UCC) 2-205—restates this rule. Thus, if Able does not want to delegate his delivery duties to Charles, or if Charles does not want these duties, the assignment contract must clearly say so.

Delegability of duties. It must first be explained that, although it is quite possible to delegate a duty, it is not possible to get rid of it. Thus: Able owes Baker $1,000. Able delegates to Charles the duty to pay Baker the $1,000, for consideration. Baker is a creditor beneficiary of the Able-Charles contract, and now has the right to collect $1,000 from Charles. But, Baker still has the right to collect $1,000 from Able if he cannot collect from Charles. Able did not get rid of his $1,000 debt by delegating the duty to pay it; the only way he can get rid of it is for Charles to pay it as agreed, or for him to pay it himself as originally agreed.

Not all duties may be delegated. In fact, many duties are nondelegable. Very simple duties performable by anyone may be delegated, but more complex duties involving a personal element are nondelegable.

Some examples of delegable duties follow.

1. Adam Manufacturing Company has a contract to sell to Baxley Company all of its requirements of widgets. Adam finds it necessary to contract its widget production, so it delegates its duties to deliver widgets to Baxley (and assigns its right to receive payment for the widgets from Baxley) to Case Manufacturing Company. Twenty-six American corporations manufacture widgets, and all widgets are substantially indentical in form and quality. If Case widgets are the same as Adam widgets, there is nothing wrong with the delegation.

2. John has a contract to buy Bill's car for $1,000 cash. John decides he does not want the car, so he assigns his rights and delegates his duties under his contract with Bill to Grant. Delivery of the car and payment are due simultaneously. This is a good delegation. It should not matter to Bill who buys the car. Since the contract does not call for a credit sale, Bill need not sell until Grant offers to pay.

Some examples of nondelegable duties follow.

1. For consideration, Ben hired Frank to collect a $1,000 debt Gene owed him. Frank decided he did not want to do this, so he delegated the duty to collect the account to Dean. Ben refused to allow Dean to contact Gene. Ben was justified in doing this. He no doubt trusted Frank—otherwise he would never have hired him to collect this account. This necessary quality of trustworthiness injects a personal element into the performance of this particular duty, and Ben is under no obligation to extend any trust to Dean.

2. Koch owned the Old Heidelberg restaurant. He had a contract with Metzger under which Metzger undertook to supply the restaurant with all the meat it needed during the calendar year 1978, the restaurant to pay on the last day of each month for all meat delivered during that month. In July 1978 Koch sold the restaurant to Ziffel, and assigned all rights and delegated all duties under the contract with Metzger to Ziffel. Metzger refused to deliver meat to Ziffel, and Ziffel claimed that was wrongful. It was not wrongful. The contract calls for sale of meat on credit. Metzger no doubt found Koch to be creditworthy; otherwise he would never have made such a bargain with him. But what does Metzger know of Ziffel's creditworthiness? The credit factor injects the personal element here.

3. Pang hired Snyder, a custom tailor, to make him a custom-made suit. Pang weighed 300 pounds, and thus had a most difficult figure for suit-making. But Snyder had made him six suits in the past, and Pang was very happy with Snyder's work. Before Snyder started on the suit, he became ill and sold his tailor shop to Schnitt,

assigning all rights and delegating all duties under his contract with Pang to Schnitt. Pang told Schnitt that he was canceling the contract, and Schnitt claimed that this was wrongful. It was not, because Pang made the contract with Snyder in reliance upon Snyder's ability to make him a good suit. Pang may not be sure that Schnitt is as competent a tailor as Snyder. Essentially, the services of a skilled craftsman are unique. The duties of such a craftsman are nondelegable.

The person to whom a delegated duty is owed must be informed of the delegation soon after it is made. If the delegated duty is delegable, the person to whom the duty is owed may make no objection. If, however, the duty is nondelegable, this person need not accept performance by the delegatee. If he chooses not to accept the delegated performance, though, he must inform the delegatee of his decision within a reasonable time after getting his notice. Silence here is agreement to accept performance by the delegatee.

Assignability of rights. Most contract rights are freely assignable. The person owing a duty generally does not care for whom he performs the duty. His interest is mainly in whether or not the other party to the contract performs the duty owed to *him*.

The assignment of certain rights, however, is forbidden by law. Among such nonassignable rights are the following:

1. The right to receive governmental pensions.
2. The right to receive alimony.
3. The right to receive child support money.
4. The right to receive welfare-type income, such as Social Security, Workers' Compensation, unemployment compensation, welfare benefits, and the like.
5. The right to receive wages from a governmental employer, under most circumstances.
6. The right to receive wages from a private employer, if the assignee is a commercial lender or a seller of goods on credit.
7. The right to receive money when the duty of the debtor to pay said money has been discharged in bankruptcy.

Contracts forbidding assignment of rights. Courts normally look with disfavor upon contract terms which seek to forbid assignment of rights. The Uniform Commercial Code (UCC 9-318) makes unenforceable provisions in contracts for the sale of goods and other contracts governed by the UCC which seek to restrict assignments of rights. In essence, rights under such contracts are freely assignable. The parties may not by contract provision change this.

It is possible to limit assignability of contract rights in non-UCC contracts—contracts for sale of land and contracts for services, for example. In order for an absolute prohibition of a contract right to stand, however, the contract must state that any assignment of rights under it is void. If the contract so provides, the courts will respect the wishes of the parties.

If, however, the contract merely says that the parties agree not to assign contract rights, the courts hold that assignment of rights is not thereby prohibited. Any assignment of rights under such a contract provision will be recognized as valid; however, the assignment will be considered to be a breach of contract by the assignor. The third party may therefore be able to sue the assignor for damages caused by the breaching assignment, if indeed the third party can prove that the assignment caused him to suffer damages. Generally, such damages are difficult to prove.

Assignment of nonexistent rights. In general, one may not assign a right which one does not possess. It does not matter here if the right assigned never will come into existence, or if it will come into existence sometime in the future. The assignment of a right which never will come into existence is of course fraudulent. The assignment of a right which does not yet exist, but which assignor believes will some day exist, is not fradulent; but it is not valid either.

For instance, Author is busy writing a novel. He has made no effort to sell it yet, but he is sure he can sell it. He borrows money from Lender to live on, and assigns to Lender 50 percent of all royalties from the sale of the novel. Later Author sells the novel to Publisher, not telling Publisher of the royalty assignment. Lender thus receives no royalties. Lender informs Publisher of his assignment and demands that Publisher pay 50 percent of the royalties to him. Publisher refuses to do this. The refusal is justified. At the time Author made the assignment, he had no royalties to assign; so the assignment, as an assignment, is invalid.

However, if Lender demanded that Author pay him 50 percent of the royalties he received, he could enforce that demand. The Author-Lender bargain could not be an assignment because there existed nothing to assign. But it could and would be interpreted as a contract to assign. If at the time of the Lender-Author bargain, Author had a signed contract with Publisher under which Publisher had agreed to publish the novel when complete and to pay Author a royalty upon each copy sold, Lender would have a valid assignment. Since Publisher was bound by contract to pay royalties to Author, Author in this case would have had a vested right to assign.

Assignable rights. The most commonly assigned contract right is the right to receive money. It does not matter whether the right being assigned is liquidated or unliquidated, nor does it matter if the assigned right is conditional. Thus, in the situation where Attorney is representing Client in litigation on a contingent fee basis, Attorney could assign his right to receive a fee from Client to Creditor. Of course, Creditor cannot be certain that he will receive anything under the assignment, because Client might not win the case. But since Attorney does have a vested contingent right here, he has something which is assignable.

A cocreditor may assign his portion of a right to receive money. Thus: Able owes Baker and Charles $1,000, Baker and Charles being co-owners of this obligation. Baker may assign his interest in this obligation to Davis.

A creditor may also assign a portion of an obligation, though this normally is not very wise. Thus: Franks owes Gibson $1,000. Gibson owes Hart $500. Gibson may assign to Hart the right to receive $500 from Franks.

A judgment is an assignable debt. It must be remembered, though, that the assignment of a judgment must be in writing to be valid, and the assignee must record the assignment in a proper public record.

Some rights other than rights to receive money are also assignable. One of these which is of interest is the right to accept an option. If Partin owns an option by which he has the right to buy Lot 6 of Zilch Addition from Quirt any time before December 31, 1981, Partin may assign the right to accept this option to Sands. Of course, it must be remembered that the sale of the right to accept the option is also the delegation of any duties falling upon the owner of the option. Thus, if the option gives Partin the right to buy the lot from Quirt on credit, Quirt would not have to recognize Sands as the owner of the option if he does not care to, because of the personal nature of the credit term of the option. However, if the option obligated Partin to pay cash for the lot, the option is freely transferrable.

The mechanics of assignment. In general, assignments may be oral or written. They may be for consideration or gratuitous. They may be evidenced by a contract or by a transfer of possession of property only.

A few types of assignments must be in writing to be valid. These were listed in the chapter on the statute of frauds; by way of review you should remember that assignments of such things as judgments, real estate mortgages, patents, copyrights, trademarks, and other such things must be written. When a writing is not required by law, an oral assignment is permissible.

The ordinary contractual assignment is made for consideration. A contractual assignment not accompanied by consideration will not be valid unless it constituted a completed gift, because a promise to make a gift is unenforceable (due to lack of consideration).

The subject of gifts will be covered in some detail in the chapter on personal property, but some mention must be made here of the requirements for a valid gift. The law recognizes two types of gifts: the gift inter vivos and the gift causa mortis. The gift inter vivos is the common, everyday gift. There are two requirements: intent on the part of the donor to make the gift and delivery of the subject matter of the gift to the donee. In this context, then, transfer of possession of the thing being assigned is absolutely essential to the validity of a gratuitous assignment.

The gift causa mortis is a gift in anticipation of death. There are four essential elements here: The donor must fear that he is going to die of some specific cause; because of this fear, he develops the intent to make the gift. He delivers possession of the gift to the donee. He then dies of what he feared would kill him. If the donor does not die of what he feared, the gift becomes revocable. Again, there can generally be no valid gratuitous assignment in the absence of a completed valid gift.

Generally, assignments for consideration are evidenced by some sort of contract, either written or oral. However, some types of rights which are evidenced by documents may be assigned for consideration simply by transfer of possession of the documents. Among the documents which may be transferred in this way are items of commercial paper (checks, drafts, and promissory notes), documents of title (warehouse receipts, bills of lading, and delivery orders), investment securities (stock certificates, bonds, and debentures), savings account passbooks, some types of insurance policies, and similar posessions.

Multiple assignments of the same right. It sometimes happens that an assignor through fraud or negligence assigns the same right to two or more assignees. The problem then arises, which of the assignments is the valid one?

If both assignments are for consideration, Texas courts follow the rule of "first in time, first in right." In other words, the first assignment takes precedence over subsequent assignments.

If the assignment involves a right which must be recorded—that is, if the assignment is of a judgment, real estate mortgage, or all or most of the accounts receivable of a business—or if it is an assignment of an item of intellectual property (a patent, copyright, or trademark), the first assignment recorded takes priority. It is thus essential for an assignee of such a property right to record his assignment as soon as possible, in order to avoid losing out to a subsequent assignee.

If a gratuitous assignment is followed by an assignment for consideration, the assignment for consideration takes precedence, unless the gratuitous assignment was a completed gift. The rationale here is that completion of a gift transfers legal title to the subject matter to the donee, so that the donor had nothing to assign when he made his subsequent assignment for consideration.

Rights of assignees. The assignee of a contract right ordinarily gets the same right to realize upon it that the assignor had—no more, no less. Thus, if the obligor (the person owing the duty the right to receive which was assigned) has a reason not to perform for the assignor, he need not perform for the assignee.

Thus: Seller sells Buyer defective goods on credit for $1,000, Buyer not knowing the goods were defective when he took possession. Seller assigned the account receivable to Assignee, Assignee not knowing of the defective goods. Assignee notified Buyer of the assignment, Buyer notified Assignee of the defective goods, and stated that he would pay only $300 for them. Buyer could prove that the goods were worth only $300. In such a case, Seller could collect only $300 from Buyer, so that is all Assignee can collect.

Or: Lender lent Junior, a minor, $500 for non-necessities. Lender assigned the account to Assignee. When Assignee demanded payment from Junior, Junior invoked his right as a minor not to pay. Assignee could not force him to pay.

Sometimes the obligor can use a claim of set-off which he has against the assignor against the assignee. Thus: Seller sells goods to Buyer on credit for $1,000. A few days later, Buyer lends Seller $500 for a week in a totally unrelated transaction. The week passes, but Seller does not repay the loan to Buyer. Buyer does not pay Seller for the goods either. Later Seller assigns the right to collect the $1,000 for the goods to Assignee. When Assignee demands that Buyer pay this, Buyer says he will pay only $500. This is all Assignee can collect. Buyer could offset the $500 Seller owes him against the $1,000 he owed Buyer; so Assignee collects only what Seller could collect.

A set-off arising after assignee is notified of an assignment cannot be used by obligor against assignee. Thus: On Monday Seller sells $1,000 worth of goods to Buyer on thirty-day open account. On Tuesday Buyer lends Seller $500, repayable on Friday. On Wednesday Seller assigns the $1,000 account receivable to Assignee, notifying Assignee of the assignment. On Thursday Assignee notifies Buyer of the assignment. On Friday Seller does not pay back the $500 as he agreed to do. When Assignee later demands $1,000 from Buyer, Buyer claims he need pay only $500. He is wrong. Since the debt Seller owed Buyer had not matured when the assignment was made, Buyer cannot use it as a set-off. Buyer must pay Assignee the $1,000, and get his $500 from Seller. Of course, the obligor may use any claim he has against the assignee as a set-off against the assignee's claim on him.

A seller of goods on credit or a lender of money who customarily assigns accounts receivable to financing institutions may try to arrange matters so that the obligor is obligated to pay an assignee even though he may be able to escape paying the assignor. This is done by including a waiver of defenses clause in the contract between obligor and assignee.

A waiver of defenses clause provides essentially that an obligor agrees not to use any reason he might have for not paying an assignor as an excuse for not paying an assignee. Naturally, an obligor who has much bargaining power will not agree to such a clause. These clauses get into contracts because a would-be assignor has bargaining power superior enough to get them included.

The use of such a clause in a consumer contract is now banned by a trade regulation rule of the Federal Trade Commission. Under this rule, consumer contracts must contain a legend in conspicuous type stating that consumer may use any defense to payment he possesses against any assignee of the right to collect his payment. Thus, an assignee of a consumer account receivable will never get better rights to collect the account than his assignor had. However, use of the waiver of defenses clause is still legitimate in commercial contracts.

Effect of modification of assigned contract right by assignor and obligor without assignee's consent. The assignee of a contract right in a sense acquires a vested right at the moment he is informed of the assignment. However, the assignee needs to perfect his vested right by telling the obligor of the assignment, especially if the contract giving rise to the assigned right is executory (totally unperformed).

Thus: On Monday seller contracts to sell a car to Buyer, Seller to deliver and Buyer to pay on Friday. On Tuesday Seller for consideration assigns the right to collect the purchase price to Assignee. On Wednesday Assignee informs Buyer of the assignment. On Thursday Buyer asks Seller if he could postpone payment until Monday. Seller agrees. This does not bind Assignee; since Buyer knows of the assignment the contract cannot be modified without Assignee's consent. However, had Buyer not been informed of the assignment, the payment date would have been changed to Monday. If the change damaged Assignee in any way he could recover damages from Seller.

If the contract is partially performed, the assignee's rights are totally vested, and no modification of the contract is possible without his consent. Thus: Seller delivers a car to Buyer on Monday, and Buyer promises to pay $400 for it on Friday. On Tuesday Seller assigns the right to collect to Assignee. On Thursday Buyer asks Seller to change the payment date to next Tuesday and Seller agrees, Buyer being unaware of the assignment. This does not bind Assignee, who is entitled to enforce the original agreement and to collect on Friday unless he agrees to the modification.

When assignment becomes binding on obligor. Obviously, an obligor will not know about an assignment until someone tells him of it, or until he finds out about it in some other way. An obligor is thus under no obligation to perform for an assignee until he learns of the assignment. Assignees should therefore inform obligors of their assignments as soon as possible. Failure by assignees to do this may result in grave difficulties.

Thus: Debtor owes Creditor $5,000. Creditor assigns the right to collect this to Assignee on Monday. Assignee does not tell Debtor about this. On Thursday Debtor pays Creditor the $5,000, Creditor taking the money and not mentioning the assignment. On Friday Assignee informs Debtor of the assignment and demands his money. Debtor refuses to pay again. Debtor's position is correct. He paid in good faith to the party he thought he was supposed to pay, so his obligation is discharged.

On the other hand, had Assignee in the above example told Debtor of the assignment on Tuesday, and had Debtor still paid Creditor on Thursday because he did not want to be involved with Assignee, Debtor could be required to pay again. In this case he deliberately paid a person he knew he was not supposed to pay.

The same sort of problem can arise with respect to multiple assignments of the same right. Thus: Ard owes Boggs $1,000. On Monday Boggs assigns the right to collect this to Cass. On Tuesday Boggs assigns the same right to Dowd, both assignments being for consideration. On Wednesday Dowd tells Ard about his assignment, and Ard pays him. On Thursday Cass tells Ard about his assignment, and, when Ard explains that he has already paid Dowd, Cass demands that he pay again. To be sure, Cass's assignment had priority over Dowd's, but how was Ard to know about Cass if no one told him? Ard paid in good faith here, so his obligation is discharged.

Situations may arise where the obligor is not sure who he must pay. Thus: Smith owes Tutt $1,000. Tutt assigns the right to collect this to Verk, and Verk informs Smith of the assignment. Then, Tutt demands $1,000 from Smith. Smith tells Tutt he will not pay, because Verk has told him of the assignment. Tutt says that Verk is a liar, that he, Tutt, has made no such assignment. Smith is now in an uncomfortable position. Should he believe

Verk, or should he believe Tutt? If Verk has something in writing signed by Tutt proving the assignment, Smith could safely pay Verk. If Verk has no such writing, Smith takes a risk in paying either claimant.

Smith may escape his dilemma in one of two ways. He could refuse to pay either claimant, and wait until one of them sues him. He can then use as a defense the claim of the other to the money. The other claimant may then be made a party to the case, and the court will decide to whom the $1,000 is owing.

Smith's other escape route is to file an interpleader complaint against both claimants, alleging in essence that he owes $1,000 to either Tutt or Verk, but he is not sure which, and that he asks the court to tell him to whom the money is owed. Tutt and Verk will be the defendants; they fight it out as to who gets the $1,000.

The obligor may face the same problem when multiple assignments have been made; two or more assignees may claim to be the first assignees. The obligor may also resolve these situations as described above.

Rights of competing assignees among themselves. When two or more assignments of a right have been made, but the obligor has not yet performed his duty, priority among the assignees is determined according to the rules of priority described above: first in time, first in right, assignment for consideration prevails over gratuitous assignment, or first to record, first in right. When the obligor has paid one of the assignees, though, these rules may not apply. If the obligor has paid one of the assignees in good faith, his obligation is discharged.

If the obligation is one in which recording of assignments is mandatory or advisable, the obligor should check the public records before he pays anyone. Everyone is presumed to know what is in the public records, so payment to a subordinate assignee is by definition payment in bad faith and is thus not a discharge of the obligation. If the obligation is one in which recording of assignments is not done, the obligor knows nothing about assignments which have not been communicated to him. If he pays in good faith, he has paid, even though the assignee he paid has rights which are in truth inferior to those of another assignee. The rights of the competing assignees among themselves must then be considered.

The rule here is that an assignee who collects upon a claim in good faith keeps the proceeds of his collection, even when his right to collect upon the claim is inferior to that of another assignee. Thus: Black owes Brown $1,000. Brown assigns the right to collect this to Tann. He then assigns the same right to White. White informs Black of the assignment to him, and Black pays him. Tann then informs Black of the assignment to him, and gets the bad news that Black has already paid White. Tann cannot collect from Black, because Black has paid White in good faith. Could Tann then collect from White? The answer is negative, because White collected the amount in good faith, not knowing of the assignment to Tann. Had White known of the prior assignment to Tann when he collected from Black, Tann could recover the payment from him, because White would have collected in bad faith.

Here again, if assignments of the claim have been recorded, a subordinate assignee who collects upon a claim does so in bad faith, because he is expected to know what is in the public records. So if the records show that the subordinate assignee's claim is truly subordinate, they show that the subordinate assignee has in essence no right to collect.

Warranties of an assignor. If an assignee is unable to collect upon the assigned claim from the obligor, can he collect from the assignor? The answer depends on the circumstances. An assignor makes two implied warranties to his assignee:

1. That the right assigned actually exists.

2. That the assigned right is worth the agreed face value and is not subject to defenses, off-sets, etc.

Examples of the applicability of these warranties include:

1. Blue owed Green $1,000. Blue paid this obligation to Redd, Green's agent, who had authority to collect it. Green, not knowing of Blue's payment to Redd, assigned the account to Orange. When Orange sought to collect, Blue showed him his receipt from Redd, showing the debt paid. Orange therefore demanded $1,000 from Green. He collected. The assigned obligation did not exist any more at the time of assignment.

2. Black owed Gray $1,000 for goods purchased on credit, or so Gray claimed. Black claimed he owed only $400 for these goods because they were defective. Gray assigned the right to collect $1,000 from Black to White. When White sought to collect the $1,000, Black tendered him $400. White refused to take this and sued for $1,000. Black used defective goods as a defense and won the case, so he paid $400. White now demanded $600 from Gray. He also collected, since Gray had breached his implied warranty that the claim was good for $1,000.

An assignor does not warrant that the obligor is solvent. He also does not warrant that the obligation is collectable. Thus, if the obligor is discharged from his debts in bankruptcy before the assignee can collect from him, the assignee takes the loss.

Of course, the assignor will be liable to the assignee in damages if fraudulent acts by the assignor prevent the assignee's realization upon the assigned claim. If the assignor makes two assignments of the same claim, only one assignee will be able to collect. The other will have recourse against the assignor.

The warranty liability of the assignor may of course be varied by contract. In cases where the assignee has superior bargaining power, he may be able to get the assignor to guarantee collectability of the assigned claim. In such a case, the assignor will be obligated to pay the assignee if the assignee is unable to collect from the obligor.

On the other hand, if the assignor has superior bargaining power he may be able to get the assignee to agree to an assignment without recourse. In such a case the assignor makes no warranties to the assignee. If the assignee cannot collect from the obligor he is completely out of luck, unles the assignor committed fraud in the assignment or some similar problem arises.

Subassignments. The law does not prevent an assignee from making a further assignment of an assigned claim. Such an assignment is a subassignment, and the second assignee is a subassignee. A subassignee acquires the collection rights of the assignee. The assignee also makes the implied warranties to the subassignee. However, the original assignor makes no warranties to a subassignee.

Thus: Redd assigns his $1,000 claim against Scarlett to Pink. Scarlett has already paid off this obligation to an agent of Redd, but Redd does not know this. Pink then assigns the right to collect to White. White asks Scarlett to pay. Scarlett refuses, proving that he has already paid. Scarlett being off the hook, White demands $1,000 from Redd because of breach of warranty. White cannot collect, because Redd did not assign the claim to White. White has a breach of warranty claim only against Pink, and Pink in turn will have a breach of warranty claim against Redd.

Enforcement of partial assignments. Suppose that Azul owes Rojo $1,000. Rojo owes Blanco $500. In order to pay Blanco, Rojo assigns to him the right to collect $500 from Azul. Blanco informs Azul of the assignment. Azul refuses to pay Blanco anything, because, he says, he does not really owe Rojo anything. Blanco therefore files suit against Azul for $500. Azul moves to dismiss the case because Rojo is not involved as a party. The result will either be that Rojo will be joined as a party to the case, or that Blanco's complaint will be dismissed. The reason for this is that, originally, Azul owed one debt to Rojo. When Rojo assigned the right to collect a part of it to Blanco, he in essence split the one debt into two debts. Azul is not obligated to defend himself in two lawsuits brought to collect one debt. He is entitled to have both of his creditors facing him in court here, so that he may get the question of whether or not he owes this obligation settled once and for all.

This illustrates the great disadvantage of partial assignments of a claim. Such an assignment splits one debt of the obligor into two. The claim may now not be resolved in court without bringing both creditors before the court. This can cause complications.

Acceptance of an assignment by assignee. Technically, an assignee is not bound to accept the benefit of an assignment, but since it is to his advantage to do so, no question usually arises as to whether or not he has accepted. Silence by the assignee upon receipt of notice of an assignment is considered to be acceptance. However, an assignee may disclaim the benefits of an assignment. When the assignee does this, he gives up all benefits conferred by the assignment.

16

Performance and Discharge of Contracts

Performance of Contracts

In general, each party to a contract has the obligation to do exactly what he promised to do at the time and place at which he promised to do it. Failure to perform exactly as one has agreed to perform is a breach.

A question may arise as to whether a breach by one party will excuse the other from the obligation to perform, thus in effect discharging the contract. Although it may seem at first glance that any sort of breach should result in a termination of the victim's duties under the contract, such a rule does not always make sense.

Whether a breach will result in a discharge of the entire contract will in essence depend upon two things: the nature of the breach and the wording of the contract. An obligation may be worded as a condition, in which case a breach of it discharges the contract. Or it may be worded as a promise, in which case a breach of it may not necessarily discharge the contract.

Conditions may be express—spelled out in the contract. They may also be implied by the nature of the bargain. A condition may be a condition precedent, in which case the contract would not come into being until the condition is met; or it may be a condition subsequent, in which case an existing contractual obligation may be discharged if the condition is not met.

Conditions precedent. Certain "magic words" will indicate the presence of a condition precedent in the contract. Among these are the words "if," "to be," "to go (depart, etc.)," "provided that," "on condition that," and "when."

Examples of the use of these words and phrases include:

1. Able promises to pay $500 for Baker's car on January 15, 1980 "on condition that Baker deliver the car to Able with four new tires properly mounted thereon on or before January 9, 1980."

2. Boss agrees to hire Cypher as his chief bookkeeper for a year beginning July 1, 1980, "if Cypher receives his degree in accounting from Podunk State University at the end of the spring semester of 1980."

3. Eagle of Houston agrees to ship goods by water to Fields of Kingston, Jamaica aboard the *USS Seawitch*, "said vessel to depart from the port of Houston no later than January 22, 1980."

4. Goss contracts to buy a described machine from Harvey, the machine "to be delivered by the said Harvey on the railway siding at the Goss factory in Pearland, Texas, no later than January 15, 1980."

5. Jackson contracts to buy a racing car from Kinney on March 1, 1980, "provided that if said car fails to finish any race between now and March 1, 1980, due to mechanical defect this agreement shall be of no force and effect."

6. Lord for consideration promises to pay Monk $5,000 "when I sell Lot 12 of Zilch Addition, located in Podunk, Texas."

If the expressed condition is not complied with, there is no contract. However, if the condition is not met because of the wrongdoing of the party who wants release from the bargain, the bargain will be enforceable despite the nonfulfillment of the condition. Thus, in example 5 above, if the car in question breaks down during an auto race in January, 1980, because Jackson sabotaged it, Kinney could still enforce the contract of sale against Jackson.

If parties want to include a condition precedent in their contract, they must carefully word the provision containing it so that there is no doubt that the provision is a condition. Courts are reluctant to declare the nonexistence of a contract due to nonfulfillment of a condition precedent. They will seize upon any available excuse to find that the contract does not contain any condition.

When contract provisions are not stated as conditions—when the contract states, "It is agreed that," or "Creditor promises that," or words to that effect—a breach of the promise will not result in the nonexistence of the contract. Whether or not the breach will excuse the victim's performance will depend upon whether or not the breaching party has given substantial performance of his bargain, a matter which will be discussed later in this chapter.

Conditions subsequent. Conditions subsequent are relatively rare. The three most common kinds are:

1. A provision commonly found in life insurance policies that any person with a claim under a policy must sue upon it within two years of the death of the insured; otherwise the insurer is under no obligation to pay the claim.

2. A provision commonly found in fire insurance and similar policies that, in case the insured suffers a loss covered by the terms of the policy, he must file a proof of loss within a certain number of days of the loss; otherwise the company will be under no obligation to pay the claim.

3. A provision sometimes found in contracts for the sale of goods, that if buyer has any claim against seller relative to the quality of the goods or the like, he must make it within two years of the date of the sale, otherwise seller shall not be responsible.

The occurrence of the condition subsequent—nonfiling of a claim or proof of loss within the prescribed time period—extinguishes a contract right which existed up to that time.

The "expert's certificate" condition in construction contracts. The usual construction contract provides that the customer who has contracted for erection of a building or other structure will make progress payments to the general contractor as the work of construction progresses. It also provides that the customer will make the final payment after construction is completed. The customer is ordinarily not obligated to make this final payment until the general contractor produces a certificate of approval of his work from an architect or other expert, stating that the construction contract has been complied with. Production of this certificate is a condition precedent with respect to the contractor's right to receive the final payment.

Normally, if the expert refuses to issue the certificate the contractor will not be paid the final payment. However, there are circumstances under which the contractor is entitled to payment despite the refusal of the expert to issue the certificate. These circumstances are:

1. The expert's refusal is arbitrary and unreasonable. In case of litigation, of course, the contractor must prove that the expert was arbitrary and unreasonable, which is difficult.
2. The expert died before completion of the building, or he was physically or mentally incapable of performing his final inspection.
3. The expert's refusal to issue the certificate was made in bad faith, because of collusion with the customer, refusal to exercise honest judgment, fraud, or the like.
4. The expert made a mistake of fact in evaluating contractor's work—discrepancies he complained about were not discrepancies at all.
5. The contractor has substantially performed the contract—he has done 95 percent or more of his work according to the terms of the contract.

If the expert refuses to issue the certificate in good faith, or if he bases his refusal to issue upon an error of judgment (and not an error of fact) it is too bad for the contractor—he will not be able to get his final payment.

The implied condition of payment in legal tender. Unless a contract for sale says otherwise, the buyer of whatever is the subject matter of the contract must pay in legal tender. With respect to contracts for the sale of goods, this is expressly provided for in TB&CC (UCC) 2-511. It is provided for in the common law in other cases.

Legal tender is essentially lawful money of the United States—in other words, cash. A seller need not accept payment, then, in the form of a check, or in foreign currency, or in a commodity. Unless the contract expressly calls for payment in cash, however, a buyer does not breach if he tenders payment in the form of a check or the like. The seller has the right, though, to refuse the check and to demand cash. But, if the seller chooses to demand payment in cash he must give the buyer a reasonable time to obtain said cash before he claims breach.

Implied concurrent conditions of delivery and payment. Unless a contract expressly provides for delivery of subject matter at one time and payment at another, it is assumed that delivery and payment are due at the same time. When this is the case, a party cannot complain about another's nonperformance unless he himself has tendered performance.

Thus: On Monday Seller and Buyer agree that Seller will sell his car to Buyer for $400, Seller to deliver the car at noon Friday, and Buyer to pay cash for it at that time. Neither party contacts the other at noon Friday, and neither says a word to the other all weekend. Seller now wants to file suit against Buyer for breach on Monday. He is wasting his time. Buyer was wrong not to offer to pay for the car, as he agreed; but Seller was also wrong not to tender delivery of the car, as he agreed. So, Seller has no claim against Buyer, and Buyer has no claim against Seller.

Had the bargain provided that Buyer would take possession of the car on Monday and he would pay for it on Friday; and had Seller actually delivered on Monday without Buyer paying on Friday, Seller could of course sue on the next Monday because he had already performed his end.

Suppose the bargain provided that Seller would deliver the car on Friday, and that Buyer would pay the next Thursday. Seller did not deliver on Friday and the parties did not contact each other all weekend, so Buyer wanted to file suit on Monday. Here, Buyer may sue, even though he has not tendered payment. This is so because his tender of payment is not due yet. He may sue without tender of payment if he does so before Thursday; if he waits until Thursday or later to sue, though, he must tender payment first.

Time of performance. It might seem logical that a party to a contract must perform his obligation on or before the agreed time for performance, and that otherwise breach has occurred. This, though logical, is not always true. The true rule is that performance is due on or before the agreed time, or within a reasonable time thereafter, unless time is of the essence. If time is of the essence, then, performance which is one minute late is a breach. If time is not of the essence, performance which is three days late may not be a breach. Time is of the essence under the following circumstances:

1. When the parties to the contract agree that it is. If they so agree, they should insert a "time is of the essence" clause in the agreement.
2. In contracts for the sale of goods.
3. In contracts for the sale of securities.
4. In charter parties (contracts for the charter of a vessel).
5. In option contracts.

In contracts for sale of goods and securities, courts will insist upon timely delivery of the subject matter. They do not hesitate to call late delivery a breach. They are somewhat more broad-minded about late payment. The logic behind this distinction is this: A seller is not likely to suffer any great damage if he does not get paid on time, but a buyer might suffer considerable damage if he does not get his goods or securities on time. The buyer might have an immediate need for the goods, and the price of securities can change very rapidly.

In other sorts of contracts where time is of the essence, any performance which is late is generally a breach.

Time generally is not of the essence in the following sorts of contracts:

1. Contracts for work or labor.
2. Contracts for personal services.
3. Construction contracts.
4. Contracts for purchase of land.

Remember, though, that the parties may make time of the essence in these if they agree to do so and if they insert the proper clause in the written agreement.

Most insurance policies provide that time is of the essence in filing of claims and the like. However, since insurers do not bargain with the insured on policy terms, courts are reluctant to construe "time is of the essence" clauses in insurance policies strictly. They give the insured the benefit of the doubt when they can.

Contracts requiring performance "to personal satisfaction." When the parties agree that one will perform to the personal satisfaction of the other, problems may arise. If the promisee says he is not satisfied, but the promisor says that he should be satisfied, has a breach occurred?

If the contract is for the doing of something involving the personal taste of the promisee, and the promisee says he is not satisfied, there is a breach. In such cases a subjective standard is used—if the promisee is not satisfied, he is not satisfied, and that is that. Types of contracts to perform "to personal satisfaction" where the subjective standard is used include:

1. Painting of portraits.

2. Making of sculpture.
3. Tailoring custom-made clothing.
4. Cooking and baking.
5. Landscaping.
6. Hair styling.
7. Making of photographs.
8. Interior decorating.

If the contract involves the doing of work not involving personal taste "to personal satisfaction," an objective standard is used to evaluate the work if the promisee says he is not satisfied. In other words, the work is evaluated by experts, and if they say the work is properly done and the promisee should be satisfied, there is no breach. Among those types of contracts in which the objective standard is used are the following:

1. Tuning up a car, changing its oil, lubricating it, or the like.
2. Mowing a lawn.
3. Constructing a building.
4. Filling a tooth.
5. Removing an appendix, etc.
6. Harvesting a crop.

To sum up here: if the contract is to perform services "to personal satisfaction" which do not involve personal taste, no additional burden is imposed upon the person agreeing to do the work. If he does a good workmanlike job, his customer should be satisfied, so he can be made to pay even if he says he is dissatisfied.

If the contract is to perform work involving personal taste "to personal satisfaction," the promisor takes a sizable risk in agreeing to such a term. He must do his work in a manner which pleases his customer, with the customer as sole judge as to whether or not he is pleased. If promisor does not want to assume the risk of dealing with a particular customer who can never be pleased, he can refuse to agree to perform "to personal satisfaction." If there is no "to personal satisfaction" agreement in the contract, the promisor's work will be judged by objective standards, and he may be able to collect payment even if his customer is not satisfied if he did an objectively good job. The ultimate protection is to refuse to work for customers who are too particular.

Effect of breach of an installment contract. An installment contract is one which is to be performed in segments rather than all at once. For instance, if Able agrees in February that he will mow Baker's lot every other Monday for six months beginning the first Monday in March for $4 per mowing, we have an installment contract.

A problem can arise when an installment is breached. Is this to be considered as a breach of the installment only, or is it a breach of the entire contract? The resolution of the problem can make quite a difference to the parties. If a breach of an installment is a breach of the whole contract, the victim may cancel the balance of the contract and sue for damages for breach of the balance. If on the other hand the breach is only a breach of the installment, the victim may claim damages for the breach of the installment, but the unperformed balance of the contract remains in force.

Generally, a breach of the first installment of such a contract will be considered a breach of the whole bargain. After all, if the breaching party will not even perform the first installment as agreed, how can the victim be sure he will perform subsequent installments? Cancellation of the whole contract would be quite justifiable here. However, breach of a later installment may not be considered a breach of the whole. For instance, if Able in the above example diligently mows Baker's yard as agreed during March, April, and May, but he does not do the first mowing in June, Baker cannot assume that he intends to abandon the contract at this point, since he has already performed half of it as agreed. However, if Able also does not come to do the second mowing in June, it now looks like he intends to abandon the contract; at least, he has shown himself to be so unreliable that his ability to perform in the future is now in serious doubt. Nonperformance of two consecutive installments would certainly be grounds for cancellation.

Substantial performance. In the performance of complex contracts, such as construction contracts, it sometimes happens that the contract is almost, but not quite, perfectly performed. The question then arises as to whether or not the almost-perfect performance is enough of a breach to relieve the other party of the duty to perform.

If the discrepancy is due to the deliberate act of the performing party, it is treated as a breach. However, if the discrepancy is inadvertent, and performance by the party who made the error is not a condition of the other party's obligation to perform, the doctrine of substantial performance applies. The discrepancy is then considered a breach in that the other party is entitled to recover damages for it. However, it is not such a breach as to excuse the performance of the other party.

Thus: Builder contracts to construct a house for Owner. He complies with the contract in all respects, except that he inadvertently paints a bedroom the wrong color. Owner cannot escape making the final payment due to this, but he may deduct from the payment the cost of getting the room repainted. Or, perhaps, Builder will repaint the room at his own expense.

If the construction of the building is only 90 percent according to specifications, a court probably would not call this substantial performance. In such a case the builder cannot require his customer to make the final payment of the contract price, and the customer is excused from further performance. This does not necessarily mean that the customer need not pay builder anything more. If the customer is allowed to obtain the rest of the builder's work free of charge, the customer may well be unjustly enriched at the builder's expense. So, though customer is excused from paying contract price for the improperly constructed building, he may be forced to pay the builder the fair value of his work. Of course, the customer may deduct from that damages for the builder's breach of contract.

Anticipatory breach. If a party states in advance of the time his performance is due that he will not perform, anticipatory breach has occurred. The other party may legitimately react to this in one of two ways: He may take the breaching party at his word, and treat the contract as breached. He may then sue for damages, or exercise any other remedy for breach which might be available to him. Or, he may inform the other party that he will not accept his statement as a breach, and he still expects the other party to perform as agreed. In such a case, the contract still exists and is in full force and effect. Each party will then be expected to perform when the performances are due.

The victim of an anticipatory breach is bound by his initial response to it. If he accepts the anticipatory breach as a breach, the contract is dead and can only be revived by mutual consent. If he refuses to accept it as a breach, he has waived his right to call it a breach. Any effort on his part to back out now will in and of itself be a breach.

Discharge of Contracts

The usual method of discharge of contractual obligation is by performance—that is, each party to the contract does what he obligated himself to do. When all duties are performed, the contract of course no longer exists. However, contractual obligations may be discharged in ways other than by performance. There are numerous ways in which contracts may be terminated by act of the parties other than performance. There are also numerous ways in which these obligations may be discharged by operation of law, without any act of the parties.

We shall first consider the methods of discharge by act of the parties, and afterward the methods of discharge by operation of law.

Excuse for nonperformance created by other party or by circumstances. Several sorts of occurrences may create an excuse for nonperformance. Among these are the following:

1. A condition precedent did not occur. Buyer contracted to hire Pharmacist to manage a named drugstore, on condition that Owner sold him the store. Owner did not sell. Therefore, Buyer has no store for Pharmacist to manage. The condition did not occur.

2. A condition subsequent did occur. Owner had fire insurance upon the goods in his house. Some of these were burned in a hostile fire, but Owner did not file a proof of loss with his insurer within sixty days of the loss, as his policy required. The insurer refused to pay the claim. His duty was discharged by the occurrence of the condition subsequent. The proof of loss was not filed on time.

3. One party breached before the other's performance was due. Buyer and Seller made a contract on Monday that Seller would deliver his car to Buyer on Tuesday, and Buyer would pay on Friday. Seller did not deliver on Tuesday. Buyer's duty to pay is discharged.

4. One party deliberately prevented the other from performing. On Monday Seller contracted to sell a vase to Buyer on Friday, delivery and payment due Friday. On Thursday Buyer paid Ruff to go to Seller's and smash the vase, which Ruff did.

5. Performance was tendered too late when time was of the essence. On Monday Seller and Buyer contracted that Seller would sell his car to Buyer for $700, Seller to deliver the car on Tuesday, Buyer to pay on Friday, Buyer specifying that he had to have the car on Tuesday. Seller did not tender delivery until Wednesday, and Buyer refused to take it.

6. An anticipatory breach has occurred, and the other party has accepted it as a breach.

Mutual rescission. Mutual rescission occurs when the parties to the contract agree to rescind. Mutual assent is necessary, and consideration is also necessary. If the contract is executory, consideration will be present if there is mutual assent, because each party will be giving up his right against the other. If the contract has been completely performed on one side, though, additional consideration will be necessary. The party who has already received performance has no right to give up.

There is no requirement that the rescission be in writing, even though the contract to be rescinded is in writing. An oral rescission of a written contract is perfectly binding—the only problem may lie in proving the mutual agreement to rescind.

Unilateral rescission. Under some circumstances one of the parties to a contract may rescind it without the other party's consent. There are three major types of circumstances in which this is possible.

The first of these is the contract of employment or agency where no set period of employment or agency has been agreed to. The employment or agency relationship will then last only as long as both parties desire it to last. Unless otherwise agreed, an employee may quit his job at any time he feels like it, and an agent may resign his employment as agent any time. The right of a principal to fire an agent is also almost unrestricted, unless the agency contract provides otherwise. The right of an employer to fire an employee may be more restricted, due to antidiscrimination laws of one sort and another. This will be discussed in some detail in the chapter on employment.

Another circumstance under which unilateral rescission is possible is in the situation where a party enters into a contract under duress or undue influence, where he has been defrauded, where he is a victim of violation of a fiduciary relationship, or where a mutual mistake as to the nature of the subject matter exists. In all of these cases, the victim may unilaterally rescind.

The third situation in which unilateral rescission is possible—and the situation requiring the most explanation—is the situation where a consumer signs a contract to buy consumer goods at a place other than the seller's place of business. The consumer may well have the right to unilaterally rescind such a contract, at least for a few days after he signed it. The rescission right is provided by both federal law and Texas state law. The federal law is an administrative regulation of the Federal Trade Commission—16 CFR 429. The Texas state law is found in Chapter 13 of the Consumer Credit Code—RCS 5069-13.01 et seq. The provisions of the federal regulation and the state law are essentially the same, with a few minor exceptions.

The consumer has the right to rescind a contract for purchase of goods or services made at a place other than the seller's place of business if:

1. The consideration for the goods or services to be purchased exceeds $25, and
2. The salesman is not calling to complete negotiations begun at seller's place of business, and
3. The salesman is not calling in response to an emergency request from consumer for goods or services needed immediately, and
4. The bargain has not been negotiated by mail or telephone, with no personal contact between consumer and seller before seller's agent calls to deliver the goods or perform the services, and
5. The salesman has not come at consumer's request to perform repair or maintenance service upon consumer's property, and
6. The transaction does not involve rental of real estate or the sale of securities or commodities.

In short, for the rescission right to exist there must be more than $25 involved in the transaction; the sale must involve purchase of goods, services, or real estate (but not rental of real estate or purchase of securities or commodities); the seller must have initiated the contact leading to the making of the contract; and there must not have been a contact made by mail or telephone before personal contact was established between salesman and consumer.

If the contract is one in which the rescission right exists, the seller must include certain disclosures in the contract in order to limit the consumer's rescission right to within three business days of the making of the contract. It is also required that the seller write his contract in the language used in the making of the sales pitch. Thus, if the salesman makes his presentation in Spanish, the contract must be in Spanish; if the sales pitch is in German, the contract must be in German; and so forth.

Assuming that the contract is written in the proper language, it must make the following disclosures:

1. That the consumer may cancel the contract without penalty by mailing notice on a form attached to the contract to the seller at an address disclosed upon the form.
2. That any trade-in, down payment, or other consideration made by consumer will be returned by seller within ten days of receipt of notice of cancellation.

3. That consumer must make available to seller at his residence any goods that he received from seller, in the event of cancellation.
4. That, if consumer does not make the above-mentioned goods available to seller, the contract will remain in full force.
5. That, if seller does not pick up the above-mentioned goods within twenty days of the date of cancellation, consumer is free to use or dispose of the goods as he sees fit.
These disclosures must be printed in the contract in a conspicuous manner.

Seller is also obligated to inform consumer orally of his rescission right. The nature of the right must not be misrepresented in any way. The seller must not assign any contract right under such a contract before midnight of the fifth business day after the making of the contract. If consumer rescinds, seller must return the down payment or trade-in within ten business days, as provided in the contract, and seller must inform consumer within ten days of rescission as to whether or not he will repossess any goods delivered to consumer under the contract.

If the required disclosures—both written and oral—are not made, consumer may rescind at any time; the contract is void. If the proper disclosures are made, notice of rescission must be sent by midnight of the third business day after the making of the contract to the address specified in the contract. Sundays and holidays do not count as business days for this purpose.

Consumer has the right to sue seller for damages if the law here is not complied with, the right to sue being granted by Texas law, not by federal law. Consumer may be liable to seller in damages if he does not make available to seller the goods delivered under a rescinded contract, or if he did not properly care for these goods.

Remember that the three-day rescission right applies only to contracts signed at places other than the seller's place of business. It also applies only to consumer contracts, not to commercial contracts.

Accord and satisfaction. This is a bargain by which the parties to a contract agree that one of them may substitute one performance for another. Thus: On Monday Able contracts to sell a named car to Baker for $1,000, delivery of the car and payment for it due on Friday. On Thursday Able tells Baker that he does not want to deliver the car on Friday, and he offers instead to pay Baker $200 on Friday. Baker agrees to take the $200 instead of the car.

When Baker agrees to Able's proposal, an accord has been reached. However, the making of an accord alone will not discharge a contractual obligation. There must also be satisfaction, which in our example will consist of Able's payment of the $200. Accord plus satisfaction equals discharge. Should Able not pay Baker the $200 on Friday as promised, Baker has two avenues of recourse. He may sue Able for $200 for breach of the accord, or he may sue for damages for breach of the contract to sell the car. Whichever alternative Baker chooses, he is justified.

Account stated. When a debtor and a creditor agree that, as of now, debtor owes creditor an agreed sum, an account stated has been agreed upon. The purpose of the arrangement may be to convert an unliquidated debt into a liquidated debt, or it may be to merge several separate debts into one debt. Thus: Redd claims that Pink owes him $1,000 for services rendered. Pink says that the services were worth only $500. After long argument, the parties agree that Pink will pay Redd $800. The agreement has created a new liquidated debt of $800. Redd can no longer claim that Pink owes him $1,000, while Pink can no longer claim that he owes only $500.

Or: Blue owes Green for several separate purchases of goods. Blue has made five purchases from Green within the past six months—one of $500, one of $700, one of $300, and one of $1,000—all of which are undisputed. Blue also made a fifth purchase of goods from Green; Blue claimed these goods were defective, but Green denied the defectiveness of the goods and claimed Blue owed him $800 for this purchase. Blue claimed he owed only $250 because of the defects. The parties, after negotiation, finally agree that Blue owes Green $3,000, all told, on all accounts. At this point Blue no longer owes five debts; he owes only one.

Since an account stated creates an entirely new contract between debtor and creditor, a new statute of limitations begins to run with its making. The making of an account stated is therefore a good way to extend the statute of limitations, where unliquidated debts or multiple accounts exist.

Material alteration of a written contract. When a party in possession of a written contract alters it in some way, the alteration may result in a discharge of the contract. Before such an alteration is a discharge, however, three things must be true of it. First, it must be deliberate—that is, the party doing the altering must intend to do it. Accidental alteration, such as accidental erasure, or accidental mutilation, is not a discharge. Second, it must be fraudulent—that is, the alteration must be done with the intent to deceive the other party to the contract, and it must damage him in some way. Third, it must be material. It must change the obligations of the parties in some way, and must work to the disadvantage of the other party. However, the other party may ratify a material alteration by agreeing to be bound to the contract as altered.

Unauthorized completion may also be a discharge, but it is much harder to prove. Unauthorized completion occurs when a written contract is signed which contains blanks which are not filled in; later a party fills in the blanks in a manner not agreed upon by all parties. If this is fraudulent and material, discharge results.

The intelligent person who enters into a written contract will take steps to ensure that material alteration and unauthorized completion are not likely to occur. He should make certain that a contract contains no blanks not filled in when he signs. Then, once the contract is signed, there should be two copies of it, one to be possessed by each party to the bargain. If a witness or two signs both copies, this is even better—but the witness or witnesses should familiarize themselves with the contents of the contract before they sign; and they should of course be trustworthy.

The courts will presume that all blanks in the contract were filled in before it was signed. The party who claims unauthorized completion must show that the blanks were not filled in at the time he signed, and that the contract as it reads does not represent the true agreement of the parties. It is most difficult to get a judge or jury to buy such an argument, when the other party will swear that all blanks were completed when the contract was signed.

In material alteration cases, proof is fairly easy when the alteration is sloppily done. If it is carefully done, there will be problems. If there is only one copy of the contract, and it was carefully altered, proof of the alteration will be very difficult. If there are two copies, and these are not identical, the case can boil down to one party's word against the other's as to which is the true, unaltered copy. It is in this situation that honest witnesses come in handy. They can give unbiased testimony as to which copy is the true one.

Surrender or cancellation of formal contract. A formal contract is a contract of specified form, such as a check, draft, promissory note, document of title, or investment security, which is transferred by transfer of possession of the document itself. Such a contract may be discharged by:

1. Surrender of the document to the person being discharged. Debtor owes Creditor $500, the debt evidenced by a promissory note. Creditor says he is excusing Debtor from the duty to pay, and gives Debtor possession of the note. This is a good discharge.
2. Cancellation with intent to discharge. If, instead of Creditor in the above example surrendering the note to Debtor, he merely marks it "Paid," it is cancelled and the debt is discharged.
3. Destruction with intent to discharge. If, instead of surrendering the note to Debtor or marking it "Paid," Creditor in the above example tears up the note with intent to discharge it, it is cancelled and the debt is discharged.

The above means of discharge would also work with respect to any written contract contained in a single document which spells out all of the obligations of the parties. However, they would not work to discharge contracts evidenced by informal memoranda, such as an informal note spelling out the terms of sale of a car not signed by both parties to the bargain.

Destruction of a written contract will not always discharge the underlying bargain. For a destruction to be a discharge, it must be deliberately done with intent to discharge. Accidental destruction is therefore not a discharge. Of course, accidental destruction of the written contract may make it more difficult to enforce, especially if it was of a sort which the law requires to be in writing. In case of litigation, the plaintiff must be able to prove that the written contract at one time existed, and he must also be able to prove its terms. Finally, he must prove that the destruction of the document was accidental.

Novation. A novation is generally a three-cornered bargain in which one party is discharged from a contractual obligation and another party becomes obligated to the original obligee.

The most common novation situation is exemplified by the following: Black owes White $1,000. Black, White, and Gray agree that in exchange for White's discharging Black from the obligation to pay him $1,000, Gray will assume and agree to pay the $1,000 debt. In such a case, Black is no longer liable to White. The bargain might also provide that Gray will deliver a $2,000 car to White in exchange for White's paying Gray $1,000 on a named future date and White's discharging Black from the $1,000 obligation.

A written contract may be discharged by an oral novation, unless the novation is itself a contract required to be in writing because of its terms—the sale of real estate, for example.

Arbitration and award. When the parties to a contract agree that they will submit their disputes under the contract to arbitration and that they will accept the award of the arbitrators as binding, they open the door to discharge of their contractual obligations in this manner.

Remember that, under the provisions of the Texas Uniform Arbitration Act, RCS 224–236, contracts to submit contractual disputes to arbitration are binding unless one of the circumstances described on page 165 ("arbitration" section of chapter 9 on special court procedures) prevails. If parties to a collective bargaining agreement agree to arbitrate differences, this arbitration agreement is enforceable by federal law.

In situations where the agreement to arbitrate is binding, the party claiming breach of contract must go to arbitration; he cannot sue in the courts. The decision of the arbitrators has the effect of a court judgment, though a party dissatisfied with it may appeal it to the courts. Once the decision of the arbitrators becomes final, the original contract duties which were the subject of the arbitration are discharged, and replaced by the duties imposed by the arbitrators' decision. Thus, a part or all of the old contract is replaced by the award.

Bankruptcy of one of the parties. We come now to the situations under which contractual obligations may be discharged by operation of law. The bankruptcy of one of the parties will discharge some contractual obligations, but not others. The exact effect of bankruptcy upon contractual obligations will be discussed more fully in the chapter on bankruptcy, but in general the following is true:

The obligation to pay most debts is discharged in bankruptcy, though some debts are nondischargeable. Discharge of a dischargeable debt relieves the debtor of the duty to pay it.

The duty to deliver goods or the like will be discharged if the bankruptcy renders the delivery of the goods impossible—because of a liquidation of the assets of the bankrupt's business, for instance.

A duty to perform services may be discharged by bankruptcy, or it may not be. If a business which is being liquidated in bankruptcy was to perform the services, the obligation would be discharged. But, if the services are to be performed by the bankrupt himself, and the bankruptcy will not affect his ability to perform, the obligation will not be discharged.

Expiration of the statute of limitations. Technically, expiration of the statute of limitations will not discharge a contractual obligation. The expiration of the statutory period does supply the obligor with a defense to liability, however. The obligation still exists, but the obligee cannot enforce it in the courts if the obligor makes use of this defense.

The obligor may give up his defense by promising in writing, after expiration of the statutory period, to perform the obligation. He may also give up his defense by not raising an argument that the statute of limitations has expired when obligee sues to enforce the obligation.

Subsequent illegality. If performance of a contract which was legal when made becomes illegal because of a change in the law, the contractual obligations under the now-illegal contract are discharged.

Thus: Blue owns a liquor store in Podunk, Texas, and has a contract to buy all of his requirements of liquor, at least $1,000 worth per month, from Central Texas Liquor Wholesalers, during the years 1979, 1980, and 1981. In mid-1980 the Podunk area votes itself "dry," so that operation of Blue's liquor store is now illegal. Blue's contract with the liquor wholesaler is discharged. Of course, Blue must still pay for the liquor he bought while the operation of his business was lawful. The contract is discharged as of the moment operation of Blue's business became unlawful.

Death of one of the parties. The death of an individual will discharge some of his contractual obligations, but it will not discharge others. The major sort of obligation that is not discharged by death is the obligation to pay money. Our debts do not expire with us; our creditors have the right to collect their claims out of the assets of our estates, and, if our assets are insufficient to pay off our liabilities, our heirs become responsible for these obligations.

Nonpersonal contractual obligations involving duties other than the payment of money are also not discharged by death. Thus: In January 1977 Able sold Baker an option under which Baker was to have the right to buy Lot 6 of Zilch Addition, Podunk, Texas, from Able for $15,000 at any time before December 31, 1977. Able died in June of 1977.

In October of 1977 Baker told Charles, executor of Able's will, that he has decided to exercise the option. Charles says the option is unenforceable, because the duty to honor the option died with Able. Charles is wrong. There is nothing personal about delivering a deed to a city lot. This obligation survived Able's death.

Contracts involving personal duties are discharged upon the death of one of the parties. Thus, in June 1977 Artist contracted to paint a portrait of Model, the painting to begin in August. In July 1977 Artist died, by will leaving all of his assets to his nephew Kunstler. Kunstler wants to perform the Artist-Model contract. Model may consider the contract discharged, since it involved Artist's unique artistic talents. If Model died, by will leaving all of her assets to Poseur, and Poseur demanded that Artist paint her portrait under the Artist-Model contract, Artist could choose to treat the contract as discharged. The duty to be the subject of a painting is just as personal as the duty to paint it.

Some sorts of contracts involve personal duties on one side and nonpersonal ones on the other. In such case, the death of the party owing the personal duty would discharge the contract, but the death of the party owing the nonpersonal duty would not discharge it. Thus: In early 1980 Reich hires Workman to landscape the grounds of his mansion during the summer of 1980, the parties working out an exact plan as to how this is to be done. Workman dies before the job is completed. Workman's nephew Digger, his sole heir, says he will complete the job. Reich refuses to let him do it. Reich is within his rights; he contracted for Workman's unique landscaping abilities when he made this bargain.

On the other hand, suppose that Reich died before Workman's job was completed. Goldman, Reich's heir and new owner of the mansion, tells Workman to continue his landscaping just as if Reich was alive. Workman says he will not finish the job because he had contracted with Reich and no one else. Workman is wrong. Reich's obligation under the contract was to pay for services rendered, and there is nothing personal about a duty to pay money. Workman's obligation is not discharged.

A contract involving a duty of a seller to sell goods to a buyer for cash will not be discharged by the death of either party, unless the goods are to be custom-made goods. If the goods are custom-made, the death of the seller will certainly be a discharge. The death of the buyer would also be a discharge if the goods are for buyer's personal use. A contract involving a duty of a seller to sell goods to a buyer on credit would be discharged by the death of the buyer, since the personal element of the buyer's credit is involved here. The death of the seller probably would not discharge such a contract, if the seller's heir can produce the required goods as easily as could the seller.

Extreme danger to property. When performance of a contractual obligation would subject the property of one of the parties to almost certain loss or confiscation, the contract is discharged. Thus: In January 1917 Yank made a contract to ship certain goods to Deutsch of Hamburg, Germany, the goods to arrive in July 1917. In March 1917 the U.S. declared war on Germany, so Yank never shipped the goods. In March 1919, after the war was over, Deutsch wanted to sue Yank for breach of this contract. He could not win. Even if the U.S. Government had permitted Yank to ship the goods, the German government would never have allowed Deutsch to pay. The declaration of war discharged the contract.

Another example: In early 1975 Yank made a contract with Minh, a Vietnamese of Saigon, to deliver named goods to Minh in Saigon in January 1976. Later in 1975 the North Vietnamese and Viet Cong occupied Saigon, so Yank refused to ship the goods. Minh escaped from Saigon, came to America, and sued Yank for breach. He could not win. If Yank shipped goods into the Saigon of early 1976, how could he be sure that the communists would not confiscate the goods? And how could he be sure that the communists would allow Minh to pay? The contract was discharged.

Extreme danger to the life or health of one of the parties. If performance of the contract would cause one of the parties to submit himself to physical hazards which did not exist when the contract was made, this may result in a discharge of the contract. Thus: In early 1978 Ace Company contracted with Boss that Boss would manage Ace's department store in Managua, Nicaragua, for a year, beginning on September 30, 1978. In late August and early September domestic violence broke out in Nicaragua which threatened to become all-out civil war. So Boss says he is not going to Managua, contract or no contract. In all probability his obligation is discharged. He cannot be blamed for not wanting to venture into such a work environment.

Destruction of the subject matter of the contract before the contract was made. It is obviously impossible to sell property which does not exist, and which never will exist. When a contract for the sale of nonexistent goods is made, a very basic mutual mistake has been made, which voids the contract. Of course, when one of the parties knows that the subject matter does not exist, but he makes a contract involving it anyway, he is guilty of a form of deceit. His act would not make the contract enforceable, of course, but it does constitute the commission of a tort for which the other party may recover damages.

Destruction of the subject matter after the making of the contract, but before performance. The result of the destruction of the subject matter after the making depends upon the nature of the contract. In contracts for the sale of goods, the effect of such destruction depends upon who has the risk of loss with respect to the goods. Sometime between the time the contract is made and the time when performance is completed, risk of loss with respect to the goods will pass from the seller to the buyer. Just when this occurs depends upon the contract terms.

If the destruction occurs while the seller still has risk of loss, the result will be the discharge of the contract, unless the seller has caused the destruction himself, or unless the goods have not been identified yet by the seller as being the goods he will deliver to buyer under the contract. If the destruction occurs while the buyer has risk of loss, there is no discharge. Buyer may pay for the goods he now will not get. If some other party, such as a common carrier, was legally responsible for the destruction, buyer must pursue his remedy against that party. This issue will be discussed in more detail in the materials on sales of goods.

If the contract is for the sale of improved real estate—land with buildings on it—the signing of the sales contract imposes risk of loss with respect to the improvements upon the buyer, unless the contract provides otherwise. If on June 1 Buyer signs a contract with Seller, buying Lot 1 of Lakefront Addition; Buyer intends to move into the house on the lot on July 1; and the house burns down on June 25, it is Buyer's problem. The contract of purchase is not discharged.

A contract to perform work on a structure is discharged by the total or partial destruction of the structure. Thus: Ace Roofing Company has a contract to replace the roof on Hart's house. Before Ace starts work, Hart's house catches fire and the existing roof is severely damaged. Ace's roofing contract is discharged due to the radically changed circumstances.

A contract to erect a structure is not discharged by destruction of the structure before construction is complete. Unless the construction contract provides otherwise, the contractor bears the risk of loss of such a misfortune. If this occurs, the contractor must start his work over without demanding increased compensation. However, since a contractor normally has more bargaining power than does his customer, the normal construction contract contains a "force majeure" clause stating, in effect, that if the contractor's efforts are hindered by circumstances beyond his control, such as damage to or destruction of the structure in course of erection, contractor is not obligated to start over with no increase in compensation. Under a force majeure clause destruction of the structure might discharge the entire contract, or it might obligate the owner to pay the contractor extra compensation for having to start over.

Even in the absence of a force majeure clause, however, if destruction of the structure before completion takes place because the plans and specifications for the structure are defective, this will cause a discharge of the contract. Since the contractor does not normally draw up the plans and specifications, he cannot be blamed for such defects. (Of course if the contractor did act as architect it is another matter entirely.)

Performance of the contract is objectively impossible. If there is no way in which the contract can be performed, the contract is discharged. Thus: In mid-1941 Seller agreed to sell to Buyer a quantity of Malayan rubber, the rubber to be shipped from Singapore to the U.S. in April 1942. In December 1941 World War II came to Southeast Asia, and by the beginning of March 1942 the Japanese had occupied all of Malaya. Thus, the supply of Malayan rubber to the United States was cut off, and there was no way for Seller to ship the rubber. The contract was discharged.

A more common sort of objective impossibility is illustrated by the following: Painter agrees to paint Owner's house, Painter to do the job by himself and to finish the job in ten working days. Painter starts the job as agreed, but on the second working day he falls off his ladder and breaks a leg. This accident discharges the contract, because it is now physically impossible for him to get the job done by himself within ten working days.

A distinction is drawn between situations in which there is no possible way to perform the contract, and situations in which changed circumstances make performance of the contract very difficult, or very unprofitable. The latter situations are situations of subjective impossibility—impossibility existing mainly in the mind of the party who wishes for a discharge. Subjective impossibility is generally no ground for discharge.

Thus: Haricot is a grincho bean farmer. In the fall of 1976 he contracts to sell his 1977 bean crop to Vert Cannery for $3 per bushel. 1977 turns out to be a very bad year for grincho bean farmers throughout the United States. But Haricot produces an excellent crop, the drought and disease which so damaged the crop elsewhere not hurting him. At the time he harvests his crop, there is such a shortage of beans that the going market price is $6 per bushel. Haricot claims he should not have to sell to Vert for $3 per bushel because it would be unfair to make him sell for only 50 percent of market value. Haricot is stuck. When one makes long-term contracts for the purchase or sale of such commodities, the risk of wild swings in price should be taken into account. He could have hedged against this risk by buying a contract to buy beans amounting to the equivalent of his crop on a commodity exchange; what he lost on the crop he would have gained on the futures contract.

Or: In 1976 Haricot contracts to sell Very Cannery 10,000 bushels of grincho beans thirty days after completion of the 1977 bean harvest in his area. Haricot intends to grow the 10,000 bushels of beans on his farm, but the contract with Very does not state that the beans are to come from his farm. Haricot has a bad harvest; his farm yields only 7,000 bushels of beans. He wants Very to take the 7,000 bushels in fulfillment of his contractual obligation. Very demands that he either come up with 10,000 bushels or pay damages for breach of contract. So long as beans are available on the open market Very has the best of this argument, because Haricot could buy 3,000 bushels to resell to Very. If the crop is bad all over so that there are no beans to be had, Haricot has the best of the argument. In the former case, subjective impossibility exists; Haricot can perform, though it will be more difficult and expensive than he had anticipated. In the latter case, objective impossibility exists; there is no way for Haricot to perform. Of course, had the original contract provided that the 10,000 bushels of beans would come from Haricot's farm, there would be objective impossibility, since the farm did not produce 10,000 bushels.

Prospective inability to perform or impossibility of performance. If one party finds out that the other probably will be unable to perform, that party may delay his performance until he learns whether or not the other party will be able to perform.

Thus: Buyer has a contract to buy a tract of land from Seller. Buyer is to pay 25 percent of the purchase price to Seller on April 15; Seller is to deliver a deed to the land on May 15; and Buyer is to pay the balance of the purchase price then. On April 1 Buyer learns that a third party has filed suit against Seller to have himself declared the owner of the land Buyer has contracted to buy. Seller files an answer to the third party's complaint, denying that third party has any interest in the land. Under these circumstances Buyer refuses to make the 25 percent down payment on April 15. Seller says that is a breach of contract.

Seller is wrong. It is possible that the third party might win his suit against Seller and be declared the owner of the land. In that case, Seller would not be able to sell the land to Buyer at all. Buyer has the right to defer his payment here until he is sure that Seller will be able to sell.

Insolvency of one of the parties. The insolvency of one of the parties to a contract may discharge the contract, or it may not. It depends, of course, on whether or not the insolvency will impair that party's ability to perform.

Insolvency of the buyer will not affect any cash transaction in goods or services. The seller is entitled to payment when he delivers the goods or services. If the buyer does not tender payment, the seller does not have to deliver; seller thus need not perform if buyer does not, so the contract still exists. There is no discharge.

If the seller in a cash bargain becomes insolvent, however, this might result in discharge. Thus: On March 1 Deuce makes a contract to buy an Ace color TV set from Trey TV Sales for cash, Deuce to pick up the set on March 15 and Deuce to pay for it then. On March 9 the IRS seizes all the assets of Trey's business because of Trey's tardiness in paying federal taxes, and on March 11 Trey files bankruptcy. At this point Trey's liabilities far exceed his assets. Since either the IRS or the bankruptcy court now has control over Trey's inventory, Trey is hardly in a position to sell Deuce a TV set on March 15. Certainly, Deuce can claim here that he may delay performance due to Trey's potential inability to perform. Had Trey not filed bankruptcy, but instead permitted IRS to sell off his inventory in order to collect the delinquent taxes, this would excuse Deuce's tender of performance for certain.

If a buyer in a cash transaction becomes insolvent, there will be no discharge of duties. If the buyer cannot pay, the seller need not sell. If the buyer does pay, the seller must sell. If the buyer in a credit transaction becomes insolvent, the result is the discharge of the credit portion of the bargain. A seller cannot be expected to deliver goods to a buyer who might not be able to pay for them in the future. However, if the buyer tenders cash for the goods the contract is not discharged, and the seller must then sell for cash.

Frustration of the purpose of the contract. If performance of a contract is not rendered impossible, but the circumstances surrounding the contract have so changed that the value of the contract has been destroyed, frustration of purpose has occurred.

The classic type of frustration case will involve something like this: A parade through the streets of Podunk is scheduled for a certain day. Able owns a building on the parade route. He rents out space in the rooms facing the parade route to spectators who want to watch the parade from a high vantage point. He makes many bargains with such spectators during the days before the parade. Unfortunately for Able, on the day of the parade a tremendous tropical storm strikes Podunk, causing much damage to the city. As a result, the parade is totally canceled. This, of course, destroys the whole purpose of the contracts Able made with the would-be parade spectators, and discharges all of these contracts.

Texas courts are reluctant to declare contractual duties discharged because of frustration of purpose. The case must be an extreme one in order to justify a discharge in this state.

Merger. An obligation is discharged by merger when it is swallowed up by another obligation. Thus, when Ace sues Deuce for damages for breach of contract; a jury decides that Deuce is guilty of breach; and the court awards Ace a judgment against Deuce, Deuce's duties under the breached contract are terminated. They are replaced with Deuce's new duty to pay off the judgment. The judgment thus swallows up the contract.

An obligation may also be discharged by merger when an obligor pays an obligation with a check, promissory note, or other form of commercial paper. However, the rule of UCC 3-802 applies—that when, for instance, a debtor pays a debt with a check, the check is a conditional payment that suspends the original obligation while it goes through the clearing process. If the check is honored, the debt is paid and discharged. If the check is dishonored, the creditor may sue the debtor on the check to force him to make it good, or the creditor may sue on the original obligation. If, however, the parties agree that a check is payment of the debtor's debt, the giving of the check (and its acceptance by the creditor) discharges the debt. If the check is then dishonored, creditor's recourse is to sue on the check. The debt has been merged into the check.

Merger can also take place in this manner: Spade owes Clubb a debt of $1,000. Spade assigns the right to collect this to Diamond. Diamond then assigns the right to collect it to Hart. Before the obligation matures, Hart assigns the right to collect it to Spade. The obligation is now discharged, since Spade has bought the right to collect $1,000 from himself. Merger could also take place in this example if Hart gave the right he had bought from Diamond to Spade as a gift. Again, Spade ends up owning the right to collect $1,000 from himself.

17

Remedies for Breach of Contract

The common-law legal system provides only one major remedy for breach of contract. This remedy is damages—the recovery of money from the breaching party as compensation for that loss caused by the breach.

Under limited circumstances two other remedies are available: restitution and specific performance. Restitution may be sought when the victim of the breach has performed, or partially performed, his obligations. Restitution permits the victim of the breach to recover his consideration, or the value thereof. When specific performance is granted, the breaching party is ordered to perform as he agreed to perform. This remedy will not be granted unless monetary damages would be inadequate to compensate the plaintiff for the breach.

Several kinds of damages may be sought for breach of contract. We shall discuss these and their measurement first.

Compensatory damages. The victim of a breach almost invariably seeks recovery of compensatory damages. These are designed to compensate the plaintiff for the loss caused him by the breach. The method of measurement depends upon the nature of the contract which was breached, and the party who did the breaching.

In contracts for the sale of goods, one almost universal measure of damages is used when the breaching party is the seller and the breach consists of nondelivery of the goods. If the goods are obtainable elsewhere (as they usually are), the buyer must obtain them elsewhere if he is going to obtain them at all. Buyer's measure of damage, then, is the difference between the cover price (what buyer had to pay to obtain the goods elsewhere) and the contract price (what buyer would have had to pay seller had seller not breached). If buyer chooses not to cover (obtain the goods elsewhere), the measure of damage is the difference between market price (what buyer would have had to pay to get the goods elsewhere) and contract price.

If seller's breach consists of the delivery of defective goods, buyer may reject the goods or revoke his acceptance of them, send them back to seller, and use the same measure of damages as if seller had not delivered at all. Or buyer may choose to retain the defective goods, in which case a basic element of computation of damages is the difference between the value of the defective goods and their value had they not been defective. This will be discussed more thoroughly in the chapter on remedies for breach of contract for sale of goods.

If seller's breach consists of nondelivery of goods which may not be obtained elsewhere, buyer may obtain specific performance—that is, force seller to deliver.

In the event of breach by the buyer, the measure of compensatory damages will depend on the nature of the contract and the nature of the breach. If the contract is a contract for sale of manufactured goods, the measure of damages will depend on how far the manufacturing process has gone at the time of breach. If manufacture has not yet been begun, seller will essentially recover the lost profit on the anticipated sale. He will recover the contract price less his estimated (and provable) costs of manufacture. If manufacture has been begun but not completed at time of breach, seller has essentially two options: to stop manufacture or to complete manufacture. If he chooses to stop manufacture, he may either scrap the partially completed goods, or sell them for whatever they are worth.

If seller completes manufacture and then sells the goods, the measure of damages is contract price (what buyer would have paid had be bought the goods) less resale price (what seller obtained when he sold the goods to a third party). If seller completes manufacture and then cannot resell the goods due to lack of market, seller may be able to recover the contract price, if completion of manufacture was the most practicable solution to seller's problems caused by the breach.

If seller halts the manufacturing process and sells the partially completed goods for what they are worth, the measure is contract price of the completed goods less the resale price of the partially completed goods. If seller halts the manufacturing process and scraps the incomplete goods, the measure is contract price less cost of complete manufacture.

Remember, though, that the victim of a breach is always under a duty to mitigate damages. He is under an obligation to react to the breach in a way that will minimize the damages which the breaching party must pay; he must not proceed in a way which will increase the potential damages recoverable. Thus, in these cases of breach while manufacture is in process, the seller must follow the alternative which will minimize his damages.

If the breach does not occur until the manufacture is complete, the measure of damages is the same as that involving any breach of contract for sale of completed goods by a buyer. That measure is either contract price less resale price (when seller sells the goods to someone else) or contract price less market price (when seller chooses not to resell the goods at the moment).

If the victim seller is a seller of goods out of inventory (such as a retailer) and the buyer has contracted to buy one or more of an item of which the seller has many in inventory, the buyer's breach essentially causes the seller to lose a sale. In such a case the seller may recover his lost profit on the missed sale from the buyer.

There are three circumstances under which the seller may recover the contract price from a breaching buyer. The first of these has been touched upon already: it is the situation in which the buyer has contracted to buy nonresalable goods—essentially, goods for which there is no regular market. If buyer refuses to buy such goods, seller cannot sell them. In such a case, the only fair remedy for seller is to essentially force buyer to buy.

If seller delivers the goods called for under the contract of sale to buyer, and buyer refuses to pay for them, the second situation has arisen under which seller may collect contract price from buyer. Obviously, if buyer has the goods and means to keep them, he should pay contract price for them.

When goods are damaged or destroyed while risk of loss is on the buyer, seller may collect the contract price from buyer; this is the third circumstance under which this is possible. The question of when risk of loss passes from seller to buyer is a complex one which will be covered in the chapter on title and risk of loss; essentially, in a contract for sale of goods in which time will elapse between the making of the contract and the completion of its performance, risk of loss with respect to the goods will be on seller until he completes his performance under the contract. When seller's performance is complete, buyer gets risk of loss, even though he may not yet have possession of the goods. When some mishap befalls the goods while risk of loss is on the buyer, it is essentially the buyer's problem. Buyer must pay for the goods he will not be receiving (or will be receiving in damaged condition) and settle matters with the third party who caused the damage to the goods (if any).

When a breach of contract for sale of securities takes place, the measure of damages is contract price less market price (if buyer breached) or market price less contract price (if seller breached). If, however, the securities in question are so closely held that there is no market for them, specific performance would be a proper remedy.

In case of breach of contract to lend or borrow money, the measure of damages in case of breach by the lender is borrower's interest cost in obtaining the loan elsewhere, less the interest borrower would have had to pay lender had lender not breached. If borrower is the breaching party, lender may recover the interest he lost because borrower did not borrow, less the interest lender earned by lending the funds to someone else.

When a contract to perform personal services is breached by an employer, the victim employee or agent may recover the wages or other compensation he lost due to the breach, plus the contract value of services performed but not paid for. If an agent or employee is the breaching party, the employer may recover whatever he lost due to the breach. If the breaching party was an employee, the loss will be mainly inconvenience, which is difficult to reduce to dollars and cents; in case of breaches by some sorts of agents, the same thing is true. If the breaching party is an independent contractor and the employer must hire another independent contractor to do his work, the measure of damages will be what the employer had to pay the new contractor less what he had agreed to pay the breaching contractor.

In case of breach of a lease by the tenant, the landlord's measure of damages is the balance of the rent called for under the lease, less rental the landlord obtains by renting out the premises to a new tenant. In any event, the landlord recovers rent from the tenant for the time the leased premises stood vacant after tenant's breach. Damages recoverable from a landlord because of his wrongful eviction of a tenant from the premises will basically be the difference between the rent tenant was obligated to pay landlord for the balance of the lease and the rent tenant has to pay his new landlord for the balance of the old lease period.

When a construction contract is breached by the contractor, the owner of the premises may generally recover as damages the cost of finishing the job the contractor did not finish, or the cost of repairing the defective work done by the contractor. If the cost of finishing the unfinished job or of repairing the defective work is prohibitive, the owner gets as damages the difference between the value of the performance he contracted for and the value of the performance he got. If the owner breaches a construction contract, the contractor recovers that portion of the contract price he has not been paid as yet. (He will have already received part of the contract price as progress payments.)

Incidental damages. Whenever a breach causes the victim to incur expenses which he would not otherwise have incurred, the victim has suffered incidental damages. These are always recoverable, if they can be proven. Examples of incidental damages include:

1. Telephone bills a seller runs up trying to find another buyer for goods a buyer unjustifiably refused to buy.

2. Telephone bills which a buyer runs up trying to find "cover" for goods a seller was supposed to sell him, but did not.

3. The brokerage fee a seller has to pay a stockbroker to sell stock for him which a buyer unjustifiably did not buy.

Nominal damages. When a breach of contract has occurred, but the victim of the breach has incurred no provable damages, the victim may recover nominal damages—one dollar or some such sum. Obviously, hardly anyone would go to the trouble of suing for nominal damages. Such damages are generally assessed when plaintiff sues defendant for damages for breach of contract, plaintiff convinces the jury that there was a breach, but jury decides that the breach did not cause plaintiff to suffer damages. Plaintiff then collects his one dollar in nominal damages as a sort of "booby prize."

Special or consequential damages. When the victim of a breach suffers damage which a reasonable man without knowledge of the victim's special situation could not foresee, special or consequential damages have been suffered. When a buyer of goods suffers personal injury as a result of a defect in the goods, consequential damages have also been suffered.

If a breach of warranty has been committed with respect to goods which have been sold, and this breach has caused personal injury, these consequential damages are certainly recoverable. However, if the special damages are not personal injury damages, they are not recoverable unless the breaching party knew or should have known that his breach might cause such damage.

Thus: Seller has a contract to sell 1,000 bushels of wheat to buyer for $2.50 per bushel. Buyer has a contract to resell this wheat to a flour mill for $3 per bushel, but seller does not know that. The market price of the wheat was $2.75 per bushel on the delivery date in the contract, and seller did not deliver. Buyer lost his contract to sell wheat to the flour mill because of this, since he could not come up with replacement wheat in time. Buyer therefore demanded $500 (50¢ per bushel) damages from seller. He will not get that much. What he will get is 25¢ per bushel, or $250, in compensatory damages (market price less contract price). The other $250 is special damages, not recoverable in this case because seller did not know about buyer's contract with flour mill. On the other hand, had buyer informed seller about the flour mill contract, seller would have known that his breach would cause special damages to buyer, and buyer could have collected his entire claim.

Punitive damages. When a defendant is assessed damages over and above those that the plaintiff can prove that he has suffered, he is being assessed punitive damages, or exemplary damages. The purpose of such an award is to punish the defendant for his wrongful conduct. Such damages are not recoverable for breach of contract. On the other hand, when plaintiff is induced to enter into a contract by fraudulent conduct by defendant, plaintiff has been a victim of the tort of deceit, or fraud. He may sue for damages for commission of the tort, and seek punitive damages as a part of his recovery.

Speculative damages. The only damages which are recoverable for breach of contract are those which may be computed with some degree of certainty. The methods of computing compensatory damages which we have observed all lend themselves to exact computations, since most market prices, costs of doing business, and other expenses are capable of exact proof. Expenses recoverable as incidental damages must be proven exactly. Where special damages are recoverable, these must also be proven exactly.

Efforts have been made to recover damages in breach of contract cases for mental suffering caused by the breach. So far, courts have refused to permit such recoveries. There is no way to compute with exactitude the amount of money one has lost because of mental suffering. Computation of such damages is an excursion into the realm of guesswork.

Claims for lost profit due to a breach of contract are frowned upon for similar reasons. Though lost profits are recoverable as compensatory damages under the limited circumstances already discussed, these are otherwise normally not recoverable, because they are so incapable of exact proof. Thus: Seller had a valid contract to sell 100 shares of Quatz Company stock to buyer for $50 per share, Quatz being listed on the New York Stock Exchange. When delivery of the stock fell due, it was selling for $53 per share, so seller refused to deliver. Buyer therefore sued seller for $1,500 damages, arguing that good news about company prospects had made it inevitable that the price of the stock would rise to $65 per share and that seller's breach had therefore caused buyer damages of $15 per share, or $1,500 all told. Buyer has no basis for recovering $1,500. How does he know that the stock will rise to $65? How can anyone know that for certain? Of course, buyer can prove damages of $3 per share here, or $300 all told. That is all he can recover.

Liquidated damages. The parties may provide in their contract that, in the event of a breach, the breaching party shall be liable to the other party for a specified sum in liquidated damages. Such a liquidated damages clause will be enforced by the courts if it is found to be reasonable. The main usefulness of such a clause is that it will eliminate the necessity to prove actual damages in litigation about the contract. If plaintiff can prove defendant's breach, he will be automatically entitled to recover the damages specified in the liquidated damages clause. Such clauses may reduce contract litigation. If there is no doubt about the existence of a breach and no doubt about the reasonableness of the liquidated damages clause, the breaching party might as well pay the stipulated damages and be done with it.

Liquidated damages clauses are not always enforceable, however. The amount of damages payable stipulated in the contract must approximate the damages which would actually be caused by a breach. If the agreed figure is too high, the courts will refuse to enforce it because it is a penalty. If the agreed figure is too low, the courts will refuse to enforce it because it is unfair. Whether or not a liquidated damages clause is fair is a question of law to be determined by the judge. When a party to litigation involving a contract with a liquidated damages clause feels that the clause is unreasonable, he must raise the question early in the proceedings. If the court rules that the clause is reasonable, the plaintiff need not prove damages in order to prevail; he must only prove breach. If the court rules the clause to be unreasonable, the plaintiff must proceed as in the normal breach of contract case; he must prove both breach and damages in order to recover.

Suppose that seller and buyer have made a contract under which seller agrees to sell his 1978 Thunderbird to buyer for $8,000, delivery and payment due at times specified within the contract. The contract also provides that, in the event of breach, the breaching party will pay the other party liquidated damages of $5,000. This liquidated damages clause would be unenforceable as a penalty since $8,000 is not far removed from the fair market value of a 1978 Thunderbird and 1978 Thunderbirds are not rare automobiles. A breach of this contract certainly would not cause the victim to suffer anywhere near $5,000 in damages.

If the contract provides that the breaching party will pay the victim $100 in liquidated damages, this would probably not be enforced because it is unfair. It is probable that a breach of this contract would cause considerably more than $100 in damages. The existence of this clause might thus provide an incentive to breach, since the consequences thereof are so minimal. If the contract sets the liquidated damages at $1,000, chances are that the courts would permit the liquidated damages clause to stand. A breach of this contract might well cause damages of somewhere in the vicinity of $1,000 to the victim. The amount is eminently reasonable.

The duty to mitigate damages. The victim of a breach is obligated to do all within his power to minimize the damages he will suffer because of the other party's breach. Thus, if he may reduce his damage by taking some sort of affirmative action, he will be obligated to do so. Failure to mitigate damages may result in a court's denying the right to the victim to recover any damages at all. Where buyer has contracted to buy a carload of lettuce from seller, and buyer tells seller not to deliver before seller has shipped the produce, seller is under the obligation to find another buyer for the lettuce before it spoils. If he finds another buyer, he may collect damages of contract price less resale price. If he tries to find another buyer but is unsuccessful, he may collect the contract price. If he does not try to find another buyer and lets the lettuce spoil, he collects nothing.

Consider the case where Prof has a contract to teach Mandarin Chinese at University for the school year 1980-81. University unjustifiably discharges Prof at the end of October 1980. Prof is under an obligation to start hunting for another job teaching Mandarin Chinese. Because of the nature of university scheduling, he would be very lucky to find such a job to begin before January, but he would have to try. If he finds such a job, he may recover from University the salary he was not paid while he was jobless. Also, if the salary per month on his new job is lower than was his University salary, he would recover the differential per month for the period of effectiveness of his old contract. If he tries hard to find another teaching job for the spring semester but is unsuccessful, he recovers his entire salary under the University contract. If in his job search he is offered a position as clerk in the registrar's office of College, and he turns this down because he wants something better, University cannot complain. The duty to mitigate damages here does not require Prof to take any job which comes along. He may continue to seek a job of the same general nature as that from which he was wrongfully dismissed.

Rescission. A plaintiff may ask a court to declare a contract rescinded—that is, totally discharged. This remedy is available to the victim of a breach if the victim has not yet performed all his obligations. It is also available to the victim of fraud, duress, undue influence, violation of fiduciary relationship, or mutual mistake.

Reformation. A plaintiff may under some circumstances ask the court to amend the contract judicially so that it accurately states the bargain between the parties. Plaintiff may desire this procedure in the situation in which defendant has materially altered a written contract, but plaintiff does not want to rescind. In this case he wants the bargain enforced as it originally stood.

Plaintiff may also seek this procedure in the situation in which the parties have made what looks to be an integrated written contract, but plaintiff, who is not a well-educated person, made the contract in reliance upon certain oral agreements between the parties being part of the contract. Defendant claims the parol evidence precludes inclusion of these oral dealings in the bargain. Plaintiff argues that these oral dealings were a part of the basis of his bargain. A court may order the contract reformed to accord with the basis of plaintiff's bargain.

Restitution. When victim has performed his obligation in whole or in part before the other party to the contract breaches, the victim may wish to recover the value of his performance from the breaching party. When he seeks this recovery, he seeks restitution.

Generally, the plaintiff seeking restitution is limited to a recovery of money. Thus, if he is seeking restitution of a down payment or deposit, he gets back what he has paid. If he is seeking restitution for delivery of property, though, he normally would not get his property back; he will have to settle for recovery of the fair value of the property, in money. Plaintiff may obtain restitution of property only when the property is irreplaceable.

Thus: Plaintiff and defendant make a contract for the sale of named stock by defendant to plaintiff for $5,000, plaintiff paying $1,000 down when the contract was made, with plaintiff to pay the balance and defendant to deliver the stock at a specified later time. Defendant refuses to deliver the stock. Plaintiff sues for restitution of his $1,000 down payment. He may of course recover.

Suppose that plaintiff in the above case made his down payment in the form of law books worth $1,000; upon defendant's breach, plaintiff sues to recover the law books. If the law books are current publications obtainable from publishers and dealers, plaintiff cannot get his books back. He may, however, recover the value of the books. Suppose that plaintiff instead made his down payment in the form of an antique suit of armor which he now wants to recover. In all probability, plaintiff will succeed here—antique suits of armor are one-of-a-kind items.

There is one important limitation on the remedy of restitution. One may not claim both restitution and damages in breach of contract situations. When it is possible to claim both restitution and damages, one must choose between the two available remedies.

Thus, suppose that the market price of the above-mentioned stock was $55 per share on the date of breach. If plaintiff sued for compensatory damages, he could recover $500, the market price less contract price. If he sues for restitution of his down payment, he may recover $1,000. But there is no way he can have it both ways and recover $1,500, the down payment plus the damages. Obviously the wisest course in this situation is to sue for restitution.

Specific performance. There are a few situations in which a plaintiff may force the defendant to perform his contract. This is the remedy of specific performance. Specific performance is available in six types of situations. The first of these is when a contract for sale of land or an interest therein is breached by the seller. Since no two tracts of land are alike, buyer may obtain no exact equivalent of land a breaching seller refuses to sell. A court will therefore order the breaching seller to deliver a deed to the property.

Construction loan agreements are the second sort of agreement for which specific performance may be obtained. Since refusal of a lender to make an agreed-upon construction loan may cause long delay in the commencement of the construction project and subsequent loss to both the contractor and the owner of the premises upon which the construction is to be done, avoidance of such loss would justify forcing the reluctant lender to perform his agreed-upon bargain.

The third type of specifically performable contract is the contract for sale of stock in a closely held corporation. For such a contract to be specifically performable, the stock in question must not be listed on a stock exchange, nor must it be traded over the counter. If the stock is listed or traded over the counter, a market for it exists and the buyer could acquire it elsewhere. If it is not so listed or traded, the buyer will have great difficulty obtaining it if he cannot get it from the seller.

A contract for the sale of a controlling interest in a corporation is the fourth sort of specifically performable contract. Since a controlling interest in a corporation is a unique thing—by definition only one may exist—if buyer cannot obtain it from seller he cannot obtain it at all. Damages here would of course be a totally inadequate remedy.

Contracts for one-of-a-kind items of personal property are the fifth sort of contract for which specific performance may be obtained. Thus, if seller has agreed to sell to buyer the original manuscript of the Beethoven Ninth Symphony, and seller later refuses to deliver, buyer will not get the manuscript. Since only one of it exists, if seller will not sell it, buyer cannot get possession of it. Thus, a court would compel seller to sell. The same principle justifies granting of specific performance of contracts for the sale of works of art, antiques, and the like.

The last sort of contract enforceable through specific performance is the contractual agreement not to do something. Thus: Brown went to work in the R&D department of Whiz Company, Brown holding a Ph.D. degree in chemistry. Brown signed a contract when he went to work for Whiz that he would not go to work for a competitor of Whiz within one year after leaving the employ of Whiz. Later Brown quit his job with Whiz. Six months after quitting, Brown accepted a job in the R&D department of Snapp Company, a competitor of Whiz. Whiz filed suit against Brown seeking an injunction forbidding him to work for Snapp. Whiz should obtain the injunction: the court will force Brown to keep his agreement not to work for a competitor of Whiz within a year of leaving Whiz.

Specific performance would not be granted in any of the six contract types if the plaintiff has imposed an unfair contract on the defendant, and the defendant has breached because of the unfairness. This is an application of the maxim, "He who seeks equity must do equity." In short, he who expects a court to be fair to him must have treated the other party to the case fairly. If no fraud or other illegality is involved in the contract, however, plaintiff might recover damages for defendant's breach.

Of course, if plaintiff has been guilty of any illegality, fraud, or the like with respect to the contract, a court will grant him neither specific performance nor damages, illustrating the maxim, "He who seeks equity must come into court with clean hands." If the plaintiff seeking specific performance has soiled his hands with illegality, the courts will not help him.

Courts will not order specific performance of contracts for the sale of goods or securities for which a market exists. If the buyer who complains about a seller's refusal to deliver such goods or securities, monetary damages will put him in a position to buy what he seeks on the market without loss. Thus, there is no necessity for forcing seller to sell to buyer: the monetary remedy is adequate.

Specific performance of contracts for personal services will also not be ordered, with the exception of contracts of enlistment in the armed forces of the United States. So long as the military service desires the service of the enlistee for the term of the enlistment, the enlistee has the unpleasant choice of serving out the enlistment or of risking criminal punishment for his refusal to do so.

Other contracts for personal service will not be enforced because enforcement would be involuntary servitude. Also, such enforcement would not necessarily be to the advantage of the other party or of society. The worker working against his will would not be a very efficient, loyal, or diligent worker. It should be noted, though, that such contracts might be specifically enforced against an employer when the termination of an employee violates civil service regulations, tenure agreements of teachers, a collective bargaining agreement, or something similar.

No specific performance is available for construction contracts. Two reasons for this exist. First, construction is a form of personal service. Second, construction contracts are complex bargains which require a long time to perform. Judges say that they are reluctant to undertake the burden of supervising performance of such contracts. Thus, if your general contractor quits when your building is 70 percent completed, no court will make him finish the job. The recourse is to hire another contractor to finish, and make yours pay for it.

Quantum meruit. When a party partially performs a contract, but his performance is so inadequate that it cannot be called substantial performance, a quantum meruit situation may arise. The victim of the breach is excused from performing his duty under the contract, and he has a claim against the breaching party for damages due to the breach.

However, if the victim of the breach is excused from paying anything for the partial performance which he has received, the victim might be unjustly enriched at the expense of the breaching party. In order to avoid this, the breaching party is given a claim for the fair value of his performance. The victim of the breach has a claim for damages. The two claims are balanced against each other, one party collecting the difference from the other.

For instance: Contractor has a contract to erect a building for Owner for $100,000. Contractor quits the job when the building is 85 percent complete, for no good reason. At this point Contractor has collected $70,000 in progress payments from owner. Owner of course refuses to pay any more money to Contractor. He instead hires Builder to finish the building, which Builder does for $30,000. Because of the delay in completion of the building, Owner has lost $10,000 in rental receipts. The Owner-Contractor contract had a "time is of the essence" clause, and Owner had informed Contractor that, if the building were completed late, Owner would stand to lose rent receipts.

Owner therefore sues Contractor for $40,000—$30,000 compensatory damages for the obligation Owner incurred to Builder to get the building finished, and $10,000 in special damages for loss of the rental receipts. Contractor filed a counterclaim for the $30,000 progress payment he never received. How would the matter be resolved?

Owner's $40,000 claim is well founded, if he can prove his special damages. Contractor's counterclaim is not. Since he did not complete the building, he is not entitled to the contract price (85 percent performance of a construction contract not being substantial performance). But, Contractor did perform 85 percent of his obligation in exchange for 70 percent of the contract price, which may not be quite fair. If Contractor is entitled to the contract price of the work he did, he is entitled to another $15,000. Since he did not wholly perform his obligations, however, he is not necessarily entitled to this. He is, however, entitled to the fair value of the work that he did. If the fair value of this is over $70,000 (as it probably is), he is entitled to something on his counterclaim, the something being somewhat less than $15,000. Owner therefore ends up recovering $40,000, less the value of Contractor's counterclaim.

Quasi-contract damages. The measure of damages in a quasi-contract case is very similar to that used in quantum meruit situations. The purpose of quasi-contractual recovery is the prevention of the unjust enrichment of the defendant at the expense of the plaintiff.

The jury in a quasi-contract case must determine the fair value of the performance the plaintiff gave to the defendant. Plaintiff is awarded a judgment against defendant for that sum. This fair value is not necessarily the value plaintiff places upon the performance. The jury may use its own wisdom in making an evaluation—within reason, of course.

PART IV

Personal and Property Relationships

18

Agency

A person may sometimes find it necessary to transact business at two places at once, or at a location in which he cannot be present at the proper time. Under these circumstances he may appoint another to do the business for him.

When appointing another to do business for you, it may be essential to give him the authority to make a contract in your name. In such a case, you have appointed an agent to do this for you, and you have become the agent's principal. There is nothing very out of the ordinary or unusual about appointing an agent. Owners of all but the smallest businesses cannot tend to all aspects of their business alone. If they could not appoint agents, their businesses could not exist. Corporations, not being individuals, must transact all of their business through agents; otherwise they could accomplish nothing.

Creation of agency relationships. Appointment of an agent is very simple. No writing is necessary, unless an agent is being appointed to sell real estate. If no sale of real estate is involved, no written contract is required. The agent need not give any consideration for his appointment. The mere fact that the principal has appointed him is sufficient to make him an agent.

A principal must have contractual capacity in order to appoint an agent, but an agent need not have contractual capacity in order to serve as one. The capacity of the agent depends upon the capacity of the principal; the capacity of the principal depends upon his own status, not upon the capacity of his agent. Thus, a minor may appoint an adult agent, but the contracts the agent makes for him are voidable. An insane person with a guardian may try to appoint a competent agent, but his effort will fail. If he cannot make a contract, he cannot appoint an agent and clothe him with authority to make a contract. On the other hand, an adult may appoint a minor his agent and clothe him with full authority. The validity of the resulting contracts will not be judged by the limited capacity of the agent, but by the full capacity of the principal.

Authority delegable to an agent. A principal may give an agent authority to do almost anything which he may legally do. There are, however, a few items, the authority to do which may not be delegated to agents:

1. The duty to swear an oath. Anyone who swears an oath may be prosecuted for perjury if he swears falsely; the duty is so personal that the performance may not be delegated.

2. The duty to testify in court in response to a subpoena. What is wanted here is the testimony of the person to whom the subpoena is directed. Since no person knows everything that another knows, this is another duty which is too personal to be delegated.

3. The right to vote in political elections. For obvious reasons, delegation of the right to vote for public officials could result in the subversion of the democratic process.

4. The right to sign a will. A valid will must be signed by the testator himself. Here again, what is involved is so personal that the testator must do it for himself.

5. Delegation of personal contractual duties. This has already been discussed in detail in the materials on the assignment of contract rights.

Certain types of duties which at first glance seems to be very personal may be delegated. For instance, a person intending to be married may appoint an agent (called a proxy) to represent him in the marriage ceremony. If the appointment, attendance, and identity of the proxy are made known to the other spouse and to the person performing the marriage ceremony, the marriage will be perfectly lawful and bind the principal, not the proxy.

The right to vote in other than political elections may sometimes be delegated. The main sort of voting right generally recognized as delegable is the right of a corporate shareholder to vote his shares. Most corporate shares, in fact, are not voted by their owners; the owners appoint agents (again called proxies) to exercise this right for them. However, a corporate director may not delegate his right to vote in a directors' meeting in this manner.

Express authority of agents. An agent has express authority to do that which his principal appointed him to do. The express authority of an agent may be very broad; it may be very narrow; or it may lie somewhere in between.

A principal may find it expedient to appoint a universal agent, and to clothe him with authority to do almost anything that the principal himself could lawfully do. Universal agents are more common in civil-law lands than in those governed by common law. In civil-law countries business owners sometimes confer upon business managers a procura, giving the manager sole authority to run the business. Needless to say, an owner must have unlimited trust in his manager to confer such authority upon him.

In our country, military personnel being sent overseas to points where family members cannot go, or naval personnel going on sea duty sometimes give their spouses a general power of attorney, conferring upon the spouse what is virtually the power of a universal agent. Depending upon the wording of the power, the spouse is given authority to sign the absent spouse's name to virtually any contract the spouse could enter into himself.

A principal desiring to confer upon an agent wide authority to manage a business enterprise will make that manager a general agent. The general agent has wide authority in a broad area of activity, but he will be given no agency authority outside the scope of his job. The principal wishing to appoint an agent to accomplish a narrow purpose, such as the sale of one specific item of property, will give that agent authority as a special agent—the authority to do one narrow thing, perhaps to act as agent in one single transaction.

Implied authority. Generally speaking, an agent has implied authority to do all things necessary to the accomplishment of his express authority. In order to avoid ambiguity, it is advisable for a principal to go into considerable detail when spelling out the extent of his agent's authority. But since principals cannot foresee all possible contingencies, the boundary of an agent's express authority may well be fuzzy. The extent of an agent's implied authority depends upon the nature of the agency; the agent's implied authority under specific circumstances will be discussed shortly.

Apparent authority. An agent has apparent authority to do what a reasonable man would expect him to have authority to do. Implied authority stems from the actuality of express authority, while apparent authority stems from the appearance of express authority.

Thus, an agent may have apparent authority to do that which he has no express or implied authority to do, particularly when the principal appoints him to a position of generally wide authority but limits him in an unusual manner without making this publicly known. An agent may also have apparent authority to do what he no longer has express authority to do. Whenever a principal terminates the authority of an agent, he must notify all persons with whom the agent has been dealing of the termination. If this is not done, the third party may justifiably assume that the agent remains an agent, and that he still has the authority which he originally possessed.

A person may also appear to be an agent when he actually is no agent at all. This can occur when he is seen under circumstances which would lead a reasonable person to assume that he is an agent, even if the principal has given him no authority whatsoever.

Authority by estoppel. A person (A) will acquire authority by estoppel when another person (B) by his action or inaction leads a third party (C) to believe that the person (A) is his agent. Thus, if Able says in Baker's presence that he has appointed Baker as his agent for a particular purpose, Able speaking to Charles at the time, and Baker does not deny this, Charles may assume that Able has spoken the truth. Also, if Baker tells Charles in Able's presence that Able has appointed him as an agent for a named purpose, and Able does not deny it, Charles may again assume that Baker is telling the truth. In both cases, Able may not now deny that Baker is his agent as described.

Authority of the real property manager. Anyone who appoints an agent to manage a piece of real estate, including an apartment building or business building, gives to the manager a wide field of authority. Such a manager usually has authority to rent the apartments or offices upon customary terms. He may collect the rent (he is of course under the obligation to remit the proceeds to his principal). He may make contracts for the repair and maintenance of the premises, and insure the premises against all perils against which such premises are generally insured.

The property manager will have implied authority to do all of the above, even if he has no express authority to do it all; and he will have apparent authority to do all these things even if his express authority denies him the power to do some of them. In short, if the property manager is not to have the authority to do all these things, the restrictions will not be effective unless all persons with whom he deals know of the limitations upon his authority.

Authority of the business manager. The business manager has the widest implied authority of all general agents. If the business involves the buying and selling of goods, the manager has implied authority to do the necessary buying and selling. However, the manager will have no implied authority to buy inventory on credit or to sell goods out of inventory on credit. Express authority is necessary to confer the power to do this.

If the business is large enough that the manager cannot run it all by himself, the manager will have implied authority to hire and fire employees to determine their wages and working hours. He will have implied authority to contract for necessary equipment and repairs to the business premises—again, on a cash basis. Here also, the manager has no authority to commit the principal's credit unless he has express authority.

The power to buy inventory and equipment and the power to contract for repairs necessarily include the authority to pay for all these in cash. A manager may not write checks, however, without express authority. Since checks are very common vehicles of payment, the business manager has authority to accept checks from his customers and to endorse these checks and deposit them in a bank account in his principal's name.

The manager has no authority to borrow money or to draw commercial paper otherwise in his principal's name, unless express authority to do this exists. The apparent authority of the business manager extends to the limits of the normal implied authority. Thus the manager has no apparent authority to buy inventory on credit or to borrow money.

Authority of the real estate broker. The real estate broker normally has very limited authority. He is to find a buyer for his principal's property, and no more. He may not negotiate terms with the buyer, he may not make representations about the property, and he may not sign any contract with the buyer. If the broker is to have more authority than this, it must be express authority.

Authority of the agent to sell land. Since a contract appointing an agent to sell land must be in writing, all aspects of the agent's authority must be in writing. Such agents generally have very limited implied authority; almost all their authority is granted by the contract of appointment. Their implied authority is limited to the power to perform the ministerial acts (such as drafting documents) necessary to the accomplishment of their express authority.

Authority of auctioneers. Auctioneers have implied authority to refuse to sell for the high bid, unless the auction is advertised as being "without reserve." (In "without reserve" auctions, the goods must be sold to the high bidder.)

The auctioneer also has implied authority to make statements of fact about the goods he puts up for sale, and to make warranties with respect to the goods. He has authority to collect the purchase price—in cash only, unless he has express authority to sign a memo of sale, as written evidence of the completion of the contract of sale with the high bidder.

Authority of factors. A factor is a professional selling agent who takes possession of goods belonging to his principal and seeks to sell them. He has authority to bargain with customers about the selling price and to make warranties with respect to the goods. He need not sell for cash: he may arrange credit terms, or he may take other property (trade-ins) in partial or full payment.

A factor thus has very wide implied authority. His apparent authority is just as wide, unless his customers know of limitations placed upon this authority by the principal.

Authority of the traveling salesman. The ordinary traveling salesman is no true agent. If he does not have possession of what he is selling, he has no implied authority to bind his principal to contracts. Thus, he also has no implied authority to collect money. His sole function is to solicit orders from his customers.

The salesman who carries with him a sample kit has no implied authority to sell any of the samples. Again, he has no authority to bind his principal to contracts or to collect money. He does, however, have authority to make warranties with respect to the goods, in that a seller who induces a buyer to buy by showing him a sample makes an express warranty that the goods sold will comply with the sample. Beyond that, such salesmen have no implied warranty-making authority.

The salesman who actually has possession of an inventory of goods for sale naturally has implied authority to sell his goods and to accept payment for them. He will not have implied authority to sell on credit, however, unless it is the custom in his industry to give salesmen such authority. Such a salesman of course has authority to make a sales pitch about what he is selling, and to make warranties with respect to the goods.

Authority of the store clerk. The authority of the sales clerk in a store will vary from business to business. Basically the sales clerk has implied authority to sell goods from his principal's inventory for cash, and to make warranties with respect to what he is selling.

The clerk generally has no implied authority to bargain with the customer about price, and he has no authority to sell in exchange for a check, or on credit. (If the proprietor of the business normally permits his clerks to accept checks or to sell on credit, their authority is thereby broadened.)

Authority of other selling agents. A selling agent normally has implied authority to sell those goods belonging to his principal of which he has possession. However, mere possession of another's goods does not confer apparent authority to sell. There must be other evidence of the agent's authority.

There is considerable ambiguity about the extent of the implied authority of such an agent. When appointing one, the principal should, to be safe, put the appointment into writing and spell out in detail just what the authority of the agent shall be. He should make clear whether the agent is to be merely a solicitor of offers to buy or whether he can actually sell. He should state the extent of the agent's powers with respect to price—whether the agent must sell for a specified price, or whether he has authority to bargain. And he should state the extent of the agent's authority with respect to negotiation of payment terms. Can he sell on credit? Can he accept a trade-in? Can he accept a check or other commercial paper as payment?

Authority of the debt collector. The implied authority of a debt collector is ordinarily very narrow. He normally is to collect, not to negotiate. His job is to get the debtor to pay up in full and in cash, unless he is given express authority to collect payment in other forms. If the debtor wants to argue, negotiate, or compromise, he should be referred to the principal.

Of course a debt collector may be given broader authority. If he has express authority to accept commercial paper in payment, or to negotiate compromises of the debt, all well and good, but debt collectors generally have no implied or apparent authority to do this.

Authority of the attorney. An attorney normally has a very narrow area of implied authority to represent his client. This authority extends to procedural matters only. An attorney may not commence litigation without the express authorization of his client. Once that authorization is given, however, the attorney may make certain commitments for his client on his own. These are limited to agreements setting trial dates, obtaining continuances, and the like.

The attorney has no implied authority to negotiate an out-of-court settlement of his client's case, or to reduce a client's claim for damages, or anything of that nature. In esssence, the attorney may not commit his client to anything affecting the basis of his client's case. Of course, a client may grant to his attorney express authority to negotiate a settlement of a case or to act for his client in other ways. But no such authority exists unless it is express authority.

More about apparent authority. A person may not whip up apparent authority to act as an agent out of thin air. Thus, the person who says that he is an agent does not possess apparent authority as an agent on his unsupported say-so; he needs some supporting proof. As mentioned above, someone who has possession of someone else's goods has no apparent authority to sell them; the possessor needs to have other proof of his status as an agent. He could merely be a thief, finder, or bailee. Someone who has possession of a promissory note has no apparent authority to collect it from the maker. Again, the possessor might be a thief or finder.

Someone from whom a debtor has borrowed money or bought goods on credit has no authority to collect the account, if the debtor knew that he was dealing with an agent when he borrowed the money or bought the goods. Just because the agent was an agent of the creditor at the time the loan was made or at the time the goods were purchased does not mean that he is still an agent of the creditor. However, the agent from whom a debtor has borrowed money does have apparent authority to collect the account if he has possession of the promissory note the debtor signed when he borrowed. The fact that the lending agent still possesses the note is good circumstantial evidence that he has authority to collect it.

When a principal hires a new agent to manage his business or his property, parties who have had dealings with prior agents may assume that the new agent has the same authority that the prior agents had, if two or more of the prior agents had identical authority. This would not be true if the principal makes changes in his agent's authority every time a new agent is appointed.

A third party may assume that an agent's authority continues to exist until he knows, or has reason to know, that it has been terminated. Thus, the terminated agent will have apparent authority with respect to those who knew of his express authority until they know or should know of his termination. The principal must inform such persons of the termination in order to end this apparent authority, or he must give them notice in some other manner.

A customer of a retail store may assume that a person dressed like a clerk who stands behind the counter and acts like a clerk in a clerk. Such a person will have apparent authority to sell goods from the store inventory. Of course, if the person behind the counter is not dressed like a clerk, or if the customer knows that the person behind the counter is not a clerk, there is no apparent authority.

PRINCIPAL AND THIRD PARTIES

A principal will be liable to a third party upon a contract made for him by a duly authorized agent, or by an agent with apparent authority or authority by estoppel. A principal is not liable upon contracts made in his behalf by would-be agents with no authority at all to make them.

Ratification. A principal may choose to be bound by a contract made for him by an unauthorized agent. If the principal knows that the would-be agent has made an unauthorized contract for him, and that the third party intends to perform his portion of it, silence by the principal is ratification. In this situation the principal has a duty to disaffirm if he is to escape liability.

If the principal did not know about the making of the unauthorized contract when it was made, but found out at a later time, his silence then might not be interpreted as ratification. In this case, if the principal then tells the third party that he ratifies, or if the principal actually begins performance of the bargain, ratification has occurred. Thus, if the third party learns that the agent with whom he made a contract had no authority to make it, and the third party wants to escape liability under it for that reason, he should inform the principal of the situation as soon as possible and make clear to him that he chooses not to be bound. He then cuts off the possibility of ratification.

Undisclosed principals. A principal may hire an agent to perform an act and instruct the agent not to disclose that he is acting as an agent, or not to disclose the identity of his principal. If the agent follows instructions and does not disclose that he is an agent, no fraud is committed, so long as the ultimate contract made by the agent is fair to all concerned.

Since the resulting contract is in the name of the agent, the third party may hold the agent liable for breach of it. On the other hand, the undisclosed principal may enforce it against the third party in case of breach by revealing his identity. Once the identity of the undisclosed principal becomes known to the third party, the third party may enforce the contract against him. In case of breach of such a contract by the principal, the third party may hold either the principal or the agent liable for a breach. If the third party has begun a suit against the agent before he finds out about the principal, he may drop his action against the agent in order to sue the principal.

An undisclosed principal may not be held liable upon commercial paper signed by an agent. If the signature by the agent on the check, note, or other paper does not disclose the name of the principal, there is no way to hold the principal to liability. Normally, no one may be held liable upon commercial paper whose name does not appear upon it.

The undisclosed principal suing to enforce a contract made in his behalf essentially stands in the shoes of an assignee of a contract right. Thus, if any reason exists as to why the third party should not be liable to the agent upon the contract, the third party would not be liable to the principal either.

Knowledge of agent. Any knowledge acquired by the agent relative to the purpose of the agency is imputed to the principal, so that the principal is assumed to know that which the agent knows. An agent is therefore obligated to inform his principal of knowledge he acquires relative to the agency relationship. When an agent receives notice of a fact relevant to the agency relationship, the notice is deemed given to the principal. Thus, when the customer of a retail business notifies the manager thereof of a breach of warranty with respect to goods purchased from the business, the principal has notice of the breach. When an agent is given notice that a check taken in by the business has been dishonored, the time limit for giving notice of dishonor to endorsers starts to run, though the principal does not yet personally know of the dishonor.

The only time in which the knowledge of the agent is not imputed to the principal is when the agent is not acting in the principal's interest, when the agent is plotting to defraud the principal, when he is assisting someone to take advantage of the principal, or something of the kind.

Principal's liability upon contract of subagents. Generally, an agent has no authority to appoint a subagent. Therefore, a principal is not liable upon the contract of an unauthorized subagent.

However, some agents do have authority to appoint subagents—notably business managers. When the business managed involves sale of goods from inventory, and the business is too large for the manager to manage alone, the manager has implied authority to hire employees. At least some of these employees must be given authority to sell goods from inventory. These are essentially subagents who have authority to bind their principal (the owner of the business) to contracts.

AGENT AND THIRD PARTIES

The authorized agent acting for a disclosed principal is not liable to third parties upon the contracts he makes, so long as he acts within his authority and commits no fraudulent acts in the process of contract negotiation. There are circumstances, however, under which liability to third parties is imposed upon agents.

Agents of undisclosed and partially disclosed principals. As discussed above, the agent of an undisclosed principal is personally liable to the third party upon contracts he negotiates for his principal. Since the third party believes that the agent is the principal (unless he knows otherwise), he may act upon this belief. Even if the third party learns that the agent was acting for an undisclosed principal, and he knows the identity of the principal, he may proceed against the agent if he chooses.

The same rule applies to the agent for a partially disclosed principal. In this situation, the agent discloses that he is an agent, but he does not disclose the identity of the principal. Here again, the third party may treat the agent as the principal. After all, the third party cannot very well sue the principal for breach if he does not know his identity.

Agents for nonexistent principals. It sometimes happens that an agent negotiates a contract on behalf of a principal who does not exist. In such a case, the agent will be held liable upon the contract, since otherwise the third party would have no recourse.

The most common type of nonexistent principal situation is that in which a promoter makes a contract with a third party in the name of a corporation in process of formation. The as yet nonexistent corporation, of course, has no capacity to appoint an agent. If the corporation never is organized, there will be no principal; if it is organized, it is not bound by the contract of the promoter, since the principal did not exist at the time of contracting. If the corporation ratifies the contract, it becomes bound. If it does not ratify, it is not bound. In cases of nonratification, the recourse of the third party is against the promoter agent.

He who acts as agent for a party with no contractual capacity, such as an incompetent person for whom a guardian has been appointed, is also an agent for a nonexistent principal. Unless the principal's guardian ratifies the contract, the agent will be liable for the inevitable breach. He who acts as agent for a deceased person also acts for a nonexistent principal. The death of the principal terminates an agency by operation of law. The authority of the agent to bind the principal ends when the principal dies—not even apparent authority survives the principal's death. Thus, the estate of the deceased principal would not be bound to contracts made by the agent after the principal's death. Unless the estate ratifies, the agent is liable upon such contracts.

Agents for persons with limited contractual capacity. An agent for a principal with limited contractual capacity, such as a minor, will not normally be liable to the third party if the minor disaffirms. The agent is under no duty to inform the third party that the principal is a minor, unless the third party shows by his action that he assumes that the principal is an adult. In such a case, the agent must set the third party straight.

The agent, then, does not warrant the capacity of his principal. But he does in a sense warrant his existence.

Agent's liability for fraud. An agent is personally liable for any fraud he commits against a third party in the course of his negotiations. This is true even if he commits the fraud upon the instruction of his principal. The principal is of course also liable to the third party for such fraud. The principal cannot escape liability by arguing that he had not authorized the agent to commit fraud. Both parties have committed a tort here, and both may be held liable for punitive damages.

The agent who misrepresents his authority to make a contract is also guilty of fraud. The principal would not be bound by the contract, unless the agent had apparent authority to make it. The principal would not be liable for the fraud either, since the agent's fraudulent representation of authority is outside the scope of his true authority. The agent may be held liable upon the fraudulently made contract, and he is also liable for damages for commission of the tort of deceit (or fraud).

Power of agent to sue on behalf of his principal. Generally, the agent of a disclosed principal may not sue a third party for breach of contract. Only the principal may do so. But if the principal is undisclosed, the agent may enforce the contract.

Selling agents may not sue buyers of the goods they sold in order to collect the purchase price, unless given express authority to do so. There are two exceptions here: auctioneers and factors have implied authority to sue to collect the purchase price of what they sell.

An agent who has the right to possess his principal's goods has the duty to protect them from harm. Such agents therefore have the right to sue third parties who damage the goods. They also have the right to sue to recover the goods from third parties who have no right to possession.

PRINCIPAL AND AGENT

It must be remembered that the principal-agent relationship is a fiduciary relationship. It is thus governed by all of the rules applicable to such relationships.

Agent's fiduciary duties to principal. Within the scope of the agency relationship, the agent must work for the welfare of his principal and for no one else—neither for third parties nor for himself. Thus, an agent must not:

1. Act as agent for two or more principals having opposing or differing interests, unless he has the knowledge and consent of all principals.
2. Buy from his principal or sell to his principal without the knowledge and consent of his principal. This is true even when the agent takes no monetary advantage of the principal.
3. Conceal facts relative to his performance of his agency responsibilities from his principal.
4. Mix his principal's property or money with his own.
5. Deposit his principal's money in his own bank account.
6. Use his principal's property or money for his own use, even if he pays rent for the property or interest upon the money.
7. Conceal conflicts between his own personal interests and the interests of his principal.

The agent who violates these fiduciary duties loses any claim to compensation he may have against his principal. If his violation of fiduciary duties causes financial loss to the principal, he will also be liable for these damages.

Agent's obligation to follow instructions. Normally, an agent is expected to follow orders: he is not expected to think for himself. The agent may act upon his own discretion only when he is authorized to do so.

Certain sorts of agents have more discretion than others. The business or property manager must have wide discretion in order to be able to do his job properly. On the other hand, the selling agent may be given detailed, rigid instructions from which he must not deviate. If the agent's disobedience damages his principal, the agent is liable for the consequences. But if his deviation benefits the principal, the benefits go totally to the principal, unless the principal chooses to share them.

The one circumstance under which an agent may use unauthorized discretion is when an emergency arises and fast action is required, but the principal is unavailable for consultation. If the agent cannot contact the principal for instructions, he may use his own best judgment. So long as his judgment is reasonable under the circumstances, he will not incur liability to the principal for the result of his actions in the emergency.

The agent's right to compensation. Unless otherwise agreed, an agent is entitled to compensation for his services. The compensation will be the fair value of the services, unless principal and agent agree upon specific compensation. Compensation to the agent is not necessary only when both principal and agent agree that no compensation is payable.

The compensation is normally payable after the agent completes his mission. It should be noted, though, that the mission of a selling agent is to commit a buyer to a contract to buy. The agent has earned his commission when the contract is made, even if the contract is never performed. The mission of the real estate broker and of similar brokers is the finding of a buyer who is "ready, willing, and able" to buy. If the principal chooses not to enter into a contract with such a buyer, the broker does not lose his right to a commission.

A principal desiring to sell something may appoint as many agents as he sees fit. He must be careful about giving more than one agent authority to bind him to a contract to sell the desired item, however. If he does not carefully coordinate the activities of his agents, he could end up with two or more contracts to sell one item.

The principal who desires to sell something does not give up the right to sell it himself by appointing an agent to sell it. The principal may in essence compete against the agent in a race to sell, and if the principal wins and sells first, he has no obligation to pay a commission to the agent.

If a principal grants to an agent an exclusive agency, he thereby binds himself not to hire other agents. If he does hire another agent, and that other agent sells the property, the exclusive agent is entitled to a commission, as is the actual selling agent. On the other hand, the principal who appoints an exclusive agent does not thereby give up the right to try to sell the property himself. If the principal succeeds in selling, the exclusive agent gets no commission. Should the principal grant an agent an exclusive right to sell, however, the principal gives up the right to sell. Under such an agreement, the agent is entitled to a commission if the property is sold, even if the principal did the selling.

If the agent incurs reasonable expenses in his efforts to carry out his mission, he is entitled to reimbursement from his principal. Reimbursable expenses might include such items as advertising expenses, travel expenses, and so on. The attorney is entitled to reimbursement of filing fees for documents and the like. The agent of an undisclosed principal who gets involved in litigation due to the principal's breach is entitled to reimbursement of his litigation expense. But an unreasonable expense, such as a speeding ticket incurred by the agent while carrying out his mission, does not qualify for reimbursement.

Termination of the principal-agent relationship. The principal-agent relationship generally ends when the agent has accomplished his mission. However, the relationship may otherwise be terminated by acts of the parties, or by operation of law.

Normally, the principal-agent relationship may be unilaterally terminated by one of the parties. If the agreement creating the relationship does not provide otherwise, the relationship exists at the will of the parties. Thus, the agent may resign at any time, and the principal may terminate the agent at any time. No mutual consent is required. If one of the parties wants to end matters, he may do so by informing the other of his decision. (Remember, though, that terminating the apparent authority of the agent will not be as easy.)

If the contract appointing the agent provides that the agent will serve for a specified length of time or that he will serve until a certain mission is accomplished, the parties no longer have the right to terminate the arrangement early, except by mutual consent. The parties may always mutually agree to rescind the appointment. The agent still has the power to resign whenever he wishes, and the principal still has the power to terminate the agent whenever he wishes; when principal or agent desire to use this power, the other party cannot prevent it. But the early resignation or termination will be a breach of contract, rendering the breaching party liable for damages (if the other party can prove that the resignation or termination caused him to suffer damages).

When the appointment of an agent is coupled with an interest held by the agent in the subject matter of the agency, the principal has neither the power nor the right to terminate the agency. In such a case, the agent has an absolute right to continue being an agent until his interest ends. A typical example is the situation where Borrower borrows money from Lender to erect an apartment building. Lender does not trust Borrower's ability to manage an apartment building, so Lender insists that Borrower hire him to manage the building until Lender's loan to Borrower is repaid. Lender has an agency coupled with an interest. The only way in which Borrower can get rid of Lender as his apartment manager is to pay off the loan in full and thus end Lender's interest in the building.

One way in which an agency is terminated by operation of law has been discussed—termination by the death of the principal. The death of the agent also automatically terminates the relationship. The agent's personal representative will have no authority of any sort to bind the former principal to contracts.

The bankruptcy of the principal probably terminates an agency. Since bankruptcy normally results in the liquidation of the bankrupt's business, the basis for the agency will end. Bankruptcy of the agent may terminate the agency. If the agent is a businessman—a professional agent—and the bankruptcy terminates the business, the agency is terminated. If the bankruptcy does not destroy the agent's ability to carry out the purpose of the agency, though, the agency continues to exist.

The insanity of the principal terminates an agency, since the agent no longer has a principal who has contractual capacity. The insanity of the agent will not have like effect, though, because an agent does not need contractual capacity. But as a practical matter the principal will probably hasten to terminate the relationship.

When the purpose of the agency becomes illegal, the basis for the agency is destroyed, and the agency is thus terminated. When a professional agent such as a real estate broker or attorney loses his license to practice his profession, his agency relationships are terminated. Essentially, these relationships are no longer legal. One may not, for instance, practice law without the proper license.

Agency relationships within the family. No family member is an agent for any other family member just because of the family relationship. A spouse has no authority to act as an agent for a spouse, and a child has no authority to act as agent for a parent, unless express authority exists.

On the other hand, a family member may subject another family member to quasi-contractual liability. A spouse is under an obligation to support a spouse, and parents are under an obligation to support their children. Thus, when a child buys necessities on credit, its parents become liable for the fair value of the necessities. Also, if a housewife buys necessities on credit, her husband becomes liable for their fair value. This quasi-contractual liability extends only to necessities. It also extends only to the fair value of the necessities, not necessarily to their contract price.

19

Employment

The employer-employee relationship is one that is similar in some ways to the principal-agent relationship; it is also different in some ways. An employee may be an agent, as is the retail store clerk. But an agent—such as a real estate broker hired by a customer to sell a tract of land for him—may not be an employee. And an employee (such as a laborer) may not be an agent.

An employee is hired for the purpose of doing a job under close supervision; an agent is hired for the purpose of making contracts. The person hired to make contracts under close supervision is both an employee and an agent.

For the purposes of this chapter the difference between an employee and an independent contractor must be kept in mind. When an employer hires an employee he generally tells the employee what work to do, and how and when to do it. The employee is subjected to more or less strict on-the-job discipline. He works fixed hours, and has a supervisor closely overseeing his work. On the other hand, the employer who hires an independent contractor tells the contractor only what work to do and when the work must be finished. Within these limitations the contractor does the work in his own way and at his own pace.

The more control the employer exercises over a person's work, the more likely it is that the person is to be an employee. The less control exercised by the employer over the work, the more likely the person is to be an independent contractor. The great advantage to hiring employees rather than independent contractors is the possibility of subjecting the hired persons to strict on-the-job discipline. However, along with this advantage comes the disadvantage of the need to comply with all the legislation enacted to protect employees. The advantage of hiring independent contractors is that the employer thereby avoids becoming subject to employee protection legislation. The disadvantage is that he gives up the possibility of subjecting his work force to much organization and discipline.

It must also be remembered that an employer is liable for torts committed by his employees in the line of duty. The employer of independent contractors is not so liable, unless he has hired the contractor in question to do extremely dangerous work.

Equal employment opportunity. All employers of fifteen or more employees during any twenty weeks of a calendar year are subject to the Equal Employment Opportunity

Act, 42 USC 2000e et seq. This legislation forbids employers to discriminate in employment practices on the basis of race, religion, sex, or national origin. For purposes of this legislation, employment practices include hiring, termination, laying off, payment, promotion, job assignment, assignment of seniority, and retirement.

Some types of discrimination on grounds of age are rendered unlawful by the Age Discrimination in Employment Act, 29 USC 621 et seq., to be discussed later. Discrimination upon the basis of membership or nonmembership in a labor union is to an extent forbidden by the National Labor-Management Relations Act, 29 USC 141 et seq., which will also be discussed later.

Persons or firms holding federal procurement contracts in excess of $2,500 in value are forbidden to discriminate in employment practices on the basis of physical or other handicaps (29 USC 793). Such discrimination will cause loss of the contract. Government contractors are also subject to other stringent antidiscrimination statutes and regulations, which are beyond the scope of our inquiry.

The antidiscrimination commands of the Equal Employment Opportunity Act are to a large degree a Congressional response to pressures generated by the civil rights movement and the women's liberation movement. They are intended to correct injustices of long standing and duration. These provisions of law of course do not eliminate all discrimination in the making of employment decisions. Among the bases for discrimination which remain legal and which are very common are:

1. Citizenship.
2. Legal status of an alien.
3. Sexual preference.
4. Criminal record.
5. Credit rating.
6. Employment record.
7. Personal appearance.
8. Personal life-style.
9. Education.
10. Grades (GPA).
11. Family and personal connections.

For positions in defense industries, security clearances are often required. Citizens of certain nations (such as the USSR and the German Democratic Republic) would find it virtually impossible to obtain such clearances. Aliens illegally present in the United States have no right to be here; they certainly have no right to work here. Some aliens legally present here may not work here, and they may of course be legally denied employment.

Discrimination against homosexuals is both legal and widespread.

It is a common practice for an employer to refuse to hire a job applicant who has been convicted of a felony. Some employers refuse to hire anyone who has been convicted of any criminal offense other than a minor traffic violation.

The conventional wisdom of American culture holds that a person who does not pay his bills as they fall due is to a degree irresponsible. Since no employer wants irresponsible employees, discrimination on the basis of credit ratings does exist. Conventional wisdom also holds that a person who has worked for many employers for short lengths of time is to a degree irresponsible. He is not "settled" and is therefore not worth training for assumption of responsibility. This sort of discrimination is very common.

All of us discriminate in our personal relationships on the basis of personal appearance. Since customers judge a business in part by the personal appearance of the employees with whom they have contact, employers often choose employees to place in customer contact positions with an eye to preserving a favorable company image. The overweight, the unattractive, the inarticulate, the shy, those with no taste in selecting clothing, and others with similar problems eternally bear the brunt of discrimination.

Society still expects its members to behave according to accepted norms. An employer may think twice about hiring a person who spends each weekend in an alcoholic stupor, or who lives with fifty other true believers in a cultish commune. Conventional wisdom equates possession of diplomas with intelligence and worthiness. Employers therefore frequently require specified levels of education for holders of specified positions. A large corporation, for instance, might refuse to hire any person as a management trainee who does not possess the M.B.A. degree. If Ace Corporation refuses to hire persons other than possessors of the M.B.A. as management trainees, it may also evaluate its applicants with M.B.A. degrees on the basis of the grades they earned in graduate school. The applicant with a 3.9226 GPA would be preferred to the applicant with 3.1429.

Discrimination in employment on the basis of connections is as old as the human race. If Ace Corporation's personnel manager is a graduate of Harvard Business School, he might hire every possessor of a Harvard M.B.A. who comes in the door while turning away possessors of M.B.A.s from Podunk State. If Deuce Company's personnel manager belonged to Alpha Beta Gamma while he earned his degree at Podunk State, he might be inclined to take a chance on any Alpha Beta Gamma brother who applies for a job at Deuce. Able, personnel manager of Trey Corporation, may have been ordered by his wife to find a job for Gil Gooch, her nephew, when he comes to file an employment application. In the interest of maintaining domestic peace, Able may do as he is told.

There is no legal objection to the use of these forms of discrimination, unless they serve to conceal discrimination of the unlawful type. If an employer doing business in an area of high black unemployment uses criminal records as a screening device for employment applicants, and many unemployed blacks in the area have criminal records, the use of this screening device may be branded a form of racial discrimination. The employer in such an area who requires all his ordinary laborers to be high-school graduates may be accused of racial discrimination, if many unemployed blacks do not have high-school diplomas and a high-school education is not an essential element in the ability to do the job.

The employer in an area inhabited by many Chicanos who expects employment applicants to fill out application forms in English and who refuses to hire job applicants who cannot do an acceptable job of filling out such forms may be guilty of discrimination on grounds of national origin. The screening device discriminates against applicants who do not read or write well in English, and many Chicanos have this difficulty.

The employer who imposes height and weight requirements for types of work which persons shorter and lighter than the requirements are capable of doing may be guilty of sex discrimination. Since women are on the average shorter and lighter than men, such requirements may well discriminate against women.

The employer located in an area inhabited by many poorly educated blacks and Chicanos who require applicants to pass a basic intelligence test may well discriminate both on grounds of race and on grounds of national origin, since persons who are fairly literate in English have a better chance to do well on these than persons who are not. Black applicants who are functionally illiterate may do badly on these. Chicanos who do not read English well will also do badly.

The traditional division of the world of work into "men's work" and "women's work" is now frowned upon. The employer who refuses to hire female truck drivers, coal-mining trainees, electricians, civil engineers, etc., is probably guilty of sex discrimination. The employer who refuses to hire male nurses, airline cabin attendants, secretaries, telephone operators, etc., is also probably guilty of such discrimination.

Another traditional notion which the law now frowns upon is the idea that a woman is a less reliable employee than a man, and is therefore not worthy of promotion, on-the-job training to improve job skills, and other benefits. The basis of the notion is that a woman may choose to marry, become a mother, and drop out of the work force, while a man cannot exercise such a choice. Regardless of how male executives feel on this question, discrimination against women on the basis of such considerations is wrongful.

A serious issue in this area has been the question of whether or not a female employee could be discharged because of pregnancy or denied benefits under company disability insurance programs when she bears a child. Congress settled this argument by enacting 42 USC 2000e-2(k), which provides that discrimination on the basis of pregnancy, childbirth, or related medical conditions is unlawful sex discrimination.

Any sort of discrimination is justifiable, on the other hand, if exercise of discrimination is necessary in order to find persons qualified to do a job. The owner of a Japanese restaurant who wishes to maintain a Japanese atmosphere in his establishment could probably refuse to hire Caucasian waitresses since a blue-eyed blonde would look out of place in a Japanese kimono. The restaurant owner might have trouble justifying a refusal to hire Vietnamese or Korean waitresses, though, unless ability to speak Japanese was deemed essential in waitresses. The Armenian restaurant owner whose specialty of the house is various forms of Armenian cuisine could insist that his cook be an Armenian. How many non-Armenians know anything about Armenian cooking?

The employer who imposes height and weight requirements upon applicants for jobs involving heavy physical labor would not be guilty of unlawful discrimination if persons who do not meet the requirements are physically incapable of doing the work. And Avon Cosmetics may justifiably refuse to hire Avon men. How many men are qualified to sell cosmetics to women?

Ace Corporation may require applicants for secretarial positions to demonstrate ability to write acceptable English. And Deuce Corporation may require applicants for posts as cashiers in its supermarkets to have no criminal records.

If employers were perfect judges of human character and ability, there would be no need for legislation to forbid discrimination in employment. The employer could judge his employees on their ability to do a job, and no other considerations would be taken into account. Employers, however, are not perfect judges of human character, and they are usually well aware of that fact. For this reason all employers use the discriminatory screening devices we have been discussing. Old habits of thought die hard, and, despite the mandate of the Equal Employment Opportunity Act, claims are still made that the employers of the nation continue to discriminate on the forbidden bases.

There are those who argue, therefore, that it is insufficient for the law to require that employers not discriminate against minorities and that in order to completely avoid discrimination against these minorities, employers must be forced to discriminate in favor of them. This is the rationale of affirmative action programs against forbidden sorts of discrimination. Opponents of affirmative action argue that such programs discriminate against the majority. Proponents argue that they insure absence of discrimination against minorities. The ongoing debate on the merits of affirmative action raises the question of whether or not discrimination can ever be eliminated from the world of employment. The answer seems to be negative: so long as employers are not perfect judges of ability to do a job, screening devices will be used. So long as the devices are used, efforts will be made to regulate their use.

Under the Age Discrimination in Employment Act, discrimination in employment practices against persons between the ages of forty and seventy is forbidden, except where age has a bearing upon the ability to do a job. Employees may not be forced to retire before age seventy, unless they become incapable of doing their work competently. It is unlawful to discriminate because of age in hiring because one prefers a young work force, or because large numbers of older employees raise insurance and pension plan costs.

Under the National Labor-Management Relations Act, union affiliation or the lack thereof should have no bearing on employment decisions. In states where the union shop is lawful, an employer may be forced to terminate a new employee who does not become a union member within thirty days of hiring, but no other form of discrimination based upon union membership is lawful. Under the provisions of the Texas Right-to-Work Law, even this form of discrimination is unlawful. No person may ever lose his job in the state of Texas because he refuses to join a union.

Equal pay. The Equal Pay Act, 29 USC 206, provides that an employer shall not discriminate in pay on the basis of sex, when members of both sexes are doing the same work. Job classifications which artificially segregate men and women who are doing essentially the same work to provide a basis for unequal pay are unlawful. Pay differentials between persons doing the same work are permissible if the differential is based on seniority (length of time on the job), merit (ability to do the job), piecework (productivity), or similar rational criteria other than sex. The Equal Employment Opportunity Act forbids discrimination in pay on the basis of race, religion, sex, and national origin, but allows it on the basis of these criteria.

The minimum wage. The Fair Labor Standards Act, 29 USC 201 et seq., requires most employers to pay most of their employees the federal minimum wage—$2.65 per hour in 1978, $2.90 in 1979; $3.10 per hour in 1980, and $3.35 per hour thereafter, as per 29 USC 206(a)(1). The following employers must pay the minimum wage to covered employees:

1. Businesses having minimal contacts with interstate commerce grossing over $250,000 per year, this figure to have risen in stages to $362,500 by 1982.
2. Laundries, dry cleaners, and similar businesses, regardless of gross sales.
3. Construction firms, regardless of gross sales.
4. Hospitals, nursing homes, schools, and institutions of higher learning operated by private organizations.
5. Farmers using more than 500 man-days of labor per year.
6. Employers of domestics for more than eight hours per week or fifty hours per calendar quarter.

Employees of public hospitals, nursing homes, schools, and institutions of higher learning are not entitled to the minimum wage. The U.S. Supreme Court held, in *National League of Cities vs. Usery*, that the federal government has no authority to force state or local governments to pay the minimum wage to their employees.

The following employees are not entitled to the minimum wage, even if they work for covered employers:

1. Executives, professionals, and administrators.

2. Salesmen paid on a commission basis.
3. Casual laborers (but not permanent part-time workers).
4. Domestics working less than eight hours per week and fifty hours per quarter.
5. Several other types of workers.

An employee who earns tips as part of his compensation may be paid as little as 60 percent of the minimum wage, if tips account for more than 40 percent of his wages. Should the tips account for less than 40 percent of his compensation, he should be paid a sum that, together with his tips, will equal the minimum wage.

An employer may pay students, learners, apprentices, and handicapped persons less than the minimum wage. However, these persons must be paid at least 85 percent of the minimum wage, and the number of these persons on a payroll must not exceed limitations set by Department of Labor regulations; if too many such employees are on a payroll, they must be paid 100 percent of the minimum wage.

Time and a half for overtime. The average employee who must be paid the minimum wage must be paid time and a half for any hours more than forty that he works during a single week. Anyone who works more than eight hours in a day is not entitled to overtime pay, unless he works more than forty hours per week. Certain employees, however, are not entitled to time and a half. Among these are:

1. Those who are not entitled to the minimum wage—executives, commission salesmen, and so on.
2. Parts men and mechanics of motor vehicles and the like not working for vehicle manufacturers.
3. Farm workers.
4. Taxi drivers.
5. Live-in domestics.
6. Movie-theater employees.
7. Other categories of employees listed in 29 USC 213.

Child labor prohibitions. Employers subject to the Fair Labor Standards Act may not hire children under sixteen except as:

1. Entertainers.
2. Newspaper delivery persons.
3. Employees of their parents.

Children between the ages of sixteen and eighteen may not be hired for dangerous work. They may not work in mining or manufacturing, nor may they work with explosives, woodworking machinery, etc., or as drivers.

Remedies for violations of above legislation. For violation of the Equal Employment Opportunity Act, the remedies provided by 42 USC 2000e-5 are injunctions to stop violations, orders to employers to reconsider the applications of persons not hired due to discrimination, and awards of back pay and job reinstatement in cases of wrongful firing and the like.

Generally, the victim of a violation of this act must complain to the Equal Employment Opportunity Commission (EEOC) and let that organization go to bat for him. If EEOC will not do this, he may file suit as an individual. But action by the EEOC is the most common enforcement mechanism.

For violations of the Fair Labor Standards Act (FLSA), injunctions may be obtained, along with back pay and sometimes a sum equal to the back pay as damages. The Wages and Hours Division of the Department of Labor may sue on behalf of injured employees, or the employees may sue. If the government chooses to sue, the employees must step aside and allow it to do so.

The best course for a victim of an FLSA violation to follow is to complain to the Wages and Hours Division of the Department of Labor about it. Government intervention in the matter may induce the employer to set things right without any necessity for litigation. If litigation is necessary, it would save difficulty to let the government take action, if it is willing. Otherwise, the individual may sue for himself.

The Texas minimum wage law. Before 1969 Texas had no state minimum wage legislation. The current legislation, RCS 5159d, was enacted in 1969 and became effective on September 1 of that year. It has not been significantly amended since.

RCS 5159d-5 provides that the state minimum wage is $1.40 per hour. RCS 5159d-4 provides for numerous exemptions, the most important of which are the following:

1. Employers and employees covered by the Federal Fair Labor Standards Act.
2. Students under twenty years of age.
3. Nonstudents under eighteen years of age.
4. Executives, administrators, and professionals.
5. Outside salesmen paid on a commission basis.
6. Domestics not covered by the federal law.
7. Farm labor employed by farmers using less than 300 man-days of labor per year.

RCS 5159d-9 provides that handicapped persons and persons over the age of sixty-five may be paid as little as 60 percent of the Texas minimum wage, which means that such persons working at jobs not covered by federal law but otherwise covered by state law may be paid as little as 84 cents per hour.

RCS 5159d-11 obligates all Texas employers to furnish their employees on payday an itemized statement containing, in addition to the employee's name:

1. His rate of pay.
2. His gross earnings during the pay period.
3. Itemization of all deductions from his pay.
4. His net pay.
5. Hours worked during the pay period.

RCS 5159d-12 provides that the furnishing of a false statement to employees with intent to deprive them of wages is a misdemeanor, for which the punishment shall be imprisonment in the county jail for no less than five nor more than thirty days, or a fine of no less than $100 nor more than $500, or both.

The civil remedy for nonpayment of the minimum wage is a suit by an injured employee on behalf of himself and others similarly situated for the amount of underpayment of wages, plus an equal amount as damages, plus court costs and attorney fees, as per RCS 5159d-13.

Texas child labor legislation. The various sections of RCS 5181 contain the state legislation upon this subject, the legislation essentially applicable to those employers not covered by federal law.

This legislation in essence makes it unlawful to employ children under seventeen years of age in dangerous work. It also provides that children under fifteen cannot work full-time, and children over fourteen cannot work full-time without a work permit issued by the county judge. These prohibitions do not apply to the hiring of nursemaids, yard servants, or others for work around the home. They also do not prohibit a farmer, rancher, or dairyman from hiring his own children. In general, violations of these laws are punishable as misdemeanors. Violators may be fined no less than $25 nor more than $500, or may be imprisoned for up to sixty days, or both.

Payday legislation. RCS 5155 provides that virtually all private employers (including persons, most companies, and all corporations) must pay their employees at least twice a month. Wages must be paid to a date not more than sixteen days prior to the date of payment. Thus, it is unlawful for an employer to pay only once a month. It is lawful not to pay an employee on the first payday after he starts work, but he must be paid on the second payday for his earnings during the first pay period.

RCS 5156 states that an employee who is not paid on payday for a legitimate reason must be paid in full on six days' demand. An employee leaving his job, or an employee who is discharged, must also be paid in full upon six days' demand.

The penalty for violation of the above two sections is a civil penalty of $50 per violation payable to the state of Texas (RCS 5157). Only the Texas Commissioner of Labor Statistics, the attorney general, or a local county or district attorney may sue for the penalty.

Payroll tax obligations of employers. Texas employers may be required to withhold two taxes from the wages of their employees: federal income tax and the employee's Social Security tax. These employers are also responsible for paying three payroll taxes: the employer's Social Security tax on the employee's wages, the federal unemployment tax, and the Texas unemployment tax.

Section 3401 of the Internal Revenue Code (IRC) requires employers to withhold income tax from the pay of all persons on the payroll except:
1. Independent contractors.
2. Partners and sole proprietors.
3. Agricultural labor.
4. Domestics.
5. Casual labor—employees grossing less than $50 per quarter.
6. Life insurance salesmen paid on a commission basis.
7. Several other categories of employees.

The Internal Revenue Service furnishes withholding tables which employers should use in computing these withholdings. The amount of withholding depends upon the employee's pay and the number of dependents he claims. Employees are required to file a W-4 form with the employer in which the number of his dependents is disclosed.

IRC 3102 requires the withholding of the employee's Social Security tax, except from the wages of employees exempted from it by IRC 3121. The major exemptions from Social Security withholding are:
1. Independent contractors.
2. Partners and sole proprietors.
3. Agricultural laborers earning less than $150 per quarter from any one employer, or not working more than twenty days per year for any one employer.
4. Domestics earning less than $50 per quarter from any one employer.
5. Casual labor earning less than $50 per quarter from any one employer.
6. Several other classes of employees.

Employers are required to file returns quarterly (by January 31, April 30, July 31, and October 31) with the IRS, accounting for these withholdings and the employer's Social Security contribution for his employees. The withholdings themselves must be paid more often, unless the employer has $200 or less in withholdings per quarter. How often payment is necessary depends on how much in withholdings the employer accumulates. If he accumulates $2,000 or more per week, for instance, he must pay every week.

If the employer has more than $200 per quarter in withholdings, he must deposit his accrued withholdings periodically (depending upon amount) with a bank designated by the

IRS as a depository for these withholdings. The bank issues a depository receipt in the amount of the withheld deposits to the employer. The employer attaches these depository receipts to his quarterly return as proof that he has made the required deposits.

Failure to file a quarterly return is a criminal offense punishable by a fine of up to $10,000 and imprisonment of up to one year (IRC 7203). Filing a return and failing to pay the tax subjects one to the same fine, but the imprisonment can run as high as five years (IRC 7202). Failure to withhold carries the same penalty.

In addition, IRC 6651 provides that a penalty of 5 percent will be added to the tax due for each month of delay in filing a required return, up to a maximum penalty of 25 percent. Unpaid but overdue taxes accrue interest at a rate of about 9 percent per year, the exact interest rate depending on the current prime rate charged by commercial banks. In addition, a penalty of .5 percent per month is assessed upon unpaid balances, up to a maximum penalty of 25 percent in toto (IRC 6601, 6621, and 6651). IRC 6656 imposes a penalty of 5 percent on late deposits.

If payment is made with a bad check, IRC 6657 provides that a penalty of 1 percent of the amount of the check may be imposed. If the check is for less than $500, the penalty shall be the lesser of $5 or the value of the check, unless the taxpayer can prove that he tendered the check in good faith, with every expectation that it would clear.

The IRC gives to the IRS a large arsenal of weapons for use in collection of taxes from reluctant taxpayers. Should the employer be reluctant to file required returns, IRC 6020b permits an IRS representative to file a return for him, estimating his liability. The only way the employer can escape such a liability is to produce his books and records and prove the IRS estimate wrong.

Should the IRS wish to examine the payroll records of an employer in order to determine his liability, it may serve an administrative summons upon the employer, ordering him to produce his records at a named time and place. Failure to comply may be punished by contempt proceedings brought in federal district court.

If returns are properly filed, but the tax is not properly paid, IRC 6331 permits IRS agents to seize property in the hands of the employer sufficient to satisfy the tax. The IRS agents may also padlock the business pending inventory of assets and sale of enough of them to pay the tax.

IRS may also seize property belonging to the taxpayer held by third parties, such as bank accounts, accounts receivable, and so on. The process is very simple. The IRS revenue officer merely serves a document called a notice of levy upon the third party informing him of the seizure, and the bank, debtor, etc. becomes obligated to turn the property he holds belonging to the taxpayer over to the government—property sufficient to pay the tax, that is.

IRC 6321 et seq. permit the IRS to file a federal tax lien in the public records of counties where the employer has assets. The effect of this is the same as the recording of an abstract of judgment against a debtor.

If the employer is a corporation which has become insolvent before payment of the tax, the IRS may institute 100 percent penalty proceedings against the person or persons who made the decision that the corporation should not pay the tax as required, and hold them personally liable for said taxes, penalties, and interest. As a last resort, the government may file suit against the taxpayer and thereby reduce its claim to a judgment.

IRC 6051 requires employers to furnish W-2 forms to both the IRS and the employee, giving the employee a statement of the amounts of federal income tax and Social Security withheld from his pay during a taxable year. These must be furnished by January 31 of the year following the withholdings. Should the employee leave the employer's work force before the end of the taxable year because the employer has gone out of business, or because the employee quit, was fired, or was laid off, the W-2 should be furnished within thirty days of the issuance of the employee's last paycheck. IRC 6674 provides that the employer shall be subject to a civil penalty of $50 for failure to furnish a proper W-2 form, or for furnishing an inaccurate one. In such situations, each late or inaccurate form constitutes a separate offense.

The federal unemployment tax and the Texas unemployment tax are closely related obligations. Both taxes are for the purpose of supporting the unemployment compensation system. The federal tax is payable annually to the IRS, and the state tax is payable quarterly to the Texas Employment Commission. The federal obligation is the smaller.

The tax amounts to 3.2 percent of the first $6,000 paid to employees during the calendar year, except for the following employees:

1. Insurance salesmen paid solely on a commission basis.
2. Employees of nonprofit organizations exempt from income tax.
3. Government employees, generally.
4. Students employed by their schools.
5. Agricultural laborers unless the employer paid $20,000 in wages to such employees during the last calendar year, or unless the employer employed at least ten agricultural laborers on each of twenty calendar days during the year.
6. Domestic laborers, unless the employer paid wages of over $1,000 per quarter for such labor.
7. Student nurses and interns.
8. Numerous other categories of employees.

The state tax amounts to 2.7 percent of the first $6,000 of the wages of covered employees, minus an experience rate deduction. The fewer the allowed claims for unemployment compensation chargeable to the account of an employer, the higher will be his experience rate deduction; the more allowed claims, the less his deduction.

If the employer pays his state tax in full as it falls due, he is given a credit against his federal tax of 2.7 percent of $6,000 for all covered employees. If the employer is delinquent on his state tax payments, he may not be allowed this credit upon his federal tax, thus raising the federal tax due.

The IRS may use all of the previously described weapons against taxpayers delinquent in their federal unemployment tax payments.

The taxpayer falling behind on his state tax payments may run into three difficulties:

1. He will lose his federal credit for state tax paid.
2. The Texas Employment Commission (TEC) may sue for delinquent taxes and obtain a judgment against him. Note that the TEC may not do anything toward collecting the tax before it obtains judgment. It must sue within three years of the filing of the return showing the delinquency.
3. If the employer is slow about paying the judgment obtained by the TEC, the TEC may withdraw his right to hire employees, which may well result in putting the employer out of business (unless he pays the judgment).

Unemployment compensation claims. A person who has lost his job may apply for unemployment compensation to his local Texas Employment Commission office. He must file the required claim forms, which will ask him for, among other things, his employment

history and the reason he lost his last job. According to RCS 5221b-2, an applicant is qualified for benefits if he meets the following requirements:
1. He has been working in covered employment for a substantial period of time in the recent past, not necessarily for the same employer throughout that time. Eligibility under this criterion is determined by a rather complex formula.
2. He has registered for work at a TEC office.
3. He has filed a proper claim for benefits.
4. He is able to work.
5. He is available for work.
6. He has been unemployed for a waiting period of seven days.

RCS 5221b-2A provides that a person otherwise qualified for benefits shall not be denied them because:
1. He entered upon a job training program approved by the TEC, or
2. Because he now lives outside the state of Texas, or
3. Because of pregnancy or termination of pregnancy.

RCS 5221b-3 provides that a person otherwise qualified to draw benefits may be disqualified for a period to be determined by the TEC, of no less than one week or no more than twenty-five weeks, because:
1. He quit his work voluntarily, without good cause connected with the work.
2. He was discharged for misconduct from his last job.
3. He failed to accept a suitable job found for him by the TEC.
4. He is unemployed because of a labor dispute, either because his union is on strike or because he refuses to cross a picket line. If he is willing to work, but the strike has caused the employer to lay him off, he may draw benefits.
5. He was paid severance pay. In such a case, he would not be considered unemployed until the period for which he was paid severance pay expires.
6. He is drawing Workers' Compensation benefits.
7. He is drawing Social Security or similar benefits.

Right after a claim is filed, the TEC contacts all employers listed on the claim form to verify the employment of the claimant. In contacting the last employer, the TEC will of course also verify the reason for which claimant left his last job. If the employer has any reason to contest the payment of benefits, RCS 5221b-4 provides that he must notify the TEC of his objection within twelve days of the mailing of the notice of filing of the claim. When an objection is filed, the matter is referred to a TEC examiner, who determines the validity of the claim. Anyone unhappy with his determination may appeal his decision if notice of appeal is filed within twelve days of the mailing of the notice of the examiner's decision. Appeals may be carried up to the full TEC, and from there to the courts, if necessary or desired.

The benefits received will be no less than fifteen dollars per week, and no more than eighty-four dollars per week. Benefits are normally payable for a period of twenty-six weeks, but this period is extended if the level of unemployment in the nation exceeds 4.5 percent, as it has for a long period recently. The maximum period now usually extends thirty-nine weeks, and may extend even longer. RCS 5221b-1 now provides that the maximum benefit shall rise seven dollars per week and the minimum one dollar per week whenever the manufacturing production worker's average wage rises ten dollars per week above the level prevailing in 1976, as determined by the TEC. Thus, an escalator has been built into the law to keep maximum benefits abreast of the inflation rate.

Employee pension plan regulation. This area was not subject to legal regulation until 1974, when Congress enacted the Employee Retirement Income Security Act (ERISA), 29 USC 1001 et seq. The scheme of regulation contained in the act is complex; space considerations preclude a detailed discussion of its provisions. The act does not require an employer to maintain a pension plan. If the employer chooses to provide one, however, its operation is subject to the provisions of ERISA.

29 USC 1052 requires that all employees who have worked for the employer at least one year, and who are at least twenty-five years of age, be covered. If the plan provides for 100 percent vesting of rights after ten years of participation, three years of service may be required for coverage.

Contributions to the plan may consist of amounts deducted from the employee's pay, or amounts contributed by the employer, or both. Employee contributions must be totally vested—that is, the employee must have the right to withdraw his contributions when he leaves the employer. Employer contributions must become vested according to one of three formulae contained in 29 USC 1053, either:

1. 100 percent vesting after ten years of service, or
2. 25 percent vesting after five years of service with the percentage of vesting growing thereafter until 100 percent vesting takes place after fifteen years of service, or
3. By use of the Rule of Forty-five. When the employee's age plus years of service equal forty-five, there must be 50 percent vesting, increasing annually until age plus years of service equal fifty-five—at which time there is 100 percent vesting.

The employer has free choice as to which of these formulae to use. Once the decision is made, however, it is very difficult to change.

29 USC 1055 requires the employer to permit the employee to set up his pension on a joint and survivorship basis, so that the employee's spouse may continue to draw a pension under the plan after the employee's death. If the employee does not set up his pension on a joint and survivor basis, his vested interest in the plan may be forfeited when he dies.

The amount of pension payable under the plan should be determined according to actuarial standards. There should be enough contributions coming into the plan to actuarially assure that the benefits to become vested can be paid.

Benefits under these plans may not be assigned, except that voluntary and revocable assignments of up to 10 percent of any benefit payment are permitted. Benefits under these plans may not be reduced because of increases in Social Security benefits or Railroad Retirement benefits (29 USC 1056).

29 USC 1101 et seq. govern the management of the assets of the plan. In short, these assets should be managed by an independent trustee. The trustee must invest assets as a prudent man would do, making his first objective the preservation of principal and the secondary objective the realization of income. The security holdings of the trust fund must be diversified. No more than 10 percent of the fund may be invested in employer securities, and the fund must not purchase more than 25 percent of any single issue of employer securities.

29 USC 1301 et seq. governs the Pension Benefit Guaranty Corporation, a federal corporation established for the purpose of insuring beneficiaries of pension funds against loss due to the insolvency of a fund or the insolvency of the employer. The PBGC has the responsibility of continuing to pay benefits to the beneficiaries of insolvent plans.

The U.S. Department of Labor and the IRS share responsibility for supervising these plans. Of these the IRS has more authority, simply because contributions by an employer to a properly constituted plan are a tax-deductible employer business expense. Should the plan not be properly operated, the IRS can refuse to permit the deduction of the contributions from the employer's taxable income.

Occupational safety and health. This area of employer responsibility was subject to little regulation until Congress enacted the Occupational Safety & Health Act (OSHA), 29 USC 651 et seq, in 1970. The act created the Occupational Safety and Health Administration of the Department of Labor, and in essence gave to it the authority to set safety standards for all of the workplaces of the nation.

The safety standards are enforced through the mechanism of inspection of workplaces by OSHA inspectors. 29 USC 657 gave to OSHA inspectors the right to enter workplaces without possession of any warrant. However, the U.S. Supreme Court declared this procedure unconstitutional. Today, the inspector may be forced to obtain a warrant before his visit.

These inspections may be of two kinds. The most usual is the routine unannounced inspection. The other is the special inspection made by request of employees. Employees who fear that their employer is violating established safety standards have the right to request such inspection.

When an inspector finds a violation, he gives the employer a citation for it. The citation contains three items of information, usually:

1. The nature of the violation, and a statement of whether or not it is "serious."
2. The penalty the inspector proposes to assess for the violation. If the violation is not serious, the inspector may suggest no penalty, but he can suggest one of any amount of money up to $1,000. Should the violation be serious, the inspector must suggest a penalty—again, of any amount up to $1,000.
3. The time allotted to the employer to correct the violation.

The citation may be issued at the moment of discovery of the violation or later, but no citation may be issued more than six months after discovery of the alleged violation (29 USC 658).

When the employer receives notice of a citation and proposed penalty, he has fifteen working days within which to appeal the citation to the Occupational Safety and Health Review Commission (OSHRC). If he files no appeal, the penalty must be paid and the violation corrected. If he does appeal, the OSHRC conducts a hearing to give him a chance to explain why he should not be penalized for the violation. The act provides no defenses for the employer to use in these hearings, but the OSHRC has come to recognize a few defenses, some of which are:

1. The citation was issued more than six months after the inspector's visit.
2. The standard in question was actually not violated.
3. The equipment which supposedly violated the standard in question is no longer in use.
4. The employer uses a safety procedure which, though not in accordance with the standard, is safer than that provided by the standard.
5. The employer has promulgated instructions to employees pursuant to the standard in question, but the employee who violated the standard was not following instructions, although he knew better.

If the OSHRC upholds the employer, the employer has escaped the penalty. If OSHRC upholds the citation, the employer either must pay or appeal to a federal circuit court of appeals. If a violation is not corrected by the deadline date contained in the citation, the employer may be penalized $1,000 per day that he is late in correcting the violation.

If a willful violation of any standard causes an employee to be killed on the job, the employer may be criminally prosecuted and is subject to a fine of up to $10,000 or six months in prison or both. For a second or subsequent offense, this punishment may be doubled—a fine of up to $20,000, or imprisonment of up to one year, or both (29 USC 666).

The act does not provide for enforcement by individual suits against employers. All penalties payable under the act go to the U.S. government. The act applies to all employers in the United States. Thus, an employer of even one employee is obligated to obey the OSHA safety standards applicable to his workplace. This act is obviously an extremely far-reaching piece of legislation.

Workers' Compensation. RCS 8306 contains the text of the Texas Workers' Compensation Law, an act designed to provide compensation for those employees who are injured on the job. The act covers almost—but not quite—all employers and employees within the state. It also covers almost—but not quite—all on-the-job injuries.

The following sorts of employees do not have a Workers' Compensation claim for on-the-job injuries (RCS 8306-2):

1. Domestics
2. Casual employees working around a residence.
3. Farm laborers.
4. Ranch laborers.
5. Railway laborers.

The exemption of railway workers is due to the fact that they are governed by the Federal Employer's Liability Act. The other exemptions leave these workers uncovered by any sort of Workers' Compensation.

It should also be noted that certain other types of employees are not covered by this legislation, notably federal government employees and seamen on vessels, both of whom are covered by special legislation.

RCS 8309a-1a states that an employer may elect to cover the following under Workers' Compensation:

1. Sole proprietors.
2. Partners.
3. Corporate executive officers.

Unless the employer affirmatively chooses to cover these persons, they are not covered. Corporate directors may not be covered in their capacity as directors.

The following sorts of on-the-job injuries are not covered (RCS 8309-1):

1. Injuries caused by acts of God, unless the employee's job is such that he is more exposed to injury through acts of God than ordinary individuals.

2. Injury caused by the act of a third person intended to injure the employee, if the third party was angry with the employee as a person, not as an employee of the employer.

3. Employee was intoxicated when he was injured.

4. Employee was willfully trying to injure himself.

5. Employee was willfully trying to injure someone else. (Thus injuries incurred as a result of fights or practical jokes are not covered.)

Of course, injuries not incurred within the scope of the employee's employment are not covered. Injuries incurred while traveling to and from work are thus not covered, unless the employer furnished the transportation and an employee of the employer was driving the conveyance carrying the injured person when the injury occurred. Also, of course, injuries incurred while the employee was supposed to be working but was actually off on "a frolic of his own" will not be covered. On the other hand, injuries which the employee suffers because of his own negligence will be covered, and injuries suffered by the employee while on the job due to the negligence of third parties will also be covered.

RCS 8306-3 provides that the benefits accorded employees under the Workers' Compensation law are exclusive; when an employee is injured on the job, he has no recourse against his employer other than that given him by this legislation. Thus, in Texas, a covered employee may not sue his employer for damages because of an on-the-job accident.

Any employer of one or more employees other than domestic, casual household, farm, or ranch employees, is subject to the provisions of this legislation. Should his employee be injured on the job in a covered accident, the employer must pay all benefits out of his pocket. The employer of course can, and should, take out insurance to protect himself against these liabilities. Should the employer wish, he may qualify with the Industrial Accident Board as a self-insurer. Those employers covered by insurance, or registered as self-insurers, get the benefit of the administrative procedure of the Industrial Accident Board in the settlement of claims. Those who are neither insured nor registered as self-insured may not use the IAB.

Persons who suffer on-the-job injuries covered by the act are entitled to the following benefits:

1. Medical aid—a doctor and his service.
2. Hospital services, when needed.
3. Nursing services, when needed.
4. Medicines.
5. Chiropractic services when needed.
6. Prosthetic appliances when needed.
7. Vocational rehabilitation when needed.

All of these are to be paid for, of course, by the employer's insurer or by the employer himself, if he is a self-insurer.

Should the injured employee suffer either temporary or permanent disability, he is entitled to monetary compensation. The basis for computation of the compensation is two-thirds of the employee's average weekly wage, taking into account, generally, his earnings over the 210 days before his injury. The maximum compensation is at present seventy-seven dollars per week, the minimum fourteen dollars per week, subject to the same escalator which applies to the fixing of the unemployment compensation rate. For each increase in the average Texas manufacturing employee's weekly wage of ten dollars over the level prevailing in 1974, the maximum workers' compensation weekly benefit is increased seven dollars per week, and the minimum increased one dollar per week (RCS 8306-29).

In case of total and permanent disability, defined in RCS 8306-11a as loss of both eyes, loss of two extremities (hands, feet, or one of each), paralysis of two limbs, or incurable brain damage resulting in insanity or imbecility, the compensation shall be 401 times the weekly compensation due.

In case of less than total permanent disability, the compensation payable depends upon the severity of the disability: for loss of a fourth finger, fifteen times the weekly compensation; for loss of a hand, one hundred and fifty times the weekly compensation; and so on. RCS 8306-12 sets forth twenty-four types of permanent disability and the allowable compensation for each.

In case of temporary disability the injured party may draw his weekly compensation for the period of disability. He will draw nothing for his first week, but if his disability lasts as long as four weeks he will be compensated for that first week. The maximum duration of temporary disability benefits is 300 weeks.

Benefits are also payable to victims of occupational diseases. In order to be able to recover such benefits, however, the employee will have to show that his disease resulted from his work environment. Sometimes this is hard to prove, especially when the medical condition claimed to be an occupational disease can be caused by factors not connected with the job.

When an employee is killed on the job, funeral expenses of up to $500 are payable. Weekly compensation may be payable to the heirs of the deceased according to the following schedule:

1. If deceased was married at the time of death, the spouse may draw weekly compensation until death or remarriage. If the spouse remarries, he is entitled to a closing payment of two years of compensation (104 weeks).
2. If the closest relative of deceased was a child, he shall draw benefits until his eighteenth birthday, or as long as he remains a dependent, or until his twenty-fifth birthday if he stays enrolled in an accredited institution of higher learning until that time.
3. The parents and stepmother of deceased, if they or one of them are the closest relative, may draw a benefit of 360 times the weekly compensation.
4. If dependent brothers and sisters, grandparents, or grandchildren are the closest relatives, they draw the same compensation as parents or stepmother.
5. If deceased left none of the close relatives described above, no death benefit is payable.

Of course, a spouse may not draw these benefits if he or she had abandoned the deceased before his or her death. The death benefit is payable directly to the beneficiaries, so it is not a part of the estate of the deceased and it is not subject to any creditor claims. Benefits payable to an injured party are likewise not subject to creditor claims.

If the death of the deceased on the job was caused by the willful act or omission of the employer or of his agent or employee, or by his gross negligence, a surviving spouse, child, or grandchild may sue the employer for punitive damages, regardless of any compensation they may receive under the Workers' Compensation Act, according to RCS 8306-5. This is the only circumstance under which an employer who has proper insurance coverage may be sued.

When an employee is injured on the job due to the act of a third party, the question arises as to whether the employee can both file a Workers' Compensation (WC) claim and sue the third party for damages. This can be done, if it is done properly.

RCS 8307-6a provides that, if the employee sues before filing his WC claim, he loses his claim. If he files the WC claim, however, the insurer is subrogated to the employee's rights against the third party. The insurer may then file suit against the third party in the name of the employee to recover what it paid out on the employee's claim. If the employee can recover damages in this suit over and above what he received under his WC claim, he is entitled to keep these. The insurer of course recovers what it paid on the original claim.

In case a borrowed employee is injured on the job, (that is, an employee who is on the payroll of one employer but working for another) the employer who supervises the employee's work is liable for paying compensation. An employee who is injured on the job should report his injury to his employer as soon as possible. In any event, RCS 8307-4a requires that the injury be reported within thirty days; otherwise the employee will lose his claim.

RCS 8307-7 requires all employers to report injuries to the Industrial Accident Board within eight days of the date the employer learned of the injury. Failure to do this can subject the employer to a $1,000 civil penalty, which can be assessed if the attorney general of Texas or a local district or county attorney chooses to sue to collect it. The employer or his insurer must decide whether or not to honor the claim. If the insurer decides not to honor it, he must inform the injured party. Should the injured party want to contest the matter, he must then file a complaint with the Industrial Accident Board within six months of his injury.

Notice of the complaint is given the employer and the insurer, and they may of course contest the claim. The case will be assigned to a prehearing officer of the IAB, who will try to work out a settlement. If this effort does not succeed, a hearing will be necessary before a member of the IAB. The administrative procedure of the IAB must be followed until the board makes a final decision on the claim. If either party is unhappy with the final IAB decision, it has twenty days within which to file notice of its unhappiness with the board (RCS 8307-5). Once such a notice is filed, the complaining party then has an additional twenty days to take the matter to court. The proper court will normally be a Texas district court, but it will depend upon the amount of money involved in the claim. Venue would be the county where the employee was injured, or the county where the employer does business. An entire new trial is held in court, the decision of the IAB being thrown out.

When an employee of an uninsured employer is injured on the job, and the employer refuses to pay the employee's claim, the employee may file suit directly against the employer for the benefits he is entitled to under the law. Should a farm worker, ranch worker, casual household employee, or domestic be injured on the job, they are of course not covered by Workers' Compensation, they are therefore not entitled to any of the benefits of this act.

Such employees must file suit against their employer in a court of proper jurisdiction. RCS 8306-1 provides that the employee may not recover unless he can prove that negligence on the part of the employer or his agents or other employees caused the injury.

The employer may not use any of the following as defenses:
1. That employee's contributory negligence was a partial cause of the injury.
2. That the negligence of a fellow employee of the injured party caused the injury.
3. That the injured party assumed the risk of getting hurt by taking the job in question.

The employer may use the following defenses:
1. The employee deliberately sought to injure himself.
2. The employee was intoxicated when he was injured.

In all other respects, a case of this sort is handled as a normal personal injury case.

Employer liability for torts of employees. Under the doctrine of respondeat superior—"let the superior respond"—the common law holds an employer responsible for the torts of his employees which are committed within the scope of his employment.

A plaintiff attempting to hold an employer liable for the tort of an employee will need to prove at least three items to the satisfaction of a court or jury. First, he must prove that the employee committed the tort. The proof here is essentially that required in any tort litigation. Second, he must prove that the person who committed the tort is truly the employee of the defendant. Third, he must prove that the employee was acting within the scope of his employment when the tort was committed.

Proof of employer-employee relationship. There is no such thing as apparent authority to commit a tort. Though a person who is not an employee or agent may bind a principal to a contract if appearances are right, the ostensible employee can never subject his apparent employer to tort liability. If the person who committed the tort was not an employee of the defendant, even though it appeared to a reasonable man that he was so employed, the defendant is not liable. Appearances are of no importance here; the reality is of supreme importance.

If the person who committed the tort does work for the defendant, and did so when the tort was committed, this is not enough to render the employer liable. It must normally be shown that the person who committed the tort is an employee rather than an independent contractor. The same factors count in this situation as when tax liability or Workers' Compensation liability is in question. The more control the employer exercises over the tort-feasor, the more likely it is that he is an employee. It is possible in rare cases for an employer of an independent contractor to be liable for the contractor's torts. This is true when the contractor is hired to do extremely dangerous work, such as blasting. However, if the contractor merely washes windows or something similar, the employer will not be responsible for his torts.

The borrowed-servant doctrine sometimes has a bearing upon the outcome of these cases. If Charles works for Able, and Able tells Charles to work for Baker for a week because he, Able, has no work for Charles to do, but Able continues to pay Charles's wages, a question could arise as to the identity of the true employer of Charles. If Charles injured Diggs on the job, and Diggs sought to sue Charles' employer, would he sue Able or Baker? The rule here is that the true employer is he who controls the employee's on-the-job work. Thus, Baker would be liable for Charles's torts during this week, despite the fact that Able signs Charles's paycheck.

The same rule would apply if Boss asks Manpower, Inc. to send over some temporary help. Manpower will pay these people their wages, but Boss will control what they do on the job. If they commit torts on the job, Boss will be liable, not Manpower.

The immediate supervisor of an employee is not liable for that employee's torts, even if that supervisor hired the employee. If both employee and supervisor work for the same employer, the employer is responsible for the employee's torts; no one else is responsible (except the employee himself). Thus, if Chef manages Sitzer's drugstore, and Chef hires Flunkey to work in the store pursuant to his authority to hire employees, Sitzer is responsible for Flunkey's on-the-job torts; Chef is not responsible.

Proof of scope of employment. Scope of employment is just as important a matter in tort cases as it is in Workers' Compensation cases. If an employee commits a tort while he is on the job, his employer is liable for it. If he commits a tort while not on the job, the employer is not liable.

If Heiss, a clerk in Schuh's shoe store, gets into a political argument with a customer inside the store and punches the customer in the nose, the customer could hold Schuh liable for the assault. To be sure, it is not part of Heiss's job to punch customers in the nose; he has no authority to do such a thing. Nevertheless, Schuh owes a duty to his customers not to hire such irascible persons to deal with them.

If Heiss is on coffee break in the lounge in the back of the store, where he gets into an argument with the plumber Schuh hired to fix a leaky water faucet, and Heiss punches the plumber in the nose, it might well be that Schuh could escape liability. Heiss was not on duty while in the lounge. This, however, would be a borderline case.

If Heiss went to the restaurant next door on coffee break and committed a tort there,

Schuh would definitely not be liable. But if Heiss went to the restaurant on Schuh's orders to fetch him a cup of coffee, and he committed a tort there, Schuh would be liable because Heiss was on duty at the time that he committed the tort.

Most problems in defining the scope of employment involve drivers of motor vehicles. The employer is liable for the negligence of his driver if the driver was on duty when he was negligent. The problem here is that drivers work under their own supervision, so they are able to "goof off" in ways not available to less mobile employees.

If Chef, an employer located in downtown Dallas, tells his delivery man Fahrer to deliver a package to an address in University Park, and Fahrer negligently gets into an accident near the SMU campus, Chef would probably be responsible. The campus is no doubt somewhere near where Fahrer had to deliver the package.

If Chef told Fahrer to deliver a package to the Texas Instruments plant on the North Central Expressway north of the LBJ Freeway, and Fahrer does this but stops at the North Park Shopping Center just off the expressway to do a little unofficial shopping, and negligently causes a wreck in the shopping center parking lot, a borderline case arises. The shopping center is just off Fahrer's most direct route back to his workplace, but Fahrer had no authorization to go there. He should have driven directly back to work. This situation would give a plaintiff's attorney ground to argue that Fahrer was within the scope of his employment. It would give a defense attorney grounds to argue that he was not.

If, after Fahrer delivers the package to the TI plant, he drives over to the Dallas-Ft. Worth Airport to pick up his girlfriend who is flying in from Los Angeles that afternoon and negligently causes an accident there, Chef is definitely not liable. Fahrer's trip to the airport has taken him far away from the most direct route back to downtown Dallas. He was on a frolic of his own over there.

The mere fact that an employee drives his employer's vehicle, then, is not grounds for holding the employer liable for the employee's negligent driving. The fact provides fair evidence that the driver is an employee, and fair evidence that he is acting within the scope of his employment, but the employer may explain away the two inferences with proper evidence.

Effect of employee admissions upon employer liability. A plaintiff may not prove the existence of an employer-employee relationship solely by the word of the employee. He will need other evidence to be able to establish this.

A plaintiff may, however, use the admission of fault by the employee as proof of liability by the employer. The admission of fault standing alone does not render the employer liable for anything, of course. The plaintiff must still prove that the employee is an employee, and that he was acting within the scope of his employment when the misfortune occurred.

20

Union-Employer Relations

Since employer-employee relations may be distinctly colored by the presence of a labor union as collective bargaining representative for some or all of the employees of a business, some discussion of the law in this area is in order. The major piece of federal legislation on the subject—and most of the controlling law—is found in the National Labor-Management Relations Act, 29 USC 141 et seq. The federal administrative agency with great authority here is the National Labor Relations Board (NLRB).

The rules of law to be discussed in this chapter do not apply to the labor relations of governments, federal reserve banks, or railways and commercial airlines. The labor relations of railways and airlines are governed by the National Railway Labor Act; those of governments and the federal reserve banks are governed by various other statutes.

The NLRB has, by administrative regulation, refused to accept jurisdiction over certain types of businesses, regardless of size (such as race tracks and gambling casinos). It also refuses to accept jurisdiction over certain small businesses, such as retailers grossing less than $500,000 per year, and hotels and motels with gross revenues of under $500,000 per year and over 75 percent of residents permanent rather than transient. We shall not discuss the law relative to unionization of small firms outside NLRB jurisdiction.

Union certification. An employer is not obligated to engage in collective bargaining until a union is certified by the NLRB as the bargaining representative of a group of employees. A union may obtain such certification in three ways:

1. Voluntary recognition by the employer.
2. Forced recognition by the NLRB, without an election and without the employer's consent.
3. Union victory in a certification election.

If the employer desires to recognize a union, he must simply notify the NLRB. After the union completes the required paperwork, it is certified. If the employer obstructs a union organizing campaign in unlawful ways (see below), the NLRB may force the employer to recognize the union as punishment for his unlawful conduct.

The most common method of attaining recognition is victory in a certification election. If 30 percent of the employees in a proposed bargaining unit favor an election, the NLRB will call for one. The 30 percent may be determined in two ways:

1. Signatures on a petition to the NLRB calling for an election.

2. Union authorization cards signed by 30 percent or more of the employees in the bargaining unit; these cards often look like applications for union membership.

The employer also has the right to ask for an election. If he does, no petitions or authorization cards are necessary. If the union initiates the organizing activity through petition or authorization cards, the union must satisfy the NLRB that 30 percent of the employees in the unit desire an election. If the employer agrees to an election, it is scheduled. If he does not agree (because, for example, he doubts that 30 percent of the employees in the union actually want an election, or because he wants to play a stalling game), an administrative hearing on the question of holding the election must be held before an NLRB administrative law judge. Resolution of the matter takes time, which is why managements sometimes stall organizing efforts by requesting these hearings.

Another important question to be resolved is the matter of the composition of the proposed bargaining unit. If union and employer agree on this, the matter is resolved quickly. If they disagree, the preelection hearing will have to resolve the matter.

Production and maintenance bargaining units—covering all plant production and maintenance workers—are common. Guards and security personnel must not be included in bargaining units with other employees. If such personnel desire to unionize, they must have their own unit.

Professionals—doctors, attorneys, accountants, scientists, and others—must not be included in bargaining units with nonprofessionals without their consent. They must vote in favor of such inclusion in a special election held for the purpose; they usually form their own unit if they want to unionize.

Certain types of workers may ask not to be included in production and maintenance units, and their wishes are generally respected. These include:
1. Technicians—draftsmen, electronic and other specialists.
2. Skilled craftsmen—machinists, tool and die makers, etc.
3. White-collar workers—office clerks, secretaries, etc.
4. Workers in a separate part of the plant—warehousemen, for example.
5. Driver-salesmen.

Those employees who worked in the bargaining unit as of the end of a specified pay period generally may vote in the election. This includes permanent part-time employees. Temporary employees, relatives of the employer, management trainees, and the like may not vote. Temporarily laid-off employees may vote; permanently laid-off employees may not. Employees hired since the end of the specified pay period may not vote; neither may employees who quit after the end of the specified pay period.

There are few restrictions upon the union in the election campaign. It may not use violence or other forms of coercion or campaign in work areas during work hours. Otherwise, it may do as it wishes. Management's campaign is subject to more restriction. It cannot threaten dire consequences if the union wins, or promise great benefits if the union loses. It cannot grant pay raises or benefits during the campaign. It cannot electronically bug union campaign meetings or otherwise spy on them. Essentially all it can do is attempt to convince the employees that they are better off without unionization. A very common reason for the NLRB to recognize a union without an election and without the employer's consent is unfair and unlawful electioneering by the employer.

Second and third unions may get on the ballot in such elections by convincing the NLRB that they have support within the bargaining unit. The 30 percent requirement does not apply to such unions.

The NLRB prints the ballots for the election and in general supervises it. The NLRB also counts the votes and announces the result; all sides are entitled to have poll watchers at the polling places. Any poll watcher may challenge the right of a would-be voter to vote. The challenged person is permitted to vote, but his ballot is placed in a separate envelope and is not counted with the others. Challenged votes are not counted unless they could influence the outcome of the election.

Of all the choices on the ballot, one must be the choice of 50 percent plus one of the voters for the election to be decisive. If no choice gets a majority, there must be a runoff between the two most popular choices. One choice in such elections is always "no union." The other choices are specific unions. If no choice gets the required majority, but "no union" finishes first or second in the balloting, "no union" will be one of the runoff choices.

If it is necessary to count challenged votes to determine the outcome, the NLRB election supervisor must hold informal hearings on each challenge and decide whether or not to count each challenged vote. Anyone unhappy with his decision may ask for a full administrative hearing to review it; the result of this hearing may be appealed. Thus, in close elections which may be influenced by challenged votes, the entire outcome may be stalled for long periods while vote challenges are litigated.

Anyone unhappy with the declared result of an election may challenge it with the NLRB within five business days after the election. Such objections are generally over unfair campaigning or something of that sort. Because of such challenges, the NLRB may throw out the result of an election and order a rerun. In a rerun, the same choices appear on the ballot as before, but a new list of eligible voters is used. In a runoff, the old voter list used in the first election is used. Thus, no one is eligible to vote in a runoff who was ineligible to vote in the first election (though an eligible voter who did not vote in the first election may vote in a runoff).

If the final result of an election is a tie between a union and no union, the union loses. If it is a tie between two unions, a further runoff is held to break the tie. If the union wins, it is certified as the official bargaining representative, and cannot be decertified for at least one year. If the union loses, a new certification election may not be held in the bargaining unit for at least a year.

It is very possible, of course, for an employer's work force to be unionized in part and to be nonunion in part. It is also quite possible to have two or more unions representing various classes of employees of an employer in collective bargaining.

Union security. Dedicated trade unionists believe that a union cannot do an effective job of representing employees in collective bargaining unless it has the power to compel all members of the bargaining unit to join it, thus giving it the power to collect dues from all unit members and to subject all members to union discipline.

Before 1947 it was federal policy to permit unions to require such membership. When the Taft-Hartley Act was enacted in that year, the states were authorized by Section 14b, 29 USC 164(b) to outlaw compulsory union membership. The Texas legislature has taken advantage of that authorization to enact the Texas Right-to-Work Law, RCS 5154g. That statute says simply that the right of a person to work shall not be denied or abridged due to membership or nonmembership in a labor union. In Texas, the open shop is the only authorized form of union security agreement.

From the union point of view, of course, the open shop provides very little security. The union may neither compel workers in the bargaining unit to join nor collect dues or the equivalent from unit members who choose not to join. In effect, the union must do such a good job of representing the interests of its members that they desire to join. It must represent all workers in the bargaining unit in any case.

Some twenty other states of the United States have enacted right-to-work laws. In the thirty or so states that have not adopted right-to-work laws, union membership may be required. The most stringent permissible security arrangement in these states is the union shop. Under this arrangement, the employer may hire nonunion employees. However, such employees must join the union within thirty days of going to work in the union shop. Any employee who refuses to join must be terminated. However, if the employee offers to join, but the union refuses to admit him, he may not be terminated.

Under a maintenance of membership arrangement, no employee is compelled to join the union. However, when an employee does join, he may not thereafter resign his membership. If he resigns, he must be terminated. Under an agency shop arrangement, no employee is required to join the union, but all workers in the bargaining unit must pay the equivalent of dues to the union. Union members pay dues; nonmembers pay a representation fee equal to the dues of the members.

Two sorts of arrangements are unlawful throughout the United States. One of these is the closed shop, under which employer and union agree that the employer will not hire nonmembers of the union. The other is the "yellow-dog contract," under which the employer forces all employees to agree not to join a union, union membership being grounds for termination.

Unions naturally would like to have an arrangement with employers by which union dues are deducted by the employer from employee paychecks and paid over to the union. This may be done only if the member agrees in writing that the employer should do it. No employee may be compelled to consent to the dues checkoff.

An employer is permitted to agree with a union that he will hire all his employees through a union hiring hall. For the arrangement to be lawful, however, the union must permit nonunion job seekers to use the hall, and the employer must demonstrate by his hiring practices that he does not discriminate against nonunion men.

Decertification of a union is accomplished through a decertification election. The decertification procedure is begun by the filing of a petition with the NLRB containing the signatures of 30 percent of the employees working in the bargaining unit, asking for such an election. Such a petition must be filed less than ninety days before expiration of a collective bargaining agreement, and more than sixty days before its expiration. It may also be filed when no agreement of collective bargaining is in force. If, however, the term of the collective bargaining agreement is more than three years, a decertification petition may be filed any time after the agreement has been in effect for three years.

The NLRB processes decertification petitions in the same way as recognition petitions, and decertification elections are conducted in the same way as certification elections.

Collective bargaining. The major reason for unionization is to permit the employees to bargain with the employer as a unit over some aspects of the employer-employee relationship, and to give employees some contractual protection with respect to certain aspects of their work.

The major subjects of collective bargaining are of course wages, hours, and working conditions. Among those items which are considered to involve pay are the following.

1. Hourly pay.
2. Overtime pay.
3. Shift differentials.
4. Holiday and vacation pay.
5. Severance pay.

6. Pension plan.
7. Profit-sharing plan.
8. Stock purchase plan.
9. Merit pay raises.

Among those items involving hours are:
1. Mandatory work hours.
2. Work schedules.
3. Sunday and holiday work.
4. Overtime in general.

Among those items involving working conditions are:
1. Grievance procedure.
2. Layoffs.
3. Discharges.
4. Sick leave.
5. Work rules.
6. Seniority.
7. Retirement.
8. Plant safety.
9. Promotions and transfers.

Management may legitimately refuse to bargain upon such matters as:
1. Volume of production.
2. Product price.
3. Expansion policy.
4. Dividend policy.
5. Discontinuation of business.

Unions and management must not bargain on the following:
1. Agreements intended to damage employer's competitors.
2. Discrimination in employment on grounds of race, age, sex, or union affiliation.
3. Secondary boycotts.
4. Closed shop (also union shop, agency shop, and maintenance of membership in Texas).

Collective bargaining agreements are in a sense contracts between the employer and the union. The procedure for dealing with breaches of the agreement depends upon the nature of the breach. If the agreement calls for arbitration of disputes, the agreement is binding in that regard, and the parties must arbitrate as agreed. If a breach constitutes an unfair labor practice as defined in the National Labor-Management Relations Act, the victim must file administrative charges with the NLRB. If the breach is not an unfair labor practice and is not subject to an agreement to arbitrate, it may be taken to the courts.

Section 301 of the Taft-Hartley Act, 29 USC 185, provides that labor unions have the capacity to sue and to be sued in federal and state courts. Unions and employers may be held liable in damages for collective bargaining agreement breaches.

Employer unfair labor practices. 29 USC 158, Sec. 8 of the NLMRA, defines unfair labor practices of employers and unions. The following are labeled employer unfair labor practices by this statute:

1. Interfering with, restraining, or coercing employees engaged in exercising rights under NLMRA. This includes interfering with employee efforts to unionize, spying on union meetings, using unfair campaign methods in union recognition election campaigns, and other such practices.

2. Unlawfully assisting a union, as by providing financial assistance, taking part in union organization, pressuring employees to join the union, etc.

3. Discrimination in employment, as by refusing to hire union members or nonunion members, or by subcontracting out work done by a unionized department of one's plant, etc.

4. Discriminating because of use of NLRB procedures, as by firing or disciplining employees who file unfair labor practice charges, or firing or disciplining employees who testify in NLRB proceedings.

5. Refusal to bargain collectively.

The employer and the union are required to maintain a relationship which is somewhat similar to the relationship between the government party and the opposition party in the British House of Commons. The employer of course is the government and the union is the opposition.

In the House of Commons the government party has the power to run the nation, and the responsibility to do it properly. The opposition has the power and responsibility to criticise the government's stewardship, but it cannot share either the power or the responsibility of governing. Of course, in British politics the opposition may win a national election and become the government, but the American union has no possibility of doing this; the union is a permanent opposition.

Management must, therefore, not enter into a close relationship with the union. Such a close relationship would destroy the basically adversary relationship between the parties. Management must also in essence not exert so much power against the union opposition that its effectiveness as an opposition is destroyed.

Union unfair labor practices. 29 USC 158 labels the following sorts of conduct as union unfair labor practices:

1. Interfering with, restraining, or coercing employees engaged in exercising rights under the NLMRA. Employees not only have the right to engage in pro-union activity (which management must not interfere with); they also have the right to engage in anti-union activity (which the union must not interfere with).

2. Restraining or coercing an employer with respect to his choice of collective bargaining representative or grievance adjustment representative. Such coercion interferes with the gentlemanly adversary relationship which should exist between management and union.

3. Causing employer to discriminate in employment.

4. Refusal to bargain collectively.

5. Coercing employers to enter into hot cargo agreement, or inducing employees to perform acts intended to induce an employer to enter into such an agreement. This will be discussed later.

6. Forcing, or attempting to force, an independent contractor or employer to join a union or employer organization. Such persons should not be coerced to join an organization they do not care to join.

7. Engaging in secondary boycotts (which will be discussed below).

8. Picketing or otherwise coercing an employer to recognize a union when the employer has a collective bargaining agreement in force with another union for that bargaining unit.

9. Engaging in jurisdictional disputes (which will be discussed below).

10. Charging excessive or discriminatory dues and initiation fees.

11. Featherbedding (which will be discussed below).

12. Picketing a nonunion plant for more than thirty days without petitioning the NLRB to call an election, or picketing an employer for recognition when employees in the plant have voted down a union less than twelve months previously.

The obligation to bargain. At contract renewal time, both union and employer are required to make a good-faith effort to negotiate a new contract. As long as one party desires to bargain, the other must comply with the desire. The subject matter for such bargaining is of course limited to those matters about which there may legitimately be bargaining. The union may not demand that management bargain about the price of its product, for example.

Both parties must take a flexible position at the beginning of bargaining; neither must assume a "take it or leave it" position. Such flexibility does not mean, however, that the parties are obligated to agree. It often happens that, after give-and-take on both sides, the parties still find themselves in disagreement. If no further concessions are forthcoming, an impasse has been reached. At this point the parties may agree to suspend bargaining for a period. In such a case neither is guilty of refusal to bargain. But if one side indicates willingness to resume talks, the other must go along.

Hot cargo agreements. Suppose that the United Production Workers of America (UPWA) represents the production and maintenance workers of Ace Company in collective bargaining. Ace Company buys raw material from Deuce Company. UPWA has been trying to organize the production and maintenance workers of Deuce, with no success. UPWA blames Deuce's management for this, and demands in collective bargaining that Ace stop doing business with Deuce. UPWA is demanding that Ace enter into a hot cargo agreement with it.

Such agreements are legal when they involve the contracting or subcontracting of work at a construction site, or when they involve the performance of the parts of an integrated production process in the garment industry. Otherwise, they are illegal.

Secondary boycotts. Suppose that the UPWA has organized the production and maintenance workers at Clubb Company. The Factory Workers' Brotherhood of America (FWBA) has organized the production and maintenance workers at Hart Company. Hart buys raw materials from Clubb. The FWBA is on strike against Hart, but Hart is keeping its plant going by using supervisors as production workers. The FWBA local at Hart asks the UPWA local at Clubb for assistance. The UPWA people comply by refusing to load shipments of raw materials bound for Hart. This is one example of a secondary boycott.

Coercive activity by a union directed at an employer other than the employer with a collective bargaining agreement with the union is normally unlawful. Secondary boycotts are lawful under very limited circumstances. For instance, if in the above example Clubb and Hart were both subsidiaries of Spade Corporation, the secondary boycott described above would be perfectly legal.

Jurisdictional disputes. These are disputes between two unions over which union should do specified work. If a participant in such a dispute attempts to coerce the employer to assign the work to it instead of to the other disputant, the coercion is normally unlawful. If no binding agreement exists between the employer and one of the disputing unions as to which should do the work, coercion by either disputant is an unfair labor practice. The proper method of resolution is to ask the NLRB to settle matters.

If the employer has agreed with one of the disputants to let it do the work, a different situation prevails. If the employer has agreed to let Union A do the job, and Union B protests by picketing, Union B is guilty of an unfair labor practice. If the employer has agreed to let Union A do the work, but it then assigns the work to Union B, the employer has breached its bargaining agreement with A. A may well protest, and its protests will be quite lawful if properly conducted.

Featherbedding. Unions occasionally seek to force employers to pay their members for work not done. In theory, it is an unfair labor practice for unions to make such demands, but in practice it occasionally occurs.

A union may not seek to force an employer to keep surplus employees on the payroll for whom there is no work. However, a union can require an employer to keep employees on the payroll who do unnecessary busywork. The union might also require the employer to pay a full day's pay to workers who report for work in the morning but who are sent home because there is no work to be done.

It must be emphasized that no employer is required to agree to this sort of thing. The union may demand it in collective bargaining, but management is under no obligation to grant all union demands. If management gives in to such demands, it has itself to blame for the resulting inflated payroll costs.

Administrative procedure in unfair labor practice cases. The party complaining of commission of an unfair labor practice must file charges with the NLRB within six months of the commission of the practice. A field representative of the NLRB conducts an investigation of the charge, and the charge and investigation report are then referred to the general counsel of the NLRB for evaluation.

If the general counsel decides that the complaint is well-founded, he will issue a formal complaint against the violator. If he decides that the charge is unfounded, no complaint is filed and the matter ends. If a complaint is issued, an effort is made to settle matters informally. If that effort is unsuccessful, an administrative hearing is held before an NLRB administrative law judge on the matter. The administrative law judge hands down a written decision, which either party may appeal to the full NLRB. The full NLRB may also review these decisions on its own motion. The final NLRB decision may then be appealed to the courts.

The NLRB may prescribe the following administrative remedies:
1. The cease and desist order—an order to stop wrongdoing.
2. The order to bargain, in refusal to bargain cases.
3. The order to arbitrate, in appropriate cases.
4. Reinstatement with back pay, in wrongful firing cases.
5. Disestablishment of a union, if it was wrongfully recognized.

The NLRB has no power to enforce its orders. This must be done through the courts, by contempt proceedings.

Economic strikes. The most common type of strike called by a union is the economic strike. The most common reason for the calling of an economic strike is that the collective bargaining agreement has expired and no new bargaining agreement has been finalized.

If either party to a collective bargaining agreement wants to make changes when renewal time comes around, it must give notice of its intent to seek changes at least sixty days before expiration of the existing agreement. If there is a possibility that the old agreement will expire before a new agreement is finalized, the union must notify federal mediation services of a possible strike at least thirty days before the strike begins.

So long as the old agreement is in effect, the union may not strike simply because no new agreement has been finalized. However, once the old agreement has expired, the union may—and usually does—strike. The maxim "No contract, no work" still has great force in management-union relations. The union may strike without calling for a vote on the matter by the membership, unless the union constitution requires approval by the membership.

The employer is not obligated to close down while a strike is in progress. He may continue operations by using supervisory personnel as production workers or the like. He may also hire outside labor to keep the plant going.

The strikers will inevitably establish a picket line around the struck plant. The presence of the pickets will dissuade pro-union persons from accepting work in the struck plant, but workers to whom picket lines have no significance may well accept work in the plant. The strikers are technically still employees. They may not draw unemployment compensation while on strike. Furthermore, once the strike is settled the employer must give preference to strikers in filling job vacancies. The employer need not discharge employees hired during the strike in order to make room for strikers, however. If the employer has no further need for some of the strikers after the strike, that is their misfortune. Since this is true, the union will doubtless use all its bargaining muscle to ensure that all strikers get their jobs back upon the settlement of the strike and the effectiveness of the new contract.

Under the provisions of the Norris-LaGuardia Act, 29 USC 101-105, the courts may not interfere with a lawful strike by handing down injunctions against the strikers. So long as the conduct of the strikers is lawful, the work stoppage must be allowed to run its course. However, when a strike would, in the mind of the president of the United States, endanger the national economy, 29 USC 176 authorizes the president to appoint a board of inquiry to ascertain whether or not the strike would truly endanger the economy. If the board determines that it would, 29 USC 178 authorizes the attorney general to seek an injunction forbidding the strike for a cooling off period of eighty days. If the strike is not settled sixty days after the injunction becomes effective, the board of inquiry is reconvened to consider the issues. If no solution is arrived at within the next fifteen days, the union members must be given a chance to vote by secret ballot upon the question of acceptance of management's last offer. If this is voted down, the strike may be resumed after the eighty days have expired.

The employer unfair labor practices strike. When the employer commits an unfair labor practice and refuses to offer adequate redress, the union may respond to the provocation with a strike. This is true even if a collective bargaining agreement is in force.

The employer may replace strikers during the strike, but he must rehire all strikers after the strike is settled, even if that means terminating new employees hired during the strike.

Remember that a breach of the collective bargaining agreement is not necessarily an unfair labor practice. If it is, a strike in protest is lawful. If the breach is not an unfair labor practice, a protest strike may be unlawful. If the collective bargaining agreement contains a no-strike clause, a strike in protest here would be a violation. (The only sort of strike which does not violate a no-strike clause is an unfair labor practices strike.) If there is no no-strike clause in the contract, but the parties have agreed to arbitrate differences, the union must arbitrate management's alleged breach before striking.

Unlawful strikes. Several types of strikes are unlawful. Among these are the following:
1. Sit-down strikes, in which the strikers occupy the employer's premises in order to stop all work.
2. Wildcat strikes—spontaneous strikes called by a minority of the union's membership without the consent of the union officers.
3. Jurisdictional strikes, if committed as part of an unfair union labor practice as described earlier.
4. Secondary strike, if it is part of an unlawful secondary boycott as described above.
5. Partial strike, which may be a strike in only a part of the employer's plant, a refusal to perform certain assigned work, a deliberate work slowdown, or something similar.

6. A strike for recognition of Union B, when the employer has already lawfully recognized Union A.

Picketing. Picketing is intended to convey a message to the public. So long as picketing accomplishes this objective and no more, the picketers are merely exercising their First Amendment right to free speech and are normally doing nothing unlawful.

Mass picketing—picketing by huge masses of persons who by their number obstruct ingress and egress from the employer's premises and intimidate onlookers—is unlawful. Violent picketing is of course unlawful. Picketing an organized employer to try to induce him to recognize a union other than the one already recognized is unlawful. Picketing an unorganized employer to try to get him to recognize a union is unlawful if an election has been held at the plant within the past twelve months.

Picketing an unorganized employer for more than thirty days without petitioning the NLRB to call an election there is unlawful. Informational picketing in which the pickets bear signs conveying untrue information is unlawful. The passing out of handbills is lawful unless the message borne by the handbills is untrue.

Picketing to influence consumers is more often lawful than not. If the union is on strike against the picketed establishment, the picketing is lawful. If the union is on strike against a supplier of goods to the picketed firm, the picketing is lawful if the struck firm supplies only a small part of the picketed firm's inventory. If the struck firm supplies a large part of the picketed establishment's inventory, so that the picketing might severely damage the business of the picketed party, the picketing is unlawful.

Common-site picketing in the construction industry is presently unlawful. This occurs when employees of a subcontractor on a construction site are on strike. The strikers may want to picket the entire site, in the hope that all union workers on the site (even employees of the general contractor and other subcontractors) will honor the picket line and shut down the project. Legislation was introduced in Congress in 1977 to legalize such picketing; though it acquired considerable support, it did not pass.

Certain large employers may have various subcontractors working on their grounds. A strike by employees of a subcontractor might result in picketing of the entire plant site and the shutting down of the large employer's operation due to refusal of his employees to cross the picket line. This may be avoided by the large employer's assigning one gate to his property for the use of subcontractors and their employees. If this is done, picketers representing struck employees of a subcontractor may picket only the reserved gate; they may not picket the other gates used only by the large employer's employees.

Under most circumstances, employees have the right to refuse to cross a picket line. Employers may not terminate employees who refuse to cross such a line unless the employer's business is being seriously damaged by the situation. Employees who are discharged for refusal to cross a picket line have the same rights to reinstatement in their jobs as do economic strikers.

When the picketing is secondary—that is, when the union picketers are not on strike against the picketed concern—employees of the picketed concern who refuse to cross the picket line may be terminated.

Lockouts. A lockout is management's economic weapon similar to the union's strike. Management simply closes down the plant temporarily and refuses to permit the union employees to work.

Offensive lockouts are generally unlawful. Defensive lockouts are generally permitted. Usually, an employer may not lock out solely to preempt a strike. The usual argument advanced in favor of such lockouts is that, since a strike can cause severe economic loss to the employer, the employer should have the option of exercising some control over when the loss will be incurred. The courts normally will not buy this argument: such a pre-emptive lockout would be allowed only when the employer stands to suffer a much more severe economic loss due to a strike than that which is normally suffered by employers who are strike victims.

If the collective bargaining agreement has expired but the union has not struck, and the bargaining negotiations reach an impasse, management may lock out. Such a situation is rare; normally the union strikes upon expiration of the bargaining agreement.

If the union commences a partial strike against the employer—calling out only the employees in a key section of the employer's plant—management may respond by closing down the entire plant. Since partial strikes are unlawful, a lockout is a legitimate response.

The most common lockout situation occurs when the collective bargaining agreement in a multi-employer bargaining unit has expired and the union chooses to strike some, but not all, of the employers included in the unit. The employers who are not struck may choose to lock out, resulting in a shutdown of the entire unit. The lockout is not a legitimate weapon to be employed in organizational disputes: employers may not lock out to inhibit an organization drive by a union, to force employees to join a union, or to prevent decertification of a union the employer favors.

Regulation of union internal affairs. Generally, the internal affairs of a union are of no concern to the employer. The employer must not intervene in these in any way. These matters are, however, a legitimate concern of union members and of the government.

The Landrum-Griffin Act, 29 USC 401 et seq., contains the statutory law in this area. The statute attempts to ensure that the unions are run in a democractic manner.

29 USC 411 sets forth a "bill of rights" for union members. Among the rights guaranteed by the statute are:
1. The right to nominate candidates for union office.
2. The right to run for union office, subject to reasonable qualifications spelled out in the union constitution.
3. The right to cast a secret ballot for union officers.
4. The right to attend membership meetings.
5. The right to speak out on matters of interest at union meetings.
6. The right to approve changes in dues and fees, either directly by referendum vote, or indirectly by vote of convention delegates elected by union members.
7. The right to sue the union for damages in appropriate cases.
8. The right to due process in union disciplinary proceedings (except for matters involving nonpayment of dues), including the right to a hearing before an unbiased tribunal and the right not to be punished for exercising rights granted by this statute.

International union officers may serve terms of no longer than five years but may be reelected. Local officers may serve terms of up to three years but may be reelected. No person may serve as a union officer who has been convicted of a felony within five years of conviction or five years of release from prison, whichever is later.

Union officers owe fiduciary duties to the union and to its membership, with all the duties and obligations implied by those duties. Union officers may have no close associations—financial, business, or personal—with the employer or executives of the employer's business.

A national or international union may impose a trusteeship upon a local union in order to remedy corruption, undemocratic practices, etc. The local self-government is essentially suspended until the local is ready to manage its own affairs again.

21

Bailments

A bailment occurs when a person acquires possession of personal property and control over that property without acquiring ownership of the property. The person acquiring possession and control is called the bailee. The person creating the bailment—that is, the person entitled to reclaim the property from the bailee—is the bailor.

The bailor is usually, but not always, the owner of the property. Any person who has possession of property may create a bailment and become a bailor. A bailment may be created for one of several purposes. Examples of transactions which create bailments include:

1. Pal lends his leather jacket to Buddy for an evening.
2. Ace agrees to let Deuce keep his car in his, Ace's, garage while Deuce spends the summer in Europe.
3. Spade rents an automobile for the weekend from Clubb Auto Rentals.
4. Diamond takes his automobile to Hart Garage for repairs.
5. Gray ships goods to Black via White Trucklines.

Most bailments are voluntary bailments. These arise out of a contractual relationship between the bailor and the bailee. There are also involuntary bailments, however, which occur when a person comes into possession of another person's property without the consent of the owner. Thus, thieves, finders, and buyers from thieves and finders may well become involuntary bailees, whether they know it or not.

Types of bailments. There are three types of voluntary bailments. The most common and most important is the mutual-benefit bailment. Here, both bailor and bailee get a benefit from the bailment. Property rentals, property repairs, property storage for consideration, and shipment of goods by professional carrier are all examples of mutual-benefit bailments.

The bailee is authorized only to use the bailed property for the purpose of the bailment. He is under an obligation not to be negligent in his use of the property or his care of it though some types of bailees are held to a higher standard of care than others. He is under an obligation to return the property to the bailor at the end of the bailment in the same condition as it was when he got it, except for normal wear and tear.

The second sort of bailment is the bailment for the benefit of the bailee. Here, the bailor permits the bailee to take possession of the property without requiring any consideration in return. A typical example of such a bailment occurs when Sylvia lends Donna a party dress to wear to a party without asking Donna to pay rent for it. Donna may use the dress only to wear to the party; she must use great care to preserve its good condition since she will be liable for the slightest damage that cannot be attributed to normal wear and tear.

The third sort of bailment is the bailment for the benefit of the bailor. Here, the bailee takes possession of the bailor's property in order to do a favor to a friend. The bailee assumes the burden of caring for the property without any payment of storage charges or maintenance. A typical example of such a bailment is Betty's agreeing to care for Cynthia's house plants while Cynthia is on vacation, Betty taking the plants to her house to care for them. Betty's obligation only extends to not being grossly negligent in caring for the plants. If she forgets to water them once in awhile, so that they are not as healthy when Cynthia comes back as they were when she left, Cynthia has no legal complaint. If Betty puts them outside during a warm winter afternoon but negligently forgets to take them in in the evening, and they are killed by an expected frost, Cynthia might have a legal complaint; arguably, Betty was grossly negligent to leave the plants outside all night in winter.

If the bailee in any of these three bailment situations does not return the bailed property to the bailor in the condition it was in at the beginning of the bailment (with allowance for wear and tear), the bailor may sue the bailee for damages. All the bailor needs to prove in his suit is that he delivered the bailed property to the bailee, that the bailee took possession of it, and that the bailee either did not return the property at all or returned it in damaged condition. The bailor will also have to prove the value of the property at the time of the making of the bailment, and its value when he got it back (if he got it back). He does not have to prove that bailee negligence had anything to do with the nonreturn or damage.

If the bailor can prove these things, the bailee will be held liable for the bailor's damages unless he can prove that the nonreturn or damage was not due to his negligence. Thus, the major burden of proof in suits by bailors against bailees lies upon the defendant bailee.

Liability of nonbailee possessors. Anyone who voluntarily takes possession of another's property subject to a contract with the lawful possessor of that property is usually a bailee. But if the possessor does not also get control of the property, there is no bailment.

Thus, when Able parks his car in Baker's parking lot, a bailment might or might not be created. If Baker requires his customers to leave their keys in the car or with the lot attendant, there is a bailment—Baker has control of the car. If, on the other hand, Baker instructs his customers to lock their cars and take their keys with them, Baker has no control of the car, and there is no bailment.

When Black, a customer of White's restaurant, gives his coat to a hat-check girl and receives a claim check in return, the restaurant assumes control over the coat and a bailment exists. However, if Black takes the coat into White's cloakroom and hangs it on a hanger himself—the cloakroom being run on a self-serve basis—White assumes no control over the coat and no bailment exists.

A nonbailee possessor has the obligation to use due care to preserve the possessed property from damage. However, such a possessor will not be held liable for loss of or damage to property unless the owner can prove that negligence by the possessor was the cause of the loss or damage. In these nonbailment cases, then, the plaintiff has the true burden of proof if he wishes to recover damages.

Bailments of containers. The bailee of a container normally assumes responsibility for its contents. The bailment of the container is a bailment of the contents. However, there is an important limitation upon the liability of the bailee for contents. He is liable for the contents he knows of and that he has agreed to accept responsibility for. He is not liable for contents that he does not know about and that no reasonable person would expect to find in the container. He is liable for contents he does not know of specifically, but which he could expect to be in the container.

The bailee who accepts a suitcase for storage could reasonably expect clothing to be inside. He would be responsible for the clothing, whether he knew it was there or not. However, if the suitcase contained jewelry, the bailee could not be responsible for it unless the bailor told him that the jewelry was there and the bailee agreed to accept responsibility.

The parking lot which accepts responsibility for an automobile will accept responsibility for the spare tire in the trunk, because virtually all cars have a spare tire in the trunk. It will accept responsibility for parcels on the front seat of the vehicle, because these are in plain view of the attendant when the vehicle is parked, so long as the parcels contain what normal parcels obtained on a shopping expedition might contain. But if the glove compartment contains $1,000 in cash, the lot would not be responsible for it. A reasonable person would not expect so much cash to be in such a place.

The restaurant checkroom assuming responsibility for an overcoat is probably not responsible for a billfold in the coat pocket. The drycleaner assuming responsibility for a pair of trousers would not be responsible for the twenty-dollar bill in the rear pocket.

Variation of normal bailee liability. The law imposes a heavier burden of liability upon common carriers and innkeepers than it does upon other bailees; they are made insurers of goods entrusted to their possession. Innkeeper liability will be discussed later in this chapter, and an entire chapter is devoted to carrier liability.

A bailee who breaches his contract of bailment becomes liable as an insurer of the bailed property. Such a bailee cannot escape liability for loss or damage by proving lack of negligence; if the bailor can prove the breach, the bailee cannot escape liability.

A bailee may by contract reduce his liability if he makes the bailor aware of the reduction before the bailment is created, and if his reduction of liability is not contrary to public policy. The usual reduction of liability maneuver is to disclaim liability for negligence in caring for the bailed property. Carriers, warehousemen, and innkeepers may not make such disclaimers effective, but most other bailees are permitted to do this. If the bailee's disclaimer of negligence liability does not constitute any sort of danger to the general public, it is permissible. Generally, there is no objection to the effort by a parking lot owner to disclaim liability for damage to autos parked in his lot.

However, bailees will not be permitted to disclaim responsibility for their own gross negligence. Even the bailee who seeks to avoid responsibility for negligence must use all the basic precautions to preserve the bailed property. A disclaimer of liability for negligence must be called to the attention of the bailor before the bailment is created. It is best if the bailee writes his disclaimer into his contract with the bailor, and then verbally calls the disclaimer to his customer's attention. The bailee may also post large signs in his establishment calling attention to his disclaimer, but he should call the signs to the attention of his customers verbally. If the disclaimer is buried in small print on the back of a claim check, it will be ineffective.

Liability of third-party to bailor for damage to bailed property. If bailed property is damaged by the negligence of a third party while in the hands of the bailee, the bailor may recover the damage from the third party. (The bailor may not normally recover from the bailee because the bailee's negligence did not cause the damage.)

If the bailed property is destroyed or damaged in an accident in which both the bailee and the third party were negligent, Texas law now permits the bailor to sue both the bailee and the third party for damages. The jury will decide how much responsibility each party bears for the damage, and the damages will be apportioned accordingly.

Before 1975, a bailor could not recover from a third party in such a case unless the third party was more negligent than the bailee. However, in 1975 the Texas Supreme Court decided that the negligence of the bailee would henceforth not be imputed to the bailor, thus making the third party liable for his share of the damages even if he was less negligent than the bailee.

Liability of bailor for injury caused by defect in bailed property. When a bailor knowingly creates a bailment of defective property, he is liable for any damage caused by that property. It does not matter whether or not the bailor got consideration for the bailment. Thus, if Buddy lends a car with defective brakes to Pal, knowing that the brakes are defective, and the brakes go out while Pal is driving, injuring Ace, Ace may hold Buddy liable for damages.

If the bailor did not know of the defect in the bailed property, he will not be liable for damage caused by it if he got no consideration for the bailment. If Buddy had not known about the bad brakes, he would not be liable to Ace.

If the bailor rents the defective property to the bailee, he is liable for any damage it causes, whether he knows of the defect or not. Thus, if Pal paid Buddy rent for the car in the above case, Buddy is responsible for the damage done because of the bad brakes, whether he knew of the defect or not.

Responsibility for repair and maintenance of bailed property. If the contract of bailment contains provisions with respect to responsibility for repair and maintenance of the bailed property, these provisions are binding. If the contract does not contain such provisions, the following rules apply:

1. Bailee must pay for fuel to keep bailed property in operation.
2. Bailee must pay normal operating expenses.
3. Bailee must pay for minor repairs.
4. Bailor must pay for major repairs.

In fact, the necessity for major repairs gives the bailee the right to rescind the contract of bailment, or to demand that the bailor replace the defective bailed property. However, in a noncommercial car rental contract, the bailee would be required to pay for the gasoline he used while in possession. He would also be responsible for any oil changes or lubrications that became necessary during the rental period and for replacing broken fan belts, burned-out lights, defective windshield wipers (if they were not defective at the beginning of the bailment), or other parts.

Sub-bailments. A bailee may not lend out or rent the bailed property to anyone else. When he does this, he creates a sub-bailment. The creation of such a sub-bailment is a breach of the bailor-bailee contract, and gives the bailor grounds for rescission of the bailment and recovery of the property from the sub-bailee. The bailee is also liable as an insurer to the bailor for the bailed property, while the property is in the hands of the sub-bailee. If any damage occurs to the property during the sub-bailment, the bailee is responsible.

Thus: Black lends his car to Gray for the weekend. Gray then lends it to Blue for

Saturday evening, and the car is damaged through the negligence of Pink. In this case, Black would have recourse against either Gray or Pink. Pink would be liable because of his negligence, while Gray would be liable because of the sub-bailment. If Black forced Gray to pay, Gray would of course have recourse against Pink. Since Blue had no contract with Black, and since Blue was not negligent, he is in no way liable here.

Liability of the bailor to persons injured by his property. A bailor is not liable to third parties injured by a bailee using his property just because he is a bailor. As discussed above, if the bailed property is defective and the defect causes injury, the bailor may well be liable, depending upon the type of bailment and whether bailor knew or should have known of the defect.

If the injury to the third party is caused by bailee negligence rather than by a defect in the bailed property, the bailor normally will not be liable for the defect. A bailee is not an agent or employee of the bailor just because he is a bailee. The bailor is thus not liable for the bailee's torts. However, if the bailor was negligent in giving the bailee possession of the bailed property, or if the bailee was an agent of the bailor, bailor liability will exist. Examples of situations in which the bailor will be liable for injuries to a third party caused by bailee negligence include the following:

1. Pal tells Bud to drive his, Pal's, car to the liquor store to buy him a fifth of bourbon. Bud negligently injures Idd in an accident. Idd may recover damages from Pal, since Bud was on an errand for Pal.
2. Pal lends Bud his car for a weekend. Bud negligently injures Idd in an auto accident. Bud has no driver's license. Idd may recover from Pal here because Pal was negligent in lending his car to an unlicensed driver.
3. Bud wants to borrow Pal's car to drive to a fraternity party. Pal knows that Bud is a heavy drinker, that he often drives while under the influence, and that much alcohol will probably be consumed at the party. Pal lends Bud the car anyway. After the party Bud, driving while intoxicated, negligently injures Idd. Idd may recover from Pal because of Pal's negligence in lending the car to a driver who will almost certainly be incompetent to drive before the bailment is terminated.

Responsibility of bailee for release of the property. Generally speaking, the bailee may not give up possession of the bailed property to anyone but the bailor, unless repair, storage, or something of the kind becomes necessary. The bailee must assume that the bailor is the owner or rightful possessor of the property. There are some circumstances, however, in which a bailee may give up possession of the bailed property to someone other than the bailor without incurring liability. Some examples include:

1. Baka checks a suitcase in a bus station checkroom, receiving a claim check from the clerk on duty there. Many suitcases are checked there, and several clerks are on duty. Baka loses the claim check. Gluck finds it, takes it to the checkroom, and claims Baka's suitcase. Baka claims the bus line is liable to him for wrongful release of the suitcase. He is wrong. The only way to identify the owner of an item in such a bailment is by the claim check. If the bailee releases the goods to the holder of the claim check, its release is rightful, unless Baka had notified the buslines that the claim check had been lost before Gluck obtained the suitcase.
2. Poseur takes a wristwatch to Jeweler for repair. Ehrlich later observes Jeweler working on the watch, and asks Jeweler where he got it. Jeweler asks Ehrlich why he wants to know. Ehrlich explains that his house had been burglarized three months ago and a watch like the one in question had been stolen. Ehrlich examines the watch and claims that it is his stolen watch. Since Ehrlich provides good proof of ownership,

Jeweler lets him take it. Poseur claims Jeweler was wrong to release the watch. He is wrong. If a bailee releases goods to the true owner he incurs no liability to the bailor.
3. Slink rented his car to Ami for a month. Unknown to Ami, Slink was making payment on the car to Grinch. Slink was behind on his payments, and Grinch had a security interest in the car, entitling him to repossess it if Slink missed payments. Slink never caught up on the payments. A week before the end of the bailment term, Grinch decided to repossess. Ami let Grinch take the car; Slink claimed that was wrongful. Slink of course was wrong. Grinch, as a secured party, had the right to repossess, even from a bailee. Ami could have committed the crime of hindering a secured creditor by giving Grinch difficulty.

When two persons—the bailor and a third party—claim to be the owner of the bailed property, the bailee can be placed in an uncomfortable position. If he releases the property to the third party, and the third party's claim of ownership turns out to be false, he will be liable to the bailor for wrongful release. If he releases the property to the bailor and the third party's claim turns out to be right, he may be liable to the third party for conversion. If the case is doubtful, the bailee will incur less risk by releasing the property to the bailor than by releasing it to the third party. In order to resolve all doubt, the bailee could file an interpleader suit against both claimants and let a court decide the issue.

Artisan's liens. A bailee who performs repair work or any service upon property acquires an artisan's lien upon the property for the value of his work. He need not release the property to the bailor until he is paid for his services. If the bailor refuses to pay, he will not get his property back.

If a period of time has passed and the bailor still has not paid the repair bill, the bailee is entitled to foreclose his lien by selling the goods to a third party in order to collect the bill. If the bailor feels that the repair bill is too high or that the bailee performed unauthorized and unnecessary repairs, he is of course under no obligation to pay. But if he wants to get his property back he will have to let a court resolve the issue of the legitimacy of the bailee's bill.

Generally, the artisan's lien is a possessory lien—that is, the artisan has a lien upon the repaired goods so long as he keeps them in his possession. He need not normally relinquish possession until his bill is paid, but if he does release the goods before payment of the bill, he loses his lien. According to RCS 5503(a), it does not matter whether the bailor and the artisan have agreed upon a price for the repairs in advance. Even if there has been no such agreement, the artisan may retain possession of the goods until the reasonable, customary, and usual compensation for the repairs is paid in full.

RCS 5506b provides that any person repairing, altering, cleaning, pressing, dyeing, or laundering a garment or article of apparel may retain the article until the legitimate charges for the service are paid.

With respect to motor vehicles, RCS 5503(b) provides that, should a garage, mechanic, or repairman who has done work upon a motor vehicle release it in exchange for a check or draft, and should payment on the check or draft be stopped, the artisan's lien upon the vehicle will continue to be effective. The garage or mechanic could then bring suit to repossess the vehicle, unless the owner in the meantime has sold it to a bonafide purchaser.

The existence of the artisan's lien upon a repaired automobile may cause some inconvenience to the vehicle owner who feels that he has been "gouged" by a garage or mechanic. The vehicle owner of course need only pay for repairs and parts which are a part of the contract between the two parties. If the garage performs unauthorized repair work, the owner may be able to escape paying for it. If the garage performs unnecessary repair work, or if it bills for repair work which was never done or for parts which were never installed, it is guilty of violating the Texas Deceptive Trade Practices Act and is liable for triple damages to the owner. The difficulty from the owner's point of view is that the garage has possession of the vehicle while the argument about the legitimacy of the bill proceeds. The owner may refuse to pay the bill and let the garage keep the vehicle, or he may pay in order to regain possession of his vehicle and then sue to get his money back. Either alternative may be unpleasant.

In order to avoid such unpleasantness, of course, one should deal only with reputable garages or mechanics. When taking the vehicle in for repairs, one should be very specific in telling the garage what one wants done, and insist that the garage obtain specific authorization before doing any additional work. To require this may well slow up the repair job, but it might prevent arguments later.

The best guarantee against this sort of gouging is to know as much about motor vehicles and their engines as your mechanic. If you do, you should have some understanding of the nature of your problem before your vehicle gets to the garage, and you will know whether the mechanic's diagnosis makes sense and whether his proposed cure is reasonable. If you do not understand that much, your ignorance leaves you exposed to the ignorance or dishonesty of the mechanic.

RCS 5504 and RCS 5506b-2 provide a procedure for foreclosure of artisan's liens upon repaired goods and wearing apparel. After the artisan has had possession of the goods for sixty days after accrual of the unpaid charges, he must send the bailor a notice to come in and pay up within ten days. If the bailor does not do this, the artisan must give him another notice that the goods will be sold at auction to collect the unpaid charges. The notice must include the time and place of the auction, the time set at least twenty days after the sending of the second notice. The proceeds from the sale are to be applied to the unpaid charges and to the expense of arranging the sale. If anything is left over it must be remitted to the bailor. The artisan should therefore notify the bailor of the result of the sale and account to him for the proceeds.

The buyer of the goods at the auction gets good title to them, even if the artisan followed improper procedure in foreclosing. However, improper procedure in the foreclosure renders the artisan liable to the bailor for conversion of the goods. The artisan must obviously be careful to follow the specified procedure.

The 1979 session of the Texas Legislature enacted RCS 5504a, which provides a special procedure for foreclosure of a mechanic's lien upon a motor vehicle. When the lienholder has had possession of the vehicle for thirty days after the repair bill becomes payable, he must send notice of the amount of charges, requesting payment, to the owner and to all lienholders whose interests are recorded on the certificate of title to the vehicle. The notice must be sent by certified mail, return receipt requested. Should the repairman not know the names of lienholders recorded upon the certificate of title, he may learn the names and addresses of these parties by writing to the Texas Highway Department.

If the charges are not paid within thirty days of the mailing of the notice of amount of charges, the repairman may proceed to sell the vehicle at public sale. The proceeds are applied to the expenses of the sale and to the repairman's bill; anything remaining belongs to other lienholders or to the owner.

The buyer at the auction is entitled to a new certificate of title in his name if his application is accompanied by a bill of sale from the foreclosing lienholder and proof of the mailing of the notice of charges required by RCS 5504a. The sale wipes out all security interests and other liens upon the vehicle, and entitles the buyer to a clear title. The buyer's major risk is, of course, that the owner who incurred the repair bill did not have good title to the vehicle. Otherwise, the buyer should have no title problems.

The new statute does not mention that the lienholder must inform the owner and other lienholders that the vehicle will be sold if the charges are not paid within thirty days, but it would be wise to include this in the notice. The statute also does not require that the owner and lienholders be sent notice of the time and place of sale, but it would also be wise to furnish them with such notice.

Hotels, motels, apartment hotels, and boarding houses as bailees. Under common law the innkeeper was an insurer of the baggage of his guest. If the baggage was lost or damaged at the establishment through no fault of the guest, the innkeeper was liable for the loss or damage. Texas has changed this rule by statute. RCS 4592 permits the innkeeper to reduce his insurer liability to fifty dollars by:
1. Furnishing a metal safe or vault in which guests may deposit their valuables for the duration of the stay, and
2. Posting a notice of the availability of the safe and of the innkeeper's limited liability on the door of each room, and
3. Putting suitable locks and bolts on doors, and suitable fastenings on windows and transoms.

If a guest loses any such valuables, the hotel will be liable for up to fifty dollars, if the loss was not due to the negligence of the guest. Of course, if negligence by the innkeeper, his agents, or his employees causes the loss, the fifty-dollar limitation of liability does not apply. Also, if the guest offers to put his valuables in the safe and the innkeeper refuses to accept them for storage, the innkeeper becomes an insurer of the valuables.

RCS 4593 provides that a gratuitous bailment (bailment for the benefit of the bailor) is created between an innkeeper and a guest for baggage belonging to the guest when:
1. The guest checks out of the inn and leaves baggage behind without checking it in a checkroom, or
2. The guest sends baggage to the inn which arrives before he does, or
3. A departing guest checks baggage in a checkroom and does not come back to pick it up within a week of checking out or otherwise departing.

The innkeeper has only the obligation not to be grossly negligent in caring for such baggage.

RCS 4594 provides that when a guest checks out of an inn and leaves baggage or other personal property behind, owing room rent or restaurant bills or the like to the innkeeper, the innkeeper has a lien upon this property for the amount of unpaid charges. The guest cannot recover possession of the property unless he pays the charges.

Under the provisions of RCS 4595, the innkeeper may sell this property in order to collect his bill if the guest does not redeem the property within thirty days. He must send the guest a notice of the time and place of the sale, and he must also post a notice of the sale in three public places within the county where the inn is located. The sale must take place at least ten days after the mailing and posting of the required notices. From the proceeds of the sale the innkeeper may keep his bill plus the costs of arranging the sale. If any money remains after this, the innkeeper must hold it for sixty days in case the guest comes to claim it. If the guest does not show up within this sixty-day period, the innkeeper must turn the funds over to the county treasurer, who will then hold them for a year. If the guest does not claim the funds within the year, the county treasurer must pay them into the state treasury; the funds then become state property.

Liens of warehousemen and carriers. A warehouseman who stores goods for consideration has a lien upon the goods for unpaid storage charges. The carrier who transports goods for consideration has a lien upon them for unpaid transportation charges. The procedure for foreclosure of a warehouseman's lien is contained in Article 7 of the Texas Business & Commerce Code. Procedures for foreclosing a carrier's lien on an intrastate shipment is governed by the Federal Bills of Lading Act. These liens and the foreclosure thereof are described in detail in the chapters on transportation of goods and documents of title.

Termination of bailments. The usual way in which a bailment is terminated is through accomplishment of its purpose—the bailee restores the goods to the bailor. The destruction of the bailed goods before bailee returns them to bailor will of course also terminate the bailment. As mentioned above, the bailee will normally be liable for the value of the destroyed goods, unless he validly disclaimed liability for them, or unless he can prove that his negligence did not cause the destruction.

If the contract of bailment contains no termination date, a bailment at will exists, and either bailor or bailee may end the bailment at any time. If the contract contains a termination date, the bailment must continue until that date, unless both parties agree to an earlier termination. No unilateral termination is possible in this situation.

The death or insanity of either bailor or bailee will normally result in the termination of the bailment by operation of law.

Involuntary bailments. A possessor of lost or stolen goods holds said goods as an involuntary bailee for the true owner. Therefore, the possessor is liable for any damage caused to the goods through his negligence.

Such an involuntary bailee may not cause an artisan's lien to be created upon the goods which will bind the true owner. Thus: Dieb picks Tor's pocket and lifts Tor's pocket watch. After a month Dieb is upset because the watch quit running, so he takes it to Bijou the jeweler for repairs. Tor finds out Bijou has the watch after Bijou has repaired it. Tor demands the watch from Bijou, and has good proof of ownership. Bijou will not release the watch until Tor pays the repair bill. Tor claims he does not have to pay. He is correct. Bijou has no lien upon the watch because Tor, the owner, did not authorize the repairs.

Bijou of course may collect his bill from Dieb. He also might have a quasi-contractual claim against Tor, if the watch was not in operating condition when Dieb brought it in but Bijou has restored it to running condition. Bijou could claim that Tor would be unjustly enriched at his expense unless he were made to pay the fair value of the repairs. A court might or might not buy such an argument.

22

Personal Property

In this chapter we will be concerned with the law governing ownership of various sorts of personal property. We shall not be concerned with bailments, sales, shipments, etc., or with such types of intangible personal property as commercial paper, securities, patents, and so on. It must also be remembered that land—real property—is governed by many unique rules of law.

Ownership of animals. The law divides animals into two categories: domestic and wild. Domestic animals are those which are normally found in the possession of owners: horses, cattle, hogs, dogs, cats, etc. Wild animals are those which are seldom, or never, found in the possession of owners: rattlesnakes, alligators, coyotes, vultures, and so on. Of course wild horses exist, as do domestic alligators; but generally those animal species which are normally wild are considered by the law to be wild, while those species which are normally domestic are generally considered to be domestic.

A wild animal living in a state of nature has no owner. A person may become the owner of such an animal by taking possession of it. A person who takes possession of a wild animal retains ownership of it only as long as he retains possession of it. If the animal escapes and goes back to its natural habitat, it will be considered wild again. An exception to this rule arises when the creature goes back to its natural habitat, but returns to its old home upon occasion, perhaps seeking a handout of food.

It should be noted that the natural habitat of a wild animal is the place where it is normally found in the wild state. Thus: Jones captures an opossum in the East Texas pine woods and brings it into town as a pet. If it then escapes, goes back to the pine woods, and never returns to Jones's house, it is a wild animal again.

On the other hand, if Smith buys a duckbill platypus from an animal dealer and makes a pet of it, and the platypus escapes to the East Texas pine woods, the animal has not become wild. Since the natural habitat of this creature is Australia, it is far away from its natural habitat. It remains the property of Smith, if he can ever find it again.

Many questions with respect to ownership of wild animals arise with regard to hunting them. The hunting of wild animals is stringently regulated by state and federal legislation.

The Federal Endangered Species Preservation Act (16 USC 668 aa et seq.) forbids the hunting of any species which the secretary of the interior has classified as endangered or threatened. Other more specific federal legislation forbids the hunting of named species of wildlife and hunting from airplanes. Violations of these statutes are criminal offenses. Texas legislation governing hunting is contained in the Texas Parks and Wildlife Code, which contains provisions relative to hunting licenses and fishing licenses, seasons for hunting certain species, bag limits, etc. Violation of these statutory prohibitions is also a criminal offense.

Any animal killed by a hunter in violation of Parks and Wildlife Code provisions is the property of the state of Texas. Whenever a person is found by state officers to have such unlawfully killed animals in his possession, the animals will be confiscated and the possessor will be given a citation for violating the law.

Any wild animal killed by a hunter upon land where the hunter has no permission to hunt is the property of the landowner. This is true even if the animal is shot on land where the hunter had permission to hunt, but moves to property where the hunter has no permission to be and dies. In cases where the animal is killed legally upon land where the hunter has permission to hunt, it becomes the property of the first person to reduce it to his possession. This will generally be the hunter who dealt it its mortal wound.

Since domestic animals normally have owners, the owner of such will not lose title if the animal escapes and "goes wild." However, if a domestic animal has been in a state of nature for so long that no one can identify its owner, it is in essence wild. On the other hand, a person who keeps a herd of normally wild animals such as bison has essentially reduced them to domesticity.

When farm animals escape from their owners, they become subject to the estray legislation enacted by the Texas legislature. RCS 6911 et seq. provide the estray rules for horses, mares, geldings, fillies, colts, mules, jacks, jennets, and work oxen. Whenever a citizen has observed a stray animal of these types upon his land for a year or more, he may begin estray proceedings. He must, in order to estray, first post notices containing a description of the animal or animals at three public places within the county in which he lives, one of these places being the courthouse door of that county. He must also give a copy of the notice to the county clerk, who must post it in his office.

If no one claims the animal within twenty days of the posting of notices, the citizen must then go before a justice of the peace and file an affidavit stating that the animal has been on his land for a year, that he has not altered or disfigured any brands upon the animal, that he has posted the notices required by law, and that no owner has been found. The JP then appoints two persons to appraise the value of the animal or animals, these persons being no relatives of the citizens seeking to estray. After the appraisal, the citizen must post a bond of double the appraised value of the animal or animals with the court.

After this is done, the finder may proceed to use the animal or animals as his own, within reason. He may keep them and use them for twelve months, or until the true owner shows up and claims them. If the owner shows up and claims the animal, he must pay the finder the reasonable expenses of caring for the creature, unless the owner is a resident of the same county as the finder and has his brand or mark recorded in that county. In such case, the finder is not entitled to expense money.

If no one claims the animal within twelve months of the posting of the bond, title to the animal automatically vests in the county. The finder must then auction off the animal for cash at the courthouse door as soon as possible, after giving advance notice of the time and place of sale by posting notices in three public places within the county.

Seventy-five percent of the proceeds of the sale must be given by the finder to the county treasurer. The finder may retain the other 25 percent. Of course, nothing prevents the finder from buying the animal himself at the sale. The original owner of the animal may reclaim the 75 percent of the sale proceeds given to the county if he applies to collect within a year of the sale. If he does not do this, the funds become county property. In any case, the owner cannot reclaim the 25 percent of the sale price retained by the finder.

RCS 6919 provides that hogs, sheep, goats, or cattle other than work oxen may also be estrayed, but the rules are a bit different for these. These animals need be on the finder's land only four months before application to estray may be made. After appraisal and posting of bond, the finder need keep these only six months before sale. At the sale there must be three adult bidders present other than members of the finder's family. If any estrayed animal is sent out of the county before sale, or injured due to excessive use, the true owner may claim damages out of the posted bond. If the estrayed animal dies before sale, the county clerk must be notified. Sales of estrayed animals may be held only on the first Monday of each month, between the hours of 1 P.M. and 3 P.M.

Notice that the estray laws do not apply to any sort of fowl (chickens, ducks, etc.) or to dogs and cats. The finder of this sort of stray is subject to the ordinary rules of law applicable to finders, which is discussed below.

Abandoned, lost, and misplaced property. Property is abandoned when its owner places it somewhere where his intent to give up ownership of it is obvious. Items of personal property at the city dump are obviously abandoned: no one puts things there for other reasons. Property in garbage bins of apartment complexes and business buildings is also obviously abandoned. Property found in a ditch at the side of a road is most probably abandoned. However, one may not abandon property on one's own land. Thus, property found in a vacant lot may or may not be abandoned; it may belong to the lot owner, in which case it is definitely not abandoned. The person who placed it there might not have intended to place it there, in which case it is lost rather than abandoned. (Of course, property found in the ditch at the side of the road might also be lost rather than abandoned.) Finally, one does not abandon property by putting it in a garbage can located upon one's own property. The true abandonment will not occur until the trash collectors come and haul the garbage away.

The person who takes possession of abandoned property becomes its true owner if he takes possession with intent to assume ownership. In case his ownership is questioned, though, he must prove that the former owner has truly abandoned the property. This can be difficult to prove, particularly if the property was found somewhere other than in a dump or garbage bin.

Property is lost when the owner has unintentionally parted with possession but the property is in a place where the loser is not likely to come back and reclaim it. Property located in a ditch at the side of a road, in a vacant lot, on a sidewalk, on the floor of a business establishment, etc., is fairly obviously lost.

The finder of such property does not become the owner of it, because the loser has not abandoned it. The finder is in essence an involuntary bailee who has better rights to the property than anyone else other than the loser. If the true owner of the property is identifiable from the property, the finder must make every reasonable effort to return it to the loser. If he does not do this he commits the crime of theft and the tort of conversion. If the owner is not identifiable from the property, and if the finder does not know the identity of the loser, he is under no obligation to do a lot of detective work. He is however under the obligation of a bailee to take care of the property. If the finder damages it, the true owner reclaims it, and the finder cannot prove that his negligence did not cause the damage, the owner may recover damages from the finder.

If the finder retains possession of the property for two years, he obtains title to it by adverse possession. This is because RCS 5526 provides that an action against a person for detaining the personal property of another and converting it to his own use, or an action for taking or carrying away the personal property of another, must be commenced within two years of the detaining or carrying away.

The finder may sell the property before he obtains title to it by adverse possession. If he does this, he sells only the title he has, which is the right of possession. Once the finder and his buyer together have had possession for two years, the buyer gets title by adverse possession. Thus: On April 3, 1978, White loses a valuable ring which has no identification on it. On April 6, 1978, Gray finds it. He advertises that he has found it, but receives no response. On May 12, 1979, Gray sells the ring to Black, who does not know who the loser was. On June 15, 1980, White learns that Black has the ring and demands that Black give it up. Black need not do so. Since it has been more than two years since Gray found the ring, it is now Black's by adverse possession.

Property is misplaced when the owner unintentionally parts with possession in a place he is likely to return to when he finds the property missing. Property found on the counter of a business establishment, on the seat of a taxicab or barbershop, under a desk in a classroom, or buried in the ground, is fairly obviously misplaced. The owner of the premises upon which misplaced property is found has a better claim to it than does the finder: the reason for this is that the owner will probably be back looking for his property, and the owner of the premises is in a better position to return it to him than is the finder. If an employee of the owner of the premises finds misplaced property, he must turn it over to his employer.

If the owner of misplaced property does not reclaim it from the owner of the premises where it was found within two years, the owner will get title by adverse possession. However, as is the case with lost property, if the loser is identifiable from the property, or if the owner of the premises knows who the loser is, he must return the property or be guilty of theft and conversion.

Buried treasure and the like will generally belong to the owner of the land where it is found, because such property is almost certainly misplaced. No one buries treasure without intending to come back and reclaim it some day, so the treasure is certainly not abandoned or lost.

Valuable property found hidden inside a rented house is also considered misplaced. If it belongs to the landlord or to a former owner it was certainly not abandoned, since you cannot abandon anything on your own property. If it belongs to a former tenant it is certainly misplaced, since you do not lose things in your own residence. The contents of a container go with the container. If the container is misplaced, so are the contents. If the container is abandoned, so are the contents.

A thief cannot get title to property which he stole by adverse possession. However, if the thief sells stolen property to someone who does not know that it is stolen, the buyer from the thief will get title by adverse possession after he has possessed the property for two years.

A bailee also cannot get title to the bailor's property by adverse possession. However, a buyer of the property from the bailee who does not know that he has bought bailed property will get title by adverse possession on the second anniversary of the bailment, unless the bailor has earlier demanded the return of the property. This is due to the provisions of Texas Business & Commerce Code 24.05(a), which provides that when the bailee of personal property or someone claiming under the bailee has possessed the property for two years, and the bailor has made no effort to recover the property within that two years, the possessor is the owner so far as purchasers from him or his creditors are concerned. So long as the bailee retains the property, however, he will never get title by adverse possession. He thus has the power to confer title upon someone else, but has no title himself and can never acquire title.

If the possessor of lost or misplaced property himself loses or misplaces it, he will have a better right to possession than any subsequent finder or property owner. A first finder, then, may recover possession of such property from a second finder.

Accession. When a possessor of personal property changes its form and adds to its value, a problem may arise as to who now owns the improved property. This depends upon the relationship between the owner of the property and the possessor, and also upon the nature of the improvements.

If the possessor is a thief, he must return the improved property to the true owner without compensation for his improvements. If the possessor is a bailee, he must do likewise. Both of these know they are dealing with property which is not their own; they have no right to change the nature of the property and they know it. If the possessor is an innocent converter, he need not return the improved property, but he must pay the true owner the value of the unimproved property.

If a thief or bailee sells the unimproved property to a good-faith purchaser, and the good-faith purchaser makes improvements, he is in the position of the innocent converter. He keeps the improved property, but is liable for the value of the unimproved property. Thus: Black and White own adjacent cornfields, with no fence separating them. Black, while harvesting his corn, deliberately harvests some of White's too. He grinds the corn into cornmeal. Then White discovers the dastardly deed and demands possession of the cornmeal made from his corn. His demand is justified; Black is a thief.

If Black harvested some of White's corn because of a good-faith error on his part as to the location of the boundary between the two fields, Black is an innocent converter. If he grinds the corn into cornmeal, he may retain all of the meal, but he must pay White the value of the unground corn that he converted to his own use.

If Black deliberately harvested some of White's corn and sold it to Gray; Gray, not knowing that the corn was stolen, ground it into cornmeal; and White found out about it all, then Gray must pay White the value of the stolen corn. Again, he may retain the cornmeal.

Sometimes the true owner of improved stolen property may recover only damages from the thief. Thus, if Black steals lumber from White and erects a barn with it, White cannot remove the barn and put it on his land. He also cannot make Black tear down the barn to recover his lumber. He may only recover damages for the conversion of his lumber. He may of course also obtain the pleasure of Black's prosecution and conviction on charges of theft.

Sometimes a thief steals items from several owners and combines them into one piece of property. Thus: Green steals an auto engine from Redd, an auto body from Brown, a chassis and transmission from Blue, tires from Black, and paint from Gray, and combines all of these into an automobile. Once Gray's paint has been applied to the car, there is no way to recover it. The engine, body, and chassis are worth more as a running vehicle than they are separately, probably, so no court would demolish the car to permit recovery of these components. On the other hand, if the tires are removed and restored to Black, the value of the auto will not be greatly diminished. In such a case the auto would be given to the owner of its most valuable component—probably Redd. Green would be required to pay to the owners of the other components the value of those components, plus any damages that he caused them to suffer. Other than that, all parties might get pleasure from Green's criminal prosecution.

Confusion. Confusion occurs when fungible goods belonging to two or more owners are mixed together. The rules for untangling the confusion vary, depending upon the circumstances.

If the ownership of the components of the confused mass can be proven, the solution is simple: every owner gets his property back. If the ownership of the individual components of the confused mass cannot be proven, resolution of the problem depends upon why the confusion occurred in the first place. If the mix-up was caused by the deliberate act of one of the owners of the mass, he recovers nothing except those components of which he can prove ownership. If he can positively identify none of the mass as his, he gets nothing back; all of it goes to the innocent party or parties. If ownership of individual components cannot be proven and the confusion was accidental, the mass will be divided in accordance with the number of components each co-owner contributed to the mass.

Suppose that 500 cattle belonging to Earp get mixed with 400 cattle belonging to Dillon. If all of the cattle are branded, untanglement is simple. Earp gets back the cattle with his brand and Dillon gets back the cattle with his. If the cattle are not branded and they are all of the same breed, and Earp deliberately caused the confusion, Dillon will get all of the cattle except those that Earp can prove are his. Of course, if they are unbranded and all of the same breed, Earp might have difficulty proving ownership of any of them. If he has trouble, of course, it is his own fault. He should not have caused the confusion to start with.

If the cattle are not branded, they are all of the same breed, and the confusion was accidental, Earp will get back 500 of the cattle and Dillon will get back 400. The mass will not be divided the same as it was before the confusion; Earp will doubtless get some of Dillon's animals and Dillon will doubtless get some of Earp's. But if the individual animals are not identifiable, that is the best that can be done.

If some of the cattle die before the confusion is untangled, risk of loss falls as follows: If the ownership of the dead animals is determinable, the owner takes the loss. If ownership is not determinable, but the confusion was deliberate, whoever caused the confusion takes the loss. If ownership is not determinable, but the confusion was accidental, the loss is borne ratably by the co-owners, each in proportion to his ownership of the mass.

A bailee of fungible goods belonging to many owners, such as a grain elevator owner, has the right to deliberately create confusion. He may mix goods belonging to many owners into one mass. All of the owners of a part of the mass are co-owners of the whole. Since such a bailee is not required to return exactly the same goods he accepted for bailment, but only the bailed quantity of equivalent goods, no harm is caused by this.

Inter vivos gifts. This subject was introduced in the chapter on assignment of contract rights. It will be considered in more depth here.

The giver of a gift is called the donor; the recipient is the donee. An inter vivos gift is one which is not given by the donor in anticipation of his own death. Two things are required for validity of an inter vivos gift: intent by the donor to make the donee the owner of the gift, and delivery of the gift to the donee or to his agent.

Anyone who gives another person possession of property may do so with intent to make a gift, or he may do so with intent to create a bailment. Usually there is no difficulty in ascertaining the intent of the donor—we merely ask him what his intent was. Under normal circumstances, what he says settles the question.

If the donor dies after transferring possession, or if he loses his contractual capacity after transferring possession, difficulty may arise in proving his intent. Since he now cannot speak for himself, others must try to divine his intentions. Often the divination of intent boils down to a contest of one person's word against another's. Thus: Ernest lends Slick a book. Before Slick returns it, Ernest dies. Ehrlich, executor of Ernest's will, asks Slick to return the book. Slick says he will not do so, because Ernest had said he could keep it. Ehrlich doubts this, but he can find no one who saw Ernest give Slick the book, and Ernest told no one about it except his housekeeper. The housekeeper says Ernest told her he lent the book to Slick. So it is Slick's word that Ernest gave him the book against the housekeeper's words that Ernest loaned him the book. If the argument gets into court, who will win? No one can predict. It all depends on which story the judge or jury decides to believe.

Delivery consists of transferring possession of the gift to the donee or to his agent. If the gift is something which is readily deliverable, such as a piece of jewelry, delivery is transfer of the gift itself. If the donee possesses it, and there is no question about the donor's intent, the gift is completed.

Delivery to an agent can sometimes cause problems. Delivery to an agent is not delivery to the donee unless the agent is the donee's agent. If the agent is deemed to be the donor's agent, there is of course no delivery. Thus: Fred wants to give a watch to Jean. He gives it to his brother Jack and tells Jack to give it to Jean. Before Jack delivers, Fred changes his mind and tells Jack to return the ring, which he does. Jean knows of Fred's intent to give her the ring, and she knows Fred gave the ring to Jack and took it back again. Jean demands the ring from Fred because, she says, he delivered it when he gave it to Jack. Jean is wrong, of course. Fred appointed Jack his agent for the purpose of delivery, but he revoked the agency before its purpose was carried out. The entire proceeding was perfectly legitimate.

Suppose that Fred gave the ring to Jean's sister Polly and told her to give it to Jean. Then Fred changed his mind and asked Polly to give back the ring while she still had it in her possession. Polly refused to give it back, instead giving it to Jean. Fred demands the ring from Jean. This is a questionable situation. Since Fred gave the ring to Polly to deliver, Polly is in a sense his agent. However, since Polly is Jean's sister, there is good reason to argue that Polly is Jean's agent, not Fred's. But, again, Jean never appointed Polly her agent to make delivery of the ring. Fred appointed her an agent to make delivery of it. So, whose agent is Polly? A jury may be called upon to decide. Of course, if Fred gave the ring to Jerry, Jean's attorney, to deliver, the gift is delivered when Fred gives it to Jerry. Jerry pretty obviously is Jean's agent here, not Fred's.

The gift of a container is a gift of the contents, unless the contents are such that no reasonable man could believe that the donor meant to give them away. The donor must check the contents of the container before parting with them.

Some gifts are by their nature incapable of physical delivery; symbolic delivery of these is sufficient. If one wants to make a gift of the contents of a wall safe, one could do so by giving the donee the combination or key to the safe. The key or combination provides access to the contents. The gift of the contents of a bank account may be completed by giving the passbook to the donee. The donor should also inform the bank of his intentions, but the gift will be complete without this.

On the other hand, the gift of the contents of a safe-deposit box is not complete until the bank is notified. This is due to the fact that the bank must assist in opening the box. A safe-deposit box has two locks: one can be opened by the owner with his key, and the other must be opened by the bank with its key. The bank must be informed of the ownership change before it is obligated to use its key for the new owner.

If the donor opens a bank account in the donee's name and makes a deposit therein, the gift is not complete. The donor must inform the donee of what he has done so that the donee can sign the bank's signature card. If the donor opens the account in the names of both the donor and the donee, the donee becomes a co-owner of the account when he is informed. However, if the donor and the donee both have withdrawal rights, the donee is only a co-owner of the balance in the account at any given moment. If the terms of the account allow either co-owner to make withdrawals upon his own signature, the donor may reduce the balance in the account—and the donee's ownership—at any time. If the donor opens an account for the donee in the name of "Donor as trustee for Donee," the donee becomes the beneficiary of this trust when the donor informs him of what he has done.

For the gift of a motor vehicle to be completed, the donor must deliver a certificate of title to the vehicle to the donee. In this case, delivery of the subject matter of the gift itself is insufficient. The same is true if the gift is a mobile home, trailer, or boat.

If the donor makes a gift to the donee with the intent to hinder, delay, or defraud his creditors, the gift is void as against these creditors. This is true even if the donee had no knowledge of the donor's evil intent, and the donor actually meant to make the donee the owner of the property. Of course if the gift is only a pretended gift and the donee knows the donor has no intent of permanently giving up the property, there is no gift at all.

Gifts causa mortis. The gift causa mortis is a gift in anticipation of death. The donor of such a gift must have a reasonable fear that he will soon die of some peril. He must, because of this fear, have the intention to make a gift. He must then deliver possession of the gift to the donee or to his agent, and then die of that cause which he feared.

The major difference between the inter vivos gift and the gift causa mortis is this: When the donor makes delivery of the inter vivos gift with the intent to make a gift, the delivery is final. The donor cannot undo what he has done and reclaim the gift. The gift causa mortis is, on the other hand, voidable. If the donor does not die of what he feared, he may revoke the gift and take it back. If the donor dies, but he does not die of that which he feared, the gift becomes voidable and the executor or administrator of the donor's estate may revoke it. Thus: Angst is scheduled for open-heart surgery and fears that he will not survive the operation. He gives his stamp collection to Freund because he wants Freund to have it after he dies. Angst undergoes the surgery, recovers, and returns home. He wants Freund to return the stamp collection. Freund must do so. Suppose that Angst survives the surgery and is discharged from the hospital. Then, on the way home from the hospital, he dies in an auto accident. Goodman, the executor of his will, demands that Freund return the stamp collection. Freund must do it, since Angst did not die of that which he feared. Had Angst died on the operating table, the gift would have been completed and Freund could have kept the stamp collection.

Conditional and voidable gifts. The ordinary inter vivos gift is irrevocable. But, under certain conditions such gifts are revocable.

Thus, the minor's gift is voidable, just as his contracts are. If he changes his mind about having made the gift, he may reclaim it from the donee. If, however, the donee has sold the gift to a bona fide purchaser, it is gone, and the minor cannot reclaim it. If the donee has given it away, though, the minor can reclaim it.

If an insane or incompetent person with a guardian makes a gift, the gift is void. The guardian may reclaim it from the donee.

The gift of an engagement ring is the most common sort of conditional gift. Boy essentially gives this to Girl on condition that she marry him. If the marriage never takes place, Boy may be able to reclaim the ring. Whether Boy can reclaim depends essentially on why the marriage never took place. If the couple mutually agrees to cancel the engagement, Boy does recover the ring. If Girl breaks the engagement for no good reason, Boy can recover the ring. But if Boy breaks off the engagement for no good reason, Girl may keep the ring.

Recoverability of the ring depends not only upon who broke off the engagement, but also upon why. Thus, if Boy breaks the engagement because Girl insists upon dating one of her old boyfriends during the engagement period, Boy had a good reason to back out, so he may get the ring back. If Girl breaks the engagement because she wants Boy to agree to have children after the marriage, but he does not want children, Girl could probably keep the ring.

Taxability of gifts. The person who makes gifts of considerable value must realize that he could incur federal tax liability. Before 1976 there existed a separate federal gift tax upon such gifts.

In the Tax Reform Act of 1976, Congress unified the gift tax and the estate tax into one unified tax. Large gifts may still subject the donor to federal tax liability, but the taxability of gifts is now so closely intertwined with the taxability of the estate of a deceased person that it is best to discuss the tax on gifts at the same time as the tax on estates. Both of these taxes will therefore be discussed in the chapter on estate planning.

23

Co-Ownership of Property

It is quite possible for two or more persons to share ownership of the same piece of property. The relationship between the co-owners, and their rights and duties with respect to the co-owned property, will depend upon the type of co-ownership.

Five types of co-ownership of property are recognized in the various states of the United States, four of which are recognized in Texas. These five are:
1. Tenancy in common.
2. Joint tenancy.
3. Tenancy in partnership.
4. Tenancy by the entireties.
5. Community property.

All of these except the tenancy by the entireties are recognized in Texas.

Tenancy in common. This is the most common form of co-ownership when the co-owners are not married to each other. It is the type of co-ownership which arises when a testator's will provides, "I leave my farm Blackacre to my sons, Bill and Jody, and my daughters Hilda, Jean, and Bonita, share and share alike." The five heirs will each be said to own an undivided one-fifth interest in Blackacre.

Within broad limits, a tenant in common may do what he pleases with his interest in the co-owned property. He may sell it; he may mortgage it; his heirs may inherit it upon his death. The other co-owners may not interfere with his management or disposal of his interest.

The ownership interests in a tenancy in common are more often than not equal, but they need not necessarily be equal. Thus, Able may own a 90 percent interest in property as a tenant in common, Baker owning the other 10 percent.

No tenant in common may dispose of the interest of another tenant in common. Thus, in the situation where Bill, Jody, Hilda, Jean, and Bonita own Blackacre as tenants in common, if Sam wants to acquire 100 percent ownership of Blackacre he must buy out all five of the tenants in common. If all of the co-owners except Jody want to sell out to Sam, there is no way Sam could get 100 percent. Those co-owners who want to sell to Sam may do so, of course, but Sam would end up owning 80 percent of the property while Jody still owns his 20 percent.

It is possible to eliminate the minority interest of a co-owner through the complex and sometimes unsatisfactory process of partition. But any discussion of partition must be preceded by a discussion of the rights and duties of tenants in common with respect to possession and management of the co-owned property.

Theoretically, all tenants in common have equal rights with respect to the use and enjoyment of the co-owned property. In practice, the existence of these equal rights may cause great difficulty, unless the co-owners work out an agreement as to who will be able to do what with the property. For instance, if Art, Bill, and Clint own an automobile as tenants in common, they all have the right to drive it. But if all three want to drive it at the same time, someone must of necessity be disappointed.

Suppose that Art, Bill, and Clint agree that Clint shall have the possession and use of the car. The rights and duties of the boys would be as follows, unless they all agree otherwise: All three boys must share in the cost of license plates for the car. If they live in a jurisdiction that levies a personal property tax upon automobiles, each would be liable for one third of the tax. Clint would be under no obligation to pay rent to Art and Bill. Clint, on the other hand, cannot make Art and Bill pay for gasoline or other expenses. So long as Clint puts the car to reasonable use, Art and Bill have nothing to say in this area.

Clint must maintain the auto as a reasonable owner would, so that the interests of the other co-owners do not unreasonably depreciate in value. If this is not done—if Clint is negligent about making required oil changes, or if he never washes the car—Art and Bill could take steps to end his possession. Clint would of course have no right to mortgage the car without the consent of Art and Bill. He could mortgage his one-third interest in it without their consent, of course; but a one-third interest in an automobile would make rather unsatisfactory collateral.

Clint could not rent out the car without the permission of Art and Bill, since a nonowner is thereby being given the use of the co-owned property. If Art and Bill consent to such a bailment, the rental proceeds are to be divided among the co-owners ratably, according to the interest of each (equally, in this case).

Should Clint want to make a major change in the car—installing a new engine, changing its body style, etc.—he may not compel Art and Bill to pay for any of this if they do not want to. In fact, they could veto such a change if it was not to their liking. If they do not object to Clint's making this major investment and the value of the auto is thereby increased, all three co-owners benefit from it. In short, if Clint spends his cash to increase the value of the co-owned property all of the co-owners benefit.

If the three co-owners have irreconcilable differences as to the control and management of the car—should Art and Bill, for example, be unhappy about the way Clint is using the car while Clint is unwilling to change his ways or give up the car—the tenancy in common can be terminated. This may be done by mutual agreement of the co-owners. If the co-owners cannot agree on how it should be done, a court may do the job. The co-owners may voluntarily end a tenancy in common through a buy-out agreement, one or more of the co-owners simply buying out the interests of the others. It could also be ended with the co-owners selling the property to a third party and dividing the proceeds according to their interests. If a court is called upon to do the job, the court will order the property sold and the proceeds divided. Obviously, it is better for the co-owners to voluntarily terminate a tenancy in common than it is for a court to do it.

If the co-owned property is divisible, a tenancy in common may be terminated by division of the property itself among the co-owners. If the property consists of fungible goods, shares of stock, etc., this can be done. If the property is something nondivisible, such as an automobile, that option is clearly not open.

With respect to real property there are other rules of law to be taken into account; these will be covered in the materials on real property.

Joint tenancy. The major difference between a joint tenancy and a tenancy in common is that, upon the death of a tenant in common, his interest passes to his heirs, as determined by his will or by the applicable law if there is no will; upon the death of a joint tenant, his interest passes to the other joint tenant or tenants. Hence, the joint tenancy is often called "joint tenancy with right of survivorship." Actually, there can be no such thing as a joint tenancy without the right of survivorship.

No joint tenancy can exist unless the four "unities" are present. These are time, title, interest, and possession.

Unity of time exists if the joint tenants acquired their interests in the property at the same time. Thus, if Jim owns 100 shares of General Motors stock, and he seeks to transfer a half-interest to Bob as a joint tenant, no joint tenancy will exist, because Jim acquired his interest in the stock before Bob acquired his. On the other hand, if Jim and Bob pool their cash to buy 100 shares of General Motors stock as joint tenants, the unity of time would be present.

Unity of title exists if the would-be joint tenants acquired their interests as a result of the same agreement. Usually, the unity of time and the unity of title go together; if one exists, the other does also. However, assume Sam desires to make Jim and Bob joint tenancy owners of his 100 shares of General Motors stock. He gives Jim a written statement that he is making him a joint tenant in the shares with Bob, and gives Bob another written statement that he is making him a joint tenant of the shares with Jim. Arguably there is no unity of title in this case, although the problem would be solved if General Motors issued a certificate to these shares in the names of Jim and Bob as joint tenants.

Unity of interest exists if the joint tenants have equal ownership interests in the property. Where there are two joint tenants, each must own an undivided half-interest in the property. If the would-be joint tenants own unequal interests, there is no joint tenancy. Unity of possession requires that the joint tenants have equal rights to possession and use of the co-owned property. If the other unities are present, this one usually is also.

If one of the required four unities is not present, no joint tenancy exists. If an attempted joint tenancy fails because of the absence of one of the unities, the result is normally the creation of a tenancy in common.

In the state of Texas a husband and wife may not own community property as joint tenants. This is because the Texas Constitution defines community property (Article 16, Section 15), and states that community property is inheritable. For that reason, the Supreme Court of Texas decided, in the case of *Hilley vs. Hilley*, 342 S.W. 2d 565, that husband and wife may not change the constitutionally mandated inheritability of community property by changing the ownership of it to joint tenancy.

It is, however, possible for a married couple to buy U.S. Savings Bonds with community funds and to take title as joint tenants. The U.S. Supreme Court decided that the federal regulations which permit the ownership of U.S. Savings Bonds in joint tenancy take precedence over any state legal provisions forbidding this. It is also possible for married persons to become joint tenants of property that was not community property at the time the joint tenancy was established. Thus, father Jed could buy 100 shares of General Motors stock and give it to son Tom and daughter-in-law Sandra as joint tenants.

It would not be possible, though, for a married person to directly convert separate property into joint tenancy property. If Tom owned 100 shares of General Motors stock when he married Sandra, and he wanted to make Sandra a joint tenant of the stock with him, he would be unable to do so directly because the unity of time would be missing—Tom acquired his interest in the shares before Sandra acquired hers. Tom could accomplish his objective indirectly, however, by selling his 100 shares of General Motors and then buying another 100 shares with the proceeds and taking title to these in his name and Sandra's, as joint tenants.

A joint tenant has the right to dispose of his interest in the joint tenancy property without the consent of the other joint tenant. The result is the severance of the joint tenancy. The buyer becomes a tenant in common, not a joint tenant. Thus: Suppose Jim and Tom own property as joint tenants. Jim sells his interest to Bob. Jim may do this; Tom cannot stop him. Tom and Bob are now tenants in common. If Bob later dies and wills all of his property to Alvin, Tom and Alvin become tenants in common in the property.

When there are more than two joint tenants, a sale of his interest by a joint tenant can create some complex ownership situations. Suppose that Ann, Dee, and Joyce own property as joint tenants. Joyce sells her interest to Nancy. The result is that Ann and Dee are still joint tenants with respect to two-thirds of the property, while Nancy is a tenant in common with them with respect to one-third. If Ann now dies, Dee acquires her third regardless of any contrary provision in Ann's will because of the right of survivorship. Dee now owns a two-thirds interest, while Nancy owns one-third.

Returning to the original example: Ann, Dee, and Joyce own property as joint tenants. Joyce sells her interest to Dee; she does not want to sell to Ann and Dee, because she does not like Ann. Result: Ann and Dee are joint tenants with respect to two-thirds of the property, while Dee is a tenant in common with respect to the other third. If Dee dies, by will leaving her property to Polly, Polly inherits the third-interest which Dee owned as a tenant in common, while Ann gets the third-interest Dee had as a joint tenant. Ann ends up with a two-thirds interest in the property and Polly ends up with a one-third interest, the co-owners being tenants in common.

There is one great advantage to ownership of property as joint tenants, and there is one great disadvantage. The advantage is the right of survivorship: the joint tenancy property passes directly to the survivor upon the death of a joint tenant. It will not be subject to probate as a part of the deceased owner's estate, and will not come under the jurisdiction of the probate court during the estate settlement process.

The disadvantage is a tax disadvantage. The entire value of property owned as joint tenants is considered to be a part of the estate of the deceased joint tenant for federal estate tax purposes, unless the surviving joint tenant can prove that he contributed some of the consideration used to purchase the property. The amount of the value taxable as part of the deceased's estate will be reduced by the amount of consideration furnished by the survivor. If the property is of no great value, this will be no great disadvantage. But if the value of the property is more than $100,000, there may well be a tax disadvantage to this type of ownership.

The rights and duties of joint tenants with respect to the co-owned property are essentially the same as those applicable in the tenancy in common.

Tenancy in partnership. This will be discussed in detail in the materials on partnership. In brief, when two or more persons operate a business as co-owners for profit, and they have not incorporated the business, they are operating a partnership. Their business assets are owned in tenancy in partnership.

Since a partnership is not a legal entity for most purposes, partnership assets are owned by the partners, not by the firm. However, the partners are under an obligation to use firm assets for firm purposes, not for personal use.

A firm asset held as part of the firm's inventory, for sale in the normal course of firm business, may be sold by a partner in the normal course of business. A firm asset not held for sale in the normal course of business may not be sold by a partner unless he has express authority to sell it. Under no circumstances may a partner sell his interest in a firm asset. The only way a partner may dispose of his interest in a firm asset is by selling his interest in the firm itself. The buyer thereby acquires the seller's equity in the firm and its assets, but he does not become a partner.

Upon the death of a partner, his interest in firm assets passes to the surviving partners, while his interest in the firm passes to his heirs. The heirs may acquire an interest in some firm assets by forcing dissolution and liquidation of the firm, but there is no way in which they may acquire an interest in any particular assets.

Tenancy by the entireties. This is the only form of co-ownership not recognized in Texas. Since it does exist in other states, however, students should know something about it.

Only persons who are married to each other may own property as tenants by the entireties. In many ways this form of ownership is similar to a joint tenancy. The main similarity here is that, upon the death of a spouse, the survivor automatically acquires full ownership of the property.

A tenant by the entireties may not dispose of his interest in the property without the consent of his spouse. Creditors of one spouse may not levy upon the property, whereas creditors of both spouses may do so. When the marriage of tenants by the entireties terminates, so does the tenancy by the entireties. The ex-spouses will then own the property as tenants in common, unless the court terminating the marriage makes some other disposition of the property.

Married Texans who own real property in a state recognizing tenancy by the entireties may well be tenants by the entireties. For instance, married persons owning real property in the state of Indiana own it as tenants by the entireties, unless the deed by which they got title specifies some other form of co-ownership.

Community property. This is a form of co-ownership recognized by only eight of the fifty states of the United States. The eight community property states are Texas, Louisiana, New Mexico, Arizona, Nevada, California, Washington, and Idaho. The general principles of community property are the same in all eight states, but the details of community property law will differ from state to state. Only married persons may own community property, but not all property owned by a married person is community property. That which is community property is owned by both spouses, each spouse in a sense owning an undivided half-interest in it. A married person may also own separate property. A married person's spouse has no interest whatsoever in separate property.

The Texas Constitution and Texas Family Code define what is separate property, and state that all property owned by a married person which is not separate is community. TFC 5.01 defines separate property as:

1. Property owned or claimed by a person before marriage, and
2. Property acquired during marriage by gift or inheritance, and
3. Recoveries for personal injuries sustained by a person during marriage, except for recovery for loss of earning capacity during marriage.

All other property owned by a married person is community property. Separate property will not lose its character by changing its form. If Tom owns a tract of real estate when he marries, the realty is his separate property. If he sells the land for cash, the proceeds of the sale are separate property. If he then invests the proceeds in IBM stock, the stock is separate property.

The following sorts of property are community property:
1. The earnings of a married person after his or her marriage (postmarital earnings.)
2. Interest earned by money in a separate bank account, or invested in a separate bond, or whatever.
3. Cash dividends paid upon separate stock.
4. Rentals earned by separate real estate or other separate property.
5. Profits earned by a separate business.
6. Personal injury damages recovered as compensation for loss of earnings or loss of earning capacity.

The following sorts of property are separate, in addition to those already mentioned:
1. Royalties on oil and gas leases, mineral leases, patents, copyrights, and the like.
2. Stock received as a stock dividend, if no retained earnings were capitalized to cover the dividend. (If retained earnings were so capitalized, the stock dividend is similar to a cash dividend and is community property.)
3. Stock received as a stock split, if no retained earnings were capitalized.
4. Cash received in a corporate distribution in partial liquidation.

All property owned by a married person is presumed to be community property, according to TFC 5.02. Therefore, if there is any question as to whether marital property is separate or community, the burden of proof rests upon the party claiming that it is separate. If separate and community property are commingled, the mass becomes community unless proof exists as to how much of the mass is separate. Separate and community property may become commingled in many ways. A few examples follow.

Tom has a savings account at Texas Savings & Loan Association when he marries. The contents of the account on his wedding day are his separate property. However, the interest the account earns after his wedding day is community. The longer he permits the interest to accumulate in the account, the more of the account becomes community. Also, if Tom deposits funds earned by himself after his marriage in the account, those funds are community funds. Should Tom desire to preserve the separateness of the original contents of the account, he must keep meticulous records with respect to the account's contents.

Dick owns a business when he marries. The business is his separate property, but the profits the business earns are community property. If he reinvests profits in the business for expansion purposes, a part of the net worth of the business will become community property. Should Dick wish to preserve the separateness of a part of the net worth of the business, he will need to keep meticulous records.

Harry owns a house when he marries. The house is his separate property. If, after his marriage, he uses some of his postnuptial earnings in order to repair the roof, or to finance the addition of another room, a part of the house becomes community property. Again, Harry needs to keep meticulous records to preserve the separateness of his interest.

Gene owns 100 shares of IBM stock when he marries. These are his separate property. A year after his marriage he sells the stock. He then adds to the proceeds money from a savings account containing his postnuptial earnings and invests in 400 shares of Ford Motor Company stock. The Ford stock is partially community, because it was purchased with a mixture of separate money and community money. It is with respect to this type of commingling that meticulous record-keeping is most important, if Gene wants to preserve his separate interest in the stock.

It should be remembered that property may be community property even if the record title to it is in the name of only one spouse. Thus, if Dianne buys 100 shares of General Motors stock with her postnuptial earnings and gets the certificate in her name only, the stock is nevertheless community property since it was purchased with community funds. On the other hand, if assets purchased with separate funds are placed in the names of both spouses as record owners, the assets no longer belong 100 percent to the spouse who furnished the funds for their purchase. Depending upon how the title to the assets is worded, the spouses may own the assets as tenants in common, or as community property.

Management of marital property. A married person has sole power of management, control over, and disposition of his or her separate property, as per TFC 5.21.

A married person has sole power of management, control over, and disposition of the community property that he or she would have owned if single (TFC 5.22), including:

1. Personal earnings, and
2. Revenue from separate property (interest, dividends, rent, profit) and
3. Recoveries for personal injuries, and
4. Increasing mutations of, and revenue from, all property subject to his or her sole management, control, and disposition.

Thus, if Mary keeps a savings account in her name containing her surplus postmarital earnings, the funds in the account are community property co-owned by John, her husband, but Mary may spend the money as she pleases. John may own some of it, but he has no right to tell Mary what to do with it.

The only sorts of community property which are under joint management and control are:

1. Community property to which the record title is in the names of both spouses, such as a joint bank account.
2. Community property consisting of commingled community property under the sole management and control of each of the two spouses. Thus, if John and Mary pool their postnuptial earnings to buy a car, and they take legal title to it in John's name, it is community property under joint control because both spouses contributed community property under sole control to its purchase.

So far as third parties are concerned, they may assume (unless they know otherwise) that property standing in the name of a married person is under the management and control of that person, as per TFC 5.24. Thus, John could sell good title to the car in example 2 above to a buyer who did not know the car was under joint control. But the proceeds of the sale would be community property under joint control.

Under unusual circumstances, a spouse may petition a court to grant to him or her the power to manage, control, and dispose of community property which is under the control of the other spouse. TFC 5.25 enumerates four such unusual circumstances:

1. The controlling spouse is unable to manage or control the community property under his control (perhaps due to mental incapacity, illness, or accident).
2. A spouse disappears and his whereabouts are unknown, unless he is in the public service of the United States, in which case TFC 5.26 provides special rules which will be covered later.
3. A spouse permanently abandons the other spouse.
4. The spouses are permanently separated.

A petition seeking control of such property must be filed in a Texas district court not less than sixty days after the happening of the event justifying the filing. The judge will appoint an attorney to represent the other spouse. A date will be set for a hearing, and the missing spouse will be served a notice of the hearing in person (if his whereabouts are known) or by publication (if his whereabouts are unknown). First publication must take place at least twenty days before the date set for the hearing.

23/ Co-ownership of Property

Notice, then, that if the controlling spouse's whereabouts are unknown, the giving of the required notice will take time—at least three weeks must elapse between the filing of the petition and the hearing. If the controlling spouse's whereabouts are known, the hearing may be expedited, particularly if he offers no objections.

When a married person has been deprived in this manner of his control over community property of which he normally had control, he may obtain control again if:

1. His mental incapacity disappears, or
2. He reappears and thus ends his disappearance, or
3. The abandonment or permanent separation ends.

With respect to the special provisions for spouses on the public service of the United States (prompted by the Vietnam war), TFC 5.26 states that when a person in public service is declared to be a prisoner of war or declared to be missing in action, the other spouse may, not less than six months after the missing spouse is declared to be a prisoner or missing, file a petition in Texas district court seeking control over the community property under the control and management of the missing party. A hearing will be necessary before the petition can be granted. If the missing person returns, he may again obtain control over the property in question.

Property agreements. An engaged couple may vary these rules by entering into a premarital property agreement. It should be in writing; if real estate is involved, it must be recorded in the real property records of all counties where affected real estate is located. For such an agreement to be effective, it must be made and recorded before the marriage occurs. TFC 5.41 authorizes these agreements.

TFC 5.42 permits married persons to partition all or part of their existing community property between themselves, converting it into separate property. Such agreements must be in writing, and, if real estate is involved, must be recorded in the real property records of all counties where the affected real estate is located.

Such an agreement is effective only with respect to currently owned community property. There is no way in which spouses may partition future community property.

Sale or encumbrance of a homestead. TFC 5.81 provides that a homestead may not be sold or encumbered without the signatures of both spouses. It does not matter whether the homestead is separate or community property. It also does not matter who has record title to the property. It is possible for one spouse to obtain the right to sell or encumber the homestead, under the same circumstances and by following essentially the same procedure as that normally provided for gaining control of community property under the control of the other spouse.

Marital property liabilities. The rules here are contained in TFC 5.61. With respect to liabilities incurred by a person before he married, his creditors have access to:

1. The separate property of that person.
2. Community property under the sole control of the debtor.
3. Community property under the joint control of both spouses.

With respect to contractual liabilities incurred by a debtor after marriage, the creditor has access to:

1. The separate property of the debtor.
2. Community property under the sole control of the debtor.
3. Community property under joint control of both spouses.

With respect to tort liabilities incurred by a spouse during marriage, the creditor has access to:

1. The separate property of the debtor.

2. All community property of the marriage, no matter whose control it is under. If both spouses are liable on the debt in question, the creditor of course has access to all property of both spouses—both separate and community.

Ownership of multiple-party accounts. Problems often arise with respect to the rights of co-owners of various types of accounts in financial institutions. To clarify the law in this area, the Texas legislature in 1979 added Sections 436 through 450 to the Texas Probate Code. The statute applies to co-owned checking accounts, savings accounts, and certificates of deposit in banks, savings and loan associations, credit unions, etc. It does not apply to partnership, joint venture, or other business accounts; it also does not apply to securities accounts with brokerage firms or similar organizations.

The new statute does not change the Texas law of community property in any way. Community funds deposited in a co-owned account remain community funds, no matter who the co-owners are. Thus, if Dick and Jane Brown open a savings account as co-owners, and they deposit postmarital earnings therein, they own the account as community property.

If Dick Brown opens a savings account in the names of Dick and Jane Brown, husband and wife, with separate funds of his, the account will not be a community account. It will be a tenancy in common account, unless Dick makes some other arrangement with the financial institution involved. Dick could set it up as a community account if he wished; he could also set it up as a joint tenancy with right of survivorship. If he deposits separate funds in an account standing in the names of Dick Brown and Don Brown, brothers— these being the funds with which the account is opened—the account will again be a tenancy in common. Dick could, however, elect to set it up as a joint tenancy with right of survivorship. If Dick sets up this account as a tenancy in common with brother Don and then deposits postmarital earnings in the account, his wife Jane now has an interest in the account. She does not lose her community property interest in these earnings just because they were deposited in an account which does not bear her name as a co-owner.

A multiple-party account may be set up so that no funds may be withdrawn except upon the signatures of all co-owners. Such arrangements are rather rare, however; usually each co-owner has the right, as an individual, to make withdrawals. The right of a co-owner to make withdrawals is not necessarily related to the extent of his contributions. However, if a co-owner withdraws more than he contributes, and his co-owners object, he may be forced to make restitution.

Unless otherwise arranged, co-owners of a multiple-party account do not own equal shares in it: ownership is determined by individual deposits and withdrawals. In other words, the equity of a co-owner in the account is normally measured by his deposits less his withdrawals. If his withdrawals exceed his deposits he has no equity at all; he owes a debt to the other co-owners. The ownership interest of each co-owner may be determined precisely from the bank records of deposits and withdrawals. It is assumed that all deposits made by a co-owner are deposits of his money, and all withdrawals made from the account are made for the use of the withdrawing party. In case of disputes about ownership, these assumptions about the nature of deposits and withdrawals may be overturned by appropriate evidence.

Questions of proportionate ownership generally arise upon the death of one of the co-owners. Thus: Black and White are co-owners of a nonbusiness savings account. Black dies. The balance in the account is $2,700. How much of this belongs to White, and how much to Black's heirs?

The record of deposits and withdrawals shows that Black made deposits of $4,900 to the account, and withdrawals of $3,700 from it. White has made deposits of $3,000 to it and withdrawals of $1,500 from it. Black's deposits exceed withdrawals by $1,200, while White's deposits exceed withdrawals by $1,500. Therefore, $1,200 is part of Black's estate, while $1,500 belongs to White. (In real life the arithmetic here would be complicated by allocating accrued and paid interest to the co-owners.) If the account had been set up as a joint tenancy with right of survivorship, the account balance would of course belong to White as survivor.

If there are three or more co-owners and there is no joint tenancy with right of survivorship, the above rules of determining ownership apply. When there is a joint tenancy with right of survivorship, a unique rule for determining ownership is applied by Texas Probate Code 439. Assume that Black, Gray, and White own a savings account as joint tenants with right of survivorship. At Gray's death the account contains $6,600. According to the reckoning of deposits less withdrawals, Black's equity in the account is $3,300, Gray's is $2,200, and White's is $1,100. The statute provides that the interest of the deceased is divided equally between the surviving co-owners, even if the prior interests of the co-owners are not equal. Thus, Black's equity in the account becomes $4,400 ($3,300 + $1,100), and White's becomes $2,200 ($1,100 + $1,100).

It is also possible to set up a multiple party account on a "P.O.D." basis (the initials stand for "Payable on death"). Thus, Redd could set up an account of which he is sole owner as long as he lives, but on his death the balance could be payable to Pink. Redd and Pink could set up an account of which they are joint tenants with right of survivorship, and provide that upon the death of the last survivor the account is payable to Green.

Essentially, the P.O.D. account is a nontestamentary way of disposing of property upon one's death. A P.O.D. payee of an account becomes the owner of it on the death of the last living owner. The balance in the account is not subject to administration as part of the deceased's estate unless the deceased died insolvent. If sums in the account are needed to pay off the liabilities of the deceased, the creditors take precedence over the P.O.D. payee, as per Section 442 of the Probate Code.

Multi-party accounts may also be set up as trusts. Blue may thus set up a savings account, "Blue in trust for Orange." Blue is trustee of the account while Orange is beneficiary. Unless it is otherwise agreed, this would be a revocable trust; Blue would have the free use of the funds in the account while he lives. Upon his death Orange would become owner as beneficiary.

If Blue set this up in the form of an irrevocable trust, however, Blue would deprive himself of the right to use the funds in this account for his benefit during his lifetime. He would still have the right to make withdrawals, but the withdrawn funds would have to be used for the benefit of Orange.

It must be emphasized that co-owners of multi-party accounts may by contract vary the rules for determining ownership. Remember also that the new statute does not change any prior rules of law with respect to ownership of community property. One should be very careful about depositing community funds in a multi-party account of which one of the co-owners is not a co-owner of the community property.

24

Suretyship and Guaranty

The law of suretyship and guaranty involves the promise of one person to be responsible for the obligation of another. The obligation involved is usually a contractual obligation, but it can also be a tort obligation. There are three parties involved in a suretyship or guaranty relationship.
1. The principal, the debtor who truly owes the debt.
2. The surety or guarantor, the party promising to be liable upon the principal's debt.
3. The creditor, the person to whom the debt is owing.

Obligation of sureties and guarantors. We loosely speak of both sureties and guarantors as sureties. In many contexts in this chapter the terms "surety" refers also to guarantors. However, a basic difference does exist between the obligation of a surety and the obligation of a guarantor, and there are also two distinct types of guaranty.

The promise of a surety essentially is, "I'll pay the principal's debt." The surety is assuming the same liability upon the debt as the principal debtor. His liability is primary, and comes into being upon the due date of the principal's obligation.

The first type of guarantor is the guarantor of payment. His promise essentially is, "I'll pay the principal's debt if the principal doesn't." His liability is secondary, and comes into being when the principal defaults. The second type of guarantor is the guarantor of collection. His promise essentially is, "I will pay the principal's debt if you cannot collect from the principal." His liability is also secondary, but it does not normally come into being until the creditor has sued the debtor, gotten a judgment against him, and been unable to collect it. His liability can come into being earlier, however, if it is obvious that the creditor cannot collect from the principal.

With respect to the extent of obligation, there are several types of guaranties, all of which may be guaranties of payment or guaranties of collection. There is the general guaranty, in which the guarantor promises, "I will pay for all goods which the principal buys from you and does not pay for." This guaranty of payment is limited neither in amount nor in time. There is the guaranty limited in time but not in amount, e.g., "I promise to pay for all goods which the principal buys from you during the month of June 1980 and does not pay for." Then there is the guaranty limited in amount but not in time, e.g., "I promise to pay for up to $10,000 worth of goods which the principal buys from you and does not pay for." Of course, the guarantor's maximum liability here is

$10,000. A guaranty may be limited in both time and amount, e.g., "I promise to pay for up to $10,000 worth of the goods which the principal buys from you during the month of June 1980."

All of these types of contracts of suretyship and guaranty must be distinguished from contracts of indemnity. An indemnitor essentially promises, "If you will guarantee to pay for all goods which White will buy from Black and will not pay for, I will guarantee that you will not suffer any loss due to your promise." The indemnitor is not promising to pay someone else's debt; he is merely promising to protect someone against suffering a specified potential loss. Thus, the law of suretyship and guaranty does not apply to such a promise.

Consideration in contracts of suretyship and guaranty. A surety (or guarantor) must receive consideration in order for his promise to be binding. The form of the consideration will depend on whether the surety's obligation is part of the principal-creditor contract—that is, whether the bargain is three-way or whether the surety's obligation is contained in a separate contract. Many suretyship obligations are created in three-way contracts involving surety, principal, and creditor. Some are created in subsequent two-way bargains between surety and creditor. Sometimes the principal knows of the subsequent suretyship bargain and sometimes he does not. A few such obligations are created in two-way bargains between surety and debtor.

If the surety's (or guarantor's) obligation is created by the same contract as the principal's, the surety need not receive separate consideration in order to be bound. His consideration is simply that the creditor sold goods to the principal on credit, or that the creditor lent the principal money. If the surety's (or guarantor's) obligation is created in a separate contract, the surety must receive separate consideration. If he got no consideration, he is not bound by his promise.

The need for written contracts of suretyship, guaranty, and indemnity. Since contracts of suretyship and guaranty are contracts to pay the debt of another, they are governed by the statute of frauds provision, with a few variations.

A contract of suretyship must be in writing if the creditor knows that he is dealing with a surety. When two or more persons are actually benefitting from the contract of the creditor, no suretyship relation is involved; all parties dealing with the creditor are co-principals. Contracts involving joint debtors need not be in writing; the creditor who believes that he is dealing with two joint debtors (though there is actually only one debtor and a surety) may make a binding oral contract with both parties if he does not know that one of them is a surety. If the creditor does know that one of the parties is a surety, he must get that person's written promise to pay; otherwise the surety is not bound.

A contract of guaranty need not be in writing if:
1. The bargain is three-way, and the guarantor is involved primarily to benefit himself, or
2. The bargain is a creditor-guarantor bargain, which guarantor has made primarily to benefit himself, or
3. The bargain is a debtor-guarantor bargain, no matter why the guarantor made it.

On the other hand, a contract of guaranty must be in writing if the bargain is a guarantor-creditor bargain and the guarantor is making it mainly to benefit the principal debtor. A contract of indemnity need not be in writing, since it is not a contract to pay the debt of another.

Offer and acceptance. The general rules of offer and acceptance apply with respect to contracts of suretyship and guaranty, with one general exception. Suppose Green writes Redd, "I promise to pay you for up to $1,000 worth of the goods you sell to Pink during the month of June 1980, if Pink does not pay. /s/ Green." This is, of course, an offer to act as Pink's guarantor. May Redd accept the offer simply by selling goods to Pink during June 1980, or must he inform Green that he is accepting? The Texas view is that no notice of acceptance is necessary here. Redd may accept by selling goods to Pink during the month of June 1980.

Defenses of the surety. If the creditor seeks to enforce the obligation of the surety (or guarantor) after the principal has refused to perform, the surety may escape liability if he has a proper defense. In general, if the principal debtor has a defense to liability if the creditor sues him, the surety may also use that defense. Thus, if the creditor has breached the principal-creditor contract, the surety is discharged (unless the breach is of a minor nature and the principal has notified the creditor that the contract is still in full force and effect). Or, if the principal has been a victim of fraud, duress, undue influence, or mutual mistake, the surety has a defense. If the creditor has materially altered the principal-creditor contract, this is also a defense for surety. Finally, if the principal-creditor contract has been discharged by operation of law, the surety has a defense.

However, if the principal is a minor or a person of limited contractual capacity and he chooses to disaffirm his obligation to the creditor, the surety is still liable. If the principal is discharged from his obligation in bankruptcy, the surety is still liable. If the statute of limitations has run out on the principal's obligations, the surety may also still be liable.

If the original bargain was three-way, one statute of limitations applies to it. If time has run out on the principal's obligation, it has run out on the surety's also. If there are two separate bargains—the principal's and the surety's—a separate statute of limitations will be applicable to each. Thus, if there are two separate bargains, the expiration of the principal's statute of limitations will not be a defense to the surety.

The surety is entitled to a defense of his own, for example, if the surety is a minor or a person of limited contractual capacity, he may disaffirm his obligation. If the surety obtains a discharge in bankruptcy from his debts, his suretyship obligations are discharged. The surety's obligation might also be discharged by operation of law. If the surety has been defrauded into entering the contract he may use this as a defense to liability, under certain circumstances, depending on who defrauded him and the nature of the claimed fraud.

If the bargain is three-way and the principal defrauds both creditor and surety, the surety has a defense. If the suretyship bargain is a principal-surety one and the principal has defrauded the surety, the surety is still liable to the creditor, unless the creditor knows of the principal's fraud. If the suretyship bargain is a creditor-surety one and the creditor defrauds the surety, the surety will usually have a defense. In negotiation of a creditor-surety contract, though, the creditor is not required to provide any information as to the principal's solvency unless the surety inquires, in which case the creditor must tell the truth as he knows it; if the surety does not inquire, the creditor may remain silent. (The surety would be very remiss not to ask, of course.) If the creditor knows that the principal is a minor or other person of limited contractual capacity, and that the surety is ignorant of the fact, he must disclose this information. However, if the surety appears to be aware of such information, the creditor need not say anything. If the principal has defrauded the creditor and the creditor is aware of it, he must disclose this information to the surety, and the surety of course will immediately refuse to become bound as surety.

Under most circumstances, the creditor is not bound to disclose material facts about the principal which he learns after the surety has become bound. Thus, if when creditor and surety are negotiating the contract, the principal has defrauded the creditor but the latter is unaware of the fraud, the principal can hardly disclose this to the surety. If the creditor finds out about the fraud after the surety is bound, he need not disclose it—and the surety may not use it as a defense to escape liability to the creditor. There are, however, two circumstances under which the creditor must keep the surety informed as to material facts he learns about the principal. One is the case where the employer has taken out a fidelity bond on an employee. Any dishonesty on the part of a bonded employee must be reported to the bonding company at once. The other occurs when a continuing guaranty exists such as: "I promise to pay you for all goods you sell to Brown if Brown does not pay. /s/ Black." Black has committed himself to an open-ended obligation here. So long as Brown continues to buy goods from the creditor, Black will be obligated as guarantor of payment. So the creditor must keep Black informed as to how well Brown is performing his obligation.

The surety of course has the right to set off claims he has against the creditor upon whatever obligation he might have to him. Thus: Blue owes Redd $1,000, and Green is Blue's surety. Blue defaults, so Redd demands $1,000 of Green. At the time of the demand, Redd owes Green $500 on an overdue loan. Green may pay Redd $500 and clear the obligation.

The surety may not use a claim which the principal has against the creditor as a set-off unless the principal consents. Thus: Blue owes Redd $1,000, and Green is his surety. At the time the debt matures, Redd owes Blue $500 on an overdue loan, but Blue defaults upon the larger obligation. Redd demands $1,000 of Green. Green wants to pay only $500, but that sum is insufficient without Blue's permission. It will be to Blue's advantage to give permission, however, since if Green must pay the entire $1,000, Green will then have a claim against Blue for $1,000.

Discharge of the surety. There are five different acts of the creditor which may result in a discharge of the surety's obligation. First, if the surety tenders payment of the principal's obligation after it has matured, and the creditor refuses the tender, the surety is discharged. Thus: White owes Black $1,000, due March 15, and Gray is White's surety. Gray contacts Black on March 16 to ask if White has paid, and Black says he has not, so Gray offers to pay. Black says, "No, you keep your money. I am going to collect from White if I can." Black's refusal to take Gray's money discharges Gray.

In the second case, if the creditor releases the principal debtor from his obligation to pay, he releases the surety. The only way the creditor may release the principal without releasing the surety is to reserve his rights against the surety or to get the surety to agree to the release of the principal. If the surety agrees to the release, he remains liable while the principal is discharged. If the creditor releases the principal and reserves his rights against the surety, the principal is not really released. The creditor cannot now force the principal to pay, but after the creditor has collected from the surety the surety is entitled to reimbursement from the principal. So the principal ends up paying after all; but a release of the principal without the surety's consent and without reservation of rights against the surety releases the surety also.

The third situation occurs when the creditor and the principal modify their contract in a way that increases the surety's risk, such as by extending the maturity date of the principal's obligation. The principal will be liable on this modified contract, but the surety will be discharged. The only way to avoid this would be by getting the surety's consent to the modification, or by the creditor's reserving his rights against the surety.

The fourth case arises if the creditor received collateral from the principal when the original contract was made, and he releases this collateral to the principal before the principal's obligation was performed, without consent of the surety and without reservation of rights against him. In this situation, the surety's obligation is discharged up to the value of the released collateral, resulting in either a total or partial discharge of the surety. Suppose Spade borrowed $5,000 from Clubb. Hart agreed to be Spade's surety here, and Spade also gave Clubb a first lien upon his 1975 Cadillac. At a time when Spade has paid Clubb $2,000 back on the loan, he acquired a chance to sell the Cadillac if he could sell a clear title to it, so he asked Clubb to release his lien upon the car, which Clubb did, without consulting Hart. Spade sold the car for $5,000 cash and skipped town. Clubb then demanded $3,000 from Hart; but Hart owes nothing. If the value of the car was $5,000, the value of the collateral exceeded the amount of the obligation, and the release of the collateral was a total discharge. Had the car been sold for $1,000 in this situation, and had that been its fair value, Clubb could recover $2,000 from Hart. Hart was discharged to the extent of the value of the released collateral only—$1,000.

Finally, when the creditor releases a co-surety without the consent of the others, the remaining co-sureties are partially discharged. So if Ace owes King $1,000, Deuce and Trey are his co-sureties, and King releases Trey from liability as a co-surety without Deuce's consent, the result is a partial discharge of Deuce's obligation. If Ace does not pay at maturity, so that King demands payment from Deuce, Deuce will normally be liable for only $500—that is, Deuce will only be liable for his portion of the obligation. If, however, Trey had been discharged from all of his debts in bankruptcy by that time, Deuce would be liable for the whole $1,000, on the theory that King would have been unable to collect anything from Trey, discharge or no discharge.

Surety's remedies—exoneration. In case the principal does not perform as he agreed, the surety has five remedies at his disposal. The first of these is exoneration: the surety's right to force the principal to perform as promised.

A surety exercises the right of exoneration by filing suit against the principal, thereby seeking a court order directing him to perform. The surety's right to exoneration comes into being only when the creditor acquires an enforceable right against him. For example, Spade borrows $1,000 from Clubb, due on March 15, Hart being Spade's surety, and Spade and Clubb agree to extend the due date of the loan to June 15. Hart objects to this, but Clubb reserves his rights against him. Hart wants to make Spade pay on March 15, as originally agreed, but since Clubb cannot make Spade pay, he cannot make Hart pay either. Since Clubb has no right to make Hart pay, Hart therefore has no right to make Spade pay. Hart must wait until June 15 and hope that Spade pays then. If he does not, Hart may then use his remedy of exoneration.

Surety's remedies—reimbursement. The surety has the right to recover from the principal debtor all outlays which reduced the principal's obligation to the creditor. In addition, if the surety was bound with the approval of the principal, he may claim reimbursement for all expenses incurred in trying to reduce his own and the principal's liability. The surety need not pay the principal's debt in full to become eligible for reimbursement. A partial payment of the obligation entitles him to reimbursement. However, the surety's claim for reimbursement does not mature until the creditor's claim against the principal matures. If the surety pays off the principal's debt early, he cannot claim reimbursement until the original maturity date of the debt.

If the principal has a defense to payment of his obligation to the creditor, he may use that defense in order to avoid reimbursing the surety. Of course, most such defenses may also be used to avoid paying the creditor. If the surety does not use the defense, it is his loss. If the creditor charges the principal usurious interest upon a loan, the surety may use the usury as a defense to paying all or part of the loan, depending on the extent of the usury. If the surety pays the loan and the usurious interest, he will not be able to obtain total reimbursement from the principal; the principal need pay him only what he would have had to pay the creditor. If the principal has a defense to liability which the surety cannot use (such as the principal's discharge from the obligation in bankruptcy), the principal need not pay the creditor, but the surety must. If the surety pays, he has no right of reimbursement. If the debt is discharged, the discharge stands, no matter who is demanding payment.

If the surety was contracted at the request of the principal, the principal must disclose to him any defenses to liability which he has. If he fails to do this and the surety pays the debt, the principal cannot use the undisclosed defense to escape reimbursing him. But, if the surety was contracted at the request of the creditor, the principal owes the surety no duty to disclose defenses, and in that case the surety must find them out for himself.

When the surety pays a part of the principal's debt in exchange for being discharged from liability for the remainder, the surety is of course discharged. The discharge of the surety does not discharge the principal, unless the creditor agrees to discharge the entire obligation, not just the surety. Whether the principal is discharged by the agreement or not, the surety is entitled to reimbursement for what he paid. When the creditor sues the surety, and the surety incurs legal fees in an effort to assert a defense to liability that would also reduce the principal's ultimate liability, the surety may or may not be entitled to reimbursement for these expenses. If the surety was contracted with the principal's consent, he is entitled to reimbursement; otherwise, he is not.

A surety may never recover more from the principal by way of reimbursement than he actually paid out. In no way may a surety use the remedy of reimbursement to profit at the principal's expense.

Surety's remedies—subrogation. When a surety pays the principal's obligation in full, so that the obligation is discharged, he thereby acquires a package of legal rights against the principal and other parties. The surety acquires:

1. The creditor's legal rights against the principal.
2. The creditor's rights to any collateral put up by the principal to secure payment of the obligation.
3. The creditor's legal rights against third parties also liable to the creditor upon the principal's obligation.
4. The creditor's rights against co-sureties and any collateral they may hold.

If the creditor has a judgment against the principal at the time that the surety pays for the amount of the obligation, the surety acquires the creditor's rights under the judgment. If the creditor holds collateral put up by the principal at the time that the surety pays the principal's debt in full, the creditor must give up the collateral to the surety.

If Spade and Clubb borrowed $1,000 from Hart; Diamond was Clubb's surety upon this obligation but not Spade's; and Diamond pays off Hart in full, Diamond acquires Hart's rights against Spade, even though Diamond is not Spade's surety. If Deuce borrowed $1,000 from Ace; Trey and King agreed to be his co-sureties; Deuce gave King collateral as assurance that he would pay Ace; and Trey ends up paying Ace the $1,000, Trey thereby acquires Ace's rights against King and any collateral held by King.

It must be remembered that the surety has no right of subrogation unless he pays off the principal's obligation in full.

Sureties will not usually acquire subrogation rights in judgments. When the creditor sues the principal to collect his claim, the surety must be joined in the suit as a defendant, so that if the creditor wins his suit, he gets a judgment against both principal and surety.

It sometimes happens that the creditor sues the principal and it is impossible to join the surety in the suit at that time because, for example, he is in Europe. The creditor prevails and obtains a judgment against the principal, but has trouble collecting, and has collected nothing when the surety returns from Europe. The creditor then informs the surety of what has happened.

The surety should be advised that the creditor's judgment is not good against him under these circumstances, but that the creditor might nevertheless file suit and obtain a judgment against him. The creditor is sure to do just that if he cannot collect from the principal. So, the surety pays off the judgment in full. This does not discharge the judgment; under the provisions of TB&CC 34.04, the surety is now subrogated to all of the creditor's rights under the judgment. He has the right to use all weapons available to judgment creditors against the principal. If creditor has obtained a judgment against the principal and, say, three co-sureties, and one of the co-sureties pays off the judgment, it is similarly not discharged. Under TB&CC 34.04, the paying surety is now subrogated to all of creditor's rights against both the principal and the other two co-sureties. Such judgments, then, will not be finally discharged until they are paid off by the principal himself.

Surety's remedies—contribution. If there are co-sureties upon the principal's debt, the creditor generally may collect the entire amount of the debt from one of the co-sureties. The co-sureties are liable among themselves, as co-debtors are liable among themselves. If there are two co-sureties, each is liable to the others for half of the debt; if there are four co-sureties each is liable to the others for one quarter of the debt, and so forth. A co-surety may enforce his right of contribution against other co-sureties if he pays more than his share of the obligation.

The amount recoverable as contribution is influenced by several factors. The contracts of the co-sureties may provide that they are not liable among themselves for an equal share of the principal's debt, though equality of obligation prevails unless a contract provides otherwise. A co-surety may use a defense available to him against the creditor as a defense against contribution. Thus: Spade owes Clubb $1,000 and Diamond and Hart are Spade's co-sureties. The loan was made for an illegal purpose; all parties know this. In spite of this knowledge, Hart paid Clubb the $1,000. Spade has no assets, so Hart demands $500 of Diamond. Diamond need not pay, because Hart did not have to pay.

If there are more than two co-sureties, and at the time one or more of them is insolvent or beyond the jurisdiction of a court, the remaining co-sureties may be held liable for his share by way of contribution. Thus: Uno has borrowed $100,000 from Dos. Tres, Cuatro, Cinco, Seis, and Siete are co-sureties for Uno. When the loan matures, Uno has been discharged from his debts in bankruptcy. Siete then pays Dos the $100,000, and looks to the co-sureties for contribution. At this time Cuatro is somewhere in Mexico; his exact whereabouts are unknown. Siete therefore demands $25,000 each of Tres, Cinco, and Seis. They claim they should only pay $20,000, since it is not their fault that Cuatro cannot be sued at the moment. It might not be their fault, but it is their problem. Since Cuatro is not present to pay his $20,000, the other co-sureties must pay for him. When and if he returns, contribution may then be enforced against him.

Other factors may influence the liability of co-sureties among themselves for contribution. The subject can become quite complex.

Surety's remedies—the right to demand that creditor sue principal. In about half of the fifty states, as soon as he learns of the principal's default upon his obligation to the creditor a surety may demand of a creditor that the creditor file suit against the principal as soon as possible in order to force him to pay. In those states which allow this, failure by the creditor to follow this instruction will discharge the surety's obligation.

TB&CC 34.02 provides that a surety has this right in Texas. He must, however, put his request into writing. The request will not cause a discharge under any circumstances if the creditor is under a legal disability (such as having a guardian). It can cause discharge if the creditor does not file suit soon, or if, having filed suit, he does not press the suit to a conclusion. In those states which do not recognize this remedy, the surety's only recourse in case of a default by the principal is the exercise of his right of exoneration.

Necessity for giving notice of default by creditor. If the principal does not perform at the time he is obligated to, the creditor need not give notice of default to a true surety. Since the surety is as liable upon the obligation as the principal is, the principal's default does not affect his obligation.

A guarantor is entitled to a notice of default, however. Since a guarantor of payment is liable only upon the principal's default, he is entitled to know that his liability will be asserted. The guarantor of collection, though not yet liable upon the principal's default, is entitled to know of it so that he may take steps to protect himself.

Effect of nonaction by creditor in collecting from principal. A surety or a guarantor of payment will not be discharged by a creditor's lack of action to collect from a defaulting debtor. If neither creditor nor surety takes action after the default, and the principal gets discharged in bankruptcy a year after the obligation matured, the creditor may still collect from the surety. To be sure, the creditor was negligent for not pursuing the principal, but the surety was just as negligent: he could have exercised his remedies of exoneration or demand that creditor sue principal. Thus, a surety or guarantor of payment must take affirmative action to protect himself if the creditor refuses to act.

The position of the guarantor of collection is different. He is not liable upon his guaranty just because the principal has defaulted, so he has no right of exoneration. He does have his right to demand that creditor sue, as provided by TB&CC 34.02, and he would be wise to use that right. If he does not use it, and collection from the principal becomes impossible due to the creditor's negligence in not trying to collect when he could, the guarantor of collection will not be discharged.

Litigations and judgments on contracts involving sureties and guarantors. In any litigation involving obligations in which there are sureties and guarantors of payment, the sureties and guarantors are essential parties to the litigation. If the creditor seeks to sue the surety alone, the surety has the right to join the creditor as a party to the suit, or to demand that the complaint be dismissed. Also, should the creditor sue the principal alone, the surety or guarantor must be joined as a party to the suit. The only circumstances in which all parties will not be brought before the court at one time is the situation where one of the essential parties is beyond the jurisdiction of the court—that is, his location is unknown, or he is outside the state of Texas. Should there be co-sureties, all of them must be brought before the court.

When a judgment is rendered in the matter it will be binding upon all the parties involved, and repetitious litigation will be avoided. If both the principal and the surety are parties to the case, and the creditor prevails, he of course has a judgment against both parties. In collection of such a judgment, however, TB&CC 34.03 requires that the sheriff must make every effort to collect by levying execution upon the principal's property first; recourse against the surety's property should be had only if insufficient property belonging to the principal can be found to satisfy the judgment.

If it is impossible to join all parties to the contract in one proceeding, problems may arise as to the effect of a judgment in one case upon the prosecution of another. For instance, Creditor sues Surety to collect upon an obligation after Principal has defaulted. Principal was out of state and could not be joined. Surety raised the defense that the entire bargain was illegal. This argument prevailed, and Surety obtained a summary judgment in his favor. Later Principal returned and Creditor sought to sue him upon this obligation. Principal claimed the contract action should be dismissed. It will be, because the determination in the first trial that the bargain was illegal cannot be questioned in other litigation.

On the other hand, if the trial resulted in victory for the creditor because the contract was legal, the surety would of course have to pay the judgment. When the principal returned later, the surety could then demand reimbursement from him—and, if he refused to pay, sue to collect reimbursement. If the principal alleged as a defense that the creditor had defrauded him in the making of the contract, though, the principal would get a hearing upon that defense. If the jury believed him, the result would be a judgment for the principal, and the surety would be stuck.

Suppose that Creditor sues Principal upon an overdue obligation upon which Principal has a surety, but the surety is beyond the jurisdiction of the court at the time of trial. Principal's defense is that Creditor breached their contract by selling him defective goods. The jury does not believe this, and Creditor gets a judgment for the amount of his claim. Before the judgment is paid, the surety returns, so Creditor files suit against him. The surety raises exactly the same defense that Principal did. Creditor can probably have this defense dismissed without a trial because the question of the defectiveness of the goods has already been litigated and is now settled. The surety must come up with another defense if he is to escape liability.

Of course, a judgment obtained by a creditor in a suit against a principal alone does not bind the surety. The existence of such a judgment will give the creditor no right to have garnishment levied upon the surety's bank account or other assets. The creditor must obtain a judgment against the surety himself before forcible collection action against the surety's property will be justified.

Fidelity bonds. Anyone who hires an employee to perform the sensitive work of handling his funds—managing his store, selling goods and collecting payment for them, managing his apartment building and collecting rent from tenants, etc.—may well want this employee to be bonded. He will accomplish this by obtaining a fidelity bond upon the employee from a bonding company. If the bonding company issues the bond, it becomes a surety for the employee's honesty. If the employer suffers a loss due to the employee's dishonesty, the bonding company will make it good.

The bonding company will not issue a fidelity bond before it finds out some facts about the background of the employee. It obtains leads for learning this information by having the employee fill out a detailed application form and having company investigators verify the information so provided. If the employee answers some of the questions on the form falsely, with intent to conceal derogatory information about himself, fraud has been committed. If the company issues a bond in reliance upon the truth of the information contained in the form and it later learns of the falsity of some of that information, it may revoke the bond. If it waits too long after learning of the fraud to cancel the bond, though, it may be held to have waived its right to do so.

As mentioned earlier, the employer is under a duty to inform the bonding company of any act of dishonesty committed by the employee. If the employer does not live up to this duty, the bonding company will have grounds for refusing to pay a claim against it under the bond. Thus: Boss hires Workman to be his store manager, and bonds him with Ace Bonding Company. Workman embezzles $500 from Boss, and Boss finds out. Workman has a tear-jerking sob story to justify his evil act, so Boss says nothing to anyone about it, and Workman pays back the $500. Three years later, Workman steals $20,000 from Boss and flees. Boss files a claim with Ace. Ace learns of the prior unreported embezzlement and refuses to pay the claim, which is within its rights. Boss will not collect his $20,000, and he might have trouble bonding other employees.

Fidelity bonds do not cover losses caused to employers by the negligence of the bonded employees. Insurance may be obtained against some types of employee negligence, but this is an insurance matter and not related to bonding.

Construction bonds. Anyone who hires a general contractor to perform work upon a structure runs some risk that the contractor might become insolvent before the job is complete, or that he will fail to complete the job for some other reason. This sort of failure by the contractor subjects the owner of the structure to two appreciable perils. First, if the contractor quits before the job is finished, there is no way the owner can make him finish. The owner must hire another contractor to finish, which might be difficult and expensive. Second, if the contractor quits without paying off subcontractors, laborers, and materialmen (suppliers of building material), these may file mechanic's liens against the owner's property. Any person who performs work upon a structure or contributes materials to the structure may file such a lien if he is not paid, and he may have the property sold at auction to collect his claim.

Contractors are bonded by owners as a means of protection against these perils. Two types of bond are required to assure full protection. To obtain protection against the contractor walking off and leaving the job half done, a performance bond is necessary. The bonding company stands surety for the contractor's performance of the contract, and if the contractor will not finish the job, the bonding company sees to it that it gets finished.

To obtain protection against the mechanic's liens of unpaid subcontractors, laborers, and materialmen, the payment bond is needed. The bonding company here stands surety for the general contractor's obligation to pay all of these people, and the company pays if the contractor does not.

PART V

Commercial Paper

PART V

Commercial Paper

25

Money and the Law

Types, Negotiability, Interpretation, and Transfer of Commercial Paper

Money and the Law

Commercial paper is, in a sense, used as a substitute for money in the business world. Items of commercial paper possess some, but not all, of the attributes of money. Commercial paper is a hybrid of money and contract right. How the law of commercial paper differs from the law of contracts and contract rights may perhaps be best understood if we begin with a discussion of the law of money.

What is money? Two sorts of money circulate in most nations of the world: coins and paper money. Of these two types, coins are by far the older. Originally, coins were made of precious metal, and had value according to the intrinsic worth of the metal itself. For most of history since the invention of coinage, only government authority could operate a mint for the creation of coinage, making it a governmental monopoly. During the twentieth century the nature of coinage has changed. The demonetization of gold during the Depression era and the rise in the price of precious metals since 1950 have caused governments to stop making coins from precious metals. The intrinsic value of the metal from which today's coins are made is considerably less than the face value of the coins; instead, coins today are valuable only because the government decrees that they are money.

Paper money has been used in large quantities only during the last two centuries or so; the development of banking on a large scale was required before use of paper money in large quantities became practicable. Paper money was originally a sort of warehouse receipt issued by a bank for precious metal on deposit in the bank. Though paper has no intrinsic value, such receipts had value because they were redeemable in something valuable—precious metal.

Until the twentieth century, many banks had the power to issue bank notes, which were redeemable in precious metal. However, state-chartered banks had this right taxed to death by a prohibitive federal tax in 1865, and national banks other than the federal reserve banks lost this right during the twentieth century. Today, federal reserve notes are printed by the U.S. Treasury, though they are issued by federal reserve banks. They are no longer redeemable in anything; again, they are money because the government decrees them to be money.

Only the coins struck by United States mints and paper money printed by the U.S. Treasury are lawful money in the United States today. Checks and other forms of commercial paper, though in some sense the equivalent of money, are not money. These coins and bills are also the only legal tender in the United States. The concept of legal tender is of importance for this reason: a party obligated under a contract must pay his obligation in legal tender unless his contract permits him to pay in another medium, or unless his creditor accepts payment in another medium. Tender of payment in a medium other than legal tender may be refused.

If a debtor tenders payment in legal tender and the creditor refuses to accept it, certain legal consequences may follow. If the debt is owed only by the one debtor, tender of payment which is refused will not extinguish the debt. If the tender is made before maturity of an interest-bearing debt, the creditor's refusal to accept tender will not even stop interest from accruing. If tender of payment of an interest-bearing debt is made after maturity, however, refusal of the tender will stop further accrual of interest. If a surety or guarantor tenders payment in legal tender after maturity and the creditor refuses the tender, the surety or guarantor is discharged if the creditor cannot collect later from the principal. If a joint debtor tenders payment in legal tender, refusal of the tender by the creditor will discharge him.

All national governments, of course, issue money. Such money is legal tender in the nation of issue, but it is not legal tender in the United States. The Mexican debtor who tenders payment of his obligation to his American creditor in Mexican pesos is not tendering payment in legal tender, unless he tenders payment in Mexico. Though foreign money is truly money in the nation of issue—and though its value in the nation of issue does not change—its value in terms of U.S. dollars may not be stable. Until the early 1970s a system of fixed exchange rates reigned in the world of international finance: the value of one national currency in terms of another was fixed by international agreement. Major changes could come about only through devaluation or revaluation by individual governments. Since the collapse of the fixed-rate system, however, the floating-rate system prevails. The value of one currency in terms of another is now determined by market forces: the law of supply and demand prevails. As a result, foreign exchange rates are much more unstable and, to a degree, more unpredictable than before.

It is perfectly legal for parties to a contract to agree upon a price payable in foreign currency. If the agreed price is in Mexican pesos and is payable in Mexico, the buyer must actually pay in Mexican pesos. If the price is in Mexican pesos but is payable in the United States, the price is payable in the U.S. dollar equivalent of the specified number of Mexican pesos as of the date of payment of the debt, unless the contract provides otherwise. (The contract could provide its own exchange rate, or it could require payment in Mexican pesos even if the debt is payable in the United States, or it could provide some other mutually satisfactory arrangement.)

Negotiability of money. Money is the most negotiable medium of payment. So long as the creditor gives consideration for the cash he receives in payment of an obligation, he does not need to be concerned with where the debtor obtained his cash. If the creditor obtains the cash for consideration in good faith, without knowledge as to wrongdoing by the debtor in obtaining it, it is his. It does not matter if the cash was obtained from proceeds of a bank robbery committed by the debtor an hour before payment, if the debtor found it on the street fifteen minutes before payment, or if the debtor swindled it away from Sam Sucker the morning of the day of payment. The creditor becomes the owner of cash he accepts for consideration in good faith.

Since this is true, the possessor of cash must treat it with great care. Once the owner of cash loses possession of it, it will almost inevitably end up in the hands of someone who acquires it for consideration in good faith, and without knowledge of its history. If I lose a $100 bill on the street, and Gus Gluck finds it, takes it to the local Safeway store, and buys groceries with it, I cannot recover the bill from Safeway. If I know that Gus Gluck found my lost bill, and I confront him and demand that he return it to me, theoretically I could force him to give it up. My problem is that I must be able to prove that he found my bill. Without witnesses, proof of that will be virtually impossible. If he denies finding a $100 bill, it is my word against his, and my story will not be particularly plausible. I have the same problem if Sal Slink picks my pocket and filches my wallet and its contents. Once Sal spends my money, it is lost and gone forever. If he is caught before he spends it, I might be able to recover it, if I can prove he is the one who picked my pocket or if he admits picking my pocket.

If I lose cash or have it stolen from me, and I do not know the identity of the finder or the thief, my cash is truly gone. As the courts are fond of saying, money has no earmarks. Normally, coins are totally unidentifiable. Bills are identifiable by the serial numbers, but almost no one keeps a record of the serial numbers of the bills in his billfold, and without such a record bills are also unidentifiable. Even if I did keep a record of the serial numbers of the bills in my billfold, the record would be of limited value in case my cash were lost or stolen. It would enable me to recover the cash from the finder or thief if he were caught with my bills in his possession; but once the bills were spent by the finder or thief, the new possessor would be the owner if he took the bills for consideration in good faith. This is true even if I could identify my former bills in this third party's possession.

Counterfeit money. Counterfeit money is essentially money manufactured by someone other than the U.S. Treasury. Such paper is not money, though it appears to be money. (We say "paper" because counterfeit coins are very rare; their value is so small that they are not worth the trouble of counterfeiting. The counterfeiting of bills, on the other hand, can be quite profitable.)

If my creditor pays me a debt in counterfeit money, he has not given me genuine money, so in truth he has not paid the debt. This may not cause a problem if I use the counterfeit bills to pay a debt I owe my creditor and he takes them, so long as he passes them on to someone else. However, if Debtor pays his $100 debt to me with a $100 bill, I take it to the bank to deposit it in my checking account, and the teller refuses to accept it because it is counterfeit, I now have a problem. The teller will confiscate the bill, and I have lost $100. My recourse is to demand that Debtor pay me another $100. If Debtor accepts my sad tale and pays me again, I have suffered no damage. However, if Debtor says to me, "So, you got a counterfeit $100 bill. But how do you know the bill I gave you was the counterfeit?" I now have an extreme difficulty. How do I prove Debtor gave me the counterfeit? If I can prove it to the satisfaction of a court or jury I can get my $100 back; if I cannot, it is my loss. If I use Debtor's counterfeit $100 bill to pay a debt I owe Creditor, and Creditor learns that it was counterfeit, he of course may demand that I pay my debt again. If I pay him, I may then demand that Debtor pay me again. Of course, the success of these demands again depends on my being able to prove the source of the counterfeit bill. The larger the bill, the easier this is to prove; the smaller the bill, the harder it is to prove.

Another sticky problem may arise in the following manner: One of Sam Shopkeeper's customers buys $100 worth of goods from him one morning and pays with five $20 bills. Sam takes one of these bills with him at lunch time to pay for his lunch. The clerk at the restaurant where he takes his meal refuses to accept the $20 bill because it is counterfeit—and he proves this to Shopkeeper's satisfaction, keeping the counterfeit bill. He informs Shopkeeper that this is one of many counterfeit $20 bills in circulation that have the same serial number. Shopkeeper returns to his shop, examines the $20 bills in the cash register, and discovers that four of them in truth have the same serial number. What should he do?

The bills are obviously counterfeit. Shopkeeper may of course turn them in at his bank, but if he does so he loses $80. He could keep them and use them as change to give his customers who pay with large bills—$50s or $100s—or he could give them to his customers who cash checks at his shop. The difficulty here is that it is a criminal offense to knowingly pass counterfeit bills. Since Shopkeeper now knows that these bills are counterfeit, he runs the risk of criminal prosecution by keeping them in circulation. Shopkeeper has another alternative, of course: if he can remember who gave him the counterfeit bills, he can ask that person to pay him again in genuine money. But he must remember where he got the bills and be able to prove it to a court's satisfaction if the customer contests the accuracy of Shopkeeper's memory. Unless he can remember who gave him the counterfeit bills, Shopkeeper will have to bite the bullet and take a $100 loss in order to avoid the risk of criminal prosecution.

Tracing. Much of the cash owned by individuals and businesses is not in the form of bills and coins, but in the form of credit balances in bank accounts. In a sense, bank account credit balances are not money, since they are usually disbursed in the form of checks, which are not legal tender. In another sense they are money, since one may obtain cash for them upon demand.

Suppose that Mugg mugs Goodman and takes his billfold and the contents thereof. Goodman knows that his billfold contains $700 in cash. Mugg takes this $700 cash and deposits it in his checking account with First Bank. A friend of Goodman's is a teller at the bank, and tells Goodman that Mugg deposited $700 in his checking account on the day of the mugging. Goodman therefore demands $700 of First Bank. What are his chances of recovery? In theory, at least, Goodman has a possibility of recovery, if he can prove three things:

1. That Mugg took his $700 unlawfully, and
2. Mugg deposited this in his account at First Bank, and
3. The unlawfully taken $700 is still in Mugg's account.

The first is easiest to prove, though of course Goodman's evidence is not infalliable. (If Goodman was the only witness to the mugging, it might be his word against Mugg's.) The second could be proven, normally, only through circumstantial evidence: if Mugg mugs Goodman at 1 P.M. on a Thursday and steals $700, and if at 2:30 P.M. Mugg deposits $700 in his checking account, the deposited $700 must surely be the money he took from Goodman. The third must be proven by showing that Mugg has not yet spent the stolen $700. If the stolen money is no longer in Mugg's account, it cannot be recovered from First Bank.

The rule of "first in, first out" is used to determine whether the stolen money is still present in the account. For instance, if the account had a balance of $800 when Mugg made his deposit, and $600 worth of checks have been honored since the deposit, all of Goodman's money is deemed to be still present in the account (if it can be proven that it was deposited there in the first place). The $600 disbursed is deemed to have been a part of the $800 in the account when the unlawfully taken money was deposited. On the other hand, if there is a $300 balance in the account when Goodman establishes the theft and deposit, there was $800 on deposit when the stolen $700 was deposited, and $1,200 has been disbursed from the account since then, Goodman may claim only $300 from First Bank.

If there was $800 in the account when Mugg made his deposit of the stolen $700 and Mugg later made an honest deposit of $500, if $300 remained in the account when Goodman made his demand upon First Bank, Goodman would recover nothing. Here, the money Mugg stole from Goodman has been completely disbursed: none of it remains in the account.

More complex problems arise when an account contains funds stolen from two or more individuals. The rule of "first in, first out" (FIFO) still determines which funds are in the account, but the presence of several potential claimants complicates matters. Thus: At a time when Mugg has $800 in his account, he deposits the $700 he stole from Goodman. The next day he deposits $500 which he stole from Victim. When his wrongdoing comes to light, $600 remains in the account. According to the rule of FIFO, $100 of this belongs to Goodman and $500 belongs to Victim. On the other hand, if Mugg had made a deposit of $1,200, consisting of the $700 taken from Goodman and the $500 taken from Victim, and $600 remains in the account when the wrongdoing is discovered, Goodman will have a claim to seven-twelfths of the $600 and Victim will have a claim to five-twelfths of it. The reason is that the balance in the account is the remainder of that $1,200 deposit—seven-twelfths of which was Goodman's money and five-twelfths of which was Victim's.

If Goodman cannot recover his money from First Bank through tracing because Mugg has already spent it, this will not destroy Goodman's claim against Mugg himself. Mugg's mugging of Goodman amounted to commission of the tort of conversion (as well as the commission of the crime of theft), so Goodman may sue Mugg for the $700. (It probably would not do him any good, though, since if Mugg has spent the stolen cash he probably has no assets from which Goodman could collect a judgment.) If Mugg is a frugal mugger and invests Goodman's cash in Zilch Corporation stock, Goodman could later recover the stock from Mugg. The theory of recovery here is that Mugg holds the stock as constructive trustee for the benefit of Goodman, so that Goodman, by calling the situation to the attention of a court, could have the trust executed and get possession of the stock. This will be discussed in more detail in the chapter on trusts.

Types of Commercial Paper

There are three basic types of commercial paper: the promissory note, the check, and the draft. These types of paper serve three purposes. Some are used as a substitute for cash—for payment, essentially; checks and sight drafts serve this purpose. Some are used for provision of short-term credit; time drafts and short-term promissory notes accomplish this. Some, such as with promissory notes, are used for the provision of long-term credit.

Promissory notes. The promissory note is two-party paper. The parties are the maker—the debtor or borrower—and the payee—the lender or creditor. The most elementary of promissory notes could take this form:

"Dallas, Texas, July 19, 1979. One year after date I promise to pay to the order of Sam Spade $1,000, with interest at 10 percent per annum. /s/ Calvin Clubb."

Clubb is of course the maker; Spade is the payee. The note is a lump-sum note. Many notes provide for payment of installments by the maker; these are installment notes. Many others provide that the payee shall have a lien upon some asset or assets owned by the maker until the note is paid in full; these are collateral notes.

Drafts. The draft is three-party paper. The parties are the drawer, the drawee, and the payee. The drawer draws the draft. He is generally a creditor. The drawee is the person directed to pay the draft. He is generally a debtor of the drawer. The payee is the person to whom the drawee is directed to pay. He is generally a creditor or an agent of the drawer; in fact, he may even be the drawer himself. A very elementary draft might look like this:

"Dallas, Texas, July 29, 1979. To Hal Hart: On sight, pay to the order of Dick Diamond $500. /s/ Sam Spade."

Spade here is the drawer, since he signed the draft. Hart is the drawee: he is the party being ordered to pay. Diamond is the payee: the party Hart is ordered to pay. The obligations of parties to drafts will be discussed at length in the materials on liability of parties to commercial paper.

Checks. The check is a specialized form of draft. The check is also three-party paper. The drawer writes the check. He is a debtor—that is, he writes the check in order to pay an obligation. The drawee is always a bank, specifically the bank in which the drawer (one hopes) has a checking account. The payee is the person to whom the check is payable. He is the drawer's creditor. Since virtually everyone is familiar with the form of a check, no example need be given.

Cashier's check. A cashier's check is a check drawn upon a bank by itself; the issuing bank is both drawer and drawee. Such a check, being an obligation of a bank, is more acceptable as payment of an obligation than a personal check. A personal check may be dishonored due to insufficient funds in the drawer's account or because of the drawer's stop-payment order, while banks do not draw checks upon insufficient funds. The purchaser of a cashier's check has no right to stop payment. Thus, the risk of dishonor of this type of instrument is so negligible as to be almost nonexistent.

Certified check. A certified check is a check upon which the drawee bank has agreed to assume liability, though it is a personal check in origin. The certified check is more acceptable as payment than the uncertified check, because the certifying bank is liable upon it; the original drawer may not stop payment.

Trade acceptance. A trade acceptance is a draft drawn by a drawer upon itself, which is then accepted by the drawer-drawee. When the drawee of a draft accepts it, he assumes the same liability as that possessed by the maker of a promissory note. Thus, a trade acceptance is essentially as reliable as is the credit rating of the acceptor.

Bank draft. A bank draft is a draft drawn by a bank upon itself, or upon another bank. Since both drawer and drawee are banks, the payee is virtually certain that the draft will be honored. Such drafts are very reliable media for the transfer of funds.

Private money orders. Private money orders are sold by banks, or by other financial companies. They are similar to cashier's checks in that the issuer is the party liable upon the order, not the purchaser. Some of these money orders are worded in a manner which imposes upon the purchaser the liability of the drawer of a check or draft and gives the issuer the liability of the drawee of a draft or check, which is to say almost no liability except to the drawer. Payment may not be stopped by the purchaser of the former sort of money order, but payment may be stopped by the purchaser of the latter.

Postal money orders. Postal money orders are issued by the U.S. Post Office; they are not issued for sums exceeding $100. They are worded in such a way as to be nonnegotiable. They may be endorsed just once, and the transferee gets only the same rights to collect as the transferor. Payment may not be stopped upon such orders.

Traveler's checks. Traveler's checks are sold by banks and financial companies (such as American Express Company). They are sold only in round amounts—$10, $20, $50, and $100 denominations, generally. They are obligations of the issuer. The purchaser is required to sign each check when he buys it. He then countersigns each check when he spends it. The payee may thus compare the two signatures to assure himself that he is dealing with the true buyer of the checks. Payment may not be stopped upon a traveler's check.

Rights of holders in general. The rights of holders of commercial paper will be considered in detail in subsequent chapters. A few general remarks on the subject are in order here, however.

If the possessor of commercial paper is also the owner, he generally has the right to collect from the party obligated to pay, unless that party has a good reason not to pay. With respect to uncertified checks and promissory notes, the party obligated to pay is the debtor and the issuer of the paper. If the debtor has reason not to pay the debt, then, the holder may not be able to collect. However, the debtor is not the issuer of items of commercial paper such as cashier's checks, traveler's checks, and money orders. The issuer of such paper may not refuse to honor it because the debtor who purchased it originally had a good reason not to pay his debt. This is why it is said that one may not stop payment upon such paper.

If the issuer of such paper has good reason not to honor it, however, the holder will not be able to collect. An issuer may have good reason not to honor because, for instance, blank forms of its instruments were stolen, without authorization, completed and put into circulation. If the possessor of the paper is not the owner, the issuer need not honor. A finder or thief of any sort of commercial paper will not be the owner. The finder or thief of bearer paper may make another the owner by transferring it under circumstances that would make the other a holder in due course. This cannot be done with order paper, which may only be negotiated through endorsement of the former owner and subsequent delivery. Any endorsement by a finder or thief is either a forgery or unauthorized, and therefore ineffective.

Thus, if any sort of commercial paper is lost or stolen, the owner should notify the issuer, who may then have grounds not to honor the paper when it is presented for payment. But, if the paper is bearer paper in the hands of a holder in due course, the issuer must still pay.

Negotiability of Commercial Paper

Commercial paper may be negotiable or nonnegotiable, as previously mentioned. Nonnegotiable paper has the attributes of a contract right. It may be assigned, but the assignee will only get the collection rights that the assignor had, unless the paper has a valid "waiver of defenses" clause in it. Negotiable paper will have some of the attributes of money.

Commercial paper which is drawn up by filling in blanks on a printed form will almost certainly be negotiable; in fact, such forms are drafted with the intention of making the completed instrument negotiable. Checks, most drafts, and most commercial promissory notes are negotiable. It is the homemade piece of commercial paper which may be nonnegotiable. When a person sets out to draft a promissory note or draft on his own, then, he must make certain that his creation meets all the requirements of negotiability.

If it falls short in even one respect, it is nonnegotiable. A discussion of the requisites of negotiability follows.

Writing and signature. It goes without saying that all commercial paper must be in written form. It must also be signed by the maker or drawer. The necessary signature usually appears at the end of the paper, and is in the signer's own handwriting. The signature need not be at the end—if the maker or drawer wrote his name in his own handwriting in the body of the paper, that is sufficient. Thus, if I draft a promissory note in my own handwriting which begins, "I, Don Alan Evans, promise to pay to the order of _____." the note is considered to be signed even if I do not formally sign at the end.

The signature need not be in the maker or drawer's own handwriting. A signature by an agent who has express authority to sign commercial paper is a valid signature. Also, many businesses use mechanical signatures on their commercial paper. A mechanically reproduced signature, whether stamped or printed, is valid if the person or organization ordinarily signs its commercial paper that way.

The signature need not be the name of the maker or drawer. Illiterate persons may sign with an "X," so long as the signature is properly witnessed.

Must contain promise or order to pay. UCC 3–104(1)(b) provides that negotiable paper must contain a promise or order to pay. A note must contain the words "I promise to pay" or the equivalent. A check or draft must contain the words "Pay to the order of," or "Pay to bearer," or the equivalent. "I owe Joe Doakes $50" is therefore a nonnegotiable promise. "Please do me the favor of paying to the order of Joe Doakes" may well not be negotiable.

Promise or order must not be conditional. UCC 3–105 defines the concept of conditionality for this purpose. Whether or not the promise is unconditional depends upon its wording. "I promise to pay, if _____" is obviously conditional. "I promise to pay, on condition that _____" is also obviously conditional, as is "I promise to pay, subject to the terms of _____." This essentially means that the maker's obligation to pay depends upon the terms of an agreement which may well be contained in some document other than the note; if this agreement is not properly performed, the maker will not pay.

"I promise to pay, out of the proceeds of _____" is conditional. This is a promise to pay out of a particular fund. The maker would not have to pay if the fund did not come into existence. If a note says that it is payable "from the proceeds of the sale of my lot in Lufkin, Texas," it will never become payable if the maker never sells the lot.

"The City of Podunk, Texas, promises to pay _____, out of the proceeds of the sale of obsolete sewage disposal equipment" is negotiable; when the maker is a government, notes payable out of a particular fund are negotiable.

"Brown & White Drugs promises to pay _____, this being payable only from the assets of Brown and White Drugs" is negotiable. Here the maker is a partnership, and the note is said to be payable from the assets of the firm—a particular fund. When the fund in question is all of the assets of a business, the note is negotiable.

"I promise to pay _____, in full payment for _____" is unconditional and negotiable. The "in full payment for" clause is merely a statement of the consideration for which the note is given. "I promise to pay _____, as per the terms of _____" is unconditional and negotiable. This is another type of statement of consideration only. It makes a big difference whether the note is payable "subject to" the terms of a contract, or "as per" the terms of a contract. "I promise to pay _____. Charge to Advertising Expense," is also unconditional and negotiable. The "Charge to" clause is merely a posting instruction for the maker's bookkeeper.

Promise must be payable in money. UCC 3–107 provides that commercial paper must be payable in money to be negotiable. The money need not be U.S. dollars; commercial paper payable in the recognized currency of any nation would be negotiable. A note for 2,000 Swiss francs will be payable in U.S. dollars equivalent in value to 2,000 Swiss francs as of the date of payment. If the maker desires to be paid in the foreign currency itself rather than in its dollar equivalent, he must specify this in the paper—perhaps with a clause reading, "This note is payable in Swiss francs only."

If the note is payable in a currency issued by a government that is no longer recognized, it will be valueless. Thus, a note payable in South Vietnamese piasters—the money of pre-1975 South Vietnam—will be worthless.

If the paper by its terms is payable in something other than money, it is nonnegotiable. It does not matter whether the paper is payable in commodities or money, or simply in commodities, but it may be difficult to determine the value of paper thus payable. A note payable in "U.S. $2,000 or twelve ounces of gold" may be paid either with U.S. $2,000 or with the twelve ounces of gold. A note payable in "U.S. $2,000 worth of gold" is payable with either $2,000 cash or with the amount of gold that $2,000 will buy at the date of payment. A note payable in "Twelve ounces of gold" is payable either in gold or in the cash value of twelve ounces of gold at maturity. Such paper represents a valid contract, but it is not negotiable.

The sum payable must be certain. UCC 3-106 provides that the amount payable must be certain, but that the sum payable is certain even if:
1. The paper is interest-bearing, or
2. It bears interest at one rate before maturity and at another rate after maturity, or
3. It provides for a discount for early payment, or for a penalty for late payment, or both, or
4. It is in a foreign currency, it contains a formula for converting the foreign currency into dollars, and for addition or deduction of the costs of the currency exchange, or
5. It provides that the maker will be liable for court costs, holder's attorney fees, or both, in case of default.

The paper must be payable at a definite time. UCC 3-107 provides that commercial paper is payable at a fixed time if it is payable:
1. On or before a fixed date, or at a stated time after a fixed date.
2. At a fixed period after sight (thirty days after sight).
3. At a fixed period after acceptance (thirty days after acceptance).
4. At a fixed date subject to acceleration. Commercial installment notes often contain a provision that, if the maker misses a payment, the holder may declare the total unpaid amount to be at once due and payable. Some commercial installment notes contain a provision that the holder may declare the total unpaid amount to be immediately due and payable if he feels himself insecure, even if the maker has missed no payments. Such acceleration clauses are permissible, and do not render these notes nonnegotiable.
5. At a fixed time, subject to extension of the option of the holder. Such notes are negotiable because the holder controls the time of payment in case he decides to extend.
6. At a fixed time, subject to an extension to a later fixed time at the option of the maker or acceptor, or upon the happening of a specified act or event. So long as there exists an ultimate due date upon which the paper must mature, it is negotiable. On the other hand, if the paper's maturity may be extended indefinitely at the option of the maker or acceptor, maturity could be postponed indefinitely; such paper is nonnegotiable.

Paper payable upon the occurrence of an event which may never happen is nonnegotiable; an example would be a note payable "When Edward M. Kennedy is inaugurated as president of the United States." Paper payable upon the occurrence of something which is certain to happen, but the date of which happening is uncertain, is nonnegotiable. An example is a note payable "Six months after the death of my cousin Dominic Moneybags." Neither the inauguration of Edward M. Kennedy as president nor the death of Dominic Moneybags would render the above notes negotiable. They would remain nonnegotiable until maturity, but of course the former might never mature.

The following note would be negotiable, however: "Sixty years after date I promise to pay to the order of _____, but if my cousin Dominic Moneybags dies before the maturity date of this note, then this note will mature six months after the date of his death." This is another useful type of acceleration clause.

Demand paper. Commercial paper is payable on demand if it says that it is so payable, or if it is payable at sight. A note payable at a definite time subject to extension of maturity at the option of the holder becomes demand paper if the holder decides to extend. Also, a note or other commercial paper with no maturity date, or commercial paper upon which the maturity date has been omitted, is demand paper. (If it is obvious to the reader of the note that a maturity date has been omitted, the note is incomplete and therefore nonnegotiable, but it may be rendered negotiable when a date is provided.) Demand paper is generally negotiable because the holder may demand payment at any time he sees fit. UCC 3-108 contains the UCC provisions relative to demand paper.

The paper must be payable to order or to bearer. UCC 3-104(1)(d) contains this provision. Thus a note worded, "I promise to pay John Jones fifty dollars on demand, /s/ Bill Brown," is nonnegotiable.

Order paper. Commercial paper is order paper when it is made payable to the order of:
1. A named person or corporation.
2. Two or more named persons or corporations—e.g., payable "to the order of Bill Brown and Joe Smith," or "to the order of Bill Brown or Joe Smith."
3. An estate, trust, or fund—in which case it is payable to the order of the executor or administrator of the estate, the trustee of the fund, etc. The person holding that position is the person who may deal with the paper.
4. An office or to an officer by his title—paper may be made payable to the order of "the treasurer of Zilch Corporation," or to "Fred Goldman, treasurer of Zilch Corporation." In either case it is payable to Zilch Corporation, but the incumbent treasurer may deal with it as the agent of the corporation.
5. A partnership or unincorporated association—in which case any partner (or the partner or partners given express authority to endorse commercial paper) or officer of the association with authority to endorse commercial paper may deal with it.

Bearer paper. UCC 3-111 states that commercial paper is bearer paper when:
1. It is payable to bearer or to the order of bearer, or
2. It is payable to a specified person or bearer, so long as the words "or bearer" are handwritten or typed. If they are printed, the paper is order paper.
3. It is payable to "cash."

Incomplete paper. UCC 3-115 provides that paper which is obviously incomplete is unenforceable. However, this applies only when the missing provision is essential to determination of the obligation of the maker, drawer, or acceptor of the paper.

If a date is missing, this may render the paper incomplete, or it may not. If the paper is payable on demand, on a fixed date, or at a fixed number of days after acceptance, the paper is not incomplete. If it is payable thirty days after date, but there is no date, then obviously the paper is incomplete.

If the time or place of payment is not specified, this will not necessarily render the paper incomplete. Many items of commercial paper do not contain a place of payment. If no time of payment is specified, the paper is simply considered to be demand paper. However, if blank spaces appear for time or place of payment, the paper is obviously incomplete. If the face value of the paper or the name of the payee is missing, the paper is also obviously incomplete.

If nothing appears about interest, the paper is simply non-interest-bearing. If the fact that the paper is interest-bearing is mentioned, but no rate is noted and no blank space for an interest rate appears, the paper bears interest at the legal rate. If, however, a blank appears where a rate should be filled in, the paper is incomplete.

When an incomplete instrument is completed, it is enforceable as completed if the completion is authorized. If the completion is unauthorized, the maker or drawer may be able to escape honoring it; this subject will be discussed more thoroughly in the section on defenses to payment. It should be noted here that when a maker or drawer claims that an instrument has been completed without authorization, he must prove the unauthorized completion. This is very hard to do; in close cases, a jury is very likely to decide for the holder and enforce the paper as written. It is therefore most unwise to sign incomplete commercial paper.

Antedated and postdated commercial paper. UCC 3-114 provides the rules on this subject. There is nothing unlawful about either antedated or postdated commercial paper; the paper is simply effective according to the date.

Provisions not affecting the negotiability of commercial paper. UCC 3-112 provides that the addition of certain terms to commercial paper will not affect negotiability. Among these are:

1. Provisions relative to collateral, including provisions describing the collateral and providing the right to repossess collateral in case of default, and provisions for maintaining and increasing collateral, etc.

2. "Cognovit" provisions. A cognovit note authorizes the holder to file suit against the maker in case of default, to hire an attorney to represent the maker in the litigation, and to instruct the attorney to confess a judgment in the litigation in favor of the holder. The maker thus is not served with citation and gets no chance to defend himself; the holder may obtain a judgment against him without his knowledge. Such provisions are illegal and unenforceable in Texas, and their federal constitutionality is at least questionable, but they may still be found in promissory note forms in some states.

3. Provisions waiving the benefit of laws protecting the obligor. A very common type of provision of this nature is one by which endorsers waive presentment and notice of dishonor as prerequisites to their liability. A provision obliging the maker to waive the benefit of consumer protection legislation will be very closely scrutinized, however, since many such provisions are either illegal or unconscionable.

4. A term on a draft providing that the act of cashing the draft is satisfaction of all claims holder has against drawer.

Interpretation of Commercial Paper

Instruments may be drawn in such a way as to create confusion regarding their true meaning. UCC 3-118 provides some rules for clarifying some of these ambiguities.

Nature of instrument unclear. If it is not clear from the wording of the instrument whether it is a note or a draft, the holder may treat it as either. But a draft drawn by the drawer upon himself is treated as a note.

Resolving conflicting provisions of commercial paper. On occasion an instrument will contain inconsistent provisions. Which of the provisions prevails?

When the conflict is between a printed provision and a typewritten or handwritten provision, the typed or handwritten one prevails, since it is more likely to state the true intent of the parties. For example: A check form has printed on it the legend, "THIS CHECK NOT VALID FOR MORE THAN FIFTY DOLLARS." The face value as typed is two hundred dollars. The true face value is $200.

When the conflict is between a typewritten provision and a handwritten provision, the handwritten provision prevails, so long as the handwriting does not constitute unauthorized completion or material alteration. For example: A blank form of interest-bearing note is filled in by typing. The rate of interest is stated to be 6 percent, but a handwritten provision in the handwriting of the maker states that the interest rate is 10 percent. The true interest rate is 10 percent.

When there is a conflict between the face value of the paper as stated in words and the value as stated in figures, the words normally prevail. For example: A check is made out for $115.60 in figures and for "One hundred fifty and sixteen one-hundredths dollars" in words. It is worth $150.16.

However, if the amount is ambiguous, the amount in figures controls. For example: A check is made out for $799.00 in figures and for "Seven ninety-nine dollars" in words. The "Seven ninety-nine" might mean $7.99 or $799.00. The presence of the figure resolves the ambiguity. Usually, however, a bank will not honor a check upon which the face value in words and figures is inconsistent. Instead it will usually check with the drawer in order to determine his intentions. This should also be done with ambiguous drafts and notes.

Use of oral evidence to prove that an instrument does not mean what it says. Courts are very reluctant to admit oral evidence on the meaning of commercial paper. Instruments may not be orally amended, but oral evidence may of course be used to show unauthorized completion, material alteration, extension of maturity date, acceleration of maturity date, and so on. Any oral agreement affecting the nature of the paper or of the liability of a party to it will not be binding upon a holder in due course who does not know of the agreement.

Use of separate written document to show amendment. Such written amendments are valid for the parties to the amendment and other parties who know of the amendment. They are not valid, however, for holders in due course who did not know of them when they acquired the paper.

Ambiguities with respect to liability of signers. This causes little difficulty. A signer is liable in the capacity in which he signs; inconsistent wording in the body of the instrument will not affect this liability. For example: A note reads, "I promise to pay fifty dollars to bearer on demand. /s/ Al Able. /s/ Ben Baker." The holder asks Baker to pay. Baker says he is not liable because the "I" in the body of the note is Able, not Baker. Baker is liable. He signed as a maker, so he is liable as a maker.

Often one or more of the signers of instruments are acting as sureties or guarantors for other signers. If the way in which the parties signed does not indicate the existence of the suretyship relation, the surety will not be allowed to prove his status with oral evidence. This will be discussed in more detail later.

Signatures by agents. An agent who has express authority to sign commercial paper will bind his principal and not himself if he signs properly. However, there exists no implied or apparent authority to sign commercial paper, except in one very limited area. The signature of an unauthorized agent will not bind the principal to anything, regardless of the form of the signature.

Assume that Paul Pepper has given Al Ace express authority to sign commercial paper for him. Ace's methods of signing are five in number, three of which can cause difficulty and only one of which is correct. Examples follow.

1. /s/ Al Ace. The agent has merely signed his own name. There is nothing to indicate that he is signing as an agent, so he is in effect liable as the principal.
2. /s/ Paul Pepper. Here the agent has signed the principal's name. Since the agent has the authority to do this, this binds the principal but not the agent. However, for those who are familiar with Pepper's signature, this will look like a forgery; someone may well question its validity.
3. /s/ Al Ace, Agent. Here Ace indicates that he is an agent, but we do not know who the principal is. Thus, we have a partially disclosed principal; in such cases in this state the agent is liable and the principal is not.
4. /s/ Al Ace. /s/ Paul Pepper. Ace signs both his name and his principal's name, with no indication of any agency relationship. Here, both parties are liable; but someone may well question the validity of the Pepper signature.
5. /s/ Paul Papper, by Al Ace, Agent. This is the correct way for the agent to sign. Here there is no question as to the relationship between the parties. Pepper is liable; Ace is not.

Corporate commercial paper must always be signed by an agent. The agent must be sure to indicate that he is signing as an agent; otherwise he will be held liable as a co-maker. Assume that Ted Terry is treasurer of Zilch Corporation and has authority to sign commercial paper for the corporation. Two examples of possible signatures are:

1. /s/ Zilch Corporation. /s/ Ted Terry. Terry does not indicate his agency here; he is liable as a co-maker.
2. /s/ Zilch Corporation, by Ted Terry, Treasurer. This is the proper way to sign, since there is no question here—Terry has signed as an agent.

Transfer of Commercial Paper

Commercial paper is legally transferrable in two ways: by *negotiation* and by *assignment*. Negotiation is the preferred method. Anyone who acquires negotiable paper by negotiation may, if he meets all requirements, become a holder in due course and get better collection rights than the party he gets it from. Anyone who acquires negotiable paper by assignment acquires only the rights of the party he gets the paper from. If one acquires negotiable paper by assignment from someone who has holder in due course rights, one acquires holder in due course rights. There is no advantage to acquisition of nonnegotiable paper by negotiation. Although nonnegotiable paper may be freely transferred, it can have no holder in due course.

Requirements for negotiation. UCC 3-202 sets out the requirements for negotiation. What is necessary depends on whether the paper is order paper or bearer paper. To determine whether paper is order or bearer, first look to see if there are endorsements on the back of it. If there are, look at the last of these: if it names the person to whom the paper is now payable, e.g., "Pay to the order of Bill Brown, /s/ Joe Smith," the paper is order paper. If the last of the names is merely a signature, the paper is bearer paper, unless the signature is obviously that of an accommodation endorser. If the last endorsement is an accommodation endorsement, one must look to the next-to-last endorsement to determine the character of the paper. A signature is an accommodation endorsement if it obviously does not fit into a "chain of title" to the paper.

An obvious case of an accommodation endorser is the note payable to the order of Jim Brown with two endorsements on the back, the first reading "Pay to the order of Sam Skelly, /s/ Jim Brown," and the second reading "/s/ Oswald Ottinger." Obviously, Oswald Ottinger was never an owner; he signed to lend his credit to the note. Since the last endorsement is an accommodation endorsement and the next-to-last names the current owner, the note is order paper.

If the only endorsement on the paper is an accommodation endorsement, which would be the case if a note payable to the order of Jim Brown were endorsed only by Oswald Ottinger, or if there were no endorsements on the paper, one would look at the face of the paper to determine its nature as order or bearer. Remember that paper may be changed from order to bearer or from bearer to order by endorsement.

In order to negotiate order paper, two things are necessary. The transferor must endorse the paper, and he must deliver it to the transferee. A transfer of order paper by delivery without endorsement is a valid transfer, but it is only an assignment. The transferee does become the owner of the paper, and he acquires the right to make the transferor endorse; but the transferee cannot become a holder in due course until the transferor endorses (UCC 3-201).

In order to negotiate bearer paper, only one thing is necessary: delivery by the transferor to the transferee.

Assignment of commercial paper. Several types of transfers are deemed assignments rather than negotiations. One that has already been mentioned is the transfer of order paper by delivery only. Another means of assignment is by means of an endorsement such as "Pay to the order of Jack James, this endorsement to operate as an assignment only and not as a negotiation. /s/ Gene Goslar." Another kind of assignment is the partial transfer, as when Gene Goslar endorses a $1,000 note as follows: "Pay $700 of this to the order of Jake Johnson, /s/ Gene Goslar." Note that such a transfer is a valid transfer, but if the maker does not pay the sum at maturity, both Goslar and Johnson would have to sue as plaintiffs to force the maker to pay (UCC 3-202).

The transfer of the entire value of the note in unequal parts is an assignment; an example would be the endorsement of a $1,000 note, "Pay $700 of the above to the order of Jake Johnson, and pay $300 of the above to the order of Sam Spade, /s/ Gene Goslar." Such an assignment would also create collection problems if the maker did not pay at maturity.

UCC 3-302(3) declares that certain unusual types of transfers of commercial paper are assignments. First, anyone acquiring commercial paper in a bulk sale which is outside the normal course of business of the seller takes by assignment. The usual situation here is that of a seller transferring all the assets of his business, including commercial paper, for consideration.

When a creditor seizes assets of his debtor under legal process, any commercial paper so seized is acquired by assignment. This could involve, for example, a seizure by a sheriff under a writ of execution, or a levy by the IRS upon the assets of a business. Should the sheriff or the IRS then auction off the seized commercial paper, buyers at the sale would also take by assignment.

When commercial paper is transferred because of the insolvency of the holder, the trustee in bankruptcy or the assignee for benefit of creditors takes by assignment. Should the trustee or assignee auction off such commercial paper, the buyers would take by assignment. When commercial paper is transferred because of the death or incompetence of the holder, assignment occurs. The guardian, executor, or administrator takes by assignment. When the decedent's estate is ultimately divided among the heirs, the heirs take by assignment.

Types of endorsements and the effects thereof. Some types of transfers are voidable or void; before we consider them we must consider the types of endorsements used on commercial paper—the *blank*, the *special*, the *restrictive*, and the *qualified*—and the effect of each.

The *blank endorsement* consists merely of the signature of the transferor. This will convert order paper into bearer paper, as per UCC 3-204(2).

The *special endorsement* names the transferee of the paper, as in: "Pay to the order of Gus Grump, /s/ Joe Schmoe." This will convert bearer paper into order paper. A transferee himself may convert a blank endorsement into a special endorsement. Thus, Joe Schmoe endorses a promissory note to Gus Grump by signing his name on it. Gus Grump then writes above Schmoe's signature the words, "Pay to the order of Gus Grump," as per UCC 3-204 (1), (3).

The *qualified endorsement* contains the words "without recourse." A qualified endorsement may be blank, as "Without Recourse, /s/ Joe Schmoe." It may also be special, as: "Pay to the order of Gus Grump, without recourse, /s/ Joe Schmoe." This form of endorsement is an effort by the endorser to disclaim liability upon the paper if it is not paid at maturity. As you will see, this effort is not always successful. A qualified endorsement which would relieve the endorser of all liability might be: "Pay to the order of Gus Grump, without recourse and all warranties disclaimed, /s/ Joe Schmoe."

The *restrictive endorsement* is found in several varieties, all of which seek to limit the rights of the transferee in some way. They are described in UCC 3-205 and 3-206. All of these are most often special; some are always special.

The endorsement purporting to stop further negotiation is the first of these we will cover. The usual form is, "Pay to the order of Gus Grump only, /s/ Sam Schmoe." The idea is to prevent Gus Grump from transferring the paper further. However, it is a waste of effort and ink to write such an endorsement, as it will not stop further transfer of the paper. Its effect is that of an ordinary special endorsement.

The "For Deposit Only" endorsement is no doubt the most commonly used of the restrive endorsements. In its special form it specifies the bank and perhaps the account number into which the paper must be deposited, e.g., "Pay to Podunk State Bank, for deposit only in Acct. #21-5606-7. /s/ Skinch Drugs, by Pete Pilroller, Mgr." Businesses use some form of this to endorse checks taken in during the business day. No bank may legitimately cash a check bearing such an endorsement.

The "For Collection Only" endorsement is used when the owner wishes to transfer the paper to a collection agent. It will be a special endorsement to the agent, e.g., "Pay to Gus Grump, for collection only, /s/ Joe Schmoe." Grump of course has no legal title to paper so endorsed: he holds it only as Schmoe's agent. Should Grump seek to transfer it further, he may only transfer the rights he has, unless Schmoe is paid the face value of the paper.

The conditional endorsement is rare, and always special. An example would be: "Pay to the order of Gus Grump, on condition that the TV set I am buying from Gus Grump with this instrument operates to my satisfaction. /s/ Joe Schmoe." Grump here has good title only as long as the TV set works. If it breaks down fairly soon Schmoe could reclaim the paper from Grump, or from whomever Grump might transfer it to.

The trust endorsement is also rare. It looks like this: "Pay to the order of Gus Grump, for the benefit of Ezekiel Esel, /s/ Joe Schmoe." Here Grump gets title to the paper as trustee for Esel's benefit, so he must use the paper and its proceeds in a way that will benefit Esel. If Grump sells this for cash he could pass on full title to it, so long as the buyer believes that Grump will use the proceeds for Esel's benefit. But if Grump uses it to pay a personal debt, or to buy property for his personal use, the buyer will not get clear title because he will know Grump is violating his duty as a trustee by using the paper in this way.

When commercial paper is used as collateral for a loan the debtor may not endorse it over to the creditor, or he may merely put a blank endorsement on it. He could also put a special restrictive endorsement on it showing that it is being transferred as collateral, e.g., "Pay to the order of Gus Grump, until I repay the $5,000 I have borrowed from Gus Grump this day /s/ Joe Schmoe."

An accommodation endorser signs his name on the paper to lend his credit to it. He has the normal liability of an endorser unless he is obviously an accommodation endorser, in which case there are some special defenses to liability available to him which are not available to other endorsers.

The "Payment Guaranteed" and "Collection Guaranteed" endorsements change the normal liability of the endorser. Their meaning will be discussed later.

Forged and unauthorized endorsements. An endorsement by an agent who has no authority to endorse commercial paper—or a forged endorsement—will normally transfer no title to the paper. The owner of the paper remains the person whose name was forged, or the victim of the unauthorized agent, no matter how many times the paper is transferred after the forgery. The owner may recover the paper, or its proceeds, from any subsequent buyer. There are, however, three circumstances under which a forged endorsement will pass good title to commercial paper, as per UCC 3-405:

1. Raggs tells Sapp that he is Moneybags, a millionaire. He says he is strapped for cash and needs a $1,000 loan, so Sapp writes out a $1,000 check payable to the order of Moneybags and gives it to Raggs. Raggs endorses the name of Moneybags on it and transfers it to Brown for value, Brown buying it in good faith. Brown owns the check; Sapp must make it good. His negligence in permitting himself to be "taken" by an impostor is costly.

2. Crooks, treasurer of Simp Company, has sole authority to write company checks. He writes one for $10,000 payable to the order of Goodman, to whom Simp owes nothing. Crooks writes the name of Goodman on the back of the check and obtains $10,000 for it and skips town. Simp Company is out $10,000; it suffers for its negligence in giving Crooks too much authority.

3. Bragg, payroll manager of Arx Company, has sole authority to make up the weekly company payroll. The check-writing department of the company writes up payroll

checks on Bragg's authority. Bragg puts on the payroll the names of Owsley, Hawke, Crow, and Jay, none of whom work for the company. The check-writing department writes up payroll checks for these people. Bragg obtains these checks, writes the names of the payees on them, and obtains cash for them. Arx Company must honor these checks; it is negligent for not having someone check the accuracy of the payroll before the payroll checks are written.

Voidable transfers. Any transfer of commercial paper which would result in a voidable contract, were commercial paper not involved, is a voidable transfer. Thus, a sale of commercial paper by a minor would be voidable. Also, any transfer where the transferor is a victim of fraud, misrepresentation, duress, undue influence, or the like is voidable. But if a person who obtains commercial paper in a voidable transaction transfers it to a holder in due course, the holder in due course gets complete title.

Void transfers. A finder does not get good title to commercial paper which he finds. A thief does not get good title to commercial paper which he steals.

The finder or thief of order paper may not negotiate it. Since the endorsement of the owner is necessary to negotiate order paper, the thief or finder would have to commit forgery to provide the necessary endorsement, so any transfer of a lost or stolen order instrument is void.

On the other hand, the finder or thief of bearer paper may negotiate it by delivery only. Thus, it is possible for a finder or thief who has no title to bearer paper to negotiate it by delivery to a holder in due course, who would have full title to it.

Limited transfers. When commercial paper has a restrictive endorsement upon it—"For Collection Only"—or a conditional endorsement or trust endorsement, potential buyers should beware: they may only be getting the limited title which their transferor had.

Endorsement by person whose name is misspelled. The payee or transferee whose name is misspelled may endorse the paper with his name spelled as written upon the paper, or with his true name. Either endorsement is correct. However, UCC 2-302 gives a subsequent holder the right to require an endorsement in both names—the name as misspelled on the paper and the true name. It is best for the person whose name is misspelled to endorse in both names when transferring the paper; this may save some later difficulty.

26

Holder in Due Course

Defenses to Payment

Holder in Due Course

The holder in due course of commercial paper may have better rights to collect upon it than had the person he got it from. There can be no holder in due course of nonnegotiable paper. Anyone who would be a holder in due course must acquire the paper by negotiation rather than by assignment.

One need not be a holder in due course to be able to collect, however. If the party obligated to pay has no good reason not to pay—that is, he has no defense to payment—then any owner of the paper may collect. If the party obligated to pay does have a defense to payment, his defense may either be *real* or *personal*. If his defense is real, it does not matter whether the owner of the paper is a holder in due course, because a real defense is good against everyone. If the defense is personal, as most defenses are, it is not good against someone with holder in due course rights, but it is good against someone without holder in due course rights. Thus, the advantage of having holder in due course rights is that one may collect upon the paper even though the party obligated to pay has a personal defense to payment.

The subject of defenses to payment will be covered in the second half of this chapter.

The holder. In order to have a chance to qualify as a holder in due course, one must first be a holder. The possessor of bearer paper is the holder of it. The possessor of order paper is the holder of it if he is the payee, or if it has been endorsed to his order. The holder is presumed to be the owner; in litigation involving commercial paper a holder need not prove ownership—he need only introduce the paper itself into evidence. The burden of proof lies at the doorstep of the defendant who claims that the holder is not the owner.

It is possible, of course, for a holder not to be an owner. The holder of bearer paper can be a finder or a thief. The endorsement making order paper payable to the ostensible holder may be a forgery. But the burden of proof of nonownership is on the defendant.

The holder who would be a holder in due course must meet six separate and distinct requirements, as set out in UCC 3-302. He must:

1. Give value.

2. Act in good faith in acquisition.
3. Not know the paper is overdue.
4. Not know the paper has been dishonored.
5. Not know of any defense to payment.
6. Not know of any claim of ownership of the paper by a third party.

Giving value. UCC 3-303 spells out the requirements. Value is given for commercial paper when:

1. A reasonable price is paid for it in goods, money, or services.
2. The paper is taken as collateral for a loan. If the amount of the loan is less than the face value of the paper, however, the holder is a partial holder in due course only—just for the amount of the loan.
3. The paper is taken as payment of a preexisting debt.

Value is not given when:

1. The buyer promises to pay for the paper in the future. In such a case, value is not given until the buyer actually pays.
2. The buyer pays an unreasonably low price for the paper.

When buyer makes a down payment on the paper when he takes possession and agrees to pay the balance due later, he may become a partial holder in due course to extent of his down payment.

Taking in good faith. UCC 1-201 defines this concept. The main requirement is that the buyer be acting honestly in his purchase. Thus, if the buyer of the paper defrauds the seller, uses duress upon him, or something of that sort, he is not acting in good faith.

The buyer is expected to have read the paper and all of its endorsements before buying. If the buyer knows or should know that the seller is breaching a fiduciary obligation or that his sale is contrary to the terms of a restrictive endorsement, the buyer is not buying in good faith. Examples of such bad faith follow:

1. Sapp buys a check from Idd which has been endorsed, "For Deposit Only, Saggs Drugs, by J. Goodman, Manager." Idd could hardly have obtained this in an honest transaction.
2. Sapp buys a note from Idd which is payable to Simp Corporation, and Idd has endorsed, "Simp Corporation, by Ike Idd, Treasurer," and Sapp knows that Idd is going to use the proceeds at the gambling tables in Las Vegas.
3. Sapp accepts a note from Idd in payment of a debt Idd owes Sapp, which is payable to "Ike Idd as trustee for Idabelle Idd."

In the first case, Sapp may well have bought holdup loot. In the second case Idd obviously is misusing a corporate asset. In the third case, Idd certainly is not using this trust asset for the benefit of the named beneficiary.

Knowing that the paper is overdue. UCC 3-304 contains the law here. Normally, one may tell whether an instrument is overdue or not simply by reading it. If the stated maturity date has passed, it is overdue. However special problems arise with respect to demand instruments, instruments containing acceleration clauses, and installment instruments.

The longer demand paper has been outstanding, the more likely it is that a court will consider it to be overdue. Of course, non-interest-bearing demand paper should have a shorter life than interest-bearing demand paper.

A check is deemed to be payable within thirty days; therefore a check which is more than thirty days old is presumed to be overdue. The thirty-day measuring stick would seem to be a good one for non-interest-bearing notes and drafts also.

Once a paper containing an acceleration clause has been accelerated, it is overdue. However, the fact of acceleration is not noted on the paper itself. A buyer of paper containing an acceleration clause is under no duty to ask about acceleration. If a buyer knows that acceleration has occurred, he knows he is buying overdue paper. If he does not know of the acceleration, he does not know it is overdue.

The amount and due date of each payment of an installment note is written into the note. As payments are made, they are noted on the paper. Thus, one may determine whether payments have been missed simply by reading the note.

If payments are in arrears, the note may or may not be overdue. If the payments are credited to both principal and interest, the note is overdue if payments are in arrears; but if the payments are credited to interest only, the note is not overdue if payments are in arrears.

Knowing that the paper is dishonored. UCC 3-304 also deals with this subject. Usually knowledge or lack of knowledge as to whether or not the paper is dishonored is unimportant; it is dishonored if the party liable upon it has been asked to pay and has refused to pay. A draft may also be dishonored when it is presented to the drawee for acceptance and the drawee refuses to accept. Normally the dishonored paper is also overdue, and the knowledge that it is overdue is enough to prevent the buyer from being a holder in due course.

However, demand paper and time drafts may have been dishonored without being overdue. It is generally possible to identify a dishonored check: The fact that the check has been dishonored may well be stamped upon its face; if the check has had to travel through banking channels, the back will show that endorsements by various banks have been canceled. However, no evidence of dishonor will appear upon demand notes and time drafts or sight drafts. The buyer will either know that these have been dishonored, in which case he cannot be a holder in due course, or he will not know, in which case he can be a holder in due course. In any event, the buyer is under no obligation to ask whether or not the paper has been dishonored.

Knowing of defenses to payment. UCC 3-304 also governs here. Obviously, if a buyer of an instrument knows that the maker, drawer, or acceptor has some legally sufficient reason not to pay at maturity, he knows of a defense to payment. If the paper is obviously incomplete, or if it contains signs of material alteration, the buyer knows of a defense to payment. Also, if the buyer is a financial institution that works very closely with a seller who has a history of sharp and shady dealings with his customers, the buyer may well be said to know of a defense to payment.

However, when the buyer of the paper has no such intimate business relationship with the seller, the buyer must know for certain that a defense to payment exists before he is deprived of holder in due course status. Mere knowledge that a defense might exist is not enough to deprive a buyer of that status. Also, the buyer is again under no obligation to inquire about the existence of possible defenses to payment.

Knowing of adverse claims. UCC 3-304 also covers this subject. A buyer knows of an adverse claim when he knows that someone other than his transferor claims to own the paper. The adverse claim might arise because of the loss or theft of the paper, or because a previous transferor was a minor, or because a previous transferor was defrauded into transferring the paper, or something similar. Usually, the paper itself will not disclose the existence of an adverse claim. The buyer either will or will not know of adverse claims; there is no obligation on the part of the buyer to ask about them.

26/ Holder in Due Course

Knowledge that will not stop a buyer from being a holder in due course. UCC 3-304(4) provides that knowledge of the following does not constitute knowledge of a defense to payment or of an adverse claim:
1. That the paper is antedated or postdated. There is nothing illegitimate about such paper.
2. That it was issued or negotiated in return for an executory agreement. If the agreement has been performed or will be performed, no defense will exist. Of course, if it is not performed as agreed, a defense will exist.
3. That it was accompanied by a separate agreement. No defense will exist unless the separate agreement has been breached.
4. That any party has signed for accommodation. There is nothing illegitimate about that.
5. That an incomplete instrument has been completed, unless buyer knows the completion is unauthorized. There is nothing wrong with an authorized completion.
6. That any person negotiating the paper is or was a fiduciary. A fiduciary may negotiate paper for the benefit of his beneficiary; if he does, there is no impropriety.

If a buyer learns of a defense to payment or adverse claim after he has acquired an instrument and paid value for it, his knowledge will not destroy his status as a holder in due course.

An owner of a limited interest may be a holder in due course. A person who has possession of an instrument under a trust endorsement, "for collection only" endorsement, etc. may of course be a holder. He has the right of a holder to enforce the instrument, and he has the rights of a holder in due course if he qualifies as a holder in due course.

Payee as holder in due course. In most transactions involving commercial paper, no problems arise with respect to the holder in due course status of a payee. If the maker or drawer has no defense to payment of the paper, it does not matter whether the payee is a holder in due course or not. If a defense to payment does exist, some sort of wrongdoing by the payee is usually the reason, so the payee is not a holder in due course. However, it is possible for a defense to payment to exist of which the payee has no knowledge. In such a case the payee may well be a holder in due course.

For example: Crook tells Sapp that he can get a new auto for Sapp very cheaply from Dealer. The car has a sticker price of $10,000, but he, Crook, can get it for $8,000. All Sapp needs to do to take advantage of this golden opportunity is to give Crook a check for $8,000 payable to the order of Dealer, and he, Crook, will take care of the rest. Sapp believes this tale and writes up and delivers the check to Crook. It happens that Crook owes Dealer a debt of $8,000. Crook uses the Sapp check to pay this debt. He tells Dealer that Sapp has lent him $8,000 in this form, and Dealer believes it. Meanwhile Sapp learns that he will get no car from Dealer, so he stops payment on the check, which is dishonored. Dealer demands $8,000 from Sapp. Sapp has been had; he must pay. Dealer qualifies as a holder in due course because he knew nothing of the fraud perpetrated by Crook and meets all other requirements for holder in due course status.

Federal limitations upon holder in due course rights in consumer transactions. Pursuant to the expanded rule-making authority conferred upon the Federal Trade Commission by the Federal Trade Commission Improvement Act of 1975 (15 UCS 57), the FTC has promulgated a Trade Regulation Rule limiting the rights of holders in due course of promissory notes signed by consumers. This rule, at 16 CFR part 433, provides that a seller of goods on credit to any individual for personal, family, or household use, violates the Federal Trade Commission Act unless the contract signed by the debtor contains the following notice, in at least 10-point boldface type:

NOTICE
ANY HOLDER OF THIS CONSUMER CREDIT CONTRACT IS SUBJECT TO ALL CLAIMS AND DEFENSES WHICH THE DEBTOR COULD ASSERT AGAINST THE SELLER OF GOODS OR SERVICES OBTAINED PURSUANT HERETO OR WITH THE PROCEEDS HEREOF. RECOVERY HEREUNDER BY THE DEBTOR SHALL NOT EXCEED AMOUNTS PAID BY THE DEBTOR HEREUNDER.

Should the consumer finance his purchase through a commercial lender, having the lender pay the seller for the goods, the seller violates the Federal Trade Commission Act when he accepts any of the proceeds of the consumer loan unless he makes certain that the contract between the lender and the consumer contains a similar provision. Sellers failing to have this notice inserted in consumer credit contracts may be assessed a $10,000 civil penalty by the FTC for commission of a deceptive trade practice.

The insertion of the required notice in a consumer credit contract makes it impossible for the holder of the contract to acquire holder in due course rights. The holder has exactly the same right to collect that the original seller had, and no more. The FTC Rule also makes holders of these notes liable to the maker for money the maker has paid on the note, when under the UCC the debtor could rescind his contract with the seller and get back all of his consideration. This will be covered in the material on sales. The rule applies only to consumer promissory notes and to nonnegotiable contracts containing waiver-of-the-defenses clauses. It does not apply to consumer checks or drafts. The rule also does not apply to promissory notes which are a part of commercial, agricultural, or real estate transactions. It does apply to consumer notes given in exchange for services, or as consideration for leases of personal property.

Holder through a holder in due course. UCC 3-201 provides that the transferee of commercial paper shall receive at least the rights that his transferor had under normal circumstances. Thus, if one acquires commercial paper by some type of valid transfer from a holder in due course, one thereby acquires the rights of a holder in due course.

Thus, a holder may have holder in due course rights even though he is not a holder in due course himself. For example: Smith sells Jones a defective car for $500, Jones having no way to spot the defect before buying, Jones paying with a $500 check. Jones soon discovers the fraud and stops payment on the check. Meanwhile Smith negotiates the check to Green, a holder in due course. Green then negotiates it to White, who knows of Smith's fraud against Jones. Jones's bank dishonors the check. White demands that Jones make it good. White can win, since he acquired holder in due course rights from Green.

Even a nonholder may have holder in due course rights, if he obtained the paper in question from someone with holder in due course rights in a valid transaction. For example: By fraud Black induces Gray to sign a negotiable note promising to pay $500 to the order of Black on demand, Gray knowing that he has signed a promissory note. Black negotiates the note to Blue by special endorsement, Blue being a holder in due course. Blue sells the note to Redd for value without endorsement. Redd asks Gray to pay. Gray refuses because of Black's fraud and also because the note by its endorsements is payable to Blue, not to Redd. Result: Redd can collect, if he can prove that he bought the note in a valid transaction from Blue, and if he can prove that Blue was a holder in due course.

There are two circumstances under which a person who acquires commercial paper from a holder in due course will not himself get holder in due course rights. One of these is where the transferee is acquiring the paper for the second time, and he was not a holder in due course the first time he had it. One may not "launder" commercial paper by negotiating it to a holder in due course and later getting it back.

The other circumstance is where the transferee participated in the wrongdoing which caused the maker, drawer, or acceptor to have a defense to payment. For example: Black and Gray collaborate in selling White a counterfeit Zilch Corporation bond. White pays with a negotiable note promising to pay $5,000 to the order of Black on demand. Black specially endorses and negotiates the note to Pink, a holder in due course. Pink specially endorses and negotiates the note to Gray. Gray does not get holder in due course rights, even though Pink had such rights, because of his participation in the original fraud against White.

Defenses to Payment

The maker or drawer of an item of commercial paper is obligated to honor it at maturity, unless he has some good reason for not honoring it. If he has a good reason, it is said that he has a defense to payment.

Some defenses to payment are good against anyone, even holders in due course or holders through a holder in due course. Such defenses are called *real* defenses. Other defenses are good against persons who do not have holder in due course rights, but are not good against persons who do have holder in due course rights. If the maker or drawer has a *personal* defense, then, he may or may not have to pay the item; it depends on the status of the holder.

UCC 3-305(2) lists most of the real defenses. UCC 3-306 lists some, but not all, of the personal defenses. We shall consider the possible defenses one at a time, beginning with the real defenses.

REAL DEFENSES

The real defenses are those which are good against anyone, even persons with holder in due course rights. Anyone who has a real defense need not pay, no matter who is seeking payment.

Minority. UCC 3-305(2)(a) states that infancy is a real defense to the extent that it is a defense to a simple contract. A person becomes an adult in Texas upon his eighteenth birthday. Minors in this state may disaffirm virtually all sorts of contracts in which issuance of commercial paper is involved. However, disaffirmance of checks or the like given in payment of medical or dental bills may not be permitted, since these services are considered to be necessities. Disaffirmance of checks given in payment for food, clothing, or shelter may also be difficult if the item purchased is considered to be a necessity.

Incapacity. A person who has been declared incompetent by a court and who has a guardian appointed by the court has no capacity to make a contract. He therefore has no capacity to issue items of commercial paper. Such items are void; neither the incompetent nor his guardian may be compelled to honor them. This is true even if the paper is issued in exchange for a necessity. Other sorts of incapacity are merely personal defenses.

Extreme duress. A person who signs an item of commercial paper because of a razor held to his throat, a revolver aimed at his head, or any like form of duress has a real defense to payment. If he signed in fear of his life, he need not honor the paper. If he signed in fear for the life of his loved one, the same rule holds true. All other sorts of duress constitute personal defenses.

Usury. Whenever the maker or drawer of commercial paper has been charged excessive interest, he has a real defense to payment. Private lenders in Texas may not charge more than 10 percent annual interest. The maximum which commercial lenders may charge is governed by the type of lender, type of borrower, and the nature of the transaction. If the borrower has been charged double or more than double the maximum interest rate, the paper is void; the maker or drawer has a complete defense. If the interest charged is less than double the maximum, he has a partial defense; he must pay the face value less a usury penalty.

Fraud in the execution. Whenever the maker or drawer has been tricked into signing an item of commercial paper not knowing what he is signing, and without a reasonable opportunity to find out what he is signing, he may claim this defense. Before this defense will hold up, the maker or drawer must show that he had no reasonable opportunity to find out what he was signing before he signed. A person could claim this defense, of course, if he is blind, illiterate, or unable to read the English language (assuming that the check or note is written in English). If he cannot read without his glasses, and he has no glasses available, the defense will hold. If he is a victim of a fast switch—that is, he reads the document he thinks he is to sign, but his attention is distracted and a document that looks similar is substituted—he has a defense. Or if his signature on the commercial paper is a carbon signature, put there when he signed an original document that was not an item of commercial paper, he has a defense. However, if he could have found out what he was signing by use of due care, or if someone (other than the person committing the fraud) could have read or translated what he was signing without much difficulty, there is no defense at all.

Discharge in insolvency proceedings. The only sort of court proceeding which results in a discharge of debts is a bankruptcy proceeding. When a bankruptcy court declares an obligation represented by an item of commercial paper to be discharged, the maker or drawer is given a complete defense to payment.

Discharge of which the holder has notice when he takes the paper. A person who acquires an item of commercial paper, knowing that a former holder has discharged the liability of the maker or drawer to pay, is acquiring an item that he will be unable to collect. If the acquirer knows of the discharge, it is valid with respect to him.

Forgery. No person is liable upon commercial paper unless his name has been signed thereon by himself or by his authorized agent. A forged signature is one placed upon the paper by a person with absolutely no authority to act as the purported signer's agent. According to UCC 3-404, such a signature is totally ineffective. The signature is assumed to be genuine if the signer is alive and competent; thus the burden of proof is upon the person who claims the signature to be a forgery. If the alleged signer is dead or incompetent, the questioned signature is not presumed to be genuine; in this case the burden of proof is upon the party who claims that it is genuine.

Negligence (by the person whose name was forged) that contributes to the making of the forgery will operate to prevent the victim from using the defense. Thus, if a person uses a mechanical means of signing commercial paper, such as a signature stamp, he must use care to make certain that unauthorized persons do not get access to the stamp. The stamped signature will appear to be genuine, of course, no matter who wields the stamp.

If a person knows that some of his blank personalized checks have been lost or stolen, he is under an obligation to notify his bank as soon as possible. The finder or thief may have the intention of forging the victim's name to some of them, and warning of the loss or theft of the checks will put the bank on guard to look out for them.

The person or firm mailing out checks is under an obligation to make certain that the check is mailed to the proper individual. Mailing the check to the wrong individual could constitute negligence. For instance: Ace Company owes money to Samuel J. Spade. Ace Company has lost Samuel's address, so it looks him up in the telephone directory. It finds a Samuel J. Spade listed there, living at 123 Easy Street. Therefore the check is mailed to Samuel J. Spade at that address. However, the Samuel J. Spade residing at 123 Easy Street is not the individual to whom the company owes money; the latter individual lives at 456 Lullaby Lane, but has an unlisted telephone number. The Samuel J. Spade on Easy Street wonders why Ace Company is sending him a check, but he is not one to look a gift horse in the mouth. He cashes the check at Second Bank. Second Bank sends the check over to First Bank, Ace's bank, which honors it. Meanwhile the Lullaby Lane Spade asks Ace where his money is, and the error comes to light. Ace claims Second Bank did wrong by honoring a check with a forged endorsement. It is forged in the sense that the intended payee did not endorse it, but it is apparently endorsed correctly. Ace Company has no recourse against the banks. Ace's negligence in mailing the check to the wrong Samuel J. Spade has caused the whole problem. (The Samuel J. Spade of Easy Street may of course be forced to disgorge his windfall.)

Ultra vires issue by a government or government agency. The power of governments and government agencies to make expenditures and to borrow money is strictly regulated by constitutional provisions, statutes, and administrative regulations. The courts enforce them rigidly, since it would not be in the interest of taxpayers to permit the easy evasion of such legal provisions.

For a government or governmental agency to spend or borrow money in violation of applicable restrictions is of course illegal. If the expenditure or borrowing is evidenced by some form of commercial paper, the illegality will constitute a real defense to payment. If this were not so, illegal borrowings and expenditures could be made by issuing commercial paper and making certain that the paper came into the hands of a holder in due course.

Unauthorized signature. A signature properly placed upon commercial paper by an agent possessing authority to do so binds the principal in the same way as if the principal had signed himself. The signature by an agent having no authority to sign commercial paper does not bind the principal. An agent normally must have express authority to sign commercial paper for his principal as maker, drawer, or acceptor. There is no such thing as implied authority to do this, and apparent authority to do it almost never exists.

The one situation in which apparent authority will exist is exemplified by the following: White has hired Black to manage his drugstore, and has given him authority to sign checks on the store checking account. Later White fires Black and revokes his check-writing authority, but he does not inform the bank of this fact. So far as the bank is concerned, Black still has apparent authority to write checks upon the account, because it does not know of the termination of his express authority. If Black has had express authority to borrow money in the name of the drugstore, the store owner should inform the banks with which Black has dealt in this capacity that he no longer has such authority. If this is not done, Black may still retain apparent authority to make such borrowings.

Possessor has no title to the paper. If the possessor of an item of commercial paper is neither its owner nor an authorized agent of its owner, he has no right to collect upon it.

If the possessor is a holder—that is, if the paper is bearer paper, or if it is order paper endorsed or originally drawn to the order of the possessor—the possessor is presumed to be the owner. The maker or drawer may prove that he is not the owner by proving that an endorsement essential to his title is a forgery, or that it is unauthorized.

Proof that an endorsement is forged or unauthorized will destroy the possessor's status as a holder and also destroy his legal title to the paper. It must be remembered, though, that this is the only way in which the title of any holder of the paper may be challenged.

It must also be remembered that certain sorts of forged endorsements will operate to pass good title to the paper, as discussed earlier. If the forged endorsements are made possible due to the negligence of the maker or drawer in being "taken" by an imposter, the fraud of the dishonest agent who has sole check-writing authority, or the fraud of dishonest agents padding the payroll or padding the accounts payable, then the possessor of the paper—if it is duly endorsed to him—will be the holder, and the maker or drawer will suffer for his negligence. Of course, if the person seeking to collect is not a holder—if the paper is order paper not drawn or endorsed to the possessor's order—the maker or drawer need not pay until the possessor can prove ownership or authority to collect.

Material alteration. When a completed item of commercial paper is altered, a provision of it is changed. If the alteration changes the contract of any party to the paper in any respect, it is a material alteration. The contract of a party to the paper may also be changed by the addition or deletion of terms to or from an already completed instrument. UCC 3-407 defines the effect of this alteration upon the obligation of the maker or drawer.

Unless negligence by the maker or drawer contributed to the material alteration, the paper is not enforceable as altered. A holder in due course may enforce it as it was originally drawn, while a non-holder in due course may not enforce it at all. The material alteration will not be a defense unless it was done by the holder or by a person acting for a holder. A material alteration by a disinterested third party (such as, for instance, a meddling child) has no effect. The alteration must be done with intent to defraud if it is to be a defense. Usually, the intent to defraud is fairly obvious, as when the value of the instrument is altered upward. But in borderline cases the party claiming the defense will have to prove the fraudulent intent of the altering party.

If negligence by the maker or drawer in drawing the instrument made the task of the altering party easy, the alteration will not be a defense to payment (UCC 3-406). Such negligence could consist of writing the instrument in pencil rather than in ink, or in leaving blank spaces beside essential portions of the paper in which altering material may be inserted. For instance, consider the following check:

FIRST NATIONAL BANK OF PODUNK

Podunk, Texas _____ July 7 _____, 1978 _____

Pay to the
Order of _____ Sam Slink _____ $ 100.00 _____

_____ One Hundred and no/100 _____ Dollars

_____ Dan Dimwit _____

If Sam Slink is clever at imitating other people's handwriting, or if he owns a typewriter with the same style of type of type as was used in writing this check (if we assume that it was typewritten), Sam can add a figure "1" before the $100.00, and he can write in the words "One thousand" before the words "One hundred," making these two lines look like this:

Pay to the
Order of _____Sam Slink_____ $1100.00_____
_____One thousand One Hundred and no/100_____ Dollars

Should this check as altered get into the hands of a holder in due course, or a person with holder in due course rights, Dan will be liable for $1,100 on it, his negligence having made the alteration very easy. Of course, Dan should have completed the amount lines in this way:

Pay to the
Order of _____Sam Slink_____ $100.00_____
_____One Hundred and no/100_____ Dollars

This sort of elemental precaution can save much grief (and cash).

On the other hand, it is not negligence not to use check-writing machines for drawing checks; not all of us can afford them. It is also not negligence to not use tamper-proof paper for the printing of checks. It is certainly very difficult to successfully alter checks printed upon such paper, but such paper is also more expensive than the ordinary paper used for checks.

Expiration of the statute of limitations. Under the provisions of RCS 5527, a person entitled to enforce an obligation evidenced by a written promise may sue to enforce the obligation within four years of the obligation's arising. Thus, generally, one may sue to enforce commercial paper in Texas within four years of the maturity of the paper. However, this four-year period may be extended by various causes, such as the obligor's spending time outside the state of Texas during the four-year period. The defense, when usable, is a real defense.

PERSONAL DEFENSES

The personal defenses are those which will permit the maker or drawer to escape paying a person who does not have holder in due course rights. The defenses will not hold against those who do have holder in due course rights; if the person seeking payment can prove that he has holder in due course rights, then the maker or drawer must pay, despite the existence of the defense.

UCC 3-306 lists some of the personal defenses available to makers, drawers, or acceptors of commercial paper, but the listing is nowhere near complete. Many of the personal defenses exist as matters of judge-made law, and the drafters of the UCC thought it unnecessary to list them all.

Breach of contract. This is one of the most common personal defenses. If the payee did not perform his obligations under his contract with the maker or drawer, the maker or drawer is relieved from his performance obligation, so long as the paper has not gotten into the hands of a person with holder in due course rights.

Lack of consideration. If the maker or drawer got no consideration for the issuance of the paper, he need not pay anyone without holder in due course rights. In connection with this, UCC 3-408 provides that when a negotiable instrument is given in payment of a debt or in settlement of an obligation, consideration is given for it.

Nonperformance or nonoccurrence of a condition precedent. If the contract of the maker or drawer provides that he shall not be obligated unless a condition precedent occurs, and it does not occur, a personal defense exists. Thus, if the maker of a promissory note given in payment for a racing car has agreed with the seller that the note shall be void and the sale cancelled if the car does not place at least sixth in the Podunk 500 auto race, and the car finishes ninth, the condition is not fulfilled and a personal defense exists.

Fraud in the inducement. If a person is tricked into signing a check, draft, or promissory note through false representations by another, but he knows what he is signing when he signs, he is a victim of fraud in the inducement. This is a personal defense to payment when it is grounds for rescission of a contract. Before there is a defense to payment the fraud, justifiable reliance by the victim upon the truth of the fraudulent statement, and damages caused to the victim must all exist.

Duress. Any duress of a lesser nature than the fear for life that constitutes extreme duress is a personal defense to payment. A threat to commence a civil lawsuit, or a threat to do that which one has the legal right to do (other than commence a criminal prosecution) is not duress.

Undue influence. Conduct that would enable a person to rescind a contract because of undue influence constitutes a personal defense to payment of commercial paper. This includes taking advantage of a fiduciary relationship, of the need for love and affection of the very old or very infirm, or of the emotional turmoil of a person facing a grave crisis.

Mistake. The sort of mutual mistake as to the nature of the subject matter that provides grounds for rescission of a contract comprises a personal defense to payment of commercial paper. Mutual mistake as to the value of the subject matter is no defense. Unilateral mistake is likewise no defense, unless the other party as a reasonable person should have been aware of the mistake.

Unconscionability. The victim of an unconscionable contract has a personal defense to payment with respect to any commercial paper which he signed when he made the contract. If the paper which he signed is a promissory note, and if he is a consumer, he may escape paying the note altogether due to the FTC regulation discussed in the materials on holders in due course, which prevents any buyer of a consumer promissory note from being a holder in due course.

Limited contractual capacity. As discussed earlier, minors and persons declared incompetent for whom guardians have been appointed have real defenses to payment to commercial paper which they have signed. Incompetent or retarded persons for whom no guardian has been appointed have a personal defense to payment of their commercial paper if it has not been given as consideration for a necessity and if the person dealing with them knew or should have known of their incompetence. In the case of necessities, or when the other party did not know and could not be expected to know of the mental infirmity, no defense at all exists.

Illegality. Any sort of illegality other than usury or ultra vires issuance of the paper by a government constitutes a personal defense to payment in Texas. Thus: Jones pays his poker losses to Smith in the form of a check and then stops payment upon the check; Smith negotiates the check to Adams, a holder in due course. Jones will be required to make the check good, even though it was given in payment of a gambling debt.

Unauthorized completion. If one issues an item of commercial paper containing blanks which are not filled in, and the blanks are filled in in an unauthorized manner, a personal defense to payment exists.

Thus: Sapp wants to buy 100 shares of Quatz Corporation stock from Broker. Broker agrees to deliver the stock, but tells Sapp he is not sure what the price will be—only that it will be somewhere around $4,000. Sapp signs a blank check payable to Broker's order, telling Broker to fill in the exact price when he finds out what it is. Broker fills in the amount as $9,500 and negotiates the check to Third Bank, a holder in due course. Sapp finds out what Broker did and stops payment. Sapp has been had; he must pay Third Bank the $9,500 and try to recoup his loss from Broker.

Prior payment. When a person pays off a promissory note or draft in full he acquires a personal defense to payment of it. If he acquires possession of the instrument, or if he has it cancelled or destroyed, the defense is good against the world, because the instrument will no longer circulate. However, if one pays such an instrument in full and does not reacquire it or have it canceled or destroyed, it can still circulate. If the paid-off holder gets it into the hands of someone with holder in due course rights, the maker, drawer, or acceptor may be made to pay again. This is true even if the former holder gave a receipt for the payment.

Thus, when paying off a note or draft before its maturity, one must either get the paper from the holder or have it canceled or destroyed. If one is paying after maturity, the danger is not so great, since a buyer of an overdue instrument is not a holder in due course. However, if the party who collects payment is someone other than the original payee, he might be a holder in due course. If so, he could transfer the paper to a holder through a holder in due course; so even in this situation prudence commands that one take the proper precautions when making full payment.

Partial payment. When one makes a partial payment upon a promissory note, one may not, of course, ask to obtain the note. Since the note is not fully paid, one may not ask for its cancellation. The partial payment is a partial defense to liability upon the note, but it is only a personal defense. If the current holder sells the note to a buyer who qualifies as a holder in due course or holder through a holder in due course and who does not know of the partial payment, one may be forced to make that payment again, even though he has a receipt showing that the payment has been made and accepted. The only way to avoid this possibility is to make certain that the fact that partial payment has been made is noted on the face of the note itself.

Discharge other than payment or bankruptcy. The existence of a discharge from liability to pay other than payment or bankruptcy constitutes a personal defense. The question of what constitutes such a discharge will be discussed in the chapter on discharge of commercial paper.

Nondelivery. Generally, the maker or drawer of commercial paper must deliver it into the hands of the payee or his authorized agent before he becomes obligated. The maker or drawer may make delivery personally, or he may do it through an authorized agent. If the payee gets possession of the instrument in an unauthorized manner (as by simply taking it from the drawer's desk without permission), a personal defense to payment exists.

Delivery for a special purpose. When an instrument is given to a payee for a special purpose, but the payee does not use it for that purpose, a personal defense to payment arises. Thus: the treasurer of Alpha Beta Gamma fraternity draws a check on the fraternity checking account payable to the order of brother Omega, telling Omega to cash it and use the proceeds to buy refreshments for the Saturday night party. Omega cashes it and is seen no more, so the treasurer stops payment. Omega cashed it at First Bank, so First Bank demands that the fraternity make it good. Alpha Beta Gamma has been had: the bank will qualify as a holder in due course unless it knew of Omega's evil intentions (which it almost certainly did not).

When commercial paper is issued for a special purpose, the purpose should be noted upon the paper. This is no guarantee against misappropriation, but it will stop certain types of buyers from becoming holders in due course. The notation would not have prevented First Bank from becoming a holder in due course if Omega had cashed the check there; the teller need not ask a person cashing a check what he intends to do with the proceeds. On the other hand, if Omega had used the check to make a payment upon a loan he had outstanding at the bank, the bank would not be a holder in due course; it would have known that Omega was misappropriating the fraternity's funds.

Breach of fiduciary duty. If the maker, drawer, or acceptor of an instrument knows that the person seeking payment obtained the instrument from someone who breached a fiduciary duty or knows that a former holder transferred in breach of fiduciary duty, he has a personal defense to payment. Again, how good the defense is depends on the status of the collecting party.

Thus: Goodman gives a check to Gard, guardian of Pobre, telling Gard to use the money to buy Pobre a new suit. The check is payable to "Gard for the benefit of Pobre." Gard endorses the check, "Gard, guardian of Pobre," and gives it to Wolf, a creditor of his, in payment of a debt. Goodman finds out Gard did this and stops payment. Wolf cannot collect here; he knows of Gard's breach of his fiduciary duty to Pobre. However, if Wolf negotiated the check to First Bank as a payment on a loan, the bank would have no way of knowing of Gard's wrongdoing. The bank would be a holder in due course and could collect upon the check.

Payment inconsistent with terms of restrictive endorsement. If the maker, drawer, or acceptor knows that his payment would be contrary to the terms of a restrictive endorsement, he has a personal defense. If the holder of the paper also knows this, he is not a holder in due course and cannot collect. It is not possible to become the owner of an instrument endorsed "for deposit only" and qualify as a holder in due course unless the owner is a bank. It is also not possible to obtain clear title to an instrument bearing a conditional endorsement if the condition has not been met. It is possible, however, to become a holder in due course of an instrument bearing a trust endowment, even if the trustee has breached his trust.

Thus: Baker borrowed money from Able, giving Able in return a negotiable note payable to Able's order. Able negotiates it to Gard for the benefit of Pobre, endorsing "Pay to Gard for the use of Pobre." Gard negotiates it to Wolf in payment of a debt he owes Wolf, endorsing "Gard, trustee for Pobre." Wolf negotiates it to Goodman in payment of a debt he owes Goodman, using a normal special endorsement, Goodman being a holder in due course. Baker finds out about Gard's breach of trust and therefore refuses to pay Goodman when the note matures. His defense will not hold up; he must pay Goodman. Had Wolf been the one to present the note for payment, this defense would have been good. Wolf, knowing of Gard's breach of trust, would not be a holder in due course.

Theft. If the instrument has been stolen during its life, the person obligated to pay has a personal defense to payment. If the stolen paper is order paper, it will either bear a forged endorsement (if it is endorsed to the current possessor) or the current possessor will not be the holder because it is not endorsed to him. If the paper is bearer paper, though, the possessor will at least appear to be the holder.

If the bearer of such bearer paper is not a holder in due course, the defense will hold against him. If he is a holder in due course, however, the obligor must pay.

26/ Defenses to Payment   393

Loss. If the instrument has been lost during its life, the person obligated to pay has a personal defense to payment. The conditions surrounding the availability of the defense are essentially those discussed above with respect to theft.

Setoff. If the maker, drawer, or acceptor has a claim against the payee arising out of the same transaction as the instrument to be paid, a personal defense exists to the extent of the claim.

Thus: Seller sold goods to Buyer, and Buyer paid the purchase price in part with a negotiable promissory note. Buyer claimed the goods were not fit for normal use and thus did not comply with the warranty of merchantability. Seller negotiated the note to Moneybags. Buyer refused to pay Moneybags because of the breach of warranty of merchantability. If Moneybags is a holder in due course the defense will not hold. If he is not a holder in due course, Buyer may claim the setoff.

Suppose that, in the above case, the face value of the note Buyer gave Seller was $5,000, and there was no breach of warranty by Seller. Seller negotiated the note to Moneybags. When Moneybags asked Buyer to honor the note, he owed Buyer $3,000 on an overdue loan. Buyer said he would pay only $2,000 on the note. Buyer can get away with this because the maker, drawer, or acceptor may claim as a setoff any claim he has against the holder of the paper who is demanding payment.

Counterclaim. If the maker, drawer, or acceptor of a negotiable instrument has a claim against the payee that is not related to the transaction giving rise to the note, he has a personal defense to payment to the extent of the counterclaim. The rules governing availability of this defense are essentially those applicable in the case of setoff.

MATTERS WHICH ARE NOT DEFENSES

There are cases that might appear to the uninitiated to be good defenses to payment but that are not recognized as defenses at all. We shall close this chapter by considering some of these.

Inability to pay. If the person obligated to pay an instrument does not have the funds with which to pay, the holder obviously cannot force him to pay—"you cannot get blood out of a turnip." However, this will not prevent the holder from suing the obligor and getting a judgment against him. The holder must then wait until the obligor acquires the ability to pay, at which point he may forcibly collect if necessary.

The paper is nonnegotiable. Students may get the idea that an instrument which is nonnegotiable cannot be enforced. This is a very erroneous notion. The big difference between negotiable and nonnegotiable paper is that there can be no holder in due course of nonnegotiable paper. Thus, any defense to payment of nonnegotiable paper is good. However, if the obligor has no defense, he must pay.

A third party has a better right to the paper. If the possessor of the paper is not a holder, the obligor need not pay unless the possessor can prove legal title or authority to collect. If the possessor is ostensibly a holder, the obligor need not pay if an essential endorsement is a forgery which does not pass legal title, or if the holder is not a holder in due course and the paper is lost or stolen.

Under circumstances other than these, the obligor cannot escape paying by arguing that someone else has better rights to the instrument. However, the obligor might be able to interplead the third party with a supposedly better claim and let him make his own case, or he might convince the third party to intervene in the case to make his own plea. Thus: Gray owned a negotiable note by which White promised to pay $5,000 to his order. Black defrauded Gray into negotiating the note to him. Black refused to return the note, so Gray told his sad tale to White and asked White not to pay Black when the note matured. White refused to pay as requested and Black threatened to sue. White cannot escape paying Black unless Gray is made a party to the suit to press his claim of ownership. Gray must do this for himself; White cannot do it for him.

The payee does not exist. No obligor may escape paying an instrument by proving the nonexistence of the payee. According to UCC 3-413, the obligor admits the existence of the payee when he signs an instrument payable to the order of the payee.

Thus: Idd does business as Zapp Corporation, though he has never organized Zapp Corporation. Slink buys goods from Idd and pays for them with a check payable to the order of Zapp Corporation. Slink stops payment upon the check, arguing that he owes the corporation nothing because it does not exist. Essentially, Zapp Corporation does exist as far as Slink is concerned: he admitted that it does when he wrote the check.

The payee has no (or limited) contractual capacity. The obligor of an instrument admits the full contractual capacity of the payee by signing the instrument payable to the order of the payee. He may not escape payment by arguing the payee's lack of capacity.

Thus: Simp buys goods from Nemo, paying for them with a check. Simp does not know that Nemo has been declared incompetent by a court, and that Watchman has been appointed his guardian. Simp learns this the hard way when Watchman demands the return of the goods, because Nemo has no capacity to sell them. Simp therefore stops payment on the check, since Watchman tells him that Nemo did not give it to him. Meanwhile Nemo has negotiated the check to Merchant in payment for goods, Merchant not knowing of Nemo's incapacity. Merchant demands that Simp honor the check. Simp claims Merchant has no title to the check because Nemo had no capacity to negotiate it to him. Simp is wrong. It is true that, normally, Nemo could not negotiate a check. But he can negotiate this check, because Simp admitted his capacity to do so by writing the check in the first place.

The instrument does not mean what it says. The parol evidence rule is most stringently applied to commercial paper. Oral evidence may not be admitted that contradicts the plain meaning of the instrument. It may be used to clear up ambiguities in the wording of the instrument, however, or to show the existence of defenses to payment.

Payment will cause a hardship. Just as one may not escape an ordinary contractual obligation by arguing that performance would cause hardship, or escape paying a debt by arguing that one cannot afford to pay it just yet and payment now would cause hardship, one may not escape paying commercial paper by arguing hardship.

It may well be that the debtor was improvident to sign the paper in the first place. It may even be that the holder has a moral obligation not to press for immediate payment. But, as in so many other areas of the law, moral obligations are not necessarily legal obligations, and individuals are held responsible for their improvidence.

Payment of the instrument has been stopped. The drawer of a check has the right to instruct his bank not to honor it, and the bank will generally obey the instruction. The check will then be dishonored. This does not mean, however, that the drawer need not honor the check. If the drawer gave his bank the stop payment order because he had a defense to payment, he may be able to escape liability. That will, of course, depend on the nature of the defense and the status of the holder. However, the making of a stop payment order is not a defense to payment, in and of itself.

The stop payment order given by a customer to his bank upon a check is the most common sort of stoppage of payment. However, a drawer could ask an acceptor not to pay a draft he has accepted, or a payee could ask a maker not to honor a promissory note.

Again, the recipient of such a request may honor it, but the fact that he has received a request to stop payment does not provide him with a defense to payment. Stoppage of payment without a good defense to payment merely invites litigation.

Issuance of the instrument was an ultra vires corporate act. The powers of corporations are limited by law and by their articles of incorporation. However, corporations may not escape liability upon commercial paper by arguing that the instrument should not have been issued because it was beyond the power of the corporation to issue. If the issuance was truly ultra vires, and if it causes loss to the corporation, those who authorized it will be liable to the corporation for the loss, but the corporation must honor the instrument.

27

Liability of Parties

Discharge of Commercial Paper

Liability of Parties

No party is liable upon commercial paper unless he has signed it, unless his signature has been placed upon the paper by an authorized agent, or unless he has transferred the paper for consideration.

Persons who sign commercial paper may incure *primary* liability, *secondary* liability, *guarantor of payment* liability, or *guarantor of collection* liability. Persons who transfer commercial paper for consideration, whether they endorse or not, may incur *warranty* liability. Persons who present commercial paper for payment or acceptance may also incur *warranty* liability, whether they endorse or not.

UCC 3-413(1) describes the characteristics of primary liability. A person with such liability is expected to pay the instrument he signed upon maturity, without being asked. If he does not pay at maturity, he may be sued without prior notice. Those parties with primary liability include makers of notes, acceptors of drafts, and certifying banks on certified checks. Accommodation makers and accommodation acceptors also have primary liability.

Liability of makers of notes. If a note has only one maker and no endorsements, it is not necessary to hunt up the maker and ask him to pay at maturity. If he does not pay he may be sued at once. As a practical matter, though, it obviously pays to ask the maker to pay before filing suit. If he pays, the note is discharged and no unpleasantness is necessary.

If a note has one maker and one or more endorsers, it will be necessary to ask the maker to pay as soon as possible after maturity. This need not be done to fix the liability of the maker, but UCC 3-501 provides that endorsers may not be held liable unless presentment is first made to the maker, presentment being the act of asking the maker to pay. If the maker shows reluctance to pay, the holder may then seek to force him to pay or he may take action to collect from the endorsers.

If a note has two or more makers, the co-makers have joint and several liability upon it, unless the note by its terms provides for some other sort of liability. Thus, the holder may demand payment from one or more of the co-makers. If the holder finds it necessary to sue to collect, he need not name all co-makers as defendants; he may sue some now and others later.

If one of the co-makers is an accommodation maker, this will not affect his liability to the holder unless the note itself indicates that the co-maker is a guarantor of collection or something of the kind. Should the accommodation maker be a surety or a guarantor of payment, he will have essentially the same liability as his principal debtor.

The liability of the co-makers among themselves will of course be influenced by their relationship. Suppose Redd lends $1,000 to Black and White, and Black and White sign as co-makers a note promising to pay $1,000 to Redd on demand. And suppose that White pays the $1,000 on demand. What recourse has White against Black? If the loan was to Black and White as partners, joint venturers, or the like, Black and White have equal liability. Therefore White can force Black to pay his share of the note—$500. If the loan was to Black, and White signed as accommodation maker, White is in the position of a surety exercising his right of reimbursement against his principal debtor. He can collect $1,000 from Black. If the loan was to White, and Black was White's accommodation maker, White has no claim against Black. Here, since the principal debtor has paid the debt, the surety is discharged.

When the note is an interest-bearing note, interest continues to accrue until the note is paid. Accrual of interest does not stop at maturity. The maker who desires to stop the accrual of interest must search out the holder and pay off the note. Inaction by the holder in trying to collect will normally not stop accrual of interest.

If the note in question is a domiciled note, though, the rules are a bit different. A domiciled note is payable at a named bank. If the maker has sufficient funds on deposit at the bank to pay the note plus accrued interest at maturity, the maker is said to have tendered payment and the accrual of interest stops. According to Texas Business & Commerce Code 3-121, when a domiciled note is presented for payment at the named bank, the bank may treat the note as a check drawn upon its customer's account. It may thus honor the note without informing the maker beforehand.

Notice that a note which says that it is payable through a named bank is not a domiciled note. The named bank in such a case is not obligated to pay anything on the note. Such wording merely authorizes the bank to act as a collection agent upon the note, as per the provisions of UCC 3-120.

Liability of acceptors of drafts. The acceptor of a draft also incurs primary liability. It must be remembered, however, that all drafts do not have acceptors.

There are two basic categories of drafts—sight drafts and time drafts. Sight drafts are generally worded, "To John Jones. On sight pay $100 to the order of Bill Smith. /s/ Ben Black." The sight draft is essentially demand paper. Black will give the draft to Smith. Smith will then take it to Jones and ask him to pay it. There is no reason for the drawee of a sight draft to accept it. He will either pay it upon presentment, or he will not.

Should Jones refuse to pay this sight draft, he cannot be held liable upon it, because he has never signed it. His refusal to pay may well be a breach of contract, however, and he may be sued for damages upon that theory.

There are two types of time drafts. All time drafts are payable at a fixed time. Some of these require the making of an acceptance in order to fix the maturity date. An example is a draft worded this way: "June 3, 1980. To John Jones: 30 days after acceptance pay to the order of Bill Smith $100. /s/ Ben Black."

Black will give this draft to Smith, in all probability, and Smith will then be obligated to present it to Jones for acceptance. Should Jones wish to accept, he will do what is required by UCC 3-410. The best way to accept this draft is for Jones to write upon its face, "Accepted, June 5, 1978. /s/ John Jones." By making this acceptance Jones has agreed to pay the draft on July 5, 1980, as drawn. Jones has thereby incurred the primary liability of an acceptor. Should Jones refuse to accept, he may not be held liable for nonpayment of the draft due to the fact that he has never signed it. But, if his refusal to accept is a breach of contract, the victim of the breach may sue him on that basis.

When a drawee accepts a draft, he becomes liable upon the paper as it read when he accepted it. It does not matter if the draft had been materially altered before acceptance, or if the drawer's signature upon it was a forgery. By accepting, the drawee waives the benefit of the defense of forgery of the drawer's signature, or of material alteration. The acceptor also may not use a breach of contract by the drawer as a defense to payment.

The mere signature of the drawee will operate as an acceptance. The acceptance need not be dated. The holder of a draft with an undated acceptance may supply a date of acceptance, if he does so in good faith. An acceptance must be written upon the face of the draft itself. Thus, an oral acceptance is invalid, as is a written acceptance on a piece of paper separate from the draft.

The second type of time draft requires no acceptance in order to fix the maturity date. An example would be a draft such as the following: "June 3, 1978. To John Jones: On July 15, 1980, pay to the order of Bill Smith $100. /s/ Ben Black." This draft already specifies a maturity date; there is therefore no absolute necessity for anyone to ask Jones to accept this. The holder could simply wait until July 15, 1980, and then ask Jones to pay it. However, if Jones does not pay then the only recourse would be a suit against Jones for breach of contract.

The holder may want to find out Jones's intentions with respect to payment. These may be ascertained simply by presenting the draft to Jones for acceptance. If Jones means to pay this, he should not object to accepting it. If he refuses to accept it, though, that is a sure indication that he will not pay.

Refusal to accept or to pay a time draft, or refusal to pay a sight draft, constitutes dishonor. Upon such dishonor, the holder should immediately take the necessary steps to fix the secondary liability of the drawer, which will be discussed when we reach the subject of secondary liability.

The drawee is under no obligation to make his decision whether or not to accept at once. He has the right to defer his decision until the close of the next business day after presentment (UCC 3-506). The holder may grant the drawee an additional day within which to decide, without prejudicing his rights against the drawer or endorsers. Should the drawee not return the draft after expiration of his time for consideration of acceptance, his silence is not deemed to be acceptance. However, he is guilty of conversion of the draft and may be sued for that, the damages being the face value of the draft as per UCC 3-419.

It may be that the drawee is willing to accept the draft, but not on the terms written into the paper. An acceptance by the drawee which alters the terms of the draft is called a draft-varying acceptance. According to the provisions of UCC 3-412, the holder has an option as to whether or not to permit the drawee to make a draft-varying acceptance. If he permits it, he must obtain the agreement of the drawer and all endorsers to the alteration of terms; otherwise the drawer and all endorsers endorsing before the making of the draft-varying acceptance are discharged from liability. If he refuses to permit it, the draft is at that point dishonored, and the holder must immediately take the necessary steps to fix the secondary liability of the drawer and endorsers.

An accommodation acceptor has the same primary liability as any other acceptor.

If the party he accommodated is the drawer, he will have greater liability toward the holder than does his principal debtor. However, the accommodation acceptor who pays a draft does of course have recourse against the party he signed to accommodate.

Liability of certifying bank on checks. When a bank certifies a check, it performs essentially the same act as a drawee does when he accepts a draft. The bank incurs the primary liability of an acceptor. The other ramifications of the certification of checks will be discussed in the material on checks and bank deposits.

Prerequisites for fixing secondary liability. Parties with secondary liability upon commercial paper may be called upon to pay it when the parties who are supposed to pay it do not pay. Secondary parties do not become liable until the preliminary requirements of presentment, notice of dishonor, and (sometimes) protest are complied with.

The requisites for presentment are contained in UCC 3-503, 504, and 505. A note is presented by asking the maker to pay, or, in the case of the domiciled note, presenting it for payment at the specified bank. A draft is presented by asking the drawee to accept or to pay, as the case might be. A check is presented by asking the drawee bank to honor it, either by using banking channels or by making a direct presentment at the bank by going there to cash it.

Presentment can be made in person, by mail, through banking channels, or through a clearinghouse. If the paper specifies that it must be presented at a certain place (as does a domiciled note), presentment must be made at that place. If no place is specified, a note or draft may be presented at the place of business or residence of the maker, drawee, or acceptor.

Presentment must be made at a reasonable time, normally during business hours. The person to whom presentment is made has the right to ask the presenter to show him the paper which he is being asked to accept or pay. He may also ask the presenter for identification, and for proof that he is the owner of the paper. A maker or acceptor may delay payment until the close of business on the day of presentment, in order to check his records to ascertain whether or not he should pay.

Presentment is excused under the following circumstances:
1. When the paper contains a provision under which endorsers waive presentment as a precondition to liability, or
2. The maker, drawee, or acceptor is dead or involved in an insolvency proceeding such as bankruptcy or assignment for benefit of creditors, or
3. The maker, drawee, or acceptor cannot be located with use of due diligence, or
4. The secondary parties know that the maker of acceptor will not pay (because, for example, one of them breached a contract with the maker or drawer).

After presentment has been duly made (or excused), the next step is the giving of notice of dishonor to the secondary parties against which the holder wants to proceed. UCC 3-508 contains the requirements.

A notice of dishonor must be timely. The deadlines for giving one are very short. A non-bank holder must give notice to all the secondary parties he wishes to hold liable by midnight of the third business day after dishonor—Saturdays, Sundays, and holidays not counting as business days. If dishonor occurs on Monday, the non-bank holder must give notice of dishonor by midnight Thursday. If dishonor occurs on Thursday, the deadline is midnight Tuesday.

A bank holder must give notice by midnight of the next business day after dishonor. Thus, if dishonor occurs on Monday, the bank's deadline is midnight Tuesday.

A nonholder secondary party, usually an endorser, may want to give notice of dishonor to endorsers who endorsed before he did in order to preserve recourse against them if he is called upon to pay the instrument. The deadline for such a party is midnight of the third business day after he got notice of dishonor.

Notice of dishonor may be given orally or in writing. The best way to give it is by registered or certified mail, delivered to addressee only, return receipt requested, so that proof of mailing and proof of receipt will exist. Ordinary mail will suffice, but proof of mailing will be more difficult. Oral notice will also suffice, but proof of giving is more difficult. Oral notice is effective when given. Mailed notice is effective when sent, if mailed in good faith to an address the giver believes to be good.

Notice of dishonor is excused when:

1. The paper contains a provision stating that endorsers and other such parties waive notice of dishonor as a precondition for liability. Usually these clauses provide for waiver of both presentment and notice of dishonor.
2. The person to whom notice ordinarily would be given is the person who is responsible for the dishonor.
3. The holder does not know that the instrument is due, usually because a former holder accelerated the due date and did not inform the present holder when he transferred the paper.
4. The notice was given late, due to circumstances beyond the giver's control, but he gave the notice as quickly as he could.

With respect to international drafts—drafts drawn in the United States payable outside the United States or drafts drawn outside the United States payable inside the United States—a protest will also be required before secondary parties may be held liable. A protest is a document sworn to before a U.S. consul, vice-consul, notary public, or any other official having authority to administer oaths, and bearing the official's seal, containing:

1. A description of the dishonored instrument, and
2. Facts as to how, when, and where presentment was made, and
3. A statement that the instrument was dishonored by nonacceptance or nonpayment, and
4. The signature and seal of the attesting official.

The instrument must be presented to the proper official before the deadline for giving notice of dishonor. The official may either prepare the protest at that time or note the instrument for protest and prepare the protest later, but the instrument must at least be noted for protest before the notice of dishonor deadline. UCC 3-509 deals with protests. The making of the protest is excused by the same sorts of circumstances which will excuse the making of presentment or the giving of notice of dishonor.

It must be remembered also that unreasonable delay in presenting an instrument for payment will discharge secondary parties in case of dishonor.

Secondary liability of drawers. Dishonor of a draft when presented either for acceptance or payment will cause the drawer to become liable. Improper procedure in making the presentment or protest (where required) or in giving notice of dishonor will not completely discharge the drawer; he will be discharged only to the extent that the delay or improper procedure causes him to lose his recourse against the drawee for not accepting or paying, as the case might be. Except in cases involving the death, insolvency, or disappearance of the drawee during the period of unnecessary delay in presentment, improper procedures will not discharge the drawer of a draft.

Improper procedure in presenting a check for payment or in giving notice of dishonor is even less likely to discharge the drawer of a check. The only circumstance under which this will occur is when the bank the check is drawn upon becomes insolvent during the period of unnecessary delay; this very seldom occurs. Thus the drawer of a check can hardly ever escape liability due to such technicalities.

Secondary liability of endorsers. Delays and improper procedures with respect to presentment, notice of dishonor, and protest will operate to cause discharge of endorsers. The procedures described above must be strictly followed when preservation of endorser liability is desired.

Endorsers are liable upon the paper in the order of endorsement. Unless accommodation endorsers are involved, an endorser can never be held liable to anyone who endorsed after he did. However, an endorser may be liable to someone who endorsed before he did.

A holder seeking recourse against endorsers is not limited to recourse from his immediate transferor. He may "pick his victim" from all prior endorsers. An endorser held liable to a holder also has recourse against all those who endorsed before he did.

An endorser of a check cannot be held liable as an endorser unless the check is presented for payment and dishonored within seven days of his endorsement. If the dishonor occurs more than seven days after the endorsement, the endorser is discharged.

Accommodation endorsers have the same liability as other endorsers, unless the accommodation character of the endorsement is obvious. In such a case, the endorser may be able to use one of the three suretyship defenses in order to escape liability.

Accommodation endorsements are often not identifiable as such; since the endorser usually merely signs his name, the endorsement looks like an ordinary blank endorsement. However, they are identifiable in two situations. One is exemplified by the check or note payable to the order of Walt White, which has on the back the signatures of Gus Gray and, following Gray's signature, the signature of Walt White. Gus Gray is obviously an accommodation endorser. Why else would he have endorsed?

The other sort of identifiable accommodation endorser is exemplified by the situation of the check or note payable to the order of Gerald Green, which has on the reverse the following endorsements:

1. Pay to the order of Ben Blue, /s/ Gerald Green.
2. /s/ Paul Pink.
3. /s/ Ben Blue.

Paul Pink is obviously an accommodation endorser here, since, according to the chain of endorsements, Pink never owned the paper.

The three suretyship defenses are:

1. The party the endorser signed to accommodate has been discharged from liability without the endorser's consent and without reservation of rights against said endorser. (The endorser may prove by oral evidence the identity of the party he signed to accommodate.)
2. The party accommodated has been given an extension of time to pay without the endorser's consent and without reservation of rights.
3. The holder has damaged the accommodation endorser's recourse against the accommodated party without the accommodation endorser's consent, by releasing collateral put up by the accommodated party, or something of that nature.

The accommodation endorser may also raise these defenses against a nonholder in due course of the paper who knows of the accommodation relationship. Accommodation makers and acceptors may also make use of these defenses under these circumstances.

Liability of a guarantor of payment. The guarantor of payment endorses, "Payment

Guaranteed, /s/ Jim Jones." According to UCC 3-416, he has more than normal secondary liability. If the party obligated to pay does not pay on the maturity date, the guarantor of payment may be sued on the next day, without need for presentment, notice of dishonor, or protest.

Liability of a guarantor of collection. The guarantor of collection endorses, "Collection Guaranteed, /s/ Jim Jones." According to UCC 3-416, he has less than normal secondary liability; he becomes liable only when collection from the party obligated to pay is virtually impossible. Normally, a judgment must be obtained against that party from which collection cannot be made. However, if the party obligated to pay is dead, discharged from his debts in bankruptcy, etc., the guarantor of collection becomes liable.

Liability of a person endorsing after maturity of the paper. Such a person has normal secondary liability, except that there may be a greater than average possibility of his incurring liability. Such an endorser is not entitled to presentment, notice of dishonor, and protest as prerequisites to liability. He has virtually the liability of a guarantor of payment.

Warranty liability of one presenting instruments for acceptance or payment. UCC 3-417(1) imposes three warranties upon such persons, whether they endorse at the time of acceptance or payment or not. The warranties are as follows:

1. The warranty of title. The person warrants that he is the owner of the instrument, or that he has authority to act for the owner. Violators of this warranty could be persons holding the paper under a forged endorsement, unauthorized agents, thieves, or finders.
2. The warranty that presenter has no knowledge that the signature of the maker or drawer is unauthorized or is a forgery. This warranty is not made by a holder in due course acting in good faith to the maker of a note (because the maker of a note should certainly know his own signature) or to the bank a check is drawn upon (because the bank is expected to know the signature of its customer).
3. The warranty that the paper has not been materially altered. This warranty is not made by the holder in due course acting in good faith to the maker of a note or to the acceptor of a draft, because these parties should remember the terms of their outstanding notes and drafts.

He who breaches one or more of these warranties in the process of collecting payment of an instrument can be made to give back the payment. He who breaches one or more of these warranties in the process of obtaining acceptance of a draft is liable in damages to the acceptor, the damages in all probability amounting to the face value of the draft.

Warranty liability of a transferor of instruments for consideration. He who receives no consideration for his transfer of commercial paper makes no warranties to his transferee. However, UCC 3-417(2) imposes five warranties upon the transferor for consideration:

1. The warranty that the transferor is the owner of the paper, or that he has authority to transfer ownership, and that his transfer is rightful. A violator might be a holder under a forged endorsement, a thief, a finder, an unauthorized agent, a dishonest trustee, or something of the sort.
2. The warranty that all signatures are genuine or authorized. If any signature on the paper is forged or unauthorized there exists a breach of this warranty, whether the transferor knows about it or not.
3. The warranty that the paper has not been materially altered. If the paper has been materially altered, there is a breach, whether the transferor knows of it or not. Note that this is not a warranty against unauthorized completion.
4. The warranty that no defense to payment is good against the transferor—that is,

that he has every right to collect the value of the paper himself. The qualified endorser, the endorser "without recourse," merely warrants that he knows of no defense to payment which is good against him, that so far as he knows he has every right to collect upon the paper.

5. The warranty that the transferor knows of no insolvency proceedings (essentially bankruptcy proceedings) involving the maker, drawer, or acceptor. Note that the transferor does not warrant that no such proceedings exist; he merely warrants that he knows of no such proceedings.

The transferor who endorses makes these warranties to all subsequent holders of the paper. The transferor who does not endorse makes the warranties only to his transferee (the person to whom he is transferring).

When a breach of warranty becomes known, a party damaged by it may sue upon it at once; it is not necessary to wait until the paper matures to make the claim.

The transferor for consideration does not, you will notice, warrant that the instrument will be paid. If it is not paid, but no breach of warranty has occurred, the transferor will not be liable unless he endorsed.

Interplay between endorser and warranty liability. The transferor of commercial paper may incur both endorser and warranty liability. He may incur endorser liability but no warranty liability. He may incur warranty liability but no endorser liability. Or he may incur no liability at all. If he endorses and receives consideration for his transfer, he will incur both liabilities. If he endorses and gives the paper away, he makes no warranties, but is liable as an endorser. If he does not endorse but receives consideration for the transfer, he is not liable as an endorser but he does make the warranties. If he gives the paper away and does not endorse, he incurs no liability at all. He who endorses "without recourse" disclaims endorser liability; but if he gets consideration for his transfer, he still makes warranties. He who endorses, "Without recourse, and all warranties disclaimed" disclaims all liability upon the paper.

Discharge of Commercial Paper

In this chapter we are concerned with actions that will terminate the liability of parties who have signed commercial paper. In considering the subject of discharge we must keep in mind the difference between acts discharging the instrument, which terminate the liability of all parties to the instrument at once, and acts terminating the liability of certain parties to the instrument while leaving the instrument itself still in force. We shall first consider the methods of discharge of the entire instrument, then proceed to consideration of methods for discharge of individual parties.

Payment. Obviously, most items of commercial paper are discharged by payment. The maker, drawer, or acceptor pays the holder, and everyone is happy. However, problems may arise when the holder is not the owner. In such situations, UCC 3-603 provides that payment to the holder is normally a discharge. This provision preserves a debtor from the necessity of acting as judge in a dispute between two would-be creditors as to the true ownership of the paper.

Example: White lent Green $1,000 for a year, taking back a negotiable note by which Green promised to pay $1,000 to White's order a year from date. Three months later White made a contract with Brown and endorsed the note to Brown as part of the bargain. A dispute arose between White and Brown, White accusing Brown of breach of contract and fraud, and Brown denying the charge. So White told Green not to pay Brown when the note matured. Green did as White requested, but Brown threatened to sue to collect. At that point Green paid Brown. White claimed that was wrongful; it was not. The White-Brown dispute is White's problem, not Green's. The note is discharged.

In this situation, Green of course could not discharge the note by paying White. Payment to a nonholder will not be a discharge. Had White wanted to prevent Green from paying Brown, he could have done so in one of two ways. First, he could have given Green an indemnity in exchange for Green's promise not to pay Brown. This would force Brown to sue Green in order to collect. Had Brown won the suit, though, Green could have paid out of the indemnity. Since Green himself has no defense to payment, Brown will win, unless White is made a party to the case so that he may present his claim in court.

White's other alternative would be to go to court and obtain an injunction forbidding Green to pay Brown. The injunction would remain in effect until Brown and White litigate their dispute and true ownership of the note is determined.

There are two circumstances under which payment to the holder will not discharge an instrument. The first of these occurs when the maker or drawer makes payment in bad faith to a person who acquired the paper by theft, or in bad faith pays a non-holder in due course who acquired the paper through a thief. Examples follow:

1. Sadd owns a negotiable note, unendorsed, by which Debtor promises to pay $1,000 to Bearer on demand. Thief steals the note. Sadd informs Debtor of the theft, not knowing the identity of the thief. Thief presents the note to Debtor for payment, and Debtor pays without asking any questions or making any comments. Thief is the bearer of the note, but of course he has no legal title. Debtor paid in bad faith because he should have known that the bearer of this stolen note might well be the thief. The payment is not a discharge.

2. Suppose Thief presented the note for payment before Sadd notified Debtor of the theft. This could be said to be payment of the holder in good faith; a good discharge has therefore been made.

3. Thief stole the note, and Sadd informed Debtor of the theft. Thief gave the note to Creditor in payment of a debt he owed Creditor without endorsement, Creditor asking no questions and Thief saying nothing as to how he obtained the note. Creditor presented the note to Debtor for payment, and Debtor paid without asking questions or making comments. Here it could be said that Debtor paid in bad faith because he did not ask how Creditor came to have possession of the note. However, since Creditor got the note by negotiation and was a holder in due course, Debtor paid the legitimate holder and the note was discharged.

4. Suppose that Thief in example 3 above had given the note to Pal as a gift, and Debtor had paid Pal without asking any questions. Pal was the holder, but since he was not a holder in due course because he gave no value, and since Debtor paid in bad faith, the payment is no discharge.

The other circumstance under which payment to the holder will not be a discharge arises when the paper has a restrictive endorsement upon it and the payment is made contrary to the terms of the endorsement, so long as the paying party is not a payor bank or intermediary bank.

Example: Ace Company pays Workman his weekly wage with a check drawn upon First Bank. Workman endorses the check, "For Deposit Only, /s/ Wes Workman," and starts off for the bank. Mugger mugs him and steals this check and other items. Mugger takes the check to First Bank and asks the teller there to cash it. She does. The check is not discharged; the bank should not have paid out cash upon a check so endorsed.

It should be noted that UCC 3-603 does not say that payment to a finder or to one who holds through a finder is not a discharge. If the finder or the person holding through him is a holder, payment to him would apparently be a discharge. Payment by an accommodation maker or acceptor will not be a discharge, since the accommodation party still has his right of reimbursement against his principal debtor.

A person other than the maker or acceptor may pay an instrument, if the holder consents to his doing so. Such a payment will discharge the right of the holder against the maker, drawer, or acceptor; but the holder must surrender the paper to the stranger, and the stranger will succeed to the rights the holder possessed against the maker, drawer, or acceptor. The stranger in essence becomes another holder.

Payment to the holder, it must be remembered, may well not discharge the paper unless the holder surrenders the paper to the paying party upon payment, or unless the paper is cancelled, destroyed, etc. Otherwise, if the paper has not matured, the holder could negotiate it to a holder in due course, who could collect upon it again. If the paper has matured and the holder is a holder in due course, he could negotiate to a holder through a holder in due course, who could collect again. The only situation where no danger of this exists is where the holder is not a holder in due course and the paper is paid after maturity. However, prudence dictates that one should never pay a draft or promissory note in full without getting the instrument back from the holder, or watching it canceled or destroyed.

Payment to a nonholder will ordinarily be no discharge; however, under some circumstances such a payment will operate as a discharge. This will be true, essentially, when the nonholder is the true owner of the paper, or when he is an agent with authority to collect upon the paper.

If the holder of the paper is a thief, a non-holder in due course, or a nonholder through a holder in due course who got the paper from a thief or through a thief, the holder does not have an enforceable claim to the paper. Payment to the true owner would probably stand up as a discharge. However, it will not be a discharge if the current holder would transfer the paper to a holder in due course. If the current holder has no holder in due course rights and the maturity date of the paper has passed, however, this problem could not arise.

The collecting agent may or may not be a holder. If the named payee is designated an agent, or if the agent holds under a "For Collection Only" endorsement or something of the sort, payment of the agent is payment of the holder. If the paper is payable to the agent's principal, however, one should not pay the agent without first ascertaining the agent's authority to collect.

Mere possession of the paper will not clothe the agent in apparent authority to collect. However, if the debtor negotiated the transaction which led to the creation of the paper in question in the presence of the agent, and he has no knowledge that the authority of the agent has since been terminated, the agent still has apparent authority to collect. Also, if the agent has the paper he seeks to collect and a receipt for payment signed by his principal, the agent has authority to collect.

Payment to an "agent" who does not have possession of the paper he seeks to collect is very dangerous. If he does not have express authority to collect, payment to him will not be a discharge. Furthermore, even if he has express authority to collect there is no guarantee that the paid note will not be further negotiated into the hands of a holder in due course.

Renewal notes as discharges. The giving of a renewal note at the maturity date of an existing note may or may not operate as a discharge of the old note; it depends upon the intent of the parties. If the holder of the old note surrenders it in exchange for the new, the new operates as a discharge of the old, including the liability of all endorsers of the old. If the holder of the old note retains it and also takes possession of the new note, this indicates that the holder is taking the new note as collateral for the old. In such a case the old note is not discharged.

Contractual discharge of commercial paper. Any sort of bargain which will discharge a simple contractual liability will also discharge a commercial paper obligation. Thus, an accord and satisfaction, an account stated, a novation, or a similar form of contractual arrangement will operate as a discharge. The discharge need not necessarily involve the substitution of a new piece of commercial paper for the discharged piece.

Cancellation and renunciation as discharge. UCC 3-605 provides that either a cancellation or renunciation made with the intent to discharge a piece of commercial paper will operate as such a discharge.

Cancellation may be accomplished in two ways: by deliberate destruction of the instrument, or by marking it "Paid," "Canceled," or the like. No consideration need be received for the act of cancellation, but the act must be deliberate; accidental destruction of an instrument or accidental cancellation will not operate as a discharge. Cancellation is by its very nature an irrevocable act.

Renunciation may also be accomplished in two ways. One is by surrender of the instrument to the party to be discharged, a surrender to the maker, drawer, or acceptor being a complete discharge. The other is by delivery of a signed writing stating the facts of the renunciation to the party to be discharged. Renunciation by surrender is an irrevocable discharge; renunciation in a separate writing may not be a discharge, because a renunciation of this nature will not be binding upon a holder in due course who has no knowledge of it.

Reacquistion by maker or acceptor. UCC 3-601(3) provides that when an instrument is reacquired by its maker or its acceptor, the instrument is discharged. The maker or acceptor is essentially paying it off early.

The same will hold true if the instrument is reacquired by one of several co-makers before maturity. This will not discharge the obligations of the co-makers among themselves, or the obligation of an accommodated party to an accommodation party, but it will discharge the other obligations on the instrument.

Discharge of a maker or acceptor. The discharge of a party to an instrument will discharge the entire instrument if that party had no recourse against any of the other parties. Discharge of a maker or acceptor will then result in discharge of the entire instrument.

A discharge of one (or of less than all) co-maker will have the same effect, due to the general rule that a discharge of one debtor in a joint and several obligation is a discharge of all.

This completes the list of actions that will discharge an entire instrument. We will now consider those actions which have the result of discharging some of the parties to the instrument.

Tender of payment. A tender of payment is made when a party liable on the instrument offers to pay it. A tender of payment before maturity may be refused; refusal will not affect the accrual of interest or the liability of any party. Tender of payment after maturity does have definite legal consequences.

Refusal of a tender of payment will not discharge the instrument. It does discharge the accrual of interest, and all obligations of the tendering party to pay court costs and attorney fees in case of suit upon the instrument. If the tender is made by a maker or acceptor, refusal discharges all endorsers. If the tender is made by an endorser, refusal discharges all endorsers who endorsed after the tendering party. Remember that tender of payment on a domiciled note is made if the maker has enough money on deposit in the named bank to pay the note on the maturity date.

Discharge of party with reservation of rights. As mentioned earlier, discharge of a maker or acceptor results in the discharge of the entire instrument. This consequence of a discharge of a maker or acceptor may be avoided if the holder reserves his rights against the other parties he does not expressly include in the discharge. The reservation of rights must be contained in the document of discharge, but it need not be communicated to those against whom rights are reserved.

The discharge of an endorser without reservation of rights will also discharge all who endorsed after the discharged endorser; those who endorsed before him will not be discharged. However, rights may be reserved against subsequent endorsers in this sort of situation.

Of course, a discharge of a party with reservation of rights will not operate as a complete discharge. For example: Blue lent $1,000 to Green for a year, taking back a negotiable note by which Green promised to pay $1,000 to the order of Blue a year from date. Blue later endorsed and negotiated the note to Redd, and Redd later endorsed and negotiated it to Brown, who later endorsed and negotiated it to Gray. Green was unable to pay at maturity, so notice of dishonor was given by Gray to all endorsers. Blue gave Gray such a hard-luck story that Gray discharged him from liability, reserving his rights against the other endorsers. Redd paid $1,000 to Gray, and demanded $1,000 from Blue. Blue claimed he was not liable to Redd because Gray had discharged him. He was wrong. Gray discharged Blue from liability to himself, but when he preserved the liability of the other endorsers to him, he also preserved Blue's liability to them. Thus, Blue did not get a complete discharge.

It must also be remembered that only the holder of an instrument has the power to discharge parties to it. No one else may do so.

Extension of time to pay as discharge. An agreement by the holder with the maker, drawer, or acceptor to extend the maturity date of an instrument will have the effect of discharging endorsers, unless the endorsers consent to the extension or unless rights are reserved against the endorsers as described above.

The holder's taking of a renewal note as collateral upon the old note is of course such an extension of time. Thus the holder must either obtain the consent of the endorsers of the old note to the renewal, or reserve his rights against them.

Impairment of collateral as discharge. The holder of a collateral note has a security interest in the collateral as well as ownership of the note. The holder has the obligation to do all he can to preserve and perfect his rights in the collateral, both for his benefit and for the benefit of the other parties to the note who may be called upon to pay it.

The presence of the collateral may reduce the probability of endorsers of the note being called upon to pay, since the holder could foreclose upon the collateral. Also, if endorsers are compelled to pay the note they acquire by subrogation the rights of the holder to the collateral. It is therefore only logical that impairment of collateral by the holder without the consent of other parties may result in a discharge of the other parties. Such impairment may consist of a failure by the holder to perfect a security interest in the collateral, thus permitting the security interest to be lost to a third party. This could be caused, for example, by the failure to note a lien on a motor vehicle upon the certificate of title to the vehicle.

Impairment may also consist of the holder's releasing collateral to the maker of the note without the consent of the other parties. UCC 3-606 contains all the provisions relative to impairment of collateral, extension of time as a discharge, and discharge of parties as a complete discharge.

Reacquisition by a prior party as discharge. UCC 3-208 provides that the reacquisition of an instrument by a former owner will result in a partial discharge of some endorsers.

For example: Jones lends Smith $1,000 for a year, Smith giving Jones a negotiable note promising to pay $1,000 to Jones's order a year from date. Jones negotiates and endorses the note to Blue; Blue negotiates and endorses to Green; Green negotiates and endorses to Redd; and Redd negotiates and endorses back to Blue. If Blue is the holder at maturity and has trouble collecting from Smith, he will have no recourse against Green and Redd because they endorsed after Blue. However, if Blue now endorses and negotiates the note to Pink, and Pink has trouble collecting from Smith, Pink would have recourse against Green or Redd. Green or Redd would then have recourse against Blue, since his first endorsement preceded theirs.

Material alteration by holder as discharge. UCC 3-407 provides that material alteration of an instrument by the holder discharges the maker, drawer, or acceptor and all prior endorsers. However, if the guilty party further negotiates the instrument so that it is acquired by a holder in due course, the holder in due course may enforce it against all parties in accordance with its original tenor—that is, according to its terms before alteration.

Those who endorse or accept an instrument after material alteration has taken place are liable upon the instrument as altered. The alteration is in no way a discharge for such parties.

Certification of a check by someone other than the endorser as a discharge. UCC 3-411 provides that certification of a check by someone other than the drawer will discharge the drawer from liability, along with all others who endorsed before certification. A certification by the drawer, on the other hand, will discharge no one.

Effect of accidental destruction, loss, or theft of instruments. Accidental destruction, loss, or theft of commercial paper does not result in discharge; the holder may enforce the instrument as it was written. His main problem, of course, is to prove that the instrument existed, the nature of its provisions, what happened to it, and his ownership of it. UCC 3-804 provides that the court hearing the case may, within its discretion, require the plaintiff to put up a bond indemnifying the defendant against damage caused by other potential litigation on the instrument.

Effect of commercial paper upon the underlying debt. The taking of an instrument in payment of an obligation is not in and of itself a discharge of the obligation, unless a bank is the maker, drawer, or acceptor of the instrument and there is no recourse under the instrument against the debtor. Thus, a cashier's check or bank draft, or a check certified by someone other than the drawer, will operate as a discharge. An ordinary check, note, or draft will not be a discharge.

UCC 3-802, which provides for the above, also provides that the payment of an obligation with an instrument will suspend the obligation until the instrument is due or, if the instrument is a demand instrument, until presentment. If the instrument is dishonored, the holder may sue either upon the instrument or upon the underlying obligation. A discharge of the instrument will also be a discharge of the debt.

Reminder of miscellaneous discharges. Remember that the following will cause discharge of parties to commercial paper:

1. The making of a draft-varying acceptance. If the holder of the draft allows this without obtaining the consent of the drawer and of prior endorsers, the drawer and prior endorsers are discharged.

2. The unexcused delay in presenting an instrument for payment or acceptance. This will discharge endorsers before maturity. It will also discharge drawers who can prove that the delay caused them to suffer a loss.

3. Improper presentment, notice of dishonor, and protest by a holder, unless these are excused. Impropriety here will discharge endorsers. It may also discharge drawers, if they can prove that the impropriety has caused them to suffer a loss.

4. Dishonor of a check more than seven days after the date an endorser endorses. The secondary liability of an endorser of a check lasts only seven days. Dishonor of the check must occur during this seven-day period for the endorser to be liable.

28

Checks and Bank Deposits

The relationship between the owner of a checking account and his bank is governed for the most part by Article 4 of the UCC. It is a debtor-creditor relationship, governed by contract. The contract in question is drafted by the bank and signed by the customer when he opens his checking account.

Under the contract the bank promises to honor checks drawn by the customer, unless it has a good reason for dishonoring such checks. It also promises to pay money out of the account only upon the customer's order, unless payment to another is required by law, or unless the bank exercises its right of offset. It further promises to use due care in processing items chargeable to the account and to stop payment on checks at the customer's request if he follows proper procedures.

The customer promises to pay the service charges levied upon him. He also agrees to use the printed personalized checks (bearing his account number in magnetic ink) which he must buy through his bank. He further agrees to use due care in checking his cancelled checks for improperly paid items.

Liability of parties to checks. The drawer of a check incurs secondary liability upon it. As is the case with the drawer of a draft, he may not be sued until the check has been presented for payment at the drawee bank and dishonored, and he has been given notice of dishonor. The three-day deadline for giving notice of dishonor is not applicable, unless the delay in giving notice causes the drawer to suffer a loss; this rarely occurs.

The bank upon which a check is drawn has no liability upon it unless it is certified. Since most checks are not certified, their holders have no claim against the drawee. The act of certification of a check has the same legal effect as the acceptance of a draft, the certifying bank assuming primary liability upon it. The mechanics of certification will be discussed later.

The legal nature of payment by check. Anyone who accepts payment of an obligation in the form of an uncertified check cannot be completely certain that the check will be honored. In the first place, the drawer of a check does not assign any of the money in his account to the payee (UCC 3-409). Thus, the payee has legal title to the piece of paper which is the check, but no legal title to anything else. The check will not be honored if the drawee has a legally sufficient reason for dishonor and acts upon it.

Since the check is not the equivalent of cash, payment by check is only provisional. UCC 3-802 states that the taking of the check merely suspends the obligation to the extent of the face value of the check, pending the decision of the drawee to honor or to dishonor. Honor results in the discharge of the obligation to the extent of the payment; dishonor revives the obligation, and also gives the holder the right to sue upon the dishonored check.

Provisional and permanent credit upon deposits. When the customer of a bank deposits cash to his account, he receives a permanent credit, and may draw checks against that credit at once. When the customer deposits checks to his account, the credit he is given is provisional only (UCC 4-201). The reason for the provisional nature of the credit is of course that the check may be dishonored.

A bank is under no obligation to permit its customer to draw checks against a provisional credit; it may dishonor checks which are so drawn. On the other hand, it is also under no obligation to dishonor such checks. If the customer is a regular customer who ordinarily does not deposit checks that are later dishonored, he may well be allowed to draw against provisional credits. If he is a new customer, or one whose credit rating is not reliable, he may not be given this privilege.

The check collection process. It may take a considerable length of time to obtain the honor of a check deposited to a checking account. The length of time required will depend upon the distance of the drawee bank from the depository bank, the bank holding the account to which the deposit is made.

Suppose that John Jones of Podunk, Texas, does his banking with the Republic State Bank of Podunk. He deposits to his account a check drawn by Bill Smith upon *his* account with the Republic State Bank of Podunk. In banking terminology this is an "on us" check. Republic State Bank will determine whether to honor it or dishonor it after the books are closed on the day of deposit; this is a simple matter of determining whether the balance in Smith's account is sufficient to cover the check.

Next, suppose that Jones deposits in his account a check drawn by Rip Redd upon his account with Lone Star National Bank of Podunk, Texas. This is a "city" check. At the close of business on the day of deposit, Republic State Bank assembles all the checks drawn upon Lone Star National and the other banks of Podunk which it has accepted for deposit or cashed. These are taken to the clearing house and exchanged for those checks drawn upon Republic State which have been accepted for deposit or cashed by the other banks of Podunk. The next day Lone Star will determine whether or not to honor this check. If it honors, it will make no announcement of the fact—over 99 percent of all checks which are written are not dishonored. If Lone Star dishonors, the check will be returned via the clearinghouse at the close of business on that day, and Republic State will receive the notice of dishonor on the next day. Thus, if a city check is deposited on Monday, word of dishonor may not be received before Wednesday.

Next, suppose Jones deposits to his account a check drawn by Ben Black upon his account with the Petroleum State Bank of Oil City, Texas. This is a "country" check. Republic State may handle its collection in various ways. It may well send it to the Federal Reserve Bank of Dallas, where it maintains an account. If Petroleum State also maintains an account with the Dallas Federal Reserve, Dallas Federal would credit its Republic State account and debit its Petroleum State account for the amount of the check, and send the check along to Petroleum State for honor. If Petroleum State chose to dishonor, it could send the check back to Dallas Federal for transmission to Republic State, or it could send the check directly to Republic State. In any event, if the check were deposited on Monday it might be Thursday or Friday before word of the dishonor reached Republic State.

Next, suppose Jones deposits a check drawn by Gus Green upon his account with Redwood State Bank of Timber City, California. In this case, Republic State might well send the check to the Federal Reserve Bank of Dallas. Dallas Federal would then transmit it to San Francisco Federal. San Francisco Federal would transmit it to Redwood State. If Redwood State dishonors, it would retrace its path through San Francisco and Dallas to Podunk, or, again, Redwood State might send it directly back to Republic State.

If Jones deposits a check drawn by Hans Herrmann upon his account with the Neuburger Stadtbank of Neuburg, Switzerland, the collection process would of course be more complex; it could well take two or three weeks for the check to travel to Switzerland and return in case of dishonor.

Generally, the temporary or provisional credit granted upon the deposit of a check will be permitted to become permanent when no notice of dishonor of the check is received within the time during which such notice could be expected. Of course, if notice of dishonor is received, the provisional credit is revoked and the dishonored item is returned to the depositor.

The collection process may be avoided by taking the check to the drawee bank and asking it to "cash" it. In such a case, the teller at the drawee bank may well check the identification of the person seeking to cash the check, to make certain that he is its owner. The teller will then check the latest computer printout showing the balance in the drawer's account, and, if there are sufficient funds there to cover, will honor the check on the spot. If there are not sufficient funds there to cover, the teller will say so and that will end the matter. Obviously, this alternative is practicable only with "city" checks. The travel involved in taking a "country" check to the drawee bank is usually more trouble and expense than it is worth.

Provisional credits, dishonors, and overdrafts. Suppose that John Jones moves to Newtown, Texas, and opens a checking account at First State Bank with a check for $1,000 drawn on Sixth National Bank of Oldburg, Ohio, plus $300 cash. He then draws a check upon this account the same day to pay a month's rent, $200, to his landlord. The landlord takes the check to First State Bank the next day and presents it for payment. Of course, First State Bank should honor it.

On the day the landlord cashes the $200 check, Jones buys $300 worth of lumber from Smith Lumberyard and pays for it with a check on this new account. Smith Lumberyard deposits the check in its account with First State that evening; the next day First State dishonors the check. It has every right to do so, since the Oldburg, Ohio, check has not had enough time to clear, and the cash deposit is now insufficient to cover the Smith check.

After Jones has established his reputation as a good customer of First State Bank, the bank lets him draw upon provisional credits to his account. Because of that, the following occurs: At a time when Jones has a permanent credit of $50 in his account, he deposits a check for $600 drawn upon a New York City bank. That same day he draws a $200 check upon this account, payable to his landlord for the month's rent. The landlord presents the check for payment the next day, and the bank honors it. Later that week, First State Bank gets the word that the New York check has been dishonored. The $600 credit is therefore revoked, and the $450 credit balance in the Jones account has become a $150 overdraft. First State Bank now demands $150 from Jones at once. This is of course an enforceable demand. If Jones does not make good the overdraft, the bank may take legal action against him.

This sort of thing may also happen: At a time when Jones has a permanent credit of $100 in his account, he deposits a check drawn by Smith to his order for $900, Smith drawing the check upon Second State Bank of Newtown. Jones then draws a check for $500 payable to Baker of Dallas and mails it. Second State Bank dishonors the Smith check for insufficient funds, so First Bank revokes the $900 provisional credit given for that check. Before Jones reacts to the news, the Baker check arrives for payment at First Bank through banking channels. First Bank of course dishonors it for insufficient funds; Jones must now seek to get Smith to make his check good, and he also has the embarrassing task of making explanations to Baker.

Some banks offer a plan to their depositors under which they undertake to honor all overdrafts within limits, automatically lending their customers sufficient funds to cover. The bank of course has the right to charge interest upon such loans. It must be remembered, though, that banks are not required to furnish this service: some have chosen to do so, most have not. With respect to those which have not, creation of an overdraft can be a serious matter—much more serious than an overdue car payment, for example.

The right of offset. Jones maintains a checking account with First State Bank, and he also borrows from the bank on occasion. He has borrowed $500 for a month, promising to repay the principal with appropriate interest. The due date of the loan has come and gone, and the bank has heard nothing from Jones as to when he will pay. His checking account contains a permanent credit of $200, and his savings account contains $3,000. The bank decides to collect this loan through self-help. It debits the checking account $200 and the savings account $300 plus accrued interest upon the loan, and declares the loan paid. By doing this, the bank has exercised its right of offset. It has the right to do this without notice to its debtor-depositor.

Generally, the bank may do this only when the depositor is delinquent in his loan payments. It must be remembered that commercial loan contracts made by banks often contain acceleration clauses which provide that, if the debtor misses a payment, the bank may declare the entire unpaid balance to be immediately due and payable. If the unpaid balance has been accelerated, the bank may offset for this entire sum.

Some commercial loan agreement forms contain a more stringent acceleration clause, which provides that the bank has the right to accelerate and demand immediate payment whenever it in good faith deems itself insecure with respect to the loan, even if the debtor is not delinquent in his payments. Under such a clause the bank could accelerate when, for instance, the IRS files a federal tax lien against the debtor because he is delinquent in paying the IRS withholdings from the wages of his employees. The bank might also accelerate under such a clause because it has discovered that the debtor has accepted employment in another locality, and it fears that he might skip town without paying off his loan. In any event, if the bank chooses to accelerate under such a clause, it may at once exercise its right of offset for the total unpaid balance.

Right of other creditors to seize bank accounts. A creditor who has obtained a judgment against the owner of a checking account may, by following proper procedure, levy a garnishment upon the account and have the proceeds applied to his judgment. The bank of course has no choice but to comply with the demands of a garnishment.

In Texas, two creditors may have access to a checking account without the necessity of court action. After the IRS has assessed a tax delinquency (an administrative declaration that the tax is owing but unpaid) against a debtor, it may serve a notice of levy upon the bank, commanding that it pay over all amounts belonging to the debtor, up to the amount of tax owed. Failure to comply with the demand can subject the bank to suit.

When a businessman who sells goods subject to the Texas sales tax is delinquent in his tax payments, the Texas State Comptroller's office may serve a document upon the bank demanding that the accounts of the debtor be frozen for a period of sixty days. The bank is under no obligation to pay over any of the funds in the account, but it must not permit the debtor to make withdrawals. Of course, if the comptroller's office obtains a judgment against the taxpayer before the sixty-day period expires, it may then levy a garnishment upon the tied-up account and collect the delinquent sales taxes.

No other tax collecting agency has authority to seize or tie up a bank account without going through the courts.

Stop-payment orders. UCC 4-403 gives the bank's customer the right to order the bank to stop payment upon checks which he has written. The version of this section in effect in most states provides that a stop-payment order may be oral or written. However, the version of the section enacted by the Texas legislature (TB&CC 4-403) provides that a stop-payment order shall not be effective unless it is in writing and describes with certainty the item upon which payment is to be stopped. Thus a bank in Texas is under no obligation to obey an oral stop-payment order; it may do so if it chooses, but it incurs no liability if it disobeys.

In order for the order to describe the check to be stopped with certainty, it should contain the following information:
1. The number of the check.
2. The date of the check.
3. The name of the payee.
4. The amount of the check.
5. The name of the drawer.
6. The drawer's account number.

The stop-payment order does not become binding upon the bank at the moment it is given. It becomes effective only when the bank has had time to inform all its personnel who handle incoming checks—tellers, posting clerks, etc.—of its existence. This will require from two hours to half a day. Thus, if the customer gives his bank a stop-payment order at 9:30 one morning, and a teller cashes the check at 10 that same morning, the customer has no complaint, since the stop-payment order was not yet effective.

The order is ineffective under the following circumstances:
1. If the check had been honored before the order was given.
2. If the check was honored after the order was given, but before the bank had informed all employees of its existence.
3. If the check had been certified before the order was given, or before all employees had been notified of it.

Since a bank assumes primary liability upon a check when it certifies, it cannot thereafter use any defense to payment of the customer to escape liability. Therefore it cannot legally obey a customer's stop-payment order upon certified checks.

If a bank negligently ignores an effective stop-payment order, the question arises as to whether or not the customer may claim damages for the error. Although it might seem that the customer could always claim damages in such a situation, that is not the case. The customer may claim no damages from the bank in such a case unless he can prove that he has suffered damages. Remember that a customer does not have a defense to payment upon a check merely because he has stopped payment upon it. He will be excused from liability upon the check only if he has a defense to payment which is good against the holder. Thus: Buyer purchases goods at Seller's store and pays for them with a check. Later that day he decides he should not have spent the money for the goods, and asks Seller to take the goods back. When Seller refuses to do this, Buyer stops payment upon the check.

Buyer has no valid reason to stop payment. If the bank honors the stop-payment order and dishonors the check, Seller could force Buyer to make the check good. Buyer would also be open to a criminal charge of theft by check if he sought to retain the goods; one may not legitimately breach a contract by stopping payment upon a check in this manner.

If the bank ignores Buyer's stop-payment order in this situation, it has in effect done its customer a favor by unintentionally ensuring that he perform his contractual obligation. The bank error would cause the customer no loss, so the customer could collect no damages.

If on the other hand the goods Seller had sold Buyer were defective, and Seller had refused to remedy the defect, Buyer would have had a defense to payment of the check. Had the bank ignored the stop-payment order, Buyer would have suffered damages and would have cause to make a claim on the bank. Again, had the goods been defective; had Seller refused to remedy the defect; had Buyer stopped payment on the check; had Seller negotiated the check to Financer as part payment on a loan, Financer knowing nothing of the origin of the check; and had the bank ignored the stop-payment order and honored the check, the customer would have suffered no loss and would have no claim. Buyer's defense to payment—breach of contract—is a personal defense. Financer would be a holder in due course of the check and this defense would be no good. Since Financer could have forced Buyer to honor the check had the stop order been obeyed, the customer has no complaint.

Death or incompetence of the bank's customer. UCC 4-405 deals with the effect of the death or incompetence of the bank's customer upon its authority to accept, pay, or collect items upon the customer's account.

The death of the customer will not affect the bank's authority until it learns of the death and has a reasonable time to act upon the knowledge. Even if the bank knows of the customer's death it may normally continue to certify or honor checks written upon the account prior to his death until ten days after the death.

The bank is not expected to know of the death of its customer until it is informed. The law will not hold the bank responsible for not learning about the death until it is printed in the local newspaper or until the bank is similarly informed. The bank, then, is not responsible for any item it honors after the customer's death but before it learns of the death. It also is not responsible for any item it honors within ten days of the death, even if it knows of the death, if the item was drawn before the death.

A problem could arise here with respect to a check drawn upon the account by an authorized agent. If the agent drew the check before the principal's death, the bank may honor it within ten days of the principal's death. If the agent drew the check after the principal's death, the bank must not honor it if it knows of the death. The reason for this is, of course, that the death of the principal terminates the agency relationship and ends the agent's authority to draw checks upon the account.

Upon the death of the bank's customer, all persons claiming an interest in the checking account acquire the right to stop payment upon checks written by the customer. Among persons acquiring this right are the executor or administrator of the customer's estate, the customer's heirs, or the customer's creditors. Whenever such a person seeks to exercise this right, the bank is not likely to question him very much. The obligation of the bank to honor this sort of stop order is the same as its obligation to honor those submitted by its customer.

When a person is declared incompetent and a guardian is appointed for him, that person's authority and power to draw checks upon a checking account ends. As soon as a bank receives notice of the incompetence and appointment of a guardian, and informs its check-handling employees, its authority to honor checks drawn by the incompetent ends. Also, the guardian of the incompetent has the power to stop payment upon checks drawn by the incompetent prior to the declaration of incompetence.

The bank's liability for disregard of the duties described here is essentially the same as its liability for ignoring a valid stop-payment order from its customer. If the error caused a loss to the estate of the deceased customer or to the incompetent, the bank is liable to the extent of the loss. If the error causes no loss, there is no liability.

Collecting bank as a holder in due course. When a bank is accused of wrongfully honoring an item (by ignoring a valid stop-payment order, for example) and the drawer or drawer's estate has a personal defense to payment of the item, the liability of the bank for wrongful dishonor will turn upon the question of whether or not the party the bank paid when it honored the item had the rights of a holder in due course. If a holder presented the item for payment at the drawee bank, he may not have been a holder in due course. But if the item was presented for payment through banking channels, the party presenting for payment was a bank, and hence probably a holder in due course.

The collecting bank will of course have no knowledge of how the person collecting a check has obtained it, and no knowledge of defenses to payment. The one thing that might prevent it from acquiring holder in due course status is the possibility of its not having given value for the check. If the customer of the collecting bank obtained cash for the check, this is of course giving value on the part of the bank. If, however, the collecting bank accepted the check for deposit in its customer's account, it may not have given value.

According to UCC 4-209, the rule of "first in first out" is used to determine whether or not the collecting bank has given value in such a case. The first funds deposited to an account are deemed to be the first funds paid out as a bank honors its customer's check. Thus: At a time when Jones has $500 in his checking account, he deposits a $500 check written by Smith. Jones then draws a $300 check on the account, which is duly honored. The Smith check is then dishonored. Jones's bank is not a holder in due course; the $500 credit granted when he deposited the Smith check has not been drawn upon.

Had Jones drawn an $800 check upon this account, had the bank honored it, and had the Smith check then been dishonored, the bank would have permitted Jones to draw $300 against the Smith deposit. The bank would be a holder in due course of the Smith check to the extent of $300. In such a situation, however, the bank would be unlikely to take action against Smith. It would merely charge back the Smith check to Jones, creating a $300 overdraft in the Jones account. It would then demand $300 from its customer, and let Jones deal with Smith.

If a depositor cashes a check, then closes his account and disappears, and the cashed check is then dishonored, the bank may have occasion to take action against the drawer of the dishonored check. In this situation the bank has of course given value (in the form of cash) for the check, so it would qualify as a holder in due course.

Bank liability for wrongful dishonor of checks. UCC 4-402 provides that a bank is liable to its customer for damages proximately caused by the wrongful dishonor of an item. If the dishonor is caused by mistake, the damages recoverable are limited to those the customer can prove, including damages caused by his arrest or prosecution.

Such a dishonor is of course wrongful if the bank has no good and lawful reason for it. A dishonor for insufficient funds caused by the revocation of a provisional credit after dishonor of a deposited check is not wrongful, but a dishonor due to a bookkeeping error by the bank is. More often than not, the damages caused by a wrongful dishonor are limited to the amount of the wrongfully dishonored item. If the customer's credit rating has been damaged by the wrongful dishonor, and the customer can prove it, damages for that are recoverable. Of course, if the dishonor results in charges of theft by check or of passing a bad check being brought against the customer, damages are also recoverable for that.

No punitive damages are recoverable in this sort of situation unless the bank's act of dishonor is willful or malicious. No one may make a damage claim against a bank for wrongful dishonor other than the drawer. Since the drawee of an uncertified check is not liable to the holder on the check, it is also not liable to the holder for wrongful dishonor.

Checks bearing forged or unauthorized drawer's signatures. When a check has not been signed by the drawer or by his authorized agent, the drawer has a real defense to payment unless his negligence has contributed to the forgery. Thus, if the bank honors a check bearing such a signature, it has not paid out the customer's money pursuant to his order. If this causes the customer to suffer a loss, the customer may have a claim against the bank.

The bank is expected to recognize the signature of its customer, because of the specimen signature it obtained when the customer opened his checking account, and because of its obligation to pay out the customer's money only upon his order. However, as a practical matter the bank's personnel do not have time to check the signatures on all of the checks they process. Thus, it is in essence the duty of the customer to catch and report forgeries and unauthorized signatures to the bank. UCC 4-406 provides that the customer must exercise reasonable care and promptness in checking canceled checks received in his bank statement. To be on the safe side, one should examine one's canceled checks for forgeries immediately upon receipt of a bank statement and report any problems to the bank at once. Normally, this will be sufficient to obligate the bank to restore the amount paid on the forgery to the account.

If a delay by the customer in reporting the forgery causes the bank to suffer a loss by making restoration—when the forger is unidentified and the delay makes it more difficult to catch him, or when the forger is identified but has disappeared after the forgery—the bank is excused from making such restoration. If negligence by the customer—leaving a signature stamp out where unauthorized persons can get access to it or not reporting lost or stolen blank check forms to the bank, for example—has made the forger's task easy, the bank is likewise under no obligation to make restoration.

If the same wrongdoer has forged more than one check upon the customer's account, delay by the customer in reporting the forgeries to the bank may be extremely costly. UCC 4-406(2)(b) provides that the bank is under no obligation to make restoration for any of a series of forgeries unless the customer reported the first of the series to the bank within fourteen days of receiving the statement containing the first of the series. Thus, if Crook forges a check against Sapp's account on June 3 and cashes it, then forges another against the account and cashes that on June 10, and these forgeries are contained in a bank statement received by Sapp on June 20, Sapp must report the forgeries to the bank by July 4. If he does so, the bank will in all probability be required to make restoration.

However, if Sapp does not examine this statement at all; Crook forges and cashes another check on June 26, another on July 2, and another on July 9; these are included in the bank statement Sapp receives on July 20; and Sapp immediately spots these and calls them to the bank's attention, Sapp takes the loss with respect to all five forgeries. His negligence in not catching and reporting the first two by July 4 renders him responsible for all five.

If negligence by the bank played a part in the honoring of the forgeries, the bank will be required to make restoration despite the negligence of the depositor in reporting the forgeries. But proof of such negligence is difficult.

The same principles apply with respect to checks bearing the signatures of unathorized agents, or checks bearing the signatures of agents who are obviously exceeding their authority or breaching their fiduciary duties. The customer must report these as soon as possible to the bank in order to receive restoration, unless bank negligence was partially responsible for the wrongdoing. Bank negligence is easier to spot and prove here. For instance, if a trustee or agent draws a check upon the agency payable to the order of himself, an obvious breach of fiduciary duty exists. The honor of such a check by the bank is almost certainly negligent.

It must be remembered that an agent has apparent authority to draw checks upon a checking account after his express authority to do so has been revoked, until the bank is informed of the revocation of his check-writing authority. It is not negligence for a bank to honor a check written by a formerly authorized agent if the bank has not been notified of the termination of his authority.

Materially altered checks. A bank has no way of knowing for how much the depositor writes his checks. It has no way of spotting a material alteration unless the alteration was so sloppily done that it is obvious. Nevertheless, the bank which honors a materially altered check can be forced to restore some or all of the face value of such a check to the depositor's account, subject to the same conditions as apply to forgeries and unauthorized signatures.

If the party obtaining payment had the rights of a holder in due course, the customer is liable for the original face value of the check; the bank need restore only the amount by which the check was altered. If the party obtaining payment had no holder in due course rights, the customer is not liable upon the check at all, and the bank must restore the entire face value.

If negligence by the customer made the alteration easy, so that the alteration would not be a defense to payment (as by writing the check in pencil, or by leaving blank spaces which invite alteration), no duty to restore exists. Also, if late reporting of the alteration causes the bank to suffer a loss if restoration is made, no restoration is necessary.

Checks bearing forged endorsements. When a bank honors a check which bears a forged endorsement, the customer's money is very likely being paid to someone who has no right to it. This is a violation of the bank-depositor contract, so the customer may obtain restoration of the money so paid under most conditions.

The bank will have no way to determine whether or not all endorsements upon a check are genuine. The customer who wrote the check will also have no way of determining this. Thus, forged endorsements cannot be reported to the bank until the customer knows of them himself. An owner of a check who loses it or has it stolen from him should inform the drawer or the person he got the check from as soon as possible. As soon as the drawer learns of the loss or theft of a check which he wrote, he should check his latest bank statements to determine whether or not the check has already been honored. If he possesses the check already, he must report the situation to his bank; he may then normally obtain restoration of the check's value to his account. If he does not yet possess the canceled check, he should contact the bank to determine whether or not it has been paid. If it has been, he may at once demand restoration. If it has not been, he should at once stop payment upon it, which should prevent its honor.

Remember that if the forged endorsement was made easy by the drawer's negligence (because he was taken in by an impostor, or because he has given a dishonest agent too much check-writing authority, or because he is a victim of a padded payroll or padded accounts payable), the party who cashed the check is deemed to be the owner thereof if he had holder in due course rights. The bank has therefore done nothing wrongful in honoring such checks.

Checks with missing endorsements. If at the time a check is presented for payment it is order paper, the endorsements should be part of a chain of title leading back to the payee. If the chain is unbroken, there are no missing endorsements. If the chain is broken, however, there are missing endorsements, and the party who obtained payment upon the check may well have had no legal title to it.

Two sorts of missing endorsement situations could arise. One involves the check drawn by John Jones payable to the order of Bill Smith, which has the following endorsements on the back:

Pay to Sam Brown.
/s/ Bill Smith.

Pay to Edmund Black.
/s/ James East.

/s/ Edmund Black.

If a bank permitted Edmund Black to cash this check, or to deposit it in his account, it would commit a serious error. Since Bill Smith endorsed the check to Sam Brown, one would expect the next endorsement to be that of Sam Brown. It is not; Sam Brown has never endorsed. Therefore, James East appears to have had no title to the check, and could not transfer it to Edmund Black. It is possible that Brown assigned the check to East without endorsement, of course, but no proof of that appears upon the check. East could have stolen the check from Brown for all we know.

A more common missing endorsement situation is the following: Ross Redd draws a check payable to the order of Pat Pink and Gus Gray. Pat Pink signs his name on the back of the check and cashes it. The bank permitting Pink to do this made an error, because Guy Gray is a co-owner of this check. He has never endorsed, so Pink's cashing of the check was illegitimate. If Pink paid Gray his half of the proceeds, no harm has been done, but if Pink has not done this, harm has been done. Here, however, the most Redd could recover by way of restoration is half the face value of the check. Since Pink owned a half-interest in the instrument, he owns half of the proceeds; payment of half of the proceeds to him is therefore rightful.

Statute of limitations on claims against a bank. Since forged or unauthorized drawer's signatures, material alterations, or missing endorsements on checks can be spotted by the bank's customer at once, these must be reported as soon as possible and in any event no more than one year from the time the statements containing them are made available to the customer, as per UCC 4-406(4).

Since the customer will not know of a forged endorsement until someone else informs him, the customer is given three years to report these after the statement containing them is made available to him (same section).

Payor bank's right to recover improper payments from other parties. When a bank is required to restore to its customer's account funds which were improperly paid out, a question will arise as to whether the bank has recourse against the party improperly paid.

If the party improperly paid has been guilty of breach of one of the warranties made by a party presenting an instrument for payment or acceptance spelled out in UCC

4-207(1), the bank will have recourse. In the case of a forged or unauthorized drawer's signature, the bank may have trouble. UCC 4-207(1)(b) provides that a party presenting an item to a bank warrants that he has no knowledge that the signature of the maker or drawer is unauthorized. Furthermore, if the item is a cashier's check or a certified check, the warranty is not made at all by a holder in due course acting in good faith. (However, anyone presenting a check for payment in the knowledge that the drawer's signature is forged or unauthorized would hardly be acting in good faith.) In order for the bank to recover the improper payment, then, it would be required to prove that the party obtaining payment of the check knew of the irregularity of the signature. That would be difficult, unless, perhaps, the presenting party was the forger or one of the forger's confederates.

The case of material alteration is easier for the bank. UCC 4-207(1)(c) provides that the person obtaining payment warrants that the check has not been materially altered (but not necessarily that he has no knowledge that it has been materially altered). The warranty is not made to the drawer of a cashier's check; the bank should remember the original face value of its cashier's checks. The warranty is not made to a certifying bank with respect to alterations made after certification, or on alterations made prior to certification if the party collecting is a holder in due course and took the check after certification with no knowledge of the certification. A non-holder in due course, however, makes the warranty without exception.

The forged endorsement case is also easy for the bank. UCC 4-207(1)(a) provides that the party presenting an item for payment warrants that he has title to the item, or that he has authority to collect for a principal who has title. Anyone who obtains an item with a forged endorsement has no title to it, unless the endorsement is one of those which passes good title. If the bank can prove that one of the endorsements on the item was forged, it has proven breach of warranty of title, and can therefore recover.

Time of receipt of item. A bank is generally deemed to have received an item on the calendar day of actual receipt. It is also deemed to have received a payment on that date.

However, the process of accounting for all of the day's transactions may prove to be a lengthy one. In order to speed up this process, UCC 4-107 permits a bank to close its books for the day before it closes its doors to its customers. A bank may establish a cutoff hour of 2 P.M. or later for this purpose. Though the UCC does not require it, the bank should post notice of the existence of such a cutoff hour, if it has one. If the bank uses 2 P.M. as its cutoff hour, a check deposited to an account at 1:55 P.M. Monday has been deposited on Monday, but a check deposited at 2:05 Monday afternoon has been deposited on Tuesday. A loan payment made at 2:05 P.M. Monday could also be treated as having been made on Tuesday.

The bank's midnight deadline. A bank which holds a dishonored item must give notice of dishonor to prior holders before its midnight deadline if it desires to hold these parties liable upon their endorsements. UCC 4-104 (1)(h) states that this midnight deadline falls at midnight upon the banking day after the receipt of the item or after the time for taking action starts to run.

Thus, if the item is received at 12 noon on Monday, notice of dishonor must be given before midnight Tuesday. If it is received at 2:30 P.M. Monday and the bank uses 2 P.M. as a cutoff hour, the deadline for giving notice is midnight Wednesday. Sometimes, however, clearinghouse rules or federal reserve regulations extend this time. Such extensions are quite legitimate. Failure of the bank to give timely notice of dishonor prevents it from holding prior parties liable upon their endorsements, but will not prevent it from making breach of warranty claims.

Stale checks. UCC 4-404 provides that a bank need not honor a check that is more than six months old. However, if the bank honors such a check in good faith, the customer has no legal complaint. Most often, a bank will not honor such a check without making inquiry of its customer, unless the check is a dividend check or similar sort of check which the bank knows its customer will wish it to honor.

The safest way to insure that one's bank will not honor a stale check is to stop payment on it. This way, if the bank inadvertently honors the old check and thereby causes the customer a loss, the bank will be liable for replacing the funds paid out.

Limitation upon liability of endorsers of checks. UCC 3-503(1)(b) provides that a reasonable time for presentment of a check for payment with respect to an endorser is within seven days of the date of his endorsement. Under UCC 3-502(1)(a), when presentment is delayed beyond the time at which it is due, any endorser is discharged. If a check is presented within seven days of the date the endorser endorsed, the holder may demand payment of the endorser if the check is dishonored and if proper and timely notice of dishonor is given. In fact, initiation of the bank collection process—that is, deposit in the holder's account—is sufficient to meet this requirement.

When one acquires a second-party check—one which has been endorsed and transferred by the payee—it is inadvisable to hold it for more than six days. If the check carries more than one endorsement, the advisable holding period is even shorter.

These rules do not apply to certified checks and bank checks such as cashier's checks. They also would not apply, probably, to postdated checks. So long as the bank collection process upon such a check is initiated within seven days of the date of the check, endorsers who endorsed prior to that date would not be discharged.

Overdue checks. A person who obtains an overdue check may not be a holder in due course (though, of course, if he obtains it from a holder in due course, he may become a holder through a holder in due course). According to UCC 3-304(3)(c), a purchaser of a check has knowledge that it is overdue if it is drawn and payable within the states and territories of the United States and the District of Columbia and is more than thirty days old. Such a check will not be deemed overdue if the holder can prove that there exists a very good reason for its still being outstanding. Of course, the thirty-day period is measured from the date of the check.

Bank liability on multiple-party accounts. Banks offer multi-party accounts to their customers as a convenience. Because of the complexities inherent in the ownership of such accounts and the difficulty outside parties have in supervising the conduct of account co-owners, bank liability for wrongful payouts from these accounts is limited.

When the signature of all co-owners is required for withdrawals, the bank must not permit a withdrawal which all co-owners have not signed. When the signature of only one co-owner is required, however, the bank is not required to question any co-owner who desires to make a withdrawal. If one co-owner withdraws the entire balance of the account (to cite the most extreme case), the bank may assume that the withdrawal is legitimate. If the co-owner skips town with the proceeds, depriving his colleague of his interest in the funds in the account, the bank is not responsible (Texas Probate Code 444).

When a bank becomes aware of the death of a co-owner of a multi-party account, it must not permit any person to make withdrawals on behalf of the estate of the deceased without proof of authority to withdraw. Thus the bank should not permit an alleged executor or administrator of the deceased's estate to make withdrawals without seeing proof of his appointment. It should not permit an alleged heir to make withdrawals without satisfying itself that the heir truly is an heir possessing an interest in the account. If the account is a joint account with right of survivorship, no one but the survivor or survivors should be permitted to make withdrawals.

When the last owner of a P.O.D. account dies, the P.O.D. payee or payees become the legal owners of the account. Once the bank learns of the death of the last owner, it must not permit anyone but the P.O.D. payee or payees to make withdrawals. Beneficiaries of trust accounts normally have no authority to make withdrawals; a bank must therefore not permit them. The only time a bank may justifiably permit withdrawal by a beneficiary of a trust account is when the bank receives proof that all trustees are dead.

A co-owner of a multi-party account may file a written request with the bank that other co-owners not be permitted to make withdrawals. The effect of this is essentially the same as that of a stop-payment order on a check. If the bank permits a withdrawal in violation of such an order, and the giver of the order is thereby damaged, the bank is liable for the loss.

Electronic fund transfers. Futurists tell us that the time of the cashless, checkless society will soon arrive. When (and if) that time does arrive, most fund transfers will be accomplished by electronic impulse—communication between computer terminal and computer, or between computer and computer.

Though our society has not yet arrived at that point, electronic fund transfers do occur upon occasion. Four sorts of electronic fund transfer mechanisms are now found. These are:

1. Twenty-four-hour bank teller machines, which enable customers of banks to make deposits and withdrawals from accounts at any hour of the day or night, or to transfer funds from account to account at any hour.
2. Pre-authorized direct deposit and payment arrangements, under which paychecks, Social Security checks, etc. are electronically deposited to a person's account, while utility bills, rent, etc. are automatically paid from an account on specified days of the month.
3. Pay-by-phone systems, under which a consumer may phone his bank and order it to pay obligations through electronic fund transfer.
4. Point-of-sale transfers, under which a merchant may set up a computer terminal connected to a bank's computer, so that consumer customers of the merchant may, through the terminal, automatically transfer payment for goods from their account to the merchant's account.

Legal regulation of electronic fund transfer at the state level is spotty; no legislation of the subject yet exists in Texas. Some regulation now exists at the federal level, though, in the form of the Electronic Fund Transfer Act, 15 USC 1693–1693r. A part of the act has been effective since February of 1979; the balance became effective on May 10, 1980. When a bank's customer signs up to take advantage of the EFT services which his bank offers, the bank must disclose to him the terms and conditions of the service, including service charges and possible liabilities.

For access to twenty-four-hour tellers, the customer will be issued an "access device," usually a plastic device similar to a credit card. Whoever has possession of the device will have access to the customer's accounts, so the customer must guard the access device with care. The bank must furnish the customer with monthly statements showing EFT activity in his accounts and he must monitor these carefully to catch errors. It is with respect to monitoring statements of activity and care of the access device that customers run risks with EFT. 15 USC 1693g(a) provides that a customer may recover an unauthorized EFT transfer from his account if he reports it to the bank within sixty days of transmittal of the statement showing the transfer. Failure to report the transfer within sixty days results in the loss of the funds so transferred.

Should the customer lose his access device or have it stolen from him and not report the loss or theft to the bank within two business days, the customer is liable for up to $500 worth of unauthorized transfers from the account if an earlier report would have enabled the bank to prevent the loss. If earlier report was impossible (due to travel, hospitalization, or the like) the late report is excused. Should the customer report the loss or theft of his device to the bank before two business days expire, he will be liable for up to $50 worth of unauthorized transfers made before the reporting of the loss or theft.

15 USC 1693f provides procedure for resolution of claims of error by the customer. Such errors must be reported to the bank within sixty days of receipt of a statement allegedly containing the error, as mentioned above.

Upon receipt of a claim of error, the bank may do one of two things. It may either give the customer provisional credit for the amount of the alleged error and then take forty-five days to investigate the problem; otherwise it must completely resolve the matter within ten days. If the bank decides that there was an error, it must correct it within one business day of making its determination (by making a previously granted provisional credit permanent, or otherwise). If the bank decides that there was no error, it must notify the customer within three business days of its decision, explaining thoroughly the grounds for its decision.

If the bank decides that there was no error, the customer's only recourse would be litigation. The bank is liable for triple damages if it knowingly and willingly determines that no error exists when good evidence of commission of the error does exist. It is also liable for triple damages for not following the prescribed error resolution procedure.

An access device may be issued only in response to an application, or to replace an expiring device. Unsolicited access devices may also be mailed out, but these must not become effective until the recipient takes affirmative steps to validate them. The validation procedure must be spelled out in literature accompanying the mailing.

An access device must carry upon it a means of identifying the owner. This may be a photograph, a signature block, or a thumb print.

Since payment of an obligation by an EFT is instantaneous, there is of course no possibility of stopping such a payment. On the other hand, when the customer preauthorizes payment of monthly obligations (such as rent, car payments, utility bills, etc.) by EFT, he has the right to stop payment. He may do this by notifying the bank either orally or in writing, no more than three days before the payment is to be made.

If ignoring such a stop order damages the customer, or if the bank fails to honor an outstanding pre-authorization and this damages the customer, the bank is liable for the damages caused.

Should the bank's EFT system malfunction, all obligations of customers which would be paid if the system had not malfunctioned are suspended until the malfunction is corrected. Thus, if a creditor of a customer is not paid on time due to system malfunction, the customer may not be penalized.

Dormant and inactive accounts. One of the problems faced by commercial banks in the conduct of their business is that of the account that is ignored by its owner for a long period of time. Many state legislatures have solved this problem by enacting legislation declaring that accounts that remain inactive for one year (in some states) or two years (in some other states) or for other designated periods of time are forfeited to the bank where they are maintained.

The Texas legislature has enacted no such statute; the Texas solution to the problem is found in RCS 3272b. Section 2 of this statute makes it unlawful for a bank to transfer or reduce a dormant or inactive account to its own use or ownership. The remainder of the statute provides procedure for the disposing of such accounts.

When an account has been dormant or inactive for seven years (that is, if no deposit has been made to it and no funds removed from it for seven years) and the bank has no knowledge of the whereabouts of the depositor or owner, during the month of May of the eighth year of inactivity the bank must cause to be published in a local newspaper a notice that the account has been inactive for more than seven years, and that—if the balance in the account is not claimed within the next nine months—the account balance shall be remitted to the Texas State Treasurer.

After remission, the owner of the account may reclaim the funds by filing a proper claim with the state treasurer. If the amount is never claimed, it remains the property of the state. Thus, no bank may become the owner of an unclaimed deposit or account within the state of Texas.

Bank records and the confidentiality thereof. The Federal Banking Secrecy Act, P.L. 91-508, requires banks and other financial institutions to keep and retain certain records with respect to the identity of owners of various financial accounts. Section 101(d) authorizes the secretary of the treasury to require, by administrative regulation, that banks make a microfilm or other reproduction of each check, draft, or other instrument drawn upon it and presented to it for payment. It also requires the bank to make such reproduction of all checks, drafts, or other instruments presented to it for deposit or collection, with an identification of the party to whose account the instrument was deposited or collected. The secretary of the treasury is also given authority to require banks to maintain other sorts of records. The period of retention of these records is also to be set by administrative regulation, but may be no more than six years.

Section 221 of this act gives the secretary of the treasury the authority to require banks and other financial institutions to keep records of such domestic currency transactions as the secretary may by regulation require, and to report such transactions to the treasury department.

These records and other bank records (such as account ledgers, for example) are to an extent confidential. No bank may divulge the contents of these records to private parties, except in response to a proper subpoena. Wrongful disclosure to a private party subjects the disclosing bank to liability for damages. On the other hand, until very recently there was no statutory provision restricting the access of government agencies to these records and the information contained therein. This situation has been changed to a degree by the Right to Financial Privacy Act of 1978, P.L. 95-630. The act is a lengthy piece of legislation. In general Section 1102 of the act provides that no government agency may have access to any financial records of a customer of a financial institution unless the records are described with reasonable certainty and:

1. The customer authorized the disclosure, or
2. The disclosure is in response to a proper administrative subpoena, or
3. The disclosure is in response to a proper search warrant, or
4. The disclosure is in response to a proper judicial subpoena, or
5. The disclosure is in response to a formal written request which meets legal requirements.

Section 1104 of the act provides that a customer may authorize disclosure of his financial records with a financial institution by furnishing to both the institution and the government agency desiring the information a document which:

1. Identifies the records to be disclosed, and
2. Authorizes disclosure for a period not to exceed three months, and
3. Reserves to the customer the right to revoke the authorization at any time, and
4. Specifies the agency to which the records may be disclosed and the purpose for which they may be disclosed.

The institution may not require its customer to give such consent as a prerequisite for doing business or opening an account.

Under Section 1105, a government agency may obtain financial records under an administrative subpoena or summons if:

1. The records sought are relevant to a legitimate law-enforcement inquiry (not part of an agency "fishing expedition"), and
2. The subpoena or summons was served upon the customer on or before the date it was served upon the financial institution, and
3. The subpoena or summons informs the customer that he may file a motion objecting to release of the information within ten days of the service of the subpoena or within fourteen days of the mailing of the subpoena, and
4. Ten days have passed since the service of the subpoena and fourteen days have passed since the mailing of it and no motion to object has been filed.

Section 1107 provides essentially the same ground rules for obtaining access to financial records under a judicial subpoena. Section 1106 provides that, if a government agency obtains a search warrant entitling it to examine financial records, the search warrant may be enforced without notice to the customer. The customer must, however, be informed of the issuance of the warrant within ninety days of its issuance, unless the agency convinces the court issuing the warrant that notification should be delayed up to 180 days. The customer thus has no opportunity to stop the authorized search, but he may later argue in court that the search warrant was wrongfully issued (because, for instance, it was not issued due to a legitimate law enforcement inquiry).

A government agency may request records under Section 1108 if:

1. There is no authority available to the agency for obtaining a subpoena, and
2. Administrative regulations authorize the agency to request the records, and
3. The procedure with respect to subpoenas of records is otherwise followed.

The agency desiring the records may obtain from a court an order delaying giving notice to the customer of the examination if notice to the customer will result in:

1. Endangering the life or property of any person, or
2. Flight from prosecution, or
3. Destruction of or tampering with evidence, or
4. Intimidation of potential witnesses, or
5. Jeopardizing the success of an investigation or delaying the start of a trial or official proceeding.

If the customer files a motion to quash a subpoena or request for records and the government opposes the quashing, a hearing on the matter must be held in federal district court. The judge decides the matter himself, and his decision is not appealable.

An agency obtaining financial records under this procedure may transfer them to another agency as part of a legitimate law-enforcement inquiry. The customer must be given appropriate notice of the intended transfer, and the customer may make a motion in court to oppose the transfer.

Various sections of the act exempt certain sorts of government investigations from this procedure. Among those exempted are:

1. Foreign intelligence or counterintelligence investigations.
2. Secret Service investigations.
3. Disclosures when the customer and the government are adverse parties in litigation or in adjudicatory administrative proceedings.

A financial institution divulging information wrongfully, or a government agency obtaining information wrongfully in violation of this act, is liable for the civil penalties contained in Section 1117 of the act. These are:

1. $100, plus
2. Actual damage caused the customer by the violation, plus
3. Punitive damages if the violation is willful or intentional, plus
4. Court costs and plaintiff's attorney fees.

Section 231 of P.L. 91-508 requires anyone transporting monetary instruments of a value of $5,000 or more into the United States from abroad, or out of the United States, to report to the secretary of the treasury the amounts, types, origins, and destinations of the instruments transported. The act also requires anyone receiving such instruments within the United States (such as a bank) to make such reports. Failure to make such a required report renders the violator liable for a civil penalty of up to the value of the monetary instruments not reported.

The purpose of all of this disclosure legislation is, of course, more effective enforcement of the Internal Revenue Code. The existence of the legislation makes it more difficult to move unreported taxable income about through the banking system, or into or out of the United States via banking channels. In the interests of law enforcement, there is really very little bank secrecy in the United States. Bank records are virtually public records so far as government is concerned.

Rights of private parties to examine bank records. A bank has no right to disclose information about the affairs of its customers to private parties, except under two circumstances.

When two private parties are involved in civil litigation, and the bank records of one are relevant to the subject matter of the case, the records would of course be subject to judicial subpoena. They would also be subject to discovery. Since there is no right to subpoena before litigation has commenced, though, prelitigation examination of bank records by a private party would be unlawful.

If a customer borrows money from the bank in which he maintains his checking account, the bank is to a degree entitled to answer questions of credit bureaus and other creditors of the customer about the customer's credit rating. In such a situation the bank may disclose how well the customer shoulders his burden of making timely loan payments. However, information about transactions that are run through the customer's checking account would be irrelevant to such an inquiry; the bank could not legitimately disclose that information.

Any disclosure by the bank of information on a customer's checking account transactions which is not in accord with the circumstances described here is unlawful.

PART VI

Sale and Transportation of Goods

29

Formation of Contracts for Sale of Goods
Title, Risk of Loss, and Insurable Interest

Formation of Contracts for Sale of Goods

Most of the law regarding contracts for the sale of goods is contained in Article 2 of the Uniform Commercial Code, enacted by the Texas legislature as Article 2 of the Business and Commerce Code.

The law contained in Article 2 is applicable only to contracts for the sale of goods. It is not applicable to contracts for sale of services, real estate, securities, intangibles, and the like. For the most part it is also not applicable to non-sales transactions.

Nature of contracts for sale of goods. These agreements may be very simple or very complex. They may involve very small amounts of money or very large amounts. In any case, such a contract may be a more complex undertaking than the layman would ordinarily imagine.

Many factors must be taken into account in the negotiation of such a contract. A contract may exist if seller and buyer have agreed upon only two of these essential factors:

1. The definition of the goods to be sold.
2. The quantity of goods to be sold.

If the parties have agreed on exactly what it is that seller is to sell to buyer, a contract may be said to exist. There are of course many more elements of the bargain that must be ascertained. Some of these are:

1. The price buyer is to pay.
2. How the price is to be paid—cash, check, letter of credit, etc.
3. When price is to be paid—in advance, upon delivery, open account, etc.
4. Where payment is to be made—at place of delivery, at seller's place of business, etc.
5. How delivery is to be made—delivery by seller to buyer, shipment by carrier, buyer to pick up, etc.
6. When delivery is to be made—the time at which buyer will get the goods.
7. Where delivery is to be made—the point at which buyer will get control of the goods.
8. The nature of the guarantees with respect to quality, quantity, title, and other such assurance given by seller to buyer.

9. Procedure for resolving disputes between the parties as to performance—arbitration and problems of this kind.

The well-drafted contract for sale of goods should have provisions governing all these factors as well as any other factors which might be important to buyer and seller in the performance of the contract. However, the parties often do not think of all these factors.

Within very broad limits, buyers and sellers of goods are free to make their own bargains in any way that they see fit. With respect to areas where there exists no contract provision, however, the UCC in effect fills in the blank. We shall now consider some of the UCC rules with respect to important terms in contracts for sale of goods.

Identity of goods. UCC 2-204 provides that parties have entered into a contract when their conduct shows their intention to enter into a contract, and when they have agreed upon enough of the subject matter so that an appropriate remedy may be fashioned. The essential thing here is the identification of the nature of the goods which will be the subject matter. *What* is to be sold?

Quantity of goods. Some sort of agreement upon quantity of goods will be essential in order to lay a groundwork for an adequate remedy in case of breach. Least ambiguous is for the parties to spell out a quantity—e.g., "1,000 gallons of Zippo regular gasoline." However, more indefinite expressions of quantity are acceptable—"about 1,000 gallons" or "1,000 gallons, more or less" would be permissible.

The quantity deliverable may also be expressed in terms of output or requirement— that is, seller may agree to sell to buyer all of his output of the subject goods over a period of time, or buyer may agree to buy from seller all of his requirements of the subject goods for a period of time. UCC 2-306 provides that the obligated party must take the output produced in good faith, or provide the requirements generated in good faith. Under these contract provisions buyer may not be required to take the unreasonably high output, nor may seller be required to meet an unreasonably high requirement.

Price of goods. UCC 2-305 provides that if the parties do not agree upon a price and they do not agree upon a method of fixing the price, the price shall be a reasonable price at time of delivery. This would normally be the fair market value of the goods at time of delivery.

The parties may agree that the price shall be fixed by the seller alone, or by the buyer alone. In such a case the fixed price must bear a reasonable relationship to current market prices. When it is agreed that one party should fix the price, but he fails to do so, the other party may either fix a reasonable price himself or cancel the contract.

The parties may also agree that if they cannot agree upon a price, there will be no contract. If a portion of the contract is performed before the parties discover that they cannot agree upon a price, each must return to the other the consideration received. Remember, though, failure to agree upon a price will not cancel the contract unless the parties have expressly agreed to the cancellation.

Time of delivery. UCC 2-309 provides that when the contract does not specify a time for delivery, delivery is due within a reasonable time after the making of the contract. What is a reasonable time will depend upon such factors as whether the goods are identified or not; whether the seller has them in inventory or must obtain them from a supplier; whether or not the seller must manufacture the goods before selling them; when a crop will be harvested; and other such considerations.

Place of delivery. UCC 2-308 provides that if the contract does not specify a place of delivery, the place is the seller's place of business, or, if he has none, his residence. If the goods are identified goods located at a place other than the seller's residence or the seller's place of business, the place of delivery is the place where the goods are.

29/ Formation of Contracts for Sale of Goods 431

Quantity to be delivered. UCC 2-307 provides that seller must deliver all goods called for under the contract at once. Delivery in installments is not proper unless the contract specifically authorizes such delivery.

Time and place of payment. UCC 2-310 provides that payment is due at the time and place where buyer receives the goods, unless the contract provides otherwise. Thus, buyer need not pay in advance, nor must seller grant buyer credit. Of course, payment must be in full unless the contract grants credit to buyer.

Method of payment. UCC 2-511 provides that payment may be made in any commercially reasonable manner in the absence of agreement upon medium of payment. Thus buyer may offer a personal check in payment. However, seller has the option to ask for payment in legal tender. Since checks are not legal tender, seller may refuse to accept payment in the form of a check. But seller cannot refuse to take a check and then accuse buyer of breach for not paying in legal tender. If seller does not want to take the check he must give buyer a reasonable time to come up with some legal tender (that is to say, cash).

If seller wishes to be paid in some specific medium of payment, he should of course make his wishes a part of the contract.

Guarantees with respect to the goods. The UCC imposes two implied warranties upon sellers of goods who are not merchants. UCC 2-311 imposes a warranty of title upon most sellers; this is a warranty that buyer is getting valid title to the goods he is buying, and that the goods are not subject to any security interest or other lien that buyer does not know about. In addition, UCC 2-315 imposes upon the non-merchant seller a warranty of fitness for the buyer's purpose, if the buyer has in mind a specific use for the goods and the seller knew what that use was and selected the goods fit for that use.

Merchant sellers make these two implied warranties, and two more. UCC 2-312 imposes upon the merchant seller a warranty against infringement—a warranty that buyer will not be subject to patent infringement claims or the like due to his purchase. Most important, UCC 2-314 imposes upon the merchant seller the warranty of merchantability—a warranty that the goods sold are fit for normal use. Sellers make these warranties unless the contract between the parties limits or disclaims them in some way. The subject is important; an entire chapter in this section will be devoted to warranties.

Remedies for breach. The UCC provides a wide range of remedies for both buyer and seller in case of breach. These will be considered in detail in the chapter on breach and remedies. Any applicable remedy may be sought by a victim of breach unless the contract has limited the availability of such remedy. UCC 2-719 permits this modification or limitation.

Statute of limitation for suit on breach. UCC 2-725 provides that suit may be commenced upon a breach of contract within four years after occurrence of the breach. The parties may shorten this period to as little as one year but they may not extend it beyond four years.

Arbitration. Under the UCC there is no requirement that parties to a contract for sale of goods submit disputes arising under the contract to arbitration. Agreements to arbitrate are enforceable, but no obligation to arbitrate exists unless both parties have agreed to it.

Contract formation under Article 2. Prior to enactment of the Uniform Commercial Code, contracts for the sale of goods were formed in the same manner as other contracts—by exchange of an offer and a "mirror image" acceptance. In order for a response to an offer to be an acceptance, it had to agree to all terms of the offer and to add nothing to the offer. The nonconforming acceptance was deemed to be no acceptance at all. The law treated it as a counteroffer.

The mirror image rule made sense before the Industrial Revolution and the evolution of large-scale business enterprise; it still makes sense in commercial transactions where buyer and seller bargain face-to-face in the negotiation of the terms of a contract. But it does not make much sense in routine, large-scale commercial transactions.

Consider the situation of Ace Company, a manufacturer of widgets. Ace often orders raw materials used in the manufacture of widgets from various suppliers. It also has occasion to order factory equipment, packing supplies, office supplies, and equipment from suppliers. The company may well have on its payroll a purchasing agent and staff to handle these ordering chores. Probably the ordering of most of these items is a routine matter; the various operating departments of the firm tell Purchasing what they require, and Purchasing orders the goods from the best source.

Since it would be very time-consuming for Ace's purchasing staff to compose an individualized letter for each order that is sent out, the company has no doubt devised and had reproduced a standard purchase-order form for use in sending out orders. The form contains a lot of small print which, it is hoped, will comprise the purchase contract to be entered into between Ace and its suppliers. The small print was very likely drafted by an attorney hired by Ace for this purpose, and will contain terms very favorable to buyers.

Since Ace must sell the widgets it manufactures, it may well receive numerous orders for its product from its customers. These orders will also be processed in a routine manner. Since Ace's business is the selling of widgets, it naturally wants to fill all orders which it receives. These orders being offers to buy, Ace will naturally desire to accept them. Since the normal commercial practice is to acknowledge receipt of an order before shipping goods, Ace will respond to orders by mailing to the ordering firm an acknowledgment form. The form is used because, again, it saves more time than writing individualized letters of acknowledgment. The typical acknowledgment form is a promise to deliver. It also contains much small print which, it is hoped, will comprise the terms of a contract of sale. The small print in the acknowledgment form was also very likely drafted by an attorney. However, since Ace is a seller here, the terms in the acknowledgment form will be quite different from the terms in the purchase-order form. The terms here will most likely be very favorable to sellers.

Other firms the size of Ace will conduct their purchasing and shipping operations in the same manner. Thus, when Ace orders items from Deuce Office Supply, Ace will send Deuce its order on its probuyer purchase order form. Deuce will respond to the offer with an "acceptance" on its proseller acknowledgment form. At the same time, when Trey Widget Sales orders widgets from Ace, it will use its probuyer purchase-order form for its order. Ace will "accept" the order with its proseller acknowledgment form.

Under the pre-UCC law, no contract would exist in either of the above examples. In both cases, the acceptance is not the mirror image of the offer, so it is truly a counteroffer. The pre-UCC law therefore ignored commercial realty: Deuce Office Supply would, after receipt of Ace's offer and the dispatch of its acknowledgment, ship exactly the supplies that Ace ordered. Ace would receive these in due course and pay for them. The supposedly nonexistent contract would be fully and fairly performed.

Normally, it is to the advantage of business firms to honor their commitments. Therefore, in the past, the vast majority of these nonexistent contracts were performed without a hitch. However, when difficulties did arise in the performance of a contract under pre-UCC law, the results of litigation could be surprising.

For example: Trey would order widgets from Ace on its standard probuyer purchase order form. Ace would "accept" the offer with its standard proseller acknowledgment form, and would then ship the widgets as ordered. But, meanwhile, Trey had found a cheaper source of widgets, so it refused to accept or pay for Ace's shipment. Ace would accuse Trey of breach of contract. If Ace were so foolish as to sue in this situation, it would lose. Since the terms of the purchase-order form and the acknowledgment form were not identical, the acknowledgment was no acceptance; it was a counteroffer. When Trey rejected the shipment, it rejected the counteroffer. There was no contract; therefore there was no breach.

Or this could happen: Cinque Widget Sales would order widgets from Ace, its purchase form stating, "Seller guarantees the goods sold under this contract against all defects in manufacture for a period of one year." Ace promises to ship the widgets, its acknowledgment form stating, "Seller guarantees the goods sold under this contract for a period of thirty days." Ace ships the widgets, and Cinque accepts and pays for them. Defects in them are discovered by Cinque ninety days after receipt. Cinque claims this is a breach of contract. Ace claims it isn't. Here, of course, a contract did exist—Ace shipped the widgets and Cinque accepted and paid for them. The problem was, what were the guarantee terms of the contract?

Under pre-UCC law, Ace would win the argument. The acknowledgment was not an acceptance of Cinque's offer; it was a counteroffer. Ace's shipment of the widgets was another manifestation of the counteroffer. Cinque's acceptance of and payment for the widgets was acceptance of the counteroffer, so the contract was on Ace's terms.

Or this could happen: Ocho Widget Sales would order 1,000 #9 widgets from Ace for immediate resale to Diez, Ocho pointing out in its order that it needed immediate delivery of the #9 widgets to meet its commitment to Diez. Ace had no #9 widgets in stock, and would not have any for a week. It did have 1,000 #12 widgets available, though, so it immediately shipped Ocho 1,000 #12 widgets without sending any acknowledgment first. When Ocho received the shipment it rejected it, because Diez could not use #12 widgets. Diez then accused Ocho of breach of contract for not delivering the #9 widgets, and Ocho blamed Ace for its problem because—had it known Ace had no #9s—it could have sought #9s elsewhere. Under pre-UCC law, Ocho had been "had." Ace made a counteroffer by shipping the #12s. Ocho's rejection of the shipment was a rejection of the counteroffer. Therefore, there was no contract and no breach.

The above examples should give the reader some notion about the defects in the pre-UCC law of contract formation. Because of the "battle of the forms" between buyer and seller, the exchange of purchase order and acknowledgment seldom, if ever, resulted in the making of a binding contract. Yet seller and buyer behaved as if there was a binding contract. If seller and buyer behave as if there is a contract under these circumstances, should the law not recognize that a contract exists?

There also exists the notion rooted in basic ideas of fairness, that the offeror should be the master of his offer. The offeror-buyer initiates the majority of commercial transactions. Since the offeree-seller would not make many sales if offeror-buyers did not send orders, the offeror-buyer should have the majority of the control over the terms of the contract of sale. Under pre-UCC law, it did not work out that way; ultimate control of contract terms rested with the offeree-seller. The acknowledgment form comprised a counteroffer, and if the seller then shipped goods and the buyer accepted them, he was accepting the counteroffer.

The UCC rules on contract formation, then, are intended to do two things. First, they recognize the existence of a contract when buyer and seller by their behavior act as though a contract exists. Second, they provide a set of rules for determining the content of a contract which, to a large degree, assures that the offeror does remain the master of his offer.

Offer and acceptance—the offer to buy goods for prompt shipment. When buyer sends seller an offer worded, "Please ship me _____ as soon as possible," the question may arise as to whether the seller may accept the offer by shipping goods, or whether he must promise to ship the goods in order to make his acceptance. Pre-UCC law held that the only proper way to accept such an offer was to make a promise to ship, and that shipment alone was not an acceptance.

UCC 2-206 changes this rule. A seller may now accept an offer such as the above either by shipping goods or by sending a promise to ship. One result of this rule is that if seller responds to the offer by shipping goods other than those buyer ordered, the act of shipment is both an acceptance of the offer and a breach of the resulting contract.

Should an offeror desire that his offer be accepted by a promise to ship rather than by shipment of goods, he should specify in the offer that acceptance must take the form of a promise to ship. Should an offeree desire to ship goods other than what offeror ordered in response to such an offer, he should inform the offeror that the goods are being shipped not as an acceptance of the offer but as an accommodation to the offeror. This makes the shipment a counteroffer. If the offeror does not want the substitute goods there is no contract and no breach.

Offer and acceptance—terms of contract when offer and acceptance are not identical. UCC 2-207 provides that an acceptance of an offer to buy or sell goods is normally a valid acceptance, even if the terms of the acceptance are not the same as the terms in the offer. This will be true unless the parties act in such a manner as to indicate that they do not recognize the existence of a contract.

The problem in such a situation is that of determining what the terms of the contract are. For this purpose, it makes a difference whether or not both parties to the bargain are merchants. If neither is a merchant, or if only one party is a merchant, the contract consists of those terms upon which offer and acceptance are in agreement. With respect to the conflicting terms, it will be as if the contract made no mention of them at all. Thus, the UCC rules for filling in blanks in the contract will be used to provide the missing terms, unless both parties eventually agree to terms.

If both parties are merchants, the outcome will depend upon whether the acceptance merely adds terms to those contained in the offer, or whether the acceptance materially alters the terms of the offer. If the acceptance merely adds terms to the offer, silence by the offeror is agreement to the added terms, and the ultimate contract will be on the offeree's terms. The only way the offeror can avoid being bound to the additional terms is to notify the offeree that he objects to them. This will result in the contract being on the offeror's terms. Essentially, the added terms are merely proposals for addition to the contract, and the offeror need not agree to them. If the acceptance contains terms that materially alter the terms contained in the offer, silence by the offeror does not constitute agreement. These terms will not become part of the contract unless the offeror expressly agrees to be bound by them. Silence by the offeror here is rejection of the added terms; the result is the existence of a contract upon the offeror's terms.

There is some uncertainty as to what sort of extra terms in an acceptance constitute additions, and what sort constitute material alteration. To begin with, if a term in the acceptance contradicts a term in the offer, material alteration exists. Thus, if offeror offers to buy on credit and offeree accepts, but says he is shipping C.O.D., the C.O.D. term is a material alteration. Offeror is not bound to the C.O.D. term unless he agrees to it. If the acceptance contains a term which the offer does not contain, the additional term may be an addition, or it may be an alteration. Thus, if offeror offers to buy on credit, and offeree accepts the offer but states that interest will accrue on invoices more than thirty days old at

10 percent per annum, this would be construed as an addition. Silence by offeror would be agreement. If the offer merely says, "Please ship at once," and the acceptance says, "Am shipping via Rusty Railroad," this would be an addition. Shipment by rail is consistent with the request for shipment at once. If the offer mentions nothing about dispute resolution under the contract, while the acceptance provides for arbitration of differences, this would probably be considered an addition.

If the offer mentions nothing about claims for goods damaged in transit, while the acceptance says that claims for transit damage must be made within fifteen days of receipt of the goods, this is another example of addition. On the other hand, if the offer does not mention guarantees of quality, while the acceptance says that the goods are sold "as is, with all faults," a material alteration of the terms of the bargain the buyer had in mind exists. The seller is trying to disclaim the UCC-implied warranties of merchantability and fitness for the buyer's purpose here. The offeror should not be bound to such a bargain without his express consent.

If the offer does not specify the method of payment, and the acceptance says that the goods are being shipped C.O.D., a material alteration of the buyer's expected bargain is being attempted. Normally, a buyer has the right to inspect the goods he is ordering before he pays, but under C.O.D. terms the buyer must pay before he inspects. The buyer should not be deprived of his inspection right without his express consent.

From this discussion it should be clear that UCC 2-207 provides a fairly logical method for distilling contract terms from the contradictions generated from the battle of the forms. To a degree, the mechanism provided for this loads the dice in favor of the offeror: when the offeree wants to accept an offer but also wants to change its terms, his task is made quite difficult. The rules are designed to insure, to a large degree, that the offeror shall be the master of his offer.

The rules of UCC 2-207 still leave scope for maneuver in the battle of the forms, however. Though the offeree can no longer materially change the terms of a bargain without the express consent of the offeror, the offeror must still be on guard with respect to additional terms in an acceptance. An offeror, to protect himself, should scan every order acknowledgment he receives for additional terms. Failure to do this might mean acceptance of and agreement by silence to the additional terms.

Additional insurance against such surprises may be taken out through provisions in the purchase-order form. If it is more important to the offeror that his contract with the offeree be on his terms than it is that he get goods from the offeree, he may word his offer this way: "This offer is made on the condition that you agree to all terms and conditions contained herein." Any "acceptance" of this that seeks to alter it or change it will be a counteroffer, not an acceptance. A milder form of insurance would be wording of this nature: "Any terms in your acceptance which are in addition to or in alteration of the terms of this order are hereby objected to." Any sort of acceptance of this will indeed be an acceptance, and it will be an acceptance of the offeror's entire package of terms.

Offerees must now be aware of the fact that a normal, customary acknowledgment of an offer is quite likely an acceptance of the entire package of terms contained in the offer. Offeree might try to slip additional terms past offeror in his acceptance, hoping that offeror will not notice them and will remain silent about them. But offeree cannot get a binding contract with offeror and at the same time materially change the terms of the offer, unless offeror agrees to the changes. Offeree's alternatives now are to deal with offeror on offeror's terms, or not to deal with him at all.

If offeree does not like offeror's terms, he still has available the option of rejecting the offer. He also has the option of making a counteroffer. A third possibility is to respond as follows: "We accept your offer on condition that you agree to the following:——" This is in essence a polite form of counteroffer. There will not be a contract here unless offeror accepts offeree's terms.

UCC 2-207 has also changed the law with respect to the following situation: Ace orders goods from Deuce, both being merchants, Ace using his probuyer purchase order form. Deuce does not like Ace's terms, so he sends back a proseller acknowledgment form which says at the end, "This acknowledgment form operates as an acceptance of your offer only on condition that you agree to be bound by all the terms and conditions hereof." Ace does not like the terms in the acknowledgment, so he makes no response to it. At this point, no contract exists.

Deuce then ships to Ace the goods which Ace ordered. Ace accepts the goods and pays for them. This of course creates a contract. Ace later claims the goods are defective. Under the terms of Ace's offer the goods are to be guaranteed for a year. Under the terms of Deuce's acceptance the goods are sold "as is, with all faults." Which provision prevails?

In this situation, neither does. The contract was created by the shipment and acceptance of goods, not by the exchange of forms. Therefore, the contract consists of those terms upon which the two forms agree. With respect to the terms upon which the forms disagree, the forms are completely disregarded and the UCC rules for filling in blanks supply the missing terms. The result is that Deuce made the warranty of merchantability to Ace, because Ace never agreed to Deuce's disclaimer of it. Ace therefore has a good claim.

Review of UCC provisions relative to formation, modification, and assignment of contracts for sale of goods. These were presented in Part III, Contracts, but a short review is in order here. Remember that when a merchant puts a firm offer into writing—an offer he promises to hold open for a specified length of time—he must hold it open for the specified time or for three months, whichever is shorter (UCC 2-205).

Contracts for the sale of goods for $500 or more must be in writing, unless:
1. The bargain is between merchants; one sends the other a letter confirming the bargain and spelling out its terms; and the recipient of the letter does not object to the existence of a contract within ten days of receipt of the confirmation, or
2. The contract is for nonresalable goods, and seller has irrevocably committed himself to performance, or
3. Buyer has taken possession of the goods, or
4. Buyer has paid the purchase price in full, or
5. The goods are nonfungible, and buyer has made a partial payment, or
6. Buyer admits the making of the oral contract, either on the witness stand in court or in a court pleading (UCC 2-201).

Oral contracts for the sale of $500 or more worth of fungible goods become enforceable when partially performed to the extent of the partial performance—that is, to the extent of the partial payment made by the buyer or to the extent of the partial delivery made by the seller. A contract for the sale of goods may be modified if the parties agree to the modification, even if both parties did not receive consideration for the modification (2-209).

An assignment of a right for sale of goods under an executory contract is also a delegation of the corresponding duty, unless the contract of assignment itself provides otherwise.

A contract interpretation problem may arise when two merchants make a contract for sale of more than $500 worth of goods over the telephone, and one of the merchants later sends the other a letter of confirmation of the bargain. A contract will exist if the recipient of the confirmation does not object to the existence of a contract within ten days. Will the contract which comes into existence be the contract described in the confirmation?

The answer is, not necessarily. The letter of confirmation, if not objected to, will prove that a contract exists. However, if the receiving merchant claims that some of the provisions in the letter are not accurate and do not truly describe the bargain made, he may introduce oral evidence in court to prove his point.

It also can happen that both merchants involved in the above bargain send letters of confirmation to each other. What happens if the two confirmations disagree as to some of the terms of the bargain? The answer there is as follows: The contract contains those terms upon which the confirmations agree. With respect to those upon which they disagree, oral evidence would be admissible in court to attempt to prove which of the conflicting provisions are the true ones. No rule exists to provide an automatic solution to this problem.

Title, Risk of Loss, and Insurable Interest

Before a contract for the sale of goods is made, the buyer has no interest in the goods whatsoever. After a contract for the sale of goods has been completely performed, the buyer has complete ownership of the goods, and all interest of the seller in them has been terminated. When the contract is made and performed at the same time, the buyer acquires complete ownership of the goods immediately, and the seller loses all of his interest immediately. When the contract is made at one time and performance extends for a long period afterward, it becomes important to know when certain interests and obligations come into being and are transferred. Sometime during the process of performance, the buyer will acquire an insurable interest in the goods. Before buyer has this, he may not insure his interest in the goods against loss or damage. After he has it, he may take out insurance.

Sometime during the process of performance, risk of loss will pass from seller to buyer. If the goods are damaged or destroyed while risk of loss is on the seller, the seller bears the loss, and the buyer will not be required to pay for the goods. If the goods are damaged or destroyed while risk of loss is on the buyer, however, the buyer will be obligated to pay for the goods. The buyer takes the loss. Sometime during the course of performance, title will pass from seller to buyer. While the seller has title, creditors of the buyer have no claim against the goods. When title has passed to the buyer, creditors of the buyer do have claim against the goods, while creditors of the seller no longer have such claims.

When the buyer acquires his insurable interest, and when title and risk of loss pass, both depend upon the nature of the seller-buyer transaction. We shall examine various types of sales transactions and discuss when these interests pass, but first we shall examine the UCC provisions relative to these interests.

Insurable interest. UCC 2-501 contains the relevant provisions. Buyer obtains an insurable interest:

1. In existing and identified goods when the contract is made.
2. In goods existing but unidentified when the contract is made, when the goods are identified. Identification may take place in any manner upon which the parties agree.

In the absence of agreement, identification occurs when goods are shipped, marked, or otherwise designated by seller as the goods to which the contract refers. If the contract calls for sale of part of a mass of fungible goods, the goods are considered to be identified when the contract is made. No special act of identification is necessary, unless the parties agree otherwise.

3. Future goods—goods that do not exist when the contract is made—are identified when they come into existence and are identified in the contract. When the contract is for the sale of a crop to be harvested within twelve months of the making of the contract, identification occurs when the crop is planted. If the contract is for the sale of unborn young animals to be born within twelve months of the making of the contract, identification takes place when the young are conceived.

Identification is usually a unilateral act by the seller. Even if the seller identifies nonconforming goods to the contract, the buyer has his insurable interest in them. No identification is final unless the seller informs the buyer that he has made a final identification, or unless the seller becomes insolvent. Until then the seller may substitute other goods for those identified. The seller retains an insurable interest in the goods until the title passes to the buyer and any security interest which the seller has retained in the goods is discharged.

Title. UCC 2-401 governs passage of title, except for those goods such as motor vehicles and aircraft which are subject to special registration of title statutes. It provides that title to goods shall pass from seller to buyer as the parties shall agree. In the absence of agreement the rules are as follows:

1. In existing and identified goods which are not to be moved, when the contract is made, so long as no document of title is to be delivered.

2. In existing and identified goods which are not to be moved, but for which a document of title is to be delivered, when the document is delivered.

3. In existing but unidentified goods which are not to be moved after identification and for which no document of title is to be delivered, when the goods are identified.

4. When the goods are to be moved by the seller, when seller has completed all of his performance with respect to delivery. If contract requires shipment but not delivery at destination, title passes at time and place of shipment. If contract requires delivery at destination, title passes upon tender of delivery at destination.

5. In contracts for sale of part of a mass of fungible goods, buyer becomes a tenant in common of the mass with seller to the extent of his purchase at the time the contract is made.

Title to motor vehicles, house trailers, motorcycles, aircraft, ships, and small boats. Proof of ownership of motor vehicles, house trailers, and motorcycles other than motor-driven bicycles is governed by the Texas Motor Vehicle Certificate of Title Act, RCS 6687-1. The provisions of this act are set forth in some detail in the chapter on motor vehicle law. It is sufficient here to say that the owner of such vehicles is required to obtain a certificate of title for the conveyance from the Texas Highway Department, and that any transfer of ownership of such a vehicle must be accomplished by transfer of the certificate of title in proper form. Any purported sale of such a vehicle without transfer of the certificate of title is void. Thus, title to such vehicles passes only with transfer of the title certificate.

Parks and Wildlife Code 31.045 et seq. provide for issuance of certificates of title for motorboats and outboard motors. The ownership of new motors and outboard motors is evidenced by a manufacturer's certificate of origin or an importer's certificate, unless the boat is fourteen feet long or less, or unless the motor is rated at less than twelve horsepower (HP). Ownership of these small boats and motors when new may be evidenced by the above-mentioned documents. The ownership of motorboats and outboard motors which are not new must be evidenced by a certificate of title, unless the boat is fourteen feet long or less, or the motor is less than twelve HP. Ownership of such small boats and motors may be evidenced by certificate of title.

These small boats and motors may be transferred without transfer of a manufacturer's certificate of origin or of a certificate of title. However, a transfer of a motorboat more than fourteen feet long or of an outboard motor of twelve HP or more must be accompanied by transfer of a proper manufacturer's certificate of origin, a proper certificate of title, or sufficient information from seller to enable buyer to apply for and obtain a proper certificate of title. Buyer must then apply for a proper certificate of title in his name. A buyer will not get title to a motorboat more than fourteen feet long or to an outboard motor of twelve or more HP until he either has a proper certificate of title issued in his name or receives a manufacturer's certificate of origin with all proper endorsements. Boats and outboard motors require separate certificates.

Transfer of title to aircraft is governed by federal law; the applicable statutes are found at 49 USC 1401 et seq. Conveyances of title to aircraft must be in writing, and, for the conveyance to be effective against third parties, must be recorded with the U.S. Secretary of Transportation. A seller may transfer valid title to a buyer by written conveyance, but until the buyer records his conveyance, the seller could deprive him of his title by selling the aircraft to a third party who records his conveyance. As with any recording system, the first conveyance recorded takes priority over subsequent conveyance of the same right. Registration records of aircraft are also maintained by the Department of Transportation, and conveyances are noted upon registration records, but the registered owner of an aircraft is not necessarily the legal owner. The legal owner in essence becomes the registered owner only when his conveyance is recorded.

Any vessel flying the American flag which operates on the navigable waterways of the United States or on the high seas must be registered with the Collector of Customs in its home port. According to 46 USC 1012, any bill of sale transferring title to such a vessel must be recorded with the Collector of Customs of the vessel's home port to be valid against third parties. As with sale of an aircraft, the buyer gets title upon transfer of a bill of sale to the vessel, but he should record his bill to perfect his title with respect to the outside world.

Risk of loss. UCC 2–509 governs passage of risk of loss when no breach of contract has occurred, and UCC 2–510 describes the effect of a breach upon risk of loss. The parties may make any contract provisions they choose with respect to passage or allocation of risk of loss. When the parties have made no such provision, the following rules apply:

1. If goods are in the possession of seller and are not to be shipped by carrier, when risk passes depends upon whether or not seller is a merchant. If he is a merchant, risk of loss passes upon delivery to buyer. If he is not, risk passes upon tender of delivery to buyer.

2. If goods are in the hands of a bailee, buyer gets risk of loss upon receipt of a negotiable document of title for the goods, or upon acknowledgment by the bailee of the buyer's right to possession, or upon delivery of a nonnegotiable document of title or delivery order addressed to bailee after buyer has had an opportunity to notify bailee of his possession of the nonnegotiable document of title or of the delivery order.

3. If goods are to be shipped by carrier, when seller delivers goods to the carrier (if only shipment is required) or when seller tenders delivery to buyer at destination (if tender of delivery at destination is required).

If seller breaches the contract of sale (as by shipping nonconforming goods or by not performing his duties under the agreed shipping term), risk of loss remains upon the seller until he cures the nonconformity or until buyer accepts the goods. If buyer breaches (by refusing to accept conforming goods, or by repudiating the contract after shipment of goods), risk of loss will rest upon the buyer for a reasonable time after the breach. The following are illustrations of the applications of these rules to specific situations.

Contract for sale of a crop. In November 1980 Buyer and Farmer make a written contract under which Buyer will buy Farmer's 1981 spring wheat crop. The crop has not yet been planted.

Since the subject matter of this contract does not yet exist, no property interests have passed. This is a contract for sale, not a sale. Buyer will get an insurable interest in the crop when it is planted. Risk of loss will lie with Farmer until he tenders delivery of the crop to Buyer after harvesting, since courts do not consider farmers to be merchants of their produce. Passage of title will depend upon the arrangements Farmer and Buyer make for delivery. If Buyer is to pick the crop up after harvesting, it could be argued that Buyer will get title upon planting, but if Farmer is to move the crop in order to deliver to Buyer, Buyer will not get title until Farmer has completed his obligations with respect to delivery.

Contract for sale of a custom-made machine. Buyer orders a custom-built machine from Manufacturer, Manufacturer to build it to Buyer's specification. Again, the subject matter of this bargain does not exist at the time of the making of a contract; therefore we have a contract for sale, not a sale. Buyer will obtain an insurable interest in the machine when Manufacturer commences the manufacturing process. The goods will be identified at that time. Risk of loss will lie with Manufacturer until the machine is delivered to Buyer, or until he completes all of his obligations under the agreed-upon shipping term if the machine is to be shipped by carrier. If Buyer is to pick up the machine at the factory, he will get title when manufacture is begun. If Manufacturer is to move the machine in the process of delivery, or if he is to ship it by carrier, Buyer will get title when Manufacturer completes his obligations with respect to moving the goods.

Contract for sale of non-custom-made manufactured goods. Builder orders five steel girders of specified dimensions from Steelmaker, Steelmaker having none of these in inventory, but these being a regular item of production for him. Steelmaker is to deliver the girders to Builder's building site.

Again the subject matter does not yet exist. Builder acquires an insurable interest here when the manufacturing process is complete and Steelmaker chooses the exact five girders which he will deliver under this contract. Since these are not unique they will not be identifiable during the manufacturing process. Risk of loss will pass when Steelmaker delivers the girders at the building site. Title will pass at the same time, since Steelmaker's obligation to move the girders will be complete at delivery.

Contract for sale of a quantity of fungible goods. Buyer contracts to buy 500 bushels of hard red spring wheat from Elevator, Elevator to deliver the wheat to Buyer and Elevator now having the wheat in inventory. Elevator has 5,000 bushels of hard red spring wheat in one of his storage elevators.

Buyer acquires a 10 percent interest as a tenant in common in the 5,000 bushels of hard red spring wheat in the elevator at the time of the making of the contract. Along with the title goes an insurable interest. Risk of loss remains with Elevator until the wheat is delivered to Buyer by him, as agreed.

Contract for sale of existing identified goods by nonmerchant. Student contracts to sell his hi-fi set to Buddy, the contract being made on Monday and Buddy to pick up the set and pay on Friday. Student offers to let Buddy take the set on Monday, but Buddy refuses. Buddy gets title to the set when the contract is made, and also gets an insurable interest. Buddy gets risk of loss on Monday, since Student tendered delivery on Monday.

Contracts for sale of existing identified goods by merchant. Buddy contracts to buy a new hi-fi set from Dealer on Monday, Buddy picking out the set he wants from Dealer's inventory. Dealer is to bring the set to Buddy's house on Tuesday. The sale is a credit sale.

Buddy gets title and insurable interest when the contract is made. Dealer keeps risk of loss until the set is delivered to Buddy's house.

Contract for sale of a motor vehicle. Student contracts on Monday to sell his car to Buddy on Tuesday. Buddy takes the car when the contract is made. Student is to sign the certificate of title over on Tuesday, and Buddy is to pay on Friday. Buddy gets an insurable interest on Monday. He also gets risk of loss, because he has taken delivery. He gets title on Tuesday, when the certificate of title is signed over.

Contract for sale of goods in the hands of a bailee, where no document of title is outstanding. Pal contracts to sell his watch to Bud, the watch now being repaired by Jeweler. Bud is to pick up the watch at Jeweler's shop later, after Bud has paid the repair bill. Bud gets title when the contract is made, and of course gets an insurable interest at that time. Pal keeps risk of loss until Jeweler informs Bud that he recognizes Bud as the owner of the watch.

Contract for sale of goods in hands of bailee where negotiable document of title is outstanding. Seller has a power lawnmower in storage in Ace Warehouse, Ace having issued him a negotiable warehouse receipt for it. Seller contracts to sell the mower to Buyer, the sale to be consummated by endorsement of the warehouse receipt from seller to buyer. Buyer gets an insurable interest when the contract is made. Buyer will get title and risk of loss when Seller delivers and negotiates the warehouse receipt to him.

Contract for sale of goods in hands of bailee when nonnegotiable document of title is outstanding. Assume the same situation as above, the only difference being that Seller's warehouse receipt is nonnegotiable. Buyer gets his insurable interest when the contract is made. Buyer gets title when the warehouse receipt is transferred. But Seller keeps risk of loss until Buyer has had a chance to take the document to the warehouse and obtain the goods.

Also, according to UCC 2-503, the buyer's title will not be secure until he informs the bailee that he is now the owner of the document and of the goods. The ramifications of this will be discussed further in the materials on documents of title and performance.

Contracts for shipment by carrier. When the goods are to be moved for a long distance and the services of a carrier are to be utilized, passage of title and risk of loss will depend upon the shipping terms contained in the contract. Title and risk of loss will pass at the same time. They will pass as follows under the various terms in common use:

Ex Factory (Mill, Warehouse, etc.): When the seller makes the goods ready for shipment. Under this term the seller need not move the goods; he must merely prepare them for shipment and notify buyer of that fact.

F.O.B. Shipping Point, C.I.F., C&F, or C.O.D.: These are all "shipping point" terms with respect to passage of title and risk of loss. Both interests normally pass when seller ships the goods.

F.A.S. Vessel: When seller delivers the goods to the dock from which the vessel will load, or, if the vessel anchors out in the harbor, when the lighter brings the goods alongside the vessel ready for loading.

F.O.B. Vessel: When seller gets the goods loaded on board the vessel.

Ex Vessel: When the goods leave the ship's tackle at the destination of the vessel.

Ex Dock: When buyer picks the goods up from the dock at the port of destination.

F.O.B. Destination, or No Arrival, No Sale: When the last carrier delivers the goods to buyer.

For risk of loss to pass under a shipping term, it must be remembered that seller must perform all of his obligations under the terms. Should seller not perform all of his obligations, breach occurs and risk of loss remains with seller.

Shipment under reservation. When seller ships goods under a shipping term which does not require him to deliver the goods to the buyer at their destination, buyer will acquire legal title to the goods before they arrive. However, if buyer has not paid for the goods in advance; seller does not give the buyer credit; and buyer is not financing the bargain by means of a letter of credit, seller may want to keep control over the goods so that he will be paid for them before the buyer obtains possession. Seller may accomplish this by shipment of the goods under reservation, thus keeping a security interest in the goods until he is paid (UCC 2-505).

If when seller ships the goods he obtains a negotiable bill of lading for them from the carrier, he has reserved such a security in them no matter who is named as consignee of the bill of lading. Whether the bill of lading names seller, buyer, or a financing agency as consignee, the seller has a security interest in the goods as long as he controls the bill of lading. If the bill names a financing agency (usually a bank) as consignee, the security interest passes to the bank when seller delivers the bill of lading to the bank. If buyer is named as consignee, seller releases the security interest when the bill is delivered to the buyer.

If seller obtains a nonnegotiable bill of lading for the goods naming himself or an agent as consignee, seller again retains a security interest in the goods. But if the buyer is named as consignee of the nonnegotiable bill, seller has no security interest.

Sale on approval, sale or return, and consignment. Special rules relative to title and risk of loss are necessary with respect to transactions in which the buyer may return goods to the seller even though the goods comply with the contract for sale. Such bargains permit the buyer to keep the goods for a specified period of time while he decides whether or not to purchase them. The rules governing these transactions are found in UCC 2-326 and UCC 2-327. If no period is specified, the trial period is a reasonable time.

If a bargain is a sale on approval, seller has title and risk of loss with respect to the goods during the specified trial period, or for a reasonable time. If buyer permits the specified time period to pass without returning the goods, or if no time period is specified, and he lets a reasonable time pass without return, his silence is acceptance of the goods.

Seller keeps title and risk of loss during the return process, but if he is a merchant, buyer must follow reasonable instructions furnished by seller as to the return. If buyer is not a merchant, he may return in any reasonable manner. He may not return some of the goods and keep others.

If a bargain is a sale or return, buyer has title and risk of loss during the trial period. Should buyer decide to exercise his return option he must do so during the specified trial period if there is one, or within a reasonable time of receipt of the goods. If a return is made, buyer has the risk of loss during the return, and must pay all expenses of the return. Buyer is permitted to return some of the goods and retain others.

The parties may determine whether their bargain is a sale on approval or a sale or return. If the bargain is not specified as one or the other, it is a sale on approval if the buyer is considering the goods for use, and it is a sale or return if buyer is considering the goods for resale.

If the owner of goods sends them to another party "on consignment" or "on memorandum" to see if the consignee can sell them, the consignor retains legal title to them and also retains the risk of loss. The consignee is a mere sales agent and bailee, having the liability of a bailee with respect to the goods.

However, creditors of the consignee may treat consignment goods as the property of the consignee, unless:

1. The goods are clearly marked as consignment goods, or
2. The consignee is known to his creditors to be substantially engaged in the sale of consignment goods, or
3. The consignor files a financing statement in the proper public records perfecting a security interest in the consigned goods.

Artists' Consignment Act. In 1977 the Texas legislature enacted RCS 9018, which became effective on August 29, 1977. The act provides that any work of art—defined in the act as painting, sculpture, drawing, work of graphic art, pottery, weaving, batik, macrame, quilt, or other recognized art form—delivered to an art dealer for purpose of exhibition or sale is not subject to the claims, liens, or security interests of the creditors of the art dealer.

The same is true with respect to the proceeds of the sale of a work of art, no matter whether the dealer himself buys the piece or a third party buys it.

Since many works of art are offered for sale by dealers holding the pieces on consignment, under prior law it was possible for the artist to lose his work or the proceeds from the sale of his work because of ignorance of the legal requirement that consignment goods be marked as consignment goods to let creditors of the consignor know that they are not part of the consignor's inventory. This provision of law exempts artists from this worry. Creditors of a dealer may not now assume that all works which are part of the dealer's inventory belong to the dealer.

30

Documents of Title

There are two major sources of law on the subject of documents of title—Article Seven of the Uniform Commercial Code, and the Federal Bills of Lading Act (Pomerene Act, 49 USC 81-124).

There are three major types of documents of title: the warehouse receipt, the bill of lading, and the delivery order. The warehouse receipt is issued by a bailee who stores goods for consideration; the bill of lading is issued by a carrier of goods, or by a freight forwarder; and the delivery order is issued by the bailor of goods for which a document of title has been issued, or by a holder of such a document.

Warehouse receipts and bills of lading serve three purposes. First, they constitute the receipt given by a warehouseman or carrier for goods received. Second, they serve as the contract between bailor and bailee. Third, they serve as documents of title for goods—one may transfer or encumber the goods by transferring or encumbering the document. A delivery order may serve as a document of title, or it may not; it does not serve either of the other purposes.

Documents of title may be order or bearer documents. A document making goods deliverable to the order of a named person is an order document, as is a document upon which the last endorsement is special. A document upon which the last endorsement is blank, or a document making goods deliverable to bearer, is a bearer document. As with commercial paper, the character of the document may be changed by endorsement.

Documents may also be negotiable or nonnegotiable. A warehouse receipt or bill of lading will state upon its face whether it is negotiable or nonnegotiable. A straight bill of lading is nonnegotiable. One must read a delivery order in order to determine its negotiability: if it makes goods deliverable to the order of someone or to bearer, it is negotiable.

As is commercial paper, a bearer document is negotiated by delivery only. An order document is negotiated by the endorsement of the transferor plus delivery to the transferee. A person to whom a negotiable document is negotiated by "due negotiation," which will be discussed later, will get better title to the document and to the goods than his transferor had. The source of these propositions is UCC 7-104 and 7-301. With respect to bills of lading governed by the Federal Bills of Lading Act, 49 USC 83, 86, 107, and 111 contain analogous provisions.

In these respects the law governing documents of title is very similar to the law governing commercial paper. In commercial paper terms, warehouse receipts and bills of lading are somewhat like promissory notes, with the bailee standing in the shoes of the maker. A delivery order is very much like a draft, with the holder in the position of the payee, the drawer in the position of the drawer, and the bailee in the position of the drawee. The drawee of a delivery order, like the drawee of a draft, is not liable upon it until he accepts it.

In the remainder of this chapter, we shall consider the three types of documents separately, beginning with the warehouse receipt.

WAREHOUSE RECEIPTS

Who may issue. UCC 7-201 provides that any warehouseman may issue a warehouse receipt. When an owner of distilled spirits or agricultural produce holds such a receipt under government bond against disposition, he may issue receipts against his inventory which shall be treated as warehouse receipts, although they are issued by an owner and not a bailee.

Terms of warehouse receipts. UCC 7-202 provides that no specific form is required for a warehouse receipt. Such a receipt must contain the following:

1. Location of the warehouse where goods are stored.
2. Date of issue.
3. Consecutive number of receipt.
4. Statement as to whether goods will be delivered to bearer, to a named person, or to a named person or his order.
5. Rate of storage and handling charges.
6. Description of goods, or of packages containing the goods.
7. Signature of warehouseman, which may be made by an authorized agent.
8. A statement that warehouseman is an owner or partial owner of the goods, if this is true.
9. A statement of advances made or liabilities incurred for which warehouseman claims a lien. If the precise amount claimed is unknown when the receipt is issued, the receipt must contain a statement that advances have been made and liabilities incurred for which a lien is claimed.

Liability of warehouseman for nonreceipt or misdescription. When a warehouseman issues a warehouse receipt, he incurs the liability of a mutual-benefit bailee for the goods described upon the receipt. If the warehouseman cannot deliver the goods described to the holder of the receipt, he will be liable to the holder for the value of the goods described, unless he can prove that his inability to deliver is not due to his negligence.

A warehouseman may disclaim responsibility for the description of the contents of a container by:

1. Describing the container and then stating, "Contents, condition, and quality unknown," or by
2. Describing the container, then stating "Said to contain _____" and proceeding with a description of contents, or by
3. Making any other reasonable statement.

Of course, if the warehouseman knows what the contents of the container are, he must put a true description on the receipt, and he may not disclaim responsibility for his description. These rules are found in UCC 7-203, and, with respect to duty of care, in UCC 7-204(1).

Limitation of liability of warehouseman. UCC 7-204(2) permits a warehouseman to limit his liability upon stored goods to a specific sum per item, so long as the bailor has the option to request in writing that the warehouseman increase his liability upon all or a portion of the stored goods in exchange for the payment of a higher storage charge. No such limitation is effective if the warehouseman converts the goods to his own use. No warehouseman may completely disclaim liability for his negligence in caring for the goods.

Unauthorized completion and material alteration of warehouse receipt. UCC 7-208 provides that when a warehouseman issues a receipt containing a blank that is not filled in, the warehouseman will be responsible for the receipt as the blank is filled in, even if the completion was unauthorized, if the person presenting the receipt for honor gave value for it and has no knowledge of the unauthorized completion.

The warehouseman is not responsible for material alteration of his receipt, however.

Fungible goods, obligation to keep nonfungible goods separate. UCC 7-207 permits a warehouseman to commingle various lots of fungible goods. The owners of all of the lots are tenants in common in the commingled mass to the extent of their respective interests. It is possible, though not lawful, for the warehouseman to issue receipts for more fungible goods than he has in storage. If this occurs, a holder of an overissued receipt who got his receipt by due negotiation becomes a tenant in common in the mass of goods.

In such a case, the tenants in common share ratably in the mass. The warehouseman is guilty of conversion with respect to any shortfall, and will be liable in damages to the extent of the shortfall. However, overissues usually come to light only upon the insolvency of the warehouseman; the civil liability of the warehouseman for conversion then becomes meaningless because he has no assets with which to pay off such a liability.

A warehouseman must keep each lot of nonfungible goods separate, so that he may at any time identify and deliver the goods called for by a receipt.

Termination of storage at warehouseman's option. UCC 7-206 provides rules for termination of storage. It must be remembered that a warehouseman has a lien upon goods stored in his warehouse, the extent of which will be discussed in the section on the warehouseman's lien. Upon termination of storage, the warehouseman may require the removal of the goods from the warehouse and payment of the charges; otherwise the warehouseman may proceed to foreclose his lien.

If the warehouse receipt provides for a set period of storage, the warehouseman may require removal of the goods at the end of the period. If no set period is specified in the receipt, the warehouseman may notify the bailor or anyone known to claim an interest in the goods that the goods must be removed before the expiration of a stated period (not less than thirty days) after the giving of notification. If the goods are not removed in accordance with the notice, the warehouseman may proceed to foreclose his lien.

If the goods become a hazard to the warehouse or to persons or property in the warehouse, and the condition creating the hazard was unknown to the warehouseman at the time he accepted the goods for storage, he may require removal of the goods in less than thirty days. He need give only a reasonable length of time for removal, considering the nature of the hazard.

If the goods threaten to decline in value to less than the amount of the warehouseman's lien upon them, he may terminate storage upon notice of less than thirty days. Again, the length of time given for removal must be reasonable, considering the condition of the goods.

Nature of warehouseman's lien. The warehouseman's lien covers storage charges, transportation charges (including demurrage), insurance, labor, and charges incurred for the purpose of preservation of the goods. A warehouseman may also claim against a bailor a lien for charges incurred with respect to other goods held in the warehouse for that particular bailor. However, if the holder of the receipt is not the original bailor but a holder of a negotiable warehouse receipt who acquired it by due negotiation, the warehouseman may enforce against him only the lien upon the goods covered by that particular receipt.

The warehouseman may also claim a lien upon the goods for money advanced. Technically this is considered to be a security interest rather than a lien; but the warehouseman may nevertheless collect these charges before releasing the lien, or the goods. A warehouseman loses his lien upon goods which he voluntarily delivers, or upon goods which he wrongfully refuses to deliver.

UCC 7-209 governs the subject matter of this section.

Enforcement of the warehouseman's lien. UCC 7-210 provides the rules for enforcement of the warehouseman's lien. If the goods are stored by a merchant in the course of his business, the warehouseman must notify all persons claiming an interest in the goods of the lien foreclosure sale. The notice must contain:

1. A statement of the amount due the warehouseman.
2. A statement of the nature of the proposed sale, which may be either a private sale or public sale.
3. If the sale is to be a public sale, the time and place of the sale.

So long as the sale is conducted in a commercially reasonable manner it is legitimate. The warehouseman may retain enough of the proceeds to satisfy his lien, but must hold the balance for the person who would have been entitled to delivery of the goods had they not been sold.

In the case of goods stored for a merchant not in the course of his business, or goods stored by a nonmerchant, the normal foreclosure procedure is more complex. Foreclosure of the warehouseman's lien upon such goods requires:

1. Notification of all persons known by the warehouseman to claim an interest in the goods.
2. Delivery of the notification in person, or by registered or certified mail, to the last known address of all such persons.
3. Notification must contain:
    a. An itemized statement of warehouseman's claim, and
    b. A description of the goods subject to the lien, and
    c. A demand for payment within a specified time not less than ten days from receipt of notification, and
    d. A conspicuous statement that if payment is not made within the specified time, the goods will be advertised for sale and sold by auction at a specified time and place.
4. After expiration of the time for payment given in the notification, the goods must be advertised for sale. The ad must be published once a week for two consecutive weeks in a newspaper of general circulation in the area where the sale is to be held. It must describe the goods, state the name of the person upon whose account the goods are stored, and give the time and place of the sale.
5. The sale must take place at least fifteen days after publication of the first ad.
6. The sale must be an auction, and it must be held at the time and place stated in the notification and ad.
7. The sale must be held at the nearest suitable place to that where the goods are held or stored.

If the goods threaten to decline rapidly in value to less than the amount of the warehouseman's lien, the warehouseman may shorten the time stated in the notification to remove the goods and pay the charges, and he may sell not less than one week after a single advertising. If the goods constitute a hazard, the warehouseman may sell at public or private sale without previous notification or advertisement.

Before any foreclosure sale, a claimant of the goods may redeem them by paying the warehouseman's charges and expenses in mailing notifications and other expenses. Once the goods are redeemed the redeemer may withdraw them from storage or leave them in storage (unless the goods have become a hazard). The warehouseman may buy the goods himself at a public foreclosure sale.

A good-faith purchaser of the goods at any lien foreclosure sale gets good title to them, and the warehouse receipt issued by the warehouseman is cancelled so far as its function as a document of title for the goods is concerned.

Should the warehouseman fail to follow the prescribed procedure in foreclosing his lien, he is liable in damages to anyone injured thereby. If the violation is willful, he may be held liable for conversion of the goods to his own use.

Obligation of warehouseman to deliver stored goods. UCC 7-403 provides that the warehouseman must deliver the stored goods to a person entitled to them under the warehouse receipt. If the warehouseman has issued a negotiable warehouse receipt for the goods, he must take up the receipt in case of full delivery, and he must note any partial delivery upon the receipt. If the warehouseman has issued a nonnegotiable receipt he need not take up the receipt upon release of the goods, and he need not note partial release upon the receipt. The warehouseman may refuse to release the goods until his lawful charges are paid.

Excuses for nondelivery by warehouseman. A warehouseman is not liable for inability to deliver goods subject to negotiable warehouse receipts when:

1. The receipt is a counterfeit.
2. The receipt is genuine, but the signature upon it is forged or unauthorized and no goods were received in exchange for its issue.
3. The goods were lost, damaged, or destroyed while in storage through no negligence of the warehouseman, and the warehouseman can prove his lack of negligence.
4. The goods are stolen goods, and they have been released to the true owner.
5. The goods were put into storage by a bailee who had no authority to store them, and the goods have been released to the original bailor.
6. Storage has been terminated and the goods have been sold in foreclosure of the warehouseman's lien.

In addition to the above instances, a warehouseman is not liable for inability to deliver goods subject to a nonnegotiable warehouse receipt when:

1. The goods have been released in good faith to another party (perhaps the original bailor).
2. A part or all of the goods have been released to holders of delivery orders against them honored in good faith.

A warehouseman will be liable in damages for inability to deliver goods to the holder of his negotiable warehouse receipt when:

1. The receipt was signed by an employee of the warehouseman who had authority to issue receipts, even though no goods were received for it.
2. The goods were lost, damaged, or destroyed while in storage due to the warehouseman's negligence.
3. The goods were released to a nonowner.

4. The goods were sold by the warehouseman at an improperly held or advertised lien foreclosure sale.

5. The goods were sold by the warehouseman to one of his customers.

6. The warehouseman released the goods to the holder of a delivery order without noting the delivery upon the receipt.

In addition to the above, the warehouseman will be liable for nondelivery to a holder of his nonnegotiable warehouse receipt when he released the goods in bad faith to a nonowner of the goods and of the receipt. Notice that a warehouseman may assume that a person asking him to store goods is either the owner or an agent who has authority to store. The warehouseman need not check into the pedigree of the goods he accepts for storage.

A warehouseman is always safe in releasing stored goods to a person who can prove that he is the true owner of the goods. However, if a person who claims to be the true owner has questionable proof and no warehouse receipt, the warehouseman should not release. In case of doubt he may require the claimant to post a bond sufficient to protect him against rightful claims by holders of warehouse receipts, or he may require the claimant to obtain an order for the release from a court of competent jurisdiction.

The warehouseman is also always safe in releasing goods to the holder of his warehouse receipt if he does so in good faith (UCC 7-404). Of course, if he knows for a fact that the goods are stolen, or a court has ordered him not to release the goods, a release to the holder of the receipt would be a release in bad faith. (This would also be true if the warehouseman knows his receipt bears a forged endorsement.)

When goods are placed in storage by a nonowner who has no authority to store, the warehouseman's lien for storage charges does not attach to the goods as against the true owner. The owner may reclaim the goods without the necessity to pay storage charges.

Lost and missing warehouse receipts. When goods are in storage under a negotiable warehouse receipt, the warehouseman must take up the receipt when he releases the goods. Thus, when a warehouse receipt is lost, misplaced, or stolen, the owner will have a problem reclaiming his goods. UCC 7-601 and 7-402 cover this contingency.

The owner of the document may always go to court and obtain an order directed to the warehouseman to release the goods. The order may require, though, that the claimant post bond with the warehouseman to protect him against a later wrongful release claim by a holder of the missing document.

The owner may induce the warehouseman to release the goods upon the posting of a proper bond, or he may induce the warehouseman to issue a replacement warehouse receipt in exchange for the posting of a bond. The new receipt must be conspicuously marked "DUPLICATE." It will become the document of title for the goods; the holder of the original will be relegated to a claim for the bond posted by the owner when the duplicate receipt was issued.

Negotiation of warehouse receipts. As mentioned earlier, negotiable warehouse receipts may be transferred so as to give the transferee greater rights than the transferor originally had. A person who obtains a negotiable warehouse receipt by due negotiation must meet the following five requirements:

1. He must give value.

2. He must act in good faith.

3. He must know of no advance claims to the document or the goods, and must know of no reason why the warehouseman would not honor the receipt.

4. He must obtain the receipt in the regular course of business or financing of the goods involved.

5. He must not be taking the receipt in payment of a money obligation.

UCC 7-501 thus establishes requirements for taking warehouse receipts by due negotiation which are similar to those for becoming a holder in due course of commercial paper. There are, however, two major differences in requirements.

The first is the requirement that the receipt be obtained in the business or financing of the goods involved. Thus, a nonbusinessman or nonfinancer could never acquire a warehouse receipt for a large quantity of goods by due negotiation. A consumer could acquire such a receipt for a small quantity of goods by due negotiation, however, if he were buying the receipt in order to acquire the goods for personal use.

The second requirement is that the receipt not be acquired in the payment of a money obligation. Warehouse receipts are not the sort of documents one normally uses for debt-payment purposes. Payment of debts with documents of title is so infrequent that the drafters of the UCC saw fit to deny creditors who accept payment in documents the right to possession through due negotiation.

Rights acquired by due negotiation. According to UCC 7-502, the party who acquires a warehouse receipt by due negotiation acquires:

1. Title to the receipt.
2. Title to the goods.
3. Ownership of the right to the warehouseman's delivery of the goods.
4. Rights to goods delivered to the bailee covered by the document after the document was issued.

The holder of the receipt obtained by due negotiation cuts off the title of former owners of the document deprived of it by fraud, duress, loss, theft, breach of duty by a fiduciary or agent, etc. Holders by due negotiation also have better title to the goods than possessors of the goods, except under two circumstances:

1. When the original bailor of the goods was a thief or a bailee who had no authority to store, or
2. When the goods placed in storage are fungible goods, and the warehouseman is a dealer in these fungible goods and sells them in the ordinary course of his business to a good-faith purchaser. The warehouseman commits conversion by doing this, but the buyer gets title to the goods, as per UCC 7-205.

Rights acquired in absence of due negotiation. When a valid transfer of a negotiable warehouse receipt is made, but the transferee does not take by due negotiation, he gets the rights his transferor had, as per UCC 7-504(1). Thus, whoever acquires a warehouse receipt from someone who acquired it by due negotiation rights gets due negotiation rights.

The transferee of a nonnegotiable warehouse receipt gets the same rights to the document and the goods which his transferor had, but he must inform the warehouseman of his purchase and obtain his recognition as the owner of the document and of the goods to perfect his position. Otherwise, he may lose title to the goods if:

1. The warehouseman releases the goods to the transferor in good faith, and the transferor sells them to a good-faith purchaser, or
2. The transferor sells the goods to a good-faith purchaser and tells the warehouseman about it, and the warehouseman recognizes the buyer as the owner of the goods, or
3. The transferor draws delivery orders against the goods in favor of other buyers, and the warehouseman releases the goods to these buyers by honoring the delivery orders.

Since the warehouseman need not take up a nonnegotiable warehouse receipt when he releases the goods—so long as he releases in good faith—it is obvious why a buyer of such a receipt must inform the warehouseman of his purchase in order to protect his rights.

Liability of endorsers of warehouse receipts. UCC 7-505 provides that an endorsement of a warehouse receipt does not make the endorser liable for the defaults of the warehouseman or of other endorsers. Thus, the endorser does not have the secondary liability of the endorser of commercial paper. However, UCC 7-507 imposes three warranties upon the transferor of a document of title (other than a collecting or intermediary bank):
1. That the document is genuine, and
2. That he has no knowledge of any fact that would impair the validity or worth of the document, and
3. That his negotiation or transfer is fully effective with respect to the title to the document and to the goods it represents.

These warranties are made only to the immediate transferee. The holder of a document of title may have recourse against the issuing bailee and the party from whom he obtained the document, but he has no recourse against other endorsers. It should be noticed also that the three warranties are broad enough so that a transferor would almost certainly have breached one of them if his transferee were unable to obtain any goods for the document.

Collecting or intermediary banks transferring documents of title as a part of the process of collecting a draft or in performance of a payment against documents transaction warrant only that they are acting in good faith and in accordance with their authority to act for the principals of the transaction (UCC 7-508).

Attachment of goods covered by negotiable warehouse receipt. Except in the case of a receipt issued to a person who had no right to put the goods in storage, no one may reach goods in a warehouse for which a negotiable warehouse receipt has been issued except by obtaining possession of the receipt or by a court order forbidding the negotiation of the receipt and ordering the holder of the document to surrender it. The judicial process provides no access to the goods except through the document (UCC 7-602). If a court has enjoined the honor of a warehouse receipt, but it is duly negotiated to a transferee who does not know of the injunction, that transferee will get clear title both to the document and the goods.

Interpleader. The warehouseman faced with conflicting claims to goods in his possession that he is unwilling or unable to resolve himself may invoke the aid of the courts to solve his problem. When one of the claimants sues to obtain the goods, he may raise the other claim or claims as a defense and ask the court to join the other claimants as defendants; or, if he desires, he may file an interpleader action against all of the claimants himself in order to bring them into court and determine the ownership of the goods (UCC 7-603).

BILLS OF LADING

Bills of lading are issued by carriers of goods for hire. They are issued by ground, air, and water carriers and by freight forwarders.

There are now two statutes which may govern a bill of lading. Bills used in interstate transactions or in export transactions are governed by the Federal Bills of Lading Act (FBLA) enacted by the U.S. Congress in 1916. Bills of lading used in intrastate transactions, and in import transactions in which the goods do not cross a state line after entry into the United States, are governed by the Uniform Commercial Code. Thus, the FBLA governs most bills of lading.

The rules of law under the UCC and the FBLA are identical or very similar in many particulars. However, there are a few important differences, which will be pointed out as we proceed.

Terms of bills of lading. The format and content of bills of lading issued by ground carriers are determined by administrative regulations of the Interstate Commerce Commission; the same form of bill is used in both interstate and intrastate transactions by ground carriers. Bills of lading issued by water carriers must comply with provisions of the Carriage of Goods by Sea Act and are uniform in nature. Bills of lading issued by air carriers have less uniformity. However, all bills of lading serve the same three purposes as do other documents of title, and all bills of lading must state upon their face whether or not they are negotiable (41 USC 83, 86).

Clean and foul bills of lading. As a bailee, the carrier has the obligation to deliver the shipped goods to the recipient in the condition in which they were received for shipment. The shipper of goods has an obligation to his customer to deliver undamaged goods.

When the recipient receives goods in damaged condition, he is not getting what he ordered, and he will want to hold someone responsible for the damage. That someone will most likely be the carrier, unless the carrier can prove that the damage did not occur while the goods were in his custody, or that the damage was due to circumstances for which he is not liable. For this reason, a carrier who receives damaged goods for shipment will note upon his bill of lading the fact that the goods were damaged when received, and the nature of the damage. A bill of lading which contains such a notation is a *foul* bill, and the carrier will obviously not be responsible for the described damage. If the bill of lading contains no description of any damage to the shipped goods, the bill is *clean*, and constitutes evidence that the goods were shipped in undamaged condition.

If goods are shipped under a clean bill of lading, but they arrive damaged, this is good circumstantial evidence that the carrier is responsible for the damage—or, at least, that the damage occurred while the carrier had possession of the goods. The burden will be on the carrier to show that the cause of the damage was something he was not liable for.

It is normally a breach of contract for a shipper to ship goods under a foul bill of lading. This may give the recipient an excuse to reject the shipment at the point of delivery under most shipping terms, and it will also give the bank issuing a letter of credit cause not to honor drafts drawn under the credit.

Liability of a carrier for misdescription of goods on a bill of lading. With respect to this, the law is essentially the same for carriers as it is for warehousemen. The carrier can disclaim responsibility for the description of the contents of a sealed container by prefacing it with the phrase "Said to contain," or other words to that effect.

When a shipment of goods is loaded by the shipper rather than by the carrier, the carrier may be called upon to issue a bill of lading for a shipment of goods which his employees have not loaded, weighed, or counted. The carrier will take the word of the shipper for the contents of the shipment (so long as it is reasonable) and place the description of the shipment furnished by the shipper on the bill of lading. Following the description will be the phrase "Shipper's weight, load, and count," or words to that effect. As per UCC 7-301 and 49 USC 101, the carrier would not be held responsible for the accuracy of the description. But, when the shipper has weighing facilities which it makes available to the carrier, the carrier must make use of these to verify the shipper's weight, and cannot rely upon the phrase "Shipper's weight, load, and count" to escape liability for the accuracy of his description.

Through bills of lading. When goods are to be transported by more than one carrier in an intrastate transaction, the receiving carrier may issue a through bill of lading which will follow the goods to the end of their journey and render the first carrier liable for the goods from the beginning of their journey to the end (UCC 7-302). The first carrier is under no obligation to issue a through bill, however.

In interstate and export shipments, the Carmack Amendment to the Interstate Commerce Act, 49 USC 20(11), makes all bills of lading through bills. The first carrier is responsible for the goods from the beginning of the journey to the end, no matter whether the bill of lading says that it is a through bill or not.

Unauthorized completion or material alteration of bills of lading. 49 USC 43 and UCC 7-306 both provide that a carrier is not liable for unauthorized completion or material alteration of a bill of lading. The bill is enforceable as issued only. Thus a carrier will suffer no ill effects from issuing a bill of lading with blanks which are not filled in.

Stoppage in transit and reconsignment. In both intrastate and interstate shipments a shipper may stop goods in transit if he meets the qualifications of UCC 2-705, which will be discussed later. If the carrier refuses to deliver goods because of a lawful stoppage in transit, he will not incur liability under UCC 7-401(1) or 49 USC 119.

In intrastate shipments, UCC 7-303 provides that the following persons may divert or reconsign a shipment:
1. The holder of a negotiable bill, or
2. The consignor of a straight bill notwithstanding contrary instructions from the consignee, or
3. The consignee of a straight bill, if there are no contrary instructions from the consignor and the goods have arrived at their destination, or if the consignee is in possession of the bill, or
4. The consignee of a straight bill if he is entitled to dispose of the goods.

The carrier may legitimately obey a reconsignment order if it comes from any of these four categories of persons in an intrastate shipment.

In interstate shipments, the FBLA has no provision similar to UCC 7-303. 49 USC 89 provides that carriers may lawfully deliver goods to:
1. Persons who are lawfully entitled to receive the goods, or
2. To the consignee named in a straight bill of lading, or
3. To the holder of an order bill of lading.

It would seem that the holder of an order bill could divert or reconsign, then, as could the consignee of a straight bill.

Problems can arise when the carrier gets conflicting instructions—reconsignment instructions from one party and instructions to deliver as ordered from another. In intrastate shipments, if the carrier reconsigns because of instructions from one of the four parties named in UCC 7-303, he has acted rightfully. In interstate shipments, the carrier must deliver to someone lawfully entitled to the goods; if he does not know for certain who is lawfully entitled to the goods, he should wait for court instruction for delivery before committing himself.

Carrier's lien. A carrier has a lien upon goods for carriage charges and the like, regardless of whether the goods were shipped by an owner or not, under UCC 7-307. The lien extends to transportation, storage, terminal, and demurrage charges. 49 USC 105 contains an almost identical provision.

UCC 7-308 provides that the carrier's lien may be foreclosed either under the short or the long procedure for foreclosure of a warehouseman's lien. The FBLA sets forth no definite procedure for foreclosure of the carrier's lien in interstate transactions. 49 USC 106 provides, though, that a carrier may lawfully sell goods in his possession under four circumstances:
1. To foreclose a carrier's lien, or

2. Because the goods have not been claimed, or
3. The goods are perishable, or
4. The goods are hazardous.

The section further provides that once the carrier has lawfully sold the goods, he shall not be liable for nondelivery of them to the holder of the bill of lading issued for them.

Excuses for nondelivery of shipped goods. With respect to bills of lading governed by the UCC (intrastate and import bills) the same excuses for nondelivery are available to carriers as are available to warehousemen. Under the FBLA, the same excuses are also available to carriers. However, with respect to interstate or export bills governed by the FBLA, a carrier must be careful about releasing goods when ownership is in question.

49 USC 90 provides that a carrier shall be liable for misdelivery when he releases goods to the holder of an order bill of lading or to the consignee of a straight bill if:

1. Persons having a property right in the goods instructed the carrier not to make delivery, or
2. The carrier had information at the time of delivery of the goods that the holder or consignee was a person not entitled to the goods.

An adverse claimant, if he has proof of his claim, can in essence stop delivery of goods for which an interstate or export bill of lading is outstanding. With respect to goods and bills of lading governed by the FBLA, then, the carrier must litigate to be safe if there is any question about ownership of the goods. Release of the goods to the wrong party can be costly, whether the wrong party was the holder of a bill of lading issued by the carrier, a thief, or an imposter.

49 USC 97 allows the carrier to bring an interpleader section against all claimants in disputed ownership situations. 49 USC 98 excuses the carrier from all liability for nondelivery until the courts tell the carrier to whom to deliver.

Lost, stolen, and misplaced bills. A lost, stolen, or misplaced bill governed by the UCC may be replaced in the same manner as is applicable to lost, stolen, or misplaced warehouse receipts. The FBLA contains no authorization for issue of duplicate bills in such situations, however.

49 USC 94 provides that a court may order a carrier to deliver goods to the owner of a lost, missing, or stolen bill of lading, and may require the posting of bond to protect the carrier. It also provides that delivery of the goods under the court order will not relieve the carrier of liability to the holder of the document, who, if he can establish ownership, will be entitled to collect the bond.

Spent bills of lading. Under the UCC, so long as a legitimately issued negotiable bill of lading exists covering goods, the owner of the document owns the goods. Under the FBLA, this is not always true. The owner of a bill of lading acquired while the carrier has possession of the goods has title to the goods, as he does under the UCC. However, a buyer of a bill of lading who acquires it after the carrier has released the goods may not have title to the goods if they find their way into the hands of a bona fide purchaser. If the release of the goods by the carrier was wrongful, as it probably was in such a case, the holder of the bill would have a claim against the carrier for wrongful release, but he could not get the goods back from a bona fide purchaser.

Thus, a purchaser of an interstate or export negotiable bill of lading runs a slight risk of not acquiring title to the goods; the buyer of an intrastate or import bill runs much less of a risk of this sort.

Freight forwarder bills of lading. When a shipment of goods is handled by a freight forwarder, there will be two bills of lading outstanding for the goods. The first will be the bill issued by the forwarder to the shipper; the second will be the bill issued by the carrier to the forwarder. In case of dishonesty in the handling of these bills, questions may arise as to which bill controls the goods.

UCC 7-503(3) provides a specific answer with respect to interstate bills. The courts have come to the same answer in interpreting the FBLA and the Interstate Commerce Act. Since the freight forwarder's bill was issued first, it is the true document of title to the goods. The carrier's bill issued to the forwarder, however, is the only bill for which the carrier is responsible. Thus, the owner of the forwarder bill is the owner of the goods, but the carrier is not liable for release of the goods to the holder of his bill.

Due negotiation of bills of lading. Any person who would acquire an intrastate or export bill of lading by due negotiation must meet the five UCC requirements. (The UCC sets out the same requirements for both bills of lading and for warehouse receipts.) A person who would acquire an interstate or export bill by due negotiation must meet the three requirements of the FBLA: 49 USC 117 provides that a person acquires a bill of lading by due negotiation if he buys it for value, acts in good faith, and has no knowledge of any breach of duty, loss, theft, conversion, fraud, or duress involved in the transfer.

Warranties of endorsers of bills of lading. Endorsers of intrastate and import bills of lading make the same warranties and are subject to the same liabilities as are endorsers of warehouse receipts. 49 USC 114 imposes essentially the same liabilities upon endorsers of interstate and export bills, though the warranties are expressed differently. The endorser or transferor for value of a bill governed by the FBLA warrants that:

1. The bill is genuine, and
2. He has a legal right to transfer it, and
3. He has no knowledge of any fact that would impair the validity or worth of the bill, and
4. He has the right to transfer title to the goods.

The fourth warranty is, among other things, a warranty that the bill is not a spent bill—that the buyer will not lose title to the goods because the carrier has already released them and they have gotten into the hands of a bona fide purchaser.

49 USC 115 provides that the endorser of a bill of lading does not guarantee performance of obligations by previous transferors or by the carrier.

Summary. With respect to the other aspects of the law as applicable to bills of lading, the UCC principles applied to warehouse receipts also apply.

The existence of two separate bodies of law governing bills of lading make the law here a bit more complex than that covering warehouse receipts. The general principles contained in the two bodies of law are virtually identical; even many of the details are identical. It is only with respect to certain unique details that the variations become important.

DELIVERY ORDERS

There is not much statutory law governing this type of document of title. The FBLA has no provisions governing them; the UCC mentions them in passing only. However, the law of delivery orders is substantially identical under both the UCC and the FBLA.

Obligation of the issuer of a delivery order. The issuer of a delivery order is not the bailee of the goods in question. He is, rather, the bailor or the holder of a document of title issued by the bailee. By issuing the delivery order he is ordering the bailee to deliver the goods called for in the order to the holder of the order.

The holder of the delivery order is in the position of the holder of a draft. Just as the drawee of a draft is not liable upon it until he accepts it, the bailee upon whom a delivery order is drawn is not liable upon it until he accepts it (if it is negotiable) or informs the holder that he recognizes him as the owner of the goods called for (if it is nonnegotiable).

However, just as the drawer of a draft has secondary liability upon it if it is not accepted or paid, the issuer of a delivery order is liable upon it if it is not honored by the bailee. The issuer will be liable to any holder of his delivery order in case it is not honored.

Liability of the bailee of a delivery order. The drawee of a delivery order is not liable upon it until he accepts it, if it is negotiable, or until he recognizes its holder as the owner of the goods called for, if it is nonnegotiable.

The drawee of a delivery order may respond to it in three ways, when presentment of it is made:

1. He may deliver the goods called for under the order.
2. He may accept the order or recognize the holder as the owner of the goods called for, as the case may be, promising to deliver later.
3. He may refuse to deliver goods and refuse to accept the order.

The drawee cannot go wrong by adopting the third alternative, since he can incur liability to no one by dishonoring the delivery order. Since it is bad business for him to do this as a matter of policy, however, he is unlikely to dishonor a delivery order unless he must do so to protect himself.

The drawee's willingness to honor a delivery order will depend to a great extent upon whether the original bill of lading or warehouse receipt outstanding for the goods is negotiable. The drawee should not, and will not, honor a delivery order against goods held under a negotiable document of title, unless he is given the opportunity to note upon the document that the delivery order has been honored or accepted.

If the document of title is nonnegotiable, on the other hand, the drawee runs no risk by honoring or accepting a delivery order, so long as he does so in good faith. A holder of a negotiable document of title who intends to sell small lots of the goods stored under the document through the issuance of delivery orders should therefore exchange his negotiable document for a nonnegotiable document before beginning to issue delivery orders.

Overissue of delivery orders. The issuer of delivery orders may, intentionally or through negligence, issue orders for more goods than he has in storage. In such a case, the holders of all of the orders will not be able to obtain goods, but the issuer will be liable to all holders of his delivery orders for the value of the goods called for. The drawee will incur no such liability if he refuses to honor and accept the excess orders. The holders of the dishonored orders will of course have no recourse against the drawee.

Should the drawee accept too many orders, or acknowledge too many holders as owners of goods, he will of course be liable to all of these parties. As to the matter of which holders get goods, the solution is as follows: If the delivery orders are negotiable, it is a matter of first come, first served—the holders who obtain goods for their orders get goods, and when the goods run out, the other holders have to be content with money. If the delivery orders are nonnegotiable, it would seem that title to goods is determined by the order in which the drawee recognizes holders of delivery orders as owners of the goods, though a holder of an order who obtained goods in good faith for the order would have better title than a holder who merely had the drawee's recognition of himself as an owner.

31

Transportation of Goods

The law of transportation of goods is complex. Although the relation between a shipper of goods and a carrier is essentially a bailor-bailee relationship, the law governing the relationship is quite different from simple bailment law.

There are three broad modes of transport of goods: overland, water, and air. Organized water transport has existed in the Western world since ancient times, and some of the law governing transport of goods by water has developed from this ancient time. Large-scale overland transport of goods became possible only with the development of the railroad during the early nineteenth century. A great competitor of the railroad for overland transit business came upon the scene with the development of the modern trucking industry during the 1920s and 1930s. The last of the major modes of transport to make its appearance was the aircraft, the major growth in air cargo carriage having taken place after the end of World War II.

Since each mode of transport is governed by its own law, we must consider the law governing each in turn.

RAILROADS

Virtually all railroads are common carriers. This means that they must serve all comers, unless good reason exists not to serve a potential customer. In general, a railroad may not refuse to handle a proffered shipment unless it is improperly packed or too hazardous for the line to handle (such as a shipment of explosives), or unless the line is not equipped to handle it.

Most aspects of railroad operation are subject to stringent government regulations, including building new truck and expanding service, contracting service, scheduling, charging freight, and so on. Interstate railroads are subject to regulation by the Interstate Commerce Commission; intrastate railroads in Texas are regulated by the Texas Railroad Commission. However, the intrastate aspects of the operation of interstate lines are under the jurisdiction of the ICC.

The Interstate Commerce Act and regulations of the Interstate Commerce Commission require railroads to determine a separate freight rate for every sort of cargo they handle. The rates also vary according to the size of the shipment, with carload lots receiving much cheaper per-unit rates than do lesser amounts.

As the common law of overland carrier liability developed, common carriers were said to be insurers of their cargo, unless the loss of or damage to cargo was caused by five specific causes. The Interstate Commerce Act permits a railroad to reduce its insurer liability to a portion of the value of a shipment. However, the railroad is required to disclose this limitation of liability in its tariffs filed with the ICC and to disclose it to the shipper in its bill of lading. The railroad is also required to give a shipper the option of holding the carrier liable as insurer for the total value of the shipment, in exchange for paying a higher shipping charge.

The Carmack Amendment to the Interstate Commerce Act, 49 USC 20(11), provides that the bill of lading issued by the carrier picking up an interstate shipment will cover the shipment until it arrives at its destination. Thus, the issuing carrier will be liable for the shipment to all persons having an interest in the bill of lading or the shipment while the goods are in transit, whether or not the issuing carrier is actually responsible for any loss or damage. Should the initial carrier be required to pay a damage claim for which another carrier was responsible, it will be able to obtain indemnity from the responsible carrier.

Aside from its right to levy a shipping charge upon a shipper, a carrier may levy two other charges which are of interest. When goods arrive at their destination, the carrier's tariff and bill of lading will provide that the goods will be stored for a certain period free of charge until they are picked up. If they are not picked up during this period, the carrier may begin charging a storage charge of a certain amount per day. Also, when a recipient is given control of a boxcar for unloading purposes, the tariff and bill of lading will give him a period of free use of the car for that purpose. Should the car not be returned to the railroad after that time, it may levy a demurrage charge of so much per day upon the recipient.

Carload lots. Usually the railroad will spot the required type of car upon a siding belonging to the shipper when the shipper informs it that it wishes to make a carload shipment. The shipper's employees then load the goods aboard the car. When the loading process is finished, the railroad takes charge of the car, seals it, and issues its bill of lading. The shipper of course tells the railroad what the cargo in the car is, and the railroad enters that description on the bill of lading, adding the notation "Shipper's weight, load, and count," or words to that effect. This legend relieves the railroad of liability for misdescription of the cargo on the bill of lading. However, Section 101 of the Federal Bills of Lading Act provides that when a carrier has facilities for weighing bulk freight (grain, coal, or similar cargo), it must weigh such cargo loaded by the shipper and enter that weight on its bill of lading; in such a case the cargo description must not carry the legend "Shipper's weight and load."

The railroad then sends the loaded car on its journey, transferring it to a connecting carrier en route if necessary. Upon arrival at its destination, the delivering railroad will spot the car on the recipient's siding, so that his employees may unload; putting the car upon the recipient's siding constitutes delivery. The recipient then must unload during the specified free time for unloading. If he does not complete the unloading within that time, he may be charged demurrage. The recipient, of course, is liable for the demurrage even if the shipper prepaid the shipping charges.

Less than carload lots. The shipper may deliver less than a carload shipment to the railroad freight terminal himself. He will then give the railroad his shipping instructions at the time of delivery. The railroad personnel will count and inspect the shipment and issue the bill of lading on the spot.

Should the shipper not be ready to issue shipping instructions at the time of delivery to the railroad, railroad personnel will deliver a receipt for the goods, but no bill of lading will be issued until shipping instructions are received. Until the shipping instructions are received, the railroad holds the goods as a warehouseman, and has the same liability for loss or damage as a warehouseman.

The railroad may pick up the goods at the shipper's residence or place of business. The ICC authorizes interstate railroads to operate motor vehicle pickup and delivery services within designated terminal areas, these comprising the city limits where the railroad has a terminal and a prescribed area beyond the city limits. If the carrier picks up the goods with its own truck, a bill of lading is issued by the truck driver who picks up the shipment. The railroad may also have a truck operated by a separate trucking company pick up the goods, if it has a contract with that trucking company to pick up and deliver its shipments within a specified area. In such a case, the trucking company may issue a railroad bill of lading as agent for the railroad, or the trucking company may issue its own bill of lading.

The shipper may also turn the goods over to a freight forwarder for shipment. The overland freight forwarder collects less-than-carload shipments, consolidates them into carload shipments, and then ships the carloads by rail or truck. The differential between less-than-carload freight rates and carload freight rates is so great that the forwarder's main source of profit is the advantage he can take of this differential. Overland freight forwarders must be licensed by the ICC to be in business. They are regulated as common carriers under Part IV of the Interstate Commerce Act, and have the same liability as a carrier. The shipper may deliver a shipment to the freight forwarder's place of business, or the forwarder may pick it up. Either way, the forwarder then issues the bill of lading.

If the goods are identifiable when shipped, the bill of lading will describe them. If they are packed in sealed containers, the bill will describe the containers and then state, "Said to contain _____," which is a disclaimer of liability for the accuracy of the description.

When the goods arrive at the destination, the railroad may put them in its terminal and notify the recipient of their arrival, leaving it to him to come and pick them up. In such a case, the railroad tenders delivery when it notifies the recipient of their arrival. The liability of the railroad will then be reduced to warehouseman liability if the goods are not picked up within a reasonable time after tender of delivery.

The railroad may deliver the goods to the recipient in its own motor vehicle. In such a case, it tenders delivery when the goods arrive at the recipient's location, so long as the delivery is made during normal business hours. The carrier's liability is reduced to warehouseman liability if the delivery is not accepted; storage charges upon the goods may then begin to accrue.

The railroad may also deliver via a motor truck belonging to a motor carrier with which it has a contract for operation of pickup and delivery service. If delivery is not accepted in this case, the motor carrier will hold the goods in its warehouse until they are picked up. It will then be able to levy storage charges and will have warehouseman liability.

If the shipper turned the goods over to a freight forwarder for shipment, the carrier will turn the car upon which the goods were shipped over to the forwarder (or to another forwarder designated by the shipping forwarder) at the destination. The receiving forwarder then unloads the car and delivers the goods to the recipients, having essentially the same liabilities in the process as the railroad.

Liability of railroad for loss or damage in transit. Railroads are liable for any damage to goods in transit, or for their loss, unless the damage or loss is due to one of five reasons:
1. An act of God.
2. An act of public enemies.
3. An act of government authority.
4. An act of the shipper.
5. Inherent vice.

An act of God is a natural catastrophe. If the train carrying the goods is damaged or destroyed by flood, earthquake, tornado, landslide, etc., the railroad is not liable for loss or damage. It should be noted, though, that fire is not considered to be an act of God, even if a natural phenomenon such as lightning started it.

An act of a public enemy is an act of the armed forces of a nation with which the United States is at war. No such enemy has attacked the soil of the continental United States since a Japanese submarine shelled a California oil refinery early in 1942, and Japanese incendiary bombs carried by hot-air balloon started small forest fires in Oregon and Washington in 1944 and 1945. Acts of organizations such as the Popular Front for the Liberation of Palestine, the Symbionese Liberation Army, or the Mafia, are not acts of public enemies for this purpose. Neither are acts of individual criminals or terrorists.

An act of government authority is a seizure of a shipment by a government agency. Shipments of agricultural produce may be seized by agents of state departments of agriculture if they are found to be pest-infested. Shipments of adulterated or misbranded foods, drugs, or cosmetics may be seized by the United States Food and Drug Administration, and shipments of unregistered pesticides may be seized by the United States Environmental Protection Agency. Shipments of goods passing through a disaster area may be seized by local authorities for the use of victims of the disaster. A railroad or other carrier is required to give prompt notice of such governmental actions to the persons named on the carrier's bill of lading, so that they may contest the legality of the government action should they choose to do so.

An act of the shipper in this case is essentially improper packaging, marking, or labeling. It could consist of shipping glass containers in flimsy packaging, not marking shipments of glass containers "Fragile," not marking shipments of goods going north in winter which could be damaged by freezing "Do Not Freeze," using shipping labels which fall off the package in transit, etc. In general, shippers must realize that freight gets rough handling in transit, and they must pack it accordingly.

Inherent vice is essentially the spoilage of perishable goods. Some types of goods, such as agricultural produce, are likely to deteriorate with time no matter what measures are taken to protect them. If they do deteriorate, it is not the railroad's fault.

If loss or damage in transit is due to a combination of an exempted cause and carrier negligence, the carrier will be held liable for the damage. A railroad is obligated to move goods it is responsible for quickly, and by the most direct practicable route. The railroad must also take reasonable steps to keep perishable goods from spoiling, by using refrigeration, for example. The railroad may well be responsible for loss or damage not caused by its negligence, since losses by fire, theft, criminal activity, or riot do not fall within the five traditional exemptions from liability.

Filing of claim for loss, damage, or misdelivery. A shipper or consignee who has a claim against a railroad for loss, damage, or misdelivery may not sue on the claim immediately. Instead, he must file a claim with the issuer of his bill of lading.

The Carmack Amendment does not state in so many words how long a claimant has to file such a claim, but it does state that no carrier may by bill of lading provision reduce the claim filing time to under nine months. Virtually all railroads therefore include in their bills of lading a provision limiting the time for filing claims to within nine months of receipt of a damaged shipment or within nine months of the date a lost or misdelivered shipment should have been delivered.

The filed claim must be in writing, must identify with particularity the shipment for which the claim is being made, must state specifically that it is a claim for money (a mere notice of damage is not a claim), and must be for a specific amount of money. ICC regulations (49 CFR 1005) forbid a carrier to pay a claim for an indefinite sum of money.

The claim may be filed with the receiving carrier, the delivering carrier, or the intermediate carrier believed to be responsible for the loss or damage. It may also be filed with the carrier issuing the bill of lading. All of these are safe to file with, except the intermediate or connecting carrier believed to be responsible. If it turns out that that carrier was not the one responsible, it might be too late to file with the responsible carrier. In any case, a filing with the receiving carrier, the delivering carrier, or the carrier issuing the bill of lading will be sufficient.

The ICC regulation at 49 CFR 1005 provides directions as to how a railroad or other ICC-regulated carrier must respond to a claim. It must acknowledge receipt of the claim within thirty days of receipt; it must establish a claim file immediately. If documentation is desired to support the claim, this should be requested of the claimant at the time of acknowledgment. It must promptly investigate the claim. If the claim is for loss of an entire package or shipment, the carrier may require the consignee to file a sworn statement that the shipment or package has not been received from another source. (This is to protect against the possibility that another carrier got custody of the shipment through error and delivered it to the consignee.)

Normally, the carrier must either pay, deny, or offer to compromise the claim within 120 days of filing. If it cannot do this, it must notify the claimant of this fact within the 120-day period after filing. It must then notify the claimant of the status of the claim every 60 days thereafter until the matter is finally settled.

Once the carrier denies the claim, the claimant may go to court to sue upon it. The Carmack Amendment forbids carriers to give claimants less than two years after denial of a claim to file suit, so carrier bills of lading almost inevitably provide that period of limitation. The two-year period starts with the giving of notice of denial of the claim.

If the shipment is covered by inland transit insurance, the claimant may well prefer filing an insurance claim to filing with the railroad. However, the insurance company will not normally consider a claim under inland transit policies unless a carrier claim has been filed.

In a suit on a claim against a railroad, as in any suit against a bailee, the plaintiff makes out a case against the carrier by proving that goods were shipped in good condition and that they were received in damaged condition, or not received at all. The burden is then the carrier's to prove lack of liability.

MOTOR CARRIERS

Interstate motor carriers have been under ICC jurisdiction since the enactment of the Motor Carriers' Act of 1935. The scheme of regulation is very similar to that of railroad regulation, but there are a few differences.

The biggest difference is that there are three types of motor carriers in operation:

common carriers, contract carriers, and private carriers. A common motor carrier serves the public much as a railroad does, holding itself out as a public servant, usually operating scheduled service, serving all comers, and not having the right to reject a shipment except for good reason.

A contract motor carrier does not operate scheduled service, and does not hold itself out to the public as a server of all comers. The contract carrier picks and chooses its own customers, and makes a haul when it has a contract.

The private carrier does not serve others at all: it hauls its own goods; a firm that hauls its own goods in its own vehicles is thus a private carrier. The firm that rents or leases vehicles and uses them to haul its own goods is also a private carrier.

The motor common carrier operating interstate needs a certificate of public convenience and necessity issued by the ICC in order to serve a particular city; it cannot obtain the certificate unless it can show that motor freight service to that city is inadequate, that it can make such service more adequate, and that it is financially responsible. It must file its rate schedule with the ICC, and charge only what its tariffs permit for its services.

The interstate contract carrier needs a permit in order to operate. The main consideration which must be met in order to get such a permit is financial responsibility. Contract carriers must file and get approval of minimum rates with the ICC, but are permitted to charge as much above their minimum as they wish.

The private carrier, since it hauls only its own goods, needs no permit to operate as such. However, the private carrier must not haul goods belonging to other shippers. If it does this, it is operating as a contract carrier and needs an appropriate permit.

The contract carrier issues no bill of lading for the goods it hauls. It has the liability of a bailee only, which of course means that it is not liable for loss of or damage to the goods it hauls unless it is negligent. Of course, in suits against contract carriers the burden of proof is essentially upon the carrier to prove lack of negligence if it seeks to escape liability.

The common motor carrier operates under the same sort of rate schedule as does the railroad. It too charges much lower rates for truckload shipments than it does for less-than-truckload shipments. As with the railroads, the shipper often loads a truckload shipment; when it does, the bill of lading will contain the disclaiming phrase "Shipper's weight, load, and count" after the description of the goods. The consignee will often unload a truckload shipment. When he does he may be charged demurrage for keeping the carrier's trailer out of circulation too long.

Less-than-truckload shipments are loaded and unloaded by carrier personnel, as are analogous railroad shipments. Shippers making use of trucklines for less-than-truckload shipments can and do make use of overland freight forwarders, who proceed in the same manner with respect to truck shipments as they do with rail shipments, and are subject to the same liabilities.

The Carmack Amendment applies to motor freight common carriers, which means that they are subject to the same rules of liability for lost, misdelivered, or damaged shipments as are railroads.

Common carriers involved in the transportation of household goods are subject to certain ICC regulations on this subject which are of interest. 49 CFR 1056.2 requires such carriers to quote shipping rates only in terms of price per 100 pounds weight. A customer of a common carrier of household goods may request an estimate of cost of a move from the carrier. The carrier must inspect the goods before making the estimate, which must be in writing (49 CFR 1056.8). If the customer then decides to use the carrier's services, he may request from it a notification of actual weight and charges for the shipment. When the shipper makes this request he must furnish a telephone number or address to which the information must be delivered, and the carrier must deliver that information at its expense as soon as it has ascertained the true weight and charges.

49 CFR 1056.9 requires the carrier to furnish the shipper an order for service before picking up a shipment of household goods. This document must contain, among other things, the agreed pickup and delivery dates, the amount of estimated service charges, and a statement as to whether or not the shipper has requested notification of charges. Of course, the location at which the goods are to be picked up and the location to which they are to be delivered, and some other essential information, must be included. A bill of lading or receipt will be issued by the carrier upon receipt of the goods.

The goods must be transported with reasonable dispatch, meaning that the pickup and delivery dates in the order for service must be complied with, unless force majeure prevents this. If pickup or delivery is to be late, the carrier must notify the shipper. Such notices must be given as soon as the carrier knows of a delay. The carrier must preserve a record of the giving of such notification (49 CFR 1056.12).

According to 49 CFR 1056.13, the carrier must not tender delivery of a shipment early, except upon the concurrence of the shipper. Should the shipper not wish to accept an early delivery, the carrier may put the shipment into storage in a warehouse near the destination, at its own expense. It must then notify the shipper of what it has done. The carrier remains responsible for the shipment until it picks it up from the warehouse and makes proper delivery.

The carrier may of course require the shipper to sign a receipt for the goods upon delivery. However, 49 CFR 1056.14 forbids the carrier to place any language in the receipt discharging it from liability. The receipt may, however, state that the property has been received in apparent good condition except for discrepancies noted on the receipt. The recipient should therefore inspect the shipment for damage before signing the delivery receipt, and he should make certain that all apparent items of damage are noted upon the receipt.

Carriers of household goods must not sell insurance to their customers upon their shipments. Such carriers may, however, procure their own insurance; if they wish to fully insure their shipments themselves in favor of their customers, they may do so, if they inform the ICC of their insurance arrangements.

The nine-month rule for filing claims with ICC-regulated overland carriers applies also to household goods carriers. The carriers must acknowledge receipt of a claim within 30 days of receipt. It must pay, deny, or offer to compromise within 120 days of receipt. If it cannot settle within 120 days, it must give the claimant a status report upon his claim every 30 days thereafter, as per 49 CFR 1056.20. With respect to filing suit on a rejected claim, the general rule that this must be done within two years of rejection of the claim applies. Any violation of these rules by a carrier should be reported by the shipper to the ICC at once. The ICC may then take administrative sanctions against the violator.

The same ICC regulations with respect to filing of claims, processing of claims, and bringing of suit that apply to the railroads apply to the common motor carriers. When an interstate shipment is to be handled by more than one interstate motor carrier, the bill of lading issued by the originating carrier is a through bill, just as with the rail shipment.

It sometimes happens that a shipment of goods via motor carrier will also be handled by a railroad for part of the journey. This can occur when the motor carrier has an arrangement with the railroad for "piggyback" transport of its semitrailers. In such a case, the truckline's through bill of lading covers the goods while they are being transported by rail; if the goods are damaged while in the custody of the railroad, the railroad will be just as liable for the damage as it would have been had it issued the bill of lading.

CARRIAGE OF GOODS BY AIR

Domestic carriage of goods by air. Airlines are not subject to regulation by the ICC. Interstate airlines are subject to regulation by the Civil Aeronautics Board, under the provisions of the Civil Aeronautics Act. Intrastate airlines in Texas are under the jurisdiction of the Texas Aeronautical Commission. Two types of airlines handle freight: the scheduled passenger airlines and the cargo airlines. Both are subject to the same rules of liability.

When a shipment of goods is made via air freight, the shipper may take the goods to the air terminal. If this is done, of course, the airline issues its waybill—the airline term for a bill of lading—at that point. Airlines are also permitted by the CAB to operate pickup and delivery service within twenty-five miles of the airports they serve. This radius of service is sometimes extended further by CAB permit. When the airline picks up the shipment, it issues its bill of lading at that point. At the other end of the journey, the recipient may pick up the goods at the air terminal, or the airline may deliver to the recipient.

The shipper may also use the facilities of a freight forwarder for sending a shipment. The ICC authorizes freight forwarders licensed by it under Part IV of the Interstate Commerce Act to arrange for air shipments. However, no freight forwarder may arrange domestic air shipments without a permit from the CAB. Thus, a freight forwarder wishing to be able to arrange both overland and air shipments must be licensed both by the ICC and the CAB. The freight forwarder arranging air shipment does essentially the same things as the forwarder arranging an overland shipment.

No particular statute regulates the liability of the domestic air carrier. This regulation has been left to the courts and the CAB. The courts have decided that the liability of the domestic airline is essentially bailee liability. Thus, an airline is not responsible for loss, damage, or misdelivery of freight unless it was negligent in handling the shipment. Air carriers are also allowed to limit their liability upon any particular freight shipment in accordance with tariffs filed with the CAB. However, they must give the shipper the option to hold the carrier liable for full value by paying a higher shipping charge.

No statute regulates the filing of claims against air carriers for loss of or damage to cargo, and no statute sets time limits upon suing after a claim is denied. The air carriers may provide their own time limitations in their tariffs filed with the CAB. Their customers must be informed of these limitations in the airline bill of lading, and the customers are bound thereby. The time limits may vary from airline to airline, but all require the filing of a claim in writing before they will even consider any payment.

When damage to an air shipment occurs on the ground, even if the shipment is being transported on the ground by a motor vehicle belonging to the carrier, the carrier is not liable for the damage unless it was negligent.

The authority of the CAB in matters relative to air cargo has been greatly diminished by congressional enactment of the Air Cargo Deregulation Act, P.L. 95-163. Prior to its enactment, the CAB had sought to expand the liability of air carriers for loss of or damage to shipments by administrative regulation. Subsequent to the enactment of the deregulation statute the CAB repealed its regulations in this area.

The CAB has now lost its regulatory authority over air freight with respect to rate-fixing and has given up its authority with respect to regulation of handling cargo in most respects.

The congressional enactment provides for further progressive deregulation of the airline industry, and the eventual abolition of the CAB. At some point in the future, then, regulation of airlines as we presently know it will terminate. Apparently, liability of airlines for loss of or damage to shipments is once again a matter for the courts.

International carriers of goods by air. The main difference between the liability of the domestic air carrier and the liability of the international air carrier is that the Warsaw Convention, to which the United States is a signatory, limits the liability of an international air carrier to approximately $8.16 per pound for lost cargo on an international shipment. The shipper may hold the carrier to liability for the value of the shipment in toto by declaring extra value and paying a higher shipping charge, but in the absence of such declaration and payment, the carrier's liability is so limited.

The only time the carrier cannot take advantage of the limitation of liability is if the carrier or its agent acting in the scope of his authority is guilty of willful misconduct. In the absence of this, the carrier will not be liable at all if:

1. It took all steps necessary to prevent the damage that occurred, or
2. It was impossible to take steps against the occurrence of the damage, or
3. The damage was due to an error in piloting, handling of the aircraft, or navigation.

Notice, then, that under the Warsaw Convention the airline is not responsible for the negligence of the pilot or navigator in the management of the aircraft.

Sometimes the shipper of goods by air makes use of the services of an international air freight forwarder. Such freight forwarders must be licensed by the CAB. The international freight forwarder usually acts as the agent of an airline; therefore it does not issue its own bill of lading and it is not liable itself for loss of or damage to a shipment. On the other hand, if the forwarder acts as the agent of the shipper, it is liable for the safety of the shipment. If the forwarder is acting as agent for an airline, it must disclose this fact to the shipper.

The Warsaw Convention contains some specific rules relative to the making of damage and loss claims. A claim must be made in writing on the document of transportation or by separate written document. A damage claim with respect to goods must be sent to the appropriate carrier within seven days of the receipt of the goods. A delay claim must be sent within fourteen days of the day on which the goods should have been placed at the disposal of the person entitled to delivery. No time limit is provided in the Warsaw Convention for the making of loss claims.

A suit against a Warsaw Convention carrier must be filed within two years of the date the goods were delivered to the consignee by the carrier, or within two years of the date the goods should have been delivered. If no notice of damage is given to the carrier within the seven-day or fourteen-day limitations described above, no suit against the carrier is possible except for fraud. The damage notice is a necessary preliminary to the filing of suit.

CARRIAGE OF GOODS BY WATER

Domestic carriers of goods by water. Domestic water carriers are either intracoastal or intercoastal. The intracoastal carrier carries goods between ports on one coast of the United States, along the Intracoastal Canal, between ports of the Great Lakes, or along the navigable rivers of the United States. Intercoastal carriers carry goods from the Atlantic coast to the Pacific Coast or vice versa, from any continental port to Hawaii, Alaska,

Puerto Rico, or any other place outside the continental United States where the U.S. flag flies. Both types of domestic carriers are under the jurisdiction of the ICC to a degree. There exist common, contract, and private carriers in this trade, and all are subject to essentially the same regulation as are similar overland carriers.

All water carriers, even intrastate ones, are subject to federal jurisdiction. Since admiralty law is a matter of federal law, no water carrier is exempt from federal jurisdiction. The Carmack Amendment does not apply to domestic water carriers, however. The rules of liability for shipments are therefore not the same as those with respect to overland shipments.

A water carrier loads either from a dock or from lighters which ferry the goods out to where the vessel is anchored in the harbor. Usually the cargo is delivered to the dock, no matter where the vessel loads. If the dock is owned by and under the control of the shipping line, a bill of lading will be issued for the goods when they are received for shipment at the dock. If the dock is managed by a port authority or by an independent dock operator, a dock receipt will be issued when the goods are delivered at the dock. In such a case, when the operator of the dock turns the goods over to the water carrier, the carrier issues a bill of lading. If the carrier issues a bill of lading at the dock, this is called a *received-for-shipment bill*. If the carrier does not issue the bill until the goods are loaded on board the vessel, this is called an *on-board bill*. The shipping company may convert a received-for-shipment bill into an on-board bill by stamping it to signify that the goods have been loaded on board the vessel in good condition.

The water carrier takes responsibility for the shipment when the goods pass into its control; it loses responsibility for the shipment when the goods pass out of its control. The carrier does not lose responsibility for the goods when they are unloaded from the vessel, unless the contract between shipper and shipping line provides that delivery shall be made to the consignee when the goods leave the ship's tackle. Most shipping contracts do not provide for this. When they do not, the shipping company must offload the goods onto a safe wharf and hold them there for a reasonable time until they are picked up. While the goods are on the wharf, they remain the responsibility of the shipping company.

Numerous federal statutes permit the water carrier to limit its liability for loss of or damage to cargo. The Fire Statute, 46 USC 182, declares that a shipowner is not liable for cargo damage caused by fire unless the fire is caused by the design or negligence of the owner (including his employees, the crew of the ship). The Limited Liability Statute, 46 USC 181, 183–189, limits the liability of the owner of a vessel to his interest in the vessel itself plus the freight charges earned by the vessel on the voyage in question. The Harter Act, 46 USC 190–196, contains some limitations upon liability of owners and vessels in addition to the above.

46 USC 190 provides that no owner of a vessel may insert in a bill of lading provisions exempting the owner or the vessel from liability for negligence in loading, stowing, custody, or delivery of cargo. 46 USC 191 forbids an owner or employee of a vessel to insert in a bill of lading provisions disclaiming liability of the owner for failure to furnish a seaworthy vessel. But 46 USC 192 provides that, if the owner furnishes a seaworthy vessel and due care is taken to stow cargo properly, there shall be no liability imposed upon the owner or upon the ship for loss of or damage to cargo caused by:
1. Navigation errors or management errors with respect to the ship.
2. Dangers of the sea.
3. Acts of God.
4. Public enemies.

5. Inherent vice.
6. Insufficiency of packaging.
7. Seizure under legal process.
8. Act of shipper.
9. Saving or attempting to save life or property at sea.

Thus, under these statutes the liability of the owner of the domestic water carrier is considerably less than the liability of the railroad or other overland carrier. Essentially, two overriding duties are imposed upon domestic water carriers: the duty to furnish a seaworthy vessel, and the duty to stow the cargo properly aboard the vessel and to properly care for the cargo while it is in its custody before it is loaded aboard the vessel and after it is unloaded from the vessel.

The liability with respect to handling and stowage of cargo is negligence liability; due care must be used. With respect to the seaworthiness of the vessel, the owners must provide a vessel which is sufficiently supplied, sufficiently manned, and in good enough general condition to make the voyage in question as of the beginning of the voyage. The beginning of the voyage is the port from which the vessel departs upon its journey. Thus, if a vessel meets the tests of seaworthiness upon departure, the owners are not responsible if it becomes unseaworthy later in the voyage.

Provided that the cargo is properly cared for and the vessel is seaworthy, the owners are not liable for cargo damage caused by the five circumstances in which overland carriers are exempt from liability plus three other exemptions of importance.

Open water can be a dangerous place for water craft, even under good weather conditions, hence the exemption for damage caused by dangers of the seas. Waves can break over the prow of a vessel even in good weather, and water might find its way into the holds. The danger always exists of collision with almost submerged floating objects, and there are conditions where the difference between "Act of God" and "Danger of the sea" becomes indistinct, e.g., where vision is impeded by heavy fog or mist. In any event, if damage is caused by a danger of the sea, the owners may disclaim liability for it in their bill of lading.

The owners may also disclaim liability for damage to cargo caused by attempts to save life or property at sea. It has always been a primary duty of seafaring men to do everything within their power to succor shipwreck victims and any persons in danger at sea. This duty still takes precedence over timely delivery of cargo. There are also practical reasons for the exemption extending to the saving of property at sea. The sinking of a vessel normally causes the vessel and its cargo to be totally lost to the world. It is easy enough to salvage what can be salvaged from a wrecked overland vehicle; but if anything is to be salvaged from a shipwreck, the rescue must be accomplished before the vessel sinks or is permanently rendered useless by the waves. Furthermore, when a vessel is abandoned at sea by its crew, its owners lose ownership rights in it. If anyone later takes control of the vessel and its cargo, they as salvors become the owners. Whatever goods of value are realized from the salvage operation become the property of the salvors. Hence, there are economic possibilities inherent in the effort to salvage property at sea.

The last of the exemptions seems foreign to general principles of the law of agency and employment, under which an employer is liable for the negligence of his employees. This general rule does not apply with respect to a seagoing vessel; the owners are not responsible for negligence by officers or crew in the navigation and management of the vessel. Here, admiralty law draws a distinction between negligence by the owners in not hiring an adequate crew in numbers and skill to properly man the vessel, and negligence by the crew of the vessel in doing their jobs. For negligence in manning, the owners are liable. For negligence in navigation and management by a competent crew, they are not liable. Notice, however, that owners are not completely exempted from responsibility for negligence by members of the crew. Owners may be held liable for negligence by the crew in improper stowage of cargo, in permitting a fire to break out on board ship, or in negligently fighting the fire once it has broken out.

Mention must also be made of that institution peculiar to maritime law, general average. When a vessel encounters such grave difficulty at sea that a sacrifice of part of the vessel or part of the cargo seems necessary to save the rest, the captain may order cargo to be thrown overboard, or he may order that part of the vessel be thrown overboard, or both. If the sacrifice enables the vessel to complete its voyage, the owners of the sacrificed cargo and the sacrificed portion of the ship have a claim against the owners of saved cargo and the owners of the ship for part of their loss. Essentially, the owners of the sacrificed goods need only bear that proportion of the loss of their goods that the value of their goods bears to the value of the venture.

For example: Able has shipped cargo worth $100,000 aboard a vessel. The vessel gets into trouble at sea not caused by its own unseaworthiness, and the captain orders Able's goods thrown overboard. This sacrifice saves the vessel, so that the other cargo aboard reaches its destination. The factors taken into account in computing Able's general average claim are the following:
1. The value of Able's goods.
2. The value of all goods aboard at the beginning of the voyage, including Able's.
3. The value of the ship itself.
4. The freight charges paid the shipowners by the shippers of cargo.

Suppose, then, that Able's goods were worth $100,000; all cargo aboard was worth $8,500,000; the ship was worth $1,000,000, and the cargo owners have paid freight charges of $500,000. The total value of cargo, vessel, and freight charges is therefore $10,000,000. Able thus owned 1 percent of the dollar value of the venture. The sacrifice of his 1 percent interest in the venture saved the entire venture. Therefore, each participant in the venture is made to bear a 1 percent loss, so that Able will recover 99 percent of the value of what he sacrificed. He has a claim for $84,000 against the other cargo owners in proportion to the interests of these owners in the total cargo, and he has a claim for $15,000 against the shipowners—1 percent of the value of the ship and 1 percent of the value of the freight charges.

This example of general average is of course grossly oversimplified. In the usual general average situation, cargo belonging to more than one owner is sacrificed, and, very often, no owner loses all of his cargo. The computation of who has a claim against whom for how much becomes very complex—so complex that a firm of general average adjusters is usually called in to take care of it.

No general average claim may be made, however, unless three conditions prevail:
1. The captain or another appropriate ship's officer ordered the sacrifice because he believed that the ship was in imminent danger, and
2. The sacrifice was made pursuant to that order, and
3. The sacrifice was successful; vessel and cargo eventually arrived at the planned destination.

Since domestic water carriers are to an extent subject to the Interstate Commerce Act, the provisions of that legislation apply with respect to time limits on filing suit against carriers for damages. The ICC regulations with respect to time limits upon filing claims for damages also apply. The process of filing suit against a water carrier is a bit more complex than is the process of filing against the land carrier. A suit for damages for cargo damage may be filed either against the ship carrying the cargo, or against the owners of that ship. Under the principles of admiralty law, a ship is an entity in and of itself which may sue and be sued. However, a suit against a ship cannot be begun unless the ship is within the jurisdiction of the court hearing the case; a suit against the owners is not subject to that limitation. However, the liability of the owners may be limited under the Limitation of Liability Statute to the extent of their interest in the ship and its cargo.

A shipper of goods by domestic water transport may use the services of an ocean freight forwarder. More often than not, these operate as agents of ocean shipping companies and are therefore not liable as carriers. An ocean freight forwarder which does consolidate small shipments into large ones and issues bills of lading to its customers in its own name is liable to its customers as a carrier.

Since the Carmack Amendment does not apply to domestic water carriers, these are not obligated to issue through bills of lading for their shipments, and are thus not responsible for shipments not in their custody unless they have voluntarily issued a through bill of lading and assumed such responsibility.

A problem sometimes arises when goods are shipped domestically to a destination requiring some overland movement and some water movement. An overland carrier's through bill of lading covers the goods under the water portion of their journey, just as it covers them on the overland portion of the journey. However, the issuing carrier assumes only the liability of a water carrier for the water portion of the journey, unless the issuing carrier's bill of lading provides otherwise. It will not provide otherwise, in all probability, because the water carrier performing the water carriage will have only its usual liability for the shipment.

International carriers of goods by water. International water carriers are under the regulatory jurisdiction of the Federal Maritime Commission, as are international ocean freight forwarders. The freight rates charged by these carriers must be approved by the FMC.

The liability of the international water carrier to owners of cargo is governed primarily by the Carriage of Goods by Sea Act (COGSA), 46 USC 1300-1315, enacted in 1936. Secondarily, the Harter Act also governs their liability. Essentially, the Harter Act governs the international water carrier from the time it takes custody of a shipment until the shipment is loaded on board the vessel, and from the time the shipment is offloaded from the vessel until the shipment is delivered. The Harter Act thus imposes the same obligations with respect to care and delivery of cargo on shore upon international carriers as it imposes upon domestic carriers.

The COGSA requires two things of a carrier: that it furnish a seaworthy ship, and that it care properly for the cargo. 46 USC 1303(1) requires the carrier, before and at the beginning of the voyage, to exercise due diligence to:
1. Make the ship seaworthy.
2. Properly man, equip, and supply the ship.
3. Make the holds, refrigerating and cooling chambers, and all other parts of the ship in which goods are carried, fit and safe for their reception, carriage, and preservation.

These requirements apply only before and at the beginning of the voyage. Before the ship sails, then, the owners must use due diligence to see to it that the ship itself is in condition to make the voyage, that sufficient supplies are on board, that necessary equipment is aboard and in good operating order, that the crew is sufficient in number and competence; and that all parts of the ship where cargo is carried are in condition to receive and preserve the cargo.

46 USC 1303(2) provides that the carrier must properly and carefully load, handle, stow, carry, keep, care for, and discharge the goods carried. This essentially is a requirement that the cargo be properly stowed, cared for, and delivered.

Under 46 USC 1304(1), the owners or the ship are not responsible for loss or damage caused by unseaworthiness unless the owners did not carry out their obligations under 46 USC 1303(1). There is no liability, then, for unseaworthiness arising after the beginning of the voyage. If there is any debate about whether or not the ship was seaworthy, the burden of proof is on the owner to show seaworthiness.

46 USC 1304(2) declares that the owners and the ship are not liable for loss or damage caused by sixteen specific things:

1. Negligence in navigation and management of the ship.
2. Fire, unless caused by carrier negligence or privity (including negligence of the crew).
3. Perils of the sea and other navigable waters.
4. Acts of God.
5. Acts of war.
6. Acts of public enemies—pirates, for example.
7. Arrest or restraint by governments, or seizure under legal process.
8. Quarantine restrictions.
9. Acts and omissions of the shipper.
10. Strikes and lockouts, except lockouts by the carrier itself.
11. Riots and civil commotion.
12. Saving or attempting to save life or property at sea.
13. Inherent vice.
14. Insufficiency of packing.
15. Insufficiency of marks.
16. Latent defects not discoverable by due diligence.

The section, then, exempts the ship and the owners from loss or damage due to any cause arising without the fault or privity of the carrier, but the burden of proof in such a case would be on the carrier to prove lack of negligence.

46 USC 1304 (4) provides that the carrier is not liable for loss or damage caused by any reasonable deviation from course by the vessel. Reasonable deviation is defined, specifically but not exclusively, as deviation for purposes of saving or attempting to save life or property at sea. Deviation for purposes of loading or unloading passengers or cargo is defined prima facie as unreasonable: the carrier would have to show a very good reason for deviation for that purpose to have a court consider it reasonable. Of course, a deviation to get a seriously ill passenger to a hospital on shore would be reasonable. Deviation to avoid a war zone, to avoid severe weather conditions, to avoid a port where longshoremen are on strike, or any equally compelling deviation, would be quite reasonable.

46 USC 1304(3) and (6) contain provisions relative to possible liability of the shipper to the carrier. When goods of an inflammable, explosive, or dangerous nature are shipped, their nature should be disclosed to the carrier. If such goods are shipped without disclosure of their nature, the carrier may land, destroy, or render harmless the goods without compensation to the shipper; if the goods cause damage to the ship or to other cargo, the shipper will be liable for such damage. If such goods are shipped after disclosure of their nature to the carrier, the carrier may still land, destroy, or render harmless the shipment if in the judgment of the captain they constitute a danger to the ship or to other cargo, except that the owner of the cargo may then have a general average claim. The shipper would not be liable for damage caused, though, if the nature of the cargo has been disclosed.

Under no other circumstances shall the shipper be liable to the carrier for damage caused by shipped goods, unless shipper negligence is involved in the damage.

46 USC 1304(5) limits the liability of the carrier subject to COGSA to $500 per package of goods shipped, or, if the goods are the sort that are not shipped in packages, $500 per commercial unit. If the shipper wishes to hold the carrier liable for more than this sum, he may do so by agreement with the carrier if he pays extra shipping charges. In any event, the shipper must disclose the nature of his shipment and its value to the carrier. False and fraudulent misstatement of the nature or value of a shipment will absolve the carrier from all liability for loss or damage.

The Limitation of Liability Act applies with as great force to COGSA carriers as it does to Harter Act carriers. Therefore, the carrier's liability with respect to a shipload of goods may be limited to its interest in the ship plus its interest in the freight charges earned by the ship.

46 USC 1303(6) contains the COGSA provisions relative to damage claims and damage suits. When the person entitled to delivery of goods shipped on a COGSA carrier accepts delivery, he should inspect the goods for signs of damage or of noncomformity with the bill of lading description. Should any damage be noticed, agents of the carrier should be informed at once, in writing. Should the damage not be immediately visible, notice of it should be given in writing to the carrier within three days of delivery. Failure to give notice of damage is evidence that the goods were delivered in good condition.

Suit against a COGSA carrier for damage to, loss of, or misdelivery of a shipment must be brought within one year of the date of delivery, or within one year of the date the shipment should have been delivered. Thus, it is most important that a shipment received by a COGSA carrier be promptly inspected for damage, and that notice of the damage be given at once. What counts under COGSA is not the filing of a formal claim—it is merely the giving of notice of claim.

REGULATION OF EXPORT AND IMPORT TRANSACTIONS

Regulation of the foreign trade of the United States is another subject so complex that many books have been written about it. Yet foreign trade is becoming so common in the American business community that students should have some notion of the basic operation of the regulatory mechanism. This section will provide a brief introduction to the subject.

Reasons for export regulation. It is in the national interest of the United States to regulate the export of goods, services, and technology from this nation. William P. Streng states, in his *International Business Transactions Tax and Legal Handbook*, that export controls serve three useful purposes:

1. National security.
2. Furtherance of the political objectives of the United States.
3. Protection of the national economy.

For purposes of national security, the export of weaponry, particularly sophisticated weaponry, is closely regulated. For purposes of international politics, trade with certain foreign nations, such as Cuba, Vietnam, and Rhodesia, is forbidden. Trade with many other nations is limited more or less severely. For purposes of protection of the domestic economy exports of crude oil and foodstuffs are closely controlled.

General nature of export regulation. The basic mechanism of export regulation is contained in the Export Administration Act, 50 App. USC 2401 et seq. The major administrative agency having jurisdiction in this area is the Office of Export Control of the U.S. Department of Commerce.

Exports are regulated both on the basis of items and on the basis of nations. Export of some commodities is absolutely forbidden while export of certain commodities is permitted to some nations, but not to others. The export of still other commodities is unrestricted.

The Office of Export Control maintains a Commodity Control List, which states the current restrictions (if any) upon export of all commodities from this nation. The would-be exporter must then check the status on the list of any commodity he desires to export. Since the content of the list changes often, the exporter must make certain that his information as to the exportability status of any commodity is current.

With respect to certain commodities, exportability is regulated by agencies other than the Office of Export Control. The Office of Munitions Control of the State Department must be consulted about arms and ammunition export. The Justice Department has jurisdiction over the export of narcotics, and the Nuclear Regulatory Commission controls exports of nuclear materials.

Exports to Canada as a nation are unrestricted (though commodity restrictions may apply). Other nations are divided into groups for regulatory purposes. Streng lists the current groupings as follows:

Group Q—Romania.
Group S—Rhodesia.
Group T—All nations of the Western Hemisphere except Cuba (and Canada, which belongs to no group).
Group W—Poland.
Group Y—Albania, Bulgaria, Czechoslovakia, East Germany, Outer Mongolia, People's Republic of China, and the USSR.
Group Z—North Korea, Vietnam, and Cuba.
Group V—All other nations except Canada.

In general, exports to Groups V and T are subject to the fewest restrictions. Groups Q and W are subject to more, Group Y to still more, while trade with Groups S and Z is virtually forbidden.

Specific export procedure. Exports to all nations except Canada must be licensed. Two types of licenses exist: the general license and the validated license.

The exporter must check with the Office of Export Control (or some other governing agency) after receipt of an export order to determine whether or not the order may be lawfully filled, and, if so, what sort of license is needed. If export of the item to the ordering nation is forbidden, no license may be issued, and the exporter cannot lawfully fill his order. If the export is of a commodity of the right dollar value to the right nation, a general license for the export may exist. If so, no application for a specific license is required; the transaction may be consummated under the authority of the general license.

If the export is not specifically forbidden, but no general license for it exists, the exporter must apply for a validated license, which is a specific permit to engage in a specific export transaction, or a specific permit to engage in a specific series of export transactions. These licenses are not necessarily issued for only one transaction. The nature of the license will depend upon the nature of the transaction.

The Office of Export Control (OEC) issues most of these licenses (unless some other agency governs the commodity being exported). The OEC must respond to a license application within ninety days, but that does not mean that it must make a decision on granting the license within that time. It may just make a status report on the application and take its time about rendering a final decision. If issuance of the license is denied, the export may not be made.

If the validated license is granted, the exporter may then make his shipment. He must fill out a shipper's export declaration to accompany the shipment, which must state the number of the general export license under which the shipment is being made, or must have attached thereto a copy of the shipper's validated export license.

The international carrier transporting the shipment must be given a copy of the export declaration. The U.S. Customs Service will not permit an international freight carrier to leave the U.S. until it furnishes a manifest of all cargo and proof of filing of the export declaration for all cargo.

Export shipments must also be accompanied by all of the documentation which will be required by the nation of importation. Such required documentation may include consular invoices, certificates of origin, and similar papers.

Import regulation. The major reasons for regulation of imports into the United States are fairly obvious. There is the police power purpose—prevention of importation of commodities dangerous to the well-being of the American people. There is the economic purpose—protecting American businesses from the unfair competition of foreign produce within the American domestic economy. Then, of lesser importance, there is the revenue-production purpose—the raising of tax revenue through import duties on imported commodities.

Two administrative agencies of the federal government have great authority in this area: The International Trade Commission (formerly the Tariff Commission) makes the administrative regulations implementing the U.S. system of import duties and import regulation in general, and the U.S. Customs Service is the field agency which inspects goods being imported into the nation and enforces the above laws and regulations.

General restrictions on imports. Many sorts of goods produced domestically may not be marketed in the United States unless they conform to standards established by various regulatory agencies. Thus, motor vehicles must have pollution-control and safety equipment mandated by law and by agency regulation. Motor vehicles imported into the United States must also meet these standards. If they do not, they will not be permitted to enter the nation. If a standard is applied to a domestically produced product, the imported product of that type must also meet the standard.

Several administrative agencies have the power to ban the sale of domestically produced products in the U.S., or the manufacture thereof for domestic sale. If an agency has banned the sale of such a commodity, the importation of it into the nation is also banned.

Various federal statutes forbid the importation of certain products into the United States unless the importer possesses a special import license. Such requirements exist with respect to narcotics, firearms, explosives, and other commodities. Such commodities will not be allowed into the nation unless the importer has a proper license.

The holder of a valid patent, copyright, or trademark may petition the International Trade Commission to refuse admission to the nation of commodities which infringe upon a valid American patent or copyright, or which bear a trademark which infringes upon a properly registered U.S. trademark. When imported goods are brought into the United States for the purpose of injuring or destroying an economically and efficiently operated domestic industry of the United States, the International Trade Commission may forbid the further importation of such goods. Of course, if the importer merely means to engage in fair competition with domestic producers in the U.S. market, there is no legal objection. Objections arise when the price of the imported goods is so low that domestic producers may be unable to mount effective price competition (19 USC 1337).

Customs duties in general. The enactment of customs duty schedules was formerly a matter of legislation by Congress, elaborate statutes being enacted that specified the customs duty upon every conceivable import into the United States.

For many years now, that rate-setting authority has rested in the hands of the president of the United States and of the International Trade Commission. The determination of rates of duty is now governed by U.S. obligations under the General Agreement on Tariffs and Trade (GATT) of which the U.S. is a signatory; and by principles of reciprocity. Formerly, rates of duty depended solely upon the nature of the commodity. Now they may also depend upon the nation of export and its policies on taxation of imports.

Under some circumstances, however, rates of U.S. import duty may be altered for domestic political and economic reasons, perhaps to protect a domestic industry endangered by imports, or to drive up the domestic price of cheap foreign goods "dumped" here by foreign producers and domestic importers.

Most goods imported into the United States are subject to import duty. More often than not, the duty is an *ad valorem* duty, based upon the value of the commodity in the nation of export. (In this respect, U.S. valuation is more lenient than the valuation used by most nations in the levying of import duty: The U.S. uses the FOB export point value of the commodity, while most other nations use CIF value at the point of importation, taxing the cost of transporting the commodity to the point of import and the cost of insuring it while in transit.)

Procedure for handling imports. When goods are imported into the U.S. by tourists on their person or in their luggage, the Customs Service inspects the tourist and (perhaps) his luggage at the point of entry, and levies duty if any is due. The procedure for handling commercial imports is more complex.

International freight carriers must furnish a manifest of all shipments coming into the United States to the U.S. Customs Service. This way, the Customs Service knows in advance the nature of the cargo of the carrier, and its taxability. If the goods arrive by sea, the carrier must not unload them from the vessel without Customs Service clearance.

At the time the goods enter the country, an entry form must be filed with the Customs Service. The nature of this form depends upon what will happen to the goods after entry. If the goods are to be released to the consignee for resale, consumption, or some other use at the port of entry, one type of form is used; if the goods are to transported to another point, another form is used. Also, if the goods are worth more than $500 and are subject to ad valorem duty, a special customs invoice must be filed which itemizes the goods and states their value.

If the goods are released at the port of entry, the customs duty must be paid before release. The consignee normally does this, though he may have a customs broker accept delivery of the goods and take care of the transaction. If the consignee wants to take delivery at the port of entry, but later than the arrival time, the goods may be placed in storage in a bonded warehouse without payment of duty. The warehouseman may then not release the goods before the duty is paid. If he does, he incurs liability to the Customs Service for the unpaid duty.

It may be that the goods are to be transported to an inland point before the duty is paid. In such a case they are released to a bonded carrier for transportation. The carrier must not release the goods at their destination before the duty is paid. Both the bonded warehouse and the bonded carrier will be liable to the Customs Service for duty on imported goods if the goods are lost or stolen in cases where the warehouseman or carrier would be liable to the consignee or the shipper for the value of the goods.

Before the goods are released to the consignee or customs broker, the Customs Service inspects them, comparing the goods and their value with the goods and value declared on the entry form and the special customs invoice. If the customs inspectors find goods included in the shipment which are not listed on the documents, duty is payable on the unlisted goods. If the nonlisting of goods appears to be fraudulent, the Customs Service has the right to seize the unlisted goods. Of course, if the unlisted goods are goods which may not legally be imported into the United States, these will be seized.

It is not wise to attempt to slip unlisted goods past customs inspectors. Such activity invites the confiscation of the goods, and may also be cause for criminal prosecution.

INSURANCE OF GOODS

Inland transit insurance. When goods are to be shipped by ground carrier, they may be insured by those having an insurable interest in them with inland transit insurance. This form of insurance is also sometimes called inland marine insurance. The coverage obtainable under such insurance will vary somewhat according to whether the goods are shipped by rail or truck, and will also vary somewhat according to the insurer one purchases the coverage from. In general, inland transit insurance will insure against the following perils:

1. Collision, derailment, or other such destruction of or damage to the carrying vehicle causing loss of or damage to the goods.
2. Acts of God, such as storm, flood, tornado, earthquake, and so on.
3. Theft.

Inland transit insurance will not insure against losses caused by:

1. War, riot, or civil commotion.
2. Strikes or lockouts.
3. Delay in transit.
4. Acts of public authority.
5. Acts of shipper—improper packing, for example.
6. Inherent vice.
7. Breakage, leakage, and pilferage.

The major purpose of such insurance coverage, then, is protection against acts of God, for which carriers are not liable. The coverage for losses due to damage to the carrying vehicle and theft duplicate carrier liability, but in general it is easier to collect on an insurance claim than it is to collect from a carrier.

Breakage and leakage mean what one would expect in this context. If goods are shipped in glass containers, for instance, and some of these break in transit, the loss is a breakage loss and is not covered by insurance. If goods are shipped in wooden barrels, and some of the contents of a barrel are lost because the seams spring or because a hole gets punched into the side of the barrel, this is a leakage and is not covered.

Pilferage is the theft of a portion of the contents of a package. A package for this purpose is the packing case in which goods are shipped. Thus, if a shipment of 144 cartons of cigarettes is made in 6 cases containing 24 cartons each; and all 6 cases are broken into and 5 cartons stolen from each case, we have a pilferage case which is not covered by inland transit insurance. On the other hand, if only 5 of the 6 packing cases of cigarettes arrive at their destination—the sixth being stolen—we have a theft case, which the insurance will cover.

Inland transit coverage is to an extent subject to negotiation between insured and insurer. By paying a higher premium one may obtain greater coverage. The coverage described above is generally the minimum available.

When a loss occurs, it is the obligation of the insured to notify the insurer as soon as possible. Delay in this matter may give the insurer cause to resist paying the claim. Inland transit policies usually require the insured to file a Proof of Loss with the insurer within a certain number of days after the occurrence of the loss, generally within sixty to ninety days, depending on the policy provisions. This is a detailed form spelling out what items have been lost and the values of the lost items. Failure to file the Proof of Loss within the time limit may also cause difficulty in collecting a claim.

These policies generally also contain provisions stating that suit against the company to collect upon a claim must be brought within a named period after the accrual of the claim. This period will generally be one or two years, and no longer. Courts interpret this to mean what it says.

The coverage applicable to partial losses—damage to the shipment rather than total loss or destruction—will vary according to the nature of the goods shipped and the terms of the policy. Generally, partial losses amounting to only a small percentage of the value of the item damaged will not be covered. Losses amounting to a greater percentage of the value of the damaged item may be covered. Destruction of a packing case is a total loss of that case, even if the rest of the shipment remained undamaged. Slight damage to all of the packing cases of a shipment will be considered to be a slight partial loss, and may not be covered at all.

Ocean marine insurance. When goods are to be shipped by water, those parties having an insurable interest in them may wish to insure them with ocean marine insurance. In general, ocean marine coverage insures against the following perils:
1. Acts of God.
2. Perils of the sea.
3. Fire.
4. Theft, including barratry by the officers or crew of the ship.
5. Negligence in navigation and management of the ship.
6. Collisions.
7. General average claims.
8. Explosions.

Ocean marine insurance will not cover the following sorts of losses:
1. Delay due to strikes and lockouts.
2. Riot or civil commotion.
3. Acts of war.
4. Piracy.
5. Acts of government authorities, including seizure and quarantine.
6. Acts of the shipper.
7. Inherent vice.
8. Breakage, leakage, and pilferage.

Partial losses (called *particular average* in admiralty law) are not recoverable under ocean marine coverage unless the loss is caused by stranding (the vessel running aground), sinking, burning, or collision. Even when recoverable, the recovery right would not come into effect unless the damage amounts to more than a stated percentage of the value of the package damaged, the percentage depending on the nature of the goods.

Three circumstances will lead to automatic cancellation of ocean marine coverage:
1. The fact that the vessel carrying the insured goods is unseaworthy at the beginning of its voyage.
2. The fact that the vessel carrying the goods insured deviates from its course for reasons other than the saving of lives at sea.
3. The fact that the insured goods are an illegal shipment under the law of either the sending or receiving nation, or the voyage of the vessel carrying the insured goods is illegal.

The fact that the carrying vessel is unseaworthy at the beginning of its voyage obviously increases the risk that the carrying vessel will not arrive at its destination. Deviations from the normal course of the journey by the carrying vessel also tend to increase the risk of loss of shipped goods.

It is a general principle of insurance law that insurance will not underwrite any sort of illegal venture. This principle holds here, as elsewhere.

It is possible to obtain more ocean marine coverage than that described above by payment of a higher premium. However, no private insurer will sell war risk insurance. This type of coverage must be obtained from governments, when they are willing to provide it.

Fire insurance. Fire insurance covers perils which are not too closely related to the perils encountered in transportation of goods. However, anyone with an insurable interest in stored goods may well want to take out fire insurance upon them, as might anyone who owns a building in which goods are stored.

Fire insurance protects against loss of goods due to a hostile fire. It does not protect against losses due to friendly fires; a friendly fire is a fire burning in a place where it is supposed to be, while a hostile fire is a fire burning in a place where it is not supposed to be. In the domestic context, then, a fire burning in a fireplace or in an incinerator is friendly. If a spark from the fire in the fireplace sets the living room rug afire, though, the fire has become hostile.

In a warehouse, a bonfire set by outside employees in wintertime in order to keep themselves warm is friendly, so long as it is burning in a reasonable place and the employees keep it under control. If the fire breaks out of its confinement, it becomes hostile. Thus, if warehouse employees throw stored goods into their fire for fuel, the loss is due to a friendly fire. The warehouse would be liable to the owner for the loss, due to negligence.

If insured goods are destroyed by a hostile fire, they are covered. If they are partially damaged by the fire, they are covered. If they are destroyed or damaged by foreseeable consequences of the fire, they are covered. Thus, the insurance will cover damage caused by the following, among other things:
1. Smoke.
2. Heat.
3. Water pumped in to fight the fire.
4. Theft occurring while the goods are being moved out of reach of the fire.

Ordinary fire insurance will cover damage caused by lightning, or by the consequences of lightning. It will not cover damage caused by explosion. If an explosion starts a fire and the insured goods are damaged by the fire, however, the goods are covered.

The owner of the insured premises is under an obligation to summon the fire department as soon as possible after the fire is discovered. Failure to do this will cause the insurer to have a defense to payment of claims. Once endangered goods are removed from the vicinity of the fire, the insurance no longer protects against theft. The owner will be obligated to post guards to protect the goods, or to take other measures for their protection.

Fire policies also will not cover goods destroyed by certain types of hostile fires, including those resulting from:

1. Acts of war.
2. Riot, civil commotion and civil disorders.
3. Orders of civil authority.

A fine line exists here between a fire caused by an arsonist and a fire set by a rioter. The fire set by the arsonist would cause covered damage; the fire set by the rioter would not. It makes a difference whether the fire-setter stealthily works alone or whether he works in the open as part of a larger disorder.

If a building containing insured goods is burnt or destroyed by order of the fire chief to create a firebreak to stop an advancing conflagration, the loss is not covered. This is the meaning, or one of the meanings, of the phrase "orders of civil authority." Destruction by authority in the effort to fight a fire, then, does not create an insurable loss.

In order to collect a fire insurance claim, the insured must generally notify the insurer of his loss as soon as possible after the loss occurs. He must also file a Proof of Loss with the insurer within the time limit set by the policy, usually sixty or ninety days after the loss.

Effect of negligence on insurer liability. Fire insurance is in effect a form of no-fault insurance. Negligence by the insured in permitting a fire to start would not defeat a claim. (Negligence in not promptly summoning the fire department will defeat a claim, however.)

Negligence by a shipper in packaging his shipment will defeat an inland transit or ocean marine claim. Negligence by the carrier transporting a shipment would not defeat a claim, the insured not being responsible for the carrier's negligence, in most cases. (Negligence amounting to the furnishing of an unseaworthy ship does defeat the ocean marine claim, however.)

Subrogation. The insurer who pays an insurance claim acquires all of the rights that the insured might have had against third parties. Thus, the inland transit or ocean marine insurer who pays a claim acquires the insured party's rights against the transporting carrier(s). Also, if third-party negligence caused the insured's claim to arise, the insurer acquires the insured's rights against that party. If the insurer is required to sue to enforce his subrogation rights, he generally sues in the insured's name, and the insured must cooperate in the suit.

All of these forms of insurance insure covered property for actual cash value—cost less depreciation. This may amount to considerably less than replacement cost, sometimes, but it is difficult to find insurers willing to insure property at replacement cost.

32

Bulk Sales

Sale of Goods by Nonowners

Performance of Contracts for Sale of Goods

Letters of Credit and Credit Cards

Bulk Sales

Article Six of the Uniform Commercial Code contains the law relative to bulk sales of the assets of a business.

Before bulk sales legislation was enacted by the states, the following situation sometimes arose: The owner of a business which sold goods out of inventory—a grocery store, hardware store, or other retail outlet—would buy a great deal of inventory from his suppliers on open account, the suppliers thus having no lien upon the inventory. The owner would then sell the business to a new owner for cash, the new owner not agreeing to assume and pay the debts of the old owner. The old owner would take the cash and disappear, leaving the suppliers with no claim against either the buyer or the assets of the business. Unless they could locate the seller and collect their claims from him, the suppliers were left holding a large empty bag.

The purpose of bulk sale legislation is to provide a procedure by which creditors of the seller of a business may receive notice of its sale before the sale is consummated. Article Six of the UCC as adopted by a majority of the states merely provides for the giving of notice of a bulk sale to creditors of the seller before the business is sold. There is no procedure provided under which the creditors will actually be paid before the buyer takes over.

A minority of the states, including Texas, have adopted an optional section of Article Six under which the buyer must actually pay off the seller's creditors before turning any of the promised consideration over to the seller. A smaller minority of states, *not including Texas*, have adopted another optional section of Article Six under which the buyer may deposit the agreed consideration in court, so that a court takes care of paying the seller's creditors.

Sales subject to bulk sale procedure. UCC 6-102 provides that a bulk sale is a sale in bulk and out of the ordinary course of the seller's business of a major part of the materials, supplies, merchandise, or other inventory from an enterprise whose principal business is the sale of merchandise from inventory, including those who manufacture what they sell.

Sales which are exempt from bulk sale procedure. Sections 6-102 and 6-103 provide many exemptions from bulk sale procedure. Among the exemptions are the following:
1. Sales of inventory in the normal course of seller's business.
2. Sales of assets of service-type businesses.
3. Sales of equipment only.
4. Transfers of inventory made as collateral for performance of an obligation.
5. Transfers in foreclosure upon collateral or in settlement of a lien.
6. Assignments for benefit of creditors, and transfers by such assignees.
7. Sales by executors, administrators, trustees in bankruptcy, receivers, sheriffs, tax collectors, etc.
8. Sales held pursuant to dissolution of a corporation, where notice is sent to creditors pursuant to the provisions of the Texas Business Corporation Act.
9. Sales in which the buyer assumes and agrees to pay the debts of the seller.
10. Sales pursuant to the reorganization of the enterprise, where notice to creditors has been given, the new enterprise assumes liabilities of the old, and the former owner gets nothing from the transfer except an interest in the new enterprise subject to claims of creditors of the old enterprise.
11. Sales of property exempt from execution.

Notice of a transfer exempt under 9 and 10 above may be given by publishing in a newspaper of general circulation in the locality of the enterprise once a week for two consecutive weeks a notice giving the name of the transferor, the name of the transferee, the addresses of both, and the date of the transfer.

Drug stores, grocery stores, furniture stores, and clothing stores are examples of businesses which sell goods out of inventory. Barber shops, bowling alleys, restaurants, pool halls, and beauty salons are examples of service-type businesses, the sales of which are exempt. Sales of factory machinery, showcases, advertising displays, and delivery vehicles are examples of sales of equipment, which are exempt if not combined with sales of inventory. Transfers which are part of a secured transaction are exempt, because the transaction is either not a sale or the foreclosing secured creditor probably has better legal rights in the collateral than any unsecured creditor of the former owner.

Sales by executors and trustees in bankruptcy are exempt because creditors get notice of the existence of these proceedings as provided in the laws establishing them, and they are provided a mechanism for making claims. Sales by sheriffs and tax collectors are exempt, again, because the foreclosing creditor has a better claim to the goods than does an unsecured creditor.

In a reorganization of the enterprise creditors do not stand to lose anything if the reorganization meets the exemption requirements. If the reorganization is one in which the creditors could lose, it is not exempt and the required procedure must be followed.

If the buyer has agreed to assume and pay the seller's debts, the seller's creditors are assured of all the protection they would get from having bulk sale procedure followed; hence there is no point in requiring the procedure.

Schedule of property being transferred and list of creditors. UCC 6-104 requires the following of transferor and transferee:
1. Transferor must furnish to transferee a complete list of all his creditors, including those asserting claims which are in dispute. The list must contain the name and business address of all such creditors, and the amount owed to or claimed by each. The list must be signed and sworn to by the transferor or his agent. If there are errors

in the list, the transferor bears all responsibility for them, unless the transferee knows of them.

2. Transferor and transferee must prepare a complete list of the property being transferred, in enough detail to identify it.

3. Transferee must either preserve the list and make it available to interested parties for six months after the transfer, or he must record it in the public records of the county where the business is located.

Notice to creditors. At least ten days before taking possession of the property sold, the transferee is required to send notice of the transfer to all creditors listed on the transferor's creditor list, and also to any creditors of the transferor known to the transferee but not included in the list (UCC 6-105). The notice must be delivered in person, or mailed by registered or certified mail.

The content of this notice is prescribed by UCC 6-107. If the transferor's debts are to be paid in full, a short form of notice is required, containing:

1. A statement that a bulk transfer is to be made, and
2. The names and business addresses of transferor and transferee, including all business names and addresses used by transferor within the last three years, and
3. A statement that the debts of transferor will be paid in full, and of the address to which bills should be sent.

If transferee believes that all of transferor's debts will not be paid in full, or if the transfer is in settlement of a debt or the like so that no new consideration is payable, the long form of notice must be used. In such a case the notice must also contain:

4. The location and general description of the property being transferred, and the estimated amount of transferor's debts, and
5. The location of the list of transferred property and list of creditors, and
6. Whether or not transferee is to pay any existing debts, and, if so, which debts and to whom they are owed, and
7. If new consideration is to be paid, its amount and the time and place where creditors may file claims with transferee.

Payment of debts, application of proceeds. If transferee is giving new consideration, he must pay nothing to transferor until all known debts of transferee are paid. Transferee must pay off all creditors listed upon transferor's list of creditors, plus all creditors filing claims with transferee within thirty days of the mailing of the notices to creditors. If some debts are disputed, transferee must retain the amount claimed by such creditors until the dispute is settled. If the new consideration is insufficient to pay all creditors in full, it must be divided ratably among the creditors. This is the mandate of UCC 6-106.

Liability of transferee if creditors not paid. The transferee is not liable to a creditor not listed on transferor's list of creditors if the creditor did not file a claim during the thirty-day filing period and transferee did not know about the creditor. A creditor unknown to transferee who files his claim more than thirty days after mailing of notices to creditors also has no claim against transferee. Transferee will be liable to any creditor on transferor's list who was not paid, or to a creditor known to transferee who was not listed who was not paid, or to a creditor filing a timely claim who was not paid.

According to UCC 6-111, transferee's liability to creditors ends six months after he takes possession of the transferred property, unless the transfer was concealed. In the case of a concealed transfer, creditors may collect from transferee up to six months after the date of discovery.

As per UCC 6-109, creditors of transferor who become his creditors after notice is mailed are entitled to no notice, but they still may file claims during the thirty-day filing period. Transferee is entitled to credit against his obligation for all amounts paid in good faith to particular creditors. Transferee's liability is limited to the amount he agreed to pay transferor for the transferred property.

Subsequent transfers. Creditors of the transferor may levy execution upon the purchased assets if bulk procedure is not complied with. If transferee sells such assets to a bona fide purchaser, the purchaser will get valid title to them free and clear of creditor claims. However, a purchaser who knows of the defective title of the transferee, or a person who does not give value for the assets, gets voidable title to them; the assets may be levied upon by unpaid creditors (UCC 6-110).

When the sale is by auction. UCC 6-108 provides that when a bulk sale is conducted by auction the auctioneer has all the duties of the transferee in a normal sale. The auctioneer must collaborate in making the list of property to be sold, he must mail out notices to creditors and pay off creditors with the proceeds, and he will be liable to unpaid creditors for six months after the sale to the extent of the proceeds.

Buyers at the auction get clear title to their purchases.

Sale of Goods by Nonowners

A possessor of goods may also be the owner of the goods. If he is, he is said to have *valid title* to them. A possessor of goods who has no ownership rights in them is said to have *void title*. A possessor of goods who has ownership rights which may be divested by some other person is said to have *voidable title*.

A person with valid title to goods may dispose of them in any way he sees fit and, so long as he intends to transfer his title by his disposal, he does so. A person with void title cannot ordinarily sell ownership rights that he does not possess, so a buyer of goods from someone with void title ordinarily gets void title. A person with voidable title, however, may sell valid title to a bona fide purchaser.

However, some sorts of possessors who have void title to goods may sell valid title. UCC 2-403 describes several instances of this being done, and also contains definitions of certain types of persons who have voidable title.

Persons with void title. The following sorts of persons have no legal title to goods in their possession:
1. Thieves.
2. Bailees.
3. Finders.
4. Buyers from persons with guardians (or donees from such, etc.).
5. Buyers, donees, and so on from any of the above.

It must be remembered, however, that a finder may obtain title to found goods by adverse possession, if he keeps the goods for two years (RCS 5526).

An ordinary bailee acquires the power (though not the right) to sell bailed goods after possessing them for two years, so long as the bailor has made no demand for their return (TB&CC 24.05). In addition, if a bailee sells bailed goods to a bona fide purchaser before he has had possession of the goods for two years, the buyer gets good title after the bailee's period of possession and the buyer's possession add up to two years.

A bailee for hire, such as a repairman, a carrier, or a warehouseman, acquires an artisan's lien upon the goods for the amount of his legitimate charges. Such a bailee may foreclose his lien to collect his charges; in the process of doing so, he may sell valid title to the goods to the buyer at his foreclosure sale.

A merchant may sell goods entrusted to him by others to buyers in the usual course of business, giving such buyers valid title to the goods sold. The merchant of course commits conversion; nevertheless, the buyer gets valid title to the goods. Among the merchants who may do this are repairmen who sell the goods they repair, and merchants who retain possession of goods they have already sold to customers. (They may sell the retained goods to other customers, giving them good title, but in so doing they convert the goods to their own use, since the first buyer already had title to them.)

The bona fide purchaser from a person with void title. A person is a bona fide purchaser if he meets three qualifications:
1. He gives value for the goods.
2. He acts in good faith in buying them.
3. He knows of no defect in the seller's title.

The bona fide purchaser of goods from the following parties with void title will get valid title in Texas:
1. A merchant who deals in the goods.
2. A lien-foreclosing bailee.
3. An ordinary bailee who has had possession of the goods for two years, the bailor not having demanded the return of the goods.

A bona fide purchaser from any other person with void title may obtain valid title by adverse possession if he keeps the goods for two years. If he buys from a finder who has had possession of the goods for eighteen months, he gets void title, but he will have valid title by adverse possession within six months. Thus, bona fide purchasers may "tack on" periods of adverse possession by their transferors in order to arrive at the magic number of two years of adverse possession which creates valid title.

Persons with voidable title. The following sorts of purchasers obtain voidable title to what they buy:
1. Buyers from minors.
2. Buyers from insane or incompetent persons who have no guardian, when the buyer knows or should know that he is dealing with an abnormal person.
3. Buyers who defraud their sellers into selling the goods.
4. Buyers who subject their sellers to duress to induce the sale.
5. Buyers who use undue influence on their sellers to induce the sale.
6. Buyers who induce their seller to sell by pretending to be someone else.
7. Buyers at cash sales who do not pay for the goods.
8. Buyers who pay for the goods purchased with bad checks, and do not make the bad checks good.

Any person obtaining goods from someone with voidable title who does not qualify as a bona fide purchaser will get voidable title, including:
1. A person receiving goods as a gift from a person with voidable title.
2. A person who defrauds the seller with voidable title into selling him the goods.
3. A buyer from a person with voidable title who knows that his seller has voidable title.

When a bona fide purchaser gets no title. A bona fide purchaser normally gets good title to what he buys, but he will not get good title to what he buys when:

1. He is buying stolen goods from the thief.
2. He is buying lost or misplaced goods from the finder.
3. He is buying borrowed goods from a bailee who has not yet had possession of them for two years.
4. He is buying stolen, lost, or misplaced goods from a bona fide purchaser who has not had possession long enough to have title by adverse possession.
5. He is buying goods upon which a negotiable document of title is outstanding, unless the goods are fungible goods or unless he is buying at a lien foreclosure sale held by the issuer of the negotiable document.

Afterword. Remember that anyone acquiring goods in a legitimate transaction will get at least the title that his transferor had. Thus, someone who obtains goods as a gift from someone who has valid title to them gets valid title. Someone who buys goods from a bona fide purchaser from a minor gets valid title, even if he knows his seller got the goods from a minor.

Sales of motor vehicles by nonowners. Since a sale of a motor vehicle is void in Texas unless the certificate of title is validly transferred, there can normally be no such thing as a bona fide purchaser of a motor vehicle who has not purchased the certificate of title. Thus, one cannot very well lose title to a Texas motor vehicle by entrusting it to a motor vehicle dealer.

About the only circumstances under which one may buy valid title to a Texas motor vehicle without also buying the certificate of title are when one buys the vehicle at a sale held to foreclose a lien, such as the sale of a repossessed vehicle or the sale of a vehicle by a garage in order to foreclose a mechanic's lien upon it.

Performance of Contracts for Sale of Goods

The seller of goods has one primary obligation—to deliver conforming goods to the buyer in accordance with the terms of the contract. The buyer has two primary obligations—to accept delivery of conforming goods, and to pay the agreed price.

The mechanics of the transaction may take many forms. The buyer may agree to pay in advance for the goods, in which case the payment obligation is completed before the delivery obligation becomes due. The seller may grant the buyer credit, in which case the delivery obligation is completed before the payment obligation arises. The contract may be an installment contract, in which case there will be more than one delivery and more than one payment.

Seller may agree to deliver the goods to buyer without moving them, and buyer may agree to pay on the spot, in which case buyer goes to where the goods are and picks them up, or seller may agree to move the goods to where buyer is, and buyer may agree to pay upon delivery.

The goods may be in the hands of a third-party bailee, with the seller agreeing to deliver either by furnishing a document of title to the goods or by furnishing the acknowledgment of the bailee of the buyer's right to possession of the goods. The buyer agrees to pay upon delivery of the document or acknowledgment. The seller and buyer may be at such a distance from each other that transportation of the goods by a third-party carrier is necessary. In such a case, the seller's delivery obligation will depend upon the shipping

32/ Performance of Contracts for Sale of Goods

terms agreed to by the parties. Buyer's payment obligation, in the absence of payment in advance or credit, may take one of three forms.

The parties may agree on C.O.D. (Collect on Delivery) terms, in which case the buyer must pay the delivering carrier the cost of the goods plus the shipping charges when the carrier delivers the goods. The parties may also agree to payment against documents. In such a transaction, the seller ships the goods and obtains a bill of lading for them from the carrier, the bill of course being a clean bill. The bill will ordinarily be a negotiable bill, and the goods will perhaps be consigned to the order of the seller and perhaps to the order of the seller's bank. The seller will attach to this an invoice showing the goods shipped. If the terms of the contract with the buyer require it, he will also attach proof that he has properly insured the goods against loss or damage in transit. He will then draw a draft upon the buyer for the price of the goods, making this payable to the order of the consignee of the bill of lading. The draft will usually be a sight draft, although it can be a time draft if the seller has agreed to grant short-term credit to the buyer.

If the draft and the bill of lading are drawn to the order of the seller, he will then endorse and negotiate them to his bank. If the draft and bill of lading are drawn to the order of the bank, the seller simply delivers them to the bank. In either event, the bank pays the seller the face value of the draft less a small discount, and then forwards the documents to a bank in the buyer's financial market. This bank notifies the buyer that the documents have arrived; buyer comes to the bank, inspects the documents, and, if all is in order, accepts or pays the draft as the case may be. The bank turns over to him the bill of lading, now endorsed to his order. When the goods arrive, the buyer may exchange the bill for the goods, thus completing the transaction.

The parties may also agree to a letter of credit transaction. Here, the buyer must obtain a letter of credit from a bank in his financial market. A bank, by issuing a letter of credit, essentially agrees to finance a purchase by agreeing to honor drafts drawn against it by the seller of the goods for the purchase price of the goods, provided that the draft is accompanied by documents showing that conforming goods have been shipped by the seller. Once the letter of credit is issued, the mechanics of the transaction are very similar to those of the payment against documents transaction.

The bill of lading will be negotiable, usually making the goods consignable to the order of the issuer of the credit. The draft will be a sight draft drawn upon the issuer of the credit. Insurance of the shipment by the seller is usually required. The seller will send the documents through banking channels to the issuer, which will honor the draft if the accompanying documents are in order. Issuer will then notify buyer of the arrival of the documents, buyer will reimburse issuer for the amount paid out on the draft, issuer will negotiate the bill of lading to buyer, and buyer may then exchange the bill for the goods when they arrive.

The seller may want the buyer to obtain a confirmed letter of credit. In such a case, the credit is issued by a bank in the buyer's financial market, but it must be confirmed by a bank in the seller's financial market. When the credit is confirmed, the seller may draw his drafts upon a bank in his locality; thus, he need not discount his draft.

The obligations of the parties to a letter of credit transaction will be covered in detail in the next section.

Seller's tender of delivery. Unless buyer has agreed to pay in advance or seller has granted buyer credit, delivery and payment are concurrent obligations. When this is true, seller must make a proper tender of delivery in order to trigger buyer's obligation to pay.

What constitutes tender of delivery is spelled out in UCC 2-503; the necessity of proper tender of delivery to trigger buyer's obligation to pay is found in UCC 2-507.

If buyer is to pick up the goods at seller's place of business, for example, seller must make conforming goods available to the buyer at that place and keep them available until buyer has a reasonable opportunity to pick them up. He must also notify buyer of their availability. If seller is to move the goods to buyer's place of business, he must notify buyer of the approximate time of delivery. He must make the delivery at a reasonable hour, and keep the goods available for a reasonable time. Seller has the right to expect that buyer will furnish facilities suitable for receipt of the goods. If buyer has not furnished such facilities, seller could justifiably retract his tender.

If the goods are in the hands of a bailee and are not to be moved, and if no document of title is outstanding for them, seller tenders delivery by procuring the bailee's acknowledgment of buyer's right to possession of the goods. If the goods are in the hands of a bailee and are not to be moved, and if a negotiable document of title is outstanding for them, seller may tender delivery by negotiating the document of title to buyer. Seller could also tender delivery by drawing a delivery order on the bailee ordering delivery of the goods to buyer, but buyer need not accept such a tender. In fact, the buyer should not accept such a tender unless the bailee has already accepted the delivery order, since a bailee is not obligated to deliver goods to the holder of an unaccepted delivery order.

If the bailee has issued a nonnegotiable document of title to the goods in this situation, seller may tender delivery by negotiating it to buyer. Buyer need not accept this form of tender either, and should not accept it unless it is accompanied by an acknowledgment by the bailee that he recognizes buyer's right to possession of the goods. Since a bailee who has issued a nonnegotiable document of title for goods may release the goods without taking up the document, there is no guarantee that buyer will be able to obtain goods for his document. If buyer does accept a tender in the form of a delivery order or a nonnegotiable document of title, but is unable to obtain the goods from the bailee, the tender is defective.

If the goods are to be shipped by carrier, the nature of the seller's delivery will depend upon the shipping term used by the parties; seller's obligations in this case will be discussed in detail later. In general, however, if the contract requires delivery of the goods to buyer at destination, proper tender is tender of conforming goods by the last carrier. If the contract requires shipment but not delivery, seller must see to it that proper documents are tendered to buyer as required by the shipping term used.

Buyer's tender of payment. UCC 2-325 provides that if the contract calls for payment by letter of credit, buyer must obtain an irrevocable letter of credit within a reasonable time after the contract is made. If the contract calls for a confirmed letter of credit, buyer must obtain an irrevocable letter of credit from a bank in his financial market and also obtain its confirmation by a bank in seller's financial market.

If the contract calls for payment against documents, buyer tenders payment by accepting or paying the draft accompanying the documents, as the case may be. According to UCC 2-514, buyer will be entitled to the documents upon acceptance of a draft only if the draft is payable more than three days after presentment. If it is payable three days or less after presentment, buyer must pay it in order to obtain the documents.

If the contract calls for payment at time of delivery, UCC 2-511 provides that buyer may tender payment in any commercially acceptable medium, unless otherwise agreed. However, seller has the right to demand payment in legal tender. Thus, buyer may tender payment in the form of a personal check, but seller need not accept the check. If seller refuses to take buyer's check, he may not accuse buyer of breach. Rather, he must give buyer a reasonable time within which to cash his check and obtain the required cash.

A tender of payment in the form of cash or commercial paper which is the primary obligation of a bank (a cashier's check, for example) is at the same time payment, if it is accepted. Payment in the form of a personal check does not become final until the check clears the drawee bank.

Buyer's inspection right. UCC 2–513 provides that buyer has the right to inspect tendered goods before he pays for them, unless he has given up that right. Essentially, he has the right to look over what is being delivered so that he can be sure that he is getting what he ordered.

Buyer gives up this right if he agrees to pay in advance. He also gives it up if he agrees to accept a C.O.D. shipment, or if he agrees to payment against documents. Under C.O.D. terms, the buyer must pay the carrier which delivers the goods in order to obtain the package containing the goods. Since the buyer cannot look inside the package before he gets possession, and since he must pay in order to obtain possession of the package, there is obviously no inspection possible. However, if the buyer and seller agree to "C.O.D., Inspection Allowed" terms, the buyer may open the package and inspect before he pays.

It is an improper tender of delivery for a seller to ship goods C.O.D. without the buyer's consent, unless inspection is allowed. The buyer may not be deprived of his inspection right without his consent. When the transaction calls for payment against documents, the buyer may well be called upon to pay for the goods several days before they arrive. If the term is "Payment against Documents, Inspection Allowed," the buyer may delay payment until the goods arrive and he has a chance to examine them. Otherwise, the only item the buyer may inspect are the documents.

The buyer should inspect the documents closely before paying or accepting the draft. If the documents disclose that the seller has not complied with his obligations under the contract, the buyer should not pay the draft. Payment or acceptance of the draft is a waiver of any breach of contract shown upon the face of the documents (UCC 2–605). The only safe way to pay or accept under such circumstances is to notify the seller that one reserves the right to claim damages for any defect in the delivery shown on the face of the documents.

Buyer's right to reject defective tender. A tender of delivery is defective if:
1. It deprives buyer of his inspection right without his consent, or
2. Documents are tendered rather than the required goods, or vice versa, or
3. Tender is made in the form of a nonnegotiable document of title or in the form of a delivery order, and buyer objects to such tender, or
4. The goods are not the goods which buyer ordered, or
5. The goods are damaged or otherwise not of the agreed quality, or
6. An improper quantity of goods is delivered, either too much or too little, or
7. The delivery is too late, or
8. The tendered documents indicate that seller has not performed his obligations under the contract.

If buyer means to object to an improper delivery, he must inform seller as soon as possible of his objections. The nonmerchant buyer must describe his objection in enough detail so that the seller knows what he is objecting to; the merchant buyer should explain his objections in detail. If the tender is nonconforming, the buyer may either accept the delivery and notify the seller that he is claiming breach, or he may reject the shipment.

UCC 2–601 provides that when buyer objects to an improper delivery he may accept the entire shipment (even when seller is delivering more goods than the contract calls for), reject the entire shipment, or accept some commercial units of the goods and reject others.

According to UCC 2-607, buyer must pay for accepted goods at the contract rate, but may claim damages for breach as a deduction from contract price. Thus, if seller delivers too much, and the market price of the delivered goods is higher than the contract price, buyer may accept the entire shipment and realize a windfall profit. On the other hand, if seller delivers too much and market price is now below contract price, buyer may reject the entire shipment and perhaps escape an unprofitable bargain.

Failure to inform seller of a rejection will render the rejection improper, according to UCC 2-602. When both parties to the contract are merchants, seller has the right to demand that buyer give him a detailed statement of the defects which caused buyer to reject an allegedly improper delivery. Failure to furnish such statement upon demand is a waiver of buyer's right to claim damages because of the defects (UCC 2-605). Failure by either a merchant buyer or a nonmerchant buyer to explain his reasons for a rejection will be a waiver when the defect is of such a nature that the seller could cure it if he knew about it. It goes without saying that a rejection, to be effective, must be made as soon as possible after tender of delivery.

Seller's right to cure defective tender of delivery. Under the provisions of UCC 2-508, seller may cure a defective delivery under two circumstances.

If the defective delivery is made before the time for delivery specified in the contract, seller may cure if he can make a conforming delivery before the time for delivery specified in the contract, and if he tells buyer that he is going to attempt to cure. If the second delivery is conforming, the defect is of course cured. If it is nonconforming, buyer may reject and seller may try again to cure if he can make another delivery before the delivery time specified.

If the defective delivery is made at the last minute, but seller reasonably believed that he was making a conforming delivery—so that buyer's rejection comes as a surprise to seller—seller is entitled to a reasonable time within which to cure if he notifies buyer of his intention. However, in this situation seller must be able to show that he truly believed that he was making a conforming delivery.

Buyer's right to revocation of acceptance. Under the provisions of UCC 2-608, it is possible for the buyer to revoke his acceptance of goods already accepted. This may be done under two circumstances.

If the goods appeared to be conforming when buyer accepted them, but a defect appears later that could not reasonably have been discovered upon pre-acceptance inspection—and the defect substantially reduces the value of the goods to the buyer—the buyer may revoke his acceptance. Buyer must of course do this as soon as possible after discovering the objectionable defect. If the buyer knowingly accepted defective goods upon the assurances of the seller that he would cure the defects, and if the seller has been given a reasonable time to cure the defects and has been unable to do so, the buyer may revoke his acceptance.

Any revocation of acceptance must occur before the goods decline in value due to normal wear and tear. Buyer must of course inform seller of the reasons for the revocation of acceptance, in detail if buyer is a merchant.

Buyer's duty with respect to rejected goods or goods the acceptance of which has been revoked. Buyer's duty with respect to such goods depends upon whether or not he is a merchant. If buyer is not a merchant, his duties are spelled out in UCC 2-602. After he notifies seller of the rejection or revocation of acceptance, he must keep the goods in a safe place until seller removes them. During this period buyer must not exercise any ownership rights over the goods (by using them, selling them, or whatever). Otherwise buyer will be said to have accepted them after all.

The merchant buyer has more duties with respect to such goods. UCC 2-603 provides that, after notification to seller of the rejection or revocation and the reasons for it, buyer must follow any commercially reasonable instructions of the seller for disposal of the goods. If no such instructions are forthcoming within a reasonable time, buyer may use his own judgment with respect to the goods. He could:

1. Ship them back to seller at seller's expense, or
2. Put them in storage at seller's expense, or
3. Sell them to a third party and account to seller for the proceeds, or
4. Keep them in a safe place on his own premises until seller comes after them.

If the goods are perishable or otherwise threaten to decline rapidly in value, buyer must salvage them while they still have value by selling them to a third party without waiting for disposal instructions.

When such goods are sold to a third party, buyer must inform seller how much the goods were sold for. From this sum, buyer may deduct his damages for seller's breach in sending improper goods, and his expenses in arranging the sale. If anything is left after these deductions, buyer must remit it to seller. If damages plus expenses exceed these proceeds, buyer may claim the deficiency from seller.

Any instructions furnished by seller to buyer with respect to disposal of rejected goods are not proper if they do not include a promise by seller to indemnify buyer for any expenses which might be incurred. So long as buyer acts in good faith in disposing of such goods, seller may not claim that buyer has accepted or converted them to his own use, nor may he claim any sort of damages from buyer.

Anticipatory breach. When a party announces in advance of the time for performance that he will not perform, the innocent party may:

1. Wait for a reasonable time to see if the breaching party will repent and perform; or
2. Treat the contract as breached and invoke all remedies to which he is entitled, even if he has told the breaching party that he still expects performance; and
3. Suspend his own performance.

The above provisions are found in UCC 2-601. This section also states that an anticipatory breach must substantially impair the value of the contract to the innocent party before the above measures will be justified.

According to UCC 6-111 the party committing an anticipatory breach may retract his breach if he does so before his next performance is due, unless the innocent party has cancelled the contract or otherwise changed his position because of the anticipatory repudiation. Retraction of the anticipatory repudiation must be communicated to the other party; if valid, it will restore the contract to full force and effect.

Right to assurance of performance. When a party to a contract for sale of goods has reasonable grounds to doubt the ability of the other party to perform as promised, he may demand from the other party reasonable assurance of that party's ability to perform. If the party upon whom such a demand is made does not furnish the requested assurance within a reasonable time (not to exceed thirty days), the requesting party may treat this as a repudiation of the contract.

These provisions are found in UCC 2-609. The section goes into no more detail; however, common sense provides some enlightenment. Should the solvency of a credit buyer be in question, for instance, seller might demand proof of solvency, a partial payment in advance of delivery, the furnishing of a surety, or something comparable. Should the ability of a seller to make a timely delivery be called into question, a buyer might require the seller to furnish some sort of proof of ability to deliver.

Installment contracts. An installment contract is one in which the seller has the right to deliver goods in installments rather than in one delivery. UCC 2-612 provides the law in this area. Buyer may reject any installment which is nonconforming if the nonconformity substantially reduces the value of that installment.

Furthermore, if the breach of an installment or installments substantially impairs the value of the entire contract, the innocent party may treat the breach as a breach of the entire contract. However, if the innocent party wishes to claim breach of an installment as grounds for repudiation of the entire contract, he must inform the breaching party of this fact. The innocent party may not claim that the entire contract is repudiated if he demands performance of future installments, if he brings suit only for breach of past installments, or if he accepts performance of any installment after claiming breach of the entire contract.

A court may be reluctant to recognize a breach of a late installment as a breach of the entire contract if the breaching party has a good performance record. However, a breach of the first installment might well be considered to be a breach of the entire contract. In general, the later the breached installment, the less likely it is that a breach of that installment will be considered a breach of the entire contract.

Duties of parties under shipping terms in common use. Each shipping term in common use imposes a package of duties upon each party to the contract. Each party must perform all the prescribed duties; failure in any area could be considered a breach.

Under "Ex Factory" terms (or "Ex Warehouse," "Ex Mill," etc.) the seller undertakes no obligation to ship the goods. The seller must make conforming goods available to the buyer at the named place, and inform the buyer that they are available. The buyer arranges for the shipping himself, and has all responsibility during the shipping process.

Under "F.O.B (Free on Board) Shipping Point" terms, the seller must ship conforming goods and obtain a clean bill of lading from the carrier. He must also inform the buyer of the time of shipment. The buyer must insure the goods if he wants them insured; he has risk of loss during shipment. The buyer must also pay the shipping charges—goods are generally shipped "collect" under these terms. F.O.B. Shipping Point is one of those terms, also, where payment for the goods against documents is required. If the buyer wants the seller to pay shipping charges, he may seek to have the term read, "F.O.B. Shipping Point, Freight Prepaid." The buyer may also change the payment against documents feature by negotiation.

Under C.I.F. (Cost, Insurance, Freight) terms, the price seller quotes buyer for the goods includes the cost of the goods plus the cost of shipping and the cost of insurance against loss or damage in transit. Seller must ship conforming goods, obtain a clean bill of lading from the carrier, notify buyer of shipment, prepay the shipping charges, and insure the goods while in transit. Seller must also furnish a proper invoice. Buyer is obligated to pay against documents under this term, unless otherwise agreed.

Under C&F (Cost and Freight) terms, seller assumes the same obligations as he does under C.I.F., except that he need not insure the goods. C&F also requires payment against documents.

Under C.I.F. and C&F terms, the parties may vary the obligations under the terms in certain ways. If the contract calls for payment on the basis of "net landed weight" or "delivered weight" or the like, buyer must pay for the weight of goods received, not for weight of goods shipped. If the goods are of a nature that shrink or dry out in transit, the inclusion of such a term in the contract throws the risk of loss due to shrinkage and the like onto the seller. The seller will quote a price based upon weight shipped less estimated shrinkage, but the goods must be weighed at the destination and an adjustment made according to the true landed weight.

Buyer may obtain for himself an inspection right under C.I.F. or C&F terms by getting seller to include a "Payment on Arrival" term in the contract. Buyer need not pay here until the goods arrive and he has a chance to inspect.

Under "F.A.S. Vessel" (Free Alongside Vessel) terms, seller is obligated to get the goods alongside the vessel ready for loading at his own expense. He must also obtain a receipt from the owners of the vessel for which buyer may obtain a bill of lading. Buyer must name the vessel under these terms and must also furnish the berth and sailing date. In short, buyer must tell seller where to deliver the goods at the port from which the goods will be shipped, and when to deliver there. Buyer is also responsible for getting the goods on board the vessel and for all that occurs thereafter.

Under "F.O.B. Vessel" terms, seller is responsible for getting the goods on board the vessel. As proof that he has done this, seller must obtain a clean "on board" bill of lading from the shipping company. Seller may ship the goods "collect" on the vessel, and seller is not responsible for insurance. Buyer must furnish the name of the vessel, the sailing date, and the loading berth. Normally, both "F.O.B. Vessel" and "F.A.S. Vessel" require payment against documents by buyer.

Under "Ex Ship" terms, seller must get the goods off a ship at the named port. Seller has the option of choosing the ship under these terms, unless the parties agree otherwise. Seller must pay the charges levied by the ocean carrier, and must notify the buyer of the estimated date of arrival of the ship at the named port. If any import duties are payable upon the goods, buyer must pay them. If any storage charges are levied for the time the goods are on the dock in the port of unloading, buyer must pay these.

Under "Ex Dock" terms, seller must arrange things so that buyer can pick up the goods at the dock in the named port without difficulty. Seller must pay all shipping charges; he must also pay import duties and storage charges on the dock for a reasonable time after unloading, and notify buyer of the estimated time of arrival of the goods in the destination port.

Under "F.O.B. Destination" terms, seller is obligated to deliver the goods to buyer at the named destination. Seller is responsible for all shipping and for paying all shipping charges. If the goods do not reach their destination, seller may well be liable to buyer for nondelivery.

Under "No Arrival, No Sale" terms, seller is also obligated to deliver the goods to buyer at the destination. However, if the goods do not arrive, seller is not responsible unless his actions cause the nonarrival.

Casualty to identified goods. If the goods are lost or damaged in transit or before performance of the contract is completed, the effect of the loss upon the contract depends upon who has risk of loss at the time the casualty occurs.

If it happens after risk of loss has passed to buyer, buyer must pay for the goods, even though he may not receive them at all or receive them in damaged condition. If it happens while risk of loss is on seller, the result depends upon whether or not the goods were identified when the contract was made. If the goods were so identified, total destruction of the goods discharges the contract. Partial damage or destruction gives buyer an option. He may accept the damaged goods and pay fair value for them, or he may cancel the contract (UCC 2-613).

If the goods were not identified when the contract was made, seller could identify other goods to the contract to replace the destroyed or damaged goods. Seller would be required to do this, or to pay damages for breach for improper delivery, unless identification of other goods is impossible. In such a case, the contract is discharged.

Substituted performance. UCC 2-614 provides that if the agreed manner of delivery becomes impracticable (or if the agreed berthing, loading, or unloading facilities become unavailable), but a commercially reasonable substitute is available, the substitute must be tendered and accepted.

If domestic or foreign governmental regulations make payment in the agreed manner impossible, seller may withhold performance unless buyer can furnish a commercially equivalent medium of payment. If delivery has already been made, payment by buyer in the manner allowed by the new regulations will be sufficient.

Some explanation of the provisions of this section on payment may be in order. Thus: An American exporter may have agreed to sell goods to an importer in Guatador, the contract providing for payment in U.S. dollars. After performance of the contract began but before payment was made, the government of Guatador imposed such stringent restrictions upon the ability of its citizens to buy foreign currency that payment for the goods in dollars by the importer became impossible. If the American exporter had not made delivery of the goods, and if he did not want to take payment in Guatadoran pesos, he could withhold delivery unless buyer could pay in dollars. But if the buyer had already taken delivery of the goods, the American exporter would have to accept payment in pesos if that were the only medium of payment open to the buyer.

Discharge due to unforeseen circumstances. When a seller finds himself unable to meet his delivery commitments due to totally unforeseen circumstances, he may escape some or all of his obligations by following the procedures set out in UCC 2-615. Such unforeseen circumstances might consist of unanticipated governmental regulations affecting the supply of an essential raw material; an unexpected diminution of the supply of a raw material caused, perhaps, by war in the country from which the commodity comes; a strike interfering with seller's ability to meet the demand for his product; an explosion which seriously damages seller's productive capacity; or something similar. When this occurs, seller must notify buyer of his problem and state how much of buyer's order he can deliver and when he can deliver it. By informing buyer of his problem, seller frees himself from the obligation to deliver as he had originally promised.

Upon receipt of such notice, UCC 2-616 gives the buyer two options. He may inform seller that he is canceling the contract, which notice operates as a discharge, or he may inform seller that he is modifying the contract so as to reduce seller's obligation to that delivery which seller said he could make under the changed conditions. If buyer makes no response to seller's notification of changed circumstances within a reasonable time (not exceeding thirty days), the contract is automatically discharged.

Letters of Credit

The nature of a letter of credit transaction has been described under the heading of performance of contracts for the sale of goods; the law governing letters of credit is found in Article 5 of the Uniform Commercial Code, but the code allows parties to these transactions much leeway in devising their own contract terms.

Parties to a letter of credit. There are three essential parties to a letter of credit:
1. The *issuer*—usually a bank doing business in the buyer's financial market. The issuer issues the letter of credit and agrees to honor drafts drawn under it if the drafts are properly drawn and accompanied by proper documentation.
2. The *customer*—the buyer of the goods. He procures the issuer's promise to issue the credit.
3. The *beneficiary*—the seller of the goods. The letter of credit is issued primarily for his benefit, since he is the one who has the right to draw drafts under it.

Generally, a bank in the beneficiary's financial market will also be involved in the transaction. This bank may be called the *advising bank* or the *confirming bank*. An advising bank notifies the beneficiary that he may discount drafts drawn under the draft there, or send drafts drawn under the credit through it for collection. The advising bank incurs no liability as a party to the letter of credit. A confirming bank agrees to undertake the legal responsibility to honor drafts drawn under the letter of credit. So far as the beneficiary is concerned, a confirming bank is just as liable upon the letter of credit as is the issuer.

Types of letters of credit. The liabilities, privileges, and obligations of parties to a letter of credit are governed by the provisions of the credit. There are several types and classifications of letters of credit which must be understood.

A *revocable credit* may be revoked by the issuer at any time before it honors drafts drawn under the credit, without the knowledge or consent of any other party. An *irrevocable credit* may not be revoked without the consent of the customer and beneficiary once these parties have had their rights established under it. According to UCC 5-106, the customer's rights are established when the issuer sends him notice of the issuance of the credit. The beneficiary's rights are established when he receives advice of the issuance of the credit. An irrevocable credit may be revoked or modified without notice to any party whose rights are not established.

A letter of credit is revocable unless it is expressly made irrevocable.

A *lump-sum credit* entitles the beneficiary to draw only one draft under it. The beneficiary of an *installment credit* may draw as many drafts as he pleases, so long as the total face value of the drafts does not exceed the face value of the credit. UCC 5-110 provides that a credit is an installment credit unless it provides otherwise.

The beneficiary of a *transferable credit* may assign the right to draw drafts under it. The beneficiary of a *nontransferable credit* may not do this, but he may assign the right to receive proceeds under the credit. Under UCC 5-116, a credit is nontransferable unless it provides otherwise.

The beneficiary of a *straight credit* may not transfer any of his rights under it. Drafts drawn under a straight credit must be payable to the order of beneficiary, and they must not be negotiated to anyone other than banks in the collection process.

A *notation credit* is an installment credit which provides that the issuer must not honor a draft drawn under it unless the draft is accompanied by proof that its drawing has been noted upon the letter of credit (UCC 5-108). If the installment credit is not specifically made a notation credit, it is of necessity a *nonnotation credit*, and drafts drawn under it may be honored without proof of notation.

A *clean credit* obligates the issuer to honor drafts drawn under it if they are drawn by the beneficiary and the draft does not overdraw the credit. Such credits do not require that drafts drawn under them be accompanied by any documentation. They are not used in commercial transactions to any great extent.

A *documentary credit* requires that drafts drawn under it be accompanied by specified documentation. It also provides that the issuer must not honor the draft unless it is accompanied by the proper documents in good order.

Form of credit. UCC 5-104 provides that a letter of credit must be in writing and signed by a representative of the issuer. A confirmation of a credit must also be in writing and signed by a representative of the confirming bank. A modification of a credit must also be in writing; it must be signed by a representative of the issuer and by a representative of the confirming bank if the credit is confirmed. However, there is no specified form prescribed for a letter of credit.

Consideration unnecessary. No consideration is needed either to establish a letter of credit, or to modify it (UCC 5-105).

Usual provisions. Since a contract of sale provision calling for payment by letter of credit requires that the buyer obtain an irrevocable credit—and since the seller has much more assurance of being paid under an irrevocable credit—revocable credits are none too common.

Since the letter of credit transaction is a modified form of the payment against documents transaction, a clean credit would hardly suit the purpose of the ordinary buyer. Therefore, documentary credits are used in sales transactions. The required documents may vary a bit according to the nature of the transaction; but at the minimum the draft drawn by the beneficiary must be accompanied by a clean bill of lading and an invoice showing that the beneficiary has shipped conforming goods. Usually a certificate of insurance is also required, unless the shipping term used does not require the seller to insure the goods. The buyer may require that the documents include a certificate of inspection of the goods by a reputable third party at the point of shipment. If the transaction is an international one, government regulations may require the furnishing of other documents, such as export declarations, export licenses, consular invoices, import licenses, certificates of compliance with various product quality regulations of the destination country, and so on.

The beneficiary might be anxious for the credit to be transferable—so that, perhaps, he may assign his rights under it to his supplier—while the customer may not want it to be transferable because he has no control over assignments of rights under transferable credits. The relative bargaining power of the parties will bear strongly here. Both issuer and customer would feel more comfortable if an installment credit is also a notation credit. Problems of the beneficiary overdrawing thereby would be minimized.

Error in transmission in terms. More than likely, the beneficiary will get the advice confirming his rights under the credit from the advising bank; his rights will become established at this time. According to UCC 5-107, if the advising bank makes an error in describing the terms of the credit to the beneficiary, the credit becomes established on its original terms, not on the erroneous terms transmitted by the bank. The issuer is not liable for any communication failure here. Unless otherwise provided, the customer assumes the risk inherent in all such mix-ups.

Rights of parties upon revocation of revocable credit. The issuer may revoke a revocable credit at any time. It must give notice of the revocation to the parties, but the revocation is effective when made, as per UCC 5-106. The parties have no recourse in the event of revocation, unless drafts have been honored or negotiated before notice of revocation is received by the parties involved. In such a case, the party to whom the draft has been negotiated (or the party honoring the draft) is entitled to have the draft honored by the issuer, and the issuer becomes entitled to reimbursement from the customer.

Thus, if the issuer revokes a revocable credit, it must inform the parties of its action as soon as possible so as to make the revocation effective. If the beneficiary has already discounted his draft with the advising bank, or if the confirming bank has already honored a draft drawn by the beneficiary, the revocation is too late with respect to that draft.

Transfer of rights and assignment of right to proceeds. Under UCC 5-116 the beneficiary may assign the right to draw drafts under a credit only if the credit is transferable. The transfer becomes effective only when the issuer is notified of it.

This section also provides that the beneficiary of a nontransferable credit does have the right to assign the right to receive the proceeds of the credit, unless the credit expressly denies this right (as does a straight credit). An assignment of proceeds becomes effective when the letter of credit or advice of credit is delivered by the beneficiary to the assignee. The beneficiary must also inform the issuer of the assignment in writing. Once the issuer is informed of the assignment it may legitimately refuse to honor any draft drawn under the credit which is not accompanied by the letter of credit or the advice of credit itself.

Notice that the assignment of proceeds is not an assignment of the right to draw under the credit. In a sense it is a restriction of the right of the beneficiary to make the payee of the draft anyone he chooses. Once the assignment is made and the issuer is informed, the payee of drafts drawn must be either the assignee or a person of whom the assignee approves. More often than not, the assignee of the right to proceeds under a letter of credit will be the supplier of the goods the beneficiary intends to ship his customer under the contract, the assignment being a way the beneficiary can finance his purchase of the goods.

Time allowed issuer for honor or rejection of drafts. When a draft is presented to a bank under a letter of credit, the bank need not decide immediately whether to honor or to dishonor. Without dishonor the bank may hold the draft until the close of the third business day following the presentment. It may defer its decision even longer than that if the presenter consents. These provisions are found in UCC 5-112. The issuer must check all accompanying documents before honoring the draft to ascertain that all is in order. This cannot be done in a short time.

Issuer's decision to honor or to dishonor. The issuer's decision on whether or not to honor must be based upon the compliance of the draft with the terms of the credit and upon the state of the accompanying documents. If the draft is not in compliance with the terms of the credit, the issuer must dishonor it. Thus, the issuer must dishonor if:

1. The credit is nontransferable and the drawer is someone other than the beneficiary.
2. The credit is transferable, but the drawer is someone other than the beneficiary and the issuer has not been notified of any transfer of the right to draw.
3. The credit is nontransferable, but the issuer has received notice of an assignment of the right to receive proceeds, and the draft is not drawn to the order of the assignee or accompanied by the credit or advice of credit itself.
4. The credit is a notation credit, but the draft is not accompanied by proof of notation.
5. The draft overdraws the face value of the credit.

There are, of course, other similar defects which would justify dishonor.

If the accompanying documents are deficient or defective, the issuer must dishonor. Among the reasons for such dishonor might be:

1. The fact that a required document is missing.
2. The bill of lading is foul, indicating that the goods were damaged when shipped.
3. The invoice indicates that nonconforming goods were shipped.
4. A required certificate of inspection shows that the goods are nonconforming.

5. One or more of the documents shows obvious signs of material alteration or forgery.

The customer will have great difficulty in stopping payment upon a draft if the draft itself and the accompanying documents are all in order, even though the customer knows that, for instance:

1. The beneficiary has shipped nonconforming goods, although the documents show the shipment of conforming goods.
2. The beneficiary has shipped no goods at all—the documents are forgeries.
3. The goods will not arrive because the vessel carrying them has been shipwrecked.

UCC 5-114, the section dealing with these problems, provides that the customer's only avenue of recourse here is to go to a court of competent jurisdiction and obtain an injunction forbidding the issuer to honor the draft.

Notice that the issuer is not in any way responsible for the performance of the customer-beneficiary contract. Breaches by the beneficiary are the customer's problem, so long as the documents accompanying a draft are in order.

Clever rascality by someone at the beneficiary's end of the transaction may well result in the issuer's honoring spurious drafts and being forced to dishonor legitimate ones. For example:

1. Dishonest persons forge a set of documents showing shipment of conforming goods by the beneficiary at a time when he has not yet shipped any goods. The documents appear to be in order, so the issuer honors the draft. Later, the beneficiary ships the goods and sends honest documents; the issuer dishonors this draft because the credit would otherwise be overdrawn.
2. The beneficiary assigns right to draw drafts under a transferable credit. He never informs the issuer of the assignment. Instead he draws a draft payable to himself, attaches to it proper documents, and procures honor by the issuer. The transferee then draws a draft and attaches to it proper documents. The issuer will dishonor this because it overdraws the credit, though in the short run this rewards the beneficiary's dishonesty.

When the issuer rightfully honors a draft drawn under a credit, it is entitled to immediate reimbursement by its customer. Customer has no choice but to pay. If there is a breach of the underlying contract, the customer's only recourse is against the beneficiary.

If the customer becomes insolvent after his rights become established under a letter of credit, the issuer may be unable to obtain reimbursement for honor of the draft. In such a case, the issuer may well end up taking a loss—it cannot dishonor the draft because of the customer's insolvency. It will, however, have access to the goods, so long as it still controls the accompanying documents.

If the issuer wrongfully honors a draft, the customer is under no obligation to make reimbursement. In such a case, the issuer's recourse is against the beneficiary, because UCC 5-111 imposes a warranty upon the beneficiary when he draws and transfers a draft drawn under a letter of credit that he has complied with all of the terms and conditions of the credit. If the honor was wrongful, it was probably because of some sort of noncompliance by the beneficiary.

If the issuer wrongfully dishonors a draft, UCC 5-115 provides that the holder of the draft or other person entitled to its honor may sue the issuer for damages. The holder also acquires all of the rights in the documents of a person in the position of a seller under UCC 2-707. He may, for instance, use the documents to acquire the goods and then resell the goods.

Should the issuer wrongfully revoke an irrevocable credit, the beneficiary is in the position of a seller who is a victim of an anticipatory breach of contract, and has all of the rights of such a person against the issuer.

Honor of drafts under installment nonnotation credit. The possibility exists that a nonnotation installment credit may be overdrawn. In such a case the issuer may honor drafts drawn under the credit in order of presentment until the credit is exhausted. The last drafts presented for payment will be the ones dishonored.

As between good-faith holders of such drafts, however, the order of issue determines the relative rights of the parties, not the order of presentment for payment. For example: Able is beneficiary of an $8,000 installment credit. On May 1 he discounts a $3,000 draft under the credit with First Bank. This credit is duly honored by issuer on May 5. On May 3, Able draws a draft on Issuer for $3,000 in favor of Baker for consideration. On May 5, Able draws another $3,000 draft under this credit in favor of Charles for consideration. Baker is slow about collecting upon his draft. The Charles draft reaches Issuer on May 7, and is honored. The Baker draft reaches Issuer on May 10 and is dishonored, because it overdraws the credit. Baker finds out that Charles had his draft honored by Issuer, though it was drawn after his, Baker's, draft. Baker therefore demands $3,000 of Charles. Baker recovers, because he purchased his draft before Charles purchased his.

Credit Cards

The credit card is a quite recent consumer credit device. Because of its novelty there was not much law on it for many years. That situation has now changed. In 1970 Congress added Sections 1642, 1643, and 1644 to the Consumer Credit Protection Act, providing some regulation in this area. Since that time more regulation has been added so that a substantial body of law has been created.

Two sorts of credit cards are in common use: the two-party card and the three-party card. The nature of these will be discussed first.

Two-party cards. The two-party card is often issued by a merchant to his customers when the customers open revolving charge accounts with him. The card is essentially proof that the customer has such an account; only the issuer will honor it. Thus, all transactions involving the card involve a contract between the card owner and the issuer. The Sears credit card is a typical example of the two-party card.

Three-party cards. The three-party card is more useful to the consumer than is the two-party card. It is therefore more common.

Three-party cards are issued by banks or other financial organizations. The owner may use them to buy goods on credit from merchants who have no relationship to the issuer (other than a contractual relationship). Whenever the owner of a three-party card uses it to charge a purchase, three contracts will affect the relationship of the parties involved.

The issuer and the customer enter into a contract when the card is issued. This contract will deal with ownership rights in the card, payment terms, finance charges, and so on. When the customer buys goods from the honoring merchant, he enters into the usual contract for the sale of goods with that merchant. The fact that the price of the goods was charged to a credit card account will not affect the basic contract of sale. When the issuer agrees to permit the honoring merchant to honor his credit cards, a contract comes into being between issuer and honoring merchant. This involves the terms and conditions under which issuer will reimburse honoring merchant for goods sold under the card, and the circumstances under which issuer may charge back customer purchases to the honoring merchant. Visa (formerly Bankamericard) and Master Charge are the most commonly used three-party cards.

Issuance of credit cards. Before 1970, an issuer could issue a credit card simply by mailing it to a desired customer without the customer filing any application for it. 15 USC 1642 has made that practice unlawful. Under present law, a credit card may be issued only under two circumstances:

1. In response to an accepted application for it, and
2. To replace an existing card which is about to expire.

When a card is issued, the issuer must make certain disclosures to the customer with respect to it. These include:

1. Disclosures required to be made under the Federal Truth-in-Lending Act with respect to finance charges and so on.
2. Disclosures required to be made under the Fair Credit Billing Act with respect to the customer's right to contest billing errors.
3. Disclosures with respect to the liability of the card owner in case of loss or theft of the card.

The first two matters are discussed at length in the chapter on consumer protection and will not be repeated here. The third matter will be discussed next.

Liability of cardholder in case of loss or theft. Before 1970, the liability of a card owner for unauthorized purchases on his credit card was in theory unlimited. Accrual of liability for unauthorized charges stopped when the owner notified the issuer of the loss or theft, but the owner was liable for all charges made to the account before the notice was received. 15 USC 1643 changed this. The maximum liability of a card owner for unauthorized charges to his account is now $50, no matter how much is unauthorizedly charged. In order for the issuer to be able to assert even this $50 liability, the following conditions must have been met:

1. The card must have been validly issued under 15 USC 1642.
2. The card must have been accepted by the owner—that is, he must have signed it or used it. (If it is a new card stolen from the mail, it is unaccepted and the owner is not liable upon it.)
3. The card must have on it a means of identifying the owner. Three such means of identification are acceptable:
   a. A photograph, or
   b. A signature block, or
   c. A thumb print.
4. The issuer must inform the owner of this potential liability.
5. The issuer must furnish the owner a stamped self-addressed envelope for use in informing issuer of the loss or theft of the card.

If one of the above conditions has not been met, the issuer cannot hold the customer liable for any unauthorized charges to the account. In addition, the issuer is not liable for unauthorized charges to the account made after he informs the issuer of a loss, theft, or whatever. It behooves the credit card owner to use care in guarding his card from loss, theft, or unauthorized use; it also behooves him to keep his envelope from the issuer in a safe, accessible place. He also should inform the issuer of a loss or theft as soon as possible after the misfortune is discovered.

Availability of defenses to payment of owner against issuer. Such problems as the following have concerned persons involved with credit cards since the invention of this payment medium: Hart buys goods from Knave and charges them to his Ace credit card. Knave is guilty of breach of warranty with respect to the goods, but he refuses to do anything about it. Hart therefore refuses to pay Ace for the goods. Could Ace force Hart to pay?

Two legal theories were advanced under which Hart could be forced to pay. One was that Ace was in the position of a holder in due course of commercial paper; therefore Hart's personal defense to payment should not be valid against Ace. The other was that a three-party credit card is in essence a letter of credit. Since the issuer of a letter of credit is not responsible for performance of the customer-beneficiary contract, Ace need not get involved in Hart's problem with Knave. If Ace pays Knave, Hart must pay Ace.

The courts never did speak authoritatively on this matter—Congress forestalled them in 1975. 15 USC 1666i provides that the owner of a credit card may assert defenses against the issuer under named circumstances, which are:

1. If the card is a two-party card, and the seller is the issuer, or
2. If the honoring merchant is controlled by the issuer, or
3. If the honoring merchant and the issuer are under common control (e.g., both are subsidiaries of the same parent), or
4. If the honoring merchant is a franchised dealer in issuer's products, or
5. Issuer through material mailed to the customer solicited him to buy honoring merchant's products by mail.

If none of the above circumstances prevails, the customer may still use his defense against the issuer if:

1. He has made a good-faith effort to resolve his dispute with the honoring merchant, and
2. The amount of the disputed transaction exceeds fifty dollars, and
3. The place where the disputed transaction occurred was in the same state as the card owner's mailing address, or within 100 miles of that address.

In short, the customer may use his defenses if there is a close business relationship between the issuer and the honoring merchant of one of the five sorts described by the statute. Otherwise, he may use his defenses if more than fifty dollars is involved, and, for example, a customer living in Marshall, Texas, bought his defective goods in El Paso, Texas, or Shreveport, Louisiana. Since El Paso is in Texas, the defense will hold, even though the distance between El Paso and Marshall is great. Since Shreveport is within 100 miles of Marshall, the defense will hold even though Shreveport is not in Texas. If the customer had entered into the transaction in New Orleans, however, he would have to pay, since New Orleans is not in Texas and is more than 100 miles from Marshall.

The defense cannot be asserted with respect to portions of the price of the disputed goods paid before the customer informs the issuer of his problem; it applies only to the unpaid balance at the time the issuer is informed.

Credit limits on credit cards. Issuers usually specify that the owner may have no larger balance than a specified sum outstanding upon his card. The issuer may therefore refuse to permit a charge which causes the customer to exceed his credit limit. However, increases in the limit may be applied for and granted, within the bounds of the creditworthiness of the customer.

This ceiling may of course also be reduced by the issuer, or the issuer may revoke the customer's credit altogether. Revocation for slowness in making payments is quite lawful, but revocation for other reasons could be dangerous, particularly reasons which violate the Equal Credit Opportunity Act.

The issuer-honoring merchant contract. When issuer and honoring merchant enter into their contract, the honoring merchant may advertise that he honors the issuer's card; the issuer pays the merchant for the goods the holder of the issuer's card buys at the merchant's establishment. The issuer, however, does not pay the merchant 100 percent of the amount charged to the issuer by the cardholder. Rather, these charge slips are discounted by 5 percent or more, the rate of discount determined by contract. If, therefore, Hart buys a $150 suit from King Men's Wear and charges his purchase to his Ace credit card, King may receive only $142.50 from Ace, though Ace will bill Hart for $150.

The honoring merchant must use care in honoring the issuer's cards; otherwise he runs the risk of having a sales draft charged back to him by the issuer. First, the issuer will furnish the merchant a list of numbers of revoked, lost, stolen, and expired cards. The merchant should check the number of a proffered card against this list. If he honors a card bearing a number appearing on this list, his negligence will prove costly—a chargeback is almost inevitable.

Secondly, the issuer-merchant contract will usually provide that all charges in excess of a named sum, perhaps fifty dollars, must be approved by the issuer before the sales draft will be honored. The merchant must be aware of the limit, whatever it is, and be sure to obtain approval of these large charges.

Thirdly, the merchant is under a duty to check the identity of all customers presenting credit cards. Since all cards now have signature blocks, it is a fairly simple matter to compare the customer's signature on the sales draft with the signature on the card. It is also easy to ask the customer to present some other type of identification. In any event, if the merchant negligently honors a lost or stolen card and the issuer is unable to collect the amount charged from the owner of the card, a chargeback will follow.

Fourthly, if the customer asserts a defense against the issuer, and the customer has the right to refuse to pay issuer, the issuer may charge back.

Finally, if the customer returns the goods to the merchant and informs the issuer of the return, there will obviously be a chargeback.

The issuer may not require the merchant to obtain any service from him as part of the consideration for permitting him to honor the issuer's cards. 15 USC 1666g forbids such tying arrangements. If the merchant wants to limit his relationship to the issuer to the credit card relationship, that is his privilege.

Cash discounts. Suppose that King Men's Wear honors Ace credit cards. Spade wants to buy a $200 men's suit from King. He may pay cash for it or charge it to his Ace credit card. He knows that if he charges it to the Ace card, he must pay $200 plus finance charge for the suit, while King receives only $190 from the transaction (assuming an Ace discount rate of 5 percent). So Spade asks King if he would sell the $200 suit for $195 cash. If King agrees to do this, Spade saves $5 and finance charges, while King gains $5. Ace, by losing a credit card charge, loses $10 and finance charges. Could King lawfully agree to such a bargain?

Before 1975, such action by King would have almost certainly breached his contract with Ace, since most issuer-merchant contracts contained provisions forbidding the merchant to grant cash discounts to his customers. Now, however, 15 USC 1666f renders such contract provisions unlawful. However, merchants are not required to grant such discounts: King may accept Spade's offer if he wants to, but Spade cannot legally complain if he does not.

Returns and refunds. Suppose that Spade buys a $40 gizmo from Hart and charges it to his Ace credit card account. The gizmo is defective, and Spade complains to Hart about it. Hart takes the gizmo back and gives Spade a $40 cash refund. What happens to the $40 debit to Spade's credit card account?

The answer, of course, is nothing. If Hart gives Spade cash, Spade cannot also get the $40 debit reversed; if he could, he would be making $40 from this transaction. Spade should use the $40 he gets from Hart to pay Ace. If he does not do this, finance charges will accrue upon the $40 debit until it is paid off. Spade will be in the position of having borrowed $40 cash from Ace.

Now, Hart could handle the refund to Spade in another way. Instead of giving Spade a cash refund, he could inform Ace of the return of the gizmo so that Ace could reverse the debit to Spade's account. Hart, in this case, must inform Ace of the return within five business days. Ace must then credit Spade's account for the $40 within three business days of receipt of the notice of return. Spade receives no cash this way, but the debit to his credit card account is reversed. Such a debit is not completely reversed, however. Any finance charge which accrued upon the original debit must be paid, return or no return.

Offset by card issuer. Before 1975, a bank which issued a credit card could collect delinquent payments from accounts maintained by card owners by use of the bank's right of offset. 15 USC 1666h has rendered that practice unlawful, unless the bank and its customer have entered into a written agreement permitting the bank to use it. A credit card issuer may not require a credit card applicant to agree to it as a condition for issuance of the card.

It is now becoming normal practice for a customer to agree with a bank card issuer that the bank may, through electronic fund transfer or otherwise, debit the customer's checking account for his monthly credit card payment. Such agreements are quite lawful, if they are in writing. A card owner may reverse such a payment within sixteen days of its making if the customer has bought goods and charged them to the card and later asserts a defense to payment for the goods which the card issuer must honor. If a payment has been made through the card account on the goods, and the issuer is notified of the defense within sixteen days of the making of the payment, the amount of the payment must be restored to the owner's checking account by the issuer.

If the issuer is notified of the defense more than sixteen days after debiting the owner's checking account for a payment, no recovery of the payment is possible. The defense will apply only to the amount of purchase price for the item which remains due and unpaid. In connection with this, it sometimes becomes important to know how payments to credit card accounts are applied against outstanding debits. The rule for application is:

First, all outstanding late payment charges are satisfied.

Second, all outstanding finance charge debits are satisfied.

Third, the balance of the payment is applied to purchases charged to the account in chronological order of charge.

A simple example will illustrate. Clubb opens an Ace credit card account on May 1. Ace grants a thirty-day free ride on all purchases charged to the account, so no finance charge accrues on a purchase if paid for during the month of purchase. Clubb charges a $45 gizmo to the account on May 3, a $75 whatzit on May 15, and a $60 widget on May 21. The whatzit proves defective; he tries to get the seller to correct the defect, but to no avail. Ace bills Clubb for $180 on June 1. Ace is a bank, and Clubb has agreed to EFT automatic deduction of payments from his checking account on the tenth day of each month.

On June 10 Ace deducts $20 from Clubb's checking account. On June 15 Clubb asserts his defense to payment against the seller of the whatzit and demands two things: the reversal of the $20 debit from his checking account (the restoration of his payment, in essence) and the reversal of the $75 debit to the credit card account for the whatzit. Clubb does not get the $20 back. That payment is for a portion of the charge for the gizmo, since the gizmo comprised the first charge. However, Clubb will succeed in having his credit card balance reduced by $75.

On the other hand, if Clubb had authorized Ace to deduct $180 from his checking account on June 10 and Ace had done so, Clubb would be able to recover $75 from Ace. This would be true because he made his request for reversal of debit within sixteen days of the date of debit, and the debit was for payment for an item upon which a defense to payment existed.

If Clubb authorized Ace to deduct $100 per month from his checking account on the tenth of each month; Ace did so on June 10; and Clubb made his claim of defense to Ace on June 30, the position would be as follows: Clubb could not obtain restoration of any of his $100 payment, because his notification of defense came more than sixteen days after the payment was deducted from his checking account. His claim of defense will result in a reduction of his next bill by $20 only, because $45 of his $100 payment went to pay for the gizmo, and the other $55 applied on the price of the whatzit. Since only $20 is owed now on the whatzit, that is all the defense to payment will apply to; Clubb must obtain the other $55 from the seller of the whatzit, if he can.

These rules on application of payments and result of assertion of defenses apply whether or not the card owner allows EFT deduction of payments from checking accounts. Recovery of payments is not normally possible when EFT deduction of payments from checking accounts is not authorized.

The rights of a credit card owner when the issuer makes billing errors will be discussed in the chapter on consumer protection.

33

Warranties

Product Liability

Warranties

The law of warranty and product liability has been one of the most rapidly developing areas of law throughout the second half of the twentieth century. From the decidedly pro-seller attitude of caveat emptor—"let the buyer beware"—which prevailed around the turn of the century, new legislation and new legal theories of seller liability have so transformed the situation that some now claim that the prevailing rule is caveat venditor—"let the seller beware."

Whether matters have progressed to that point is open to argument. However, it is undeniable that back around the turn of the century the law expected a buyer of goods to look out for himself, not to listen to the salesman's hard sell, to inspect thoroughly what he was buying before he bought, and—if he could not do all that—not to buy. Not all sellers were assumed to be honest, but buyers were expected to be intelligent enough and knowledgeable enough to be able to look out for themselves.

In our more technological and paternalistic time, the law has recognized that the buyer of many types of goods is in no position to be able to look out for himself. Many products have become so complex that buyers are unable to judge the quality of what they are getting. Also, with respect to many products, there is no equality of bargaining power between seller and buyer; buyer must deal with seller upon seller's terms, or not deal at all.

It can be said that current law recognizes the fact that superior power and superior knowledge are accompanied by great responsibility. If buyers can in fact not protect themselves against defective products and sharp sales practices, the law must protect them. In that sense, then, perhaps the law truly has evolved to the condition of caveat venditor.

The Uniform Commercial Code imposes five implied warranties upon various sorts of sellers of goods, warranties which sellers make to their buyers when they make sales whether they make them expressly or not. The UCC also regulates the making of express warranties, promises actually made by the seller with respect to his goods. Federal legislation—the Magnuson-Moss Act—also regulates the making of express warranties. In addition, other legislation protects the consumer with respect to the marketing of certain sorts of products, and new principles of judge-made law afford recourse to persons injured by defective products.

IMPLIED WARRANTIES

Five implied warranties are imposed upon sellers by the UCC (TB&CC in Texas):
1. The warranty of title.
2. The warranty against encumbrances.
3. The warranty against infringement.
4. The warranty of merchantability.
5. The warranty of fitness for buyer's purpose.

These will be discussed in order.

Warranty of title. UCC 2-312(1)(a) provides that the seller of goods warrants that the title to the goods sold is good, and that his transfer of the goods is rightful. It is essentially a warranty that the buyer is becoming the owner of the goods sold, and that he is acquiring the right to possession of those goods.

All sellers of goods make this warranty, except those who are obviously selling someone else's goods. Among the types of sellers who do not make the warranty of title are the following:
1. Executors and administrators of estates.
2. Trustees in bankruptcy.
3. Foreclosing lienholders, such as finance companies selling repossessed property.
4. Sheriffs selling property seized under writ of execution.
5. The IRS selling property seized from a delinquent taxpayer.
6. Pawnbrokers.

This list is of course not exclusive; any seller who is obviously not the owner of the goods being sold does not make this warranty.

Some sellers have the power to sell good title to goods they do not own, even when not foreclosing liens. Such sellers include the merchant selling goods entrusted to him, or the bailee selling goods which have been in his possession for two years. Even though such sales are wrongful, the buyer of the goods normally gets good title to them. If the buyer reasonably believes that the seller is selling his own goods, a warranty of title is made.

A seller may disclaim the implied warranty of title. The language of disclaimer must be specific, and it must be in writing if the contract of sale is in writing. The traditional way to disclaim this warranty is to state that one is selling "all of his right, title, and interest" in the goods being sold, but the effectiveness of this disclaimer is not complete—a poorly educated person might not understand the meaning of the phrase. More concise wording will serve better.

The damages recoverable for breach of warranty of title generally amount to what the buyer has paid for the goods.

Warranty against encumbrances. Under UCC 2-312(1)(b), the seller warrants that the goods shall be delivered free from any security interest or other lien or encumbrance of which the buyer had no knowledge at the time of contracting. It is essentially a warranty that no one has a lien on the goods which the buyer does not know about.

If the subject matter of the sale is a motor vehicle, the buyer will know about any existing liens because, to be valid, they must be noted upon the certificate of title to the vehicle. If the subject matter is something other than a motor vehicle, however, the buyer would not know of existing liens when he takes possession. If a lien exists which the buyer does not know of, and the buyer loses the goods to the holder of the lien, he has a claim for breach of this warranty. This is true even if the seller did not know of the existence of the lien.

Those sellers who do not make the warranty of title also do not make the warranty against encumbrances, which may be disclaimed in the same manner as the warranty of title.

The warranty against infringement. UCC 2-312(3) states that, unless otherwise agreed, a seller who is a merchant dealing regularly in goods of the kind warrants that the goods shall be delivered free of the rightful claim of any third person for infringement or the like. It also provides that, in essence, a buyer who furnishes specifications for goods to a seller makes a similar warranty to the seller.

An example of such a situation would be this: Deuce Recording Company copies a popular song from a recording made by Ace Recording Company without the knowledge and consent of Ace and markets it. Ace finds out that Trey Music Store, among other music stores, is marketing this record to the public. Ace accuses Trey of infringement of copyright. Ace had duly perfected a copyright upon the recording. Trey is guilty of infringement here, as of course is Deuce. Trey has a claim against Deuce for violation of the warranty against infringement.

This warranty, then, is a warranty that the buyer (or seller of custom-made goods built to specification) will not become involved in claims for infringement of patent, copyright, or trademark because of the contract in question. As soon as the party to whom the warranty is made learns of an infringement claim, he must notify the party making the warranty. The warrantor must then either defend his customer against the claim, or stand ready to pay any judgment which may be obtained against him.

A failure by the party to whom the warranty is made to notify the warrantor of the claim within a reasonable time relieves the warrantor of liability under the warranty. The warranty may be disclaimed by the use of proper language in the contract of sale.

Warranty of merchantability. Under UCC 2-314, sellers who are merchants of the goods being sold make an implied warranty of merchantability with respect to the goods. Generally, the warranty is that the goods sold are fit for normal use. More specifically, it is a warranty that:

1. The goods conform to the contract description, and
2. If they are fungible goods, they are of fair average quality within the description, and
3. They are fit for ordinary use to which such goods are put, and
4. They run within variations permitted in the contract of even kind, quantity, and quality within each unit and among all units involved, and
5. They are adequately contained, packaged, and labeled as the contract may require, and
6. They conform to all promises or affirmations of fact made on the container or label, if any.

This warranty is made by any merchant seller to any merchant or nonmerchant buyer. Thus it is not made only to consumers, but also to retailers and the like.

The concept of fitness for normal use includes that of safety for normal use. Therefore, a product which is dangerous to the user is not merchantable, unless the user is warned of the danger or the danger is obvious. There is no requirement that the product be accident-proof. Of course, the product must comply with safety standards imposed by legislation or by administrative agencies, but the courts recognize that accidents can occur with even the most safely designed products. On the other hand, negligence in omitting obvious safety features from a product may render a seller liable—not for breach of warranty, but for negligent design.

The warranty of merchantability is not a warranty that a product will last forever. The product should have a useful life which is comparable to that of similar products sold for similar prices. But parts do wear out and require replacement, and entire products do live out their appointed days and become useless.

A cosmetic or similar product is not considered unfit for normal use because a few users are allergic or sensitive to it. However, the larger the number of allergic or hypersensitive users, the more likely it is that a court would find the product to be unfit for normal use.

If the contract of sale requires that the goods be packaged in a specified way, the seller makes the warranty of merchantability with respect to the package or container. Even if the container is not required by the contract of sale, the seller may be held responsible for defects in it under the warranty of merchantability, especially when the container is a bottle which contains a carbonated drink.

The warranty of merchantability does not require that any particular sort of label be placed upon goods, although other legislation may specify the presence of a label making certain disclosures. If a label is present upon the product, however, the product would not be fit for normal use if the label contains false information.

The warranty of merchantability is made with respect to food and drink served for value, whether they are to be consumed on the premises where sold or elsewhere. A breach of the warranty will occur when the food contains a foreign item which causes injury to the consumer, unless the foreign item is one which a reasonable person would expect to find in the food. Fried fish, for example, may be expected to contain fish bones, unless it is advertised as boneless fillet, but a cherry pie should not contain cherry seeds, and a sandwich should not contain a piece of glass.

There is no warranty of merchantability made with respect to the furnishing of blood for use in the making of blood transfusions. The furnishing of the blood is considered to be part of a service rather than a sale, and no warranty of merchantability or other implied warranty is made with respect to provision of services.

This warranty is also applicable to contracts for the sale of second-hand goods. In such contracts the seller warrants that the goods are as fit for normal use as can be expected of goods of that age and state of wear. If the buyer has had the opportunity to examine new or used goods before buying, whether he availed himself of the opportunity or not, the warranty is not made with respect to defects in the goods which the buyer could readily have discovered upon his examination.

If the buyer understands that the seller is selling the goods "as is," no warranty of merchantability is made with respect to the goods. Should the seller wish to disclaim the warranty in that manner, he must make certain that the buyer understands what is involved, and that there is no warranty of merchantability. If the contract of sale is in writing, the writing must clearly state the disclaimer.

In written contracts of sale, the best way to disclaim the warranty of merchantability is by a conspicuous provision which expressly states that this warranty is disclaimed (UCC 2-316). The disclaimer must use the word "merchantability," and should be in larger type or in a different color from the rest of the contract. A disclaimer of this warranty will be fully effective only when the seller makes no express warranties in his written contract of sale. When the contract contains express warranties, disclaimer of the warranty of merchantability is of limited or no effect (see next section on express warranties).

Warranty of fitness for buyer's purpose. UCC 2-315 provides that any seller may make an implied warranty of fitness for the buyer's purpose. The warranty is made under the following circumstances:

1. The buyer of the goods has some special use for them in mind, and
2. The seller either knows or should know the nature of the special use, and
3. The buyer lets the seller select the goods which are to fulfill this special purpose.

Of course, the seller usually learns of the special purpose when the buyer informs him of it. The seller would not otherwise know of it unless he and the buyer are closely acquainted.

In addition, this warranty is not made unless the seller has unlimited discretion in the selection of the goods. If the buyer does the selecting, or if the buyer limits the seller's discretion by insisting upon a certain brand name, etc., there will be no warranty of fitness.

The warranty of fitness for the buyer's purpose may be disclaimed in the same ways as the warranty of merchantability. The disclaimer must be conspicuous and in writing, unless the buyer knows and understands that the goods are being sold "as is" and "with all faults."

EXPRESS WARRANTIES

UCC 2-314 provides that a seller may create express warranties in the following manner:
1. By making affirmations of facts or promises which relate to the goods and become a part of the basis of buyer's bargain.
2. By making a description of the goods that becomes a part of the basis of buyer's bargain, as in an advertisement or a catalog description.
3. By making a sample of the goods a part of the basis of the bargain.
4. By making a model of the goods a part of the basis of the bargain.

The affirmation of fact which becomes a part of the basis of the buyer's bargain may be made by the seller or his salesman in a face-to-face conversation with buyer, or it may be contained in an advertisement or catalog description. The promise may be made in the same ways.

If a salesman induces a buyer to contract to buy goods by showing him a sample of them, and the buyer desires that the goods be like the sample and makes that fact known, an express warranty comes into being that the goods are like the sample. If a salesman induces a buyer to contract to buy goods by letting him use a test model or demonstration model of the goods, and the buyer contracts to buy because of the performance of the demonstration model, an express warranty exists that the goods sold will perform as does the demonstration model.

Oral express warranties. When the contract for sale of goods is oral, it may contain oral express warranties made by the seller. If the contract of sale is in writing, oral express warranties of the seller may well not be a part of the bargain.

If a written contract appears to be a complete and exclusive statement of the bargain between the parties, it will be interpreted as the entire agreement (UCC 2-202). Thus, if the written contract does not contain the oral warranty, the warranty would not be considered part of the bargain.

Written contracts for sale of goods also frequently provide that no warranties are made by the seller with respect to the goods other than those contained in the written contract. Such provisions are generally said to mean what they say. They are good disclaimers of oral warranties not written into the contract. A buyer may try to argue around a disclaimer of oral express warranties by claiming that the making of the oral warranty and the later disclaimer of it constituted fraud. Proof of the required intent is not difficult here, but proof of justifiable reliance is difficult.

Another way out is to argue that the written contract did not contain the entire bargain between the parties, even though it said that it did. An educated person would have difficulty in arguing this, since he should know that a written agreement is generally considered to contain the entire agreement between the parties, especially if the agreement states this. An uneducated person could argue that the oral warranty was a part of the basis of his bargain despite what the written contract said and could perhaps succeed with that argument.

Written express warranties. Obviously, a written express warranty is an integral part of the contract containing it. It cannot be disclaimed. It must be realized, however, that written express warranties are by no means indicative of the notion that the seller stands behind his product. Rare is the written warranty which guarantees that the product is fit for normal use—the guarantee imposed upon merchant sellers by the implied warranty of merchantability.

The typical written express warranty is more likely to be the seller's statement of the circumstances under which the product is not guaranteed to be fit for normal use and of the circumstances under which the seller will not stand behind his product. It thus serves to narrow the seller's warranty obligations to the buyer, not to expand them. The written express warranty, then, is very likely to include disclaimers of implied warranties. If the express warranty is inconsistent with an implied warranty, UCC 2-317(c) clearly states that the express warranty displaces the implied warranty, unless the implied warranty is the warranty of fitness for the buyer's purpose.

Since written express warranties are very commonly made by manufacturers and retailers of expensive consumer goods (such as automobiles), and since these warranties are inevitably efforts by manufacturers to reduce their responsibility for defects and malfunctions of their products, federal legislation has been enacted regulating the format and, to a small extent, the content of such warranties.

This legislation is the Federal Warranty Act (or Magnuson-Moss Act), 15 USC 2301 et seq. It contains substantive provisions governing the making of consumer express warranties, and also gives the Federal Trade Commission authority to make administrative regulations in this area. The act governs consumer express warranties only—it does not apply to commercial warranties. It also applies only when the consumer product is sold for more than fifteen dollars.

Required content of the written consumer warranty. 15 USC 2302 requires that a written consumer warranty contain the following items of information:

1. Names and addresses of warrantor.
2. Identity of party or parties to whom warranty is extended—is it just to buyer, or is it extended to users, subsequent buyers, and others?
3. The product or parts covered.
4. A statement of what warrantor will do in case of defect, malfunction, or failure to conform with the warranty, at whose expense, and for what period of time.
5. A statement of what the consumer must do in such a case and the expenses he must bear.
6. Exceptions and exclusions from the warranty terms—what is not covered? When do the warranty terms not apply?
7. A statement of the step-by-step procedure consumer must follow in order to obtain his rights under the warranty—and identification of any person or class of persons (such as, perhaps, seller's authorized dealers) authorized to perform the obligations set forth in the warranty.
8. Information regarding any informal dispute settlement procedure maintained by

warrantor and a statement that, when the warranty so provides, consumer must resort to this procedure before taking any complaint under the warranty to court.

9. A brief general description of remedies available to consumer in case of breach of warranty.

10. The time at which warrantor will perform obligations under the warranty.

11. The period of time within which, after notice of defect, the warrantor will perform obligations under the warranty.

12. Characteristics and/or properties of the product which are not covered by the warranty.

13. The terms of the warranty, expressed in clear language which would not mislead the average consumer.

If the product being warranted costs the consumer less than fifteen dollars, the above requirements do not apply.

The warranty must be made available to a consumer or prospective consumer before the product is sold to him. When the fact that a product is warranted is used in advertising, the ad must state enough about the terms of the warranty to give the consumer an idea of its contents.

The warrantor must not make the existence of the warranty conditional upon the consumer's using an article or service identified by brand or trade name along with the warranted product, unless the warrantor can convince the Federal Trade Commission that the warranted product will not function properly unless the accompanying specified product or service is used. Thus, the warrantor cannot normally require that the consumer use his repair service, his spare parts, etc.

There is no requirement that any particular product be expressly warranted. There is also no requirement as to the duration of any express consumer product warranty.

Full warranty. All express warranties on consumer products costing fifteen dollars or more must be labeled either *full warranties* or *limited warranties*. The giver of a full warranty stands behind his product. 15 USC 2304 provides that a full warranty must meet at least the following standards:

1. Warrantor must agree to correct defects, malfunctions, or failures to conform to the written warranty without charge and within a reasonable time.

2. Warrantor must not impose limitations upon the duration of any implied warranties (such as the warranty of merchantability) with respect to the product.

3. Warrantor must not exclude or limit consequential damages for breach of any express or implied warranty on such product unless the exclusion or limitation appears upon the face of the warranty (and he must not seek to limit or exclude damages for personal injury at all).

4. If the product contains a defect or malfunction which warrantor is unable to correct after a reasonable number of attempts, warrantor must either replace the product without charge or grant the consumer a refund.

The warrantor may not require any action by the consumer other than notification as a condition for using his warranty rights. The warrantor may, however, require the consumer to return a product surrendered for replacement or refund free and clear of security interests and other liens.

Limited warranties. Any express warranty of a consumer product costing more than fifteen dollars which does not meet the standards for a full warranty must be labeled a limited warranty. There are no express requirements for the contents of a limited warranty; under such a warranty, the rights of the consumer may be very severely limited.

The warrantor need not commit himself to replacing a "lemon," or to making a refund when correction of a malfunction is not accomplished. Repairs and replacement of parts need not be made free of charge; the consumer may be required to pay shipping charges to get the product to the point of repair, labor charges for the making of repairs, and even a reduced cost for the parts used in making the repair. (The warranty must clearly explain the nature of the charges that the consumer must pay.) The warrantor may also impose duties upon the consumer other than mere notification to the warrantor of his difficulties. If he does impose such duties, the warranty must clearly state what these are.

Under a limited warranty implied warranties may not be disclaimed or modified. However, they may be limited in duration to the duration of the limited warranty itself. Thus, products under limited warranty are covered by the warranty of merchantability for as long as they are covered by the limited warranty; the making of even a limited warranty guarantees the product as being fit for normal use for the duration of the warranty.

Registration of warranty. The warrantor may require the consumer to register himself as a purchaser of a warranted product to assure himself coverage under a full or limited warranty. If registration is required, the warrantor should place a warranty registration card in the package containing the warranted product.

If the return of the warranty card is not required for warranty coverage, the warranty itself must so state. As a practical matter, the warranty itself usually spells out the requirements, if any, for registration. The rules on registration are found in administrative regulations of the Federal Trade Commission at 16 CFR 701.4.

Informal dispute settlement procedure. 15 USC 2310 states that it is the policy of Congress to encourage warrantors to establish informal dispute settlement procedures to handle warranty claims. The FTC has the authority to promulgate standards for the operation of such procedures. A warrantor's procedures must conform with the applicable FTC standards. If the procedure conforms, the warranty must notify the consumer of its existence. It must also tell the consumer what he must do in order to file a claim under the procedure.

The existence of the approved procedure will bar a consumer from suing in court over a breach of warranty until he has exhausted all remedies provided him by the procedure. The idea is to keep some warranty disputes out of the court system, but this does not seem to be happening. Most warrantors do not care to go to the trouble of setting up such dispute settlement mechanisms; they seem willing to rely upon informal negotiation and the courts to resolve such difficulties.

Remedies under the Magnuson-Moss Act. A consumer damaged by a failure to comply with the Magnuson-Moss Act (as by improper labeling of a warranty or something similar) or by an actual breach of express warranty or implied warranty may sue for damages in either federal or state court. If the consumer prevails in such a case, he may recover not only his damages but also his costs and expenses, including a reasonable attorney fee.

A Magnuson-Moss Act violation is also a violation of the Federal Trade Commission Act, subjecting the violator to administrative action by the FTC.

Special rules applicable to the sale of used cars. 15 USC 2309 mandates that the FTC devise administrative regulations applicable to warranties upon used motor vehicles. The FTC has devised a set of regulations governing this subject, but it has not as yet completed its rule-making procedures. When it does finish this project, the giving of warranties by sellers of used motor vehicles will be subject to detailed regulation. No such rules are yet in effect.

Defenses to charge of breach of express warranty. The warrantor may refuse to honor a warranty claim involving a warranted product when:
1. The product was damaged in the possession of the consumer, and the damage was not caused by a defect or malfunction of the product.
2. The product was damaged due to misuse by the consumer.
3. The product has not been properly maintained.

Product Liability

Since we have covered in detail the types of warranties made by sellers of goods, we must now consider how the law of warranty fits in to the broader legal area of the responsibility of sellers of products for what they sell.

A person who is damaged by a defective product may have recourse under four different theories of product liability:
1. Breach of warranty.
2. Strict tort liability.
3. Negligence.
4. Violation of statutory duty.

On rare occasions only one of these theories of liability offers recourse to the injured party; more often, two or more of the theories are usable.

Warranty theory. As already discussed, a seller of goods may make express warranties with respect to them. He may also have one or more of the implied warranties imposed upon him.

One very basic requisite of warranty liability is that there must have been a sale of the defective product. There can be no warranty unless there is a sales contract. A person injured by a defective product which he is examining while he decides whether or not to buy cannot claim to be a victim of breach of warranty.

Another problem in the warranty area is the troublesome question of whether or not the person claiming breach of warranty must actually have a contract with the person he is making the claim against. Until very recently, privity of contract has been an essential element of warranty liability; if plaintiff had no contract with defendant, defendant had made no warranty to plaintiff. The drafters of the Uniform Commercial Code wrestled with this problem in Section 2-318. The original version of the section relaxed the privity requirement to a small degree. Alternative versions of the section proposed in 1966 virtually abolish the requirement. The Texas version of the section, TB&CC 2-318, simply states that the legislature takes no position as to whether privity of contract is necessary to render a defendant liable upon a breach of warranty claim; it is up to the courts to decide the matter. There is very little case law on the point.

Privity of contract problems are of two sorts: vertical privity and horizontal privity. Problems of vertical privity involve questions as to whether only the retailer of a product makes warranties to a consumer buyer, or whether firms higher up in the distribution chain—manufacturers, wholesalers, and distributors—also make warranties. There is of course no question but that a retailer makes implied warranties to the consumer, unless he disclaims them all in a valid manner. A retailer may of course also make express warranties.

A manufacturer may also make warranties to a consumer, even though the consumer does not buy the product directly from the manufacturer. If the manufacturer advertises his product in the printed media or on radio, TV, or film, any statements of verifiable fact regarding the product contained in the ads will be construed to be express warranties. This of course makes sense, since the purpose of the advertising is to induce the consumer to buy the product. Most formal full and limited warranties with respect to consumer products are in fact made by the manufacturer, not by the retailer; a retailer incurs no liability upon such a warranty unless he agrees to be bound by it. The canner of prepared foods, for example, makes the warranty of merchantability to the consumer, even if the consumer does not buy directly from the canner. As to the liability of wholesalers, component parts manufacturers, and others under the warranty theory, there is no theoretical reason why they should not be so liable, but the matter is for the most part unclear in this state.

Problems of horizontal privity involve questions as to whether the warranties made by sellers and manufacturers apply only to the original consumer buyer of the product or extend to persons other than the original buyer who might be damaged. The original UCC 2-318 extended the protection of the warranties to members of the buyer's family and guests in his household. Those states which have adopted the more liberal later versions of this section extend the protection of the warranty to practically anyone who might be damaged by the product—employees of the buyer, buyers from the buyer, bailees, and bystanders who just happen to be around when the product malfunctions and are damaged by it. It is an open question as to how far Texas courts may go in abolition of requirements of horizontal privity.

An important limitation upon the right to sue for breach of warranty is the requirement that the claimant must notify the warrantor of the breach as soon as possible after its occurrence. This notification is mandatory: failure to give it will be a defense to liability in a breach of warranty action.

Other possible defenses in breach of warranty actions are:
1. Disclaimer of warranty liability.
2. Misuse of the product.
3. No sale of the product.

Remember that the warranty of merchantability may be validly disclaimed, as discussed earlier in this chapter. A valid disclaimer relieves a merchant of warranty liability.

The warranty of merchantability is, essentially, a warranty that a product is fit for normal use. When the product is misused, it is being subjected to abnormal use; should the product not be fit for the abnormal use to which it is put, no breach of warranty ensues. Negligence by the claimant in use of the product is no defense to warranty liability, unless the negligence consists of putting the product to an abnormal use.

A warranty of a merchant seller does not become effective until the product has actually been sold. Generally, the product has not been sold until title has passed from seller to buyer. The general rule is, "No sale, no warranty."

The victorious plaintiff in a breach of warranty action is entitled to recover 100 percent of all damages assessed against the defendant by the jury. Establishment of a defense to liability by the defendant will relieve him of all damages.

Since a breach of warranty is a breach of contract, the statute of limitations upon such claims is the contract for the sale of goods limitation period of UCC 2-725. Such suits must be commenced within four years of the making of the warranty, or within four years of the discovery of the breach (if the breach was not discoverable earlier).

Strict tort liability. During the 1960s and 1970s, the courts of most of the states have adopted the notion that any merchant who sells a defective product which is unreasonably dangerous to a user or consumer or to his property should be absolutely liable for any harm, be it personal injury or property damage, done by the product. The Texas courts too have adopted this theory.

Under this theory of product liability, it does not matter whether the merchant to be charged with liability knew of the defective and dangerous nature of the product. It also does not matter whether the merchant made any promises or warranties with respect to the product.

The plaintiff making a claim under the strict tort liability theory must essentially prove three things:

1. That the product was dangerously defective, and
2. That the plaintiff was injured or damaged due to the defect, and
3. That the defendant was part of the distribution chain of the product, and that the product was defective when the defendant parted with control over it.

Privity of contract requirements have pretty well been abolished by Texas courts in litigation under this theory. Manufacturers, wholesalers, retailers, and other parties in the distribution chain may be sued. Buyers from the buyer, employees of the buyer, bailees, lessees, and injured bystanders may all sue.

Liability under this theory is incurred only by professional sellers of products; nonmerchant sellers do not incur this liability. A merchant seller may not disclaim liability under this theory. A disclaimer of all warranties will not serve to disclaim strict tort liability.

In order to prove that a product is defective, a plaintiff must prove that the item which injured him did not comply with normal standards of fitness for use of that particular product. The product must have been in less than good operating order.

It must be remembered that many of the products we use in our daily lives are inherently dangerous, even when in perfect operating order. A power saw will remove a finger while operating properly. An automobile in perfect mechanical condition may become involved in an accident. A blowtorch which operates as it should is capable of inflicting nasty burns. So long as such a product operates as it should, no seller is liable under the strict tort liability theory for injuries or damages caused. If, on the other hand, the blade of the power saw disintegrates, the steering gear of the automobile locks and thereby causes an accident, or the blowtorch blows up, one may talk of the product being defective.

The definition of "defect" often plays an important role in litigation involving persons injured in auto accidents. The tremendous physical forces generated by automobiles in collision may twist and smash component parts of the vehicles out of shape, doing horrendous physical damage to the fragile bodies of human beings. There are those who argue that auto bodies ought to be so stoutly built that these forces cannot cause parts of the vehicle to cause personal injury. In short, automobiles should be "crashproof." Is an auto which is not "crashproof" defective? At the moment, the answer is no. We could possibly construct crashproof autos if we required them to be constructed along the lines of a Patton tank, but to require this is impracticable. It is accepted that autos are not crashproof; the fact that they are not does not mean that they are defective.

A plaintiff injured by his own auto in an accident may argue that his vehicle was improperly designed to maximize passenger safety, or he may argue that the vehicle did not comply with applicable government safety standards. Such arguments do not try to assert strict tort liability, however; they are related to other theories of product liability.

After the plaintiff has proven that the product which damaged him was defective, he must then proceed to prove that it was the defect in the product which caused his injury. This is normally not difficult. If the saw blade of a brand new power saw disintegrates, and fragments lodge in the plaintiff's cheek; if the brand new blowtorch blows up for no ascertainable reason and badly burns the plaintiff; or if the steering gear on the plaintiff's brand new auto locks and causes the auto to collide with a tree, proof of causation of injury is easy.

Two problem areas here may be illustrated by examples of auto accidents. If a brand new, properly mounted tire on Schnell's sports car blows out, causing the vehicle to collide with a tree, and the impact crushes Schnell's body against the engine of the car, which was forced back into the passenger compartment of the vehicle by the impact of the collision, what was the cause of Schnell's death? Was it the blowout of the tire, the collision of the auto with the tree, or the collision of Schnell's body with the auto engine?

In a suit by Schnell's estate against the manufacturer of the tire, the manufacturer might try to argue that Schnell's death was not caused directly by the blowout of the tire, but by an intervening matter. Courts do not receive this sort of argument with open arms, but efforts by plaintiffs to prove causation of injury by a product defect are often met with this sort of counterargument.

The second problem area may be illustrated if we change the scenario of Schnell's new-tire blowout and collision with the tree a bit. Suppose that Schnell had been driving with his vehicle open to the air and he had not fastened his seat belt. After the tire blowout and collision with the tree, Schnell met his doom because the impact of the collision had thrown his body forward out of the car, causing him to collide with the tree in person, headfirst. The manufacturer now argues in court that the defect in the tire did not cause Schnell's death, that the true cause of death is attributable to the fact that Schnell was not wearing his seat belt.

Courts throughout the nation have reacted to this situation in three different ways. Some have accepted the manufacturer's argument, making not wearing a seat belt an absolute defense to liability in cases of this nature. Others have held that not wearing a seat belt is no defense at all. Still others take a middle position, that not wearing a seat belt is no defense to liability, but the fact that the belt was not worn may serve to reduce the damages which the plaintiff may recover. The position of Texas courts on this is not yet clear.

Proof that the defendant was part of the distribution chain of the defective product is easy. If the plaintiff is suing the manufacturer, he must merely prove that the manufacturer manufactured it. If he is suing the retailer, he must merely prove that he bought the defective product from the retailer. If he is suing a wholesaler, he must prove that the product was at one time part of the wholesaler's inventory, and that the wholesaler sold it.

The last item which must be proven is that the product was defective when the defendant parted with control over it. If the defendant is a retailer, and the plaintiff bought the product from him, the plaintiff must simply prove the product was defective when he bought it. If the defendant is a manufacturer, it is a bit harder to prove that the product was defective when it left the factory. A manufacturer may escape liability if he can show that the product was rendered defective after it left his establishment.

Suppose, for instance, that Habitant bought a new gas heater for his home from Maison Appliances, a retailer. The heater emitted carbon monoxide fumes which made Habitant and members of his family ill. Habitant decides to sue Chauffage Manufacturing Company, manufacturer of the heater, for damages. Chauffage tries to argue that the heater was in perfect shape when it was sold to Maison, and that Habitant's carbon monoxide problem occurred because Maison installed the heater improperly. If Chauffage can convince a jury of this, it escapes liability. Habitant's only recourse would be to sue Maison.

A manufacturer may try to escape liability by arguing that he instructs his retailers to thoroughly inspect his products for defects before selling them to the public and that, if a defective product made by the manufacturer is sold to the public, it is because of negligence on the part of the retailer and the manufacturer should not be held responsible. This argument is not accepted by American courts. Manufacturers cannot escape liability for their defective products by delegating the task of quality control to someone down the distribution chain.

Manufacturers may also not escape liability by arguing that they are not responsible for defective components in their products which are manufactured by someone else. A manufacturer is responsible for all components of his product. If he builds into a product a defective component part manufactured by another manufacturer, he is still responsible. (The manufacturer of the component may also be held liable, unless the manufacturer of the complete product rendered the component defective in the course of his manufacturing process.) The same principle renders manufacturers responsible for defects in the containers used for packaging their products.

Two defenses are available to defendants in strict tort liability litigation. These are:
1. Misuse of the product.
2. Assumption of risk.

A plaintiff is guilty of misuse of the product when he uses it for a purpose for which it is not intended, when he uses it in an unreasonable manner, or when he violates instructions furnished by the manufacturer for use of the product.

Manufacturers should furnish instructions for the use of inherently dangerous products. The instructions should be written in simple language, so that the average user may understand them. If certain uses of the product are dangerous, and the unsophisticated user may not be aware of the danger, adequate warnings of the danger should be furnished. If a user is injured because he violated comprehensible instructions for use, or because he ignored a comprehensible warning, he is obviously guilty of misuse. If a user is injured because he used the product in a manner in which no reasonable user would use it, he is guilty of misuse even if no instruction or warning on the point was given. Thus, if someone attempts to cut sheet metal with an ordinary ripsaw, he has no one to blame but himself if he gets hurt.

Ordinary negligence in the use of a product does not constitute misuse. The person who mounts new tires on his car according to instruction and then drives 70 MPH on an interstate highway is negligent, in the sense that he is violating the law, but he can hardly be said to be misusing the new tires. If one of them blows out, causing an accident which injures the driver, he should be able to recover damages under the strict liability theory.

If a user of a product knows that the product is defective but uses it anyway, he assumes the risk of damage. Thus, if the known defect later causes him to suffer injury, he will have difficulty recovering damages.

Misuse is not an absolute defense to liability in strict tort liability cases in Texas. The Supreme Court of Texas has adapted the comparative negligence scheme of apportionment of fault in such cases, by its decision in *General Motors Corp. vs. Hopkins*, 548 SW2d 344. The court modified the scheme, however.

The jury in a product-liability case where the defense is misuse is asked to assess the plaintiff's damages. It is also asked to divide blame for his injuries between him and the defendant, taking into account the amount and nature of the plaintiff's misuse. The result is that the plaintiff recovers that percentage of his damages for which the defendant is held responsible, even if that percentage is 50 percent or less. Thus, if the jury decides that the plaintiff suffered $100,000 in damages, that the plaintiff's misuse of the product is 95 percent to blame for his injury and the defect in the product renders the defendant 5 percent responsible for the injury, the plaintiff recovers $5,000. (He would of course recover nothing in a negligence case.)

Thus, if the plaintiff meets his burden of proof with respect to the defect the defendant cannot totally escape liability with his misuse defense unless the jury apportions 100 percent of the blame for the damage to the plaintiff. Whether the same rules of apportionment of blame would apply in assumption of risk cases has not yet been decided.

The plaintiff may seek and recover punitive damages under the strict tort theory. Such damages are not recoverable for breach of warranty, since they are not recoverable for breach of contract in general.

Suits under the strict tort liability theory are governed by the personal injury statute of limitations in Texas. Such suits must therefore be commenced within two years of the date of damage or injury.

Negligence theory. The ordinary tort law of negligence extends into the field of product liability. It is not often used because the wide extent of the theory of strict tort liability makes the use of negligence as a basis for suit unnecessary. When the theory is used, ordinary comparative negligence rules apply.

The most important area in which negligence theory has vitality is that of product design. If the design of the product renders it unsafe, even if the product is not defective, a person injured by the product who attributes his injury to the unsafe design may have a case against the manufacturer.

The question of safe design is often a close one. Products such as automobiles and power tools are certainly inherently dangerous, but we manufacture and use them because their social value outweighs their inherent danger. There is no way to design an accident-proof automobile or ripsaw; but some such products may be safer than others.

If a particular make of a product sells for approximately the same price as competing similar products, but it lacks a safety feature incorporated in the competing products, the manufacturer is open to a charge of negligent design. If, however, the product in question is cheaper than the competing safer products, the manufacturer may not be open to such a charge; he may well argue that one acquires more safety by paying more.

These questions about negligence in design of products have been solved to some extent by the enactment of the Federal Consumer Product Safety Act, which will be discussed shortly. The act authorizes the Consumer Product Safety Commission to establish safety standards for most consumer products. With the promulgation of the necessary standards, product design will be a matter of compliance with the required standard.

Another area in which the concept of negligence is important is that of warning of dangers inherent in the use of the product. It is of course not necessary to warn users of obvious dangers; everyone knows that razor blades are extremely sharp, for instance. It is in the area of less obvious dangers that warnings are necessary. Failure to warn effectively of a hazard the product user may not be aware of is certainly actionable negligence.

A third area where negligence is of some importance is in product inspection. Good quality control will prevent defective and dangerous products from getting into the stream of commerce. Proof of quality control negligence is not really necessary to establish liability on the part of a manufacturer or retailer—he would be liable under the strict tort theory if he lets a defective, dangerous specimen of his product into the stream of commerce and it injures someone. Proof of negligence in inspection in such situations will often add frosting to the plaintiff's cake, however. The jury may well be willing to assess more damages against a negligent defendant than it would against a defendant who was not negligent.

The usual defenses to negligence apply in this context. If the plaintiff is guilty of negligence with respect to the use of the product, the rules of comparative negligence will apply. The two-year statute of limitations is applicable in actions for negligence in the area of product liability.

Violation of statutory duty. The most important statute imposing duties in the product liability area is the Consumer Product Safety Act, 15 USC 2051-2081. The act gives the Consumer Product Safety Commission (CPSC) the power to fix safety standards for virtually all consumer products except those which are governed by other statutes. The main categories of products which are *not* governed by the Consumer Product Safety Act are automobiles, boats, airplanes, firearms, tobacco products, pesticides, foods, drugs, and cosmetics.

Once the CPSC sets a safety standard for a product, all manufacturers of the product must comply with the standard. Manufacture and distribution of noncomplying products subjects the manufacturer to criminal and civil penalties. In addition, an individual damaged by a noncomplying product may sue the manufacturer for damages on the basis that it was noncomplying. Responsibility for noncompliance with these standards does not rest only with the manufacturer. Any businessman who sells a noncomplying product may be subjected to the criminal and civil penalties, and may be sued by individuals damaged by the product. Retailers and other distributors of products for which CPSC safety standards exist may protect themselves from this liability by obtaining written guarantees from manufacturers stating that the lot of the product being purchased is in compliance with relevant standards. If the retailer has the guarantee he is protected, unless he knows for a fact that the lot is actually nonconforming.

34

Remedies for Breach of Contract for Sale of Goods

The UCC provides an arsenal of remedies for those who are the victims of a breach of contract for sale of goods. Remedies are also provided for those who might suffer losses due to the insolvency of the other party to the contract.

Remedies of seller for breach by buyer. UCC 2-703 makes the following remedies available to seller when buyer wrongfully rejects or revokes acceptance of goods, when buyer wrongfully fails to make a payment due on or before delivery, or when buyer repudiates a part or the whole of a contract (with respect to the goods directly affected if a part and, if the breach is of the whole contract, also with respect to the entire undelivered balance):

1. Withholding of delivery.
2. Stopping delivery of goods in transit.
3. Identifying goods to the contract.
4. Salvaging unfinished goods.
5. Reselling identified goods and recovering damages.
6. Recovering damages for nonacceptance.
7. Recovering the price (in a proper case).
8. Canceling the contract.

Withholding of delivery. A default by buyer suspends seller's obligation to perform. Thus seller is under no obligation to make deliveries of goods until buyer cures his default.

Stoppage of goods in transit. UCC 2-705 provides that seller may stop in transit a carload, truckload, planeload, or larger shipment of goods due to buyer's breach if:

1. The goods have not yet been received by buyer, and
2. No negotiable document of title to the goods has been negotiated to buyer, and
3. No carrier has reshipped the goods for buyer, and
4. No carrier while acting as warehouseman and no other bailee has acknowledged to buyer that he holds the goods for buyer.

Seller must notify bailee to stop in enough time so that bailee has a reasonable opportunity to prevent delivery. Once the goods have been stopped bailee must hold and deliver the goods according to seller's instructions, and seller is liable to bailee for any charges or damages caused by the stoppage. If bailee has issued a negotiable document of title for the goods, he need not obey an order to stop in transit until the document is surrendered. Thus, if seller does not control the document he cannot stop in transit.

A carrier which has issued a nonnegotiable document of title for the goods need not obey an order to stop in transit by anyone except the consignee of the goods. If someone other than seller is named as consignee of a nonnegotiable bill of lading, seller may not stop the goods in transit unless the named consignee is willing to give an order to stop on the seller's say-so.

Notice that a less-than-carload, truckload, or planeload shipment may not be stopped in transit due to a buyer's breach.

Identification of goods to the contract. UCC 2-706 provides that if buyer breaches at a time when seller has not yet identified the goods to the contract, seller may proceed to identify goods if they are in his possession or control. If the goods which are the subject matter of the contract are in the process of being manufactured at the time of breach, seller may, if it is reasonable under the circumstances, finish the manufacturing process and identify the goods to the contract.

Once the goods have been identified, seller may make use of his remedy of resale with respect to these goods.

Salvage of unfinished goods. When the goods are in the process of being manufactured at the time of breach, seller may decide to stop the manufacturing process and sell the unfinished goods for their scrap or salvage value. Seller may do this if in his considered judgment less loss will be incurred due to buyer's breach if he so proceeds.

Resale of identified goods. Seller may sell to a third party those goods buyer wrongfully refused to buy (UCC 2-706). The sale may be public (an auction) or it may be private. Seller must conduct the resale in good faith and in a commercially reasonable manner; he must announce in connection with such a resale that the goods are being sold because of a broken contract.

If the resale is a private sale, the seller may negotiate a contract of sale with a buyer. The seller need not disclose the identity of the buyer, nor need he disclose the resale price if the goods were resold at a profit. However, he may not make a private contract for resale without notifying the original buyer in advance of his intent to resell at private sale. If the resale is a public sale, the seller must notify the buyer of the time and place of sale, unless the goods are perishable or threaten to decline in value rapidly. The sale must take place at a location customarily used for such sales. The goods must either be present at the sale, or the seller must state in his notice of sale the place at which the goods are available for inspection. The seller may buy the goods at the sale.

If the goods were not resold at a profit, the seller may then recover from the buyer the difference between the contract price and the resale price, plus his expenses in arranging the resale.

Recovery of price. UCC 2-709 provides that the seller may force the breaching buyer to pay contract price for the goods under the following three circumstances only:

1. When the buyer has accepted the goods, but has not paid for them.
2. When the goods are nonresellable goods. Goods are nonresellable when they are so unique that there is obviously no market for them, or when the seller has made a reasonable effort to resell them but cannot obtain a reasonable price.
3. The goods were lost or damaged in transit while risk of loss was on buyer.

Recovery of damages for nonacceptance. When recovery of the price is not possible, and seller chooses not to resell, seller's recourse is to recover damages under UCC 2-608. The normal measure of damages here is contract price less market price, plus expenses caused by breach less expenses saved by breach. Occasionally this measure of damages will be inadequate, particularly in the situation where the seller is a retailer selling expensive items out of inventory for a specified price.

Thus: Boss makes a contract with Furrier to purchase a mink coat for $5,000 as a gift to Secretary, delivery of the coat and payment due on December 21. Mrs. Boss discovers this early in December and makes her great unhappiness known to her husband in no uncertain terms, so Boss fires Secretary and repudiates his contract with Furrier. Furrier then sells the coat he would have sold Boss to Mrs. Richman. Furrier had six such coats in inventory at the beginning of December, three at the end of December. He sold all three for $5,000 each. He paid his supplier $3,000 for each coat. Furrier decides that he could have sold four of these coats had Boss not repudiated his contract, so he claims $2,000 damages from Boss. Boss claims Furrier suffered no damage because he obtained $5,000, the contract price, for the coat Boss did not buy. Who has the better claim? Furrier does. To be sure, the rule of contract price less market price would net Furrier no damages, but this is not realistic because the breach of Boss did cost Furrier a sale and the profit on that sale. Furrier's damages would not be quite $2,000, though—the overhead expense saved Furrier by the breach would be deducted.

Cancellation of the contract. Seller may, by informing buyer that he is canceling the contract, relieve himself of all further obligations under the bargain.

Seller's remedies on discovery of buyer's insolvency. Seller may make use of the following remedies upon discovery of buyer's insolvency, as per UCC 2-702 and 2-705:

1. Refusal to make more deliveries except for cash and payment for all goods heretofore delivered but not paid for.
2. Reclamation of goods received by buyer and not paid for.
3. Stoppage of goods in transit.

Refusal to deliver. If buyer is insolvent, seller is under no obligation to deliver goods to him on credit, even if seller has agreed to sell on credit in the original contract. Seller may thus refuse to make more deliveries until goods delivered but unpaid for have been paid for. He may also require that buyer pay cash for all future deliveries upon delivery.

Reclamation of goods. When seller discovers buyer's insolvency he may recover goods delivered on credit to buyer if he makes his demand within ten days of buyer's receipt of the goods. However, if buyer has in writing misrepresented his solvency to seller within three months of the delivery of the goods, the ten-day limitation does not apply. If the buyer has sold the goods to a buyer in the ordinary course of business or to any other bona fide purchaser; or if a creditor of buyer has obtained a lien upon the goods while they are in the buyer's possession, seller's reclamation right is cut off.

The right to stop in transit. Seller may stop any quantity of goods in transit if buyer is insolvent, so long as the other requirements of UCC 2-705 are met.

Disposal of down payments or other deposits of buyer in event of buyer's breach. When buyer has made payments upon goods, then breaches so that seller may justifiably withhold delivery of these goods, a problem may arise as to the disposition of the payments. UCC 2-718(2) provides that buyer is entitled to restitution of any amount by which the amount paid exceeds 20 percent of the value of buyer's performance under the contract, or $500, whichever is smaller. Seller may offset against this sum any damages that he can prove he suffered due to the breach, plus the value of any benefits buyer has received under the contract.

Buyer's remedies in event of breach by seller. UCC sections 2-711 through 2-717 describe the remedies available to buyer in the event of seller's repudiation, failure to make delivery, or delivery of nonconforming goods that buyer justifiably rejects or refuses to accept. The remedies may be applied to the goods involved in the breach or to the entire contract, if the breach was a breach of the entire contract. The available remedies are:

1. Cancellation of the contract.
2. Recovery of that portion of the price already paid.
3. Cover and recovery of damages.
4. Recovery of damages for nondelivery.
5. Recovery of damages for nonconformity of accepted goods.
6. Recovery of consequential damages, including damage caused to person or property by breach of warranty.
7. Specific performance.
8. Replevin.

Cancellation of contract. Buyer simply informs seller that he will not make any more performances under the contract. This discharges all remaining obligations of buyer provided for in the contract.

Recovery of that portion of price already paid. Buyer may obtain the return of any down payment or deposit, and he may seek damages in addition. The normal rule that one may not seek both restitution and damages in the same litigation does not apply here.

Cover. Buyer may purchase the goods seller did not deliver from another source of supply. If buyer covers in good faith and without unreasonable delay he may recover from seller as damages the price he paid for the covering goods less the contract price, plus expenses of cover (UCC 2-712).

Damages for nondelivery or repudiation. Buyer may choose not to cover. In such a case, the measure of damages for nondelivery or repudiation is market price less contract price (UCC 2-713). If the breach consisted of nondelivery, the market price considered is that of the day of delivery under the contract. If the breach consisted of repudiation, the market price is determined as of the day of repudiation. If the breach was an anticipatory breach, market price is determined as of the day buyer learned of the breach, as per UCC 2-723. If there is any question as to the correct market price, price reports in newspapers or trade journals may be used as evidence (UCC 2-724).

Recovery of damages for nonconformity of accepted goods. According to UCC 2-714, buyer may recover as damages the difference between the accepted goods as accepted and the value they would have had had they been conforming—or, to put it another way, contract price less actual value.

Of course, if buyer accepts the goods, seller will have a claim against him for the purchase price. Buyer has a claim against seller for the damages caused by the nonconformity. More often than not, seller will on balance have a claim against buyer, since the damages will not exceed the contract price (unless, of course, the contract price has already been paid). In cases where buyer has accepted the goods but has not paid the contract price, UCC 2-717 allows buyer to inform seller that he will deduct his damages from the purchase price.

Recovery of consequential damages, including personal injury and property damage caused by breach of warranty. UCC 2-715 allows recovery of damages caused by special circumstances of which seller was informed, or of which he should have had knowledge. A common cause of consequential or special damages is that buyer needs the goods in order to fulfill a contract he has with another party; seller's subsequent breach causes buyer to breach his contract with his customer. If seller knew or should have known of buyer's other contract, he will be liable for the consequences of buyer's breach of his contract. Should a defect in the goods cause personal injury to the buyer, or should it cause damage to the property of the buyer, these damages are recoverable.

Obviously, the sky is the limit with respect to the amount of damages recoverable for personal injury. Also, the amount recoverable for property damage is not limited to the value of the goods causing the damage.

Buyers are not the only parties who may seek damages for breach of warranty. As pointed out in the last chapter, anyone injured in his person or property may sue for damages for breach of warranty, particularly breach of the implied warranty of merchantability.

UCC 2-715 also permits a buyer to recover incidental damages from a breaching seller. These are essentially expenses the buyer has been caused because of the breach—expenses of dealing with rejected goods, expenses in effecting cover, and other such things.

Specific performance. If the goods contracted for are unique, or if the court hearing the case feels that the circumstances are proper, UCC 2-716 permits buyer to force seller to perform his contract. Essentially, then, buyer may seek to make seller deliver. Traditionally, specific performance of contracts for the sale of goods was limited to contracts involving one-of-a-kind goods—works of art, antiques, manuscripts, and other such things that could not be reproduced. The UCC seeks to relax this requirement to an extent, so that a judge hearing a case in which a buyer seeks specific performance may order the seller to deliver goods that are not unique if he feels that circumstances justify it.

The court may decree in a specific performance case such terms of payment of the price, damages, or restitution as it sees fit.

Replevin. Buyer may seek to force seller to deliver identified goods which are not unique under two circumstances.

If there exists such a shortage of the goods involved that the buyer cannot cover, or if circumstances indicate that there is no use in trying to effect cover, the buyer may obtain replevin. Here, the goods which are normally not unique become so because of the shortage: if the buyer cannot get the goods from the seller, he cannot get them at all.

If the seller has shipped the goods under reservation and the buyer has paid for them or otherwise discharged the seller's security interest, the buyer may force seller to deliver by asking for replevin.

Buyer's remedy in case of seller's insolvency. When buyer has made a partial or full payment for goods and seller becomes insolvent within ten days after his receipt of the first installment of the purchase price, buyer may recover the goods from the seller if they are identified to the contract and if buyer tenders payment of the unpaid balance of the purchase (UCC 2-502).

There are two rather severe limitations upon the buyer's right to reclaim. The requirement that the insolvency of the seller occur within ten days after his receipt of the first installment of the purchase price is the first of these. If the insolvency occurs more than ten days after such receipt, buyer's only remedy would be the filing of a claim in the insolvency proceeding for his payment.

The second limitation is the requirement that the goods be identified to the contract. Except when the contract is for the sale of already identified goods, or for the sale of a crop to be planted, the process of identification is under the control of the seller—unless, of course, the contract gives the buyer the power to identify. Unless the contract permits the buyer to identify the goods, the buyer has no right to recovery of the goods if they are not identified at the time he wishes to make his demand. If the contract calls for a cash or credit sale, the buyer will have no reclamation right at all.

Rights of a person in the position of a seller. UCC 2-707 provides that a person in the position of a seller may exercise some of the remedies of sellers, such as the right to stop goods in transit, the right to resell rejected goods, and the right to recover incidental damages. Among those who may qualify as persons in the position of a seller are:
  1. An agent of the seller who has paid for the goods and who now seeks reimbursement from the seller.
  2. A surety of the buyer who has paid the seller the purchase price of the goods because of the buyer's default.
  3. A financing agency which has acquired documents governing the goods by discounting seller's draft drawn on buyer for the purchase price.

With respect to the financing agency, UCC 2-506 provides that when such an agency acquires a draft upon a buyer for the price of goods and documents of title accompanying the goods, it acquires the rights of the shipper of the goods, including the right to enforce the draft against the buyer.

Liquidated damage clauses in contracts for sale of goods. UCC 2-718 essentially codifies the normal contract rules with respect to liquidated damage clauses. The parties may insert such a clause into a contract for sale of goods, and the courts will enforce it if it is reasonable. If the clause fixes unreasonably high damages, it is void as a penalty.

Modification or limitation of remedies. Parties may limit or modify the remedies for breach provided by the UCC. Certain remedies may be made exclusive if the parties so agree. The parties may also devise other remedies not provided for in the UCC. However, UCC 2-719 limits the power of the parties to write the remedies provided by the UCC out of their contracts in two ways.

First, if a contractually provided limited or exclusive remedy does not serve its purpose, recourse may be had to the UCC remedies. Second, a disclaimer of liability for consequential damages is acceptable only if it is not unconscionable. Any attempt to limit or disclaim liability for personal injury damages in a consumer transaction is unconscionable, though it may not be in a commercial transaction.

Also, it should be remembered that the four-year statute of limitations upon suits for breach provided by UCC 2-725 may be shortened by agreement to as little as one year, but it may not be lengthened.

Remedies for fraud. UCC 2-721 states that all of the remedies provided by the UCC for breach are available to a victim of fraud or material misrepresentation. Under this section one may both rescind the contract or reject or return defective goods and sue for damages in case of defraud or misrepresentation. In addition, the victim of fraud may seek punitive damages.

Right to sue third party for injury to goods. When a third party so damages goods which have been identified to a contract for sale of goods as to be liable for the damage, UCC 2-722 provides that either seller or buyer may sue for damages if the plaintiff has:
  1. Title to the goods, or
  2. A security interest in the goods, or
  3. An insurable interest in the goods, or
  4. Risk of loss with respect to the goods.

However, if the plaintiff did not have risk of loss with respect to the goods at the time of damage or destruction, he will hold any recovery as a trustee for the party with the risk of loss. However, the defendant will not be able to get the suit dismissed because the plaintiff did not have risk of loss.

PART VII

Secured Transactions
Motor Vehicles
Business Regulation

35

Secured Transactions

The law governing secured transactions in personal property is found in Article Nine of the Uniform Commercial Code. This article governs consensual secured transactions—that is, transactions in which the debtor voluntarily gives his creditor a lien upon certain of his property in return for the creditor's permission to purchase the property on credit, or in return for the creditor's loan of money.

The types of transactions covered by Article Nine include, but are not limited to:
1. Purchases of household goods, etc., on credit by consumers.
2. Purchases of business equipment on credit by businessmen.
3. Purchases of inventory on credit by businessmen.
4. Borrowing by a farmer to finance the planting and cultivating of the current year's crop, with the crop serving as collateral for the loan.
5. Raising cash for the purpose of meeting current business expenses in return for the sale or pledge of accounts receivable.
6. Borrowing money for personal use by a consumer who gives the creditor a lien on some of his assets as collateral.

UCC 9-104 provides that Article Nine does not govern a long list of security arrangements, including, among other things:
1. Security agreements and interests in certain types of property (ships and aircraft, for instance) governed by federal law.
2. Landlords' liens (liens landlords have against property of their tenants for unpaid rent).
3. Artisans' liens, mechanics' liens, warehousemen's liens, carriers' liens, and other such encumbrances, except as to priority against a UCC security interest.
4. Assignments of wages (which are for the most part illegal in Texas in any event).
5. Transfers by governments, governmental subdivisions, and government agencies.
6. Assignment of all accounts receivable or chattel paper of a business in connection with a sale of the business, assignments or sales of single accounts receivable, assignments of accounts for collection only, or assignments accompanied by delegations of duties.
7. Transfers of interests in or claims to insurance policies, except for proceeds and questions of priority with respect to proceeds.

8. Rights represented by judgments.
9. Rights of setoff.
10. Interests in or liens upon real estate, with the exception of fixtures.
11. Tort claims.
12. Transfers of deposit accounts, except for matters of proceeds and priorities in proceeds.
13. Federal and state tax liens.

Extensive amendments to Article Nine were proposed by the Permanent Editorial Board for the UCC in 1971. The Texas legislature has adopted these amendments; however, not all states have yet done so.

Important definitions. Article Nine makes use of some specialized terminology; familiarity with some of it is essential.

The *debtor* is the person who owes payment or performance of an obligation, or the person who owns the collateral, as per UCC 9-105(1)(d).

The *collateral* is the property subject to a security interest, as per 9-105(1)(c).

The *secured party* is the lender or seller in whose favor there is a security interest, as per 9-105(10)(m).

A *security interest* is an interest in personal property securing the payment of a debt or the performance of an obligation, as per 1-201(37).

A *security agreement* is the agreement creating or providing for a security interest, as per 9-105(1)(l).

A *purchase-money security interest* is a security interest taken by the seller of collateral to secure the payment of all or part of the price, or a security interest taken by a lender or person who has given value so that the debtor might acquire rights in collateral, if the value were so used (9-107).

Attachment and perfection of security interests. A security interest must attach to collateral before it becomes a valid lien upon the collateral as between the debtor and the secured party. According to UCC 9-203, a security interest attaches when the last of three required occurrences comes to pass:

1. The secured party takes possession of the collateral, or the debtor signs a security agreement containing a description of the collateral and—when the collateral is crops growing or to be grown, or timber to be cut—a description of the land concerned, and
2. Value has been given, and
3. The debtor has rights in the collateral.

Notice, then, that there can be no attachment of a security interest (and thus no valid security interest) unless the debtor has signed a written security agreement, or the secured party has possession of the collateral. Normally there can be no valid oral security agreement.

When a security interest attaches to named collateral, it also attaches to the proceeds of the sale or other disposal of the collateral, including insurance payable by reason of loss or damage, to the extent that the insurance is payable to a party other than a party to the security agreement, as per UCC 9-306(1) and (2).

A security interest must be *perfected* in order to be valid against third parties who might acquire an interest in the collateral. Security interests may be perfected in one of four ways, depending upon the nature of the collateral.

1. By attachment—only in the case of a purchase-money security interest in consumer goods.
2. By the secured party's taking possession of the collateral, except for accounts

receivable and other intangible assets impossible to reduce to physical possession, such as patents, copyrights, trademarks, patent licenses, etc.

3. By the filing of a financing statement in the proper public records, except for commercial paper, investment securities, negotiable documents of title, etc.

4. By notation upon a certificate of title—the only way to perfect a security interest in a motor vehicle.

A security interest may not be perfected until it has first attached.

The financing statement is the document which must be recorded in order to perfect a security interest by filing. It must contain a description of the collateral and the names and addresses of the debtor and the secured party. It must also be signed by the debtor (UCC 9-402).

Types of collateral and the means of attaching and perfecting security interests in each. Consumer goods other than motor vehicles. Consumer goods are goods used or bought for personal, family, or household purposes, as per UCC 9-109(1).

Most security interests in these goods are purchase-money security interests, under which the debtor has the use of the collateral while he is paying for it. The debtor signs a written security agreement giving the secured party an interest in the collateral. The secured party may be the seller of the collateral (if the debtor agrees to make payments to the seller until the collateral is paid for). The secured party may also be a financing agency (if the debtor has borrowed the money to pay for the collateral from the financing agency and has agreed to make payments to the financing agency). A deal with a financing agency may also be a three-way deal under which the seller delivers the collateral to the debtor, the financing agency pays the seller for the collateral, and the debtor agrees to make payments to the financing agency until the loan is repaid.

The purchase-money security interest in consumer goods becomes perfected when it attaches, except with respect to bona fide purchaser consumers, as per UCC 9-307(2), or when the consumer goods are to become fixtures. Goods become fixtures when they are built into a building so that, in a sense, they become a part of the building. If, for example, the consumer goods consist of a stove that is to be built into a residence and that will be sold if the residence is sold, once the stove is installed it becomes, for many purposes, a part of the house and thus a part of the land upon which the house sits.

If the goods are not to be attached to real estate, the secured party's security interest will be perfected without the filing of a financing statement against other creditors of the buyer who may claim liens upon the property (with the exception of claimants of artisans' liens). The secured party will also be protected if the debtor gives the collateral away or sells it to a second-hand dealer or a consumer who knows that it is not paid for. However, the debtor could cut off the security interest of the third party by selling to a consumer who gives value, acts in good faith, and does not know the goods are not paid for.

In order to perfect the security interest against bona fide purchaser consumers, the secured party must file a financing statement in the office of the county clerk of the county where the debtor resides (UCC 9-401).

If the goods are to become fixtures, the secured party must protect himself against the interests of those parties who claim an interest in the real estate of which the fixture will become a part.

Perfection of a purchase-money security interest in goods which are to become fixtures requires a *fixture filing* by the secured party either before the goods become fixtures or within ten days thereafter. A fixture filing consists of the filing of a financing statement in the real property records of the county where the real estate in which the goods to become a fixture is located, containing the usual contents of a financing statement, plus a description of the real estate to which the goods are to be attached.

A non-purchase-money security interest in consumer goods may arise when a consumer desires to borrow money and to give the lender a security interest in collateral he already owns.

If the bargain between the debtor and the secured party here is a *pledge*, the security interest will attach when the debtor gives the secured party possession of the collateral. The interest of the secured party will also be perfected as of the time of attachment (UCC 9-305).

If the bargain is not a pledge, so that the debtor will retain possession of the collateral, there will be no attachment unless the debtor signs a proper security agreement; there will be no perfection of any sort unless a proper financing statement is filed. There can be no perfection of a non-purchase-money security interest in consumer goods without either possession of collateral by the secured party or the filing of a financing statement.

Security agreements sometimes contain after-acquired property clauses. For instance, a bank may make a loan to a consumer, the consumer in return giving the bank a security interest in his household furniture. The security agreement might provide that the bank has a security interest in the furniture the consumer owns at the time of contracting as well as all household furniture he may acquire in the future before the loan is paid off. In consumer transactions such an after-acquired property clause is of little help to the secured party, because under UCC 9-204 no security interest in consumer goods will attach because of an after-acquired property clause to goods acquired by the consumer more than ten days after the secured party gives value. In addition, UCC 9-312(4) provides that a purchase-money security interest in most sorts of collateral will be superior to a non-purchase-money security interest in the same collateral if the interest was perfected when the debtor took possession of the collateral or within ten days thereafter. Thus, after-acquired property clauses in consumer security agreements have almost no effect.

Equipment. Equipment consists of goods bought for business use, or for use by a nonprofit organization or government agency. A security interest in equipment will attach either when a secured party takes possession or when a security agreement is signed, and when other requirements of attachment are complied with.

Security interests in equipment are perfected either by the secured party's taking possession (which is rarely done with equipment) or through the filing of a financing statement. Financing statements covering farm equipment must be filed with the county clerk of the county where the equipment is used. Financing statements covering other kinds of equipment must be filed with the secretary of state in Austin unless the equipment is to become a fixture.

After-acquired property clauses are often used in equipment security agreements; they apply to all after-acquired equipment. However, a purchase-money security interest in equipment takes precedence over a non-purchase-money interest coming into existence by virtue of an after-acquired property clause if it is perfected when the debtor receives the collateral or within ten days thereafter.

Farm products. Crops, livestock, and supplies used or produced in farming operations—or products of crops or livestock in their unmanufactured state—are farm products if they are in the possession of a debtor engaging in farm operations, according to UCC 9-109(3). Security interests in these become attached in the usual way. They are perfected either by the secured party's taking possession or by filing. The filing must be done in the office of the county clerk of the county where the farm is located.

A perfected security interest in a crop for new value, given not more than three months before planting to enable the debtor to produce the crop during the production season takes precedence over an older and earlier security interest if the earlier interest secured obligations coming due at least six months before the planting of the crop in question, as per UCC 9-312(2). The purpose of this provision is to make it easier for a farmer to obtain financing for his current crops if he is in debt on production loans for crops from previous years.

A buyer of farm products in the ordinary course of business takes them subject to any security interest in them held by creditors of the farmer, according to UCC 9-307(1).

Inventory. Inventory comprises goods held for sale or lease, goods to be furnished under service contracts, raw materials, work in process, or materials or supplies to be used or consumed in a business, as per UCC 9-109(4).

Acquisition of inventory is often financed by the debtor's giving his financer or supplier a *floating lien* on his inventory. Such a lien covers everything contained in the inventory at any particular time. Since floating lien agreements contain an after-acquired property clause, newly acquired inventory will become subject to the lien. However, a purchase-money security interest in new inventory will take precedence over a preexisting floating lien if it is perfected at the time the debtor receives the inventory and the purchase-money secured party gives notice in writing to the floating lienholder of his intent to sell inventory to the debtor and to claim a purchase-money security interest in it. This notice must be received by the floating lienholder before the purchase-money interest is perfected, according to UCC 9-312(3).

Buyers of inventory in the normal course of the seller's business take their purchases free and clear of the lien, as per UCC 9-307(1). A buyer not in the normal course of business (e.g., a retailer buying inventory from another retailer) will not buy free and clear of the floating lien or other security interest in the inventory.

A security interest in inventory will attach through the signing of a security agreement plus the completion of the other requirements of attachment. It will be perfected through the filing of a financing statement, since no debtor would want to give the secured party possession of his inventory. A financing statement perfecting a security interest in inventory must be filed with the secretary of state in Austin.

When inventory is repossessed by the debtor under a floating lien, the lien reattaches to the goods from the time of repossession until the repossessed goods are again disposed of in the normal course of the debtor's business, according to UCC 9-306(3).

When inventory is sold, the consideration received for the sale is proceeds, and is subject to the inventory lien. If the sale is on credit, the account receivable will be subject to the lien until collected. If the sale is for cash, the security interest will continue in the proceeds only for so long as the proceeds are identifiable; as soon as the cash becomes commingled with other cash belonging to debtor, the proceeds are no longer identifiable, according to UCC 9-306(2).

Accounts. This category of collateral comprises accounts receivable; not included are receivables represented by promissory notes or receivables represented by written contracts of sale. Essentially, then, these are accounts receivable as a result of sales on open account.

A security interest in these will not attach unless there is a written security agreement. Such an interest may be perfected only by filing a financing statement. The statement must be filed in the office of the secretary of state unless the collateral is accounts arising from or relating to sales of farm products by farmers, in which case the filing must take place with the county clerk of the county where the farm is located. Filing is necessary no matter whether the transaction involving the accounts is called a sale or an assignment. Filing theoretically is not required to perfect a security interest in an isolated assigned account, or in accounts assigned for collection only.

Accounts are freely assignable. Any provision in a contract forbidding the assignment of an account is ineffective, as per UCC 9-318(4). The assignment or sale will not obligate the person owing the account—called the account debtor—to pay the assignee until he is informed of the assignment. The account debtor may refuse to pay the assignee until the assignee furnishes satisfactory proof of the assignment, according to UCC 9-318(3).

The assignee of an account gets only the rights to collect that the assignor had, unless the contract involved contained a valid waiver of defenses clause, which open account contracts are not likely to contain.

An assignee of an account must be aware of the fact that, since the account may arise from the sale of inventory and that it thus becomes proceeds of the sale of inventory, a financer of the debtor's inventory may already have a security interest in the account as proceeds. He must also remember that, according to UCC 9-306, a security interest in collateral is also a security interest in the proceeds of the collateral, except in the unlikely case where the financing statement filed on the collateral says that proceeds are not covered.

The assignee of an account should also realize that, if another security interest in the debtor's inventory was perfected prior to the assignment of the account, that other interest will prevail if the goods sold to create the account are repossessed. Such goods become inventory again and are subject to the security interest in inventory, while the account has probably become uncollectable because of the repossession.

Chattel paper. This category of collateral consists of nonnegotiable sales contracts and sales contracts attached to negotiable promissory notes, as per UCC 9-105(1)(b).

A security interest in chattel paper could attach as a result of a written security agreement or as a result of the secured party's taking possession. The security interest in chattel paper may be perfected either by filing or by the secured party's taking possession; perfection by filing requires filing with the secretary of state.

Perfection by filing may be ineffective; according to UCC 9-308, if the paper comes into the possession of a purchaser who gives new value and takes possession in the ordinary course of his business, such a purchaser will have priority over a filed security interest in that chattel paper if he does not know of the filed security interest. He will have absolute priority over a holder of a security interest in inventory claiming the chattel paper as proceeds, even if he knows of the existence of the proceeds claim.

The only safe way to perfect a security interest in chattel paper is by taking possession of the paper. The next best method is to stamp notice of the existence of the security interest upon the contract itself; this would give notice of the existence of the interest to any buyer of the paper.

Instruments. UCC 9-105(1)(i) defines this category of collateral to include primarily commercial paper and investment securities. A security interest in these can and sometimes does attach as a result of a written security agreement, but more often it attaches by the secured party's obtaining possession; gaining possession is the only way to obtain a permanent security interest in instruments, according to UCC 9-304(1).

UCC 9-304 provides for the temporary perfection of a security interest in instruments without possession by the secured party under two circumstances. In both cases the perfection endures for only twenty-one days, and may be defeated by negotiation of commercial paper to a holder in due course or by negotiation of investment securities to a bona fide purchaser.

The first situation in which temporary perfection is possible is when a secured party, for new consideration, acquires a security interest in instruments under a written security agreement. The security interest becomes perfected when it attaches and remains perfected for twenty-one days thereafter. The debtor must deliver the collateral to the secured party during the twenty-one day period for the security interest to become permanently perfected.

The second situation where temporary perfection is possible occurs when a secured party who has perfected a security interest in the instrument by possession delivers possession of the instrument to the debtor for purposes of sale or presentment for payment. The security interest remains perfected for twenty-one days after delivery to the debtor.

In both of these situations the security interest will remain attached to the collateral after expiration of the twenty-one day period. If the debtor sells or otherwise disposes of the collateral during that period, the secured party will retain his security interest in the proceeds. But if the debtor sells the instrument to a holder in due course or sells the security to a bona fide purchaser, the secured party's rights in the collateral terminate; the secured party will be left with only his rights in the proceeds.

It should also be remembered that an inventory financer may lose his security interest in instruments received by the debtor as proceeds of the sale of inventory if the debtor negotiates the instruments to holders in due course. The financer will have a temporary perfected security interest in such instruments for twenty-one days after the debtor receives them, but the only way he could permanently perfect his security interest in such instruments is by taking possession of them.

Documents of title. This category of collateral consists of bills of lading, warehouse receipts, delivery orders, and receipts issued by bonded owners of distilled spirits and agricultural commodities, according to UCC 9-105(1)(e) and 7-201(2). The documents are governed by the same rules, whether they are negotiable or nonnegotiable.

The mechanism for attachment and perfection of security interests in documents is essentially the same as that for instruments; a written security agreement or possession of the document will be essential for attachment of the security interest. Possession of a negotiable document is the only surefire way to perfect a security interest in it, but the filing of a financing statement will also perfect a security interest, subject to the same limitations as filing on chattel paper. If the document is negotiable, perfection by filing may be defeated by negotiation of the document to a third party who is unaware of the filing and gives new value.

A temporary twenty-one day perfection of a security interest in a negotiable document is available under the same circumstances that govern such temporarily perfected security interests in instruments. Once a security interest attaches to a negotiable document by the signing of a written security agreement, the secured party's interest is perfected for twenty-one days without possession. The second situation where temporary perfection without possession is possible for twenty-one days occurs when the secured party has possession of the document and releases it to the debtor so that the debtor may sell, exchange, load, ship, process, or otherwise deal with the document or the goods. The temporary perfection without possession is subject to defeat if the debtor duly negotiates the negotiable document to someone who does not know of the interest.

If a document is nonnegotiable there is no point in perfecting a security interest in it, since the holder of the document does not control the goods. Thus, if the goods are in the hands of a bailee who has issued a nonnegotiable document of title for them (or if the bailee has issued no document at all) the ways to obtain a security interest in the goods are three in number, as per UCC 9-304(3):

1. Obtaining a document of title from the bailee in the name of the secured party, or
2. Notifying the bailee of the secured party's interest in the goods, or
3. Filing a financing statement on the goods themselves.

Once the bailee takes up a negotiable document of title and releases the goods, the perfected security interest in the document will not cover the goods unless the secured party takes possession of the goods or a financing statement has been filed on the document.

If the goods are going into the inventory of a debtor who has given another financer a floating lien on his inventory, the secured party with respect to the document must be certain to take all steps required to perfect a purchase-money security interest in the goods which will be superior to the floating lien. This involves perfecting the interest in the goods before the debtor takes possession and notifying the floating lienholder of the intent to claim a purchase-money security interest in the inventory before the debtor takes possession.

General intangibles. These are essentially rights to receive money other than accounts, chattel paper, instruments, and so on—such as assignments of the right to receive royalties from patents or copyrights. They are perfected by filing, and they attach because of a written security agreement. The place of filing is the same as that for accounts.

Motor vehicles. So long as a motor vehicle is part of a dealer's inventory, it is governed by rules applicable to inventory.

When the vehicle is sold to a user and becomes consumer goods or equipment, however, it becomes subject to the provisions of the Texas Motor Vehicle Certificate of Title Act. According to the act (RCS 6687-1), the only way to perfect a security interest in a motor vehicle is by notation on the certificate of title. Any security interest not noted there is not binding upon a third party who does not know of it, with the exception of a security interest duly perfected out of state which is not noted upon the Texas title.

Multiple state transactions. UCC 9-103 contains the rules governing situations where goods subject to a security interest cross a state line. Since the UCC has been enacted by all states except Louisiana, the procedure for perfection of a security interest is the same in all states but Louisiana, with the exception of perfection of interests in motor vehicles and other property governed by certificates of title. Problems relative to motor vehicles will be discussed later.

If goods are purchased on credit in one state and the purchaser desires to take them into another state, if the seller wishes to perfect a security interest in them he must do so in the second state. Thus: Buyer of Texarkana, Texas, buys goods from Seller of Texarkana, Arkansas, on credit. If seller wants to perfect a purchase-money security interest in the goods, he will have to file his financing statement in the public records of Bowie County, Texas, the county where Texarkana, Texas, is located.

If a resident of Texarkana, Arkansas, buys goods on credit from an Arkansas merchant, with the seller reserving a security interest in the goods by filing a proper financing statement in the proper Arkansas records, this security interest will remain perfected as long as the debtor does not move out of his Arkansas county. However, if he moves to Texarkana, Texas, the seller's security interest will be perfected against Texas bona fide purchaser consumers for only four months after the move. In order to perfect his security interest in Texas, the seller must file a financing statement in Bowie County within four months of the move. This financing statement need not be signed by the debtor; the signature of the secured party will be adequate.

With respect to collateral in which a security interest is perfected by possession, the interest will remain perfected so long as the secured party retains possession, no matter how many state lines are crossed by the debtor or the secured party.

The situation with respect to motor vehicles brought into Texas is more complex. If a vehicle is brought into Texas from a certificate-of-title state, and that state requires notation of security interests upon the certificate of title, in effect any lien shown upon the out-of-state title will remain perfected in Texas because the Texas title to the vehicle will show that lien when issued. The old title will keep the lien perfected until a new title is issued. An existing lien not shown upon the old title will not be perfected in Texas if it was not perfected in the state issuing the old title.

If the vehicle comes from a nontitle state, or from a state not requiring the notation of liens upon the certificate of title, the rules are different. If a perfected security interest exists in the other state, it will remain perfected in Texas for at least four months after the vehicle is brought into Texas, and from then on until the vehicle is registered in Texas and the out-of-state title (if any) is surrendered.

If a Texas title is issued for a vehicle brought into this state from out of state, and the Texas title shows no liens, any nondealer buyer of the vehicle who knows of no out-of-state lien will acquire the vehicle free and clear of any such perfected lien. A dealer buyer will buy subject to the lien, however, if he buys within four months of the date the vehicle is brought into Texas.

If a Texas vehicle is taken into another state while it is subject to a security interest, the interest will not of course be perfected if not noted upon the Texas title. It will remain perfected in the other state for four months, or until the vehicle is registered in the new state or the Texas title is surrendered.

If the vehicle has been taken to a nontitle state, the filing of a financing statement may well be required in order to perfect the security interest there. If the other state is a title state, noting the lien upon the new title or recording it in the proper state records will be necessary for perfection. In any event, if (through fraud or whatever) the debtor acquires a certificate of title in the new state showing that no liens exist upon the vehicle and then sells the car to a nondealer bona fide purchaser, the security interest will be cut off and the lien upon the vehicle will terminate.

Multicounty transactions. The fact that the debtor lives in one county and the secured party in another—or that the debtor takes the collateral from one county into another will not affect the perfection of the secured party's interest in the collateral if the interest is perfected by filing at the state level or by notation on a certificate of title. However, it will affect perfection of security interests in consumer goods and farm equipment, since these are perfected by recording at the county level.

The proper county for recording financing statements on such collateral is the county of the debtor's residence; if the secured party and the debtor do not reside in the same county, filing in the secured party's county does no good. If the debtor moves out of the county where the security interest is perfected and takes the collateral with him, the secured party's security interest in the collateral remains perfected for four months after the move. In order to keep the interest perfected after that time, the secured party must file a financing statement in the debtor's new county of residence. Filing in the new county more than four months after the debtor's removal there will perfect the security interest again, but only as of the date of the new filing; timely filing perfects the interest in the new county as of the date of filing in the old county.

Whether or not the secured party files a new financing statement, the security interest remains attached to the collateral. The secured party will not lose his interest even if he does not file, unless the debtor sells the collateral to a bona fide purchaser.

Perfecting security interests in aircraft and ships. Security interests in aircraft are perfected by recording them with the secretary of transportation. Recording is not necessary for attachment.

Security interests in ships are perfected by recording them with the collector of customs in the home port of the ship; in this case, recording is necessary for perfection, but not for attachment.

Priority problems—fixtures. As noted earlier, perfection of a security interest of a purchase-money nature in a fixture requires a fixture filing in the real estate records of the county where the real estate is located. UCC 9-313 provides some rather complex rules for determining the priority of a purchase-money security interest in fixtures as against a mortgage lien upon the real estate or a claim by an owner of the realty. The security interest in the fixture will have priority if:

1. It is a purchase-money security interest perfected at the time the goods became a fixture or within ten days thereafter, the interest of the encumbrancer or owner arose before the goods became fixtures, and the debtor either has an interest in the realty or possession of it, or
2. The security interest was perfected by fixture filing before the interest of the encumbrancer or owner is of record, the interest has priority over conflicting interests of predecessors in title of the encumbrancer or owner, and the debtor has an interest of record in the realty or possession of it, or
3. The fixtures are readily removable office machines or replacements of readily removable domestic appliances which are consumer goods, and a security interest in them has been perfected in any authorized way before the goods became a fixture, or
4. The conflicting interest is a lien obtained by legal proceedings after perfection of the security interest in the fixture.

Thus, it is of the utmost importance that a person claiming a security interest in a fixture do so before the goods become a fixture. With respect to electric typewriters, refrigerators, etc., ordinary perfection will do; but with respect to air conditioners, furnaces, etc., fixture filing is a necessity.

If goods become fixtures before construction of a building is completed, any security interest in them will be subordinate to the lien of the holder of a construction mortgage (a mortgage securing a loan made to construct an improvement upon real estate) unless the security interest was perfected by fixture filing before the construction mortgage was recorded, or unless the fixtures are readily removable office machines or replacements of consumer goods domestic appliances and the security interest was perfected before the goods became fixtures.

An unperfected security interest in a fixture will have a superior right to a mortgage or realty owner if the mortgagee or owner has consented in writing to the security interest or disclaimed an interest in the fixture, or if the debtor has a right to remove the fixture.

When the secured party has priority over real estate interests he may remove the fixture on default of the debtor, but he is liable to any holder of an interest in the realty other than the debtor for any physical injury done to the realty in the process of removal. A security interest in building materials terminates when the materials are built into a structure.

Refinancing. A question may arise as to the enforceability of a security interest when the debtor is unable to pay off a loan as it matures and the secured party permits him to refinance the transaction. Would a new security agreement and financing statement be necessary to preserve the security interest of the secured party in the collateral? The answer is no; the security interest will remain perfected by the old financing statement, regardless of the refinancing.

Future advances. If a security agreement and financing statement are worded properly, a secured party may obtain a security interest in the collateral for both present and future advances of financing to the debtor without the need for any new filing. If the security agreement covers future advances, it does not matter whether the advances are made pursuant to prior commitment; see UCC 9-204(3).

Priority: security interest vs. lien creditor. A lien creditor is a party who claims a lien upon property due to an attachment or execution; the Internal Revenue Service is such a creditor under a federal tax lien. Also considered to be lien creditors are trustees in bankruptcy as of the date of the filing of a bankruptcy petition, assignees for benefit of creditors as of the making of the assignment, and receivers as of the date of their appointment.

A lien creditor has priority over an unperfected security interest; he is subordinate to a secured party holding a security interest perfected before the lien attached. An attachment or execution is perfected as of the date of the attachment or execution. A federal tax lien is perfected as of the day it is filed in the public records.

A lien creditor is subordinate to a perfected security interest only to the extent of advances made by a secured party to a debtor before he became a lien creditor or within forty-five days thereafter. A person perfecting a purchase-money security interest within ten days of the date the debtor obtained the collateral will have a perfected security interest against lien creditors or transferees in bulk (buyers of goods from a debtor in a bulk sale) as of the date of attachment of his interest; these provisions are made in UCC 9-301.

Priority: security interests vs. mechanic's liens. According to UCC 9-312, a holder of a mechanic's lien or artisan's lien for services performed upon goods in the normal course of the lien claimant's business will take precedence over a perfected security interest.

Priority between conflicting security interests subject to no special rules of priority. UCC 9-312(5) provides that as between perfected security interests, if no other priority rule applies the first perfected takes priority. If both were protected by filing, the first filing has priority; if one of the competing interests was not perfected by filing, the date of perfection controls. If one of the competing interests is perfected and the other is not, the perfected interest has priority. If the conflicting interests are unperfected, the first to attach has priority. Of course neither would be effective as to third parties.

Duration of a security interest perfected by filing. Financing statements are valid for five years, except for a real estate mortgage serving also as a financing statement for fixtures (UCC 9-403). A continuation statement signed by the secured party should be filed during the six months prior to expiration of a financing statement to keep the security interest perfected.

Assignment of a security interest. When a security interest which has been perfected by filing is assigned, the assignee should make certain that a financing statement stating the name and address of the assignee and the rights being assigned is filed and signed by the original security party. It should of course refer to the original financing statement.

Failure to file such a statement of assignment will not affect the perfection of the original security interest in any way. However, filing of the statement is necessary to perfect the assignment because an assignment so perfected will take precedence over an earlier unperfected assignment. UCC 9-405 governs assignments and the filing of statements of assignment.

Termination statement. When the obligation giving rise to a secured transaction is discharged and no obligation remains to make future advances, UCC 9-404 provides that the debtor may demand that the secured party file a termination statement in the records where financing statements were filed; it should be signed by the secured party and state that the secured transaction represented by the financing statement involved in the transaction has been terminated.

A security party failing to file a termination statement upon the request of a debtor is liable to the debtor for $100 plus any damages the debtor can prove he suffered due to the failure.

Default by debtor. Default by the debtor in the performance of his obligations under the security agreement permits the secured party to repossess the collateral or to exercise the other remedies provided to him by law.

The important term *default* is not defined anywhere in the UCC; it is left up to the parties to the security agreement to define. Since creditors have all of the bargaining power in the negotiation of the typical security agreement, "default" means what the creditor wishes it to mean, within reason. The lengthy creditor-drafted security agreement which secured parties are required to sign as a part of the secured transaction will obviously always provide that the missing of a scheduled payment is default. Among other happenings which may be defined as default in security agreements are the following:

1. Failure to insure the collateral.
2. Perfection of another security interest in the collateral.
3. Failure of the debtor to pay other debts as they mature.
4. Insolvency of the debtor.
5. Dissolution of the corporate or partnership debtor.
6. Death of the individual debtor.
7. Appointment of a receiver for the collateral.
8. Decline in market value of the collateral.
9. Secured party's deeming his position to be insecure.

These examples are taken from Eugene A. Cook's article, "UCC Default Provisions and Foreclosures," contained in the State Bar of Texas publication, *Texas Consumer Law for General Practitioners*.

The security agreement and promissory note signed by the debtor will almost certainly also contain an acceleration clause. Under such a clause, the secured party has the right to declare the entire obligation owed by the debtor to be immediately due and payable upon his default. The acceleration usually is not automatic, but the secured party will obviously accelerate when he feels it to be to his advantage to do so after the debtor's default. Any acceleration must be done in good faith by the secured party, but in case of any dispute on this point the debtor has the burden of proving bad faith.

Self-help repossession. The security agreement will doubtless provide that the secured party has the right to take possession of the collateral in the case of the debtor's default (if the secured party does not already have possession). UCC 9-503 provides that the secured party may take possession without judicial action if he may do so without committing a breach of the peace; otherwise he may take possession through judicial action.

The UCC does not define the term "breach of the peace," so its definition is determined by the courts and varies from state to state. According to Eugene Cook, Texas courts generally hold that a repossessor does not breach the peace unless he uses force or violence in the repossession process. The force or violence must of course consist of more than the mere taking away of the repossessed collateral.

If the secured party desires to repossess without judicial action, he need not give advance notice of his intentions to the debtor; he may simply come and take possession of the collateral. There is nothing wrong with sending a tow truck to tow away a collateral automobile parked on a public street or with towing the auto away from the debtor's driveway. There also may not be anything wrong with taking collateral from the debtor's back yard (if it is open and unfenced) or from an open garage.

In *Gulf Oil Corp. vs. Smithey,* 426 SW 2d 262, the Dallas Court of Civil Appeals held that a repossession effected by picking a lock on the debtor's service station door was unlawful and an unauthorized use of force. Whether or not opening an unlocked door or gate to gain access to the desired property would be permissible is questionable.

If the collateral to be repossessed is inside the debtor's residence, it cannot be repossessed without judicial process or the debtor's consent. Even if the security agreement provides that agents of the secured party may enter the debtor's residence to repossess, the debtor is under no obligation to permit them to enter his residence. Refusal to admit them or to turn over possession of the collateral to them is neither a breach of contract nor a commission of the crime of hindering a secured creditor. The same principle would be applicable if the collateral is inside a building used by the debtor for business purposes.

Agents of the secured party coming onto the debtor's property to repossess an automobile from the debtor's driveway are not trespassers; interference with their work could constitute hindering a secured creditor. The debtor of course has the right to ask such persons for ID and authorization papers, but once he is satisfied as to their indentity and mission, he must let them proceed so long as they do not demand access to a building or garage.

If the property being repossessed is a "container" such as an automobile, the secured party of course has no security interest in property inside the container that is not an essential part of it. The secured party repossessing the auto has a security interest in the auto itself, the spare tire, the jack, and other such items found in the vehicle which are an essential part of it, but he has no security interest in contents of the vehicle which are not an essential part, such as packages containing goods purchased by the debtor on the day of repossession which the debtor has not removed from the vehicle.

The secured party in essence becomes a bailee of such items when he repossesses. He becomes obligated to use care to secure them against theft or damage and he may not disclaim liability in his security agreement for not exercising such care.

Judicial repossession. If the collateral is located inside a building or in other places where it cannot be reached without the use of force and violence, and the debtor refuses to surrender possession peaceably to the secured party, the only lawful avenue of repossession is judicial action.

The secured party must file suit for foreclosure of his security interest in a proper court, and, if he wants immediate possession, ask for a writ of sequestration. The requirements for obtaining this writ have been discussed in the chapter on civil procedure. It must be remembered that legal assistance will probably be necessary in preparation of the required documentation, and that a bond of an amount to be determined by the court must be posted by the secured party before the writ will issue. Expense must therefore be incurred to accomplish such repossession.

In addition, RCS 6840 provides that the debtor may recover possession of the collateral during the foreclosure suit by posting a replevy bond, and may also seek to have the writ dissolved. Should the secured party succeed in establishing in court the existence of his lien and his right to foreclose it, the property will be disposed of in the same manner as property seized in execution of a judgment.

Disposal of repossessed property or property already in possession of secured party

without repossession. UCC 9-504 provides that the secured party may dispose of the collateral after default and repossession (if repossession was necessary). UCC 9-505 provides that, under conditions to be discussed later, the secured party may keep the collateral and call the debtor's account even. Normally it is the secured's choice which alternative to follow.

If the secured party chooses to dispose of the collateral (which is what he does more often than not), he may dispose of it either by public or private sale. Public sale is sale by auction; private sale is by negotiation of a contract with a single purchaser. Either method is acceptable, so long as it is commercially reasonable.

Under UCC 9-504, the collateral may be disposed of without notice to the debtor if:
1. The collateral is perishable, or
2. The collateral threatens to decline speedily in value, or
3. The collateral is of a type customarily sold on a recognized market.

A good example of the first sort of collateral is fresh leaf lettuce. An example of the second sort is winter clothing repossessed in February. An example of the third is corporate stock, or grain. The first two sorts of collateral must be disposed of while they still have value. The existence of the recognized market provides a mechanism for selling the third sort at a fair price without the participation or knowledge of the debtor. The only sort of goods for which a recognized market exists for this purpose are securities and fungible commodities.

Notice to the debtor is required for sales of other sorts of collateral to be valid. If the sale is to be public, the debtor must be notified of the time and place thereof. If the sale is to be private, the debtor must be notified of the date when the secured party will begin seeking private buyers. The debtor may waive this right to notice if he does so in writing after his default. Any security agreement provision by which the debtor gives up the right to notice of sale is invalid, since it would have been signed before default.

The UCC requires that the notice of sale be reasonable, but no guidelines are furnished as to what is or is not reasonable. There is no legal requirement that the notice be in writing, but obviously such notice should be written. It should also be sent registered or certified mail, return receipt requested, so that delivery can be proven. There is also no exact provision governing how far in advance notice of sale must be given. Eugene Cook recommends ten days; Ray Henson, in *Secured Transactions under the Uniform Commercial Code*, suggests that five days' notice is sufficient.

Under the 1972 version of Article 9 of the UCC, adopted in Texas, only the debtor is entitled to notice of sale, unless some other party claiming an interest in the collateral has requested a notice of sale from the secured party. Thus, in Texas, the secured party is not obligated to search the public records to determine whether or not anyone else might have a security interest in the collateral.

Retention of collateral by secured party in satisfaction of debt. As mentioned above, the secured party normally need not sell the collateral. He may instead suggest to the debtor that he be permitted to retain the collateral and call the debtor's account even. The secured party may not do this if the debtor objects to it. In addition, if the collateral is consumer goods and the debtor has paid 60 percent of the cash value of the goods or 60 percent of the money borrowed upon security of the goods, the secured party may not even suggest this. The secured party must sell the goods.

Under most circumstances the debtor should not object to the secured party retaining possession. If the goods are sold, they very often do not bring fair market value. Buyers at forced sales are not noted for generosity. Also, it costs money to arrange a forced sale. The expenses so generated are paid out of the proceeds of the sale itself, which in essence means that they are paid by the debtor. In addition, if the proceeds of a sale do not equal the expenses of repossession and resale plus the amount debtor still owes upon his debt, debtor is liable for any deficiency.

Thus, retention of the goods by secured party avoids the incurring of expenses of repossession and resale, and it also eliminates the possibility of any deficiency. To be sure, debtor will lose his equity in the collateral. But he will probably lose that at a sale also.

Debtor's right of redemption. The debtor has the right to recover possession of his goods any time before a public sale is completed—or any time before the secured party makes a binding contract to sell the goods to a third party—by paying to the secured party the amount owed for the goods plus any repossession and resale expenses incurred up to the time of redemption.

Other parties holding security interests in the collateral also have this redemption right. Normally the right is of no particular value to the debtor. If his financial condition was bad enough to obligate him to miss payments to the secured party to begin with, he will not be in any position to redeem the collateral later. However, the right might be of value to second lienholders.

UCC 9-504(4) provides that a buyer at a security interest foreclosure sale obtains all of the interest of the debtor in the collateral, and that the secured party's security interest and all security interests junior to his are discharged. Thus, the second lienholder might find it advisable to redeem the collateral in order to preserve his interest in it. If he does redeem it, he may then proceed to foreclose his interest if the debtor is in default relative to him.

Commercially reasonable disposal of collateral. UCC 9-507 gives the secured party wide leeway with respect to the commercial reasonableness of the disposal method. If the goods are sold on a recognized market for the prevailing market price, the debtor has no complaint even if market conditions have produced an abnormally low price at that time. If the goods are perishable or threaten to decline speedily in value, speedy disposal is the prime consideration before the collateral loses all value.

If the sale is at public auction, there is the difficulty that buyers at forced sales do not normally pay fair market value. Though a buyer at such a sale obtains the debtor's rights in the collateral, and the secured party's security interest and all subordinate security interests are discharged; and though a buyer at such a sale cannot lose title to what he bought because the sale was unlawfully conducted (unless the buyer acted in bad faith, by participating in the illegality or simply by knowing of it), the buyer runs two sizable risks.

First, he gets no guarantee of his title to the goods. To be sure, he gets the debtor's title, but if that title is defective in some way he will normally have no recourse. Forced sellers make no implied warranty of title in these situations. Second, the buyer gets no guarantee as to the quality of the goods. The collateral is not sold subject to the warranty of merchantability if the seller is an auctioneer or a financer of the transaction which went sour, because he would not qualify as a merchant of the goods in question. Even if the seller is such a merchant, he is very likely to sell on an "as is, with all faults" basis, which of course disclaims the warranty of merchantability. Even if the goods are sold at private sale, the risks will tend to hold the selling price down.

The secured party is permitted to bid at his own public sale. If he turns out to be the high bidder there is no illegality, so long as he pays a fair price under the circumstances. The secured party is obligated to make some effort to get a fair price for the property. If he chooses to sell at private sale, he should try for the best price, taking into account the risks of buyers at such sales and the secured party's wish to get the collateral sold without unnecessary haggling. If he sells at a public sale, he should make some effort to attract bidders, and should make the collateral available for inspection before the sale, if that can reasonably be done.

So long as the secured party makes a reasonable, good-faith effort to get the best price for the collateral, he has complied with the legal requirements. It will not do debtor much good to second-guess him by arguing that he could have gotten a better price if he had held the sale on another day, at another place, or in another manner.

Effect of sale on other security interest holders. The secured party is essentially selling the debtor's equity in the collateral, but he also wipes out subordinate security interests in the collateral. Thus: Bob owned a car upon which First Bank had a first lien and Jack had a second lien. Bob got behind on his payments to First Bank, so the bank repossessed. If First Bank sold the car to foreclose its lien, the buyer would get clear title and Jack's second lien would be wiped out by the sale. The bank's first lien would be discharged and Bob's equity would be transferred. If Jack wanted to preserve his security interest in the vehicle, he would either have to redeem it before the sale (by paying what Bob owned on it, plus expenses of repossession) or he would have to buy it at First Bank's sale. By doing that, he would of course become the owner.

On the other hand, if Bob defaulted on his payments to Jack, but kept his payments to First Bank current, Jack could repossess in order to foreclose his lien. In that case Jack could not sell a clear title to the vehicle; all he could sell would be Bob's equity. A buyer at his sale would buy subject to First Bank's security interest. What Jack has to sell would not be very attractive to most buyers—he would be fortunate to find a buyer other than himself.

If First Bank foreclosed its interest in the car by choosing to keep the vehicle in full payment of Bob's account, Jack's lien would also be wiped out. The bank would be under no obligation to send Jack any notice of its repossession or intentions, but if Jack found out what the bank was up to and objected within twenty-one days of the bank's sending notice of its intent to Bob, Jack could force the bank to sell the vehicle, thus giving him a chance to buy it.

If Jack repossessed and chose to keep the vehicle and call Bob's debt to him even, he would of course acquire the vehicle subject to First Bank's lien. First Bank could force him to sell by giving the appropriate notice.

Disposal of proceeds of sale. UCC 9-504(1) provides that the proceeds of a sale of repossessed property shall be divided as follows:

1. Payment of expenses of repossession, storage after repossession, resale, etc., including—if provided for in the security agreement—legal expenses and a reasonable attorney fee incurred by the secured party.
2. Satisfaction of the debtor's indebtedness secured by the collateral.
3. Payment to subordinate lienholders in order of priority, if such lienholders have made written demand for such payment upon the secured party before distribution of the proceeds of the sale.

The expenses of a self-help repossession may not be very great. However, if repossession by judicial process was necessary the expenses will run very high. To be sure, legal expenses are not collectable out of the proceeds of a forced sale of this sort unless the security agreement provides for such collectability, but one may be very sure that a commercial security agreement will have such a provision.

Subordinate lienholders will get nothing from the proceeds of the sale unless they demand payment in writing, and unless there are funds left after the expenses and the debtor's debt to the secured party are paid. More often than not the expenses and the secured party's claim against the debtor exhaust the fund of proceeds, so that nothing is left for subordinate lienholders. However, if such a lienholder learns of a foreclosure sale by a first lienholder, it will pay him to make a demand for payment—if anything remains after the secured party is paid, the subordinate lienholder will at least obtain something in exchange for the loss of his lien.

If anything remains after all claiming lienholders are paid, it goes to the debtor. In nearly all cases, however, nothing will remain. If the sale of the collateral does not produce sufficient funds to pay off the expenses of repossession and resale plus the debtor's debt to the secured party, the debtor is liable for the deficiency. Naturally, the debtor must be informed if this occurs.

The deficiency will be in the form of a judgment if the secured party judicially foreclosed his lien. If there was no judicial foreclosure of the secured party's lien, the deficiency will be a debt rather than a judgment, but the secured party may then sue to reduce the deficiency claim to a judgment. Whether it would pay him to do this depends upon the debtor's financial situation; more often than not the debtor is in such financial difficulty that collection of the deficiency is doubtful. Many such deficiencies turn out to be uncollectable.

Penalties for improper foreclosure of a security interest. If improper foreclosure procedures cause damage to the debtor, he will have a claim against the secured party for the damages. Improper repossession, noncompliance with UCC notice requirements, and attempts to dispose of the collateral in ways which are not commercially reasonable are examples of improper procedures.

If the collateral is consumer goods, UCC 9-507 provides that the injured consumer debtor may recover a penalty equal to the credit service charge (finance charge) plus 10 percent of the principal amount of the debt, or the time-price differential plus 10 percent of the cash price. Thus: Brown bought a 1970 Cadillac from Ace Motors for a cash price of $2,000, promising to pay for the car in thirty-six monthly payments of $80.55 each (which would obligate him to pay a time-price differential of $15 per $100 per year, or a total of approximately $2,900, the maximum he could be asked to pay under Texas law). Brown defaulted and Ace unlawfully sought to foreclose its security interest. The penalty Brown could collect would be computed this way: Brown may collect the time-price differential, which is $900. In addition, he collects 10 percent of the cash price, which is $200. His total recovery is therefore $1,100.

Foreclosure against collateral other than goods. If the collateral is intangible, foreclosure may or may not be similar to the foreclosure upon goods. When collateral consists of commercial paper or securities, the secured party already possesses the collateral. He may choose to sell it, in which case he will proceed with public or private sale of the commercial paper or simply sell the securities on the established market through a broker, or he may keep the collateral and call the debtor's account even. He may then simply hold bonds or promissory notes until they mature, and hold stock until a favorable time arrives to sell.

If the collateral is documents of title, he again already has possession. He may sell the documents at public or private sale, exchange them for the goods and then sell the goods at public or private sale, or decide to keep the documents and call everything even.

If the collateral consists of accounts receivable, the secured party could sell them by public or private sale. More likely, however, the secured party will simply inform the account debtors that he is taking over the accounts, and that the account debtors should now pay him instead of the original debtor.

Generally, the secured party will have a claim against the debtor for any amount of the secured debt not collected from the account debtors. If his collections exceed the amount of the debt plus expenses, the secured party must account to the debtor for the excess. However, the secured party gets only the rights to collect from the account debtors that the debtor had and no more. Whether or not the secured party has the right to charge back uncollectable accounts to the debtor will depend upon the provisions of the security agreement.

Pawn transactions and pawnbrokers. A pawn transaction is a special sort of secured transaction entered into by the debtor with a special sort of secured party, the pawnbroker. These transactions are regulated by Chapter 51 of the Texas Consumer Credit Code—RCS 5069.

RCS 5069-51.02(b) defines a pawnbroker as any person engaged in the business of lending money on the security of pledged goods or engaged in the business of purchasing tangible personal property on condition that it may be redeemed or repurchased by the seller for a fixed price within a fixed period of time.

The pawnbroker's collateral for his loan is called *pledged goods*, which RCS 5069-51.02(c) defines as tangible personal property deposited with or otherwise delivered into the possession of a pawnbroker in connection with a pawn transaction. Pledged goods may not include securities, printed evidence of indebtedness, or the like. A pawnbroker may not make loans upon securities, commercial paper, or similar things; the pledged goods must be tangible.

No person may engage in business as a pawnbroker without a license issued by the Texas Consumer Credit Commissioner. Licensed pawnbrokers must be bonded, and must maintain a net worth of at least $25,000. The conduct of their business is subject to administrative regulations of the Consumer Credit Commissioner. Noncompliance with these regulations may cause revocation of license. RCS 5069-51.17(a) provides that the engagement in the business of operating a pawnshop without a license is a misdemeanor, subjecting one to a fine of up to $1,000 and/or confinement in the county jail for up to six months.

When a debtor pledges goods with a pawnbroker, he incurs no personal liability to the pawnbroker. RCS 5069-51.11 states that the pledgor shall have no obligation to redeem pledged goods or to make any payment on a pawn transaction. The pledgor may let the pawnbroker keep the collateral and not redeem it, or he may redeem and recover his collateral; what he does is strictly up to him.

RCS 5069-51.10 provides that the pawnbroker must give the pledgor a pawn ticket at the time of the making of the pawn transaction. The pawn ticket must contain the following:

1. The name and address of the pawnshop.
2. The name and address of the pledgor, and the pledgor's description, including his driver's license number or military serial number.
3. The date of the transaction.
4. The identification and description of the collateral, including its serial numbers, if any.
5. The amount of cash advanced or credit extended to the pledgor.
6. The amount of pawn service charge.
7. The amount which must be paid to redeem the collateral.

8. The annual percentage rate of the pawn charge.
9. The maturity date of the transaction, which must not be more than one month after the date of the transaction.
10. A statement that the pledgor need not redeem the collateral, and that the collateral may be forfeited to the pawnbroker sixty days after the maturity date.

The maturity date of a pawn transaction may be extended from month to month by mutual agreement of the pawnbroker and the pledgor. Normally, the pawnbroker must not release the pledged goods to anyone who is not the holder of the pawn ticket issued for them; only the ticketholder may redeem the goods. RCS 5069-51.14 provides that the holder of the ticket is presumed to be entitled to redeem the goods.

If the pawn ticket is lost, stolen, or destroyed, the pledgor should notify the pawnbroker in writing. Receipt of such notice by the pawnbroker will invalidate the pawn ticket unless the goods have already been redeemed (RCS 5069-51.15). Before the pawnbroker releases the collateral or issues a new ticket, he must require the pledgor to make an affidavit of the loss, destruction, or theft of the ticket.

The pawnbroker must hold the collateral for at least sixty days after the maturity date of the pawn transaction (RCS 5069-51.13). During this period the pledgor may redeem by paying the original cash advance and pawn service charge, plus an additional one-thirtieth of the pawn service charge for each day past the original maturity date. Once this sixty-day period has expired, the pawnbroker may, at his option, declare the goods forfeited and treat them as his property.

RCS 5069-51.16 forbids a pawnbroker to do several things, among which are:
1. To enter into a pawn transaction with a person under the age of eighteen.
2. To fail to use due care to protect pledged goods from loss or damage.
3. To fail to return the collateral to the pledgor upon payment of the full amount due.
4. To make any charge for insurance upon a pawn transaction.

The maximum pawn charge was discussed in the chapter on illegal contracts, as were the penalties for making unlawful pawn charges. The penalty for other violations of law by pawnbrokers in the operation of their business is a fine of up to $1,000, plus loss of license.

36

Consumer Protection

Fifteen years ago the federal and Texas statute books contained very little legislation designed to govern specifically consumer transactions. In the past few years there has been a virtual explosion in the enactment of such legislation, both at the federal and state levels, governing all facets of the consumer contract, from advertising designed to induce the consumer to enter into a contract through disclosure of information in a consumer contract to debt collection practices. Some of this legislation—particularly that covering interest rate regulation, rescission rights in home solicitation transactions, modification of the holder-in-due-course doctrine, and warranty disclosure legislation—have been covered earlier in these materials. The legislation dealing with real estate sales and landlord-tenant relationships will be covered in the section on real estate.

Credit advertising. Federal laws currently impose an all-or-nothing requirement on advertisers of credit. Should the advertiser merely advertise that he has money to lend, goods to sell on credit, or revolving charge accounts for his customers, no wrong is done, and no disclosure of credit terms in advertising is required.

However, should the advertiser disclose some of his terms, he must disclose all of them. Any advertiser of the availability of open-end credit plans (revolving charge account or credit card plans) who discloses some of his terms must disclose, as per 15 USC 1663:

1. The length of the free-ride period, if any. (That is, the time during which the customer may pay in full for a purchase without being liable for a finance charge.)
2. The method of determining the balance upon which the finance charge will be improved (beginning balance, ending balance, average balance, etc.).
3. Method of determining finance charge.
4. If periodic rates are to be used for determination of finance charge, the rate expressed as an annual percentage rate. (If the rate is expressed as 1.5 percent per month, it must also be expressed as 18 percent per year.)

15 USC 1664 requires advertisements of credit other than open-end credit to disclose rates of finance charge as annual percentage rates if these are to be disclosed at all. If the ad says anything about the amount of down payment or installment payments, the dollar amount of finance charges, the number of installments, or the period for repayment, the following must be disclosed in the ad:

1. Cash price or amount of loan, as applicable.

2. Amount of down payment.
3. Number, amount, and due date of payments.
4. Annual percentage rate of finance charge.

15 USC 1662 forbids advertisers to state terms in their ads—particularly specific loan amounts, down payments, installment payments, and other plans—unless the advertiser customarily grants these terms to customers. Violation of these provisions will render the advertiser liable to a consumer for double the finance charge of the transaction (but no less than $100 and no more than $1,000), plus court courts and a reasonable attorney's fee.

Discrimination in the granting of credit. RCS 5069-2.07 forbids lenders within the state to deny credit on the basis of sex. Violation of this provision subjects a lender to liability for actual damages caused by the discrimination or $50, whichever sum is greater. A licensed lender may also lose his license for a violation.

However, the antidiscrimination legislation with real bite in this area is the Federal Equal Credit Opportunity Act (ECOA) and the administrative regulations in effect thereunder. The ECOA is found at 15 USC 1691 et seq; the relevant administrative regulation is Regulation B of the Federal Reserve Board. The ECOA as amended in 1976 makes it unlawful for a granter of credit to discriminate in credit upon the grounds of sex, marital status, race, religion, national origin, age (so long as applicant is an adult), or receipt of public assistance. The act applies to all credit transactions, not just consumer transactions. Regulation B contains many dos and don'ts for credit granters, designed to implement the act.

Under Regulation B, a credit granter may not ask for the following information on a credit application:

1. Sex of applicant.
2. Birth control practices of applicant.
3. Child-bearing plans of applicant.
4. Fertility (ability to bear children) of applicant.
5. Race, color, religion, or national origin of applicant.

A credit granter may ask for the following information:

1. Marital status of applicant, unless the applicant can prove he is not a resident of a community property state. It is improper to ask this information of applicants who do not reside in community property states.
2. Accounts upon which the applicant is liable; the name and address in which the account is carried.
3. Other names in which applicant has obtained credit.
4. Number and ages of applicant's dependents.
5. Applicant's dependent-related financial obligations or expenditures, without requiring disclosure of sex.
6. Applicant's citizenship and, if applicant is an alien, his permanent residence and immigration status.

Also, the applicant may be asked if income stated in the application comes from alimony, child support, or separate maintenance payments, if the credit granter makes clear that the applicant need not disclose such income if he does not want the granter to consider it in determining creditworthiness. If the applicant wants this income to be so considered, however, the granter can inquire into the source of it.

A creditor also may make no oral or written statements with respect to a credit application which would lead a reasonable applicant to believe that there is no chance to obtain credit due to one of the forbidden bases of discrimination. It is okay to tell an unemployed applicant with no income that he has no chance to obtain credit, but it is not okay to tell a seventy-five-year-old applicant that he had better not apply because he is too old.

In evaluating a credit application, the creditor must not:

1. Use sex, race, age, receipt of public assistance, or any other such forbidden criteria as grounds for rejection, or even as grounds for evaluation.
2. Use assumptions or statistical probabilities of child bearing, reduction of income, or the like in evaluation.
3. Use listing of a telephone in applicant's name in evaluation.
4. Discount or exclude from consideration in evaluation income from part-time employment or retirement benefits, or income of a married woman. Amount of income and probable continuance of it may be considered, so long as probable continuance is not evaluated solely on the basis of statistical probability.
5. Consider the credit history of the applicant's spouse.

In the granting of credit, the creditor must not:

1. Deny credit upon one of the forbidden bases.
2. Refuse to allow an applicant to open an account in her maiden name, or in a combined maiden name-spouse's name surname (Ann Smith-Jones).
3. Require a cosigner if the applicant qualifies under the creditor's general standards of creditworthiness for the requested credit.
4. Refuse credit because applicant is too old to obtain credit life insurance or other credit clearance.

If a married applicant is applying for unsecured credit, and he has sufficient separate property and income to be considered creditworthy, the creditor may not require the spouse to sign any document in connection with the transaction. If the separate property is insufficient to prove creditworthiness, but the applicant has control of sufficient community property to be creditworthy, the spouse again need not be involved. If community property under the control of the other spouse must be counted in order to establish creditworthiness, however, that spouse may be required to sign an agreement making community property under his control available to the creditor in case of default. The spouse may not be required to cosign a promissory note in this situation, however.

If a married applicant asks for secured credit, the creditor may require that the spouse sign the security agreement with respect to the collateral.

Within thirty days of receipt of a completed credit application, or within thirty days of the taking of action on an incomplete application, the creditor must inform the applicant of his decision. An affirmative decision may be communicated by issuance of a credit card or some other act—or by simple notification. Negative action must be accompanied by a reason for such action, or by a statement that, should the applicant desire to learn the reason for the decision, he may contact a named person at a named place in order to find out.

Should the application be denied because of an adverse report on the applicant obtained from a credit bureau, the Fair Credit Reporting Act requires that the creditor disclose that denial was due to an adverse credit bureau report and name the bureau. He does not have to disclose the nature of the adverse information received from the bureau, however.

The victim of unlawful discrimination in granting of credit may sue for compensatory damages in federal court. He may also recover punitive damages of up to $10,000. A group of persons so victimized may sue in a class action, and obtain up to $500,000 in punitive damages, or an amount equal to 1 percent of the net worth of the violator, whichever is less. Injunctions may also be obtained against violators.

Credit bureaus and credit reporting. The creditor evaluating a credit application from a stranger may want to check the veracity of information on the credit application by asking the present and former employers of the applicant for information about him. He may also wish to check with other creditors of the applicant to see about his payment record or to get a more detailed report on the applicant from a credit bureau, a business set up especially to collect and disseminate information about people.

No law restricts the right of a creditor to make such inquiries. However, the Federal Fair Credit Reporting Act, 15 USC 1681 et seq., does regulate the process to an extent. As mentioned earlier, when a credit applicant is denied credit due to an adverse credit bureau report (or when an employment applicant is denied employment or an insurance applicant insurance upon this basis), the bureau furnishing the report must be revealed to the applicant, though not the adverse information (15 USC 1681m).

A consumer has the right to ask a credit bureau what information it possesses on him (15 USC 1681g). The consumer has no right to see his actual file, and has no right to medical information on him possessed by the bureau. But he does have the right to learn:

1. The nature of all information except medical information contained in his file.
2. The source of all such information, except sources of information contained in investigative consumer reports (field background investigations, essentially).
3. Recipients of all reports made by the bureau for employment purposes within the last two years, and for credit or other purposes within the last six months.

This right of inquiry is somewhat limited by the provisions of 15 USC 1681h. The requested information need be furnished by the bureau only during business hours and after the giving of reasonable notice. The consumer may bring one other person with him to study this information. The agency must designate a trained person to answer any questions the consumer may have with regard to the file.

If the inquiry is made within thirty days of denial of credit to the consumer because of a report by the credit bureau in question, the bureau may not levy any charge upon the consumer. If the request is made at other times, however, a reasonable fee may be charged (15 USC 1681j).

If the consumer finds anything in the report which he considers to be inaccurate, he has the right to ask the bureau to recheck that information. The bureau must do this, unless it believes that the dispute is frivolous or irrelevant, which it most often is not. The bureau must inform the consumer of the result of the reinvestigation. If the questioned information turns out to be false, or if its truth cannot be verified, the bureau must delete it from the consumer's file. If the consumer requests, the bureau must also send a report of the deletion to everyone receiving a report on the consumer for employment purposes during the last two years and to anyone receiving a report for other purposes during the last six months. The bureau may refuse to delete the disputed information if reinvestigation leads it to believe that it is true. In such a case, the consumer has the right to insert a statement of 100 words or less in the file telling his side of the dispute.

A credit bureau may not disseminate obsolete information on a consumer to its clients. There is no time limit upon age of information which may be included in reports to:
1. Employers considering hiring the consumer for a job paying $20,000 per year or more.
2. Creditors considering lending the consumer $50,000 or more.
3. Insurers considering insuring the consumer for $50,000 or more.

In other cases, the credit bureau may not report bankruptcies in which the adjudication antedates the report by more than fourteen years. Generally, other information may not be reported dealing with incidents antedating the report by seven years. It should be noted, however, that criminal convictions can be reported until seven years after conviction, parole, or release from prison, whichever occurs last. Judgments may be reported until the statute of limitations on collection runs out, which makes them reportable until they are ten years old in Texas. Tax liens are reportable until seven years after the tax has been paid off. 15 USC 1681c governs this matter.

A fertile source of information for inclusion in credit bureau files and reports is the public records of the county in which the bureau does business. There, information relative to the consumer's real estate dealings, lawsuits, arrests, indictments, tax difficulties, and so on may be found. Information found in the public records may be very misleading. For instance:
1. Judgments against a person are recorded, but payments upon a judgment are not. The record reveals the existence of the judgment; it does not necessarily reveal how little is still owed on it.
2. The beginning of a lawsuit is recorded, the end may not be. If the matter was settled out of court in the consumer's favor, the record will not reflect this outcome unless something was inserted in the case file to show the disposal of the case.
3. Indictments are recorded, as are convictions. But if an indictment does not result in a conviction, there might not be a record of the disposal of the case. The case might have gone to trial and ended in a hung jury, or the prosecutor might have had the case dismissed for lack of evidence.

Of course, every effort is made to keep court records up-to-date, and to make the records of closed cases complete. When this is properly done, correct information may be found in the record. But when—due to human error, etc.—the record is incomplete, what is found there can be very misleading and, sometimes, damaging.

When public record information is used by a bureau in a report for credit or insurance purposes, the bureau need not notify the consumer of its use; he will never find out about it unless he checks his file. However, should the bureau want to use public record information in a report for employment purposes, 15 USC 1681k imposes some obligations. When using such information for this purpose, the bureau must either inform the consumer that the information is being used in a report for a named potential employer, or it must use stringent procedures to ensure that all public record information used is complete and up-to-date. So long as the records themselves are up-to-date and accurate, of course, these stringent procedures will disclose accurate information, but if the records themselves are inaccurate, the report will be as well.

Should anyone hire a credit bureau to make an investigative consumer report—essentially a field background investigation or "snoop" report—he must notify the consumer that this report is to be compiled. He must also notify the consumer that he has a right to request information upon the nature and scope of the required investigation. Thus, 15 USC 1681d, which governs this matter, permits the consumer to find out what the snoops are investigating about him, but it does not require the party ordering the investigation to disclose what he learns. If the consumer wants to learn this, he will have to inquire of the credit bureau, where he may learn the essence of the report but not the sources of information disclosed therein, since sources of information contained in snoop reports are confidential.

The credit bureau must not use information obtained in a background investigation for the making of ordinary credit reports. It also may not use the information in other background investigation reports, unless the second report is issued within three months of the issuance of the first. In short, background investigation material must be reinvestigated every three months if it is to be used.

Credit bureaus are permitted to make reports on consumers only for credit, employment, or insurance purposes; to determine a consumer's eligibility for a government grant or license; or for other business purposes. Such reports are also legitimate if made in response to a request of the consumer, or pursuant to a court order (15 USC 1681b). It is also legitimate for a bureau to furnish information for identification purposes—name, current and past addresses and employment—to governmental agencies. They must not furnish full reports to such agencies however, except for employment, insurance, credit, or licensing purposes (15 USC 1681f).

Release of information on a consumer to an unauthorized person is a criminal offense. 15 USC 1681r provides that an officer of a bureau or an employee of a bureau guilty of the offense may be fined up to $5,000 or imprisoned up to one year or both. Anyone who obtains a credit report from a credit bureau under false pretenses also commits a criminal offense and is subject to the same punishment (15 USC 1681q).

Anyone guilty of negligent violation of the Fair Credit Reporting Act is liable to the damaged party for compensatory damages, plus court costs and attorney's fees (15 USC 1681o). Anyone guilty of willful violation of the act is liable to the damaged party for compensatory damages, court costs, attorney fees, and such punitive damages as the court may allow (15 USC 1681n).

Suits under the act may be brought in federal courts. They must be commenced within two years of the violation or its discovery. It is of course difficult to prove willful violation of this act. Negligent violation is easier to prove, but sometimes it is difficult to prove that one has suffered substantial damage due to a violation.

It must be remembered that the provisions of the act apply to any business or individual collecting information about consumers and passing it on to another business for consideration or otherwise. Credit bureaus are the main entities in this sort of activity, but any other business which passes on information about consumers received from outside sources is essentially a credit bureau subject to this act.

No potential liability is incurred by an employer who informs another employer of the work record of a former employee, or by a businessman who informs another businessman of the credit standing of a consumer with him. On the other hand, the employer who tells another employer of an employee's record with a third employer runs the risk of a violation.

It must also be remembered that a consumer may not sue a credit bureau for damages for defamation of character or invasion of privacy because of information discovered in bureau files, except for false information furnished with malice or intent to injure the consumer. 15 USC 1681h furnishes credit bureaus with almost total immunity from such liability. This immunity exists although there are no legal requirements that such bureaus accumulate only information which is relevant to the credit standing of the consumer.

Bureaus may still accumulate information on hair length, clothing styles, amusement preferences, and other such things about consumers—and creditors, insurers, and employers may base decisions having far-reaching effects on the life of a consumer upon such information.

Financial disclosure requirements. The Federal Consumer Credit Protection Act (or Truth-in-Lending Act), 15 USC 1601 et seq., and Regulation Z of the Federal Reserve Board requires lenders and sellers of goods on credit to make many disclosures of credit terms and regulations to their customers in their contracts.

The disclosure requirements apply to consumer transactions and not to business transactions. In general, the disclosure requirements do not apply in the following types of transactions (15 USC 1603):

1. Transactions by governments, government agencies, or organizations.
2. Securities and commodity transactions by broker-dealers registered with the SEC. (SEC regulations prescribe full disclosure in margin transactions with such brokers.)
3. Credit transactions other than real estate transactions where the amount financed is more than $25,000.
4. Transactions under public utility tariffs where a state regulatory body regulates the rates, late-payment charges, and so on.
5. Credit transactions made by credit unions.
6. Credit transactions for agricultural purposes when the amount to be financed exceeds $25,000.

The key items which are to be disclosed under this legislation are the finance charge and the annual percentage rate of finance charges. The finance charge constitutes the total amount of money which the consumer must pay for the privilege of borrowing, buying goods on credit, or maintaining a charge account. The annual percentage rate of a finance charge is the ratio between the annualized finance charge and the borrowed principal or cash price of goods expressed as a percentage. It is analogous to an annual percentage rate of interest, except that items other than interest may be figured into the finance charge. The APR of finance charge upon a transaction will at least equal the APR of interest, and most of the time will exceed it. Disclosure of APR of finance charge is required; disclosure of the APR of interest is not.

According to 15 USC 1605, the following items must be included in the finance charge, and must be individually itemized in the consumer's contract:

1. Interest.
2. Time-price differential—the difference between the cash price of goods and the price charged to credit borrowers.
3. Points, discounts, or other system of additional charges.
4. Service or carrying charge.
5. Loan fee, finder's fee, or any similar charge.
6. Investigation report, credit report fee, or credit insurance premium (on insurance to protect the creditor against the debtor's default).

If the creditor requires that the debtor take out credit life, accident, or health insurance, or if the creditor does not tell the debtor that he has the right not to buy such insurance, the premium for the insurance must be included in the finance charge. However, the creditor may not require that the debtor buy such insurance from him—he must give the debtor the option of buying it from other insurance agents or of assigning life insurance policies to the creditor to provide the desired protection.

Property insurance premiums—collision insurance premiums on motor vehicles, for instance—must be included in the finance charge unless the cost is revealed in another disclosure and the debtor is informed that he may purchase this insurance elsewhere.

Filing fees for financing statements and taxes need not be included in the finance charge, but must nevertheless be itemized. In real estate transactions, the following shall not be included in the finance charge, but must be itemized:

1. Title examination fees.
2. Title insurance premiums.
3. Fees for preparing deeds.
4. Escrows for future payment of taxes and insurance.
5. Notarization fees.
6. Appraisal fees.
7. Credit report fees.

The APR of a finance charge is to be calculated according to approved mathematical formulae or according to rate tables approved by the Federal Reserve Board.

The following disclosures must be made with respect to consumer loans not under open-end credit plans (15 USC 1639):

1. Amount of credit of which debtor will have use, or which will be paid to him or to another person.
2. All charges, itemized, that are not a part of the finance charge but are included in the amount of credit to be extended.
3. The total amount to be financed.
4. The amount of the finance charge with all its components itemized. (This disclosure is not required with respect to a purchase-money first-mortgage lien upon real estate.)
5. The APR of finance charge (FC). (This disclosure is not required when the FC is $7.50 or less, or when the FC is $5 or less and the amount financed is $75 or less.)
6. Number, amount, and the dates of payments.
7. Default or delinquency charges to be applied in case of late payments.
8. Description of any security interest to be given creditor as collateral, and description of said collateral.

15 USC 1639 requires that these disclosures be made before the debtor signs any contract. Disclosure in the contract itself is sufficient, so long as the debtor is familiarized with them before he signs.

In connection with credit sales of goods not under open-end credit plans, 15 USC 1638 requires the making of the following disclosures:

1. Cash price of property or service.
2. Down payment and trade-in credits.
3. Cash price less down payment and/or trade-in allowance.
4. Other charges, itemized, included in amount of credit to be extended but not included in the finance charge.
5. Total amount to be financed.
6. Total finance charge, with individual components itemized.
7. APR of finance charge (disclosure excused under the same circumstances as with consumer loans).

8. Number, amount, and due dates of payments.
9. Default or delinquency charges to be levied in case of late payment.
10. Description of any security interest to be held as collateral, and description of the collateral.

Disclosure must be made in the same manner as for consumer loans.

With respect to open-end credit plans, 15 USC 1637 requires the making of disclosures upon two occasions—when the account is opened and when bills are sent to the debtor. The following disclosures are mandatory upon the opening of the account:

1. The free-ride period, if any.
2. The method of determining the balance upon which finance charge will be imposed.
3. The method of determining the amount of finance charge, if two or more APRs may be used.
4. The APRs to be used and the range of balances to which they apply.
5. Minimum or fixed finance charges, if any.
6. Conditions under which other charges may be imposed (late payment and service charges, etc.)
7. The method of determining monthly payments to be made, and amounts of fixed or minimum payments.
8. Conditions under which creditor may acquire a security interest in any property to secure payment of advanced credits, and a description of the security interests to be acquired.

The bills sent to the debtor must contain certain disclosures, but these will be discussed in connection with the Fair Credit Billing Act later in this chapter.

15 USC 1611 provides that anyone guilty of willful and knowing violation of this legislation may be fined up to $5,000 or imprisoned up to one year, or both. The civil penalty for violation is contained in 15 USC 1640. The violator is liable to the debtor for actual damages caused plus a penalty of double the finance charge, but no less than $100 nor more than $1,000. The debtor may also recover court costs plus a reasonable attorney's fee.

15 USC 1640 also provides that a violator may escape liability by proving that his violation was unintentional and resulted from a bona fide error, notwithstanding the existence of procedures reasonably adopted to avoid such violations or the fact that the violator relied upon the provisions of a federal or state administrative regulation which has since been amended or declared invalid.

A violator may also escape liability if he discovers his violation and sends the debtor a notice of its correction, so long as he does so within fifteen days of discovery and before the debtor notifies him that he has discovered the violation. Suit for violation of this legislation must be brought within one year of the violation, in either federal or state court.

An assignee of an account is normally not liable for nondisclosure of financial terms by the assignor, or for erroneous disclosures by him. If the debtor has signed a statement stating that he has received all required disclosures from the assignor, the assignee is protected.

However, if an assignor customarily assigns all or most of his accounts to a particular assignee, or if an assignee participates in the negotiation of the bargain between the debtor and the assignor, the assignee may be held liable for the assignor's disclosure errors and omissions.

Consumer leasing disclosure. The Federal Consumer Leasing Act, 15 USC 1667 et seq., applies the disclosure principles of the Truth-in-Lending Act to consumer leasing contracts. The act applies to any contract for lease or bailment of personal property for consumer use for a period of time exceeding four months. The act does not apply to leases of property for agricultural or commercial use, and it does not apply to short-term leases. It does not matter whether the lessee is given an option to buy the leased property at the termination of the lease.

The following items must be disclosed in a consumer lease contract:

1. Description or identification of the leased property.
2. Amount of payment required of lessee at beginning of lease.
3. Amount paid or payable by lessee for official fees, registration, certificate of title, license fees, or taxes.
4. Amount of other charges, itemized, payable by lessee but not included in periodic payments.
5. If lessee is to be liable for the difference between the anticipated fair market value of the leased property and its actual value at the termination of the lease, a statement to that effect.
6. A statement as to whether or not lessee has the option to purchase the leased property, and, if he does, a statement of the price he must pay and the time during which he may exercise the option.
7. A brief description of insurance provided or paid for by lessor or required of lessee, including types, amounts, coverage, and costs.
8. A description of any security interest to be held by lessor in the property.
9. The number, amount, and due dates of payments, and the total of all such amounts to be paid.
10. If lessee is to be liable for the fair market value of the leased property upon termination of the lease, the fair market value at the beginning of the lease and the estimated cost of the lease, and the difference between these.
11. A statement of the conditions under which lessor or lessee may terminate the lease before expiration.
12. Amount of or method of determination of penalties, late payment charges, delinquency charges, and so on.

If the lessee is to be held liable for the difference between estimated market value of the leased property and actual market value, the estimated market value must be determined in a reasonable manner. If at the end of the lease the estimated market value is greater than actual market value by a sum equal to three monthly rental payments or more, and the goods have not been physically damaged or subjected to abnormal wear and tear, the estimated fair market value is presumed to be unreasonable. In such a case the lessee need not pay the difference until the lessor sues him to collect and obtains judgment. Whether the lessor wins or loses, he must pay the lessee's attorney's fee in the suit. Thus, lessor must be reasonable in computing the estimated fair market value of the property at the termination of the lease (15 USC 1667b).

15 USC 1667c provides that when a lessor advertises that he is leasing property and

includes anything about the payments required, or when he advertises that no down payment is required, his advertising must also disclose the following:

1. That a lease transaction is being advertised.
2. Payment required at the inception of the lease, or a statement that no payment is required.
3. Number, amount, and due dates of payments, and total amount to be paid under the lease.
4. If lessee is to be liable for the difference between estimated market value of leased property at termination of the lease and actual market value at that time, a statement to that effect.
5. A statement of how any liability of lessee at termination of the lease is to be determined.
6. Whether or not lessee has the option to buy the leased property at the termination of the lease, and, if so, at what price and time.

Lessors violating these provisions are subject to the usual Consumer Credit Protection Act penalty—actual damages plus double the finance charge (but no less than $100 nor more than $1,000), plus costs and attorney fees.

Correction of billing errors. The Federal Fair Credit Billing Act provides a procedure under which an open-end credit plan debtor may seek to delay billing for items erroneously charged to his account. This act is found as 15 USC 1666 et seq.

At the time a revolving charge account is opened, or when a credit card is issued, the creditor must disclose to the debtor all of his rights under the Fair Credit Billing Act. The disclosure must include the address to which a claim of billing error should be sent. If the creditor does not want the debtor to give notice of a billing error on a billing stub, the notice must so state. Otherwise, the notice must furnish the debtor a digest of the discussion which is to follow.

The creditor must also send the debtor further notice of his rights under this Act at least twice a year, and must furnish sufficient information on his monthly bills so that debtor can spot billing errors. Generally, 15 USC 1666a provides that the following must be disclosed on monthly open-end credit plan bills:

1. The balance owed at the beginning of the billing cycle.
2. Amount and date of every debit to the account during the billing cycle, with enough information to enable debtor to identify the purchase or other transaction causing the debit.
3. Itemized credits to the account (payments and returns, for example) during the billing cycle.
4. Finance charge added to the account during the billing cycle.
5. How the finance charge was computed.
6. The APR of the added finance charge.
7. Balance upon which finance charge was computed, and a statement of how that balance was arrived at.
8. Balance due at end of billing cycle.
9. Date by which payment must be made to avoid further finance charges.

Thus, the debtor should know from these disclosures what debits to his account were made and why, and what credits to his account were allowed and why. He should therefore be able to discover billing errors at once.

Under the provisions of 15 USC 1666(b), a billing error may constitute:

1. An improper charge to the account—charging debtor for what he did not buy, or charging him an improper price for what he did buy.

2. An item charged to the account which is not properly verified in the required disclosures.
3. Charges for goods not accepted by the debtor.
4. Charges for goods not delivered to the debtor as agreed.
5. Failure of the statement to reflect payments made or credits granted.
6. Computation errors or similar accounting errors.

When the debtor decides that his periodic statement contains an error, he should send notice to that effect within sixty days of his receipt of the statement to the address the creditor has furnished for purposes of making billing error complaints. The notice must not be written on a billing stub if the creditor has stated in his notice of rights that such notice is unacceptable. The notice must contain.:

1. Debtor's name.
2. Debtor's account number if any, or information sufficient for creditor to identify debtor's account.
3. A statement that the account contains a billing error of $_____.
4. A statement of debtor's reasons for belief that the error exists.

The creditor must acknowledge receipt of the notice within thirty days of receipt. Within the period of two complete billing cycles (but no more than ninety days), the creditor must decide what to do about the claim of error, and must notify the debtor of the decision. The creditor may respond in one of three ways.

He may respond (in essence), "You're right," and make the correction to the account requested by the debtor. He may respond (in essence), "You're wrong," and refuse to make the requested correction. If he does this, he must explain why. He may respond (in essence), "You're partly right," and grant the debtor a partial adjustment. When the creditor does this, he must explain why.

After a notice of billing error has been received, but before the request for adjustment has been investigated and disposed of, the creditor is under no obligation to remove the disputed amount from the debtor's bills, though he may mark the disputed amount "in dispute."

While the debtor's notice of error is pending, he is under no obligation to pay the disputed item. The creditor may not sue to collect the item, nor may he close the debtor's account or reduce the debtor's line of credit because of it. The creditor may not report the debtor to a credit bureau as delinquent because he does not pay this item.

If a creditor resolves the investigation of a debtor's claim in the creditor's favor, he may of course take all measures permitted by law to force the debtor to pay. If the debtor still thinks he does not owe the disputed amount, he may tell the creditor so. If he does, the creditor may not report the debtor to a credit bureau as delinquent in his payment of the disputed item without also telling the bureau that the item is in dispute. The debtor's only other recourse is to try to convince the creditor that he is after all right, or to convince a court that he truly does not owe the disputed amount.

If the creditor does not properly respond to a claim of billing error, he loses the right to collect the disputed amount and the finance charge thereon, except that his maximum loss for such failure is $50. Thus, if a debtor claims a billing error of $90, and his creditor does not respond properly to it, the amount in dispute is reduced to $40. Only one $50 penalty is assessed per error.

Creditors must promptly record received payments. These should be posted on the date of receipt if at all possible. It must be remembered, though, that payments sent by mail are made when received, not when sent. If such payments are delayed in the mail, finance charge accrues upon the amount paid until the mail arrives and the amount received is posted.

When a creditor grants a thirty-day free ride on new charges to the account, his bills must be received by the debtor at least fourteen days before finance charge begins to accrue upon these free-ride items.

The only penalty for violation of the Fair Credit Billing Act is the forfeiture of up to $50 for improper response to a claim of error. However, when notices of consumer rights under the act are not furnished as required, the usual penalty of double the finance charge but no more than $1,000 and no less than $100 may be collected by the debtor.

There is no Texas state equivalent to the Fair Credit Billing Act; the law here is strictly federal law.

Deceptive trade practices. In 1973 the Texas Legislature enacted the Texas Deceptive Trade Practices Act, TB&CC 17.41 et seq. Numerous amendments to the act were enacted in 1977, some strengthening the act and some weakening it. More amendments were enacted in 1979, most of which had a weakening effect. The law as it now stands is a powerful piece of consumer protection legislation, but it was more powerful before the 1979 amendments became effective.

The heart of the act is TB&CC 17.46, which forbids twenty-three specific false, misleading, or deceptive acts or practices. These are:

1. Passing off goods or services as those of another.
2. Causing misunderstanding or confusion as to source, sponsorship, approval, or certification of goods or services.
3. Causing confusion or misunderstanding as to affiliation, connection with, association with, or certification by, another.
4. Using deceptive representations or designations of geographic origin in connection with goods or services.
5. Representing that goods or services have sponsorship, approval, characteristics, ingredients, uses, benefits, or qualities which they do not have, or that a person has a sponsorship, approval, status, affiliation, or connection, which he does not have.
6. Representing that goods are original or new when they are deteriorated, reconditioned, reclaimed, used, or second-hand.
7. Representing that goods are of a particular standard, quality, or grade, or that goods are of a particular style or model, when they are not.
8. Disparaging the goods, services, or business of another with false or misleading representations of fact.
9. Advertising goods or services with intent not to sell them as advertised.
10. Advertising goods and services with intent not to supply a reasonable, expectable public demand, unless the advertisement discloses a limitation of quantity. (This and the preceding practice are the variations of the "bait and switch" gimmick—get the customer into the store by advertising one item, then try with might and main to sell him another.)
11. Making false and misleading statements of fact concerning the reasons for, existence of, or amount of, price reductions. This covers a multitude of sins. The common ad, "Regular price $2.29, our price $1.98," is a violation if the regular price is not $2.29. Closely related is the gimmick, "Suggested retail price $1.98, our price $1.79." The legitimacy of use of this device depends not only on whether or not the suggested retail price is $1.98, but also on how many retailers actually sell the product for $1.98. If most retailers sell it for less than $1.98, the ad is deceptive. If a seller says

he is selling at wholesale prices, he must either be a wholesaler or his prices must be true wholesale prices. If he says his low price is due to the fact that he has "acquired the stock of a bankrupt competitor," or because of the fact that "we lost our lease," the statements must be true.

12. Representing that an agreement confers or involves rights, remedies, or obligations which it does not have or involve, or which are prohibited by law. (This is simply misrepresentation of the terms of a contract or similar agreement.)

13. Knowingly making false or misleading statements of fact concerning the need for parts, replacement, or repair service.

14. Misrepresenting the authority of a salesman, representative, or agent to negotiate the final terms of a consumer transaction. (This covers the gimmick under which the salesman supposedly makes a deal with a customer but later tells the customer that the terms must be changed because the boss did not approve. If a salesman does not have authority to finalize a deal, the customer must be told. If he does have authority to finalize, the customer must be told that, too. This prohibition would probably also cover the situation where the salesman who has authority to close a deal tells the customer he must go get the just-worked-out deal approved by the boss. He then goes to drink a Coke, returns, and tells the customer the boss would not buy the worked-out deal and the trade-in allowance on the customer's old car must be reduced, etc.)

15. Basing a charge for repair of any item in part or in whole on a guarantee or warranty instead of on the value of the actual repairs or work done without stating separately the charges for the work and the charges for the guarantee or warranty, if any. (This forbids the giver of a guarantee or warranty upon a product from charging the customer for the giving of the guarantee or warranty by burying the charge in a repair bill. If the guarantor or warrantor expects the customer to pay for a warranty or guarantee, the cost must be fully disclosed. The theory of this prohibition is praiseworthy, but the difficulty of detecting a violation is great.)

16. Disconnecting, turning back, or resetting the odometer of a motor vehicle to reduce the mileage shown.

17. Advertising a sale by fraudulently representing that one is going out of business.

18. Using a chain referral plan in connection with offering of or sale of goods or services, under which buyer will get compensation or consideration for furnishing seller names of other prospective buyers if receipt of consideration is contingent upon occurrence of an event after buyer buys the goods. (Buyer may get his consideration, for instance, only when a prospect he steered seller's salesman to contracts to buy the sold product. Such efforts by sellers to recruit a force of unpaid salesmen may be of assistance to the seller, but the recruited buyer-salesmen rarely profit.)

19. Representing that a guarantee or warranty confers or involves rights which it does not confer or involve, unless the representation exceeds the obligations of a merchant under the UCC implied warranty of merchantability.

20. Selling or offering to sell, either directly or in connection with the sale of goods or services, a right of participation in a multilevel distributorship—that is, a plan under which an individual will receive a rebate or payment for securing or recommending other individuals to assume positions in the sales operation where the rebate or payment is not conditioned on or in relation to proceeds from the sale of goods. (This refers to pyramid sales schemes, under which a persons buys a distributorship of a product on the understanding that he may hire subdistributors and sell the product to them at a profit. This of course is a variation on the ancient chain letter scheme. The

market for a product is limited in size; thus the number of distributors of the product who may operate profitably is also limited.)

21. Representing that work or services have been performed on—or parts replaced in—goods, when the work or services were not performed or the parts were not replaced.

22. Filing suit on a consumer contract in writing signed by the defendant in a county other than where the defendant lives or that where he signed the contract, unless the defendant lives in a county of less than 250,000 population and the suit is filed in the nearest county of over 250,000 population. (The propriety of the venue of such a suit is determined by the law of venue. If the defendant lives in Jasper County, signs a consumer contract in Polk County, later breaches the contract, and finds himself being sued by plaintiff in Newton County, this prohibition is violated and the venue is improper. If the plaintiff sues the defendant in Jefferson County, the venue is still improper, but this prohibition is not violated, since Jefferson County is the nearest county of over 250,000 population to Jasper County.)

23. The failure to disclose information concerning goods or services which was known at the time of the transaction if failure to disclose such information was intended to induce the consumer into a transaction which the consumer would not have entered had the information been disclosed. (In short, concealment of a material fact violates this act if the consumer would not have entered into the transaction if the material fact had been known to him.)

The material interpreting the meaning of the sections of the Deceptive Trade Practices Act discussed above is based upon Philip Maxwell's article "Public and Private Rights and Remedies under the Deceptive Trade Practices Consumer Protection Act," found in *Texas Consumer Law for General Practitioners*, published by the Consumer Law Section of the State Bar of Texas.

TB&CC 17.50 provides that a consumer may sue under this act if:

1. He is a victim of any of the twenty-three deceptive trade practices described above, or
2. He is a victim of breach of express or implied warranty, or
3. He is a victim of an unconscionable action or course of action, or
4. He has been victimized by an act or practice in violation of Texas Insurance Code 21.21 or of administrative regulations of the Texas Insurance Board, such as misrepresentation of the contents of an insurance policy.

TB&CC 17.50A provides that a consumer may not sue for damages under the act unless he gives written notice to the violator he intends to sue at least thirty days before filing suit, indicating his specific complaint and the amount of actual damages and expenses (including reasonable attorney's fees) incurred by the consumer in asserting his claim.

The violator may lessen his damages by making a written offer of settlement to the consumer within thirty days of receipt of the consumer's notice. If the consumer accepts the offer, the matter is of course settled. If he rejects the offer, he may proceed to sue the violator. However, one of the matters the court will consider during the trial will be the question of the reasonableness of the rejected settlement offer. If the court finds it to be reasonable, the most the victorious consumer will be able to recover will be actual damages and expenses. If the rejected offer is found to be unreasonable, he may recover sums in excess of his actual damages and expenses.

TB&CC 17.50B provides that a defendant is not liable for damages under this act if he informed the consumer before the consummation of the consumer transaction (the sale of the goods) that he was relying upon the truth of certain written information in inducing the consumer to enter into the transaction. The fact that the information which the defendant regarded as true turns out to be false is a defense to liability. The written information in question may be:

1. Information from official government records, or
2. Information from another source (such as the manufacturer), or
3. Information concerning results of tests prescribed by government agencies.

If the violator used this false written information in his effort to induce the buyer to buy the product and the violator told the buyer of this use; the violator believed that the information was true; and the falsity of the information caused buyer's damage, the violator has a defense to liability. The buyer might then claim damages from the source of the false information.

The major remedy available to consumers injured by a violation of this act is a suit for damages. Remember that no suit may be commenced unless proper notice of claim is first given the violator so that he has a chance to make a settlement offer. Assuming that proper notice is given, that no settlement offer was forthcoming (or an offer was rejected), and that the 17.50B defense is not available, the plaintiff's recovery is measured as follows: If the violation was knowingly committed by the defendant, the plaintiff may recover up to three times his actual damages. If the violation was committed unknowingly, the plaintiff may recover actual damages, plus two times the portion of actual damages that does not exceed $1,000.

Thus, if a violation is knowing and the plaintiff suffers $10,000 in actual damages, the recovery is $30,000. If the violation is unknowing and the plaintiff suffers $10,000 in actual damages, the recovery is $12,000. If the violation is unknowing and damages are $100,000, the recovery is $102,000. If the violation is unknowing and the damages are $600, the recovery is $1,800. The prevailing plaintiff is also entitled to recover a reasonable attorney fee.

Additional remedies for violation of the act are:

1. Injunctions.
2. Restitution of money or property acquired by defendant in violation of the act.
3. Appointment of a receiver for defendant, if plaintiff obtains a judgment which is not satisfied within three months.

If a consumer brings a groundless suit under this act, the defendant is to be awarded court costs and attorney fees.

TB&CC 17.56A provides that suits brought under this act must be filed within two years of the commission of the violation or within two years of the time plaintiff discovered or should have discovered the violation.

The 1979 amendments to the act have had two major "watering down" effects. Prior to the amendments, most prevailing plaintiffs were entitled to recover triple damages whether the violation was knowing or not. Under present law, only the exceptional plaintiff—the victim of a knowing violation—may recover triple damages. Also, the statute of limitations under the act was shortened from four years to two. Despite this weakening, the act remains a powerful protector of Texas consumers.

Debt collection practices. Two pieces of legislation are important in this area. One is the Federal Fair Debt Collection Practices Act, 15 USC 1692a et seq., which became effective March 20, 1978; the other is the Texas Debt Collection Act, enacted in 1973 and effective in that year. Since the federal act has not completely superseded the Texas act, both must be considered here.

The federal act does not apply to all debt collectors; it applies only to professional collectors of debts owed to others, other than attorneys and the like—in short, mainly to collection agencies and creditors seeking to collect debts owed them through debt collection activity under another business name. The Texas act, on the other hand, applies to all debt collectors, even persons seeking to collect their own accounts receivable.

The economics of debt collection encourage the use of rather forcible collection methods. The situation therefore lends itself to abusive practices.

The debt collector of last resort is of course the court system. However, litigation as a method of debt collection is not very efficient. It takes time, it costs money, and it involves the creditor in dealings with attorneys. When possible it is simpler to get the debtor to pay up without recourse to courts. If the debtor is reluctant to pay, an unpleasant hassle is almost inevitable. If the transaction with the debtor is a secured transaction, the creditor may foreclose on collateral, but if the collateral is not in the creditor's possession and is not amenable to self-help repossession, it cannot be touched without the debtor's cooperation or court assistance. If the transaction is unsecured, the only recourse is to force the debtor to pay, somehow.

Large creditors have credit departments whose mission it is to deal with recalcitrant debtors. Small creditors cannot afford this luxury. Neither the large nor the small creditor can afford a ledger full of aging accounts receivable; these must somehow be converted into cash. Vigorous action by the creditor might accomplish this, litigation might do it, or professional collectors might be called in.

The creditor might assign delinquent accounts to a collection agency for a percentage of face value. In such cases the agency becomes the owner of the accounts and seeks to recoup its investment by collecting as many of them as possible. The creditor might also appoint a collection agency as its agent to make collection, the agency's compensation being a percentage of all amounts collected. The large collection agency may well hire field men to do the job of collecting, the major part of their pay being a percentage of the amounts they collect. Such a system has encouraged at least some debt collectors to operate on the principle that "the end justifies the means"; hence the existence of legislation regulating debt collection practices.

Both acts forbid harassment and abuse of debtors by debt collectors. The federal provisions are found in 15 USC 1692b, the state provisions at TB&CC 11.02 and 11.03. Both acts forbid:

1. Threats to use violence or criminal means to get debtor to pay.
2. Accusing debtor of commission of fraud or crime.
3. Threats to have debtor arrested if he does not pay.
4. Threats to have debtor criminally prosecuted if he does not pay.
5. Threats to repossess collateral not amenable to self-help repossession (such as household furniture) without court process.
6. Threats to tell a third party (e.g. an employer or credit bureau) that debtor willfully refuses to pay.
7. Use of obscene, profane, or abusive language in the collection effort.
8. Making repeated phone calls to debtor.
9. Making phone calls to debtor without disclosing the identity of the caller.
10. Causing debtor's telephone to ring repeatedly.

In addition, the federal law forbids professional debt collectors to:
1. Publish lists of delinquent debtors.
2. Advertise debts for sale by name of debtor.

Both laws forbid the use of unfair or unconscionable means against debtors to enforce collection. Federal provisions are in 15 USC 1692f, state provisions in TB&CC 11.04. Both forbid:
1. Collection of unauthorized amounts from debtor—that is, collecting from the debtor more than he really owes, or more than the debt owner authorized a professional to collect.
2. Charging long-distance phone calls, collect telegrams, etc. to debtor before informing him of the reason for the phone call or telegram.

In addition, the federal law forbids professional debt collectors to:
1. Take a postdated check from debtor dated more than five days after the date it was written, unless collector notifies debtor of his intent to deposit no more than ten days or less than three days before deposit. Such notice must be given in writing.
2. Take a postdated check from debtor in order to get an excuse to have him criminally prosecuted.
3. Deposit or threaten to deposit a postdated check before the date of the check.
4. Threaten to repossess property if collector has no right to repossess, if he does not intend to repossess, or if repossession would be unlawful.
5. Communicate with debtor about the debt by postcard.

The Texas law does not forbid these actions. Texas law does, however, forbid a creditor to seek or obtain a statement from a debtor that a debt was incurred for necessities when in reality it was not so incurred.

Both laws forbid the use of fraudulent, deceptive, or misleading representations in the collection effort; the federal provisions are at 15 USC 1692e, the Texas provisions at TB&CC 11.05. Both forbid:
1. Use of a false name in the collection effort. The collector must operate under his true individual or business name.
2. Falsely representing that collector is a credit bureau rather than a collection agency.
3. Falsely representing that collector is an attorney.
4. Falsely representing that collector has information, a prize, money, or the like for debtor, in order to obtain information (such as employer, location of bank accounts, etc.).
5. Misrepresenting the character, amount, or status of the debt.
6. Representing that collector is vouched for, bonded by, or affiliated with any government, or implying any of these.
7. Falsely representing services rendered or compensation received by a debt collector.
8. Using documents in communication with debtor which appear to be—but are not—court or government documents.
9. Falsely representing that legal documents are not legal documents and that they require no action.
10. Misrepresenting debtor's liability for court costs and attorney's fees.

In addition, the federal law forbids debt collectors to:
1. Communicate or threaten to communicate false information about debtor to third parties.

2. Fail to communicate to other parties acquiring information about debtor that a disputed debt is disputed.

Texas law does not expressly forbid these, but it does forbid:

1. Failure to disclose the name of the creditor (including an assignee) to debtor.
2. Asking the debtor to reply to a communication of the collector to an address other than the collector's true address.
3. Use of any communication which violates U.S. postal laws and regulations.
4. Representation that debt will be increased if it is not paid (other than through accrual of finance charges and the like).

The federal law imposes some additional obligations upon professional debt collectors which the state law does not apply to others. 15 USC 1692b imposes the following obligations upon debt collectors seeking location information on debtors:

1. The collector must identify himself to the party he is asking, but must not identify his employer unless asked.
2. He must not state that the debtor owes a debt.
3. He must not communicate with the person he questions more than once unless asked to by that person.
4. He must not communicate by postcard.
5. He must not disclose in any written communication with outside parties that he is a debt collector or that the communication seeking information relates to collection of a debt.
6. If he knows that the debtor has an attorney, and if he knows the name and address of the attorney, he must not communicate with any person other than the attorney unless the attorney does not respond within a reasonable time to communications from the debt collector.

15 USC 1692c restricts the collector's rights to communicate with the debtor as follows:

1. He must communicate with the debtor only at a reasonable time of day—normally between 8 A.M. and 9 P.M.
2. If the debtor has an attorney, collector must communicate with the attorney rather than the debtor, unless the attorney does not respond to communications within a reasonable time.
3. He must not contact the debtor at his place of employment, if he knows or should know that the employer objects to such contact.
4. If the debtor notifies the collector in writing that he refuses to pay, or that he refuses to communicate further with the collector, the collector must respect that wish, except that he may inform the debtor that his efforts are being terminated, that he will make use of the rights given by law to collect, or that he will invoke a specified remedy in order to collect. In short, if the debtor does not want to talk about the debt any more, the collector must not talk; but the collector still has every right to act—by filing suit, for example, in order to collect.

15 USC 1692g requires the collector to validate the debt within five days of his original contact with the debtor. Unless he did so with his original communication, he must send the debtor a written notice containing:

1. The amount of the debt.
2. The name of the creditor to whom it is owed.
3. A statement that, if the debtor does not dispute the validity of the debt within thirty days of receipt of the notice, the collector will assume that the debt is valid.

4. A statement that, if the debtor disputes the validity of the debt within the thirty-day period, the collector will check the validity with the creditor and send the debtor verification.

5. A statement that, if the debtor requests it in writing, the collector will furnish the name and address of the original creditor if the present creditor is an assignee or the like.

If the debtor requests verification, the collector must cease collection efforts until the verification is obtained. If the debtor does not dispute the validity of the debt, no court may take that fact as an admission that he owes it.

Both the federal and state laws provide that a violation which was committed as a bona fide error will not subject the violator to liability, so long as he has procedures in force designed to avoid commission of such errors. The federal law contains no criminal provisions. The state law in RCS 5069-11.09 provides that violation is a misdemeanor, subjecting a violator to a fine of $100 to $500. As to civil liability, 15 USC 1692k provides that a person injured by a violation of the federal law may recover actual damages, plus additional damages not to exceed $1,000. A plaintiff suing under the federal law may also recover court costs and a reasonable attorney's fee. RCS 5069-11.10 provides that plaintiffs suing under the Texas act may recover actual damages, plus court costs and attorney's fees.

Both statutes provide for injunctions against violators. Both also provide that a plaintiff may be required to pay the defendant's attorney when the plaintiff's suit is brought in bad faith.

Antigarnishment provisions of federal law. The Federal Consumer Credit Protection Act limits the amount of a debtor's paycheck which may be reached by garnishment, and forbids an employer to terminate an employee because of one garnishment. These provisions are of no real importance in Texas, since Texas law completely forbids garnishment of paychecks.

37

Motor Vehicle Law

The motor vehicle plays such an important role in modern American life that a large body of law has arisen to govern its ownership and operation. Some of the law is specialized and unrelated to other areas of legal regulation; the rest comes from areas which we have already covered. So important is this entire subject, however, that all of the law is gathered into one chapter and treated here as a unit.

Standards for marketing of new automobiles. Federal law imposes two types of standards upon manufacturers of and dealers in new motor vehicles. The Federal Clean Air Act, 42 USC 1857 et seq., gives to the Environmental Protection Agency (EPA) the power to impose pollutant emission standards on manufacturers of new vehicles. It also requires all new vehicles to bear a sticker certifying compliance with such standards. The EPA also conducts laboratory tests on all models of autos marketed in this country each year to determine the mileage per gallon of fuel obtained by the vehicle under laboratory conditions—one test being conducted under supposed city driving conditions, the other under country conditions. The MPG figures obtained for each model in question must be disclosed on the sticker. It must be realized, of course, that these test results are obtained under laboratory conditions and that there is no guarantee that the vehicle will get as good gas mileage in actual operation. Experience has shown that the EPA MPG figures are artificially high. In any event, it is unlawful to market a new vehicle which does not have the required EPA sticker or to market a vehicle with an altered sticker.

In addition, the National Highway Traffic Safety Act authorizes the National Highway Traffic Safety Administration of the U.S. Department of Transportation to set safety standards for new autos, and to require that all new vehicles comply with these standards. 15 USC 1397 makes it unlawful to sell or offer for sale a nonconforming new vehicle. It also requires that a certificate of conformity with these standards accompany each new vehicle; and forbids any manufacturer, dealer, distributor, or repair business to render inoperative any device required to be a part of the vehicle by any safety standard. It is permissible, however, to render inoperative safety belt interlocks or continuous buzzers designed to warn that safety belts are not in use.

The Texas Motor Vehicle Commission. RCS 4413(36) establishes the Texas Motor Vehicle Commission (TMVC), and gives it the power to regulate the distribution and sale of vehicles within the borders of Texas. No person may do business as a dealer, manufacturer, or distributor of motor vehicles in this state without a TMVC license.

RCS 4413(36) 5.01 makes it unlawful for a Texas motor vehicle dealer to:

1. Require a purchaser of a new vehicle to buy special features, equipment, parts, or accessories not ordered or desired by the purchaser, unless the items in question were already installed on the vehicle when received by the dealer.
2. Use false, deceptive, or misleading advertising. (Manufacturers and distributors are of course also forbidden to do this.)
3. Fail to perform all of the obligations imposed upon a dealer to deliver and prepare a new vehicle for retail sale.
4. Fail to live up to obligations imposed upon a dealer by the manufacturer's warranty.

These obligations of dealers are enforced primarily by the TMVC itself. However, a buyer of a new vehicle who is unhappy with the dealer's performance of his obligations under the manufacturer's warranty may complain to the commission. If the dealer still does not do as the buyer wishes, the buyer may ask the commission to hold a hearing to determine whether or not the dealer is violating the law. The commission may order the dealer to perform his obligations properly or, in an extreme case—or in a case where the dealer has defrauded the consumer—take steps to revoke the dealer's license.

Naturally, this recourse is in addition to rights given a consumer under the Uniform Commercial Code and the Deceptive Trade Practices Act. The main reason for complaining to the TMVC is that this agency can put a dealer out of business if he does not perform properly. A threat of loss of license may be more persuasive than a threat of loss of money.

The Texas Mobile Home Standards Act. RCS 5221f gives to the commissioner of the Texas Department of Labor and Standards (DLS) the power to promulgate by administrative process a Texas Mobile Home Standards Code, to which all mobile homes offered for sale in this state must comply. This code essentially enacts at the state level standards imposed upon mobile home manufacturers and dealers by the Federal Mobile Home Construction and Safety Standards Act and the administrative regulations issued thereunder by the Department of Housing and Urban Development.

Mobile home dealers are not required to have a state license under this legislation, but they are required to post bonds with the DLS to insure performance of their obligations under this act. Salespersons also must post such a bond.

All mobile homes marketed in this state must bear a certificate stating that all requirements of the Mobile Home Standards Code have been complied with. In addition, all mobile homes must be sold subject to a warranty which provides that:

1. The home complies with the code.
2. The warranty shall be in effect for at least one year after initial setup.
3. The home and all appliances and essential furnishings therein are free from defects in materials and workmanship.
4. Installation functions performed are in compliance with this act, if they have been performed by the dealer, manufacturer, or their authorized agents.
5. The manufacturer or dealer or both will take appropriate corrective action within a reasonable time after notification of defective materials or workmanship, or of lack of compliance with the code.
6. Manufacturer and dealer are jointly and severally liable to the consumer upon the warranty.

In addition, the warranty must inform the consumer of the address to which warranty claims must be sent.

A violation of the code or warranty provisions of this act is also a violation of the Deceptive Trade Practices Act, entitling the consumer to all remedies thereunder. In addition, the consumer may complain to the DLS to have administrative action taken against the violator which could result in assessment of a $1,000 civil penalty payable to the state for each violation proven. In addition, violation of this act constitutes a Class A misdemeanor.

Regulation of sale of used motor vehicles. Sellers of used vehicles need not comply with pollutant emission and safety equipment standards. There is little regulation present on this subject at the moment, though the Federal Trade Commission is considering a detailed trade regulation rule to cover the marketing of used cars. When and if this goes into effect, detailed regulation will exist in this area.

The only regulation now applicable to sales of used cars is designed to ensure that the odometer of the vehicle registers its true mileage. 15 USC 1988 requires the Department of Transportation to devise rules requiring the transferor of a motor vehicle to disclose to the transferee the cumulative mileage registered on the odometer, or to tell him that the true mileage is unknown if the odometer is known to have been tampered with. This disclosure must now be made on official forms. The statement given, of course, must be true. It is unlawful for a transferee to accept an incomplete statement.

15 USC 1983 makes unlawful the use of any device or the sale, installation, or advertising of any device which causes an odometer to register other than the true mileage driven. 15 USC 1984 forbids the disconnecting, resetting, or altering of an odometer. 15 USC 1985 makes it unlawful to operate a vehicle with a disconnected or nonfunctional odometer, if this is done with intent to defraud.

Any person violating these provisions of law is subject to criminal prosecution by federal authorities, a fine not to exceed $50,000, and/or one year imprisonment (15 USC 1990c). In addition, the federal authorities may sue in a civil action to recover penalties of $1,000 per violation. 15 USC 1989 authorizes the individual damaged by a violation to sue for three times actual damages suffered or $1,500, whichever sum is greater. It also authorizes the successful plaintiff to recover a reasonable attorney's fee.

RCS 6696b makes it a Texas state criminal offense to tamper with the odometer of a motor vehicle with the intent to defraud. For a first conviction of this offense, the maximum punishment is a fine of $1,000 and/or two years in the county jail. For a second or subsequent offense, the punishment is a fine not more than $2,000 and between thirty days and two years in the county jail. Imprisonment is thus mandatory upon conviction of a second offense.

It must also be remembered that the selling of a motor vehicle with an inaccurate odometer reading is a deceptive trade practice under the Deceptive Trade Practices Act. The victim may therefore sue for triple damages in the proper state court.

Title to motor vehicles. No motor vehicle owned by a resident of Texas may be operated upon the highways of this state until it has been registered and licensed in accordance with state law. The process involves the obtaining of license plates and a certificate of title for the vehicle. The statute governing certificates of title to Texas motor vehicles is the Certificate of Title Act, RCS 6687-1. Since the act has many sections, it will be cited in this chapter as CTA.

CTA 2 defines a motor vehicle as any motor-driven or motor-propelled vehicle required to be registered under the laws of Texas, including trailers, house trailers (mobile homes), and semitrailers. It also includes motorcycles, except those designed for use solely on golf courses; it does not include motor-assisted bicycles.

When a motor vehicle is sold for the first time within the borders of Texas as a new vehicle, the buyer must obtain a certificate of title in his name, with the seller (if a dealer) doing the necessary paperwork. The selling dealer must furnish the county official taking the application for the certificate with a manufacturer's certificate of origin showing the dealer as seller and the customer of the dealer as buyer (CTA 28). When an initial buyer buys a new vehicle outside Texas and brings it into this state for registration, he must have in his possession a manufacturer's certificate of origin issued to him by the selling dealer, showing him as the owner. It should be noted here that no certificate of title need be applied for until a dealer sells the new vehicle to a consumer.

When a dealer brings a used vehicle into Texas for purposes of resale, he must furnish an importer's certificate to the proper authorities before a Texas title will be issued to his buyer (CTA 29). When a person other than a dealer or importer brings a used car into the state of Texas with intent to establish residence here (or, if already a resident here, with intent to operate the vehicle within the state of Texas), he must obtain Texas license plates for the vehicle and must also obtain a Texas certificate of title, according to CTA 30. Before an application for a certificate of title will be accepted, the vehicle must be inspected by a peace officer, who must then sign a certificate stating the motor number and serial number or permanent identification number of the vehicle. The person seeking registration must of course have some proof of ownership of the vehicle—a certificate of title from another state—if that state has a Certificate of Title Act, or a registration certificate or bill of sale if the state from which the vehicle comes has no Certificate of Title Act.

If the applicant for the initial Texas title for the vehicle has clear title—that is, if there are no outstanding liens upon the vehicle—the original title will be issued to him and will show no outstanding liens (CTA 32). This section also provides that, if there is a lien upon the vehicle, two certificates shall be issued—an original and a duplicate original. The original will be mailed to the lienholder, who will of course hold it until the lien is discharged. The duplicate original will be mailed to the owner. CTA 32a provides that the duplicate original will serve only as evidence of ownership of the vehicle; the original must be used for purposes of transferring legal title.

Security interests in Texas motor vehicles. Anyone who holds a lien upon a motor vehicle in essence has a security interest in it, with all of the rights and privileges accorded to holders of security interests by Article 9 of the UCC (TB&CC). The only way to perfect such a security interest in a motor vehicle is by proper notation on the certificate of title, as per CTA 41.

When a security interest is satisfied, the holder of the lien shall obtain a discharge by swearing to the discharge before a notary public. If the lienholder held the original certificate of title before discharge of the lien, he would then turn that document over to the owner, together with the statement of discharge. If the lienholder did not have possession of the original title—perhaps because he was a second lienholder, or because he did not require the owner to give him the original title—he should merely furnish the statement of discharge to the owner. The owner could then apply to the Texas Highway Department for a new title showing no liens against the vehicle.

Should a person bring into Texas a vehicle against which a lien exists, and should that person obtain a Texas title for the vehicle without disclosing the existence of the lien so that the Texas title shows no liens upon the vehicle, the out-of-state security interest will become unperfected four months after the vehicle is brought into Texas. This means that a

Texas buyer of the vehicle who did not know of the out-of-state lien would buy the vehicle free and clear of it. Since the security interest would still be attached to the vehicle, however, the lienholder could enforce his lien against the original Texas owner for as long as he owned the vehicle, despite the lack of notation upon the title certificate.

Transfer of title to motor vehicles. No motor vehicle may be transferred voluntarily in this state except by transfer of the certificate of title. The seller endorses his title over to the buyer on a prescribed form printed on the back of the title certificate. The seller swears that he is the owner of the vehicle, and that no liens exist upon the vehicle except those shown on the title certificate. CTA 33 provides that no title will pass until the certificate is properly transferred; to emphasize this, CTA 53 states that all sales of motor vehicles in Texas which do not comply with the CTA are void. The endorsement of the seller on the certificate of title must be notarized to be valid.

Should a first lien exist upon the vehicle to be sold, and should the first lienholder possess the original certificate of title, the seller must of course obtain possession of this document from the lienholder in order to sell the vehicle, since a duplicate original cannot be used to transfer title. Thus, the first lienholder must be informed of the sale and must approve of it. If he does not approve, he need not give up his original title, and without the original title the owner cannot sell the vehicle.

When title to a motor vehicle is transferred involuntarily or by operation of law, there will not be any opportunity for endorsement of the title certificate from seller to buyer. Transfer of title by operation of law may take place because of the death or bankruptcy of the owner. Involuntary transfer may be due to seizure of the vehicle under a writ of execution in satisfaction of a judgment, seizure by the IRS for nonpayment of federal taxes, or foreclosure of a mechanic's lien by a repairman, etc. CTA 35 provides that the Highway Department may issue a new title to the vehicle upon receipt of valid documentation of the transfer of title—a bill of sale or a court order transferring ownership.

When a voluntary sale is made, and the seller duly endorses his title to the buyer, the buyer should of course send his old title in to the Highway Department so that a new title may be issued in his name.

Loss or theft of certificate or vehicle. When an existing certificate of title is lost or destroyed, CTA 36 provides that a certified copy may be obtained from the Highway Department on proper application. When a lien is noted upon a title certificate, the department will not issue a certified copy of the original to anyone except the lienholder.

These certified copies are plainly marked as such. A buyer of such a copy gets the title to the vehicle formerly possessed by the owner of the copy. Of course, if the owner of the copy truly lost his certificate, the buyer of the certificate copy would get good title to the vehicle. There is always the possibility, however, that an unscrupulous vehicle owner will obtain a certified copy of a certificate he has not lost so that he will have two certificates to the same vehicle. If he then sells the original, and later sells the copy, the buyer of the original will get better title to the vehicle than will the buyer of the certified copy. Of course, when the buyer of a certified copy obtains a new certificate in his name for the vehicle, his certificate will be an original.

Whenever a vehicle is stolen, the theft should be reported to the police and to the Highway Department as well, so that its file on that particular vehicle may be flagged to show the theft. Should anyone then seek to have a new title issued to the vehicle, the door will be open to its recovery.

Revocation and refusal of certificate. CTA 38 provides that the Highway Department

may refuse to honor an application for a certificate of title, and that it may revoke an existing title, when:
1. The title application contains false or fraudulent statements.
2. The applicant has not furnished all required information on his application.
3. The applicant is not entitled to a title certificate.
4. The department has reason to believe that the vehicle has been stolen or converted.
5. Issuance of a new title would be fraudulent against the true owner, or against a lienholder.
6. The registration of the vehicle has been revoked or suspended.
7. The required fees have not been paid.

When an application for a title certificate is denied or notice of revocation of a title certificate is received, anyone unhappy with the situation may ask for a hearing on the legitimacy of the refusal or revocation before the county tax assessor-collector of the county where application for registration was made. Anyone aggrieved with his decision at the hearing may then appeal the matter to the county court of the county in question (CTA 39). The county court will then conduct a whole new trial on the matter; its decision is final.

Penalties for violation of the Certificate of Title Act. CTA 62 provides that anyone guilty of violation of this act commits a misdemeanor, for which he may be fined at least $1, but no more than $100. For a second or subsequent offense a fine of no less than $2 nor more than $200 may be levied. Among the acts so punishable are:
1. The sale, offering for sale, or offering as collateral of a motor vehicle without possessing a certificate of title for said vehicle (CTA 51).
2. Making application for certificate of title upon a vehicle one knows to be stolen, converted, or concealed (CTA 54).
3. Giving a false name or false address on applications for certificates of title (CTA 59, 61).
4. Misrepresenting facts regarding the release or discharge of liens upon motor vehicles (CTA 61).

The act also contains provisions establishing special penalties for other violations. The master or captain of any ship or aircraft who accepts a motor vehicle for transportation out of Texas without first checking its ownership with the Highway Department commits a misdemeanor for which the minimum penalty is a fine of $50 and the maximum $500 for a first offense, minimum $100 and maximum $1,000 for second and subsequent offenses (CTA 61a).

Anyone who alters, forges, or counterfeits a certificate of title, or who falsifies or forges an assignment thereof, commits the crime of forgery (CTA 49a). Anyone who alters, changes, erases, or mutilates any motor vehicle identification number commits a misdemeanor punishable by a fine not to exceed $1,000 and/or two years imprisonment in the county jail (CTA 49b). Anyone who possesses, sells, or offers for sale a motor vehicle upon which identification numbers have been changed, altered, mutilated, or erased is subject to the same penalties as above, unless the vehicle is his and he did not commit the mutilation (CTA 49c).

Whenever a person is charged with any violation of CTA 49, the vehicle in question will be taken into custody. The seized vehicle will then be turned over to the true owner if he can be located. If he cannot be located, the vehicle will be declared forfeit to the state of Texas.

Junked motor vehicles. RCS 6687-2 provides that when an auto salvage dealer obtains a motor vehicle for purposes of scrap disposal, demolition, resale of parts, or other form of salvage, he must obtain the certificate of title from the owner and surrender it to the Highway Department for cancellation. Such dealers are required to keep accurate records of the source of all junked vehicles and junked parts purchased. Peace officers may inspect these records at any reasonable time; they may also inspect the inventory of such dealers at any reasonable time, and may seize, hold, and dispose of any vehicle or part thereof which has been stolen or misappropriated.

Section 10 of the Abandoned Motor Vehicle Act, RCS 6687-9, grants to cities, towns, and counties the right to enact ordinances providing for the seizure and disposal of junked motor vehicles located upon public or private property or upon public rights of way. AMVA 2(5) defines a junked vehicle as a motor vehicle which is inoperable; does not have lawfully affixed unexpired license plates and safety inspection certificate; is wrecked, dismantled, partially dismantled, or discarded; or has remained inoperable for a continuous period of more than 120 days. No such vehicle may be seized prior to the giving of 10 days' notice to the owner of the vehicle and to the owner of the premises upon which the vehicle is located. Should the vehicle not be removed during this 10-day period, the local government may remove it and have it demolished.

Abandoned motor vehicles. An abandoned motor vehicle is defined by AMVA 2(2) as:

1. A vehicle which is inoperable, more than eight years old, and left unattended upon public property for more than forty-eight hours, or
2. A vehicle which has illegally remained on public property for more than forty-eight hours, or
3. A vehicle that has remained on private property for more than forty-eight hours without the consent of the property owner or person in control of the property, or
4. A vehicle left unattended on any county, state, or federal highway right-of-way for more than forty-eight hours.

The police may take any such vehicles into custody. Within ten days of taking them into custody, notice of the seizure must be given to the owner of the vehicle shown on Highway Department records, and to all lienholders shown upon these records. An owner or lienholder may reclaim the vehicle from the police within twenty days of the notice by paying all towing, preservation, and storage charges.

If no one claims the vehicle, it may be sold at auction. Notice of the time and place of the auction must be given to the public. A buyer of the vehicle at the auction gets clear title to it; his bill of sale given by the auctioneer will entitle him to a certificate of title for the vehicle in his name. From the proceeds the police may keep the towing and other charges. The excess is held for the owner and/or lienholders for ninety days; if unclaimed it goes into a special fund for the defraying of towing expenses of abandoned vehicles when police are unable to recover the charges from anyone (AMVA 3, 4, and 5). The old title certificate is of course canceled.

If the identity of the owner and lienholders cannot be determined, or if notice sent to the address of the persons on Highway Department records is returned undelivered, notice of the seizure may be given by publication.

AMVA 6 provides that a vehicle left for more than ten days in a storage facility operated for commercial purposes after notice has been sent to the registered owner to pick it up shall be considered abandoned. Such storage facilities include parking lots, park houses, and garages. The ten-day period for determining abandonment starts with sending notice to the owner to come pick up his vehicle. The vehicle is considered to be abandoned after expiration of this period; the facility owner must notify the police within the next ten days of the presence of the abandoned vehicle. The police will then notify the owner and lienholders that the abandoned vehicle must be reclaimed and that otherwise it will be sold at auction. If the vehicle is not reclaimed, the police may then take custody of it and sell it at auction, according to the procedure described above. The garage or other storage facility recovers its charges from the proceeds of the auction, the balance being disposed of as described.

The owner of property upon which an abandoned vehicle is located may apply to the Highway Department for permission to turn the vehicle over to a salvage dealer or other demolisher. Should this permission be granted, the owner of the property may then sell the vehicle to the demolisher and keep the proceeds. The demolisher will surrender the title to the vehicle to the Highway Department, which will of course cancel it. Before permission for demolition can be granted, however, the registered owner must be notified as in the seizure cases; and permission to demolish will not be granted unless the registered owner does not reclaim his vehicle.

Licensing of motor vehicle drivers. RCS 6687b contains the statutory law relative to the licensing of motor vehicle operators in this state. These provisions are so complex that space forbids consideration in detail of the provisions of the statute. In general it provides that no one may operate a motor vehicle on Texas highways without a driver's license issued under Texas law, except certain classes of persons. It also provides that licenses may not be granted to certain classes of persons, and that licenses may be revoked (or renewal not granted) for certain specified reasons.

The following sorts of persons, among others, may operate motor vehicles in Texas without possession of a Texas driver's license (RCS 6687b-3):

1. Persons in the service of the United States operating government vehicles on official duty.
2. Persons operating farm equipment.
3. Persons operating commercial vehicles in time of emergency.
4. Nonresidents possessing valid licenses from their home jurisdictions, if they are at least sixteen years of age.
5. Nonresident military personnel having valid licenses from their home states and dependents of such personnel. (These persons may be considered nonresidents even if stationed in Texas, if they maintain voting residence, etc., back home.)

Section 4 of the driver's license statute provides that the following sorts of persons, among others, shall not be granted driver's licenses in Texas:

1. Persons under eighteen years of age, except those who have completed driver education courses approved by the Highway Department, have passed the required examinations, and are sixteen or older.
2. Habitual drunkards and drug addicts.
3. Insane or feebleminded persons, idiots, or imbeciles.
4. Persons unable to understand highway signs in the English language.
5. Persons drawing public assistance as needy blind.
6. Persons physically or mentally incapable of driving motor vehicles.

Special and restricted licenses may be issued to persons with physical disabilities (such as defective vision which can be corrected with glasses) or to persons fifteen years of age or older who need licenses for the benefit of their families.

Learner's permits are issued to those learning to drive. Learners may not obtain a regular license without first passing a written exam on knowledge of traffic law and a practical exam involving the actual driving of a vehicle, to determine driving skill. Written examinations are given in both English and Spanish, but Spanish-speaking persons must demonstrate their understanding of traffic signs written in English.

Persons moving to Texas from other states may drive in this state on their home state licenses for thirty days only. After that they must take the written exam in order to obtain a Texas driver's license.

Operators of large commercial vehicles must obtain special commercial operator or chauffeur's licenses. The requirements for obtaining these will not be discussed, but it should be remembered that commercial vehicle drivers may well be required to obtain such special licenses.

The first Texas driver's license obtained by a person expires on the birthday of the applicant occurring four years after the date of application. Renewal licenses are good for four years, always expiring on one's birthday.

Every motor vehicle operator must carry his driver's license with him; failure to do this may cause him to be charged with a misdemeanor. However, if one is accused of driving without possession of a valid license, production of a valid license in court is a defense to the charge. It is best to have the license with you while driving: if you drive, but you leave the license at home, you may be charged with the offense of driving without a license, and though you may escape conviction upon the charge, you must go to the trouble of producing your license in court.

Driving without a license is a misdemeanor. For the first offense the maximum sentence is a fine of no more than $200. For a second offense committed within one year of the first the maximum is a fine of no less than $25 and no more than $200. For a third offense within one year of the second, the maximum is a fine of $500 and six months' imprisonment. The minimum for such a third offense is a fine of no less than $25 or imprisonment of no less than seventy-two hours (RCS 6687b-13).

Suspension of driver's licenses. RCS 6687b-24 provides that a Texas driver's license shall be automatically suspended when:

1. The driver negligently kills a person while operating a vehicle.
2. The driver is guilty of DWI, or driving under the influence of drugs.
3. The driver commits a felony while driving his vehicle.
4. The driver is convicted of failure to stop, render assistance, and disclose his identity after an accident in which he was involved.
5. The driver is convicted of a charge of aggravated assault with a motor vehicle—that is, he used the vehicle as a weapon for committing the assault.

Such suspension is for a period of twelve months for the first offense; a second suspension is for eighteen months. Should the driver attempt to drive while his license is suspended, and get caught, the suspension period will be doubled.

Section 25 of the driver's license act requires any court convicting a person of an offense for which a driver's license may be suspended to report the conviction to the Highway Department at once, so that appropriate action may be taken. The Highway Department may initiate proceedings to suspend a driver's license when:

1. Driver has been responsible for an accident resulting in death.
2. Driver is an habitual reckless or negligent driver.
3. Driver has incurred four moving violations within a twelve-month period, or seven moving violations within a twenty-four-month period.
4. Driver is incapable of driving a vehicle.

5. Driver has permitted an unlawful or fraudulent use of his license.
6. Driver was involved in an accident for which submission of an official accident report was required, but he failed to submit the report.
7. Driver was responsible for an accident causing severe personal injury or severe property damage.
8. Other conduct spelled out in RCS 6687b-22(b).

Suspension of a driver's license for these reasons is not automatic. The Highway Department must file a complaint for suspension of the license in question in the JP court of the precinct where the driver resides. The driver is entitled to a hearing on the question of whether or not his license should be suspended. Should he be a resident of an incorporated city or town, the hearing must be held before a judge of the local municipal court. There is no trial by jury in these cases: the judge makes a recommendation in the matter which the Highway Department must execute. Should the case be decided against the license holder, he may appeal the matter to the county court, where he is entitled to a new trial.

A person whose license has been suspended whose capacity to drive is essential to his ability to support himself may apply to the Highway Department for a special license. Such a license may be granted if the department feels that it is necessary, but it may be subjected to various restrictions designed to protect the public.

Unlawful acts. RCS 6687b-32 declares the following acts to be unlawful:
1. Having in one's possession, or possessing or causing to be possessed, a canceled, revoked, suspended, or altered driver's license.
2. Lending, or knowingly permitting the use of, a license issued to the lender by a person other than the licenseholder.
3. Using a license not issued to the user.
4. Failing to surrender a license suspended or revoked according to law.
5. Applying for or having in possession more than one valid license.
6. Using a false and fictitious name or address, or making false statements, in applications for licenses.

Section 35 of the act forbids a person to permit his child or ward under eighteen years of age to drive a vehicle without a license. Section 36 forbids a person to permit an unauthorized person to drive a vehicle owned by him on Texas highways. Section 38 forbids a person to rent a motor vehicle in this state to an unauthorized driver, and requires the owner of a rental vehicle to inspect the driver's license of the renter before allowing him the use of his vehicle. According to Section 44, any of the above violations are misdemeanors, for which the maximum penalty is a fine of $200.

Anyone counterfeiting a Texas driver's license commits a felony, for which the maximum penalty is five years' imprisonment; the minimum penalty is two years. The same penalty applies to anyone possessing such a license with intent to sell or circulate it. Anyone counterfeiting a driver's license from another state, or having such a license in his possession with intent to sell or circulate is subject to the same penalty.

Financial responsibility of Texas drivers. Texas, unlike some other states, has not enacted a mandatory liability insurance law. Therefore, drivers of motor vehicles registered in Texas need not possess liability insurance to protect others against the consequences of their negligence.

However, Texas has enacted a Financial Responsibility Act, RCS 6701h. This essentially provides that the driver's license of a Texas driver and the registration of a

Texas motor vehicle may be revoked if the holder of the license or owner of the vehicle is involved in an accident for which he may incur liability, and he is unable to prove his ability to pay off a potential judgment arising from the accident.

In a sense, the law operates on the principle that no one need prove financial responsibility if he can avoid getting involved in accidents which may be his fault. It is only after an accident that the necessity for proving responsibility can arise.

Accident reports. Section 44 of the Uniform Traffic Act, RCS 6701d, imposes upon the Texas driver the duty to file a written accident report with the Department of Public Safety whenever he is involved as a driver in an auto accident resulting in personal injury or death, or when property damage of more than $25 is done. It does not matter whether the accident occurs on public or private property. According to Section 4 of the Financial Responsibility Act (FRA), the necessity to prove financial responsibility may arise if the accident report shows that death or personal injury occurred, or that $250 or more in property damage has occurred and that it is probable that a judgment will be obtained against the driver for these damages.

The report must be filed with the DPS within ten days of the accident. The form inquires about all the particulars of the driver's liability insurance coverage, if any. This information is essential to the proof of financial responsibility if the driver has liability insurance coverage. (If he has no such insurance, it may be good evidence of lack of responsibility.)

Proof of financial responsibility. FRA 6 provides that financial responsibility need not be proven, even if personal injury, death, or more than $250 in property damage occurs, if:

1. Only the driver and his vehicle suffered injury or damage, or
2. The driver was legally parked, or had legally stopped for a traffic signal, when the accident occurred, or
3. The driver has been released from liability, or found by a court not to be liable, or has settled all claims against him out of court. In addition, the owner of a vehicle driven by someone else need not prove responsibility if his vehicle was being driven without his permission.

FRA 5c provides that financial responsibility is proven when:

1. Driver had in effect $10,000/$20,000 liability insurance, with at least $5,000 property damage coverage. A $250 deductible under the policy is acceptable.
2. The owner had in effect such a liability policy that covered the driver.
3. The driver was covered by some other form of liability insurance.
4. The driver was employed by the U.S. Government, and at the time of the accident was within the scope of his employment.
5. The vehicle belonged to an owner registered with the DPS as a self-insurer. Any owner of twenty-five or more vehicles may apply for registration as a self-insurer under FRA 34, if he can prove financial responsibility to the satisfaction of the DPS.

If the driver claims to be covered by some form of insurance, or if he claims to have some other excuse for exemption from proof of responsibility, the DPS will check out his claims. He will, of course, not be asked to prove responsibility if it appears that he has incurred no legal liability. If it appears that he has incurred liability, and his claim of insurance is verified, the insurer becomes legally bound to pay any judgment against the driver within the bounds of $10,000/$20,000 coverage for personal injury or $5,000 property damage. The effect of this will be discussed later in the chapter under the heading of auto insurance.

If the driver is not insured and cannot prove responsibility in the ways mentioned above, and it appears that he may be legally responsible for the accident, the department may take steps to suspend the driver's license and all motor vehicle registrations in the name of the driver in question unless he deposits security of a named amount with the department, with the amount set by the department at a level sufficient to pay off the probable judgment the injured party could win upon suit.

The DPS must give the driver notice of its intent to require deposit of security or suspend licenses and registration. The notice may be served in person by employees of the department, or it may be sent by certified mail to the driver. License and registration may then be suspended unless the driver makes the required deposit within twenty days of his receipt of the notice or makes a written demand for a hearing on the matter within the twenty-day period.

When a hearing is demanded, it is held before a municipal court judge or a justice of the peace in the county and JP precinct of the driver's residence. The driver must be notified of the time and place of the hearing, which must be scheduled at least ten days after his receipt of notice. There is no right to a jury in this hearing. The JP or judge must decide whether or not there is a reasonable probability of a judgment being rendered against the driver due to the accident, and, if there is, how much the judgment might be. If the decision is that there is no reasonable probability of such judgment being rendered, that ends the matter. If the decision goes against the driver, he may appeal the matter to the county court, where a new hearing will be held.

Once it is decided that the driver is likely to have judgment rendered against him, he must either post the required security or suffer the suspensions mentioned above. The security may take the form of a cash deposit, of a surety bond issued by an acceptable bonding company, etc.

FRA 7 provides that suspension of a driver's license and vehicle registration under the provisions of this act shall remain in effect until:
 1. The required security has been deposited, or
 2. Two years have elapsed since the accident and no suit has been filed because of it, providing that driver has filed proof of responsibility (by taking out liability insurance, for instance), or
 3. The driver has been released from liability, or a court action carried to completion has determined that the driver is not liable for consequences of the accident.

FRA 12 provides that whenever a judgment is handed down against a driver as a consequence of an auto accident and the judgment is not paid within sixty days—or, as FRA 15 provides, if at least $10,000 has not been paid to the judgment creditor on a personal injury judgment of more than $10,000; at least $5,000 has not been paid to a property damage judgment creditor when judgment for more than $5,000; or $20,000 has not been paid to multiple judgment creditors with personal injury judgments totaling more than $20,000—a certified copy of the judgment or judgments must be sent to the DPS. The DPS must then suspend the driver's license and vehicle registrations of that driver until the judgment is paid in full, or at least until the amounts required by FRA 15 have been paid.

According to FRA 14b, the driver who is discharged from obligation to pay such a judgment in bankruptcy will not recover his driver's license or vehicle registration if they have been suspended. A discharge in bankruptcy is not considered to be satisfaction of a judgment for purposes of this legislation.

Effect of suspension of license and registration. Suspended driver's licenses and registration slips must be returned by the driver to the DPS within ten days of receipt of notification of the suspension. Failure to do this subjects one to a fine of no more than $200, as per FRA 32(d).

It is of course unlawful to drive with a suspended license. It is also unlawful to drive, or to allow another to drive, a vehicle upon which registration is suspended. Anyone who does this may be fined up to $500, and/or imprisoned for up to six months, as per FRA 32(c).

Anyone filing false proof of financial responsibility, or forging the same, may be fined up to $1,000 and/or imprisoned for one year, as per FRA 32(a).

Suspension of the registration of a vehicle simply means that it is unlawful to operate it on Texas highways under the canceled registration. The certificate of title is not suspended; the owner of the vehicle may therefore sell or otherwise dispose of it. If the owner does not keep up his payments, lienholders may repossess. However, the Highway Department will not recognize the validity of the transfer of ownership of such a vehicle until it is convinced that the former owner is not trying to evade the result of the suspension of his registration (FRA 30). A good-faith transfer is of course perfectly lawful.

This act applies also to out-of-state drivers who use Texas highways. Texas of course has no authority to suspend out-of-state vehicle registrations or out-of-state driver's licenses, but it may report all accidents to the home state authorities of the drivers involved; and these authorities may suspend their driver's licenses and vehicle registrations.

An out-of-state accident may cost a Texan his driver's license and vehicle registration if the other state has a financial responsibility law like ours (which most states have) and if the Texan cannot prove responsibility under that state's law. That state can report the matter to the Texas DPS, and the DPS can take authorized action.

Inspection of motor vehicles. Section 140 of the Texas Uniform Traffic Act (TUTA) provides that all motor vehicles registered in Texas and operated on the highways of Texas shall be subject to annual safety inspection. This inspection shall be performed by qualified personnel of state-licensed inspection stations. The inspection shall cover the tires, braking system, lights, horns, warning devices, mirrors, windshield wipers, front seat belts when these are original equipment, steering systems, wheel assembly, safety guards, flaps, exhaust system, and exhaust emission system. The DPS has authority to promulgate administrative standards for determining the safety of these items to be inspected, in accordance with general standards contained in several sections of the TUTA subsequent to 140.

Should an inspected auto be deficient with respect to an item or items of inspected equipment, the inspector must inform the owner of the deficiency. An inspection sticker will not be issued until the deficiency is corrected. Of course the inspector may not insist upon the correction of any deficiency by his business establishment; the vehicle owner has the right to choose where the correction shall be made. It is unlawful for an inspector to pass a vehicle having obvious deficiencies; it is also unlawful for an inspector to state that a vehicle has deficiencies which it does not have.

Inspection stations may charge $2 for their services. Should first inspection reveal a deficiency, reinspection is necessary after its correction. No charge may be made for such a reinspection.

The inspection certificate is the familiar sticker found on the windshield of all Texas vehicles. The month of inspection appears on the sticker, and the sticker expires on the last date of the month shown thereon. It is of course unlawful to operate a vehicle on Texas highways bearing an expired inspection sticker, except that TUTA 140(e) provides a five-day grace period extending into the next month.

When a vehicle is involved in so severe an accident that some of the equipment subject to safety inspection is damaged, an investigating police officer may remove the inspection sticker from the vehicle. When this is done, of course, the defective equipment must be repaired and the vehicle must be reinspected so that a new inspection certificate may be issued. The vehicle may not be lawfully driven on Texas highways until this is done, but in such circumstances operation without a certificate is permitted for thirty days after the accident, as provided by TUTA 140(c).

Violation of any provision of the TUTA regarding inspection is a misdemeanor, punishable by a fine of no less than $1 and no more than $200, as per TUTA 143.

General duty of driver in case of accident. Whenever a driver is involved in an accident on a Texas street or highway which results in damage to a vehicle, he must stop, return to the scene, and furnish the following information:

1. Name and address.
2. Registration number of his vehicle (license plate number).

He shall also show the other party his driver's license upon request, if it is available.

If the accident has caused personal injury to anyone, or has killed anyone, the police must be informed, (as they should be if more than $25 in property damage is done). Reasonable assistance must also be rendered to anyone injured—including, in appropriate cases, the summoning of an ambulance or the transporting of the injured party to a hospital.

Failure to stop at the scene of an accident when personal injury or death has occurred is a felony, punishable by up to five years in prison and/or a fine of up to $5,000 (TUTA 38). TUTA 39 provides that it is a misdemeanor not to stop at the scene of an accident in which one is involved when property damage has occurred, the punishment being the usual fine of no less than $1 nor more than $200.

When a driver strikes an unattended vehicle, he must either contact its owner and explain what happened or attach a note to the vehicle in a conspicuous place, giving his name and address and explaining what occurred. The same obligation is imposed upon a driver striking fixtures on or adjacent to a highway. TUTA 41 and 42 impose these requirements.

Driving while intoxicated. QCS 67011-1 provides that a person operating a motor vehicle on any public highway, road, or street in this state while under the influence of intoxicating liquor commits a misdemeanor, for which he may be confined in the county jail for no less than three days nor more than two years, and fined no less than $50 nor more than $500. The imprisonment may be commuted to probation of no less than six months at the court's discretion.

Once a person has been convicted of DWI, a second offense becomes a felony, according to RCS 67011-2. Such a person may be confined in the state penitentiary for up to five years, or in the county jail for no less than ten days nor more than two years. He may also be fined no less than $100 nor more than $5,000. Minors convicted of DWI may not be fined more than $100, nor may they be imprisoned; however, if their fines are not paid, their driver's licenses may be suspended until they pay, as per RCS 67011-3, 4.

Any person operating a motor vehicle within the state of Texas automatically consents to the administration of a breathalyser test when he is under suspicion of DWI. Refusal to submit to such a test may result in the suspension of one's driver's license for a year. This suspension may not take place before a hearing is held before a municipal court judge or justice of the peace with the court finding that:

1. It is probable that the driver was guilty of DWI, and
2. He was duly arrested before he was ordered to take the test, and

3. He refused to take it.

A decision suspending a license may be appealed to the county court for a new trial.

A driver may consent to a test of his blood or urine to determine alcoholic content in lieu of the breathalyser test, but no driver is obligated to consent to these. If the breath test or any other test shows an alcoholic content of the driver's blood amounting to 0.1 percent or more, it is presumed that he was guilty of DWI. The presumption of course is not conclusive; if the driver can prove his lack of guilt he can escape conviction, but it would be very difficult to escape in the face of such a test result.

Driving under the influence of drugs. TUTA 50 provides that driving on Texas highways, roads, or streets while under the influence of narcotic drugs is unlawful. It does not matter whether the driver is authorized to use the drug in question.

As per TUTA 50, the punishment for a first offense shall be imprisonment of no less than ten days nor more than two years, or a fine of no less than $100 and no more than $1,000, or both. For second and subsequent offenses, there shall be imprisonment of no less than ninety days nor more than two years, and, in the discretion of the court, a fine of no more than $1,000. Thus, the first offense under this section carries potentially greater punishment than first offense DWI; but a second offense under this section carries less punishment than second offense DWI.

Homicide by vehicle. Anyone who unlawfully and unintentionally, with a conscious disregard for the rights of others, causes the death of a person while violating a traffic law is guilty of homicide by vehicle. The offense is a misdemeanor, for which punishment is a fine of no less than $500 nor more than $2,000, or imprisonment for no less than three months nor more than one year, or both.

Venue must be in the county of the violation. A person accused of this offense must be indicted by a grand jury, although the offense is labeled a misdemeanor. The statute governing this offense is TUTA 50A.

Reckless driving. TUTA 51 singles out this traffic offense for special definition and punishment. Any person driving a vehicle in willful or wanton disregard for the safety of persons or property commits this offense; a person guilty of it may be fined up to $200, or imprisoned for up to forty days, or both.

Other traffic offenses. TUTA defines a host of other traffic offenses too numerous for discussion here. These include, for example, speeding, failing to yield the right-of-way, following too closely, improper passing, and having faulty equipment of various sorts. TUTA 143 provides that a person convicted of any of these offenses commits a misdemeanor, for which he may be fined a sum of between $1 and $200.

It should be mentioned that TUTA 185 forbids any sort of racing on public highways. It also forbids contests of physical endurance involving motor vehicles on state highways.

Fleeing or attempting to elude a police officer. Any person failing to stop his vehicle upon the order of a police officer, or any driver who attempts to flee or elude a police officer, commits this offense. TUTA 186 provides that the punishment for it shall be imprisonment for no less than thirty days nor more than six months, a fine of no less than $100 nor more than $500, or both. Playing hide and seek with the police may be an expensive sport.

Parties to traffic offenses. TUTA 145 provides that a person inducing, causing, coercing, requiring, or directing a driver to commit a traffic offense is just as guilty of the offense as is the driver.

TUTA 146 states that a vehicle owner who employs or directs a driver to commit a traffic violation, or who knowingly permits a driver to commit a traffic violation, is just as guilty of the offense as the driver.

Procedure in traffic cases. A person arrested for commission of a traffic offense must be taken before a magistrate immediately upon arrest when (TUTA 147):
1. The arrested person demands that this be done, or
2. The charge is homicide by vehicle, or
3. The charge is DWI or driving under the influence of drugs, or
4. The charge is failure to stop at the scene of an accident, or
5. The arrested person refuses to promise to appear in court at a named time and place.

The procedure to be followed in such cases will depend upon the wishes of the arrested party and the classification of the offense as felony or misdemeanor.

In other cases, the arresting officer writes out the familiar ticket, a written notice to the driver to appear in court at a named time and place containing a notice of the offense charged, the name and address of the driver, and the license number of his vehicle. The time of appearance in court must be at least ten days after the arrest. The court must be located in the city or county where the offense was committed. The driver must sign the ticket in duplicate on the appropriate blank, thereby promising to appear in court as directed. These provisions are found in TUTA 148.

Should the recipient of the citation fail to appear in court as he promised to do, he commits a misdemeanor regardless of what disposal is made of the charge for which the citation was issued. An appearance in court by the driver's attorney at the appointed time is considered to be appearance. Failure to appear may result in the magistrate's issuing a bench warrant for the arrest of the driver.

An officer making an arrest for speeding must be in uniform. He must not trap his victims by lying in wait for them, concealed. Thus, the tactic used by police officers of other states of lying in wait for speeders behind billboards is not allowed in Texas (RCS 6701d-8).

Every conviction of a traffic offense or forfeiture of bail in a traffic case, must be reported by the clerk of the court handling the case to the DPS, so that the DPS may file an abstract of the matter in the driver's individual file. In this way the DPS may keep track of the number of violations accumulated by licensed drivers in this state.

Liability of drivers and owners of motor vehicles. In general, operation of a motor vehicle in violation of the traffic laws of this state is actionable negligence. Thus, a driver who causes injury to persons or property while in violation of the law may be sued for damages by his victim, in accordance with principles of negligence discussed in the chapter on torts.

The owner of a motor vehicle may be liable to persons injured through the negligence of the driver thereof in accordance with principles of the law of agency and the law of bailments, as discussed in the sections on those subjects.

The liability of the driver of a vehicle for injuries caused by his negligence to nonpaying guests in his vehicle is to an extent limited by the provisions of the Texas Guest Statute, RCS 6701b. This statute provides that a nonpaying guest related to the driver within the second degree of consanguinity or affinity will have no claim against the driver for injuries caused by his negligence, unless the accident was deliberate, was caused by the heedlessness of the driver, or by his reckless disregard for the rights of others. A person is related to another within the second degree of consanguinity when the people in question have the same grandparent—a first cousin or closer relative would thus have no claim. Likewise, a first cousin or closer relative of the driver's spouse would ordinarily have no claim.

If, however, the driver was guilty of DWI, or had been driving 100 MPH when the accident occurred, or had been driving a gravely defective vehicle without the knowledge of his unfortunate passenger, he would not be exempted from liability by the provisions of this guest statute.

Auto liability insurance. As mentioned in the section of this chapter on financial responsibility, Texas law does not require the Texas auto owner to carry liability insurance. However, the intelligent owner will carry such insurance—both because it serves as proof of financial responsibility when required and because no driver is so perfect that he never makes a mistake while driving. The best driver may have a mental lapse; if another vehicle is in close proximity when the lapse occurs, an accident may happen for which the normally careful driver may be responsible.

Insurance is procurable from private insurers licensed to sell auto insurance within this state. Since insurance is an industry that is very strongly regulated, the form of policies and the premiums insurers may charge are also strictly controlled. However, all potential purchasers of auto insurance are not entitled to the same premiums. In general, persons under twenty-five years of age must pay higher premiums than those over twenty-five. Persons who have good driving records pay less than those with bad records.

An insurer may, in fact, refuse to accept an insurance application from an applicant who has an exceptionally bad driving record. However, FRA 25 requires the Texas auto insurance industry to make such insurance available to the worst of risks through an assigned risk plan. Under this plan, applicants with bad records will be administratively assigned to insurance companies. The insurer may of course charge high premiums to such customers due to the high risks involved, but an insurer may not refuse to insure an assigned risk.

The amount of insurance required to meet proof of financial responsibility requirements under FRA is $10,000/$20,000 coverage. This means that the insurer will pay up to $10,000 to any one victim of an accident caused by the insured and up to a total of $20,000 to all victims of such an accident. The policy must also obligate the insurer to pay up to $5,000 in toto to settle property damage claims arising from an accident.

Suppose that Able has $10,000/$20,000 personal injury liability coverage. In an accident which is entirely his fault, Baker suffers personal injury causing him $15,000 in damage, and Cass suffers $3,000 in such damage. Must the insurer pay both claims in full? No: it will pay Baker only $10,000, which is the maximum payable to any one claimant under the policy, and will pay Cass in full.

Suppose again that Able has this coverage. He causes an accident in which Xavier suffers $8,000 personal injury damage, York suffers $9,000, and Zale suffers $10,000. Total damage is $27,000, though no single injured party suffered more than $10,000 damages. The insurer must pay only $20,000 to these claimants; how much it will pay to whom is essentially up to it to decide.

If the total damages exceed the limits of the liability policy, the liability of the insurer is normally bounded by this limit; the insured is liable for the excess. Since this is true, it behooves all insured persons to have adequate coverage. At the present time, $10,000/$20,000 coverage is hardly adequate.

When an insured is involved in an accident which appears to be his fault, he may not automatically assume that his insurer will take care of things. To begin with, the insured must do all that the law requires him to do because of the accident. He must stop and give information, call the police, and file the state accident report if these things are legally required. He must also notify the insurer of the accident as soon as possible after it happened. He should not discuss the accident with the other parties. Most certainly he should not admit liability, make any promises to pay damages, or the like. He must of course file a report with the insurer, and disclose to it all the facts of the matter openly and honestly.

If the claims of the injured parties amount to less than the limits of the liability policy, settlement of the claims is a matter between the insurer and the claimants. The insurer is legally obligated to defend the insured against liability; if anybody has to pay, it will be the insurer, so the insured must simply cooperate with the insurer in all ways.

Should the insurer and the claimants be unable to agree upon a settlement, the claimants may decide to sue. In such a case, they cannot sue the insurer directly; they must sue the insured. Citation in the action will be served upon the insured, not upon the insurer. The insured must notify the insurer at once of the service of the complaint, and he must turn over all of the served papers to the insurer.

The insurer will defend the action in the name of the insured, so the latter must cooperate with the insurer's attorney in all particulars as he defends the case. If the insured does not cooperate with the insurer in the defense of the case, the interests of insured and insurer diverge; the insured violates the terms of his contract of insurance if he does not cooperate. If he breaches this contract, the insurer would be justified in refusing to pay any claim. Thus, the insured may end up paying the claims of his victims.

On the other hand, if DPS requires the insured to prove financial responsibility, and he proves it with his liability policy, his insurer is now absolutely liable for paying off the injured claimants up to the $10,000/$20,000 limits imposed by law. The insurer cannot escape paying the claimants because the insured breached the terms of his insurance policy, but, in such a case the insurer may recoup what it paid to the claimants from the insured. It therefore again behooves the insured to cooperate with the insurer in all ways.

If the insured has, for example, $50,000/$100,000 liability coverage, and he causes an accident which gives rise to a $300,000 claim against him, a further complication arises. Assuming that there is only one claimant in the case, the most the insurer can lose here is $50,000. If the claimant could get a judgment against the insured for his $300,000, the insured might end up being liable for $250,000 despite his insurance. In such a case, the interests of insurer and insured have diverged. All that the insurer can lose here is $50,000, so the insurer might be very willing to settle the case for $75,000 since, if it did so, it could avoid liability for court costs and other expenses while only losing the $50,000 it would probably lose anyway. On the other hand, this would cost the insured $25,000. If the insurer thought the claimant's case was not too strong and the claimant offered to settle for $50,000, the insurer might be inclined to refuse, because fighting the case to the finish might save it $50,000. If the insurer refused the settlement, it would be gambling $50,000 on the outcome of a trial. Of course, from the insured's point of view, a $50,000 settlement would get him off scot-free (because the insurer would pay), but a trial could cost him $250,000 if the claimant ended up with a $300,000 judgment.

In this sort of a situation, the insured should not rely upon the insurer to defend him; he should hire his own attorney to look out for his interests. However, if the insurer was permitted to represent the insured in the above case; the insurer refused the $50,000 settlement, though the insured urged it to accept; and the trial resulted in judgment for $300,000 for the plaintiff, the insured could force the insurer to pay the entire judgment because the insurer was looking out for its own interest to the prejudice of the interest of its insured. It might require another lawsuit to force this liability upon the insurer, however. Again, in this sort of situation it is better for the insured to hire his own attorney at the start, preferably one who specializes in these matters.

The usual auto liability policy covers not only the owner while he is driving his vehicle, but also anyone else driving the vehicle with the owner's permission. Thus members of the owner's family, bailees, etc. are also covered; thieves are of course not covered.

Many auto policies also cover the insured when he is driving a vehicle other than his own with the consent of the owner. One must read the policy in question in order to determine whether this coverage is included.

Auto collision insurance. Under this coverage the owner insures his own motor vehicle against damage. It is possible to obtain full coverage collision insurance, but this is very expensive. The coverage is marketed subject to deductibles of varying amounts, $100 and $250 being very popular. If one has $250 deductible collision coverage and is involved in a collision in which $500 worth of damage is done to one's own vehicle, the insurance will pay $250 on the claim. The insured must pay the rest. If only $200 in damage is done, the insured has no claim at all.

Collision coverage protects against damage done to the insured's vehicle by collision with another vehicle. It also covers against damages caused by collisions with other objects—walls, trees, etc. It does not matter whether the negligence of the insured caused the collision; so long as the vehicle is damaged in a collision, the damage (less the deductible) is covered. Collision coverage does not protect against personal injury caused by a collision; it covers only property damage.

When an insured who has collision coverage has his vehicle damaged in an accident caused by the negligence of another party, he of course has two avenues of recovery open. He may sue the other party or he may file a claim under his collision coverage. The fact that someone else is legally liable for the damage will not defeat a claim under the collision coverage. The insured may file his claim, and the insurer will pay it. The insurer then has the right to all legal remedies that the insured had against the responsible party, including suit against the responsible party in the name of the insured to recoup what it paid out. The insured will then recover his deductible.

Auto comprehensive coverage. This coverage protects a vehicle owner against damage to his vehicle caused by hazards other than collision. It also protects against loss of the vehicle due to theft. The coverage thus protects against fire, theft, storm damage, flood damage, etc. It also protects against highway hazards like broken windshields caused by gravel kicked up by a passing vehicle. This coverage is usually offered with a deductible, although full comprehensive coverage is not much more expensive than coverage with a deductible.

In case of the theft of a covered auto or parts of it (such as tires, hub caps, or batteries), the policy will require the insured to report the theft to the police. In case the covered vehicle itself is stolen, the insurer will require the insured to endorse his certificate of title over. Thus, if the auto is ever recovered, the insurer will be its owner and will be able to recoup some of its loss by selling the vehicle.

Uninsured and underinsured motorist coverage. Article 5.06-1 of the Texas Insurance Code (TIC) requires all auto insurers selling liability policies to include this coverage in the liability package. The insured may decline to purchase the coverage, but unless he affirmatively declines it it must be sold to him. This is true even of an insured assigned to an insurer under the assigned risk program. The furnished coverage must be at least $10,000/$20,000, with $5,000 property damage. But the insured must be given the option to purchase greater coverage, up to the limits of the liability insurance he has purchased.

This coverage is intended to protect the insured against personal injury and property damage caused by an uninsured or underinsured motorist, or a hit-and-run driver. To have a good claim under this coverage, the injury or property damage must have been caused by another driver, who must be unidentified, uninsured, or without sufficient insurance coverage to pay off the claim against him. Naturally the insured must report a hit-and-run incident to the police to have a claim under this coverage.

The property damage portion of this coverage may be sold subject to $250 deductible. Of course, if the insured has a good uninsured motorist claim for property damage as well as collision coverage, he cannot make two claims; he may only file a claim under the coverage with the smallest deductible. If both coverages have the same deductible, it is immaterial which coverage the claim is filed under.

It should be noted that when a collision or comprehensive claim or a liability claim is filed a friendly cooperative relationship generally exists between the insured and insurer—unless, of course, the amount of the liability claim exceeds the insurance coverage, as mentioned above. However, when the filing of an uninsured motorist claim becomes necessary, an adversary relationship may well arise between the insured and insurer. The insurer may have some incentive to argue that its insured was partly to blame for the accident in question since if it can establish this it can reduce the amount of the claim it must pay. The insurer may also want to argue that the other party was not truly uninsured. If it can establish this, it has a good defense to liability. If, however, a question arises as to whether or not the driver who caused the damage is insured, the burden of proof is upon the insurer to show that he was uninsured.

Because of this adversary relationship, if the insurer is reluctant to settle an uninsured motorist claim the insured would be well advised to hire an attorney to assist him in the matter.

No-fault personal injury protection coverage. TIC 5.06-3 requires Texas insurers marketing liability insurance in this state to include in the policy personal injury protection coverage of $2,500 for the insured, members of his family, authorized drivers even if not family members, and passengers in the vehicle. Under this coverage, the driver of the vehicle and its passengers who are injured in an accident may recover from the insurer medical, surgical, and dental expenses incurred, including ambulance, hospital, professional nursing, and funeral expenses. If the injured party is working at the time of the accident and is rendered incapable of work due to injury, he may also claim the lost income. If the injured person is not a wage earner but he or she contributes something to his family (such as housekeeping, cooking, or babysitting services) for which the family must now pay outside help, this expense is recoverable. Under this coverage, it does not matter if negligence on the part of the insured or authorized driver of the vehicle caused the accident and injury. It must also be remembered, however, that the insurer is only required to furnish this coverage up to a limit of $2,500 per injured person. Some insurers will sell a higher coverage, but they are not required to do so.

Limitations upon auto insurance coverages. Liability coverage will not protect the insured against claims arising against him out of his own deliberate acts, or deliberate acts of an authorized driver of the vehicle. It also does not cover claims by employees of the insured if these are covered by worker's compensation.

Uninsured motorist coverage also will not provide protection when a partial cause of the accident is a deliberate act on the part of the insured or his authorized driver. No-fault personal injury protection will also not protect a person who is injured by his own deliberate act. If the injury is sustained by someone in the process of commission of a felony or seeking to evade a law enforcement official, there is also no coverage. If the injury is caused by another vehicle belonging to the insured or to a member of his family which is not insured, the coverage will also not apply.

Insurance thus will not cover all the hazards involved in the ownership and operation of motor vehicles. Here, as in so many other areas of life, there is no substitute for prudence and good luck.

Auto liability within the family. The question often arises as to whether or not the owner of a family automobile is liable for the negligent driving of other family members. In many states, the courts have decided to follow the "family purpose" doctrine in order to answer this. In such states, if the family car is being driven by a family member for a family purpose, the owner of the car is liable for the torts of the driver. Texas, however, does not follow the family purpose doctrine.

In this state, the owner of the family car is not liable for the torts of a family member driver unless:

1. The driver is acting as the owner's agent—doing an errand for him, etc.
2. The driver has no driver's license, or
3. The driver is known to be a reckless driver.

The owner would be considered negligent to permit an unlicensed driver to drive his vehicle (and he would also commit a misdemeanor in doing so). He would also be negligent to let a member of his family known to be a reckless driver drive the vehicle, although this is not a criminal offense. The owner would also be negligent if he left the car keys in a place in which such unqualified drivers could get easy access to the vehicle.

The owner's liability insurance normally covers all persons driving the insured vehicle with the owner's consent. Thus, a family member who negligently causes injury while driving the owner's car with his permission is covered by his insurance. Even if the owner is not personally liable for the driver's negligence, the injured party will thus have a claim against the owner's insurer. One result of this may well be an increase in the owner's insurance premiums, even though the owner is not legally responsible for the accident in question.

Unauthorized parking in parking facilities. RCS 6701g-2 permits the removal of vehicles parked without authorization in parking facilities. The statute defines a parking facility as a commercial parking lot, a parking garage, or a parking area serving or adjacent to a business, church, school, home, or apartment complex, where the right to park is restricted to paying customers in the case of the commercial lot, or to guests, residents, students, faculty, nonpaying customers or the like with respect to other facilities. A restricted portion of an otherwise unrestricted parking facility is also included in the definition of parking facility—perhaps that part of a shopping center parking lot reserved for employees of the businesses located there.

The owner of such a parking facility may have an unauthorized vehicle removed from the facility without the consent of the owner or operator, and at the expense of said owner or operator, if.

1. A sign (or signs) specifying those persons permitted to park in the facility and prohibiting all others is placed so that it is readable day and night from all entrances to the facility (the signs need not be illuminated), and
2. The owner or operator has received notice from the owner of the parking facility that the vehicle will be towed away if it is not moved, or
3. The unauthorized vehicle is obstructing an entrance, exit, fire lane, or aisle of the facility.

An unauthorized vehicle is one parked in the facility without the consent of the facility owner.

If the unauthorized vehicle is not blocking an entrance, exit, fire lane, or aisle, and no notice has been given to its owner or operator, the vehicle may be removed only under the supervision of a peace officer or the owner or operator of the vehicle. If the vehicle is removed in accordance with the provision of the statute by an insured towing company, the owner of the parking facility shall not be liable for any damage to the vehicle caused by the removal or subsequent storage.

A towing company may remove an unauthorized vehicle from a parking facility when:
1. The signs described above are present at all entrances to the facility, and
2. The towing company has received verification in writing from the parking facility owner that notice has been given to the owner or operator of the unauthorized vehicle that it will be towed away if it is not removed, or
3. The unauthorized vehicle is obstructing an entrance, exit, fire lane, or aisle of the facility.

In other cases, the towing company may remove a vehicle only under the supervision of a peace officer or of the owner or operator of the vehicle. A towing company may not remove a vehicle from a public highway except under the supervision of a peace officer or of the owner or operator of the vehicle.

In cases of removal of unauthorized vehicles from parking facilities, the owner of the facility must not give any sort of consideration to the towing company, nor may the towing company give any sort of consideration to the facility owner. The facility owner must have no pecuniary interest in the towing company, and the towing company must have no pecuniary interest in the parking facility. The towing company will receive compensation for its services from the owner or operator of the unauthorized vehicle, who must pay all towing and storage charges. Apparently the towing company will be liable for all damage caused the towed vehicle by its negligence.

Should the facility owner and a towing company remove a vehicle in violation of the provisions of this act, the violators will be liable for damages to the vehicle owner or operator. The facility owner must pay the towing and storage charges if he is the violator. If damage is done to the vehicle during the process of improper removal, the facility operator and the towing company are liable for the damage, even if it was not caused by their negligence. In any litigation under this statute, the loser must pay a reasonable attorney's fee to the winner. In addition, violation constitutes a Class B misdemeanor.

An injunction may be obtained against a violator under the provisions of the Texas Deceptive Trade Practices Act, TB&CC 17.41 et seq.

38

Intellectual Property

The law of intellectual property deals with intangibles devised by the mind of man. There are four specific categories of intellectual property: patents, copyrights, trademarks, and trade secrets.

A *patent* is the intellectual property right granted to an inventor; it gives him the privilege of controlling the production and use of his invention.

A *copyright* is the intellectual property right granted to an author, composer, or recording or other artist, giving him the privilege of controlling the reproduction, dissemination, and performance of his creation.

A *trademark* is the intellectual property right granted to the manufacturer of a good or the provider of a service to control the brand name, etc. of the good or service.

A *trade secret* is the intellectual property right granted to a businessman to control the dissemination of confidential information essential to the functioning of the business in question.

Patents, copyrights, and trademarks are governed by statutory law; trade secrets are governed by common law only. Patents and copyrights are granted by federal agencies pursuant to federal law; trademarks are registered at the state level under the provisions of state law and at the federal level under the provisions of federal law. The common law applicable to trade secrets is essentially state law.

PATENTS

The federal statutory law governing the issuance of patents is found at 35 USC 100 et seq. This legislation was enacted by Congress in 1952.

What is patentable. The patent laws set forth seven categories of patentable inventions:

1. Processes.
2. Machines.
3. Manufactures.
4. Compositions of matter.
5. Improvements.

6. Designs.
7. Plants.

A *process* has been defined as a means for production of a given result. The means may be chemical or mechanical; it is essentially a means of accomplishing something. Thus, a method for electroplating metal, a method of extracting a metal from its ore, or a means of converting solar energy into electricity could be patentable if other requisites of patentability are met. It does not matter if the instrumentality for carrying out the process is already patented, so long as that instrumentality is not patented for the particular process.

A *machine* is essentially a mechanical apparatus with moving parts. The apparatus itself may be patentable as a machine; what the apparatus does may be patentable as a process.

A *manufacture* is a product made by changing the nature of a raw material or materials. Such items as pieces of furniture or hand tools containing no moving parts are considered to be manufactures. The use of a patentable machine for performance of a patented process could well produce as its end product a patentable manufacture.

A *composition of matter* may be a chemical compound, a chemical formula, an alloy of metals, or something similar. In a sense it is the chemical equivalent of a manufacture. The new hand tool or item of clothing, for example, is a manufacture, while the new detergent or antibiotic is a composition of matter.

An *improvement* is a change in an already patented item. To be patentable the improvement must be novel, useful, and nonobvious. If it meets these and the other criteria of patentability, the inventor receives an improvement patent, the ramifications of which will be discussed later.

35 USC 100 sets forth these five categories of patentable inventions. The remaining two categories are set forth in other sections of the patent statute.

35 USC 171 sets forth the criteria for patentability of a design. For a design to be patentable it must be new, original, and ornamental, and it must be for an item of manufacture; thus, it must be for something tangible. A design for a building would therefore not be patentable (unless the building was to be mass-produced as a prefabricated product). Such a design, which is more a work of art than an article of manufacture, could be copyrighted rather than patented.

35 USC 161 sets forth the criteria for patenting of plants. To be patentable a plant must be cultivated rather than discovered in a state of nature. It must be reproduced asexually by means other than tubers, and must be distinct and new. Relatively few plant patents are granted in the course of a year.

Novelty, usefulness, and nonobviousness. No invention is patentable unless it is new, useful, and nonobvious. Several provisions of 35 USC 102 deal with various ramifications of the novelty problem. These will be discussed in detail.

An invention is not patentable unless it is capable of being put to some practicable use—in short, it must be "good for something." It is also not useful unless it is operable—that is, unless it is capable of doing the job it is intended to do. It must work.

35 USC 103 provides that there must be enough difference between the invention to be patented and other closely related inventions so that the new invention was not obvious to anyone having ordinary skill in the art to which the invention pertains. Thus, if anyone working in the art could have devised the invention, it is too obvious to be patentable.

Nonpatentable subject matter. Kintner and Lahr, in their work, *An Intellectual Property Law Primer*, state that there are six sorts of unpatentable materials:

1. Printed matter.
2. Naturally occurring substances.
3. Methods of doing business.
4. Ideas.
5. Scientific principles.
6. Mental processes.

If printed matter is to be protected as intellectual property, it must be copyrighted. Methods of printing of course are patentable, but the printed product is generally not, unless it is printed electrical circuits or the like. Anything found in nature may not be patented, but a new process for refining or creating what occurs naturally is patentable. Bookkeeping, marketing, sales, and other methods are not patentable.

An idea all by itself is not patentable: the inventor must reduce his idea to one of the patentable forms before it becomes patentable. Thus, the inventor who decides that it is possible to build a solar-powered clock cannot patent the idea. Once he converts the idea into reality by actually building a working model of a solar-powered clock he may have a patentable invention.

A scientific principle is not patentable. The mathematician who discovers a new law of mathematics has found nothing patentable, but if he uses this new-found law to devise a new process he may have something patentable.

A mental process (as opposed to a physical process) is not patentable. It would be most difficult to patent any method for analysis of data unless the analysis is from beginning to end a physical process done by mechanical means.

When patent upon otherwise patentable invention may be denied. 35 USC 102 sets forth several circumstances under which a patent on an otherwise patentable device may be denied.

35 USC 102(a) provides that if the invention was known or used by another in this country before invention by the patent applicant, if it was patented in this country or abroad before that time, or if a description of it appeared in a printed publication here or abroad before that time, it is not patentable. If such cases, of course, the patent applicant really is not the inventor.

According to 35 USC 102(b), if the invention was patented or described in a printed publication in this or a foreign country, or if it was in public use or on sale in this country more than one year prior to application for a U.S. patent, the invention is not patentable. This is true even if the inventor himself is responsible for the public use, sale, or description in a printed publication. An inventor must therefore be wary of describing his invention in learned journals, of using it, or of offering it for sale before he files his U.S. patent application. If he must do one of these things, he must note the date accurately, and make certain that he files his application within a year of that date.

35 USC 102(c) states that an invention is not patentable if the inventor has abandoned it. Express abandonment takes places when an inventor announces his invention to the world and states that he will not patent it, or that anyone who wishes may use it. Implied abandonment occurs when the inventor does not apply for his patent within a reasonable time of the invention. The law does not set forth the length of this reasonable time, but the longer the delay in application the more likely someone is to claim abandonment.

35 USC 102(d) provides that an invention is not patentable in the United States if it has been patented in another country upon a patent application filed more than twelve months before the filing of the U.S. patent application. In order to avoid this pitfall an inventor must either file for a United States patent before filing in any other country, or he must file in the United States within twelve months of filing abroad.

In this connection it must be remembered that the nations of the world do not recognize the validity of each other's patents. Thus, a Canadian patent confers no rights within the United States, and a United States patent confers no rights within Canada. An inventor who wishes to have patent protection for his invention in both the United States and Canada must obtain patents in both countries.

The applicant for a patent must normally be the inventor himself, as per 35 USC 102(f). If more than one person did the inventing, all of the inventors must apply. The only situation in which a person other than the inventor may apply for a patent is when the inventor died or was declared incompetent before the filing. In such a case, the personal representative or guardian of the inventor may file.

The applicant must be a living human being; a corporation or other organization may not file for a patent. This is so even when the inventor is an employee of a corporation and the invention was part of his job performance.

It may happen that two or more persons make the same invention. In such a case, 35 USC 102(g) provides that the first inventor shall normally be entitled to a patent. If both inventors file patent applications, an interference proceeding will be conducted to determine who was first. The person who filed his application first usually wins in such a proceeding. However, if the second applicant can prove that he made the invention before the first applicant, he will prevail. This is difficult to prove, and in case of doubt the first applicant to file wins.

The first inventor may however lose the right to a patent to a subsequent inventor. This happens when the first inventor abandons, suppresses, or conceals the invention. If he abandoned the invention by announcing it to the world, it would not be patentable by anyone, because it has become public knowledge. But if the abandonment consisted of not applying for a patent within a reasonable time, a subsequent inventor could obtain a patent. If the first inventor chose to keep his invention secret under the law of trade secrets, a subsequent inventor could obtain a patent. Keeping an invention a secret is the most common way of suppressing or concealing it.

Procedure for obtaining a patent. The first requirement for the obtaining of a patent is that the inventor keep meticulous records of his work and of its accomplishments. Once the invention is finalized it is very helpful for the inventor to show the invention to a trusted accomplice and to have this accomplice sign a written description of it; this document should of course be dated. In case of argument it will provide evidence as to the date of the invention which can be corroborated by the testimony of the witness.

The inventor should of course contact an attorney about his patent application. If he consults an attorney in general practice, this attorney will either consult a patent attorney himself or refer his client to a patent attorney, who will then arrange for a search of patent office records to make a preliminary determination as to the patentability of the invention. The search must be conducted in Washington, D.C. The patent attorney must himself go there to do it, or a professional patent searcher must be hired to do it.

If the search discloses that the invention has already been patented, as it sometimes does, that ends the matter. If the search discloses that the invention has not yet been patented, the next step will be the filing of a patent application with the commissioner of patents at the U.S. Patent Office in Washington. A patent application is a very technical collection of documents. It should be prepared by professionals since the layman is incapable of making the drawings and of drafting the legal description of the invention.

The application, when received, is assigned to an examiner for consideration. It normally takes from four to six months for the examiner to make a response to the application. He may grant the patent in his response, but he usually rejects it, explaining why, and asking the applicant to provide arguments to show that his rejection is unjustified.

The applicant—in fact, of course, his patent attorney—then has six months to reply to the rejection, advancing arguments to try to convince the examiner to change his mind. The examiner then has another six months to consider the reply. Again, the examiner may grant the patent, or he may reject. If he rejects this time he may make the rejection final, in which case there is no more argument with him, or he may again make the rejection tentative and seek more arguments.

Usually the second communication of the examiner to the applicant is final—only with respect to complex inventions may there be three or four communications by the examiner to the applicant. In any event, the fourth communication, if the proceeding drags on so far, will be final.

If the examiner learns that two or more persons have filed independent applications for patents on the same invention, he will call an interference proceeding. The competing applications are then referred to a board of interferences, composed of three examiners, which will take evidence on the question of which applicant first invented the invention in question. As mentioned above, in interference proceedings the inventor who filed his application first is assumed to have priority unless the inventor who filed later can prove that his invention was actually made first. It is in interference proceedings that meticulous record-keeping by the inventor pays off: being able to prove the exact date of the invention can be most important.

Usually the question of whether or not a patent should be granted is of concern only to the patent office and to the applicant or applicants. Outsiders have no right to intervene. However, outsiders may intervene if the proposed invention has been in public use for more than one year prior to the filing of the patent application. In such a case the outsider may file a protest with the patent office alleging and containing evidence of the public use, and asking for the initiation of a public use proceeding to determine whether or not the inventor is entitled to the patent.

If such a protest is made and the protester has good evidence of the alleged public use, the normal patent office proceedings are suspended until the public use proceeding runs its course. If the protester can prove the public use, the patent is denied. If he cannot, the normal proceedings resume.

The grant of a patent by a patent examiner is final: no one may appeal this determination. But a final rejection by the examiner is not absolutely final: the applicant may appeal to the Patent Office Board of Appeals. The board of appeals hears arguments as to why the examiner was wrong to reject the patent, and will either grant the patent application or reject it. Again, a grant by the board is final, while a rejection is appealable to either the Court of Customs and Patent Appeals or to a federal district court for the District of Columbia. A rejection here may be appealed to a circuit court of appeals, and an adverse decision there may be appealed to the Supreme Court of the United States.

It must be noted, therefore, that a patent proceeding may be a long, drawn-out affair. The application may be in the hands of the original examiner for two years or more, and in case of interference proceedings or appeals of a rejection the matter may drag on for five years or more.

Content of the patent grant. The grant of a patent essentially confers upon the applicant a monopoly on the manufacture and use of the invention for a period of seventeen years, starting at the date of issue of the patent. This grant is not renewable.

All patents are not valid just because the patent office or the courts have seen fit to issue them, however. The federal courts have the power to second-guess patent office decisions on patentability. These courts can, and often do, declare duly issued patients to be invalid. When this occurs, the patent holder loses his monopoly.

Transfer of patent rights. Patents and patent applications are freely transferable. Since this is true, an employee who applies for a patent may transfer his application to his employer after filing it. Nothing prohibits corporations or other organizations from owning patents or patent applications.

A transfer of a patent application or patent should be recorded in the patent office within three months after the transfer is made. Failure to record such a transfer will not make the transfer invalid; however, recording is necessary to make the transfer valid against third parties. A subsequent buyer of a patent will therefore prevail over a previous buyer who did not record his purchase within three months.

Rights of employers to patents of employees. An employer has no right to inventions of employees merely because he is the employer. However, an employer does automatically have a shop right in an invention by an employee that is developed on company time with the aid of company equipment. The shop right consists of the right to use the invention free of royalties, and no more. In the absence of an employer-employee contract, the greatest right an employer can have in an employee invention is this shop right.

On the other hand, the employer and employee may by contract agree that the employer shall have greater rights in employee patents. These may extend from broader licenses to complete ownership by assignment, depending upon the contract terms.

Patents developed under government contracts. When a patentable invention is developed by an inventor doing research under a U.S. Government research grant, the contract between the researcher and the government will in all probability provide that the government is to have some sort of rights in the patent.

The contract may provide that the researcher must assign the patent to the government, or it may provide that the researcher retains title to the patent, but that he must grant the government a royalty-free license. Some other arrangement might also be spelled out. How the matter will be handled depends in large part upon which government agency made the research grant. Federal statutes and administrative regulations impose different policies on the various research-sponsoring agencies.

Patent licensing. A patent holder who wishes to grant to others the permission to make, use, or sell a patented invention while retaining legal title to the patent may accomplish this objective by granting a license. The patent holder's compensation for granting the license will be some form of royalty.

Patent licenses may take many forms. The license usually imposes limitations on the right of the licensee to make, use, or sell the invention. The limitation might be territorial, forbidding the licensee to do anything with the invention outside a prescribed geographical area. It could be a quantity limitation, under which the number of units the licensee may manufacture or sell is limited. There might be use limitations, restricting the purposes for which the invention may be used; price limitations may prescribe or limit the price for which the licensee may sell the invention.

A patent license is nonexclusive, unless it is specifically made exclusive. A patent holder may therefore grant as many licenses upon his patent as he sees fit, unless he limits his right to do this by contract. A licensee is not protected against the grant of another license to his competitors unless he has the bargaining power to induce the licensor to grant him an exclusive license.

A licensee has no right to sublicense the patent, unless his license expressly permits sublicensing (which virtually none do) or unless the license is totally exclusive. A license could be totally exclusive only if the licensor has granted virtually all of his rights to the licensee in an exclusive license.

The life of a patent license is of course limited to the life of the patent itself. When the seventeen-year patent grant expires, the license also expires. The right of the licensor to receive royalties under his license will of course also expire with his patent grant.

Patents and the antitrust laws. The possession of a patent confers a lawful monopoly upon the holder. Thus, the holder is permitted to impose restrictions on his licensees which an ordinary manufacturer could not impose on his distributors. The patent holder may dictate to his licensee the price at which the patented item shall be sold and to whom it may be sold. If the patented item is only a component part of a product, however, the patent holder may not exercise such powers.

A firm with a powerful position in a market must be careful about buying up patents. Attempting to preserve a dominant position in a market by acquiring competing technology is certainly an effective way of preserving one's position. It is in fact so effective that courts do not hesitate to call such conduct attempted monopolization, or monopolization. Weaker firms may buy up all the patents they wish without suffering adverse antitrust consequences.

The patent laws of many industrialized nations do not permit patent holders to suppress technology by "sitting on" patents. If the patent holder does not use his grant, he may be compelled to license it to someone who will use it. This notion of compulsory licensing does not exist in the United States except in a very narrow area. Normally, if the patent holder chooses not to exercise his patent rights, that is his privilege.

However, if a very large firm in a market accumulates patents and suppresses them in order to maintain a monopoly position, an American court might compel licensing in order to break up the monopoly. Usually the courts do not object to a patent holder's protecting his position by filing patent infringement suits against competitors. However, when a dominant firm in a market follows a policy of filing infringement actions against holders of similar patents, this is branded a form of attempted monopolization; it can be a powerful weapon of harassment.

Improvement patents. A person who obtains a patent upon an improvement to another patent does not quite obtain the broad package of rights described above. The rights of the improvement patent holder are subject to the rights of the original patent holder: the original patent is said to be dominant over the improvement patent, and the improvement patent is servient to the dominant original patent.

Though the holder of the improvement patent may not license it without the consent of the dominant patent holder, he is not required to give the dominant patent holder any rights in his patent unless a contract between the parties provides otherwise. As a practical matter, however, the party developing an improvement on a patent is probably a licensee of the original patent holder. If the patent license is well drafted, it will contain provisions relative to improvement patents. The license agreement may compel the licensee to assign all improvement patents to the licensor, or it might require the licensee to grant the licensor a royalty-free license upon the improvement. There are other possible arrangements also, depending upon the relative bargaining power of the parties.

The improvement patent has an independent life of seventeen years. It will therefore still be in effect when the dominant patent expires.

Patent infringement. Any act which violates the rights of a patent holder is an infringement. Though patent infringement is not a criminal offense, it is a tort; the patent holder may therefore sue to force the infringer to stop infringing, or to recover damages.

35 USC 271 defines three types of patent infringement: direct, active inducement, and contributory.

Anyone who makes, uses, or sells a patented invention without authority within the United States during the term of validity of the patent is guilty of *direct infringement*. Any making, use, or sale of an identical copy of the patented invention is of course a direct infringement if done without authority. A making, use, or sale of something which is not an identical copy of the invention but which is the equivalent of the invention is also a direct infringement. Of course it is sometimes difficult to determine whether or not something very similar—but not identical—to a patented invention is an equivalent of the invention.

One may not escape a charge of infringement merely by rearranging the components of an invention, by omitting a component or specification, or by adding components or specifications if the modified invention is still the equivalent of the original. However, the more difference there is between the original invention and the modified invention the less likely the modification is to be an infringement. Each case of direct infringement of this sort must of course by judged upon its own merits.

Active inducement of patent infringement consists of knowingly and deliberately inducing someone else to infringe directly upon a patent. There can be no active inducement to infringe without direct infringement by someone else.

Contributory infringement consists of knowingly selling an unpatented component of a patented invention, when such a component is not an ordinary article of commerce in and of itself. If the main use of the component is as a part of the patented invention, it should be sold only for that particular use and not for any other use.

The act constituting the infringement must have taken place after the patent was issued and before it expired. Although an invention for which a patent has been applied may be marked with the legend "Patent Pending," an unauthorized use of the invention before the issuance of the patent will not constitute infringement. If the use continues after the granting of the patent, it will of course constitute infringement. Since a United States patent is valid only within the territorial limits of the United States, an act committed outside the United States cannot be infringement.

Suits against patent infringers must be filed in federal court. The remedies against infringers are damages and injunctions to stop further infringement. Though it is possible to recover triple damages from an infringer, it is allowed only in extreme cases.

Another remedy is available against imports of infringing goods into the United States. The patent holder who desires to stop such importation may ask the International Trade Commission (formerly the Tariff Commission) to refuse entry of the offending goods into the United States. Another possibility, of course, is to sue the importer for his infringement.

Defenses in patent infringement cases. Suits against patent infringers must be begun within six years of the date of infringement. Delays in filing suit of less than six years may result in defeat of an infringement claim, when the delay in suing led the infringer to believe that there was no infringement and induced him to spend sums of money on his use of the invention.

A very commonly used defense in patent infringement litigation is the claim that the patent which allegedly has been infringed is invalid because it never should have been issued in the first place. The courts will hear the defendant's evidence that the patent office erred in granting the patent, and, if they find the evidence persuasive, will declare the patent invalid.

Equitable estoppel is another defense which is occasionally used; it applies in situations where the patent holder leads another party to believe that his actions do not constitute patent infringement and later changes his position and files an infringement action.

The last of the major defenses is that of "unclean hands." The defendant here alleges that the plaintiff has himself done such wrongful things as obtaining his patent by fraud upon the patent office, using superior bargaining power to overreach himself in licensing agreement provisions, by using his patent position as leverage to violate the antitrust laws, etc.

Of all of these defenses, the most devastating is the defense of patent invalidity. When a patent holder considers an infringement suit, he must always keep in mind that the defendant may raise invalidity as a defense. If the defendant can make the defense stick, the plaintiff not only receives no remedy for the alleged infringement but also loses his monopoly grant. If this defense is upheld once, the patent is dead. On the other hand, if a defendant uses the invalidity defense and loses, the implied declaration of validity by the court will not stop some other defendant from raising the defense of invalidity. Thus, no court can declare a patent valid once and for all, but a court may certainly declare one invalid once and for all.

Patent infringement by government contractors. Businesses holding R&D or procurement or supply contracts with the federal government are generally authorized by the federal government to infringe upon any or all patents necessary in order to carry out the terms of the contract. When infringement occurs under such circumstances, the patent holder may not sue the infringer; his recourse is to sue the U.S. Government.

In such a case the plaintiff may not seek an injunction to stop the infringement, since the infringement was government-authorized. Instead he must sue for monetary damages in the court of claims. Should the plaintiff prevail in the suit and the government be forced to pay damages, the government may demand indemnity from the infringer. The loss caused by this government-authorized infringement may thus fall upon the contractor rather than the government. Contractors should therefore not be too anxious to avail themselves of this government authorization to infringe upon patents.

Confidentiality of patent office records. It should be remembered that applications for patents which have been granted are public records. Anyone may learn everything that the patent office knows about the patented invention by examining the patent office record. Thus, when the patent expires anyone may examine the patent office record and duplicate the invention.

On the other hand, pending patent applications are confidential; no outsider has access to them, so inventors need not worry about a patent application causing disclosure of the details of their inventions to the public.

TRADE SECRETS

Since the law of trade secrets is not statutory law no specific legislative definition of a trade secret exists, and no specific procedure for declaring something to be a trade secret exists.

Anything which is patentable may be protected under the law of trade secrets, but items which are not patentable may also be protected. An item may be protected under the law of trade secrets when:
1. It is something unique enough to be valuable to the owner and to not be readily discoverable by others, and
2. No one other than the protector and his authorized personnel know of it, and

3. The protector makes a concerted effort to keep the secret a secret.

Items protectable as trade secrets. Kintner and Lahr list eight types of items which courts have held protectable as trade secrets.

The first such item is the *formula*. The formula may be in the nature of a chemical formula, or in the nature of a recipe; it is one of those items of intellectual property protectable either by patenting or by trade secret treatment. Since a complex formula may not be discovered through chemical analysis, trade secret protection—if surrounded by a tight enough security net—is far more effective than patent protection. The Coca-Cola Company has never patented the formula for Coca-Cola, but no one outside the company knows the formula. It has been a protected trade secret, and a secure one, for nearly a century. Recipes for food items, composition of cosmetics, and formulas for all sorts of chemical products have been held entitled to trade secret protection.

Industrial processes are the next protectable category. Here again, patent protection is available for those desiring it. The more complex the process, the more difficult it is for those not familiar with it to figure it out.

Technological know-how is the third category of protectable trade secrets. It may well not be patentable if no processes are involved. Know-how could well be defined as method or technique, as opposed to process. The less technological the know-how, the easier it is for others to divine, and the less protectable it is.

Pricing information is protectable if it is truly kept secret. Pricing code systems are protectable if the keys to the code are not obvious and security measures are taken to restrict knowledge of the code to those with a need to know. However, such pricing information as the method of determining the retail price of an item is not protectable, because business logic limits the possible ways of setting such prices.

Products are definitely protectable. A product may of course be patentable as a manufacture, machine, or composition of matter; if the nature of the product is such that a competitor may dismantle it and determine how it works, patent protection is the only feasible method of protection available. If the product is complex enough that such reverse engineering is not practicable, it could be kept secret for a long period under the law of trade secrets. One type of product which may not be patented is the computer program, which does not fit any of the statutory categories of patentability.

Customer lists are protectable if the owner takes steps to prevent disclosure, such as binding salesmen by contract not to make disclosures and forbidding them by contract to work as salesmen for competitors for a period of time after leaving the original employ.

Customer information—information on the special needs and requirements of customers—is also protectable if the owner of the information takes proper steps to prevent disclosure by employees. *Sources of supply* of raw materials and the like are also protectable when not easily divined and when appropriate efforts are made to preserve secrecy.

The courts have uniformly refused to classify merchandising methods and business information as trade secrets. Merchandising methods generally are not inherently capable of being kept secret; once they are put to use they become matters of general knowledge to outsiders who study them. Business information such as that contained in catalogs and advertising disseminated by the owner is not protectable; obviously the information is not a secret if it is publicized by advertising.

Maintaining secrecy of trade secrets. Generally, knowledge of a trade secret must be restricted to the owner and those of his agents and employees who have a need to know it. The wider the dissemination of knowledge of a secret, the less secret it is.

Affirmative action must be taken to preserve secrecy. Examples of such actions are the institution and maintenance of security programs within the plant and contracts with employees and independent contractors having access to the secret, binding them not to disclose it.

The nature of the secret must not be publicized in any manner. Advertising it or describing it in a catalog or article in a publication will destroy secrecy. Application for a patent upon it will destroy the secrecy if the patent is granted, since the patent application will then become a public record.

Sale of the secret to the public in the form of a product may result in disclosure, unless the secret is so complex that it cannot be discovered through chemical analysis, reverse engineering, or similar processes.

Methods of improper disclosure. A very common method of disclosure is disclosure by a disloyal employee or independent contractor. Whether the employee is bound by contract not to disclose the secret or not, disclosure is a violation of the employee's fiduciary duty to his employer. This fiduciary duty does not only exist while the employee is on the employer's payroll; it continues to exist even after the employer and employee have severed relations.

Independent contractors often do not owe fiduciary duties to those who employ them, though of course contractors such as attorneys do owe such duties. Disclosure by a contractor who owes no fiduciary duty is not improper, unless the contractor is bound by his contract with the owner of the secret not to make disclosure.

Acquisition of a trade secret through commercial bribery is of course improper. The party paying the bribe commits a criminal offense and also renders himself liable for damages to the owner of the secret.

Acquisition of trade secrets through industrial espionage is also improper. Such espionage usually takes the form of infiltration by a spy into the secret owner's organization to steal the secret. It can, however, take other forms, such as taking aerial photographs of the owner's unfinished new factory to learn of the design of new equipment therein.

Trade secrets and government contracts. Government agencies may require their contractors to disclose trade secret data relevant to performance of the government contract. Some agencies require no such disclosure; others require disclosure of all trade secrets concerning work under the contract; still others require disclosure under some circumstances but not others. It all depends on the policy of the agency.

When agency policy requires disclosure of trade secrets, the agency itself is under an obligation to maintain the secret and to make certain that it does not fall into the hands of competitors of the contractor. However, the government itself is not liable for wrongful disclosure of a secret; only the individual government employee who made the disclosure is liable. He is subject to criminal prosecution, and may be sued for damages by the injured contractor.

Remedies for unauthorized disclosure or acquisition of trade secrets. The basic remedies for disclosure or acquisition of trade secrets are provided by state law. Suits under the law of trade secrets are therefore generally prosecuted in state courts. The remedies are the normal ones—damages from the discloser and injunctions to stop further disclosure. Where the acquirer is an active participant in the disclosure he may also be sued for damages or enjoined.

If the acquirer has engaged in commercial bribery, he may be criminally prosecuted in Texas. If he has engaged in industrial espionage, he has committed an unfair trade practice under Section 5 of the Federal Trade Commission Act, so that the federal agency may take action against him.

COPYRIGHTS

The law of copyrights was completely revised by Congress in 1976. The new copyright law is found at 17 USC 101 et seq. The revision has changed the substantive law of copyrights in many particulars. It may well take some time before all of the changes become manifest.

Subject matter of copyrights. 17 USC 102 provides that the following sorts of original works of authorship may be copyrighted:
1. Literary works.
2. Musical works, including accompanying words.
3. Dramatic works, including accompanying music.
4. Pantomimes and choreographic works.
5. Pictorial, graphic, and sculptural works.
6. Motion pictures and other audiovisual works.
7. Sound recordings.

Literary works of course include novels, short stories, and works of nonfiction, including books and less-than-book-length articles. Musical compositions include symphonies, popular songs, and everything in between. The words to a song may be copyrighted along with the music. Dramatic works include stage plays, operas, etc.; if the dramatic work is musical the music may be copyrighted along with the words. Choreographic works include ballets and other dance works. Pictorial, graphic, and sculptural works include what we generally consider to be works of art. Videotapes are an example of audiovisual works other than motion pictures; sound recordings may of course be on records or on recording tape.

Compilations and derivative works may be the subjects of a copyright, subject to restrictions. A compilation is a collection of preexisting works combined into an original work of authorship; an anthology of poetry or a collection of short stories exemplifies the compilation. Since the original contents of the compilation are probably already copyrighted by their authors, the copyright in the compilation extends only to the work contributed by the compiler and not to the original items included.

A derivative work may be a translation of a work into another language, a motion picture dramatization of a novel, a popular arrangement of a piece of classical music, a sound recording of a musical composition, or the like. Again, the author of the derivative work is entitled to no copyright upon the preexisting material—he is only entitled to a copyright on his creation.

Registration of copyrights. Before the 1976 copyright law revision, the author of an unpublished work had no rights or protection under the federal copyright statutes. 17 USC 104(a) now provides that unpublished works are subject to statutory protection. Before an author can make any infringement claim, however, he must register his copyright (17 USC 411).

In order to register a copyright, the author or owner of the copyright must deposit with the Register of Copyrights of the Library of Congress one or two complete copies of the work to be copyrighted—one copy if the work is unpublished, two copies if it is published. The deposit must be accompanied by an application for registration, which must include eleven items of information required by 17 USC 409, including the name of the copyright owner, how he came to be the owner, the title of the work, the date of the creation of the work, and the date of publication of the work.

If the Register of Copyrights determines that the work is copyrightable, a certificate of registration is issued to the applicant. If it is determined that the work is not copyrightable (which is rare), the register notifies the applicant that registration is denied, explaining why. In the matter of registering copyrights, there are no examiners, no hearings, no great delays, no arguments, and no appeals. The application is submitted, is either granted or denied, and that is that.

Ownership of copyrights. Ordinarily the author of a copyrightable work is the owner of it. However, under some circumstances the question of ownership is complicated by the question of the identity of the true author.

If the work has more than one author—such as a textbook written by several experts—all of the authors are co-owners of the copyright. If the work is written for hire, the employer is the author, unless otherwise agreed. With respect to collective works—works in which the parts are written by various authors—each author of a portion of the work owns the copyright on the portion he wrote. The owner of the copyright on the collective work has only the right to reproduce each contribution as a part of the collection.

Copyrights are freely transferable. They may be sold or given away, and may be willed or passed by inheritance. They are not subject to seizure by any government or official so long as they are owned by the original author. However, a copyright owned by someone other than the original author can be seized by government authority.

All these provisions relative to copyright ownership are contained in 17 USC 201.

Transfer of copyright ownership. 17 USC 204 provides that any transfer of ownership rights in a copyright must be in writing and signed by the owner or his authorized agent. According to 17 USC 205, the transfer must be recorded with the copyright office within one month of execution to be valid against third parties not knowing of the transfer or against licensees not knowing of the transfer.

Exclusive rights in copyrighted works. According to 17 USC 106, the owner of a copyright owns the following rights in his creation:

1. The right to reproduce the work in copies or recordings.
2. The right to prepare derivative works (translations, abridgements, etc.) based on the copyrighted work.
3. The right to distribute copies or recordings of the work to the public by sale, rental, lease, lending, or other transfer of ownership.
4. In the case of literary, musical, dramatic, and choreographic works, and pantomimes, motion pictures, and other audiovisual works, the right to perform the work publicly.
5. The right to display in public those works described in 4 and also works of art.

In general, no one may print, otherwise copy, sell, or otherwise distribute a work without the permission of the copyright owner. Likewise, no one may convert a work into a play or motion picture script without permission.

No one may record or perform in public a copyrighted musical composition without the consent of the owner of the copyright on the composition. Nor may anyone make an arrangement of such a composition without permission. No one may reproduce a sound recording without the permission of the owner of the copyright on the recording.

This bundle of exclusive rights is subject to a complex scheme of limitations contained in 17 USC 107-116. Reproduction for classroom or library use may be permissible; performances for educational purposes may be authorized; and certain transmissions of performances by TV are also authorized. But generally no infringement upon this bundle of rights for purely commercial purposes is allowed.

Duration of copyright. Before the revision of the copyright laws of 1976, an American copyright was good for twenty-eight years, and could be renewed for a second period of twenty-eight years. The new legislation has extended this life somewhat.

17 USC 302 provides that the copyright upon works created after January 1, 1978, is valid during the life of the author and for fifty years after his death. If there are joint authors, the copyright shall endure until fifty years after the death of the last surviving joint author. The copyright upon a work for hire endures for seventy-five years after first publication, or one hundred years after creation, whichever period expires first.

Any person having an interest in a copyright may record with the copyright office a statement that an author has died, or a statement that an author is still alive as of a certain date. A statement of death must contain the date of death, if known.

Seventy-five years after publication of a work, or one hundred years after its creation, a person may inquire of the copyright office if it has any record of the life or death of the author. If the office has some record, it will make this known to the applicant. If it has not, it will notify him to that effect. A statement of no record by the copyright office entitles the inquirer to presume that the author has been dead for fifty years and that the copyright has therefore expired.

17 USC 304 provides for the extension of copyrights existing as of January 1, 1978. A copyright in its first twenty-eight-year term as of this date may be renewed during the twenty-eighth year of its life for an additional term of forty-seven years, thus giving the copyright a total life of seventy-five years. Any copyright in its second twenty-eight-year term as of January 1, 1978, is extended to a date seventy-five years after the date of the original copyright was secured.

Copyright infringement. 17 USC 506 declares that any person willfully infringing upon a copyright for purposes of commercial advantage or private financial gain commits a criminal offense for which the maximum punishment is one year in prison and/or a $10,000 fine. If the infringement involves sound recordings or motion pictures, the maximum sentence is one year and/or $25,000 for the first offense and two years and/or $50,000 for second and subsequent offenses. A criminal prosecution for copyright infringement must be commenced within three years of the infringement.

The plaintiff in a civil infringement action has several remedies available. 17 USC 502 permits a federal district court to enjoin future infringement. Under 17 USC 503 a court may impound all infringing copies of the copyrighted work while the proceeding is pending; if the court finds that infringement has indeed occurred it may then order the destruction or other disposition of the impounded items.

17 USC 504 makes two forms of damages available to the plaintiff. He may recover actual damages plus the profits the infringer realized upon his infringement, or he may elect to recover statutory damages, which may be a sum not less than $250 nor more than $10,000. If the plaintiff can prove that the infringement was committed willfully, the maximum sum recoverable as statutory damages is increased to $50,000. Under 17 USC 505, a successful plaintiff may also recover his court costs plus a reasonable attorney's fee from the defendant.

Civil actions for infringement must be begun within three years of the date of infringement.

It must be restated that one may now sue for infringement of an unregistered copyright. It does not matter whether the copyright was registered at the time of the alleged infringement, but it must be registered at the time of commencement of the suit. Also, the items of which infringement is claimed must have upon them a notice of copyright, stating the owner of the copyright and the date of copyright.

Copyrights in foreign trade. The United States is a signatory of the Universal Copyright Convention, as are some fifty nations. These nations have agreed that a copyright validly registered by one of them shall be respected by all. The United States is also a signatory of the Buenos Aires Convention of 1910, under which most of the nations of the Western hemisphere have agreed to honor each other's copyrights. This nation has also entered into a number of bilateral treaties with some other nations relative to copyright matters—some of them not being signatories of the Universal Copyright Convention or of the Buenos Aires Convention.

A U.S. copyright will be valid, then, in about seventy other nations, and copyrights registered under the laws of these seventy or so nations will be valid here. U.S. copyrights may be recorded with the U.S. Bureau of Customs. This will enable the bureau to prevent import into this country of works which infringe upon valid U.S. copyrights.

TRADEMARKS

The subject of trademarks is one governed by both federal and state law. Generally, the law applicable to trademarks used in interstate commerce is federal law. The governing statutory law at the federal level is the Lanham Act, 15 USC 1051–1127. The Texas law governing trademarks not used in interstate commerce is found in Chapter 16 of the Texas Business & Commerce Code, and in the Texas judge-made law on the subject.

Since most trademarks in use are used in interstate commerce or will some day be used in interstate commerce, the federal law will be considered first. The Lanham Act is essentially a registration statute. A trademark registered under the statute is protected against infringement, and its owner may sue in federal courts to obtain the remedies provided against infringers.

The Texas statutory provisions also provide for registration, and for remedies against infringers.

Types of marks registerable under the Lanham Act. The Lanham Act defines four registerable types of marks: trademarks, service marks, certification marks, and collective marks.

A *trademark* is defined as "any word, name, symbol, or device, or any combination thereof adopted and used by a manufacturer or merchant to identify his goods and distinguish them from goods manufactured or sold by others." A trademark must be placed directly upon the goods or on the labels, containers, or tags associated with the goods to become registerable. Use of a trademark only in advertising or catalogs will not be sufficient. 7-Up, Whirlpool, and Pontiac are examples of registered trademarks.

A *service mark* is a mark used in the sale or advertising of services to identify the services of one person and distinguish them from the services of others. These are used primarily in advertising, on signs at the locations where the services are performed, etc. Examples of service marks are MasterCharge, Jack-in-the-Box, and Motel 6.

A *certification mark* is a mark used on, or in connection with, the products of one or more persons not connected with the owners of the trademark to certify regional or other origin, material, mode of manufacture, quality, or accuracy; or to certify that the work or labor on the goods or services was performed by members of a union or other organization. A certification mark is used not on the goods or services of its owner but on goods bearing other trademarks. The seals of approval bestowed upon products by various testing agencies—such as Underwriters' Laboratories—are examples of such marks.

A *collective mark* is a trademark or service mark used by the members of a cooperative, an association, or other groups or organizations, it includes marks used to show organization membership. These do not indicate that the goods or services involved are approved by any organization; they simply indicate the source of the goods or services. Another type of collective mark is the insignia of a lodge or fraternity.

Kinds of marks registerable under the Lanham Act. The Lanham Act declares that a registerable mark may be any word, name, symbol, device, or combination of these. Actually, the categories of registerable marks extend even beyond these boundaries; registration has been allowed for marks consisting of the following:

1. Words and phrases.
2. Colors, when used as part of a distinctive design or shape.
3. Pictures and symbols.
4. Numerals and letters.
5. Label and package designs.
6. Configuration of containers and goods.
7. Slogans.
8. Sounds.

Some marks consist only of words and phrases, pictures or symbols, or numeral-letter combinations. Others of course consist of combinations of these components.

Prohibited marks. The Lanham Act forbids the registration of a few types of marks. Thus, any mark consisting of the flag or other insignia of a government may not be registered, since such official symbols may not be appropriated for private use.

The names, portraits, or signatures of living persons may not be used without the written consent of the person involved. Also, the name, portrait, or signature of a deceased president of the United States may not be used during the lifetime of his widow.

No mark will be registered which is immoral, deceptive, or scandalous. A mark will be considered deceptive if it misrepresents the nature of the goods or services to which it applies, or if it could cause such deception in the minds of the unthinking. The use of terms carrying a religious connotation upon products forbidden to adherents of the religion in question—or upon products not associated in the public mind with religious observance—has been considered to be scandalous. Whether a mark is immoral or not will depend to a large degree upon the examiners or judges called upon to consider the question.

Strength and distinctiveness of a mark. Though a registerable mark need not consist of a word or phrase especially coined for the product or service to which it is to be applied, such marks are potentially the strongest and will be granted the greatest degree of protection by the courts. The advantage of such a mark—Pepsi, Kodak, Xerox, etc.—is that it has no commonly accepted preexisting meaning and, once familiar to the public, is associated solely with its product or service.

A word or phrase adopted as a trademark which is not specially coined will have an accepted, common meaning that may well not be associated with any product or service. Such a mark will have no strength, and indeed may not even be registerable unless and until it acquires a secondary meaning which associates it with the product or service. Some of the problems which arise in this regard are discussed below.

There may be a temptation to adopt as a mark a word or phrase which describes the product or service being offered. The more descriptive the mark, the less likely it is to be registerable. Thus, "Foamy Beer" or "Stretchy Rubber Bands" would probably be totally unacceptable. What beer is not foamy? What rubber bands are not stretchable?

Geographically descriptive terms—names of towns or geographic features—are difficult to protect unless powerful secondary meaning has been generated. Examples of acceptable marks featuring geographically descriptive terms include Old Milwaukee beer and Old El Paso food products. It helps to tie the name of the geographic location to a descriptive adjective.

The trademark which consists of a surname will also be difficult to register. Again, association of the name with the product or service is essential. Of course, the business world abounds with surname trademarks—Ford automobiles, Libby's food products, Borden dairy products, Schlitz beer, Seagram's whiskey, for example. The longer the product or service has been around, the more distinctive is the surname trademark.

Trade names—essentially the names of business organizations—are not registerable. If the organization does not apply its name to its product, the trade name is not entitled to protection as a trademark. The application of the name to a product or service is what makes it a trademark.

A mark which is deceptively similar to another mark will also be denied registration. This is a prime consideration in deciding upon a new mark for use with goods or services.

Federal trademark registration procedure. Before filing application for federal registration of a trademark, it is advisable to consult an attorney specializing in this area. Among other preliminary matters, it is advisable to have a search made of registered federal marks and of the pending federal applications (these are public records, as patent applications are not). This might disclose if the mark is already registered, or if an application for its registration is pending. If it has already been registered, or if a registration application is pending, it may not be worthwhile to proceed. However, if the mark has been registered for a product or service bearing no relationship to the product or service for which one intends to use it, registration may still be possible.

This search will not always disclose that the proposed mark has already been appropriated. Matters are arranged alphabetically in these files, and since words used as trademarks may have unusual spellings coined by registrants, similar spellings should be searched. It is also possible that another party might have appropriated an equivalent word from a foreign language for use as a mark. A search would not disclose this information.

A thorough search would cost more than the average registrant might be willing to spend; nevertheless, the search procedure should not be bypassed. If it shows that the mark is already in use, much difficulty and expense will be saved.

The registration procedure is quite similar to patent procedure. The application, which must include a drawing of the mark, is filed with the patent office. It is then assigned to an examiner of trademarks for consideration. The examiner checks the application for sufficiency, and searches the records to see if the mark has already been appropriated. He will then grant the application or reject it.

Rejection procedure is also like patent procedure. The examiner explains why he feels that the application cannot be favorably considered. The applicant has six months to reply by presenting arguments as to why the examiner should change his position. The examiner will then reply; he may reverse himself and approve the application, or he may again reject, explaining why. This time he may make his rejection final, in which case the applicant must follow appeal procedure if he desires to press the application. If, however, the examiner does not make the rejection final, the applicant may reply and make more arguments. Again, he has six months after the rejection to file.

This may go on for four or five rounds, but eventually the examiner must make a final decision one way or the other. The first appeal of a final rejection must be made to the Trademark Trial and Appeal Board within six months of the rejection. This board may reverse the examiner and approve the application, or it may affirm and hold that the examiner was correct. The adverse trial and appeal board decision is appealable to the Court of Customs and Patent Appeals or to a federal district court for the District of Columbia according to the same rules as apply to patent appeals.

When two applications for registration of the same or very similar marks are pending, an interference proceeding may be commenced by the examiner involved. This works very much like a patent interference proceeding, except that only one examiner decides it. Such proceedings are rather uncommon because other ways exist to handle such problems. In situations where the same mark is sought to be registered, but it is to be used in two geographical areas that do not overlap or for two unrelated products or services, concurrent registration may be permitted, each party getting registration rights in his mark for his particular use.

Approval of an application by an examiner does not automatically entitle the mark to registration, but it does entitle it to publication in the *Official Gazette* as a mark that has been approved.

Any individual or firm desiring to prevent registration of the mark may file a notice of opposition with the patent office within thirty days of the *Official Gazette* publication. The opposer must allege that he will suffer damage if the registration is allowed. He is then given a chance to prove his arguments in a hearing before the Trademark Trial and Appeal Board. If the opposer wins, registration is denied. If the registrant wins, registration is granted. If no notice of opposition is filed within thirty days of the *Official Gazette* publication of the mark, registration is also granted.

Effect of registration. The registration supposedly confirms the registrant of the mark as owner against subsequent users. However, the owner's title to the mark may still be challenged.

Marks are contestable for five years after initial registration. Thus, any person or firm who believes that a mark should not have been registered may file a petition with the patent office to have the mark canceled. In such a case there is a hearing before the Trademark Trial and Appeal Board on the question of whether or not the mark should be canceled. The decision of the board, whichever way it goes, is appealable to the Court of Customs and Patent Appeals, or to the federal district court for the District of Columbia.

The opposer must prove that he is suffering damages from the registration. He generally needs stronger evidence of this than does the petitioner in an opposition proceeding. This is logical: why did the petitioner for cancellation not file an opposition before registration?

After five years the registrant should file an affidavit of continued use and an affidavit of incontestability with the patent office. These make the mark incontestable; no one can argue that the mark should never have been registered, and the owner may use his mark for another fifteen years.

After a mark has been registered for twenty years the initial registration expires. However, if the mark is still in use it may be reregistered, and it may be continually reregistered every twenty years until it is no longer used.

Loss of incontestable mark. An incontestable mark may be lost for one of three reasons:

1. Abandonment.
2. The mark has become a generic term for the type of goods or services it represents.
3. Misuse.

A mark is abandoned when the registered owner no longer uses it and has no intention of reusing it. 15 USC 1127(a) provides that when a mark has not been used for a period of two consecutive years, it shall be presumed that it has been abandoned. In order to escape the presumption, the owner would have to prove that he did not have the intent to abandon the mark by not using it—a matter that could be difficult to prove.

A mark becomes a generic term when it becomes associated in the public mind with a type of goods or services rather than with the particular good or service to which it was originally attached. According to Kintner and Lahr, such valid trademarks as "Thermos," "Aspirin," and "Shredded Wheat," among others, have met that fate. The possibility exists that other marks may soon join their ranks. Many people have formed the habit of referring to any cola drink as "Coke," although the term "Coke" is a trademark for Coca-Cola only, and not for Pepsi or other similar drinks. One hears all types of paper handkerchiefs referred to as "Kleenex," though Kleenex is a trademark for one specific brand. One hears talk of "Xeroxing" a copy of a document when it is copied on an electronic duplicating machine, although all such machines are not made by Xerox. Special advertising is sometimes necessary to make clear that the owner of a mark does not intend it to become a generic term and to lose its association with his product.

Misuse can take several forms. The most common is the use of a mark for the purpose of misrepresenting the source of goods or services, or for misrepresenting the nature thereof. Another form of misuse consists of permitting a licensee to use the mark without exerting quality control over his product, thus diluting the quality the public has come to associate with the mark.

Assignment and licensing of trademarks. A registered trademark may be assigned, as may be marks for which an application to register has been filed and unregistered marks. An assignment is not valid, however, unless the goodwill of the business using it is assigned along with the mark. Since the mark is associated in the public mind with the goods or services to which it attaches, separation of the mark from its particular good or service is unacceptable. Assignment of a mark without assignment of goodwill can destroy the validity of the mark.

15 USC 1060, the statutory provision requiring the assignment of business goodwill along with the assignment of a mark, also provides that an assignment must be in writing, and must be recorded with the patent office within three months after it is executed in order to be valid against third parties.

A subsidiary of the owner of a registered mark may use the mark without questions of infringement or abandonment arising. However, when the owner seeks to let an unrelated party use the mark, a licensing contract should be prepared giving the mark owner quality control rights over the goods or services to be dispensed.

The most common sort of trademark licensing occurs in the franchising situation, in which the franchiser—a firm such as Holiday Inn or Kentucky Fried Chicken—grants to the franchisee the right to use a trademark in its business. The franchiser will invariably exercise strict supervision over the franchisee's operation, even though the franchiser and franchisee are not under common ownership.

Trademark infringement litigation. The owner of a mark has the right to sue unauthorized users for infringement. If the mark is federally registered, the suit may be filed in federal court. The most common remedy for such infringement is an injunction against the infringer, forbidding his unauthorized use of the mark.

Another possible remedy is that of compensatory damages, which the plaintiff may recover if he can prove in dollars and cents the extent of the damage caused by the infringement. In cases of flagrant infringement, the plaintiff may be awarded up to three times the proven damages, though awards of triple damages are exceptional.

When the defendant has himself realized profits from his unauthorized use of the mark, the plaintiff may seek to force the defendant to turn these profits over to him. Determining the amount of these profits is often difficult, however: it may cost more to determine the amount than the amount of the profits themselves.

As is the case with the patent infringement, the defendant in a trademark case may raise the defense that the plaintiff's trademark should not have been registered by the patent office, or that the plaintiff has lost his rights in the registered mark through abandonment, misuse, or the fact that the mark has become a generic term. Thus, the plaintiff could end up losing his rights in his mark because of the unwise commencement of infringement litigation.

Trademarks in foreign trade. As in the case with American patents, a federal trademark registration gives protection only within the territory of the United States. If an owner wants to protect his mark in another country, he must register it under the law of that country.

By the same token, a trademark registered abroad is not protected in the United States. Federal registration by the foreign owner would be necessary in order to achieve such protection. The owner of a registered federal mark who desires protection against importation of goods bearing an infringing mark into this country may record his mark with the Bureau of Customs in Washington, D.C. Once this has been done, the bureau will not permit goods bearing an infringing mark to be imported.

Texas trademark registration. The user of a trademark within the confines of the state of Texas may find it advisable to register the mark with the Texas secretary of state, pursuant to provisions found in Article 16 of the Texas Business and Commerce Code. Generally, if the mark qualifies for federal registration except that it has never been used in interstate commerce, it qualifies for state registration.

The application procedure is similar to federal procedure with respect to the paperwork required. However, there is no elaborate examination of the application by examiners. If the mark is not scandalous or immoral and if it obviously does not infringe upon an already registered mark, registration will be granted. Once registered, the mark remains registered for ten years. Application for reregistration must be filed every ten years, so long as the mark remains in use.

A mark registered in Texas will take priority over a similar unregistered mark being used in Texas but will not take priority over a mark which has been registered at the federal level before the Texas mark was registered. On the other hand, a Texas registration may well have priority in Texas (but not elsewhere) over a similar mark bearing a later federal registration.

39

Regulation of Business Practices

Regulation of business practice is a subject which could easily fill a large book. Since space precludes detailed consideration here, this chapter will merely furnish an outline of the subject.

REGULATED INDUSTRIES

As a matter of policy the Congress and state legislatures have chosen to subject certain industries to stringent regulation in the interest of protecting the public from uneconomic competition and unfair practices. A brief discussion of some of these regulated industries follows.

Transportation. Regulation of the transportation industry has been discussed to a degree in the chapter on transportation of goods. The following federal agencies exercise authority in this industry:
1. Interstate Commerce Commission—over interstate railroads, interstate truck lines, all inland water carriers, all coastal water carriers, and interstate oil pipelines.
2. Civil Aeronautics Board—all interstate airlines.
3. Federal Maritime Commission—high-seas water carriers.

Generally, no carrier may serve a particular point without permission from the regulatory agency. Often service may not be discontinued without permission; schedule changes also require permission. Rates and the capital structure of the firms in the industry are regulated. No corporate combination involving firms in the industry may take place without the permission of the regulator.

Details of regulatory schemes vary from industry to industry, and from agency to agency.

The following Texas state agencies exercise authority over intrastate transportation firms:
1. The Texas Railroad Commission—railroads, trucklines, oil pipelines.
2. The Texas Aeronautical Commission—intrastate airlines.

Electric power. A complex web of regulation exists in the electric power industry. With respect to generation of electric power, the following situation prevails:

Three major methods are used for generating electricity in this nation—conventional power plants burning fossil fuel, hydroelectric plants, and nuclear plants.

At the federal level, conventional plants are subject to Environmental Protection Agency regulation with respect to pollutant emissions (smoke from burning coal, for example) and to Department of Energy regulations with respect to the fuel burned.

No hydroelectric plant may be erected which involves construction of a dam on a tributary of a navigable waterway without permission of the U.S. Army Corps of Engineers. Permission of the Federal Energy Regulatory Commission (FERC) is required for erection of the plant itself.

Nuclear plants may not be built without the permission of the Nuclear Regulatory Commission (NRC). All phases of the construction and operation of such plants are subject to NRC supervision and regulation.

When electric power is transmitted across a state line, the FERC has rate-setting authority if the generating company resells the power to another power company. This is the only situation in which federal regulatory authority has anything to say about the pricing of electric power.

The distribution of electric power to the consumer is regulated at the state or local level. Since electric power is considered to be a "natural monopoly," only one power company is permitted to furnish service to any particular area; each is granted a franchise by the local government. The retail price of the power is regulated in Texas either by the Public Utilities Commission or by the municipality.

Natural gas. The major regulation of production of natural gas is done at the state level—in Texas, by the Railroad Commission.

Before 1978 the FERC had authority to control the price of natural gas distributed in interstate commerce, but not gas sold intrastate. Now, the FERC has authority to set the wellhead price for all gas, wherever sold. The constitutionality of such federal authority to regulate the price of intrastate gas has been challenged; the outcome is still in doubt.

Interstate gas pipeline operations are also subject to FERC regulation. Retail distribution of natural gas is regulated in the same manner as the distribution of electric power, except that the federal Department of Energy has the authority to allocate scarce supplies of gas among various classes of users so as to make certain that homes will have gas available in times of shortage.

Telephone. Interstate telephone communication is regulated by the Federal Communications Commission (FCC). Its authority here extends mainly to the approval of interstate telephone rates.

Locally, the industry is regulated in the same manner as the electric power and gas industries.

Radio and television broadcasting. No firm or person may engage in the broadcasting business without a license from the Federal Communications Commission. These licenses are issued for three-year periods, subject to renewal. Each license specifies the frequency on which the station may broadcast, the hours of operation permitted, the broadcasting power of the station, etc.

Licenses may not be transferred without the consent of the FCC; changes in control of a corporate licenseholder must also be approved by the FCC. The Commission frowns upon owners of other communications media (such as newspapers) owning broadcasting licenses. It also limits the number of licenses which may be owned by any single person or entity.

The licensee is expected to use his license in the public interest; programming must conform to local tastes with respect to morality and standards. The licensee must also provide some local programming.

With respect to presentation of information on issues of public importance, the "fairness doctrine" is enforced by the FCC. If the licensee donates time to one side of a public issue or to one political candidate, it must make available equal time to the opposing side of the issue, or to opposing candidates (at least major candidates). If the licensee sells time to one side of an issue or one candidate, it should permit the other side or other candidates to buy equivalent time for an equivalent price, within reason.

The FCC has no authority to regulate broadcasting networks, since networks require no license. Regulation of networks is by indirection only, through regulation of the customers of the networks, the broadcasting licenseholders.

The FCC may revoke a license for misuse, a power it very seldom exercises. It may also refuse to renew a license, a power it makes use of on occasion.

Banking. The scheme of regulation of the banking industry is extremely complex. No corporation may operate a bank without a proper license. The license may be issued by the federal government, in which case the bank is a national bank, or it may be issued by the state, in which case the bank is a state bank. Federal bank licenses are issued by the Comptroller of the Currency; Texas bank licenses are issued by the Texas Banking Board.

National banks are required to belong to the Federal Reserve System, and to have their depositors' accounts insured by the Federal Deposit Insurance Corporation (FDIC). National banks are thus subject to regulation by three federal agencies: Comptroller of the Currency, Federal Reserve Board, and FDIC.

State banks may choose to belong to the Federal Reserve System and to the FDIC, but they are not obligated to do so. Most state banks belong to the FDIC and accept FDIC regulation. Fewer state banks choose to belong to the Federal Reserve System and accept Federal Reserve Board regulation. All Texas state banks are subject to Texas Banking Board regulation.

The regulators require banks to maintain a certain reserve of liquid assets to deposits, the reserve varying according to economic conditions. The loan policy of banks is also subject to regulation. The interest rates banks may charge their customers on loans is regulated by state usury laws. The interest rates they may pay to depositors are set by administrative regulation. The regulations specify maximum rates only; banks may pay anything less than the maximum.

Whether or not branch banking is permitted is a matter of state law. Some states, like Texas, choose to forbid branch banking. Others, like California, permit statewide branch banking. Other states take compromise positions, allowing countywide branch banking, for example.

Generally, banks are forbidden to own nonbanking businesses. They avoid this prohibition through the mechanism of the one-bank holding company. The bank organizes a parent corporation, which is given control over the bank. The parent then acquires other businesses. Such organizations are, however, subject to regulation by the banking industry regulators.

Texas has an indirect form of branch banking, the multi-bank holding company. The law permits a parent corporation to own two or more banks as subsidiaries. Again, acquisition of a bank by a multi-bank holding company must receive the approval of the appropriate bank regulating agency.

Other regulated industries. Many other less important industries are subject to stringent administrative regulation.

Such financial industries as savings and loan associations and credit unions are subject to regulation which is quite similar to banking regulation, as are consumer finance companies. Consumer finance company regulation is virtually all state regulation by the Consumer Credit Commissioner of Texas. Credit union and savings and loan regulation is done at either level of government, depending upon whether the institution is licensed at the federal or state level.

The insurance industry is stringently regulated at the state level. The regulatory scheme here is technical and complex.

Securities brokers, stock exchanges, mutual funds, and other such industries are regulated at the federal level if they operate in interstate commerce. Most such firms do, because of the necessity of access to the New York and American stock exchanges. The major regulator is the Securities and Exchange Commission.

Regulation of the petroleum industry is becoming more and more stringent, particularly with respect to certain types of pricing. The Department of Energy is the major regulator here.

Various sorts of mining are strongly regulated—open-pit mining with respect to environmental protection, underground mining with respect to miner safety.

Exporting and importing are subject to regulation in the interest of protecting the domestic economy of the United States.

REGULATION OF PRODUCT

Two major products may not be marketed in the United States without government permission: drugs and pesticides.

New drugs. A new drug may not be marketed in the United States until the Food and Drug Administration (FDA) has given permission under the provisions of the Federal Food, Drug, and Cosmetic Act, 21 USC 1471 et seq.

The manufacturer of the new product must file a New Drug Application (NDA) with the FDA. This application must disclose, among other things:

1. The chemical composition of the drug.
2. Recommended use of the drug.
3. Laboratory proof that the drug is effective for the recommended use.
4. Laboratory proof that the drug has no harmful side effects.

The FDA checks over the application and lab test results, and perhaps hires an independent testing lab to verify the manufacturer's claims. The agency will eventually either approve the drug for marketing, or will not approve it. A negative decision may be appealed within the agency, and eventually to the courts.

The new drug will be approved (if it is approved) for either over-the-counter marketing (in which case no doctor's prescription will be required) or for marketing only upon a doctor's prescription, in which case it may be distributed only to pharmacists, medical practitioners, and others so qualified. The registration of a new drug is permanent, but the FDA may, for good reason, change or revoke a registration after a hearing.

Once a new drug has been approved for marketing, other drug firms may also market it without FDA approval. Such drugs are called "me-too" drugs. Of course, "me-too" marketing could constitute patent infringement if the originating company has obtained a patent upon the new product's formula.

New pesticides. A new pesticide may not be marketed in the United States without the permission of the Environmental Protection Agency, under the provisions of 7 USC 135 et seq. Among those products considered to be pesticides are insecticides, herbicides, fungicides, and rodenticides.

An application for registration must be filed with the EPA which is quite similar to that filed with FDA on new drugs. If the EPA denies the application, the denial is appealable.

The EPA may grant three types of registration:
1. Approval for over-the-counter sale.
2. Approval for use only by licensed pesticide applicators.
3. Approval for experimental use only.

The registration need not be granted for all of the territory of the United States: the product may be approved for use in some areas but not in others or it may be given different registrations in different areas.

A pesticide registration is good for only five years, subject to renewal. The EPA may refuse to renew a registration, and it may, for good cause, revoke a registration before the five-year registration period expires (but only after an administrative hearing).

New motor vehicles. No new motor vehicle may be marketed in the United States which does not bear a sticker stating that its engine complies with air pollutant emission standards set by the EPA.

Products subject to agency safety and grading standards. Many sorts of products may be marketed in interstate commerce without prior government permission, but must meet safety and quality standards set by administrative agencies. The marketing of a non-complying product will subject the manufacturer (and perhaps other distributors) to criminal and/or civil liability.

Meat, poultry, eggs, and dairy products. Meat, poultry, eggs, and dairy products marketed in interstate commerce are subject to U.S. Department of Agriculture regulation. Animals and fowl subject to this regulation must be slaughtered in accordance with USDA regulations and inspected and graded after slaughter. Eggs must be inspected and graded before marketing. Dairy products must be inspected and tested for compliance with USDA standards on cream content, bacteria content, cleanliness, and so forth.

Other food products. Food products other than meat, poultry, eggs, and dairy products marketed in interstate commerce must meet FDA standards with respect to content. The FDA has set such standards for all processed foods. As a result, peanut butter must contain at least a stated percentage of peanuts, all-beef wieners must contain a specified percentage of beef, etc.

In addition, the FDA sets tolerances for foreign matter allowable in foods—so many parts per million of pesticide residue, so many parts per million of insect remains, etc. The agency also has the power to forbid the use of additives, such as food dyes, which are known carcinogens.

Any food product which does not comply with these standards in some way is adulterated. It is a criminal offense to knowingly distribute such a product, and the product itself may be seized without hearing by FDA inspectors (though it cannot be destroyed or otherwise disposed of without court action).

Cosmetics. The FDA has essentially the same powers over the marketing of cosmetics as it does over the marketing of foods. It may forbid the use of carcinogenic substances in cosmetics, and set tolerance standards for foreign materials in cosmetics.

Poisons and other hazardous substances. Under the provisions of the Federal Hazardous Substances Act, 15 USC 1261 et seq., the Consumer Product Safety Commission (CPSC) has the power to forbid the marketing and distribution of hazardous

substances within the borders of the United States. The CPSC has authority to ban the following sorts of substances as hazardous:
1. Poisons.
2. Corrosives (strong acids, for example).
3. Irritants.
4. Sensitizers (animal enzymes, for example).
5. Flammables or combustibles.

The power of the CPSC to ban such substances extends only to their household use; some hazardous substances are of great value in industrial processes, and cause no great danger when used by persons in industry who know what they are doing.

The CPSC also has the power to ban hazardous articles from use as toys or as household goods. The following sorts of items may be so banned:
1. Items which may generate pressure through decomposition, heat, or other means.
2. Emitters of dangerous radiation.
3. A toy or similar article presenting electrical, mechanical, or thermal hazards to children.

Under the provisions of the Toxic Substances Control Act, 15 USC 2601 et seq., the EPA has authority to regulate the manufacture and use of toxic substances in the economy as a whole. Under this legislation, the EPA may ban manufacture and distribution of a toxic chemical or may regulate its manufacture and distribution.

Flammable fabrics. Under the Federal Flammable Fabrics Act, the CPSC has authority to set standards of flammability for fabrics used in the making of clothing and interior furnishing. Manufacture or sale of a fabric which does not comply with a standard is a criminal offense.

Noise-emitting products. Under the provisions of the Federal Noise Control Act, 42 USC 4901 et seq., the EPA has authority to set noise emission standards for products that may emit noise at levels dangerous to health. Under this act, the EPA may permit the sale of products that emit noise at a dangerous level, but must set its standard at the lowest level at which production of the noise-emitting product is technologically feasible. Violation of these standards is a criminal offense.

Radiation-emitting products. The Federal Radiation Control for Health and Safety Act authorizes the Department of Health, Education, and Welfare to enact radiation emission standards for TV sets, microwave ovens, and other such products that may emit radiation in harmful quantities. Manufacture and distribution of noncomplying products is a criminal offense.

Motor vehicles, aircraft, and boats. Assorted federal legislation and administrative regulations require manufacturers of motor vehicles, boats, and aircraft to install specified safety equipment. Manufacture and sale of noncomplying products is a criminal offense.

Generality of consumer products. The Consumer Product Safety Act, 15 USC 2051 et seq., grants authority to the CPSC to enact safety standards for most consumer products. The act is discussed in the chapter on warranty and product liability.

Packaging. Two pieces of federal legislation regulate product packaging—one specific, one general.

The specific act is the Poison Prevention Packaging Act, 15 USC 1471 et seq. This legislation authorizes the CPSC to require that household products which are dangerous to children (such as over-the-counter drugs, drain openers, and so on), be packaged in child-proof packages. Such packaging generally consists of adding caps which are difficult to remove.

The general statute is the Fair Packaging and Labeling Act, 15 USC 1451 et seq., requiring that packages containing consumer products be filled as full as possible, taking into account the nature of the product.

Labeling. All of those statutes which grant to administrative agencies the power to prescribe safety or other standards for a product also grant the agencies the power to prescribe labels for the product.

The Fair Packaging and Labeling Act applies to the generality of consumer products. It requires that the label disclose the nature of the contents of the package and that the quantity of content of the package be disclosed—in ounces if liquid or solid, in square inches if paper or fabric, etc. The contents may be stated in pounds and ounces, pints and ounces, or quarts and ounces, but the total content in ounces must also be stated. The act permits packages of odd content—11 13/16 ounces are permissible—if the label accurately states the content.

Food labels must disclose the nature of the contents of the package. Ingredients must be disclosed in order of importance, but the quantity of each need not be disclosed. Vitamin and mineral fortification must be disclosed—in terms of percentages of minimum daily requirements if known, or in terms of units, micrograms, etc. Inaccuracy of labeling is misbranding, a criminal offense, subjecting the misbranded items to administrative seizure.

Drug labels must disclose both the popular and generic name of the drug, the ingredients and the quantity of each, the directions for use, the dosage, and so on. If the drug may be poisonous, if it should not be used under certain circumstances, or if it produces unexpected side effects, the label must so state. If it is for sale only on prescription, the label must so state. If a drug label does not contain all required information, the drug is misbranded.

If a noise-making product emits noise at a level dangerous to health, it must bear a label disclosing this information. If a consumer product is dangerous for any reason, the label must say so. If it is poisonous, the label must give directions for use of an antidote.

Motor vehicles must bear stickers stating that the engine complies with EPA pollutant emission standards, and giving the miles per gallon the engine made in EPA laboratory tests.

Fabric products must bear labels disclosing the fiber content—"100 percent cotton," "30 per cent wool and 70 percent polyester," or whatever. If the fabric is flammable, the label must say so. Fur products must bear labels disclosing the type of fur the product is made from.

If a product is imported, the label must say so. If the nation of origin is not obvious, the label must disclose it. Such labels must not be removed by American dealers in the product.

MARKETING THE PRODUCT

Advertising. False advertising is unlawful. Most sorts of false advertising are violations of the Texas Deceptive Trade Practices Act, subjecting the advertiser to potential triple damages. This aspect of advertising has been discussed in the chapter on consumer protection.

False advertising in interstate commerce is a deceptive trade practice under Section 5 of the Federal Trade Commission Act, subjecting the advertiser to administrative action by the FTC. In addition, false advertising of a food, drug, cosmetic, or medical device is a violation of the Federal Food, Drug, and Cosmetic Act and is a criminal offense.

Generally, the FTC does not take into account the intent of the advertiser in determining whether or not an ad is false or misleading. If the agency determines that the ad tends to deceive, or if the total impression given by the ad is misleading, the advertiser has committed an unfair trade practice. An ad is false and misleading if it contains an outright lie, such as an untruth about the composition of the product; if it fails to disclose a material fact, it is misleading. If an ad contains lies about the advertiser or about production methods used in manufacture of the product, or if material facts relative to these matters are omitted, the ad is also misleading.

In advertising, as in all sales talk, there exists a fine line between "puffing" and out-and-out fraud. An auto dealership could advertise itself as the "friendliest dealer in town" without fear; who is to say which dealer is the friendliest in town? A restaurant could advertise that it serves "the best catfish steaks in town"; who is to say which catfish steaks are best? But the car dealer who advertises, "We do our own financing—we tote your note," but assigns all of his auto purchase contracts to a finance company is guilty of false advertising. He is guilty of a blatantly false statement of verifiable fact.

Among the sorts of false advertising which violate both the Federal Trade Commission Act and the Texas Deceptive Trade Practices Act are:

1. Misrepresenting the geographic origin of a product.
2. Misrepresenting the sponsorship, approval, or endorsement of a product.
3. Misrepresenting the age of a product—saying it is new when it is really used, for instance.
4. Misrepresenting the reasons for price reductions.
5. Advertising that one is going out of business when one really is not.
6. Misrepresenting the quality, grade, or ingredients of a product.
7. Using bait-and-switch tactics—advertising a product for sale that one does not intend to sell, or advertising goods for sale at a low price without mentioning that one has in inventory only a small quantity of the advertised goods.

Endorsements and testimonials must be true. If Hank Hardtack, the great baseball player, says in a TV commercial that he uses Zilch Aftershave Lotion, the testimonial is false if Hardtack really does not use Zilch. If Bonnie Boling the movie star says that Cinch Beauty Cream keeps her skin soft, she should believe in the truth of what she says.

If an ad contains the results of tests or surveys, it must truthfully state the results of the tests or surveys. It is not legitimate to use only the part of test results that please the advertiser, and to quietly file and forget those results of the survey which are unfavorable. It is now permissible to advertise, "Product A is better than Product B because ____" if the "because" part of the ad is arguably true. It is not permissible to advertise, "Don't use Product B because ____." The latter is disparagement, which is of course unfair.

The subject of advertising is more complex than this discussion might lead the student to believe; entire books have been written on advertising law.

The FTC may commence administrative proceedings leading to a cease-and-desist order against false advertisers. It may now go directly to federal court to seek injunctions against advertisers when their false advertising could damage consumers. The penalty for violation of a federal injunction is of course the penalty for contempt. The penalty for violation of an FTC cease-and-desist order is a fine of a maximum of $10,000 per day of violation. However, FTC cease-and-desist order proceedings are time-consuming; the advertiser does not become liable for the penalty until the agency makes a final decision in the proceeding.

Monopolization. Except in the regulated industries, the law frowns upon one firm dominating a market. As a result, when competition exists within a market the competitors must not try too zealously to eliminate each other. One may compete, of course, but the vigorousness of the competition will depend upon the number of competitors. In a market containing many competitors, the chance for any one to acquire a dominant position in the market is slight, so vigorous competition is possible. In an oligopolistic market containing few competitors, a live-and-let-live policy is wise. To strive too hard to corner the market is to invite a charge of attempted monopolization, and to succeed in cornering the market may result in a charge of monopolization—both being violations of Section 2 of the Sherman Act.

Under some circumstances, monopolization is quite legal. For instance, if a firm is the only one in a market because it possesses the patent upon the monopolized product, the monopoly is legal. If a firm is the only competitor in the market because it was the first to enter the market, there can be no legal objection; someone has to be first into a market, after all. In this situation, however, one must not strive too hard to hold on to one's monopoly. Efforts to expand production to keep up with demand, to stimulate demand through advertising, to increase operating efficiency, and to keep improving the product are quite permissible; but, on the other hand, efforts to buy up all raw materials, to acquire new patents in the field, or to otherwise hinder the establishment of potential competitors would be highly unlawful.

Tying arrangements. A firm with an established product may seek to increase its sales of a not-quite-so-successful product by requiring all buyers of successful Product A to buy the not-quite-so-successful Product B along with it. Such tying arrangements are unlawful; they violate Section 3 of the Clayton Act. They are lawful only when there exists good reason for the tie-in—perhaps that Product A will not operate properly without Product B.

Distribution arrangements. The manufacturer of a product must use care in arranging for its distribution. There are some dangerous legal pitfalls to be avoided.

The manufacturer may establish his own retail outlets and in essence act as his own retailer. No legal problems arise here, unless no competing product exists and the product is not patented. In this unlikely situation, the manufacturer could theoretically be accused of violating Section 2 of the Sherman Anti-Trust Act by monopolizing the market for the product. If, however, the product is patented or there are competing products, there is no monopolization problem.

The manufacturer may wish to market the product through franchise outlets. Here, the retailers operate under the name and trademark of the manufacturer, but are actually independent contractors. The franchiser-franchisee relationship is a very complex one. The manufacturer-franchiser may well earn revenue by selling franchise rights to franchisees. The retail outlets are usually developed with capital furnished by the franchisee. The franchiser will not be liable in any way for the franchisee's operation; his main obligation is to furnish assistance to the franchisee in the development of the potential of his franchise. The franchiser is also obligated to exert supervision over his franchisees to make certain that the standard of product and service provided by the franchisee measures up to what the public expects of the franchiser's trademark.

Since the franchiser-franchisee relationship is a contractual relationship, and since the franchiser has superior bargaining power in the relationship, franchisers have in the past taken advantage of their superior bargaining power to impose unfair bargains upon their franchisees. The Federal Trade Commission is stepping into the gap by requiring franchisers to make full disclosure of the contents of their franchises to would-be franchisees before negotiations for the sale of a franchise begin.

Lastly, the manufacturer could market the product through independent distributors. If this is done, the manufacturer may not be able to exercise any control over the distributor's operations. The distributor may carry competing products or may not use his full effort to push the manufacturer's product, for example.

The manufacturer may try to control the independent distributor's operations to a degree, but there are antitrust pitfalls to be avoided. The manufacturer might want to impose an exclusive-dealing contract upon the distributor, requiring him to purchase all of his requirements of the product from the manufacturer. This prevents the distributor from dealing with the manufacturer's competitors and carrying competing product lines. There is no antitrust objection to this, unless the manufacturer occupies a large share of the market for the product in question. If a manufacturer ties up an excessive share of a product market through exclusive-dealing contracts (say, 5 percent or more), he violates Section 3 of the Clayton Act.

The manufacturer might also try to restrict the distributor's marketing of the product to particular classes of buyers, or to a particular geographic area. The manufacturer who attempts this is engaging in vertical market division, which may be a type of contract in restraint of trade and a violation of Section 1 of the Sherman Act.

If the manufacturer sends inventory to his distributor on true consignment, he may dictate how the distributor disposes of it. If he sells inventory, however, he must be careful with his restrictions.

Speaking very generally, the manufacturer must not restrict his distributor's choice of customers, either as to geographic area or as to nature. Thus, the manufacturer could not tell his distributor to sell only to consumers and to refer all business buyers to the manufacturer. On the other hand, the manufacturer could assign to his distributor an area of primary responsibility and require him to limit his advertising to newspapers and broadcasting media within that area. A manufacturer may also terminate his relationship with a distributor if he does not perform to the manufacturer's expectation within the assigned area.

Unless a manufacturer has such control over his product market as to be a potential monopolist, he has almost absolute discretion as to his choice of distributor. Refusal to deal with a distributor is not unlawful, and the severing of relationship with a distributor is not unlawful unless a breach of contract or concerted activity with other firms is involved.

Pricing. The manufacturer has very wide latitude with respect to the price at which he sells his product. In the absence of collusion with his competitors (which will be discussed later) he may set any price he chooses. He should, however, be aware of the antitrust pitfalls of engaging in price discrimination, which consists of selling the same product to two different buyers for two different prices. This is not always unlawful, but if it is unjustified and causes damage to other businesses it is a violation of the Robinson-Patman Act.

Price discrimination may cause primary, secondary, or tertiary injury. Primary injury is injury caused a competitor of the seller. Secondary injury is injury caused a competitor of the seller's customer. Tertiary injury is injury caused to a customer of a customer, or to a competitor of a customer of a customer.

Primary injury is caused by selling a product for two different prices in two different geographical markets. Suppose that Ace Company markets a product in Texas, Arkansas, Oklahoma, and Louisiana. It has a competitor, Deuce, which operates only in the Dallas-Fort Worth area. Deuce has made serious inroads into Ace's sales in that area, so Ace begins selling its product at cost in Dallas-Fort Worth, while continuing to sell above cost in the remainder of its market. Deuce's cost of manufacture is higher than Ace's, so Deuce cannot compete against Ace's price-cutting and is threatened with insolvency. Ace is guilty of unlawful price discrimination.

If selling at or below cost injures a competitor, unlawful price discrimination has occurred. If, however, there are logical reasons for selling for two prices in two different markets—such as higher transportation costs to one market than to another—and the price differential reflects exactly the transportation cost differential, there is no illegality.

There are legitimate reasons to sell goods below cost. Among these are:
1. The fact that the goods are perishable, and must be disposed of before they spoil.
2. The fact that the goods are seasonal (like winter clothing) and should be disposed of before the season ends.
3. The fact that the goods are obsolete (because of changing style, technology, etc.).
4. The fact that the goods are inventory of an outlet the seller is closing down, and costs of moving the goods to another outlet are high.

Secondary injury is caused by selling to one customer for one price, and to another customer for another price. If the two customers are competitors, the disfavored one may be injured by the discrimination.

For instance: Ace Company sells a product to two distributors in the Austin area, Spade and Clubb. Spade is owned by the son-in-law of Ace's president, so Ace gives Spade a better price than Clubb. Spade then offers Ace's product to retailers for less than Clubb can afford to offer it. Since the product is in considerable demand in Austin, Clubb cannot refuse to stock it. He is therefore damaged by this discrimination. Ace's act is unlawful.

If Ace had a rational reason for giving a price break to Spade there would be no illegality. For example, if Spade's orders are generally four times the size of Clubb's, Ace could grant Spade a quantity discount. If the discount passes along the lower costs of processing large orders, it would be justified. (There is just as much paperwork to processing a small order as there is to processing a large one.)

Quantity discounts, based upon the size of individual orders, are generally acceptable. Volume discounts, based upon the quantity of a product purchased by a customer over the course of a time period, are less acceptable. Discounts to a son-in-law or the like are not justifiable at all.

Tertiary injury is generally caused by this type of situation: Ace sells its product to several wholesalers in the Houston area for the same price. It also sells the product directly to Hart Company, a large retailer, for the same price it gives the wholesalers. It refuses to sell directly to other retailers, so Hart's competitors claim they are being damaged.

They probably are. The wholesalers cannot sell to their customers for the price Ace sells to Hart and make a profit; Hart thus has a big advantage over its competitors. Ace's act is unlawful.

The manufacturer who sells to both wholesalers and retailers must give his wholesale customers a functional discount in order to avoid this pitfall. The discount must be calculated finely to compensate the wholesaler for acting as a wholesaler, and no more.

Price discrimination problems may also arise when a price war erupts in a market. It is lawful to meet a competitor's price cut if that cut is itself lawful; it is unlawful to meet a competitor's unlawful price cut. (Thus, if your competitor starts selling below cost to run you and your other competitors out of a market, you must not copy him and sell below cost—you would both be doing an unlawful thing.) It is also unlawful to beat a competitor's price cuts, if by so doing you damage other competitors.

Suppose that King Company markets a product under the King trademark, which commands a high price. King sells exactly the same product to Knave, which markets it under the Knave trademark for a lower price. King refuses to permit smaller competitors of Knave to have this privilege; so these competitors claim unlawful price discrimination. Here nothing unlawful has occurred. So long as the King trademark has such prestige that consumers are willing to pay a high price for it, no harm has been done.

A question may also arise as to whether a manufacturer may tell his distributors at what price to sell his product. Normally this is unlawful vertical price fixing—it cannot be done.

If, however, the product is a patented product (the entire product, not just a part of it), such price-fixing is lawful. If the manufacturer sends the product to the distributor under a true consignment, so that the manufacturer keeps legal title to it, he may dictate the resale price. The manufacturer may print a retail price upon his package without penalty; so long as he merely suggests this as the retail price, there is no illegality. Some retailers will doubtless sell for less than the suggested price. Suggesting a retail price is permissible, then; requiring a retail price is not.

Problems may be caused with respect to the handling of transportation costs in pricing. When, for example, goods are shipped under F.O.B. shipping point terms, the recipient pays the shipping charges, so no problems exist. When goods are shipped C.I.F., C&F, or F.O.B. Destination, the shipping charges are paid by the seller. If these charges are passed along in toto to the recipient there is no problem. If, however, the seller absorbs part or all of the shipping charges himself, price discrimination could arise unless the seller absorbs all shipping charges without exception.

If the seller chooses to use a delivered pricing system, he is asking for trouble, unless the system is a single basing-point system, under which all customers are treated the same.

There are other aspects of the law of price discrimination which are beyond the scope of this chapter; this area is one of the most complex in antitrust law.

COLLABORATION WITH COMPETITORS

Generally, it is expected that competitors will compete, not cooperate; the businessman must therefore be somewhat careful about coexisting too cozily with competitors. Lack of care in this regard may cause one to be charged with combination or conspiracy in restraint of trade under Section 1 of the Sherman Act, or conspiracy to monopolize under Section 2 of the same act.

Pricing. Agreements between competitors as to the price at which goods will be sold, or as to the price at which raw materials will be bought, are considered horizontal price-fixing, and are wholly unlawful. It does not matter whether the price agreed upon is reasonable or not.

It is, however, legitimate for competitors to charge almost the same price for their products. Since market conditions have virtually the same economic effect upon all competitors in a market, the logic of the market mechanism will go far toward dictation of a logical market price. However, in a truly competitive market there may well exist mavericks who defy the logic of the market and charge nonconforming prices.

It may also be that, in oligopolistic markets particularly, competitors will prefer to live and let live and not to compete violently. Under such circumstances price leadership may exist, under which, when one firm changes prices, all other firms change prices by almost—but not quite—identical amounts.

It sometimes happens that competitors in a market organize themselves into a trade association in order to exchange information for the betterment of all association members. If the association collects information from all of its members on inventories, sources and prices of raw materials and labor, customers, sales, and expected demand for the products of the competitors, all members have available the same information with respect to market conditions. Under such circumstances, the logic of the market will again dictate that the prices charged by association members will be quite similar.

If similar prices are charged by competitors because of price leadership or trade association activity, nothing unlawful is occurring. If on the other hand the price leader uses coercion to ensure that its lead is followed, or if trade associations discipline their members to follow the group lead with respect to pricing, horizontal price-fixing is said to exist, and the Sherman Act is violated.

Refusals to deal. When a group of competitors refuses to deal with a supplier or group of suppliers (or a customer or group of customers) a horizontal group boycott exists. Since the purpose of such a boycott is almost invariably the exertion of pressure on the boycotted group, such conduct is deemed to be a combination in restraint of trade and a violation of Section 1 of the Sherman Act. A unilateral refusal to deal may not be harmless, but it is not a conspiracy; a group refusal to deal is by definition a conspiracy.

If a group of competitors refuses to deal with another firm or firms because it is forced to do so by the coercion of a powerful supplier or customer, a vertical group boycott exists. This is just as unlawful as the horizontal group boycott. The members of the boycotting group are just as guilty of unlawful activity as is the coercing supplier or customer.

Market division. Competitors may organize themselves into a cartel and agree not to compete against each other in certain product or geographic markets. In a spirit of live and let live, they divide some or all of the existing markets among themselves to insulate themselves against competition and to insure comfortable survival for all.

Such agreements are so obviously anticompetitive that they are violations of Section 1 of the Sherman Act. They are called horizontal market division.

Attempted monopolization. When two or more competitors in a market work together to eliminate other competitors, they are attempting to monopolize the market. They are also conspiring to monopolize the market.

The conspiring firms might buy up more raw materials than they need in order to deny them to competitors. They might buy up promising plant sites for the same reason, or engage in the various types of unlawful behavior described above in order to eliminate competition. Such activity violates Section 2 of the Sherman Act.

ANTITRUST ENFORCEMENT

Sherman Act violations are criminal offenses. For violations, the maximum penalty for individuals is a fine of $100,000 and/or five years imprisonment. For a corporation, the maximum fine is $1,000,000. Prosecutions are carried out by the Antitrust Division of the Department of Justice.

The antitrust division may bring civil actions against violators of all antitrust laws. The objective of such civil actions is the obtaining of an injunction against the violator.

The Federal Trade Commission may enforce the Clayton and Robinson-Patman acts through administrative proceedings leading to cease-and-desist orders. The FTC may also seek federal court injunctions against violators when consumer interests are involved. As in false advertising cases, the penalty for violation of the FTC cease-and-desist order is a penalty of up to $10,000 per day of violation.

Any person or firm injured by an antitrust violation may bring suit against the violator for damages in federal district court. If the plaintiff can prove the law violation and the amount of his damages, he is entitled to recover three times the amount of proven damages. The civil plaintiff may also sue for an injunction against the violator.

Criminal prosecutions of antitrust violators are rare. Suits by the government for injunctions against violators are also rare, except in cases of allegedly unlawful corporate combinations, which are discussed in the materials on corporations. FTC actions against violators are somewhat more common, particularly in case of Robinson-Patman Act violations and cases of unlawful corporate combinations. Civil actions by private parties for triple damages are growing in number, and constitute the major antitrust pitfall for small and medium-size businesses.

There is also a Texas state antitrust law, found in Chapter 15 of the Texas Business & Commerce Code. This statute renders monopolies, trusts, and conspiracies in restraint of trade unlawful. Under the Texas act, monopoly is defined in terms of corporate combinations; it will be discussed in the chapter on that subject.

A *trust* is defined as a combination of capital, skill, or acts by two or more persons to:
1. Restrict trade, commerce, pursuit of a business, or preparation of goods for market, or
2. Manipulate the price of goods, or
3. Prevent or lessen competition in business, or
4. Fix the price of goods, or
5. Limit the supply of goods.

A *conspiracy in restraint of trade* is defined as:
1. An agreement not to buy from or sell to another person, or
2. An agreement not to deal with goods produced by or belonging to another person.

Under the Texas act agreements involving price-fixing, market division, and so on are thus defined as trusts, and group boycotts are defined as conspiracy in restraint of trade. Agreements to limit to supply of goods (in order to drive the price up) are not expressly unlawful under the Sherman Act, but the Texas act does expressly make them illegal. On the other hand, the Texas act does not mention price discrimination at all.

There is a criminal penalty for violation of the Texas act which is applicable only to individuals: imprisonment for no less than two years nor more than ten years. Such criminal prosecutions are very rare.

The state may bring a civil action against violators. The remedies are:
1. A penalty of no less than $50 nor more than $1,500 per day of violation.
2. Forfeiture of the charter of a Texas corporation violating the act.
3. Forfeiture of the right of a foreign corporation violating the act to do business in Texas.

A private party may sue a violator for damages. He may seek compensatory damages or an injunction against the violation. The Texas act does not provide for collection of triples damages as does the federal law.

Some other penalties for violation of some of the other statutes covered in this chapter are worthy of mention. Violators of the Federal Food, Drug, and Cosmetic Act (sellers of adulterated or misbranded foods, drugs, and cosmetics, or of unregistered drugs) are subject to the following criminal penalties:

First offense—imprisonment of no more than one year, a fine of no more than $1,000, or both.

Second or subsequent offense, or any offense committed with intent to defraud—imprisonment for no more than three years, a fine of no more than $10,000, or both.

For false advertising of a food, drug, cosmetic, or medical device—imprisonment of no more than six months, a fine of no more than $5,000, or both.

The Texas legislature has enacted RCS 4476-5, which is a statute very similar to the Federal Food, Drug, and Cosmetic Act. Any act which is a violation of the federal act is also a violation of the state act and constitutes a misdemeanor. The penalties are:

First offense—a fine of no less than $25 nor more than $200.

Second or subsequent offense—a fine of no less than $100 nor more than $1,000, imprisonment for no more than one year, or both.

An accused who has been tried by federal authorities for violation of the federal act may not be prosecuted by state authorities for the same violation.

The unlawful sale or use of a pesticide subjects a professional dealer or user to a fine of no more than $25,000, imprisonment for no more than one year, or both. Such an offense by a private applicator subjects him to a fine of no more than $1,000, imprisonment for no more than thirty days, or both.

The seller of a product violating EPA noise emission standards is subject, for a first offense, to a fine not to exceed $25,000 per day of violation, imprisonment of no more than one year, or both. For a second or subsequent offense the penalty is doubled: a fine of no more than $50,000 per day of violation, imprisonment for no more than two years, or both.

The seller of a product in violation of Consumer Product Safety Commission safety standards is subject to a fine of no more than $50,000, imprisonment for no more than one year, or both. A violator of the Federal Hazardous Substances Act who sells a banned hazardous substance or does not put proper warnings on the label of a hazardous substance is subject to the following penalties: First offense—a fine of no more than $500, imprisonment for no more than ninety days, or both. Second or subsequent offense, or offense committed with intent to defraud—a fine of no more than $3,000, imprisonment of no more than one year, or both.

A violator of the Federal Flammable Fabrics Act (a seller of fabric not meeting CPSC flammability standards) may be fined no more than $5,000, imprisoned no more than one year, or both.

For violations of the Consumer Product Safety Act (mainly selling products not in compliance with CPSC safety standards), the agency may assess a civil penalty of $2,000 per violation if committed knowingly. Each knowing violation is a separate offense, the maximum civil penalty collectable being $500,000. The CPSC must of course sue to collect.

The EPA may sue pesticide violators to collect civil penalties. The maximum penalty for a dealer or professional applicator is $5,000; the maximum for nonprofessional violators is $1,000.

The businessman must obviously be very careful in his business practices; heavy penalties may be incurred if he is not.

THE TEXAS LIMITED SALES TAX

Any discussion of the law of business practice would be incomplete without a brief discussion of the Texas Limited Sales Tax, the law relative to which is found in Chapter 20 of the Texas Taxation Code. Most articles sold by retailers to consumers in this state are subject to this tax, and the retailer is obligated to collect the tax and pay it over to the Comptroller of Public Accounts of the State of Texas.

The tax rate is 4 percent. However, municipalities within the state are permitted to levy a 1 percent municipal sales tax if the levy is approved by the voters of the municipality in a duly held election for that purpose. In addition, areas located within the boundaries of the Houston metropolitan transit district are subject to an additional 1 percent sales tax. The comptroller collects these taxes for the municipalities and districts levying them, and remits collection proceeds to the taxing governments as required by law. Thus, the tax rate is effectively 5 percent in municipalities levying the 1 percent tax, and it is 6 percent in most of the Houston metropolitan area.

Taxation Code (TC) 20.021(C) provides that any person desiring to engage in the business of selling to consumers goods which are subject to this tax must obtain a permit from the comptroller. The businessman must file a separate application for each place of business that he operates within the state.

Upon receipt of the application in good form the comptroller will issue to the applicant a temporary permit to go into business and will inform the applicant that his temporary permit will not become permanent until he posts with the comptroller a bond of $50,000 or three times the comptroller's estimate of the average quarterly tax liability of the business, whichever is lower. The purpose of the bond is, of course, protection of the state against nonpayment of tax collections by the applicant. The bond may take the form of cash, negotiable securities, a bond issued by a licensed bonding company, or any other form the comptroller finds acceptable.

Temporary permits are issued for a limited time period—the applicant must post his bond before the temporary permit expires. After the bond is posted a permanent permit is issued.

The following sorts of items and transactions are exempt from the limited sales tax, as per TC 20.04:

1. Oil and motor fuels.
2. Water.
3. Telephone and telegraph service.
4. Receipts from sale of mixed drinks if taxable under the provisions of the Texas Alcoholic Beverages Code.
5. Sale of alcoholic beverages to holders of private club registration permits.
6. Property used in manufacturing—raw materials, component parts, tools, equipment, office equipment, and so on.
7. Wrapping, packing, and packaging supplies for business use.
8. Containers for business use.
9. Meals served by most nonprofit organizations.
10. Property to be shipped out of state, unless delivered to buyer in Texas.
11. Property sold to governments or charitable organizations.
12. Food and food products for human consumption (not including over-the-counter medicines, soft drinks, candy, or food sold for consumption on the premises).
13. Drugs and medicines sold pursuant to prescription.
14. Medical and prosthetic devices.
15. Animal life of a kind the products of which provide food for human consumption (hogs, cattle, chickens, etc.).
16. Horses, mules, and work animals.
17. Feed for animals of the sort exempted in 15 and 16 above.

18. Seeds and annual plants the products of which are used for human consumption, or which are sold for resale.
19. Pesticides for agricultural use.
20. Fertilizer.
21. Agricultural machinery to be used on farms or ranches.
22. Leases or rentals of property.
23. Vessels weighing fifty tons or more.
24. Aircraft used by licensed carriers of persons or property.
25. Gas and electricity.
26. Railway rolling stock.
27. Religious books containing teachings of the faith published and distributed by that faith.
28. Property sold from vending machines.
29. Casing, drill pipe, tubing, etc., used in oil and mineral drilling.
30. Motion picture theater admissions.
31. Services in general.

The exemption provisions are somewhat more complex than the above listing might lead one to believe, but the list provides a good idea of the items included in the exemptions.

The retailer is obligated to collect the applicable sales tax upon sales of nonexempt property unless the sale itself is exempt. When making an exempt sale of nonexempt property, the seller should obtain from the buyer a certificate of exemption which explains the reason for the exempt nature of the sale.

The retailer must add the applicable tax to the price of the goods sold. He may not include the tax in the price of the goods sold, and he must not advertise that he absorbs the sales tax himself.

Returns and payment. TC 20.05 contains provisions relative to filing of returns and computation of tax. Returns are normally to be filed quarterly—by April 30, July 31, October 31, and January 31—declaring taxes due for the calendar quarter ending one month earlier than the return due date. If the taxpayer collects more than $750 in tax per month, he must file monthly returns for the preceding month.

The basis for the tax liability is the taxable percentage of gross receipts from taxable sales made during the taxable period. Ideally, the taxpayer should fix his cash registers so that taxable transactions are recorded separately from nontaxable transactions, and train his cashiers to ring up the transactions accordingly. For those sellers who do not do this, TC 20.05 provides acceptable methods for approximating the liability. In short, if gross receipts from taxable sales in a store in a city levying the 1 percent city sales tax are $10,000, the tax liability would be $500—$500 being 5 percent of $10,000.

The taxpayer is permitted to deduct 1 percent of the tax due as compensation from the state for acting as collection agent. In addition, the taxpayer may entitle himself to an additional 2 percent deduction by prepaying his tax—if he pays his estimated liability before the fifteenth of the month if he files monthly, or before midquarter if he files quarterly. If the taxpayer does not file his returns on time he forfeits all right to a discount.

Penalties for nonpayment, underpayment, and the like. If the taxpayer does not pay the tax shown to be due by his return, he is subject to a 5 percent penalty. If the tax is not paid when thirty days have passed since the due date, he is subject to an additional 5 percent penalty. In addition, delinquent sales tax draws interest at 6 percent per annum, beginning sixty days after payment becomes delinquent.

TC 20.06 provides that, if the comptroller feels that the tax collections stated in a return are inaccurate, he may compute and determine the true tax on the basis of any information he may have in his possession. The Comptroller may also make such a determination when the taxpayer fails to file a required return. Notice of the deficiency determination must be mailed to the taxpayer. Such determination may be made up to four years after the due date of the return, or four years after the date of the filing of the return, whichever is later. (If no return was filed there is no time limitation upon the assessment of a deficiency.)

In cases of nonfiling, the comptroller may make his determination of tax due by educated "guesstimate." In nonfiling cases, 10 percent of the amount declared to be due shall be added to the tax as a penalty.

In any deficiency case in which the comptroller feels that the taxpayer is guilty of fraud or of intent to evade payment of the tax, a penalty of 25 percent may be added, in addition to other penalties.

TC 20.08 states that a taxpayer served with such a notice of deficiency may petition the comptroller for redetermination within thirty days of his receipt of the notice of deficiency. The taxpayer is then entitled to an oral administrative hearing on his petition; at this time the burden of proof is on him to show that the comptroller's determination of deficiency is incorrect. If no redetermination petition is filed within the thirty-day period, the taxpayer loses his right to contest the accuracy of the notice of deficiency.

Collection of delinquent sales tax. Upon determination that a taxpayer is delinquent, the comptroller may proceed to collect the delinquency from the taxpayer's bond. If the bond is sufficient to pay off the delinquency, the comptroller may then demand that the taxpayer increase the amount of his bond by a sum sufficient to make up for the reduction caused by the forced collection.

If the bond is insufficient to pay the delinquency, or if the taxpayer does not augment the amount of the bond after collection from it, the comptroller may proceed under TC 20.021(E) to revoke the taxpayer's business permit. If this is revoked, the taxpayer loses his right to be in business.

If these measures fail, forcible collection methods may be used. Under TC 20.09(A), a notice may be sent to all debtors of the taxpayer (including banks where he keeps checking accounts) notifying them of the delinquency, and requiring them not to transfer or make any other disposition of property belonging to the taxpayer until the comptroller lifts the freeze order, or until sixty days have passed. Such freezing of assets could obviously be very damaging to a businessman.

Under TC 20.09(H), the comptroller may administratively seize nonexempt property of the taxpayer and sell it at auction. The taxpayer must of course be notified of the time and place of sale, and is entitled to any surplus funds realized at the sale over and above expenses of seizure and sale, plus the delinquent tax, penalties, and interest due.

TC 20.09(G) permits the comptroller to sue the taxpayer and reduce his claim to a judgment. The claim is considered to be liquidated. Thus the Comptroller may obtain attachment against nonexempt assets of the taxpayer right after the filing of suit.

The comptroller has three years after sales tax payments become due to collect. Suit must be filed during this three-year period. A judgment, once obtained, is good for ten years.

Transferee sales tax liability. Any purchaser of a business which sells goods subject to the sales tax should be certain that the seller owes no delinquent taxes when he takes possession. The buyer of the business may be held liable for sales tax obligations of the seller.

TC 20.09(I) provides that the buyer must withhold from the purchase price of the business sufficient funds to pay any sales tax liabilities of the seller. Since the sale is probably a bulk sale under Article 6 of the UCC, the buyer would be obligated to consider the comptroller as another creditor of the seller to be paid.

The buyer should inform the comptroller of his purchase and request that the comptroller either furnish him a certificate showing no sales tax is due from the seller or tell him how much the seller owes. If the comptroller issues a certificate showing no tax due, the funds withheld for sales tax may be released to buyer. If the comptroller says tax is due, the buyer should pay it from the withheld funds.

Sales tax permits are not transferable; a buyer of a business that collects taxes must therefore acquire a business permit and surety bond in his own name.

PART VIII

Business Organizations

40

Partnerships

Traditionally there are three types of business organization: the sole proprietorship, the partnership, and the corporation. Over time the numbers have expanded somewhat: there are now two types of partnerships, for example—the general partnership and the limited partnership. There are also two types of organizations occupying the middle ground between the partnership and the corporation—the joint stock company and the business trust. Several chapters of this work will be devoted to the law of corporations; the other business organization forms will be considered in this chapter. Of all these forms, the one deserving most of our attention is the general partnership; most of this chapter will be devoted to that form. Before taking up the general partnership, however, a brief discussion of the sole proprietorship is necessary.

Sole proprietorship. The sole proprietorship is a one-owner business. In essence, the owner is the business and the business is the owner. The owner is personally liable for every liability of the business—he risks not only his capital investment but everything he owns on its success. The business is not a separate entity; it is run in the name of the owner. He is the only person with any management authority, unless he appoints an agent or agents to help in the management task. The business is not a taxpayer: the owner is responsible for its tax liabilities.

The potential burdens of operating a business as a sole proprietorship are great enough that the proprietor should think hard about incorporating. If he incorporates, and if he runs the business properly, he may appreciably reduce his risks.

What is a partnership? The law of partnerships in Texas is to a large degree statutory law. The governing statute is the Texas Uniform Partnership Act (UPA), RCS 6132b. UPA 6 defines a partnership as "an association of two or more persons operating as co-owners a business for profit."

If two or more persons own an enterprise that conforms to this definition, they are operating a general partnership, whether they know it or not. Absolutely no formalities are required to establish a partnership. No formal partnership agreement is necessary; in the absence of a partnership agreement, all rights and obligations of the partners are defined by the UPA. The UPA will govern most aspects of the operation of the business.

It is of course possible for those who deliberately create a partnership to create their own rules for the operation of the business, within wide limitations. They may do this by entering into a written partnership agreement. It is wise for would-be partners to do this; they may tailor the ground rules of their operation to fit their needs and the nature of their enterprise.

Not all economic associations of two or more persons are partnerships. For instance, if Able and Baker own a tract of empty land as tenants in common for speculation purposes, they are not partners. The land requires no active management, so the association is not a business. If Cass and Dowd own 1,000 shares of General Motors stock as tenants in common, they are not partners. Again, this is a passive investment: The only decision to be made here is when to sell the shares. However, if Eaves and Foxx own and manage an apartment building as tenants in common, they are partners. An apartment house is not a passive investment: Someone must be on the spot to manage things.

UPA 7 provides that not all business relationships between two or more persons are partnerships. If Guff and Hixon operate a grocery store as co-owners and share profits and losses, their operation fits the UPA 6 definition and they are partners. If Guff and Hixon have agreed that they will share the profits from the store equally, but have made no agreement about losses, they are still partners since they still fit the definition. They will share losses too (whether they know it or not). But if Guff owns the store building and Hixon operates the store, having put up the capital for it and bought its inventory; and Guff's rent is a share of the store profits, there is no partnership. There is no co-ownership of the business.

If Jacobs lends Hixon the capital with which to start the store: Hixon rents the store area from Guff; and Jacobs has agreed that his interest upon the loan will be a percentage of the store profits but that he will take no part in managing the business, there is no partnership. Jacobs is a creditor here, not a partner. If Kinsey works for Hinson in the store and receives as pay a percentage of gross profits, he is not a partner. He is merely an employee.

If Marlow and Nunn operate a business as partners for a long period and Nunn dies, by will leaving all of his assets to his widow; and the widow moves out of state and plays no part at all in the business, but receives a part of the profits as an annuity because of her deceased husband, UPA 7 provides that there is no partnership. The heirs of a deceased partner are not automatically partners; Marlow has not created a situation here under which the widow Nunn would qualify as a partner.

If Oxley lends Peck the capital with which to start a business, Peck owns all of the store assets and does all of the work connected with the business; and Oxley and Peck split gross receipts one-fourth to Oxley and three-fourths to Peck, Peck paying operating expenses out of his three-fourths, there is no partnership, because there is no co-ownership.

If Quincy furnishes all of the capital of the business but Ross does all of the day-to-day managing; Quincy and Ross agree to share profits and losses equally; and Ross agrees not to make any fundamental changes in the business without Quincy's consent, a partnership does exist. Despite the inequality of the investment, Quincy and Ross are co-owners here.

The firm name. Each partnership must have a firm name. This name may disclose the names of the partners, or it may not. Any firm name which does not disclose the names of all of the partners is an assumed name, and subjects the firm to the obligations imposed by TB&CC 38.01 et seq., the Texas Assumed Name Statute. TB&CC 38.02 provides that, for a partnership, a name is assumed either when it does not include the names of all the partners or when it does include all and contains in addition the words "Company," "& Company," "& Associates," etc. These words suggest the presence of other partners.

The partnership doing business under an assumed name must record a certificate in

the county records of every county in which it does business (TB&CC 36.10). The certificate must contain:
1. The assumed name.
2. The partnership name.
3. The office address of the firm.
4. The names and residence addresses of all partners.
5. The period, not to exceed ten years, during which the assumed name will be used.
6. The fact that the business is a partnership.

The maximum term of validity of the certificate is ten years. If the firm is still in business after ten years, a new certificate must be filed. If the name of the business is changed—or if a new partner is admitted, or an existing partner dies, retires, or resigns—a new certificate must be filed to reflect the changed circumstances.

Failure to comply with this requirement is a misdemeanor. TB&CC 36.26 provides that a firm doing business under an assumed name that does not comply with the statute may be fined up to $2,000. In addition, TB&CC 36.25 provides that a firm violating this statute may not enforce any contracts in the courts of Texas before the statute is complied with. Also, if a noncomplying firm is sued in Texas courts and the plaintiff was required to go to extra expense to learn the identities of the owners of the noncomplying business, that business is liable for the extra expenses.

The partnership as a legal entity. A partnership is a legal entity for most purposes, but not all. It may own property, both real and personal, in its own name; it may sue and be sued in its own name; it may accrue liability for and pay business taxes in its own name; and it may make contracts in its own name. But since the partnership is not an individual, it must do all of these things through the instrumentality of human agents.

However, the partnership is not an entity in the sense that the corporation is: the corporation is an entity quite distinct and independent from its shareholders. The entity of the partnership is very closely bound to the identity of its partners. Partners are personally liable for partnership liabilities, while corporate shareholders are not liable for corporate liabilities. The continued existence of the corporation does not depend upon the continued existence of its shareholders, or upon the personnel of its shareholders remaining unchanged; the partnership, on the other hand, is dissolved on the departure of an old partner or the addition of a new one.

For federal income tax purposes, the partnership is not an entity. Partnership profits are taxable to the partners ratably, in accordance with the partnership agreement or the UPA. It does not matter whether profits are distributed to the partners or retained in the business—they are 100 percent taxable.

Who are partners? Any person may be a partner who has the capacity to make a contract. Thus, persons with guardians may not be partners but anyone else may be. A minor may be a partner, but he retains his right of disaffirmance; he may withdraw from a partnership at any time, regardless of the provisions of the partnership agreement.

Organizations may also be partners. For a long time there was hostility to permitting corporations to participate in partnerships, but that hostility is now passing away throughout the country. Neither Texas partnership law nor corporation law now forbids a corporation to be a partner.

Identification of the members of a Texas partnership is easy. Their names all appear in the firm name or on the certificate of doing business under an assumed name on file at the local courthouse. Any person named in the partnership agreement as a partner is a partner. Usually, but not always, all of the partners participate in the management of the business.

Usually, but not always, all partners have made financial contributions to the capital of the business. Usually, but not always, all partners are glad to be known to the public as partners.

Thus, an individual may be known to the public as a partner who takes no part in the management of the business. This is the "silent" partner. An individual who is not known to the public as a partner and who keeps his partnership affiliation a deep secret is a "secret" partner. No special name is given the partner who makes no capital contribution in the form of money or property; if the other partners are willing to let one of their number contribute services in exchange for partner status, it is a perfectly lawful arrangement.

Partners by estoppel. Normally, no person who is not a true partner may be held liable upon a partnership liability. However, a person who is not a true partner, but who leads the public or specific firm creditors to believe that he is one, will incur the liability of a partner (UPA 17); such a person is a partner by estoppel. He may incur liability under the following circumstances.

First example: Davis tells Smith that he is a member of the partnership of Able, Baker, and Cass. Smith believes this and makes contracts with Able, Baker, and Cass on the basis of the financial standing of Davis in the community. Smith may hold Davis liable as a result.

Second example: Spade tells Ace in the presence of Hart that Hart is a partner in the firm of Spade, Clubb, and Diamond. Hart does not deny this. Ace makes contracts with Spade, Clubb, and Diamond in reliance upon Hart's being a partner. So far as Ace is concerned, Hart is a partner.

Third example: Deuce runs a business as a sole proprietorship. He talks to the public as if Ace is a partner in this business, although Ace really is not a partner. Ace does not announce in public that he is a partner, and he does not say that he is not. No one asks him about it, one way or the other. So far, Ace is not a partner by estoppel; he has not done any affirmative thing to make people believe that he is. But if Deuce applies for a loan from First Bank, and tells it that Ace is his partner, Ace had better speak up. The First Bank people will now ask Ace if he is a partner, and he must deny it if he does not wish to be so considered.

Firm assets—personal property. According to UPA 8, assets are firm assets if:
1. They were contributed by a partner to the firm, either as a part of the partner's capital contribution or as a gift.
2. They are purchased in the firm name, whether with firm money or otherwise.
3. They were purchased with firm money, unless the circumstances make it obvious that the assets so purchased are not firm assets.

The first two situations need no amplification, but the third requires some explanation. Suppose Ace, partner in the firm of Ace, Deuce, and Trey, buys a desk with firm money. Ace, Deuce, and Trey are real estate brokers, so they obviously have a use for desks. The desk is a firm asset, even if Ace tries to convert it to his own use. On the other hand, suppose Deuce's wife is badly injured in an accident, and Deuce runs short of cash. He uses firm cash with which to buy his wife a wheelchair. This is obviously not a firm asset: real estate brokers have no use for wheelchairs. It is obvious from the circumstances that Deuce bought this chair for personal use.

If any doubt exists in cases like this, an asset bought with firm cash will be deemed a firm asset. The contrary proof must be very strong.

Firm assets—real estate. Partnerships may of course own land. Since title to land is a matter of public record, it makes a difference how title to the land appears in the record.

If the partnership itself has title to the property, the land cannot be sold without the consent of all of the partners unless the firm is in the business of selling land. Generally, real estate is not an asset held for sale in the normal course of business. A sale of land held in the firm name without the consent of all the partners—either as signers of the deed or as principals of the partner or partners who signed for them as agents—is void.

A partnership may also hold title to real estate in the names of all the partners. When the title is held this way, all the partners must sign the deed transferring title, or they must confer express authority upon those partners signing to sign for them. If this is not done the sale is void, unless the partnership is in the business of selling land.

A partnership may hold land in the names of less than all its partners. In such a case, those partners who hold the record title have apparent authority to sell the property. They have the power to sell good title to a bona fide purchaser, although they do not have the right to do this unless the other partners agree to the sale. Nevertheless, the bona fide purchaser will get clear title to the land; the partnership will have recourse against the partners who engage in the wrongful sale.

Tenancy in partnership. UPA 25 provides that partnership assets, both personal property and real property, are owned in tenancy in partnership. The firm owns the asset, but the partnership's members also have ownership rights of sorts.

All members of the firm have the right to use firm assets for firm business, unless otherwise agreed. No partner may use a firm asset for personal use, unless all his partners consent. No partner may ever sell, assign, or mortgage his interest in a firm asset; a partner's interest in an asset may not be separated from his interest in the firm. No creditor of an individual partner may reach that partner's interest in a firm asset. Only firm creditors may seize such assets; they are not directly subject to claims of individual creditors.

Upon the death of a partner, his interest in firm assets passes to the surviving partners. The heirs of a deceased partner acquire no interest in firm assets as such.

The interest of the partner in the firm. UPA 26 provides that a partner also owns a share in the profits and surplus of the firm, which is separate and distinct from his interest in the firm assets. This interest of the partner in the firm is to an extent transferable; upon the death of a partner it passes to the heirs of the deceased. A partner may thus dispose of such an interest by will. It may also be sold by its owner, and creditors of a partner may reach this interest if they follow proper procedure. The consequences of changes of ownership of the interest will be considered later.

When a partner has invested community funds in a partnership, his interest in the firm will be community property. The share of a married partner in the profits of the firm will be community property. Thus, even when a married partner has invested separate funds in the partnership, his share will contain a growing element of community property, unless the partnership distributes all earnings to the partners.

The spouse of a partner is not a partner just because he or she owns a portion of his or her spouse's interest in the firm. This matter will also be discussed later.

Authority of partners. UPA 9 provides that, in the absence of an agreement to the contrary, all partners have the power to bind the firm to contracts that are a part of the firm's ordinary business. In short, all partners have authority to participate in the operation of the business, and to do all things which need to be done in the course of day-to-day operations. In the absence of a partnership agreement, then, it can be said that all partners have express or implied authority in this area.

If the partners in their partnership agreement allocate express authority in the day-today management of the business in other ways, this division of authority must be made known to those who deal with the firm. Otherwise the individual partners will still have apparent authority in the day-to-day operations of the business. A person dealing with a partner may assume that the partner has authority to transact the normal business of the firm, unless he knows that particular partner has no such authority.

In defining the boundaries of the normal authority of a partner, it makes a difference whether the firm is a trading partnership or a nontrading partnership. A *trading partnership* is one that sells or manufactures goods—a partnership whose business is buying and selling goods, real estate, securities, etc. A *nontrading partnership* is one whose business is essentially the provision of services—medical care, accounting or bookkeeping service, legal advice and representation, and similar services.

An outsider may assume that a partner of either a trading partnership or a nontrading partnership has authority to:

1. Buy supplies for the firm for cash or on credit.
2. Hire and fire employees and agents within the scope of the firm's business.
3. Insure firm property.
4. Collect firm accounts receivable.
5. Pay firm accounts payable.
6. Adjust, compromise, or release claims by and against the firm, if they arise in the normal course of firm business.
7. Negotiate settlement of insurance claims of the firm.

In addition, one may assume that a partner of a nontrading partnership has authority to take on new clients for the firm, and to set the terms of payment for the services to be rendered to the client.

In addition to the apparent authority possessed by partners of both trading and nontrading firms, the partner of a trading partnership has apparent authority to:

1. Sell goods from the firm inventory, if held for sale in the normal course of firm business.
2. Make express warranties with respect to goods sold out of inventory.
3. Buy new inventory, for cash or on credit.
4. Borrow money in the firm name.

Any agreement among the partners which modifies this authority is not binding upon third parties unless they know of it.

In the making of day-to-day business decisions, the majority of the partners rules (UPA 18). The majority rules with respect to:

1. Limiting the authority of partners.
2. Defining the duties of partners.
3. Pricing policy.
4. Warranty policy.
5. Hiring and firing policy.
6. Financial policy.
7. Inventory and general purchasing policy.
8. Pay policy.
9. Other matters of short- and long-range business policy which do not alter the basic nature of the firm business.

Of course the partners may vary these rules by appropriate provision in the partnership agreement.

According to UPA 9 and 18, some things may not be done by fewer than all of the

members of the partnership unless the partnership agreement provides otherwise. These include:
1. Amending the partnership agreement.
2. Paying a partner a salary for his services.
3. Selling partnership real estate.
4. Selling partnership personal property not held for sale in the normal course of firm business.
5. Changing the basic nature of the firm business.
6. Admitting a new partner.
7. Making an assignment for benefit of creditors.
8. Filing voluntary bankruptcy for the firm.
9. Making a contract that would make continuation of the firm business impossible.
10. Making contracts of suretyship, guaranty, or indemnity.
11. Submitting a controversy involving the firm to arbitration.
12. Confessing a judgment.

UPA 11 provides that an admission by a partner in a controversy involving the firm binds the firm. If a partner admits that the firm is liable for a tort or a breach of contract, the firm has admitted liability. According to UPA 12, a notice about firm business given to a partner is notice given to the firm. Thus, a citation served properly upon a partner is service upon the firm; notice of a breach of warranty on goods sold by the firm given to one partner is notice to the firm; and notice of dishonor of commercial paper given to one partner is notice to the firm. A partner receiving any notice of this sort should communicate it to the other partners as soon as possible.

A partner who, while performing firm business, commits a wrongful act that causes loss or injury to a third party renders the partnership liable for the injury. Likewise, if a partner omits performance of an act he should have performed while on firm business and his omission injures a third party or causes him loss, the partnership is liable. Under UPA 13, a partnership is liable for torts committed by the partners while on firm business. However, the firm is not liable for torts committed by one partner against another partner.

UPA 14 provides that the partnership is liable to third parties damaged by the misapplication of funds received by a partner in the course of firm business. If a partner converts funds received by the firm to his own use and thereby damages a third party, that third party has a claim against the firm.

Duties of partners to the firm and to other partners. The partnership relationship is a fiduciary relationship. Partners owe fiduciary duties to each other and to the firm; they must not:
1. Use firm assets for personal use.
2. Compete against the firm in the firm's line of business.
3. Engage in other business activity which prevents devotion of most of their energy to the firm's business, unless they are silent partners.
4. Profit at the firm's expense, as by selling assets to the firm for more than fair value.
5. Divert a business opportunity which could be valuable to the firm to their own use without giving the firm an opportunity to take advantage of it.

UPA 21 provides that the partnership has a claim against a partner for any profits earned by him from personal use of firm assets.

Partners are of course under other duties to the firm. They must not:
1. Exceed their authority in dealing with third parties.
2. Neglect to inform other partners of notices they receive regarding firm business.

3. Be negligent in the conduct of firm business, both with respect to using due diligence in transaction of business and with respect to commission of negligent torts.

Liability of partners to the firm for violation of these duties. If a partner violates these duties to the firm and to his fellow partners, he becomes liable to the firm and to the other partners for the loss so caused. If a partner commits a tort while on firm business and causes the firm to suffer a loss, the partner is liable to the firm for the loss. If a partner exceeds his express or implied authority and thereby causes the firm to suffer a loss, the partner is likewise liable to the firm for the loss.

On the other hand, if a partner causes a loss to the firm by exercise of bad business judgment the firm will have no claim against him.

Rights of partners. UPA 18, 19, and 22 provide that partners possess several very important rights.

First: All partners have equal rights to participate in the management of the firm business, unless the partnership agreement provides otherwise. The management authority of the partners is equal even if capital contributions are unequal, unless otherwise agreed.

Second: All partners have equal rights to share firm profits and equal duties to share firm losses, unless otherwise agreed. Profits are not ratably divided according to capital contribution unless the partners have specifically agreed that they will be divided that way.

Third: All partners have the right to the return of their capital contributions upon liquidation of the firm if the firm has a surplus upon liquidation. If the firm has no surplus the partners share only those assets which remain after liquidation; there can be no full return of capital under such conditions. If firm liabilities exceed firm assets, the partners lose all capital contributions and may lose more besides, since they are personally liable for unpaid firm liabilities.

Fourth: All partners have the right to inspect the firm books whenever they wish. Should a partner be denied access to the books, he may go to court and demand a formal accounting of the firm's affairs from his colleagues.

Fifth: Should a partner lend money to the firm in excess of his capital contribution, he is entitled to interest upon the loan, payable from the date of the loan.

Sixth: Should a partner incur personal liability in the conduct of firm business or in the preservation of firm property, or should a partner use his personal funds in the course of conduct of firm business or preservation of firm property, that partner is entitled to indemnification from the firm.

Liability of partners to outsiders. UPA 15 provides that partners are jointly and severally liable upon firm obligations to outside creditors. It does not matter whether the obligation in question is a tort or contractual obligation.

Should a partner make a contract with a third party in his own name, intending to bind the firm, and should the third party not know that the contract is with a partnership, the partnership is not liable; the partnership is in essence an undisclosed principal. If the third party learns of the existence of the firm and the intent of the partner, he may then hold the firm liable. If the firm is not liable upon such a contract the nonsigning partners are not liable either.

If a partner signs or endorses commercial paper in his own name, not writing the name of the firm in his signature or endorsement, the firm has no liability upon the paper. This is because of the general rule that no party is liable upon commercial paper unless his name appears thereon, signed by the party himself or by an authorized agent.

Suits against partnerships. In order to properly enforce the joint and several liability of partners for partnership obligations, a plaintiff should name the partnership and all partners as defendants in his suit against the firm. A suit against the firm only gives the court jurisdiction over the firm and firm assets; adding the partners as defendants gives the court jurisdiction over the persons of the partners and over their personal assets.

Since the liability of partners is joint and several, it is not necessary to sue all partners along with the firm, but a judgment once obtained is good only against those partners named as defendants and properly served with citations.

It is also possible to sue one or more partners on a firm obligation without joining the partnership as a defendant. This is not normally done unless the firm is insolvent and there is no use in suing it.

Liability of an incoming partner. A new partner may be admitted only with the consent of all existing partners. One admitted, the new partner has all of the rights and duties of the old partners, with one important exception: UPA 17 provides that an incoming partner does not become personally liable upon existing firm liabilities when he joins the firm. Of course his capital contribution upon joining becomes a firm asset, and may then be taken by firm creditors. The new partner will only become personally liable upon firm liabilities incurred after he joins.

When a partner may leave the firm. Generally, a partner has the power to withdraw from his firm at any time. Whether or not he has the right to leave depends upon the provisions of the partnership agreement, if any. If there is no partnership agreement, the firm is a partnership at will, and the partners have the right to leave at any time. If there is a partnership agreement providing for a fixed term, a partner has no right to leave the firm until the fixed term expires, unless the agreement permits withdrawal upon the occurrence of certain events, upon the approval of the other partners, or upon other circumstances. The partner who unjustifiably leaves a partnership for a fixed term is guilty of breach of contract.

The partner who rightfully leaves his firm is entitled to all of his share in the firm net worth when he goes. He becomes a firm creditor for this amount, and may cause difficulties unless and until he is paid. The partner wrongfully leaving a partnership for a fixed term is also entitled to his share of the firm net worth, subject to deductions. The firm is entitled to retain the capital contribution of such a partner until the fixed term expires. In addition, the withdrawing partner is not entitled to be paid his share of the firm good will until the term expires. If the firm suffers damages because of the withdrawal for which retention of the partner's capital contribution and share of good will is inadequate compensation, the firm may claim additional damages. Thus, the partner leaving a partnership for a fixed term may subject himself to some problems.

Liability of outgoing partner to firm creditors. An outgoing partner remains liable upon firm obligations incurred while he was a partner. This is true even if the remaining partners agreed to relieve him of such liability when he left since no one other than the creditor may by contract discharge a debtor from a debt.

The outgoing partner must also be certain that those who customarily deal with the partnership know that he has departed; otherwise these persons could hold him liable as a partner by estoppel upon firm obligations incurred after his departure. The best way for the departing partner to deal with this possibility is for him to personally inform all regular clients, customers, or suppliers of the firm of his departure. He should also publish a notice of his withdrawal in a newspaper of the locality where the firm does business.

Assignment of a partner's interest in the firm. UPA 27 deals with the right of a partner to sell or otherwise assign his interest in his firm. A partner has the right to transfer his interest in the firm, but he has no right to make the transferee a partner; the assignee of a partner's interest therefore has no right to participate in the management or business of the firm. He also has no personal liability upon the firm liabilities.

The assignee of a partner's interest does have the following rights:

1. The right to the assignor's share of the firm profits.
2. The right to the assignor's share of the firm profits and surplus upon dissolution or liquidation.
3. The right to examine the firm books to the extent necessary to determine his rightful share of profits and surplus.

The assignee acquires no power to participate in the business. To an extent, the partners may ignore him. However, if the partners obstruct the assignee's right to examine the books—or if the assignee's share of profits declines because of what he says is mismanagement of the firm by the partners—he may go to court and ask for dissolution or liquidation of the firm.

The assignment by a partner of his interest in the firm may therefore create an awkward situation for both the remaining partners and the assignee. Since the assignee has no direct power to protect the safety of his investment but does have indirect power to do so, he may well be the unseen participant in all firm deliberations.

The assignability of a partner's share of the firm may be limited by the partnership agreement. The usual way of accomplishing this is for the partners to agree that, in case a partner wants to sell his interest, the partnership or the other partners will buy it for an agreed valuation. This valuation could be any reasonable sum, not necessarily the current value of the partner's share of the profits and surplus.

Rights of a creditor of a partner against the partner's interest in the firm. A creditor of an individual partner may not touch that partner's interest in specific firm assets. However, UPA 28 provides a mechanism whereby such a creditor may reach the interest of the partner in the firm if he can show that there is no other practicable way to realize his claim.

The creditor may file an action to obtain a charging order against the partner's interest in the firm. If the creditor can prove that he has a good claim, that the partner is truly a partner, and that he (the creditor) is unable to collect his claim in any other way, he will be given what he seeks.

The creditor is then in the position of a buyer of a partner's interest in the firm (an assignee). He is not a partner and is not liable for firm obligations, but he does have all the affirmative rights of assignees described above.

The creditor's rights as an assignee will terminate when he collects his claim against the debtor partner. The debtor partner may pay him off and obtain a release of the charging order, or the firm or some of the other partners may pay him off to be rid of him. Of course, if he is paid by the firm or by other partners, they have recourse against the debtor partner who originally created the situation.

When a married partner whose share in the firm is community property obtains a divorce, the divorce court may award his spouse part or all of the partner's share in the firm as part of the divorce settlement. The spouse then stands in the position of an assignee of her husband's interest in the firm. She needs no separate charging order to attain this position: the divorce decree fulfills that purpose. Her position is somewhere between that of a creditor of her ex-husband and that of a buyer of his interest. She was in essence a creditor before the division of the community property of the marriage, because of her claim upon some or all of that property, but her claim was settled with the actual property division. She is not really a buyer of her husband's interest, because she gave no consideration for it (in the sense that a buyer normally gives consideration for what he buys), and in the sense that he may not have voluntarily agreed to the transfer.

In any event, since her ex-husband now owes her no debt, the only way in which her interest as assignee may be eliminated is by buying her out or by admitting her as a partner.

Dissolution of a partnership. UPA 29 defines *dissolution* as applied to a partnership as "the change in the relation of the partners caused by any partner ceasing to be associated in the carrying-on as distinguished from the winding-up of the business." A reduction in the number of partners is the usual cause of a dissolution, but it is not the only cause.

UPA 30 provides that a partnership is not terminated by dissolution. Rather, it continues until its affairs are wound up. One must therefore keep in mind the great difference between dissolution on the one hand and winding-up or liquidation on the other. Dissolution may be the preliminary to liquidation, or it may merely signify a reshuffle in ownership of an ongoing business.

UPA 31 lists the possible causes of dissolution of a partnership. These are:

1. If the partnership was organized for a definite term or until a specified undertaking was completed, the expiration of the term or the completion of the undertaking.
2. If the partnership is a partnership at will, by the will of one of the partners. (Any partner may dissolve such a partnership at any time.)
3. By the mutual agreement of all of the partners who have not assigned their interests in the firm or had these interests subjected to charging orders.
4. When a partner is expelled from the firm in accordance with procedures contained in the Articles of Partnership.
5. When a partner chooses to breach the partnership agreement and cause dissolution.
6. If an event occurs which makes it unlawful to carry on the business, or for the members to carry it on in partnership.
7. The death of a partner.
8. The bankruptcy of any partner, or of the firm.
9. By a court decree under the provisions of UPA 32.

UPA 32 permits dissolution by decree of a court when:

1. A partner has been declared incompetent by a court, or is otherwise shown to be of unsound mind.
2. A partner has become incapable of performing his part of the partnership agreement.
3. A partner has been guilty of conduct which tends to affect prejudicially the carrying on of the business.
4. A partner willfully or persistently breaches the partnership agreement, or is otherwise guilty of such misconduct that it is not practicable to carry on business in partnership with him.
5. The business may only be carried on at a loss.
6. Other circumstances render a dissolution equitable (as where an even number of partners are deadlocked).

In addition, UPA 32 permits an assignee of a partner's interest to secure dissolution by court decree:

1. At any time after he becomes an assignee, if the firm is a partnership at will.
2. After expiration of the agreed term of years or the termination of the specified undertaking if the firm is not a partnership at will.

If dissolution is not to be followed by liquidation, a partnership may find itself suddenly obligated to pay the heirs of a deceased partner the value of the deceased's interest in the firm. This may require an expenditure which could cause considerable damage to the firm's financial position. If the cash necessary for the payment cannot be raised, the estate of the deceased partner will be in the position of an assignee of the deceased's interest. If partners will use some forethought in drafting their partnership agreement, this problem may be minimized.

It is possible for the partners to agree in advance that the value of a partner's share in the firm shall be considered to be a named sum. So long as this sum is reasonable, no court would question the valuation.

Also, since a partnership is deemed to have an insurable interest in the lives of its partners, it is possible for the firm to insure the lives of its partners. If the firm insures the lives of its partners for the agreed valuation of each partner's interest in the firm, the firm is assured that adequate cash will be available to pay to the estate of a deceased partner the value of that partner's interest in the firm.

If the firm's business is continued after dissolution, a new partnership essentially arises from the ashes of the old. The new firm possesses all of the assets of the old, and it also assumes all the liabilities of the old. Of course, dissolution of a firm absolves no one from liability to firm creditors.

Liquidation of a partnership. If after dissolution the remaining partners decide to liquidate the business, a notice of dissolution should be inserted in a newspaper in the county where the firm does business, in order to notify members of the public of the impending liquidation. Notice should also be given directly to all persons and firms who are regular customers and suppliers of the firm.

The reason for this is as follows: UPA 35 provides that the express and implied authority of partners to bind the firm to new contracts ends upon dissolution, unless the firm is continued under a new name. However, a partner still has apparent authority to bind the firm to new contracts with respect to persons who do not know of the dissolution. The newspaper notice is sufficient notice to those who have never dealt with the firm before, but personal notice is necessary to inform regular customers and suppliers. Partners of course still have express authority to make those contracts that are necessary to complete the performance of all outstanding firm obligations, and to bring about final liquidation.

The actual liquidation consists of turning all firm assets into cash and dividing this cash according to the priorities set by law. UPA 40(b) provides that the priority for distribution of assets upon liquidation is:

1. Payment of nonpartner creditors.
2. Payment of firm obligations to partners (other than capital and profits).
3. Repayment of capital contributions.
4. Division of profits.

The operation of these rules for distribution of assets will be illustrated by three examples.

Example 1: Liquidation of a solvent firm with a surplus. When Ames, Bass, and Cage decide to liquidate their partnership they have assets of $50,000. The firm owes $30,000 to outside creditors. It also owes Cage $5,000 on a loan he made to the firm. Capital contributions were Ames $4,000, Bass $3,000, and Cage $3,000. The partnership agreement said nothing as to how profits and losses were to be split. The steps in distribution of the $50,000 are as follows:

1. The outside creditors are paid $30,000, leaving $20,000.
2. The loan to Cage is repaid, leaving $15,000.
3. The capital contributions are returned, leaving $5,000.

4. This $5,000, being profit, is divided equally among the partners, since no other way of division is specified.

Example 2: Liquidation of a solvent firm which has suffered a net operating loss. Lang, Moss, Nunn, and Ott decide to liquidate their partnership, which has assets of $100,000. It owes outside creditors $70,000. Lang has lent the firm $10,000, which has not been repaid. Capital contributions were Lang $10,000, Moss $8,000, Nunn $7,000, and Ott $5,000. The partnership agreement specifies nothing about division of profits and losses. The steps in distribution of the $100,000 are as follows:

1. The outside creditors are paid $70,000, leaving $30,000.
2. Lang is repaid his $10,000 loan, leaving $20,000.
3. Since capital contributions were $30,000, but only $20,000 remains, the firm has suffered a $10,000 loss. Since losses are borne equally unless the partnership agreement says otherwise, each partner bears $2,500 of the loss. Thus:
    a. Lang receives $10,000 less $2,500, or $7,500.
    b. Moss receives $8,000 less $2,500, or $5,500.
    c. Nunn receives $7,000 less $2,500, or $4,500.
    d. Ott receives $5,000 less $2,500, or $2,500.

Example 3: Liquidation of an insolvent firm. Xavier, Yale, and Zorn liquidate their partnership. They have assets of $30,000. They owe outside creditors $36,000. No partner had lent the firm anything. Capital contributions were Xavier $16,000, Yale $8,000, and Zorn services. The $30,000 in assets must all go to the outside creditors, and it will be necessary to raise another $6,000 to go with it. Since the partners are personally liable for firm obligations, they must come up with this additional sum.

Original capital contributions were $24,000. Since there is a deficit of $6,000, the net loss is the $24,000 capital plus the $6,000 deficit, or $30,000. Since losses are borne equally, each partner's share of the loss is $10,000. Since Xavier's share of the loss is less than his original capital contribution, he is entitled to $6,000 from his partners. Yale's share of the loss is $2,000 greater than his capital contribution, so he owes an additional $2,000. Zorn of course owes $10,000, since he made no capital contribution. Thus, Zorn must contribute $10,000 and Yale $2,000 to the $30,000 in assets which remain. The $42,000 thus assembled will go $36,000 to the outside creditors and $6,000 to Xavier.

Marshaling of assets. Should an insolvent partnership decide to liquidate by filing bankruptcy, the partners in the firm should also file bankruptcy if they want to be discharged from their share of the firm obligations. This of course is due to the fact that the partners are personally liable for firm liabilities.

Since individual creditors of the partners would have access to the interest of each partner in the firm—and firm creditors would have access to individual assets of the partners—the rule of marshaling of assets is necessary in order to establish priorities. Firm creditors are therefore given prior access to firm assets, while individual partner creditors will only have access to those assets which remain after firm creditors are satisfied. Individual partners are given prior access to individual assets. Firm creditors have access only to those individual assets which remain after individual creditors have been satisfied. Had some of the partners been insolvent at the time of the bankruptcy, the solvent partners of course bear the burden of paying unsatisfied claims by firm creditors.

Suppose the firm of Pitt, Quagg, Ross, and Sims files bankruptcy, as do all of the partners. The firm had assets of $300,000. It owed outside creditors $266,000. It also owed Pitt $10,000 on a loan he had made to the firm. Capital contributions were Pitt $30,000,

Quagg $20,000, Ross $10,000, and Sims services. Not counting interests in the firm, Pitt had assets of $130,000 and liabilities of $170,000; Quagg had assets of $100,000 and liabilities of $50,000; Ross had assets of $100,000 and liabilities of $90,000; and Sims had assets of $40,000 and liabilities of $100,000. The liquidation of the firm would occur as follows:

1. The outside creditors would be paid $266,000, leaving $34,000.
2. Pitt's $10,000 loan would be repaid, leaving $24,000.
3. Since the paid-in capital was $60,000, of which only $24,000 remains, the firm suffered a loss of $36,000. Assuming the partnership agreement said nothing about how profits and losses were to be borne, the loss is borne equally, each partner bearing $9,000 of it. If all partners were solvent, Pitt would have $21,000 coming after liquidation, Quagg would have $11,000 coming, Ross would have $1,000 coming, and Sims would owe $9,000. Sims would add his $9,000 to the $24,000 in remaining assets, and the resulting $33,000 would be divided between Pitt, Quagg, and Ross as described above.

However, not all of the partners are solvent. After liquidation of the assets of the individual partners, Pitt owes his creditors $40,000. Quagg remains solvent, with assets of $50,000. Ross is solvent, with assets of $10,000. Sims is insolvent, with unpaid liabilities of $60,000. Sims is thus unable to bear his $9,000 share of the loss; the other partners must each bear $3,000 of it. Each must then bear $12,000 as his share of the firm loss. So, after adjusting for this, Pitt has $18,000 coming after liquidation; Quagg has $8,000 coming; and Ross now owes $2,000. Ross contributes $2,000 to the $24,000 in remaining firm assets, and this total is split $18,000 to Pitt and $8,000 to Quagg. Pitt's creditors, to whom he still owes $40,000, will claim his $18,000, plus the $10,000 loan repayment he received from firm assets. Since Quagg is solvent, he will retain his $8,000. Ross also remains solvent, while Sims's creditors hold the largest empty bag.

Limited partnerships. Limited partnerships in Texas are governed by the Texas Uniform Limited Partnership Act (ULPA), RCS 6132a. A limited partnership is a partnership composed of one or more limited partners and one or more general partners. A general partner is personally liable for firm obligations, as is the partner in a general partnership. The limited partner is not personally liable for firm obligations: he risks only his capital contribution to the firm. It must be remembered that a limited partnership must have at least one general partner; it is impossible for a limited partnership to exist which is composed solely of limited partners.

A limited partnership must have a written partnership agreement, which sets out the names of the limited partners and of the general partners. This must be recorded in the public records of the county in which the firm does business. Failure to record the agreement deprives the limited partners of the limitation of liability provisions of the ULPA and renders all partners liable for firm obligations (ULPA 2).

The limited partner labors under certain disabilities with respect to his participation in firm affairs. His name may not appear in the firm name; if it does appear in the firm name, he is a general partner. He also has no right to participate in the management of the firm; if he does, he becomes a general partner. On the other hand, the limited partner has the right to receive a share of the profits (an equal share with other partners, unless the partnership agreement says otherwise), the right to examine the books, and the right to dissolve the firm, as per ULPA 10.

The limited partner has no authority—express, implied, or apparent—to act for the firm in the conduct of firm business. In litigation against a limited partnership, a limited partner may not be sued as an individual.

According to ULPA 23, the assets of a limited partnership are distributed as follows upon liquidation:

1. Outside creditors.
2. Profits due to limited partners.
3. Capital contributions of limited partners.
4. Claims by general partners against the firm, other than for profits and capital contributions.
5. Profits due general partners.
6. Capital contributions of general partners.

Thus, limited partners have a liquidation preference over general partners with respect to profits and capital. In the event of the insolvency of a limited partnership, all losses will be borne by the general partners unless the loss is of so great a magnitude that the general partners cannot bear it all.

Joint stock companies. Joint stock companies are in some ways similar to corporations and in other ways similar to partnerships. This form of business organization is not too common, but examples of it do exist. It is a creature of statute in Texas: RCS 6132 et seq. govern this form of business organization.

The joint stock company is like a general partnership in that all owners of the business are jointly and severally liable for its obligations. A shareholder in a joint stock company is in many respects a partner in a partnership.

The joint stock company is like a corporation in several respects: First, the management authority is vested in a board of directors, elected by the shareholders. Only these directors have management authority—and this authority is limited to authority to choose and supervise officers. No shareholder or director has authority as an individual to bind the firm by virtue of his office. Thus, in a large sense, the shareholder in a joint stock company has liability without authority. Also, shares in a joint stock company are freely transferable. A shareholder may dispose of his interest in the firm without dissolving the firm. However, a shareholder does not get rid of his share of liability for firm obligations by disposing of his shares. On the other hand, a new shareholder does not assume personal liability for existing firm obligations merely by becoming a shareholder.

The joint stock company thus combines the corporate form of management and free transferability of shares with the personal liability of shareholders for firm obligations.

Business trusts. The business trust is sometimes called the Massachusetts trust, because this form of business organization first came into existence in Massachusetts and was most commonly used there.

Under this form of organization the investors, called beneficiaries, contribute their capital to elected managers, called trustees. The trustees own all assets in their names, and manage these assets upon behalf of the business. In those states which recognize the Massachusetts trust in its pristine form, the beneficiaries are not personally liable for firm obligations—only the trustees are, and only the trustees have authority to act for the firm in business transactions. In return for this grant of authority, the trustees assume personal liability for firm obligations. Thus, this form of organization provided the limited liability of corporate shareholders without the expensive formalities of the corporate form of business organization.

However, the Texas view of the business trust is not the conventional view. Because of the decision of the Supreme Court of Texas in the case of Thompson vs. Schmitt, 115 Tex 53 (1925), the business trust is in some ways a partnership. The beneficiaries are personally liable for firm obligations in this state, so the investor in a business trust is like a shareholder in a joint stock company. He has personal liability without authority to influence management. In fact, he is on balance worse off than the joint stock company shareholder, who has the right to elect company directors while the business trust beneficiary has no such right. Usually, the trustees of a business trust hold office permanently and are not subject to removal by the beneficiaries.

Obviously, business trusts are not very common in Texas. There is no really practical reason for organizing a business in this form today.

Joint ventures. A joint venture is a cooperative venture of two or more persons in order to accomplish a specific purpose. Joint venturers are not generally businessmen; they are much more likely to be speculators or the like.

Joint venturers buy real estate for speculation purposes, or engage in other such one-shot ventures. Since they do not operate a business as co-owners for profit, they are not general partners in a partnership. However, the courts generally apply the law of partnerships to joint ventures so far as is practicable. Thus, the authority of joint venturers to bind all of the venturers to contracts is generally governed by the law of partnerships, as are the division of profits, the liability of the joint venturers in case of loss, etc.

Real estate investment trusts. Since amendments to the Internal Revenue Code provide favorable tax treatment for certain investors in real estate, the Texas legislature enacted RCS 6138A, permitting the resurrection of the business trust, with limited beneficiary liability, for investors in real estate. It is now possible to organize a business trust for real estate investment purposes which is not subject to the regulation of a corporation but which insulates the trust beneficiaries from liability for the debts of the trust.

41

Formation and Powers of Corporations

Formation and Organization of Corporations

A corporation is an artificial person created by state law. It has many of the rights and privileges of an individual, including the right to own property and the right to sue and be sued. It has one great advantage over individuals, in that it may be immortal.

Most of the Texas statutory law governing corporations is found in the Texas Business Corporations Act (TBCA). Other federal and state statutes also govern corporations, including—on the state level—the Miscellaneous Business Corporations Act, the Uniform Commercial Code, and the Texas Securities Act. On the federal level, certain corporate activity is regulated by the Federal Securities Act and the Federal Securities and Exchange Act.

Corporations also make "law" to govern themselves. Their articles of incorporation are analogous to a constitution: they contain the fundamental law of the organization. The bylaws are the equivalent of the statutory law of the corporation, dealing with matters that are not so fundamental as those contained in the articles of incorporation.

Most corporations conducting business in Texas are incorporated under Texas state law. However, there is no absolute requirement that this be the case. Persons desiring to form a corporation may incorporate it under the laws of any one of the fifty states. The provisions of state business corporation acts vary considerably as to the leeway given corporate managements to govern the corporation as they see fit. They also vary considerably with respect to such things as reports required. In these regards, Delaware is the most liberal state in the nation. Many of the large corporations of America consequently are incorporated under the law of Delaware. Unless the organizers of a corporation expect their creation to grow into a large enterprise with many shareholders, however, there is not much advantage to be gained by incorporating outside the state of Texas.

The process of organization begins with the drafting of articles of incorporation for the proposed corporation; this should be done with the assistance of an attorney. The selection of a corporate name is also important. The name must not be deceptively similar to the name of any existing corporation licensed to do business in Texas. The corporate name must contain the words "company," "corporation," "incorporated," or abbreviations thereof, so that anyone dealing with the firm will be notified that he may be dealing with a corporation.

If it is very important that a certain name be given the corporation, its organizers may write the secretary of state and request that that name be reserved for the corporation in process of organization. If the name is available—that is, if it is not deceptively similar to the name of an existing corporation—the secretary of state will reserve it for a period of 120 days. This guarantees its availability if the articles are filed during that 120-day period.

Articles of incorporation. The articles must be submitted to the secretary of state in duplicate. They must be signed by the incorporator. TBCA 3.01 provides that only one incorporator is required for a Texas corporation; any natural person eighteen years of age or older may be an incorporator. An organization—such as a corporation, partnership, association, trust, or estate, regardless of residence or domicil—may also act as incorporator.

The articles of incorporation must contain, as per TBCA 3.02:
1. The name of the corporation, keeping in mind the considerations mentioned above.
2. The period of duration, which may be perpetual.
3. The purpose or purposes, which may be stated as "the transaction of all lawful business for which corporations may be incorporated under the Texas Business Corporations Act." (The use of this broad purpose clause is advisable, because corporations may only transact the business permitted by the purpose clause. The wider the latitude permitted by this clause, the fewer the potential problems.)
4. The capital stock structure of the corporation, including:
    a. Number of shares authorized.
    b. Classes of shares authorized, if any. Shares may be all of one class, or shares of two or more classes may be provided for.
    c. Par value of each class of shares authorized, or a statement that some or all shares are no-par shares.
    d. If classes of shares are authorized, the number of shares each class authorized.
    e. If classes of shares are authorized, the privileges, limitations, and rights of holders of each class of shares.
5. A statement that the corporation will not commence business until it has received for its shares at least $1,000 in money, labor done, or property actually received.
6. Any limitations upon preemptive rights of shareholders.
7. Any provision limiting cumulative voting rights of shareholders.
8. Any provision permitting a close corporation and providing for management of the corporation as a close corporation.
9. The post office address of the corporation, and the name of the corporate agent at that address.
10. The number of directors comprising the original board, which may be comprised of one or more persons.
11. The name and address of each incorporator.

The articles may in addition contain provisions relative to the internal affairs of the corporation, but it is generally advisable to include such matters in the by-laws. It is much easier to amend the bylaws than to amend the articles.

Prepayment of franchise tax. The 1979 session of the Texas legislature amended Taxation Code 12.06 to provide that incorporators must pay a Texas franchise tax deposit of $100 to the comptroller of public accounts. The nature of the franchise tax will be discussed later in these materials; for now it suffices to say that the tax is essentially a tax upon the privilege of a corporation to exist.

The secretary of state may not issue a certificate of incorporation for a newly organized corporation until proof of payment of this deposit is furnished. The deposit is a prepayment of a portion of the corporation's initial year tax liability. It is not subject to refund; if the corporation is dissolved soon after it is formed, this deposit is lost.

The certificate of incorporation. If the submitted articles of incorporation are in order and if the required fees are paid, the secretary of state must issue a certificate of incorporation. He may refuse to do so if the corporate name is deceptively similar to the name of an existing corporation licensed to do business in Texas, if the articles do not comply with legal requirements in some way, or if the required fees are not paid.

The corporation is born when this certificate is issued: its legal existence begins at that time. The certificate is conclusive evidence that all of the formalities of organization have been complied with. No party other than the state may attack or challenge the legality of the organization of the corporation after the certificate of incorporation has been issued (TBCA 3.03 and 3.04).

Effect of defective incorporation. If persons do business as a corporation without trying to organize their corporation, no corporation exists. The business is a sole proprietorship or a partnership, depending upon the number of owners, and the owners are personally liable for business obligations. If the owners are in the process of organizing their corporation, but have not yet sent articles in to the secretary of state, the same rule applies—no corporation exists.

If the owners have sent in their articles and a certificate of incorporation has been issued, the corporation exists, even if the articles were defective and no certificate of incorporation should have been issued. If the articles have been sent in but no certificate of incorporation has been issued because the secretary of state determined that the articles were defective, there is no corporation. The defects must first be corrected and the articles resubmitted.

If the articles have been submitted and no reply has been received from the secretary of state, it can be argued that a de facto corporation exists, because the incorporators have done everything required by law in order to organize the corporation. If there is no defect in the submitted articles, TBCA 3.03 provides that the secretary of state must issue the certificate of incorporation.

Corporation by estoppel. A person dealing with a business on the assumption that it is a corporation, when in reality it is not incorporated, may have difficulty holding the owners of the business liable to him as partners. The owners may argue that, since the claimant assumed that he was dealing with a corporation, he should be treated as though he truly was so dealing. The outcome of such a case will depend upon several factors, however, as the following examples illustrate.

1. Deuce makes a contract to supply goods to an organization he believes is Spade Corporation. He deals with Clubb, who says he is the president of the corporation. The "corporation" breaches the contract. Deuce does some investigating and finds out there is no Spade Corporation, so he sues Clubb for damages for the breach. Clubb's defense: He is not liable because, since Deuce made the contract with Spade Corporation, he cannot now deny that Spade Corporation exists. No effort was ever made to organize Spade Corporation. Deuce should win, because in a sense Clubb defrauded Deuce by saying that he was the president of the corporation. Clubb most assuredly did not have clean hands here.

2. Trey makes a contract with Hart Corporation, dealing with Diamond, who says he

is the treasurer of the corporation. The contract is of a type which a treasurer has authority to make. Diamond has been told by Knave and Jack, supposedly the president and executive vice-president of Hart Corporation, that all incorporation formalities have been complied with and that the corporation now exists and is in business. The corporation breaches; Trey investigates and finds out that no articles have been filed for Hart Corporation. Trey sues Diamond for breach. Diamond's defense is that, since both he and Trey assumed that the corporation existed when the contract was made, it would be wrong to hold him personally liable for the breach of it because he had acted in good faith—and besides, Trey admitted the existence of the corporation by contracting with it. Diamond might win here, though he was somewhat negligent for taking the word of Knave and Jack with respect to the true status of the corporation.

The doctrine of corporation by estoppel will not permit owners of a nonexistent corporation to escape personal tort liability. Since a tort claimant did not voluntarily choose to get involved with the organization, his dealings with the owners do not stop him from proving that the corporation does not exist.

Initial meeting of directors. The process of organizing the newly created corporation is carried a step farther when the directors named in the articles hold their first meeting. At this meeting, two essential items of business will be transacted: bylaws will be adopted and officers will be elected. The directors may also wish to take action with respect to contracts made by promoters on behalf of the corporation before incorporation and to take action relative to outstanding stock subscriptions.

The bylaws. The bylaws are the "statute law" of the corporation. According to TBCA 2.23, they are to be enacted and amended by the directors, unless the articles grant the power to enact and/or amend to the shareholders. Usually, power over the bylaws is left to the directors. The bylaws will contain provisions such as:

1. The titles, powers, terms, etc. of the corporate officers.
2. The time and place of the annual meeting of corporate shareholders.
3. The number, term of office, and classification of directors.
4. The time and place of regular meetings of the directors.
5. Quorum requirements for directors' meetings, if different from TBCA requirements.
6. Procedure for calling special meetings of the board of directors.
7. Authorization, if any, for an executive committee of the board of directors, and an enumeration of the powers of such a committee.

The officers. TBCA 2.42 provides that there shall be a president, one or more vice-presidents, a secretary, a treasurer, and such other officers as the directors may provide for. One person may hold more than one office, except that the offices of president and secretary may not be held by the same person.

Promoter contracts. Promoters are persons who act to get the corporation organized and functioning. They often make contracts on behalf of a corporation before the organization process is complete. They may, for instance, make contracts for rental of office space, purchase of office equipment, or acquisition of business inventory.

Principles of agency law govern the liability of the parties to these contracts. The promoter making a contract for an as yet nonexistent corporation is in the position of an agent for a nonexistent principal. Since no agent may bind a nonexistent principal, the corporation is not liable upon these contracts; the promoter is liable as the principal, unless the contract absolves him from liability. However, if the contract absolves the promoter from liability, it is no contract at all: the law regards it as a continuing offer made by the third party to the corporation, which the corporation may accept or reject after it comes into existence.

The corporation is not liable upon such contracts until it ratifies them. The directors of the corporation, at their initial meeting, may well consider whether or not to ratify these preincorporation contracts. When the corporation ratifies, the promoter is discharged from personal liability. When the corporation votes not to ratify, the promoter has the option of performing himself or of being liable for damages for breach.

Nonaction by the directors upon such contracts is not ratification, unless the corporation accepts the benefits provided for in the contract. Thus: Promoter Deuce contracts with Spade to rent office space for Ace Corporation. The Ace directors do not ratify the contract, but Ace sets up shop in the rented premises. Ratification by estoppel has taken place; Ace cannot now deny that it has ratified, because it has taken advantage of the privilege provided in the contract.

Subscription agreements. There is no point to organizing a corporation if no one will buy shares in it. If no one buys shares, there is no capital and no funds with which to do business. One of the duties of promoters is to make certain, as nearly as possible, that the necessary capital will be forthcoming. This is done by solicitation of subscription agreements from would-be shareholders. Since a nonexistent corporation has no shares which can be sold, the promoters are essentially soliciting offers to buy corporate shares when they solicit subscriptions.

TBCA 2.14 provides that a subscription is in essence a firm offer to buy shares in the future corporation. The subscriber may not revoke his offer for six months after it is made. The acceptance occurs when the articles of the corporation are filed with the secretary of state, if a list of the subscriptions to be accepted is filed along with the articles. Included in the list must be the name of the subscriber, his address, the number of shares he subscribed to, and how much (if anything) he has paid upon his subscription.

Any subscription not so filed is rejected. Once the certificate of incorporation is issued, then, the corporation may proceed to collect payment from the subscribers. Subscriptions are payable upon demand of the directors; in order for the necessary capital to be accumulated as soon as possible, it behooves the directors to make the demand at this first meeting.

Once the corporation has come into existence, subscriptions may still be solicited. However, such subscriptions are not firm offers—they are merely ordinary offers which are open until accepted or terminated. Such subscriptions must be accepted by resolution of the board of directors. Any pending subscriptions should be accepted at the first meeting of directors.

Solicitors of subscriptions must be aware of the fact that too wide a solicitation will be a violation of Texas and federal legislation regulating sale of securities by a corporation; this will be discussed in more detail later. Briefly, solicitation of more than thirty-five individuals for subscriptions is a violation of the Texas Securities Act, unless the securities being subscribed to are first registered with the Texas Securities Board. Solicitation of subscriptions from individuals in other states (other than sophisticated investors) will be a violation of the Federal Securities Act unless the securities are registered with the Federal Securities and Exchange Commission.

Subscribers do not become shareholders just because their subscriptions are accepted. The shares must be paid for in full before the subscriber is entitled to the status of shareholder. Recognition of a subscriber as a shareholder before his shares are fully paid for will result in imposition of liability upon both the shareholder and the directors who voted to recognize the subscriber as a shareholder if the corporation should become insolvent before the shares are paid for.

Powers of Corporations

The powers of Texas corporations are not unlimited. The limitations on corporate powers are contained in several sections of the TBCA and of the Miscellaneous Business Corporation Act (MBCA). The general grants of power to Texas corporations are also contained in the TBCA.

Several types of corporations are governed by special legislation. Among these are nonprofit corporations (charitable, religious, benevolent, and similar organizations), professional corporations (corporations organized to practice law, medicine, dentistry, etc.), banks, insurance companies, savings and loan associations, and abstract and title insurance companies. We shall not consider these special sorts of corporations here.

Forbidden business combinations. TBCA 2.01B(3) forbids the organization of corporations to carry on two types of business combined, as follows:

1. Raising cattle and meat packing, although the combination of operating feed or feeding lots and meat packing is permitted.
2. Producing oil and operating oil pipelines.

Restrictions of powers of corporations to own land. Texas corporations do not have unlimited powers to acquire and own land. MBCA 4.04 provides that no Texas or other corporation whose main purpose of business is the acquisition or ownership of land shall be permitted to acquire land in Texas by purchase, lease, or otherwise.

No corporation of any sort may acquire Texas land, except to enable the corporation to do business in this state, or when the land is purchased in the due course of business to secure payment of a debt (MBCA 4.01). Thus, land acquisition is permissible in connection with carrying on the corporate business, so long as the business is not land acquisition. If a corporation acquires land not necessary for the operation of its business, it must dispose of such land within fifteen years of acquisition (MBCA 4.02).

Should a corporation hold onto surplus land for more than fifteen years, MBCA 4.06 authorizes the attorney general of Texas to bring suit against the corporation to require forfeiture of the land in question to the state of Texas.

A major exception to the prohibition against corporations organized for the purpose of acquiring and holding land is provided by MBCA 4.05. Corporations may be organized for the purpose of leasing, purchasing, selling, and subdividing real estate within the city limits of incorporated localities and two miles beyond their corporate limits, or in unincorporated cities, towns, and villages within two miles of the courthouse or depot nearest the center of the locality. Real estate development corporations are thus not forbidden.

General corporate powers. TBCA 2.02 grants Texas corporations twenty broad powers:

1. The power to endure forever, unless the articles limit the duration of the corporation.
2. The power to sue and to be sued in the corporate name.
3. The power to have a corporate seal.
4. The power to acquire and own land, subject to the limitations discussed above.

5. The power to dispose of any of its property or assets.
6. The power to lend money and otherwise provide assistance to its employees, but not to its officers or directors.
7. The power to acquire and own securities of all sorts, both of governments and of other corporations, including the right to vote shares of other corporations.
8. The power to reacquire its own securities, subject to the limitations contained in TBCA 2.03, to be discussed later.
9. The right to borrow money, issue debt securities, mortgage its assets, and otherwise make contracts.
10. The power to lend money for corporate purposes, to make investments, and to take mortgages and the like upon real estate as collateral.
11. The power to carry on its business both within and without the state of Texas.
12. The power to elect or appoint officers and agents, to define their duties, and to fix their compensation.
13. The power to adopt and amend bylaws for the internal government of the corporation.
14. The power to make charitable contributions.
15. The power to transact any lawful business which the directors find will be in aid of government policy.
16. The power to indemnify officers or directors for expenses incurred in connection with legal actions in which these persons became involved because of their service as officers or directors, except those actions in which the officer or director in question is found guilty of negligence or misconduct; and the power to purchase liability insurance for such officers and directors.
17. The power to pay pensions and to establish pension plans, stock option plans, profit-sharing plans, and other benefits for officers, employees, or both.
18. The power to be an incorporator of another corporation and to be a member of a partnership, joint venture, or similar enterprise.
19. The power to dissolve voluntarily.
20. The power to exercise all powers necessary for the conduct of the corporate business.

The articles of incorporation may limit these powers. In the absence of such limitations, though, the powers of the Texas corporation are wide indeed.

The defense of ultra vires. When a corporation performs an act which is beyond the power granted to it by its articles or by state law, it performs an ultra vires act. A corporate act which is ultra vires is not illegal. TBCA 2.04 states that the corporation may not use the fact that an act is ultra vires as a defense in any sort of legal proceeding.

A shareholder may file suit to enjoin the performance of a corporate ultra vires act. The suit must involve all of the parties to the contract and, if the court finds it equitable to enjoin performance of the act, it may award damages to any party adversely affected.

The corporation itself, or its shareholders in a shareholder derivative suit (the nature of which will be discussed later), may sue officers or directors for damages caused by their causing corporate performance of ultra vires acts.

The attorney general of Texas may file suit to dissolve a Texas corporation for repeated performance of ultra vires acts. He may also sue to prevent the transaction of ultra vires business, or to force divestment of real property held in violation of the applicable provisions of the MBCA discussed earlier.

Right of the corporation to purchase its own shares. The right of a corporation to purchase its own shares (granted by TBCA 2.02) is somewhat limited by the provisions of TBCA 2.03.

So long as the purchase will not render the corporation insolvent or cause liabilities to exceed assets, the corporation may purchase its own shares for the following four purposes:

1. To eliminate fractional shares (which may come into existence because of small stock dividend distributions, etc.).
2. To collect or compromise indebtedness owed by or to the corporation (in order to settle litigation out of court, in order to avoid litigation, etc.).
3. To pay dissenting shareholders who have exercised their appraisal and payment rights granted under the TBCA.
4. To purchase or redeem redeemable shares.

Normally, a corporation may not purchase its own shares for other than the above purposes unless it has earned surplus sufficient to cover the purchase, the directors approve the purchase, and there are no preferred stock dividends in arrears.

Purchase of a corporation's own shares out of capital or reduction surplus is possible if the articles of incorporation permit it. It is also possible for a corporation to purchase its own shares out of capital surplus if the directors and two-thirds of all shares vote in favor of the purchase. Such purchased shares are considered to be treasury stock. Treasury stock is issued and outstanding stock, but it of course has no voting rights and no right to dividends. It is not carried upon the corporation's books as an asset.

On the other hand, it may be reissued by the corporate directors at their discretion. It cannot be given away: it must be sold for consideration, although the consideration may be less than par value, or less than the declared value of no-par shares. The realized consideration should bear some reasonable relationship to the true value of the shares, however.

The directors may also choose to cancel treasury shares. When this is done, these shares are no longer issued and outstanding. They become instead authorized but unissued shares.

42

Corporation Finance

Investment Securities

Financing the Corporation: Capital Structure, Dividends, and Taxation

Only part of the capital structure—the equity security structure of the corporation—must be spelled out in the articles of incorporation. However, it must be remembered that there are two legitimate ways for corporations to raise capital: through the sale of equity (ownership) and through borrowing.

Since all Texas corporations have inherent authority to borrow money, it follows that they have the power and the right to issue debt securities without provision for these being made in the corporate articles, and without consultation of shareholders.

For short-term borrowings corporations may issue commercial paper. Such paper usually takes the form of short-term promissory notes. Short-term funds may also be raised through the sale of trade acceptances, which are drafts drawn by the corporation upon itself and accepted by itself. The obligations assumed by corporate sellers of such paper are essentially the obligations of the maker of a note or of the acceptor of a draft; these have been discussed in the material on the law of commercial paper.

Bonds. For long-term borrowing, the corporation will issue bonds. In the process of issuing bonds, a trust indenture will be drawn up granting to the bondholders a mortgage upon named corporate assets. A trustee will be appointed under the indenture to represent the bondholders in dealings with management, and to look out for the interests of the bondholders in general.

Bonds may be registered, in which case the owner for most purposes is the person registered upon the corporate books as the owner. They may also be bearer, in which case the corporation keeps no records as to their ownership. The owner of the piece of paper which is the bond is the owner of the bond for all purposes.

The bondholders, of course, are corporate creditors; they therefore have no say in corporate management. They are, however, entitled to be paid interest upon their investment. The interest becomes due and payable no matter whether the corporation earns a profit or not. If interest payments get so far into default that the trustee loses patience with corporate management, he may of course take steps to foreclose upon the collateral provided in the trust indenture. Another possibility in case of default is that the trustee and other creditors could file for a reorganization of the corporation under Chapter XI of the Federal Bankruptcy Act, which could result in the bondholders becoming shareholders at the expense of existing shareholders.

Debentures. These are unsecured debt securities. Debenture holders are essentially unsecured creditors, in about the same position as holders of corporate notes and trade acceptances. Because debenture holders have no mortgage upon any corporate assets, the corporation must pay a higher interest rate upon these securities.

Convertible debentures are often marketed. These are convertible into a specified number of corporate shares after the passage of a specified length of time. By issuing convertible debentures, corporate management will make the debenture more salable, and it may get rid of the obligation to pay interest upon these securities early if the stock performs well enough to make conversion profitable. Bonds may also be made convertible. However, convertible debentures are more common than convertible bonds.

Bonds may be marketed without registration under Federal or Texas securities legislation if they are sold to financial institutions and other institutional investors. Debentures are more likely to require registration because they are more often sold to the general public. However, if the debenture issue is sold to institutional investors, no registration will be necessary.

Preferred stock. Preferred stock is an equity security. The owner of it is a part owner of the corporation. Preferred stock is almost always par value stock. It may carry voting rights or it may not. Its preference is either with respect to assets upon liquidation, with respect to dividends, or both.

A preferred stock which is preferred as to assets upon liquidation will entitle its holders to be paid the full par value of their shares upon liquidation before common shareholders are paid anything. Preferred stock is not automatically preferred as to assets upon liquidation; it has no such preference unless the articles of the corporation so provide.

The usual preference of preferred stock is preference as to dividends. The shares will be entitled to an annual dividend, usually stated as a percentage of par value. The right to this dividend may be:

1. Cumulative, or
2. Cumulative if earned, or
3. Noncumulative.

A cumulative preferred stock is entitled to its dividend for each accounting period, whether the corporation earned profits during that period or not. The directors need not declare and pay the preferred dividend at the end of any accounting period, but if the preferred dividend is not declared and paid, no dividend upon the common stock may be declared and paid. In addition, the right to receive the dividend cumulates, so that if dividends upon a cumulative preferred stock are in arrears the arrearage must be made up before the common shareholders may be paid a dividend.

For example: Ace Corporation has outstanding an 8 percent cumulative preferred stock. Ace declares and pays dividends quarterly when it pays dividends. Ace declared and paid the normal dividend on this preferred every quarter up to and including the last quarter of 1978. Business became so bad thereafter that no dividend of any sort was declared and paid during 1979. No dividend was declared or paid for the first quarter of 1980. However, business has so improved by June of 1980 that management would like to declare a dividend at the end of the second quarter of 1980. In this situation, the cumulative preferred has received no dividend for five quarters. Therefore it must be paid a dividend for six quarters before the common shareholders could be paid a dividend. The required dividend per quarter would be 2 percent of par value, so a 12 percent dividend to the preferred will be necessary before the common will be entitled to anything.

Holders of a cumulative-if-earned preferred are entitled to a dividend for accounting periods during which the corporation earns enough earned surplus to cover the dividend. If the dividend is not paid during an accounting period, it cumulates. But if the corporation does not earn enough during an accounting period to cover the dividend, the right to it is lost.

For example: Deuce Corporation declares and pays dividends upon an annual basis. It has outstanding a 6 percent cumulative-if-earned preferred. The last time a dividend was paid on this was at the end of 1974. The corporation operated at a loss during 1975 and 1976. It earned profits in 1977 which were barely sufficient to cover a preferred dividend, but management saw fit not to declare and pay the dividend. The company operated at a loss in 1978, and paid no dividend. It earned large profits in 1979, so management would like to pay a dividend. In this situation, the preferred must be paid a 12 percent dividend if the common is to receive anything, since the preferred dividend for 1977 was earned but not paid. The preferred is entitled to no dividends for 1975, 1976, and 1978 because these were not earned.

Holders of a noncumulative preferred are not entitled to a dividend at the end of an accounting period unless the directors see fit to declare it. Their only preference is this: If any dividend is to be paid to common shareholders at the end of an accounting period, the perferred shareholders must first be paid their specified dividend. However, if the preferred receives no dividend for an accounting period, its right to that dividend is lost.

A preferred stock may also be participating or nonparticipating. A nonparticipating preferred is entitled only to its specified dividend for an accounting period, and no more. The holders of a participating preferred are entitled to participate in any dividend the common shareholders receive that is larger than the specified dividend of the preferred. The formula for determining the method of participation must be spelled out in the articles of incorporation since there are many possible means of determining it.

A preferred stock is cumulative unless the articles specify that it is not. A preferred is nonparticipating unless the articles specify the fact that it is participating and the method of determining participation.

Preferred stock may or may not be voting stock. Preferred shareholders may be allowed to elect a certain number of directors themselves, or their votes may be counted along with the votes of the common shares in the election of directors. Even though the preferred may be nonvoting, it will still have voting rights with respect to extraordinary matters; this will be discussed in the section on shareholders' rights.

Common stock. Common stock may be par-value or no-par stock. It may also be voting stock or nonvoting stock. Par-value stock must be initially sold by the corporation for at least par value. This is also true of par-value preferred. No-par common stock must be sold for at least the consideration determined by the board of directors. The required consideration for no-par shares is usually determined by the board of directors at its initial meeting.

A corporation must issue at least one class of voting common stock; it must therefore have at least two classes of common stock if it is to issue a nonvoting common. Common stock has no absolute right to be paid a dividend. Payment of dividends to common stock is within the discretion of the board of directors, as we will see later.

Allocation of corporate control. Corporate insiders may well want to rig things so that they are certain to control the corporation—even if, perhaps, they have not contributed a majority of the capital. There are many ways of accomplishing this, some of which we shall now explore.

One method is to issue voting stock to the insiders, and to sell debt securities to other investors. This has the advantage that only the insiders have voting rights, but the disadvantage that the outsiders are creditors who can make trouble if their interest payments are not made on time.

Another method is to issue voting common stock to the insiders, and to issue nonvoting preferred stock to the outsiders. This has the advantage of eliminating the necessity to pay interest to bondholders, but the preferred would probably have to be cumulative—or at least cumulative-if-earned—to be marketable. A holder of a noncumulative nonvoting preferred really is not much preferred, as knowledgeable investors are aware. The obligation to pay cumulative dividends to preferred shareholders could become onerous to insiders. The preferred could also be made more appealing to investors by putting into the articles a provision that preferred shareholders become entitled to elect a minority of the directors if they receive no dividends for a specified period of time.

Still another method is to issue voting common stock to the insiders and to issue nonvoting common to the outsiders. Theoretically this offers every advantage to the insiders. Practically, how good an investment is a nonvoting common? There are two possible variations upon the latter theme, both of which share the same advantages and disadvantages of nonvoting common. The corporation could issue many shares of a low par-value common to insiders and fewer shares of a high par-value common to outsiders, giving each share of each class one vote for directors. This assures the insiders a majority of the votes. But, if the company has outstanding a $1 par-value class of common and a $100 par-value class of common, a buyer of the first gets 100 votes per $100 invested, while a buyer of the second gets one vote per $100 invested. What outsider would want to take a hand in this game, considering how the deck is stacked? A similar method is to issue a class of common with, for example, 100 votes per share to insiders and another class with one vote per share to outsiders. There is no requirement of "one share, one vote" in the TBCA; but, again, the class of shares reserved for outsiders might be hard to market.

There are two other methods of assuring insiders control of a corporation that do not require the issuance of two or more types of securities, but do require that the insiders control a majority of the voting power of the corporation. There are the voting trust and the pooling agreement.

The members of a *voting trust* transfer their shares to a trustee under the provisions of a written agreement. The trustee then votes the shares and distributes the dividends ratably to the trust members. TBCA 2.30A requires that a copy of the trust agreement be filed at the corporate headquarters. It also provides that the maximum duration of the trust shall be ten years, subject to renewal. If the trust members own a majority of the voting power of the corporation, then the trustee has a majority of the votes and thus complete, or almost complete, control.

A *pooling agreement* is a written contract between shareholders under which the signatories agree to vote their shares as the majority of the signers direct. According to TBCA 2.30B, a copy of the pooling agreement must be filed at the corporate headquarters; the maximum duration of the agreement shall be ten years, subject to renewal.

Under a pooling agreement, the shareholders who are members retain legal title to their shares. They also have some say in how their shares are voted, which of course is not the case with the voting trust, when the trustee decides how to vote by himself.

Some basic corporate accounting. Texas corporations may not make distributions to shareholders unless surplus exists out of which the distribution may be made. Dividends on common stock may only be paid out of earned surplus. Dividends on preferred stock may be paid out of capital surplus if the preferred is cumulative preferred. Stock dividends to either preferred or common shareholders must usually be covered by capitalizing either earned or capital surplus. Distributions in partial liquidation must be made from either reduction surplus or capital surplus.

Earned surplus cannot exist unless the corporation has operated profitably, and some of the earnings have been retained in the business. Capital surplus is created in two basic ways. When par-value shares are issued by the corporation for more than par, the excess consideration above the par value is credited to capital surplus. When no-par shares are issued by the corporation for more than the value set by the board of directors, the excess consideration is credited to capital surplus. Also, when no-par shares are sold for the value determined by the board of directors, the board has the right to allocate up to 25 percent of the consideration so received to capital surplus.

Capital surplus has several important uses: It may serve as a source of dividends for cumulative preferred stock, and may justify the payment of stock dividends to common shareholders. Also, it may be used to eliminate a deficit in the earned surplus account by debiting capital surplus the desired amount and crediting that amount to earned surplus.

Reduction surplus is created by reducing the stated capital of the corporation. This may be done in three ways:

1. By reducing the par value of par-value shares. This would require an amendment to the articles of incorporation.
2. By reducing the stated value of no-par shares. This requires a resolution of the board of directors and approval of a majority of the outstanding shares at a meeting of shareholders.
3. By cancellation of treasury shares held by the corporation. This requires only a resolution of the board of directors.

Distributions to shareholders from reduction surplus are not considered to be dividends: they are in a sense a return to shareholders of a part of their investment. Such distributions are called distributions in partial liquidation. The required procedure for authorizing these will be discussed later.

Revaluation surplus arises when an asset which has appreciated in value is revalued on the firm books to reflect the appreciation. The legitimacy of this from an accounting viewpoint is questionable. In any event, such surplus may not be considered to be earned surplus; therefore it cannot be used to cover payment of dividends upon common stock.

It should be noted that not all states follow the rule that dividends may be paid to common shareholders only out of earned surplus. There are some states that permit payment of dividends to common shareholders out of capital surplus, so long as the payment does not render the corporation insolvent. Still other states permit payment of dividends during a year in which the corporation has earned a net profit, even though there is a deficit in the earned surplus account. Generally, such dividends must be declared and paid during the year after the profits are earned—that is, if an earned surplus deficit exists.

Cash dividends. As discussed earlier, a Texas corporation may declare and pay dividends to common shareholders when it has earned surplus sufficient to cover the dividend. It may pay a dividend to preferred shareholders when it has either earned surplus or capital surplus sufficient to cover the dividend.

When the corporation is legally able to declare and pay a dividend, it is not legally obligated to do so. If management sees fit to retain earned surplus for reinvestment in the corporate business, it may do so. However, if the corporation does not pay dividends when it is legally able, TBCA 2.38C provides that one-third of the outstanding shares may petition the directors to make a written justification of their dividend policy. When such a demand is made, the directors must comply.

If the shareholders feel that the justification of dividend policy by the directors is weak, they may file suit in a Texas district court to compel the payment of dividends. It is very difficult for shareholders to win such a suit, since courts are very unwilling to second-guess management policy in such areas. However, if the reason for nonpayment of dividends is to oppress minority shareholders, or to reduce the income tax liability of the majority shareholders, the courts may provide relief.

A dividend is declared by resolution of the board of directors. The dividend is declared to be payable on a certain date to shareholders of record as of some earlier date. Thus, the dividend may be declared on May 15 and be made payable on June 30 to shareholders of record as of June 15. Anyone who owned shares of the declaring corporation of the class for which the dividend was declared on June 15 will be entitled to the dividend. A shareholder who sold his shares on June 17 would still be entitled to the payment, but anyone buying shares in the company on June 17 would not be entitled to payment.

A declared cash dividend becomes a corporate liability when declared. The corporation may not revoke the declaration of a cash dividend, unless the declaration was illegal (usually due to lack of the required surplus).

The declaration of a dividend may be attacked by court action of a shareholder when:
1. The surplus required to cover it does not exist, or
2. The dividend violates the dividend preference of preferred shareholders, or
3. The dividend discriminates as between holders of the same class of shares. All shareholders holding the same class of shares must be treated alike.

When such an attack is justified, the court will enjoin the payment of the dividend.

Property dividends. Occasionally a corporation will make a dividend payable in property rather than in cash. The property might be the product produced by the corporation; it might be shares in another corporation owned by the declaring and paying corporation; or it may consist of any other kind of property.

The legality of a property dividend is determined by the same rules which govern declaration and payment of cash dividends.

Stock dividends. A stock dividend is a dividend payable in the stock of the declaring company. It is lawful for a Texas corporation to declare and pay a stock dividend when it has sufficient earned or capital surplus to cover the payment of the dividend, or when it owns sufficient treasury stock so that the entire dividend may be paid by distributing this.

When a stock dividend is paid out of authorized but unissued shares, then, there must be a credit to the capital stock account entered upon the corporate ledgers. When par-value shares are distributed, the capital stock (paid-in capital) account must be credited with the par value of the shares issued. The earned surplus or capital surplus account will be correspondingly debited, depending upon the resolution of the directors declaring the dividend. When no-par value shares are distributed, the directors must vote to debit the appropriate surplus account an appropriate sum, and to credit paid-in capital with that sum.

When a stock dividend is paid out of treasury stock, no change in the paid-in capital account is necessary, because there was no adjustment made to the account when the treasury stock was acquired. Thus, a corporation may declare and pay a stock dividend out of treasury stock when it has no surplus.

42/ Corporation Finance

Stock dividends are declared in the same way as are cash dividends. The dividend is usually declared as a percentage—for example, a 10 percent stock dividend. When a corporation declares a 10 percent stock dividend, each holder of the class of shares upon which the dividend was declared receives ten new shares for each hundred old shares that he owned.

The shares may not be directly issued to the shareholders, however. The corporation may choose to issue one right per share of stock held by a shareholder, each right being worth one-tenth share of stock. The shareholder could then redeem his rights for shares. A holder of, say, five shares, would receive five rights. Since five rights would be worth only one-half share of stock, the shareholder would either have to acquire another five rights in order to entitle himself to a new share or sell his five rights to someone else so that the buyer could accumulate enough rights to entitle himself to a share. Of course, the value of a right depends upon the stock dividend percentage declared.

The declaration of a stock dividend by the board of directors is not irrevocable. The board may revoke the declaration at any time before the payment date.

Stock splits. A stock split is a distribution of shares to the shareholders that does not involve a distribution of treasury stock and does not require the making of any change in the stated capital account. A stock split may thus be declared when the corporation has no surplus.

A stock split is usually declared in terms of a ratio—two for one, five for one, three for two, five for four, etc.

The only way to split par-value shares without distributing treasury stock or crediting paid-in capital with the par value of the shares distributed is by splitting the par value of the shares themselves. This, of course, requires amending the corporate articles.

No-par value shares may be split by resolution of the board of directors, so long as there are enough authorized but unissued shares to cover the split. In the process of declaring the split, the directors simply change the stated value of the no-par shares in order to adjust for the issuance of many new shares.

Distributions in partial liquidation. The corporate directors may decide to distribute cash to common shareholders out of capital or reduction surplus. Such distributions are called distributions in partial liquidation.

In order to authorize this, a resolution of the board of directors is necessary. The resolution must then be approved by two-thirds of all the shares of the corporation, plus two-thirds of all the shares in each class of shares issued. Of course, if reduction surplus is to be used as the source of payment, that surplus must first be created by following proper procedure.

Even if proper procedure is followed and a distribution in partial liquidation is authorized, it will not be lawful if (TBCA 2.40):

1. It will impair the ability of the corporation to conduct its business, or
2. Dividends on cumulative preferred stock are in arrears, or
3. The distribution would reduce net assets below preferential payments required upon voluntary dissolution (to preferred shareholders with liquidation preferences, perhaps), or
4. Full disclosure is not made to shareholders as to the source of the payment.

Taxation of corporations—basic federal income taxation. A corporation, being a legal entity, is also normally subject to federal income tax. The tax is levied upon net profits, according to the following rate schedule:

On the first $25,000 of net profits—17 percent.

On net profits exceeding $25,000 and less than $50,000—20 percent.
On net profits exceeding $50,000 and less than $75,000—30 percent.
On net profits exceeding $75,000 and less than $100,000—40 percent.
On all net profits over $100,000—46 percent.

If net profits are taxable to the corporation at all, they are taxable whether or not they are paid out to the shareholders as dividends. It is possible for some net profits not to be taxable if, for instance, they are earned outside the United States and taxed by the host nation, but the complexities of determining taxable corporate net profits are beyond the scope of this work.

Dividends paid by the corporation to its shareholders are taxable to the shareholders as ordinary income, except that the first $100 of dividends received by an individual during a taxable year are excluded from taxable income. This is the reason why it is so often said that corporate profits are subject to double taxation. The profits are taxable to the corporation during the year earned, and they are again taxable to the shareholder during the year in which he receives them in dividends.

The existence of the double taxation of funds paid out in dividends by corporations is of little concern to the person who invests in stocks for income. He is counting upon dividends for a portion of his living expenses. To be sure, the dividends are taxable, just as income earned upon the job is. For such investors the income tax is perhaps unpleasant, but inescapable. For the wealthier investor who is not dependent upon dividend income to meet a portion of his living expenses, the existence of the double taxation is a cause for concern. Most individuals wealthy enough to own substantial amounts of stock are in the 50 percent tax bracket. For a person whose earnings as a practitioner of a profession or as a corporate executive place him in these tax brackets, dividends are not all that welcome. These individuals, when they serve as corporate directors, have a rather strong incentive not to vote to pay out corporate profits in dividend form.

For personal income tax purposes, it makes more sense to the large shareholder for the corporation to distribute its earnings in the form of stock dividends. The advantage of the stock dividend, income tax-wise, is that it does not become taxable unless and until the stockholder sells it and realizes a profit. The taxable profit is figured as in this example: Ace owns 1,000 shares of Zilch Corporation stock for which he paid $10 per share. Two years later Zilch declares and pays a 10 percent stock dividend, so that Ace now owns 1,100 shares of Zilch. This dividend will not become taxable to Ace until he sells those shares. If the fair market value of Zilch stock was $20 per share as of the day that it went ex-dividend—that is, as of the first day that a buyer of Zilch shares would not be entitled to the 10 percent dividend on the day of distribution, the basis of the dividend stock would be $20 per share. If Ace holds the dividend for fifteen months and then sells those 100 shares for $30 per share, he would realize a long-term capital gain of $10 per share. This would then be taxable to Ace during the year in which he sold the shares. But, since long-term capital gains are taxable at much lower rates because only 40 percent of them count as taxable income, Ace has done well with respect to taxes on his stock dividend. Had Ace sold all 1,100 of his Zilch shares at once, he would be considered to have paid $12,000 for his 1,100 shares—the $10,000 he paid for the original 1,000 shares and the $2,000 market value of the 100 dividend shares as of the day he became entitled to them. He would then realize a long-term capital gain of $18,000, less brokerage commissions and expenses—$9,000 of which would be taxable.

The tax aim of the investor in stock is to realize long-term capital gains when selling out. One must now hold stock for twelve months before selling it if the profit is to qualify for long-term capital gain treatment. Retention of earnings and reinvestment of them in the corporate business is one very good way to make the market value of shares grow—the "open sesame" to the long-term capital gain.

If it were that simple, the fairly wealthy person would have at his disposal a handy and virtually foolproof method of reducing his tax liabilities: he could simply incorporate his economic activities and see to it that his corporation paid virtually no dividends. As the net worth of his enterprises increased, the value of his stock in the enterprise would increase, so that some day he could sell out at a fat profit which would be all long-term capital gain and thus virtually 60 percent tax-free.

This will not work, however. Congress has rammed two very stout plugs into these potential loopholes: the personal holding company tax and the accumulated earnings tax.

Personal holding companies. A personal holding company is in a sense an incorporated personal investment program, or an incorporated mutual fund with a handful of investors. Such incorporated ventures are not illegal, but they must pay out most of their earnings in dividends. If they do not, the government will tax them very heavily.

The corporate earnings will be taxed once to the corporation when earned, and they will be taxed a second time that year, whether paid out in dividends or not. If distributed to shareholders, they are taxed to the shareholders at normal personal income tax rates. If not distributed to shareholders, they are subjected to a 70 percent penalty tax payable by the corporation.

The personal holding company penalty tax applies only to undistributed personal holding company income of a personal holding company. IRC 541 provides that a corporation is a personal holding company if:

1. At any time during the last half of the taxable year more than 50 percent in outstanding value of the corporation's stock was owned by less than six individuals, and
2. At least 80 percent of the corporation's gross income was personal holding company income.

With respect to the first test, most close corporations would qualify as personal holding companies. After all, if the corporation has ten or fewer shareholders more than 50 percent of the shares must be owned by less than six persons. A corporation with many more than ten shareholders might also fit the classification. A company might have a thousand shareholders, but if five of these own more than 50 percent of the stock the company would be a personal holding company.

Also, for purposes of this test IRC 544 provides that a person is deemed to own not only the corporate shares standing in his name, but also those standing in the names of his partners and his family—including spouse, brothers and sisters of the whole or half blood, lineal descendants (children, grandchildren, etc.), and lineal ancestors (parents, grandparents, etc.). Thus it does little good to split up personal holding company stock among your close relatives, since the IRS considers it to be all yours for purposes of determining whether or not the company is a personal holding company.

The second qualification is the one that matters for the close corporation. IRC 543 defines personal holding income to include:

1. Dividends.
2. Interest.
3. Royalties.
4. Rents, unless rental income less depreciation and expenses of generating the income equal 50 percent of corporate gross income, which they probably will not unless the corporation is essentially in the property rental business.

Banks, insurance companies, and small loan companies are specifically exempt from the personal holding company provisions of the internal revenue code. Companies whose primary business is the rental of personal property are also exempt. Companies whose main business is collection of royalties upon minerals, oil, gas, or copyrights may also be exempt if complex qualifications are met.

A corporation engaged partially in the investment business and partially in another type of business may or may not be considered to be a personal holding company, depending on the relationship between the gross income generated by investments as against the gross income generated by the other business or businesses. If the active business generates 40 percent or more of corporate gross income, the company is not a personal holding company. This is true even if the active business operates at a loss and the investments generate large profits. The personal holding company penalty is assessed against undistributed personal holding company income; this means that, in order to avoid the penalty, the management of such a company should distribute all such income to the shareholders as dividends.

This discussion of personal holding companies is of necessity incomplete. Competent professional advice is essential for management with problems in this complex and complicated area.

The accumulated earnings penalty. If a corporation accumulates earnings for no reasonable business purpose, IRC 532 permits the IRS to assess accumulated earnings tax against the earnings unreasonably accumulated. The rate of tax is 27.5 percent of the first $100,000 of unreasonably accumulated earnings accumulated annually, and 38.5 percent of any excess.

Earnings accumulated for a reasonable business purpose are not subject to the tax; in any event, a corporation may keep up to $100,000 in retained earnings without being subject to this tax. This does not mean that the first $100,000 in retained earnings in any year is automatically exempt. It simply means that a company will not be subject to this tax if it has retained earnings of $100,000 or less.

Whether the corporation will be subject to this tax depends upon whether the accumulation of earnings is for a reasonable business purpose, or simply for the purpose of tax avoidance by its shareholders.

Reasonable accumulation of earnings may be for such purposes as:
1. Expansion of the business.
2. Acquisition of another business enterprise.
3. Retirement of a bona fide business debt, such as a bond issue, debenture issue, commercial paper issue, etc.
4. Accumulation of working capital to expand inventory or something of the sort.
5. Making of new business-related investments.

Unreasonable reasons for such accumulations include:
1. Making loans to shareholders.
2. Making loans to friends or relatives of shareholders.
3. Making loans to corporations in unrelated businesses that are controlled by the shareholders of the accumulating business.
4. Making investments unrelated to the main company business.
5. Providing against "unreasonable" hazards—the IRS and, ultimately, the courts having the final say as to what sorts of hazards are unreasonable to provide against.

A personal holding company is not subject to this tax. A corporation with many shareholders is less likely than one with fewer shareholders to be assessed this tax because an accumulation of earnings for tax avoidance purposes would be less likely (unless a handful of large shareholders control the corporation). On the other hand, an investment company or a holding company will be very suspect with respect to its retained earnings, even if it has too many shareholders to qualify as a personal holding company.

Multiple corporations. Prior to the passage of the Tax Reform Act of 1969 there were tax advantages to be gained by separately incorporating small portions of a corporate business in order to take advantage of the low tax rates on the first $25,000 of corporate income. The rules were complex, but a large business earning net profits of $200,000 per year, for instance, could under some circumstances be divided into ten small corporations, each earning net profits of $20,000 per year; the tax savings were substantial. Congress plugged the loophole in 1969, however, gradually phasing the advantage of the multiple corporation out of existence. The advantage ended in the taxable year 1974.

It is still legitimate to divide a business into multiple corporations when the division serves a useful business purpose. However, the IRS will ignore multiple corporations when it deems that the only purpose for the multiplicity of corporations is tax avoidance.

Subchapter S corporations. The management of a small corporation may choose to arrange things so that the corporation does not pay any federal income taxes; the profits of the corporation are then taxable directly to the shareholders as if the corporation were a partnership. This way of arranging matters may be especially advantageous to the owners of a small business who earn most of their income from the business. The profits of the business are taxable only once—to the shareholders.

It should be noticed that all profits of a Subchapter S corporation are taxable to the shareholders, not only those profits distributed as dividends. Thus, tax considerations need not be taken into account in deciding whether or not to declare and pay dividends. On the other hand, since shareholders are taxed upon their proportionate share of the corporate profits, the corporation will need to distribute enough earnings to the shareholders so that the individual income taxes may be paid.

There is one area in which payment of dividends makes a difference as to shareholder tax liability. If the corporation uses a fiscal year which does not end on December 31, undistributed profits are taxable to the shareholders for the calendar year during which the last day of the corporate fiscal year fell. Dividends are taxable to the shareholder for the calendar year during which they were received. Only those shareholders are liable for tax on undistributed profits who are shareholders on the last day of the corporate fiscal year.

IRC 1371 spells out the requirements which must be met by a corporation for it to qualify as a Subchapter S corporation.

1. It must be organized under the laws of the United States, or of a state or territory thereof.
2. It must not be a subsidiary of another corporation.
3. It must not have more than ten shareholders. For computing this, shares owned by a husband and wife are considered to be owned by one shareholder, unless each spouse owns shares separately and no shares are owned jointly. With respect to shares jointly owned by persons other than married couples, each co-owner counts as a shareholder.
4. All shareholders must be individuals or estates of deceased persons. If any shareholder is a corporation, partnership, trust, or the like, the corporation does not qualify for Subchapter S tax treatment.
5. It must have only one class of stock outstanding.
6. It must not earn more than 20 percent of its income through passive investments—

dividends, interest, rent, royalties, and so on—subject to some complex qualifications.

7. At least 20 percent of its income must be earned within the confines of the United States.

In order to avail itself of Subchapter S status, the corporation must notify the IRS during the first month of the taxable year for which the status is claimed, or during the month before that. All of the shareholders must agree to this election, and their written consent must be filed with the IRS.

Once the status is achieved, it is kept until it is lost. The status may be lost by:

1. An election to revoke the Subchapter S status, which must be agreed to in writing by all shareholders. Such a revocation will not be effective for the taxable year within which it is filed, unless it is filed during the first month of that year.

2. The corporation becomes ineligible for Subchapter S status. This could be caused by a corporation's becoming a shareholder or its acquiring more than ten shareholders, by the issue of a second class of stock, or in many other ways.

A voluntary election to revoke Subchapter S status may be changed again the next year, if the shareholders wish. If the corporation involuntarily is deprived of the status, however, it loses it as of the first day of the year during which the disqualification occurred, and may not reapply for Subchapter S status until five years after the disqualification. The reapplication will not be granted unless at least 50 percent of the applying shareholders were not shareholders at the time of the involuntary disqualification. It is thus not too advisable to lose Subchapter S status through disqualification.

Investment Securities

The law on investment securities is contained in Article Eight of the UCC. Included in the category of investment securities are those types of paper normally traded by securities brokers. The most common types are stocks and bonds, but also included in the category are debentures, warrants, rights, and similar securities. Commercial paper is not a type of investment security; nor are commodity future contracts, currency future contracts, or other contracts of this type.

All investment securities are negotiable. A bona fide purchaser of an investment security will thus have rights similar to those of a holder in due course of commercial paper, or to those of a person who acquires a document of title by due negotiation.

Investment securities may be in registered or bearer form. The ownership of a registered security is a matter of record upon the books of the issuing corporation. It is transferable only upon the endorsement of the owner and delivery to the transferee. A bearer security is transferable by delivery only. The issuing corporation keeps no records as to the ownership of bearer securities.

In the United States and in most English-speaking countries, stock and securities derived from stock—rights, warrants, and so on—are in registered form. Bearer shares are not used. In civil law nations, however, bearer corporate stock is not uncommon. Bonds, debentures, and similar securities may be in either the registered or the bearer form.

Original issue of investment securities. A corporation may not issue investment securities without proper authorization. If, however, an issuer negligently permits unauthorized securities to get into circulation, the issuer will be liable to any good-faith purchaser for their value.

A counterfeit investment security is of course void and obligates the issuer to nothing, as per UCC 8-202(3). A security illegally issued by a governmental issuer is void, unless there has been substantial compliance with requirements of issue, or unless the issuer has received consideration for the issue. A security illegally issued by a private issuer will be to an extent valid in the hands of a good-faith purchaser not knowing of the defect in it, as per UCC 8-202(1) and (2).

Corporate bylaws authorize only certain individuals to sign investment securities. A genuine security bearing a forged signature is invalid, as is a security bearing an unauthorized signature, unless the signature was put there by a person authorized by the issuer to sign securities or by an employee of the issuer entrusted with the proper handling of the security (UCC 8-205).

Transfer of investment securities. Registered securities are transferable by endorsement of the owner and delivery. Bearer securities are transferable by delivery only. A blank endorsement on a registered security will render it transferable by delivery only. A special endorsement will make the security deliverable to a named person; a special endorsement on a bearer security will not change the bearer nature of it, but will provide an indication of ownership (UCC 8-310). A blank endorsement may be converted into a special endorsement, according to UCC 8-308(2).

When a bearer security is delivered without endorsement a good transfer has taken place. When a registered security is delivered without endorsement the transferee becomes the owner and may compel the transferor to endorse, as per UCC 8-307. An endorsement without delivery is not a transfer (UCC 8-309). An endorsement of a security need not appear upon the security itself; it may appear upon a separate paper. An endorser may transfer only a partial interest in the security. Such an endorsement will be effective to transfer the partial interest. UCC 8-308, besides containing these provisions with respect to endorsement, declares what persons may be proper endorsers. A proper endorser may be:

1. The owner as specified by the security itself or by a special endorsement, or
2. The executor, administrator, or guardian of the owner, if the owner is dead, incompetent, etc., or
3. The survivor of named joint tenants or tenants by the entireties, if some of the co-owners have died, or
4. An authorized agent of the owner, or
5. An authorized fiduciary.

The owner of the security may transfer it as he pleases, unless a restriction upon transfer imposed by the issuer is noted conspicuously upon the security. A restriction upon transfer does not bind a transferee who does not know of it (UCC 8-204).

Bona fide purchasers. The transferee of a security normally obtains all of the rights of his transferor. A bona fide purchaser acquires the security free of adverse claims. He may get better title than his transferor did if the transferor got the security by defrauding a former owner, for example. A bona fide purchaser is one who gives value for the security, purchases in good faith, and knows of no adverse claim.

A transferee from a bona fide purchaser gets the rights of a bona fide purchaser, unless he has been a party to fraud or illegality involving the security or is a former owner of that security who was not a bona fide purchaser at the time he had it (UCC 8-301 and 8-302).

Effect of forged or unauthorized endorsement. The purchaser of a security bearing a forged endorsement gets no title to it. The person whose endorsement was forged may reclaim the security from any subsequent purchaser, even a bona fide purchaser. But, if a bona fide purchaser obtains registration of the security in his name, the rights of the person whose endorsement was forged—or the true owner of the old certificate—are cut off; he will have no recourse against the bona fide purchaser (UCC 8-311).

Notice to purchaser of adverse claim. A purchaser of a security has notice of an adverse claim and is thus not a bona fide purchaser if:

1. The security is endorsed "for collection," "for surrender," or the like. Such restrictive endorsements of course limit free transferability.
2. The security is in bearer form, but has a written notation (such as a special endorsement) naming someone other than the transferor as owner.
3. The transferee knows that the transferor is a fiduciary who is breaching his fiduciary duty (as by using the proceeds of the transfer for his own use).
4. The purchaser is buying the security more than one year after the date for surrender or redemption of the security.
5. The purchaser is acquiring the security more than six months after a date set for payment of money against presentment or surrender of the security.

These provisions are found in UCC 8-304 and 8-305.

Warranties of a transferor. A transferor of a security does not warrant that the issuer will honor the security, as per UCC 8-308(4). He does make three warranties to his transferee under UCC 8-306(2), however:

1. That the transfer is effective and rightful,
2. That the security is genuine and has not been materially altered, and
3. That he knows of no fact that might impair the validity of the security.

Request for registration by transferee. The transferee of a bearer security obtains complete ownership by obtaining the security. But a transferee of a registered security must become registered upon the books of the issuer as the true owner before he acquires most rights of ownership.

With respect to registered bonds, ownership on the books of the issuer is necessary in order to collect interest. With respect to stock, the following rights belong to the registered owner:

1. The right to be paid dividends.
2. The right to vote.
3. The right to inspect the corporate books.
4. The right to a ratable share of assets upon liquidation.
5. The right to bring shareholder derivative suits.

In order to become the registered owner, the transferee must send his certificate to the issuer or its transfer agent. A new certificate will then be issued in his name, and his name will be added to the roster of shareholders.

UCC 8-316 provides that a transferee may require a transferor to furnish proof of authority to transfer. Such proof will be necessary when the transferor is not the owner named on the face of the certificate. If the transferor is an agent, for example, the issuer may require proof of the agency before making the transfer.

UCC 8-402 provides that the issuer may require proof from the transferee that the endorsements on the certificate are effective. A guarantee of the signature of the transferor will certainly be required. The guarantor of the signature must be a responsible party in the eyes of the issuer. UCC 8-312 provides that the guarantor of a signature warrants that, at the time of signing:

1. The signature was genuine, and
2. The signer was an appropriate person to endorse, and
3. The signer had legal capacity to sign.

The issuer may also require assurance of the authority of an agent to sign if the endorser was an agent, or of the appointment or incumbency of a fiduciary to sign if the endorser was a fiduciary. The transferee may furnish a guarantee of the endorsement, although the issuer may not require the furnishing of such a guarantee. According to UCC 8-312(2), a guarantor of the endorsement makes all of the warranties of a guarantor of signature, as well as a warranty that the transfer is rightful in all respects.

Duty of issuer to register. UCC 8-401 provides that the issuer must register a transfer of a security if:

1. The security is endorsed by an appropriate person or persons, and
2. Proper assurance is furnished that the endorsements are genuine and authorized, and
3. Issuer had no duty to inquire into adverse claims, or, having had such a duty to inquire, has done so, and
4. Any applicable law relative to collection of taxes (taxes on stock transfers, primarily) has been complied with, and
5. The transfer is to a bona fide purchaser or is in fact rightful.

If the transfer would be wrongful, the issuer will not transfer. Also, no transfer will be made if:

1. The certificate is counterfeit, or
2. An essential signature is a forgery, or
3. The certificate is part of an overissue, or
4. The transfer violates a conspicuous restriction upon transfer, or the transferee is not a bona fide purchaser and knows of the restriction, or
5. The security has been completed without authorization or materially altered.

In the case of unauthorized completion or material alteration, the security should be registered according to its original terms. The security completed without authorization should be registered to a person with bona fide purchaser rights as completed, unless overissue will result. A certificate that is part of an overissue will not be registered, unless only a portion of it is overissue, in which case it will be registered to the extent that it is not overissue.

A bona fide purchaser of a certificate that cannot be registered due to overissue, material alteration, or something of the sort will be entitled to monetary damages from the issuer equal in value to the value of the security he thought he had purchased.

Duty of issuer to inquire into adverse claims. UCC 8-403 provides that the issuer must inquire into the existence of an adverse claim when a written notice of adverse claim is received long enough before a request for reregistration of the security in question to give the issuer a reasonable opportunity to act upon it. Any notice of adverse claim must be accompanied by an address of the claimant to which communication may be directed. These notices are generally filed by a person claiming that a security was lost, stolen, or wrongfully transferred under the provisions of UCC 8-405(1).

The issuer must conduct the inquiry in a reasonable manner. It may simply notify the adverse claimant by registered or certified mail at the address furnished with the notice of claim that the disputed security has been presented for reregistration, and that the issuer will reregister unless the claimant furnishes a restraining order or injunction from a proper court within thirty days of the mailing of the notification; or unless the claimant posts an indemnity bond in an amount requested by the issuer, sufficient to protect the issuer against any claims by a bonafide purchaser for wrongful refusal to register.

If the issuer required a transferee to furnish a copy of a will, trust agreement, partnership agreement, or corporate bylaws in order to prove the authority of an endorser to endorse, the issuer is charged with knowledge of everything in the document relative to the authority of the parties concerned. Possession by the issuer of a copy of such a document will impose upon it a duty to inquire about an adverse claim when the possibility exists that a signature on the document might be unauthorized. In the absence of a filed notice of adverse claim or issuer possession of a document, the issuer need not inquire into the extent of a fiduciary's authority.

The issuer's duty to inquire into an adverse claim does not require it to act as judge in a dispute over the ownership or rightfulness of transfer of the shares or security. If there is no doubt of the validity of the adverse claim and no doubt that the transferee is not entitled to be registered as owner of the security, the issuer may refuse to register. If there is doubt, the issuer may simply notify the claimant of its intent to transfer unless the claimant posts an indemnity bond or obtains a court order enjoining the transfer.

Issuer liability or nonliability for registration. A registration is rightful if the endorsements upon the security are in order and no notice of adverse claim has been filed, or if the issuer has properly inquired into a notice of adverse claim.

When the issuer transfers a security to someone not entitled to it the true owner is entitled to receive a like security from the issuer or—if issuance of a like security would cause overissue of the security—the monetary equivalent of the security, as per UCC 8-404. However, if the true owner has not filed a notice of adverse claim with the issuer as of the time of transfer, the true owner loses his right to the security and the transfer is rightful so far as the issuer is concerned, as per UCC 8-405(1).

Issuer's duty on notice of claim received before application of transfer received. As discussed earlier, when the owner of a certificate loses it, has it stolen from him, or feels that it has been wrongfully taken from him—or when it has been destroyed—he must file notice of this fact with the issuer as soon as possible. The owner will normally ask the issuer to replace the shares. Issuer must replace the shares upon request if:

1. No application for transfer has been received, and
2. The owner posts a proper bond with the issuer, and
3. The owner complies with any other reasonable request by the issuer.

These requirements are found in UCC 8-405(2). If an application for registration has already been received, the issuer may treat the notice of loss as a notice of adverse claim and proceed accordingly. If, however, the notice is received after registration has been granted, the notice is too late; the issuer must simply tell the owner that the security has been registered and the notice is too late.

The bond requirement protects the issuer against the possibility of the old security turning up in the hands of a bona fide purchaser. If the old security is presented for registration by a bona fide purchaser after a new security has been issued to the old owner, the issuer must reregister as per UCC 8-405(3), unless the reregistration would result in overissue. The bona fide purchaser in that case would be entitled to the monetary value of the security, payable out of the posted indemnity bond. If the issuer reregisters the security, the bond becomes payable to the issuer as consideration for the issue.

In such a case the issuer may also recover the replaced security from the old owner (since he really was not entitled to replacement if it is now owned by a bona fide purchaser), or from anyone he transferred it to except a bona fide purchaser.

Action against purchaser based upon wrongful transfer. UCC 8-315 provides that a person wrongfully deprived of a security may recover the security from any subsequent purchaser except a bona fide purchaser if the security has not been reregistered. If the security has been transferred on a forged or unauthorized endorsement, it may be recovered even from a bona fide purchaser before reregistration.

If it has been transferred upon a forged or unauthorized endorsement, and a bona fide purchaser has obtained reregistration, the security may not be recovered from a bona fide purchaser, although it may be recovered from a person without bona fide purchaser rights (UCC 8-311). A reregistered security may be recovered from a non-bona fide purchaser. Reregistration will not "wash the security clean."

Whenever the issuer reregisters a security bearing a forged or unauthorized endorsement, the reregistration is wrongful as against the true owner, unless the true owner was negligent about reporting the loss or similarly negligent.

Warranty of a presenter for registration or payment. A person presenting a security for reregistration or payment warrants to the issuer that he is entitled to the registration or payment. The bona fide purchaser who receives a new reregistered security warrants only that he has no knowledge of any unauthorized (or forged) endorsement, as per UCC 8-306(1).

Thus, a nonowner of a bond who obtains payment of it from the issuer is guilty of breach of warranty and can be made to return the money. However, a bona fide purchaser of a stock certificate bearing a forged endorsement who does not know of the forgery and who obtains a new certificate in his name is not guilty of any breach of warranty.

Liability of guarantor of endorsement. The guarantor of endorsement makes his warranties to all persons dealing with a security in reliance upon the guarantee. Thus, if a guaranteed endorsement is not genuine and an issuer or transferee or agent of either suffers a loss as a result, the guarantor may be held liable for the loss.

Duties of authenticating trustees, transfer agents, and registrars. UCC 8-406 provides that when an issuer delegates its responsibilities with respect to issue, transfer, and registration of securities to agents such as registrars and transfer agents, these have the same obligations with respect to the holders of securities as the issuer as regards the function the issuer has appointed the agent to perform. Notice to such an agent is notice to the issuer when relevant to the function performed by the agent.

Brokers. A buyer and seller of a security are not likely to deal face to face, unless the security is one issued by a small corporation whose shares are not publicly traded. Trades in securities in publicly held corporations are more likely to be handled through brokers, professional dealers in securities.

The usual procedure is that a seller informs his broker that he wishes to sell his 100 shares of Zilch Corporation. A buyer wishing to buy 100 shares of Zilch Corporation informs his broker that he wishes to buy. If Zilch is listed on a stock exchange, there are so many would-be sellers and buyers of Zilch Corporation stock that trades in it are taking place upon the floor of the stock exchange during virtually every minute of the day. Orders to buy and orders to sell are transmitted to the exchange floor by brokers as received, and personnel on the floor match up buy and sell orders very quickly.

If Zilch is not listed on an exchange but is publicly traded, the buy and sell orders will be matched by the brokers through the facilities of the over-the-counter market. If your would-be seller of Zilch and our would-be buyer both use the same brokerage firm, the firm, acting as agent for both seller and buyer, consummates the transaction. If no customer of the seller's broker has put in an order to buy 100 shares of Zilch, the seller's broker must contact other brokers in search of a buyer. When a broker having a potential buying customer is located, the transaction is consummated.

A person who buys and sells securities through a broker may ask his broker to procure registration of the securities he buys in his name, and to have the securities delivered to him (the buyer), or he may choose to let the broker retain the certificates.

Duties of brokers when customer takes delivery of securities. A seller of a security through a broker must deliver the sold security, properly endorsed, to the broker. The seller's broker then must deliver the security, properly endorsed, to the buyer's broker. The seller fulfills his obligation when he delivers to his broker; his broker fulfills his obligation when he delivers to the buyer's broker (UCC 8-314).

Delivery to the buyer occurs when the buyer's broker acquires a security specially endorsed to the buyer, or when the broker gives him confirmation of his purchase and identifies a security in his possession as the security belonging to the buyer.

When publicly traded securities are traded through brokers, regulations of the Securities and Exchange Commission provide that the seller has seven days after his sale to make delivery of a security to his broker, and the buyer becomes the owner on the buyer's broker's books seven days after the purchase, the buyer being obligated to pay at that time.

The buyer's broker normally procures registration of the security in the buyer's name. The broker (or the issuer) will deliver the security when registration formalities are completed, a process that requires several weeks.

Duties of brokers when customer does not take delivery of securities. If a buyer permits his broker to retain his securities, the buyer is still owner of the securities on the broker's books. However, the broker may obtain registration of the security from the issuer in its name. Thus, the broker is the owner of the security so far as the issuer is concerned. The broker therefore possesses the right to vote, the right to receive dividends, and the other rights that go with stock ownership.

The broker is of course obligated to credit all dividends received to the buyer's account. He must submit all proxy materials received from the issuer to the buyer, and he must follow the buyer's instructions in voting the shares. In short, as between issuer and broker, the broker owns the shares; but as between broker and customer, the customer owns the shares.

When an owner of securities who has let his broker retain the securities wishes to sell, he simply gives his broker an order to sell, and the broker does so. No paperwork is required of the seller. Such a sale through a broker may not result in any transfer of a security. If the buyer of the security is another customer of the broker, the only paperwork required will be a change in ownership of the security upon the broker's books.

Securities litigation. The holder of a security has essentially the same advantages in litigation as does the holder of a negotiable instrument (UCC 8-105). The genuineness of a signature is not to be questioned unless it is called into question in the pleadings of the parties. Once the validity is called into question, the signature is presumed to be valid (genuine or authorized) until proven otherwise.

A holder of a security—the bearer of a bearer security or the person to whom a registered security is endorsed—is presumed to be the owner; the defendant must prove deficiency in the holder's title. Once the defendant has proven the existence of a defect in the holder's title, the holder will have to prove bona fide purchaser status if that will override the defense or defect.

Attachment or levy upon security. UCC 8-316 provides that the only way to levy upon a security is for the creditor, sheriff, etc., to get physical possession of the security itself. A court order will usually be necessary in order to accomplish this.

43

Rights and Duties of Shareholders, Directors, and Officers

Rights and Duties of Shareholders

The corporate shareholder is in some ways in the position of the citizen of a governmental unit. Just as the governmental unit exists for the benefits of its citizens, the corporation exists for the benefit of its shareholders. And, just as the citizen has only indirect control over what his government does for his benefit, the shareholder has only limited control over what the corporate management does for his.

However, this analogy may be carried only so far; the ties of the citizen to his government are much stronger than the ties of the shareholder to his corporation. If we as citizens do not like the way our city or state is run, and we feel that we do not have the power to change things, we can move, which may cause much dislocation in our personal lives. If we as shareholders do not like the way our corporation is run, and we feel that we do not have the power to change things, we may simply sell our shares. We as citizens have equal voting rights—in matters governmental, the rule is "one person, one vote." In matters corporate, however, the rule is "one share, one vote," so there is no equality among shareholders—some shareholders are much more powerful than others. Keep these matters in mind as we consider the rights and duties of that corporate citizen, the shareholder.

The right to hold and participate in shareholders' meetings. The annual meeting of shareholders is, in a sense, the town meeting of the corporate citizens. Here management must account to the shareholders for its stewardship over the past year, and it is here that the directors submit themselves to the will of the shareholders as they seek reelection.

TBCA 2.24 provides that an annual meeting must be held each year at the time and place specified in the bylaws. Notice of the meeting must be given personally or by mail to those shareholders entitled to vote at the meeting. It must be sent no more than fifty days nor less than ten days before the date of the meeting (TBCA 2.25). The notice must contain the date, place, and hour of the meeting.

If the directors do not call the annual meeting, this will not cause them to lose their authority to manage the corporation. However, if an annual meeting is not called within thirteen months of the date of the last annual meeting, any shareholder may petition a

Texas district court in the county where the principal office of the corporation is located to call the annual meeting. The court may summarily do this when satisfied that no meeting has been called within thirteen months.

A quorum of shares must be present at the annual meeting in person or by proxy before any business may be transacted. Fifty percent plus one of the shares of the corporation entitled to vote constitutes a quorum, unless the articles or bylaws specify some other percentage. The articles and bylaws may not authorize a quorum of less than one third of those shares entitled to vote.

In determining the number of shares authorized to vote, all authorized and issued voting shares are counted except treasury shares and shares owned by subsidiary corporations.

If no quorum is present at the meeting, no business may be transacted. The shares present may vote to adjourn the meeting to another time (and to another place, if authorized by the bylaws). If a quorum is present, business may be transacted. The vote of a majority of those shares voting may then settle any matter coming before the meeting, unless state law or the articles or bylaws require a greater vote.

If a quorum is present at the beginning of the meeting, all business scheduled to come before the meeting may be transacted, even if no quorum is present later on in the proceedings. Loss of a quorum, then, does not compel the adjournment of the meeting.

The usual purpose of the annual meeting is the election of directors for the coming year and the presentation of financial reports and the like for the fiscal year just passed. If any other business of import is to be transacted at the meeting, the shareholders would be so notified when the notice of the meeting is sent out. However, the annual meeting is not limited to considering matters contained in the notice mailed to shareholders.

Special meetings of shareholders may be summoned during the year by the president, board of directors, holders of 10 percent of the shares entitled to vote, or any other person or persons authorized by the articles or bylaws to summon such a special meeting (TBCA 2.24C). Special meetings may be called for purposes such as:
1. Amending the articles.
2. Approving a merger, consolidation, sale of assets, or something similar.
3. Approving a reduction in stated capital.
4. Approving a distribution in partial liquidation.
5. Approving a proposal for dissolution of the corporation.
6. Removing a director or directors from office.

The notice requirements that must be met are the same as those for annual meetings, except that the notice must contain the purpose of the meeting. If a merger or consolidation is to be voted upon, the notice must be sent at least 20 days before the date of the meeting.

The quorum requirements are the same for special meetings as for annual meetings, but the agenda at the special meeting is limited to those matters mentioned in the notice to shareholders.

TBCA 9.10 provides that shareholders may act without a meeting if all consent in writing to the action to be taken. Acquiring such unanimous written consent may be easy in small corporations, but the more numerous the shareholders, the more difficult it is to acquire such consent.

The right to vote at shareholders' meetings. The right of a holder of shares to vote them at a shareholders' meeting depends upon several factors. First and foremost, it depends upon whether or not the shares are voting shares. Voting shares may be voted upon any proposition legitimately presented at the meeting.

Nonvoting shares normally may not be voted at a meeting. However, nonvoting shares do have the right to vote upon questions of vital import to the holders of those shares, such as:
1. Mergers and consolidations.
2. Sales of all assets.
3. Voluntary dissolutions.
4. Amendments to the articles, if the amendments affect the rights of the nonvoting shareholders.

Nonvoting shares may thus be voted on some amendments to the articles, but not others. For example: A corporation has outstanding a class of nonvoting cumulative preferred stock. An amendment to the articles is proposed which would make the preferred stock noncumulative. The preferred shareholders may vote on this, because their rights are involved. On the other hand, if an amendment is proposed which will increase the number of authorized common shares, the preferred shareholders would normally have no vote; the success or failure of the amendment would have no effect on their rights.

Holders of voting shares are entitled to vote on this matter, however. Various considerations determine the voting rights of holders of voting shares. First, some voting shares may not be voted. Treasury stock may not vote, because corporate management could vote it for itself. Voting stock owned by subsidiary corporations may not be voted, because these shares are ultimately under the control of the management of the parent corporation. With respect to other voting shares, the call for the shareholders' meeting generally provides that shareholders of record as of a certain date may vote. The meeting may be held on June 30, and the notice may provide that those shareholders of record as of June 15 have the right to vote. In such a case, a shareholder who sold his shares after June 15 could vote at the meeting, but a shareholder who bought shares after June 15 would have no voting rights.

In certain situations, special rules govern the right to vote. If shares are jointly owned—by tenants in common, joint tenants, or something of that sort—all of the holders of record must agree upon how to vote. If the co-owners do not agree, the shares cannot be voted. If the shares are community property but only one spouse is the record owner, the shares may be voted by the record owner.

If the shares are pledged to a creditor as collateral for a loan, the debtor (and not the creditor) has the right to vote, unless the debtor has transferred the shares into the name of the creditor. Shares owned by corporations are voted by the person named in the corporate bylaws. If there is no bylaw provision on this point the board of directors determines how the shares should be voted by majority vote.

The shares of a deceased shareholder are voted by the executor or administrator of his estate until transferred to his heirs. The shares of a person who has a court-appointed guardian are voted by the guardian. Shares in the name of a person or corporation in receivership or bankruptcy are voted by the receiver or trustee in bankruptcy if the court appointing the trustee or receiver gave him such voting power.

Remember that shares bought through a broker and left in the custody of the broker are in the name of the broker; the broker therefore has the right to vote them.

Proxies. A shareholder who will not attend the shareholders' meeting in person may appoint an agent to attend and cast his votes for him. He does this by giving a proxy to a proxyholder. The proxy must be in writing and signed by the shareholder or by his authorized agent (TBCA 2.29).

The shareholder may give his proxy discretion as to how to vote his shares, or he may give his proxy instructions on how to vote. If the shareholder gives instructions, the proxyholder—as a good agent—must follow them. In the absence of instruction the proxyholder may vote the shares at his discretion.

Corporate management of all but the very smallest corporations will solicit proxies from shareholders before the annual meeting, and will ask each shareholder to give the proxyholder instructions to vote his shares for the management candidates for directors and for the management position on other issues to come before the meeting. These materials are distributed at corporate expense.

Opponents of management also have the right to solicit proxies from shareholders, but in all but the smallest corporations these opponents operate at a grave disadvantage. First, they may not know the names and addresses of all the shareholders. This they may learn by invoking their right to inspect the company books, but management may stall their request in various bureaucratic ways. Second, their communications must be sent to shareholders at their expense, at fifteen cents per letter that expense soon adds up.

When the corporation is big enough to have its shares registered with the Securities and Exchange Commission under the provisions of the Securities and Exchange Act, proxy solicitation comes under SEC jurisdiction; this will be discussed in the chapter on federal and state securities regulation.

Once given, a proxy is good for eleven months after the date of issue, unless revoked sonner or expressly made irrevocable. The courts look with disfavor on irrevocable proxies, which they uphold only in the case of a proxy coupled with an interest. A pledgee of shares may, for instance, require as a condition of making a loan and taking corporate shares as collateral that the pledgor debtor give him an irrevocable proxy to vote the pledged shares at his discretion until the loan is repaid.

A revocable proxy expires or is generally revoked under one of four circumstances:
1. Eleven months expire after the date of issue.
2. The shareholder informs the proxyholder in writing that he is revoking the proxy.
3. The shareholder grants another proxy to someone else. When two proxies are outstanding on the same shares, the last one granted has priority.
4. The shareholder himself attends the meeting and seeks to vote his shares. This effectively revokes his proxy.

Cumulative voting. Cumulative voting is a method of casting votes for directors which will permit minority representation on the board of directors. Under this voting system the shareholder may cast as many votes for director as the number of votes his shares entitle him to times the number of directors to be elected. The shareholder then divides these votes among the candidates for director in any way he chooses. If Ace owns 1,000 shares of Zilch Corporation stock, each share has one vote, and there are eleven directors to be elected, Ace may cast 11,000 votes for directoral candidates. He may give all 11,000 votes to one candidate, or he may split them up in any way he sees fit.

When cumulative voting is used, a minority with a sizable number of votes which is less than a majority may assure itself of some seats on the board. If the minority knows how many votes will be cast as a whole and how many votes it controls, it will be able to figure out how many directors it can elect and divide its votes accordingly. For example: Zapp Corporation's annual meeting is attended by holders of 100,000 of its voting shares, in person and by proxy. Nine directors are to be elected. Management probably controls a majority of these shares, but a minority faction knows it has the votes of 25,000 shares. How many directors can the minority elect?

There will be 900,000 votes cast for directoral candidates altogether (9 x 100,000). The minority controls 225,000 of these votes (9 x 25,000). In order to elect one director, one-tenth plus one of all votes cast are required. (No ten candidates could get one-tenth plus one of all of the votes—only nine candidates at the most can do that, so any candidate mustering that figure is sure of election.) Ten percent of 900,000 is 90,000, so it will take 90,001 votes to elect one director, 180,002 to elect two, and 270,003 to elect three. Our minority is thus sure of electing two directors. If it can round up the votes of 5,001 more shares, its leaders can elect a third director.

Cumulative voting will also permit a fairly large shareholder to elect himself a director, no matter how other shareholders vote. In the situation described above, if shareholder Spade owns 10,001 shares of Zapp, he could elect himself a director. His 10,001 shares would give him 90,009 votes, more than enough to secure election.

TBCA 2.29D provides that shareholders in a Texas corporation have cumulative voting rights unless the articles deprive them of that right. More often than not, the articles do just that, since majority factions of shareholders find minority representation on the board annoying, to say the least.

When cumulative voting is permitted, it still will not be allowed at any one shareholders' meeting unless at least one shareholder informs the corporate secretary in writing on or before the day preceding the election of his intent to vote cumulatively. If one shareholder announces his intent to do this, all shareholders have the right to do it.

There are ways in which the effects of cumulative voting may be diluted, even when it is allowed. One method of dilution is to make the board of directors small. The fewer the directors, the more votes it takes to elect one. Another way is to classify the board, so that its members serve terms of more than one year and not all directors come up for reelection at the same meeting. Another way is to have most of the work normally done by the directors done by an executive committee, elected by majority vote of the directors. The minority can be deprived of representation on this committee.

Of course, when cumulative voting is not used in elections of directors, the election is an all-or-nothing proposition when there is a contest. The majority rules; the winning side takes all.

The right to remove directors from office. A director may be removed from office by the shareholders for cause. A director may not be removed from office without cause unless the articles or bylaws permit this (TBCA 2.32). A special meeting of shareholders must be called in order to bring about a removal. That means that either the president or a majority of the board must be in favor of the removal, so that the management will call the required meeting; or 10 percent of the voting shares must be in favor of it, so that these persons will call the required meeting.

If cumulative voting is not used in the election of company directors, a majority of shares voting on the question of removal must vote to remove. If cumulative voting is used in the election of directors, an extraordinary majority must vote for removal. If a number of shares sufficient to elect the director to office vote to retain him in office, he is not removed. Thus, in case a director of Zapp Corporation in the above example is the target of a removal effort, if 100,000 shares vote on the question of his removal he needs only 10,001 votes to remain in office.

Distinction must be made between removal for cause and removal not for cause. Removal for cause means removal because the director is not doing his job properly. Perhaps he makes illegal proposals, violates his fiduciary duties to the corporation, never shows up for meetings, or something of that sort. Removal of a director not for cause essentially involves removal for political reasons. Perhaps the majority of directors or shareholders disagrees with his ideas about how the corporation should be run; perhaps they simply no longer want him.

To repeat: Removal for cause is always authorized; removal for other reasons is not possible unless expressly allowed in the bylaws.

The right to inspect corporate books and records. TBCA 2.44 provides that shareholders of record for six months or longer, or shareholders owning 5 percent or more of the company shares, have the right to inspect books and records for a proper purpose. Shareholders not meeting these requirements may obtain a court order permitting the inspection if they can show good cause. Among good reasons for inspection are:

1. A desire to obtain a list of shareholders for use in soliciting votes for director.
2. A desire to check the accuracy of financial information disseminated by management.
3. A desire to check on possible illegal conduct by officers or directors, if there is good reason to believe that such illegality exists.

Unacceptable reasons for inspection might be:

1. A "fishing expedition" into the company books to find out if there might be illegality in management when there is no reason to believe that any illegality exists.
2. A desire to obtain a list of shareholders for use as an advertising mailing list for the shareholder's own company.
3. A desire to inspect to have something amusing to do.

Preemptive rights. These are the rights of existing shareholders to purchase enough of a new issue of shares to maintain their proportion of ownership in the company. TBCA 2.22 provides that shareholders have this right, unless the articles limit or deny it.

Even if the articles do not eliminate preemptive rights, there are circumstances under which they do not exist in a stock issue. Preemptive rights in new shares do not exist when:

1. The new shares are issued for services or property.
2. The shares are to be sold to employees, under a plan earlier approved by the shareholders.
3. The shares are not of the same class.

When the rights do exist, they exist with respect to both authorized and unissued shares and with respect to treasury shares.

The right to freely dispose of one's shares. This right exists unless restricted by the articles. TBCA 2.22 provides that transferability may be restricted if the restrictions are conspicuously noted upon each share certificate subject to them, and if the restrictions are reasonable. If the restrictions are complicated and lengthy, TBCA 2.19 provides that they may be filed in the office of the secretary of state and notice placed upon the share certificates that their transfer is subject to restrictions so filed. Among the permissible restrictions are:

1. Shareholder must offer his shares to the corporation before offering them to other parties. The corporation may buy or not buy as the directors see fit.
2. The shareholder must offer the shares to the corporation if he desires to sell, and the corporation must buy.
3. The shareholder must offer his shares to the other shareholders before selling them to third parties, the other shareholders having the option to buy or not to buy. This is not enforceable if the corporation has more than twenty shareholders.
4. The shareholder must offer the shares to the other shareholders, and the other shareholders must buy them. This is also unenforceable if the corporation has more than twenty shareholders.

5. The shareholder must give the corporation first right of refusal to buy shares for a price negotiated between the shareholder and a third person. The third person cannot buy for the agreed price unless the corporation refuses.
6. The shareholder must not sell his shares to any named person or class of persons, so long as the prohibition is not unreasonable.
7. The shareholder may not sell his shares unless the corporation or its shareholders approve.
8. Upon the death of the shareholder the corporation shall have the option to buy the shares of the deceased.
9. The shareholder shall make no transfer which would jeopardize the close corporation or Subchapter S status of the corporation.

Where options to buy or sell and obligations to buy or sell are included in the restrictions, a provision determining the price of purchase and sale will also be included. This price could be market value, par value, book value, or any other reasonable measurement. If the set price is reasonable, the restriction will be reasonable.

Options to buy should have a time limit of reasonable duration placed upon them. If no limit is set in the restriction, the option endures for a reasonable time only. Where shareholders or directors are given veto power over a disposition, the veto must be exercised in a reasonable manner. A restriction may not entirely forbid the transfer of the shares.

The right to bring shareholder derivative suits. A shareholder has the right to sue to enforce a claim by the corporation against a third party when the corporation refuses to press the claim itself. The reasoning behind this is as follows: If the corporation does not press the claim, the interest of the shareholder in the corporation may be damaged. Therefore the shareholder should have the right to sue in order to protect the corporation and himself. If the suit is won, the recovery goes to the corporation, not to the suing shareholder, but the shareholder's attorney is paid out of the proceeds of the suit.

Before a court will entertain a shareholder derivative suit, the shareholder must demand of the directors of the corporation that they sue, and the directors must either refuse to sue or do nothing in response to the demand. The making of the demand is excused if the shareholder can show that making it would be futile.

The suit may involve a claim by the corporation against an outsider for commission of a tort or for breach of contract. It is more likely to be against a corporate insider who by unlawful acts has damaged the corporation but who has enough power in the corporate hierachy to prevent action by the corporation directly. The nature of the wrongs for which such a suit might be brought will be covered in the discussion on the duties of directors and officers.

The plaintiff shareholder must have been a shareholder at the time of the commission of the wrong complained of, or he must have acquired his shares by operation of law thereafter.

The plaintiff may be required to post a bond with the court to secure payment of expenses which will be incurred by the defendant in the suit. This is to protect defendants against the filing of nuisance suits by plaintiffs. If the plaintiff prevails, his bond is refunded.

The plaintiff shareholder stands in the shoes of the corporation in this sort of suit. If the defendant has a defense that would be good against the corporation, the defense is also good against the plaintiff. Any out-of-court settlement in such a case will not be binding until approved by the judge hearing the case.

Duties of shareholders. Since ordinary shareholders owe no fiduciary duties to other shareholders or to each other, they are not under any duties with respect to the corporation, its management, or each other.

The controlling shareholder, however, does owe fiduciary duties to ordinary shareholders. In many respects the controlling shareholder stands in the shoes of a director or officer. In fact, he is very likely to be a director or officer. If he is, he of course has all the duties and obligations which go with such a position. If he is not, however, he may influence directors and officers to perform unlawful acts. If he does, he is just as responsible for the consequences as they are.

The major situation where controlling shareholders get into difficulty as controlling shareholders is when they sell their shares—and thus control of the corporation—causing damage to minority shareholders. The controlling shareholder owes a duty to the other shareholders not to sell control of the company to a person who will not look out for the minority interest. If Jones sells a controlling interest in Ace Corporation to Smith, knowing that Smith will loot the corporation of valuable assets to the detriment of the other shareholders, the other shareholders will have a good claim against Jones (and against Smith, for that matter).

If Jones were unaware of Smith's evil intentions, and Jones had no reason to question Smith's character, Jones of course would not be liable. If Jones did not know of Smith's intentions in this case, but did know or should have known that Smith was a person of bad character, Jones would be liable.

Controlling shareholders may also violate their duties to minority shareholders when they try to deprive them of their chance to participate in the business of the corporation. Here, however, a fine line exists.

The majority may use all sorts of political tactics to deprive the minority of representation on the board of directors. It may electioneer against the minority in proxy fights, and finance its campaign with corporate funds. It may dilute the effects of cumulative voting by reducing the number of directors or by classifying the board, so that all directors are not elected at the same time. If it controls more than two-thirds of the voting shares it may amend the articles to abolish cumulative voting altogether. If it controls two-thirds of the voting shares, it may amend the articles to permit removal of minority directors from the board without cause, and then, if cumulative voting has been abolished, use its majority voting power to eliminate the minority representation.

There are other tactics that the majority may not use, however. Any sort of tinkering with the integrity of the corporate electoral process—vote-buying, padding the list of qualified voters, miscounting the votes, etc.—is not allowed. The selling of treasury stock to majority members or supporters without offering the minority a chance to purchase is not allowed. Deliberately pursuing a no-dividend policy in order to induce the minority to sell out is also not allowed.

Most reprehensible of such tactics, perhaps, is the freeze-out, whereby the majority seeks to reorganize the corporation in such a way as to deprive the minority of such influence and ownership as it possesses. The majority shareholders in Black Corporation, for instance, may incorporate White Corporation and subscribe to all its shares themselves. They then cause Black to sell all of its assets to White. The result is that Black's minority shareholders are effectively frozen out, since White now owns the business. If the Black majority has more than two-thirds of the voting shares of Black, it may now voluntarily liquidate Black and thereby sever all business connections with the Black minority.

In cases such as these, the minority may recover substantial damages from the majority, and may also be able to get a court to enjoin the majority from carrying out its schemes.

Questions of violation of fiduciary duties by majority shareholders have also arisen when a majority of shareholders or a group of shareholders constituting a majority sell their shares at a premium over market value. Minority shareholders on occasion have tried to force the majority to share this premium. These efforts have so far been unsuccessful. The courts seem to take the position that a controlling interest in a corporation does command a premium in the marketplace, because, after all, a controlling interest is a one-of-a-kind thing.

Rights and Duties of Directors and Officers

Directors are in a sense the legislators of the corporation. Theoretically they make general policy and choose and supervise the executives (the officers). Their duty is to run things in the best interest of the constituents who elected them (the shareholders). Sometimes it works out this way, and sometimes it does not.

Election and qualifications of directors. The initial directors of a corporation in Texas are named in the articles. They hold office until the first annual meeting of shareholders, at which time permanent directors are elected. From that time forward, the directors are elected by the shareholders at each annual meeting.

Directors need not be shareholders or residents of Texas, unless the articles or bylaws provide otherwise. Directors serve one-year terms, unless the board consists of nine or more members and the bylaws call for a classified board. If the board consists of nine or more members, TBCA 2.33 permits the classification of the board into two or three classes, with the two or three classes being as nearly equal in numbers as practicable, the members of each class serving two- or three-year terms, and members of only one class standing for election each year.

Should the annual meeting not be held, or should it be unable to elect directors for some reason, those directors whose terms expired at that meeting continue to hold office until their successors are elected and qualified.

The number of board members is set out in the bylaws. If the number of directors is reduced through a bylaw amendment, the reduction does not become effective until the next annual meeting. Directors may not be removed from office by reducing the size of the board.

If the number of directors is increased through amendment of the bylaws, the vacancies must be filled by the shareholders, acting either at the annual meeting or at a special meeting called for the purpose of electing the new directors. If a vacancy occurs on the board due to a death or resignation, the remaining directors, acting at a meeting, may fill the vacancy.

Meetings of directors. The time and place of regular meetings of the board is spelled out in the bylaws, as is the procedure for calling special meetings. No notice of regular meetings is needed unless the bylaws require it; notice of special meetings is required.

A quorum of the board must be present before business can be transacted. Unless the articles or bylaws provide otherwise, a quorum consists of one more than half the members. Bylaw or article provisions may make the required quorum larger, but they may not make it smaller. A directors' meeting may transact only one type of business without an initial quorum. If a majority of the board has resigned or has otherwise become dissociated from the corporation, the remaining directors may fill the vacancies.

If a quorum is present at the beginning of the meeting, but enough directors leave so that a quorum is no longer present before all business is transacted, the meeting may be forced to adjourn for lack of a quorum. Whether or not this is necessary depends upon why those directors who departed left. If they departed with the intent of breaking the quorum and making it impossible for the meeting to continue, the meeting may continue, quorum or not; but if their departure was not with the intent to force adjournment such adjournment will be necessary.

Directors must attend meetings in person in order to be counted as part of a quorum. Proxy voting by directors is not permitted. Directors may not agree among themselves in advance how they will vote. Informal agreements of this sort are certainly made and kept, but the law will not enforce them.

Director actions without a meeting. TBCA 9.10 permits directors to take action without holding a formal meeting under two circumstances.

First, if all directors are willing to consent in writing to a proposed action, that action is the act of the board. The consent must be unanimous. If all directors will not consent in writing, approval of the action must be obtained in another manner.

Second, it is possible to hold a "meeting" by conference telephone call. If a quorum of the board participates in the conference call, the act of the majority is the act of the board.

Executive committee. TBCA 2.36 permits the board of directors to delegate some of its functions to an executive committee if the articles or bylaws permit. Such a committee must be elected by the directors by majority vote, and it must consist of at least two members.

The executive committee may transact routine business for the board. However, TBCA 2.36 provides that certain board functions may not be delegated to the executive committee. Among other things, the executive committee may not:

1. Appoint officers for the corporation.
2. Remove officers of the corporation.
3. Fill vacancies on the board of directors.
4. Propose amendments to the corporate articles.
5. Amend the bylaws.
6. Propose voluntary dissolution of the corporation.
7. Propose a merger or consolidation.
8. Propose a sale of all corporate assets.
9. Authorize issue of authorized but unissued shares.
10. Purchase treasury shares.
11. Sell treasury shares.
12. Declare dividends.

The members of the full board are responsible for anything the executive committee does, just as if they had voted in its favor; the board may not avoid responsibility by delegating it to such a committee. On the other hand, since minority shareholders may be denied membership on an executive committee, the minority of the board may be deprived of some power to obstruct through the authorization and creation of such a committee.

Duty of care owed corporation and shareholders by directors. Directors owe a fiduciary duty to the corporation, but they do not owe such a duty to the shareholders.

Directors are expected to devote as much care to supervising the management of their corporation as they would devote to the management of their own businesses. Directors are therefore expected to take an active interest in corporate affairs. Should they choose to leave the management of the firm to officers and merely rubber-stamp officer requests with their approval, they run a definite risk. Nobody argues with success; if the business prospers under the direction of an officer the directors never challenge, no one is likely to complain so long as the dominant officer treats all concerned fairly. But if the dominant officer is not operating the business soundly, or if he is operating it unfairly with respect to minority shareholders, the directors who acquiesce in his actions are courting trouble. Directors may be held liable to the corporation and to the shareholders for wrongdoing by officers if director diligence could have prevented the wrongdoing from taking place or if it could have prevented the wrongdoing from going too far.

On the other hand, the law does not expect each corporate director to possess a crystal ball in good operating order. No matter how well we plan, life is still unpredictable; the best-laid plans of businessmen do go astray. Directors are not held responsible for bad business judgment, either that of their elected officers or their own.

Directors must be very careful when they enter into contracts with their corporation. It is best if directors do not enter into any contractual relationships with their corporation at all, but sometimes such contracts are advisable or necessary. Since the director-corporation relationship is a fiduciary relationship, the director must not profit at the expense of the corporation in any way. If the contract is fair to the corporation, it will stand the strongest judicial scrutiny. If it is unfair, a court will void it. This is true even if a disinterested majority of directors has approved the contract, and even if a majority of shareholders have ratified it.

Problems usually arise with respect to director sales of goods or services to the corporation, or director purchases of goods or services from it. Among the factors taken into account in assessing the fairness of such contracts are:

1. The need of the corporation to enter into the contract. Does the corporation get something needed from it?
2. The financial position of the corporation. Could it really afford this bargain?
3. The adequacy of consideration given the corporation. Did it get market value for what it sold, or did it get less? Did it pay market value for what it bought, or did it pay more?
4. Alternatives available. Could the corporation have bought what it bought from someone else for less, or could it have sold what it sold to someone else for more?
5. Full disclosure. Were the consenting directors aware of all of the material facts of the bargain?

When a director becomes aware of a business opportunity which would be beneficial to his corporation and also beneficial to himself, he must give the corporation first crack at taking advantage of the opportunity. If he takes advantage of the opportunity himself and makes a profit from it, the corporation may compel him to turn the profit over to the corporation, or a shareholder may compel this by filing a shareholder derivative suit against him on behalf of the corporation.

The director should make the corporate management aware of the existence of the opportunity. The corporate board of directors may then decide whether or not to take advantage of it. Should the directors decide to pass up the opportunity, however, the refusal may be scrutinized just as thoroughly as any contract between the corporation and a director. There must be a very good reason for the refusal to take advantage, and full disclosure of all material facts must have been made to the directors.

Statutory liability of directors to corporation. TBCA 2.41 provides that assenting directors will be liable to the corporation for damages caused by:

1. Declaration and payment of illegal dividends.
2. Unlawful purchase by the corporation of its own shares.

3. Illegal distribution of assets to shareholders during liquidation.
4. Making of loans to directors and officers.
5. Commencing business before $1,000 is paid in.
6. Illegal payments to shareholders from reduction surplus.

Those directors who assented to these illegal acts would be jointly and severally liable to the corporation for the consequences.

The following rules determine which directors assented to an illegal action:

1. If the minutes of the directors' meeting reveal that the illegal action was approved by a voice vote, and no record exists of who voted "yes" and who "no," all are deemed to have voted "yes" who were present at the meeting.
2. Those who voted "yes" on a record vote are liable.
3. Those who voted "no" on a record vote are not liable.
4. Those who were present but did not vote are liable. Silence here is essentially assent.
5. Those who were absent from the meeting and who had a good excuse for not being there are not liable.
6. Those who were absent who are habitual absentees are liable—they are negligent in carrying out their duties.
7. The assenting nonprofessional director has an available escape hatch. If he voted in favor of the illegal act upon advice of a knowledgeable professional that the action was legal, he is not liable. However, if he knew as much about the professional's field as the professional, so that he could exercise his own professional judgment, he is liable if he voted "yes."

Directors who assent to the following may well be liable to the corporation, though the TBCA does not directly impose liability:

1. The sale of corporate shares for promissory notes or for promises to perform future services.
2. The issue of corporate shares that are not fully paid for.
3. The issue of corporate shares as fully paid for, for inadequate consideration.

Federal and Texas securities legislation imposes other liabilities upon directors of corporations subject to such legislation. That liability will be taken up in the materials on securities regulation.

Powers of officers. The titles and authority of officers are generally spelled out in the bylaws. An officer has authority to do what the bylaws say he can do. He also has implied authority to do everything necessary to carry out his express authority. Officers also have apparent authority with respect to third parties who are unfamiliar with the express authority granted the officer by the bylaws.

The president has only the apparent authority to preside over meetings of officers and employees. He does not have apparent authority to preside over meetings of the directors; that is the function of the chairman of the board, who strictly speaking is not a corporate officer.

Vice-presidents have only the apparent authority to act for the president in his absence. The secretary has apparent authority to keep the corporate records and to certify actions of the board and of the shareholders. The treasurer has apparent authority to receive and keep corporate funds, arranging their deposit, etc.

Appointment, term, and removal of officers. The officers are appointed by the directors, unless the bylaws delegate the choice to someone else. The directors may enter into employment contracts with officers for terms exceeding the terms of the appointing directors. The terms of officers, then, are determined by the bylaws or by the appointing contract.

Officers may be removed from office by the directors or by the appointing officer, unless the bylaws provide otherwise. They may be removed without cause. Essentially, they hold office for as long as they retain the confidence of the appointing authority.

Officers hired for definite terms of office may thus be removed before their terms expire, but such removal is a breach of contract unless made for cause. The officer who is the victim of such removal may sue the corporation for damages for breach of contract, but he may not sue to retain his job.

Compensation of officers. Officers are of course paid salaries. The salary must be reasonable, considering the business, profitability, and size of the corporation. For tax avoidance purposes, officers may receive their compensation, or a part of it, as deferred income, in stock options, or something similar. The legalities of the various forms of deferred executive income are beyond the scope of this work.

Salaries of officers are of course deductible business expenses for the corporation under the Internal Revenue Code. Payment of high executive salaries may seem to be a device for reducing the income tax liability of the corporation. However, the payment of unreasonably high salaries to officers who are major shareholders may be attacked by the IRS upon the ground that the salary is in truth a concealed dividend. If the IRS can make such a determination stick, the salary is not completely deductible by the corporation, and the funds so expended are subject to the double taxation which is the fate of dividends.

Duties of officers. Officers are subject to essentially the same duties and the same liabilities to the corporation as directors. Officers too owe fiduciary duties to the corporation. Contracts between officers and the corporation are therefore subject to the same scrutiny as are contracts between directors and the corporation. Officers must also give the corporation first shot at business opportunities which may prove profitable to the corporation.

Since officers do not declare dividends or vote to buy treasury stock, they are not subject to the liability of directors for such actions. On the other hand, officers are presented with more opportunity to violate their fiduciary duties to the corporation by using corporate employees to perform private labor for them, using corporate equipment for personal use, or using corporate funds for personal use.

Duties of promoters. Though a promoter is not a director or an officer, he does owe a fiduciary duty to the corporation because he acts as its agent. Thus, a promoter is under a duty not to profit at the expense of his corporation.

Promoters sometimes violate their fiduciary duties by transferring property to the corporation for an unfair price. If a promoter transfers to the corporation property which he owned at the time the promotion of the corporation began, he may transfer it at fair market value and earn a profit for himself. If he transfers it for more than fair market value, he violates his fiduciary duty. If he obtained the property after the promotion began, however, he must not profit by the transfer. He should transfer it to the corporation at his cost or less.

The promoter may retain his profit if:
1. The full facts of the situation were known to the corporate directors who approved of the transfer, and
2. The approving board was not dominated by the promoter, or
3. All of the original subscribers and shareholders ratify the bargain, and
4. The promoter committed no fraud in the bargain.

44

Texas and Federal Securities Regulation

When corporate securities are sold or otherwise distributed to the investing public, the securities and the corporation itself become subject to federal and state regulation. Federal regulation does not come into play unless the corporate securities are owned—or it is proposed that they be owned—by persons in more than one state. Texas state regulation comes into play when corporate securities come into the hands of more than a few owners.

The state statute regulating distribution of securities within Texas is the Texas Securities Act; the regulating authority is the Texas Securities Board. Two federal statutes regulate securities distribution and corporations at the federal level—the Federal Securities Act and the Federal Securities and Exchange Act. The regulating authority is the Securities and Exchange Commission.

Under both Texas and federal law, certain types of securities are not subject to regulation, and certain transactions in certain securities are exempt from regulation. In general, corporate management must become concerned with Texas securities regulation when it contemplates offering corporate securities to so many offerees that, if all offers are accepted, the corporation will have thirty-five or more security holders. Management must become concerned with federal securities regulation when it contemplates distributing securities to persons outside the state of Texas.

We shall first consider the scheme of regulation of the state of Texas.

Securities exempt from state regulation. The Texas Securities Act comprises Section 581 of RCS. It has numerous sections. The act will be cited as TSA and the section number. TSA 6 lists exempt securities. Eleven types of securities are exempted from Texas Securities Board regulation, many pertaining to government securities and securities issued by nonprofit corporations. The exemptions of concern to us here are:

1. Securities issued by national banks or federally chartered corporations.
2. Securities issued by railroad corporations or public utilities.
3. Securities listed on the New York Stock Exchange, the American Stock Exchange, or any other stock exchange approved by the Texas Securities Board (TSB).
4. Securities issued by Texas state banks.
5. Commercial paper maturing in twenty-four months or less.

Any transactions in nonexempt securities which are not in and of themselves exempt transactions are unlawful unless the security has been duly registered with the TSB. All transactions are nonexempt for nineteen types of exempt transactions listed in TSA 5.

Exempt transactions in Texas securities. The major exemptions provided for transactions in nonexempt securities are:

1. Sales by executors, administrators, guardians, conservators, sheriffs, receivers, or trustees in bankruptcy.
2. Sales by pledgees or mortgagees—essentially foreclosure of security interests in securities.
3. Sales by investors who are not in the business of buying and selling securities.
4. Sales by insurance companies of securities held as investments.
5. Distribution of securities as stock dividends.
6. Distribution of securities as part of a corporate reorganization.
7. Issue or sale of securities by one corporation to another as part of a corporate combination duly approved by shareholders of both.
8. Exchanges of stock by a corporation and its shareholders where shareholders need give no consideration other than other securities of said corporation.
9. Sales of securities to institutional investors—banks, insurance companies, etc.
10. Most sales by dealers—the nonexempt dealer sales do not concern us here.
11. Sales of shares under approved employee stock option plans.
12. Any sale by issuing corporation so long as no public advertising of the sale was made and the sale does not increase the number of security holders of the corporation beyond thirty-five.
13. Sales by issuer to not more than fifteen persons during the twelve-month period before the sale in question, exclusive of other exempt transactions. Notice of all sales claimed to be exempt under this provision must be filed with the TSB at least five days before consummation of the sale.

Planning for security distribution. From this list, it is obvious that all securities likely to be issued by a small Texas corporation are not exempt from TSA regulation, except commercial paper maturing in twenty-four months or less. Any sale of long-term commercial paper, bonds, debentures, or stock may be subject to regulation. It is also obvious that most security distributions and sales which are exempt are sales by persons other than the issuer. Other than security distributions by issuers as stock dividends or security exchanges or as part of a corporate combination or the like, the major exemptions are sales to institutional investors and sales to small numbers of buyers.

So long as the total number of security holders is kept below thirty-five, all sales will be exempt. If it is desired to raise the number above thirty-five, exemption may be maintained by selling only to institutional investors or to no more than fifteen noninstitutional investors in any twelve-month period. Obviously, these restrictions make it difficult to distribute any large numbers of securities to large numbers of buyers. If management truly wishes to go public and bring in a large number of security holders, registration of the security with the TSB will be mandatory. The TSA provides for three methods of registration—qualification, notification, and coordination.

Qualification. TSA 7A sets forth the requirements for qualification. An issuer or a dealer licensed by the TSB to deal in securities must file with the TSB a sworn statement containing, among other things:

1. The names, addresses, and residences of issuer's officers and directors.
2. The location of issuer's principal offices and of all Texas branch offices.
3. Copies of the issuer's articles, bylaws, and director resolutions relative to the securities to be qualified.
4. Description of the security issue to be sold.

5. Promotional fees and commissions to be paid, to whom these are to be paid, and how they are to be paid.
6. Copies of the security to be sold.
7. Copies of prospectuses and other sales materials to be used in the distribution of the security.
8. Detailed balance sheets and profit and loss statements of issuer for latest accounting periods.

The TSB will examine these materials and decide whether or not to approve the sale. A permit to sell will be issued by the TSB if:
1. The required information is provided, and
2. Issuer's plan of business is just, fair, and equitable, and
3. Commissions to be paid to promoters are fair, and
4. No fraud will be worked upon the purchasers of the issue.

The TSB has authority to take into account whether or not the security is a good buy. If TSB feels that it is a bad investment, it may refuse to issue a permit to sell. If TSB does issue a permit, this does not constitute a recommendation of the security to the public, and the issuer must not use the permit as a sales aid.

The permit is valid for one year. If the entire issue qualified is not sold within a year, the issuer must apply for renewal of the sales permit to the TSB.

TSA 9 also permits the TSB to issue conditional permits to sell. The TSB may issue such a permit when the security is not such a bad investment that the marketing of it should not be allowed but is not such a good investment that an unrestricted permit is justified. Under a restricted permit the TSB will require all proceeds of the sale—less those necessary to finance the sales effort—to be deposited in a financial institution approved by the TSB until an amount of the issue specified by the TSB is sold. When and if the required amount is sold, the TSB will permit the depository to release the impounded funds to the issuer.

If the required amount of securities is not sold within two years (assuming, if the sales effort took that long, that the TSB granted the issuer a renewed permit for the final year's sales effort), the TSB will order the impounded funds returned to the buyers of the issue. In such a case, of course, the buyers must return their securities to the issuer for cancellation.

Notification. TSA 7B permits the registration of a new security issue by notification when:
1. Issuer has been in operation for at least three continuous years, and
2. If the issue is to be one of interest-bearing securities, during those three years issuer had net annual earnings equal to at least 150 percent of the annual interest payable on those securities to be issued plus outstanding interest-bearing securities of the same type, or
3. If the issue is to be one of fixed dividend securities such as preferred shares, the issuer has had annual net earnings at least equal to 150 percent of the annual dividends required for these shares and for all similar shares now outstanding, or
4. If the security is one for which no fixed dividend is specified (a common stock), the issuer has had sufficient annual earnings over the past three years to pay a dividend of 5 percent of the maximum offering price of these securities upon all outstanding stock of the same rank plus the stock to be marketed.

The registration materials to be filed with a notification registration must include:
1. Name and business address of issuer, and location of issuer's principal office in Texas, if any.

2. Title of security being registered and total amount of security to be offered.
3. Price at which security is to be offered to the public.
4. Brief statement of facts showing entitlement to registration by notification.
5. Name and business address of applicant filing statement.
6. Financial statements for last three years prior to registration statement, including a certified profit and loss statement, a certified balance sheet, and a certified statement of surplus for each year, the latest set of statements reflecting the financial condition of issuer no more than ninety days prior to the filing of the registration statement.
7. A copy of the prospectus describing the securities, if any.

The registration statement becomes effective five days after its receipt by the TSB, unless the board permits it to become effective sooner. If the TSB decides that the information in the registration statement does not entitle the security to registration by notification, the board may require the use of the slower qualification procedure.

If the TSB discovers false or fraudulent material in the registration statement after it has been approved, it may take steps to stop the sale of the security to the public.

This registration, like the one by qualification, is valid for one year, but may be renewed if all of the security is not sold during the one-year period.

Coordination. Registration by coordination is provided for by TSA 7C, and is used when the issue to be registered is also being registered at the federal level with the Securities and Exchange Commission. The registration statement filed under this section must comprise:
1. Three copies of the prospectus filed with the SEC, plus all amendments thereto.
2. The amount of securities to be offered in Texas.
3. The states in which a registration statement has been or will be filed.
4. Any adverse order, judgment, or decree issued with respect to this security by any court or by the SEC.
5. A copy of the issuer's articles and bylaws, a copy of the security, and a copy of any other contract affecting the issue (such as a trust indenture of a bond issue, or the underwriting agreement if the issue is to be marketed by professional underwriters).
6. Any other documents filed with the SEC that the TSB may request.
7. A promise to forward all amendments to the federal registration statement promptly.

The TSB examines the registration statement as soon as it is filed. The board may refuse registration if it does not meet the four qualifications set out in the section on qualification. If the registration is not denied it becomes effective when the federal registration becomes effective, so long as the registration statement has been on file with the TSB for at least ten days and other specified requirements are met. The issuer must notify the TSB of the effective date of the federal registration and of the offering price.

Consent to service of process by out-of-state issuers. Issuers organized under the laws of states other than Texas and Texas corporations doing most of their business outside the state must include with their Texas registration statements a statement that they are authorized to do business in the state of incorporation or state of operation, and that they are not delinquent with respect to taxes or assessments levied by that state. The statement must be certified by an appropriate officer of the state in question.

The out-of-state issuer must also file a statement with the TSB appointing the Texas Securities Commissioner its agent for service of all court process in actions brought under the TSA. These statements are required by TSA 8.

Criminal liability for TSA violations. TSA 29 makes it a felony to:

1. Sell, offer to sell, or deal in unregistered securities in nonexempt transactions.
2. Use fraud or deceit in order to sell any security within Texas, registered or not.
3. Make false statements in documents filed with the TSB.

The maximum penalty for each of the first two offenses is a fine of $5,000 and imprisonment for ten years. The maximum penalty for the third violation is a fine of $2,000 and imprisonment for not more than two years. The act also makes some other conduct criminal.

Civil liability of violators of the TSA. TSA 33 provides that:

1. Sellers or offerors of unregistered securities for sale are liable to buyers for the value of the security sold if the buyer still owns the security at the time of suit (or for damages if the buyer no longer owns the security at the time of suit) if the transaction was a nonexempt transaction.
2. Sellers, issuers, and buyers of securities who are guilty of fraud or misrepresentation in the purchase or sale of such securities are liable for restitution or damages to the innocent party plus a reasonable attorney's fee, unless the other party knew of the fraud or misrepresentation, or the party committing the misrepresentation did not know and could not reasonably be expected to know of the untruthfulness of his statements.

Sellers, of course, include selling issuers. The fraud or misrepresentation includes any sort of false or misleading pitch in sales material put out by the issuer with respect to the sale.

A seller may escape being sued for selling or offering to sell an unregistered security by offering to refund to the buyer the purchase price of the security plus 6 percent interest from the date of payment, less any income received on the security. If the buyer still owns his security, his acceptance of the refund or his failure to reject within thirty days of receipt will cause him to lose his right to sue. If the buyer no longer owns the security, his acceptance of the offer or his failure to reject it in writing within thirty days of receipt will cause him to lose his right to sue.

Remember that the antifraud provisions of the TSA, both criminal and civil, apply not only to fraud committed in the sale of registered securities, but also fraud in the sale of any security.

General observations on intrastate security offerings in Texas. An issuer need not grow very large in order for dealings with the TSB to become necessary. Registration of an issue with the TSB, though not an extremely complex undertaking, will probably require professional assistance.

The TSB does not require the preparation of a prospectus to accompany the sales effort to distribute an issue, which is a cost saving. If the marketing of the issue is to be done by the issuer, that is also a cost saving. If the marketing effort is a sizable one, however—if, for example, an effort is to be made to sell the issue to large numbers of buyers—professional marketing assistance may well be necessary. The issuer may decide that the assistance of an underwriter is advisable.

An *underwriter* is a professional securities marketing firm. It may be only in the underwriting business, or it may be a brokerage firm which also does underwriting. When an underwriter is used in the marketing effort, the issuer and the underwriter agree, for a suitable consideration, that the underwriter will use its best efforts to sell the security in question to the public, and that if it cannot sell the entire issue it will itself purchase the unsold balance from the issuer.

When the marketing is to be done through an underwriter, a copy of the contract between underwriter and issuer must be filed with the TSB as part of the registration statement.

A danger of a large intrastate securities offering. So long as a Texas issuer offers securities for sale only to Texans, it technically need not register the issue at the federal level. However, once a securities issue enters interstate commerce, federal registration becomes necessary unless federal exemptions apply. The Texas issuer must make certain, if he can, that the issue does not cross a state line, or he must register it with the SEC.

Policing the distribution of a large intrastate issue is difficult, to say the least. No offer to sell across a state line must be made; therefore all offerees must be residents of Texas. A legend should be printed upon each security that it is part of an intrastate offer not registered with the SEC, and that it therefore cannot be sold outside the state of Texas. Every effort should be made to keep the issue out of the hands of persons who might move outside the state of Texas within the year after issue.

If any of the intrastate issue "leaks" outside the borders of Texas, the issue must be registered with the SEC, unless it escaped the confines of Texas in a federally exempt transaction. Otherwise, the issuer has violated federal securities laws and is subject to heavy penalties.

Exempt securities and exempt transactions under federal law. Section 3 of the Federal Securities Act (FSA) sets up exemptions for securities which are very similar to the list of exempt securities contained in the TSA. Governmental securities, securities of nonprofit organizations, and securities issued by banks and other corporations subject to regulation by federal administrative agencies (such as railroads and savings and loan associations) are exempt. Securities issued as part of a corporate reorganization are exempt, as are securities issued as part of an exchange within the issuer. A stock dividend—or any other distribution of securities by an issuer that is not a sale—is exempt. Commercial paper having a maturity period of nine months or less is exempt. (Notice that twelve-month commercial paper is an exempt security under the TSA, but is nonexempt under the FSA.) And, of course, securities distributed intrastate are exempt.

Section 4 of the FSA details the exempt transactions. Here again the federal law and the Texas law are similar, though the federal exemption list is much shorter. The federal exemption list comprises:

1. Sales by persons other than issuers, underwriters, and dealers.
2. Private offerings.
3. Certain sales by dealers of no concern to us here.
4. Sales through brokers, except when a controlling shareholder disposes of his shares through a broker. This will be discussed in detail later.

FSA 3(2) also provides for a partially exempt issue—an issue of a value of less than $1,500,000. This is called the "Regulation A" exemption.

The federal registration process. If an issuer desires to market a new issue of a nonexempt security in interstate commerce, and he proposes to offer it for sale to the public in an amount of more than $1,500,000 (the public comprising many persons who are not sophisticated investors), the full federal registration process must be completed.

A registration statement and a prospectus must be prepared and filed with the SEC. FSA 5 requires the filing and FSA 6 prescribes the contents.

The prospectus is a document that must ultimately be furnished to every buyer of the issue. Twenty-one items of information must be presented in the prospectus, including a description of the issuer's business; information about his management; a summary of his earnings for the last five fiscal years; a description of the security being registered; the plan of distribution for the security (who the underwriters are and so on); the use to be made of the proceeds of the issue; names and addresses of principal holders of the issuer's securities; remuneration of officers and directors of the issuer; and current financial statements, together with certifications by auditors as to their accuracy.

The registration statement must contain up to seventeen additional items of information not contained in the prospectus, which will not be released by the SEC to potential buyers of the issue. This information includes marketing arrangements, recent sales of unregistered securities (through exempt transactions, of course), subsidiaries of the issuer, accounting treatment of proceeds of the issue (how much will be allotted to paid-in capital and how much to capital surplus), and certain supplemental information. The information required to be included in the registration statement is often very bulky, so that the completed statement is a volume containing several thousand pages.

The assistance of expert accountants and attorneys is absolutely necessary in the preparation of these documents. Months of work by professionals and clerks may be needed to assemble the necessary data, and the expense of preparation may run to hundreds of thousands of dollars.

Any issue of a security that will require federal registration will certainly also require state registration unless the security is listed upon an exchange. Before the federal registration statement is filed, no offers of the security may be made in interstate commerce, and no intrastate offer may be made by mail, under federal law. Under state law, however, no offers for sale may be made until the state registration is in effect, so the Texas issuer should make no offers at all before the statements are filed.

After the filing of the federal documents, federal law permits the making of offers to sell in interstate commerce and by mail; it also permits advertising of the offer through "tombstone ads" which disclose very basic facts with respect to the offered issue. Texas state law has no objection to the tombstone ads, but it does forbid the making of offers for sale before the state registration becomes effective. Remember that the state registration of an issue to be marketed interstate will be by coordination, so the state registration will not be effective before the federal registration.

The processing the SEC gives the filed documentation will take one of four forms, depending upon the state of the documentation and the experience of the SEC in dealings with the issuer. These are customary (full) review, cursory review, summary review, and deferred review.

Customary review is complete review. SEC personnel look over the documentation thoroughly, to be as certain as they can that the documentation discloses the truth, the whole truth, and nothing but the truth about the issue. If they find deficiencies in the documentation (as they usually do) a letter of deficiency is drafted and sent to the issuer, who will then usually amend his documents to correct the deficiencies. If the SEC is happy, the statement will be permitted to become effective and the registration process is complete.

FSA 8(a) provides that a registration statement automatically becomes effective twenty days after filing if it is complete when filed. The SEC will not complete review, particularly customary review, within twenty days. Thus, the issuer files a slightly incomplete statement, leaving out the final offering price and sometimes some other information. This way there is time for the SEC to check out the documentation and there is time for the issuer to correct deficiencies. When the deficiencies are corrected, the issuer furnishes the offering price and the statement is permitted to go into effect. The SEC has the authority to accelerate effectiveness, so that when the registration statement is finally complete the issuer need not wait twenty more days.

The SEC gives first registration statements customary review. It will also give the full treatment to issuers who had difficulty in clearing a first statement, or to issuers who do not do as careful a job on their documentation as the agency thinks they should.

The agency may choose to give a registration statement *cursory review*. This is done with respect to registration statements by smaller concerns with which the agency has had no great prior difficulties. Agency personnel examine the documentation to some degree, but not thoroughly. Deficiencies may be found and brought to the issuer's attention, but the issuer is notified that the examination was not thorough and is informed that if there are defects in the registration statement which were not discovered on cursory review the issuer is responsible for them. The issuer and its chief executive officer must inform the SEC in writing that they understand this, and that they realize they may incur liability due to such an unspotted and uncorrected defect. The statement is then permitted to become effective after the selling price is provided.

Summary review is generally given to registration statements of large issuers with whom the SEC has many dealings and no great difficulties. The agency assumes that the documentation is properly prepared, so it is very summarily examined in order to look for obvious defects. Deficiencies are not often spotted on this type of review. The issuer is informed of the summary nature of the review, and the same statement from the issuer is required here as on cursory review. Statements given this type of review go into effect very quickly.

Deferred review is actually little or no review. If when SEC personnel look over a registration statement they find many obvious defects without having to search, they send the issuer what is known in the business as a "bedbug" letter. The letter informs the issuer that the registration statement is so full of defects that the issuer should discard it and begin preparation of the documentation all over again.

Meanings of effectiveness of a registration statement. Once the registration statement is effective, the issuer may proceed to accept offers to buy the security. A copy of the prospectus must be furnished to all buyers.

The SEC has no power to evaluate the investment potential of a security. It may not deny registration to a security that is not a good buy. The SEC's mission is to be certain that the issuer has made full disclosure of all material facts surrounding the issue to the public in the prospectus and in the registration statement. A buyer of a registered security knows, then, that the issuer has probably told the truth, the whole truth, and nothing but the truth about the security in the prospectus and registration material. But the SEC puts no stamp of approval on the security as a good buy.

Stop orders. The effectiveness of the registration statement is not permanent. If the SEC discovers that a registration statement or prospectus contains false or misleading material, or that material omissions of fact have been made, the agency may stop further sales of the security without notice or hearing.

It usually suggests to the issuer that sales be stopped, and the issuer usually complies. The public image of an issuer suffers a grave blow when the SEC issues a stop order against its securities. It obviously gives the impression to the investing public that dishonest things go on within the issuer's management.

The issuer has the right to challenge the validity of a stop order in administrative proceedings and in court, but that is a losing battle: the issuer gets bad publicity no matter what the outcome.

Shelf registration. Generally speaking, an issuer may only register securities it plans to market in the near future. There would be no point in permitting registration of securities to be marketed a year from now, since by the time of marketing much of the information contained in the prospectus and registration statement would be obsolete. Shelf registration is permissible under limited circumstances, among which are the following:

1. When an issuer is using its stock as consideration for stock of other corporations to be acquired through tender offers and the like, or
2. When the issuer has outstanding rights or warrants entitling the holders to stock at their option.

In both of these situations, distribution of the stock is subject to more uncertainty than that provided by the ordinary marketplace. Where shelf registration is allowed, the issuer must keep his registration statement up to date and accurate by filing amendments with the SEC when necessary.

When the marketing of a new registered issue proceeds slowly, problems similar to those of shelf registration may arise. Information contained in the registration statement and prospectus may become obsolete.

In such a case, the issuer should amend his registration statement and prospectus to remove the obsolete material. He will not incur liability to anyone for issuing a false registration statement if he does not do this, so long as the statement is true when it becomes effective; that is all that is required. However, the issuer would be guilty of fraud for not disclosing those facts that have made portions of the registration statement untrue.

In addition, a prospectus more than nine months old may not contain information more than sixteen months old. Thus, if a portion of an issue remains unsold nine months after the issuance of the prospectus, the prospectus must be amended to delete the old information, and the more current information must be disclosed. Generally, it is not necessary to draft and print an entire new prospectus to accomplish this; it may be done by amending the existing prospectus.

The Regulation A exemption. FSA 3(2) permits the SEC to exempt an interstate issue involving $2 million or less from the full registration process, but not from registration altogether (the statutory authorization was raised to $2 million late in 1978). The SEC has chosen to extend the exemption to offerings of $1.5 million or less only (the exemption was only $500,000 prior to 1978). The issuer need file only a short-form registration statement and a short-form prospectus, called an offering circular. These documents are much shorter than those required for full-scale registration, and are much cheaper to prepare. They are not given the full review accorded to full-scale registration statements upon customary review.

If the issue amounts to less than $100,000, no offering circular is required. The short-form registration statement is sufficient. When the issue amounts to $100,000 or more, the offering circular must of course be furnished to all buyers of the issue.

Only one Regulation A offering may be made in any twelve-month period, for obvious reasons. There may well be less paperwork involved in several Regulation A offerings than in one full-scale offering.

The private offering exemption. The private offering exemption from registration is the most commonly used exemption. A new issue of securities may be marketed in interstate commerce with no registration if it is offered only to institutional and other sophisticated investors.

No public advertising of such an issue is permitted. Mail advertising is allowed only if it is directed solely to sophisticated investors. The issuer must diligently monitor his advertising campaign to make certain that no advertising gets into unsophisticated hands.

Seminars and similar sessions may be held to promote sale of the issue, but the issuer must make sure that no unsophisticated investors attend such seminars.

The issuer must inform the SEC of its intent to make use of this exemption, and buyers of the issue must inform the agency of their purchases by filing investment letters. The letter must inform the SEC of the details of the buyer's purchase, and must contain a statement that the purchase is for investment purposes only. The resale of securities issued under this exemption is severely restricted. Securities issued under the exemption should carry upon them a conspicuous notice that they are unregistered and that resale is therefore restricted.

An owner of such securities may dispose of them to another sophisticated investor without limitation. Difficulty arises only when an effort is made to sell the shares to the public. The right of the holder of such shares to sell them to the public is limited by the provisions of SEC rule 144 and by general law.

If the owner can get the issuer to register the securities, free sale becomes possible. Prior to 1976 it was difficult to convince an issuer to do this because of the necessity for preparation of a full-scale SEC registration statement. Since 1976 registration of such stock has become much simpler, provided that the issuer has already issued and registered a class of securities with the SEC under the Federal Securities and Exchange Act (to be discussed later) and is complying with the reporting requirements of that act. In such a case, the issuer may register securities issued under the private offering exemption by filing Form S-16 with the SEC—a form only three or four pages in length which incorporates by reference financial information already on file with the SEC. The time and expense involved in preparing and filing this form is minimal, so issuers should be much less reluctant to register such securities. However, unless the issuer has contractually agreed to register the securities upon the request of the holder, it may refuse to register. The holder then has no recourse.

The holder is permitted to sell some or all of an issue of unregistered securities to the public under the provisions of SEC Rule 144. Formerly this privilege was subject to severe limitation, but recent SEC amendments to the rule have very much broadened the resale privilege.

If the holder is a nonaffiliate (not a parent or subsidiary) of the issuer and has been for three months; the securities are not listed on a stock exchange; the prices thereof are not quoted by the NASDAQ system for quotation of prices of over-the-counter securities; the issuer is registered with the SEC under the Federal Securities and Exchange Act and is making the reports to the SEC required under that act; and the holder has owned the unregistered securities for four years, the holder may sell all of its holdings to the public without registration and without volume limit.

If the unregistered securities are part of an issue listed upon a stock exchange, or if the price of the issue is quoted by NASDAQ, and if other of the requirements are met, the holder may unrestrictedly sell the issue to the public after owning it for three years. If the owner is an affiliate of the issuer, or if the owner has not owned the unregistered security for the required three or four years (depending upon stock-exchange listing, etc.), the holder may sell limited quantities of his holdings to the public without registration. The requirements here are as follows:
 1. Holder must have owned the issue for at least two years, and
 2. There is current public information available about the issuer, and
 3. Sales are immediately reported to the SEC.

Under these circumstances, the holder may sell a portion of its holdings to the public once every three months. The amount which may be sold during a three-month period is limited to the greater of:
1. One percent of the outstanding securities of the class of which the unregistered securities are a part, or
2. The average weekly trading volume of the security on stock exchanges or the over-the-counter market during the four weeks immediately preceding the sale.

Sales of unregistered securities under Rule 144 must be made only through securities brokers or through market-makers such as stock exchanges. Such sales may not be made directly to an unsophisticated buyer.

Thus, the buyer of a securities issue through a private placement runs a considerable risk. He is locked into his investment for a period of two years unless he can dispose of it to a sophisticated investor or unless the issuer registers his holdings. His capacity to unload during the third year (and possibly the fourth year) is limited. By the time unlimited disposal of the issues becomes possible, the value of the investment may well have been severely impaired.

On the other hand, such a buyer may be the recipient of unusually great capital gains. These issues are sold at a discount with respect to market price, in order to compensate buyers for their extra risk; if the price of the issue rises, the risk is more than compensated for.

Many buyers of securities through such private offerings are institutional investors, such as mutual funds, pension funds, and the like. The majority of these buyers are investing funds which they manage for their clients.

Since investment managers are fiduciaries, they are expected to use great prudence in the handling of the funds entrusted to their care. Under the money management rules of yesteryear, it would have been deemed most imprudent to commit the funds of clients to this sort of illiquid investment.

Today, however, the objective of the investment manager must be the pursuit of the elusive capital gain. Otherwise, the purchasing power of the carefully preserved dollars comprising the investment fund melt away like snow in the heat of today's inflation.

Thus, the investment manager is attracted by the great potential capital gain inherent in the private placement. The rewards may be great—but the risks may be equally great.

The controlling person and Rule 144. When a corporation decides to sell shares to the public, the security issue sold to the public must ordinarily be registered. Things are generally arranged so that the former owner of the small company gets enough shares during the expansion to retain control. These shares should be registered for the later convenience of the controlling person, but often they are not so registered.

An owner of such shares is in the position of a person who has bought shares of the issuer under the private placement exemption. Before the controlling person can sell these shares to the public, he will have to get them registered, sell to sophisticated investors only, or sell under the limitations of Rule 144. So long as he does not want to sell, he has no problem; but if he dies and his heirs want to sell a definite problem exists.

Criminal liability for violation of FSA. FSA 24 provides that anyone willfully violating any provisions of the FSA, or anyone willfully making an untrue statement of fact in a registration statement or omitting material facts from a registration statement shall be, upon conviction, fined not more than $5,000 or imprisoned not more than five years, or both.

The major criminal violation of the FSA is violation of the fraud provisions of FSA

17, which state that it is unlawful to use the mails or any instrumentality of interstate commerce to fraudulently induce a person to buy a security. The section not only applies to securities subject to the FSA but to any and all securities. The section, however, applies only to fraud by sellers; it does not govern fraud by buyers. The offering for sale, or sale, of unregistered securities in a nonexempt transaction would also be a criminal offense.

Persons using fraudulent methods of selling securities in interstate commerce may also be guilty of mail fraud if they use the U.S. mails for their schemes. Makers of false registration statements commit the offense of making a false official statement, for which one may be fined up to $10,000 and imprisoned up to ten years. Two or more persons working together upon such a scheme commit the crime of criminal conspiracy, carrying a maximum fine of $10,000 and maximum imprisonment of five years.

Civil liability for FSA violations. FSA 11 has to do with the civil liability of those involved in the filing of a false registration statement. Those liable for this are liable for an amount up to the price the buyer paid for the security when it was issued. Plaintiffs under Section 11 are essentially trying to get their money back.

Those liable for the falsity of registration statements include:
1. The issuer.
2. All persons who signed the registration statement. FSA 6(a) requires that the president (or other chief executive officer), the treasurer (or other chief financial officer), the comptroller, and a majority of the directors sign.
3. Directors who did not sign the registration statement, and persons about to become directors who are named in the registration statement.
4. Each accountant, engineer, appraiser, and other professional who is named in the statement as having certified any professional opinion.
5. The underwriter.
6. Any person controlling any of the above.

The issuer has no defense to liability. If there are false statements in the registration statement, or if material facts have been omitted, the issuer cannot escape liability.

Directors and signers of the statement can escape liability if they resign their office as soon as they learn of a falsity in the registration statement and inform the SEC of what they know, and—if they resign after the statement is effective—if they make a public announcement as to why they resigned. With respect to parts of the statement certified by an expert, a nonexpert may escape liability by showing that he had no reason to doubt the certification of the expert. Of course the director who is an accountant might have trouble arguing that he signed a registration statement containing false financial data because he had no reason to doubt the certification of the statement by an expert CPA.

Professional experts are of course liable only for their own certifications. An accountant could hardly be held responsible for a false certificate of appraisal by a professional appraiser. Underwriters have no escape hatch available. Attorneys who are board members also have few escape hatches; they have more specialized knowledge and are better equipped to spot falsities than are nonattorneys.

The plaintiffs do not have to be original owners of the securities in question. Any owner may sue. Damages recoverable are compensatory damages; the plaintiff recovers the difference between the price the security was issued for (in the case of the original buyer) and the worth of the security at the time the suit was brought.

FSA 12(1) provides that a buyer of an unregistered nonexempt security from a seller in a nonexempt transaction may rescind his purchase and recover his consideration less income received on the security from his seller. An original buyer can get his money back from the issuer, and a buyer from the original buyer can get his money back from that original buyer or from the issuer.

FSA 12(2) provides that any person who uses fraud in the sale or offering for sale of a security by mail or by use of any other medium of communication in interstate commerce shall be liable to his buyer for rescission of the sale and return of the buyer's consideration, or for the compensatory damages if the buyer no longer owns the security. The section applies to any fraudulent sale or offer of sale of a security by mail or by medium of communication in interstate commerce, not just to securities which are registered or should be registered. Agents are not liable under this section; only the issuer or the former owner of a security could incur liability, except that persons controlling the issuer could be held liable. Under this section a buyer has recourse only against his seller or against persons who control his seller.

Statutes of limitations. Criminal prosecutions for FSA violations must be brought within five years of the commission of the offense. Civil suits must be brought within one year after discovery of the offense or within three years after the first issue to the public, or—in the case of fraud—three years after the fraudulent sale, whichever period expires first being the determining factor.

Registration requirements under the Federal Securities and Exchange Act. A corporation must register an issue of nonexempt securities with the SEC under the FSEA when:
1. The security is traded upon a recognized stock exchange, or
2. The issuer is:
    a. Engaged in interstate commerce, and
    b. Has at least 500 holders of a class of equity securities, and
    c. Has total assets of over $1 million.

FSEA 12(a) requires registration of issues listed upon exchanges. FSEA 12(g) requires registration of the corporation when the above qualifications are met.

A corporation registers under the FSEA by providing the SEC with essentially the same information required in a FSA registration statement. FSEA registrations become effective sixty days after filing. The SEC may require correction of deficiencies—but the agency is not as technical about examining FSEA statements as it is about FSA statements, and difficulties are all ironed out during the sixty-day period.

Reporting requirements of registered corporations. Registered corporations must file three types of reports with the SEC after registration becomes effective.

FSEA 13(2) requires the filing of annual reports. These must be filed within 90 days of the end of the corporate fiscal year, except for financial information which must be filed within 120 days of the end of the fiscal year.

The annual report must contain:
1. The number of equity security holders.
2. Increases and decreases in outstanding equity securities.
3. Changes in parents and subsidiaries of registrant.
4. Changes in registrant's business.
5. Principal holders of voting securities.
6. Directors of registrant.
7. Remuneration of directors and officers.
8. Options to purchase securities outstanding.
9. Interest of management and others in corporate transactions.
10. Financial statements and exhibits, which must be audited and certified.

Quarterly reports must be filed within forty-five days of the end of the quarter of the fiscal period. These are essentially condensed statements of profit and loss and of capitalization. They must be in comparative form showing the results, for example, of the first quarter of 1980 as compared to the first quarter of 1979. These figures must be prepared in accordance with accepted accounting principles, but they need not be audited or certified.

Special reports must be filed when any special event occurs. The report must be filed within ten days of the end of the month within which the special event occurred. There are thirteen such special events, the prompt reporting of which is required:

1. Changes in control of registrant.
2. Significant acquisitions or dispositions of assets (involving 15 percent or more of assets or income).
3. Material legal proceedings, including receivership proceedings, proceedings where a corporate insider is an adverse party, and suits for damages by or against the registrant where the damages sought amount to more than 15 percent of assets or income.
4. Material changes in terms of securities.
5. Material changes in security (collateral) for registered securities.
6. Defaults upon senior securities if these amount to 5 percent or more of assets. Such defaults include failure to make interest payments on bonds and failure to declare dividends upon preferred stock.
7. Increases in amount of securities outstanding, if more than 5 percent of the class.
8. Decreases in amounts of securities outstanding, including any acquisition of treasury stock and any other decrease amounting to over 5 percent of a particular class.
9. Granting and exercise of options to purchase securities, if more than 5 percent of a class is involved.
10. Material revaluation of assets or restatements of stated capital account (reductions in stated capital, for example).
11. Submission of matters to vote of shareholders, other than uncontested reelection of directors.
12. Other materially important events, such as mineral discoveries and large casualty losses.
13. Financial statements in case acquisitions are made.

Reporting requirements for corporate insiders. Officers, directors, and ten percent shareholders must file with the SEC a statement of their shareholdings in a registered corporation at the time of registration. Persons becoming officers, directors, or ten percent shareholders must file such reports within ten days of acquiring this status. The first report filed must show all changes in share ownership for a period of six months before insider status was acquired.

A person losing his insider status must continue making the reports until six months have passed after his loss of the status.

Whenever an insider changes his shareholdings in the registrant, he must report the change within ten days of the end of the month is which it occurred. All of this reporting is required by FSEA 16(a).

Prohibitions on insider share transactions. FSEA 16(c) prohibits officers, directors, and ten percent shareholders from selling stock in their companies short. When a person sells shares short, he borrows shares from another shareholder or from his broker and sells them, hoping to be able to buy them back and repay the loan at a time when the price of the shares is lower. The profit of the short seller is basically the difference between what he sold the borrowed shares for and the price he had to pay to buy them back. So long as the latter is less than the former, a profit is made. Short sellers are seeking to profit from the distress of an issuer of securities. This being the case, it would certainly be a violation of fiduciary duties for a corporate insider to seek to profit from his company's misfortunes.

Any officer, director, or 10 percent shareholder should hold securities in his company for six months or more before selling them. If such a person sells shares he has held for less than six months at a profit, the corporation or shareholders acting for the corporation may sue to force the insider to turn his profit over to the corporation, as provided by FSEA 16(b). Liability will accrue here even if the insider did not sell the identical shares he bought within six months of a purchase.

Liability for fraud under FSEA 10b and SEC Rule 10-b-5. SEC Rule 10-b-5 makes it unlawful to use any instrumentality of interstate commerce, the U.S. mail, or the facilities of a national securities exchange to employ a device or scheme to defraud; to disseminate untrue statements of fact or to conceal material facts; or to engage in any act, practice, or course of business that would defraud or deceive any person in connection with the purchase or sale of a security.

The antifraud effect of this is much broader than the antifraud provisions of the FSA. As with the FSA, 10-b-5 applies to fraud in connection with the purchase or sale of any security, not only registered securities. It applies, however, as much to fraudulent buyers as to fraudulent sellers. The courts have held that the rule prohibits all sorts of questionable conduct in the purchase and sale of securities.

For instance, the inclusion of false information in FSEA registration statements in annual or quarterly corporate reports under this statute, or in special event reports would be a violation, as would the failure to make a timely special event report. Since the information contained in such reports is essential to permit investors to evaluate fully the prospects of securities they deal in, false information in these reports will prevent members of the investing public from having essential information at hand in dealing in the registrant's securities. Issuers will not be directly liable for such violations unless they buy and sell their own securities directly after the violation has taken place. However, corporation insiders who have reason to know what was not disclosed to the public can most certainly be held liable when they act upon the true, undisclosed facts.

Insiders, of course, will always have access to facts knowledge of which is temporarily denied to outsiders. Personnel in the company accounting department who assemble the data from which financial statements are prepared may well know about company financial trends before anyone else. Personnel in the office of the corporate general counsel know about potential litigation involving the company before anyone else does. Officers know about delicate preliminary negotiations involving a potential acquisition before anyone else. Personnel of the company's R&D department know about potentially valuable technological breakthroughs before anyone else. Personnel in the office of the company geologist know more about potential mineral discoveries on company lands than anyone except the field personnel making the surveys and drilling the test wells. We tend to think of the knowledgeable insider as a director or officer, but obviously there are situations where lower-placed company personnel know some things the higher-ups do not yet know.

Should we attempt to prevent these insiders from using their advance information to profit in dealings in the securities of their company? This question was at least in part answered in the affirmative in the case of *SEC vs. Texas Gulf Sulphur Company*, 401 F.2d 833 (1968). Geologists working for the company discovered huge mineral reserves on a tract of company land in Ontario, Canada. The discovery was duly reported to the company. The company delayed in reporting it to the SEC and to the public, and downgraded the magnitude of the discovery when it did report. Meanwhile, insiders loaded up on the stock, and when the true magnitude of the discovery came to light the price of the stock soared, enabling the insiders who had bought early to realize a large profit. However, when the SEC learned of the early suppression of the news, it went to court to compel the profiting insiders to disgorge their profits.

In this case, not only directors and officers were made to disgorge—employees and members of their families were also compelled to do so. All defendants found guilty of violation of Rule 10-b-5 were ordered to pay into the treasury of Texas Gulf Sulphur Company the difference between the price they paid for the questionable stock when they bought it and its market price the day after the true news became public, or to give up the stock itself to the company. The fund so created was to be used to pay compensation to those who sold Texas Gulf Sulphur stock between the time the discovery was made and the time the true news of it became public.

Those employees and others who passed along information of the discovery to friends and relatives (tippees) were made liable for the profit earned by these tippees as well as their own to the extent that their tips could be traced. It should be noted, though, that the SEC did not go after the tippees themselves.

Any corporate insider, then—be he officer, director, or employee—who uses inside information available to himself but not to the public to profit in transactions in his company's stock may be made to give up his profits. Any seller or buyer who is directly defrauded in a security transaction would appear to have recourse under this rule. The defendant in such a case need not have dealt with the plaintiff. The defendant needs only to have done things that caused the defendant loss through his—the defendant's—wrongful actions. For instance: Able sells his Zilch Company shares to Baker at a low price, feeling that there is not much chance for Zilch to climb in price. Shortly thereafter the price of Zilch soars because of good publicity. Later Able learns that the news which was contained in the publicity release had been deliberately suppressed by Charles, president of Zilch, until after Able had sold his shares. Able would have a good claim against Charles, even though he had had no dealings with Charles and even though Baker had been as ignorant of Zilch affairs as Able. (Of course, had Baker had knowledge of the suppressed news and not told Able, Able would have a case against Baker also).

The remedy of the plaintiff is usually compensatory damages. When a defrauded buyer sues his seller, the buyer may also ask for rescission of the contract and return of the purchase price.

The statute of limitations on 10-b-5 cases is the state statute of limitations for fraud, normally two years in Texas.

Proxy regulation. FSEA 14 gives the SEC power to regulate solicitations of proxies in connection with corporations registered with the SEC under the FSEA—that is, companies whose stock is listed on an exchange, or companies in interstate commerce having more than $1 million in assets and 500 holders of their equity securities.

Any solicitation of proxies must be accompanied by a proxy statement, containing twenty-one items of required information. This statement must be filed with the SEC at least ten days before distribution to shareholders. Solicitation of proxies by management for election of directors and other business at an annual meeting of shareholders must be accompanied by a current annual report of the corporation, including financial statements which meet SEC standards.

Stockholders have the right to submit proposals to shareholders in management's proxy materials, except for nominations for director and proposals censuring management. If management decides to support a stockholder proposal, the proposal goes in the proxy statement with management's blessing. If management opposes the proposal, it must still be included in the proxy statement, together with a 200-word statement by the proponents in support. Of course management will make clear in its statement that it opposes the proposal.

Management may refuse to include a proposal in its statement when:
1. It is illegal—it would require the corporation to violate federal, state, or foreign law if adopted.
2. It is a personal proposal, relating to enforcement of a personal claim against the corporation or its management, or to the adjustment of a personal grievance against these.
3. It is irrelevant—it is not significantly related to the corporation's business, or it is beyond the corporation's power to effectuate (a tax reduction or social reform, for example).
4. It relates to the ordinary business operations of the corporation (such as size of the work force, quantity of production, etc.).
5. It relates to specific amounts of dividends.
6. It is either counter to a proposal by management or similar to a proposal of another shareholder that is to be included by management in the proxy statement.
7. It is moot (the proposal has already been put into effect, for example).
8. The proposal (or one substantially identical to it) has been previously submitted within the last five years and has received only a small percentage of affirmative votes (how small depending upon when and how many times previously submitted).

Management may not exclude a proposal from the proxy statement upon its own initiative. It must inform the SEC of the submission, and of its opposition. If the SEC agrees to the exclusion, the proposal is excluded. If the SEC orders inclusion, management must include it—and may also include its arguments against the proposal.

The scope of such shareholder proposals is severely restricted, of course, by these limitations. Essentially, the shareholders may not intrude upon management's discretion to handle the day-to-day operations of the corporation. On the other hand, shareholders may not use the shareholders' meeting as a forum for sounding off on political issues and other matters unrelated to corporation business. This mechanism makes it easier for shareholders to propose changes in corporate government and policy within those areas which are subject to shareholder jurisdiction.

When there is a contest for election of directors, the contestants must file with the SEC a list of the participants in the contest. Both management and the opposition must do this. Participants include the directorship candidates, members of shareholder committees either opposing management or supporting it, campaign contributors paying $500 or more to either side, and those who finance a campaign effort through making loans or lending credit. Information on the background of the participants and on their interest in the securities of the corporation must be filed along with the list, the inclusion of this information in the proxy statements being mandatory.

The opposition's communication with shareholders is in a sense at the mercy of management. Management may either send out the opposition's proxy statements at opposition expense, or it may furnish the opposition with a shareholder list and the

44/ Texas and Federal Securities Regulation

opposition may then send out its own materials. If management will not do the opposition the favor of sending out its campaign materials, the opposition must set up its own organization for doing so; this can be expensive.

Under the FSEA, then, management cannot be forced to part with a list of shareholders. The opposition may go to court and force management to issue such a list; this can be done under the TBCA. It is of course time-consuming and expensive.

Remedies for proxy rule violations include injunctions and damages. Opposition shareholders may obtain an injunction forbidding a shareholder meeting when management has obstructed the opposition by proxy rule violations. The result of a meeting held after such rule violations may be declared void and a rerun of a contested election may be granted. Also, the presence of false statements in a proxy statement or the nondisclosure of material information therein is a violation of rule 10-b-5, under which aggrieved shareholders may recover damages.

Tender offer regulation. Any person making an offer to acquire 10 percent or more of an equity security registered under the FSEA must file a copy of his offer with the SEC and with the issuer before making it. He must also file a statement with the SEC containing the following information:

1. The identity of the offeror.
2. The source of the funds to be used to buy the offered shares.
3. Intentions of the offeror as to liquidation of the target company, etc.

A tender offer usually states that the offeror will buy up to so many shares of the target company for a named price, if a named number or percentage of shares are deposited with the offeror or his agent on or before a named date. If too few shares are tendered, the offeror does not buy at all. If more than the maximum are tendered, the offeror buys ratably from all tendering offerees.

The usual purpose of a tender offer is the acquisition of control of the target company by the offeror. The incumbent management has nothing to say about the making of the offeror. Management may counter the offer by sending out materials to its shareholders advising them not to accept the offer, but such materials must be cleared with the SEC before dissemination. Management may also counter a tender by offering to buy up target company shares itself. If it does this, it too must file the same materials with the SEC as are required of the original offeror.

The making of false statements or omission of material facts from these materials is a 10-b-5 violation, entitling victims to damages. Violation of these rules may also be cause for obtaining an injunction to stop the tender offer procedure. FSEA 14(d), (e), and (f) govern tender offers.

Going private. A registered corporation under the FSEA may cancel its registration and relieve itself of FSEA reporting requirements by reducing the number of its equityholders below 300, and, of course, by delisting its stock from security exchanges in the process.

This reduction in the number of equityholders can come about through larger shareholders buying out smaller ones, little by little, or by the mechanism of the company itself making a tender offer to its shareholders. If management decides to go the tender offer route, this sort of offer is subject to the tender offer rules. Some managements find it a relief to be rid of the FSEA reporting requirements and of the continuing supervision of their firms by the SEC.

Effectiveness of securities regulation. The essential purpose of securities regulation is disclosure of information to the investing public. It is intended to force corporate insiders to share some of their knowledge with those who stand outside the corporate world, looking in.

No nation requires more information disclosure of its corporate managers than does the United States. The American investor has access to immeasurably more information than does the shareholder of any other nation. It must be remembered, however, that no set of laws or regulations can equalize the positions of corporate insider and corporate outsider. The insider acquires information first, simply because he is an insider. When one adds to this the fact that the insider possesses understanding which the outsider has little opportunity to acquire, the inequality becomes more apparent.

The law labels the relationship between directors and officers on the one hand and shareholders on the other as a fiduciary relationship, assuming that insiders have enough interests in common with outsiders so that they will work together for the common good. This assumption does not always hold. Despite the existence of the fiduciary relationship, insiders and outsiders do have divergent interests.

Outsiders may feel that the insiders would have no firm to manage without their capital investment and that the insiders should therefore be duly grateful for the opportunity to hold their jobs. Insiders may feel that outsiders could not possibly collect their dividends and capital gains without the dedication and hard work of the insiders. In addition, corporate insiders are like all human beings in that they want to be free to work with a minimum of outside interference. Shareholders may definitely be seen as a source of outside interference, and they may be resented accordingly.

The law's insistence upon disclosure of so much financial information could give the unsophisticated outsider the notion that he truly has his finger upon the financial pulse of his corporation. To be sure, he does—to a small degree. He must realize, however, that accounting is not an exact science. The various numbers which are combined into income statements and balance sheets may be manipulated in order to appear in the light desired by management.

Let us consider some examples.

Business equipment—assets used for purposes of producing income—are assets which normally decline in value as they are used. They are therefore subject to depreciation. Depreciation is treated in accounting as a noncash expense; it reduces profit without influencing cash flow. Management must determine the useful life of a depreciable asset—the number of years over which it will be depreciated. Management must also decide whether to use the straight-line method of depreciating the asset—providing for equal depreciation allowances for each year of useful life—or to use one of the accelerated methods, resulting in large allowances during the early years of life of the asset and smaller allowances later in its life. A large element of discretion enters into these decisions. A short useful life and accelerated depreciation in the short run increase expenses and reduce profits. Long useful life and straight-line depreciation do the opposite.

Inventory may be valued by the FIFO (first-in-first-out) method, or by the LIFO (last-in-first-out) method. If FIFO is used, items in inventory are considered to be the last ones purchased. If LIFO is used, items in inventory are considered to be the first ones purchased. In these inflationary times, FIFO produces a higher inventory valuation than does LIFO. LIFO produces a higher cost-of-goods-sold figure, and so reduces profit. FIFO does the opposite. Which method to use? It is solely a matter of discretion, though the IRS frowns upon rapid changes in method.

If technological change renders a valuable asset obsolete before its useful life has expired, the asset is now worth less than its book value. To carry it on the books at book value overstates the value of corporate assets, and also overstates the corporate net worth.

The situation could be rectified by writing off the asset—writing it down to its scrap value, for example. The big result of the write-off will be a large expense charge against current income. During the accounting period in which the write-off is taken, profit will be reduced or wiped out. When does the corporation "take the bath"? Within limits, it will be done when management decides to do it. If such an asset is one of great book value, a sword of Damocles hangs over the corporate income statement from the time that management begins to realize that a write-off is becoming necessary. The existence of the sword probably will not become known to the outsiders until management chooses to let it fall; potential write-offs are not disclosed in corporate financial statements until the sword is about to fall or has fallen.

Accounts receivable are carried on the corporate books as assets, though some of them will prove to be uncollectable. Uncollectability of small accounts may be taken care of in accounting through the reserve for bad debts account. Uncollectability of large accounts cannot be accounted for through this procedure, however; someone must make a final determination that a large account is uncollectable, and at that point write it off. When the write-off occurs, profit is diminished. In the absence of the bankruptcy of the debtor, the date of the write-off is a matter of management discretion. The existence of a potential write-off of this nature will not be shown on a financial statement.

Other examples of this sort could be cited. Once the outsider realizes the limitations of accounting as a measure of the financial condition of a corporation, he is in a position to make very good use of the information. Understanding is very important here; someone who is able to recognize reality when he sees it is in a position to deal with it intelligently.

45

Close Corporations

Creditors' Rights

Corporate Combinations and Divisions

Close Corporations

TBCA 2.30 provides a mechanism by which corporations owned by only a few shareholders may simplify the process of corporate government. The procedure for acquisition of this close corporation status is explained below.

Required provisions of the articles. TBCA 2.30-1 requires that the articles of the close corporation contain the following:
1. A statement that the corporation is a close corporation.
2. A statement that no shares of the corporation shall be issued by any public offering, solicitation, or advertisement.
3. A statement that the shares of the corporation are subject to restrictions upon transfer which are to be set out in the articles or in a document incorporated by reference into the articles.
4. A statement that the total number of shareholders of the corporation shall not exceed a fixed number not to exceed thirty-five; under this provision a husband and wife who co-own corporate shares shall count as one shareholder. (The maximum number of shareholders, of course, could be set at five, twenty-five, or any number less than thirty-six).
5. If ownership of corporate shares is to be restricted to a certain class of persons, or if a certain class of persons is to be denied the right to own shares in the corporation, the articles must so state.

When a corporation is organized as a close corporation, all of the shareholders and subscribers to shares must sign the articles as incorporators. If they do not, the corporation does not have close corporation status.

If an existing corporation desires to become a close corporation, it must amend its articles to include the provisions required by TBCA 2.30-1. All shareholders must agree to the amendment in writing; otherwise close corporation status is not achieved.

Management of the close corporation. The close corporation shall be managed by directors and officers as are other corporations, unless the articles provide otherwise.

However, the articles may provide that the shareholders rather than the directors shall manage the corporation. In such a case no directors are elected; all shareholders are deemed to be directors and to have the duties and responsibilities of directors.

The shareholders shall in such a case manage the corporation by holding meetings as directors do. Proxy votes are permitted at such meetings, and votes at the meetings are distributed on a basis of one share, one vote unless the articles provide for some other distribution of voting power. The unanimous written consent of the shareholders without a meeting is binding upon the corporation, as is the result of a meeting held by conference telephone call.

A close corporation managed by shareholders may amend its articles to provide for management by directors. A close corporation managed by directors may amend its articles to provide for management by shareholders.

Special agreement of shareholders. TBCA 2.30-2 provides that the shareholders of a close corporation may enter into a special agreement varying the provisions of the TBCA in the following particulars:

1. Management may be delegated to one or more shareholders or to one or more persons to be selected by the shareholders; or divisions of management authority otherwise not allowed under the TBCA may be provided for.
2. Any reasonable restrictions upon transfer of shares may be provided for.
3. Voting requirements and divisions of voting power may be used which are ordinarily not allowd by the TBCA.
4. Terms and conditions of employment of any shareholder, director, officer, or employee may be spelled out, regardless of the length of time of such employment.
5. Those persons who may be or shall be directors and officers of the corporation.
6. Declaration and payment of dividends or division of profits.
7. Arbitration of issues in case of deadlock among shareholders or directors.
8. Treatment of the business and affairs of the corporation as if it were a partnership.

This agreement may be made part of the articles or part of the bylaws, or it may be a separate and distinct agreement. In any event, the consent of all shareholders is necessary to adopt it, and the consent of all is necessary to amend it.

The agreement must be printed upon the face or back of every share certificate issued by the corporation; otherwise a notice must be placed upon each certificate that it is subject to a shareholders' agreement on file at a given place.

Loss of close corporation status. A corporation may lose close corporation status if, among other things:

1. It acquires more than thirty-five shareholders, or
2. It offers shares to the public by public advertising or solicitation.

It will also lose this status if provisions of the articles or of the special shareholder agreement are breached, and nothing is done to cure the breach.

If something occurs that would cause loss of close corporation status, the corporation must—within thirty days of the occurrence of the disqualifying event or thirty days of the discovery of the event, whichever is later—file a statement with the secretary of state setting forth the breach. A copy of the statement must also be sent to all shareholders.

Within sixty days after the filing of the statement, corrective action—such as refusing to complete a wrongful transfer of shares or beginning a suit to prevent loss of close corporation status—must be taken. If these things are not done, close corporation status is lost. When the corrective action is complete, a statement must be filed with the secretary of state making the correction a matter of record.

Suit to prevent loss of close corporation status. TBCA 2.30-3 provides that when it is threatened with loss of its close corporation status a corporation—or any shareholder or person who is a party to or bound by agreements among the shareholders of the corporation—may file a petition in the Texas district court of the county where it has its principal offices to have the court issue all orders to prevent loss of close corporation status. These may include injunctions to keep threatened acts which will destroy close corporation status from taking place or to set aside acts which have caused the loss of close corporation status.

Defendants in such actions may ask the court to appoint a receiver for the corporation instead, or to involuntarily dissolve it. The court may do this if it feels that such action is justified.

Appointment of provisional director. When the directors or the shareholders of a close corporation are deadlocked so that they cannot make management decisions, the corporation, a shareholder, or a party to a shareholder agreement may petition a court to appoint a provisional director. This person must not be a shareholder or creditor of the corporation. He has the power of an ordinary director or shareholder; in essence he becomes the breaker of the deadlock, serving until a majority of the directors or shareholders terminate his powers, or until the court that appointed him terminates the appointment. These provisions are found in TBCA 2.30-4.

Power of shareholder to dissolve a close corporation. TBCA 2.30-5 provides that the articles of a close corporation may grant any shareholder, or the holders of any specified number or percentage of shares, the option to have the corporation dissolved at will or upon the occurrence of a specified event or contingency. When the option is exercised, notice must be sent to all shareholders. After thirty days pass, voluntary dissolution shall begin.

All certificates of a close corporation of which shareholders have this option must set forth conspicuously the existence of the option, its terms, and its conditions.

Advantages of close corporation status. The ordinary mechanism for the government of the business corporation is designed for the large corporation with many shareholders. This mechanism is too complex for small operations. Close corporation status that dispenses with directors gives the 100 percent shareholder the power to manage his business just about as a sole proprietor would. It gives the controlling shareholder true control, and bypasses much unnecessary ritual.

In corporations with larger numbers of shareholders, it provides much scope for the invention of forms of governance which suit the peculiar business situation of a particular corporation. In those situations where the form of government mandated by the TBCA is a straitjacket, the straitjacket may be shed and thrown away.

Close corporation status is valuable for many small corporations; it is one of those situations in which small can be beautiful.

Creditors' Rights

Since the main purpose of the organization of a business in corporate form is the insulation of shareholders from personal liability for business obligations, it follows that the usual recourse of corporate creditors for satisfaction of claims is to corporate assets. Creditors will normally not be able to collect claims from shareholders, directors, or officers. Creditors do upon occasion have access to remedies devised to give them the power to force the corporation to do their will; upon occasion creditors may be able to hold shareholders, directors, and officers liable upon corporate obligations.

Pre-incorporation contracts. As previously discussed, pre-incorporation contracts are made by promoters before the corporation exists. If the corporation is formed, and if it ratifies the contract either by formal act of ratification or by taking advantage of its benefits, the corporation is liable upon it. If the corporation never comes into existence or never ratifies, the third party has recourse to the promoter for damages for breach.

Contracts of defectively formed corporations. As previously discussed, shareholders of a defectively organized corporation are liable to firm creditors as partners unless they have sent in to the secretary of state articles of incorporation in good form, or unless circumstances are such that the creditor is estopped to deny the existence of the corporation.

Torts by defectively formed corporations. Tort claimants against a defectively formed corporation may recover against shareholders under the same conditions that contract claimants can, except that no tort claimant can ever be estopped to deny the existence of the corporation.

Creditors of solvent corporations. Creditors of solvent corporations are generally limited in collection of their claims to actions against the corporation. If the corporation has the assets with which to pay the claim, the rights of the claiming creditor are essentially the rights of any creditor seeking to collect a claim from a debtor. If the debtor corporation cannot pay, or if it will not pay and forcible collection methods are unavailing, other remedies against shareholders, directors, and the corporation itself may be available.

Extraordinary remedies against the corporation itself. There are four extraordinary remedies against a debtor corporation of which creditors may make use. The first of these is initiation of a *receivership*. Receivership proceedings may be commenced when (TBCA 7.05):

1. The creditor has a judgment against the corporation which he is unable to collect, or
2. The corporation has admitted in writing its inability to pay the creditor's claim, or
3. Other good grounds for institution of receivership proceedings exist, such as protection of corporate assets from dissipation by current management.

Under a receivership, the corporate management is deprived of some or all of its management authority. The court hearing a petition for appointment of a receiver is usually a Texas district court. If the judge is convinced that a receiver should be appointed for the corporation, a person unaffiliated with the corporation or pertitioning creditor is appointed and given management powers that are spelled out in the order of appointment.

The receiver usually retains the current management in office—who knows better the business of the corporation? But of course management now functions under his supervision and control.

The receiver seeks to rehabilitate the corporation from the condition or conditions which made the receivership necessary. If he succeeds—one measure of success being that the creditor who petitioned for his appointment is satisfied—this receivership is terminated and control of the corporation is restored to management. If he fails, liquidation or reorganization is necessary.

The creditor may also seek *involuntary dissolution* of the corporation. This remedy may be sought only when a petitioning creditor can convince the judge of a Texas district court that immeasurable damage will be caused to unsecured creditors as a class if there is no dissolution. The result, if the petition is granted, is liquidation.

Also, the creditor may take steps to file a petition in federal district court for a *Chapter XI reorganization* of the corporation. This is a bankruptcy proceeding which will be discussed in detail in the chapter on bankruptcy. Three creditors are required to file such a petition. The result is usually a reorganization of the financial structure of the debtor corporation in which, quite often, the creditors become shareholders.

If the corporation is in such bad financial condition that there is little hope for successful reorganization, the creditor may, with the collaboration of two other creditors, file an *involuntary bankruptcy petition* against the debtor corporation. The objective of such a petition is the complete liquidation of the corporation. If the court agrees that rehabilitation of the debtor is next to impossible, the petition will be granted and the liquidation will follow, assets being distributed according to the priorities established by federal law.

Creditors' remedies against shareholders—piercing the corporate veil. Under several circumstances corporate creditors are permitted to disregard the separate existence of the corporation and assert their claims directly against shareholders. A very common example of this is the "alter ego" situation, in which a shareholder who owns 100 percent of the stock of a corporation is careless about keeping corporate affairs separate and distinct from personal affairs. So far as the management of the corporation goes, the addition of the TBCA amendments permitting close corporations simplified matters for the 100 percent shareholder. He may simply arrange things so that he, the shareholder, manages the business, and he may go about the business of managing as if he were a sole proprietor.

He must remember, however, that his personal insulation from corporate liabilities exists because the corporation is an entity separate and distinct from himself. He must therefore always keep the corporation separate from himself: he must keep complete and accurate books on the corporation's operation and, most important, he must keep corporate assets and personal assets strictly segregated. If he confuses his affairs with the corporation's affairs, no court will try to straighten out the confusion. A creditor will have little difficulty in persuading a court to treat the corporation and the shareholder as one entity.

The corporate veil will also be pierced when a controlling shareholder seeks to use the corporate entity as a means of profiting by his own unlawful conduct. Perhaps the classic situation is illustrated by this example: Ace Company owns a building which is insured against fire. Deuce owns 75 percent of the stock of Ace. Deuce sets the building on fire; it is totally destroyed. Deuce then has Ace file a fire insurance claim. If the fact becomes known that Deuce set the fire, the claim will be disallowed. To be sure, Ace did not set the fire, and Deuce was not acting as Ace's agent when he set it. But the proceeds of the claim will indirectly benefit the controlling shareholder—Deuce. So Deuce will not be allowed to profit from his arson.

Sometimes a controlling shareholder seeks to use a corporate entity as a vehicle for defrauding his creditors. A common example: Slick owns a business as a sole proprietorship. The business is in financial difficulty, and Slick fears that he will lose it. Slick therefore causes Slippery Corporation, of which he owns 100 percent of the shares, to be organized. He transfers the assets of the business to the corporation as consideration for the corporation issuing him its stock, and he makes certain that the contract of transfer provides that Slippery Corporation does not assume and agree to pay any of Slick's liabilities. Slick now claims that his creditors cannot touch any of Slippery's assets because it is not liable for his obligations. It will not work, of course, since the whole purpose of organizing Slippery was to enable Slick to put some of his assets beyond the reach of his creditors.

A variation upon this theme is the use of corporate entities by controlling shareholders as a vehicle for escaping the obligations of an unprofitable contract. For example: Spade Corporation has a contract to buy all its supplies of an essential raw material from Hart Company for the next two years. The price of the raw material has declined so that Spade management feels that it is now paying an exorbitant price to Hart. Spade tries to get Hart to modify the contract, but Hart will not agree to do so. So, Spade shareholders cause Clubb Corporation to be organized. Spade shareholders control Clubb as they do Spade. They have Spade transfer all its assets to Clubb, and they carefully provide in the transfer instrument that Clubb does not assume the obligations of Spade. Clubb then stops buying the raw material from Hart and finds a new, cheaper source. Hart claims this is a breach. Clubb denies it because it has no contract with Hart. Meanwhile the controlling shareholders liquidate and dissolve Spade.

This whole transaction of course causes Spade to breach its contract with Hart. But the controllers of such a deal are careful to arrange things so that Spade has no assets of any value left after the transfer to Clubb. So, if the creditor Hart is to have any recourse, it must have it either against Clubb or against the controlling, masterminding shareholders themselves. Courts are quite sympathetic to creditors in Hart's position. They are very likely to hold that Clubb is the "alter ego" of Spade and hold that Clubb is bound by Spade's contracts—by this particular contract, anyway.

Still another variation upon this theme is the following sort of situation: Knave Corporation acquires an essential raw material from Queen Corporation. Knave Corporation acquires enough of Queen's voting stock to obtain control of Queen. Knave and Queen then enter into an output contract under which Knave agrees to buy all of Queen's output of the raw material for a price far below cost of production. From that time on, of course, Queen runs up gigantic operating losses. Knave lends it the money to survive, taking back a mortgage on Queen's productive assets. The end result of all of this will be that Knave will treat Queen as the spider treats the fly caught in its web, draining Queen dry of assets. When the draining process is complete, Knave could then dissolve the empty shell of Queen and Queen's unsecured creditors would get nothing from the liquidation. In such a case, courts do not fear to hold Knave liable for Queen's obligations, even though a parent corporation is not normally liable for the obligations of its subsidiaries. Parent corporations do not normally milk their subsidiaries dry, however.

Courts may also pierce the corporate veil in this sort of situation: Able Corporation wants to branch out into a new line of business operations, but the new venture appears to be very risky. Able causes Baker Company to be organized to conduct the venture. Able management figures Baker will need $5 million in working capital to conduct this venture, so Able management has Baker issue all of its stock to Able for consideration of $500,000. Able then lends Baker the other $4.5 million required working capital, taking back a mortgage on Baker's assets of value. The venture is a failure. Baker ends up losing the $5 million in working capital and owes outside creditors another $2 million for equipment, supplies, services, and so on. Able claims the remaining valuable assets because of its mortgage. The other creditors claim the assets because, they say, Able undercapitalized Baker and caused the difficulty in the first place.

The creditors should win the argument. The 90 percent debt security-10 percent equity security financing scheme was certainly unreasonable for a risky venture. Able management was trying to set up a "Heads I win, tails you lose" situation as against Baker's outside creditors. At best, the court will subordinate the claim of Able to the remaining Baker assets, giving the outside creditors first shot at them and giving Able anything left over. At worst, if the remaining Baker assets are inadequate to compensate the outside creditors for their losses, the courts would look favorably upon a suit by these creditors against Able to collect the balance of their claims. The undercapitalization of Baker by Able may well result in Able's being held liable for some of Baker's obligations.

The last example of a situation where the corporate veil might be pierced is this: Venture Company owns a large department store. Its controlling shareholders know that such businesses may incur all sorts of liabilities due to defects in products sold, accidents to customers and employees on store premises, etc. The shareholders of Venture Company therefore cause to be incorporated a host of subsidiaries to operate the various store departments. One is given title to the store building and leases parts of it out to the various operating subsidiaries. The sporting goods department is a subsidiary, the pharmacy is another, the grocery another, the furniture department another, and so on.

A defective lawn mower sold by the nursery and gardening subsidiary badly injures a user. The user sues for $1 million in damages, but discovers that the nursery and gardening subsidiary has assets of only $200,000. He therefore wants to join Venture Company as a defendant, but Venture's management claims it is only the parent of a subsidiary and cannot be held liable for the obligations of subsidiaries. Here it is quite likely that the court would impose liability upon the parent. The main reason for establishment of so many subsidiaries in this case would appear to have been insulation of the parent from liabilities such as this. Multiple corporate entities can be disregarded if the main reason for their existence is the insulation of a parent or controller from liability. It must be remembered, however, that courts disregard the separateness of a corporation only under unusual conditions. If there is no misuse of the corporate entity, it will not be disregarded.

Shareholder liability to creditors not based upon disregard of the corporate entity. TBCA 2.21 is the only section of the TBCA imposing any liability directly upon shareholders for the benefit of creditors. The section provides that the only liability a shareholder shall have to the corporation or to its creditors shall be to pay the full consideration for his shares, as determined by law.

A shareholder may be held liable to creditors, then, for the amount of consideration for his shares which is unpaid if the corporation itself becomes insolvent and is unable to pay its obligations.

Creditors could hold a shareholder liable upon unpaid-for shares under three circumstances. The first situation is that where the corporation issued the shares in exchange for a promissory note, or in exchange for the promise of the shareholder to perform personal services in the future. Such issue is unlawful under TBCA 2.16. If the note has not been paid or adequate services have not been performed, the shareholder may be held liable for the original consideration agreed upon for the shares.

The second situation would be that in which the corporation issued, for example, shares with a par value of $200,000 to a shareholder in exchange for $150,000 cash, carrying on the books a "stock consideration receivable" account showing that this shareholder owed $50,000 on his shares. The creditors may, in essence, collect upon this receivable.

The third situation is that in which the shareholder holds "watered" stock. Watered stock could come into being under several circumstances, some of which are:

1. The corporation at one time agreed to give buyers of shares of preferred stock a

free share of common for each purchased share of preferred, the common being issued from authorized but unissued shares. Able bought 100 shares of the preferred and so obtained 100 shares of free common. The common is watered.

2. Baker bought common with a par value of $200,000 from the corporation and paid $150,000 for it. The corporation's books show Baker's stock as being fully paid for.

3. Charles "bought" stock from the company with a par value of $100,000 by performing services worth $50,000. The corporation itself valued the services at $50,000, but carried Charles's stock on its books as fully paid.

Creditors may hold Able, Baker, and Charles liable for the "water" in their stock. They may collect the par value of the unpaid-for common from Able, or its stated value if it is no-par common. The "water" in the shares of both Baker and Charles is $50,000; each may be held liable for that amount by the creditors.

Had the directors of the corporation valued the services performed by Charles at $100,000, Charles would have no more liability upon the shares, so long as the directors placed that value upon his services in good faith. Had the directors acted in bad faith in valuing the services at $100,000, Charles could still be held liable. TBCA 2.16C provides that the valuation placed upon property or services given in exchange for shares by the directors is conclusive in the absence of fraud by either directors or shareholders.

Assignees or transferees of unpaid-for or watered shares are not liable upon them in any way, unless they know the shares were unpaid-for or watered. Pledgees of shares that are unpaid-for or watered are not liable upon them in any way. Executors, administrators, guardians, trustees, receivers, etc. are not personally liable upon unpaid-for or watered shares which they hold as fiduciaries, but the estate, trust funds, or similar entities may be held liable.

Liability of directors to creditors. Directors may be held directly liable to creditors upon dissolution of a corporation for unlawful distributions out of reduction surplus if the corporation became insolvent after the payment. They are liable only to those who were creditors at the time of the improper payment and to those who became creditors within thirty days thereafter.

Those directors held liable for this may claim contribution from the shareholders who received the improper payments, but the creditors have no direct claim against these shareholders.

Liability of shareholders and directors to trustees in bankruptcy and assignees for benefit of creditors and receivers. It must be remembered that trustees in bankruptcy, receivers, and assignees for benefit of creditors stand in the shoes of the corporation. They therefore may enforce any and all claims which belonged to the corporation. Thus, these persons may proceed against directors for:

1. Voting to declare and pay illegal dividends.
2. Voting to make illegal purchases of treasury stock.
3. Voting to make corporate loans to directors and officers.
4. Voting to make improper distributions out of reduction surplus.
5. Voting to commence business before $1,000 in capital was paid in if the $1,000 in capital was in fact never paid in.

These persons may proceed against shareholders for:

1. Holding watered or unpaid-for shares, if creditors could hold these persons liable for this.
2. Receiving unlawful distributions from reduction surplus.

Corporate Combinations and Divisions

Corporate managements sometimes find it advisable to combine corporations. They also sometimes find it advisable to divide them. This section deals with the types of combinations and divisions, and the required procedures for carrying them out.

Merger. A merger occurs when Baker Company is absorbed into Able Company. Before the merger, two independent corporations existed—Able and Baker. After the merger only one remains—Able.

TBCA 5.01 provides that the merger process shall begin with the adoption of identical resolutions by the boards of directors of the merging corporations, containing:

1. The name of the merging corporations.
2. The name of the surviving corporation.
3. The terms and conditions of the merger.
4. The manner and basis of converting the securities of each corporation into shares or securities of the surviving corporation—and, if some securities are not to be converted into securities of the surviving corporation, what consideration is to be given these security holders for their securities.
5. A statement of any changes in the articles of the surviving corporation to be effected.
6. Any other provisions which are necessary and desirable.

The merger must be submitted to a vote of the shareholders of the merging corporations at either a regular or special meeting. The holders must be given notice of the proposed merger at least twenty days before the meeting, and must be given a copy or summary of the merger plan at that time.

All shares including nonvoting shares have the right to vote upon this proposal at the meeting. Two-thirds of the outstanding shares of each corporation must vote in the affirmative for the merger to be approved. Two-thirds of the shares of any class of shares entitled to vote as a class or two-thirds of the shares of any class whose rights will be changed by the merger in some way must also be obtained. TBCA 5.03 contains the provisions relative to shareholder approval.

When all participating corporations have approved the merger, articles of merger are filed with the secretary of state by all participating corporations. When these are filed and found to be in order, the secretary of state issues a certificate of merger to the surviving corporation, as per TBCA 5.04. Once the certificate is issued, the merger is effected (TBCA 5.05). The surviving corporation acquires all of the assets and assumes all of the liabilities of the combining corporation. It also acquires all of the rights and privileges of the combining corporations (TBCA 5.06).

Any shareholder of any of the merging corporations who is unhappy with the merger may dissent from it and demand that he be paid the fair value of his shares if he follows proper procedure. The proper procedure, according to TBCA 5.12, is:

1. He must inform his corporation before the shareholders meeting to approve the merger that he objects to it and that he will dissent if it is approved.
2. He must not vote in favor of the merger at the meeting.
3. He must, within ten days of receipt of notice from his corporation of approval of the merger (which must be sent out within ten days of the approval) make written demand upon the surviving corporation for payment of the fair value of his shares.
4. He must surrender his share certificate to the surviving corporation within twenty days of making his demand for payment.

He is entitled to be paid the value of his shares as of the day before the shareholders approved the merger. If the shareholder and the corporation cannot agree on this value, TBCA 5.12 provides elaborate rules for resolving the controversy. Once the controversy is resolved, the shareholder is entitled to be paid the fair value of his shares in cash.

Consolidation. A consolidation occurs when Able Corporation and Baker Corporation combine to form Charles Corporation. Before the consolidation, Able and Baker existed as independent entities. After the consolidation, both Able and Baker cease to exist, but a new entity—Charles—arises to replace them.

The directors of the corporations proposing to consolidate must adopt identical resolutions containing the following (TBCA 5.02):
1. The names of the consolidating corporations.
2. The name of the new corporation into which they will consolidate.
3. The terms and conditions of the consolidation.
4. The basis and manner of converting securities of the old corporations into securities of the new corporation—and, if any security holders of any of the old corporations are not to be security holders of the new consolidated corporation, the consideration to be paid them for their securities.
5. A statement on behalf of the new corporation of everything required to be included in the articles of incorporation.
6. Any other provisions that are necessary or advisable.

Once these resolutions are adopted, the procedure is identical with that for effecting a merger. The shareholders of the old corporations have the same dissent, appraisal, and payment rights as in mergers.

Sales of assets. A corporate combination may effectively occur when Able Corporation acquires all or substantially all of the shares of Baker Corporation. For Baker Corporation this is a very fundamental transaction, because the very nature of Baker will be affected by a sale of all of its assets.

Baker must follow the following procedure on this, as per TBCA 5.10:
1. The Baker directors must adopt a resolution authorizing the sale and recommending that the shareholders approve it at a regular or special meeting.
2. Notice of the proposed sale must be given all shareholders before the meeting in the manner provided for giving notice of matters to be considered at regular or special meetings of shareholders.
3. The shareholders may determine the terms and conditions of the sale at this meeting. Approval requires consent of two-thirds of all shares of the corporation, nonvoting as well as voting. If any class of shares is entitled by the articles to vote as a class upon this matter, two-thirds of the shares of that class must also approve. If the articles do not grant any class the right to a class vote here, no class has a class vote.

Shareholders unhappy with the proposed sale of assets have the same dissent, appraisal, and payment rights as shareholders who dissent from a merger or consolidation.

Assets for cash combinations. Able Corporation may wish to acquire the assets of Baker, and it may wish to pay for them with cash or in Able debt securities.

On Able's side, all that is required is a resolution of the board of directors authorizing the purchase. On Baker's side, a resolution of the directors and shareholder approval are required. From Baker's point of view, a decided disadvantage of this could be the realization of a taxable capital gain upon the sale of its assets. If such a capital gain is realized, Baker will be subject to the appropriate income tax liability. Able accomplishes the desired objective of controlling Baker's assets, without changing its ownership structure in any way.

Baker is essentially transformed into an investment company. It may liquidate and distribute the Able cash or debt securities to its shareholders, draw interest on the Able debt securities, or invest the Able cash in another business.

In any event, Able and Baker continue to exist as separate entities, so Able need not concern itself with Baker's liabilities.

Assets for stock combinations. Able may desire to purchase the assets of Baker Corporation and to pay for them with Able Corporation stock.

If Able has sufficient treasury stock or authorized but unissued shares, a resolution of its board is all that is required from it. If Able has insufficient treasury shares or authorized but unissued shares to pay the required consideration, it must either buy up sufficient shares from its shareholders or amend its articles to authorize more shares.

An effort to buy up shares from the shareholders would require the making of a tender offer; if Able or Baker is large enough to be registered with the SEC, SEC tender offer requirements would have to be complied with. If Able is not that large, the SEC need not be involved.

An amendment to the articles to authorize issuance of more shares will require consultation with the shareholders and a two-thirds vote of all voting shares of the corporation. On Baker's side, the requirements are the same as in the assets for cash combination.

Baker realizes a decided advantage from this type of deal. The receipt of stock for assets does not result in a taxable capital gain, so long as the Able stock is voting stock. Baker will owe no income tax on this transaction until the Able stock is sold. The disadvantage to Baker is that it is now a holding company with one major asset—Able stock. Baker will have to sell the stock and pay the resulting capital gains tax before entering into another business unless it liquidates and distributes the Able stock to its shareholders.

From Able's point of view, its ownership structure has changed: it has a new shareholder of some power. Depending upon the magnitude of the stock issue required to pay for the Baker assets, Baker will have some influence upon Able's affairs from now on.

Acquisitions through purchase of stock. Another way in which Able Corporation may acquire control of Baker Corporation's assets is by acquiring enough Baker stock to reduce Baker to the status of a subsidiary of Able. This does not require the direct purchase of any Baker assets; all that is required is the purchase of Baker stock. It also requires no dealings with Baker's directors or officers. It merely requires dealings with Baker's shareholders.

Stock for cash combinations. Able may wish to pay for the Baker stock it proposes to buy with cash or Able debt securities. In such a case Able management need only deal with Baker shareholders, without consulting its own shareholders.

If Baker has a few large shareholders, Able may accomplish its objective through a few interpersonal negotiations. If Baker has no large shareholders, or if those it has are opposed to Able's intentions, Able must contact the small shareholders, and, if there are many of these, a tender offer will be necessary. Again, if either Able or Baker is large enough to be registered with the SEC, compliance with SEC tender offer procedures will be necessary.

From the point of view of Baker management, the consummation of Able's intentions might be a grave threat. Once Able obtains control of Baker, Able will likely wish to install its own management team there. This could mean that the Baker managers will be out of a job unless they make peace with their new overlords. They may, therefore, decide to fight Able's effort.

Those selling Baker shares will realize taxable capital gain when they dispose of their shares. If this is an important consideration to a Baker shareholder it may cause him to have second thoughts about accepting the tender offer.

From Able's point of view, there is the risk that an insufficient number of Baker shares will be tendered; this will mean failure of the acquisition effort. Then, if the effort does succeed, Able still will have a minority interest in Baker to contend with—unless it can buy up 100 percent of the shares of Baker, which is most doubtful. If Baker's articles allow cumulative voting, these people will be able to elect some of Baker's directors. Even if the minority cannot elect directors, it can question Able's management of Baker and make its presence felt in other ways.

Stock for stock combinations. Able may want to acquire control of Baker by inducing enough Baker shareholders to exchange Baker shares for Able shares so that Able can elect a majority of Baker's directors. Unless there are enough Able treasury shares and authorized but unissued shares to serve as consideration here, Able must amend its articles to authorize more shares in order to accomplish this. Again, an Able tender offer will be needed unless Able can accomplish its objective by dealing with a few large Baker shareholders.

From the point of view of the Baker shareholders, Able shares may be more welcome as consideration than cash, because a stock for stock exchange is nontaxable until the Able shares are sold, so long as the Able stock is voting stock. The former Baker shareholders now become Able shareholders. If they got voting stock in the exchange they will now have some influence upon Able management. This situation may or may not be welcome to the Able shareholders.

Corporate combinations—summary. Of the six possible combination methods, only two result in a true combination—the merger and the consolidation. Only when the combination takes one of these two forms does the acquiring firm (or the new firm, in the case of the consolidation) end up becoming directly responsible for the liabilities of all parties.

Four of the methods result in no tax liabilities. Mergers and consolidations are generally tax-free to all parties. Only when the transaction involves the purchase of assets or stock is tax liability almost certain.

Under four of the methods, shareholders of at least some participants will have appraisal and payment rights. This is true of the merger, consolidation, and both acquisition of assets methods.

In five of the methods, the acquiring company will have some sort of continuing relationship with the shareholders of the acquired company. In mergers and consolidations, a sort of marriage between the two groups of shareholders occurs: all have an interest in the new venture. The same thing occurs in stock for assets and stock for stock combinations, except that in the stock for assets combination the target company becomes a shareholder rather than some of the shareholders of the target company. In the cash for stock type of acquisition, the target company shareholders who did not sell out remain as minority shareholders of the new subsidiary of the acquiring company and must be dealt with as such.

Merger of a subsidiary into a parent. TBCA 5.16 provides a simple procedure for a subsidiary to be merged into a parent when the parent owns at least 90 percent of each of the outstanding classes of shares of the subsidiary.

The directors of the parent adopt a resolution approving the merger. The officers of the parent prepare articles of merger similar to the resolutions of merger adopted in a normal merger. The articles of merger are then filed with the secretary of state, who issues a certificate of merger. And that ends it—almost.

If there are minority shareholders of the subsidiary, these need not be consulted before the merger; they are merely informed of the merger within ten days after it is finalized.

They then have appraisal and payment rights, unless cash was to be paid for their shares under the merger terms. If a cash price was set for their shares in the merger terms, they may in essence argue about the price by seeking appraisal and payment.

Corporate division in general. There are times when it becomes necessary, in the minds of corporate management, to divide the enterprise. This may be because two groups of shareholders within the enterprise are in conflict and a "divorce" is desired without one group's having to buy out the other. Or it may be because the enterprise is engaging in or desires to engage in two businesses, one of which has proven successful, the other of which is questionable. The management may want the speculative business to be separate from the successful one so that it will not drag the successful one down to destruction in case of failure.

There are four ways of accomplishing this objective:
1. Organization of a new subsidiary.
2. The spin-off.
3. The split-off.
4. The split-up.

Organization of a new subsidiary. This is the simplest method. The parent simply acts as incorporator of a new corporation. The parent then acquires all of the stock of the newborn subsidiary in exchange for the capital to begin a new venture, or in exchange for the assets of the business operation to be transferred to the subsidiary.

So long as the subsidiary is adequately capitalized, and so long as the management of the parent is not seeking to defraud creditors or breach contracts, the division will be legitimate and the parent will be insulated from the liabilities of the subsidiary.

The spin-off. Black Company owns two businesses. It desires to transfer one of these to a new company, but its management does not want a parent-subsidiary relationship to exist between the two companies, although it does want both businesses to be owned by the same shareholders.

Black Company causes Redd Company to be organized. Black then transfers one of the businesses to Redd in exchange for Redd's stock. So far Redd is a new subsidiary of Black. To effect the spin-off, Black now distributes the Redd shares ratably to its shareholders as a dividend in kind. Result: The Black shareholders have the same interest in Redd as they do in Black, but Redd is now not a Black subsidiary.

The split-off. The situation where the split-off is possible is essentially the same situation as that where the spin-off is used; the procedure is different, however. Again, Black causes Redd Company to be formed. The Black shareholders, or some of them, give part of their shares to Redd in exchange for Redd stock. Thus, Redd's initial assets consist of Black stock. Black then essentially repurchases its stock with the assets of the business it desires to transfer to Redd.

In a split-off the shares of the new corporation need not be owned by all of the shareholders of the old corporation, and the proportion of ownership need not be the same. On the other hand, at least some of Redd's shareholders will also be Black shareholders.

The split-up. This division method brings about a true divorce between antagonistic shareholder groups. Here, Black Company causes two new companies to be organized—Redd Company and Green Company. Black then transfers one business to Redd in exchange for its stock and transfers the other to Green in exchange for its stock. Black is then voluntarily liquidated, and its assets, the stock of Redd and Green, are divided among the shareholders by agreement, one group getting the Redd shares and the other the Green shares. The two businesses and two groups of shareholders are thus completely separated.

Tax consequences of corporate division. In general, the tax considerations here are too complex to be discussed in this work. Any one of the division methods can be tax-free if done properly or taxable if not done properly. Expert advice is necessary in planning such a division.

CORPORATE COMBINATIONS AND THE ANTITRUST LAWS

Clayton Act Section 7. Section 7 of the Clayton Act provides that any corporate combination which restrains trade or tends to create a monopoly is unlawful. The prohibition is one that need not concern managements of small corporations unduly, but it most certainly does concern managements of larger corporations.

The lawfulness of a corporate combination depends upon the business relationship of the combining firms. For purposes of analysis courts and legal scholars write of seven types of corporate combinations:

1. Horizontal.
2. Vertical.
3. Geographic market extension.
4. Product market extension.
5. Preferred access.
6. Joint venture.
7. Pure conglomerate.

Horizontal combinations. Horizontal combinations are combinations between direct competitors, firms operating in the same product market and the same geographical market. A good hypothetical example of a horizontal combination would be a combination between Ford Motor Company and American Motors. Such a combination would reduce the number of large American auto makers from four to three, and increase the industrial concentration in an already concentrated industry. The government would almost certainly challenge the legality of such a combination under the Clayton Act, and the challenge would almost certainly be upheld.

Horizontal combinations are likely to be challenged if both of the combining firms occupy more than 1 percent of the relevant market, unless one of them is a *failing company* (about to become insolvent and cease competing) or a *wasting assets company* (a mining company or something similar).

Vertical combinations. A vertical combination is a combination between a supplier of a product and a user of that product—that is, between two firms which have, or might have, a seller-buyer relationship. A good hypothetical combination of this sort would be one between United States Steel Corporation and General Motors Corporation. Since auto bodies are in part made of steel, a seller-buyer relationship could exist between these firms.

The economic objections to such a combination are fairly easy to discern. If United States Steel and General Motors combined, USS would have a large captive customer for its steel and GM would have a large captive source of supply for steel, all of which could work to the detriment of both the competitors of USS in the steel industry and the competitors of GM in the auto industry. If both combining firms occupy a fairly large portion of their respective product markets, a challenge to such a combination may be made, and the courts are likely to sustain the challenge.

Geographic market extension combinations. A combination between two firms in the same product market but in different geographic markets is a geographic market extension combination. Such a combination does not directly reduce the number of competitors in a market, nor does it foreclose competition in any market directly by creating captive customers or captive suppliers. This sort of combination does, however, indirectly influence the competitive situation in a market.

Suppose Ace Supermarkets operate only in Texas, and Deuce Supermarkets operate only in Louisiana. Ace wants to absorb Deuce so that it can invade the Louisiana market. If Ace went into Louisiana in competition against Deuce, the number of competing supermarkets in Louisiana would be increased by one. Since Ace wants to invade Louisiana by absorbing Deuce, this increase in competition will not take place. Rather, Ace will be a stronger competitor in the market than Deuce was, because the Ace-Deuce combination will have more competitive muscle than Deuce alone had. This might be damaging to competition among supermarkets in Louisiana.

Combinations of this sort are not always challenged by the government, and the courts do not always sustain the challenges. The result will depend upon the size of the combining firms, the level of competition in the involved markets, etc.

Product market extension combinations. A combination between two firms which market similar but not identical products is a product market extension combination. The classic case involved a proposed combination between Procter & Gamble, the great soap and detergent maker, and Clorox, the bleach maker.

Procter & Gamble marketed many soaps and detergents but no laundry bleach. It wanted to add a bleach to its product line. It could have developed its own bleach, but it decided instead to acquire an already established bleach—hence its effort to acquire Clorox. Procter & Gamble was, and is, a very large, diversified firm. Clorox was the nation's largest bleach maker, but was not very large in terms of total assets.

The government challenged the validity of the acquisition, because it would destroy the independence of Clorox and force the competitors of Clorox in the bleach market to find "corporate spouses" among the nation's large firms to be able to compete against the huge advertising revenues and power of Procter & Gamble.

The Supreme Court upheld the challenge and found the combination to be unlawful, in the case of *Federal Trade Commission vs. Procter & Gamble*, 386 US 568, decided in 1967.

Preferred access combinations. Consolidated Foods Corp. owned and operated food processing plants and wholesale and retail grocery stores. It bought large quantities of processed foods from food processors for use as inventory in its retail outlets.

Consolidated Foods acquired Gentry Company, a manufacturer of dehydrated onion and dehydrated garlic, components of some processed foods. The acquisition permitted Consolidated to put subtle pressure upon its food processor suppliers—"If you'd like to continue having us as your customer, we suggest that you buy your dehydrated onion and dehydrated garlic from Gentry."

This is the classic preferred access, or reciprocal dealing, combination. It was challenged, and the challenge was upheld in the case of *Federal Trade Commission vs. Consolidated Foods Corp.*, 380 US 592, decided in 1965.

The major factor to be evaluated in such situations is the size of the small acquired firm in its markets. If it occupies a fairly large portion of its market, the combination could be severely damaging to its competitors.

Joint ventures. When two competing corporations decide to invade a market in which neither presently competes by organizing a jointly owned new corporation to undertake the task, a joint venture is created. The competitors essentially agree not to compete against each other in the new market, but to join forces in competing against the other firms in the new market.

Before 1965 it was uncertain whether or not a joint venture was a type of corporate combination which could reduce competition or tend to create a monopoly under Section 7 of the Clayton Act. The Supreme Court decided that it could, in the case of *United States vs. Penn-Olin Chemical Co.*

Pure conglomerate combinations. Combinations between totally unrelated firms are pure conglomerate combinations. The Supreme Court has never had the opportunity to decide a case relative to the legality of such combinations. Government challenges to these have been rare; all have either been lost in lower courts and not appealed or settled out of court.

Pure conglomerate combinations have been numerous in recent years, and several large conglomerate empires composed of unrelated corporations have come into existence. Some of the larger empires are Transamerica, Textron, Tandy, LTV, and ITT.

Premerger notification requirements. Twenty years ago corporate managements planning corporate combinations were under no obligation to inform anyone of their intentions. Announcement of plans would not be made. The public would know nothing of the combination until it was completed.

With the enactment of the Williams Act regulating tender offers, it became necessary for corporations intending to acquire control of other corporations through making offers to public shareholders to buy their shares to tip their hands by announcing their intentions to the SEC. However, no advance notification was required for combinations to be accomplished other than via tender offers.

In 1976 Congress enacted the Hart-Scott-Rodino Act, 15 USC 18a, requiring the Federal Trade Commission to promulgate premerger notification rules for mergers or other corporate combinations involving large corporations. The administrative regulations went into effect in September 1978; they are found at 16 CFR 801.1 et seq.

A proposed combination must be prenotified when:
1. The larger firm has consolidated assets or annual sales of $100 million or more (counting all corporations under unified control) and the smaller firm has consolidated assets or annual sales of $10 million or more, and
2. The acquisition exceeds $15 million in value or 15 percent of the stock or assets of the acquired company.

The statute and regulations require prenotification of mergers, consolidations, acquisitions of assets, and acquisitions of stock if the dollar and/or percentage of stock or assets requirements are met. Also covered are tender offers in which the offeror seeks more than 15 percent of the stock of the target company and stock acquisitions to be consummated through stock purchases on the open market or through negotiations with individual shareholders. Even acquisitions of large blocks of stock for investment purposes by insurance companies, mutual funds, and trusts are covered. (Remember the high dollar thresholds that trigger the prenotification requirement, though.)

If the acquisition is a merger, consolidation, acquisition of assets, or other bargain in which a contract is made between the acquiring firm and the acquired firm, no notification is either required or possible until the contract is finalized. After this is done both companies must send notification of the combination to the FTC and to the antitrust division of the Department of Justice.

If the acquisition is to be accomplished by a tender offer, the offeror must make the notification after announcing its offer. Once the target company learns of the offer, it must also file notification, even if it opposes the tender offer. The notification must contain detailed information about the company's business and markets.

The acquisition must not be consummated until thirty days after notification is sent. A tender offer must not be activated until fifteen days after the offeror's notification is sent. Either the FTC or the antitrust division (but not both) may request additional information of either or both companies. If this is done, the waiting period is extended ten days in the case of the tender offer or twenty days in the case of other types of acquisition.

The whole purpose of premerger notification is to give the FTC or antitrust division extra time within which to decide whether or not to oppose the combination.

Enforcement of prohibition against unlawful combinations. As suggested above, both the FTC and the antitrust division of the Department of Justice have authority to enforce Section 7 of the Clayton Act, the FTC having this power because a violation of this statute also violates Section 5 of the Federal Trade Commission Act.

The major remedy in such cases is the injunction to stop the consummation of an unlawful combination, a cease-and-desist order forbidding such a combination, or an injunction compelling the breakup of an already consummated unlawful combination.

Since it is easier to prevent a combination from taking place than it is to "de-combine" a combination that has already occurred, it is to the advantage of antitrust enforcers to be able to bring suit against unlawful combinations before they are consummated. This is the major reason why the Hart-Scott-Rodino Act was enacted.

It is also possible for a private party to sue for an injunction against an unlawful corporate combination. Since such suits do not often redound to the direct economic benefit of such a plaintiff, however, this kind of suit is rare.

46

Dissolution and Liquidation of Corporations
Foreign Corporations
Texas Corporate Franchise Tax

Dissolution and Liquidation of Corporations

The corporate entity, once formed, continues to exist until the span of its existence expires (if it was formed for a specified length of time) or until its existence is terminated. The corporation given perpetual existence by its articles will endure forever, or until legal steps are taken to terminate it.

The legal procedure by which the existence of a corporation is terminated is called dissolution. Once the corporation's existence ends through dissolution, its assets must be divided among those legally entitled to them—its creditors and shareholders. This process is called liquidation.

The dissolution of the corporation may be voluntary, caused by the corporation itself or its shareholders and directors; or it may be involuntary, caused by minority shareholder action, creditor action, or the action of the state.

Voluntary dissolution. There are three voluntary dissolution procedures provided by the TBCA: one for dissolution by incorporators, one for dissolution by the act of all shareholders, and one for dissolution by act of the corporation.

Under TBCA 6.01, a corporation may be dissolved by its incorporators or directors when:
1. It has issued no stock, and
2. All monies paid in by stock subscribers, less expenses, have been repaid, and
3. No business has been commenced by the corporation, and
4. The corporation has no outstanding liabilities.

Under these circumstances a majority of the incorporators or directors may dissolve. Articles of dissolution signed by the incorporators or directors favoring the dissolution are filed with the secretary of state; if he finds everything to be in order, he issues a certificate of dissolution, which ends the life of the corporation.

Under TBCA 6.02, a corporation may be dissolved by the unanimous consent of the shareholders. Once the shareholders have consented in writing, the procedures necessary for dissolution by act of the corporation must be followed with respect to collection and distribution of assets and so on.

TBCA 6.03 sets forth the procedure for dissolution by act of the corporation, the most commonly used method of dissolution. First the directors adopt a resolution recommending dissolution and directing that the question of dissolution be submitted to the shareholders at a regular or special meeting. If it is to be considered at a regular meeting, advance notice of this agenda item must be furnished to all shareholders. If it is to be considered at a special meeting, the procedure for calling special meetings must be followed.

At the meeting, all shares of the corporation, including nonvoting shares, have the right to vote upon this question. Two-thirds of all of the shares of the corporation must vote in favor of the dissolution. In addition, in case the corporate articles give any class of shares the right to vote as a class upon dissolution, two-thirds of that class or those classes of shares must vote in favor.

If the dissolution is approved, TBCA 6.04 requires that the following be done:
1. The corporation must cease transacting new business. It still may continue to transact old business in order to complete performance of existing contracts, etc.
2. Written notice of intent to dissolve must be sent by registered mail to all creditors of and claimants against the corporation.
3. Assets must be collected, and, when necessary, liquidated (turned into cash).
4. Liabilities must be paid.
5. If any assets remain after liabilities are paid, these must be distributed to shareholders.

When dissolution is accomplished by act of the shareholders or the corporation, articles of dissolution must be filed with the secretary of state containing the following, as per TBCA 6.06:
1. The name of the corporation.
2. The names and addresses of its officers.
3. The names and addresses of its directors.
4. A statement that all liabilities have been paid or provision for payment of them has been made, or, if corporate liabilities exceed corporate assets, that assets have been distributed as far as they will go in a fair and equitable manner and that no assets have been distributed to shareholders.
5. If assets exceeded liabilities, a statement that those assets remaining after payment of liabilities were distributed to shareholders in accordance with their rights and preferences.
6. A statement that there are no suits pending against the corporation in any court, or, if suits are pending, that provision has been made for payment of any liabilities that may be created as a result of the suit.
7. Proof that proper approval for dissolution by consent of shareholders or dissolution by act of corporation exists.

Under TBCA 6.07, the articles of dissolution must be filed with the secretary of state. If he finds all to be in order, he will issue a certificate of dissolution, which will terminate the corporate existence.

Under TBCA 6.05, a corporation may revoke dissolution procedures any time before issuance of the certificate of dissolution by following essentially the same procedure as that required for initiation of dissolution proceedings.

Involuntary dissolution. A corporation may be involuntarily dissolved by administrative decree of the secretary of state, or by a court order.

TBCA 7.01B provides that the secretary of state may dissolve a Texas corporation when:
1. It has failed to file reports required by law, or has failed to pay franchise tax, fees, or penalties as required by law.
2. It has failed to maintain a registered agent in Texas, as required by law.

Before ordering dissolution, the secretary of state must send notice of the delinquency or omission by registered mail to the corporate registered office, principal place of business, or last known address of any officer or director, or to any other known place of business of the corporation, notifying it of the delinquency and informing it that it will be dissolved in ninety days if the delinquency is not corrected.

If the delinquency is not corrected within the ninety-day period, the secretary of state issues a certificate of involuntary dissolution, at least temporarily ending the corporate existence. The dissolved corporation may be reinstated within twelve months of dissolution if the situation that caused the dissolution is corrected and proper application for reinstatement is made.

TBCA 7.01F provides that the attorney general may bring suit for the involuntary dissolution of a Texas corporation without any advance notice to the corporation when the corporation or any of its high managerial agents has been convicted of a felony connected with the business of the corporation.

The court may dissolve the corporation if it finds that:
1. The corporation or a high managerial agent of the corporation acting in its behalf has engaged in a persistent course of felonious conduct, and
2. Dissolution is required to protect the public against such future conduct.

Under this section, then, a corporation could be involuntarily dissolved if it persistently violates federal or state antitrust laws, habitually commits security act violations, etc.

The attorney general may bring suit for dissolution of a Texas corporation after giving advance notice of his intentions if:
1. The corporation or its incorporators have not done everything required in order to incorporate (such as filing articles with the secretary of state or paying the filing fee, or
2. The articles of the corporation were obtained through fraud, or
3. The corporation habitually commits ultra vires acts, or
4. The corporation has made false statements or misrepresented material facts in documents required to be filed under the TBCA.

Under TBCA 7.02, the secretary of state must periodically report to the attorney general the names of all Texas corporations that have given cause for involuntary dissolution. The secretary of state must send notice to each corporation so reported of the fact that it has been reported and the reason for the report. If the corporation does not remedy the situation within thirty days after the mailing of notice to the corporation, the attorney general may bring suit to dissolve.

The TBCA provides several opportunities for the corporation to cure its delinquencies before final judgment of dissolution is entered against it. If it does not take advantage of these, it will be dissolved.

Private parties may not sue directly for involuntary dissolution of a Texas corporation, except in the case of a suit by a creditor alleging that immediate liquidation is necessary to prevent irreparable damage to the unsecured creditors, as per TBCA 7.06A(4). Shareholders and creditors, however, normally must sue for the appointment of a receiver to rehabilitate the corporation. Dissolution will ensue only if the receivership proves unsuccessful.

As mentioned in the chapter on creditors' rights, creditors may seek appointment of a receiver when the creditor has a judgment against the corporation which it is unable to collect or when the corporation has admitted its liability to the creditor in writing; in both cases, the corporation must be insolvent.

A shareholder may seek appointment of a receiver when:
1. The corporation is insolvent or in immediate danger of insolvency, or
2. The directors are deadlocked in the management of the corporation, the shareholders are unable to break the deadlock, and the situation threatens irreparable injury to the corporation, or
3. The acts of the directors or controlling shareholders are illegal, oppressive, or fraudulent, or
4. The corporate assets are being misapplied or wasted, or
5. The shareholders are deadlocked in voting power and have failed for a period including two annual meetings of shareholders to elect successors to directors whose terms have expired, as per TBCA 7.05A(1).

TBCA 7.07 provides that a receiver shall be appointed by the court with which the petition seeking a receivership was filed. The receiver may be an individual or a corporation qualified to act as a receiver in Texas. He must post bond of an amount to be determined by the appointing court. The receiver shall have the right to sue and be sued in his own name, and shall have such other powers as are normally held by receivers, plus such powers as the appointing court may grant.

The receiver essentially manages the corporation under the supervision of the appointing court. Generally the incumbent management continues to do the routine work of running the business, with the receiver supervising operations and making the big decisions. The receiver is given twelve months to solve the problems which caused his appointment, or to formulate a plan by which the corporation may eventually solve its problems. As soon as the problems are solved, the receivership may be terminated and the management given control of the corporation again.

If no solution to the problems is in sight after twelve months of receivership, the court may order liquidation and dissolution of the corporation, as per TBCA 7.06.

In cases of involuntary dissolution by court order, the court does the dissolving by handing down a decree of dissolution. A copy of this is then filed with the Secretary of State, as per TBCA 7.09 and 7.10.

Order of distribution of assets upon liquidation. The TBCA does not go into detail on this subject. However, when an insolvent corporation is liquidated the assets are by definition insufficient to pay off liabilities in full, so the question of which creditors shall be preferred when the assets are divided becomes important. Also, if the corporation is solvent but has more than one class of shares outstanding, questions may arise as to priority in assets among shareholders.

When receivership preceded liquidation, the costs of the receivership must be paid first. These include:
1. Court costs.
2. The fee of the receiver himself.
3. Fees of the receiver's attorneys.
4. Claims of persons who furnished goods and services to the receiver for use in administration of the receivership.

Next in order of priority come claims of secured creditors. These are creditors who hold security interests or liens upon specific corporate assets. Their preference extends only to the assets in which they have security interests or upon which they have liens. If the corporation went through receivership before liquidation and its assets are insufficient to pay the costs of the receivership, the secured creditors will of course lose out.

Next come the expenses of operating the business during the receivership. This category includes items such as tax liabilities incurred during the receivership period and obligations incurred by the receiver to suppliers, employees, and the like during the receivership.

Next come federal taxes incurred before establishment of the receivership and debts owed the United States before the receivership. 11 USC 91 is the federal statute providing for this priority. The U.S. Government has a priority claim here for judgments it holds against the corporation; contract claims by government agencies against the corporation; income, employment, and excise taxes due and unpaid, etc.

Next in priority are claims of state and local governments against the corporation for taxes and the like accrued before commencement of the receivership. At the end of the line of creditors come the unsecured creditors for their claims arising before the commencement of the receivership. If any creditors lose out because of the insolvency of the corporation, these of course are the victims.

If any assets remain after the creditors are paid, they will go to the shareholders. As between classes of shareholders, there is no liquidation preference unless it is provided for in the articles. Thus, preferred shareholders have no automatic preference as to assets upon liquidation unless the articles say they do, and cumulative preferred shareholders whose dividends are in arrears upon liquidation have no preference as to these unless the articles say they do.

It is possible that a shareholder may also be a creditor. If the shareholder takes no part in management, this causes no difficulties. Such a creditor-shareholder is treated the same as any other creditor. However, when a shareholder who has taken part in management is also a creditor, a harder look will be taken at his situation. If his actions leading to his becoming a creditor were good-faith actions, if he is not guilty of any sort of mismanagement (other than bad business judgment), and if he has not sought to take advantage of other creditors or of the minority shareholders, he will be treated as are the other creditors. But if his claim as a creditor arises because he and other controlling shareholders deliberately undercapitalized the corporation, or if he in other ways sought to use his position as a controlling shareholder and creditor to the detriment of other creditors and shareholders, his creditor claim will be subordinated to the claims of other creditors. If the corporate liabilities exceed its assets he will be the one who is not paid.

If the corporation has contingent liabilities (such as liability as an endorser of a long-term promissory note), assets must be withheld upon liquidation to pay off the liability in case it materializes. If, for instance, the maker of the note pays it at maturity, the contingent liability of the endorser is discharged, and the funds set aside to cover the potential liability may be distributed to shareholders.

If upon liquidation a creditor or shareholder entitled to funds cannot be located, TBCA 7.11 directs that the cash to which this person is entitled is to be turned over to the state treasurer, together with a statement giving the name of the person entitled to the funds, his last known address, the amount due him, and any other information the treasurer may require. If the owner of this fund does not claim it within seven years, the state treasurer must publish notice of this fact one time in a newspaper of general circulation in Travis County. If no one then claims the fund within two months of the publication of the notice, the fund escheats to and becomes the property of the state of Texas.

Limited survival of corporation after dissolution. RCS 1302-2.07 provides that a corporation dissolved by issuance of a certificate of dissolution, by court decree when liquidation has not been completed, or by expiration of its period of duration, survives for a period of three years after dissolution for the following purposes:
1. Prosecuting or defending in the corporate name any legal proceeding by or against the corporation.
2. Permitting the survival of any remedy not barred by a statute of limitation available to or against the corporation or its officers, shareholders, or creditors for any right or claim existing or liability incurred before dissolution.
3. Holding title to and liquidating any assets or property not liquidated and distributed during the process of liquidation.
4. Settling other affairs not completed prior to dissolution.

During this three-year period the directors of the corporation at the time of dissolution, their survivors, or the successors selected by them have the power to manage the corporation for these four purposes. They hold any assets that come into their hands as trustees for the shareholders and creditors, and are jointly and severally liable for such assets.

If at the end of the three-year survival period there still exists an unresolved legal proceeding involving the corporation, the corporation will continue to exist for the limited purpose of resolving it until it is finally resolved. A corporation which has been dissolved because its period of duration has expired may be revived during the three-year period after dissolution by amending its articles to extend its period of duration or to perpetuate itself.

Foreign Corporations

With respect to place of organization, Texas law divides corporations into three categories:
1. *Domestic* corporations, which are corporations organized under the law of Texas.
2. *Foreign* corporations, which are corporations organized under the law of other states or territories of the United States.
3. *Alien* corporations, which are corporations organized under the law of another nation.

An alien corporation, being in essence a foreigner, has no constitutional right to do business in the United States in general or in Texas in particular. Texas law does not discriminate against alien corporations in any significant way, but federal law does. Texas treats alien and foreign corporations alike.

Generally, those things which federal law forbids aliens to do in this country are also forbidden to alien corporations. Thus, alien corporations may not, under federal law:
1. Own broadcasting licenses.
2. Own a domestic airline.
3. Own ships carrying cargo between two U.S. ports.
4. Own any license for use of nuclear materials.

A foreign corporation, on the other hand, is an American citizen. Texas may, and does, restrict the right of a foreign corporation to conduct intrastate business in Texas. Texas may not, however, forbid a foreign corporation to transact any sort of business in

Texas. A foreign corporation may, according to TBCA 8.01B, carry on the following activities in Texas without any obligation to obtain official permission:
1. Suing or being sued, engaging in arbitration or administrative proceedings, or settling claims or disputes to which it is a party.
2. Holding directors' or shareholders' meetings.
3. Maintaining bank accounts.
4. Maintaining offices or agencies for the transfer, exchange, and registration of its securities.
5. Voting stock of corporations.
6. Effecting sales through independent contractors.
7. Borrowing money or mortgaging real or personal property.
8. Collecting debts and foreclosing liens upon property.
9. Conducting interstate transactions.
10. Conducting isolated intrastate transactions if completed within thirty days and not in the course of a number of like transactions.
11. Other transactions of a similar nature.

A foreign corporation desiring to transact other business in Texas must obtain a certificate of authority from the secretary of state. The application must contain essentially the same information as the articles of incorporation of a domestic corporation.

The foreign corporation must maintain a registered office within Texas, and it must have a registered agent at that location. The location of the office and the name of the agent are two of the essential items that must be filed with the secretary of state.

A duly issued certificate of authority is valid for ten years, and may be renewed. The foreign corporation then becomes liable for Texas franchise tax, and its officers and directors become subject to the same duties, restrictions, penalties, and liabilities as officers and directors of Texas corporations. On the other hand, Texas thereby acquires no authority to regulate the internal affairs of the foreign corporation (TBCA 8.01 A and 8.02).

A foreign corporation may lose its Texas Certificate of Authority for essentially the same kinds of wrongdoing that would cause the involuntary dissolution of a Texas corporation, as per TBCA 8.16.

The major penalty suffered by a foreign corporation doing business in Texas without a certificate of authority is that it may not use Texas courts as a plaintiff. Thus, for example, it may not sue to collect accounts receivable. Such corporations may defend themselves in Texas courts, and they may enter into contracts here. The problem is that they cannot sue to enforce such contracts, although others may sue to enforce the contracts against them.

A further minor penalty is that the corporation becomes liable to the state of Texas for the franchise tax it would have had to pay had it obtained the proper certificate of authority. TBCA 8.18 contains the statutory provisions on doing business without authority.

A foreign corporation may be sued in a Texas state court even if it has no certificate of authority to do business here and no assets here. If it makes a contract in Texas with a Texan and then allegedly breaches it, or if it commits a tort in Texas against a Texan, the Texas courts have jurisdiction to hear the case under the Texas "Long Arm" statute— RCS 2033e.

Problems of the Texas corporation doing business outside Texas. All state business corporation acts contain provisions similar to those of the TBCA requiring a foreign corporation to obtain a certificate of authority (or similar document) before engaging in intrastate transactions within that state. The Texas corporation may of course do business with persons in other states without so qualifying by making certain that all such transactions are interstate transactions.

So long as the Texas corporation opens no business office in the other state, hires employees to carry out the normal business of the corporation in that state, or does any other such things, no certificate of authority will be required. All states have long-arm statutes such as RCS 2033e, however. Thus, engaging in business activity—even interstate activity—in another state may subject the Texas corporation to suits in the state courts of that state.

Most states impose corporate income taxes on corporations doing business within their boundaries. If a Texas corporation engages in intrastate activity in such a state, it will almost certainly become liable for the other state's income tax on its profits earned within that state. Texas is one of the few states imposing no such tax.

A state may not impose its corporate income tax on profits earned by foreign corporations outside the boundaries of the state, but the Texas corporations doing business within a state imposing an income tax must keep accurate records of business done within that state in order that its profits from operation within that state may be ascertained. For corporations operating in several taxing states, the accounting and compliance burden can become heavy.

It must be remembered, in general, that if you conduct business in another fellow's ballpark, you must play according to his rules. With respect to forms of taxation other than income tax, consumer protection, employment, and so on, other states may have more stringent regulation than does Texas. These must be obeyed while doing business there.

For some corporations, there are advantages to be gained by doing business abroad. The market for the firm's goods and services is immeasurably expanded, and there may well be federal tax benefits to be derived from export trade. It should be remembered, however, that, even if all transactions by the firm with its foreign customers are international transactions, there will be contact with an alien legal system, and, perhaps, an alien language and an alien culture.

There is no way in which a Texas firm may do business abroad and completely insulate itself against such contacts. The Texas corporation in Brownsville that makes a contract with a Mexican customer in Matamoros may find contact with the Mexican legal system to be necessary if the Mexican breaches the contract. If the contract was made in Brownsville the American may sue the Mexican for breach in a Texas state court, but if the Mexican has no assets in Texas that will not do a lot of good. Mexico will not enforce the Texas judgment until it becomes a Mexican judgment, which will require legal action in a Mexican court.

If the contract was made in Matamoros, of course, there would be no possibility of suit for breach in Texas unless the Mexican owned assets here. The Texas corporation would be required to sue in Mexico if it wanted to sue. This would of course mean long contact with the Mexican civil-law system and the Spanish language, unfamiliar to most Texas businessmen.

Should our Texas corporation wish to export goods into Mexico, this will require official dealings with the Mexican customs service, and perhaps with other Mexican government personnel. And should it decide to establish offices in Mexico, the hiring of Mexican employees will almost certainly be necessary, which will require person-to-person intimacy with Mexican culture and the Spanish language, and also close contact with elements of Mexican law with which the Texans would have no familiarity, such as the law governing employer-employee relations.

The U.S. tax advantages of the set-up could be very attractive; and, if the international dealings of the Texas corporation are properly managed, they may become very profitable indeed, perhaps more profitable than dealings in the domestic markets of the United States.

Texas Corporate Franchise Tax

All corporations incorporated under Texas law and all foreign corporations operating within the state of Texas are subject to the Texas corporate franchise tax, as per the provisions of Chapter 12 of the Texas Taxation Code, unless they belong to one of the categories of exempt corporations set forth in Taxation Code (TC) 12.03.

Exempt corporations. TC 12.03 exempts eighteen types of corporations from the franchise tax. Among the more important exemptions are the following:

1. Insurance companies; surety, guaranty, or fidelity companies; transportation companies; or sleeping car companies or others that are now required to pay an annual gross receipts tax.
2. Nonprofit corporations organized for the purpose of religious worship.
3. Nonprofit corporations organized for the purpose of providing places of burial.
4. Nonprofit corporations organized for strictly educational purposes, including those organized for the sole purpose of providing a student loan fund or scholarships.
5. Nonprofit corporations organized for purely public charity.
6. Savings and loan associations.
7. Open-end investment companies (mutual funds, essentially).
8. Nonprofit corporations exempt from paying federal income tax.
9. Corporations engaged in manufacturing, selling, or installing solar energy devices.

The rate of tax. TC 12.01(1) provides that the tax shall be computed by three methods, and the tax shall be that computed by the method yielding the greatest liability. The three methods are:

1. $4.25 per $1,000 or fractional part thereof of stated capital, surplus, and undivided profits. If the corporation does business in more than one state, this taxable capital is allocated among the states according to a mathematical formula contained in TC 12.02, so that only that taxable capital allocated to Texas is used in computing the Texas tax.
2. $4.25 per $1,000 or fraction thereof of the assessed value for ad valorem tax purposes of the real and personal property owned by the corporation within the state.
3. $55.

TC 12.01 also provides that certain types of corporations shall pay a reduced franchise tax, and that certain others shall be able to make specified deductions from taxable capital.

Taxable year and return due date. The taxable year for franchise tax purposes runs from May 1 to April 30. The tax is due and payable on the following June 15 (TC 12.065). Newly organized corporations and foreign corporations newly registered to do business in Texas may be required to pay their initial franchise taxes on other dates, depending upon the date of organization or date of qualification. When a tax payment becomes thirty days overdue, a 5 percent penalty is assessed. When it becomes more than sixty days overdue, an additional 5 percent is assessed. Interest at an annual percentage rate of 6 percent begins to accrue upon payments which are sixty days overdue. These penalty and interest provisions are found in TC 12.14(1).

Forfeiture of right to do business in Texas. TC 12.14(2) provides that, if the franchise tax is not paid in full by September 15, or within ninety days of the due date of an initial payment, the corporation shall forfeit its right to do business in this state. This forfeiture may be administratively declared by the Texas comptroller of public accounts, the public officer to whom the tax is payable.

A corporation that has forfeited its right to do business in Texas may not use Texas state courts as either plaintiff or defendant. It thus may not sue to collect debts or defend itself against claims filed against it. The taxpayer corporation may have its right to do business (and thus its right to sue and defend itself) restored simply by paying the delinquent taxes, plus penalties and interest.

TC 12.14(3) provides that, in the event of forfeiture of a corporation's right to do business, the officers and directors become liable for all debts of the corporation, including franchise taxes, as if they were partners. However, an officer or director may escape liability for such debts if he can show one of two things:

1. That the debt was created over his objection, or
2. That the debt was created without his knowledge, if by the use of reasonable diligence he could not have discovered the management's intention to create the debt.

TC 12.15 requires the comptroller of public accounts to mail a delinquency notice to corporations that have not made timely payment of the tax within forty-five days of June 15, or within forty-five days of the due date of an initial tax payment, stating that forfeiture of the right to do business will occur on September 15, or upon the ninetieth day after the due date of the payment, unless payment of all tax, penalties, and interest is made before that date. If the notice is properly sent, the forfeiture will be automatic in the case of nonpayment. No further notice is necessary.

Forfeiture of the charter of delinquent taxpayers. TC 12.15 further provides that if a corporation whose right to do business in Texas has been forfeited for nonpayment of franchise tax does not pay the tax and gets its rights restored within 120 days after forfeiture (by January 15, normally), the comptroller shall report it to the attorney general of Texas and to the secretary of state of Texas so that steps may be taken to forfeit the charter of the delinquent taxpayer.

There are two methods by which forfeiture of a corporate charter for nonpayment of franchise tax may be accomplished. The attorney general of Texas may bring suit to accomplish this under the provisions of TC 12.16; this method is used when the corporation has assets out of which the delinquent franchise tax may be collected. The comptroller of public accounts has the authority under TC 12.13 to file tax liens in all counties where the corporation owns property, giving the state a lien upon such assets for the taxes due. This is done after the forfeiture of the corporation's right to do business.

The suit under TC 12.16 has two objectives, one being the forfeiture of the articles of the delinquent corporation; the other is the recovery of the delinquent tax. Suit may be brought either in the Texas district court of the county where the corporation has its principal office, or in a district court of Travis County. If no corporate officer or agent may be located upon whom to serve citation in such a case, the citation may be served upon the Texas secretary of state.

If the secretary of state determines that a corporation whose right to do business has been forfeited has no assets with which to pay the delinquent franchise tax, and the corporation has not revived its right to do business by January 1 following the forfeiture, he may administratively declare the forfeiture of the charter of the corporation.

Should the delinquent corporation be a foreign corporation, Texas authorities may not declare its charter forfeited. In such a case the right of the corporation to do business in Texas is already forfeited, and Texas authorities can do no more to the delinquent.

The legal consequences of the forfeiture of the charter is that the corporation has ceased to exist. Should its management continue its business, they will be liable as partners for all business obligations; the disqualification from use of Texas courts as plaintiff or defendant will continue.

Another consequence could be that other persons could organize a new corporation under the name of the old. Since the old does not exist any longer, its name is subject to appropriation by others.

Restoration of charter. TC 12.17 provides a procedure by which a corporate charter which has been forfeited for nonpayment of franchise tax may be restored. The first step is that all delinquent franchise tax returns must be filed and all delinquent tax, penalty, and interest paid. Any shareholder, director, or officer may do this.

Then, if the corporation was judicially dissolved, a petition for bill of review of the dissolution must be filed in a Texas district court of Travis County asking for restoration of the forfeited charter. If the court is satisfied that the delinquent taxes are all paid—and if the corporate name has not been appropriated by a newly organized corporation—the charter is restored. If the old corporate name is no longer available, the corporate shareholders must amend the articles to change the name.

If the charter was administratively declared forfeit by the secretary of state, application must be made to him for restoration. Again, if the Secretary of State is convinced that all delinquent taxes, penalties, and interest have been paid—and the corporate name is still available—he will administratively restore the charter. If the corporate name is no longer available, the corporate Articles must be amended to provide a new name.

The amounts of money involved in franchise tax liabilities is normally not great. However, this brief summary of the law in this area should convince the reader that ignorance of this tax liability could involve the owners and managers of corporations in rather unpleasant difficulty.

PART IX

Real Property

47

Estates in Land

Real estate law is the area of United States law most encrusted in tradition; it is based upon the land law of medieval England. Technicalities still abound in American land law which are survivals of the age of feudalism. Although many of the feudal remnants of English land law were abolished in England in 1925, some of these technicalities still survive in American states.

Since the original sovereign of the soil of Texas was the king of Spain, the original land law of Texas was Spanish civil law. When Mexico obtained independence from Spain, the Spanish land law was essentially kept in effect here. The act of the Congress of the Republic of Texas which adopted the English common law as the basis of Texas law in a sense replaced the Spanish land law with English law, and since the Anglo-Saxon colonists of Texas were opposed to feudal privilege and unnecessary legal complexity, some of the more obscure feudal technicalities of English land law were kept out of the land law of Texas.

The transfer of title to land is a very formal matter. When land is voluntarily transferred by a living owner, the transferor (called the grantor) must deliver to the transferee (called the grantee) a formal document of transfer, a *deed*.

Since ownership of land is of great public interest, public records are maintained within each county from which ownership of all tracts of land within the county may be determined. In order to keep these records up-to-date—and also in order to protect his ownership—a grantee should properly record his deed as soon as possible after receiving it.

When ownership of land is transferred by death, this act must be memorialized by the recording of a written document. When the deceased has left a will, the transfer is made a matter of record by recording a copy of the will. When the deceased left no will, the probate court will hand down a decree specifying the transfer of ownership mandated by the Statute of Descent and Distribution, and that decree will be recorded.

When ownership of real estate is involuntarily transferred because of seizure and sale by a judgment creditor of the former owner or something of that kind, the selling agency—sheriff, tax authority, etc.—will give a deed of a special sort to the buyer indicating his new ownership.

Ownership of real estate carries with it a large package of rights and interests. These may be concentrated in the hands of one person, or they may be divided among two or more persons in various ways. These divisions will be the subject of much of the material in this section.

First, ownership of the surface may be severed from ownership of the subsurface. The subsurface estate is often called the *mineral estate*. Thus, Jones may own the surface of a tract of real estate, while Smith owns the subsurface minerals. Ownership of the subsurface minerals may also be divided: Smith might own the subsurface mineral estate, but transfer the right to remove coal from a certain subsurface rock stratum to Brown. Smith might also transfer the right to drill oil wells and remove underlying oil and gas to Anderson.

Secondly, ownership of the land in time may be divided. Thus, Able may deed a tract of land to "Ben Baker for the term of his life, remainder to Cal Cass and his heirs." Able is in essence dividing ownership between Baker and Cass, the nature of the division being that Baker obtains present ownership and retains it for as long as he lives while upon his death his interest terminates and Cal Cass or his heirs become owners. There are several ways by which ownership of land may be temporally divided; we shall soon proceed to a discussion of these.

Thirdly, present ownership may be divided among two or more persons or organizations in one of the forms of co-ownership discussed in the section on personal property.

Fourthly, a portion of the package of surface rights may be transferred by the surface owner to someone else. Thus, Jones, owner of the surface estate, may grant Blake the right to build a road across his property, along with the right to use that road. He might also grant to Green the right to dig sand out of a surface sand deposit on the property. He might also grant to Redd the right to fish in the lake on his property, and the right to take home all the fish he catches. He might further grant to Blue the right to graze cattle on the pasture that is part of the property.

Land is also subject to several sorts of items or security interests, interests granted to creditors of the owner to secure his payment of various sorts of obligations. A person who borrows money from a savings and loan association to finance the erection of a building on a piece of real estate will be required to grant the association a trust deed lien upon the property. If the loan is not properly repaid, the association may foreclose its lien and extinguish the ownership interest of the borrower. By the same token, those governments with authority to levy and collect real property taxes are granted liens upon the land subjected to taxation until the assessed taxes are paid. Should the taxes not be paid, the agencies may foreclose their liens in order to collect.

The landlord who rents or leases his property to a tenant also divides the package of ownership rights in various ways. Generally the tenant obtains possession and use of the property in exchange for the obligation to pay rent. Nonpayment of rent by the tenant may give the landlord legal cause to evict the tenant and to terminate his rights.

Present and future interests. If all temporal interests in a piece of land are united in one owner, we say that he owns a *fee simple absolute estate.* He owns the entire temporal interest—he may convey it away while he lives, and he may pass it on to his heirs when he dies. He may use the land as he pleases, subject to the rights of others who may have special rights in the surface (such as the right to build and use a road).

If the present temporal right of the paramount owner is limited in some way, the temporal ownership is split in two or more ways. Thus, if the present paramount owner has ownership of the property for the term of his life only, someone else will acquire paramount ownership rights upon his death; that someone else possesses a future interest.

Since the fee simple absolute estate represents complete temporal ownership, no future interest coexists with it. Whenever the present paramount owner has less than a fee simple, he does not possess total temporal title. The portion of the title that he does not own is the corresponding future interest.

Most tracts of land are owned in fee simple absolute; the complications of creating divided temporal ownership should discourage anyone from the creation of such ownership. However, testators often provide for divided ownership in their wills, in order to prevent use of their land for undesired purposes, to provide for heirs who might be unable to look out for themselves, to attempt to control the lives of their heirs, or for some other reason. Creation of divided ownership of this nature by deed is less common, but it does occur—and for some of the same motives as guide the testator.

The fee simple absolute. The nature of the estate granted in a will or deed depends upon the wording of the operative part of the will or deed. Word usage was all-important in medieval England: it is not much less important in the present-day United States. It is perhaps a bit less vital in Texas than in some other states, but in the matter of conveyance of land it is still of the utmost importance to say what you mean and to mean what you say.

Traditionally, if one wanted to will a fee simple absolute to one's heirs or sell a fee simple absolute to one's buyer, the deed or will had to state that, for example, John Jones, seller, was conveying the land to "Sam Smith and his heirs forever," or words to that effect. The use of the magic words "and his heirs" was necessary to make clear that Sam Smith was to have the right to pass the land along to his heirs upon his death. Under Texas law, however, RCS 1290 provides that words of inheritance are not necessary to the creation of a fee simple absolute estate. If the wording of the deed or will makes clear the intention of the grantor or testator to create a fee simple absolute estate, and if the grantor or testator has a fee simple absolute to transfer, his words will be given their plain meaning.

The fee simple determinable and the possibility of reverter. It sometimes happens that a transferor of land wants to restrict the use to which the land may be put or to impose some other restriction upon the transferee. It is then possible for him to word his deed or will in such a way that, if the transferee violates the restriction, his ownership ends there and the transferor or his heirs reacquire the property.

A deed may accomplish this if it is worded, "To Sam Jones and his heirs and assigns forever, so long as said premises are used for agricultural purposes, and no longer." Another possibility might be, "To Sam Jones and his heirs, so long as no intoxicating liquor is sold upon these premises and no longer."

Sam Jones has almost complete temporal ownership here. The interest he has may be sold, given away, mortgaged, or willed to his heirs; but the restriction will remain against the property forever, in theory. Any violation of it by Sam Jones, his heirs, or his assigns will terminate the fee simple determinable estate.

Let us assume that Jim Smith conveyed the land to Sam Jones and created this fee simple determinable. The right to retake the land in case of violation of the restriction has been retained by Smith. This future interest is called a *possibility of reverter*. It too may be sold, given away, or willed to heirs. If Jones violates the restriction, his ownership automatically ends. Smith is now the owner, and Jones is merely a trespasser. Smith may now reclaim the property by filing an action against Jones and proving the violation of the restriction. The court will then decree that Smith is the owner, and order Jones to give up possession. There is no time limit on the making of Smith's claim because, in fact, he became the owner as soon as the restriction was violated.

The fee simple subject to condition subsequent and the right of entry. A transferor of land who wishes to impose restrictions upon the transferee may word his deed or will in such a way that the transferee's ownership does not automatically end upon the violation of the restriction; instead the transferor may go to court to have the transferee's ownership terminated. Sam Jones might accomplish this by wording a deed as follows: "To Jezebel Jones and her heirs forever, on condition that Jezebel Jones not marry Ahab Able." Another example of such a restriction would be, "To Barry Biznotch and his heirs forever, on condition that the playground for children located at the northeast corner of these premises never be removed." Jezebel Jones and Barry Biznotch obtain a fee simple subject to a *condition subsequent*. The future interest retained by Sam Jones is a *right of entry* for condition broken.

A right of entry does not automatically ripen into legal title upon violation of the condition. The owner of the right of entry does have the right to file an action against the violator to have himself declared the owner. If he prevails, he will become the owner as of the time the decision of the court becomes final.

Since the owner of the right of entry merely acquires a legal cause of action upon breach of the condition, he must file his action within four years of the violation of the restriction. If he does not do this, the statute of limitations runs out on his action, and the violator now has essentially a fee simple absolute. As with the fee simple determinable, the condition may endure forever. And, as with the possibility of reverter, the right of entry may exist forever.

The fee simple upon executory limitation and the executory interest. Jim Jones might deed land to his daughter Jenney, the deed reading in part, "To Jenney Jones and her heirs forever; but if Jenney Jones marries any son of Frederick Farmer then to Jeremy Jones and his heirs." Or Jim Jones might deed land to Pete Pollok, the deed reading in part, "To Pete Pollok and his heirs, but if Pete Pollok shall not be survived by any child of his then to Dan Duncan and his heirs." Or Jones might deed land to Ed Eads, the deed reading in part, "To Ed Eads and his heirs, but if the land ever be used for purposes other than one-family residential purposes then to Frank Fannin and his heirs."

One thing that is common to all of these conveyances is the fact that the land will pass to a third party in case of violation of the restriction. Jim Jones has given up all of his rights, retaining no interest at all. The interest passed to all of these third parties is called an *executory interest*. The interest which is subject to the restriction is a fee simple upon executory limitation.

The executory interest ripens into full ownership when the restriction imposed upon the owner of the fee simple is violated. As with the possibility of reverter, the holder of the executory interest need merely go to court and seek the ejectment of the former fee owner as a trespasser. The executory interest is also an interest which may be transferred or inherited.

The life estate, reversion, and remainder. Suppose that Jim Jones deeds a tract of land "to Abe Ardo for the term of his life." Abe Ardo acquires a *life estate*—the right to possess and use the land so long as he lives. Abe's interest is not an inheritable interest, though: it terminates upon his death. Abe may, for most purposes, treat the land as his own while he lives. He may use it in almost any way he sees fit. He may mortgage his interest, or even sell it.

Since Jim Jones did not specify in his deed what was to happen to the interest he did not convey to Abe Ardo, Jim kept that for himself. Jim's interest is a *reversion*, since title to the land will revert back to Jim or his heirs upon Abe's death. The reversion, too, may be sold, mortgaged, inherited, etc.

Had Jim Jones made his deed read, "To Abe Ardo for the term of his life, remainder to Bob Burkey and his heirs," Jim would have disposed of all of his ownership. Jim would have no reversion, because he conveyed the right to ownership after the death of Abe Ardo to Bob Burkey and his heirs. The future interest obtained by Bob Burkey is a *remainder*. There are several classifications of remainders; they will be discussed shortly.

Had Jones made his deed read, "To Abe Ardo for the term of his life, remainder to Bob Burkey and his heirs if Bob Burkey survives Abe Ardo," three interests are created. Abe Ardo has his life estate. Bob Burkey has a remainder, contingent upon his being alive at the death of Abe Ardo. Jim Jones has a reversion: the property will revert back to him upon the death of Abe Ardo if Bob Burkey is not alive at that time.

The use to which a life tenant may put land is to an extent limited. The life tenant may not use the land in a way that would injure the interest of the owner of the reversion or remainder. Since the life tenant will not own the place forever, he must have some concern for the rights of his successor in ownership. He may not commit waste upon the property. For instance, if he is a farmer he must use farming methods that will minimize soil erosion. If there is standing timber on the property, he may cut as much as he requires for personal use, but he may not cut the timber and sell it without the consent of the owner of the remainder or reversion. If there are buildings on the property, the life tenant must keep them in repair at his expense.

The life tenant is responsible for payment of the real property taxes levied upon the land. However, the owner of the reversion or remainder must make certain that the taxes are kept current. If a taxing government forecloses its lien upon the property in order to collect delinquent taxes, the entire title will be sold, and the future interest will be wiped out. The holder of the future interest should therefore pay the taxes if the life tenant does not. In such a case the future interest owner may recover what he paid from the life tenant.

If the life tenant makes any permanent improvements upon the property, they will go to the future interest holder in the end. Should the life tenant wish to build a new house upon the property, then, it will become part of the property and pass to the future interest holder upon the life tenant's death. Despite this, the life tenant may not force the future interest holder to pay any part of the cost of building the house or of making other improvements. A life tenant therefore has no great incentive to make such permanent improvements.

The life tenant alone may not sell any mineral rights (assuming that the mineral rights are owned by the persons who own the surface rights). He may not grant any oil and gas leases or other mineral leases. He may not grant any easements or anything of the kind. All owners of interests in the property must join in such transactions. Thus, if the life tenant wants to grant an oil and gas lease to Goop Oil Company, but the owner of the remainder does not want to do so; Goop Oil gets no lease and there is nothing the life tenant can do about it, short of buying out the remainderman.

The life estate pur autre vie. Suppose Jim Jones deeds land "To Bob Baker for the term of the life of Billie Jones Baker." Bob Baker gets a life estate here, and Jim Jones keeps a reversion. The measuring stick of the duration of Bob Baker's life estate is not his life, however; it is the life of another person, Billie Jones Baker. A life estate the duration of which is measured by the life of some person other than the life tenant is a life estate *pur autre vie*—the phrase is Old French for "for another life."

A life estate pur autre vie is also created when Les Link sells his life estate in a tract of land to Mike Murphy. All Les Link can sell, of course, is what he owns. If he owns a life estate measured by the term of his life, that is all he can sell. So Mike Murphy gets a life estate measured by the life of Les Link. Upon the death of Les, Mike's interest ends.

The life estate pur autre vie may be inherited. If Les Link conveys his life estate to Mike Murphy, and Mike Murphy dies before Les Link, the life estate is not terminated, because the measuring life—that of Les Link—has not ended. Mike Murphy's life estate for the life of Les Link therefore passes to his heirs; only the death of Les Link will terminate that interest.

Complex combinations of life estates, remainders, and reversions may be erected. For instance: Ben Baker deeds land "to Cal Collins for the term of his life, remainder to Don Doll and his heirs." Collins has a life estate; Doll has a remainder. Collins then deeds his interest to "Ernie Evers for the term of his life, remainder to Frank Forbes and his heirs." Evers has a life estate pur autre vie in the property. Forbes has a remainder in the life estate. The possibilities are numerous here. If Collins dies before either Evers or Forbes, the life estate and the remainder in the life estate both terminate and the property goes to Doll. If Evers dies before Collins, the property goes to Forbes, who will have a life estate pur autre vie measured by the life of Collins. If Forbes then dies and wills all of his property to Goss, Goss will acquire a life estate measured by the life of Collins.

Classification of remainders. The law recognizes four classifications of remainders. These are convenient tools for analysis, and they also have some legal significance. Examples of these four classifications follow.

1. Ned Nelson deeds land to "Pete Parker for the term of his life, remainder to Otto Obetz and his heirs." Otto Obetz has a totally vested remainder. Upon the death of Parker, only Obetz and his heirs have any interest in the property.

2. Rick Ryan deeds land to "Stan Senff for the terms of his life, remainder to the children of Sonia Senff Barlow." Sonia Senff Barlow has one son, Tim. Sonia is thirty-two years of age and is married to Bob Barlow. Tim Barlow has a vested remainder subject to partial divestment. He is sure to obtain an interest in this property after the death of Stan Senff, but the size of his interest is open to question. It will depend upon how many more children are born to his mother.

3. Ken Katz deeds land to "Lonnie Lunk for the term of his life, remainder to Melinda Murgg and her heirs, but if Melinda Murgg should not survive Lonnie Lunk then to Nora Norpig and her heirs." Melinda Murgg has a vested remainder subject to total divestment here. If she is alive upon the death of Lonnie Lunk, the property is hers. But her death will terminate her interest. Nora Norpig's interest is not a remainder at all—it is considered to be an executory interest.

4. Ulysses Unch deeds land to "Vern Vigosh for life, remainder to the child of Vern Vigosh who has the most living children upon the death of the said Vern Vigosh." Contingent remainders are created in the children of Vern Vigosh here. It would normally be impossible to determine at the time of Unch's conveyance to Vern Vigosh which of Vern's children is likely to have the most living children at Vern's death. But, so long as Vern has at least one child, and that child has at least one living child at Vern's death, some child of Vern's will meet the terms of the remainder and obtain the property. The possibility also exists that no one will meet the necessary qualification. Since that is true, Ulysses Unch retains a reversion here.

This classification of remainders is significant for several purposes. First, if ownership of land is divided between a life tenant and remaindermen, it is possible for these persons together to convey full fee simple absolute title to the property if the life tenant and the remaindermen together own fee simple absolute title. Thus in example 1, Pete Parker and Otto Obetz together could convey a fee simple title to a buyer. In example 2, conveyance of full title will be difficult so long as Sonia Senff Barlow is alive. The difficulty is that an unborn child of Sonia's would have an interest in the property on Stan Senff's death. Stan Senff and Tim Barlow together could not convey full title to the property because of the contingent interests of the unborn children of Sonia Senff Barlow.

In example 3, Lonnie Lunk, Melinda Murgg, and Nora Norpig together could convey full title. If all three would not agree to convey their interests, full title could not be assembled before Lonnie Lunk's death unless Melinda Murgg were to die before Lonnie Lunk. The death of Melinda would terminate her interest; at that point, Lonnie and Nora together could convey full title. In example 4, no conveyance of full title would normally be possible before the death of Vern Vigosh, unless Vern is no longer able to father children and Vern, his children, and Ulysses Unch all join in the conveyance.

In lawsuits involving property—such as eminent domain suits or trespass to try title suits—all persons claiming an interest in the property must normally be joined as plaintiffs or defendants before the judgment will be effective with respect to all. Owners of vested interests must certainly be joined if they can be located and served with citation. Unborn children and other contingent claimants may be represented by parents, guardians, or— where the claimants are members of a class (such as children of a named person)—by other members of the class. It may, however, be impossible to join totally contingent claimants.

A third situation where classification of a remainder is important arises when a long period of time will lapse before the remainder results in possession. A remote contingent remainder may be cut off by the *rule against perpetuities*, which will be discussed later. Vested remainders are not influenced by this rule.

Powers of appointment. Suppose that Jim Jones deeds land as follows: "To Quincy Quarles for the term of his life, remainder to such person as Quincy Quarles shall by will appoint." Quarles obviously has a life estate here, but he also has more: He has the right to determine who gets the property upon his death, if he will bother to leave a will appointing someone to receive it. He possesses in addition a general power of appointment exercisable by will. Since the possibility exists that Quarles will die intestate, Jim Jones possesses a reversion.

The deed from Jim Jones might read, "To Quincy Quarles for the term of his life, remainder to such of the brothers and sisters of Quincy Quarles as he shall by deed or will appoint." Again, Quarles has a life estate. Again, he also has a power of appointment. But this one is both broader and narrower than the one in the prior example. It is broader in the sense that it may be exercised either by deed or by will. It is narrower in that the persons Quarles may appoint to take title are limited to Quincy's brothers and sisters. This is a special power of appointment exercisable by deed or by will. Again, Jim Jones has a reversion: Quarles may never deed away the remainder, and he may die intestate.

The deed from Jim Jones could read, "To Red Raffish for life, remainder to such persons as Ted Tucker shall by deed or will appoint, and, should Ted Tucker not exercise this power of appointment before the death of Red Raffish, then to Urs Unch and his heirs." Here Raffish has a life estate; Ted Tucker has a bare general power of appointment, exercisable by deed or will, and Urs Unch has an executory interest.

A *power of appointment* is the power to determine who shall have title to a piece of property upon the termination of a prior interest. The power exists independently of any ownership interest; it may be held by a person who has no other interest in the property whatsoever. The right to exercise the power is personal to the owner. Only the owner may exercise: he may not dispose of it in any manner, and it is not subject to seizure by his creditors. If he dies without exercising it, it is lost; no one else may inherit it.

If a power of appointment is special, the members of the class eligible for the appointment have no interest whatsoever in the property. They are in the position of the probable heir of a living property owner; they have an expectancy that is entitled to virtually no legal protection.

Leasehold estates. The possessory owner of real estate has the power to lease or rent the premises. Most of the law relative to such arrangements is in essence the law of landlord and tenant, which will be discussed in Chapter 49. There are four types of leasehold estates:

1. The term of years.
2. The periodic tenancy.
3. The tenancy at will.
4. The tenancy on sufferance.

The last three tenancies are essentially matters of landlord-tenant law, as are most aspects of the term of years. The duration of a term of years may be a period of less than one year or a term of many years. A formal deed is not required for the creation of such an estate, but if the term is to be more than one year the lease must be in writing. The lessor of a term of years is a landlord; the lessee is a tenant. The lessor's interest in the property is also called a reversion.

The duration of the lessee's term may be affected by the nature of the lessor's interest. The lessee from a holder of a fee simple absolute estate has no worry on this count, but a lessee from a holder of less than a fee simple absolute may have some worries. If the estate of the lessor is terminated by a breach of restriction, the estate of the lessee terminates also. If the lessor holds a life estate only, the duration of the lessee's interest is limited not only by the term of the lease but also by the duration of the lessor's life estate. When the life estate terminates, so does the lease.

Ambiguities in conveyances. The lack of clear thinking by drafters of deeds and wills, and some technical remnants of English feudal law in American court decisions, have combined to create difficulties that can madden law students first exposed to property law.

One such troublesome matter occurs, for example, when Sam Smith by will leaves property "to Tim Tucker for the term of his life, remainder to the heirs of Tim Tucker." Does Tim Tucker have a life estate and his heirs a vested remainder, or does Tim Tucker have a fee simple absolute? The literal interpretation of the words used would favor the life estate; but an English court determined, in *Shelley's Case, 1 Co. Rep. 93b, (1579–1581)*, that such a conveyance gives Tim Tucker a fee simple absolute. Because of the decision in Shelley's Case, this was the law of Texas until the Texas legislature abolished the rule in 1963; RCS 1291a now provides that this rule is no longer law in this state. This sort of conveyance is now interpreted literally again.

Another such complication is illustrated by this example: Al Able deeds land "to Ben Baker for the term of his life, remainder to the heirs of Al Able." Literal interpretation of this would lead to the conclusion that Ben Baker gets a life estate and the heirs of Al Able get a vested remainder. However, English courts devised the *doctrine of worthier title* to govern such situations. By this doctrine the heirs of Al Able get no interest because they would stand to inherit the right to take the land upon Ben Baker's death in any case—and a title received through inheritance is worthier than one received through the operation of a conveyance such as this one. Under this doctrine, then, Ben Baker got a life estate and Al Able retained a reversion, which he could dispose of during his lifetime. This, too, was the law in Texas until 1963. RCS 1291a also abolishes the doctrine of worthier title in this state.

Another complication is illustrated by this example: Pat Patman deeds land "to Ripp Ruggles and the heirs of his body forever." The meaning of such a conveyance has varied under English law, but from the year 1285 until quite recent times it was held that Ripp

Ruggles had a *fee tail estate* in the property. If Ruggles died without lineal descendants, which is what "heirs of his body" means, the land would revert back to Pat Patman. But if Ruggles did produce heirs of his body who survived him, the land would remain the possession of these heirs until the line of direct heirs of Ripp Ruggles died out, a process that might take centuries. All of the heirs of the body of Ripp Ruggles who came into title to this property would own a fee tail estate in it and would be totally unable to transfer its ownership to anyone but the heirs of their bodies.

Needless to say, this aristocratic notion of tying up land in one family forever did not take too well in the United States. Most American states, including the state of Texas, do not recognize a fee tail estate. A few states do recognize it, but not in its medieval English form. In Texas, such a conveyance is given its plain meaning. A conveyance such as that in the example above would certainly be interpreted as giving Ripp Ruggles a fee simple absolute. However, if the deed read, "To Ripp Ruggles for life, remainder to the heirs of his body," Ruggles would get a life estate, while the heirs of his body would have a remainder.

A fourth complication is illustrated by this conveyance: Frank Farkle deeds land "to Gus Gosling for the term of his life, remainder to the first child of Gus Gosling to reach his twenty-first birthday." Assuming that no child of Gus's has become twenty-one at the time of the making of this deed, all of Gus's children have contingent remainders. Frank Farkle has a reversion, because of the possibility that Gus Gosling might die childless, or that none of Gus's children would live until their twenty-first birthday. The complication arises as follows: Suppose that Gus Gosling died at the time his eldest child was seventeen years of age, and, four years later the child celebrated his twenty-first birthday. Upon Gus's death, title to the property would have reverted back to Frank Farkle. But, would this child of Gus—let us call him Gene—get title from Frank upon his twenty-first birthday?

English courts would have answered this in the negative. Under the *doctrine of destruction of contingent remainders* a contingent remainder which did not vest upon the termination of the previous estate was destroyed, and never could vest. Texas courts have not seen fit to accept this notion, however. Gene Gosling would acquire title to this property from Frank Farkle upon his twenty-first birthday with no difficulty. RCS 1296 reinforces this conclusion, since it provides that an estate may be granted by deed *which will commence in the future.*

Problems may arise with respect to definition of terms used in a conveyance. Three such troublesome terms are "children," "issue," and "heirs." The problem with respect to "children" often is, does the term include adopted children and illegitimate children? The intention of the grantor or testator as it appears in the will or deed may answer the question. But in the absence of such guidance, if the children are the children of the grantor or testator, adopted children are included, but not illegitimate children. (Remember, though, that the child of an unwed mother is her legitimate child.) If the children are someone else's children, adopted and illegitimate children generally are not included.

"Issue" generally refers to lineal descendants. Primarily, a person has issue when he has children. But if the children all predecease their parent, leaving children of their own, the grandchildren still qualify as issue of their grandparent.

"Heirs" generally refers to those persons who would inherit from someone who dies intestate. Heirs may thus be any blood relatives of a person; one's spouse may also be one's heir. The only circumstance under which a person would die without heirs is when he dies leaving no spouse and no known blood relatives.

Class gifts. Suppose that Danny Dunn deeds land as follows: "To Frank Farkas for life, remainder to the brothers and sisters of Frank Farkas." Here the brothers and sisters are not mentioned by name. The remainder therefore belongs to a group—the siblings of Frank Farkas.

Two sorts of problems can arise here. Suppose that, at the time of Dunn's deed to Farkas, Frank has one living brother, Festus, and one living sister, Freda. Festus dies before Frank, leaving three children. Would the children of Festus inherit his share? The answer is negative: Frank's three nephews are not his brother (their father).

Suppose that, after Dunn's deed and before Frank's death, Frank's parents beget another son, Fred. Would Fred obtain a portion of this property upon Frank's death? Yes, he would: the membership of the class may increase while Frank still lives. Suppose, then, that at Frank's death he is survived by Freda and Fred, Festus having predeceased Frank. Freda and Fred now own the property as tenants in common. Now suppose that Frank's parents beget another child, Ferdinand. Is Ferdinand entitled to a one-third interest in this property? The answer is negative: the class closed at Frank's death. Of course this outcome would have been different had the deed read: "To Frank Farkas for life, remainder to Festus and Freda Farkus, share and share alike." The remainders of Festus and Freda would have been vested. The children of Festus would have received his interest, while Fred and Ferdinand would receive nothing.

The rule against perpetuities. Suppose that Joe Jomini leaves a will which provides: "I bequeath my residence to my eldest son Jerry for the term of his life; then to my grandson Japheth, eldest son of Jerry, for the term of his life; then to the eldest son of Japheth for the term of his life; then to the eldest son of the eldest son of Japheth for the term of his life; and to the eldest son of the eldest son of the lineal descendants of Japheth Jomini until the line of direct descandants runs out; remainder to the Salvation Army." Joe Jomini is creating a chain of life estates which could endure forever. The chain begins with a life estate in Jerry Jomini. Japheth Jomini has a vested life estate remainder, and the other life estates are contingent upon Japheth's having an eldest son and all of these subsequent eldest sons having eldest sons.

Joe Jomini could not erect such a structure—this land would be effectively removed from the market for generations. The mechanism which prevents it is the *rule against perpetuities*. This rule was devised by the English courts and adopted by the courts of most American states. It provides that no contingent interest—a contingent remainder or an executory interest—shall be valid unless it vests within a life in being at the time of the conveyance or death of a testator plus twenty-one years.

Assuming that both Jerry and Japheth are alive at the time of Joe's death, their interests are vested. The interest of Japheth's eldest son, though contingent, would vest within twenty-one years of Japheth's death; if he has an eldest son, the son would be born while he still lives, or, at the latest, within nine months of his death. Japheth's eldest son might not have an eldest son within twenty-one years of Japheth's death. That interest and all which follow it are too remote in vesting, and would be outlawed by the rule.

The rule in its common-law form has been adopted by the Texas courts. Problems arise, however, with respect to what should be done with conveyances which violate the terms of the rule. Should the entire conveyance be avoided? Should those portions that do not violate the rule be enforced and those which violate it avoided? The Texas answer is contained in RCS 1291b. This statute provides that those portions of the conveyance that do not violate the rule shall be enforced, and that those parts which do violate it shall be reformed so as to carry out the intent of the grantor or testator, within the bounds of the rule.

Probably a Texas court would permit the first three life estates to exist under this conveyance; then, upon the death of the eldest son of Japheth, the property would go to the Salvation Army.

The rule as interpreted and applied may produce surprising results. For instance, if Abner Akins deeds land to "Betsy Botkins for life, remainder to the first child of Betsy Botkins to reach the age of twenty-one," Betsy's children will have contingent remainders. If Betsy has one or more children over twenty-one when she dies, the eldest will acquire this property. If she has children, but none are twenty-one at the time of her death, title to the land will go back to Abner Akins until one of Betsy's children becomes twenty-one. If all die before they reach twenty-one, Abner reacquires a fee simple absolute in the property. However, despite the contingencies, a good contingent remainder exists.

On the other hand, if Abner's deed reads, "To Betsy Botkins for life, remainder to the first child of Betsy Botkins to reach the age of thirty-five," the remainder is void because of the rule. The logic of this is that the life in being at the time of the conveyance is Betsy's; there is no assurance that any child of Betsy's will reach thirty-five within twenty-one years after Betsy's death.

If Zeke Zarbles wills land "to Yale York and his heirs, but if Edward M. Kennedy becomes president of the United States, then to Vince Vann and his heirs," Yale York has a fee simple upon executory limitation and Vince Vann has an executory interest. Vann's interest, though contingent, would not violate the rule because Edward M. Kennedy is alive today, and Vann's interest would vest, if it ever did, during a life in being.

On the other hand, if Ken Kruppler wills land "to Mike Murphy and his heirs, but if the New Orleans Saints ever win the Super Bowl, then to Ned Needles and his heirs," we have a different situation. The same pair of interests exists as in the above example, but no one knows when, if ever, the New Orleans Saints might be victorious in the Super Bowl. This may not occur for a century—but it may occur next year. In fact, it may never occur at all. Thus, there is no certainty that this interest of Needles's will vest during a life in being plus twenty-one years; the Needles executory interest is therefore void.

Another pitfall is illustrated by this example: Amos Todd Renfrew wills land "to my son Amos Todd Renfrew, Jr. for the term of his life, remainder to the first of my grandchildren to bear the name of Amos Todd Renfrew." The grandchild of course has a contingent remainder, unless a grandchild by that name is alive when old Amos Sr. dies. If no grandchild of Amos's by that name is living when Amos Sr. dies, the remainder would still be valid, because the children of Amos Jr. would all be alive at Amos Jr.'s death or within nine months thereafter. The remainder would thus vest within the life in being plus twenty-one years. If the remainder portion of the will read, "Remainder to the first of my grandchildren to acquire a net worth of ten million dollars," however, the remainder would be invalid. There is no guarantee that the first child of a child of Amos to acquire a net worth of ten million dollars would do so within twenty-one years of the death of Amos's last child living at his death.

Thus, the operation of the rule seems quite technical and to some extent unpredictable, until one acquires the "feel" of it.

Restraints upon alienation. The restrictions placed upon owners of fee simple determinables, fee simples subject to condition subsequent, and fee simples upon executory limitation usually deal with the use of the property. Restrictions upon use are generally upheld.

Sometimes the restriction is a restriction upon *alienation*, the right to transfer or encumber the property. Courts take a long hard look at such restrictions. More often than not, a restriction of this type is found to be invalid.

As an example, consider the following conveyance by Bob Burk: "To my son Benjamin Burk and his heirs, but if Benjamin conveys or encumbers this property during his lifetime, or if Benjamin's creditors obtain liens upon it, then to my son Bernard Burk and his heirs." Bob here seeks to forbid Benjamin to dispose of the property. He also seeks to insulate the property from the claims of Benjamin's creditors. This cannot be done, at least not in this way. Restrictions of this sort which absolutely forbid alientation are void and unenforceable. Benjamin would possess a fee simple absolute estate here.

The only way in which Bob could give Benjamin an interest in the property and at the same time insulate it from the claims of Benjamin's creditors would be for him to establish a spendthrift trust of which Benjamin would be beneficiary. That subject will be discussed at length in the chapter on trusts.

Less than total restraints upon alienation may be valid. A total restraint for a limited period of time will be held invalid, but a restraint under which the grantee must offer to sell the property to the grantor for market value before selling to a third party would be upheld. Such a restriction does not absolutely forbid the transfer of the property.

A restriction that was very common in deeds before 1948 was like this one, or one of its many variants: "To Calvin Cord and his heirs, on condition that the ownership or possession of this property does not come into the hands of a person not of the white Caucasian race." Such restrictions were enforced until 1948. In that year the U.S. Supreme Court declared, in the case of *Shelley vs. Kraemer*, that the Fourteenth Amendment to the U.S. Constitution forbids the states to enforce such restrictions, because in so doing the states deny equal protection of the law to persons not of the Caucasian race.

In 1969 the Texas legislature enacted RCS 1293a, which provides that any restriction upon property providing that the property not be sold, leased, transferred to, or used by any person because of race, color, religion, or national origin is void and unenforceable.

Restraints upon marriage. A testator may in his will seek to influence the options of his beneficiaries with respect to marriage. For instance, the will of Lucas Little might leave a tract of land to "My daughter Lavinia Little and her heirs, but if Lavinia marry while her mother Melinda Maxwell Little lives, then to my son Lafe Little and his heirs." Probably Lucas wants Lavinia to stay home and care for her mother while her mother lives, and he fears that if Lavinia marries her duties to her husband would prevent this.

A court would not look with favor upon this; it comes very close to being a total restraint upon marriage—how total of course depending upon the ages of Lavinia and Melinda. In all probability a court would decide that Lavinia has a fee simple absolute here.

On the other hand, Abe Alder might will land to "My wife Alice Barnes Alder for the term of her life, remainder to such of her children as she shall by will appoint, but if Alice Barnes Alder remarry, then to my son Aloysius Alder and his heirs." Abe here seeks to keep Alice from remarrying. She stands to lose her right to the use and disposal of this property if she does remarry.

The chances are that a court would uphold the validity of this restriction. Restraints upon the remarriage of widows usually pass scrutiny. However, in this era of expanded rights for women, this view could change.

Then there are sometimes will provisions like this one in the will of Paul Parsons, leaving property to: "My daughter Darlene Parsons and her heirs, but if Darlene marry James Jacobs then to my son Randall Parsons and his heirs." Obviously Paul does not want Darlene to marry James Jacobs, and he is giving her some incentive not to do this. Since this does not totally forbid Darlene to marry, courts probably would not disturb it. After all, it merely reduces by one Darlene's possible choices of mate. Partial restraints upon marriage are generally upheld, but the nearer they come to being total restraints the more likely they are to be disallowed.

Mineral estates. The ownership of the surface of a tract of land and the ownership of the subsurface minerals may be held by the same person. However, it is possible to sever the ownership of the minerals from the ownership of the surface rights. A provision in a deed stating "Reserving all minerals to the grantor hereof" is sufficient for this—or, more simply, "Reserving all minerals."

After such severance has taken place the surface owner has no rights in the subsurface minerals. The surface owner must share the use of his estate with the mineral estate owner, to the extent that the mineral owner can only get access to the minerals through the surface. Thus, the mineral owner has the right to such use of the surface as will permit him to reach his minerals.

If the minerals are oil and gas, the surface owner must permit the necessary well drilling. If the mineral is silver, the surface owner must permit the sinking of a mine shaft. The mineral owner, in the process of exploiting his minerals, must use care not to damage the surface unduly, as by polluting surface water or anything of that kind.

Oil and gas. Texas regards oil and gas in their natural formations under the earth as being part of the earth. They belong to the surface owner when the surface owner owns all minerals and to the owner of the minerals if the surface and mineral estates have been severed.

Once oil is removed from its natural formation under the earth, it becomes personal property. Thus, if an oil spring exists upon a tract of land, the oil issuing from it belongs to the surface owner of the land where the spring is located. If it flows across a boundary line onto someone else's property, it becomes subject to the rule of capture; if the owner of the property upon which it is flowing takes possession of it, it is his. Furthermore, the owner of the property upon which the spring exists cannot follow the oil onto the other land and reclaim it. The same principle holds true when oil leaks onto the ground from a producing well and when oil leaks out of a producing well through a broken casing or the like underground.

The drilling of oil and gas wells in this state is to a large extent governed by administrative regulations of the Texas Railroad Commission. The spacing of such wells is also so governed, as is the production from them.

When the surface and mineral estates are held by the same owner, that owner has every right to drill a well if he gets the proper permits. When the ownership of surface and minerals have been severed, the mineral owner may drill without the consent of the surface owner, though he must be careful not to damage the surface any more than necessary. More often than not, though, oil and gas wells are drilled by professionals other than the surface and mineral owners. Oil companies generally do not own the land upon which they drill: they acquire the right to drill by obtaining an oil and gas lease upon the property.

When ownership of property is divided, questions arise as to who may grant an oil and gas lease. If surface and mineral estates have been severed, the mineral owner may enter into a lease alone. The company may get a damages release from the surface owner, but no more is required.

If a life tenant is in possession of the property, he may not enter into such a lease alone. The remainderman or reversioner must join in. If the possessor has a fee simple determinable, fee simple subject to a condition subsequent, or a fee simple upon executory limitation, he may lease the property alone: the owner of the future interest has no say. If the possessor is a tenant, the landlord may be able to grant a lease without his consent. Whether or not this is true depends upon the terms of the lease. If the drilling of wells will not interfere with the tenant's use of the land, the tenant's joinder in the lease is not necessary. If the drilling will interfere, then the tenant must consent. Generally, if the tenant is using only the surface—as for farming or ranching—his consent is not necessary.

If the property is owned by co-owners, tenants in common, or joint tenants, any one co-tenant may enter into a lease, without the knowledge or consent of the others. The other co-owners cannot object. However, the leasing co-owner must share all income with the other co-owners in proportion to their interests.

Texas regards the oil and gas lease as a conveyance of a fee simple determinable in the oil and gas to the lessee oil company. The typical oil and gas lease conveys a right to drill for a primary term of a stated number of years and, if oil and gas is produced upon the property, for a secondary term of as long as oil and gas is so produced. The compensation of the grantor of the lease is a delay rental payment of an agreed sum per year so long as there is no production, or a royalty of one-eighth of the production if there is production.

If a lease grants the oil and gas to the lessee for five years or as long as oil or gas is produced from the property, the lessee is essence has five years within which to drill a producing hole upon the property. The lessee is under no obligation to start drilling right away: he could wait until the fifth year to drill if he wanted to. But if there is no production from the property as of the first anniversary of the lease, the lessee must pay the agreed delay rental or lose his lease. The same will be true on the second, third, and fourth anniversaries; if there is no production as of the fifth anniversary, the lessee is liable for the delay rental, but the lease is terminated.

If production is begun, the lessee's obligation to pay delay rental ends. He must now pay royalty for as long as production continues. The lease will of course continue until production is terminated. The lessor may take his royalty in kind—in oil or gas—or in cash. the value of his one-eighth of the production.

The lessee is generally not required to maximize production. His production could be limited by Texas Railroad Commission regulations, or he might decide to limit it because of market conditions. The lessor has nothing to say about this; the lessee may use his discretion with respect to deciding how much to produce (unless the lease provides otherwise).

Problems sometimes arise with respect to drilling upon property by persons without a proper lease. The trespasser who drills a producing well without authority is liable to the mineral owner for the value of the oil and gas produced. If the trespasser acted in good faith, he may deduct his drilling costs. If he acted in bad faith he gets no deduction.

If the trespasser drills a dry hole, the most he could be liable for is the value of a lost lease. The landowner could argue that, if the trespasser had not drilled his dry hole, it might have been possible to grant a lease to some legitimate driller. In the case of a well drilled upon Jones's land but slanted so as to remove oil from Smith's, Smith is the victim of a bad-faith trespass and may recover accordingly. If, however, the well is entirely upon Jones's land, but oil is drawn from under Smith's land, no trespass has occurred. Smith's only recourse is to drill his own well upon his land, or to grant a lease upon his land.

Easements—in general. When a person has the right to use land belonging to another for a specified purpose, he has an easement. An easement is a recognized property right. It is created by deed or by will, just as are most other property rights. It is transferable and inheritable. It may be encumbered. Estates such as life estates may exist in it.

Easements in gross. An easement may grant the right to use a tract of land for a certain purpose that is not related to ownership by the easement holder of any other tract of land.

For instance: If the Podunk Telephone Company wants to erect a line of telephone poles across a 160-acre tract belonging to Sam Jones, it must obtain an easement from Jones for this purpose. The easement will describe the strip of Jones's land across which the power line may run, and will probably describe the nature of the power line. Or, if Interstate Pipeline Corporation desires to run a natural gas pipeline across Able Anson's farm, it must obtain an easement from Anson describing the strip of land across which the pipeline is to run.

Easements in gross may belong to individuals, but they are far more likely to belong to public utilities. If a public utility desires to obtain an easement across a landowner's property for power line purposes, the landowner may not like the notion, but he may be compelled to grant the easement. Public utilities generally have the power to use eminent domain proceedings to obtain those easements which they desire. They must of course pay fair compensation.

Appurtenant easements. Appurtenant easements are generally rights to use a tract of land for the benefit of another tract of land. For example: In the Lott Addition of Podunk, Texas, Lot 6 borders upon a public street. Lot 7 does not border upon any public street, but the developer of the tract required that the owner of Lot 7 have the right to use a specified strip of Lot 6 for ingress and egress. The owner of Lot 7 thus has an easement across a specified strip of Lot 6. The easement is appurtenant to Lot 7: it cannot be separated from the ownership of Lot 7.

Lot 7 here is said to be the *dominant* estate, since its owner has the easement right across Lot 6. Lot 6 is said to be the *servient* estate, since it is burdened by the rights of the owner of Lot 7. In order to have access to the street, the easement in our example will provide that the Lot 7 owner has the right to use a driveway across Lot 6. The location of the driveway will be specified in the easement. If we assume that the owner of Lot 7 has the sole right to use this driveway, he will also have the sole responsibility for maintaining it. Though it runs across Lot 6, the owner of Lot 6 will have no direct responsibility for it.

On the other hand, the owner of Lot 6 must use his lot in a way which will not interfere with the right of the owner of Lot 7 to use the driveway. He must not, for instance, build a fence across the driveway that unduly interferes with Lot 7's rights. He could put a locked gate across the drive, for instance, only if he gives the Lot 7 owner the key and does not interfere with his use of it. The Lot 6 owner also must not permit a condition to exist upon his lot which could damage the driveway, such as an excavation so near the boundary of the easement that the lateral support of the driveway is threatened.

When the servient estate is sold or otherwise transferred, it is transferred subject to the easement. When the dominant estate is sold or transferred, the easement should be transferred with it. The ownership of the easement may not be severed from the ownership of the dominant estate; any effort to do that will extinguish the easement. Thus, if Sam Jones owns Lot 7 and the easement, he could not sell the lot to Bill Smith but reserve the easement for himself—the effort might well extinguish the easement.

An appurtenant easement may also be extinguished when the dominant estate and the servient estate come under common ownership. When that happens, there is no reason for the easement's continued existence. If the ownership is ever severed again, the easement must be reestablished by the new deed.

An appurtenant easement may also be lost by abandonment, which is essentially nonuse. There is no prescribed period of nonuse that will result in abandonment, however: if the easement owner fails to use it for a long enough period that it appears that he does not intend to use it again, it is abandoned.

Easements by necessity. When a tract of land has no access to a road, the owner of the property is entitled to an easement across adjoining property sufficient to provide him with access to the outside world. Since the servient estate owner cannot deny an easement to the owner of the dominant landlocked estate, he may as well grant the easement across an area that is mutually acceptable to all concerned. If this is not done, the necessary easement may be created by other means, by court order if necessary.

Easements by prescription. The unpermitted use of a right-of-way, road, path, or the like across a tract of land for a period of ten years will cause the creation of an easement by prescription, legitimizing the unauthorized use. For this reason, a landowner who is aware of such unauthorized use of his property would be well advised to erect a fence or other barrier across the used area. By doing this he announces to the world that the unauthorized use lacks his permission.

The unauthorized users are of course trespassers, and legal measures may be taken against them as such. Such action would not be necessary in order to frustrate the obtaining of an easement by prescription, however; the fencing-off of the area in question would be sufficient to accomplish that.

Profits a prendre. When a landowner gives to another the right to remove some naturally occurring material from the surface of his property—sand, gravel, etc.—he has granted to the other a profit a prendre. The owner of the profit of course has the right to such ingress and egress as will permit him to exploit his profit, whatever it might consist of.

Since a profit is essentially a right to remove a portion of a tract of land, the creation is a sale of an interest in the land. It must therefore be in writing.

Licenses. The owner of a license has permission to use the land of another for a specified purpose. He may also have the right to remove something from the land which is not attached to the land. Thus, a landowner may give another person permission to camp upon his property during the summer months. He may also give to another permission to hunt upon his land, and to remove all of the game successfully hunted.

Since a license is not a sale or transfer of an interest in the land, it need not be in writing. Licenses are neither exclusive nor transferable. Thus, if Brown permits Green to camp upon his land, he may also permit Black to camp there, even though Green and Black may not be the best of friends. If Brown permits Redd to hunt deer upon his land during the deer season, this will not stop him from giving Gray the same right. However, if Redd has permission to hunt upon Brown's land, he cannot give Pink permission to hunt there. A license is personal to the grantee: the grantee cannot assign his rights without the permission of the grantor.

48

Transfer of Ownership of Real Property

Ownership of real property may be transferred voluntarily (by sale or gift), involuntarily (by foreclosure of a trust deed lien, mechanic's lien, tax lien, judgment lien, etc.), or by operation of law (through inheritance, for example). Ownership may also be lost due to adverse possession—permitting a person or persons who are not the legal owners to occupy the premises for the length of time provided in the statute of limitations governing such matters.

We shall first consider the mechanics of the ordinary sale of a tract of real estate, and then proceed to a consideration of some of the other methods of transfer.

The ordinary sale of real estate. The would-be seller of real property may himself advertise his property for sale and handle the negotiations leading to the sale, or he may hire a real estate broker or other professional to do this for him.

In any event, the seller and the buyer will eventually negotiate and sign a contract for the sale and purchase of the property. Since the statute of frauds requires all contracts for the sale of real estate to be in writing, this contract must be in writing to be enforceable. Once the contract is signed, the buyer must buy the property in accordance with the terms of the contract, and the seller must sell in accordance with those terms.

Legal title to the land does not pass with the signing of this contract, however. The seller performs his part of the contract by delivering a deed of the type specified in the contract to the buyer, along with proof that he has good legal title to the property. The buyer performs his end by tendering payment in the form agreed to in the contract.

The entire bargain may involve only two parties—when the buyer agrees to pay cash for the property or the seller grants the buyer credit in some form. On the other hand, three or more parties may be involved when the seller does not grant the buyer credit and the buyer finances his purchase through a financial institution or a third individual.

The parties to the contract may deal with each other face-to-face; this is what is usually done in small localities. They may employ a third party to act as stakeholder and coordinator of the transaction, as is often done in larger cities. This third party, called an escrowee or escrow company, makes certain that the final contract is not performed on any side until all parties have carried out their contractual obligations.

We shall now consider the details of various phases of the transaction.

The contract of sale. In many respects, the negotiation of a contract for the sale of land is governed by the same considerations as the negotiation of any other contract. However, the fact that a fairly large amount of money is generally at stake dictates that the parties proceed with care.

A very important consideration is the matter of the buyer's financing of the purchase. If the buyer proposes to pay cash—and if it is obvious that he has in his possession sufficient cash to carry out his commitment—there is no cause for great concern. However, the ordinary buyer is not so blessed with this world's goods: he will need credit in order to make the purchase.

If the seller chooses to be the primary financer of the purchase, he may proceed in one of three ways. First, he could sell on a *land contract* basis, under which the buyer pays off the agreed purchase price in monthly installments. The buyer gets possession of the property, but the seller retains legal title until the purchase price is paid in full. The seller is under no obligation to deliver a deed until the buyer has paid in full, which normally occurs years after the contract is made. These land contracts generally provide that, should the buyer default upon his payment obligations, the seller may void the contract and evict the buyer from the land, the buyer thereby forfeiting all of the payments he has made up to the point of forfeiture.

Secondly, the seller may agree to deliver to the buyer a *title deed* to the property in exchange for the buyer's naming him as beneficiary of a trust deed upon the property given to secure payment of the purchase price. Under this arrangement the buyer has equitable title to the property; legal title is held by the person or corporation named as trustee in the trust deed. The trustee holds the legal title for the benefit of the seller, the beneficiary of the trust deed. Should the buyer default in his obligation to make payments upon the trust deed, the trustee may then take steps to foreclose the lien upon the property and extinguish the buyer's title to the property.

Thirdly (and very uncommonly), the seller may give the buyer a deed to the property reserving a vendor's lien upon it, and not requiring the buyer to name him as beneficiary of a trust deed. Instead, he merely requires the buyer to make specified monthly payments upon the purchase price of the property. If the buyer defaults, the seller may then go to court in order to enforce his vendor's lien on the property and thereby extinguish the buyer's title. Since the seller's interests are very well protected under a land contract or under a trust deed, but not so well protected under the vendor's lien, few sellers on credit choose to travel this third route.

From the seller's point of view, it is less risky to require cash from the buyer and force him to obtain his financing from a financial institution or from a third individual. In this age of government-guaranteed home loans (through the Federal Housing Administration, the Veterans' Administration, etc.) credit-worthy realty buyers should have no great difficulty in obtaining the required credit. The seller may, and often does, require of the buyer that he obtain the required financing from outside parties if he wishes to buy.

It sometimes happens that the seller is just as interested in selling soon as he is in avoiding financial ties to the buyer after the sale. In such a case, he may be willing to grant the buyer credit for part of a down payment so that the buyer may be able to borrow most of the purchase price from a financial institution. In such a case the financing institution is given a first trust-deed lien upon the property and the seller takes a second trust-deed lien.

The buyer is generally required to put down as *earnest money* a specified percentage of the agreed purchase price of the property on or before the signing of the formal contract. The buyer should not put up any earnest money until he has the seller's signature on a contract for sale. Otherwise, if the bargain falls through, the buyer might have problems getting his money back. The contract of sale invariably provides that if the sale is not completed through no fault of the seller he may retain the earnest money as liquidated damages for breach.

It must be emphasized that a contract to sell real property is not enforceable unless a written memorandum of its terms exists which is signed by the party to be charged with a breach. Oral contracts for the sale of realty are normally not enforceable, even if the buyer has already made a deposit of earnest money.

Texas courts will enforce an oral contract for the sale of real property only where the buyer has taken possession of the property in reliance upon the validity of the contract and has materially changed his position in reliance upon its validity—by making valuable improvements upon the property, for example, or by making binding contracts to make such improvements.

Procedure after signature of the contract. The contract may or may not permit the buyer to take possession of the property before delivery of the deed. The contract provisions control on this point.

Whether the buyer takes possession or not, the law considers that he has equitable title to the property. Should the seller breach the contract of sale, the buyer may go to court and obtain specific performance of the contract. In such a case a court would order the seller to deliver a deed to the property as he had agreed to do.

Since the buyer has equitable title to the property, he also has an insurable interest in it. He may therefore take out fire insurance and the like upon it. Since the seller still has legal title, he too has an insurable interest. Should the property be damaged after the signing of the contract but before the delivery of the deed, both seller and buyer would have good claims under their respective insurance policies (if they have insurance, of course), but the combined insurance claims would not exceed the value of the property. Each insurer would be liable only for the value of the interest of its insured in the property.

As between buyer and seller, the buyer acquires risk of loss with respect to the property as of the signing of the contract unless the contract provides otherwise. If the building on the property burns down after the buyer signed a contract of purchase but before the seller delivered a deed, the buyer will still be obligated to pay full contract price for the property—the occurrence of the fire will not discharge or alter the contract. It therefore behooves such a buyer to purchase fire insurance on the property effective as of the signing of the contract unless he has sufficient bargaining power to get a clause into the contract changing the allocation of the risk of loss.

The seller is under an obligation to prepare and sign a deed to the property of the sort required by the contract. He must also furnish proof of merchantable title. The buyer is of course under the obligation to come up with the agreed purchase price of the property, or—if the seller is to grant him credit—to produce that part of the purchase price that will not be financed by the seller.

The contract will provide that all of the obligations are to be performed by a named date. Upon that date, the seller must tender delivery of the deed and the proof of merchantable title and the buyer must tender proof of payment. As with other sorts of contracts, one party may not complain about the other's lack of performance unless the first party has duly tendered his own performance. Time is normally not of the essence in real estate contracts, unless a contract provision states otherwise. Slightly late performance is therefore not normally a breach.

Any amendment of a real estate contract must of course be in writing. However, as with other written contracts, oral rescissions are quite valid if they can be proven.

Deeds. A deed is a formal legal document by which title to real estate is transferred.

In some states, deeds are long, complexly worded documents. The required form for a deed in Texas is somewhat simpler. In RCS 1292 the Texas legislature provided a form of deed sufficient to transfer title to realty when the seller chooses to guarantee that the buyer is getting clear title to what he is buying. An example of the form follows:

The State of Texas
County of Podunk
  Know all men by these presents, that I, Barry Biznotch, of the city of Podunk, county of Podunk, state of Texas, for and in consideration of ten dollars and other good and valuable consideration to me in hand paid by Manfred Murgg, have granted, sold, and conveyed, and by these premises do grant, sell, and convey, unto the said Manfred Murgg of the city of Funk's Thicket, county of Funk, state of Texas, Lot 53 of Podgorny Addition of the city of Podunk, Texas. To have and to hold the above premises, together with all and singular the rights and appurtenances thereto in any wise belonging to the said Manfred Murgg, his heirs or assigns forever. And I do hereby bind myself, my heirs, executors, and administrators to warrant and forever defend all and singular the premises unto the said Manfred Murgg, his heirs, and assigns, against any person whomsoever, lawfully claiming or to claim the same, or any part thereof.
                   Witness my hand, this 28th day of February, 1980.
                   /s/ Barry Biznotch.
                   Signed and delivered in the presence of
                   /s/ Peter Perkins
                   /s/ Rudolf Riepers.

This is a *general warranty deed*, one of the three types of deeds used in real estate transfers. Essentially, the grantor of such a deed guarantees that he had good title to the property to transfer, and that—if he or any of his predecessors in title did anything that would cause the grantee to lose his title later on—the grantor would be responsible. The warranty of the general warranty deed is made not only to the grantee but to the grantee's successors in title. The vast majority of deeds used in voluntary transfers of real property are general warranty deeds.

Should the grantor not want to make the broad general warranty, and should he have sufficient bargaining power to make the grantee agree to the purchase of his property without the protection of a general warranty, a *special warranty deed* may be used. The type of warranty made by the grantor of such a deed will depend upon how the deed is drafted. Probably the most common sort of special warranty is the warranty that the grantor has himself done nothing that would damage the title to the property he is conveying to the grantee. His position, in layman's language, is, "I think that I have good title, and I believe that I've done nothing which would damage your title. If I have done something which damages your title, I'll be responsible, but I'm not responsible for anything those who owned this property before I did may have done."

Should the grantor not want to guarantee title at all, he will give the grantee a *quitclaim deed*. The position of the grantor of a quitclaim deed is, essentially, "I'm conveying to you all of my right, title, and interest in this property. I'm not certain that I have any interest at all. I don't guarantee that I have any. If it turns out that I don't have any, I'm not responsible." The quitclaim deed is normally used to clear up possible title defects to property when a person who may have an interest conveys it to someone with a greater interest in order to eliminate the possibility of the grantor's having an interest. Very rarely is it used as a mechanism for conveyance of complete title, since the grantee receives no guarantee of title whatsoever under such a deed.

No deed will be valid as a conveyance of title to real estate unless it is either signed by the grantor in the presence of two credible subscribing witnesses, or signed and acknowledged by the grantor before an officer authorized to take acknowledgments (such as a notary public) and properly certified by that officer for registration (RCS 1294).

Before a deed becomes a valid conveyance it must also be delivered to the grantee. The simplest form of delivery is of course accomplished by the grantor's handing the document to the grantee. Delivery by the grantor to an authorized agent of the grantee is a valid delivery, but delivery by the grantor to a person who is neither the grantee nor an authorized agent of the grantee is of course no delivery.

Unsigned deeds are invalid as conveyances, as are unwitnessed and unnotarized deeds. However, an unwitnessed or unnotarized deed that is not effective as a conveyance of title to property will be considered to be a valid contract for the conveyance of the property, so long as it has been duly delivered (RCS 1301). A deed signed by an authorized agent of the grantor will be a good conveyance. A deed signed by an agent who had no authority to sign has no effect as a conveyance. A deed bearing the forged signature of the grantor is also ineffective.

Recording of deeds. Deeds and other documents affecting the title to real property—such as leases, trust deeds, and mortgages—should be recorded in the public records of the county where the real estate is located. Failure to do this renders the document of no force and effect as to subsequent creditors and bona fide purchasers of the property who have no notice of the existence of the documents in question (RCS 6627). However, this statute further provides that unrecorded documents of this nature are effective as to the parties and their heirs, and as to creditors, purchasers, and others who have knowledge of their existence.

It is therefore of great importance that a grantee record his deed as soon as possible after he receives it. A deed is not effective against bona fide purchasers and the like until it is recorded (RCS 6631).

So long as the grantor of an unrecorded deed is an honest man who does not convey the property again to a bona fide purchaser, and so long as he informs all of his heirs of the transfer so that they do not convey the property to bona fide purchasers after his death, no loss will be caused by failure to record a deed. However, the risks inherent in not recording are so great that the grantee would be very unwise not to record.

For instance, suppose that Black deeds land to Pink in 1970. Pink does not record his deed. In 1971 Black deeds the same land to Redd, who does not know of Black's deed to Pink. Pink does not live on the property. Redd records his deed. Pink finds out, and claims that Redd does not own the property. He is wrong: Redd does own it now. Or suppose that Redd knew of Pink's unrecorded deed from Black; Redd would not be the owner, because he is not a bona fide purchaser. But Redd recorded his deed anyway, and then sold the land to Gray, who knew nothing of Pink's deed, Gray—as a bona fide purchaser—would now have better title than Pink.

Remember, though, that the definition of a bona fide purchaser here is the same as that of a bona fide purchaser of personal property: the purchaser must give value, act in good faith, and know nothing of unrecorded deeds and the like involving the property. In addition, the bona fide purchaser of real estate must meet one more requirement. He must inspect the property to find out if persons he does not know of might be in possession.

Thus: Black sells land to Pink and Pink moves onto the property but does not record his deed; Black later deeds the land to Redd. Redd is deemed to have knowledge of Pink's claim to title because Pink possesses the property. If Redd inspects the property and finds evidence of Pink's possession, he will be expected to contact Pink and inquire why Pink is there. At that point he will learn of Pink's unrecorded deed. If he does not inspect, he is still charged with knowledge of Pink's possession because he was negligent for not inspecting in the first place.

The recording system and the chain of title. The recording system provides a public record from which the ownership of every piece of property located within the geographical area in which the system operates may be determined with a reasonable degree of accuracy. The feature that makes this work in practice is the indexing system. So many documents are recorded in even the smallest Texas counties that some form of indexing is absolutely necessary in order to enable one to find a particular document.

Deeds and the like are normally indexed according to the last names of the grantor and of the grantee. By use of the grantor index the ownership of a tract of land may be traced from the original sovereign of the soil up to the present owner. Every piece of real estate in private hands located within this state was at one time the property of the sovereign of the soil. But at some time in the past the King of Spain, the government of the Mexican Republic, the government of the Republic of Texas, or the government of the state of Texas granted that land to a private owner. This grant was the beginning of the chain of title to the property—the first link in a chain extending without break to the present day.

The mechanism of tracing the chain is essentially this: Suppose that the tract in question was granted by the government of the Republic of Texas to Ben Booker in 1841. The searcher then begins searching the grantor index of the county beginning in 1841, hunting for the document by which Ben Booker transferred the land to someone else. It is discovered that Booker sold the land to Tim Tyler on July 31, 1869. Beginning with July 31, 1869, the grantor index is searched for the document by which Tim Tyler transferred the land. It is found that Tim Tyler sold it to Hank Harpp on May 19, 1888, so the grantor index is searched for documents involving Hank Harpp after that. And so it goes up to the present day.

Once one understands the concept of the chain of title, the importance of prompt recording of documents involving title to real estate becomes more obvious. A document that is part of the chain of title can be discovered by a title searcher and will influence the title; a document which is not a part of the chain of title cannot be discovered by a title search, and will not influence the title. The examples that follow will clarify this point.

In June 1970 Ben Black deeds a tract of land to Pat Pink. Pink does not record his deed, nor does he take possession of the property. In October 1970 Ben Black deeds the same land to Gus Gray, and Gus Gray records his deed. In January 1971 Pat Pink deeds the land to Vic Violet, and Vic Violet records his deed. Both Gray and Violet acted in good faith. An argument arises between them as to who owns the land. Who does?

Gus Gray does. Gray's deed is part of the chain of title; Violet's is not. A title searcher will discover that Black deeded the land to Gray in October 1970. Violet's deed, though recorded, would never be found by a title searcher, because the Black-Pink deed was never recorded. The title searcher would have no reason to hunt for Pat Pink's name in the grantor index, because he never shows up in the record as a grantee of this land.

If Pat Pink had recorded his deed in June of 1970, Vic Violet would be the owner. In this case, Gus Gray's deed would never show up in the chain of title because the record would show that Ben Black deeded the land to Pat Pink in June 1970; the searcher would therefore stop looking for deeds from Ben Black as of June 1970 and search for deeds from Pat Pink after that time. He would thus never find the deed to Gus Gray.

The chain of title concept of course does not provide a perfect, foolproof record of the title to a tract of land. A document which should be part of the chain of title may never show up there, for instance, because of human error in the recorder's office. If the employees there never index a deed, searchers can obviously never find it. If they index it improperly, it will also never be found. For instance, if the grantor is Pat Pink and a clerk enters the deed in the grantor index under the name "Pat Punk," the deed is lost. The county clerk commits negligence by making errors of this sort; Pat Pink—or anyone else damaged by this mistake—may hold the county clerk liable in damages.

It is also possible for deeds to show up in the chain of title that are totally ineffective as a transfer of property. The county clerk has no way of knowing whether the signature of a grantor upon a particular deed is genuine. Most such signatures are genuine, but forged deeds do get recorded upon occasion. Also, the county clerk has no way of knowing whether a deed signed by an agent was signed by an authorized agent. The signatures of most agents are of course authorized, but some deeds are signed by unauthorized agents. The position of a person who possesses a deed giving him title to a tract of real estate is thus very similar to that of the person possessing a certificate of title to a motor vehicle. In all probability he is the owner of the property, but the picture given by the chain of title might be wrong. If it is, he is not the owner despite his deed and good chain of title.

The title searcher must not only examine the record of documents transferring legal title to real estate, he must also examine the record for documents showing the existence of liens upon the property or of other legal claims against it. These matters will be discussed later in this chapter.

The job of searching title to real estate is rendered immeasurably easier by the work of abstract companies and title insurance companies. The county clerk's records are usually indexed only according to grantor and grantee. The record would be much more accessible if the indexing were on a tract basis, so that all documents affecting a particular piece of land would be indexed in the same place. This job is done by abstract companies and title insurance companies who obtain copies of all documents recorded in the county records and then index these both as to grantor and grantee and as to tract. They are thus able to keep track of all deeds and documents affecting a particular tract of land.

The abstract company combines copies of all relevant documents, or summaries of longer relevant documents, into a thick document called an *abstract*. It makes no evaluation of the documents it assembles: it merely makes available copies of each. The owner of the tract in question keeps the abstract; when he wishes to sell the property he takes the abstract to the abstract company to have it brought up to date. He then furnishes the abstract to the attorney for the buyer and perhaps also to the attorney for the buyer's lender for examination. The attorneys then need not go to the courthouse to begin a new search of the title from scratch: all of the relevant documents are part of the abstract. If the abstract company neglected to include a relevant document it is negligent and will be liable to anyone injured by the omission.

Title insurance companies are in the business of selling insurance on real estate titles to those interested in the purchase of such protection. Particularly in large cities, savings and loan associations and the like may be unwilling to make real estate loans unless the title to the property involved is insured by a title insurance company. From its records the title insurance company makes up a title report, and in its policy it insures the state of the title as revealed by the report. Should the title not be as shown by the report—because of a forged deed, for example—the company will compensate the insured for the loss so caused. As with any sort of insurance, however, the liability of the insurer may well be limited by the provisions of the policy. The insured should read his policy thoroughly, or have his attorney read it for him. Only in that way may he understand the nature and extent of his protection.

Escrow. As stated earlier, in larger cities the parties to a real estate transaction may use the mechanism of the escrow as a means for coordinating the transaction and making certain (as near as is humanly possible) that all obligations of all parties will be performed at approximately the same time. The escrowee or escrow company acts as the stakeholder in the transaction.

The seller draws up the deed to the property and delivers it to the escrowee for delivery to the buyer upon certain terms and conditions. The buyer delivers his agreed consideration to the escrowee for disbursement to the seller upon certain terms and conditions. If a third-party lender is involved in the transaction it will deliver the proceeds of its loan to the escrowee for disbursement to the seller upon certain terms and conditions. There may well also be a fourth-party lender involved in the transaction—particularly when the seller has given one savings and loan company a trust deed upon the property while the buyer is financing his purchase through a second savings institution. In such a situation the second S&L will lend the buyer much of the consideration he is to pay for the property, and some of this money will be used to pay off the seller's debt to the first S&L. The first S&L will deliver to the escrowee releases of its trust deed lien upon the property, to be delivered to Buyer upon certain terms and conditions.

The escrowee will generally deliver nothing to anyone until all parties to the transaction have delivered to it all documents and monies called for in the transaction. When all such obligations have been performed, the escrow will "close," and the escrowee will distribute all documents and monies to those entitled to them.

It should be noted that there are two deed deliveries when a real estate transaction is conducted in escrow. The first delivery occurs when the seller delivers the deed to the property to the escrowee. The escrowee here is not considered to be acting as the agent of the buyer, so the first delivery does not clothe the buyer with legal title to the property. If all conditions of the escrow are not met, the escrowee will return the deed to the seller and the sale may never be consummated. If, however, the escrow never closes due to the misconduct of the seller, the seller has breached the seller-buyer contract. The buyer may then sue for specific performance of the contract and, if justice in the case demands it, the court will decree the buyer to be the owner of the property as of the date of the first delivery. Should the seller die before the escrow closes, the courts will consider that the deed was delivered to the buyer upon the first delivery, in order to avoid arguments about whether or not the death of the seller revoked the authority of the escrowee to act as his agent.

Normally, though, the buyer does not get true legal title to the property until the second delivery, when the escrow closes and the escrowee delivers (among other things) the deed to the buyer.

The Real Estate Settlement Procedures Act and real estate closings. Since the paperwork involved in the processing of a real estate purchase is quite complex, and since the buyer may not be sophisticated enough to know what is going on and to protect himself against being charged excessive fees by the various parties involved in the transaction,

Congress enacted the Real Estate Settlement Procedures Act (RESPA) in 1974 to provide some protection to buyers.

The act is found at 12 USC 2601 et seq. It applies to all real estate transactions involving a federally insured or regulated mortgage loan. Since virtually all realty purchases involve mortgage loans, and since virtually all mortgage loans made on residential property are either federally regulated or federally insured, this legislation applies to virtually all purchases of residences.

12 USC 2603 requires that the Department of Housing and Urban Development of the federal government develop a uniform settlement statement which must be completed by the person conducting the settlement (generally the escrowee) and made available to the buyer at or before settlement. The form must clearly and conspicuously itemize all charges imposed upon the buyer and all charges imposed upon the seller with respect to the settlement. It must also disclose whether any title insurance premium included in the closing costs protects only the lender's interest in the property, the buyer's interest, or both interests.

12 USC 2604 requires lenders to distribute information booklets informing buyers of the closing mechanism of real estate transactions and informing them of their rights in the conduct of such transactions.

12 USC 2609 is a rather complex provision limiting the amount of money that a buyer may be compelled to place in escrow for future taxes, insurance premiums, and other charges. In general, the required amount must not exceed one-sixth of all such charges to come due during the next year.

12 USC 2610 forbids preparers of the disclosure statements required under this law to charge a fee for their preparation. Since a statement of borrowing costs must also be prepared by the lender under the terms of the Federal Truth-in-Lending Act and furnished to the buyer, no charge may be levied for the preparation of that statement either.

Other provisions of the RESPA protect the buyer against collusion against him by other participants in the transaction. The buyer may be required to purchase title insurance as a part of the transaction, but he may not be required to buy it from any particular insurer; he may choose his own insurer.

No fees may be divided between participants in the transaction, nor shall fees be collected for services not performed, nor are kickbacks authorized as compensation for referral of business. Fees levied for services actually rendered are of course legitimate. A real estate broker may not charge a fee for steering lending business to a lender, nor may the lender "kick back" compensation to the broker. Escrow companies must not make kickbacks to lenders or brokers, and title insurers may not make kickbacks to sellers or lenders. Such kickbacks are criminal offenses, subjecting the participants to fines of up to $10,000, imprisonment of up to one year, or both (12 USC 2607). In addition, violators are liable to the buyer for triple the bribe, kickback, split fee, etc.

Description of the property conveyed. A deed must contain a description of the property being conveyed. Accuracy in the description is essential to the proper performance of the transaction.

Description of urban or suburban property is generally simple. Most such property has been subdivided; a tract of property is surveyed and subdivided into lots, and a map showing the subdivision is placed in the records of the county of subdivision. Each tract so subdivided is given a name, and the lots into which it is subdivided are given numbers. "Lot 19 of the Brown Addition of the city of Podunk, Texas" is a common type of urban real estate description. The description may well contain the book and page number of the county records where the plat of Brown Addition is recorded. It is then a simple matter to examine this official map and determine the location of the lot in question.

Rural property is not generally so subdivided. A description of a tract of rural land is generally a description of the boundaries of the tract—a *metes and bounds* description. It might read like this: "Beginning at the point where the center line of the bed of Turtle Creek intersects the east line of the right-of-way of Parker Road; thence due north four hundred sixty feet to a point; thence due east seven hundred feet to a point; thence south two hundred seventy-seven feet to a point at the center line of Turtle Creek; thence southwestward along the center line of Turtle Creek to the point of beginning." A surveyor who could locate the intersection of the center line of Turtle Creek with the east line of the right-of-way of Parker Road could determine the boundaries of this tract with no difficulty. The only factor which might cause a problem is the determination of the location of the center line of Turtle Creek.

Older metes and bounds descriptions can cause much more trouble. Take for example: "Beginning at the cypress stump four hundred sixty feet due south of the southwest corner of the Abe Anson house; thence south about five hundred feet to the big pine tree; thence east about six hundred feet to the big spring; thence north about five hundred feet to the cornerstone of the old Hamilton barn; thence west about six hundred feet to the cypress stump, the point of beginning." Here, if the cypress stump, the big spring, the cornerstone of the old Hamilton barn, and the big pine tree still exist, the boundaries of this tract can be determined. But if one or more of these monuments no longer exists there will be difficulty.

Other problems can also arise. If the described tract is not a regular rectangle, the description might not "close"—that is, the end point of the description might not be the same as the beginning point. If one of the boundaries of the tract is a stream, the stream might have changed its location since the last survey. Most such descriptions are perfectly accurate, but it must be kept in mind that deed descriptions of tracts of rural property may be uncertain and ambiguous.

The doctrine of after-acquired title. The grantor who transfers real estate by a general or special warranty deed warrants that he is conveying to the grantee the quantum of land ownership specified in his deed. The grantor may convey only that which he owns; if he does not own what the deed states that he is conveying, he is conveying only what he has. If he owns less than what he is purportedly conveying, he is liable for damages for breach of warranty.

Suppose, though, that the grantor later acquires that interest which he has supposedly already transferred to the grantee. Title to this after-acquired property automatically passes to the grantee, the grantor automatically performing his obligation to the grantee, however late the performance. For example: Brown deeds to Green Lots 2 and 3 of Ace Addition of the city of Podunk, Texas. Brown owned Lot 2, and he thought he owned Lot 3; but he truly did not own Lot 3. Green now has title to Lot 2, but he has no title to Lot 3 since Brown did not own it. The true owner of Lot 3 was Pink. Later Pink deeds Lot 3 to Brown. Brown dies, by will leaving all of his property to Gray. Gray and Green now both claim they own Lot 3. The true owner is Green; when Pink deeded Lot 3 to Brown, Brown's title automatically vested in Green due to Brown's warranty deed to Green.

Of course, the problem in this form is not likely to occur. Had Green had a title search run on Lots 2 and 3 before accepting Brown's deed, he would have known that Brown did not own Lot 3, and he never would have accepted the deed to it. Instances in which the *doctrine of after-acquired title* can operate will thus be rather rare.

The doctrine will not apply against a grantor who has conveyed by quitclaim deed. The quitclaim grantor, remember, makes no warranties to his grantee: the grantee knows, or should know, that he is getting only the grantor's present interest in the property, if any.

Adverse possession. A nonowner of land who peaceably and openly occupies it adversely to the rights of the owner may obtain good title to it by adverse possession. This may be accomplished without payment of consideration or possession of any deed or other evidence of ownership.

It must be remembered, though, that the possession of the nonowner must be totally adverse to the rights of the true owner. Thus, if the nonowner came into possession with the owner's consent, he may never get title by adverse possession. The life tenant may never get title by adverse possession against the reversioner or the remainderman, then, since the life tenant has a legal right to possession which is not adverse to the rights of the reversioner or remainderman. The tenant who retains possession of rented or leased property after the expiration of his lease or tenancy cannot get title by adverse possession against his landlord, since the landlord originally gave the tenant the right to possession of the property. The tenant in common or other co-owner of property cannot obtain complete title by adverse possession against the other co-owners, because all co-owners have equal possession rights. This is true even if the possessing co-owner is in possession without the consent of the other co-owners.

Anyone who could obtain title to property by adverse possession therefore must be in the position of a squatter. In the majority of cases he knows he has no right to the property, but he squats there anyway. In the minority of cases, he thinks he has the right to be there but actually has no such right. It therefore behooves the owner of vacant real estate to inspect his property upon occasion to find out whether squatters are in open possession of it. If he finds that unauthorized persons are in possession, he must take action to have them evicted as trespassers. Failure to discover squatters or failure to take action against known squatters may cost the negligent landowner his property.

How long must the squatter remain in possession to get title by adverse possession? It depends upon the status of the legal owner of the property and upon whether the squatter has any claim to ownership of the property in question. The Texas legislature has enacted four adverse possession statutes, applicable to four different situations. An adverse possessor who has almost perfect title to property will get title by adverse possession after only three years on the land. RCS 5507 provides that, in order to get title after three years of adverse possession, the adverse possessor must either hold a deed that is part of a chain of title from the sovereign of the soil or have color of title. RCS 5508 provides that a person holds land under color of title when he has a deed that is part of an irregular chain of title from the sovereign of the soil—the irregularity consisting of an unrecorded deed, an improperly recorded deed, or something of that sort.

A possible application of the three-year statute could be this situation: Black in Dallas deeds El Paso County land to Redd. Redd neither records his deed in the El Paso County records nor takes possession. Black later deeds the same land to Green. Green does not know of the deed to Redd; he goes out to El Paso County and inspects the land, finding it vacant. He then records his deed but does not take possession. Redd then goes out to El Paso County and takes possession, never recording his deed. Four years later Green conveys the land to Pink. Pink inspects it and finds Redd there. He sues to evict Redd as a trespasser. Pink will probably lose. Redd is certainly there under color of title—his unrecorded deed. So long as he has been there three years, Green's negligence in not watching the property will prove costly.

The three-year statute does not apply if the possessor is guilty of fraud or anything similar. It also does not apply when a part of the possessor's title or color of title depends on a forged deed, or a deed signed under a forged power of attorney.

Under RCS 5509, an adverse possessor may gain title after five years of adverse possession if:
1. He is claiming under a deed which has been duly recorded, and
2. The deed is not a forgery or one signed under a forged power of attorney, and
3. The possessor has paid the real property tax, if any, upon the property.

Under this statute it does not matter whether the recorded deed is part of a chain of title, so long as it is not forged. But it does matter very much whether or not the possessor is paying the property taxes.

An example of the applicability of this statute might be this: Henry Hawk owns real estate in Podunk County. He has made a will naming his son Harvey his sole heir. Henry is very ill; Harvey makes a deal with Ben Botkins that he will sell Botkins a tract of land Botkins is interested in as soon as Henry dies. Henry in due course does die, so Harvey gives Botkins a deed to the property. Botkins takes possession and records his deed. Unfortunately for Harvey, though, it turns out that Henry made a secret will shortly before his death, naming his daughter Cindy Hawks Bently of New York as his heir. This turns out to be Henry's true will, so Cindy inherits his property, not Henry. Cindy does not come back to Podunk to look at her property for six years. Ben Botkins happily treats the property he "bought" from Henry as his own and pays the property taxes on it. Cindy then comes back home and finds Botkins on her land. She sues to get him off, claiming that he is a trespasser. She loses: Botkins's deed is not a forgery; it is recorded; he has paid the property taxes; and he has been in possession for more than five years. Cindy's return was too late.

Under RCS 5510, the ordinary squatter who has no deed or other evidence of ownership may gain title to property after an adverse possession of ten years. The squatter need not have paid any taxes—the only requirement, really, is ten years of open, peaceful, and adverse possession. The maximum quantity of land which a squatter may claim under RCS 5510 is 160 acres, unless he has in his possession some sort of written document other than a deed that has been recorded and that purportedly transfers to the squatter more than 160 acres. In such a case, he may claim all of the land included in the description if he is occupying it and using it.

Another fairly common situation in which a landowner may lose land by adverse possession under RCS 5510 is the following: Able and Baker are adjoining landowners. Able builds a fence which he says is on the boundary between the two tracts of land. The fence is not on the boundary, but Baker does not know that. Actually, it is twenty feet on Baker's side of the boundary, giving Able the use of a strip of Baker's land. Eleven years later Baker discovers this discrepancy and demands that Able move the fence or pay him for the wrongfully appropriated land. Baker cannot enforce his demand—he should have discovered this long ago.

Easements may also be acquired under the terms of this statute. If a landowner allows the public to take a shortcut across his property for a period of ten years, an easement in favor of the public will arise by prescription, and the landowner will not be able to block the path and deprive the public of its use.

The clock begins to run upon the statutes of limitations contained in these legislative provisions when the adverse possession begins. However, RCS 5518 provides that the clock will not start to run at the beginning of the adverse possession if:
1. The record owner is under twenty-one years of age, or
2. The record owner is a member of the U.S. armed forces and the nation is at war, or
3. The record owner is of unsound mind, or
4. The record owner is in prison.

The clock does not start until these conditions no longer apply.

Under the provisions of RCS 5519, an adverse possessor who has been in possession for twenty-five years will get title to the possessed property by adverse possession even if the record owner is a minor, insane, in prison, etc. Nothing will stop the clock on this statute. These statutes of limitations do not apply, however, when the record owner of property is a government. Title to government land—federal, state, city, county, school district, or whatever—cannot be obtained by adverse possession. RCS 5517 provides the exemption for state and local government, while federal law simply makes no allowance for adverse possession of federal lands.

Finally, it must be remembered that the same adverse possessor need not be in possession of the claimed land for the entire statutory period. If one adverse possessor transfers his rights to another, the two periods of possession are added together. Thus: Haggin squats upon land owned by Dillon without Dillon's knowledge or consent, and stays there for two years. Haggin then gives Dooley a deed to the property and Dooley takes possession. Dooley stays there four years and deeds the land to Kallikak. Kallikak stays there five years. Neither Dooley nor Kallikak recorded his deed, and none of the three adverse possessors ever paid any property taxes. Dillon then discovers Kallikak on the land, and seeks his removal. He cannot get it: Haggin, Dooley, and Kallikak together have been in possession for more than ten years.

On the other hand, suppose that Bloke squats on land belonging to Reich for four years, with no deed whatsoever. Bloke moves away, and the land sits vacant for a year. Then Slink moves onto the land, not knowing who it belongs to, though he knows Bloke had been there. He stays for seven years; then Reich discovers him. Reich may evict him— since Slink and Bloke never had any dealings and since there was a gap in their combined period of possession, Slink does not have title by adverse possession.

Suits to set aside defective deeds. RCS 5523a provides that, should a person desire to bring suit to set aside a defective deed because it was not properly acknowledged or notarized, or because it was defectively signed by corporate agents, he must do so within ten years of the date upon which the deed could have been recorded, which essentially means within ten years of the date of execution. Generally, then, a deed bearing such a defect becomes fully effective after the passage of ten years.

49

Landlord and Tenant

When the owner of a piece of real estate permits another person to take possession of the premises for a limited period of time and for consideration, a *landlord-tenant-relationship* comes into existence. This chapter will discuss the rights and duties of landlords and tenants under Texas state law.

The four types of tenancies. A tenant may hold possession of the premises as one of four categories of tenant.

The lessee holds a *term for years* (if he holds under a long-term lease) or a *leasehold* (if he holds for a year or less). A lease is a formal agreement entered into between landlord and tenant. If the term of the lease is to be more than one year, the agreement must be reduced to writing as commanded by the statute of frauds (TB&CC 26.01). If the term is to be one year or less the lease may be oral, though it is wiser to put it in writing in order to avoid disputes over terms. The lease expires when its terms ends.

The tenant is a *periodic tenant* if he took possession of the property under a lease, remained there after the lease expired, and continued to pay the landlord rent which the landlord accepted. The period of the tenancy is the same as the period of the lease except that if the lease ran for more than a year the periodic tenancy runs only from year to year. The periodic tenancy expires when its terms ends; the party desiring to terminate it must give notice of his desire to terminate at least one rental period before termination. Thus, if rent is payable monthly, landlord or tenant must give one month's notice before terminating the tenancy.

A tenant is a *tenant at will* if it is agreed between landlord and tenant that either party may terminate the tenancy at any time. Hotel and motel rooms are often rented on this basis. The tenant is a *tenant by sufferance* if he is in possession of the premises after the expiration of his tenancy, and he has either not offered to pay more rent or has offered to pay and been refused by the landlord. The tenant by sufferance has no right to occupy the property; the landlord may evict him by filing a forcible detainer action against him.

Contents of a lease. A written lease will of course contain the names of the landlord and the tenant, and a description of the property that is being leased. It will also spell out the term of the lease. There will be a provision with respect to rent, the due dates of rental payments, and the amounts of these payments. If the tenant is to have the right to possession only for specified purposes, the lease must explain these.

Unless the lease says otherwise, the landlord's obligation to make repairs is essentially limited to an obligation to keep the property minimally livable: the landlord must not allow the property to deteriorate to the point that the tenant no longer enjoys quiet possession of it. If the tenant wants the landlord to assume more responsibility for repairs, he must get a proper covenant to repair inserted into the lease. Unless the lease says otherwise, the landlord has no right to come onto the premises without the tenant's knowledge and consent. However, if the landlord covenants to make repairs, he obviously must have the right to come onto the property to make them.

Whether the lease mentions a covenant of quiet enjoyment or not, the landlord makes such a covenant to the tenant. The covenant is an agreement by the landlord not to interfere with the tenant's peaceable and quiet possession of the premises. The scope of this is to a degree limited, however. The landlord or his successors in title to the property must not interfere with the tenant's use of the property. If they do, they breach the lease. But if outside parties interfere with the tenant's quiet enjoyment, the landlord is not responsible.

The tenant may make such uses of the natural resources of the property as are reasonable for his own enjoyment. He would be entitled to cut timber growing upon the property for firewood, but he could not cut the timber and sell it to others for use as firewood. If the lease is for agricultural purposes, the tenant must do all within his power to preserve the fertility of the soil and to prevent erosion and other problems. In short, the tenant must do nothing to reduce the value of the landlord's reversion.

The obligation of the tenant to pay rent is independent of the obligation of the landlord to provide quiet enjoyment of the premises. The fact that the landlord interferes with the tenant's peaceful use of the property will not excuse the tenant from his obligation to pay rent although the tenant could sue the landlord for breach of the lease. The tenant's obligation to pay rent is also independent of the landlord's obligation to leave the tenant in possession until the end of the term of the lease. Thus, if the tenant gets behind on his rent the landlord's recourse is to sue to collect the delinquent payments. However, if the lease itself provides that nonpayment of rent is cause for termination of the lease and eviction of the tenant, the lease provision will stand.

Houses and apartments may be rented *furnished* or *unfurnished.* If the dwelling is rented furnished, the landlord provides the furniture and the major appliances—refrigerator, stove, etc. In such a case, these items are the landlord's property; he is obligated to keep the appliances in good working order and to replace worn-out furniture, unless the lease provides otherwise. By the same token, the tenant is in essence a bailee of the furniture and appliances, and is obligated to use due care in using them. A dwelling rented unfurnished may or may not contain major appliances. In any case, the tenant must provide what furniture there is.

With respect to utility service, one of three situations might prevail. The landlord may rent on the *all bills paid* basis, in which case the tenant need have no contact with the gas and electric companies; the cost of utility service is absorbed in the rent. The lease may be on a *no bills paid* basis, in which case the tenant must obtain his utilities directly from the utility companies. The lease may also be on a *pay all bills to the landlord* basis, in which case each apartment has its own utility meters, but the utility bills the landlord rather than the tenants, and each tenant must then pay the landlord for the gas, electricity, etc. he used.

Formerly, the "all bills paid" basis was most common. However, it provides no incentive to tenants to conserve gas and electricity and, in this time of energy scarcity and rising energy costs, it makes little economic sense. The other two methods are becoming more common. From the landlord's point of view, "no bills paid" is best, because he does not need to get involved with utility companies on his tenants' behalf. From the tenant's viewpoint, "pay all bills to the landlord" is better, however, because public utility rate schedules offer cheaper power to large users through quantity discounts. A whole apartment complex would qualify for these cheaper rates, while individual tenants could not, and the landlord could pass savings generated by the discount along to his tenants.

The lease might well contain a provision with respect to tenant pets. The landlord may not want pets on his property. (If he does not like dogs and cats, that is his privilege.) The lease might provide that no pets are authorized, and that the presence of an unauthorized pet is grounds for termination of the lease and eviction. The landlord may allow pets, but require a large security deposit from the pet owner to protect himself against damage the pet might do to the dwelling.

The landlord will almost certainly require the tenant to make some sort of security deposit as protection against the tenant's unduly damaging the premises during his tenancy, or against the tenant's absconding while owing back rent.

Duty of landlord to keep premises habitable. The tenant's obligation to pay rent continues until the end of the term of the lease even if the landlord breaches the lease, unless the lease itself provides otherwise. A sore spot in this area has been—and still is—the question of the extent to which the landlord is obligated to go in order to keep his premises in good repair.

Many states answer this question by imposing an implied warranty of habitability upon the landlord. If he allows his premises to deteriorate to the point at which they are no longer fit to live in, the tenant may treat this as a breach and perhaps withhold rent or move out.

Until 1978, Texas recognized no such warranty. However, in that year the Texas Supreme Court decided that a Texas landlord does make an implied warranty of habitability to his tenant, to the extent that he must not allow his premises to deteriorate so that they are unsafe. The court decision was very vague as to the borders of this newly recognized warranty. In order to clear up some of the ambiguity—and to water down the economic threat perceived by landlords as represented by such a warranty—the 1979 session of the legislature enacted RCS 5236f.

The heart of the act is RCS 5236f Sec. 2(a), which provides that a landlord shall have a duty upon actual notice to make a diligent effort to repair or remedy any condition which materially affects the physical health or safety of an ordinary tenant. This duty, however, is hedged about by numerous qualifications and restrictions, and may even be waived by the tenant.

Some of the qualifications of the duty are:
1. The landlord is not required to repair or remedy any condition caused by the tenant or his family, guests, or invitees.
2. The landlord is not obligated to furnish utility service if utility lines from the utility company are not reasonably available.
3. The landlord is not obligated to furnish security guards for the premises.
4. The landlord is not obligated under this act to repair breakages, malfunctions, or other conditions which do not materially affect the physical health or safety of an ordinary tenant.

If a condition materially affecting the physical health or safety of an ordinary tenant develops due to normal wear and tear, the landlord must repair or remedy it. If such a condition develops as a result of an insured casualty loss (fire, hail, smoke, explosion, or the like), the landlord is under no obligation to commence repair until he collects some insurance proceeds (RCS 5236f Sec. 4).

A tenant may make use of his remedies provided by the act only if the following conditions prevail, as per Sec. 3:
1. Notice of the condition has been given to landlord by giving it or sending it to the person or place where rent is normally paid, and
2. Tenant is not delinquent in his rent, and
3. The condition materially affects the health or safety of an ordinary tenant, and
4. The landlord has failed to make a diligent effort to repair or remedy the condition, and
5. The landlord has had a reasonable time to repair or remedy, taking into account the availability of material, labor, and utilties, and the nature of the problem.

Sec. 5 of the act provides that the tenant may terminate the rental agreement if the conditions of Sec. 3 are met and the tenant has given the landlord written notice that he will terminate if the condition is not remedied within seven days. Sec. 6 makes some judicial remedies available to the tenant. The tenant may sue if the conditions of Sec. 3 are met, and if he notifies the landlord in writing that he will sue in case the condition is not remedied within seven days. The judicial remedies are as follows:
1. A court order to the landlord to repair or remedy the condition.
2. A court order for partial rent reduction until the condition is remedied, the reduction being proportional to the reduction in rental value of the premises because of the condition.
3. A monetary penalty of one month's rent plus $100.
4. A court order awarding actual damages to the tenant.
5. Recovery of court costs and attorney's fees, unless the claim involves personal injuries.

Section 7 forbids the landlord to retaliate against the tenant for giving a repair notice by:
1. Filing unjustified eviction proceedings against the tenant, or
2. Unjustifiably depriving the tenant of the use of the premises, or
3. Decreasing services to the tenant, or
4. Terminating the rental agreement or raising the rent within six months of the tenant's action.

If the landlord can prove that these actions were taken not for purposes of retaliation but for other legitimate reasons, he incurs no liability.

A landlord may evict a tenant without being guilty of retaliation if:
1. The tenant's rent is delinquent, or
2. The tenant or his family, guests, or invitees deliberately caused property damage, or
3. The tenant or his family, guests, or invitees have threatened the personal safety of the landlord or his employees, or the safety of other tenants, or
4. The tenant has materially breached the rental agreement, or
5. The tenant has held over after termination of the rental agreement or notice of intent to evict, or
6. The tenant is holding over though landlord had notified him of termination of the rental agreement, and the notice of termination was given prior to tenant's notice to repair, or

7. The tenant is holding over and the landlord has in good faith terminated his rental agreement in the belief that the tenant, his family, his guests, or his invitees may adversely affect the quiet enjoyment by other tenants of their premises; that they may adversely affect the health and safety of the landlord, other tenants, or neighbors; or that they may cause damage to property of the landlord, other tenants, or neighbors.

The tenant's judicial remedies for retaliation are:
1. A penalty of one month's rent plus $100, and
2. Reasonable moving costs, and
3. Court costs and attorney's fees.

Sec. 8 of the act provides that a tenant must not withhold rent in retaliation for nonremedy of a condition covered by the act. The landlord must inform the tenant in writing of the penalty for doing this; he may then sue the tenant for a penalty of one month's rent plus $100, recovering in the process court costs and attorney's fees.

Under Sec. 12 of the act a landlord may legitimately respond to a repair notice or a threatened repair notice by closing down the premises. If he gives the tenant notice of the closing before the tenant files a repair notice, the tenant will have no rights under this act. If the closing notice is given after the repair notice, the landlord must pay the tenant's moving expenses (if reasonable), refund his security deposit, and give him a rebate of unearned rent.

The other core provision of this act is contained in Sec. 13. The provisions of the act may be waived if:
1. There exists a written rental agreement, and
2. The waiver is underlined or in bold print in the rental agreement, or in a separate written addendum to the rental agreement, and
3. The waiver is specific, listing with clarity what duties are being waived, and
4. The waiver is made knowingly, voluntarily, and for consideration.

This waiver provision may well eviscerate the entire piece of legislation. Though the act as written imposes no particularly onerous burden upon landlords, the burden may still be one which landlords do not care to bear. If the landlord wants the provisions of the act to be waived by his tenants, he should have little difficulty accomplishing this goal. Rental agreements are, for most tenants, contracts of adhesion. If the tenant wants to rent the landlord's apartment, he must sign the landlord's rental agreement form. Most tenants are probably not aware of the fact that they have the right to bargain over rental terms. Besides, even if the tenant were inclined to bargain, the landlord probably would not be willing to consider modifications of his standard agreement. As to the requirement of consideration, the landlord might well inform the tenant that his rent will be less if he agrees to waive the protection of this act, or that his security deposit will be lower if he agrees to the waiver.

There are those who claim that this legislation is a welcome codification of the law of landlord's warranty of habitability. There are others who claim that this legislation is a sugar-coated abolition of the warranty of habitability so unwelcomely injected into Texas landlord-tenant law by the Texas Supreme Court. There are logical grounds for support of both arguments.

Constructive eviction. When residential premises are rendered uninhabitable by fire, explosion, or other catastrophe, RCS 5236f Sec. 4 provides a solution to ensuing problems. If the premises are rendered totally uninhabitable, either landlord or tenant may terminate the rental agreement. The tenant is then entitled to a rebate of paid but unearned rent, and a refund of his security deposit. If the premises are rendered partially uninhabitable, the tenant is entitled to a partial rent reduction depending upon the degree of reduction of habitability. If the landlord and tenant cannot agree upon the amount of the reduction, the tenant may apply to a court for resolution of the matter.

If a professional office or storeroom is rendered totally unusable by a catastrophe, the tenant might well claim that the catastrophe has frustrated the purpose of his lease and thereby discharged it. If he cannot conduct his business or practice his profession there, the premises are of no use to him. An apartment tenant might use a similar argument to obtain discharge of his lease.

If the farmhouse on a 400-acre rented farm is destroyed by a catastrophe, however, this may well not discharge the lease. The use of the land is probably much more valuable to the tenant than is the use of the farmhouse, so the value of the lease is not greatly damaged.

When the tenant is renting a city house, a borderline case arises. Is the use of the lot upon which the house sat of any value to the tenant? If it is of value, there is just a partial discharge. If it is not of value, there is a total discharge.

Assignments of leases and subleases. Black leased a house to Brown for five years, the lease being in writing. Two years later Brown was transferred to another state by his employer. Brown therefore conveyed the remainder of his rights under the lease to Gray. But when Gray sought to move into the house, Black refused to let him do so. Gray claimed that was unlawful. Was it?

Brown made an effort to assign his rights under the lease to Gray. However, in Texas such an assignment is invalid unless the landlord agrees to it (RCS 5237). If the landlord, Black, did agree to the assignment, Gray would now have the obligation to pay rent to Black. However, if Gray did not pay on time Black would have the right to force Brown to pay. Here the contract law principle applies: You do not get rid of a duty by delegating it to someone else.

Suppose that Orange rented an apartment to Redd for a year, beginning in January. Redd decided to go to Europe that summer, so he got Blue to agree to live in the apartment while Redd was gone, Blue to pay his rent to Orange. Orange refused to allow Blue to move in. Could he legally do this? In this case Redd has made an effort to sublease his apartment to Blue. Such subleases are also made invalid by RCS 5237, unless the landlord agrees. If the landlord agrees, he may collect his rent either from the tenant (Redd) or from the subtenant (Blue).

It follows, then, that a tenant may not escape his obligation to pay rent to his landlord unless the landlord agrees. It also follows that one may not rent premises from a tenant; one must deal with the landlord or with his authorized agent. On the other hand, a landlord may ratify an unauthorized assignment or sublease by accepting rent from the assignee or subtenant.

Tenant's liability for rent when he abandons the premises. If the tenant moves out of the premises before the lease has expired, he remains liable to the landlord for the agreed rental, unless the landlord agrees to discharge him from such liability or the landlord rents the premises to another tenant.

In such a situation the Texas landlord is under no obligation to mitigate his damages—that is, he need not make an effort to find another tenant. On the other hand, the doctrine of anticipatory breach does not apply to the abandonment of the premises by the tenant. If the landlord wants to sue to collect all of the rent payable under the lease, he must wait until the lease expires and then sue, letting the premises remain vacant in the meantime. If the landlord rents to another tenant before the breached lease expires, the tenant's obligation to pay rent ends. However, the tenant remains liable for the agreed rental for the period during which the premises were vacant.

Thus: Student rents an apartment for a year from Landlord under a written lease, to run from September 1 until the next August 31, the rental to be $200 per month. Student moves out on November 30 without informing Landlord, having paid rent on September 1, October 1, and November 1. Landlord, being under no obligation to find another tenant, could let the apartment stay vacant until the next September 1 and then sue Student for $1,800, the nine months' rent which Landlord has not collected. On the other hand, if Landlord rents the apartment to Pupil on February 1, the Landlord-Student lease would be terminated as of February 1, and Student would be liable only for $400 in rent, for the two months during which the apartment was vacant. If Landlord rented the place to Pupil for $190 per month, the question could arise whether Student would be liable for $10 in damages per month until August 31. The answer is no; once Landlord rerents the property, Student's obligation for future rent or damages ends.

Landlord's lien for rent. When a tenant gets behind on his rent, RCS 5236d provides that the landlord shall have a lien upon all of the tenant's property within the dwelling and upon all property stored by the landlord for the tenant in a storage room for the unpaid rent. However, the statute further provides that thirteen specific types of property belonging to the tenant are exempt from this lien:

1. All wearing apparel.
2. Tools, apparatus, and books of a trade or profession.
3. School books.
4. One automobile and one truck.
5. Family library and all family portraits and pictures.
6. One couch, two living room chairs, one dining table, and all dining chairs.
7. All beds and bedding.
8. All kitchen furniture and utensils.
9. All food and foodstuffs.
10. All medicine and medical supplies.
11. All goods known by the landlord or his agent to belong to persons other than the tenant or other occupiers of the dwelling.
12. All goods known by the landlord or his agent to be subject to recorded financing statements.
13. All agricultural implements.

The scope of the exemptions is obviously so broad that most of the tenant's possessions would be exempt from the lien. Excess furniture and works of art are the most obvious sorts of things that would be subject to this lien.

In addition, RCS 5236d Sec. 4 provides that this lien shall not be enforceable unless it is provided for in a written rental agreement between landlord and tenant. This statute further provides that the portion of the agreement referring to the lien must be either underlined or printed in conspicuous type.

If the tenant has abandoned the premises, the landlord has the right to remove all of the tenant's property from there, including exempt property. Formerly, the landlord could enforce his lien upon nonexempt property through distress warrant proceedings, which would result in the landlord's seizure of the tenant's property subject to the landlord's lien without any sort of judicial hearing. Though RCS 5227 and RCS 5239 authorize this, at least one Texas court of civil appeals has found the procedure to be unconstitutional (*Stevenson vs. Cullen Center, Inc.*, 525 S.W.2d 731). It would appear that foreclosure of the lien cannot be accomplished without a judicial hearing, at which the tenant has the right to contest the validity of the lien.

If the landlord proceeds illegally with his claim of a lien upon a tenant's property, RCS 5236d Sec. 7 permits the tenant to sue the landlord for actual damages plus one month's rent and reasonable attorney's fees. The landlord may of course counterclaim for delinquent rent.

Interruption of utility service by landlord. If the tenant is renting the premises on a "no bills paid" basis, the landlord has no right to interfere with his utility service (RCS 5236c, Sec. 1). Since there exists a direct contractual relationship between the tenant and the utility company, the landlord has no right to interfere.

It would seem, however, that if a tenant is renting on the "all bills paid" or the "pay all bills to landlord" basis, the landlord could cut off utility service to the tenant for such good cause as nonpayment of rent. Here the tenant has no contractual relationship with the utility company; the landlord is the utility company's customer. Of course, a utility company has the right to cut off service to its customer for such good cause as nonpayment of bills.

RCS 5236c Sec. 4 provides that if a tenant is a victim of a wrongful termination of utility service by the landlord, he may terminate the rental agreement. He may also sue for actual damages plus one month's rent and a reasonable attorney's fee, less any landlord counterclaim for unpaid rent, etc.

Wrongful exclusion of tenant from the premises. A landlord may not prevent the tenant from entering the premises, except through judicial process. The landlord may not, for example, change locks upon the premises and refuse to provide a key until the tenant pays his delinquent rent (RCS 5236c Sec. 2). The landlord may change locks if he desires, but he must post a notice on the door of the premises informing the tenant of this, and telling the tenant where and from whom he may pick up a key. The key must be made available to the tenant on demand, regardless of the hour, whether the tenant pays the delinquent rent or not.

Obviously, the only benefit the landlord obtains from changing locks is that the delinquent tenant must show himself in order to get the new key. At that time the landlord may demand to know when the delinquent rent will be paid—and he may speak some harsh words on the subject of deadbeat tenants. Should the landlord wrongfully exclude the tenant, the tenant has all the remedies of RCS 5236c Sec. 4 described above, plus the right to recover possession of the premises.

Landlord's refusal to return security deposit. It is standard procedure for a landlord to require a tenant to deposit a specified sum of money with him as a security deposit to insure that the tenant will comply with the rental agreement and will use due care to preserve the rented premises from excess damage. The deposit is normally refunded in full if the tenant leaves the premises in good condition when he moves out.

However, difficulties may arise when the landlord deliberately or through negligence does not return the deposit after the tenant moves. In order to aid the tenant who must wrestle with this problem, the Texas legislature enacted RCS 5236c, which became effective September 1, 1973.

Suppose Ehrlich leases an apartment at Armadillo Gardens from Grinch, the landlord, for twelve months at $200 per month. Ehrlich is given a written lease to read and sign; it informs him, among other things, that he must pay the first and last months' rent upon moving in, plus a security deposit equal to one month's rent, plus a special deposit of $100 per pet. Since Ehrlich owns a Chihuahua, he observes that it will cost him $700 to move into Armadillo Gardens, although the rent is only $200 per month. The lease provides that it is automatically renewable for another year, unless landlord or tenant gives notice of intent not to renew at least thirty days before the lease expires, and that if the tenant moves out without giving the required notice the landlord may keep the last month's rent payment and the security deposit as liquidated damages. This is printed in bold type; it is all quite legal.

As the end of the eleventh month of Erhlich's lease draws near, he decides that he does not want to renew the lease. He informs Grinch of his intent. Since the twelfth month will be the last month of the lease, he need make no rental payment on the first day of the twelfth month, since he already paid rent for that month when he moved in. At the end of the twelfth month, Ehrlich moves out. When he returns the apartment key to Grinch, he gives Grinch his new address, and asks Grinch for the return of the security deposit. Grinch says he cannot return it until he has a chance to inspect the apartment and that he will mail a check to Ehrlich's new address.

On the twenty-ninth day after Ehrlich moves out, he receives in the mail a check from Grinch for $300. Though Erhlich is peeved at Grinch for keeping his deposit so long, he has no legal complaint. Grinch has complied with the law. If Ehrlich had not given Grinch a forwarding address, Grinch would only have been obligated to hold the deposit until Ehrlich came after it. Failure by the tenant to furnish his new address does not permit the landlord to keep the deposit; it just excuses him from making any affirmative efforts to make the refund.

If Ehrlich received a letter from Grinch stating, "I've retained your $300 deposit because your dog so badly chewed up the couch in the living room that it is useless as a piece of furniture. It had a reasonable value of $150. In addition, the dog discolored and ruined carpeting with a fair value of $75, and two dining-room chairs with a fair value of $40 were smashed. It will cost me $100 to give your apartment a thorough cleaning—had a more civilized tenant lived there for a year the cleaning bill would be only $50. I'm therefore retaining your $300 deposit," he would have no complaint. If the landlord chooses to retain all or a part of the security deposit, he must furnish a detailed, itemized explanation of his reasons for doing so; in this case Grinch has done that.

If, on the other hand, Grinch had merely said in his letter, "I'm retaining your $300 deposit because your apartment was a shambles when you moved out," the landlord would be asking for trouble. If he simply did not bother to send a check to Ehrlich's new address within thirty days after Ehrlich moved out, Grinch would also be asking for trouble. When the landlord has the tenant's new address but does not refund the deposit within thirty days or explain why he retained all or part of it, the statute presumes that the landlord is acting in bad faith. The tenant may sue the landlord for $100 plus three times the amount of the wrongfully withheld deposit plus a reasonable attorney's fee. The landlord may escape liability altogether if he can prove that he did not violate the statute. If he cannot prove innocence of violating the law, but he can prove that he acted in good faith in not making a proper refund, he will not be liable for anything but the wrongfully withheld deposit—that is, the tenant will not collect the $100, the triple damages, or the attorney's fee. But since everyone is expected to know the law, a landlord would have difficulty proving that he withheld a deposit in good faith.

If the tenant owes unpaid rent when he moves out, the landlord may retain a portion of the security deposit sufficient to cover the rent without obligation for documentation, so long as landlord and tenant are in agreement as to the rent due and owing.

If the tenant refuses to pay all or a part of the last month's rent because he wants to use his security deposit as the rent, he is in violation of RCS 5236c. If he moves out without paying the last month's rent or a part of it, landlord may sue him for triple the wrongfully withheld rent plus a reasonable attorney's fee. The tenant may escape the triple damages and the attorney's fee liability by proving that he withheld the rent in good faith, but the burden lies upon him to prove good faith; this is difficult, since the tenant should know that one cannot count a security deposit as part of the last month's rent.

If ownership of the premises changes (except because of a mortgage or trust deed foreclosure), the new landlord is liable for refund of deposits paid to the former landlord. The former landlord also remains liable for these deposits. If a mortgage or trust deed lienholder becomes owner through foreclosure proceedings, only the former owner is liable for these deposits.

Eviction of tenants. If a tenant remains on the landlord's property after breaching his lease, and the breach is grounds for eviction, the landlord must proceed to remove the tenant by court action. "Self-help" eviction is not authorized by Texas law.

Whether or not grounds for eviction exist will depend upon what sort of tenancy exists and what sort of wrong the tenant has committed. If the tenant holds under a term of years, and the term has not yet expired, grounds for eviction will not normally exist no matter what the tenant has done. Remember that nonpayment of rent by a lessee is not grounds for termination of the lease and eviction unless the lease says otherwise.

If the lease has expired, the tenant has tendered rent for a period after the expiration, and the landlord has accepted it, a periodic tenancy exists, and the landlord has lost his right to evict. When a periodic tenancy exists, its duration is usually measured by the length of the rental period. Either party may terminate the tenancy by giving a notice of one rental period. Thus, in a month-to-month periodic tenancy, if the landlord gives the tenant thirty days' notice to get out, but the tenant is still there on the thirty-first day, grounds for eviction exist. When a tenancy at will exists, if the landlord gives the tenant a one-rent-period notice to get out, and the tenant does not do so, grounds for eviction exist.

In short, whenever the possessory rights of the tenant are reduced to tenancy at sufferance (because the tenant's right to be there has expired), eviction is possible.

The first step in the eviction process is the sending of a letter to the tenant demanding that he vacate the premises. If the demand is sent by registered or certified mail, it may state that if the tenant does not vacate within ten days a forcible detainer suit will be filed against him. It may further state that if the tenant does not vacate and forces the landlord to sue, the landlord will seek judgment for eviction, attorney's fees, court costs, and for delinquent rent, if the delinquency is for less than $500. If the landlord is in a rush to get the tenant evicted, the letter may demand that the tenant vacate after three days and state that otherwise suit will be filed. In such a case, the landlord may not seek attorney's fees. RCS 3975b authorizes the ten-day letter, RCS 3975a the three-day letter.

The landlord's next step is to file his complaint of forcible detainer in the justice of the peace court for the JP precinct in which the premises are located. If the landlord is in a rush to get the tenant out he may, along with his complaint, file a possession bond in the amount of probable damages to the tenant and court costs as determined by the JP hearing the case. This is authorized by Rule 740 of the Texas Rules of Civil Procedure (TRCP). Notice of filing of the suit and notice of filing of the bond may be served upon the tenant at the same time.

After notice of filing of suit and bond have been served upon the defendant tenant, TRCP 740 gives him three choices:

1. He may do nothing. If he chooses this alternative, a constable or sheriff may evict

him any time after six days have passed since service of citation. If the citation and notice of filing of bond are served upon the defendant tenant on May 7, the sheriff or constable may evict him on May 14.

2. He may demand a trial within six days of the service of citation and notice of bond.

3. He may file a counterbond equal to court costs plus damages accruing to the landlord because of the tenant's wrongful possession, as determined by the JP hearing the case. In such a case he will have until ten days after service of the citation to file an answer to the landlord's complaint. A trial will be held later, and the tenant may continue in possession of the premises until the trial is resolved.

Of course, the tenant has a fourth choice not mentioned by TRCP 740: he may simply move out.

If a trial is necessary, the date shall be set by the JP. As in other civil matters, there will be a jury trial unless neither party asks for one. The trial may be postponed up to six days for good cause, or by agreement of both attorneys. The only question to be decided at the trial is whether or not the tenant's possession of the premises is lawful, unless the landlord is also seeking to collect delinquent rent. If collection of rent is at issue, it must be decided how much delinquent rent—if any—the tenant is liable for.

If the decision is for the plaintiff landlord, he is entitled to a judgment for possession of the premises, damages, delinquent rent (if any) and a fee for his attorney (if the requirements of RCS 3975b are met). If the defendant tenant does not appeal the result to the county court within five days, the court will issue a writ of restitution to the landlord, and a constable or deputy sheriff will evict the tenant. If the decision is for the defendant tenant, the tenant will receive judgment against the landlord for costs and damages.

Either party may appeal from the final judgment within five days after rendition of the judgment. Ordinarily the appealing party must post an appeal bond covering costs and damages assessed against him. However, TRCP 749a provides that the appealing party may escape posting the bond by filing a pauper's affidavit with his appeal, alleging that he cannot afford to post a bond. If the other party feels that the appealing party is not a pauper, he may ask for a hearing on the matter within five days of the filing of the affidavit. If the JP decides that the appealing party is a pauper, he will permit the appeal without the bond; if he decides that the appealing party is not a pauper, the appealing party may appeal this decision to the county court. After a hearing, the county judge will then decide whether or not the appealing party is a pauper. If he decides in the negative, the party must either post bond or drop the appeal. If he decides in the affirmative, the case moves to the county court.

In all tenant appeals, the tenant remains in possession pending the disposition of the appeal. There is an entirely new trial on the matter in the county court, in which there will be a jury if either party wishes. The decision in the county court is final; no further appeal is authorized. If the tenant loses, he must get out within five days of the decision or submit to being evicted. Of course, the tenant will be liable for rent during the period in which he remained in possession.

Forcible detainer proceedings thus may move rather slowly if the tenant takes advantage of all opportunities to stall. Such stalling may prove expensive in the end, however, because of the potential liability for court costs and attorney's fees. On the other hand, the reluctant tenant who has no assets and little or no income may want to drag things out to the bitter end. After all, if he has nothing he can be made to pay nothing.

50

Liens on Real Property

Since land is among the most valuable of assets, it is also among the most acceptable forms of collateral for loans—and the most favored targets of creditors, when accessible to their claims. Furthermore, much of the tax revenue of local governments is raised through the taxation of real property.

Land as collateral—the mortgage. The traditional way of financing a purchase of real estate—and the traditional way of using land as collateral for a loan—is use of a mortgage. When a purchase of land is financed by a mortgage transaction, the seller delivers a deed to the property to the buyer. The buyer then delivers a mortgage upon the property to the financing lender. The buyer, or *mortgagor*, retains legal title to the property. The lender, or *mortgagee*, acquires a mortgage lien upon the property.

If the mortgagor defaults on his payments or otherwise defaults on his obligations under the mortgage the mortgagee has the right to foreclose the mortgage. He is in some ways in the same position as the holder of a security interest in personal property, in that foreclosure of his lien does not give him title to the collateral. Rather, by foreclosing he becomes obligated to sell legal title to the collateral and collect his claim against the mortgagor from the proceeds of the sale.

The great disadvantage of the mortgage as a financing device from the lender's point of view is this: At common law, and in most states that commonly use this device, nonjudicial foreclosure of the mortgage lien is not possible. Foreclosure requires court action, which makes it slow and expensive. Another disadvantage is the existence of the mortgagor's right of redemption. For a period of time after foreclosure—a period that varies from state to state—the mortgagor can redeem his property from the buyer at the foreclosure sale by paying off what he owes on the property plus the expenses of foreclosure. Thus, the buyer at a mortgage foreclosure sale does not get clear title to what he is buying until the time limit for exercise of the right of redemption has expired.

If a borrower of funds seeks to put up land he owns as collateral, he gives the lender a mortgage upon the land. In this situation the lender is again subject to the disadvantages of being a mortgagee.

Land as collateral—the trust deed. In many states of the United States, efforts have been made to devise methods of using land for collateral which are more advantageous for creditors than the mortgage. The notion of adapting some of the features of the law of trusts to this area has resulted in the invention of the *trust deed*, a method of financing that is now used in several states, including Texas. In fact, so popular is the trust deed here that the mortgage is a rare specimen indeed.

The trust deed is a three-party document. The parties are:

1. The *trustor*—the buyer of the land the purchase of which is being financed or the borrower of the money for which land is being put up as collateral.
2. The *beneficiary*—the lender, the party for whose benefit the trust deed is being executed.
3. The *trustee*—a third party whose only connection with the transaction is that he will be granted legal title to the land to hold for the benefit of the beneficiary until the loan is paid off.

The trust deed must be signed by the trustor. It must of course contain the names of the trustee and the beneficiary. It will also spell out the obligations of the parties to each other, and will contain a description of the land being put up as collateral. It will also provide that in case of default by the trustor the trustee may dispose of the land by nonjudicial process, without right of redemption, and that if the foreclosure does not net enough proceeds to pay off the trustor's debt to the beneficiary plus expenses of foreclosure the trustor will be liable for any deficiency.

The usefulness of the trust deed has been destroyed in many states by court decisions holding that a trust deed is a form of mortgage which may be foreclosed only through judicial process. In Texas, however, it is settled law that the trust deed is not a mortgage and that nonjudicial foreclosure and denial of a right of redemption to the trustor are perfectly lawful.

In order for the trust deed to be effective as a lien upon land, it must be recorded. An unrecorded trust deed is not effective against subsequent purchasers of the land involved or against subsequent creditors of the trustor, unless these purchasers or creditors have notice of the existence of the trust deed and its lien.

It is possible for a trustor to execute more than one trust deed against land he owns or is buying. In such a case, the priority of the trust deeds depends upon the order in which they were recorded. The rule normally is "first in time, first in right," but this order may be changed by provisions in the trust deeds themselves. If a trust deed provides that the lien created by it shall be subordinated to the lien created by another trust deed, the provision will be enforced regardless of the order of recording.

It is also possible for the beneficiary of a trust deed to assign his rights. Again, such an assignment must be recorded for it to be effective against subsequent assignees without notice. Normally, when two or more assignments of the same beneficial right are made the first to be recorded has priority. This would of course not be true if the first assignee to record had notice of a prior unrecorded assignment.

When foreclosure of the trust deed becomes necessary, the procedure provided in RCS 3810 must be followed. Notice of the foreclosure must of course be given the trustor. The foreclosure sale must be by public auction and must be held upon the first Tuesday of the month between the hours of 10 A.M. and 4 P.M. Notice of the time and place of the sale must be posted at three public places within the county where the land is located for three consecutive weeks before the sale. One of these public places must be the courthouse door of the county in question.

The foreclosure sale will wipe out all liens upon the property junior to the lien being foreclosed; it will not, however, wipe out liens senior to those being foreclosed. There is thus no guarantee that the buyer at the sale will get clear title to the property. The would-be buyer should run a title search on the property before bidding in order to ascertain just what title the trustor possessed and what other liens are outstanding against the property. If, for example, a first trust-deed beneficiary forecloses, and a second trust deed is outstanding, foreclosure of the first lien will wipe out the second lien. The second lienholder would have to buy the property himself at the sale in order to protect his interest. However, if the second trust-deed beneficiary forecloses, the buyer at his sale will buy subject to the first trust-deed lien. The first lien will not be disturbed by the sale.

Of course, the buyer at the foreclosure sale must consider non-trust-deed liens which might exist against the property—property tax liens, judgment liens, mechanic's liens, federal tax liens, and so on. If some of these are senior to the trust deed lien being foreclosed, the buyer will buy subject to them. One matter which the buyer need not normally worry about is the regularity of the foreclosure proceedings up to the time of sale. So long as the buyer knows of no such irregularity, he is deemed to be a bona fide purchaser. The trustor may not have the sale set aside because of such irregularities, but he may of course sue those responsible for the irregularities for damages.

The proceeds of the sale are divided according to law. The expenses of foreclosure and sale come off the top, the balance being divided among lienholders in accordance with their respective priorities. If anything remains after the lienholders are all paid, the trustor gets it. If the proceeds are insufficient to pay off all lienholders, the trustor remains liable for the deficiency.

The state laws exempting the property of a debtor from the claims of his creditors do not apply to foreclosure of trust deeds and the like except in one particular. A non-purchase-money lien upon a homestead may not be foreclosed (RCS 3839). Remember the difference between a purchase-money lien and a non-purchase-money lien. If funds are lent to the borrower for the purpose of financing his purchase of the homestead, the resulting lien upon the property is a purchase-money lien which may be foreclosed. If the money is lent for a purpose other than the purchase of the homestead, the lender has probably wasted his time in obtaining a lien upon the homestead; even if the debtor defaults flagrantly, the creditor cannot foreclose his lien.

RCS 3837 provides that publicly owned property in the state of Texas shall not be subject to forced sale. It would thus be useless for a creditor of a governmental unit to accept a trust-deed lien upon a piece of publicly owned real estate.

Mechanic's, contractor's, and materialman's liens. Whenever a property owner contracts to have construction or repair work performed on any house, building, or improvement on his property, he is responsible for seeing to it that everyone who contributed labor or material to the job is properly paid. Should anyone who made such a contribution not be paid, that party may be able to claim a lien upon the property itself and may take steps to foreclose the lien if he is not paid.

A lien may be claimed only for labor or materials furnished in compliance with the contract for the construction or repair work; it cannot be claimed for unauthorized work. If the work done is authorized, RCS 5452 provides that the lien may be claimed for:

1. Labor used in direct prosecution of the work.
2. Material, machinery, fixtures, or tools incorporated in the work; consumed in the process of performing the work; or ordered and delivered for incorporation or consumption.
3. Rent at a reasonable running rate and actual running repairs at a reasonable cost for construction equipment used in the direct prosecution of the work, or reasonably required and delivered for such use.

4. Power, water, fuel, and lubricants when consumed, or ordered and delivered for consumption, in the direct prosecution of the work.

According to RCS 5453, original (or general) contractors, subcontractors, lumber dealers, artisans, laborers, and mechanics may claim mechanic's liens if not properly paid.

It is normal procedure in construction for the general contractor on a job to contract for purchase of supplies, hire of labor, etc. The owner of the site pays the general contractor as the work progresses, and the general contractor pays the subcontractors and laborers. It is also normal procedure for the general contractor to be bonded with a payment bond, so that a bonding company will be obligated to pay subcontractors, materialmen, and laborers if the general contractor does not pay them. The owner is thus not likely to become involved in mechanic's lien claims by subcontractors and suppliers.

RCS 5469 authorizes the owner to retain 10 percent of the contract price of the work for thirty days after completion of the job, for use as a fund to pay claims of subcontractors, materialmen, and laborers who claim they have not been paid by the general contractor. In addition, if the owner receives a notice of nonpayment from a subcontractor or supplier before the work is completed, RCS 5463 authorizes him to withhold sufficient funds from any progress payment falling due after receipt of the notice in order to pay off the claim.

A claimant of a mechanic's lien may not file his lien until his claim has *accrued* as provided by RCS 5467. A general contractor's claim accrues when the owner breaches or terminates the contract, or on the tenth day of the month following the month of completion of the contract (except for the 10 percent of the contract price which may be withheld for another thirty days). A laborer's, artisan's, or mechanic's claim accrues at the end of the calendar week during which his work was performed. A subcontractor's claim accrues on the tenth day of the month following the month in which his work was completed. A materialman's claim accrues on the tenth day of the month following the month in which his material was furnished.

In order for a general contractor to claim a mechanic's lien, he must file an affidavit claiming the lien in the office of the county clerk of the county where the property involved is located within 120 days of the accrual of his claim. Other mechanic's lien claimants are required to give notice of their claims to the general contractor and the owner before filing affidavits with the county clerk. When a laborer, mechanic, or materialman has not been paid by a subcontractor, he must give written notice of his claim by registered mail to the general contractor not later than thirty-six days after the tenth day of the month following the month during which the work was done or materials furnished. If the general contractor is the party indebted to the claimant, the claimant must file his notice with the owner rather than with the contractor. He must then file his affidavit with the county clerk not later than ninety days after his claim accrues.

The filing of the affidavit perfects the lien, since the county clerk is required to record the document in the county real estate records. RCS 5459 provides that the lien is deemed to have attached when the work commenced (not when the affidavit of lien was recorded). It is possible for the lien to attach even earlier if the construction agreement itself—or an affidavit of the existence of a contract to perform work upon the property—was recorded earlier.

If the lien is upon urban property, it attaches to the lot or lots upon which the building or other improvement is located (RCS 5458). The statute also provides that if the improvement in question is on rural land, the lien attaches to a maximum of fifty acres of the land.

The lien may only be foreclosed after judgment is rendered in a court proceeding seeking foreclosure (RCS 5472); though no court procedure is required to perfect the lien, it is thus impossible to have the property sold without a court procedure and a judgment. The foreclosure sale must be held pursuant to the law governing execution sales.

The lien is subject to all liens which were perfected against the property prior to the attachment. Essentially, then, all liens recorded against the property prior to the attachment of the mechanic's lien are superior to it. A buyer of the property at the lien foreclosure sale will then buy subject to these prior liens. On the other hand, the holders of these prior liens need not be made parties to the foreclosure suit.

If two or more mechanic's liens are filed against the same property, they all have equal standing. Under RCS 5468, the proceeds of the sale held to foreclose a mechanic's lien go first to satisfy all outstanding mechanic's liens against the property. Other lienholders may collect something only if the proceeds exceed the total of the outstanding mechanic's liens. If the proceeds are less than the total of all outstanding mechanic's liens, they are to be divided ratably among the claimants; the party beginning the foreclosure action gets no preference.

If the property upon which the improvements were made is a homestead, this procedure for perfecting a mechanic's lien is insufficient. RCS 5460 provides that, in order for it to be possible to obtain a mechanic's lien upon a homestead, the general contractor or person primarily responsible for furnishing labor or materials must enter into a written contract with the owner to do the work before the work is commenced. The contract must spell out all the terms of the bargain; it must be signed by both the owner and his spouse; and it must be recorded. If the contract between the owner and the general contractor is recorded, subcontractors and others may later file their mechanic's liens if they are not paid.

Mechanic's liens upon oil and mineral property. RCS 5473 et seq. provide a mechanism whereby contractors, materialmen, laborers, and others who provide material and labor for drilling wells or operating mines, quarries, and the like may obtain mechanic's liens upon the property in question. These liens differ from ordinary mechanic's liens in that they attach only to the oil and gas lease if the work was done on an oil or gas well, or to the mineral estate if the work was done on a mine or quarry. They will attach to the surface estate only if the surface owner commissioned the work.

The rules for attachment, priority, and foreclosure of such liens are very similar, but not identical to, the rules governing other types of mechanic's liens upon real property.

Judgment liens. A plaintiff who obtains a judgment for money in a civil lawsuit may acquire a lien upon the defendant's real estate by recording an *abstract of judgment* with the county clerk of every county in which the defendant owns real property. The plaintiff does not automatically obtain this lien when his judgment becomes final. He must ask the clerk of the court that rendered the judgment for an abstract, and he must then have this recorded in the office of the county clerk.

The lien is perfected as of the date of recording. It is junior to all liens recorded prior to this date and will be senior to liens recorded after it. When the ten-year statute of limitations for collecting a judgment expires, the lien also expires. When a judgment is renewed before the statute expires, the recording of a new abstract is necessary. RCS 5447 et seq. contain the law on these matters.

RCS 5451 provides that abstracts of federal court judgments may be recorded in the same manner as state court judgments, and that such abstracts have the same force and effect as abstracts of state court judgments.

Real property tax liens. The law relative to the assessment and collection of real property taxes in Texas is relatively complex, as is the law relative to the Texas real property tax lien and the foreclosure thereof. A brief summary of the law here follows.

Real property is subject to taxation by the state of Texas, counties, cities, school districts, and any other district or corporation given power by the legislature to levy real property tax. The major tax-assessing and collecting governmental units are the county, the school district, and the city. Numerous categories of real property are exempt from taxation, according to RCS 7150 et seq. Among types of real property exempt from taxation are:

1. Church and private school property.
2. YMCA and YWCA buildings.
3. Cemeteries.
4. Most government-owned property.
5. Property owned by public charities.
6. Art galleries.
7. Boy Scout and Girl Scout property.
8. Texas Federation of Women's Clubs property.
9. Veterans' organization property—American Legion, VFW, etc.
10. Fraternal organization property.
11. Garden club property.
12. Church parsonages.

RCS 7150h provides that property owned by a disabled veteran, his spouse, or his surviving minor child shall be partially exempt from taxation. In addition, Section 1-d-1 was added to Article VIII of the Texas Constitution by the state's voters in November 1978; it provides for the partial exemption of homesteads from taxation.

The procedure for assessment and collection of property taxes described below is that which applies to county taxation, but the same or very similar rules apply to school district and municipal taxation.

Between January 1 and April 30, the property owner must *render* his property for taxation with the county tax assessor-collector by filing with that officer a statement containing a description of the property owned by him, its true and full value, and his name and address. The taxing entity may use full market value as the basis for taxation, or it may follow a policy of multiplying this value by an *assessment ratio*, a percentage of full market value, to determine the assessed value. If an assessment ratio is used, it should be uniform throughout the county. The constitutional amendment of 1978 provides that agricultural land is to be rendered and assessed on the basis of productive capacity rather than market value. However, since the amendment also provides that this procedure must be enacted by the Legislature before it goes into effect, the basis for assessment will remain market value until such legislation is enacted.

RCS 7211 permits the tax assessor-collector to raise the valuation of property rendered for taxation if he believes that the owner did not render it at fair cash value. Any property that is not rendered for taxation may also be valued by the assessor-collector himself, under authority granted by RCS 7205.

Between the second Monday in May and the first of June, the county commissioners' court must meet as a board of equalization for the county. At this time the assessor-collector must turn over to the commissioners all of the records of property subject to taxation in the county and the valuations placed upon each parcel by the owner or by the assessor-collector. The commissioners must then adjust these valuations so that all property in the county is valued properly, like properties being valued in a like manner. If the commissioners acting as the board of equalization raise the value of any property above the value rendered by the owner, they must notify the county clerk, who must then notify the property owner.

In cases in which the assessor-collector himself changes the valuation of rendered property under the authority of RCS 7211, the owner has the right to appeal this change to the board of equalization. Such cases are considered during the month of May, when the commissioners' court is acting as the board of equalization. If a property owner is dissatisfied with the value placed upon his property by the board of equalization, he may appeal its decision to a Texas district court within forty-five days after the tax roll containing the disputed valuation is approved by the taxing authority (which will occur after the board of equalization completes its work).

The appeal must be filed in the county where the land is located, and the county where the board of equalization made its decision. The plaintiff is entitled to a jury trial if he wants it. The issue in the case is the proper valuation of the property. If the court or jury decides that the valuation of the board of equalization is in error, then it may fix its own valuation. The statute governing this appellate procedure—RCS 7345f—provides that the valuation set by the board of equalization must prevail if the owner failed to use good faith in rendering his property—that is, if he deliberately and knowingly understated its value.

The actual tax payable upon the property is determined by three factors. The first is the valuation of the property. The second is the assessment ratio: if, for instance, the taxing authority determines that the value for taxation purposes shall be 60 percent of actual market value, a property with a market valuation of $100,000 would be valued at $60,000 for taxation purposes. The third factor is the actual tax rate, usually expressed in terms of mills (tenths of a cent) per dollar. The only one of these factors which the property owner may argue about as an individual is the valuation of his property in terms of cash or market value. The determination of the tax rate and the assessment ratio are essentially political matters; the control that the taxpayer has over these is his power as a voter.

The assessor-collector should compute the tax due upon each parcel of property by the first of October. RCS 7255 provides that collection shall begin October 1; the tax becomes delinquent if not paid by the following January 1. When the tax is paid before it becomes delinquent, the property owner is entitled to a discount of up to 3 percent if the taxing government has chosen to make the discount available to its taxpayers. The taxpayers may also obtain an extension of the due date until June 30 of the following year if he pays at least 50 percent of the taxes imposed upon his property before November 30 (RCS 7336). If the taxpayer does not pay 50 percent of the tax by November 30, he must pay it all by January 31 or be subject to a penalty. In such a case, the penalty is 1 percent of the tax if he pays in February, 2 percent if he pays in March, 3 percent if he pays in April, 4 percent if he pays in May, 6 percent if he pays in June, and 8 percent if he pays thereafter. If he pays 50 percent by November 30 but does not pay the other 50 percent by June 30, he must pay the 8 percent penalty when he pays the balance, the penalty being computed only on the unpaid balance. In addition, the tax liability accrues interest at the rate of 6 percent per year after it becomes delinquent.

RCS 7324 requires that the assessor-collector mail notices of delinquency to property owners during the month of July if their property taxes have not been paid in full earlier. Duplicates of these notices must be sent to the local county or district attorney. If the delinqency is not paid within thirty days of the date of the notice, the proper attorney shall have the duty to file suit against the taxpayer as soon as possible to foreclose the property tax lien (RCS 7326). This duty shall not apply, however, if the taxpayer is sixty-five years of age or older, and the property upon which the tax is due is his homestead. In such a case, RCS 7329a provides that the collection of delinquent tax may not be accomplished through foreclosure of the tax lien. The taxpayer is still personally liable for the tax, and the tax lien still attaches to the property, but the lien may be foreclosed only when the property ceases to be the homestead of a person sixty-five years of age or older.

In the tax foreclosure suit, the taxing agency shall sue for all tax, penalty, and interest due up until the date of rendition of judgment (RCS 7326a). All record lienholders must be named as defendants in the suit, along with the record owner of the property (RCS 7328). In addition, RCS 7345b provides that the plaintiff taxing agency should join as defendants all other taxing agencies with power to levy real property taxes against the property in question, so that all tax liens against the property for real property taxes may be foreclosed at the same time.

The owner's defenses in such a suit are severely limited. RCS 7329 provides that only the following three defenses are available.

1. The defendant was not the owner of the property at the time of the filing of the suit.
2. The taxes sued for have been paid.
3. The taxes sued for are excessive—have never been assessed, are in excess of that tax limit allowed the taxing agency by law, etc.

In addition, if suit is erroneously filed to foreclose upon the homestead of a person sixty-five years of age or older, the defendant may have the suit dismissed by offering proof of his age and of the fact that the property is his homestead.

Once the plaintiff has obtained a judgment of foreclosure (which it almost always does), the land must be sold at auction to foreclose the lien. The sheriff must announce in advance the time and place of the sale. It is not likely that a buyer will appear at this sale, because RCS 7284a and 7284b provide that the purchaser at such a sale shall not have the right to possess the property until two years after the date of the sale, and that during this two-year period the owner shall have the right to redeem his property by paying the buyer double the amount paid at the sale. Thus, a purchaser will not get clear title to the property at the time of sale, nor will he get possession. He can, however, speculate on doubling his money if the former owner redeems.

Under the provisions of RCS 7345b Sec. 12, the owner may redeem directly from the buyer at the foreclosure sale if he is redeeming during the first year after the sale, by paying what the buyer paid for the property plus subsequent taxes, penalties, interests, costs, and recording fees, plus 25 percent of the aggregate. If redeeming during the second year after foreclosure, the above plus 50 percent of the aggregate must be paid.

The buyer at the foreclosure sale will normally be the state of Texas, the purchaser if no one else bids. It is also possible for the taxing unit bringing the foreclosure suit—or some other taxing unit involved in the case—to purchase. The buyer may resell the property at any time after purchase, or it may choose to keep the property for its own use and for the use of the other governments holding tax liens upon it. Any taxing government may compel the sale of the property if it has not been resold by the purchasing taxing agency within six months of the expiration of the original owner's right of redemption. The resale may be at public or private sale, but if it is compelled by a taxing agency other than the purchasing agency at the original sale it must be a public auction presided over by the sheriff of the county where the land is located.

The second buyer obtains "good and perfect" title to the property, if proper procedure was followed in the sale. If proper procedure was not followed he gets all the rights in the property that the taxing agencies had, meaning that he has a lien which he may now foreclose. The only liens not discharged by such sales are certain liens against irrigable lands held by water improvement districts or the like.

Under the provisions of RCS 7345a, it is possible for a government to sell its tax lien upon real estate to a third party in exchange for the payment of the delinquent taxes by that party. The buyer of the lien may not foreclose it within twelve months after his purchase, and the owner may redeem the property from him during this period. After the expiration of the twelve months the buyer may foreclose, but at the sale he buys subject to a twelve-month redemption period. The owner, then, retains his two-year redemption period.

Municipal real property taxation. Texas municipalities are permitted to assess and collect their own property taxes. Each municipality may elect or appoint its own assessor-collector. City dwellers must then render their taxable property within the city limits to this municipal official.

The municipal council may act as a board of equalization for the city, exercising essentially the same powers as the county board of equalization. The municipal council may also appoint three commissioners to serve as the board, if it wishes (RCS 1048). Collection of delinquent taxes is essentially by the same procedure as that used by counties.

Independent school district real property taxation. The governing body of a Texas independent school district is a board of trustees elected by the voters of the district. The trustees have the authority to appoint a tax assessor-collector for the district, according to Texas Education Code (TEdC) 23.93. This person may be independent of any other tax-collecting agency within the territory of the district. On the other hand, TEdC 23.94 permits the trustees to designate the county assessor-collector of the county within which the district is located as the district assessor-collector. If the district is located entirely or partially within the borders of an incorporated municipality, the trustees may also appoint the city tax assessor-collector as the district assessor-collector (TEdC 23.96).

The trustees also have the power to appoint a board of equalization for the district. If the district is located in whole or in part within the boundaries of an incorporated municipality, the district may appoint the city board of equalization to serve as its board. TEdC 23.97 permits two or more districts to appoint the same person to serve as assessor-collector.

Since independent school districts do not have district attorneys as such, TEdC 23.98 permits such districts to hire attorneys to collect delinquent real property taxes for them. The attorney must use the procedures counties use under RCS 7345b Sec. 6.

The Texas Property Tax Code. The 1979 session of the Texas legislature took action which radically changes the law of property taxation as of January 1, 1982. Upon that date the new Texas Property Tax Code goes into effect. This section summarizes the important changes in the law which this will bring about.

First: The new code directs the establishment of countywide appraisal districts in each of the state's 254 counties. The appraisal district will have authority to appraise property for ad valorem tax purposes within the county for all taxing governments except the county itself, and county governments have the option of contracting out their appraisal function to the appraisal district. Thus, there will be no more than two appraisal authorities per county, and there may be only one.

Second: The exemption statutes have been rewritten, although there have been no changes of importance in the substantive law of exemptions.

Third: Property subject to taxation shall be rendered under the new law to the chief appraiser of the county, to the county assessor-collector, or to both, between January 1 and April 1.

Fourth: If the appraised value of any rendered property is to be raised $1,000 or more, a notice of the new appraised value must be sent to the taxpayer by April 15 or as soon thereafter as possible.

Fifth: Assessment ratios are forbidden under the new code. All property must be assessed on the basis of 100 percent of appraised value.

Sixth: A taxpayer unhappy with the appraised value of his property may protest to the appraisal review board of the county appraisal district, or to the county commissioner's court acting as the board of equalization if the county does its own appraising. A county government may, however, delegate the board of equalization function to the appraisal review board by contract. Protests must be filed before May 11, or within twenty days after the appraisal records are submitted by the appraising authority, whichever is later. The taxpayer is entitled to a hearing on his protest, and the appraisal review board or board of equalization must hand down a written decision on the matter. Should the taxpayer wish to appeal the decision on the protest to the courts, he must file notice of appeal within fifteen days of the handing-down of the decision, and he must file his petition for review with the district court within forty-five days of its handing-down. The court review is by trial de novo; the result of the administrative process is disregarded and the court decides the matter on its own. The district court decision is appealable under the law and rules applicable to ordinary civil cases.

Seventh: The governing body of a taxing government must announce its tax rate. It cannot increase this rate without public announcement and a public hearing. In addition, if the proposed increase in the tax rate exceeds 5 percent, a procedure is set forth in the new code under which dissatisfied taxpayers may petition for a popular referendum on the tax increase. If a proper referendum petition is filed, the increase may in effect be vetoed by a majority of persons voting at the referendum.

Eighth: Though payment dates, early payment discounts, the split-payment option, and delinquency dates remain the same under the new code, penalties for late payments change. Under the new code, a penalty of 4 percent of the delinquency will be assessed for the first month of delinquency. A penalty of 1 percent will be assessed for each subsequent month. The maximum penalty will be 8 percent. In addition, interest at the rate of 0.75 percent per month will accrue on delinquent tax balances.

Ninth: Sending a notice of delinquency to the taxpayer will no longer be a prerequisite to the filing of suit to foreclose the tax lien. It will be possible to file a foreclosure action any time after the tax becomes delinquent.

Tenth: Tax sale and redemption procedure will remain the same under the new code, except that it will apparently no longer be possible for a taxing government to sell its lien to a private party. The taxing governments must now foreclose their own liens.

Federal tax liens. Whenever delinquent federal taxes—be they ordinary income taxes, withholding taxes, etc.—are not paid by a federal taxpayer when due, the Internal Revenue Service may proceed to assess the delinquent taxes against the taxpayer. Making the assessment gives the IRS a lien upon most of the taxpayer's property.

The IRS may make the lien a matter of public record by recording a notice of federal tax lien in the records of counties in which the taxpayer owns real estate, under the provisions of IRC 6323. The lien may be recorded before any court action is taken by the IRS. In general, the lien has the effect of a judgment lien upon real property. It is junior to private liens recorded before it, and also junior to all real property tax liens. It is senior to all private liens recorded after it and to all private liens held by parties who knew of the existence of the IRS tax claim against the taxpayer at the time of recording their liens.

The IRS has the right to foreclose its lien by a nonjudicial seizure and sale of the property. The buyer at the IRS sale gets all of the taxpayer's interest in the property, but he buys subject to all liens senior to the IRS lien. Thus, the would-be buyer of property at an IRS tax sale should run a title search before bidding in order to be sure what he is buying.

51

Public Rights in Private Property

The rights of an owner of real estate in his property may be limited by public authority. Public authority may regulate the use of real estate through exercises of the police power, the most common such exercise being zoning. Public authority may also take private property for public use. When this is done as an exercise of the police power—as in the abatement of a public nuisance—it is done without compensation to the landowner. When it is done in order to appropriate the property to an essential public use—as in the construction of a highway—compensation is required. This is done through exercise of the power of eminent domain. It is that power which we will consider first in this chapter.

EMINENT DOMAIN

Possessors of eminent domain powers. Governments and government agencies possess eminent domain powers. The Texas legislature has also granted eminent domain powers to the following private types of corporations (among others): cemetery associations, electric power companies, gas companies, pipeline companies, railroad companies, telephone companies, water companies, and canal companies.

Preliminary negotiations. The public authority or private corporation wishing to condemn a tract of private property for public use must approach the owner and try to negotiate an acceptable purchase price. Whenever an owner of private property is approached in this manner, he should realize that he is about to lose the property the condemnor is seeking, since any governmental or private body having eminent domain powers has the absolute right to condemn private property for public use. The only way in which the property owner may preserve his property is by arguing that the proposed taking is not for public use. This is almost impossible to prove—the number of public uses for private property in the last third of the twentieth century is legion. Among the possible public uses to which condemned property may be put are roads, government buildings, public schools, university dormitories (for state universities), parking lots adjacent to government buildings or schools, public airports, public boat docks, parks, recreation areas, wilderness areas, dam sites, power line rights-of-way, pipeline rights-of-way, and publicly owned sports arenas. This list does not begin to exhaust all of the possibilities.

The landowner may question the wisdom of the public use the condemnor has in mind for his land, but the wisdom of a public project is generally not a legal question. If the condemnor has followed proper procedure in getting approval for its project, it is not a matter to be argued in a court or other tribunal; it is a political matter, to be argued through the political process. In short, the only way to save the property is to attempt to prove that the proposed taking is not for a public use, which is normally futile. Political resistance may well bear more fruit than resistance in the courts, but the chances of success in that endeavor are also none too good.

The argument between condemnor and landowner—if any—will therefore not be over whether or not the condemnor may take the land. That point is settled before negotiations ever begin. The only point of argument is: How much will the condemnor pay for the property?

According to RCS 3265, if the condemnor takes the whole of a tract or parcel of land, it must pay the market value of the property in the area of its location. Of course, reasonable minds may well differ as to the market value of a tract of land. If the condemnor is taking less than all of a tract or parcel, the arithmetic gets more complex. The condemnor must pay the fair market value of what it is taking, but it also must take into account the effect of the taking upon the remainder of the owner's property. If the result of the condemnation will be to increase the value of the remainder of the tract or parcel, the market value of the portion taken must be reduced by this appreciation. If the value of the remainder of the property will be decreased, these damages must be added to the market value of the property taken.

The law requires the condemnor and the landowner to negotiate, but it does not compel them to agree. If the owner demands too much, or the condemnor offers too little, the parties may agree to disagree. At this point the condemnor may set the wheels of the eminent domain legal process in motion.

The special commissioners. If the condemnor and the landowner cannot agree upon a price, the condemnor must file a petition for condemnation with a proper court. Originally the proper court was the county court, but today RCS 3266a requires that the petition be filed with the district court of the county where the land is located, unless that county has a county court at law which has been given jurisdiction by the legislature in eminent domain cases.

The petition must include a description of the land to be condemned, a statement of the purpose for which condemnation is requested, the names of all parties owning an interest in the land, and a statement that the parties have been unable to agree upon the value of the property or the damages.

RCS 3266a and RCS 3264 require that the judge of the court in which the petition is filed must appoint three special commissioners to determine the value of the property to be taken and the damages involved. These special commissioners must be freeholders of the county in which the land is located. If the condemnor and the landowner can agree on three persons to serve in this capacity, the judge shall appoint those persons; otherwise the judge may use his discretion in this matter.

The commissioners must set a time and place for a hearing on the case. They must send notice of the time and place of the hearing to all interested parties, and these notices must be served upon the parties at least ten days before the date set for the hearing. The commissioners have the power to subpoena witnesses, administer oaths, take testimony, and punish for contempt. If an owner's residence is unknown, if he lives outside the state, or if he cannot be located, notice may be served on him by publication, as in a civil action.

After the commissioners hear all of the evidence, they must compute the market value of the property and the damages to the best of their ability, as per RCS 3265. A majority of the commissioners may render this decision. In computing damages and benefits, they must not take into account damages suffered because of the condemnation by the community as a whole; they must consider only the effect of the condemnation upon the land of the landowner himself. The commissioners then file their decision with the court that appointed them.

RCS 3266b provides that if condemnation will require that an individual, family, business, farm, ranch, or nonprofit organization be displaced, the following must be included in the condemnation award:

1. Moving expenses.
2. Relocation payments.
3. Financial assistance to find replacement housing.
4. Rental supplements.

There are limits upon the amounts of money payable for these four purposes. RCS 3265 Sec. 7 provides that a landowner who is physically displaced and who must move permanently is entitled to a moving allowance for personal property other than machinery, equipment, or fixtures not to exceed $500, if the property is moved from a residence. If the property is to be moved from a place of business the maximum allowance is not to exceed $5,000. When it is necessary for the displaced person to acquire replacement housing or replacement business premises, the condemning agency must pay compensation like that required of federal condemnors under the federal relocation assistance programs, 42 USC 4651 et seq. These programs of compensation are discussed under federal condemnation later in this chapter.

If both the condemnor and the landowner are happy with the decision of the special commissioners, the condemnor pays the assessed sum and the proceeding ends. If one or more of the parties is not happy, an appeal may be taken.

Appeal from decision of special commissioners. According to RCS 3266 Sec. 6, a party dissatisfied with the decision of the special commissioners has until the first Monday following the twentieth day after the filing of the decision to file his objections in writing with the judge who appointed the commissioners. Once the objections are filed, citation must be served upon the other party in accordance with the rules of civil procedure, and the case becomes another piece of ordinary civil litigation. A jury trial is permitted if either party desires one. The decision of the court is appealable just as is the decision in any other action for damages.

When condemnor may take possession of property. If condemnor and landowner cannot agree upon the price to be paid for the property, so that the proceeding before the special commissioners becomes necessary, the condemnor may not take possession before the commissioners hand down their decision.

It is possible for the condemnor to take possession after the commissioners make a decision even if the landowner wants to appeal the decision; RCS 3268 sets forth the required procedure. The condemnor must either pay to the landowner the amount awarded by the commissioners, or it must deposit that sum in court subject to withdrawal by the landowner. It must also deposit in court either another sum of money equal to the award of the commissioners, or a surety bond for an equivalent sum. This additional sum is in the nature of assurance to the landowner that, if he can convince the jury on the appeal to award him additional damages or compensation, the funds for payment by the condemnor are available. If the condemnor complies with these two requirements, it may take possession of the property and commence its project without the necessity for waiting until the appeal is settled.

What interests may be condemned. In general, the condemnor may not take more of the landowner's property than is required for the condemnor's project. It also may not take a greater interest in the property than is required. Usually an easement is sufficient to provide the condemnor with the rights it requires.

If there has been a severance of the mineral estate from the surface estate, the condemnor will have no cause to condemn the minerals, since the condemnor usually requires only the right to use the surface for its desired purpose.

The condemnor may not disturb the interest of a party not cited at the beginning of the proceedings. Thus, if the property has co-owners (tenants in common, joint tenants, community property, etc.), all co-owners must be cited. If there are trust-deed liens and the like upon the property, the lienholders must be cited. If tenants occupy the property, they must be cited. If squatters or other adverse parties are in possession, these should be cited. If the condemnation will disturb the rights of easement holders, these must be cited. And if future interests exist in the property, the owners of these must be cited.

Division of the condemnation award. All parties owning an interest in the property whose interests will be disturbed by the condemnation are entitled to share in the award. When multiple owners exist, the special commissioners must apportion the award among them. If the award is appealed, the award of the jury upon appeal must be apportioned. The method of apportionment will depend upon the value of the various interests involved.

Federal condemnations. When the federal government desires to acquire land for strictly federal use, the condemnation procedure will be commenced in federal court, and the acquisition will be governed by federal law. Space does not permit a detailed description of federal eminent domain procedure, but some aspects of federal acquisition policy are worthy of consideration. 42 USC 4651 contains the uniform federal policy on real property acquisitions.

The agency desiring to acquire property by condemnation should have the desired property appraised by a professional appraiser as soon as the property has been identified. The owner should be informed of the proposed taking and of the appraisal so that he may accompany the appraiser during the appraisal. The agency should then offer to purchase the property from the owner for its fair value, the fair value of course being greatly influenced by the result of the appraisal. The amount offered by the agency for the property must be at least equal to the appraised value.

The agency should make every reasonable effort to acquire the property by negotiation. Only if there is no meeting of the minds after negotiation should condemnation proceedings be commenced.

If the project for which the property is condemned will require the person lawfully occupying the property to move his dwelling, business, or farm operation, the agency acquiring the property should give the occupier at least ninety days' written notice of the date by which the premises are to be vacated. An owner may not be required to vacate his property before he has been paid the agreed purchase price; an amount equal to the appraised value of the property has been paid into court for the benefit of the owner; or the amount awarded by the court as compensation for the taking has been so paid.

In addition to the fair value of the property being condemned, the owner of property condemned by federal authority is entitled to some additional compensation. 42 USC 4622 provides that moving and related expenses are payable as follows:

1. Actual moving expenses for the owner, his family, business, farm operation, or other personal property.
2. Actual direct losses of tangible personal property as a result of moving or discontinuing a business or farm operation, not to exceed the costs of relocating such property.
3. Actual reasonable expense in searching for a replacement business or farm.

The owner who must seek another dwelling may receive, in lieu of actual moving expenses, a moving expense allowance of no more than $300 and a dislocation allowance of $200.

The owner who must move a business or farming operation may receive, in lieu of moving losses and expenses, an amount equal to the annual net earnings of the business or farm, but no less than $2,500 nor more than $10,000. This shall not be payable unless the agency is convinced that the business cannot be relocated without substantial loss of patronage.

If tenants are ejected from dwellings as a result of a federal condemnation, 42 USC 4624 provides that they are entitled to compensation sufficient to lease or rent a decent, safe, and sanitary dwelling of a sort similar to the condemned dwelling for four years, the compensation not to exceed $4,000; or the tenant is to be awarded an amount necessary for him to make a down payment upon a dwelling similar to the one he lost, the award not to exceed $4,000. If the award so made for a down payment exceeds $2,000, the tenant must match the amount of the federal award.

If a homeowner is ejected from his dwelling by a federal condemnation, 42 USC 4623 entitles him to a payment not to exceed $15,000 to enable him to purchase another dwelling similar to the one he lost. This payment should be the difference between what he was paid for his old property and the cost to him of acquiring similar property. If he must pay interest at a higher rate on the trust deed on his new dwelling than he was paying on the old, he is entitled to an allowance to compensate for the difference.

These statutes were enacted in 1971, at a time when real estate prices and prices in general were much lower than they are today. The dollar limitations on some of the awards authorized by these statutes are now obviously unrealistic, and the compensation provided, while perhaps adequate in 1971, may not be adequate now. On the other hand, we must remember that the Texas state condemnation statutes are much less generous in the awarding of these sorts of compensation. In short, if one is so unfortunate as to lose one's dwelling or business location to a condemning agency, one will probably lose money despite the fact that the condemning government must pay compensation for what it takes.

ZONING

Zoning involves the regulation of land use by governmental authorities. RCS 1011a empowers the legislative body of cities and incorporated villages to engage in this sort of regulation.

RCS 1011c provides that these regulations should be made with the following purposes in mind:
1. Lessening congestion in the streets.
2. Providing safety from fire, panic, and other dangers.
3. Promotion of health and the general welfare.
4. Provision of adequate light and air.
5. Prevention of overcrowding of land.

6. Avoiding undue concentration of population.
7. Facilitation of provision of adequate transportation, water, sewage service, schools, parks, etc.

RCS 1011a provides that the following sorts of land use regulation are authorized:
1. Height, number of stories, and size of buildings.
2. Percentage of lot that may be occupied.
3. Size of yards, courts, and other open spaces.
4. Density of population.
5. Location and use of buildings, structures, and land for trade, industry, residence, or other purposes.
6. Preservation of the nature of areas of historic or cultural importance.

The scheme of regulation is contained in a zoning ordinance. The scheme is to be part of a rational plan for the use of all land within the community. The municipality is divided into districts, each district to have its own scheme of regulation. The regulation must be uniform within the district, but the regulations may vary from district to district.

RCS 1011f requires each municipality desiring to enact a zoning ordinance to create an administrative body to be known as a *zoning commission*. This commission is to devise the original plan, and to consider changes in the original plan once adopted. The zoning commission must hold public hearings while devising the original plan. Once it has arrived at a final plan, it must report this to the municipal legislative body, which will hold further hearings on the proposed plan before enacting the zoning ordinance.

RCS 1011h provides that the municipality may enforce the zoning ordinance in two ways. First, violation of the ordinance is declared to be a misdemeanor. Since all violations of city ordinances are Class C misdemeanors, such a violation may subject the violator to a fine of up to $200. In addition, the municipality is empowered to obtain injunctions against violators, a more powerful form of enforcement.

Amending the zoning ordinance. The municipality may amend the zoning ordinance and the restrictions and regulations applicable to a district or a portion thereof by following proper procedure. Proposed changes must first be considered by the zoning commission, which must hold a public hearing upon the changes before voting on them. Notice of a proposed change in the use classification or other classification of property must be sent to the owners of all property that is to be reclassified and to the owners of all property lying within 200 feet of the property to be reclassified. This notice must be given at least ten days before the hearing. Interested parties may appear at the hearing and make their views known to the commissioners. After the hearing the commissioners may vote upon the change. If they approve it, it is submitted to the municipal legislative body.

The municipal council must hold another hearing on the matter, unless by city ordinance the hearing before the zoning commission is also to be considered as the hearing before the council. If the owners of 20 percent or more of the land area involved (including all land within 200 feet of any land the zoning of which is to be changed) protest the change, the vote of three-fourths of all members of the municipal council will be necessary to approve the amendment.

Operation of zoning. Zoning ordinances vary in content from municipality to municipality. They generally provide for at least three types of land use: residential, commercial, and industrial. These may be further broken down into subcategories: single-family residential and multi-family residential, with perhaps a separate category for mobile home parks and the like. Areas zoned *commercial* may be broken down into subcategories consisting of various types of commercial activity—a drug store might be authorized in an area where a butcher shop might not be. Areas zoned *industrial* may be broken down into categories consisting of various sorts of industry; for example, a small clothing factory might be allowed in an area where a foundry would not be permitted. There may also be areas within the municipality zoned for agriculture. Other areas may be zoned for public uses such as schools and government buildings.

The ordinance might permit *cumulation* of uses within an area, the existence of "higher" uses alongside "lower" uses. Thus, it may permit the use of industrially zoned property for commercial or residential use, or the use of commercially zoned property for residential use. It would never permit the use of residential property for commercial use. On the other hand, the community may decide not to permit cumulation; it may choose not to allow residential use of commercial property, for instance.

Since building restrictions of various sorts are an integral part of zoning schemes, it follows that the owner of a tract of town property may not erect any sort of structure he pleases upon his property; nor may he alter existing structures upon the property as he pleases. The landowner who wants to alter an existing structure or erect a new structure may not do so before he obtains a building permit from the municipal authorities who administer the zoning ordinance. These authorities will not issue a building permit unless the structure as erected or altered will comply with the zoning law.

The ordinance may also require that anyone desiring to operate a business within the city limits must obtain a permit from the municipal authorities. The permit will be granted only if the zoning ordinance authorizes the existence of that particular business in that proposed locality.

Territorial limitations upon the zoning power of municipalities. In general, municipal governments have authority only within those areas that are part of the territory of the municipality; municipal ordinances have no extraterritorial effect. The zoning ordinance of the city of Podunk applies only to the territory that lies within the city limits of Podunk. Whenever the city of Podunk extends its corporate limits by annexation of new territory to the municipality, that territory and the inhabitants thereof become subject to all the municipal ordinances of Podunk. The city thus acquires the authority to zone all of the territory so annexed.

In this connection it must be remembered that most of the land area of the state of Texas is not within the boundaries of any municipality, and thus is not subject to any municipal zoning law. Though all of the land area of the continental United States is part of one of the 48 continental states, and all of the land area of the state of Texas is part of one of the 254 counties of the state, the same principle does not apply with respect to municipalities. One may thus escape municipal zoning by acquiring real estate in an area that is not a part of an existing municipality. However, it often happens that land which was thinly settled and distant from the borders of any town back in 1930 is now more thickly settled and very near the borders of a growing city. The more thickly settled and urbanized an area becomes, the more advantages there are for its residents in becoming part of a municipality. Access to municipal police and fire services, sewage disposal systems, etc. become desirable.

How the residents of such an area may deal with the problem can best be described through an illustration. In 1930 Sam Smiley bought a farm five miles west of the center of the town of Podunk. Back then, Sam's farm was four miles west of the Podunk city limits. Since 1930, though, much industry has located in Podunk, and the town is now a city. The western city limits are now within a half a mile of Sam's land. In 1930, Sam's neighbors were few. They were all farmers like himself. Now, most of his neighbors have sold their land to capitalize on the high land prices in a growing metropolitan area, and Sam finds himself living in what is essentially an urban area of one-family residences, even though the land is not legally part of Podunk.

The need for municipal services is growing in this area. Some residents are beginning to push for annexation to the city of Podunk. However, the Podunk city government has progressively changed the zoning of the western part of the city to encourage location of heavy industry and low-cost housing. If the area where Sam resides is to be annexed to Podunk, the city authorities may well eventually extend this sort of zoning there. Some of the residents do not mind this; others very definitely do. It bothers Sam especially because the zoning to which the area would be subject upon annexation would definitely affect the value of his land.

The problem is: How to get municipal services and at the same time avoid the association with the growing city? Sam Smiley and some others come up with a possible answer. Instead of joining the existing city of Podunk, why not incorporate a new municipality, the town of West Podunk? If this could be done, the area could form its own police and fire departments, essentially creating its own municipal services. The town of West Podunk could also enact its own zoning ordinance; if it wants to keep out the heavy industry and low-cost housing found in its big neighbor, it might be able to do so.

Assuming that Sam and those in the area who feel as he does can mobilize a majority of the public opinion in the area behind them, and assuming that they are able to comply with the requirements of state law for incorporating a new municipality, they will have accomplished their objective. This has of course been done many times in areas bordering upon the large cities of this state. Most of our metropolitan areas consist of a large city at the center, with concentric rings of suburbs extending outward to the edges of the area. The city administers its own zoning ordinance in an effort to control land use within its borders (with the exception of Houston, which has no zoning), while each suburban municipality does the same thing. The result is that, though each independent municipality follows what seems to it a rational policy with respect to regulation of its own development, there is often no rational policy with respect to the area as a whole because no authority exists to make policy for the entire area.

RCS 1011l does permit municipalities to combine their resources to create joint planning commissions. These, however, have power only to make studies and recommendations to their constituent members. RCS 1011m goes even further and permits establishment of regional planning commissions by the municipalities of part of a county, a whole county, or of two or more counties or parts thereof. These, again, only have power to conduct studies and make recommendations.

The power of each municipal government to be master in its own house with respect to zoning, the lack of extraterritorial zoning power by municipalities, and the multiplicity of municipalities in metropolitan areas render zoning schemes much less rational for wide areas than the originators of zoning first imagined.

Nonconforming uses. Whenever a formerly unzoned area is subjected to zoning for the first time or the zoning of an area is changed, the problem of nonconforming use is bound to arise. If a newly zoned area is zoned for single-family residences but some small businesses already exist within the area, what is to be done with the small businesses?

RCS 1011c specifically provides that a municipality shall not require the removal or destruction of property used in a public service business because of the enactment of a zoning ordinance. Even if this statutory provision did not exist there would be constitutional objections to the immediate elimination of nonconforming uses, on the grounds that this would be taking private property for public use without due compensation.

Zoning ordinances may deal with nonconforming uses in various ways. They often require that these uses must terminate within a certain number of years after the enactment of the provision which created the nonconformity. Such provisions are enforceable if reasonable. If the nonconforming use in question is a junkyard, slaughterhouse, or anything else approaching the category of a nuisance, a relatively short time may be provided for termination. If the use is a drug store or something similar, a considerably longer period may be required: drug stores do not normally disturb their neighbors. The ordinance may provide that a nonconforming use shall end if certain occurrences come to pass, such as a change in ownership of the business in question. Provisions of this nature are less often enforceable.

Generally, it is difficult to terminate a nonconforming use so long as the property does not change its use, and so long as the structures on the property are not altered. There can be no constitutional objection to the municipality's permitting the nonconforming use to continue until it ceases. The cessation could be due to numerous reasons, of course: the owner of a nonconforming business may die and his heirs decide to liquidate; the owner may decide to retire and liquidate; or the business may fail and be liquidated through bankruptcy proceedings.

If the building housing the nonconforming use burns down or is otherwise destroyed, the municipality may refuse to permit its reconstruction, particularly if the building did not conform with specifications for buildings in the area contained in the ordinance. Changes in ownership of a nonconforming business generally will not end the nonconforming use. The change in owner is not a change in the business, and restricting the right of the owner of the nonconforming business to sell it damages his property rights.

Alterations in the building housing the nonconforming use may be permitted under some circumstances and denied under others. Repair of deterioration caused by normal wear and tear would be permitted since it will not change the essential nature of the building. An alteration which does change the nature of the building might not be permitted. A remodeling of the interior might be one thing; the addition of another story or the enlargement of the floor area might be another. Any alteration increasing the degree of the nonconformity would not be allowed.

Under some circumstances a change in the nature of the nonconformity would be allowed; under others it would not. If a grocery store were permitted to exist as a nonconforming use in a residential area, and the owner decided to convert the grocery into a drug store, the conversion might be allowed, since there is not a huge difference between the two types of business. Should the grocery store want to sell out to a chain of dry-cleaning shops, however, there might be an objection, since the dry-cleaning establishment could emit fumes which the grocery does not and there is a danger of explosion in a dry-cleaning shop that does not exist in a grocery. If the building housing the grocery becomes vacant, so that no business exists upon the property, the nonconforming use has ended. No one would be allowed to open a new business in those premises—they must now be used as the ordinance commands.

Spot zoning. Spot zoning has occurred when one parcel—or a small handful of parcels—within a district are zoned for uses differing from those allowed within most of the district. This type of zoning may be permissible or it may not be, depending on the nature of the spot use as compared to the nature of the use generally provided.

If the spot use is consistent with the general zoning scheme of the district, it is not objectionable. A corner lot might be zoned for a grocery store in the middle of a low-cost single-family residential area without objection; the residents of the area might find it convenient to patronize the grocery. If the corner lot were zoned for a liquor store, however, the outcome might be different; many residents of the area might find the liquor store objectionable. It is probably not consistent with the general zoning scheme. To put it another way, if the spot zoning in question works for the benefit of the zoned area in general, it is not objectionable. If it seems to work only for the financial benefit of the owner of the spot-zoned property, it is definitely objectionable.

The board of adjustment. RCS 1011g permits municipalities to create a board of adjustment as part of the machinery for administration of the zoning ordinance. Since the statute is a permissive one, no municipality need create a board of adjustment if it does not desire to do so. Most Texas municipalities with zoning ordinances have chosen to create these boards.

The statute provides that the board shall consist of five members appointed for two-year terms by an appointing authority to be designated in the ordinance establishing the board. Four alternate members who may sit upon the board in the absence of regular members may also be appointed.

The board is to have the authority to do three things:
1. To hear and decide appeals from the decisions of any administrator charged with enforcement of the zoning ordinance.
2. To grant special exceptions to the terms of the zoning ordinance where authorized.
3. To allow variances from the terms of the zoning ordinance.

At least four members of the board must hear a matter brought before it, and at least four members must decide in favor of an applicant to grant him relief. Any party unhappy with a decision of the board may appeal it to a court of record within ten days of the board's decision. The court may then direct a writ of certiorari to the board, directing it to turn over copies of the record of the matter to the court for review. The court may require testimony of witnesses if it wishes, and may affirm, deny, or modify the board's decision.

Appeals of administrative decisions. Suppose a citizen applies to a proper municipal authority to obtain a permit to erect a building on a city lot he owns, presenting the authority with the plans and specifications of the proposed building. The authority refuses to grant the permit because, it says, the proposed building would be in violation of the building restrictions in effect under the zoning ordinance for that particular lot. The citizen does not interpret the ordinance as the authority does. He may appeal the authority's adjudication to the board of adjustment, since these are the sorts of administrative decisions which are appealable to it.

Special exceptions. The zoning ordinance may provide that no businesses may be conducted in residences except businesses of a nature which do not disturb neighbors, and that no such business may be conducted in a residence without the consent of the board of adjustment.

The board is thus given the authority to grant special exceptions to the general command of the zoning ordinance. Thus, if the Widow Schnitt wants to go into the clothing alteration business in her home—a sort of business that generally will not bother neighbors—she must apply to the board of adjustment for a special exception to the zoning law permitting her to do this.

Some zoning schemes would permit businesses of this sort to be conducted in residences without special exceptions. So long as the businessperson does not advertise at his residence; the street in front of the residence is not congested by customers' cars; streams of customers are not coming in and out of the residence; and the business does not create disagreeable noises, odors, or things of that sort, there is no objection.

A zoning ordinance might also provide that certain specified sorts of business may exist in a commercially zoned area. It may then specify that the board of adjustment may for good cause grant special exceptions to permit certain other sorts of business to exist in that district. Here again, someone desiring such a special exception must apply to the board.

Variances. It may be that the zoning ordinance will require a specified use for all property within a certain district, but a certain parcel of property within that district is unfit for that particular use. If the property is unfit for the prescribed use, it cannot be used at all if the ordinance is be to enforced literally. In such a situation, the property owner may ask for a variance permitting him exemption of sorts from the ordinance, in order to avoid hardship. The ordinance may require the applicant for a variance to apply to a municipal authority, giving him the right to appeal a denial of his request by that authority to the board of adjustment, or it may permit direct application to the board for a variance.

The applicant for a variance asks for permission to use his property in a way which is not authorized by the zoning ordinance. Since this is so, the request should not be granted unless special circumstances cause the property owner to suffer a hardship. For instance, the zoning ordinance may require that only single-family residences by erected in an area, and that all of them must have basements. If several lots in the area have such a high water table underlying them that it is impossible to dig basements there, the owner has an excellent reason to ask for a variance. He may ask for permission to use these lots in a manner in which the digging of a basement will not be required.

FEDERAL LAND USE REGULATION

Although the federal government has no authority to engage in zoning as such, numerous pieces of federal legislation give federal agencies authority to regulate land use. A discussion of land use regulation by government would not be complete without a brief discussion of this matter.

A detailed treatment of the subject may be found in Bosselman, Feurer, and Richter's work *Federal Land Use Regulation*, published in 1977 by the Practicing Law Institute.

Air pollution control. Two agencies are interested in land use regulation to prevent air pollution. At the federal level, the Environmental Protection Agency (EPA) exercises authority granted under the Clean Air Act (42 USC 1857 et seq.) and implements administrative regulations. At the state level, the Texas Air Control Board exercises authority granted under the Texas Clean Air Act (RCS 4477-5) and administrative regulations issued thereunder.

The EPA has authority to establish air quality standards for the various portions of the nation, and to establish tolerances for common air pollutants (such as carbon monoxide and sulphur dioxide) that may be present in the air. EPA also has the power to establish pollutant emission standards for various industries.

Anyone intending to use land for an industry that may cause emission of pollutants into the atmosphere must check into appropriate EPA and Texas Air Control Board regulations in order to ascertain that pollutant emissions will not constitute a violation of federal or state law. The EPA also has authority to promulgate regulations involving use of land for parking lots, airports, etc. At the moment it is not making use of that authority, but this situation could change.

Water pollution control. Two agencies are involved in land use control for the prevention of water pollution. At the federal level, the EPA acts through authority granted by the Federal Water Pollution Control Act (33 USC 1251 et seq.) and implements administrative regulations. At the state level the Texas Water Quality Control Board exercises authority granted under Sections 21.001 et seq. of the Water Code and administrative regulations promulgated thereunder.

No one may operate any sort of activity upon his land that would result in the discharge of pollutants into a waterway without first obtaining a permit to make such discharge. The permit will specify what sorts of pollutants may be discharged, and what quantity of each authorized pollutant may be discharged. At the moment the only exemptions from this requirement are applicable to certain agricultural activities.

Hazardous waste control. 24 USC 6901 et seq. gives to the EPA the authority to promulgate administrative regulations for the production and transportation of hazardous wastes. Hazardous wastes are garbage, refuse, and other things that may cause illness. Thus, ordinary garbage or refuse does not count—only those wastes more dangerous than the usual wastes are subject to regulation here. The exact state of regulation is as yet uncertain; the legislation involved was enacted in 1976, and became effective in October 1978.

In essence, however, any producer of hazardous waste will be required to report to the EPA and to obtain a special permit for his operations, the permit controlling the way in which he must dispose of his waste and containing restrictions upon their generation. This act and the regulations issued thereunder do not affect air and water pollution control measures under other legislation; they supplement these control measures.

Flood insurance and flood plain zoning. The National Flood Insurance Act, P. L. 90-448, and the Flood Disaster Protection Act, P. L. 93-234, establish a program of federally subsidized flood insurance that is to be available for landowners in flood hazard areas of the United States.

In order for landowners to be qualified to obtain such insurance, the flood plain area of the community in question must be zoned in accordance with administrative regulations issued by the Department of Housing and Urban Development. Residents of communities which have not complied with these regulations are not eligible for this subsidized insurance. The program does not directly involve HUD in local zoning, but it creates indirect involvement, since communities are under great indirect pressure to zone flood plain areas as HUD suggests.

Bridge erection. No one may erect a bridge or causeway across a navigable waterway without first obtaining a permit from the U.S. Coast Guard, as per 33 USC 401. An application for a permit must be filed with the Coast Guard commandant with jurisdiction over the area of the waterway where the construction is to take place. The Coast Guard must be assured that the proposed structure will not adversely affect navigation on the waterway before the permit will be granted.

Tall structure regulation. No one may erect a structure more than 200 feet in height without first obtaining a permit from the Federal Aviation Administration. If a proposed structure less than 200 feet in height would intrude on the takeoff and landing areas of an airport, a similar permit must be obtained. The justification for this is, of course, the preservation of navigable air space.

The FAA evaluates the proposed structure in order to determine whether or not it will be a hazard to air navigation. If it is decided that there is no hazard, the structure may be erected. If it is decided that there would be a hazard, the permit will be denied. FAA authority in this area is granted by 49 USC 1501.

Highway beautification. 23 USC 131 provides that if a state desires to obtain the full benefit of federal funding for the building of interstate highways, it must control the erection of advertising signs within 600 feet of the right-of-way of the highway in question. The state may require the owner of an offending sign to remove it. If the sign was legally erected, the owner will be paid compensation for its removal; if the erection was illegal, no compensation is payable.

23 USC 136 provides that if a state desires full interstate highway financing it must also take steps to control junkyards located within 1,000 feet of the right-of-way of such highway. Such junkyards must be either removed or screened from view from the highway by fences, hedges, etc. Texas has enacted the required legislation.

Other regulation. There are other federal regulatory programs which involve various federal agencies in other programs of direct and indirect land use control. No dam may be erected upon a navigable waterway or upon a tributary of a navigable waterway without the consent of the U.S. Army Corps of Engineers, for example, and no dredging operation may be conducted upon a navigable waterway without a similar permit.

No hydroelectric power generating station may be erected without a permit from the Federal Power Commission. No nuclear generating plant may be erected without compliance with the very complex construction and inspection regulations of the Nuclear Regulatory Commission.

As Federal programs of regulation of business activity proliferate, it is almost inevitable that federal land use control programs will also proliferate. New programs are devised at almost every session of Congress.

PART X

Trusts
Wills
Estates
Bankruptcy

52

Trusts

Trusts are property-management devices intended to help those who cannot help themselves. The usual trust arrangement involves a managing person's acquiring legal title to property and —along with the legal title—the duty to manage and use the property for the benefit of another.

Parties to a trust. There are three parties involved in the creation and maintenance of a trust:

1. The *settlor*, or trustor, who creates the trust.
2. The *trustee*, who gets legal title to the trust property (or corpus) and the management duties with respect to the property.
3. The *beneficiary*, for whose benefit the trust is created and maintained.

A trust may have multiple settlors, trustees, and/or beneficiaries; one individual may be more than one party. A settlor may establish a trust for his own benefit, appointing someone else trustee, or a settlor may appoint himself as trustee of property for the benefit of a beneficiary. However, one person may not be both trustee and beneficiary of a trust unless there are multiple trustees or beneficiaries. Thus, one may be sole trustee and cobeneficiary, or one may be cotrustee and sole beneficiary.

The trustee of the trust is said to have legal title to the corpus. The beneficiary is said to have equitable title. Since the trustee manages the property for the benefit of the beneficiary, a sole trustee and sole beneficiary would manage the corpus for the benefit of himself. Since that is what any property owner does, the sole trustee/sole beneficiary has in essence complete ownership of the corpus: therefore there is no trust.

Capacity required of parties to a trust. Any person with the capacity to make a gift or a will may be the settlor. Any person with capacity to make a contract may be a trustee, but his contractual capacity must be unlimited. A minor may therefore not be a trustee. No corporation may serve as trustee unless its articles authorize it to do so. Any person at all may be a beneficiary, as may any organization.

Express trusts and implied trusts. Express trusts are created by the deliberate act of the settlor. Implied trusts, which will be discussed at the end of this chapter, come into being by operation of law.

The governing Texas law. Much of the law governing express trusts in Texas is statutory law, contained in the Texas Trust Act (TTA). The remainder consists of common-law principles which are recognized in virtually all states. The law governing implied trusts is primarily common law.

Creation of express trusts. TTA 7 provides that an express trust may be created in one of five ways:

1. A declaration in writing by the owner of the corpus that he holds it as trustee for another person or persons, or for himself and another person or persons.
2. A written transfer by the owner of the corpus to another person as trustee for the owner or for a third person.
3. A transfer by will by the owner of the corpus to another person as trustee for a third person or persons, provided that a natural person named as trustee may also be a beneficiary (but not sole beneficiary).
4. An appointment by a person having a power of appointment to another person as trustee for the donee of the power or for a third person.
5. A promise by a person to another person whose rights thereunder are to be held in trust for a third person.

Method 3 above creates a *testamentary trust*; the other methods create *inter vivos trusts*. Methods 4 and 5 do not require a writing, though the exercise of a power of appointment is generally put into writing. However, if the corpus of the trust is to be real property, the settler must create the trust by a written document signed by himself or by his authorized agent.

A declaration of trust must identify the beneficiaries with reasonable certainty; otherwise the trust will fail. If property is transfered to a trustee without disclosing the names of the beneficiaries or otherwise identifying them with reasonable certainty, TTA 8 states that the trustee may convey it, encumber it, or in general treat it as his own property, and that no person claiming to be beneficiary under the trust can complain about it. If a declaration of trust identifies the beneficiary but does not identify the trustee, the trust will not fail. The beneficiary need only apply to a Texas district court for appointment of a trustee.

Revocability of an express trust. TTA 41 states that an express trust is revocable unless expressly made irrevocable. The testamentary trust is of course irrevocable by its very nature, as is the trust created by the exercise of a power of appointment. Otherwise, however, the settlor may retain the power to terminate the trust simply by not stating in the declaration of trust that he gives up that power.

One great advantage accrues to the settler by making a trust revocable. That advantage is that he retains ultimate control of the corpus; he can take it back by revoking the trust. This of course gives him some indirect power over the beneficiary since he may always state or imply, "If you don't do as I say, I'll revoke the trust." The disadvantage to the settlor of a revocable trust is that the trust income is taxable to him under the Internal Revenue Code, the logic of this being that he controls the corpus and thus the income which it produces. The settlor may escape this tax liability by making the trust irrevocable. In such a case, the trust itself becomes a tax-paying entity, its liability being computed under the personal tax rates but allowable exemptions and deductions being treated differently. By making the trust irrevocable the settlor parts with control over the corpus, thus losing a potential lever for controlling the behavior of the beneficiary.

Duration of an express trust. A trust may not be established so that it will endure forever, with the exception of a charitable trust. Trusts other than charitable trusts must vest the equitable or legal title within the period of the common-law rule against perpetuities—a life in being plus twenty-one years. Most of the considerations for determining whether or not a trust complies with the rule will be the same as those for determining whether or not a conveyance of real property complies.

The following will comply, of course: "Trustee shall pay the trust income to my son John for the term of his life, and upon his death trustee shall pay the income to the oldest son of the said John until said son reaches the age of twenty-one, at which time the trust shall terminate and the corpus shall be vested in the said oldest son of John." This vests within the period of a life in being plus twenty-one years.

The following will not comply: "Trustee shall pay the trust income to my daughter Bonita for the term of her life. Upon her death trustee shall pay said trust income to the eldest daughter of the said Bonita for the term of her life. Upon the death of the eldest daughter of the said Bonita trustee shall pay the trust income to the eldest daughter of the eldest daughter of the said Bonita for the term of her life. Upon her death the trust shall terminate, and the corpus shall be distributed to such of my needy lineal descendants as the trustee shall deem most deserving." The identity of the eldest daughter of Bonita is determinable as of Bonita's death, of course, but the identity of the eldest daughter of Bonita's eldest daughter may not be determinable within twenty-one years of Bonita's death—Bonita's eldest daughter may not have married and had a daughter by that time. That part of an express trust which complies with the rule against perpetuities will be given effect; only that part which does not comply will not be given effect. This trust will therefore be valid with respect to Bonita and her eldest daughter, but it would terminate upon the death of the eldest daughter of Bonita.

The honorary trust. Two types of trust declarations most commonly try to create an honorary trust. One type is exemplified by this will provision: "I leave my 10,000 shares of General Motors stock to the First National Bank of Podunk, Texas, upon the following trust: The bank shall use the income from these securities to erect and maintain upon the front yard of my Podunk, Texas, mansion a monument depicting the glories and accomplishments of my illustrious greatgrandfather Silas Shylock, and of his descendants." The purpose, of course, is in the creation of a family memorial in perpetuity.

The other type of trust declaration creating, or seeking to create, an honorary trust is in this form: "I leave my 10,000 shares of General Motors stock to the First National Bank of Podunk, Texas, upon the following trust: The bank shall use the income from these securities to support my 191 beloved cats in the style to which they have become accustomed while a part of my household. Upon the death of the last of my beloved feline companions, the trust shall terminate and the securities shall become the property of my daughter Ophelia."

The law of the state of Texas does not recognize honorary trusts. Such trusts will not be established, and the corpus will be disposed of as if the trust had terminated. In the first instance, then, the settlor apparently thought that he was establishing a perpetual trust, so he made no mention of what was to happen to the corpus upon termination. In such a case, the corpus would go to the heirs of the testator, probably under the residuary clause of the settlor's will. In the second case, daughter Ophelia becomes the owner of the corpus—perhaps to her surprise, undoubtedly to her pleasure.

The dry trust. A dry trust is one in which the trustee has no duty to perform as holder of the legal title to the corpus. If the trustee's only function is to hold legal title to the corpus for the beneficiary's benefit, Texas law recognizes the existence of no trust. The trust will be said to be executed, and the beneficiary will obtain complete title to the corpus.

The spendthrift trust. This is a trust in which the settlor seeks to arrange things so that creditors of the beneficiary will have no access to trust assets until the trustee pays them over to the beneficiary. The ordinary trust is not a spendthrift trust; creditors of the beneficiary may reach their debtor's interest in the trust assets before the trustee distributes them to the beneficiary.

Thus, in the situation where a trustee is to pay to the beneficiary all dividends on stock on the last day of each calendar year, the trustee will accumulate these dividends as paid to the trust during the calendar year: he will not pay them over to the beneficiary until December 31 of that year. But a creditor of the beneficiary who has a judgment against him could levy a garnishment on these funds while they are in the hands of the trustee and subject them to his claim. In this situation the creditor could not touch the stock itself; if the beneficiary is not entitled to any of the principal of the corpus, his creditors cannot touch it either. However, if the terms of the trust are such that the beneficiary does have access to principal, his creditors are entitled to the same access.

The purpose of the spendthrift trust is simply to deny access by creditors of the beneficiary to trust assets in the hands of the trustee. The creditors do have access to such assets after the beneficiary has obtained possession of them, but not before. For obvious reasons, a settlor may not create a spendthrift trust for the benefit of himself. If this were possible, it would be a handy-dandy method of insulating one's assets from the claims of one's creditors.

Three types of beneficiary creditors may reach spendthrift trust assets in the hands of the trustee:

1. Children and ex-spouses with claims for child support or alimony.
2. Sellers of necessities to the beneficiary on credit.
3. Furnishers of services to the beneficiary intended to help maintain the integrity of the trust.

The beneficiary's landlord, doctor, dentist, and other such persons thus have access to his trust assets, as would the beneficiary's attorney and other such persons. However, the ordinary creditor will have trouble breaking into a spendthrift trust.

Three specialized types of trust are also considered to be spendthrift in nature. The first of these is the support trust, which normally provides that the trustee shall use the trust for the support of a named beneficiary, either for the term of the beneficiary's life, until he reaches a certain age, until a named event in his life occurs, or whatever. Until such a trust terminates, it is treated as a spendthrift trust.

The second special type of spendthrift trust is the discretionary trust. Under this trust, the trustee is authorized to make such distributions of trust assets to the beneficiary as he thinks right and proper. He need not make any distribution if he does not think it proper. The rights of the beneficiary of such a trust are none too great. His income from the trust is up to the trustee's discretion, so the beneficiary must keep on the trustee's good side. It is then logical that creditors of the beneficiary should have no greater access to the corpus than does the beneficiary himself. If the trustee chooses to distribute nothing to the beneficiary, the creditors have nothing to levy garnishment against.

The third special type of spendthrift trust is the blended trust or—as it is sometimes called—the protective trust. This is a trust usually for the benefit of a family, intended for the protection of family members while children are growing up. Creditors of the protected individuals have no access to trust assets in the hands of the trustee here.

Charitable trusts. The beneficiary of a charitable trust is not an individual. Rather, it is a charitable organization, or a cause which in some way works toward the betterment of mankind.

The beneficiary of a charitable trust might be an organization like the American Red Cross or the Salvation Army. It might also be an organization like Southern Methodist University, the Anderson Hospital of Houston, or the Humane Society of Nacogdoches County. The beneficiary may be no organization at all. The purpose of the trust might be the awarding of university scholarships to those high-school graduates the trustee deems to be most worthy.

The charitable trust differs from a noncharitable trust in two important particulars. One is that the charitable trust may endure forever; its duration is not subject to the rule against perpetuities. A trust providing that the income should be paid to the Fredonia Hills Baptist Church of Nacogdoches so long as that church shall exist, and—if it should ever cease to exist—to the American Red Cross, would be perfectly valid. If the Fredonia Hills Baptist Church were to endure for a millenium, so would the trust. If the church were to cease to exist at the end of the millenium, with the American Red Cross still with us, the Red Cross would begin receiving income payments from the trustee.

The other way in which charitable and noncharitable trusts are different is that a noncharitable trust will not be permitted to commence existence if the beneficiary cannot be identified or if the named beneficiary does not exist (is deceased, for example), whereas so long as the beneficiary of a would-be charitable trust is identified clearly enough so that a court has a good understanding of the charitable intentions of the settler, the trust will not fail for want of a beneficiary. On the other hand, if it is clear that the settler had only one beneficiary in mind, the trust will fail if the named beneficiary no longer exists.

Courts use the doctrine of *cy pres* to make certain that most charitable trusts do not fail for want of a trustee. "Cy pres" is part of a French phrase, "cy pres comme possible," which means "as near as possible." The courts will try, as nearly as possible, to carry out the intent of the settlor of a charitable trust.

Suppose a provision in a settlor's will states, "I leave $1 million to the First National Bank of Podunk, Texas, upon the following trust: The bank shall invest these funds as a prudent man would do and pay all income to the Universal Bible Church of Podunk, Texas, in order to aid the church in propagating the true doctrines of the Universal Bible Church." If, upon the death of the settlor, the Universal Bible Church of Podunk, Texas, no longer existed, this trust would not fail for lack of a beneficiary. It is clear here that the intent of the settlor is to aid in the spreading of the Gospel according to the tenets of the Universal Bible Church. If this church is part of a denomination by that name, another church of the denomination—or perhaps the denomination itself—might be named as beneficiary by a court, this coming "as near as possible" to carrying out the intent of the settlor.

If, on the other hand, a will provision says, "I leave $1 million to the First National Bank of Podunk, Texas, upon the following trust: The bank shall invest these funds as a prudent man would do, and shall pay all income from these funds to Podunk Christian College, in gratitude for the four happiest years of my life which I spent on her campus," and the college no longer exists upon the death of the settlor, this trust probably would fail for lack of a beneficiary. Here the settlor clearly has in mind one college as the object of his bounty, not private colleges in general.

Fiduciary duties of the trustee. The fiduciary duty owed by a trustee to his beneficiary is one of the most sensitive fiduciary duties in law. Since the trustee is managing valuable property for his beneficiary's good, there is more potential for wrongdoing here than in most such relationships.

The TTA contains some statutory provisions relative to certain duties of corporate trustees and noncorporate trustees. TTA 10 provides that no corporate trustee may lend trust funds to itself or to an affiliate. It also provides that noncorporate trustees may not lend trust funds to themselves or their relatives, employers, employees, partners, or other business associates. Trustees may, however, lend trust funds to beneficiaries when the trust agreement authorizes such loans.

TTA 11 allows corporate trustees to deposit trust funds awaiting investment or distribution with themselves if the deposits are insured under federal or state law, or if the trustee has in a separate fund investment securities equal in value to the trust funds so deposited. TTA 12 provides that no trustee shall buy property from the trust or sell property to the trust. Also, the trustee shall not buy from or sell to an affiliate, director, officer, employee, relative, employer, partner, or business associate for the trust.

Under TTA 14 a corporate trustee may not invest trust funds in its own securities. It may—subject to complex limitations—retain its own securities that are part of the corpus of the trust at the time it becomes trustee. A noncorporate trustee may not purchase for his trust funds the securities of corporations of which he is a director, owner, manager, officer, etc. TTA 13 forbids a trustee of two or more trusts to sell assets from one trust to another, unless the assets are securities of the U.S. government or are securities fully guaranteed by the U.S. government.

These TTA provisions are essentially statements of common-law concepts of fiduciary duty. The trustee of course must manage the corpus for the beneficiary's good, and must be content with the compensation he is paid for acting as trustee. Whenever there are contractual dealings between the trustee and the beneficiary, there must of course be full disclosure of all material facts by the trustee.

Investment powers of trustees. TTA 46 provides that trustees in their investment activities shall act as prudent men. The trustee should consider the safety of the principal and probable income when making investments. So long as no speculation takes place, the trustee may invest in land, in investment securities of all sorts, or in investment trusts and mutual funds. The fine law between prudent investment and speculation is difficult to draw. Real property is of course a prudent investment if location and price are reasonable. First mortgages on desirable real estate are also unobjectionable, but second mortgages probably step over the line into speculation—the lien of a second mortgage is none too secure.

Government and high-grade bonds are acceptable investments; lower-grade bonds may be questionable. Preferred stocks of established corporations are unobjectionable; as are the common stocks comprising the Dow-Jones Industrial Average. Probably any corporate common stock listed on the New York Stock Exchange would be acceptable, with the exception of those that are notorious as questionable investments. In general American Exchange stocks are more speculative than New York exchange stocks, and over-the-counter issues are more speculative than Amex stocks. Stocks of private corporations are, of course, the most speculative.

However, the quality of a security is not to be judged by the market upon which it is traded. There are stocks in the Dow Jones thirty industrials that are not particularly promising and others that are very promising. Stocks of some of the largest banks of the nation are traded on the over-the-counter market: most of those are safe investments. It requires some knowledge of the individual securities to be a prudent investor these days, particularly if one chooses to invest in stocks.

When one considers that the Dow-Jones Industrial Average is lower now than it was in early 1966, it becomes clear that one's capital is not necessarily safely invested in the bluest of blue-chip common stocks. When one also considers the high inflation which has persisted since 1966 the problem is compounded. The "income" which has been earned by income-producing securities has hardly kept the investor even with the inflation rate. Prudent trustees may have preserved the principal of their trust funds over the past decade by investing in bonds, but when one considers whether they have preserved the buying power of that principal in the face of inflation the situation is shown in a different light.

In the investment climate of the 1980s, how does a prudent investor preserve the buying power of his capital and at the same time earn income? How can this be done without indulging at least a little in speculation on price movements of common stock on Wall Street? The "prudent man" investment criterion is a creation of a more or less predictable, more or less stable financial market that is a creature of the past. How the courts will adapt it to present-day realities remains to be seen.

The prudent trustee is not at present liable to his beneficiaries for losses caused by inflation or adverse price moves in blue-chip stocks; he would be liable to his beneficiaries for losses caused by adverse price moves in speculative common stocks. It would seem that the safer the trustee plays it, the more certain the beneficiary is to suffer purchasing-power loss from inflation, but the less likely the trustee is to incur liability for imprudent investing. The more speculatively the trustee invests, the better (within limits) is the possibility of his earning fat capital gains, but the risk of capital losses also increases. The more capital losses the trustee generates, the more likely it is that he may be held liable for imprudence.

Management powers of the trustee. TTA 25 contains a very lengthy catalogue of management powers granted to the trustee. Without enumerating all of these in detail, it is safe to say that a trustee may exercise virtually all powers of ownership over trust assets, with the proviso that he exercise these rights in the best interest of the beneficiary rather than in his own best interest.

Allocation of assets between principal and income. Nearly all trusts authorize some payment out of income to beneficiaries. Others mandate payment of all income to them. Some trusts do not permit payments out of principal to beneficiaries; others do. The allocation of assets to income or principal is a matter of importance in the administration of virtually all trusts. It is of such great importance that several sections of the TTA contain rules for such allocation.

With respect to receipts of money or property, TTA 27 provides that rents, cash or property dividends paid in property other than shares of the issuer, and interest are *income*. The following sorts of cash and property are *principal*:
1. Proceeds from sale of trust assets.
2. Consideration for options granted to others on trust assets.
3. Repayments of loans made by the trust.
4. Distributions upon liquidation of corporations.
5. Eminent domain proceeds.
6. Insurance proceeds.
7. Profit or loss resulting from any change in form of a trust asset.

With respect to distribution of its own shares by a corporation, TTA 29 provides that stock dividends distributed when the shareholder has the right to choose to be paid the dividend in either stock or cash are income. Distributions in settlement of preferred or guaranteed dividends accrued since the trustee became owner of the shares are also income. Other such corporate distributions, including ordinary stock dividends, stock splits, and other such disbursements are principal. With respect to distributions from mutual funds and real estate investment trusts, distributions from the ordinary income of the fund or trust are income, while those from capital gains and the like are principal.

TTA 30 provides that capital gains or losses due to bond premium or discount are chargeable to principal, except for non-interest-bearing debt securities purchased at a discount. When such a discount is received or recovered it is income. According to TTA 31, when a portion of the trust principal is the capital of a business, the profit earned by the business is income, but changes in value of the business assets not bought and sold in the normal course of business are chargeable to principal.

With respect to principal held in the form of animals, the offspring necessary to maintain the original number of animals is deemed principal and all other offspring are income (TTA 32).

Contract liability of trusts and trustees. Since trustees have the power to make contracts on behalf of the trust in the process of management, the question of who shall be liable in case the trustee breaches often arises. TTA 19 contains most of the law on this point.

The recourse of the victim of the breach is normally a suit against the trustee in his representative capacity. The victim may also sue the trustee individually for damages for the breach unless the contract excludes the trustee from personal liability. If the trustee signed the contract in question "as trustee" or used other words to that effect, this is evidence of an intent to exclude personal liability.

A judgment against a trustee sued for breach of contract in his representative capacity is collectable out of trust assets. However, the plaintiff may not collect his judgment unless he can prove that he notified each trust beneficiary known to himself of the suit by mailing to him a notice of the suit by registered mail. If the plaintiff is not certain about the identity of all of the beneficiaries, he may ask the trustee for a list, and the trustee must furnish the list within ten days of the request. Any notified beneficiary may then intervene in the case as a defendant to try to defeat the plaintiff's claim.

Whether the beneficiaries would then have a claim against the trustee for the loss caused to the trust assets because of his breach of contract would depend upon the nature of the contract and the nature of the breach. If the contract was a normal contract for a trustee of this sort of trust to make, and no negligence by the trustee or violation of fiduciary duty was involved in the breach, there would be no recovery. But if the breach did involve negligence or violation of fiduciary duty, the beneficiaries could recover.

The intervening beneficiary could also use as a defense against the original plaintiff the argument that the trustee has had no authority to make the allegedly breached contract. If this is proven, the trust would not be bound to the contract and would thus not be liable for the breach. The plaintiff's recourse would be against the trustee in his individual capacity.

Tort liability of trusts and trustees. TTA 21 provides that when a trustee or his agent or employee commits a tort in the course of administration of the trust, the victim may sue the trustee in his representative capacity and collect his judgment out of trust assets if:

1. The tort was a normal incident of the kind of business activity in which the trustee was properly engaged by the trust, or
2. The tort, though not a normal incident of the business activity being engaged in, was not caused by the actionable negligence of the trustee or an officer or employee of the trust, or
3. The tort increased the value of the trust property.

The plaintiff may not collect such a judgment out of trust assets unless he gives the same notice of suit to the beneficiaries as is required in contract suits by TTA 19. As in the contract cases, the plaintiff may obtain a list of beneficiaries from the trustee. The plaintiff may, in tort actions, always sue the trustee in his individual capacity for his damages also.

The law here assumes that all business activity carries with it an inherent risk of incurring certain types of tort liability. Thus, any business that buys and sells goods might become involved in a product liability claim, since a retailer has no way to be certain that none of the items in his inventory are defective. The trust assets will be liable against claims of this type even if negligence by the trustee or his agents or employees caused the tort. With respect to other torts—those not a common risk in the trust business—the trust assets essentially may not be held liable for negligent acts by the trustee, his agents, or his employees.

If a trustee is held personally liable for a tort committed in the course of administering the trust by himself, his agent, or his employee, he is entitled to exoneration or reimbursement out of trust assets if (TTA 20):
1. He has not discharged the claim (settled it out of court, for example), and
2. The tort was a normal incident of the type of business activity in which he was properly engaged, or
3. The tort, though not a normal incident of the type of business activity being engaged in, was not caused by the negligence of the trustee or by an officer or employee of the trust.

If the tort increased the value of the trust property, the trustee is entitled to exoneration or reimbursement to the extent of the increase.

In tort situations, then, the plaintiff victim may either sue the trustee for damages in his individual capacity, in his representative capacity, or in both. If the trustee is forced to pay off a judgement out of his individual assets, he may recoup his loss out of trust assets if the tort was a normal risk of the business, if it was not a normal risk but was not caused by his negligence or that of his offers, agents, or employees.

Cotrustees. When a trust has three or more cotrustees, the decision of a majority of the trustees is the decision of the trust. However, a minority trustee who voted against a majority decision will not be liable to the beneficiaries for the consequences. If the dissenter is forced to join in the act he voted against at the direction of the majority of trustees, he may still escape liability to the beneficiaries for his actions if he expresses his dissent in writing to the cotrustees at or before the time he joins in the objectionable act (TTA 18).

If one of multiple trustees dies, the survivors may continue to exercise their powers as trustees.

Resulting trusts. A resulting trust is a type of implied trust that comes into being as a result of certain well-intentioned acts. The most common type of resulting trust is the purchase-money resulting trust, which comes into being under circumstances such as the following: Smith wants to buy property from Jones, but he does not want to take legal title in his name for some legitimate reason. So Smith gives Brown the purchase price of the property and tells Brown to buy it and take title in his name. Brown agrees to hold title to the property until Smith is ready to have it transferred into his name. If this transaction is carried out as intended, Brown acquires legal title to the property. The public records will not disclose that the property was paid for with Smith's money. In fact, they will not disclose that Smith had any interest in the property at all.

When the facts of this transaction become known to a court, the court will consider that Brown holds the property as trustee for Smith, who after all paid for it. Thus, if Brown dies before Smith takes back title to the property, the legal title will pass to Brown's heirs, but they will hold it as trustees for Smith.

The real danger to Smith in this situation is the possibility that Brown will sell the property to, say, Green, and Green will pay a fair price and have no knowledge of the Brown-Smith arrangement. The result here is that Green gets clear title to the property as a bona fide purchaser, while Brown holds the proceeds of sale as trustee for Smith.

If Smith's reason for hiding his ownership of the property is illegal or fraudulent, the courts will not recognize the existence of the resulting trust. If Smith's game is the hiding of assets from creditors, the creditors will be able to treat the property as Smith's, regardless of the legal title. If Brown sells the property to bona fide purchaser Green under these conditions, Green gets good title to the land and Brown probably keeps the proceeds, due to Smith's unclean hands in making this arrangement to begin with.

Another sort of resulting trust comes into being when an attempted creation of an express trust fails for some reason. If the failed trust is an inter vivos trust, the trustee holds title to the corpus for the benefit of the settlor until the difficulty is resolved and the trust is terminated. If the failed trust is a testamentary trust, the trustee holds the corpus for the benefit of the heirs of the settlor.

The last sort of resulting trust arises when the purpose of an express trust is fulfilled and the trust terminates. In such a case the trustee holds the corpus for the benefit of whoever is entitled to it upon termination. This trust will continue until the courts recognize the termination of the trust and order the distribution of the corpus to those entitled to it.

Constructive trusts. Whenever title to property gets into the hands of someone who should not be allowed to retain it because of wrongdoing on his part leading to its acquisition, courts may hold that the wrongdoer holds title to the property as constructive trustee for the benefit of the person who should be the owner. Numerous types of wrongdoing may result in the creation of constuctive trusts.

If Gray defrauds Pink into selling him property in such a manner that Pink would have the right to sue Gray for damages or to rescind the contract of sale, a court could impose a constructive trust upon Gray for Pink's benefit. Thus, if Gray sold the property to Blue, a bona fide purchaser, Gray would hold the proceeds of sale as trustee for Pink. If Black forced White to transfer property to him by use of duress, or if Black acquired property from White by use of undue influence or through a mutual mistake, Black could be declared constructive trustee of the property for White.

If Slink steals, embezzles, or otherwise misappropriates property from Goodman, he holds his ill-gotten gain as trustee for Goodman. Thus, if he cleverly invests the wrongfully obtained property and increases its value, the entire corpus is Goodman's as beneficiary of the constructive trust. If Greed, sole heir under the will of Victim, murders Victim in order to speed his inheritance, and the fact that Greed was the murderer was not discovered until the estate of Victim had been probated and settled upon Greed, Greed would hold the estate as constructive trustee for the persons other than Greed who would have inherited the estate had Greed died before Victim. This is, of course, due to the general rule that a murderer cannot inherit from his victim: had Greed's identity as the murderer been discovered before the final settlement of Victim's estate, he never would have been permitted to inherit.

Suppose Pal gives Bud his properly endorsed certificate for 100 General Motors shares and tells Bud to take it to his securities broker and sell it. Instead Bud phones the broker to find out the current price of GM and buys the certificate himself, getting the consideration to Pal in such a way that Pal does not know how Bud disposed of the stock. Later Pal finds out what Bud did. Pal could recover the stock on the theory that Bud held it as constructive trustee for him, since Bud violated his fiduciary duty to Pal by buying the stock instead of following Pal's instructions with respect to its disposal. Essentially, any ill-gotten gains obtained through violation of a fiduciary duty are held as constructive trustee for the person wronged. After such a trust is recognized, the court will order it executed. The constructive trustee must then deliver the corpus in its present condition to the beneficiary.

53

Wills and Decedent Estates

When a person dies his business affairs must be wound up so that his heirs may continue his business and theirs. In order to accomplish this the deceased's debts and the taxes on the transfer of his property must be paid, and his remaining assets must be distributed to his heirs. All of this is done under the supervision of the probate court, in accordance with the legislative directives contained in the Texas Probate Code (PrC).

A person may determine the disposal of his assets at his death by leaving a will. If he dies intestate—without leaving a will—his assets are distributed in accordance with the mandate of the Statute of Descent and Distribution, a portion of the PrC.

Execution of wills. A resident of Texas may make a will if he is of sound mind and at the time of the making of the will, he is:

1. At least eighteen years of age, or
2. Married, or has been married, or
3. A member of the armed forces of the United States (PrC 57).

The state of Texas recognizes three types of wills. These are the formal will, the holographic will, and the nuncupative will.

The *formal will* is usually drawn up by an attorney. It must be in writing and signed by the testator in person or by another person for him by his direction and in his presence. The testator will sign himself if he is capable of doing so; if he is illiterate, blind, or otherwise incapable of signing, someone else may sign for him by his direction and in his presence. Two or more credible witnesses above the ages of fourteen must also sign the will in their own handwriting in the presence of the testator. PrC 59, which sets forth these requirements, does not state that the witnesses must be present when the testator signs though it is a good idea to have them present. The testator, then, need not sign in the presence of the witnesses, but the witnesses must sign in the presence of the testator.

Upon the death of the testator the witnesses will be required to testify in court as to the genuineness of the will and of their signatures, unless the will is made self-proving. A will may be made self-proving by attaching to it the self-proving affidavit set forth in PrC 59. The affidavit must be signed by the testator and the witnesses in the presence of a notary public or other officer authorized to administer oaths and must be attached to the will. The affidavit need not be executed at the same time as the will; it may be executed any time before the death of the testator or one of the witnesses. The advantage of the attachment of the affidavit is that the witnesses need not testify in court—the will proves its own genuineness. Of course, this does not mean that its genuineness may not be contested. It merely means that it is presumed to be genuine unless someone can prove otherwise.

PrC 60 provides that a *holographic will*, a will written wholly in the handwriting of the testator, need not be witnessed. It may be made self-proving by attachment of the proper affidavit, which needs to be signed only by the testator. The holographic will must be signed by the testator, although the signature need not be at the end of the will. So long as the testator wrote his name in his own handwriting somewhere in the will, it is signed. It should also be dated, and contain the location at which it was written.

A *nuncupative will* is an oral will. PrC 65 provides that a nuncupative will shall not be valid unless:

1. It is made during the last sickness of the testator, and
2. It is made at his home or at the place where he has resided for ten days prior to the making of the will; or if he is taken sick away from home and dies prior to returning home, at the hospital or other place where he is ill, and
3. It is witnessed by three credible witnesses.

A testator may not dispose of real property under a nuncupative will. Such wills are valid only for personal property.

Considerations in the execution of a will. The decision as to what should be done with one's property upon one's departure from this world is sometimes an unpleasant one. The factor making it so unpleasant is, of course, the contemplation of one's own death; we like to assume that we are immortal, and for most of us consideration of the sad fact that we are not is depressing.

Whether a person makes a will or not, upon his death his property will be distributed to his heirs. This may be done according to the wishes of the current owner or according to the mandate of the state contained in the Statute of Descent and Distribution. The advantage of making a will is that the current owner acquires some control over the inheritance process. The complexity of the problems that can arise upon a person's death is often underestimated. A skilled attorney can advise a person of some of these complexities and induce him to think about them while there is time to do something about them. A few such complexities are described below.

If one owns a residence, automobile, boat, or other item that is not paid for, how will it be paid for if one dies before the final payment is made? Credit life insurance, or mortgage life insurance, is the best way to solve this problem; if the debtor dies before the debt is paid, the insurance company pays it. In the absence of such insurance, the creditor will be a claimant in the probate proceedings and his heirs may lose the residence, car, or other object in order to pay the creditor.

If one owns much of an estate at death, there are tax liabilities that must be taken care of. If one was working or otherwise earning income during the last calendar year of life, there will be a personal income tax liability. If one's estate is of any size at all, there will be a Texas inheritance tax liability imposed upon one's heirs. If the estate is of fair size, there will also be a federal estate tax liability. The larger the estate, the more one must be concerned about these tax liabilities. For anyone who is not anxious to see governments acquire large amounts of his assets in taxes, planning is the best way to reduce these liabilities.

If one has minor children, one must consider the question of what is to become of them in the case of one's untimely death. We tend to think, "Well, if something happens to me, my spouse will still be here to care for them," but it is possible that both parents could perish in a common disaster—an auto accident, for instance. A properly drawn will should contain a provision appointing a guardian for the children in case of such a catastrophe. If both parents die intestate in a common catastrophe, the courts will certainly appoint a guardian, but the guardian may not be the person the parents had in mind.

In the process of settling an estate a personal representative of the deceased is appointed; he has the responsibility for doing what needs to be done. If the decedent leaves a will, this person is called an *executor*. If there is no will he is called an *administrator*. In a will one may name one's own executor. If one does not leave a will, the court might not always appoint the person one had in mind as administrator. The personal representative should be a person in whom the testator and his family have the utmost confidence. By making a will one may make certain that a trusted person has charge of settling one's estate.

Perhaps the most important reason for making a will is yet another consideration. The estate of an intestate person must be settled under the supervision of the probate court; this requirement adds red tape and costs. PrC 145 makes it possible for a testator to avoid both by providing for an independent administration of his estate. The independent executor may make many important decisions in the settlement process without court permission, with a great saving to all concerned in time, money, and wear and tear on nerves. It must be remembered that there can be no independent administration without a will.

In the process of preparing the will itself, the testator must carefully determine what property he owns, and which persons he wants to have it after him. He must also keep in mind that one or more of the objects of his bounty may depart this world before he does. He should therefore consider naming alternate recipients for his possessions. The well-drawn will always ends with a residuary clause, in which the testator leaves everything not otherwise disposed of in the will to a named person. This is the provision which should tie up all loose ends.

Amendment of wills. PrC 63 provides that a will may be negatively amended by the testator's destroying or canceling a portion of it. Such cancellation could consist of removing the part to be deleted from the will, or blotting it out so that it becomes illegible. Merely crossing out what is to be deleted so that it is known that someone sought to cross it out will not work if the crossed-out portion is still legible.

An affirmative amendment to a will—an amendment that adds something or removes something and adds something else—must be accomplished with the same formality as was required for the making of the original will. An amendment to a formal will is called a *codicil*. The codicil must also be in writing, signed, and witnessed, although the same persons need not witness the codicil as witnessed the original will. The codicil may of course be made self-proving.

Voluntary revocation of wills. PrC 63 provides that the intentional destruction or cancellation of a will is a revocation of it. Accidental destruction is not a cancellation, unless the copy destroyed was the only existing copy.

A will may also be revoked by the making of a formal document which states that the will is being revoked. Such a document must be prepared with all of the formality required for the making of the will. A formal revocation of a formal will must therefore be in writing, signed, and witnessed. An oral statement of revocation of a formal will is ineffective, as is an unwitnessed statement of revocation contained in a letter.

A will may also be revoked by the making of a subsequent will. However, a new will would not totally revoke an existing will unless the new will specifically provides that it revokes all former wills. If the new will does not state that it revokes former wills, the result is that any provision of the old will which is not contradicted by a provision in the new will stands. Suppose that Al Ace makes a valid will in 1970 stating, "I leave my residence at 123 Easy Street, Podunk, Texas, to my brother Abner Ace. I leave $1,000 cash to my friend Bill Buck. I leave $1,000 to my cousin Don Deuce. I leave the rest, residue, and remainder of my estate to my uncle Alphonso Ace." This will contains all necessary provisions about an executor and so on. Then, in 1977, Al makes another will which complies with all formalities and contains necessary provisions about executors. With respect to disposal of property it says, "I leave my residence at 123 Easy Street, Podunk, Texas, to my brother Abner Ace. I leave $1,000 cash to my friend Calvin Case. I leave $3,000 cash to my cousin Don Deuce. I leave the rest, residue, and remainder of my estate to my nephew Alphonso Ace, Jr." This second will does not say it revokes the first will. How would Ace's estate be divided under these two wills?

The wills agree that Abner Ace gets the residence, so he does get it. Bill Buck gets $1,000, since the second will does not mention him but the first will does; the second will does not revoke the gift to Buck. Don Deuce gets $3,000 rather than $1,000, since his gift is amended by the second will. Calvin Case gets $1,000 because of the gift in the second will. The residue goes to Alphonso Ace, Jr. rather than to Alphonso Ace, Sr., because in cases where the two wills contradict each other the later will applies. These difficulties may be avoided, of course, by having the later will provide that the earlier will is revoked.

A holographic will may revoke a formal will, and vice versa. A noncupative will may revoke those portions of formal or holographic wills disposing of personal property, but since a nuncupative will cannot dispose of real property it will not revoke those portions of a formal or holographic will dealing with real property.

Revocation of wills by operation of law. The PrC does not provide for any situation which will automatically revoke an entire will by operation of law, but it does provide for partial revocation under several sets of circumstances.

A testator is not obligated to include his children in a will. He may leave every single one out, if he chooses to do so. If a testator is childless when he makes a will and he later becomes the parent of a child, either by birth or by adoption—or his wife is pregnant when he dies—PrC 67(b) provides that his will shall have no effect during the life of the child and shall be void as of the child's first birthday unless it dies during its first year of life. This shall not occur, however, if the principal beneficiary of the will is the spouse of the testator who is the parent of all his children (except adopted children).

If a testator has a child or children at the time he makes his will, but more children are born to him or adopted by him after the making of the will—or if a child is born to him after his death—the children born or adopted after the will was made are entitled to the share of the estate of the testator they would have inherited if the testator had died without a will. Again, such children will not inherit if the principal beneficiary of the will is the spouse of the testator who is the parent of all his children, as per PrC 66 and 67(a). When the testator is divorced after making a will, all parts of the will pertaining to the ex-spouse are voided. The ex-spouse will not inherit, or become executor or guardian of the testator's children (PrC 69).

Effect of marriage upon a will. The marriage of a testator has no immediate effect upon the validity of a will under Texas law. Marriage will however have a long-term effect.

When the will of a testator does not mention his spouse, the spouse is entitled to half of the marital community property despite the provision of the will. Thus, community property acquired after the marriage belongs half to the spouse even if the testator's will was made before marriage. When testator and spouse become parents and the will is not changed, the will is voided by operation of TPC 67(b), since neither spouse nor child would then be mentioned in the will.

When the testator's will purportedly leaves all community property of the marriage to someone other than the spouse, but leaves separate property to the spouse, the spouse is put to the *widow's election*. The spouse is entitled to her half of the community property if she wants it, but in such a case she would not get the separate property left her in the will; or, the spouse may elect to let the will stand "as is," taking the separate property left her in the will, and letting the community property go as the will directs. It must be remembered that the spouse cannot have it both ways. She cannot claim both her half of the community property and the separate property left her in the will. On the other hand, if the testator chooses to leave to his spouse her share of the community property plus other property, the spouse is entitled to whatever the will provides. No election is necessary.

Contract to make a will. A contract to make a will is not a will unless it is executed with all the formality of a will. Before September 1, 1979, however, such a contract was enforceable as a contract if it met the requirements for a valid contract. Contracts to make wills made before September 1, 1979 are still so enforceable. Thus, if the party contracting to put certain provisions in his will did not do so, he breached his contract. The other party to the contract could then take legal action against the estate of the breaching party for the breach.

The 1979 session of the legislature added Section 59A to the Texas Probate Code, changing the law with respect to contracts to make wills entered into on and after September 1, 1979. Such contracts made after September 1, 1979 can be proven in court only by provisions of a will stating that such a contract exists and giving the provisions of the contract. Suppose that, back in 1977, Hank Hawkins, age seventy-five, wanted to marry Henrietta Hussey, age twenty-five. Hank was known to be a multi-millionaire. Henrietta had no particular love for Hank Hawkins the man, but she had great love for the contents of Hank's bank accounts. She told Hank she would marry him if, and only if, he would make a will bestowing a large portion of his estate upon her after his death. Hank finally agreed to make a will leaving $10 million of his separate property to her.

This bargain having been made, Hank and Henrietta married in December 1977. Hank made the required will, but the will did not mention the premarital contract. In 1978 Hank got angry at Henrietta and made a new will, leaving all his separate property to the Salvation Army and only the community property of the marriage to Henrietta. Hank did not tell Henrietta about this will. In 1979 Hank died, and Henrietta learned of the existence of the new will. She also learned that Hank's estate consisted of $1 million in community property and $15 million in separate property. Though Henrietta was assured of being a millionaire widow under the new will, she could have been a multi-millionaire widow under the old will. She felt betrayed. What could she do?

She could take what she got under the new will, and not make waves, but she did not want to do that if she could help it. She could also try to contest the second will; that possibility will be discussed later in this chapter. Her most promising alternative would be to sue Hank's estate for damages for breach of contract. So long as Hank had put his promise to make a will in writing, she would have a case. If it was not put into writing, she would have no case, since the statute of frauds requires that a contract in consideration of marriage be in writing. Her damages would be the difference between what she would inherit under the new will and what she would have inherited under the old will—$9 million in this example.

If Henrietta had made this bargain with Hank after September 1, 1979, she would have had to get Hank to actually make a will leaving her $10 million of his separate property, and the will would have had to recite that this bequest was being made pursuant to the terms of a premarital contract. Apparently the contract itself would not need to be in writing so long as its terms were spelled out in the will. If this were done, Hank's effort to revoke the old will by making a new will would not save his estate from liability to Henrietta for breach of contract. She could use the old will as proof of the existence of the premarital contract, and the new will as proof of its breach. If Hank did not mention the contract in his will, however, the contract would be totally unenforceable under the new law if the bargain were made after September 1, 1979.

Joint and mutual wills. Sometimes two persons—usually a husband and wife—execute one will to dispose of all their property. Such a will is a joint will.

Either party to such a will may revoke his assent to it while both parties live. If one of the parties makes his own individual will, this will operate as a revocation of the joint will. After the death of the first party to a joint will, however, the survivor may revoke the will only at peril of suit for damages for breach of contract. The survivor has a contractual obligation to the heirs of the first party not to change the terms of the joint will. The survivor may make a new will, however, to dispose of property he acquired after the death of the first party.

The effect of TPC 59A upon joint wills executed after August 31, 1979 is a bit questionable. It would be wise to put a provision into such a will that it is made pursuant to a contract between the parties; if this is not done it may well be that the surviving spouse could revoke such a will after the death of the first spouse without incurring any liability.

When two or more persons make a contract that each will execute an individual will disposing of his property in specified ways, and each then executes a will in accordance with the terms of the contract, mutual wills exist. With respect to mutual wills executed before September 1, 1979, a revocation after the death of one of the parties to the contract is a breach of the contract. Mutual wills executed on or after September 1, 1979 must contain a provision reciting that they are executed in accordance with the provisions of a contract, and must then recite the provisions of the contract.

Witness to a will as a beneficiary. It is not wise to make a beneficiary of a will serve as a witness to the will. If matters do not go well, the witness may be placed in the unpleasant position of having to give up his rights as a beneficiary in order to make certain that the will is admitted to probate.

PrC 61 provides that when a witness to a will is also a beneficiary of it, he cannot inherit under it if his testimony is necessary to prove its validity. However, if he would have inherited from the deceased had the deceased left no will, he inherits either what was left him in the will or what he would take under the Statute of Descent and Distribution, whichever is less. Also, PrC 62 provides that if the testimony of the witness can be corroborated by one or more disinterested and credible persons, he may still inherit under the will.

Lapse. When a beneficiary of a will dies before the testator, the heirs of the beneficiary do not receive his gift upon the death of the testator. Rather, the gift lapses and will be disposed of under the residuary clause of the will.

However, PrC 68 provides that a gift to a descendant of the testator shall not lapse if the descendant dies leaving descendants of his own. Thus, if Al Ace leaves $1,000 to his son Abner Ace in his will, and Abner dies before Al, leaving behind two children, Adelbert and

Adeline, the $1,000 gift to Al will not lapse: Adelbert and Adeline will each get $500. However, if Abner died childless and his sole heir was his wife Amity, Amity would take nothing and the gift would lapse.

The testator may avoid lapse simply by stating in the will provision concerning the gift, "This gift shall not lapse."

Ademption. If the testator no longer owns an asset which is the subject of a gift, the legatee of the asset takes nothing. Thus, if the will of Al Ace provides, "I leave my 1972 Cadillac to my cousin Joe Jeeps," and Al traded the 1972 Caddy for a 1978 model before his death, Joe does not get the newer Caddy. He gets nothing, because Al did not own a '72 Caddy when he died. This would be true even if Al had sold the '72 Caddy for cash, and that very cash were on deposit in a bank account.

Another sort of problem arises when Al Ace's will says, "I leave my 100 shares of Zilch Corporation common stock to my sister Adelle." Suppose that before Al died, Zilch split its common two for one, so Al owned 200 shares of Zilch when he died. Would Adelle inherit 100 shares of Zilch, or would she inherit 200? Here she would inherit 200, because the 200 shares are substantially the same as the 100 shares mentioned in the will. On the other hand, had Zilch paid a 25 percent stock dividend before Al's death, Adelle would not inherit the 125 shares; the 25-share dividend would not be considered part of the original 100.

If Al's will stated, "I leave my Cadillac to my brother Alexander," and Al owned a 1972 Caddy when he made the will and a 1978 Caddy when he died, Alexander would inherit the new car because it is, after all, a Cadillac. But if Al owned a '78 Lincoln when he died, having given up on Cadillacs earlier, Alexander would not inherit the Lincoln, because it is not a Cadillac. Of course, if the will merely stated, "I leave my automobile to my brother Alexander," there would be no problem: Alexander would get the Lincoln.

The moral of this is, of course, that one must be specific in making bequests of specific assets, and one should review one's will and inventory of assets on occasion to spot possible ademptions.

Abatement. A legatee named in a will may not inherit anything because the assets of the testator were insufficient to pay off his liabilities and still make all bequests in the will. This problem will be discussed in detail when distribution of the estate is covered later in the chapter.

Descent and distribution. PrC 45 provides that when a married person dies intestate without children or descendants, all community property goes to the surviving spouse. Should there be children, half of the community property goes to the surviving spouse and the other half is divided among the children and their descendants, per stirpes.

Thus, if Al Ace dies intestate having never had children, his widow Adelle surviving, Adelle inherits all the community property. If at Al's death his widow Adelle and sons Bill and Clem survive, Adelle gets one-half of the community property and Bill and Clem take one-quarter each. If at Al's death he is survived by his widow Adelle; sons Clem and Bill; grandson Don, who is the son of Bill; and granddaughters Evelyn and Francine, daughters of his deceased daughter Joan, the community property would be divided one-half to Adelle, one-sixth to Clem, one-sixth to Bill, one-twelfth to Evelyn, and one-twelfth to Francine. Don would get nothing. The half of the property going to the children is split three ways, one portion for each child. Joan's portion is divided between her two daughters. Don gets nothing because his father Bill is alive to claim his share.

PrC 38 describes what happens to the separate property of a person who dies intestate. PrC 38(a) sets forth the rules for an unmarried intestate, PrC 38(b) for the married intestate. We will consider the case of the unmarried person first.

If the deceased left children, they inherit all of the estate, per stirpes. If one or more of the children died before the decedent, the share of the deceased child is divided among his children. If the deceased left no children but both of his parents are alive, his father and mother each inherit half of the estate. If there are no children and only one living parent, that parent inherits one-half. The other half goes to the brothers and sisters of the deceased, per stirpes, so that if one or more of the brothers or sisters is deceased the nieces and nephews who are the children of the deceased sibling split his share.

If there are no children and no parents, the brothers and sisters and nephews and nieces inherit per stirpes. If there are no children, parents, brothers, sisters, or their descendants, the estate is split into two parts. One part goes to the paternal grandparents or their descendants (uncles and aunts, first cousins, and so on) and the other goes to the paternal grandparents or their descendants, all per stirpes. If there are no paternal grandparents or their descendants, the whole estate goes to the maternal grandparents and their descendants, and vice versa.

If neither set of grandparents—and none of their desceandants—is alive the estate is split into four portions, one for each set of greatgrandparents and their descendants (great-uncles and aunts, second cousins, and so on) according to the same rules. The process could in theory by carried back through the generations of ancestors of the decedent until some blood relative were located. But there are practical limitations. If no blood relative of the deceased can be located, his heir is the state of Texas.

With respect to the separate property of the married intestate, the rules are as follows: If there are children, the spouse takes one-third of the personal property that was the separate property of the intestate and the children split the other two-thirds per stirpes. With respect to the separate real estate, the children get it all, except that the spouse takes a life estate in one-third of it, with the remainder to the children. If there are no children, the spouse takes all of the separate personal property. Half of the real property is then disposed of as if the deceased had been unmarried; the other half goes to the surviving spouse. However, if the deceased was not survived by parents, brothers, sisters, nephews, nieces, or their descendants, the spouse takes all of the real property.

Some examples will illustrate the operation of these rules.

First: Consider the case of Hank Hardy, a lifelong bachelor, who dies intestate. Surviving him are his father Hal Hardy, his mother Betty Hardy, and his sister Bonita Hardy Brown. In this case, Hank's parents split the estate fifty-fifty and Bonita inherits nothing.

Second: Consider Belinda Burke, never married, who dies intestate at age thirty-three. Surviving her are her mother Celia Burke Cash (a remarried widow), her brother Sam Burke, her sister Evelyn Burke English, her nephew Don English (son of Evelyn), and her niece Tanya Trubbles, daughter of her deceased sister Dolores Burke Trubbles, In this case, Celia inherits one-half of the estate as surviving parent. Sam gets one-sixth, Evelyn gets one-sixth, Don gets nothing (because his mother is alive), and Tanya gets one-sixth (her deceased mother's share, per stirpes).

Third: Consider the case of Van Vurk, unmarried, who died intestate. Surviving him are his uncle Karl Vurk, brother of his father; his first cousin Glen Vurk, son of Karl; his aunt Petunia Purley, sister of his deceased mother; and his first cousin Lee Lunk, son of his deceased aunt Letitia Lunk, who was also the sister of his mother. Here the estate is split into two equal portions—one for the descendants of Van's paternal grandparents and one for the descendants of his maternal grandparents. Since Uncle Karl is the closest surviving relative of the paternal grandparents, he inherits one-half of the estate. Glen gets nothing because his father still lives. Aunt Petunia inherits one-quarter of the estate and Cousin Lee inherits one-quarter (as the share of the deceased Aunt Letitia) as representatives of the descendants of the maternal grandparents.

Fourth: Consider the case of Angel Ard, unmarried, who dies intestate. Surviving her are her great-uncle Tom Ard, son of the grandfather of her father; and her second cousin Sam Simpich, son of her great-aunt Julianna Jeeps, daughter of the grandfather of her mother. Here, Tom and Sam split the estate equally, as surviving representatives of the paternal and maternal lines respectively.

Fifth: Consider the case of James Jasper, married, who dies intestate. He never had children. He is survived by his widow, Joan, and two brothers, Bob and Sam. He leaves an estate of community property, separate personal property, and separate real property. Joan of course takes all the community property as surviving spouse. She also takes all the separate personal property and half of the separate real estate, while Bob takes one-quarter and Sam takes one-quarter.

It must be remembered that normally only blood relatives may inherit under the Statute of Descent and Distribution. The one exception to this is adopted children, who acquire the rights of natural children on adoption. Brothers and sisters of the half blood may inherit half the share inherited by those of the whole blood. Examples follow.

First: Consider the case of Jackie Woods Brown Gurley, who dies intestate, a widow. Surviving her are Willie Woods, a son born to her before she was married; Sam Brown, son of Jackie and Abe Brown, Jackie's first husband; Fred Gurley, son of Jackie's second husband Lem Gurley and his first wife, Thelma Tood; and Vince Gurley, son of Jackie and Lem. Here Willie Woods, Sam Brown, and Vince Gurley inherit one-third each of the estate, since all are Jackie's sons. It does not matter that Willie was born to her before she married—remember that a mother's child is always legitimate with respect to her. Fred, however, is not Jackie's natural child, and could not therefore inherit from her under the Statute of Descent and Distribution unless she had adopted him.

Second: Consider the case of widower Bill Broach, who dies intestate. Surviving him are Ben Broach, son of Bill and Burlean Bizzle, a flame of Bill's youth whom he had never married (Bill never having adopted Ben or recognized him as his son); Paul Broach, son of Bill and his only wife Lesley; and Phil Lynch, son of Lesley's first husband Dick Lynch (Bill never having adopted Phil). Paul inherits the entire estate here. Ben, being illegitimate as to his father, cannot inherit. Phil, being a stepchild, also cannot inherit.

Third is the case of Pete Poplar, unmarried, who dies intestate. Surviving him are a brother Paul, son of both of his parents; a sister Pat, daughter of his mother and her first husband (who died before she married Pete's father); and a cousin Dale, whom his parents had taken in and raised (but never adopted) after his parents died in an accident. Here Paul inherits two-thirds of the estate and Pat inherits one-third. Since Pat is only a half sister of Pete's, while Paul is a full brother, Pat inherits half of Paul's share. Dale gets nothing, since he is not a sibling.

Finally, consider the case of Jake Jarvis, who died intestate. He had no blood relatives outside his home when he died. Living with him at his death were Mary Marcus, mother of Jake's deceased wife JoAnn; Tom Tucker, JoAnn's son by a prior marriage to Ted Tucker, which had ended in divorce; and Penny Partridge, daughter of JoAnn's deceased sister Jenny, taken in by Jake and JoAnn after Jenny's death. Jake had never adopted Tom or Penny. In this situation, Jake's heir is the state of Texas. Mary is Jake's mother-in-law, not a blood relative. Tom is a stepson, not a blood relative, and Penny is a foster daughter, again not a blood relative. For lack of blood relatives, the state inherits.

Survival of heirs and beneficiaries. If persons closely related die in a common catastrophe—or if they die of unrelated causes within a few days of each other—inheritance problems may arise. Well-drafted wills contains provisions as to what should be done in such a case. However, if the will has no such provision and this problem arises, TPC 47 contains the rules for solution. If the problem arises with respect to a person who has died intestate, TPC 47 again provides the solution.

Essentially, TPC 47 provides that a person who dies within 120 hours of another is deemed not to have survived the other, unless application of that rule would cause the estate of the first deceased to escheat to the state of Texas.

With respect to intestate persons, the following example illustrates the operation of the rule. Bill Brown and his married sister Becky Brown Burk go for a ride in the country. Both are killed in an auto accident. Bill leaves no will. Other than Becky, his nearest blood relative is his second cousin Jock Jackson. Becky has no children—the person closest to her is her husband Ben. Under TPC 47, Jock Jackson inherits Bill's estate, because the law deems Becky not to have survived Bill, and Ben Burk is no blood relative of Bill's. If the accident had occurred on Sunday, Bill had died on Monday, and Becky had died on Thursday, the result would be the same, since Becky would not have survived Bill by 120 hours. If, on the other hand, Bill had died on Monday and Becky had died the next Sunday, Ben Burk would end up inheriting Bill's estate. Becky, having survived Bill by 120 hours, would inherit Bill's estate, and Ben would then inherit Becky's.

If Bill had no blood relative other than Becky, Ben Burk would end up with his estate. Since the estate would escheat to the state if Becky were not deemed to have survived Bill, Becky would be Bill's heir, and Ben would inherit as Becky's heir.

Suppose that, in this case, Bill had left a will leaving his farm to Becky and the residue of his estate to the Salvation Army. In this case, the death of Bill and Becky in a common catastrophe would cause the farm to go to the Salvation Army; if Becky is deemed not to have survived Bill, the gift to her lapses and goes into the residuum of the estate and the Salvation Army as residuary legatee gets the farm. If Becky survives Bill by 120 hours, though, the gift does not lapse, and, assuming that Becky died intestate, Ben Burk ends up with the farm as Becky's heir.

In short, if a beneficiary of a will does not survive the testator by 120 hours, the beneficiary will be deemed to have died before the testator. Unless the beneficiary is a direct descendant of the testator, this will cause his gift to lapse. It will then go to the residuary legatee of the will.

If a married couple die in a common catastrophe, separate property is disposed of as if neither had survived the other. Community property is disposed of half as if the husband had survived and half as if the wife had survived. Half thus becomes part of the husband's estate, and half becomes part of the wife's. If one of the spouses survives the other by 120 hours, however, the survivor will inherit under the general law governing inheritance of community property.

If joint owners of property die within 120 hours of each other, the property goes half to the estate of one co-owner and half to the estate of the other. If the insured under a life insurance policy and the beneficiary of that policy die within 120 hours of each other, the beneficiary is deemed not to have survived the insured. The result of that situation is discussed in the chapter on estate planning.

Murderers as heirs. It is a generally accepted principle of the common law that a murderer may not inherit from his victim. In order for such an heir to be disqualified to receive his inheritance it is necessary for him to be convicted of the murder of the decedent. If he were never brought to trial for the murder, or if he were tried and acquitted, he could of course inherit.

Generally a convicted murderer will be deemed to have died before the decedent, his victim. The victim's estate would be divided accordingly.

Out-of-state property. A will is sufficient to dispose of all property of the deceased, no matter where located. The Texas Statute of Descent and Distribution applies to all property of a decedent located within the state of Texas, and all personal property of the decedent wherever located. It does not apply to the real property of the deceased located outside Texas. Such property is disposed of according to the statute of descent and distribution of the state or nation where located.

ADMINISTRATION OF ESTATES

Commencement of administration. PrC 76 provides that an executor named in a will or any person interested in the estate of the deceased may make application to the probate court of a county for the following:
1. An order admitting a will to probate.
2. An order for appointment of the executor named in a will.
3. An order appointing an administrator where there is no will; where the executor named in a will is dead, disqualified, or has resigned; or where no executor is named in a will.

An application for probate of a will may be combined with an application for appointment of an executor or administrator.

Duty and liability of custodian of will. PrC 75 provides that the custodian of a will shall deliver it to the clerk of the court having jurisdiction over the deceased's estate upon receiving notice of the death of the deceased. If the custodian does not do this, he may be cited and ordered to produce the will. Disobedience of such a citation without good cause may result in the imprisonment of the custodian until he obeys. If the refusal by the custodian to produce the will causes damage to anyone, the person damaged may sue the custodian in any appropriate court.

Time limitations on probate and commencement of administration. According to PrC 73, a will must be admitted to probate within four years of the death of the testator, and no will may be admitted to probate after that time unless the person presenting it can show that the delay was not due to his default or negligence.

No application for grant of letters testamentary (appointing an executor) or letters of administration (appointing an administrator) may be filed more than four years after the decedent's death (PrC 74).

A person purchasing land or personal property from an heir of the deceased more than four years after the deceased's death will get good title to what he acquired if he purchased in good faith and for value, without knowledge of the existence of a will. This is true even if, under the will, the heir who sold the property to the buyer had no title to it, or less than full title to it.

Admission of will to probate. PrC 94 provides that no will shall be effective to transfer title to real or personal property until it is admitted to probate. Before a will may be admitted to probate, its existence and genuineness must be proven.

A formal or holographic will which has a proper self-proving affidavit attached proves its own validity. The mere presentation of the document in court is sufficient proof. A formal will which is not self-proving may be proven in the following ways:

1. By the sworn testimony or affidavit of one or more of the witnesses, taken in open court.
2. If the witnesses are outside the county or the resident witnesses are unable to attend court, by deposition of one or more of the witnesses.
3. If the witnesses are dead or beyond the jurisdiction of the court, by two witnesses to the handwriting of the witnesses or of the testator, either in open court or by deposition.

A non-self-proving holographic will is proven by the testimony of two witnesses as to the testator's handwriting. The testimony is to be taken in open court if possible, otherwise by deposition.

The fact that a written will cannot be produced in court will not prevent its admission to probate. PrC 85 provides that such a will may be admitted to probate if proven genuine, as above, and if the following matters are also proven to the satisfaction of the court:
1. A good reason for nonproduction, such as an accidental destruction, and
2. The contents, to be proven by the credible testimony of a witness who read the will, or heard it read.

At least fourteen days must elapse after the death of a testator before a nuncupative will may be proven (TPC 86). Also, no testimony to prove the existence of a nuncupative will may be received more than six months after the testator's death, unless the testimony has been reduced to writing within six days of his death. If the value of the estate exceeds thirty dollars, the nuncupative will must be proven by the testimony of three competent witnesses to its making.

Contest of wills. TPC 93 provides that an interested person may commence suit to contest the probate of a will any time within two years of admission of the will to probate. However, minors and incompetent persons may commence a contest within two years after achieving adulthood or recovering full contractual capacity. Suit may be filed to cancel a will for fraud or forgery within two years of discovery of the fraud or forgery.

No provision of the Probate Code deals with will contests in any detail. The law here is mainly judge-made. Acceptable grounds for contest of a will include the following:
1. The will was improperly executed.
2. The will is not the true will of the deceased.
3. Testator lacked capacity to make a will.
4. Testator made the will under undue influence.
5. Testator made the will under duress.
6. Testator was a victim of fraud in the making of the will.
7. Testator never signed the will.

Claims that a will was improperly executed would involve claims that a witness did not sign in the presence of the testator, or of some similar procedural error.

Claims that the will is not the true will of the testator would involve such arguments as that the will in question had been revoked. The contesting party may possess another will supposedly signed by the testator which he claims is the testator's true will, or he may argue that the will being contested was revoked by operation of law.

A testator may have the capacity to make a will when he has no capacity to make a contract. In theory, if the testator knows when he makes a will what property he owns and knows who should be the objects of his bounty, he makes a valid will. The person who contests a will on the grounds of lack of testamentary capacity argues, then, that the testator did not know what he was doing when he made his will. Since the act of judging the content of a person's mind when he performed an act is a very subjective thing—especially when the person who performed the act is no longer among us to justify his handiwork—will contests on grounds of lack of capacity are very often determined by circumstantial evidence. Besides, it is difficult to get evidence of the testator's capacity into the record because the Dead Man Statute may well prevent persons who had conversations with the testator while he was alive from testifying as to the contents of the conversations. (It is particularly difficult for contestants to use this sort of evidence, because they are trying to prove the testator's lack of capacity. This works to the disadvantage of the testator's estate, and it is testimony to the disadvantage of the deceased that the Dead Man Statute helps to exclude from litigation.) Evidence of the deceased's character is, on the other hand, admissible.

The outcome of a contest on grounds of lack of capacity may to a degree depend upon the identity of the contestants and the identity of the beneficiaries of the will being contested. If a testator disinherits one or more of his children, this may well cause many to question his testamentary capacity. If on the other hand he disinherits his first cousin, this may well be perfectly normal. Eccentricity, mild intoxication, mild mental retardation, etc., do not constitute equal testamentary incapacity. Neither do such matters as mild senility or drug addiction. Insanity, on the other hand, does equal incapacity. Each case must be judged upon its own merits, and the law gives the testator the benefit of the doubt.

A will contest on grounds of undue influence involves a claim by the contestant that the testator made the will that he made because his volition was subverted by another person. It is a claim that someone subjected the testator to mental pressure in order to influence the content of the will. Again, the outcome of this sort of contest depends to a large degree upon the identity of the will beneficiaries and of the contestants. If a married testator leaves his estate to his spouse and disinherits his children, for instance, the children will hardly be able to claim undue influence. If the testator leaves all of his estate to some of his children, but disinherits other children, the children he left out will have difficulty. The question arises as to why the omitted ones were omitted. The interrelationships of the children with the testator, and of the children to each other, would be very relevant to the outcome.

If the testator disinherited his children and left his estate to the nurse who cared for him during his last illness, that of course looks quite suspicious. But if the testator's children ignored him during his illness while the nurse provided much tender, loving care, the will may well withstand a contest. If the testator disinherited his children and left his estate to his attorney (this being the attorney who drafted the will), this would most likely not survive a contest. The aura of undue influence here is almost overpowering.

When a will is contested on grounds of duress, the argument is that the testator was subject to physical or strong psychological force when he made the will. Proof of this is straightforward; physical force is not a subtle thing.

The contest on grounds of fraud of course involves the claim that the testator was tricked into making the will as he did. The fraud might well involve a misrepresentation of identity by a beneficiary. For instance, Jenny Jones may have often told her husband Pete about how much she loved her cousin Juliet Jennings. Pete had never met Juliet, but because he loved Jenny he loved those whom Jenny loved. Jenny then died, and Pete was lost without her. At this point a strange lady introduced herself to Pete as Juliet Jennings. She made Pete so happy with her reminiscences of Jenny that Pete decided to make a will leaving her all of his estate, disinheriting his brother Ken in the process. Pete then died. Some time after Pete's death Ken found out that Juliet Jennings had died a year before Jenny Jones, and that Pete's friend was actually Juliet's sister Bonita, who had grabbed a chance to make herself prosperous through a bit of acting. Ken obviously may contest Pete's will on grounds of fraud here.

The contestant on grounds of forgery claims that the testator did not sign the will in question. Proof of forgery here is like proof of forgery in any other sort of situation—testimony of handwriting experts, etc., will be necessary to resolve the question. The burden of proof lies upon those who attack the validity of the signature to the will, since it is assumed that a will once admitted to probate is entitled to probate.

No one may contest a will unless he has an interest in the estate. Generally, then, the contestant must have something material to gain from a successful contest. A person who seeks to contest a will on principle only will not succeed—the courts will decide that he has no standing to contest.

A decision in a will contest suit is of course appealable.

Appointment of executor or administrator. When the deceased leaves a will, the person named in the will as executor normally files for letters testamentary and presents the will for probate. This person will usually be appointed to serve as executor, unless the court finds him to be disqualified to do so. PrC 78 provides that the following persons are not qualified to serve as executors or administrators of estates:

1. Minors.
2. Incompetents.
3. Convicted felons, unless pardoned or restored to their civil rights.
4. Nonresidents of Texas who have not appointed a Texas agent for receipt of service of citation.
5. Corporations not authorized to act as fiduciaries in Texas.
6. Persons the court finds unsuitable.

The court will not appoint an unqualified person to act as executor. Also, if the person appointed as executor refuses to serve, he will not be compelled to serve against his will. In these cases, the court will appoint another person to serve as the personal representative of the deceased. A person so appointed is called an *administrator C.T.A.* (cum testamento annexo—with the will annexed). PrC 77 requires the court to consider persons for the post of administrator CTA in the following order:

1. The surviving spouse of deceased.
2. The principal devisee or legatee of testator.
3. Any other heir of testator.
4. The next of kin of testator, in order of relationship.
5. Creditors of testator.
6. Any person of good character residing in the county who applies for the position.
7. Any other person not disqualified to serve.

When the deceased has apparently died intestate, a close relative or the like will apply for letters of administration of the estate. The person applying will normally be appointed administrator, unless he is disqualified or unless the court chooses to appoint a better qualified person to serve under the provisions of PrC 77.

Sometimes there are conflicting applications for the post of executor or administrator. It may be that it was believed that the deceased died intestate and application for appointment of an administrator is filed, but later it is claimed that a will has been found and it is presented for probate; or two or more wills may be presented for probate. In such cases, the court must decide between the competing applications, under the rules provided in PrC 83.

The appointment of an administrator may be set aside because of the discovery of the testator's will. The appointment of an executor may also be set aside if it is determined that the will under which he was appointed is not the true, valid will of the deceased.

Normal procedure in administration of estates. The executor or administrator of the estate has essentially three obligations. He must:

1. Identify and collect all property belonging to the deceased.
2. Pay all of the lawful debts of the deceased, including applicable taxes.
3. Distribute the remaining assets of the estate to the heirs, in accordance with the terms of the will or the Statute of Descent and Distribution.

The executor will be required to post an appropriate bond with the court appointing him, unless the will of the testator exempts him from this obligation. The exemption applies only to the executor named in the will; if he is disqualified or refuses to serve, the administrator CTA who will be appointed must post bond. If the deceased died intestate, his administrator will be required to post bond.

According to PrC 250, the executor or administrator must file with the court an inventory and appraisement of all the assets of the estate. This must be done within ninety days of the appointment of the personal representative, unless the court grants a longer period. The inventory must include all real estate of the deceased located in Texas, and all personal property of the estate wherever located. The court may appoint up to three disinterested appraisers to help in the evaluation of the estate assets, although this is not mandatory.

The inventory must also include a list of all claims due or owing to the estate, including the details of each claim, as required by PrC 251. If any estate assets are discovered after the filing of the inventory and list of claims, a supplemental inventory and appraisement including these items shall be filed.

The inventory, appraisal, and list of claims must be approved by the court under PrC 255. Should the court disapprove any of these items, they must be redone within twenty days of the order of disapproval. After approval of the appraisal, inventory, and list of claims, the personal representative shall set apart all estate assets which are exempt from creditor claims under state law for the use of the widow, minor children, and unmarried daughters of the deceased. If he left no widow, minor children, or unmarried daughters, this step is not necessary.

Under PrC 272, the homestead shall be delivered to the widow, if there is one, or to the guardian of the minor children and unmarried daughters living with the family. Other exempt property is to be delivered to the widow, if any, or to the children or their guardians. If the estate does not contain much exempt property, PrC 273 authorizes the court to make a reasonable allowance to the widow and children from the estate assets in lieu of exempt property. This allowance may not exceed $10,000 in lieu of a homestead and $1,000 in lieu of other exempt property.

According to PrC 286 et seq., an allowance for the support of the widow and children shall be payable out of the estate assets monthly for a period of a year. The amount of the allowance will depend upon the standard of living of the family before the deceased's death and the assets of the estate.

The homestead is exempt from claims of creditors of the deceased, except for purchase money owed, property taxes due thereon, mechanic's liens thereon if obtained through proper procedure, and federal taxes owed by the deceased. Other exempt property, property set aside in lieu of exempt property, or property included in the family allowance, is exempt from creditor claims except for funeral expenses and expenses of the last sickness of the deceased. Such property is also subject to federal tax claims.

PrC 294 et seq. provide the rules for establishing and paying claims against the estate. The personal representative must, within one month of his appointment, publish a notice in a local newspaper requiring all persons having claims against the deceased's estate to file such claims with him. Within four months of his appointment, written notice must be sent to all persons having a claim against the estate secured by a recorded mortgage, trust deed, mechanic's lien, or the like upon real estate of the deceased. Failure to give such notice renders the representative liable to the creditors for damages, if they can be proven.

Creditors of the deceased must file claims with the personal representative if they wish to be paid out of estate assets. PrC 298 requires that such claims be presented within six months of the date of the appointment of the personal representative. Holders of claims for funeral expenses and expenses of the deceased's last sickness must file within sixty days of the appointment of the personal representative if they want exempt property and family allowances to be subject to their claims (PrC 300).

The personal representative should approve or disapprove a filed claim within thirty days. If it is approved, it is filed with the county clerk and will be paid when the court approves it. Any person who objects to such approval of a claim may make his objection known to the court before final payment; a hearing will then be held on the matter, and the court will approve or disapprove.

If the personal representative disapproves, or if he takes no action within thirty days, the creditor may file suit against the estate to collect, if he does so within ninety days of the rejection. The suit will proceed as would any ordinary civil suit, but if the plaintiff wins his judgment will simply be treated as an approved claim against the estate.

If a claim is filed late, the personal representative may pay it if he approves it, provided that the estate is still open and that funds remain with which to pay it after other properly filed claims are all paid.

Generally, all steps taken in the process of settling the estate must obtain court approval; claims may not be paid without court approval, and the payment of the family allowance and the like must also be approved. If suit against a debtor of the estate is necessary in order to collect a legitimate claim of the estate, approval is necessary. If an estate asset should be sold to raise cash, this cannot be done without following a rather complex procedure. In short, the personal representative can do almost nothing on his own initiative: court approval is required for almost everything.

When all estate assets are collected and all claims are filed, the estate is prepared for closing. It must be remembered, however, that the personal representative has some important tax duties to perform before closing.

First, he must prepare and file the final personal income tax return of the decedent. If the deceased owed federal income tax for the last year of his life, this will be one of the obligations payable out of estate assets. If the deceased was an employee subject to tax withholding, it might be that he is entitled to a refund of a portion of his withholdings. If so, this refund is an estate asset which the representative is under a duty to recover.

If estate assets earned income during the administration process, federal income tax may be payable on this income. The personal representative must therefore file a federal income tax return for the estate, and pay any tax due out of estate assets.

If the estate is of any size, filing of a federal estate tax return may be necessary. Any estate tax liability must be paid out of estate assets. The taxation aspects of the settlement of estates will be discussed in more detail in the chapter on estate planning.

Distribution of estate assets. PrC 320 and 322 contain the state law relevant to distribution of estate assets. This law is of course overridden by relevant federal law with respect to taxes, etc. The federal law provides that debts due and owing to the U.S. government shall have priority over other claims in estate settlement procedures under state law. This means that U.S. tax claims and government contract claims shall be given priority. The interaction of the federal and state law produces the following schedule of priorities for paying claims against a deceased's estate:

1. Funeral expenses and expenses of the last sickness of deceased, up to $2,000, if filed within sixty days of appointment of personal representative.
2. Allowance to widow and children, if any.
3. Expenses of administration of the estate (court costs, attorney's fees, personal representative's fees, etc.) and expenses incurred in managing, preserving, and safekeeping of the estate.
4. Secured claims—claims secured by mortgages or other liens upon estate assets, including secured federal claims.
5. Unsecured federal claims.
6. Other unsecured claims filed within six months after appointment of the personal representative.
7. Claims filed more than six months after the appointment of the personal representative.

If the estate is solvent this schedule is meaningless; if assets are sufficient to pay all liabilities, all creditors will be paid. However, if the estate is insolvent the schedule does have meaning, since some creditors will be paid and others will not. In such a case the federal creditors may obtain an advantage over other creditors—specifically tax creditors—because the IRS need not recognize state property exemptions.

If estate assets are insufficient to pay off all creditors and beneficiaries of the will, abatement will take place. If the estate is insolvent, total abatement will occur, and no assets will be available to distribute to the heirs. If some assets remain after payment of creditors, the heirs lose out in the following order:

1. The residuary legatee.
2. Inheritors of specific sums of money.
3. Inheritors of specific personal property (this may be sold to raise cash, if the cash is needed to pay creditors).
4. Inheritors of specific real estate. Land will not normally be sold in order to raise cash unless there is no personal property which can be so sold.

Ways of avoiding full administration. Full administration of an estate—with approval of everything by the court required—is cumbersome and expensive. This red tape may be avoided with a little planning, or a little luck.

Under the provisions of PrC 137 et seq., an estate having assets of less than $10,000, not counting the homestead and exempt property, may be settled without administration. Generally, an application for administration of the estate will be needed, but no administration as such will be necessary if the court is convinced that nonexempt assets are less than $10,000. The personal representative appointed must of course pay claims against the small estate out of available assets, but this may be done without clearing everything through the probate court.

PrC 145 states the circumstances under which an independent administration may be had. Generally, under independent administration the personal representative must file an inventory, appraisement, and list of claims with the court as in ordinary administration, but he may then proceed to settle the estate without asking for court approval of everything. The estate is closed by affidavit when all debts are paid and all assets remaining distributed to the heirs. Before September 1, 1977, independent administration was possible only if a testator provided in his will that there would be an independent administration, and if the executor named in the will was named executor of the estate. It is now possible to have an independent administration under other circumstances if the value of all estate assets is less than $200,000. If the will names an executor but does not provide for independent administration; if it becomes necessary to appoint an administrator CTA of the decedent's estate; or if the decedent died intestate; and if all distributees of the estate agree to independent administration, the court may declare the administration to be independent. Unless the will provides for independent administration, though, there can be none unless the assets of the estate are under $200,000, and all distributees agree to the independent administration.

PrC 155 provides that when a married person dies intestate and the community property passes to the surviving spouse (as happens when the deceased leaves no descendants), no sort of administration of the estate (at least the community portion thereof) is necessary.

Under PrC 161, if the community property is to pass in part to someone other than the surviving spouse (as it will when the deceased is survived by children and grandchildren), the surviving spouse may qualify as a community administrator. A community administrator conducts what is essentially an independent administration, being required to file only the usual inventory, appraisement, and list of claims.

A community administrator has no control over separate assets of the deceased. Therefore, there is no point to the appointment of a community administrator when the deceased possessed separate property. Community administration is useful only when the deceased's assets are all community property.

Ancillary administration. It is a general principle of the law of wills and estates that a probate court of a state has jurisdiction over the personal property of a deceased located anywhere in the world, but has no jurisdiction over out-of-state real property owned by the deceased.

Suppose that Russell Reich dies in Podunk, Texas, owning personal property in Texas, Ohio, and Switzerland and real property in Texas and Ohio. The Podunk County Probate Court will have jurisdiction over all of the personal property and also over the Texas real estate. It will, however, have no jurisdiction over the Ohio real estate.

If Russell Reich had made a valid will before he died, the will would determine the disposal of all of his property. However, a separate Ohio probate proceeding—called an *ancillary proceeding*—would be necessary to transfer Reich's Ohio real estate is accordance with his will. In this proceeding, generally, Ohio could not question the validity of Reich's will. If it is valid under Texas law, Ohio must recognize it.

If Ben Buckeye dies in Ohio, owning real estate in both Ohio and Texas and leaving a valid Ohio will, an ancillary probate proceeding will be necessary in Texas to pass the Texas real estate to Buckeye's heirs. Again, Texas will not question the validity of Buckeye's will; if it is valid under Ohio law, Texas will recognize it for this purpose.

If Reich and Buckeye had both died intestate, ancillary probate proceedings would still be necessary. Ownership of Reich's Ohio property would be determined according to the statute of descent and distribution of Ohio, not that of Texas. Ownership of Buckeye's Texas real property would be determined by the statute of descent and distribution of Texas, not that of Ohio.

Conflict of laws in real estate administration. If Ben Buckeye has a will made in Ohio, and he then moves to Texas and dies here, the validity of his will will be determined by Texas law, not by Ohio law. In other words, when a will is probated, its validity is judged by the law of the state where it is presented for probate, not by the law of the state where it was drawn up.

The same principle applies when Ace Aussie moves to Texas from Sydney, Australia, bringing his Australian will with him. If he dies here in Texas, his Australian will will not be admitted to probate in Texas unless it meets Texas standards of validity. If Ace dies here leaving a valid will, and the will leaves some of his assets to relatives in Australia, Texas law will permit the Australians to inherit. If Ace dies intestate here and his heirs under the Texas Statute of Descent and Distribution live in Australia, Texas will permit them to inherit.

A problem might occur if Pak Song Kim, an immigrant from Korea, dies in Texas, and his will leaves all of his property to his father Lee Chung Kim of Pyongyang, North Korea. A question would arise here as to whether or not the government of North Korea would allow father Kim to take possession of and enjoy this inheritance. If it is probable that the North Korean government would confiscate this inheritance, a Texas court might well refuse to allow father Kim to inherit. The will might well be declared invalid and the estate given to the young Kim's nearest blood relative in a free country.

The general rule is: Texas will permit residents of another country to inherit from Texans if that country permits Texans to inherit from its citizens, and if the government of that country will permit its citizens to enjoy inheritances from abroad.

Advisability of estate planning. The materials in this chapter have dealt with some aspects of estate planning. The astute reader should be convinced of the advisability of making a will.

There are other aspects of estate planning which have not yet been covered, including the important matters of estate, inheritance, and income tax liabilities, and of the means of reducing these. There are methods of distributing one's assets prior to one's death; there are, sometimes, advantages to such distribution. It is also possible to arrange one's affairs so that assets do not become part of one's estate after death, and so are not subject to administration and estate and inheritance taxation.

These matters, and more, will be considered in the next chapter.

54

Estate Planning

Probably most persons who give any thought at all to the subject of estate planning believe it is a matter of concern only to the rich. It is true that in this age of progressive taxation the wealthy must be concerned with estate planning if they wish to pass along a substantial part of their wealth to their heirs. But this is actually a matter all property owners should consider; since most Americans own something (at least a bank account, and perhaps a residence), most should be concerned about estate planning.

Property managers and estate planners need to consider three matters of importance:
1. Minimization of income taxation of current income.
2. Minimization of taxation of assets after death.
3. Minimization of the red tape and expense involved in the probate of the estate after death.

In addition, of course, there is the matter of seeing to it that one's property passes to those heirs one deems most worthy of receipt.

For the wage earner, not much can be done about the first concern. For the self-employed person and the well-paid executive or professional, more can be done, some of which is beyond the scope of this chapter. The other considerations will be taken up in more detail. Remember, however, that entire books have been written upon the subject of estate planning. No author may concisely describe all of the law in this area in one chapter of a general work. For the handling of specific problems, skilled professional advice will be necessary.

Life insurance. Life insurance policies are perhaps the most common of estate planning devices. For many persons, ownership of life insurance is the only practicable way of accumulating an estate to pass along to their heirs. There are many sorts of life insurance policies. For our purposes mention must be made of two: *term policies* and *ordinary life policies*.

Term life policies provide only protection against the death of the insured. Ordinary life policies not only provide protection against the death of the insured; they are also vehicles for saving, to a degree. The ordinary life policy accumulates a cash surrender value as it grows older. If the owner of the policy decides to cancel it, he then recovers this cash surrender value from the insurer. He may borrow against the cash surrender value from the insurer, paying a low rate of interest on the borrowing. Many life insurance policies furnished by employers to employees as part of the employer's package of fringe benefits are term policies. Most life policies bought and paid for by ordinary individuals are ordinary life policies.

Life insurance is a commodity that grows more expensive as you grow older. The premium payable on a life insurance policy is based upon the life expectancy of the insured, plus the face value of the policy, plus the portion of premium that will be apportioned to savings rather than protection. The younger the insured, the longer he will probably live, so the longer the insurer will have the use of his premium payments. The older the insured, the more likely he is to die soon, so the insurer may not have the use of his premium payments for as long.

Term premiums are lower than ordinary life premiums, because all of the term premium purchases protection, none of it being allocated to saving. However, the premium of an ordinary life policy remains the same for the life of the policy, while the premium of a term policy will increase as the insured grows older. Ordinary life policies are "permanent"—they endure as long as the insured lives. Term policies are only for a term of years. If the term policy is renewable, it may be renewed for another term at a higher premium. If it is not renewable, the insurer need not renew upon expiration of the term if it does not care to.

The ordinary policy is devised so that the cash value becomes equal to the face value when the insured reaches the age of 100. If he lives to be 100, premium payments will be due and payable up until that time. Ordinary life policies with other sorts of premium payment arrangements are available. There are "twenty-payment" policies under which premiums are paid for twenty years only, after which the policy is paid up and no more premiums are due, no matter how much longer the insured lives. Premium payments on these are higher than payments on ordinary policies, of course. One may also acquire a paid-up policy by paying one premium only; after paying the premium the insured is insured for the face value of the policy until his death. Endowment and annuity policies make possible the payment of benefits to the insured while he still lives.

Parties to a life policy. There are five parties to the ordinary life insurance policy:
1. The insurer—the insurance company which issues the policy.
2. The insured—the person whose life is insured.
3. The beneficiary—the person to whom the face value is payable upon the death of the insured.
4. The owner—the person to whom the cash surrender value belongs.
5. The payer of the premiums on the policy.

Normally five separate persons or organizations are not involved in the contractual arrangements here. Ordinarily, the insured owns the policy and pays the premium. This is the situation when Husband insures his own life and names Wife as the beneficiary of the policy.

If Father insures Son's life and names Wife as beneficiary of the policy, Father is the owner and premium payer, Son is the insured, and Wife is the beneficiary; the insured need not necessarily be the premium-payer.

Husband may insure his own life, naming Wife as beneficiary. Husband and Wife may then obtain a divorce, the divorce decree requiring Husband to transfer ownership of the policy to Wife. As a result, Husband is the insured and premium-payer, while Wife is owner and beneficiary. If Husband maintains the policy, Wife will collect the face value when he dies. If Husband stops making premium payments, Wife will collect the cash surrender value of the policy.

The insured is thus not necessarily either the owner or the payer of premiums; the beneficiary might be the owner and also the payer of premiums. The payer of premiums may be neither the insured, owner, nor beneficiary (which happens, for example, if Father insured Son's life and named Mother beneficiary; Father and Mother are divorced; and the court names Mother owner of the policy and orders Father to continue paying premiums).

Insurable interest. The concept of insurable interest is just as alive in the law of life insurance as it is in other areas of insurance law. No problem of insurable interest arises when one seeks to insure one's own life. We all have insurable interests in ourselves; therefore we may name anyone we wish as beneficiary of policies we purchase on our own lives.

Insurable interest becomes important when one seeks to insure another's life for one's own benefit. The owner must have an insurable interest in the life of the insured. Of course, a spouse has an insurable interest in a spouse. A parent has an insurable interest in a minor child. Persons who live together and are mutually dependent have insurable interests in each other. An employer has an insurable interest in a key employee (but not in all employees). A partner has an insurable interest in his other partners and the firm has an insurable interest in all of the partners. A corporation has an insurable interest in its key executive officers. A creditor has an insurable interest in his debtor, to the extent of the debt.

Designation and change of beneficiary. The owner of the life insurance policy has the right to designate the beneficiary. There is no right to change the designated beneficiary of a life policy unless the policy itself provides for change of beneficiary. Nearly all policies do provide this right, however. One who wishes to change the beneficiary of a life policy must inform the insurer of the change. The true beneficiary of any life policy is the beneficiary shown on the insurer's records. Thus, it is possible to change beneficiaries without notifying the beneficiaries themselves.

If the designated beneficiary dies before the insured, the policy becomes payable to the estate of the insured. There are two possible ways of preventing this. One is to designate another beneficiary upon the death of the original beneficiary. A simpler method is to designate an alternate beneficiary in the policy to begin with. The advantage to having the policy payable to a designated beneficiary is that the proceeds of the policy are payable directly to the beneficiary and do not become part of the assets of the insured's estate—or taxable as part of the estate. (If the insured is the owner, however, the proceeds will be taxable to his estate.) If the policy is payable to the estate, however, its proceeds are a part of the taxable estate and subject to administration.

Assignment of life policies. Most life policies permit the owner to assign his ownership rights to another party. Again, an assignment of this right does not bind the insurer until the insurer is informed. Ownership rights may be assigned as part of a divorce decree involving the owner, or the owner may wish to assign his rights under a policy to a creditor, etc.

The obtaining of life insurance. A person desiring to take out a life policy may contact the insurer or an agent in order to file an application, or he may himself be contacted by an agent of the insurer. The sale of life insurance is regulated in this state by the Texas Insurance Board. No person may sell life insurance in this state without a proper license issued by the board. Licensed salesmen must comply with the directives of the Texas Insurance Board and the statutory provisions of the Texas Insurance Code. Disobedience to the applicable laws and regulations is grounds for revocation or suspension of the license. It is a felony for a salesman whose license is revoked or suspended to sell insurance. It is a misdemeanor for a person without a license to sell insurance.

The applicant will fill out an application for a policy for the insurer's agent. The application will inquire as to applicant's age, occupation, state of health, and so on—and will of course also ask the identity of the beneficiary of the policy. The applicant may well be asked to furnish his first payment of premium at this time. The applicant is normally not yet insured at this point. He will be required to submit himself to a physical examination by a physician designated by the insurer. The insurer's underwriters will then examine the results of the examination and the information contained in the application and determine whether or not to insure him. If the decision is made to insure, the insurer will then issue a policy and the insured is covered. If the decision is made not to insure, the applicant's premium payment (if he made one) will be refunded.

If the application provides that the insured is insured as of the date of application, it means what it says, but the insurer may cancel the coverage by refusing to issue a policy. If the applicant dies after the date of application but before the date of issuance of his policy, it makes a big difference whether or not he is insured as of the date of application. If he is, his beneficiary recovers the face value of the policy. If he is not, the paid-in premium will be refunded, but no more.

If the applicant is not the insured, the insured of course must consent to the proposed insurance, and must take the physical exam and answer the questions about his health, age, occupation, etc.

Contestability of the life policy. Section 3.44-3 of the Texas Insurance Code provides that all life policies sold in Texas must contain a provision that the policy will be incontestable two years after issue, except for nonpayment of premiums. This means that the insurer cannot cancel the policy after it has been in force for two years except for such very good reasons as nonpayment of premiums. The policy is contestable for two years, however. During that time, the insurer may cancel the policy for good cause. Good cause might include the following:

1. Insured lied about his age on his application.
2. Insured concealed the fact that he has a dangerous occupation.
3. Insured lied about his health on his application.

Other similar sorts of fraud by the applicant are also grounds for cancellation. If the insurance company is unable to uncover such fraud within two years, it may not then cancel the policy. However, the policy is not totally incontestable after the two-year contestability period expires. If the applicant was guilty of gross fraud toward the company, such as having a stand-in take the physical exam for him, the insurer may still cancel.

If the insured lied about his age, this will be grounds for adjustment of the policy terms after the fraud is discovered. The insurer may not cancel the policy for such fraud, but it may reduce the face value of the policy to an amount of insurance which could be purchased with the insured's premiums by a person of his true age. If the insured understated his age, the amount of his insurance coverage is reduced appropriately.

When the insured or owner misses a premium payment, the insurer has the right to make adjustments in the policy even if it has been in effect for more than two years. However, TIC 3.44-2 provides that the policy must contain a provision granting the premium-payer a thirty-day grace period within which a delinquent premium payment may be made. If a premium payment is due June 30 but is not paid on time, the insurer may take no action to alter the terms of the policy until July 30. The insurer may charge interest on the late premium if it is paid during July, but he may do no more. Once the premium becomes thirty days overdue, he may take further action. If the policy has not been in effect for three years, it has accrued no cash surrender value in all probability, and may therefore be canceled. If the policy has been in effect for three years, it must have accrued some cash surrender value. In such a case, the insured has three options:

1. He may surrender the policy to the insurer and recover the cash surrender value.
2. He may retain paid-up insurance for life, the face value of which is determined by the amount of paid-up insurance the insured could purchase with his cash surrender value.
3. He may retain the policy in force at face value for the period of time the cash surrender value will pay the required premium.

In short, the provisions of TIC 3.44a protect an insured against the forfeiture of the cash surrender value of the ordinary life policy because of nonpayment of premiums.

Purchase of life insurance by minors. TIC 3.49-2 provides that a minor fourteen years of age or older may purchase life insurance, and that he may not ordinarily disaffirm his purchase because he is a minor. Such policies may insure only the life of the minor or of close relatives. If the policy insures the life of the minor, the beneficiary must be a close relative or a person in whom the minor has an insurable interest.

The policy application of such a minor must be approved by the father, mother, grandparent, or adult brother or sister of the applicant.

Insured's right to surrender policy. The insured, or the owner of a life policy, may surrender the policy to the insurer at any time. The surrender terminates the insurance coverage, and entitles the owner to recovery of the cash surrender value, if any.

Payment of death claims. Upon the death of the insured the beneficiary applies to the insurer for payment of the face value of the policy. The insurer need not pay until the death of the insured is proven to its satisfaction. TIC 3.44 provides that the insurer must pay a death claim within two months of receipt of proof of the death of the insured. The beneficiary named in the policy is entitled to receive this payment unless another claimant files an adverse claim with the insurer before it pays the claim.

There might be three grounds for the filing of such an adverse claim to the benefits of the policy after the insured's death. These could be:

1. The beneficiary murdered the insured, or was otherwise responsible for his death. In such a case, TIC 21.23 provides that the beneficiary forfeits all rights to the face value of the policy, and the policy shall be payable to the closest relative of the insured. If a question is raised as to whether or not the beneficiary was responsible for the insured's death, the insurer will not pay anyone until the matter is legally determined, until the beneficiary is tried for the murder of the insured, etc.
2. The beneficiary was changed before the insured died. In such a case, good proof of the change is needed. If the insured also owned the policy, it would seem strange that he did not inform the insurer of the change while he was still alive. Normally, the adverse claimant will have no success here.
3. The beneficiary assigned his rights to another party. When this occurs, it is up to the assignee to inform the insurer of the assignment. The assignor should do this, but the assignee should really do it to protect his interest. Since the rights of the beneficiary are assignable, notification to the insurer of a valid assignment obligates the insurer to pay the assignee.

Settlement options. The beneficiary more often than not takes payment under the policy in a lump sum. This is not the only permissible mode of settlement, however. The beneficiary may elect to take monthly payments from the insurer for a fixed period of time, or until his death, or the policy may provide for other settlement options.

In this time of high inflation, the beneficiary would generally be unwise to refuse a lump-sum settlement. However, if a creditor of the beneficiary has a judgment against him, the beneficiary would be well advised to choose an installment settlement option. TIC 21.22 provides that insurance benefits are exempt from creditor claims if payable in installments. The beneficiary, then, may deny creditors access to the proceeds by choosing an installment settlement option.

An assignment of rights to proceeds by a beneficiary of a life policy is void if the assignment was made to hinder, defraud, or delay the beneficiary's creditors.

Taxability of life insurance proceeds. Life insurance proceeds are not defined as taxable income by the Internal Revenue Code. Such proceeds are therefore not subject to income taxation.

Life insurance proceeds payable to named beneficiaries are not considered to be part of the insured's estate, unless the insured owns the policy. If the policy is payable to the insured's estate, however, the proceeds are part of the taxable estate.

Regardless of the identity of the beneficiary, however, the cash surrender value of a life policy is considered to be a part of the owner's estate. Life insurance proceeds payable to individuals are exempt from the Texas Inheritance Tax up to $40,000. If premiums were paid with community funds and the insured's spouse is the beneficiary, up to $80,000 in proceeds are exempt. Proceeds over the exempt amount may be taxable to the beneficiary.

GIFT AND INHERITANCE TAXATION

The federal gift tax. Gifts made by a donor during his lifetime may subject said donor to gift tax liability. The donor is liable for the tax, not the donee. Through proper planning, a donor may dispose of much of his valuable property during his lifetime without incurring gift tax liability, but care and foresight are required.

The federal estate tax. Federal estate tax may be payable upon the net worth of the estate of a deceased person. The tax is a liability of the estate, payable before the assets of the estate are distributed to the heirs.

The Texas inheritance tax. The Texas inheritance tax is essentially a tax upon the individual or organization inheriting property. The tax is payable by the heir, not by the estate.

The unification of the federal estate and gift taxes. Before the enactment of the Tax Reform Act of 1976, the gift tax and the estate tax were separate taxes with separate rates. Gift tax rates were lower than estate tax rates, and the making of gifts and payment of gift tax did not necessarily influence estate tax liability. A person could save estate tax by making taxable gifts during his lifetime, thus reducing the size of his taxable estate. Since the Tax Reform Act of 1976 became law, identical tax rates have existed for the two taxes. One may no longer obtain lower tax rates on gifts, and the making of gifts and the payment of gift taxes may now well have an influence on estate tax liability.

The net worth of a decedent's estate must normally exceed $100,000 before any estate tax liability will exist. Taxable gifts of more than $100,000 must be made during the taxpayer's lifetime before gift tax liability will be incurred.

Gift tax liability. A single taxpayer is permitted to make tax-free gifts of up to $3,000 per year to individual donees. A married taxpayer may make gifts of up to $6,000, tax-free, to individual donees—the $6,000 exemption applying if both spouses make the gift. Thus, a person could make $90,000 worth of tax-free gifts in a year by giving $3,000 to each of thirty different donees.

Gifts to charity are tax-free, no matter how great. Gifts to one's spouse are also tax-free, up to a point: one may make up to $100,000 worth of tax-free gifts to one's spouse during one's lifetime. When the total gifts to the spouse come to exceed this figure, they become taxable. When total lifetime gifts to the spouse exceed $200,000, the gifts over and above the $200,000 level are 50 percent tax-free. Thus, the first $100,000 in gifts to the spouse are tax-free; the second $100,000 fully taxable, and gifts exceeding $200,000 50 percent tax-free.

So long as a taxpayer makes no gifts of more than $3,000 to any donee during a year, he need file no gift tax return. He must file an annual return if he makes a gift of more than $3,000 to a donee during the year. Once his lifetime taxable gifts exceed $25,000, he must file a quarterly return during each quarter in which he makes a taxable gift.

The rate of tax is 18 percent on the first taxable $10,000; 20 percent on the second $10,000; 22 percent on the next $20,000; increasing 2 percent on each $20,000 up to $100,000. On the $100,000 to $150,000 bracket the tax rate is 30 percent; on the $150,000 to $250,000 bracket it is 32 percent; on the $250,000 to $500,000 bracket 34 percent. The $1 million to $1.5 million bracket is taxed at 41 percent; the $2 million to $2.5 million bracket is taxed at 49 percent. The progression continues, until all gifts over $5 million are taxed 70 percent. The complete tax rate schedule is found at IRC 2001.

The taxpayer need not, however, pay any tax on his early taxable gifts. The explanation of this pardox is the existence of the unified estate-gift tax credit created by the Tax Reform Act of 1976. The size of the credit was $38,000 for 1979, rising to $42,500 in 1980, and $47,000 in 1981. Until a taxpayer has made gifts upon which the total gift tax is $42,500 by the end of 1980, then, he will owe no gift tax. If the total gift tax upon his lifetime taxable gifts does not exceed $47,000 by the end of 1981, he will owe no tax. Thus, if a taxpayer's total taxable gifts during his lifetime do not exceed $175,000 by the end of 1981, he will owe no gift tax. The portion of the unified credit which is not used to offset gift tax liability may be used after death to offset estate tax liability, but there is only one credit. If it is used to offset gift tax liability, it will be gone when the taxpayer dies.

All gift tax returns filed by the taxpayer are cumulative, stating total lifetime taxable gifts, total lifetime tax due, and offsetting the lifetime credit against the tax. Tax becomes payable when the credit is exhausted. The disadvantage of making taxable lifetime gifts is, of course, that one incurs gift tax liability and begins using up the unified estate-gift tax credit. On the other hand, the making of the gift may reduce the size of one's estate at death and so reduce the estate tax liability.

The person whose earnings put him in high income tax brackets may on the other hand find it helpful to give income-producing assets away to family members (other than the spouse) with less income so that the income produced by the asset will not be taxed as heavily. (There is no income tax saving in giving an income-producing asset to one's spouse: the income is community property and taxable to both spouses no matter which spouse owns the asset. In a non-community-property state, such gifts might make sense.)

Gifts made within three years of death are considered to be gifts in anticipation of death. The value of such gifts is included in the estate of the deceased.

Gross estate of a decedent. The first step in computation of the estate tax liability of a deceased person is the determination of his gross estate. The following assets are included in the gross estate, as per IRC 2031-2044:
1. Real estate.
2. Stocks, including dividends declared but not yet paid.
3. Bonds, including accrued but unpaid interest up to date of death.
4. Mortgages receivable, notes receivable, and cash.
5. Insurance proceeds payable to the estate.
6. Cash surrender values of insurance policies owned by the deceased.
7. Joint tenancy and tenancy by the entireties property.

8. Miscellaneous receivables (accounts, judgments, royalties, etc.).
9. Personal property—crops, automobiles, livestock, and the like.
10. Gifts in anticipation of death.
11. Property transferred during the deceased's lifetime in which he retained ownership interests (life estate, revocable trusts, etc.).
12. Certain other items we need not enumerate.

Most of these assets are valued at market value, although other methods of valuation may be used under special circumstances. Joint tenancy property is all included in the estate, unless it can be proven that the decedent did not furnish all of the consideration used in the acquisition of the property. The same principle applies to tenancy by the entireties property. On the other hand, only half the value of community property is includable in the gross estate.

Adjusted gross estate. The value of all assets included in the gross estate are added together to determine the value of the entire estate. Three items are then deducted:

1. Funeral and administration expenses (administration expenses are the expenses of probating and settling the estate).
2. Debts of the deceased, including costs of his last illness, income tax payable, and other bills.
3. Losses during administration—uninsured theft and casualty losses of estate assets.

The importance of adjusted gross estate is that it has a bearing upon computation of the marital deduction, a very important deduction from the gross estate.

Marital deduction. If the deceased left property to his spouse by will or Statute of Descent and Distribution, or by a substitute for a will such as joint tenancy survivorship, all or a large amount of this property will be deductible from the adjusted gross estate, thus reducing the estate tax.

The marital deduction will consist of the lesser of the following:
1. All property left outright by the deceased to his spouse, or
2. $250,000 or 50 percent of the adjusted gross estate, whichever is larger.

Thus, if the adjusted gross estate is $240,000, and the decedent willed all of his property to his spouse, there will be no taxable estate and no estate tax liability. If the adjusted gross estate is $350,000, and the deceased willed all of his property to his spouse, the marital deduction will be $250,000 and the taxable estate $100,000. If the adjusted gross estate is $1 million and the decedent willed all of his property to this spouse, the taxable estate will be $500,000.

If the deceased made gifts to his spouse during his lifetime on which the marital deduction was more than 50 percent of the value of the gift, the estate tax marital deduction will be reduced by the amount by which the gift tax deduction exceeded 50 percent. This can only happen when the deceased's gifts to his spouse during his lifetime were $200,000 or less because, as mentioned earlier, there is no gift tax on the first $100,000 of taxable gifts by a spouse to a spouse. This decrease in the marital deduction thus can never exceed $50,000—it will sometimes be less.

For example: The deceased made gifts of $150,000 to his spouse during his lifetime. The first $100,000 of these were tax-free, the latter $50,000 fully taxable. The deceased then died, leaving all his property to his spouse. His adjusted gross estate was $250,000. Normally this would all be nontaxable because of the estate tax marital deduction. However, had the $150,000 in lifetime gifts been included in the adjusted gross estate, the estate would have consisted of $400,000 and the marital deduction would be $250,000. The gift tax marital deduction on the $150,000 in lifetime gifts was $100,000 (the first $100,000 being tax-free and the $50,000 fully taxable). Fifty percent of $150,000 is $75,000; thus the gift tax deduction exceeded the 50 percent limit by $25,000. The adjusted gross estate remains $250,000, but the marital deduction is reduced to $225,000. There is thus a taxable estate of $25,000 here.

The orphan's exclusion. When the deceased is the sole surviving parent of a child or children under the age of twenty-one, property left to such children will be deducted from the taxable estate to an extent. The deduction amounts to $5,000 per year that each child is under the age of twenty-one at the time of decedent's death, or the amount of the estate left to each such child, whichever figure is smaller.

Thus, if the deceased left $50,000 to his son, age fifteen, $30,000 of this would be excluded from the taxable estate (since the son will reach twenty-one in six years). If the deceased left only $25,000 to his son, the entire gift would be excluded, but no more. It must be remembered that if the child has a surviving parent, even if the deceased was no longer married to that parent, the orphan's exclusion would not apply to gifts left to the child.

The charitable deduction. All property included in the gross estate left by the deceased to charity is deductible from the adjusted gross estate and not subject to the estate tax. This is also true of property included in the gross estate transferred to charity during the deceased's lifetime. "Charity" for this purpose includes not only organizations like the Red Cross but also religious and public organizations. Bequests to churches, governments, and state universities would thus be deductible.

A person could render his entire estate exempt from estate taxation by leaving it all to charity. He could accomplish the same objective by leaving half his adjusted gross estate to his spouse and the other half to charity.

The taxable estate. The taxable estate consists of the adjusted gross estate less the marital deduction, the orphan's exclusion, and the charitable deduction. The tentative tax is then computed on the taxable estate from the tax table. However, it must be remembered that the total tax computed will probably not be payable by the estate, because certain credits are available to reduce this liability.

First: That portion of the unified estate-gift tax credit not used to offset gift tax liabilities is available for use as a credit here. The total credit is $38,000 for deaths which occurred in 1979, $42,500 for 1980, and $47,000 for 1981 and thereafter. Thus, the deceased who dies in 1980 has available a credit of $42,500 against his estate tax liability, less the amount of the credit that has been applied against gift tax liabilities during his lifetime.

Second: Credit is granted for state death taxes paid. A maximum credit for such state tax payments is provided for in IRC 2011. Texas state law provides that, if the tax normally payable by heirs under the Texas Inheritance Tax does not equal the amount of the maximum credit for state death taxes provided for by IRC 2011, an inheritance tax will be due the state from the estate to bring the state tax up to the level of the maximum credit.

Third: There might be a credit available for prior federal gift taxes on assets in the estate. Fourth: There may be a credit available for prior federal estate taxes paid upon assets in the estate. Fifth: If the deceased owned property abroad subject to a foreign death tax, a credit may be available against the federal estate tax for the foreign tax paid. The law relative to these last three credits is quite complex and beyond the scope of the contents of this chapter.

Examples of estate tax computations. Bert Buncom died in 1979. His assets are as follows:

1. A house worth $100,000 as of the date of death.

2. Corporate stock worth $150,000 as of the date of his death.
3. Miscellaneous personal property worth $10,000 at date of death.
4. $30,000 in cash.

The estate is thus worth $290,000. At Bert's death he owed $30,000 on his house mortgage. His last illness caused unpaid medical bills of $5,000. His funeral cost $5,000. The expenses of probating his estate were $5,000. Thus, there are $45,000 worth of deductions from the gross estate, leaving an adjusted gross estate of $245,000. Bert had never married, and he had no children. His will left all of his estate to his mother. This being the case, there is no marital deduction, no orphan's exclusion, and no charitable deduction. The entire estate is taxable.

The tax on an estate of $245,000 will be nearly $70,000. Bert made no taxable gifts during his lifetime, so he has available the entire unified estate-gift tax credit to offset some of this tax liability. Since this credit is $38,000 for 1979, his liability will be reduced to about $32,000. Also available against this liability will be the credit for state death taxes paid, which will amount here to about $1,200. The entire estate tax liability of Bert's estate will thus be approximately $31,000.

Let us consider next the estate of Calvin Crenshaw, who died in 1980. Cal was married and had three children. He died owning real estate worth $1.3 million, securities worth $1.8 million, personal property worth $500,000, and $200,000 in cash. There are $800,000 worth of mortgages on the real estate, and, since Cal bought some of the securities on margin, he owed $400,000 on them. His funeral cost $10,000, last illness bills were $5,000, and expenses of administering his estate are $35,000. The real estate and the securities are all his separate property, but the personal property and cash are community property. The gross estate therefore is valued at $3.45 million, only half the value of the personal property and cash being included. Deductions are $1.25 million (the debts and expenses), leaving an adjusted gross estate of $2.2 million.

Cal's will leaves $1 million to his spouse, $50,000 to each of the three children, and the residue to the American Cancer Society. Cal has made no taxable gifts (or any gifts) during his lifetime. His maximum marital deduction would be $1.1 million (50 percent of $2.2 million). Since the bequest to his spouse is less than the maximum marital deduction, the bequest comprises the deduction—so $1.2 million remains. Since the bequests to the children comprise $150,000 in toto, the residue going to the American Cancer Society is $1.05 million. This, being a bequest to charity, is a charitable deduction. This leaves a net taxable estate of $150,000. The unified tax credit available to Cal's estate is $42,500; an estate of more than $161,000 would be required before that much estate tax would be payable. In this case the credit exceeds the tax, and no federal estate tax is due here. This illustrates the advantage of leaving most of one's estate to one's spouse and to charity.

Finally, let us consider the case of Dale Davis, a widower with two children—Dean, age six, and Dianne, age eight. Suppose Dale dies in 1981, owning a house with an appraised value of $70,000. He owned $15,000 worth of assorted personal property, and had $10,000 cash. In addition, he and his brother Donald owned a piece of land worth $60,000 as joint tenants with right of survivorship, which Dale had paid for with money inherited from his father; this purchase was made in 1977. In addition, Dale had made a gift of $10,000 to his sister Dora in 1979. Dale also owned a $50,000 life insurance policy, under which his wife Daniela had been beneficiary. Daniela died in 1976, but Dale had never changed the beneficiary of the policy.

When Dale died, he owed $20,000 on the house and had $10,000 in other debts. Funeral expenses and last illness expenses were $5,000, as were the estate administration expenses. Dale's will left everything to Dean and Dianne, share and share alike.

The house, personal property, and the cash of course are a part of the gross estate, amounting to $95,000. The joint tenancy property, though now the property of Donald, is counted as part of the estate because Dale paid all of the consideration for it. The gift to Dora is part of the estate as a gift in anticipation of death since it was made within three years of Dale's death. The life insurance proceeds are part of the estate because they are payable to it. The gross estate is thus $215,000. From this figure the mortgage and other debts and expenses are deducted, leaving an adjusted gross estate of $175,000 ($215,000 less $40,000).

The joint tenancy property, though part of the taxable estate, is not subject to the jurisdiction of the probate court, since Donald has clear title to it as surviving joint tenant. The $10,000 gift to Dora, though part of the taxable estate, of course remains Dora's property. The life insurance proceeds are both part of the taxable estate and part of the administered estate. The net worth of the estate assets is thus $105,000. The maximum that Dianne and Dean could receive from the estate is $52,500 each. They would receive this sum unless taxes reduce it in some fashion.

Since the deceased was unmarried, there is no marital deduction here. Since he left nothing to charity, there is no charitable deduction. Because the two children are now orphans without a surviving parent, there is an orphan's exclusion available. Since Dianne is thirteen years shy of being twenty-one, there is a potential $65,000 exclusion for her. Since Dean is fifteen years shy of being twenty-one, there is a potential $75,000 exclusion for him. There will not be an exclusion of $140,000 available here because the net assets of the estate do not equal $140,000. Since the two heirs would obtain $52,500 each if taxes do not reduce this figure, the total exclusion would be $105,000. This leaves a net taxable estate of $60,000. Since the estate tax due on $60,000 would not exceed the credit available (even taking into account the gift tax on the gift to Dora, which would be deducted from the credit), no federal estate tax is due on this estate.

Dale would have been expected to pay gift tax on $7,000 of the gift to Dora. He would also have been expected to pay gift tax on the consideration he paid for the property he and Donald owned as joint tenants. However, if Dale had made no other taxable gifts in his life the unified credit would have eliminated gift tax liability on these—and the taxable gifts would have made such a small dent in the available credit that it would still be large enough to offset the estate tax liability of this estate.

The Texas inheritance tax. The law relative to the Texas inheritance tax is found in Texas Taxation Code (TTC) 41.01 et seq. The tax is levied on all property owned by a deceased Texan located within the borders of Texas, and on all intangible personal property (such as bank accounts) owned by the decedent outside Texas. All of a married decedent's separate property of this nature is taxable, as is half of the community property of his marriage. Except for some technical differences, deductible expenses and debts are substantially the same under state and federal law.

Life insurance proceeds payable to the estate are taxable, as are life insurance proceeds of more than $40,000 payable to heirs. But if the policy in question was paid for with community funds, half the proceeds are nontaxable, and the $40,000 exclusion is subtracted from the taxable half. Thus, if the decedent owned a $150,000 life insurance policy when he died, payable to his widow and paid for with community funds, $75,000 of the benefits are immediately nontaxable. The $40,000 exclusion is subtracted from the remaining $75,000, leaving $35,000 of the proceeds taxable. If the policy were payable to someone other than the widow, taxability would still be calculated this way if the premiums were paid with community property.

Gifts made by the deceased within three years of his death are presumed to be gifts in anticipation of death, but if the donee can prove that the gift was not made in anticipation of death he may keep the gift from being taxed.

The tax is a liability of the heir, not of the estate. The tax rate depends on the relationship of the heir to the decedent. The Taxation Code divides beneficiaries into five classes:

Class A—Spouse, child, grandchild, other descendant, son-in-law, or daughter-in-law.
Class B—the United States, for use in Texas.
Class C—Brothers, sisters, nieces, nephews, and descendants of nieces and nephews.
Class D—Uncles, aunts, first cousins.
Class E—Others.

Gifts to charities or to the state of Texas are totally exempt from inheritance tax. The first $25,000 of a gift to Class A and Class B beneficiaries is exempt. The tax rates run from 1 percent on the next $25,000 to 6 percent on amounts over $1 million. The first $10,000 of a gift to a Class C beneficiary is exempt. The rates run from 3 percent on the next $15,000 to 10 percent on amounts over $1 million. The first $1,000 of a gift to a Class D beneficiary is exempt. The rates run from 4 percent on the next $9,000 to 15 percent on amounts over $1 million. The first $500 to a Class E beneficiary is exempt. The rates run from 5 percent on the next $9,500 to 20 percent on amounts over $1 million.

If there is a larger estate credit against state tax for federal estate tax purposes than the Texas inheritance tax due from the heirs, an estate tax is levied on the estate itself for the balance. Thus, the Texas inheritance tax law seeks to encourage persons to leave as much of their estates as possible to charity and to close relatives. The rate differentials provide some strong incentive for this distribution.

SUMMARY OF ESTATE MANAGEMENT DEVICES

The will. The will is the essential planning and management device; through it the estate's disposal is regulated. Failure to make a will causes the estate to be distributed under the mandate of the Statute of Descent and Distribution. It may also cause a person to be put in charge of the estate in whom the planner has no confidence. It will also increase the expense of settling the estate, because of the necessity of bonding the administrator to be appointed.

The testamentary trust. If a property owner wants to provide support for someone who is incapable of managing money or property, he may create a trust of which that person is beneficiary. By appointing a competent trustee to manage the trust assets, the incapable person is provided for without burdening him with management responsibilities.

Another use of the testamentary trust is as a device to keep property out of the estate of the beneficiary of a testator's benevolence. If Jim Jones leaves property outright to his wife Juanita, the property will be a part of Juanita's estate upon her death unless she made other disposition of it while she lived. If Jim creates a trust of which Juanita is beneficiary for the term of her life, but on her death the trust is to terminate and the corpus is to be given to Joanna, daughter of Jim and Juanita, the trust assets are kept out of Juanita's estate and saved from further estate taxation.

Life insurance. The purchase of life insurance insures the availability of cash to the named beneficiaries of the policies on the death of the insured. The proceeds are not administered as part of the estate of the deceased unless the policies are payable directly to it. It must be remembered, though, that the proceeds are counted as part of the estate for federal estate tax purposes if the insured was the owner of the policies. The only way he may avoid this is by making someone else the owner of the policies.

It must also be remembered that life insurance proceeds are exempt from Texas inheritance tax only up to $40,000.

Lifetime gifts. Property given away while one is alive will not be part of one's administerable estate at death. By giving assets away while you live you get to watch your donees enjoy (or perhaps misuse) the proceeds of your generosity. By giving away income-producing assets, you may reduce the amount of income subject to taxation. If you, the donor, are in a high income tax bracket while your donee is in a lower bracket, this advantage may be gained. In any event, you reduce your own taxable income (and your income tax).

Of course you may incur gift tax liability through the making of gifts, but if you make gifts only to charity or to your spouse, or if you keep the amount of gifts to any one donee below $3,000 per year, you avoid such liability (until your lifetime gifts to your spouse exceed $100,000). Remember too that gifts made within three years of your death are considered gifts in anticipation of death, and their value included in your estate for estate tax purposes.

Joint tenancy property. The advantage of owning property in joint tenancy is that the property is not part of your administerable estate. It becomes the property of the surviving joint tenant(s) automatically upon the death of a joint tenant. Remember, though, that one may not create a joint tenancy in community property under Texas law unless the property is conveyed to a third party and the third party conveys it back to the spouses in joint tenancy. Joint tenancy may, however, be created in separate property. Again, if the donor is to be one of the joint tenants he must convey to a third party, and the third party must convey back to the joint tenants.

The great disadvantage of this sort of ownership is that if the donor is the first joint tenant to die, the entire value of the property is a part of his estate for estate tax purposes. If the donee is first to die, the property is not taxed as part of his estate of course: the donor becomes sole owner again.

Conveyance of a life estate. Bob Burk wants to make certain that his mother has a house to live in while she lives. Bob owns a rental house he wants to use for this purpose, so he conveys the property to his mother for the term of her life, keeping a reversion for himself. Bob's future interest in this property will be part of his taxable estate if he dies before his mother. His conveyance of the life estate will be taxable as a gift to the extent of the value of the estate conveyed.

Conveyance of a remainder. Earl Eck owns a house. He wants his son Egbert to have it when he dies, so he conveys the property to Egbert, reserving a life estate for himself. Earl preserves his right to use and occupy the house for as long as he lives, and he has made certain that Egbert gets the property when he dies.

This has the effect of a testamentary conveyance. The entire value of the property will be a part of Earl's estate for estate tax purposes. Thus, there is little in the way of tax advantages in this situation. However, Egbert automatically becomes the owner of the property on Earl's death; it will not be subject to administration as part of his estate.

Creation of an irrevocable trust. A good way of making a gift to a person incapable of managing property is to create an irrevocable trust of which he is the beneficiary. The corpus of such a trust is no longer an asset of the donor. The income earned by the corpus is taxable to the trust, not to the donor.

The corpus of the trust may be part of the settlor's estate for estate tax purposes, however. It will be if the corpus is to revert to the settlor upon the death of the beneficiary. If, however, the settlor gives up all ownership rights in the corpus, if will not be taxable to him on his death.

Creation of a revocable trust. If the settlor of a trust wants the power to revoke the trust and regain possession of the corpus during his lifetime, he will establish the revocable trust.

Such a trust creates no income tax savings: the income earned by the corpus is taxable to the settlor. It creates no estate tax savings: the corpus is part of the settlor's estate for estate tax purposes. The corpus will not be part of the settlor's administerable estate, however. It will remain under the management of the trustee for the benefit of the beneficiary. This is the major advantage of such a trust.

Creation of a reverter trust. If Richard Rich wants to put some valuable assets in a place where the income they earn will not be taxed to him, but where he may regain ownership of them later (perhaps when his income is less and he is in a lower income tax bracket), the reverter trust may serve his purpose. The settlor of such a trust must convey the corpus to an outside trustee for the benefit of another beneficiary for at least ten years or for the life of the beneficiary. He may then provide that, upon the expiration of the specified time period or upon the death of the beneficiary, the trust will terminate and the corpus will revert to the settlor.

This device is essentially for avoidance of income tax. The settlor has parted with enough control over the corpus so that trust income is taxable to the trust or to the beneficiary rather than to him. For estate tax purposes there is no saving here: at least the reversionary interest will be taxable as part of the settlor's estate.

Summary. For persons with few assets, the principles of this chapter may be of little importance. However, continuing inflation increases the dollar value of all our assets. Inflation alone may raise the value of our assets to a point at which estate and inheritance tax liabilities become possible. Inflation also pushes many of us into progressively higher income tax brackets. Thirty years ago it could have been said that estate planning problems were problems of the rich. This is no longer so. Middle income persons ignore the law here at their risk—and at the risk of their loved ones.

55

Bankruptcy

When a debtor gets into a situation in which he cannot pay his debts as they come due, he quickly finds himself in a very uncomfortable position. Creditors generally treat a debtor with consideration so long as they are convinced that he is trying to solve his problems, and so long as there seems to be some possibility of success in this effort.

The impatience of a single creditor may precipitate the end of this time of tolerance, however. If one creditor files suit against a debtor to collect his claim, the lack of confidence will prove contagious. If the debtor owes a liquidated debt to the aggrieved creditor, that creditor may levy attachment on some of the debtor's nonexempt assets right after filing his complaint, to some extent depriving the other creditors of the right to look to these assets for payment. The result may well be that the other creditors will now also take action against the debtor. The race of diligence has begun: the first creditors to obtain liens upon the debtor's nonexempt assets will be the first to be paid. The race of diligence among creditors to carry off the debtor's assets in a sense resembles the flocking of vultures around a piece of carrion; only the swift are rewarded.

There are, however, orderly procedures that may be resorted to in such situations in order to spare the debtor and his creditors the strain of the race of diligence. These alternatives are the composition of creditors, the receivership, the assignment for benefit of creditors, and bankruptcy proceedings.

Composition of creditors. The composition of creditors is a common-law contractual procedure. The debtor enters into a contract with some—or all—of his creditors providing that, in exchange for the debtor's paying each creditor a stated percentage of his claim, all creditors release the debtor from the balance of their claims.

The procedure is simple; it is simply a matter of negotiation. It is cheap; it can be accomplished without the assistance of legal counsel or the courts. If the matter is at all complex, all parties involved would be well advised to hire counsel; still, no court procedure is necessary. A disadvantage to this procedure is the fact that no creditor may be compelled to participate. The adjustment of claims in the composition of course is not binding upon persons not parties to the composition. If too few creditors are willing to participate, the composition will not solve many of the debtor's problems.

Receivership. When a business or very valuable piece of property is being incompetently managed, creditors may under some conditions petition a Texas district court for the appointment of a receiver to manage the property or business. A receivership is intended to be a rehabilitation procedure. The idea is to get the debtor business back on its feet again through competent management. If the court chooses to appoint a receiver, the receiver must post a bond to assure the faithful performance of his duties. The court order appointing him will describe his authority. Generally, the receiver will have less authority to run the business than the debtor had; his capacity to borrow money and to buy inventory on credit may be limited, for instance.

The receiver will run the business under court supervision for a period to determine whether or not rehabilitation is possible. If the business shows improvement, the receivership may later be terminated. If rehabilitation proves to be difficult or impossible, the receiver013 will end and some form of liquidation will ensue—dissolution and liquidation of the partnership or corporation, assignment for benefit of creditors, or bankruptcy.

Assignment for benefit of creditors. The assignment for benefit of creditors is the liquidation procedure provided by state law. The procedure is essentially the following: The debtor assigns all of his nonexempt property to an assignee. The debtor also furnishes to the assignee a complete list of all his creditors and the amount that he owes each. He must also disclose all security interests and the like upon the assigned property and must furnish a complete list of the assigned assets and his estimate as to the value of the property assigned.

The assignee then sends a notice of the assignment to all of the named creditors. Any creditor desiring to collect something out of the value of the assigned assets must file a claim with the assignee stating the nature and amount of his claim. The assignee proceeds to liquidate the assigned assets and distribute them ratably among the creditors who filed claims. Once the assets are liquidated and distributed, the procedure ends.

There are two types of assignments for benefits of creditors used in Texas. The basic procedure described above is used in both, but the details of procedure differ under the two schemes. The less commonly used is the statutory procedure found in Chapter 23 of the Texas Business and Commerce Code. The advantage to using it is the provision of TB&CC 23.10 that an assigning debtor's debt to a creditor is discharged if the creditor received at least one-third of his claim from the assignee. However, this provision is in all probability inoperative; since the U.S. Constitution reserves to the federal government the right to enact bankruptcy legislation, a court may well hold that TB&CC 23.10 is a state bankruptcy provision and is thus unenforceable.

For this reason, most Texas assignments for benefit of creditors are contractual, common-law assignments. The assignment of his nonexempt assets by the debtor is easily accomplished by contract. The inventory of assets and list of creditors furnished along with the assignment is essential to the operation of the scheme.

The notice of assignment sent by the assignee to the creditors will provide that, if the creditor files a claim with the assignee, he agrees to accept whatever he receives out of the assignment proceeding in full settlement of his claim. If the creditor will not agree to accept what he gets as full settlement, he will not be allowed to participate. Thus, the debtor will be discharged from the debts he owes participating creditors due to the contracts between the assignee and each participating creditor.

Obviously secured creditors need not file claims with the assignee. The assignee takes the collateral of the secured transaction subject to the creditor's security interest. All that the assignee has to dispose of with respect to such collateral is the debtor's interest (equity) in it.

All creditors do not stand upon an equal footing when the assets are liquidated and the proceeds are distributed. First priority is assigned to administrative expenses—compensation for the assignee and his attorney and other such things.

Second in priority stand claims of the federal government. These may be (and usually are) tax claims by the IRS, but they may also include claims of a contractual nature held by other federal agencies.

Third in priority stand tax claims of the state of Texas and of local government bodies. Only after these are paid in full do unsecured creditors collect anything.

Again, it must be remembered that unsecured creditors who file no claims get nothing from the proceeding. These creditors are not compelled to participate; their claims are not discharged. And they may bring the assignment to a screeching halt by filing involuntary bankruptcy against the debtor.

Bankruptcy—in general. The Ninety-fifth Congress almost completely rewrote the federal bankruptcy law in the Bankruptcy Reform Act of 1978. This landmark legislation was signed into law by President Carter in November 1978. Most of it became effective on October 1, 1979. Under previous law, bankruptcy matters were handled by the federal district courts, and by referees appointed by federal district judges. Under the new law special bankruptcy courts are established to handle bankruptcy matters, staffed by bankruptcy judges who hear no other types of cases.

The new law provides for three major types of proceedings. There is the Chapter VII proceeding, a liquidation proceeding, and the Chapter XI proceeding, a business rehabilitation proceeding (under previous law there were two business rehabilitation proceedings—Chapter X for corporations, and Chapter XI for small businesses. These two proceedings were combined into one). Then there is the Chapter XIII proceeding, for rehabilitating the individual debtor who has large debts.

There is also a Chapter IX proceeding for insolvent municipalities, and special provisions for railroads, stockbrokers, and commodity brokers.

The new law has been codified at 11 USC 101 et seq.

Filing voluntary bankruptcy. 11 USC 301 provides that any entity that may be a debtor under 11 USC 109 may file for voluntary bankruptcy. The debtor filing voluntary bankruptcy must specify whether he is filing under Chapter VII, Chapter XI, or Chapter XIII.

The following sorts of debtors may not file for liquidation under Chapter VII:
1. Railroads.
2. Domestic or foreign insurance companies.
3. Domestic or foreign banks, savings banks, and similar institutions.
4. Domestic or foreign savings and loan associations.
5. Domestic or foreign credit unions.

Insolvent railroads may file for rehabilitation under Chapter XI, but may not be liquidated under Chapter VII. Insurance companies, banks, and other financial institutions are liquidated or rehabilitated under other statutes when they become insolvent.

Any debtor who may file for a Chapter VII liquidation may file for a Chapter XI rehabilitation except:
1. An individual who is not a businessman.
2. A stockbroker.
3. A commodity broker.

The only debtors who may file for a Chapter XIII rehabilitation are individuals with regular income owing liquidated, noncontingent, unsecured debts of under $100,000 and liquidated, noncontingent, secured debts of under $350,000.

11 USC 302 permits a husband and wife to file a joint petition for liquidation or rehabilitation, as the case might be. In case of a joint filing for Chapter XIII, the debts of the spouses combined must not exceed $100,000 in unsecured debts and $350,000 in secured debts. If one of the spouses is a stockbroker or commodity broker, however, the couple may not file under Chapter XIII.

The debtor who files for voluntary bankruptcy is considered a bankrupt as of the time he files. His person and his assets come under the jurisdiction of the bankruptcy court as of that time; no formal court order is necessary to accomplish this.

Filing involuntary bankruptcy. Creditors of a debtor may force him into bankruptcy court. Creditors are permitted, under 11 USC 303, to commence either a Chapter VII liquidation proceeding or a Chapter XI rehabilitation proceeding against the debtor. Any debtor who could file a voluntary petition under Chapters VII or XI may be filed against, except farmers and corporations which are not moneyed, business, or commercial corporations. Thus, farmers and nonprofit corporations may voluntarily come into bankruptcy court, but they may not be forced into bankruptcy.

If the debtor has more than twelve creditors who have noncontingent claims against him, any three creditors with claims totaling $5,000 may file against him. Each individual creditor need not have a $5,000 claim: the three combined may have claims adding up to $5,000. If the debtor has twelve or fewer creditors with noncontingent claims against him, any one creditor with a $5,000 claim may file against him. If the debtor is a partnership, one or more of the general partners may file against the firm.

The complaint filed by the creditors will be served upon the debtor as in an ordinary civil lawsuit. The debtor will have twenty days after service of citation to respond to the complaint. If he does not respond, an order for relief will be entered against him by default, and he and his assets will come under the jurisdiction of the bankruptcy court.

The debtor has a possible defense with which he can escape the proceeding. If he is paying his debts as they come due, and if no assignee, receiver, secured party, or the like has taken charge of all or substantially all of his assets within 120 days of the filing of the complaint, the debtor may file an answer to the complaint and get the filing dismissed after a trial. Of course, if the debtor is not paying his debts as they mature; or if all or substantially all of his assets are under the control of an assignee or receiver, he has no defense. He would be wasting time and money contesting the filing.

If the debtor succeeds in getting an involuntary bankruptcy complaint against him dismissed, he is entitled to a judgment against the complaining creditors for the costs of the proceeding, a fee for his attorney, and any damages he suffered. In addition, he is entitled to a judgment for punitive damages if he can show that the creditors filed against him in bad faith. On the other hand, if the debtor cannot substantiate his defense, an order for relief will be issued to the creditors, and the debtor and his assets will come under the jurisdiction of the court.

Effect of filing of bankruptcy petition on other legal proceedings involving the debtor. 11 USC 362 provides that the filing of a bankruptcy petition operates as an automatic stay of the following sorts of legal procedures involving the debtor:

1. Commencement or continuation of suits to collect claims against the debtor arising before the filing of the petition.
2. Enforcement of judgments obtained against the debtor before the filing of the petition.
3. Acts to obtain property of the debtor (repossessions, for example).
4. Acts to create, perfect, or enforce liens against debtor's property (foreclosures of mechanic's liens, for example).

5. Numerous other proceedings of lesser importance.

The filing of a bankruptcy petition will not stay or affect the following:
1. Criminal prosecutions of the debtor.
2. Collection of alimony or child support from the debtor.
3. Actions by governments to enforce their police or regulatory powers (actions to abate public nuisances, to revoke professional licenses, etc.).
4. Enforcement of judgments, other than money judgments, obtained by governments or government agencies to enforce police or regulatory powers (enforcement of injunctions against water pollution, for example).
5. Issuance to the debtor of a notice of tax deficiency.
6. Other proceedings of lesser importance.

The types of legal proceedings that may be stayed by a bankruptcy proceeding are precisely those used by creditors against debtors when the race of diligence begins. Thus, the debtor faced with a race of diligence situation may run for cover by filing bankruptcy. Also, creditors who get a late start in the race of diligence may slow up their competitors by filing involuntary bankruptcy against the debtor. These facts explain why so many troubled debtors end up in bankruptcy court.

General duties of debtors. After the filing of a voluntary bankruptcy petition (or, to save time, along with such a petition), or after an order for relief is handed down in an involuntary bankruptcy case, 11 USC 521 requires the debtor to file with the court a list of all of his creditors. Also, he is required to file a complete schedule of assets and liabilities, and a statement of his financial affairs (unless the court orders otherwise, which it most likely will not do).

In a Chapter VII proceeding, the debtor must surrender to the jurisdiction of the court all his assets that are not exempt by law from the proceeding. The debtor need not surrender all of his assets; 11 USC 522(b) says that the debtor may retain as exempt property either:
1. The eleven specific categories of property listed in 11 USC 522(d), or
2. Property that is exempt from claims of creditors under the law of the state where the debtor resided for most of the 180 days immediately preceding the filing of the bankruptcy petition, and any joint tenancy or tenancy by the entireties property in which he may own an interest that is exempt from claims of creditors.

The eleven federal exemptions provided by 11 USC 522(d) are as follows:
1. Debtor's interest in his residence, up to a value of $7,500.
2. Debtor's interest, not to exceed $1,200, in one motor vehicle.
3. Debtor's interest, not to exceed $200 per item, in household furnishings, household goods, wearing apparel, appliances, books, animals, crops, musical instruments, etc., held for personal, family, or household use of debtor or his dependent.
4. Debtor's aggregate interest, not to exceed $500 in value, of jewelry held primarily for the personal, family, or household use of debtor or his dependent.
5. Debtor's aggregate interest, not to exceed $400 plus any unused amount of the exemption in 1 above, in any property.
6. Debtor's aggregate interest, not to exceed $750 in value, in implements, books, or tools of his trade or profession, or of his dependent's trade or profession.
7. Any unmatured life insurance contract owned by debtor, other than a credit life contract.
8. Debtor's aggregate interest—not to exceed $4,000 in value less property of the estate transferred to pay premiums—in the accrued dividends on, interest under, or loan value of any unmatured life insurance policy owned by debtor under which the

insured is the debtor or one of his dependents. (The major exemption here is essentially the cash surrender value of life policies up to $4,000.)
9. Professionally prescribed health aids for the debtor or his dependents.
10. The following sorts of income:
   a. Social Security benefits.
   b. Unemployment compensation.
   c. Welfare benefits.
   d. Veteran's benefits.
   e. Disability or illness benefits.
   f. Alimony, child support, or maintenance necessary for support of debtor and his dependents.
   g. Certain types of retirement benefits.
11. The following sorts of payments:
   a. Awards under crime victim reparation laws.
   b. Damages collected on account of the wrongful death of a person upon whom debtor was dependent for support, to the extent necessary for debtor's support and the support of his dependents.
   c. Life insurance proceeds from policies insuring persons of whom debtor was a dependent, to the extent needed for support of debtor or his dependents.
   d. Personal injury damages not to exceed $7,500, not counting damages for pain and suffering or for compensation for actual pecuniary loss, of debtor or of a person of whom debtor is a dependent. (Pain and suffering damages, or damages in compensation for actual pecuniary loss, are totally exempt.)
   e. Payments in compensation for loss of future earnings of debtor, or of a person of whom debtor is or was a dependent, necessary for support of debtor or of any dependent of his.

The Texas debtor must make a choice between claiming the federal exemptions listed above or the Texas state exemptions described in the chapter on civil procedure. The exemptions provided by Texas law are almost always more generous. The federal $7,500 homestead exemption is niggardly compared to the Texas exemption. The federal $1,200 motor vehicle exemption is niggardly compared to the complete Texas exemption; it becomes more niggardly when one considers that an auto and a truck may both be completely exempt under Texas law. The federal household goods exemption could be valuable if one owned many items of such goods—an entire library might be exempt under that provision, for instance, if each book were counted as a separate item and no individual book were worth $200. The other areas where the federal law is more generous are the area of cash surrender value of life insurance policies and awards of damages. The great majority of Texas debtors will be able to save more assets from the grasp of the bankruptcy court by electing the Texas exemptions over the federal ones.

If all assets of the debtor are deemed exempt, there will be no property to surrender to the court. If there are nonexempt assets, though, appointment of a trustee will be necessary. In such a case, the debtor must surrender all of his nonexempt assets and all records relevant to these assets to the trustee. He must also cooperate with the trustee in all particulars until the proceeding is closed.

The first meeting of creditors. The court will notify all creditors on the debtor's list of the filing of the petition and the granting of the order for relief. 11 USC 341 requires that a meeting of creditors be held within a reasonable time after the granting of the order for relief. In Chapter VII cases, two major things may occur here—examination of the debtor on his financial affairs, and selection of a permanent trustee (if one is needed).

The debtor must appear at this meeting and is required to submit himself to questioning by the creditors. He must answer all questions, unless a question would require him to furnish information that could be used against him in a criminal prosecution. In situations in which the debtor may legitimately "take the fifth" and avoid answering a question, application may be made for a grant of immunity from prosecution with respect to the answer to the question. If the immunity is granted, the debtor may then be compelled to answer. The giving of false answers by the debtor can of course result in his prosecution for perjury. Refusal to answer when not justified may result in his punishment for contempt. Noncooperation by the debtor may also result in a denial of his discharge from debts.

If the debtor has nonexempt assets, the court must appoint an interim trustee to take charge of them until the first meeting of creditors. At this meeting the creditors may elect another person as permanent trustee. If the creditors do not elect anyone, the interim trustee becomes the permanent trustee.

Powers of the Chapter VII trustee. The Chapter VII trustee is to manage and liquidate the nonexempt assets of the debtor and to distribute the proceeds according to law. As the personal representative of the debtor's bankrupt estate, he also has the power to sue and to be sued.

If the debtor is a business, the trustee may obtain authority from the court to operate the business until its affairs are wound up. If so, he may make contracts in the course of the business activity. He may sell assets, and—if authorized—he may borrow money or obtain credit, although this would be rare in a Chapter VII case.

With respect to the debtor's existing contracts at the time the order for relief is granted, the trustee may choose to perform these as made, or he may reject them and refuse to perform them. If he chooses to reject, he must inform the other party of his decision. The other party may then file a claim for damages for breach in the proceeding. The trustee has the same option with respect to the debtor's unexpired leases. He may continue in possession of the leased premises and pay the agreed rent, or he may terminate the lease and let the landlord file a damages claim. 11 USC 365 contains some rather complex provisions applicable to specific sorts of contracts and leases.

The trustee also has the power to collect the debtor's accounts receivable as of the granting of the order for relief. Under 11 USC 544, the trustee is in the position of being a lien creditor of the debtor as of the commencement of the case. He essentially will hold a security interest in all estate assets perfected as of the date of the beginning of the case, or a judgment lien obtained as of the beginning of the case. He will also have the rights of a bona fide purchaser of estate assets as of the beginning of the case. He thus has an interest in estate assets superior to unperfected security interests, unrecorded judgments, unrecorded deeds, etc.

Under 11 USC 545, the trustee may avoid liens of landlords, receivers, assignees for benefit of creditors, and the like. 11 USC 547 permits the trustee to avoid certain preferences granted by the debtor prior to commencement of the case. Generally, if the debtor (while insolvent) paid off a creditor within ninety days before the filing of the petition or made a partial payment to the creditor (while insolvent) within ninety days of the filing of the petition amounting to more than that creditor would realize out of the current bankruptcy proceeding, the trustee may recover the payment from the creditor.

Such preferences to insiders—family members, partners, corporate directors of the debtor, etc.—may be avoided if made within a year of the filing of the petition if the insider had reason to believe that the debtor was insolvent at the time of the payment and the debtor actually was insolvent at that time. Purchases of goods or services for cash or payment of ordinary business debts within forty-five days of their incurring are not deemed to be preferences. Such payments by the debtor may not be recovered.

Under 11 USC 548 the trustee may avoid certain fraudulent transfers of property made by the debtor and certain fraudulent obligations incurred by the debtor. In general, the following sorts of fraudulent conveyances are voidable if made within a year of the filing of the bankruptcy petition:

1. Conveyances made with intent to hinder, delay, or defraud creditors.
2. Conveyances of property for less than fair consideration made while debtor was insolvent, or that caused debtor to become insolvent.

The following sorts of fraudulent obligations are voidable if incurred within a year of the filing of the bankruptcy petition:

1. A transaction that reduced debtor's capital to an unreasonably low level.
2. The incurring of a debt by debtor that would be beyond his ability to repay at maturity.
3. Obligations incurred by a general partnership to a partner at a time when the partnership was insolvent.

Postpetition property and debts of debtor. Generally, a debtor is required to turn over to the trustee the nonexempt property he owned at the time of an order for relief in his case was granted. In addition, 11 USC 541(a)(5) requires that he turn over to the trustee the following sorts of property acquired, or the right to which is acquired, within 180 days after the granting of the order for relief:

1. Property acquired by devise, bequest, or inheritance. If the right of the debtor to such property is established within 180 days of the granting of the order for relief, the property goes to the trustee, even though the debtor might not actually receive the inheritance until the 180 days have passed.
2. Property acquired through a property settlement with the spouse, as a result of a divorce or annulment decree.
3. Property acquired as a beneficiary of a life insurance policy or of a death benefit plan.

All other property acquired by the debtor after the granting of the order for relief—including personal earnings and the like—is his. Also, all debts incurred by the debtor after the granting of the order for relief are not under the jurisdiction of the court, and will not be discharged.

Creditors and claims. If a creditor desires to have the opportunity to collect something out of the bankrupt estate, he must file a claim with the trustee. If the creditor himself does not file, the debtor or trustee may do it for him (11 USC 501).

If the debtor is a corporation or partnership, shareholders and partners must file proofs of interest if they are to participate in the division of assets after all creditors are paid. As a practical matter, there is probably little point to filing a proof of interest in a Chapter VII proceeding, since the assets will not suffice to pay off creditors.

A claim is considered to be allowed unless the debtor, another creditor, or another party with an interest in the proceeding objects to it. If there is an objection, 11 USC 502 requires that a hearing be held on the question of allowance. The court may totally allow, totally disallow, or partially allow the claim.

Some sorts of claims must be partially disallowed if contested. These include:

1. Claims for unmatured interest. The holder of a promissory note of the debtor's

maturing in 1982 could not claim interest up to maturity, if the bankruptcy proceeding was filed in 1979.

2. Claims by insiders for services rendered, to the extent that the amount of the claim exceeds the fair value of the services.

3. Claims for fees by the debtor's attorney, if the claim exceeds the fair value of the services rendered. The attorney's claim will be allowed for a fair fee and no more.

4. Unmatured alimony and child support claims.

5. Claims for rent under a breached lease of real property. A landlord may claim only past-due rent up until the time of termination, plus either one year of future rent or 15 percent of the rent payable under the remaining term of the lease not to exceed three years, whichever figure is greater. This period is computed from the date the petition is filed or the date the landlord took possession of the premises, whichever is longer. In other words, future rent claims of landlords will be limited to no less than one year's rent and no more than three years' rent.

6. Claims for damages for breach of employment contracts are limited to accrued and unpaid back pay plus one year's future pay.

Contingent liabilities, such as liability as an endorser of a promissory note, may be handled in two ways. The bankruptcy proceeding may be held open until the note matures to see if the contingent claim will ripen into a liquidated claim, or the court may estimate the value of the contingent claim as of the present and allow it for that amount.

Unliquidated claims, such as tort claims against the debtor, may be handled in the same manner. The bankruptcy may be held open while the tort claimant sues on his claim and seeks to reduce it to judgment, or the claim may be valued by the court and allowed for the amount of value the court places on it.

Disposal and settlement of secured claims. Under 11 USC 725, the trustee may dispose of property upon which a creditor has a lien other than a tax lien. Notice of the proposed disposal must be given, and a hearing held upon its advisability. The result of the disposal will normally be that the lienholder recovers his claim in full or simply gets possession of his collateral.

Property upon which some governmental entity has a tax lien will be disposed of under 11 USC 724. Either the property itself will be divided among the claimants in the order specified by 11 USC 724, or the property will be sold and the proceeds will be so divided.

Distribution of the estate. After creditor claims have been filed and allowed, assets of the estate have been collected and liquidated, and property in which secured creditors have an interest has been disposed of, the estate is distributed to the creditors in accordance with the directives of 11 USC 507 and 726. The priority of distribution is as follows:

1. Administrative expenses—court costs, trustee's fees, and so on.

2. Claims arising in involuntary cases after the filing of the petition but before the granting of the order of relief.

3. Wage claims, salary claims, or commission claims, including vacation, severance, and sick pay earned by the claimant within ninety days of the filing of the petition or the cessation of the debtor's business, whichever happens first, but limited to $2,000 per claimant. (The claimant is an unsecured creditor for the balance, if any, of his claim.)

4. Claims for contributions to employee benefit plans arising from services rendered up to 180 days before the filing of the petition or the debtor's cessation of business, whichever is earlier, subject to several limitations.

5. Claims of individuals arising from deposits made before the commencement of the

case in connection with the purchase, lease, or rental of property—or the purchase of services for the personal, family, or household use of such individuals—that were not delivered or provided, up to a maximum of $900 per individual. (Should an individual have a claim of this sort for more than $900, he will be an unsecured creditor for the balance.)

6. Unsecured tax claims.
7. Timely filed unsecured claims, for actual monetary losses.
8. Tardily filed unsecured claims, for actual monetary losses.
9. Exemplary or punitive damage claims, and claims for fines, penalties, and forfeitures.
10. Interest at the legal rate (9 percent per annum) on allowed claims.
11. If anything remains after all this, it goes to the debtor.

Claims of one class are paid in full before claims of the subsequent class are paid. Normally, the fund from which claims are paid will be exhausted by claims in the seventh or eighth category if not before.

The debtor's discharge. The debtor will normally be discharged from all dischargeable debts at the end of a Chapter VII proceeding. However, 11 USC 727(a) provides that the debtor shall not be granted a discharge if:

1. The debtor is not an individual. (Corporations are not entitled to such a discharge, nor are other forms of organization.)
2. The debtor made fraudulent conveyances of his property within one year of the commencement of the proceeding.
3. The debtor did not turn over all of his nonexempt property to the trustee.
4. The debtor concealed, destroyed, mutilated, or falsified his business and financial records or failed to keep such records.
5. The debtor paid or received bribes in connection with the proceeding.
6. The debtor committed perjury in the course of the proceedings.
7. The debtor failed to explain satisfactorily why he did not have enough assets to meet his liabilities.
8. The debtor withheld records and other information about his financial affairs from the trustee.
9. The debtor refused to obey a lawful order of the court.
10. The debtor refused to answer a question in court when ordered to do so by the court.
11. The debtor was granted a discharge in another bankruptcy proceeding commenced within six years of the filing of the petition in the present case. (One may not obtain a discharge from debts in bankruptcy more than once every six years.)

The trustee or a creditor may object to the discharge of the debtor. If anyone objects to the discharge, the trustee may be ordered by the court to investigate whether a ground exists for denial of the discharge. If grounds are discovered, the court will deny discharge.

11 USC 524 requires that the debtor appear before the court at the time discharge is usually granted. At this time the debtor is informed that his discharge is granted, or that his discharge has been denied. If it is denied, the court must explain the reasons for denial. A discharge once granted remains revocable for at least one year, or longer if discharge is granted before the closing of the case. The trustee or a creditor may request revocation of a discharge if:

1. The debtor obtained his discharge through fraud, and the fraud was not discovered until after the granting of the discharge.
2. The debtor acquired, or got the right to acquire, property that should have been

turned over to the trustee (such as an inheritance), but he did not do so.
3. The debtor refused to obey an order of the court.

The objection on grounds of fraud must be made within a year of the discharge. The other two objections may be made within a year after discharge or within a year of the closing of the case, whichever comes later. No discharge may be revoked without notice of the proposed revocation being given the debtor, and a hearing being held on the matter.

Decisions of the bankruptcy court upon matters pertaining to discharge and revocation of discharge—and upon such other matters as allowance or disallowance of claims—are appealable. Each federal court circuit may establish appeals panels of three bankruptcy judges to handle these appeals. Should a circuit choose not to establish such panels, appeals of bankruptcy matters will run to the ordinary federal district courts. From the appeals panels or the district courts, appeals will run to the federal courts of appeal.

11 USC 523 provides that the following sorts of debts are not dischargeable in bankruptcy:

1. Most taxes (except taxes for which the debtor filed honest returns more than two years before the filing of the bankruptcy petition).
2. Debts incurred through false pretenses, false representations, or fraud—or debts so extended, renewed, or refinanced.
3. Debts incurred through use of false financial statements made with intent to deceive, upon which the creditor justifiably relied.
4. Debts not included by the debtor on his list of assets and liabilities, and debts for which the creditor was not listed on the debtor's list of creditors, unless the creditor knew of the bankruptcy proceeding and did not file a claim.
5. Debts incurred through fraud or defalcation while acting as a fiduciary, or through embezzlement or larceny.
6. Alimony, maintenance, and child support.
7. Debts incurred through willful and malicious injury to person or property of another.
8. Nontax fines, penalties, or forfeitures owed to a government, unless imposed for an incident occurring more than three years before the date of filing of the bankruptcy petition.
9. Debts incurred as educational loans, unless the loan matured more than five years before the filing of the bankruptcy petition, or unless nondischarge would impose undue hardship upon the debtor and his dependents.
10. Debts that could have been discharged in a prior bankruptcy proceeding involving the debtor but were not so discharged.

If a creditor wants to have a claim against the debtor preserved because it was incurred through fraud, false financial statement, breach of fiduciary duty, theft, embezzlement, or willful and malicious injury, the creditor must ask the court to declare it nondischargeable. The court must then hold a hearing on the matter of dischargeability and make a determination. The court's decision upon such a matter is appealable.

11 USC 524 provides that the debtor's discharge voids all judgments against him except those on undischargeable debts. It also operates as an injunction against commencement or continuation of any legal process against the debtor to collect a dischargeable debt. Debts secured by security interests or the like in exempt property which the debtor did not surrender to the trustee are of course not discharged. If the debtor retains his homestead, for instance, and the homestead is not yet paid for, he must continue to make payments on it.

Chapter XI proceedings. The purpose of a Chapter XI proceeding is the rehabilitation of the business debtor. Such a debtor may file a voluntary Chapter XI petition to try to prevent the bones of his business from being picked clean by creditors engaging in the race of diligence. An involuntary petition may be filed against such a debtor by creditors seeking to stop him from ruining his business through incompetent management.

A business debtor against whom an involuntary Chapter VII petition has been filed may ask the court to convert the proceeding into a Chapter XI proceeding. In order to accomplish this the debtor must convince the court that the business could be salvaged. Since a business is worth more as a going concern than its assets are worth upon liquidation, the welfare of all concerned would be served by rehabilitation. Thus, conversion of Chapter VII into Chapter XI would be denied only when there appears to be no hope for salvation of the ailing concern.

Upon the granting of an order for relief in a Chapter XI case, all or nearly all legal proceedings in process against the debtor are stayed. The debtor may ask to be continued as the manager of the business during the bankruptcy proceeding; he will be permitted to continue the business as "debtor in possession" unless good reason exists to turn control of the concern to someone else. If the business is a sole proprietorship or a partnership, the proprietor or partners will run the business as debtors in possession. If the debtor is a corporation, the duly chosen management will do so. If the debtor is permitted to remain in possession, the court may impose limitations on his authority, such as restrictions on borrowing money or purchasing inventory on credit.

If the debtor's debts exceed $5 million—or if a creditor or shareholder of the debtor so requests—the court may appoint an examiner to investigate the affairs of the debtor and to determine whether or not it is advisable to leave the debtor in possession. If the examiner concludes that this is not in the interests of creditors and shareholders, he will report to the court that a trustee should be appointed for the debtor and that the debtor's management authority should be terminated.

A creditor or shareholder may ask the court to appoint a trustee for the debtor on the grounds of fraud, incompetence, dishonesty, or gross mismanagement by the current management without going through the process of an investigation by an examiner. If appointment of a trustee is requested, the court will hold a hearing on the matter and make a determination. If a trustee is appointed, the debtor has no more authority to operate the business. If the business involved is a proprietorship, partnership, or small corporation, the trustee may be able to totally displace the proprietor, partners, or corporate management. If the business is a large corporation, the trustee may find himself compelled to work through the existing management, merely compelling that management to work under his authority and supervision.

The whole purpose of the Chapter XI proceeding is the implementation of a plan for curing the difficulties of the debtor. Plans may vary from the very simple to the very complicated. A small business in difficulty may be saved simply by scaling down the obligations owed by the firm to unsecured creditors. On the other hand, the only way in which a large insolvent corporation may be salvaged is by depriving the current shareholders of their equity in the concern and making shareholders of the corporate creditors. A plan might thus involve adjustments of claims of unsecured creditors or an adjustment of the various liens and security interests in firm assets held by secured creditors. In the extreme case, it might also involve radical surgery on the capital structure of the debtor.

In voluntary Chapter XI cases, the debtor will as likely as not file a proposed plan with his petition. In involuntary cases, the debtor may well propose a plan shortly after the order for relief is granted. In any case, so long as the debtor is in possession only he may file a plan within 120 days of the granting of the order of relief. If he is displaced as manager by a trustee, the trustee may file a plan. If the debtor remains in possession but does not file a plan within 120 days of the order for relief, a creditor or shareholder may then file a plan. Meanwhile, creditors and shareholders are required to file claims with the court, as in Chapter VII proceedings.

A proposed plan must be submitted to those classes of creditors, interestholders, and shareholders whose interests will be affected by it. For the plan to be accepted, 11 USC 1126 requires that a majority in number of each class of creditor, interestholder, or shareholder, and two-thirds in dollar amount of claim or value of each class must vote affirmatively.

If a proposed plan is rejected by the voters, another plan must be presented for consideration by someone; otherwise the proceeding will be converted into a Chapter VII liquidation. If a plan is accepted by the voters, notice of acceptance is given to the court, which must then call a hearing on the question of confirmation. At this hearing any interested party may ask the court to veto the plan, despite the fact that it has been accepted by the required majority of creditors and others concerned. The court must be convinced that the plan is fair to all interests concerned, that it is feasible, and that it meets the numerous other requirements of 11 USC 1129.

If the court refuses to confirm, the alternatives are formation of a new plan, or conversion of the proceeding to Chapter VII. If it is confirmed, it is binding on all creditors, interestholders, and shareholders, including those who voted against it and those who did not vote at all. Those obligations of the debtor discharged under the plan are then discharged. Those liens and security interests which are to be restructured are restructured. If existing shares of a corporation are to be canceled, they are canceled. If new shares are to be issued, the debtor is authorized to proceed with the issuance. If the plan calls for payments of money to various creditors, the payments called for in the plan become obligations of the debtor.

The plan as confirmed must be carried out. 11 USC 1142 provides that the court may order the debtor to perform required acts under the plan; failure to do so would constitute contempt of court.

If the confirmation of the plan was procured by fraud, a party in interest may request revocation of the confirmation within 180 days of the order of confirmation. Upon receipt of such a request the court may hold a hearing; after the hearing it will decide whether or not to revoke. This decision is also appealable.

Chapter XIII proceedings. The Chapter XIII proceeding is one which permits adjustment of the debts of a person with regular income without the necessity for liquidating his nonexempt assets. Only the debtor may petition for a Chapter XIII proceeding. An order for relief is considered to have been issued as of the time of filing, so that all legal proceedings against the debtor are stayed. A trustee must be appointed for the debtor under Chapter XIII, but if the debtor is a self-employed businessman he may continue to operate his business as a debtor in possession.

The debtor must file a plan with the court for the adjustment of his debts. The plan must provide for the payment in part or in full of all claims creditors may have against the debtor as of the time the petition is filed. It may also provide for the modification of security interests and the like in the debtor's assets. The essence of the plan must be that the debtor will pay a portion of his income over to the trustee, who will distribute it to creditors in accordance with the terms of the plan. The plan normally must provide for payments to terminate in three years or less, although the court may for good reason permit the plan to call for up to five years of payments. The details of plan requirements are found in 11 USC 1322.

Unsecured creditors have nothing to say about the debtor's plan. If the plan is confirmed, they are bound by it. On the other hand, secured creditors who file claims must all approve the plan. If all secured creditors do not approve, the court cannot confirm.

If the plan has been approved by all secured creditors, and the court finds it fair and believes that the debtor will be able to make all required payments and that the unsecured creditors will get more from it than they would from a Chapter VII liquidation, 11 USC 1325 provides that the court shall confirm the plan.

If confirmation of a plan is denied, the debtor must either devise a new plan or suffer its conversion into a Chapter VII proceeding. Failure to make payments provided for in the plan will also cause conversion to Chapter VII. In addition, 11 USC 1330 provides that the confirmation of a plan may be revoked due to debtor fraud in procuring confirmation. An objection must be filed within 180 days of confirmation; a hearing must then be held, after which the court decides whether or not to revoke. This decision is appealable.

Completion of all obligations called for in the plan will discharge the debtor from his dischargeable debts under 11 USC 1328. In addition, if unforeseen circumstances render the debtor's compliance with the terms of the plan impossible, the court may grant him a discharge even if all payments have not been made.

Antidiscrimination provision. 11 USC 525 forbids a governmental unit to discriminate against a person who is obtaining or has obtained relief from his debts in bankruptcy. Governmental units may not refuse to issue licenses or franchises for this reason, nor may they revoke them for this reason. They may not refuse or terminate employment for this reason, nor may they discriminate in matters of employment for such reason.

This provision, though, does not apply to private employers. Bankruptcy would still be a valid ground for refusal to hire or termination of employment for private employers.

Index

A

Abandoned Motor Vehicle Act, 572
Abandonment: easement, 749; of motor vehicle, 572, 573; of rented premises by tenant, 796, 770; of property, 333
Abatement, 828; of gift, 818
Absence without official leave (AWOL), 97
Abstract company, 757
Abstract: judgment, 150, 779; land title, 757
Abuse of process, 74, 75
Acceleration clause, 371, 382, 413, 538
Acceptance: of delivery order, 456; of draft, 398; of offer, 197-99
Acceptor, 397
Accession, 335, 336
Accident report, 576
Accommodation acceptor, 398, 399
Accommodation endorsement, 378
Accommodation maker, 397
Accord and satisfaction, 261
Account stated, 261, 262
Accounts: as collateral, 531, 532; multiple party, 348, 349, 421

Accountant-client privilege, 114
Accumulated earnings tax, 662
Ad valorem duty, 474
Ademption, 818
Adjudication hearing, juvenile court, 170
Adjusted gross estate, 838
Administrative agency: executive branch, 178; executive power, 180; independent, 177, 178; judicial power, 181-84; legislative power, 179; Texas, 178
Administrative law, 14
Administrative remedies, exhaustion of, 129, 186
Admiralty law, 94
Adoption; of child, 34, 35; of adult, 35
Adulterated commodity, 45
Adultery, as divorce ground, 30
Adversary system, 7
Adverse claim: to commercial paper, 382; as defense to payment of commercial paper, 393, 394; to investment security, 665, 666; to life insurance proceeds, 835
Adverse possession: of personal property, 333-35; of real property, 761-63
Advisory opinion, 129, 130
Affidavit: as evidence, 117, 143; of continued use, 605; of incontestability, 605; self-proving, 812, 813, 822
Affirmative action, 295, 296
Affirmative defense, 136
African law, 11

After-acquired property clause, 530
After-acquired title, 760, 761
Age Discrimination in Employment Act, 293, 296
Agent: in general, 282-90; nondelegable authority to, 281
Agency shop, 314
Air Cargo Deregulation Act, 464, 465
Air pollution control, 796
Alcoholic Beverages Code, 58-60
Alcoholic Beverages Commission, 181, 184
Alien, 213, 214
Alien corporation, 726
Allergy, as cause of product liability, 506
Allgemeine Landrecht, 6
Alter ego, 708, 709
American Bar Association, 16, 17
Amphetamines, 58, 69
Animals: injury by, 75; ownership of, 331
Annexation, 792
Annual percentage rate of finance charge, 552-56
Annulment, 25-31
Annulment, grounds for: concealed divorce, 29; duress, 28; fraud, 28; impotence, 28; mental incompetence, 28, 29; underage, 27; under influence of alcohol or narcotics, 28; valid preexisting marriage, 25, 26
Antitrust Division, U.S. Department of Justice, 620, 719, 720
Antitrust: enforcement (federal), 620; (Texas), 621; violations, 219
Appeal: administrative, 184, 185; bankruptcy, 855; civil, 145; court-martial, 98; criminal, 122; eminent domain, 788; real property appraisal, 781; zoning, 795
Appeal bond: civil, 145; forcible detainer, 774
Appellant, 15
Appraisal Review Board, 784
Apprehension, hindering of, 49
Appurtenant easement, 749
Arbitration: under federal law, 166, 167; prior agreement to, 129; under Texas law, 165, 166
Arbitration and award, 263, 264
Army Corps of Engineers, 609

Arraignment, 105
Arrest: of criminal suspect, 99-101; evasion of, 49; of judgment, 120
Arson, 38, 39
Articles of dissolution, 722
Articles of incorporation, 645
Articles of merger, 712
Artificial insemination, 35
Artisan's lien, 327-29; foreclosure of, 328, 329
Artist's Consignment Act, 443
Assault: aggravated, 54; causing bodily injury, 54; deadly, 54; simple, 54; as tort, 73, 74
Assessment ratio, 780
Assigned risk plan, 582
Assignment: for benefit of creditors, 846; of commercial paper, 376; of contract rights in general, 246; of contracts for sale of goods, 436; of copyright, 600; of lease, 769; of life insurance policy 833; multiple assignment of same right 247; of nonexistent rights, 245, 246; partial, 251, 252; of partner's interest in partnership, 637, 638; of patent, 593; recording of, 247, 250; of right to proceeds from letter of credit, 495; of security interest, 537; of trademark, 606
Assumed Name Statute, 630, 631
Assumption of risk: as defense in negligence case, 85; as defense in product liability, 515
Assurance of performance, 489, 490
Attachment: in general, 92, 93, 132, 133; of goods covered by warehouse receipt, 451; of investment security, 670; of security interest, 528; of witness, 111
Attorney-client privilege, 114
Attorney's fees, 18
Attractive nuisance, 82
Auction: by bulk sale, 482; by open bid, 197; by sealed bid, 199, 200
Audit of income tax returns, 71, 72, 98
Authenticating trustee, 669
Authority: apparent, 283, 285, 286; of attorney, 285; of auctioneer, 284; of business manager, 283; of debt collector, 285; by estoppel, 283; express, 282; of

factor, 284; implied, 282; of real estate broker, 284; of real property manager, 283; of selling agent, 284, 285; of store clerk, 285; of traveling salesman, 285

B

Bad conduct discharge, 97
Bail, 101, 102; jumping of, 50
Bailment, 322–30
Bait and switch, 558, 615
Bank account, death of owner of, 415, 416
Bank deposits, 411–24
Bank draft, 368
Bank records, confidentiality of, 424–26
Bankruptcy: claims of creditors in, 852, 853; discharge of debtor in, 854; first meeting of creditors, 850, 851; fraudulent transfer of assets in, 852; interim trustee in, 851; involuntary, 848; objection to discharge of debtor in, 854, 855; preferences in, 851, 852; trustee in, 851–58; voluntary, 847, 848
Bankruptcy Court, 98
Bankruptcy fraud, 62
Bankruptcy Reform Act, 98
Bar examination, 17
Barbiturates, 58, 69
Barratry: as crime, 50; as illegal contract, 220
Battery, 73
Battle of the forms, 432, 433
Bigamy, 27, 55
Bill of lading: in general, 452–54; clean bill, 452; foul bill, 452; material alteration of, 453; on-board bill, 466; Pomerene Act, 444–56; received for shipment bill, 466; spent bill, 454; through bill, 453, 458; unauthorized completion of, 453
Billing errors, 556–58
Blackmail, 64
Blank endorsement, 377
Blended trust, 804
Blood, warranty of merchantability with respect to, 506
Board of Adjustment, 795
Board of Equalization, 780
Board of Interferences, 592
Bona fide purchaser: of goods, 483, 484; of investment security, 665; of real estate, 755, 756
Bonds: construction, 359; convertible, 654; cost, 145; fidelity, 358, 359; investment security, 653; payment, 359, 778; performance, 359; possession, 774; registered, 653; replevy, 133; supersedeas, 145
Borrowed servant doctrine, 307, 309
Branch banking, 610
Breach: anticipatory, 258, 489; of contract, 389; of fiduciary duty, 392; of promise to marry, 229
Breakage, 475
Breathalyser test, 579, 580
Bribery: commercial, 45; as federal crime, 62; of public official or witness, 62; in sporting events, 62; as Texas crime, 47
Bridge erection, regulation of, 797
Broadcast networks, 610
Broker: customs, 474, 475; real estate, 284; securities, 669, 670
Buenos Aires Convention, 602
Buergerliches Gesetzbuch, 6
Building restrictions, 792
Bulk sales, 479–82
Burden of proof: civil, 141, 142; criminal, 111
Bureau of Customs, 602, 607
Burglary, 41; of coin-operated machine, 41, 42; of vehicle, 42
Business crimes, 68
Business trusts, 643, 644
Buyer's remedies: on seller's breach, 521,

522; on seller's insolvency, 522
Bylaws, 648

C

C&F: duties under, 490; risk of loss under, 441, 442
C.I.F.: duties under, 490; risk of loss under, 441, 442
C.O.D.: in general, 485; risk of loss under, 441, 442
Cancellation proceeding, 605
Canvassing operations, 180
Capias, 104
Capital case sentencing, 119, 120
Capital gain, long-term, 660
Capital surplus, 652, 657
Capture, rule of, 747
Carmack Amendment, 453, 458, 460, 461, 462, 466, 469
Carriage of Goods by Sea Act, 452, 469, 471
Carrier: bonded, 474, 475; common, 457, 458; international air, 465; private, 462
Carrier's lien: 330; foreclosure of, 453, 454
Cartel, 620
Case or controversy, 127, 128
Cashier's check, 368
Casualty to identified goods, 491, 492
Cease and desist order, 184, 615
Certificate of authority, 727
Certificate of dissolution, 722
Certificate of medical examination for mental illness, 156, 157
Certificate of merger, 715
Certificate of public convenience and necessity, 462
Certification election, 312, 313

Certification mark, 602
Certiorari, writ of, 95, 96
Chain of title, 756, 757
Chain letter promotion, 47
Chain referral plan, 559
Challenge for cause: civil, 141; criminal, 110
Champerty, 220
Chancery, 14
Change of venue, 107, 108
Chapter XI proceeding, 708, 855-57
Chapter XIII proceeding, 857, 858
Charging order, 638
Charitable contribution, promise to make, 212
Charitable deduction, 839
Charitable trust, 804, 805
Chattel paper, 532
Checks: in general, 368; certification of, as discharge of parties to payment, 408; certified, 368; city check, 411, 412; collection process for, 411, 412; country check, 411, 412; issuance of bad check, 44; "on us" check, 411; overdue, 420; stale check, 420; traveler's check, 368, 369
Child labor prohibitions, 297, 298
Childproof package, 613
Child support, 31, 33
Chinese law, 11
Citizen's arrest, 100
Civil Aeronautics Act, 464
Civil Aeronautics Board, 183, 464, 608
Civil appeals, court of, 93
Civil complaint, 130
Civil disorders, furthering, 65
Civil law system, 7, 728, 729
Class gifts, 734, 744
Clayton Act, 616, 617, 620, 717
Clean Air Act: federal, 566, 796; Texas, 796
Clergyman-penitent privilege, 114
Close corporation, 704-6
Closed shop, 314
Co-beneficiaries, 801
Co-maker, 396, 397
Co-sureties, 354, 356
Co-trustees, 801, 809
Coast Guard, 797

Cocaine, 57, 69
Codeine, 57, 69
Code Napoleon, 6, 12
Code of Criminal Procedure, 99–126
Code of Federal Regulations, 15
Code of Justinian, 5
Code of Professional Responsibility, 17
Codicil, 814
Coercion, of public servant or voter, 47
Cognovit note, 373
Collective bargaining, 314, 315; units of, 312
Collective mark, 602, 603
Commercial paper: assignment of, 376; forged endorsement of, 378, 379; incomplete, 372, 373; inconsistent provisions in, 374; negotiability of, 369–74; nondefenses to payment of, 393–95; overdue, 381, 382; special endorsement of, 377; ultra vires issue of, 387, 395. *See also* Defenses to payment of commercial paper; Discharge of commercial paper
Commissioner of Labor Statistics, 299
Commissioner of Patents, 591
Commissioners on Uniform State Laws, 16
Commitment, civil: of alcoholics, 158, 159; of drug addicts, 159; of the mentally ill, 157, 158; of the mentally retarded, 159–61
Common law, 5, 6
Common stock, 655
Community property, 344–46
Community service probation, 121, 122
Comparative negligence, 85
Compensation: for past official behavior, 48; for victims of crime, 174–76
Compensatory damges, 270, 272, 519, 520
Composition of creditors, 210, 845
Composition of matter, 589
Compounding, 49
Compromise of claims, 209
Compromise: of liquidated debts, 209, 210, 211; of unliquidated debts, 209–11
Comptroller of Currency, 610
Comptroller of Public Accounts, 413, 414 622–26
Condition precedent, 236, 237, 253, 254
Condition subsequent, 254

Conditional endorsement, 378
Confession, 9
Conflict of interest, attorneys, 19
Conflict of laws: civil, 139, 140; criminal, 125, 126; in estate administration, 829, 830
Confucianism, 11
Confusion, 336
Consanguinity, 27
Consequential damages, 273, 521, 522
Consideration, 207–12; extreme hardship as, 211
Consignment, 443
Consolidation, 713
Conspiracy: against civil rights of citizens, 62; criminal, 55, 56; in restraint of trade, 621
Constitutions, 12
Construction bonds, 359
Constructive eviction, 768, 769
Constructive trust, 810
Consumer Credit Code, 222–27, 260
Consumer Credit Commissioner, 222, 223, 544, 611
Consumer Credit Protection Act, 497, 552, 565; antigarnishment provisions of, 565
Consumer Leasing Act, 555
Consumer Product Safety Act, 516, 517, 613, 622
Consumer Product Safety Commission, 516, 517
Container: bailment of, 324; repossession of, 539
Contempt: administrative, 184; in giving of deposition, 104; before grand jury, 103; ordinary, 165; summary punishment of, 164, 165; in protective order proceedings, 174
Contestability: of life insurance policy, 834, 835; of trademark, 604, 605
Contingent fee, 18, 146
Contingent remainder, 739, 740
Continuing criminal enterprise, 70, 71
Contract: of adhesion, 200; anti-assignment clause in, 245; assignment of rights for, 246; assignment of rights for sale of goods, 436; cancellation of, as remedy for breach, 520, 521; delivery term, for

sale of goods, 430, 431; duress, as reason for rescission of, 204, 205; express, 191; illegal, enforceability of, 226; illegality of, for curruption of objectivity of communications media, 221; impossibility of performance of, 267, 268; injurious to governmental processes, 220; inspection of goods by buyer, 487; installment contracts, performance of, 257, 258, 490; interpretation of, 233–35; land, 752; to make a will, 816, 817; in obstruction of justice, 220; performance of, to personal satisfaction, 256, 257; for sale of land, 751–63; ultra vires, 213. *See also* Discharge of contract; Contract rights

Contract carrier, 462

Contract rights: assignable, 246; nonassignable, 245; of assignees, 248, 249; assignment of, in general, 246

Contractor's lien, 777–79

Contractual capacity, 213–16

Contribution among co-sureties, 356

Contributory infringement, 595

Contributory negligence, 85

Controlled substances, 57

Controlled Substances Act, 57, 58

Conversion, 75; by bailee (as crime), 40

Convertible bond, 654

Convertible debenture, 654

Coordination, 687

Copyright, 599–602

Corporations: in general, 645–731; annual financial report to SEC by, 696, 697; business combinations forbidden by Texas law, 650; by estoppel, 647, 648; combinations of, 717–19; control of, 656; criminal punishment for, 56; dissolution of, 707, 708, 721–26; division of, 716, 717; finance of, 653–64; foreign, 726–29; horizontal corporate combination, 717; income taxation of, 728; insiders of, 696, 697, 698; inspection of books and records of, 722, 723; liquidation of, 724, 725; multiple, 663; piercing the corporate veil, 708–10; power of, 650–52; pure conglomerate combination, 719; quarterly financial report to SEC by, 697; receivership of, 707, 723, 724; sale of assets of, 713–15; ultra vires issue of commercial paper by, 395; vertical corporate combination, 717; voluntary dissolution of, 721, 722. *See also* Directors, corporate

Cost bond, 145

Counterbond, 774

Counterclaim: mandatory, 136, 137; permissive, 137; as defense to payment of commercial paper, 393

Counterfeit: in general, 42, 65, 66; money, 365, 366

Counteroffer, 196

County court: at law, 92; constitutional, 92

Court-martial: in general, 98; special, 98; summary, 97

Courts: federal district, 94; of Appeal, 95; of civil appeals, 93; of Chancery, 13; of Claims, 96; of criminal appeals, 93; of Customs and Patent Appeals, 96, 592, 605; justice of the peace, 91, 92; juvenile, 168–71; of Military Appeals, 98; municipal, 92; of Military Review, 98; small claims, 91; Supreme Court of Texas, 93, 94; Supreme Court of the United States, 95, 96; Tax, 98; Texas district, 93; United States magistrate's, 94

Cover, 521

Credit advertising, 546

Credit bureau, 549–52

Credit cards: in general, 497–502; abuse of, 43; cash discount by merchant honoring, 500

Creditor, assignment for benefit of, 846; hindering of, 43, 44

Creditor beneficiary, 241

Crime Victims Compensation Act, 174–76

Criminal attempt, 55

Criminal charges, defenses to, 56

Criminal mischief, 40

Crinimal prosecutions, discharge due to delay, 108

Criminal simulation, 42, 43

Criminal summons, 101
Crop, contract for sale of, 440
Cross examination, 112
Cumulative voting, 674, 675
Cursory review, 691
Custodian of will, 822
Custom-made goods, 231, 440
Customary review, 690, 691
Customs: broker, 474, 475; Bureau of, 602, 607; Collector of, 439; Court of, 96; duties, 474; entry, 474; invoice, 474; violations, 66
Cy pres, 805

D

Damages: compensatory, 270-72; consequential, 273, 521, 522; duty to mitigate, 275; incidental, 272, 273; liquidated, 274; nominal, 273; nonconformity, 521; for nondelivery or repudiation, 521; for pain and suffering, in negligence cases, 86; punitive, 273; recovery of contract price for, 271, 272; reckless, 40; special, 273; speculative, 273, 274
Damages release, 747
Danger of the sea, 467
Dangerous Drug Act, 58
Dead Man Statute, 142, 143, 824
Debenture, 654
Debt Collection Act, 562
Debt collection practices, 561-65
Debtor in possession, 856-58
Deceptive business practices (as crime), 45
Deceptive sales contest, 45
Deceptive Trade Practices Act, 79, 206, 207, 558-61, 568, 614, 615

Decertification of union, 314
Declaration against interest, 115
Declaratory judgment, 130
Deed, 735, 753-63
De facto corporation, 647
Defamation, 77-79
Default judgment, 137: vacation of, 137, 138
Defenses to payment of commercial paper: adverse claim, 393, 394; breach of contract, 398; breach of fiduciary duty, 392; counterclaim, 393; delivery for special purpose, 391, 392; discharge of commercial paper, 391; discharge in bankruptcy, 386; duress, 390; extreme duress, 385, 386; forgery, 386; hardship, 394; illegality, 390; inability to pay, 393; incapacity, 385; incapacity of payee, 394; known discharge, 386; lack of capacity, 390; limited contractual capacity, 390; loss, 393; material alteration, 388; minority, 385; mutual mistake, 390; nondelivery, 391; nonexistence of payee, 394; nonnegotiability, 393; nonperformance of condition precedent, 390; partial payment, 391; personal defense to payment, 389, 393; prior payment, 391; real defenses, 385-89; set-off, 393; statute of limitations, 389; stoppage of payment, 394, 395; theft, 392; unauthorized completion, 391; unauthorized signature, 387; unconscionability, 309; undue influence, 390; usury, 386
Deferred review, 691
Delay rental, 748
Delinquent children, 168-71
Delivered pricing system, 619
Delivered weight, 490, 491
Delivery: concurrent conditions of delivery and payment, 255, 256; cure of defective tender of, 488; tender of, 485, 486; term of, in contract for sale of goods, 430, 431
Delivery order, 455, 456
Demand paper, 372
Demonstrative evidence, 115, 116
Demurrage, 446, 458, 462

Depositary receipt, 299, 300
Deposition: civil, 141; criminal, 104, 105
Depreciation, 702
Depressant, 57
Desertion, 97
Descent and distribution, 818-20
Destruction: accidental, of commercial paper as discharge, 408; of contingent remainders, 743; of subject matter of contract as discharge, 266, 267; of written contract as discharge, 263
Direct examination, 111, 112
Direct infringement, 595
Directed verdict: civil, 142; criminal, 111
Directors, corporate: actions of, without meeting, 680; classified board of, 675; election and qualification of, 679; executive committee, 675, 680; fiduciary duty of, 680, 691; initial meeting of, 648; liability of, to corporate creditors, 711; liability of, to trustee in bankruptcy, 711; meetings of, 679, 680; provisional, 706; removal of, 675, 676
Discharge of commercial paper: in general, 403-7; accidental destruction of commercial paper, 408; cancellation of contract, 406; extension of time to pay, 407; impairment of collateral, 407; of maker or acceptor, 406; material alteration, 408; payment, 403-6; reacquisition, 406, 408; renewal note, 406; renunciation of commercial paper, 406; tender of payment, 407; unauthorized completion, 262
Discharge of contract: death of party to a contract, 264, 265; destruction of written contract, 263; expiration of statute of limitations, 264; extreme danger to life or health, 266; extreme danger to property, 265, 266; frustration of purpose of contract, 269; material alteration, 262, 408; surrender or cancellation of formal contract, 262, 263; unilateral rescission, 259-61
Disclaimer of warranties, 504-7
Discovery: civil, 140, 141; criminal, 104, 105; in aid of judgment, 149

Discretionary trust, 804
Discrimination: in bankruptcy, 858; in granting of credit, 547-49; employment, 293-96
Dishonorable discharge, 97
Disparagement, 79
Disposition hearing, juvenile court, 170
Dispute resolution procedures, informal, 508-10
Disrespect to a superior, 97
Dissolution: of corporation, 707, 708; of partnership, 639
Distribution in partial liquidation, 659
Diversity of citizenship, 95
Dividends, 657-59
Divorce, 25; no fault, 30
Divorce, grounds for: in general, 30-32; adultery, 30; confinement in mental hospital, 30, 31; conviction of felony, 30; cruelty, 30; insupportability, 29, 30
Dock receipt, 466
Documentary evidence, 116
Documents: ancient, 16; as collateral for security interest, 533, 534; securing execution of, by deception, 46
Domestic animals, 331
Domiciled note, 397
Dominant estate, 749
Donee beneficiary, 241, 242
Dormant accounts, 427
Double jeopardy, 106, 107
Drafts: in general, 368; sight, 397; time, 397
Draft-varying acceptance, 398
Drawer, 400, 401
Driver's license, 570-78
Driving: financial responsibility of, in Texas, 575-77; reckless, 580; under the influence of drugs, 580; while intoxicated (DWI), 579, 580
Drug offenses, federal, 68-71
Dry area, 58
Dry trust, 803
Due negotiation: of bill of lading, 455; of warehouse receipt, 449, 450
Dues checkoff, 314
Duress: as annulment ground, 28; as defense to payment of commercial

paper, 390; as reason for rescission of contract, 204, 205; in will contest, 824
Duties: delegation of, 244; nondelegable, 244, 245
Dying declaration, 115

E

Earned surplus, 657
Earnest money, 752, 753
Easement: appurtenant, 749; in gross, 748, 749; by necessity, 749, 750; by prescription, 750
Economic strike, 318
Education Code, 783
Electronic fund transfers, 422, 423, 502
Electronic Fund Transfer Act, 422, 423
Embezzlement, 40
Emergency: public, 81; private, 81; involuntary commitment of mentally ill person, 156, 157
Eminent domain: federal, 789, 790; Texas, 93, 786-89
Employee Retirement Income Security Act, 303, 304
Endangered Species Preservation Act, 331
Endless chain scheme, 46, 47
Endorser of commercial paper, liability of, 401
Enlistment in foreign service, 64
Enticing a child, 55
Environmental Protection Agency, 460, 566, 609, 611, 613, 614, 622, 796
Equal Credit Opportunity Act, 500, 547
Equal credit opportunity, 547-49
Equal employment opportunity, 292
Equal Employment Opportunity Act, 292-96

Equal Employment Opportunity Commission, 181, 183, 297
Equal pay, 296
Equal Pay Act, 296
Equipment, as collateral in secured transaction, 530
Equitable estoppel, 233
Equitable title, 753
Equity, 13, 14
Escape, 49
Escrow, 758
Estate: administration of, 814, 822-30; ancillary administration of, 829; community administration of, 829; independent administration of, 814, 828, 829; taxable, 839
Estate tax, federal, 836-42
Estray, 332
Eviction of tenant, 773
Ex dock: duties under, 491; risk of loss under, 442
Ex factory: duties under, 490; risk of loss under, 441
Ex ship: duties under, 491; risk of loss under, 442
Examiner system, 182
Examining trial, 102
Exclusive agency, 290
Exclusive dealing contract, 617
Exclusive right to sell, 290
Execution, writ of, 149
Executory contract, 243, 244
Executory interest, 738, 740
Exempt securities: federal, 689; Texas, 684
Exempt bulk sale transactions, 479, 480
Exoneration: of surety, 354; of trustee of trust, 809
Expert certificate, 254, 255
Explosives, dealing in, 63
Export: license, 472, 473; regulations, 471
Export Administration Act, 471, 472
Export Control, Office of, 472
Express contract, 191
Express trust, 801-11
Express warranty, 507-11
Extortion, 40; in extension of credit, 64
Extradition, 125

F

Failure to appear, 50
Failure to identify as witness, 49
Fair Credit Billing Act, 498, 556, 558
Fair Credit Reporting Act, 548, 549, 551
Fair Labor Standards Act, 296-98
Fair Packaging and Labeling Act, 614
Fairness doctrine, 610
False alarm or report, 51
False imprisonment: as crime, 38; as tort, 74
False report to police officer, 48
False statement to obtain property or credit, 43
False weight or measure, 45
Family auto liability, 585, 586
Family Code, 167-74, 344
Family purpose doctrine, 586
Family violence proceeding, protection against, 122-24
Farm products, as collateral in secured transaction, 536, 537
Featherbedding, 318
Federal Administrative Procedure Act, 179
Federal Arbitration Act, 166, 167
Federal Aviation Administration, 75, 797
Federal Banking Secrecy Act, 424
Federal Bills of Lading Act, 444-56
Federal Communications Commission, 609, 610
Federal Deposit Insurance Corporation, 610
Federal Energy Regulatory Commission, 609
Federal Food, Drug, and Cosmetics Act, 611, 614, 621
Federal Hazardous Substances Act, 613, 622
Federal Housing Administration, 752
Federal Register, 15, 179, 180
Federal Reporter, 15

Federal Reserve Board, 547, 552, 553, 610
Federal Securities Act, 645, 649, 689-703
Federal Securities and Exchange Act, 645, 674, 693
Federal Supplement, 15
Federal Trade Commission, 181, 248, 260 383, 384, 508, 510, 614-16, 620, 621, 719, 720
Federal Trade Commission Act, 79, 510, 598, 614, 675
Federal Trade Commission Improvement Act, 383, 384
Federal Truth-in-Lending Act, 759
Federal Warranty Act, 508-11
Federal withholding tax, 300
Fee simple: absolute, 736, 737; determinable, 737, 748; upon executory limitation, 738; subject to condition subsequent, 737, 738
Fee tail, 743
Felony: capital, 36; penalties for, 36; penalties for repeat offenders, 36, 37
Fence, 40
Feudalism, 5
Fidelity bond, 358, 359
Fiduciary duty: of agent, 289; of attorney, 45; of controlling shareholder, 678, 679; of directors, 680, 681; of promoters, 683
Fiduciary relationship, 203, 204
Field background investigation, 550, 551
Finance charge, 552-54, 556
Financial Responsibility Act, 575, 582
Financing statement 529-45
Fire insurance, 477
Fire Statute, 466
Firearms: dealing in, 63, 64; unlawful transfer of, 52
Firm offer, UCC, 195, 436
First-in-first-out: inventory valuation method, 702; tracing, 366, 367
First in time, first in right, 247
Fixture filing, 529
Fixtures, 529, 536
Floating lien, 531
Flood Disaster Protection Act, 797
Flood insurance, 797
Flood plain zoning, 797

Food and Drug Administration, 180, 181, 183, 460, 611, 612
Force: deadly, 57, 81; use of, as justifiable, 56, 57
Force majeure clause, 267
Forcible detainer action, 773, 774
Foreclosure: of artisan's lien, 328, 329; of carrier's lien, 453, 454; of federal tax lien, 785; of mechanic's lien, 779; of mortgage, 775; of real property tax lien, 781, 782; of security interest, 539, 540; of trust deed, 776; of warehouseman's lien, 447, 448
Forfeiture: of pay, 97; of right to do business in Texas, 730; of corporate charter, 730, 731
Forged endorsement: of commercial paper, 378, 379; of investment securities, 665; of warehouse receipt, 449
Forgery: as crime, 42; as defense to payment of commercial paper, 386; unauthorized completion as, 42; in will contest, 825
Forum non conveniens, 140
Franchise tax, 727–31; forfeiture of corporate charter for nonpayment of, 730, 731; forfeiture of right to do business in Texas for nonpayment of, 730
Franchising, 606, 616
Fraud: as annulment ground, 28; in destruction, removal, or concealment of writing, 46; as ground for refusal of discharge in bankruptcy, 854, 855; as ground for rescission of contract, 202, 203; mail fraud, 67; in insolvency, 44; "puffing," 615; revocation of bankruptcy rehabilitation plan for, 857, 858; remedies for, in contracts for sale of goods, 523; under SEC Rule 10-b-5, 698, 699; as tort, 77; in transfer of assets, in bankruptcy, 852; in will contest, 824
Fraud in the execution, 386
Fraud in the inducement, 390
Fraudulent conveyance, 150
F.A.S. Vessel: duties under, 491; risk of loss under, 442
F.O.B. Destination: duties under 491; risk of loss under 442
F.O.B. Shipping Point: duties under, 490; risk of loss under, 441, 442
F.O.B. Vessel: duties under, 491; risk of loss under, 442
Freeze-out, 678
Freight forwarder: air, 464; international air, 465; liability on bill of lading, 455; ocean, 469; overland, 459
Friendly fire, 477
Fugitives from justice, 66, 67
Full warranty, 509
Functional discount, 618
Fungible goods, 231, 336, 440, 441, 446
Future advances, 537

G

Gambling: communicating information of, 53; as crime, 52; keeping a place of, 53; promotion of, 52, 53
Garnishment, 92, 93, 149
General Agreement on Tariffs and Trade, 474
General arbitration statute, Texas, 165, 166
General average, 468
General average adjustors, 468
General denial, 136
Generic term, 606
Geographic market extension, 717, 718
Germanic tribal law, 5
Gift, abatement of, 818; causa mortis, 247, 338; conditional, 339; delivery of, 337, 338; intent to make, 336; inter vivos, 247, 336; to public servant by person subject to his jurisdiction, 48; voidable, 338

Gift tax, federal, 836-42
Going private, 701
Good conduct time, 123
Good Samaritan, 83
Good Samaritan statute, 192
Grace period, 834, 835
Grand jury, 102, 103
Grant of immunity, 113
Gratuitous assignment, 247
Gross estate, 837, 838
Group boycott, 620; horizontal, 620; vertical, 620
Guarantee of collection, 251
Guarantor: of collection of commercial paper, 402; of endorsement, 669; of payment, 350; of signature, 666
Guardian: of estate, 154; of person, 154
Guardian ad litem, 24
Guest Statute, 581

H

Habeas corpus, 9; federal, 164; Texas, 162-64
Habitability of rental premises, 766-68
Hallucinogenic drugs, 57
Hamurrabi, king of Babylon, 4
Harassment, 51
Hart-Scott-Rodino Act, 719, 720
Hardship, as defense to payment of commercial paper, 394
Harter Act, 466, 469, 471
Hazardous waste control, 797
Health and Welfare, Department of, 613
Hearsay evidence, admissible: admission of party, 115; statement of party, 142; statement of party contrary to interest, 142

Heroin, 57, 69
Highway beautification, 797, 798
Hindu law, 11
Hiring hall, 314
Holder, 380
Holder in due course: collecting bank as, 416; in consumer transactions, 383; payee as, 383; requirements for, 380-82
Holder through a holder in due course, 384
Holding company, personal, 661; income of, 661, 662
Holographic will, 813, 823
Home solicitation sales, 260, 261
Homestead: rural, 147; sale or encumbrance of, 347; urban, 147
Homicide: by vehicle, 580; criminally negligent, 38
Homosexual conduct, 38
Honorary trust, 803
Hospitalization of mentally ill persons, temporary, 156
Hostile fire, 477
Hot cargo agreement, 317
Household goods, transport of, 462
Housing and Urban Development, Department of, 567, 797
Hung jury, 118, 124
Hunting, 331
Husband-wife privilege, 114
Husband-wife relationship, 31
Hydroelectric power plants, 609

I

Identification of goods to contract, 437, 519

Illegal aliens, 214
Illegality, as defense to payment of commercial paper, 390
Illusory promise, 208
Immorality, contracts promoting, illegality of, 220
Impeachment, 112
Impersonating a public servant, 49
Implied contract, 191
Import regulations, 473
Improper influence, 47
Improvement patent, 594
In rem jurisdiction over assets, 132
Inactive accounts, 423, 424
Inadequacy of consideration, 208
Incidental beneficiary, 242
Income of trust, 807, 808
Income tax withholding, 299
Incompetence of customer, effect upon bank accounts, 415
Incompetence to stand trial, 123, 124
Incontestability, affidavit of, 605
Incorporation: certificate of, 647; defective, 647
Incorporator, 646
Incurred risk, 85
Indemnity, 351
Independent contractor, 292, 299
Indictment, 103, 104; defective, 106
Industrial Accident Board, 182-84, 186, 308
Influence-peddling, 220
Information, 104
Infringement: copyright, 601; patent, 594, 595; trademark, 606
Inherent vice, 460
Inheritance tax, Texas, 841, 842
Injunctions, 93, 95
Injunction bond, 135
Injury: primary, 617, 618; secondary, 618
Inland marine insurance, 475
Inland transit insurance, 475
Innkeeper, 329
Inquisitorial system, 8, 9
Insanity defense, 124, 125
Insiders in bankruptcy, 851, 852
Insolvency as discharge of contract, 268
Institutional bias, 183

Institutional decision, 185
Instruments, as collateral in secured transactions, 532, 533
Insurable interest: in general, 218; buyer of real property, 753; in goods, 437; life insurance, 833
Insurance: auto, 584; fire, 477; flood, 797; inland marine, 475; inland transit, 475; ocean marine, 476, 477. *See also* Insurance, life
Insurance, life: in general, 833, 834, 855; adverse claim to proceeds of, 835; alternate beneficiary of, 833; assignment of policy, 833; credit, 552, 553; as estate management device, 843; ordinary, 831-36; settlement options, 835, 836; surrender of policy, 835; term, 831, 832
Insurance Code, 560, 574, 833-44
Intangibles, 534
Integrated bar, 16
Integrated contracts, 235
Intelligency Division of the IRS, 71
Intended beneficiary, 240, 241
Inter vivos trust, 802
Interference: with child custody, 55; with contractual relations, 80; with federally protected activity, 62, 63
Interference proceeding, 605
Interim trustee in bankruptcy, 851
Interpretation of contracts, 233-35
Interpleader, 250, 327, 457
Interrogatories, 140
Internal Revenue Code, 71, 72, 179, 180, 299-304, 426, 644, 669-83
Internal Revenue Service, 71, 72, 98, 148 149, 179, 180, 182, 299-304, 414, 537, 662, 663, 683, 784, 785
International Trade Commission, 96, 473, 595
Interstate Commerce Act, 177, 453, 457, 458, 468
Interstate Commerce Commission, 177, 457, 462, 466, 468, 469, 608
Intoxication: as defense to criminal charge, 56; driving while intoxicated (DWI), 579, 580; limiting effect upon contractual capacity, 214
Invasion of privacy, 79, 80

Inventory: as collateral in secured transaction, 531; valuation, 702
Investigative detention, 8
Investment security: in general, 664–69; adverse claim to, 665, 666; forged endorsement of, 665; issuer of, 493–97; material alteration of, 667; unauthorized completion of, 667; unauthorized signature on, 665
Invitee, 82
Irrevocable trust, 802, 843, 844
Islamic law, 10
Issue, 743
Issuer (of investment security), 493–97

J

Japanese law, 11
Joint obligations, 238, 239
Joint and several obligations, 240
Joint stock company, 643
Joint tenancy, 342, 343
Joint tenancy property, as estate management device, 843
Joint will, 817
Joint venture, 644, 718, 719
Judgment lien, 149, 150, 779
Judgments, 144; federal, 150; out-of-state, 150, 151
Jurisdiction: federal criminal, 61; primary, 129, 186
Jurisdictional dispute, 317
Jurisdictional strike, 319
Jury: in general, 6–8; civil charge to, 141, 143, 144; criminal charge to, 117, 118; hung jury, 118, 124; selection of (civil), 141; selection of (criminal), 109, 110
Juvenile court, 168–71; adjudication hearing, 170; disposition hearing, 170; informal rehabilitation proceedings, 169; transfer hearing, 169

K

Kidnapping, 38; aggravated, 38
Koran, 10, 11

L

Labeling, 614
Labor and Standards, Department of, 567
Land contract, 752
Landlord's lien, 770, 771
Landrum-Griffin Act, 321
Lanham Act, 602, 603
Lapse, 817, 818
Last clear chance, 85, 86
Last in, first out, 702
Law: finding the law, 14; origins of, 3; Texas, development of, 11, 12
Law School Admission Test, 17
Leading questions, 111, 112
Leakage, 475
Learner's permit, 573, 574

Lease, 764–66; all bills paid (by landlord), 765, 771; assignment of, 769; no bills paid (by landlord), 765, 771; pay all bills to landlord, 765, 766
Leasehold estates, 742
Leash laws, 76
Legal ethics, 17–21
Legal tender, 255, 364, 431
Legitimacy, 32
Letter of credit: in general, 485–97; assignment of right to proceeds from, 495; clean, 493; confirmed, 485, 493; documentary, 494; installment, 493; irrevocable, 493; lump sum, 493; nonnotation, 493; nontransferable, 493; notation, 493; overdrawn, 497; revocable, 493; revocation of, 494, 495; straight, 493; transferable, 493
Liability, primary, 396
Libel, 77, 78
License to use land, 750
Licensee, 82
Licensing laws, contract in violation of, 317
Lie detector test results as evidence, 116
Liens: carrier's, 330; contractor's, 777–79; floating, 531; judgment, 149, 150, 779; landlord's, 770, 771; materialman's, 777–79; purchase-money, 148; real property tax, 780–84; vendor's, 752; warehouseman's, 330
Life estate, 738, 739, 740; conveyance of, as estate management device, 843; pur autre vie, 739, 740
Life tenant, 739
Lifetime gift, as estate management device, 843
Limited guardian, 155
Limited Liability Act, 466, 471
Limited partnership, 642, 643
Limited transfer of commercial paper, 374
Limited warranty, 509, 510
Liquidated claim, 132
Liquidated damages, 274
Loan-sharking, 64
Lockout, 320
Long Arm Statute, 132, 727, 728
Loss, as defense to payment of commercial paper, 393
Lost profit, recovery of, 520
Lost property, 333
Lottery, 52, 53, 218
Louisiana law, 12
LSD, 57, 69
Lump sum letter of credit, 493

M

Machine, 589
Magnuson-Moss Act, 503, 508, 510
Mail fraud, 67
Mailing threatening communication, 64
Maintenance, 220
Maintenance of membership, 314
Malicious prosecution, 74
Malpractice: medical, 192; professional, 83
Management of marital property, 346
Managing conservator, 32
Mandatory counterclaim, 136, 137
Mandatory supervision, 123
Manslaughter: involuntary, 37, 38; voluntary, 37
Manufacture, 589
Manufactured housing standards, 567
Manufacturer's Certificate of Origin, 438, 439, 569
Marijuana, 57, 58, 69, 70
Marital deduction, 838, 839
Marital duties, contract to perform, 221
Marital property, 31, 347, 348
Maritime Commission, federal, 469, 608
Market division, 620; horizontal, 620; vertical, 617
Marketing regulation, 614–19

Marriage: brokerage contracts, 221; ceremonial, 22; ceremony, 24; common-law, 24, 25; contracts injurious to, 220; license, 22-24; proxy in, 23, 24; putative, 26; restraints upon, 746; void, 25; voidable, validation by death of spouse, 29
Marshaling of assets, 641, 642
Material alteration: as forgery, 42; of bill of lading, 453; as defense to payment of commercial paper, 388; of investment security, 667; of warehouse receipt, 446; as discharge of contract, 262, 408; as discharge of commercial paper, 408
Materialman's lien, 777-79
Mass picketing, 320
Maximum interest, 222-28
McNaghten Rule, 56
Mechanic's lien: in general, 148, 149; affidavit, 778; foreclosure of, 779; on personal property, 327; on real estate, 777-79; versus security interest, 537
Mechanic's lien affidavit, 778
Mental distress, infliction of, 74
Mental Health Code, 155-58
Mental Health and Mental Retardation, Department of, 124, 125, 155, 160
Mentally Retarded Persons Act, 159
Meretricious relationship, 26
Merger: of corporations, 712, 713; as discharge of contract, 269; of dominant and servient estate, 749
Mescaline, 57, 69
Metes and bounds description, 760
Microfilm of bank account records, 424
Midnight deadline, 420
Minor: contract liability of, 215, 216; tort liability of, 73, 83, 215, 216
Minority, as defense to payment of commercial paper, 385
Mineral estate, 736, 747
Minimum wage: federal, 296, 297; Texas, 298
Mirror image rule, 197, 198
Misapplication of fiduciary property, 46
Miscellaneous Business Corporation Act, 645-52
Misconduct, willful and wanton, 86
Misdemeanors, penalties for, 36; penalties for repeat offenders, 37
Mislabeled commodity, 45
Misplaced property, 334
Misprision of felony, 61, 62
Misrepresentation, 203
Mistrial, 117, 118
Misuse: as defense in strict tort liability cases, 515, 516; of official information, 50
Mitigation of damages, 271, 275
Mobile Home Construction and Safety Standards Act, 567
Modification of contract, 212
Money, 363-65
Money order, 368
Monopolization, 615, 616; attempted, 620
Moot case, 128
Moral obligation as consideration, 211
Mortgage, 775
Motions: to disqualify judge, 107; for judgment notwithstanding the verdict, 144; for new trial, 144, 145; to set aside verdict, 144
Motor carriers, 461
Motor Carriers Act, 461
Motor vehicle: abandonment of, 572, 573; accidents, duties of driver involved in, 579; certificate of title of, 568-71; as collateral in secured transaction, 534, 569, 570; damage to or destruction of, 65; importer's certificate, 569; inspection certificate, 578, 579; junked, 571, 572; safety inspection, 566, 578, 579; sales regulation, 568; sale by nonowner, 484; transfer of title to, 570; unauthorized use of, 41; warranties, 510
Motor Vehicle Certificate of Title Act, 438, 534, 568, 587
Multi-bank holding company, 610
Multi-level distributorship, 559, 560
Munitions control, office of, 472
Murder: in general, 37; capital, 37
Murderer: as beneficiary of life policy upon his victim, 835; as heir, 821

Mutual rescission, 259
Mutual wills, 817

Notification, 686, 687
Novation, 263
Nuclear Regulatory Commission, 472, 609
Nuisance, 76, 77

N

O

National Highway Traffic Safety Act, 566
National Highway Traffic Safety Administration, 566
National Labor Management Relations Act, 293, 296, 311-21
National Labor Relations Board, 181, 183, 184, 187, 311-21
Negligence: in general, 83; by drawer of commercial paper, 386, 387; effect of, on fire insurance claim, 478; *per se*, 83; in product design, 516
Negligent confinement, 74
Negotiability, commercial paper, 369-74
Net landed weight, 490, 491
Net worth, method of proving tax evasion, 72
Next friend, 28, 29
No Arrival, No Sale: duties under, 491; risk of loss under, 442
Noise Control Act, 613
Nolo contendere, 105
Nonconforming use, 793, 794
Nonresidents of Texas, suits against in Texas courts, 132
Nonresident motorist statute, 132
Norris-La Guardia Act, 319
Notice and comment procedure, 179, 180
Notice of delinquency, real property tax, 781
Notice of default in suretyship, 357
Notice of dishonor, 399, 400
Notice of levy, IRS, 300
Notice of opposition, 605

Obscenity, commercial, 51, 52
Obstruction of highway or other passageway, 51
Occupational disease, 307
Occupational safety and health, 304
Occupational Safety and Health Act, 179, 182, 304
Occupational Safety and Health Administration, 304
Occupational Safety and Health Review Commission, 182, 304
Offer, 193-97; published statement as, 194
Offering circular, 692
Officers of corporation, 648, 682-88
Official Gazette, 605
Official misconduct, 50
Official oppression, 50
Oil and gas, 747, 748; lease, 748
One bank holding company, 610
One hundred percent penalty, 300
Open shop, 313
Opiate drugs, 57
Opinion evidence rule, 114, 115
Opposition proceeding, 605
Option, 195, 197, 198
Order for relief, 848
Order for service, 463
Order of civil authority, 478
Order of indefinite commitment, 157, 158
Order paper, 372
Order of protective custody, 157

Orphans' exclusion, 839
Overdraft, 412, 413
Overissue: of corporate stock, 667; of delivery orders, 456; of warehouse receipts, 446
Overtime pay, 297

P

Packaging, 613, 614
Parasite (Soviet law), 10
Parent-child relationship, nature of, 31, 32
Parks and Wildlife Code, 332, 438
Parol evidence rule, 235-37
Parole, 123
Partial strike, 319
Particular average, 476
Particular fund, 370
Partition: of tenancy in common property, 341; of community property, 347
Partnership: in general, 629-41; assignment of partner's interest in, 637, 638; dissolution of, 639; nontrading, 634; trading, 634
Passing off of goods, as deceptive trade practice, 558
Past consideration, 209
Patent: active inducement of infringement, 395; assignment, 593; nonpatentable items, 589, 590
Patent Office, 96, 591
Patent Office Board of Appeals, 592
Patentable inventions, 588-89
Patents and antitrust, 594
Paternity suits, 167
Pauper's affidavit, 145, 774
Pawn ticket, 544, 545

Pawn transactions and pawnbrokers, 544, 545
Paydays, 298, 299
Payment: as discharge of commercial paper, 403-6; concurrent conditions of delivery and payment, 255, 256; inconsistent with terms of restrictive endorsement, 392; method of, 431; tender of, for goods, 486, 487
"Payment on Arrival", 491
Payment against documents, 485
Payment bond, 359, 778
Payment term, 431
Penal Code, 36-60
Pension Benefit Guaranty Corporation, 303
Pension plan regulation, 303
Peremptory challenge: civil, 141; criminal, 110
Perfection of security interest, 528, 529
Performance bond, 359
Periodic tenancy, 764
Perjury, 48, 68; aggravated, 48
Permanent credit to checking account, 411
Permanent guardianship, 153, 154
Permanent injunction, 134
Personal bias, 183
Personal property: exempt from execution, 148, 149; lease disclosures, 555
Per stirpes inheritance, 818, 819
Peyote, 57, 69
Phenobarbital, 69
Physician-patient privilege, 114
Picket line, 320
Picketing, 320
Pickpocket, 40
Pilferage, 476
Plaintiff, no remedy for, 129
Plea in abatement, 136
Plea bargaining, 106
Plea of privilege, 136
Pledge, 530
Pledged goods in pawn transactions, 544
P.O.D. account, 349, 422
Poison Prevention Packaging Act, 613
Police: discretion, 99, 100; fleeing or attempting to elude, 580
Pollution: air, 796; new auto pollutant

emission standards, 566; water, 796, 797
Pomerene Act, 444–56
Pooling agreement, 656
Possession of gambling device, 53
Possession bond, 774
Possessor, nonbailee, 323
Possessor has no title, 387, 388
Possibility of reverter, 737
Postal losses, false claim for, 65
Postal money order, 368
Power of appointment, 741, 742
Power of attorney, general, 282
Power of corporations, in general, 650–52
Power plant: conventional, 609; nuclear, 609
Preemptive rights, 676
Premarital physical exam, 23
Premarital property agreement, 347
Premarital serological exam, 23
Premerger notification, 719
Pretrial conference, 141
Preferences in bankruptcy, 851, 852
Preferred access combination, 718
Preferred stock, 655
Prejudicial information: civil, 143; criminal, 117
Preliminary injunction, 134, 135
Presentment, 399
Presumption of death, 26, 27
Presumption of innocence, 116
Price discrimination, 617–19
Price fixing: horizontal, 619; vertical, 619
Price leadership, 619
Price term, 430
Price war, 618
Principal of trust, 807, 808
Priority: in conflicting security interests, 537; security interest vs. fixture, 536; security interest vs. lien creditor, 537; security interest vs. mechanic's lien, 537
Private offering exemption, 692–94
Privilege, as defense to tort liability, 81
Privity: horizontal, 512; vertical, 511, 512
Probate jurisdiction, 92, 93
Probate Code, 348, 349, 421, 812–30
Probation, 119, 121; in drug cases, 58; community-service, 121, 122
Proceeds: security interest in, 528, 531, 532, 533; disposal from sale, 542, 543
Process, 589
Procura, 282
Product liability: defenses to, 515; negligence theory of, 516; strict tort theory of, 512–16; violation of statutory duty, 517; warranty theory of, 511, 512
Product market extension combination, 718
Product regulation, 611–13
Production and maintenance unit, 312
Profit a prendre, 750
Promise to pay, 370
Promises enforceable without consideration, 211, 212
Promissory estoppel, 211
Promissory note, 367
Promoter, 288, 683
Promoter contracts, 648, 649
Proof of interest, 852
Proof of Loss, 476
Proof of negligence, 83, 84
Property, abandoned, 333
Property description, 759, 760
Property Tax Code, 783, 784
Property taxation: independent school district, 783; municipal, 783
Prosecution, hindering of, 49
Prospective inability to perform contract as discharge, 268
Prospectus, 689–92
Protective order, temporary ex parte, 172, 173
Protective trust, 804
Protest, 400
Provisional credit to checking account, 411
Proximate cause, 84
Proxy: in general, 282, 673, 674; in marriage, 23, 24; coupled with interest, 674; federal regulation of, 699, 700
Prudent man rule, 806, 807
Public laws, 14
Public policy, contract contrary to, 220
Public use proceeding, 592
Public Utilities Commission of Texas, 186, 187
Public Utility Regulatory Act, 187
Punitive discharge, 97

878 Index

Purchase-money resulting trust, 809, 810
Pyramid sales scheme, 559, 560

Q

Qualification, 685, 686
Qualified endorsement, 377
Quantity discount, 618
Quantity term, 430
Quantum meruit, 277, 278
Quasi-contract, 192, 193
Quasi-contract damages, 278
Question cases, federal, 94, 95
Question of fact, 144, 145
Question of law, 145
Quiet enjoyment, 765
Quitclaim deed, 754, 755
Quorum: at directors' meeting, 679, 680; at shareholders' meeting, 672

R

Race of diligence, 845
Radiation Control for Health and Safety Act, 613
Rail shipment: carload lot, 458; less than carload lot, 458, 459
Railroads, 457

Rape, 38; aggravated, 38
Rate-making, 186, 187
Reacquisition as discharge of commercial paper: by maker or acceptor, 406; by prior party, 408
Real defenses to payment of commercial paper, 385-89
Real estate closings, 758, 759
Real estate investment trusts, 644
Real Estate Settlement Procedures Act, 14, 758, 759
Real property tax, 148, 780, 784
Real property tax liens, 780-84
Reasonable man standard, 83
Receivers, 93
Receivership, 134; of corporation, 707, 723, 724; as insolvency proceeding, 845, 846
Receiving stolen or embezzled property, 40
Reckless damage or destruction, 40
Reclamation of goods: from insolvent buyer, 520; from insolvent seller, 522
Reconsignment, 453
Recording of assignment, 247, 250
Recording system, 755, 756
Recovery of contract price, 519
Redemption: real property, 775; in secured personal property transaction, 541
Reduction surplus, 652, 657
Refinancing, effect on security interest, 536, 537
Reformation, 275
Refusal to deal, 620
Register of Copyrights, 599, 600
Registered bond, 653
Registrar, 669
Registration of common-law marriage, 25
Registration statement: federal, 689-95; Texas, 685-88
Regulated industries, 608-11
Regulation A exemption, 692
Regulation B, 547
Regulation Z, 552
Rehabilitation plan: Chapter XI, 856, 857; Chapter XIII, 857, 858
Reimbursement: of issuer of letter of credit, 496; of surety, 354, 355
Rejection of offer, 195, 196; revocation

of, 198, 199
Rejection of goods, 488
Release of collateral as suretyship defense, 401
Remainder, 739; conveyance of, as estate management device, 843; contingent, 739, 740; totally vested, 740; vested subject to partial divestment, 740; vested subject to total divestment, 740
Remainderman, 739, 740
Removal, of directors, 675, 676
Renewal note, as discharge of commercial paper, 406
Renunciation of commercial paper as discharge, 406
Replevin, 522
Replevy bond, 133
Repossession, 44, 538, 539
Res ipsa loquitur, 84
Res judicata, 151, 152
Resale of identified goods, 519
Rescission, 275
Rescue doctrine, 86
Resisting arrest or search, 49
Respondeat superior, 308
Restraints upon alienation, 745, 746
Restraints of trade, contracts creating, 219, 220
Restrictive endorsement, 377
Restitution, 275, 276
Resulting trust, 809, 810
Retaliation, 48
Retention: of collateral by secured party in satisfaction of debt, 540, 541; of down payment, 520
Return of service, 131
Revaluation surplus, 657
Reversion, 738, 739
Reverter trust, 844
Revised Civil Statutes, 15
Revocable trust, 802; as estate management device, 844
Revocation: of acceptance of goods, 488; of letter of credit, 494, 495; of offer, 195
Rigging: of publicly exhibited contest, 45, 46; of sporting events, 45, 46
Rights of assignees, 248, 249

Right of entry, 737, 738
Right to Financial Privacy Act, 424–26
Right to work law, 313
Riots: inciting, organizing, participating in, etc., 65
Ripeness for decision, 128
Risk of loss: in general, 271, 272; in sales of goods, 439; in sales of real estate, 753
Robbery, 41; aggravated, 41; of bank, 67
Robinson-Patman Act, 617, 620, 621
Roman law, 4
Rule of capture, 747
Rules of civil procedure, Texas, 127
Rule of Forty-five, 303
Rule 144 of SEC, 693, 694
Rule against perpetuities: as to real property, 741, 744, 745; as to trusts, 802, 803
Rule of 78, 226
Rule in Shelley's Case, 742

S

Safe deposit box, 337, 338
Safety inspection of motor vehicles: 578; of new autos, 566
Sale of assets (of corporation), 713–15
Sale of children, contract for, 221
Sale of collateral in secured transaction, 540
Sale on approval, 442, 443
Sale or return, 442, 443
Sales tax, Texas limited, 622–26
Salvage, 467; of unfinished goods after breach, 519
Salvors, 467
Scope of employment, 309

Seaworthy vessel: under Carriage of Goods by Sea Act, 469; under Harter Act, 466, 467
Search and seizure, 108, 109
Search warrant, 108, 109; on bank records, 424–26
Seat belts, 514
Secondary boycott, 317
Secret partner, 632
Secretary of state (Texas), 645, 646
Secured transactions: in general, 527, 528; consumer goods as collateral in, 529, 530; exempt, 527, 528; instruments as collateral in, 532, 533; motor vehicles as collateral in, 534, 569, 570; multiple-county, 535, 536; multiple-state, 534, 535; sale of collateral in, 540
Securities and Exchange Commission, 522, 611, 649, 674, 684, 687, 689, 714
Securities regulation, Texas: coordination, 687; notification, 686, 687; qualification, 685, 686
Security agreement, 528–45
Security deposit, 766
Security interest: in general, 528–45; assignment of, 537; foreclosure of, 539, 540; improper foreclosure of, 543; non-purchase-money, 530; perfection of, 528, 529; priority in conflicting security interests, 537; in proceeds, 528, 531, 532, 533; purchase-money, 529
Self-incrimination, privilege against, 9, 72, 112–14, 142
Seller, person in position of, 523
Selling goods below cost, 618
Sentencing, 118, 119
Separate property, 344–46
Sequestration, 44, 92, 93, 133, 134, 539
Service mark, 602
Servient estate, 749
Session laws, 14
Service of citation, 130
Service by publication, 131
Set-off: 248; by bank, 413; by credit card issuer, 501, 502; as defense to payment of commercial paper, 393; in suretyship and guaranty contracts, 353
Settlement options, life insurance, 835, 836

Settlor, 801
Several obligations, 240
Shareholders: appraisal and payment rights of, 712, 713; controlling, 694; derivative suits of, 677
Shari'a, 10, 11
Shelf registration, 691, 692
Sherman Antitrust Act, 616, 617, 621
Shipment under reservation, 442
Shipper's export declaration, 473
Shipper's weight, load, and count, 452, 462
Shop right, 593
Shoplifting, 40
Short merger, 715, 716
Sight draft, 397
Signature on commercial paper, 370
Silent partner, 632
Sit-down strike, 319
Slander, 78, 79
Slander *per se* 78, 79
Smuggling, 66
Snoop report, 550, 551
Social Security Administration, 181, 186
Social Security withholding, 299
Sole proprietorship, 629
Southwestern Reporter, 15
Soviet law, 10
Sovereign of the soil, 756
Special Commissioners, eminent domain, 787, 788
Special endorsement of commercial paper, 377
Special power of appointment, 741
Special event report to Securities and Exchange Commission, 697
Specific performance, 276, 277, 522
Speculation (Soviet law), 10
Spendthrift trust, 804
Spin-off, 716
Split-off, 716
Split-up, 716, 717
Spontaneous exclamations, 115, 142
Spot zoning, 794, 795
Squatter, 761–63
Standing to sue, 128
Stare decisis, 5–7, 13; in administrative law, 186
State Bar of Texas, 16

Statute of Descent and Distribution, 735, 812, 813
Statute of Frauds, 228–33
Statute of Limitations: in adverse possession of real property, 761–63; in civil actions, 138, 139; in contest of will, 823; in criminal actions, 109; as defense to payment of commercial paper, 389; in federal securities violations, 696; in judgments, 150; in sales of goods, 523; in suit to set aside defective deed, 763
Statutes, in general, 12, 13
Stay of proceedings against debtor, 848, 849
Stimulants, 57
Stock: common, 655; dividend of, 658, 659; nonparticipating preferred, 655; nonvoting common, 655; nonvoting preferred, 655; no-par common, 655; par value common, 655; participating preferred, 655; preferred, 655; rights, 659; splits of, 659; unpaid for, liability of holder and owner of, 710; voting common, 655; voting preferred, 655; watered, 770, 771
Stolen goods, transporting and receiving, 67, 68
Stoppage in transit, 453, 518, 519
Stop order of SEC, 691
Stop-payment order, 414, 415
Stoppage of payment as defense to payment of commercial paper, 394, 395
Stranding, 476
Strike, 318, 319
Subagent, 287
Subassignment, 251
Sub-bailment, 325
Sublease, 769
Subchapter S corporation, 663, 664
Subpoena: administrative, 184; of bank records, 424–26; of witnesses, civil, 142; of witnesses, criminal, 111; duces tecum, 111, 113; by grand jury, 103
Subrogation: of fire insurer, 478; of surety, 355
Subscription agreement, 649, 650
Subsequent illegality, 264
Substantial evidence, 185

Substantial performance, 258
Substituted performance, 492
Suggested retail price, 619
Suits against nonresidents of Texas in Texas courts, 132
Summary review, 691
Supersedeas bond, 145
Support trust, 804
Suppression of competition, contracts for, 219, 220
Suppression of evidence, 108, 109
Suretyship defenses: discharge of accommodated party, 401; extension of time, 401; release of collateral, 401
Surrender or cancellation of formal contract as discharge, 262, 263
Surrender of life insurance policy, 835
Survival of beneficiary, 821
Survival of heirs, 821
Swindling, 40
Sworn account, 146

T

Taft-Hartley Act, 313
Tall structures, regulation of construction of, 797
Tampering with: or fabricating physical evidence, 48; governmental records, 48, 49; witness, 47
Tape recordings as evidence, 116
Target company, 701, 719
Tax: federal, willful failure to collect, account for, or pay, 71; willful failure to file returns, keep records, or supply information, 71

Index

Tax evasion: bank deposit method of proof, 72; cash expenditure method of proof, 72; evidence of, 72; federal, 71
Tax liens: federal, 300, 537, 784, 785; foreclosure of, federal, 785; foreclosure of, real property, 781; real property, 780-84
Tax Reform Act of 1976, 339
Taxable estate, 839
Taxation Code, 622-25, 646, 729-31, 842
Temporary injunction, 135
Temporary restraining order, 135
Tenancy at sufferance, 764
Tenancy at will, 764
Tenancy in common, 340-42
Tenancy by the entireties, 344
Tenancy in partnership, 343, 633
Tender of delivery of goods, 485, 486
Tender offer, 701, 714, 715, 719, 720
Tender of payment: as discharge of commercial paper, 407; for goods, 486, 487
Term for years, 764
Term life insurance, 831, 832
Termination of parent-child relationship, 33-35
Termination of storage, 446
Termination statement, 538
Tertiary injury, 618
Testamentary trust, 802; as estate management device, 842
Testimonial, 615
Texas Administrative Procedure and Texas Register Act, 179
Texas Aeronautical Commission, 464, 608
Texas Air Control Board, 796
Texas Banking Board, 610
Texas Board of Medical Examiners, 181
Texas Business Corporation Act, 480, 645-52
Texas Employment Commission, 181, 301, 302
Texas Highway Commission, 132
Texas Highway Department, 569, 570, 572-75
Texas Insurance Board, 560, 833
Texas Mobile Homes Standards Act, 567 568

Texas Motor Vehicle Commission, 566, 577
Texas Public Utilities Commission, 609
Texas Railroad Commission, 177, 457, 608, 609, 747
Texas Register, 15, 179, 180
Texas Reports, 15
Texas Securities Act, 645, 649, 684-89
Texas Securities Board, 684-89
Texas Trust Act, 801-11
Texas Youth Council, 170-72
Theft, 40, 41; as defense to payment of commercial paper, 392; by false pretext, 40; by check, 40, 41; of services, 40; of trade secret, 40
Time draft, 397
Time of the essence, 256
Time-price differential, 552
Tippees, 699
Title insurance companies, 757, 758
"Tombstone ad," 690
Tort, defined, 73
Tort claim, survival of, 88
Tort liability, contracts exonerating from, 220
Tracing, 366, 367
Trade acceptance, 368
Trade association, 619, 620
Trade name, 603
Trade secrets, 596-98
Trademark: in general, 602-7; assignment of, 606
Trademark Trial Appeal Board, 604, 605
Traffic offenses, 60, 580, 581
Tranquilizers, 58
Transfer agent, 669
Transfer hearing, juvenile court, 169
Transportation of goods, "piggyback" transport, 463, 464
Transportation, Department of, 439
Transmission of wagering information, 64, 65
Treasury stock, 652, 658, 678, 714
Trespass, 75; criminal, 42
Trespasser, 82
Trust deed, 775-77
Trust indenture, 653

Trust endorsement, 378
Trustee: in bankruptcy, 851–58; of trust, 801–11; of trust deed, 776, 777; of trust indenture, 653; of voting trust, 656
Trusts: blended, 804; business, 643, 644; charitable, 804, 805; constructive, 810; corpus of, 801; discretionary, 804; dry, 803; express, 801–11; foreclosure of deed to, 776; honorary, 803; income of, 807, 808; inter vivos, 802; irrevocable, 802, 843, 844; principal of, 807, 808; protective, 804; purchase-money resulting, 809, 810; real estate investment, 644; resulting, 809, 810; reverter, 844; revocable, 802, 844; spendthrift, 804; support, 804; testamentary, 802, 842; voting, 656
Truth in Lending Act, 498, 552

U

Unauthorized completion: of bill of lading, 453; as defense to payment of commercial paper, 391; as discharge of commercial paper, 262; as forgery, 42; of investment security, 667; of warehouse receipt, 446
Unauthorized endorsement, 378
Unauthorized parking in parking facility, 586, 587
Unauthorized practice of law, 19
Unauthorized signature: as defense to payment of commercial paper, 387; on investment security, 665
Unavoidable accident, 84, 85
Ultra vires act, 651

Ultra vires contract, 213
Ultra vires issue of commercial paper: by corporation, 395; by government, 387
Unconscionability, 206; as defense to payment of commercial paper, 390
Underwriter, 688, 689, 695
Undue influence: as defense to payment of commercial paper, 390; as ground for rescission of contract, 204; as ground for will contest, 824
Unemployment compensation, 301, 302
Unemployment tax: federal, 301; Texas, 301
Unfair labor practices: employer, 315, 316; union, 316, 317; strike, 319
Unforeseen circumstances, 492
Unification, of federal estate and gift tax, 836
Unified estate-gift tax credit, 837
Uniform Arbitration Act, 263
Uniform Code of Military Justice, 97, 98
Uniform Criminal Extradition Act, 125
Uniform Declaratory Judgments Act, 130
Uniform Limited Partnership Act, 642
Uniform Partnership Act, 629–44
Uniform Traffic Act, 576, 578–80
Unilateral mistake, 206
Unilateral refusal to deal, 620
Unilateral rescission, as discharge of contract, 259–61
Union: authorization cards, 312; certification, 311; member's "bill of rights," 321; security, 313; shop, 314; trusteeship, 321
United States Code, 14
United States Reports, 15
Unity: of interest, 342; of possession, 342; of time, 342; of title, 342
Universal Copyright Convention, 602
Unliquidated claim, 133
Unseaworthy vessel, effect upon ocean marine insurance coverage, 477
Unsolicited merchandise, 200, 201
Usury: in general, 221–27; as defense to payment of commercial paper, 386
Utility service of tenant, interruption by landlord, 771

V

Variances, 796
Vendor's lien, 752
Venue: civil, 136; criminal, 107, 108
Verdict: civil, 144; criminal, 118
Vested rights of intended beneficiaries of contracts, 241, 242
Veterans' Administration, 752
Void transfer, 379
Voidable transfer, 379
Volume discount, 618
Vote-buying, illegality of contract for, 221
Voting: common stock, 655; cumulative, 655; preferred stock, 655; by proxy, 672, 673; in shareholders' meeting, 672, 673
Voting trust, 656

W

W-2 form, 300
W-4 form, 299
Wages and Hours Division, Department of Labor, 297, 298
Wagers, legal, 218, 219
Waiver of defenses clause in contracts, 248
Warehouse, bonded, 474, 475
Warehouse receipt, 445–51
Warehouseman, 445–49
Warehouseman's lien: in general, 330; foreclosure of, 447, 448
Warranty: against encumbrances, sales of goods, 504, 505; of fitness for buyer's purpose, sales of goods, 506, 507; against infringement, sales of goods, 505, 506
Warranty liability: of assignor of contract right, 250, 251; of presenter of commercial paper for acceptance or payment, 402; of presenter of investment security for registration or payment, 669; of transferor of bill of lading for consideration, 455; of transferor of commercial paper for consideration, 402, 403; of transferor of investment security for consideration, 666; of transferor of warehouse receipt for consideration, 451
Warranty of merchantability, 505, 506, 512
Warranty of title: presenter of commercial paper for acceptance or payment, 402; seller of goods, 504; transferor of commercial paper for consideration, 402
Warsaw Convention, 465
Water carrier: domestic, 465; international, 469
Water Code, 797
Water pollution control, 796, 797
Water Pollution Control Act, 796, 797
Water Quality Control Board, 797
Watered stock, 770, 771
Waybill, airline, 464
Weapons: forbidden, 53, 54; unlawful carrying or possession of, 53
West Publishing Company, 15
Widow's allowance, 826
Widow's election, 816
Wild animals, 331
Wildcat strike, 319
Wills: contest of, 823–25; execution of, 812, 813; formal, 812, 813, 822, 823; holographic, 815; incapacity to make, 823, 824; mutual, 817; nuncupative, 813, 823; self-proving, 812
Withholding of delivery, 518
Withholding taxes, 299, 300
Witness, compensation of, 20
Workers' compensation, 305–8
Workers' Compensation Law, 305–8
Write-off: of accounts receivable, 703;

of assets, 703
Written interrogatories, 105
Wrongful death actions, 88
Wrongful exclusion of tenant, 771

Y

"Yellow-dog" contract, 314

Z

Zivilgesetzbuch, 6
Zoning, 790–96
Zoning Commission, 791